AA Pet Friendly Places to Stay 2009

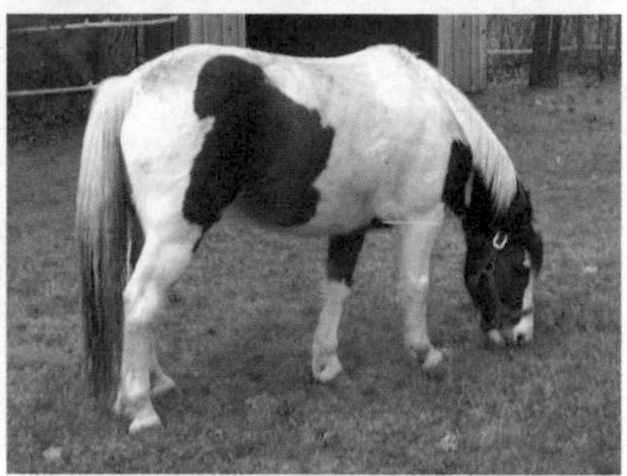

The AA strives to ensure accuracy in this guide at the time of printing. Due to the constantly evolving nature of the subject matter the information is subject to change. The AA will gratefully receive any advice from our readers of any necessary updated information.

Please contact Advertisement Sales: advertisingsales@theaa.com
Editorial Department: lifestyleguides@theaa.com
AA Hotel & Guest Accommodation enquiries: 01256 844455
AA Campsite enquiries: 01256 491577

Main cover photograph courtesy of Simon Page; bl Photolibrary Group; br Phoebe Haynes; back cover: l Leona Mundin; m Colin Bean; r Julie Hill.

Typeset/Repro by Servis, Manchester
Printed in Italy by Printer Trento SRL, Trento.

Directory compiled by the AA Hotel Services Department and generated from the AA establishment database.
www.theAA.com

Published by AA Publishing, a trading name of Automobile Association Developments Limited, whose registered office is Fanum House, Basing View, Basingstoke, Hampshire RG21 4EA.
Registered number 1878835

A CIP catalogue record for this book is available from the British Library

ISBN: 978 0 7495 5875 8
A04071

Contents

Welcome to the Guide

This guide is perfect for pet owners who are reluctant to put their animals into kennels or catteries while they go on holiday. In these pages you can find not only places where dogs and cats are welcome, but also where horses can be stabled on site or very close by.

Hints on booking your stay

As this guide shows, there are a great many hotels, bed and breakfasts and campsites that offer a warm welcome and an extensive range of facilities to both pet lovers and their animal companions. Though all the establishments listed have told us they are happy to admit animals, some go out of their way to make you and your pet feel at home, offering animal welcome packs, comfortable dog baskets, water bowls, special blankets, home-made treats and comprehensive information on local country walks.

Do remember though, that even the pet-friendliest of proprietors appreciate advance warning if you intend to bring your animal with you. See pages 12-17 for helpful hints and tips on planning your trip. While summer is an obvious time to book a holiday, you might like to consider taking an off-peak break when animals – dogs in particular – are more likely to enjoy cooler temperatures and crowd-free destinations.

And just a friendly word of warning. On sending us information for this guide many establishments stated that they very much welcome pets but they must be accompanied by well behaved owners!

How to Use the Guide

❶ **Locations** The guide is divided into countries. Each country is listed in county order and then alphabetically in town/village order within a county.

❷ **Map reference** Each town/village is given a map reference for the atlas section at the back of the guide. For example:
MAP 03 SY29
03 refers to the page number of the atlas section at the back of the guide
SY is the National Grid lettered square (represents 100,000sq metres) in which the location will be found
2 is the figure reading across the top or bottom of the map page
9 is the figure reading down each side of the map page
Campsites (and some B&Bs) include a 6-figure National Grid reference as many are located in remote areas.
A county map appears before the atlas section at the back of the guide.

❸ **Which pets are accepted** Five symbols show at a glance what type of animal is welcome – dogs, cats, small caged animals, caged birds and horses. indicates places that provide kennels.

❹ **Establishment rating & name** For further information on AA ratings and awards see page 10. If the name of the establishment appears in italic type this indicates that not all the information has been confirmed for 2009.
Within each location hotels are listed first, in descending order of stars and % score, followed by B&Bs in descending orders of stars, then campsites in order of their pennant rating (see page 10).

❺ **Contact details**

❻ **Directions** Short details of how to find the establishment or campsite.

❶ **AXMINSTER** — **MAP 03 SY29** ❷

❸

❹ ★★★ 74% HOTEL
Fairwater Head Hotel ⓯
Hawkchurch EX13 5TX
☎ 01297 678349 01297 678459

❺ **e-mail:** stay@fairwaterheadhotel.co.uk
web: www.fairwaterheadhotel.co.uk

❻ **Dir:** *off B3165. Hotel signed to Hawkchurch*

❼ **PETS: Bedrooms** (8GF) unattended **Charges** charge for damage **Public areas** except dining room (on leads) **Grounds** accessible on leads disp bin **Exercise area** surrounding countryside **Facilities** food (pre-bookable) food bowl water bowl dog chews dog scoop/disp bags leads pet sitting cage storage walks info vet info **On Request** fridge access torch towels

❽ **Resident Pets:** Mocca (Springer/Cocker Spaniel)

⓮

This elegant Edwardian country house provides a perfect location for anyone looking for a peaceful break. Surrounded by extensive gardens and rolling countryside, the setting guarantees relaxation. Bedrooms are located both within the main house and the garden wing; all provide good levels of comfort. Public areas have much appeal and include lounge areas, a bar and an elegant restaurant. ⓭

❾ **Rooms** 12 en suite 4 annexe en suite (8 GF) S £80-£115; D £140-£210 (incl. bkfst & dinner)✻ **Facilities** Wi-fi available Xmas New Year **Parking** 30 **Notes LB** Closed 1-30 Jan

⓫ ⓬ ❿

❼ Pet facilities **(PETS:)**
Bedrooms GF Ground floor bedrooms; **unattended** indicates that the establishment allows a pet to be left unattended in the bedroom; **sign** indicates that a sign is provided to hang on the door stating an animal is in the room.

Sep accomm (separate accommodation) some places have kennels or outbuildings available. Do ask for more information when you book to check that this is suitable for your pet.
Charges £ (€ Republic of Ireland) Some establishments charge a fee for accommodating a pet: the price shown is the charge per animal per night and/or per animal per week (unless otherwise stated).
Grounds Establishments may allow pets access to their gardens or grounds, or in the case of campsites there may be specified areas for exercise.
Exercise area The type of area available (ie fields, beach, coastal path etc) and the distance from the establishment (ie 100yds).
Facilities Information and specific facilties that guests who are staying with their pets might find useful. Campsites may sell certain pet related items in their on-site shop.
Other Additional information supplied by the establishment.
Restrictions Certain establishments have rules on the number of pets, or the size or the breed of dog allowed.* We strongly advise readers to check with the hotel, B&B or campsite at the time of booking that their pet will be permitted to accompany them during their stay.

*Some establishments have stated that they do not accept 'dangerous dogs'. The following breeds are covered under the Dangerous Dogs Act 1991 – Pit Bull Terrier, Japanese Tosa, Dogo Argentino and Fila Brazilierio.

8 **Resident Pets** Lists the names and breeds of the proprietors' own pets.

9 **Rooms** The number of bedrooms, and whether they are en suite, family or ground floor rooms. **Prices** These are per room per night. These are given by the proprietors in good faith, and are indications only, not firm quotations. (✻ indicates 2008 prices). At the time of going to press up-to-date prices for campsites were not available. Please check the AA website **www.theAA.com** for current information. Smoking is not permitted in the public areas of hotels and guest houses, but some bedrooms may be set aside for smokers. If either the freedom to smoke or to be in a non-smoking environment is important to you, please check with the establishment when you book your room.

10 **Facilities** **Leisure facilities** are as stated in the entries. **Child Facilities** (Ch fac), these vary from place to place so please check at the time of booking that the establishment can meet your requirements.

11 **Parking** Shows the numbers of spaces available for the use of guests. This may include covered, charged spaces.

12 **Notes** This section can include the following:
No Children followed by an age indicates that a minimum age is required (ie No children 4yrs)
RS (Restricted Service) Some establishments have a restricted service during quieter months and some of the listed facilities may not be available.
LB Some establishments offer leisure breaks.
Dinner (**B&Bs only**) indicates that an evening meal is available, although prior notice may be needed. **Licensed** (**B&Bs only**) indicates that the establishment is licensed to serve alcohol.
Payment The majority of establishments in this guide accept credit and debit cards. If they don't this is indicated in the guide.

13 **Decription** This is written by the AA Inspector at the time of their visit.

14 **Photograph** Establishments may choose to include a photograph in their entry.

15 **Hotel logo** If a symbol appears in the entry it indicates that the hotel belongs to a group or consortium.

Symbols and Abbreviations

Key to symbols

	Dogs
	Cats
	Small caged animals e.g, rabbits, hamsters
	Caged birds
	Kennels available
	Horses (stables or paddock)
★	The best hotels (see page 10)
★	The best B&Bs (see page 10)
★	Hotel and B&B rating (see page 10)
%	Merit score (see page 10)
U	AA Rating not confirmed (see page 11)
	AA Rosette Award for quality of food
►	Campsite rating (see page 11)
	Holiday Centre (see page 11)
	No credit cards
✳	2008 prices
	Indoor swimming pool
	Heated indoor swimming pool
	Outdoor swimming pool
	Heated outdoor swimming pool
	Tennis court/s
	Croquet lawn
	Golf course
	Entertainment

Bed & Breakfast only

	A very special breakfast, with an emphasis on freshly prepared local ingredients
	A very special dinner, with an emphasis on freshly prepared local ingredients

Key to abbreviations

Air con	Air conditioning
BH/bank hols	Bank Holidays
Ch fac	Special facilities for children
D	Double bedroom
Etr	Easter
Fmly	Family bedroom
Fr	From
FTV	Freeview television in bedrooms
GF	Ground floor bedroom
hrs	Hours
incl. bkfst	Including breakfast
LB	Special leisure breaks
m	Miles
mtrs	Metres
mdnt	Midnight
New Year	Special New Year programme
No Children	No children can be accommodated
rdbt	Roundabout
RS/rs	Restricted services
S	Single bedroom
STV	Satellite television in bedrooms
Spa	Establishment has own spa facilities
Whit	Whitsun Bank Holiday
Wi-fi	Wireless network access
wk	Week
wkend	Weekend
Xmas	Special Christmas programme

Bed & Breakfast only

Cen ht	Full central heating
Last d	Last time dinner can be ordered
pri facs	Bedroom with separate, private facilities
rms	Bedrooms in main building
Tea/coffee	Tea & coffee making facilities
TVB	Television in bedrooms
TVL	Television lounge

AA Classifications and Awards

Hotel and Guest Accommodation Ratings

In 2006 the AA, in association with the National Tourist Boards, introduced new common standards for rating accommodation. All Hotels and B&Bs in this guide have received an inspection under these standards.

Hotel Ratings

If you stay in a **one-star** hotel you should expect a relatively informal yet competent style of service and an adequate range of facilities. The majority of the bedrooms are en suite, with a bath or shower room always available. A **two-star** hotel is run by smartly and professionally presented management and offers at least one restaurant or dining room for breakfast and dinner, while a **three-star** hotel includes direct-dial telephones, a wide selection of drinks in the bar and last orders for dinner no later than 8pm. A **four-star** hotel is characterised by uniformed, well-trained staff, with additional services, a night porter and a serious approach to cuisine. A **five-star** hotel, offers many extra facilities, attentive staff, top quality rooms and a full concierge service.

The Merit Score (%) AA inspectors supplement their reports with an additional quality assessment of everything the hotel offers, including hospitality, based on their findings as a 'mystery guest'. This results in a overall Merit Score. Shown as a pecentage score beside the hotel name, you can see at a glance that a hotel with a percentage score of 69% offers a higher standard than one in the same star classification but with a percentage score of 59%. To gain AA recognition initially, a hotel must achieve a minimum quality score of 50%.

Red stars The very best hotels within each star category are indicated by red stars.

There are six descriptive designators for establishments in the Hotel Recognition scheme:

HOTEL Formal accommodatiom with full service. Minimum of six guest bedrooms but more likely to be in excess of 20.

TOWN HOUSE HOTEL A small, individual city or town centre property, which provides a high degree of personal service and privacy.

COUNTRY HOUSE HOTEL A rurally and quietly located establishment with ample grounds.

SMALL HOTEL Has less than 20 bedrooms and is personally run by the proprietor.

METRO HOTEL A hotel in an urban location that does not offer dinner.

BUDGET HOTEL Inexpensive group lodge accommodation, usually purpose built by main roads and motorways and in town or city centres.

Guest Accommodation Ratings

Stars in the AA Guest Accommodation scheme reflect five levels of quality, from one at the simplest level to five offering the highest quality. The criteria for eligibility is guest care plus the quality of the accommodation rather than the choice of extra facilities. Guests should receive a prompt, professional check in and check out, comfortable accommodation equipped to modern standards, regularly changed bedding and towels, a sufficient hot water supply at all times, well-prepared meals and a full continental breakfast.

Yellow stars The top 10% of three, four and five star establishments are indicated by yellow stars.

There are six descriptive designators for establishments in this scheme:

B&B A private house run by the owner with accommodation for no more than six paying guests.

GUEST HOUSE Run on a more commercial basis than a B&B, the accommodadtion provides for more than six paying guests and there are more services.

FARMHOUSE The B&B or guest house accommodation is part of a working farm or smallholding.

INN The accommodation is provided in a fully licensed establishment. The bar will be open to non-residents and provide food in the evenings.

RESTAURANT WITH ROOMS This is a destination restaurant offering overnight accommodation, with dining being the main business, and open to non-residents. The restaurant should offer a high

standard of food, and restaurant service at least five nights a week. A liquor licence and maximum of 12 bedrooms.

GUEST ACCOMMODATION Any establishment that meets the minimum entry requirements is eligible for this general category.

AA Rosettes

The AA awards Rosettes for the quality of food. These range from one Rosette for food prepared with care, understanding and skill, up to five Rosettes for the very finest cooking that stands comparison with the best cuisine in the world.

AA Campsite Ratings

AA sites are classified from one to five pennants according to their style and the range of facilities they offer. **1 pennant** – these parks offer a fairly simple standard of facilities. **2 pennants** – offer an increased level of facilities, services, customer care, security and ground maintenance. **3 pennants** – have a wide range of facilities and are of a very good standard. **4 pennants** – these parks achieve an excellent standard throughout that will include landscaped grounds, natural screening and immaculately maintained toilets. **5 pennant Premier Parks** – the very best parks with superb mature landscaping and all facilities, customer care and security will be of exceptional quality.

Campsites have shortened entries in this guide. For more detailed information visit our website **www.theAA.com** and follow the 'Places to Stay' link.

Holiday Centres

This category indicates parks which cater for all holiday needs including cooked meals and entertainment.

U A small number of establishments in the guide have this symbol because their star or pennant rating was not confirmed at the time of going to press. This may be because there has been a change of ownership, or because the establishment has only recently joined one of the AA rating schemes.

To find out more about AA ratings and awards please visit our website **www.theAA.com**

Useful Information

Britain

Fire Regulations

The Fire Precautions Act does not apply to the Channel Islands, Republic of Ireland, or the Isle of Man, which have their own rules. As far as we are aware, all establishments listed in Great Britain have applied for and not been refused a fire certificate.

Licensing laws

These laws differ in England, Wales, Scotland, Northern Ireland, the Republic of Ireland, the Isle of Man, the Isles of Scilly and the Channel Islands.

Public houses are generally open from mid morning to early afternoon, and from about 6 or 7pm until 11pm, although closing times may be earlier or later and some pubs are open all afternoon. Unless otherwise stated, hotels listed in this guide are licensed. (For guest accommodation, please refer to the individual gazetteer entry. Note that licensed premises are not obliged to remain open throughout the permitted hours.) Hotel residents can obtain alcoholic drinks at all times, if the licensee is prepared to serve them. Non-residents eating at the hotel restaurant can have drinks with meals. Children under 14 (or 18 in Scotland) may be excluded from bars where no food is served. Those under 18 may not purchase or consume alcoholic drinks. A club licence means that drinks are served to club members only. 48 hours must elapse between joining and ordering.

Prices

The AA encourages the use of the Hotel Industry Voluntary Code of Booking Practice, which aims to ensure that guests know how much they will have to pay and what services and facilities that includes, before entering a financially binding agreement. If the price has not previously been confirmed in writing, guests should be given a card stipulating the total obligatory charge when they register at reception.

The Tourism (Sleeping Accommodation Price Display) Order of 1977 compels hotels, travel accommodation, guest houses, farmhouses, inns and self-catering accommodation with four or more letting bedrooms, to display in entrance halls the minimum and

maximum prices charged for each category of room. Tariffs shown are the minimum and maximum for one or two persons but they may vary without warning.

Facilities for disabled guests

The final stage (Part III) of the Disability Discrimination Act (access to Goods and Services) came into force in October 2004. This means that service providers may have to consider making permanent physical adjustments to their premises.

For further information, see the government website **www.direct.gov.uk/en/disabledpeople/index.htm**.

We indicate in entries if an establishment has ground floor rooms, and if a hotel tells us that they have disabled facilities this is included in the description. The establishments in this guide should all be aware of their responsibilities under the Act. We recommend that you telephone in advance to ensure that the establishment you have chosen has appropriate facilities.

Useful websites:

www.holidaycare.org.uk
www.dptac.gov.uk/door-to-door

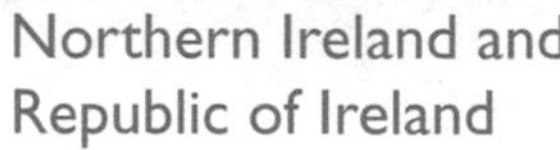

Northern Ireland and Republic of Ireland

Licensing Regulations

Northern Ireland:

Public houses open Mon-Sat 11.30-23.00. Sun 12.30-22.00. Hotels can serve residents without restriction. Non-residents can be served 12.30-22.00 on Christmas Day. Children under 18 are not allowed in the bar area and may neither buy nor consume liquor in hotels.

Republic of Ireland:

General licensing hours are Mon-Thu 10.30-23.30, Fri & Sat 10.30-00.30. Sun 12.30-23.00 (or 00.30 if the following day is a Bank Holiday). There is no licensed service (except for hotel residents) on Christmas Day or Good Friday.

Fire Regulations

The Fire Services (NI) Order 1984. This covers establishments accommodating more than six people, which must have a certificate from the Northern Ireland Fire Authority. Places accommodating fewer than six people need adequate exits. AA inspectors check emergency notices, fire fighting equipment and fire exits here.

The Republic of Ireland safety regulations are a matter for local authority regulations. For your own and others' safety, read the emergency notices and be sure you understand them.

Telephone numbers

Area codes for numbers in the Republic of Ireland apply only within the Republic. If dialling from outside check the telephone directory (from the UK the international dialling code is 00 353). Area codes for numbers in Britain and Northern Ireland cannot be used directly from the Republic.

For the latest information on the Republic of Ireland visit the AA Ireland's website: **www.AAireland.ie**

Useful websites for pet owners:

www.thekennelclub.org.uk The Kennel Club provides lots of information on microchipping and runs a pet reunification scheme. The website also includes information on lost micro-chipped pets: The European Pet Network has access to several animal databases from various European countries.

If a lost micro-chipped and registered pet is found, the EPN aims to find the owner.

www.missingpetsbureau.com A national missing pets register.

www.defra.gov.uk/animalh/quarantine/index.htm for details of the Pet Travel Scheme and for comprehensive information and advice on travelling with your pet.

www.rcvs.org.uk website of the Royal College of Veterinary Surgeons that will help you find a vet near your holiday destination.

Bank and Public Holidays 2009

1st January	New Year's Day
2nd January (Scotland)	New Year's Holiday
10th April	Good Friday
13th April	Easter Monday
4th May	May Day Bank Holiday
5th May	Spring Bank Holiday
4th August (Scotland)	August Holiday
31st August	Late Summer Holiday
25th December	Christmas Day
26th December	Boxing Day

Pet Patrol

At first, the prospect of taking your pet away with you may seem a little daunting. There is their welfare to think of and the responsibility of trying to ensure they fit comfortably into their new surroundings. Many proprietors have cats and dogs of their own and will quickly build up a good rapport with your pet. This can play a vital role in the success of your holiday, and if all goes well, owners who are genuine animal lovers will be welcoming you back year after year. On the whole, proprietors report favourably on their pet guests, often commenting that their behaviour is at least as good as their owners!

We all love our pets and want to give them the care they deserve, but holidays can mean a certain amount of stress for us and also for our pets. Changes in routine can upset an animal as much as its owner. So keep them to their regular mealtimes if possible, take plenty of water for them on your journey, especially in hot weather.

Planning ahead

Always remember to advise the proprietor when booking that you intend bringing your pet with you. This gives you both the opportunity to establish whether the accommodation really is suitable for your pet's needs. Some establishments impose restrictions on the type, size or number of animals permitted; for example, those that accept dogs may not accommodate the larger breeds. Many estabishments can provide foods but is it advisable to take the food your pet is familiar with.

Not all rooms will necessarily be available to guests with animals and some rooms may be set aside for people with allergies.

When booking, you should also check the establishment's supervision policy. Some may require your pet to be caged when unattended, or may ask you not to leave your pet alone at all.

The gazetteer entry in this guide indicates whether you should expect to pay an additional charge or deposit for your pet, but we recommend that you confirm the amount when booking.

The countryside

For your family holiday to be a complete success, you'll need to do a little research and planning. As well as finding somewhere suitable to stay, you might like to contact the tourist board for leaflets and brochures on pet-friendly places of interest, or you might find the ideal place listed in the AA Days Out guide. Remember to 'Mind that Pet!' and keep your dog under tight control when visiting local attractions.

Time to adjust

Remember that an animal shut in a strange hotel room for long periods may become distressed. We have stories from our hotels and B&Bs of dogs chewing up furniture or howling mournfully while their owners are out and these are symptoms of boredom and separation anxiety, particularly if your pet is a rescue animal.

On arrival, give your pet time to adjust to the new surroundings and if you think he will be upset and bark or howl, don't leave him alone in your room.

Watching our pets let off steam in a different environment is one of the pleasures of a good holiday, but although they are cherished members of the family who provide many hours of fun and enjoyment, owners have a duty to ensure that their pet is kept under proper control at all times.

In the case of dogs, allowing them to socialise with people and other animals from an early age means that, under your supervision, they will be at ease with other residents and their pets during your stay. It's not uncommon to end up swapping dog stories with guests or even members of staff. Lasting friendships are sometimes formed this way!

House rules

Unless otherwise indicated by the management, please don't allow your pet on the furniture, or in the bed. If he or she likes to sleep on the bed, remember to take a sheet, a blanket or a bedspread of your own, unless the proprietor provides one. Remember also to take an old towel to dry your pet after a walk in the rain and don't use the bath or shower for washing your animal.

Clean up after your pet immediately – inside the room and out – and leave no trace of them on departure. Take a supply of supermarket carrier bags with you and poop scoop anywhere in the hotel or grounds. Management will advise on disposal of the bags – some hotels/B&Bs have an animal toilet area and provide bags. If something has been damaged by your pet, notify the management immediately. It's really a case of simple common sense.

If the hotel/B&B allows you to take animals into public areas, be sure that you keep your pet under control at all times. Keep dogs on leads, especially when around small children. Your dog may be easily distracted by the sights and smells of unfamiliar surroundings, and may not respond to your commands as well as at home.

Bear in mind that dogs need to be exercised regularly – even on holiday – and time should be set aside for this as often as possible, especially if they have been travelling with you in the car for most of the day. Most country hotels and B&Bs will have plenty of good walks on the doorstep, which makes the chore of exercising your dog that much more enjoyable.

A lot of the establishments listed in this guide are surrounded by farmland so please remember to keep your dog under strict control near livestock – even letting your dog walk in the same field as farm animals may be considered as "worrying". (Remember a farmer is entitled to kill your dog if it is worrying livestock).

Just in case

One final tip is to check your insurance for the level of cover it offers before taking your pet away. Pet insurance may not cover personal liability but your house insurance might. Should your pet chew the furniture or take a nip at a passing ankle, you would be well advised to have covered this eventuality by having the appropriate, up-to-date insurance policy.

The AA offers Pet Insurance.
Please visit **www.theAA.com** or call **0800 294 2713** for further information.

The Pet Travel Scheme (PETS)

Pets are on the move. They now travel more often with their owners in the United Kingdom and, because of changes in quarantine regulations, pets can now be taken abroad and then return to the UK, subject to certain conditions. This guide includes over 1,400 pet-friendly hotels, guest houses and campsites throughout the UK, solving the problem of what to do with your pet when you want to go on holiday. But what happens if you plan to go further afield – abroad perhaps? What are the regulations?

The Pets Travel Scheme gives information about the countries involved in the scheme; regulations; documentation required; microchip ID tags; help finding a vet; guidance on looking after pets during transportation; bringing your pet from a long-haul country; authorised routes; approved transport companies; charges; a latest news section and lots more besides.

Pets that are resident anywhere in the UK can travel unrestricted within Britain, and are not subject to quarantine regulations or to the PETS rules unless they are entering this country from overseas. There are no requirements for pets travelling directly between the UK and the Republic of Ireland.

The PETS scheme, which only applies to dogs (including assistance dogs), cats, ferrets, and certain other pets, enables pets resident in the UK to enter, without quarantine restrictions, certain (listed) countries throughout the world and then return to Britain. Thanks to the relaxation of quarantine controls in this country, they can go straight home on arrival. In order to bring your pet into, or back into, the UK from one of the listed countries the scheme requires that your pet must be fitted with a microchip, be vaccinated against rabies, pass a blood test and be issued with a pet passport (or hold a valid pet certificate dated before 1/10/2004). Before entering the UK, your animal will also need to receive both tapeworm and tick treatments. Naturally, careful thought should be given to the welfare of your pet and whether a holiday abroad is appropriate, but if you decide to go ahead, remember it is necessary for your pet to have passed a satisfactory blood test at least 6 calendar months before travel commences. Your pet cannot travel under this scheme unless this time has elapsed.

For detailed information about the PETS scheme contact:

PETS Helpline: 0870 241 1710
(8am-6pm (UK time) Monday to Friday)
E-mail: quarantine@ animalhealth.gsi.gov.uk
(Please include your postal address and daytime telephone number in your e-mail).
Website: www.defra.gov.uk/animalh/quarantine/pets/

Remember, whether in the UK or abroad animals can die if left in a vehicle in direct sunlight or high temperatures.

England

BEDFORDSHIRE

ASPLEY GUISE — MAP 04 SP93

★★★ 72% HOTEL

Best Western Moore Place

The Square MK17 8DW

☎ 01908 282000 📠 01908 281888

e-mail: manager@mooreplace.com

web: www.bespokehotels.com

Dir: *M1 junct 13, take A507 signed Aspley Guise & Woburn Sands. Hotel on left in village square*

PETS: Bedrooms (16GF) **Stables** nearby **Charges** charge for damage **Public areas** (on leads) **Grounds** accessible on leads disp bin **Exercise area Facilities** cage storage walks info vet info **On Request** fridge access torch **Restrictions** largest breeds (i.e. Great Danes) restricted to 1 per room

This impressive Georgian house, set in delightful gardens in the village centre, is very conveniently located for the M1. Bedrooms do vary in size, but consideration has been given to guest comfort, with many thoughtful extras provided. There is a wide range of meeting rooms and private dining options.

Rooms 35 en suite 27 annexe en suite (16 GF) S £65-£130; D £85-£195* **Facilities** Wi-fi in bedrooms Xmas New Year **Parking** 70 **Notes LB** RS 27-31 Dec

BERKSHIRE

ASCOT — MAP 04 SU96

★★★★ 78% HOTEL

Macdonald Berystede Hotel & Spa

Bagshot Rd, Sunninghill SL5 9JH

☎ 0844 879 9104 📠 01344 872301

e-mail: general.berystede@macdonald-hotels.co.uk

web: www.macdonald-hotels.co.uk

Dir: *A30/B3020 (Windmill Pub). Continue 1.25m to hotel on left just before junct with A330*

PETS: Bedrooms (33GF) unattended sign **Stables** nearby (1m) **Charges** £10 per night £70 per week charge for damage **Public areas** except restaurant (on leads) **Grounds** accessible on leads disp bin **Exercise area** 0.5m **Facilities** walks info vet info **On Request** fridge access **Restrictions** small & medium dogs only

This impressive Victorian mansion, close to Ascot Racecourse, offers executive bedrooms that are spacious, comfortable and particularly well equipped. Public rooms include a cosy bar and an elegant restaurant in which creative dishes are served. An impressive self-contained conference centre and spa facility appeal to both conference and leisure guests.

Rooms 126 en suite (61 fmly) (33 GF) S £80-£239; D £80-£239 (incl. bkfst) **Facilities Spa** STV Gym Wi-fi in bedrooms Leisure complex including thermal & beauty treatment suites Xmas New Year **Services** Lift **Parking** 250 **Notes LB**

★★★★ 77% COUNTRY HOUSE HOTEL

Ramada Plaza The Royal Berkshire

London Rd, Sunninghill SL5 0PP

☎ 01344 623322 📠 01344 627100

e-mail: sales.royalberkshire@ramadajarvis.co.uk

web: www.ramadajarvis.co.uk

Dir: *A30 towards Bagshot, right opposite Wentworth Club onto A329, continue for 2m, hotel entrance on right*

PETS: Bedrooms (8GF) **Stables** nearby (Ascot nearby) **Charges** £10 per night £70 per week charge for damage **Grounds** accessible **Exercise area Facilities** walks info vet info **On Request** fridge access torch towels

Once occupied by the Churchill family, this delightful Queen Anne house is set in 14 acres of attractive gardens on the edge of Ascot. Public areas include a comfortable lounge bar, an attractive restaurant that overlooks the rear gardens and extensive conference facilities. The main house offers smart, well-equipped bedrooms.

Rooms 63 en suite (8 fmly) (8 GF) S £101-£156; D £101-£272 (incl. bkfst)* **Facilities** STV Wi-fi in bedrooms Xmas New Year **Parking** 150 **Notes LB**

FINCHAMPSTEAD — MAP 04 SU76

►►► California Chalet & Touring Park

(SU788651)

Nine Mile Ride RG40 4HU

☎ 0118 973 3928 📠 0118 932 8720

e-mail: enquiries@californiapark.co.uk

web: www.californiapark.co.uk

Dir: *From A321 (S of Wokingham), right onto B3016 to Finchampstead. Follow Country Park signs on Nine Mile Ride to site*

PETS: Charges £1 charge for 2+ dogs per night **Exercise area** adjacent woods **Facilities** walks info vet info **Other** prior notice required

Open all year Last arrival 17.00hrs Last departure noon

A peaceful woodland site with secluded pitches among the trees, adjacent to the country park. Several pitches have a prime position beside the lake with their own fishing area. A 5.5-acre site with 30 touring pitches, 30 hardstandings.

Notes No ground fires, no ball games

ENGLAND

HUNGERFORD MAP 04 SU36

★★★ 81% @@ HOTEL

Bear

41 Charnham St RG17 0EL
☎ 01488 682512 📠 01488 684357
e-mail: info@thebearhotelhungerford.co.uk
web: www.thebearhotelhungerford.co.uk

Dir: *M4 junct 14, A338 to Hungerford for 3m, left at T-junct onto A4, hotel on left*

PETS: Bedrooms (24GF) unattended **Public areas** (on leads) **Grounds** accessible **Exercise area** canal & common nearby **Facilities** food (pre-bookable) bedding walks info vet info **On Request** fridge access **Resident Pets:** Bear (cat)

Situated five miles south of the M4 this hotel dates back as far as early 13th century and was once owned by King Henry VIII. It now has a contemporary feel throughout. Bedrooms are split between the main house, the courtyard and Bear Island. The award-winning restaurant is open for lunch and dinner, and lighter snacks are available in the bar and lounge. Guests can enjoy a sun terrace in the summer and log fires in the winter.

Rooms 13 en suite 26 annexe en suite (2 fmly) (24 GF) S £85-£150; D £95-£190* **Facilities** FTV Wi-fi in bedrooms Xmas New Year **Parking** 68 **Notes** LB

★★★ BED & BREAKFAST

Beacon House

Bell Ln, Upper Green, Inkpen RG17 9QJ
☎ 01488 668640 📠 01488 668640
e-mail: l.g.cave@classicfm.net
web: www.beaconhouseinkpen.com

Dir: *4m SE of Hungerford. Off A4 S into Kintbury, left onto Inkpen Rd, 1m over x-rds, right to common, 3rd left after Crown & Garter pub*

PETS: Bedrooms unattended **Charges** charge for damage **Grounds** accessible on leads disp bin **Exercise area** 100yds **Facilities** food (pre-bookable) food bowl water bowl bedding feeding mat leads washing facs cage storage walks info **On Request** fridge access torch towels **Restrictions** One pet only **Resident Pets:** Bilbo & Sevie (Cocker Spaniels), Jennie (donkey)

This large house is set in peaceful countryside. Bedrooms are comfortably furnished and overlook fields. As well as the lounge, there is usually an art exhibition and sale featuring watercolours, textiles, printmaking and pottery in the adjoining Gallery. Guests are always invited to view.

Rooms 3 rms S £34; D £68 **Facilities** TVB Cen ht TVL **Parking** 6 **Notes** LB

MEMBURY MOTORWAY SERVICE AREA (M4) MAP 04 SU37

BUDGET HOTEL

Days Inn Membury

Membury Service Area RG17 7TZ
☎ 01488 72336 📠 01488 72336
e-mail: membury.hotel@welcomebreak.co.uk
web: www.welcomebreak.co.uk

Dir: *M4 between junct 14 & 15*

PETS: Bedrooms Public areas only for access to bedrooms **Grounds** accessible **Exercise area**

This modern building offers accommodation in smart, spacious and well-equipped bedrooms, suitable for families and business travellers, and all with en suite bathrooms. Refreshments may be taken at the nearby family restaurant.

Rooms 38 en suite S £39-£59; D £49-£69*

NEWBURY MAP 04 SU46

★★ 78% HOTEL

Hare & Hounds

Bath Rd, Speen RG14 1QY
☎ 01635 521152 📠 01635 47708
e-mail: reservations@hareandhoundsnewbury.co.uk
web: www.hareandhoundshotel.net

Dir: *Turn off A34 onto A4 signed for Speen. Hotel 300yds on right*

PETS: Bedrooms (11GF) sign **Charges** charge for damage **Public areas** reception & bar only (on leads) **Grounds** accessible on leads disp bin **Exercise area Facilities** food (pre-bookable) dog walking cage storage walks info vet info **On Request** fridge access torch towels **Restrictions** medium-sized dogs & must be well-controlled

A privately owned, historic hotel just a few minutes from the centre of Newbury. The hotel offers bedrooms in the coach house and in the mews, and all are modern and tastefully decorated. There is a relaxed, informal restaurant offering regularly changing menus, and the bar is popular with locals and guests alike.

Rooms 7 en suite 23 annexe en suite (3 fmly) (11 GF) S £48-£78; D £65-£108 (incl. bkfst)* **Facilities** New Year **Parking** 64 **Notes** LB

READING MAP 04 SU77

BUDGET HOTEL

Ibis Reading Centre

25A Friar St RG1 1DP

☎ 0118 953 3500 📠 0118 953 3501

e-mail: H5431@accor.com

web: www.ibishotel.com

Dir: *Turn off A329 Friar Street. Hotel 2 min from central train station*

PETS: Bedrooms Charges £10 per night charge for damage **Exercise area**

Modern, budget hotel offering comfortable accommodation in bright and practical bedrooms. Breakfast is self-service and dinner is available in the restaurant.

Rooms 182 en suite S £39-£90; D £39-£90*

RISELEY MAP 04 SU76

►►► Wellington Country Park *(SU728628)*

Odiham Rd RG7 1SP

☎ 0118 932 6444 📠 0118 932 6445

e-mail: info@wellington-country-park.co.uk

web: www.wellington-country-park.co.uk

Dir: *Signed off A33 between Reading and Basingstoke, 4m S of M4 junct 11*

PETS: Stables nearby (1m) **Charges** £1 per night disp bin **Exercise area** on site **Facilities** on site shop vet info

Open Mar-Nov Last arrival 17.30hrs Last departure 13.00hrs

A peaceful woodland site set within an extensive country park, which comes complete with lakes, nature trails, deer farm and boating. Ideal for M4 travellers. An 80-acre site with 72 touring pitches, 10 hardstandings.

Notes No open fires

STREATLEY MAP 04 SU58

★★★★ 75% ⊛⊛ HOTEL

The Swan at Streatley

High St RG8 9HR

☎ 01491 878800 📠 01491 872554

e-mail: sales@swan-at-streatley.co.uk

web: www.swanatstreatley.co.uk

Dir: *from S right at lights in Streatley, hotel on left before bridge*

PETS: Bedrooms (12GF) unattended **Charges** £15 per night charge for damage **Public areas** except restaurant (on leads) **Grounds** accessible disp bin **Exercise area Facilities** walks info vet info

A stunning location set beside the Thames, ideal for an English summer's day. The bedrooms are well appointed and many enjoy the lovely views. The hotel offers a range of facilities including meeting rooms, and the Magdalen Barge is moored beside the hotel making an unusual, yet perfect meeting venue. A motor launch is available for hire from April to October. The spa includes an indoor heated mineral pool and offers a range of treatments. Cuisine is accomplished and dining here should not be missed.

Rooms 45 en suite (12 GF) S £115-£130; D fr £150 (incl. bkfst)* **Facilities Spa** STV supervised Fishing Gym Wi-fi available Electric motor launches for hire Apr-Oct Xmas New Year **Parking** 170 **Notes LB**

WINDSOR MAP 04 SU97

★★★ GUEST HOUSE

Clarence Guest House

9 Clarence Rd SL4 5AE

☎ 01753 864436 📠 01753 857060

e-mail: clarence.hotel@btconnect.com

web: www.clarence-hotel.co.uk

Dir: *M4 junct 6, dual-carriageway to Windsor, left at 1st rdbt onto Clarence Rd*

PETS: Bedrooms Exercise area Facilities walks info vet info **On Request** towels

This Grade II listed Victorian house is in the heart of Windsor. Space in some rooms is limited, but all are well maintained and offer excellent value for money. Facilities include a lounge with a well-stocked bar, and a steam room. Breakfast is served in the dining room overlooking attractive gardens.

Rooms 20 en suite (6 fmly) (2 GF) S £45-£72; D £55-£82 **Facilities** FTV TVB tea/coffee Licensed Cen ht TVL Wi-fi available Sauna Steam room **Parking** 4

BRISTOL

BRISTOL MAP 03 ST57

★★★★ 70% HOTEL

Novotel Bristol Centre

Victoria St BS1 6HY

☎ 0117 976 9988 📠 0117 925 5040

e-mail: H5622@accor.com

web: www.novotel.com

Dir: *at end of M32 follow signs for Temple Meads station to rdbt. Final exit, hotel immediately on right*

PETS: Bedrooms unattended **Charges** £8 per night **Public areas** not in food areas (ex assist dogs) (muzzled or on leads) **Exercise area** 5 mins walk **Facilities** walks info vet info **On Request** towels

This city centre hotel provides smart, contemporary style accommodation. Most of the bedrooms demonstrate the latest Novotel 'Novation' style with unique swivel desk, internet access, air-conditioning and a host of extras. The hotel is convenient for the mainline railway station and also has its own car park.

Rooms 131 en suite (20 fmly) S £59-£149; D £59-£149* **Facilities** STV Gym Wi-fi available **Services** Lift **Parking** 120 (charged) **Notes LB**

★★★ 77% HOTEL

Berkeley Square

CLASSIC BRITISH HOTELS

15 Berkeley Square, Clifton BS8 1HB

☎ 0117 925 4000 🖹 0117 925 2970

e-mail: berkeley@cliftonhotels.com

web: www.cliftonhotels.com/chg.html

Dir: *M32 follow Clifton signs. 1st left at lights by Nills Memorial Tower (University) into Berkeley Sq*

PETS: Bedrooms (4GF) unattended **Public areas** except restaurant **Grounds** accessible **Exercise area** adjacent to park **Other** Please telephone for further details

Set in a pleasant square close to the university, art gallery and Clifton Village, this smart, elegant Georgian hotel has modern, stylishly decorated bedrooms that feature many welcome extras. There is a cosy lounge and stylish restaurant on the ground floor and a smart, contemporary bar in the basement. A small garden is also available at the rear of the hotel.

Rooms 43 en suite (4 GF) **Facilities** Use of local gym and swimming pool **Services** Lift **Parking** 20

★★★ 72% HOTEL

Arno's Manor

470 Bath Rd, Arno's Vale BS4 3HQ

☎ 0117 971 1461 🖹 0117 971 5507

e-mail: arnos.manor@forestdale.com

web: www.forestdale.com

Dir: *From end of M32 follow signs for Bath hotel on right side of A4 after 2m. Next to ITV West television studio*

PETS: Bedrooms unattended **Charges** £7.50 per night **Public areas** except restaurant/bar **Exercise area**

Once the home of a wealthy merchant, this historic 18th-century building is now a comfortable hotel and offers spacious, well-appointed bedrooms, and some have spa baths. The Chapel Lounge has many original features and is a great place to relax, while meals are taken in the decorative and stylish courtyard restaurant.

Rooms 73 en suite (5 fmly) (7 GF) S £103-£109; D £133-£139 (incl. bkfst)✳ **Facilities** Wi-fi in bedrooms Xmas New Year **Services** Lift **Parking** 200 **Notes** LB ®

★★ 74% ❁ HOTEL

Rodney Hotel

4 Rodney Place, Clifton BS8 4HY

☎ 0117 973 5422 🖹 0117 946 7092

e-mail: rodney@cliftonhotels.com

Dir: *off Clifton Down Rd*

PETS: Bedrooms (2GF) **Charges** charge for damage **Grounds** accessible **Exercise area Facilities** food (pre-bookable) walks info vet info **On Request** fridge access **Restrictions** small dogs only

With easy access from the M5, this attractive, listed building in Clifton is conveniently close to the city centre. The individually decorated bedrooms provide a useful range of extra facilities for the business traveller; the public areas include a smart bar and small restaurant offering enjoyable and carefully prepared dishes. A pleasant rear garden provides additional seating in the summer months.

Rooms 31 en suite (1 fmly) (2 GF) S £44-£95; D £62-£108✳ **Facilities** Wi-fi in bedrooms **Parking** 10 (charged) **Notes** Closed 22 Dec-3 Jan RS Sun

★★★ GUEST HOUSE

Washington

11-15 St Pauls Rd, Clifton BS8 1LX

☎ 0117 973 3980 🖹 0117 973 4740

e-mail: washington@cliftonhotels.com

Dir: *A4018 into city, right at lights opp BBC, house 200yds on left*

PETS: Bedrooms (10GF) **Charges** charge for damage **Public areas** except breakfast room (on leads) **Grounds** accessible **Exercise area Facilities** food bowl water bowl **Other** only certain bedrooms available for large dogs & birds; check when booking if pets can be left unattended in bedrooms

This large terrace house is within walking distance of the city centre and Clifton Village. The bedrooms, many now refurbished, are well equipped for business guests. Public areas include a modern reception lounge and a bright basement breakfast room. The property has secure parking and a rear patio garden.

Rooms 46 rms (40 en suite) (4 fmly) (10 GF) S £35-£69; D £44-£87✳ **Facilities** STV TVB tea/coffee Direct dial from bedrooms Licensed Cen ht Wi-fi available Reduced rate pass for local health club **Parking** 16 **Notes** Closed 23 Dec-3 Jan

ENGLAND

BUCKINGHAMSHIRE

AYLESBURY MAP 04 SP81

★★★★ ◎◎◎ HOTEL

Hartwell House Hotel, Restaurant & Spa

PRIDE OF BRITAIN HOTELS

Oxford Rd HP17 8NR

☎ 01296 747444 📠 01296 747450

e-mail: info@hartwell-house.com

web: www.hartwell-house.com

Dir: *from S - M40 junct 7, A329 to Thame, then A418 towards Aylesbury. After 6m, through Stone, hotel on left. From N - M40 junct 9 for Bicester. A41 to Aylesbury, A418 to Oxford for 2m. Hotel on right*

PETS: Bedrooms (10GF) unattended **Grounds** accessible disp bin **Exercise area Facilities** cage storage walks info vet info **On Request** fridge access torch towels **Other** pets allowed in Hartwell Court suites only

This beautiful, historic house is set in 90 acres of unspoilt parkland. The grand public rooms are truly magnificent, and feature many fine works of art. The service standards are very high, being attentive and traditional without stuffiness. There is an elegant, award-winning restaurant where carefully prepared dishes use the best local produce. Bedrooms are spacious, elegant and very comfortable. Most are in the main house, but some, including suites, are in the nearby, renovated coach house, which also houses a fine spa.

Rooms 30 en suite 16 annexe en suite (10 GF) S fr £160; D fr £260 (incl. bkfst)✳ **Facilities Spa** STV supervised Gym Wi-fi in bedrooms Sauna treatment rooms Steam rooms Xmas New Year **Services** Lift **Parking** 91 **Notes LB** No children 6yrs RS Xmas/New Year

BUCKINGHAM MAP 04 SP63

★★★ 72% HOTEL

Best Western Buckingham Hotel

Best Western

Buckingham Ring Rd MK18 1RY

☎ 01280 822622 📠 01280 823074

e-mail: info@thebuckinghamhotel.co.uk

Dir: *Follow A421 for Buckingham, take ring road S towards Brackley & Bicester. Hotel on left*

PETS: Bedrooms (31GF) unattended **Charges** £10 per night **Exercise area Facilities** vet info **On Request** torch **Restrictions** small dogs only

A purpose-built hotel, which offers comfortable and spacious rooms with well designed working spaces for business travellers. There are also extensive conference facilities. The open-plan restaurant and bar offer a good range of dishes, and the well-equipped leisure suite is popular with guests.

Rooms 70 en suite (6 fmly) (31 GF) S £40-£80; D £55-£110✳ **Facilities** STV supervised Gym Wi-fi in bedrooms Xmas New Year **Parking** 200 **Notes LB**

GAYHURST MAP 04 SP84

★★★ FARM HOUSE

Mill Farm *(SP852454)*

MK16 8LT

☎ 01908 611489 & 07714 719640 📠 01908 611489

Mrs K Adams

e-mail: adamsmillfarm@aol.com

web: www.millfarmgayhurst.co.uk

Dir: *B526 from Newport Pagnell, 2.5m left onto Haversham Rd, Mill Farm 1st on left*

PETS: Bedrooms Stables on site **Grounds** accessible disp bin **Exercise area** 20yds **Facilities** food (pre-bookable) food bowl water bowl dog scoop/disp bags leads dog walking washing facs cage storage walks info vet info **On Request** torch **Resident Pets:** Peter (Terrier), Hector (Dachshund), Alfie (Labrador)

Within easy reach of Newport Pagnell and the M1, this historic farmhouse has a peaceful setting with wonderful views over farmland. Bedrooms are decorated in a homely style and have a host of thoughtful extras. The sumptuous lounge-dining room is enhanced with fine antiques, and the extensive grounds include a tennis court.

Rooms 3 rms (2 en suite) 1 annexe en suite (1 fmly) (1 GF) S £30-£35; D £50-£60 **Facilities** TVB tea/coffee Cen ht TVL Fishing **Parking** 13 **Notes** 550 acres mixed

MARLOW MAP 04 SU88

★★★★ 84% ◎◎ HOTEL

Macdonald Compleat Angler

MACDONALD HOTELS & RESORTS

Marlow Bridge SL7 1RG

☎ 0844 879 9128 & 01628 484444 📠 01628 486388

e-mail: compleatangler@macdonald-hotels.co.uk

web: www.macdonald-hotels.co.uk

Dir: *M4 junct 8/9, A404(M) to rdbt, Bisham exit, 1m to Marlow Bridge, hotel on right*

PETS: Bedrooms (6GF) unattended sign **Stables** nearby (3m) **Charges** £10 per night charge for damage **Grounds** accessible **Exercise area** 400mtrs **Facilities** dog chews cage storage walks info vet info **On Request** fridge access

This well-established hotel enjoys an idyllic location overlooking the River Thames and the delightful Marlow weir. The bedrooms, which differ in size and style, are all individually decorated and are equipped with flat screen TVs, high speed internet and air conditioning. Bowaters Restaurant offers modern dishes and has a terrace for dining alfresco when the weather permits. Staff throughout are keen to please and nothing is too much trouble.

Rooms 64 en suite (6 GF) D £180-£280 (incl. bkfst) **Facilities** STV Fishing Wi-fi in bedrooms Fly and course fishing River trips (Apr-Sep) Xmas New Year **Services** Lift **Parking** 100 **Notes LB**

MILTON KEYNES MAP 04 SP83

★★★ 73% HOTEL

Novotel Milton Keynes

Saxon St, Layburn Court, Heelands MK13 7RA
☎ 01908 322212 01908 322235
e-mail: H3272@accor-hotels.com
web: www.novotel.com

Dir: *M1 junct 14, follow Childsway signs towards city centre. Right into Saxon Way, straight across all rdbts, hotel on left*

PETS: Bedrooms (40GF) **Charges** £10 per night **Grounds** accessible on leads disp bin **Exercise area** 50mtrs **Facilities** vet info

Contemporary in style, this purpose-built hotel is situated on the outskirts of the town, just a few minutes' drive from the centre and mainline railway station. Bedrooms provide ample workspace and a good range of facilities for the modern traveller, and public rooms include a children's play area and indoor leisure centre.

Rooms 124 en suite (40 fmly) (40 GF) **Facilities** Gym Steam bath **Services** Lift **Parking** 130 **Notes** LB

★★★ 67% HOTEL

Swan Revived

THE INDEPENDENTS HOTEL ASSOCIATION

High St, Newport Pagnell MK16 8AR
☎ 01908 610565 01908 210995
e-mail: info@swanrevived.co.uk
web: www.swanrevived.co.uk

Dir: *M1 junct 14 onto A509 then B526 into Newport Pagnell for 2m. Hotel on High St*

PETS: Bedrooms (2GF) unattended **Charges** charge for damage **Public areas** except restaurant **Exercise area** 2 min walk **Facilities** water bowl walks info vet info **On Request** fridge access

Once a coaching inn and dating from the 17th century, this hotel occupies a prime location in the centre of town. Well-appointed bedrooms are mostly spacious, individually styled and have good levels of comfort. Public areas include a popular bar and a restaurant offering a variety of freshly prepared dishes.

Rooms 41 en suite (2 fmly) (2 GF) S fr £58; D fr £78 (incl. bkfst)✳ **Facilities** STV Wi-fi available ♫ **Services** Lift **Parking** 51 **Notes** LB RS 25 Dec-1 Jan

U

Holiday Inn Milton Keynes

500 Saxon Gate West MK9 2HQ
☎ 01908 698541 01908 698685
e-mail: reservations-miltonkeynes@ihg.com
web: www.holidayinn.co.uk

Dir: *M1 junct 14. Straight on at 7 rdbts. At 8th (Saxon South) turn right. Hotel after lights on left*

PETS: Bedrooms sign **Charges** £10 per night charge for damage **Exercise area Facilities** cage storage walks info vet info **On Request** fridge access torch towels **Restrictions** no Great Danes or similar size; no Rottweilers

At the time of going to press the rating for this establishment was not confirmed. This may be due to a change of ownership or because it has only recently joined the AA rating scheme. For further details please see the AA website: www.theAA.com

Rooms 166 en suite (17 fmly) S £49-£191; D £49-£191 (incl. bkfst)✳ **Facilities** Gym Wi-fi available ♫ **Services** Lift air con **Parking** 85 (charged) **Notes** LB

BUDGET HOTEL

Campanile Milton Keynes

Campanile HOTEL RESTAURANT

40 Penn Rd - off Watling St, Fenny Stratford, Bletchley MK2 2AU
☎ 01908 649819 01908 649818
e-mail: miltonkeynes@campanile.com
web: www.envergure.fr

Dir: *M1 junct 14, follow A4146 to A5. Southbound on A5. 4th exit at 1st rdbt to Fenny Stratford. Hotel 500yds on left*

PETS: Bedrooms Charges £5 per night **Public areas Exercise area** canal walk nearby **Other** Please telephone for further details

This modern building offers accommodation in smart, well-equipped bedrooms, all with en suite bathrooms. Refreshments may be taken at the informal Bistro.

Rooms 80 en suite

ENGLAND

NEWPORT PAGNELL MOTORWAY SERVICE AREA (M1) MAP 04 SP84

BUDGET HOTEL

Welcome Lodge Milton Keynes

WELCOMELODGE

Newport Pagnell MK16 8DS

☎ 01908 610878 01908 216539

e-mail: newport.hotel@welcomebreak.co.uk

web: www.welcomebreak.co.uk

Dir: *M1 junct 14-15. In service area - follow signs to Barrier Lodge*

PETS: Bedrooms unattended **Grounds** accessible **Exercise area Facilities** walks info vet info

This modern building offers accommodation in smart, spacious and well-equipped bedrooms, suitable for families and business travellers, and all with en suite bathrooms. Refreshments may be taken at the nearby family restaurant.

Rooms 90 en suite S £39-£59; D £49-£69*

TAPLOW MAP 04 SU98

★★★★★ COUNTRY HOUSE HOTEL

Cliveden Country House Hotel

von Essen hotels A PRIVATE COLLECTION www.vonessenhotels.com

SL6 0JF

☎ 01628 668561 01628 661837

e-mail: reservations@clivedenhouse.co.uk

web: www.vonessenhotels.co.uk

Dir: *M4 junct 7, follow A4 towards Maidenhead for 1.5m, turn onto B476 towards Taplow, 2.5m, hotel on left*

PETS: Bedrooms (8GF) unattended **Stables** nearby (2m) **Charges** charge for damage **Public areas** except restaurants (on leads) **Grounds** accessible on leads disp bin **Exercise area** on site woodland walk **Facilities** food (pre-bookable) food bowl water bowl bedding pet sitting dog walking washing facs cage storage walks info vet info **On Request** fridge access **Other** charge for pet food

This wonderful stately home stands at the top of a gravelled boulevard. Visitors are treated as house-guests and staff recapture the tradition of fine hospitality. Bedrooms have individual quality and style, and reception rooms retain a timeless elegance. There are two restaurants - at the time of going to press the rosette award for Waldo's was suspended due to a change of chef. Please see the AA website, www.theAA.com, for up-to-date details. The Terrace, with its wonderful views, has two rosettes. Exceptional leisure facilities include cruises along Cliveden Reach and massages in the Pavilion.

Rooms 39 en suite (8 GF) **Facilities** Squash Gym Wi-fi available Full range of beauty treatments, 3 vintage launches **Services** Lift **Parking** 60 **Notes** LB

CAMBRIDGESHIRE

BURWELL MAP 05 TL56

►►► Stanford Park *(TL578675)*

Weirs Drove CB25 0BP

☎ 01638 741547 & 07802 439997

e-mail: enquiries@stanfordcaravanpark.co.uk

web: www.stanfordcaravanpark.co.uk

Dir: *Signed from B1102*

PETS: disp bin **Exercise area** on site

Open all year Last arrival 20.00hrs Last departure 11.00hrs

A secluded site on the outskirts of Burwell set in four large fields with several attractive trees. The amenities are modern and well kept, and there are eight hardstandings hedged with privet. A 20-acre site with 100 touring pitches, 20 hardstandings.

Notes No group bookings

CAMBRIDGE MAP 05 TL45

★★★★ 81% HOTEL

Hotel Felix

Whitehouse Ln CB3 0LX

☎ 01223 277977 01223 277973

e-mail: help@hotelfelix.co.uk

web: www.hotelfelix.co.uk

Dir: *N on A1307, right at The Travellers Rest*

PETS: Bedrooms unattended **Charges** charge for damage **Grounds** accessible on leads **Exercise area** field behind hotel **Facilities** cage storage walks info vet info **On Request** fridge access **Other** Please telephone for details

A beautiful Victorian mansion set amidst three acres of landscaped gardens, this property was originally built in 1852 for a surgeon from the famous Addenbrookes Hospital. The contemporary-style bedrooms have carefully chosen furniture and many thoughtful touches, whilst public rooms feature an open-plan bar, the adjacent Graffiti restaurant and a small quiet lounge.

Rooms 52 en suite (5 fmly) (26 GF) S £145-£199; D £180-£290 (incl. bkfst)* **Facilities** STV Wi-fi in bedrooms Xmas New Year **Services** Lift **Parking** 90 **Notes** LB

ENGLAND

★★★★ TOWN HOUSE HOTEL

Hotel du Vin Cambridge

15-19 Trumpington St CB2 1QA

☎ 01223 227330 01223 227331

e-mail: info.cambridge@hotelduvin.com

web: www.hotelduvin.com

Dir: *M11 junct 11 Cambridge S, pass Trumpington Park & Ride on left. Hotel 2m on right after double rdbt*

PETS: Bedrooms (6GF) unattended **Stables** nearby (5m) **Charges** £10 per stay per night charge for damage **Public areas** reception & lobby only (on leads) **Exercise area** 500mtrs **Facilities** food bowl water bowl bedding feeding mat cage storage walks info vet info **On Request** fridge access torch

This beautiful building, which dates back in part to medieval times, has been transformed to enhance its many quirky architectural features. The bedrooms and suites, some with private terraces, have the company's trademark monsoon showers and Egyptian linen. The French-style bistro has an open-style kitchen and the bar is be set in the unusual labyrinth of vaulted cellar rooms. There is also be a library, specialist wine tasting room and private dining room.

Rooms 38 en suite 3 annexe en suite (6 GF) D £140-£400* **Facilities** STV Wi-fi in bedrooms Xmas New Year **Services** Lift air con **Parking** 24 (charged)

★★★★ 73% HOTEL

De Vere University Arms

Regent St CB2 1AD

☎ 01223 273000 01223 273037

e-mail: dua.sales@devere-hotels.com

web: www.devere.co.uk

Dir: *M11 junct 11, follow city centre signs for 3m. Right at 2nd mini rdbt, left at lights into Regent St. Hotel 600yds on right*

PETS: Bedrooms Charges charge for damage **Public areas** except restaurant & bar (muzzled or on leads) **Exercise area** nearby **Facilities** food (pre-bookable) food bowl water bowl cage storage walks info vet info **On Request** torch towels **Restrictions** no more than 30kg; no Rottweilers, American Bulldogs or dangerous breeds (see page 7)

Built in 1834, the University Arms has an enviable position in the very heart of the city, overlooking Parker's Piece. Public rooms include an elegant domed lounge, a smart restaurant, a bar and lounge overlooking the park. Conference and banqueting rooms are extensive, many with oak panelling. Given the hotel's central location parking for guests is a bonus.

Rooms 120 en suite (2 fmly) **Facilities** Wi-fi available Reduced rate at local fitness centre **Services** Lift **Parking** 56

★★★ 79% HOTEL

Best Western The Gonville Hotel

Gonville Place CB1 1LY

☎ 01223 366611 & 221111 01223 315470

e-mail: all@gonvillehotel.co.uk

web: www.bw-gonvillehotel.co.uk

Dir: *M11 junct 11, on A1309 follow city centre signs. At 2nd mini rdbt right into Lensfield Rd, over junct with lights. Hotel 25yds on right*

PETS: Bedrooms (5GF) **Charges** charge for damage **Grounds** accessible on leads **Exercise area** adjacent **Facilities** vet info

A well established hotel situated on the inner ring road, a short walk across the green from the city centre. The air-conditioned public areas are cheerfully furnished, and include a lounge bar and brasserie; bedrooms are well appointed and appealing, offering a good range of facilities for both corporate and leisure guests.

Rooms 73 en suite (1 fmly) (5 GF) S £89-£140; D £99-£170* **Facilities** FTV Wi-fi available New Year **Services** Lift **Parking** 80 **Notes** LB RS 24-29 Dec

★★★ 78% HOTEL

Royal Cambridge

Trumpington St CB2 1PY

☎ 01223 351631 01223 352972

e-mail: royal.cambridge@forestdale.com

web: www.forestdale.com

Dir: *M11 junct 11, signed city centre. 1st mini rdbt left into Fen Causeway. Hotel 1st right*

PETS: Bedrooms sign **Charges** £7.50 per night **Public areas** except restaurant (on leads) **Exercise area Facilities** food food bowl water bowl cage storage walks info vet info

This elegant Georgian hotel is situated in the heart of Cambridge. The bedrooms are well equipped and provide great comfort. The stylish restaurant and bar are a popular choice with locals and guests alike. Complimentary parking proves a real benefit in the city centre.

Rooms 57 en suite (9 fmly) S £115-£129; D £145-£159 (incl. bkfst)* **Facilities** Wi-fi available Xmas New Year **Services** Lift **Parking** 80 **Notes** LB

CAMBRIDGE CONTINUED

►►► Cambridge Camping & Caravanning Club Site *(TL455539)*

19 Cabbage Moor, Great Shelford CB2 5NB

☎ 01223 841185

web: www.thefriendlyclub.co.uk

Dir: *M11 junct 11 onto A1309 signed Cambridge. At 1st lights turn right. After 0.5m follow site sign on left*

PETS: Public areas except in buildings disp bin **Exercise area** on site **Facilities** walks info vet info **Other** prior notice required

Open 2 Apr-2 Nov Last arrival 21.00hrs Last departure noon

A popular, open site close to Cambridge and the M11, surrounded by high hedging and trees, with well-maintained toilet facilities. The large rally field is well used. An 11-acre site with 120 touring pitches.

Notes Site gates closed 23.00hrs-07.00hrs

ELY MAP 05 TL58

★★★ GUEST HOUSE

Castle Lodge

50 New Barns Rd CB7 4PW

☎ 01353 662276 🖷 01353 666606

e-mail: castlelodgehotel@supanet.com

Dir: *Off B1382 Prickwillow Rd NE from town centre*

PETS: Bedrooms unattended **Charges** £5 per stay per night **Public areas** except restaurant (on leads) **Exercise area** field nearby **Facilities** food (pre-bookable) food bowl water bowl pet sitting dog walking cage storage walks info vet info **On Request** fridge access

Located within easy walking distance of the cathedral, this extended Victorian house offers well-equipped bedrooms in a variety of sizes. Public areas include a traditionally furnished dining room and a comfortable air-conditioned bar lounge. Service is friendly and helpful.

Rooms 11 rms (6 en suite) (3 fmly) S £32.50-£55; D fr £75* **Facilities** TVB tea/coffee Direct dial from bedrooms Licensed Cen ht TVL Dinner Last d 9pm **Parking** 6 **Notes** No coaches

HUNTINGDON MAP 04 TL27

★★★★ 75% HOTEL

Huntingdon Marriott Hotel

Marriott HOTELS & RESORTS

Kingfisher Way, Hinchingbrooke Business Park PE29 6FL

☎ 01480 446000 🖷 01480 451111

e-mail: mhrs.cbghd.front.office@marriotthotels.com

web: www.marriott.co.uk

Dir: *on A14, 1m from Huntington centre close to Brampton racecourse*

PETS: Bedrooms (45GF) unattended sign **Stables** nearby **Charges** charge for damage **Grounds** accessible **Exercise area** park nearby **Facilities** walks info vet info **On Request** torch towels

With its excellent road links, this modern, purpose-built hotel is a popular venue for conferences and business meetings, and is convenient for Huntingdon, Cambridge and racing at Newmarket. Bedrooms are spacious and offer every modern comfort, including air conditioning. The leisure facilities are also impressive.

Rooms 150 en suite (5 fmly) (45 GF) S £124-£134; D £134-£144* **Facilities** supervised Gym Wi-fi available Sauna Steam room Xmas New Year **Services** Lift air con **Parking** 200 **Notes** LB

►►► Huntingdon Boathaven & Caravan Park *(TL249706)*

The Avenue, Godmanchester PE29 2AF

☎ 01480 411977 🖷 01480 411977

e-mail: boathaven.hunts@virgin.net

web: www.huntingdonboathaven.co.uk

Dir: *S of town. Exit A14 at Godmanchester junct, through Godmanchester on B1043 to site (on left by River Ouse)*

PETS: Public areas except shower block **Exercise area** on site area set aside from site **Facilities** vet info **Other** prior notice required

Open all year open in winter when weather permits Last arrival 21.00hrs

A small, well laid out site overlooking a boat marina and the River Ouse, set close to the A14 and within walking distance of Huntingdon town centre. Clean, well kept toilets. A pretty area has been created for tents beside the marina, with wide views across the Ouse Valley. Weekend family activities are organized throughout the season. A 2-acre site with 24 touring pitches, 18 hardstandings.

Notes no cars by tents

►►► The Willows Caravan Park *(TL224708)*

Bromholme Ln, Brampton PE28 4NE

☎ 01480 437566

e-mail: willows@willows33.freeserve.co.uk

web: www.willowscaravanpark.com

Dir: *Exit A14/A1 signed Brampton, follow Huntingdon signs. Site on right close to Brampton Mill pub*

PETS: Charges 1st dog free, 50p per extra dog per night, £3 per extra dog per week **Public areas** except playground & amenities block (on leads) **Exercise area** adjacent **Facilities** washing facs walks info vet info **Other** prior notice required **Restrictions** no Rottweilers, Pit Bull or Staffordshire Terriers, German Shepherds or Dobermans **Resident Pets:** cat

Open all year (rs Nov-Feb 10 pitches only plus 6 storage spaces) Last arrival 22.00hrs Last departure noon

A small, friendly site in a pleasant setting beside the River Ouse, on the Ouse Valley Walk. Bay areas have been provided for caravans and motorhomes, and planting for screening is gradually maturing. There are launching facilities and free river fishing. A 4-acre site with 50 touring pitches.

Notes ⊜ No cars by tents. Dogs must be on leads, ball games on field provided, no generators, one-way system 5mph, no groundsheets.

PETERBOROUGH — MAP 04 TL19

★★★ 77% ❁ HOTEL

Best Western Orton Hall

Orton Longueville PE2 7DN

☎ 01733 391111 🖷 01733 231912

e-mail: reception@ortonhall.co.uk

Dir: *off A605 E opposite Orton Mere*

PETS: Bedrooms (15GF) **Charges** £15 per night charge for damage **Public areas** except restaurants (on leads) **Grounds** accessible **Exercise area** on site **Facilities** water bowl **On Request** towels

An impressive country-house hotel, set in 20 acres of woodland on the outskirts of town, that has undergone extensive improvements. The building work is due for completion in June 2008 when the swimming pool and leisure facilities will be finished. The spacious and relaxing public areas have many original features that include The Great Room and 17th-century oak panelling in the Huntly Restaurant. The Ramblewood Inn is an alternative, informal dining and bar option.

Rooms 72 en suite (2 fmly) (15 GF) S £70-£120; D £80-£160* **Facilities** STV ⓢ Gym Wi-fi available Sauna Steam room Xmas New Year **Parking** 200 **Notes** LB

BUDGET HOTEL

Travelodge Peterborough Alwalton

Great North Rd, Alwalton PE7 3UR

☎ 08719 846 003 🖷 01733 231109

web: www.travelodge.co.uk

Dir: *on A1, southbound*

PETS: Bedrooms Charges £10 per night **Grounds** accessible on leads disp bin **Exercise area** 1700yds

Travelodge offers good quality, good value, modern accommodation. Ideal for families, the spacious en suite bedrooms include remote control TV, tea and coffee-making facilities and comfortable beds. Meals can be taken at the nearby family restaurant.

Rooms 32 en suite S fr £29; D fr £29

ST NEOTS — MAP 04 TL16

►►► St Neots Camping & Caravanning Club Site *(TL182598)*

Hardwick Rd, Eynesbury PE19 2PR

☎ 01480 474404

web: www.thefriendlyclub.co.uk

Dir: *From A1 take A428 to Cambridge, 2nd rdbt left to Tesco's, past Sports Centre. Follow International Camping signs to site*

PETS: Public areas except in buildings disp bin **Exercise area** adjacent areas **Facilities** walks info vet info **Other** prior notice required

Open 2 Apr-2 Nov Last arrival 21.00hrs Last departure noon

A level meadowland site adjacent to the River Ouse on the outskirts of St Neots, with well maintained and modern facilities, and helpful, attentive staff. An 11-acre site with 180 touring pitches, 33 hardstandings.

Notes Site gates closed 23.00hrs-07.00hrs

SIX MILE BOTTOM — MAP 05 TL55

★★★ 82% HOTEL

Swynford Paddocks

CB8 0UE

☎ 01638 570234 01638 570283

e-mail: info@swynfordpaddocks.com

web: www.swynfordpaddocks.com

Dir: *M11 junct 9, take A11 towards Newmarket, then onto A1304 to Newmarket, hotel 0.75m on left*

PETS: Bedrooms unattended **Charges** £15 per night charge for damage **Public areas** except restaurant **Grounds** accessible **Exercise area** on site 2 acres of garden

This smart country house is set in attractive grounds, within easy reach of Newmarket. Bedrooms are comfortably appointed, thoughtfully equipped and include some delightful four-poster rooms. Imaginative, carefully prepared food is served in the elegant restaurant; service is friendly and attentive. Meeting and conference facilities are available.

Rooms 15 en suite (1 fmly) S £75-£165; D £75-£205 (incl. bkfst & dinner)✻ **Facilities** STV Wi-fi in bedrooms **Parking** 100 **Notes LB**

WISBECH — MAP 05 TF40

►►► Little Ranch Leisure *(TF456062)*

Begdale, Elm PE14 0AZ

☎ 01945 860066 01945 860114

web: www.littleranchleisure.co.uk

Dir: *From rdbt on A47 (SW of Wisbech) take Redmoor Lane to Begdale*

PETS: Charges £1 per night disp bin **Exercise area** on site 10-acre orchard **Facilities** washing facs vet info

Open all year

A friendly family site set in an apple orchard, with 25 fully-serviced pitches and a beautifully designed, spacious toilet block. The site overlooks a large fishing lake, and the famous horticultural auctions at Wisbech are nearby. A 10-acre site with 25 touring pitches, 25 hardstandings.

Notes

CHESHIRE

AUDLEM — MAP 07 SJ64

★★★★ FARM HOUSE

Little Heath Farm *(SJ663455)*

CW3 0HE

☎ 01270 811324 Mrs H M Bennion

e-mail: hilaryandbob@ukonline.co.uk

Dir: *Off A525 in village onto A529 towards Nantwich for 0.3m. Farm opposite village green*

PETS: Bedrooms Charges £5 per night **Grounds** accessible on leads disp bin **Exercise area** on site on farm **Facilities** water bowl walks info vet info **On Request** fridge access torch

The 200-year-old brick farmhouse retains much original character, including low beamed ceilings. The traditionally furnished public areas include a cosy sitting room and a dining room where guests dine family style. The refurbished bedrooms are stylish, and the friendly proprietors create a relaxing atmosphere.

Rooms 3 en suite (1 fmly) S £30-£45; D £50-£65 **Facilities** TVB tea/coffee Cen ht TVL **Parking** 6 **Notes LB** 50 acres mixed Closed Xmas & New Year

BURWARDSLEY — MAP 07 SJ55

★★ 81% HOTEL

Pheasant Inn

Higher Burwardsley CH3 9PF

☎ 01829 770434 01829 771097

e-mail: info@thepheasantinn.co.uk

web: www.thepheasantinn.co.uk

Dir: *from A41, left to Tattenhall, right at 1st junct and left at 2nd to Higher Burwardsley. At post office left, hotel signed*

PETS: Bedrooms unattended **Public areas** at manager's discretion (on leads) **Grounds** accessible on leads **Exercise area** surrounding countryside **Facilities** water bowl washing facs cage storage walks info vet info **On Request** fridge access torch towels

This delightful 300-year-old inn sits high on the Peckforton Hills and enjoys spectacular views over the Cheshire Plain. Well-equipped, comfortable bedrooms are housed in an adjacent converted barn. Creative dishes are served either in the stylish restaurant or in the traditional, beamed bar. Real fires are lit in the winter months.

Rooms 2 en suite 10 annexe en suite (2 fmly) (5 GF) S £65-£95; D £85-£130 (incl. bkfst)✻ **Facilities** FTV Wi-fi in bedrooms **Parking** 80

CHESTER MAP 07 SJ46

★★★★ GUEST ACCOMMODATION

Hamilton Court

5-7 Hamilton St CH2 3JG

☎ 01244 345387 📠 01244 317404

e-mail: hamiltoncourth@aol.com

Dir: *From town centre, All Saints church on left, 2nd turning on left*

PETS: Bedrooms (1GF) **Charges** charge for damage **Exercise area** 500yds **Facilities** feeding mat cage storage walks info vet info **On Request** fridge access torch towels

Hamilton Court is a family run establishment, only 10 minutes walk from the city centre. All bedrooms are en suite and have useful facilities. Children are welcome and pets can be accommodated by arrangement.

Rooms 11 en suite (4 fmly) (1 GF) S £35-£45; D £65-£75* **Facilities** FTV TVB tea/coffee Cen ht Wi-fi available **Parking** 4 **Notes** Closed 24 Dec-3 Jan

DELAMERE MAP 07 SJ56

►►► Delamere Forest Camping & Caravanning Club Site *(SJ555704)*

Station Rd CW8 2HZ

☎ 01606 889231

web: www.thefriendlyclub.co.uk

Dir: *M56 junct 12 take B5152 towards Frodsham. Site on left before rail station*

PETS: Exercise area Facilities on site shop washing facs walks info vet info **Other** prior notice required

Open all year Last arrival 21.00hrs Last departure noon

This park is adjacent to Delemere Forest, with its miles of walking and cycling trails, and well-placed for visiting Chester. Excellent toilet facilities in a purpose-built, wood-clad block, spacious pitches and attractive landscaping and planting are some of the desirable features here. A 6-acre site with 80 touring pitches, 45 hardstandings.

Notes Site gates closed 23.00hrs-07.00hrs

DISLEY MAP 07 SJ98

★★★ 72% HOTEL

Best Western Moorside Grange Hotel & Spa

Best Western

Mudhurst Ln, Higher Disley SK12 2AP

☎ 01663 764151 📠 01663 762794

e-mail: sales@moorsidegrangehotel.com

web: www.moorsidegrangehotel.com

Dir: *Leave A6 at Rams Head, Disley continue along Buxton Old Rd for 1m, turn right onto Mudhurst Lane, hotel on left*

PETS: Bedrooms unattended **Stables** nearby (3m) **Charges** £10 per night £70 per week charge for damage **Public areas** (on leads) **Grounds** accessible disp bin **Exercise area Facilities** water bowl dog scoop/disp bags walks info vet info **On Request** fridge access torch towels

Spectacular views of the moors above Higher Disley are one of the attractions of this large complex. The hotel has excellent conference and function facilities, a well-equipped leisure centre and two tennis courts in the extensive grounds. Suites, and bedrooms with four-poster beds, are available.

Rooms 98 en suite (3 fmly) S £49.50-£160; D £49.50-£180* **Facilities** Spa supervised Squash Gym Wi-fi in bedrooms Xmas New Year **Services** Lift **Parking** 250

FRODSHAM MAP 07 SJ57

★★★ 78% HOTEL

Forest Hills Hotel & Leisure Complex

THE INDEPENDENTS HOTEL ASSOCIATION

Overton Hill WA6 6HH

☎ 01928 735255 📠 01928 735517

e-mail: info@foresthillshotel.com

web: www.foresthillshotel.com

Dir: *at Frodsham turn onto B5151. After 1m right into Manley Rd, right into Simons Ln after 0.5m. Hotel 0.5m past Frodsham golf course*

PETS: Bedrooms unattended sign **Stables** nearby (0.25m) **Charges** £5 per night charge for damage **Grounds** accessible on leads disp bin **Exercise area** 40mtrs **Facilities** cage storage walks info vet info **On Request** fridge access

This modern, purpose-built hotel is set high up on Overton Hill with wonderful panoramic views. There is a range of spacious, well-equipped bedrooms, including executive rooms. Guests have a choice of bars and there is a split-level restaurant, conference facilities and a very good leisure suite and gym.

Rooms 58 en suite (4 fmly) S £70-£90; D £100-£120 (incl. bkfst)* **Facilities** Gym Wi-fi in bedrooms Nightclub Dance studio Aerobics/pilates Xmas New Year **Parking** 350 **Notes** LB

GLAZEBROOK MAP 07 SJ69

★★★ 75% HOTEL

Rhinewood Country House

Glazebrook Ln, Glazebrook WA3 5BB

☎ 0161 775 5555 📠 0161 775 7965

e-mail: info@therhinewoodhotel.co.uk

web: www.therhinewoodhotel.co.uk

Dir: *M6 junct 21, A57 towards Irlam. Left at Glazebrook sign, hotel 0.25m on left*

PETS: Bedrooms Charges charge for damage **Grounds** accessible on leads disp bin **Exercise area** 5 min walk **Facilities** cage storage walks info vet info **On Request** torch towels

A warm welcome and attentive service are assured here. This privately owned and personally run hotel stands in spacious grounds and gardens, and is located between Warrington and Manchester. Facilities include conference and function rooms, and the hotel is licensed for civil wedding ceremonies.

Rooms 32 en suite (4 fmly) (16 GF) S £50-£75; D £75-£95 **Facilities** STV Wi-fi in bedrooms Complimentary membership to nearby health spa Xmas **Parking** 120

KNUTSFORD MAP 07 SJ77

★★ 80% HOTEL

The Longview Hotel & Restaurant

55 Manchester Rd WA16 0LX

☎ 01565 632119 📠 01565 652402

e-mail: enquiries@longviewhotel.com

web: www.longviewhotel.com

Dir: *M6 junct 19 take A556 W towards Chester. Left at lights onto A5033, 1.5m to rdbt then left. Hotel 200yds on right*

PETS: Bedrooms (5GF) unattended **Charges** £10 per night charge for damage **Exercise area** 20mtrs **Facilities** vet info **On Request** fridge access torch towels

This friendly Victorian hotel offers high standards of hospitality and service. Attractive public areas include a cellar bar and foyer lounge area. The restaurant has a traditional feel and offers an imaginative selection of dishes. Bedrooms, some located in a superb renovation of nearby houses, are individually styled and offer a good range of thoughtful amenities, including broadband internet access.

Rooms 13 en suite 19 annexe en suite (1 fmly) (5 GF) S £62-£89; D £85-£118 (incl. bkfst)* **Facilities** Wi-fi in bedrooms **Parking** 20 **Notes** Closed Xmas

LYMM MAP 07 SJ68

★★★ 73% HOTEL

The Lymm Hotel

Whitbarrow Rd WA13 9AQ

☎ 01925 752233 📠 01925 756035

e-mail: general.lymm@macdonald-hotels.co.uk

web: www.macdonald-hotels.co.uk

Dir: *M6 junct 20, B5158 to Lymm. Left at junct, 1st right, left at mini-rdbt, into Brookfield Rd, 3rd left into Whitbarrow Rd*

PETS: Bedrooms (11GF) **Charges** £20 per night charge for damage **Grounds** accessible on leads **Exercise area Facilities** walks info vet info

In a peaceful residential area, this hotel benefits from both a quiet setting and convenient access to local motorway networks. It offers comfortable bedrooms equipped for both the business and leisure guest. Public areas include an attractive bar and an elegant restaurant. There is also extensive parking.

Rooms 24 en suite 38 annexe en suite (9 fmly) (11 GF) S £60-£110; D £60-£110* **Facilities** STV Wi-fi available Xmas New Year **Parking** 75 **Notes** LB

MACCLESFIELD MAP 07 SJ97

★★★★ 74% HOTEL

Barceló Shrigley Hall Hotel, Golf & Country Club

Shrigley Park, Pott Shrigley SK10 5SB

☎ 01625 575757 📠 01625 573323

e-mail: shrigleyhall@barcelo-hotels.co.uk

web: www.barcelo-hotels.co.uk

Dir: *off A523 at Legh Arms towards Pott Shrigley. Hotel 2m on left before village*

PETS: Bedrooms unattended sign **Stables** nearby (2m) **Charges** £15 per stay per night **Public areas** except dining room (on leads) **Grounds** accessible on leads disp bin **Exercise area** on site **Facilities** cage storage walks info vet info **On Request** torch towels

Originally built in 1825, Shrigley Hall is an impressive hotel set in 262 acres of mature parkland and commands stunning views of the countryside. Features include a championship golf course. There is a wide choice of bedroom size and style. The public areas are spacious, combining traditional and contemporary decor, and include a well-equipped gym.

Rooms 148 en suite (11 fmly) S £75-£165* **Facilities** supervised 18 Fishing Gym Putt green Wi-fi available Beauty salon Hydro centre Xmas New Year **Services** Lift **Parking** 300

►►► Capesthorne Hall *(SJ840727)*

Siddington SK11 9JY

☎ 01625 861221 🖹 01625 861619

e-mail: info@capesthorne.com

web: www.capesthorne.com

Dir: *On A34, 1m S of A537*

PETS: Public areas except gardens, hall & café **Exercise area** on site parkland **Facilities** vet info **Other** prior notice required **Restrictions** no dangerous breeds (see page 7)

Open Mar-Oct Last arrival 16.30hrs Last departure noon

Set in the magnificent grounds of the historic Capesthorpe Hall, with access to the lakes, gardens and woodland walks free to site users. Pitches in the open parkland are spacious and can take the larger motorhomes, and the clean toilet facilities are housed in the old stable block. The beautiful Cheshire countryside is easily explored. No tents or trailer tents. A 5.5-acre site with 30 touring pitches, 5 hardstandings.

Notes

NANTWICH MAP 07 SJ65

★★ 71% HOTEL

Best Western Crown Hotel & Restaurant

High St CW5 5AS

☎ 01270 625283 🖹 01270 628047

e-mail: info@crownhotelnantwich.com

web: www.crownhotelnantwich.com

Dir: *A52 to Nantwich, hotel in centre of town*

PETS: Bedrooms Public areas (on leads) **Exercise area Facilities** cage storage walks info vet info **On Request** fridge access towels **Resident Pets:** Bertie (dog)

Ideally set in the heart of this historic and delightful market town, The Crown has been offering hospitality for centuries. It has an abundance of original features and the well-equipped bedrooms retain an old world charm. There is also a bar with live entertainment throughout the week and diners can enjoy Italian food in the atmospheric brasserie.

Rooms 18 en suite (2 fmly) S £68-£76; D £84-£86* **Facilities** Putt green Wi-fi in bedrooms **Parking** 18 **Notes LB**

RUNCORN MAP 07 SJ58

BUDGET HOTEL

Campanile Runcorn

Lowlands Rd WA7 5TP

☎ 01928 581771 🖹 01928 581730

e-mail: runcorn@campanile.com

web: www.envergure.fr

Dir: *M56 junct 12, take A557, then follow signs for Runcorn rail station/Runcorn College*

PETS: Bedrooms (18GF) **Exercise area** on site grassed area **Other** Please telephone for details

This modern building offers accommodation in smart, well-equipped bedrooms, all with en suite bathrooms. Refreshments may be taken at the informal Bistro.

Rooms 53 en suite

TARPORLEY MAP 07 SJ56

★★★ 78% COUNTRY HOUSE HOTEL

Willington Hall

Willington CW6 0NB

☎ 01829 752321 🖹 01829 752596

e-mail: enquiries@willingtonhall.co.uk

web: www.willingtonhall.co.uk

Dir: *3m NW off unclass road linking A51 & A54, at Clotton turn off A51 at Bulls Head, then follow signs*

PETS: Bedrooms unattended **Stables** nearby (nearby) **Grounds** accessible disp bin **Exercise area Facilities** cage storage walks info vet info **On Request** fridge access torch towels

Situated in 17 acres of parkland and built in 1829, this attractively furnished country-house hotel offers spacious bedrooms, many with views over open countryside. Service is courteous and friendly, and freshly prepared meals are offered in the dining room or in the adjacent bar and drawing room. A smart function suite confirms the popularity of this hotel as a premier venue for weddings and conferences.

Rooms 10 en suite S £80; D £120-£130 (incl. bkfst) **Facilities** STV Fishing Riding New Year **Parking** 60 **Notes LB** Closed 25 & 26 Dec

TARPORLEY CONTINUED

★★★★ FARM HOUSE

Hill House Farm *(SJ583626)*

Rushton CW6 9AU

☎ 01829 732238 01829 733929 Mrs C Rayner

e-mail: aa@hillhousefarm-cheshire.co.uk

web: www.hillhousefarm-cheshire.co.uk

Dir: *1.5m E of Tarporley. Off A51/A49 to Eaton, take Lower Ln, continue E for Rushton, right onto The Hall Ln, farm 0.5m*

PETS: Bedrooms Stables on site **Charges** please call for details per night **Public areas** if well behaved **Grounds** accessible disp bin **Exercise area** on site **Facilities** food bowl water bowl bedding dog chews feeding mat leads washing facs cage storage walks info vet info **On Request** fridge access torch towels **Resident Pets:** Ruby & Milly (Springer Spaniels), Bridie & Lexi (Labradors), Mavis (Patterdale Terrier), Grommit (cat), horses

This impressive brick farmhouse stands in very attractive gardens within 14 acres of rolling pastureland. The stylish bedrooms have en suite facilities, and there is a spacious lounge and a traditionally furnished breakfast room. Catherine Rayner was a finalist for the AA Friendliest Landlady of the Year 2008 Award.

Rooms 3 en suite 1 annexe en suite (1 fmly) S £45-£60; D £75-£95* **Facilities** TVB tea/coffee Cen ht TVL Wi-fi available **Parking** 6 **Notes LB** 14 acres non-working Closed Xmas & New Year

---

WARRINGTON MAP 07 SJ68

★★★★ 77% HOTEL

The Park Royal Hotel

QHOTELS

Stretton Rd, Stretton WA4 4NS

☎ 01925 730706 01925 730740

e-mail: parkroyalreservations@qhotels.co.uk

web: www.qhotels.co.uk

Dir: *M56 junct 10, A49 to Warrington, at lights turn right to Appleton Thorn, hotel 200yds on right*

PETS: Bedrooms (34GF) **Stables** nearby (2m) **Charges** £10 per stay per night charge for damage **Grounds** accessible on leads **Exercise area Facilities** walks info vet info **On Request** torch **Restrictions** small dogs only

This modern hotel enjoys a peaceful setting, yet is conveniently located just minutes from the M56. The bedrooms are modern in style and thoughtfully equipped. Spacious, stylish public areas include extensive conference and function facilities, and a comprehensive leisure centre complete with outdoor tennis courts and an impressive beauty centre.

Rooms 146 en suite (2 fmly) (34 GF) S £75-£149; D £85-£159 (incl. bkfst)* **Facilities Spa** STV Gym Wi-fi available Dance studio Xmas New Year **Services** Lift **Parking** 400 **Notes LB**

★★ 74% HOTEL

Paddington House

514 Old Manchester Rd WA1 3TZ

☎ 01925 816767 01925 816651

e-mail: hotel@paddingtonhouse.co.uk

web: www.paddingtonhouse.co.uk

Dir: *1m from M6 junct 21, off A57, 2m from town centre*

PETS: Bedrooms (6GF) unattended **Charges** £5 per night charge for damage **Grounds** accessible on leads disp bin **Exercise area Facilities** water bowl vet info **On Request** fridge access towels **Restrictions** no large dogs

This busy, friendly hotel is conveniently situated just over a mile from the M6. Bedrooms are attractively furnished, and include four-poster and ground-floor rooms. Guests can dine in the wood-panelled Padgate Restaurant or in the cosy bar. Conference and function facilities are available.

Rooms 37 en suite (9 fmly) (6 GF) S £45-£65; D £50-£75 (incl. bkfst) **Facilities** FTV Wi-fi in bedrooms New Year **Services** Lift **Parking** 50 **Notes LB**

BUDGET HOTEL

Travelodge Warrington

Travelodge

Kendrick/Leigh St WA1 1UZ

☎ 0871 984 6180 01925 639432

web: www.travelodge.co.uk

Dir: *M6 junct 21, follow A57 towards Liverpool & Widnes to Warrington town centre, through Asda rdbt, lodge next left at lights*

PETS: Bedrooms unattended **Charges** £10 per stay per night **Public areas Grounds** accessible **Exercise area** park over road **Facilities** cage storage walks info vet info **On Request** fridge access towels **Other** cats must be in cages

Travelodge offers good quality, good value, modern accommodation. Ideal for families, the spacious en suite bedrooms include remote-control TV, tea and coffee-making facilities and comfortable beds. Meals can be taken at the nearby family restaurant.

Rooms 63 en suite S fr £29; D fr £29

WYBUNBURY MAP 07 SJ64

★★★ FARM HOUSE

Lea Farm *(SJ717489)*

Wrinehill Rd CW5 7NS

☎ 01270 841429 Mrs J E Callwood

e-mail: leafarm@hotmail.co.uk

Dir: *1m E of Wybunbury village church on unclassified road*

PETS: Bedrooms Sep Accom outdoor kennel, barns **Stables** on site **Charges** £2 per night charge for damage **Grounds** accessible on leads disp bin **Exercise area** adjacent **Facilities** food bowl water bowl bedding washing facs cage storage walks info vet info **On Request** fridge access torch towels **Resident Pets:** Lucy (Collie)

This working dairy farm is surrounded by delightful gardens and beautiful Cheshire countryside. The spacious bedrooms have modern facilities and there is a cosy lounge. Hearty breakfasts are served in the attractive dining room, which looks out over the garden, with its resident peacocks.

Rooms 3 rms (2 en suite) (1 fmly) S £29-£35; D £48-£56 **Facilities** TVB tea/coffee Cen ht TVL Fishing Pool Table **Parking** 24 **Notes** 150 acres Dairy & beef

CORNWALL & ISLES OF SCILLY

ASHTON MAP 02 SW62

►►► Boscrege Caravan & Camping Park

(SW595305)

TR13 9TG

☎ 01736 762231

e-mail: enquiries@caravanparkcornwall.com

web: www.caravanparkcornwall.com

Dir: *From Helston on A394 turn right at Ashton next to Post Office. 1.5m along lane signed Boscrege Caravan & Camping Park*

PETS: disp bin **Exercise area** on site 6-acre meadow **Facilities** washing facs walks info vet info **Other** prior notice required

Open Mar-Nov Last arrival 22.00hrs Last departure 11.00hrs

A quiet and bright little touring park divided into small paddocks with hedges, and offering plenty of open spaces for children to play in. The family-owned park offers clean, well-painted toilets facilities and neatly trimmed grass. In an Area of Outstanding Natural Beauty at the foot of Tregonning Hill. A 12-acre site with 50 touring pitches and 26 statics.

BLACKWATER MAP 02 SW74

►►► Chiverton Park *(SW743468)*

East Hill TR4 8HS

☎ 01872 560667 📠 01872 560667

e-mail: chivertonpark@btopenworld.com

web: www.chivertonpark.co.uk

Dir: *Exit A30 at Chiverton rdbt (Little Chef) onto unclass road signed Blackwater (3rd exit). 1st right & site 300mtrs on right*

PETS: Charges £2.15 per night £15 per week disp bin **Exercise area Facilities** on site shop walks info vet info **Other** prior notice required **Resident Pets:** Tolley (German Long-haired Pointer), Grogley (Golden Retriever)

Open 3 Mar-3 Nov (rs Mar-May & mid Sep-Nov limited stock kept in shop) Last arrival 21.00hrs Last departure noon

A small, well-maintained site with some mature hedges dividing pitches, sited midway between Truro and St Agnes. Facilities include a good toilet block and a steam room, sauna and gym. A games room with pool table, and children's outside play equipment prove popular with families. A 4-acre site with 12 touring pitches, 10 hardstandings and 50 statics.

Notes No ball games

ENGLAND

BODMIN MAP 02 SX06

►►► Bodmin Camping & Caravanning Club Site *(SX081676)*

Old Callywith Rd PL31 2DZ

☎ 01208 73834

web: www.thefriendlyclub.co.uk

Dir: *A30 from N, at sign for Bodmin turn right crossing dual carriageway in front of industrial estate, turn left at international sign, site left*

PETS: Public areas except in buildings & children's park disp bin **Exercise area** on site small area on site **Facilities** walks info vet info **Other** prior notice required

Open 2 Apr-2 Nov Last arrival 21.00hrs Last departure noon

Undulating grassy site with trees and bushes set in meadowland close to the town of Bodmin with all its attractions. The site is close to the A30 and makes a very good touring base. An 11-acre site with 130 touring pitches, 12 hardstandings.

Notes Site gates closed 23.00hrs-07.00hrs

BOSCASTLE MAP 02 SX09

★★★★ GUEST ACCOMMODATION

Old Coach House

Tintagel Rd PL35 0AS

☎ 01840 250398 🖹 01840 250346

e-mail: stay@old-coach.co.uk

web: www.old-coach.co.uk

Dir: *In village at junct B3266 & B3263. 150yds from petrol station towards Tintagel*

PETS: Bedrooms (2GF) **Charges** £5 per stay per night charge for damage **Grounds** accessible disp bin **Exercise area** 250mtrs **Facilities** walks info vet info **Resident Pets:** Pearl (Whippet), Finn (Border Collie), Smirnoff (cat)

Over 300 years old, the Old Coach House has lovely views over the village and the rolling countryside. The comfortable bedrooms are well equipped and include two rooms on the ground floor. A hearty breakfast is served in the conservatory, which overlooks the well-kept garden.

Rooms 8 en suite (3 fmly) (2 GF) S £32-£50; D £54-£64✻ **Facilities** TVB tea/coffee Cen ht TVL **Parking** 9 **Notes LB** Closed Xmas

BRYHER (ISLES OF SCILLY) MAP 02 SV81

★★★ ®® HOTEL

Hell Bay

TR23 0PR

☎ 01720 422947 🖹 01720 423004

e-mail: contactus@hellbay.co.uk

web: www.hellbay.co.uk

Dir: *access by helicopter or boat from Penzance, plane from Bristol, Exeter, Newquay, Southampton, Land's End*

PETS: Bedrooms (15GF) unattended **Charges** £12 per night **Grounds** accessible on leads **Exercise area Facilities** food bowl water bowl feeding mat cage storage walks info vet info **On Request** fridge access torch towels **Resident Pets:** Suzie (Springer Spaniel)

Located on the smallest of the inhabited islands of the Scilly Isles on the edge of the Atlantic, this hotel makes a really special destination. The owners have filled the hotel with original works of art by artists who have connections with the islands, and the interior is decorated in cool blues and greens creating an extremely restful environment. The contemporary bedrooms are equally stylish and many have garden access and stunning sea views. Eating here is a delight, and naturally seafood features strongly on the award-winning, daily-changing menus.

Rooms 25 annexe en suite (3 fmly) (15 GF) S £162.50-£600; D £260-£600 (incl. bkfst & dinner)✻ **Facilities** STV ⛱ ⛳7 Gym Wi-fi available Boules **Notes LB** Closed Nov-Feb

BUDE MAP 02 SS20

★★ 74% SMALL HOTEL

Penarvor

Crooklets Beach EX23 8NE

☎ 01288 352036 🖹 01288 355027

e-mail: hotel.penarvor@boltblue.com

Dir: *From A39 towards Bude for 1.5m. At 2nd rdbt right, pass shops. Top of hill, left signed Crooklets Beach*

PETS: Bedrooms Charges £6 per night charge for damage **Public areas** except restaurant (on leads) **Grounds** accessible on leads disp bin **Exercise area Facilities** vet info **On Request** fridge access **Resident Pets:** Bonnie (Old English/ Border Collie cross), Charlie (Cocker Spaniel)

Adjacent to the golf course and overlooking Crooklets Beach, this family owned hotel has a relaxed and friendly atmosphere. Bedrooms vary in size but are all equipped to a similar standard. An interesting selection of dishes, using fresh local produce, is available in the restaurant; bar meals are also provided.

Rooms 16 en suite (6 fmly) **Parking** 20 **Notes LB**

★★★★ GUEST HOUSE

The Cliff at Bude

Maer Down, Crooklets Beach EX23 8NG

☎ 01288 353110 & 356833 🖷 01288 353110

web: www.cliffhotel.co.uk

Dir: *A39 through Bude, left at top of High St, pass Somerfields, 1st right between golf course, over x-rds, premises at end on left*

PETS: Bedrooms (8GF) unattended **Stables** nearby (10 mins) **Charges** £2.50 per night **Grounds** accessible disp bin **Exercise area Facilities** cage storage walks info vet info **On Request** fridge access torch towels **Resident Pets:** Janus & Crystal (Boxers), 13 rabbits

Overlooking the sea from a clifftop location, this friendly and efficient establishment provides spacious, well-equipped bedrooms. The various public areas include a bar and lounge and an impressive range of leisure facilities. Delicious dinners and tasty breakfasts are available in the attractive dining room.

Rooms 15 en suite (15 fmly) (8 GF) S £41.40-£47.40; D £69-£79* **Facilities** TVB tea/coffee Direct dial from bedrooms Licensed Cen ht TVL Dinner Last d 7pm Gymnasium Pool Table **Parking** 18 **Notes LB** No coaches Closed Nov-Mar

►►► Willow Valley Holiday Park *(SS236078)*

Bush EX23 9LB

☎ 01288 353104

e-mail: willowvalley@talk21.com

web: www.willowvalley.co.uk

Dir: *On A39, 0.5m N of junct with A3072 at Stratton*

PETS: Charges £1.50 (Jul-Aug), £1 (Sep-Jun) per night disp bin **Exercise area** on site field available **Facilities** on site shop food vet info **Other** prior notice required

Open Mar-Dec Last arrival 21.00hrs Last departure 11.00hrs

A small sheltered park in Strat Valley with a stream running through and level grassy pitches. The friendly family owners have improved all areas of this attractive park, which has direct access off the A39, and only 2 miles from the sandy beaches at Bude. A 4-acre site with 41 touring pitches and 4 statics.

Notes

CALLINGTON — MAP 02 SX36

★★★ BED & BREAKFAST

The Olive Tree Bed & Breakfast

Maders PL17 7LL

☎ 01579 384392 🖷 01579 384392

e-mail: kindredspirits@blueyonder.co.uk

Dir: *From M5 junct 31 A38 Plymouth A388 Callington through town up hill on left*

PETS: Bedrooms (3GF) **Public areas** except breakfast room at breakfast time **Grounds** accessible disp bin **Exercise area** on site field available **Facilities** water bowl dog scoop/disp bags leads pet sitting washing facs dog grooming cage storage walks info vet info **On Request** fridge access torch towels

A warm welcome is assured at this single storey property, a mile north of Callington. The attractive accommodation is spacious, and well equipped with numerous extras. At breakfast an interesting choice is offered, featuring home produced eggs from the hens in the garden.

Rooms 3 rms (2 en suite) (1 pri facs) (3 GF) S £30; D £55* **Facilities** TVB tea/coffee Cen ht Dinner Last d 24hrs Wi-fi available Massage & reflexology available on site **Parking** 10 **Notes LB**

CARLYON BAY — MAP 02 SX05

►►► East Crinnis Camping & Caravan Park

(SX062528)

Lantyan, East Crinnis PL24 2SQ

☎ 01726 813023 🖷 01726 813023

e-mail: eastcrinnis@btconnect.com

web: www.crinniscamping.co.uk

Dir: *From A390 (Lostwithiel to St Austell) take A3082 signed Fowey at rdbt by Britannia Inn, site on left*

PETS: Charges 1 pet free; 2+ pets £1 per night **Public areas** except children's play area & shower block disp bin **Exercise area** on site walks in wildlife area with large pond **Facilities** walks info vet info **Other** prior notice required

Open Etr-Oct Last arrival 21.00hrs Last departure 11.00hrs

A small rural park with spacious pitches set in individual bays about one mile from the beaches at Carlyon Bay. The friendly owners keep the site very clean, and the Eden Project is just 2m away. A 2-acre site with 25 touring pitches, 6 hardstandings.

Notes Dogs must be kept on leads at all times

ENGLAND

CAWSAND MAP 02 SX45

★★★ GUEST ACCOMMODATION

Wringford Down

Hat Ln PL10 1LE

☎ 01752 822287

e-mail: a.molloy@virgin.net

web: www.cornwallholidays.co.uk

Dir: *A374 onto B3247, pass Millbrook, right towards Cawsand & sharp right, 0.5m on right*

PETS: Bedrooms (4GF) sign **Sep Accom** kennel **Stables** nearby (0.5m) **Charges** £4 per night £25 per week charge for damage **Grounds** accessible on leads disp bin **Exercise area** on site **Facilities** washing facs cage storage walks info vet info **On Request** fridge access torch towels **Resident Pets:** Daisy (Golden Retriever), Sylvester, Truffle, Toffee (ponies), Billy & Baby (cats), ducks

This family-run establishment has a peaceful location near Rame Head and the South West Coast Path, and is particularly welcoming to families. There is a nursery, swimming pool, games room, and gardens with play areas. A range of rooms, and some suites and self-catering units are available. Breakfast and dinner are served in the dining room.

Rooms 7 en suite 4 annexe en suite (8 fmly) (4 GF) S £45-£55; D £70-£100* **Facilities** TVB tea/coffee Cen ht TVL Dinner Last d 8pm Wi-fi available Pool Table **Parking** 20 **Notes LB** ch fac

CRACKINGTON HAVEN MAP 02 SX19

★★★★ GUEST HOUSE

Bears & Boxes Country Guest House

Penrose, Dizzard EX23 0NX

☎ 01840 230318

e-mail: rwfrh@btinternet.com

web: www.bearsandboxes.com

Dir: *1.5m NE of St Gennys in Dizzard*

PETS: Bedrooms (1GF) unattended **Public areas Grounds** accessible disp bin **Exercise area** 100yds **Facilities** food (pre-bookable) food bowl water bowl bedding dog chews feeding mat dog scoop/disp bags leads pet sitting dog walking washing facs cage storage walks info vet info **On Request** fridge access torch towels

Dating in part from the mid 17th century, Bears & Boxes is a small, family-run guest house situated 500yds from the coastal path. Guests are welcomed with a tray of tea and home-made cake, and the caring owners are always around to help and advise about the locality. The cosy bedrooms have numerous thoughtful extras, and evening meals, using the very best of local ingredients and cooked with flair, are served by arrangement.

Rooms 3 en suite 1 annexe rms (1 annexe pri facs) (1 fmly) (1 GF) S fr £32; D fr £64* **Facilities** FTV TVB tea/coffee Cen ht TVL Dinner Last d noon Wi-fi available **Parking** 6 **Notes** No coaches

COVERACK MAP 02 SW71

►►► Little Trevothan Caravan & Camping Park *(SW772179)*

Trevothan TR12 6SD

☎ 01326 280260

e-mail: sales@littletrevothan.co.uk

web: www.littletrevothan.co.uk

Dir: *From A3083 onto B3293 signed Coverack, approx 2m after Goonhilly ESS right at Zoar Garage on unclass road. Across Downs approx 1m then take 3rd left. Site 0.5m on left*

PETS: Charges £1.50 per night **Public areas** except children's play areas disp bin **Exercise area** on site fenced off area **Facilities** on site shop washing facs walks info vet info **Other** prior notice required **Restrictions** no Rottweilers or Pit Bull Terriers **Resident Pets:** 2 Weimaraners, 2 cats, 2 rabbits

Open Mar-Oct Static vans open Mar-Dec Last arrival 21.00hrs Last departure noon

A secluded site near the unspoilt fishing village of Coverack, with a large recreation area. The nearby sandy beach has lots of rock pools for children to play in, and the many walks both from the park and the village offer stunning scenery. A 10.5-acre site with 70 touring pitches, 4 hardstandings and 40 statics.

Notes Dogs must be kept on a lead & waste picked up

CRANTOCK MAP 02 SW76

►►► Crantock Plains Touring Park

(SW805589)

TR8 5PH

☎ 01637 830955 & 07967 956897

e-mail: matthew-milburn@btconnect.com

web: www.crantock-plains.co.uk

Dir: *Leave Newquay on A3075, take 2nd right signed to park & Crantock. Site on left in 0.75m on narrow road*

PETS: Charges disp bin **Exercise area** on site **Facilities** on site shop dog scoop/disp bags

Open all year Last arrival 22.00hrs Last departure noon

A small rural park with pitches on either side of a narrow lane, surrounded by mature trees for shelter. The family-run park has modern toilet facilities appointed to a good standard. A 6-acre site with 60 touring pitches.

Notes No skateboards, dogs on lead at all times

FALMOUTH MAP 02 SW83

★★★ 78% HOTEL

Best Western Falmouth Beach Resort Hotel

Gyllyngvase Beach, Seafront TR11 4NA

☎ 01326 310500 📠 01326 319147

e-mail: info@falmouthbeachhotel.co.uk

web: www.bw-falmouthbeachhotel.co.uk

Dir: *A39 to Falmouth, follow seafront signs*

PETS: Bedrooms unattended **Charges** £10 per night **Grounds** accessible on leads **Exercise area** coastal paths; beach in winter only **Facilities** vet info

Enjoying wonderful views, this popular hotel is situated opposite the beach and within easy walking distance of Falmouth's attractions and port. A friendly atmosphere is maintained and guests have a good choice of leisure, fitness, entertainment and dining options. Bedrooms, many with balconies and sea views, are well equipped and comfortable.

Rooms 120 en suite (20 fmly) (4 GF) S £53-£76; D £106-£152 (incl. bkfst)* **Facilities Spa** FTV supervised Gym Wi-fi available Sauna Steam room Hair & beauty salon Xmas New Year **Services** Lift **Parking** 88

★★★ 77% HOTEL

Green Lawns

THE INDEPENDENTS HOTEL ASSOCIATION

Western Ter TR11 4QJ

☎ 01326 312734 📠 01326 211427

e-mail: info@greenlawnshotel.com

web: www.greenlawnshotel.com

Dir: *on A39*

PETS: Bedrooms (11GF) unattended **Charges** £12.50 per night **Exercise area** 0.25m **Facilities** food food bowl water bowl cage storage walks info vet info **On Request** fridge access torch towels

This attractive property enjoys a convenient location close to the town centre and within easy reach of the sea. Spacious public areas include inviting lounges, an elegant restaurant, conference and meeting facilities and a leisure centre. Bedrooms vary in size and style but all are well equipped and comfortable. The friendly service is particularly noteworthy.

Rooms 39 en suite (8 fmly) (11 GF) S £60-£115; D £70-£190 (incl. bkfst) * **Facilities** Squash Gym Wi-fi in bedrooms Sauna Solarium Spa bath New Year **Parking** 69 **Notes LB** Closed 24-30 Dec

★★★ 75% HOTEL

Falmouth

RICHARDSON

Castle Beach TR11 4NZ

☎ 01326 312671 & 0800 448 8844 📠 01326 319533

e-mail: reservations@falmouthhotel.com

web: www.falmouthhotel.com

Dir: *take A30 to Truro then A390 to Falmouth. Follow signs for beaches, hotel on seafront near Pendennis Castle*

PETS: Bedrooms unattended **Charges** £8 per night **Grounds** accessible **Exercise area** countryside; beach (winter only)

This spectacular beach-front Victorian property affords wonderful sea views from many of its comfortable bedrooms, some of which have their own balconies. Spacious public areas include a number of inviting lounges, beautiful leafy grounds, a choice of dining options and an impressive range of leisure facilities.

Rooms 69 en suite (17 fmly) S £60-£70; D £98-£240 (incl. bkfst)* **Facilities Spa** STV FTV Gym Putt green Wi-fi available Beauty salon & Therapeutic rooms Xmas New Year **Services** Lift **Parking** 120 **Notes LB**

ENGLAND

FALMOUTH CONTINUED

★★★ 72% HOTEL

Penmorvah Manor

Budock Water TR11 5ED

☎ 01326 250277 📠 01326 250509

e-mail: reception@penmorvah.co.uk

web: www.penmorvah.co.uk

Dir: *A39 to Hillhead rdbt, take 2nd exit. Right at Falmouth Football Club, through Budock and hotel opposite Penjerrick Gardens*

PETS: Bedrooms (10GF) **Charges** £7.50 per night **Public areas** except restaurant (on leads) **Grounds** accessible disp bin **Exercise area Facilities** water bowl cage storage vet info **On Request** torch towels **Resident Pets:** Millie (Cocker Spaniel), Toffee & Minky (cats)

Situated within two miles of central Falmouth, this extended Victorian manor house is a peaceful hideaway, set in six acres of private woodland and gardens. Penmorvah is well positioned for visiting the local gardens, and offers many garden-tour breaks. Dinner features locally sourced, quality ingredients such as Cornish cheeses, meat, fish and game.

Rooms 27 en suite (1 fmly) (10 GF) S fr £65; D fr £100 (incl. bkfst)✱ **Facilities** Xmas **Parking** 100 **Notes LB** Closed 31 Dec-31 Jan

★★★★ GUEST ACCOMMODATION

The Rosemary

22 Gyllyngvase Ter TR11 4DL

☎ 01326 314669

e-mail: therosemary@tiscali.co.uk

web: www.therosemary.co.uk

Dir: *A39 Melvill Rd signed to beaches & seafront, right onto Gyllyngvase Rd, 1st left*

PETS: Bedrooms Public areas except dining room (on leads) **Grounds** accessible **Exercise area** 400mtrs **Facilities** walks info vet info **On Request** fridge access **Resident Pets:** Rifca (Black Labrador)

Centrally located with splendid views over Falmouth Bay, this friendly establishment provides comfortable accommodation. The attractive bedrooms are thoughtfully equipped and some enjoy the benefit of the views. Guests can relax in the lounge with a drink from the well stocked bar. Also available is a sunny decking area at the rear in the pretty garden, facing the sea.

Rooms 10 en suite (4 fmly) S £37-£43; D £64-£76✱ **Facilities** FTV TVB tea/coffee Cen ht Wi-fi available **Parking** 3 **Notes** Closed Nov-Jan

►►► **Pennance Mill Farm Touring Park**

(SW792307)

Maenporth TR11 5HJ

☎ 01326 317431 📠 01326 317431

web: www.pennancemill.co.uk

Dir: *From A39 (Truro-Falmouth) follow brown camping signs towards Maenporth Beach. At Hill Head rdbt take 2nd exit for Maenporth Beach*

PETS: Charges £2 (dogs) per night **Public areas** except playground **Exercise area** on site field **Facilities** on site shop walks info vet info **Other** prior notice required **Resident Pets:** 9 farm cats

Open Etr-Xmas Last arrival 22.00hrs Last departure 10.00hrs

Set approximately half a mile from the safe, sandy Bay of Maenporth this is a mainly level, grassy park in a rural location sheltered by mature trees and shrubs and divided into three meadows. It has a modern toilet block. A 6-acre site with 75 touring pitches, 8 hardstandings and 4 statics.

Notes

FOWEY MAP 02 SX15

★★★ 83% HOTEL

Fowey Hall

von Essen hotels A PRIVATE COLLECTION www.vonessenhotels.com

Hanson Dr PL23 1ET

☎ 01726 833866 📠 01726 834100

e-mail: info@foweyhallhotel.co.uk

web: www.vonessenhotels.co.uk

Dir: *In Fowey, over mini rdbt into town centre. Pass school on right, 400mtrs right into Hanson Drive*

PETS: Bedrooms Charges £7 per night **Public areas** except restaurant (on leads) **Grounds** accessible **Exercise area** beach **Facilities** food bowl bedding **Other** max 2 dogs in hotel at any time; pets allowed in cottage bedrooms only

Built in 1899, this listed mansion looks out on to the English Channel. The imaginatively designed bedrooms offer charm, individuality and sumptuous comfort; the Garden Wing rooms adding a further dimension to staying here. The beautifully appointed public rooms include the wood-panelled dining room where accomplished cuisine is served. Enjoying glorious views, the well-kept grounds have a covered pool and sunbathing area.

Rooms 28 en suite 8 annexe en suite (30 fmly) (8 GF) **Facilities** Wi-fi available Table tennis Basketball Trampoline ch fac **Parking** 40 **Notes LB**

★★★★ GUEST ACCOMMODATION

Trevanion

70 Lostwithiel St PL23 1BQ

☎ 01726 832602

e-mail: alisteve@trevanionguesthouse.co.uk

web: www.trevanionguesthouse.co.uk

Dir: *A3082 into Fowey, down hill, left onto Lostwithiel St, Trevanion on left*

PETS: Bedrooms unattended **Exercise area** Directly across road **Facilities** food bowl water bowl **Other** Please telephone for further details **Resident Pets:** Poppy (parrot)

This 16th-century merchant's house provides friendly, comfortable accommodation within easy walking distance of the historic town of Fowey and is convenient for visiting the Eden Project. A hearty farmhouse-style cooked breakfast, using local produce, is served in the attractive dining room and other menu options are available.

Rooms 5 rms (4 en suite) (1 pri facs) (2 fmly) (1 GF) S £35-£40; D £55-£70 **Facilities** TVB tea/coffee Cen ht Wi-fi available **Parking** 5 **Notes** LB

►►► Penmarlam Caravan & Camping Park

(SX134526)

Bodinnick PL23 1LZ

☎ 01726 870088 🖷 01726 870082

e-mail: info@penmarlampark.co.uk

web: www.penmarlampark.co.uk

Dir: *From A390 at East Taphouse take B3359 signed Looe & Polperro. Follow signs for Bodinnick & Fowey, via ferry. Site on right at entrance to Bodinnick*

PETS: Stables nearby (4m) **Public areas** only assist dogs allowed in toilet & shower block disp bin **Exercise area** adjacent **Facilities** on site shop food dog chews cat treats dog scoop/disp bags washing facs walks info vet info **Resident Pets:** Rusty (Border Terrier), Pippa (Collie cross)

Open Apr-Oct Last departure noon

A tranquil park set above the Fowey Estuary in an Area of Outstanding Natural Beauty, with access to the water. Pitches are level, and sheltered by trees and bushes in two paddocks, while the toilets are well maintained. A 4-acre site with 65 touring pitches and 1 static.

GOONHAVERN

MAP 02 SW75

►►►► Penrose Farm Touring Park

(SW795534)

TR4 9QF

☎ 01872 573185 🖷 01872 571972

web: www.penrosefarmtouringpark.com

Dir: *From Exeter take A30, past Bodmin and Indian Queens. Just after Wind Farm take B3285 towards Perranporth, site on left on entering Goonhavern*

PETS: Stables nearby **Charges** £2 per night Jul-Aug only disp bin **Exercise area** on site field **Facilities** on site shop food food bowl water bowl dog chews walks info vet info **Other** prior notice required

Open Apr-Oct Last arrival 21.30hrs

A quiet sheltered park set in five paddocks divided by hedges and shrubs, only a short walk from the village. Lovely floral displays enhance the park's appearance, and the grass and hedges are neatly trimmed. Four cubicled family rooms are very popular, and there is a good laundry. A 9-acre site with 100 touring pitches, 17 hardstandings and 8 statics.

Notes No skateboards/rollerskates. Families & couples only

►►► Roseville Holiday Park *(SW787540)*

TR4 9LA

☎ 01872 572448 🖷 01872 572448

web: www.rosevilleholidaypark.co.uk

Dir: *From mini-rdbt in Goonhavern follow B3285 towards Perranporth, site 0.5m on right*

PETS: Stables nearby (1m) **Charges** £1-£2 per night in high season disp bin **Exercise area** on site field **Facilities** vet info **Restrictions** no Rottweilers or Pit/Staffordshire Bull Terriers

Open Whit-Oct (rs Apr-Jul, Sep-Oct shop closed) Last arrival 21.30hrs Last departure 11.00hrs

A family park set in a rural location with sheltered grassy pitches, some gently sloping. The toilet facilities are modern, and there is an attractive outdoor swimming pool complex. Approximately 2 miles from the long sandy beach at Perranporth. An 8-acre site with 95 touring pitches and 5 statics.

Notes Families only site

GORRAN MAP 02 SW94

►►► Treveague Farm Caravan & Camping Site *(SX002410)*

PL26 6NY

☎ 01726 842295 🖷 01726 842295

e-mail: treveague@btconnect.com

web: www.treveaguefarm.co.uk

Dir: *From St Austell take B3273 towards Mevagissey, past Pentewan at top of hill, turn right signed Gorran. Past Heligan Gardens towards Gorran Churchtown. Follow brown tourist signs from fork in road*

PETS: disp bin **Exercise area** on site field available **Facilities** on site shop food food bowl water bowl vet info

Open Apr-Oct Last arrival 21.00hrs Last departure noon

Spectacular panoramic coastal views are a fine feature of this rural park, which is well equipped with modern facilities. A stone-faced toilet block with a Cornish slate roof is an attractive and welcome feature of the park. A footpath leads to the fishing village of Gorran Haven in one direction, and the secluded sandy Vault Beach in the other. A 4-acre site with 40 touring pitches.

Notes

GORRAN HAVEN MAP 02 SX04

►► Trelispen Caravan & Camping Park *(SX008421)*

PL26 6NT

☎ 01726 843501 🖷 01726 843501

e-mail: trelispen@care4free.net

web: www.trelispen.co.uk

Dir: *B3273 from St Austell towards Mevagissey, on hilltop at x-roads before descent into Mevagissey turn right on unclass road to Gorran. Through village, 2nd right towards Gorran Haven, site signed on left in 250mtrs*

PETS: Exercise area nearby lane **Facilities** vet info

Open Etr & Apr-Oct Last arrival 22.00hrs Last departure noon

A quiet rural site set in three paddocks, and sheltered by mature trees and hedges. The simple toilets have plenty of hot water, and there is a small laundry. Sandy beaches, pubs and shops are nearby, and Mevagissey is two miles away. A 2-acre site with 40 touring pitches.

Notes

GWITHIAN MAP 02 SW54

►►► Gwithian Farm Campsite *(SW586412)*

Gwithian Farm TR27 5BX

☎ 01736 753127

e-mail: camping@gwithianfarm.co.uk

web: www.gwithianfarm.co.uk

Dir: *Exit A30 at Hayle rdbt, take 4th exit signed Hayle, 100mtrs. At 1st mini-rdbt turn right onto B3301 signed Portreath. Site 2m on left on entering village*

PETS: Stables nearby (0.5m) **Charges** £1 per night £7 per week **Public areas** except shop & shower block disp bin **Exercise area** 100mtrs **Facilities** on site shop food walks info vet info **Resident Pets:** Spud (Black Labrador), Charcoal & Barnaby (Pygmy goats)

Open 31 Mar-1 Oct Last arrival 22.00hrs Last departure 17.00hrs

An unspoilt site located behind the sand dunes of Gwithian's golden beach, which can be reached directly by footpath from the site. The site boasts a superb toilet block with excellent facilities including a bathroom and baby-changing unit. There is a good pub opposite. A 7.5-acre site with 87 touring pitches, 4 hardstandings.

HELSTON MAP 02 SW62

►►► Poldown Caravan Park *(SW629298)*

Poldown, Carleen TR13 9NN

☎ 01326 574560

e-mail: stay@poldown.co.uk

web: www.poldown.co.uk

Dir: *From Helston follow Penzance signs for 1m then right onto B3302 to Hayle, 2nd left to Carleen, 0.5m to site*

PETS: Charges £1 per night **Exercise area** adjacent **Facilities** washing facs walks info vet info **Other** prior notice required **Resident Pets:** 1 dog (Retriever)

Open Apr-Sep Last arrival 21.00hrs Last departure noon

A small, quiet site set in attractive countryside with bright toilet facilities. All of the level grass pitches have electricity, and the sunny park is sheltered by mature trees and shrubs. A 2-acre site with 13 touring pitches and 7 statics.

Notes

►►► Skyburriowe Farm *(SW698227)*

Garras TR12 6LR

☎ 01326 221646

e-mail: bkbenney@hotmail.co.uk

web: www.skyburriowefarm.co.uk

Dir: *From Helston take A3083 to The Lizard. After Culdrose naval airbase continue straight at rdbt, after 1m left at Skyburriowe Lane sign. In 0.5m right at Skyburriowe B&B/Campsite sign. Continue past bungalow to farmhouse. Site on left.*

PETS: Stables nearby (4m) (loose box) **Exercise area** adjacent **Facilities** walks info vet info **Other** prior notice required **Resident Pets:** Finlee & Candy (Golden Retrievers)

Open Apr-Oct Last arrival 22.00hrs Last departure 11.00hrs

A leafy no-through road leads to this picturesque farm park in a rural location on the Lizard Peninsula. A newly built toilet block offers excellent quality facilities, and most pitches have electric hook ups. There are some beautiful coves and beaches nearby. A 4-acre site with 30 touring pitches.

Notes Dogs must be kept on leads, quiet after 23.00hrs

HOLYWELL BAY — MAP 02 SW75

Trevornick Holiday Park *(SW776586)*

TR8 5PW

☎ 01637 830531 📠 01637 831000

e-mail: info@trevornick.co.uk

web: www.trevornick.co.uk

Dir: *3m from Newquay off A3075 towards Redruth. Follow Cubert & Holywell Bay signs*

PETS: Charges £3.45 - £3.75 per night £24.15 - £26.25 per week **Exercise area** designated fields for dog walking **Facilities** on site shop food food bowl water bowl dog chews cat treats dog scoop/disp bags walks info vet info **Other** prior notice required; free dog scoop on arrival

Open Etr & mid May-mid Sep Last arrival 21.00hrs Last departure 10.00hrs

A large seaside holiday complex with excellent facilities and amenities. There is plenty of entertainment including a children's club and an evening cabaret, adding up to a full holiday experience for all the family. A sandy beach is a 15-minute footpath walk away. The park has 68 ready-erected tents for hire. A 20-acre site with 593 touring pitches, 6 hardstandings.

Notes Families and couples only

KENNACK SANDS — MAP 02 SW71

►►► Chy Carne Holiday Park *(SW725164)*

Kuggar, Ruan Minor TR12 7LX

☎ 01326 290200 & 291161

e-mail: enquiries@camping-cornwall.com

web: www.camping-cornwall.com

Dir: *From A3083 turn left on B3293 after Culdrose Naval Air Station. At Goonhilly ESS right onto unclass road signed Kennack Sands. Left in 3m at junct*

PETS: Charges 50-75p per night **Public areas Exercise area** on site 2.5 acre field **Facilities** on site shop food food bowl water bowl dog chews litter tray dog scoop/disp bags washing facs dog grooming walks info vet info **Other** prior notice required **Resident Pets:** Armstrong (Labrador), Bordeaux & Murphy (cross), Misty & Sky (Collies), Polly, Candy & Tiger (cats)

Open Etr-Oct Last arrival dusk

Small but spacious park in quiet, sheltered spot, with extensive sea and coastal views from the grassy touring area. A village pub with restaurant is a short walk by footpath from the touring area, and a sandy beach is less than 0.5 miles away. A 6-acre site with 14 touring pitches and 18 statics.

Notes

►►► Silver Sands Holiday Park *(SW727166)*

Gwendreath TR12 7LZ

☎ 01326 290631 📠 01326 290631

e-mail: enquiries@silversandsholidaypark.co.uk

web: www.silversandsholidaypark.co.uk

Dir: *From Helston follow signs to Goonhilly. 300yds after Goonhilly Future World turn right at x-roads signed Kennack Sands, 1.5m, left at Gwendreath sign, site 1m*

PETS: Stables nearby (2m) (loose box) **Charges** £1.50 - £2.20 per night **Public areas** except in toilet block & reception disp bin **Exercise area** on site field available **Facilities** food bowl water bowl dog scoop/disp bags washing facs walks info vet info **Other** prior notice required **Resident Pets:** Chrissie & Puff Fluff (cats)

Open Etr-Sep Last arrival 20.00hrs Last departure 11.00hrs

A small park in a remote location, with individually screened pitches providing sheltered suntraps. A footpath through the woods from the family-owned park leads to the beach and the local pub. A 9-acre site with 34 touring pitches and 16 statics.

Notes No groups

LANIVET MAP 02 SX06

►►► Mena Caravan & Camping Park

(SW041626)

PL30 5HW

☎ 01208 831845 ⎙ 01208 831845

e-mail: mena@campsitesincornwall.co.uk

web: www.campsitesincornwall.co.uk

Dir: *Leave A389 N signed Lanivet & Bodmin. In 0.5m take 1st right & pass beneath A30. Take 1st left signed Lostwithiel, Fowey. In 0.25m turn right at top of hill. 0.5m, then 1st right into our lane. Entrance 100yds on right.*

PETS: Sep Accom day kennels **Charges** £1-£2 per night £7-£14 per week disp bin **Exercise area** on site adjacent fields & woods **Facilities** on site shop food washing facs walks info vet info

Open all year Last arrival 22.00hrs Last departure noon

Set in a secluded, elevated location with high hedges for shelter, and plenty of peace. This grassy site is about four miles from the Eden Project, and midway between north and south Cornish coasts. On site is a small coarse fishing lake. A 15-acre site with 25 touring pitches, 1 hardstanding and 2 statics.

LANLIVERY MAP 02 SX05

★★★ INN

The Crown Inn

PL30 5BT

☎ 01208 872707 ⎙ 01208 871208

e-mail: thecrown@wagtailinns.com

web: www.wagtailinns.com

Dir: *Signed off A390, 2m W of Lostwithiel. Inn 0.5m down lane into village, opp church*

PETS: Bedrooms (7GF) unattended **Charges** charge for damage **Public areas** except restaurant **Grounds** accessible **Exercise area** footpath adjacent **Facilities** water bowl dog chews dog scoop/disp bags washing facs cage storage walks info vet info **On Request** fridge access torch towels **Resident Pets:** Eve (Springer Spaniel)

This character inn has a long history, reflected in its worn flagstone floors, aged beams, ancient well and open fireplaces. Dating in part from the 12th century, the Crown has undergone a faithful restoration. Dining is a feature and menus offer a wide choice of fresh fish, local produce and interesting dishes. The bedrooms are more contemporary and are attractively and impressively appointed. The garden is a delight.

Rooms 2 en suite 7 annexe en suite (7 GF) S £39.95-£79.95; D £39.95-£79.95✻ **Facilities** FTV TVB tea/coffee Cen ht Dinner Last d 9pm Wi-fi available **Parking** 50

LISKEARD MAP 02 SX26

★★★★ BED & BREAKFAST

Redgate Smithy

Redgate, St Cleer PL14 6RU

☎ 01579 321578

e-mail: enquiries@redgatesmithy.co.uk

web: www.redgatesmithy.co.uk

Dir: *3m NW of Liskeard. Off A30 at Bolventor/Jamaica Inn onto St Cleer Rd for 7m, B&B just past x-rds*

PETS: Bedrooms unattended **Public areas** except at breakfast **Grounds** accessible disp bin **Exercise area** adjacent **Facilities** food bowl bedding dog chews dog scoop/disp bags leads washing facs cage storage walks info vet info **On Request** fridge access torch towels **Restrictions** no Rottweilers, Rhodesian Ridgebacks, German Shepherds or Pit Bulls **Resident Pets:** Sinbad (Cocker Spaniel)

This 200-year-old converted smithy is on the southern fringe of Bodmin Moor near Golitha Falls. The friendly accommodation offers smartly furnished, cottage style bedrooms with many extra facilities. There are several dining options nearby, and a wide choice of freshly cooked breakfasts are served in the conservatory.

Rooms 3 rms (2 en suite) (1 pri facs) S fr £45; D fr £70✻ **Facilities** FTV TVB tea/coffee Cen ht **Parking** 3 **Notes LB** No children 12yrs Closed Xmas & New Year

LOOE MAP 02 SX25

★★★ 79% HOTEL

Trelaske Hotel & Restaurant

Polperro Rd PL13 2JS

☎ 01503 262159 ⎙ 01503 265360

e-mail: info@trelaske.co.uk

Dir: *B252 signed Looe, over bridge signed Polperro. Follow road for 1.9m, hotel signed off road on right.*

PETS: Bedrooms (2GF) unattended sign **Charges** £5 per night **Grounds** accessible on leads disp bin **Exercise area Facilities** food bowl water bowl dog chews cat treats feeding mat walks info vet info **On Request** fridge access torch towels **Resident Pets:** Moe (Blue Fronted Amazon Parrot)

This small hotel offers comfortable accommodation and professional yet friendly service and award-winning food. Set in its own very well tended grounds and only minutes away from Looe and its attractions.

Rooms 3 en suite 4 annexe en suite (2 fmly) (2 GF) **Facilities** Wi-fi available Mountain bikes for hire **Parking** 50

ENGLAND

★★ 76% HOTEL

Fieldhead

THE INDEPENDENTS HOTEL ASSOCIATION

Portuan Rd, Hannafore PL13 2DR

☎ 01503 262689

e-mail: fieldheadhotel@bluebottle.com

web: www.fieldheadhotel.co.uk

Dir: *In Looe pass Texaco garage, cross bridge, left to Hannafore. At Tom Sawyer turn right & right again into Portuan Rd. Hotel on left*

PETS: Bedrooms (2GF) unattended sign **Charges** £5 per night charge for damage **Grounds** accessible on leads **Exercise area** adjacent **Facilities** water bowl walks info vet info **Restrictions** small dogs preferred **Resident Pets:** Trudy (King Charles Spaniel), Connie & Pippa (Guinea Pigs)

Overlooking the bay, this engaging hotel has a relaxing atmosphere. Bedrooms are furnished with care and many have sea views. Smartly presented public areas include a convivial bar and restaurant, and outside there is a palm-filled garden with a secluded patio and swimming pool. The fixed-price menu changes daily and features quality local produce.

Rooms 16 en suite (2 fmly) (2 GF) S £40-£65; D £80-£160 (incl. bkfst) **Facilities** FTV ⸙ Wi-fi in bedrooms New Year **Parking** 15 **Notes LB** Closed 1 day at Xmas

★★★★ GUEST HOUSE

South Trelowia Barns

Widegates PL13 1QL

☎ 01503 240709

e-mail: madley.cornwall@virgin.net

Dir: *A387 W from Hessenford, 1m left signed Trelowia, 0.75m down lane on right*

PETS: Bedrooms Charges £2 (Etr-Oct) per night **Public areas Grounds** accessible disp bin **Exercise area Facilities** food bowl water bowl bedding dog scoop/disp bags washing facs cage storage walks info vet info **On Request** fridge access torch towels **Resident Pets:** Daisy (Terrier cross), Henry & Victor (cats)

Set in a very peaceful rural location, this home offers a relaxing environment and is full of character. The proprietors provide a warm welcome and guests are made to feel at home. The comfortable bedrooms have lots of extra facilities. Cooking is accomplished and features home-grown and local produce.

Rooms 1 en suite 1 annexe en suite (2 fmly) S £30-£37; D £50-£54 **Facilities** TV1B tea/coffee Cen ht TVL Dinner Last d 10.30am **Parking** 6 **Notes LB** No coaches

★★★ GUEST HOUSE

Little Harbour

Church St PL13 2EX

☎ 01503 262474

e-mail: littleharbour@btinternet.com

web: www.looedirectory.co.uk

Dir: *From harbour turn right into Princess Sq, on left*

PETS: Bedrooms Charges charge for damage **Public areas Exercise area Facilities** water bowl washing facs walks info vet info **On Request** fridge access towels **Resident Pets:** Katamia Gingerbean (Persian cat)

Little Harbour is situated almost on Looe's harbourside in the historic old town; it has a pleasant and convenient location and parking is available. The proprietors are friendly and attentive. The bedrooms are well appointed and attractively decorated. Breakfast is served freshly cooked in the dining room.

Rooms 5 en suite (1 fmly) S £20-£30; D £40-£60* **Facilities** STV FTV TVB tea/coffee Cen ht **Parking** 3 **Notes LB** No children 12yrs

►►► **Camping Caradon Touring Park**

(SX218539)

Trelawne PL13 2NA

☎ 01503 272388 🖷 01503 272858

e-mail: enquiries@campingcaradon.co.uk

web: www.campingcaradon.co.uk

Dir: *Site signed from B3359 near junct with A387, between Looe and Polperro*

PETS: Charges £1-£2 per night **Public areas** except shop, bar & club room disp bin **Exercise area** 0.25m **Facilities** on site shop food food bowl water bowl dog scoop/disp bags leads walks info vet info **Resident Pets:** rabbit

Open all year (rs Nov-Mar by booking only) Last arrival 22.00hrs Last departure noon

Set in a quiet rural location between the popular coastal resorts of Looe and Polperro, this family-run park is just 1.5m from the beach at Talland Bay. The owners have upgraded the bar and restaurant, and are continuing to improve the park. A 3.5-acre site with 85 touring pitches, 23 hardstandings.

ENGLAND

LOOE CONTINUED

►►► Polborder House Caravan & Camping Park *(SX283557)*

Bucklawren Rd, St Martin PL13 1NZ

☎ 01503 240265

e-mail: reception@peaceful-polborder.co.uk

web: www.peaceful-polborder.co.uk

Dir: *Approach Looe from E on A387, follow B3253 for 1m, left at Polborder & Monkey Sanctuary sign. Site 0.5m on right*

PETS: Stables nearby (2m) (loose box) **Charges** £1 per night disp bin **Exercise area** 10yds **Facilities** on site shop food food bowl water bowl dog scoop/disp bags washing facs walks info vet info **Other** prior notice required

Open all year Last arrival 22.00hrs Last departure 10.00hrs

A very neat and well-kept small grassy site on high ground above Looe in a peaceful rural setting. Friendly and enthusiastic owners. A 3.5-acre site with 31 touring pitches, 18 hardstandings and 5 statics.

LOSTWITHIEL MAP 02 SX15

★★★★ GUEST ACCOMMODATION

Penrose B&B

1 The Terrace PL22 0DT

☎ 01208 871417 01208 871101

e-mail: enquiries@penrosebb.co.uk

web: www.penrosebb.co.uk

Dir: *A390 Edgecombe Rd, Lostwithiel onto Scrations Ln, 1st right for parking*

PETS: Bedrooms (2GF) **Grounds** accessible on leads disp bin **Exercise area** 0.25m **Facilities** pet sitting washing facs cage storage walks info vet info **On Request** fridge access torch towels **Resident Pets:** Chocky (cat)

Just a short walk from the town centre, this grand Victorian house offers comfortable accommodation and a genuine homely atmosphere. Many of the bedrooms have original fireplaces and all are equipped with thoughtful extras. Breakfast is a generous offering and is served in the elegant dining room, with views over the garden. Wi-fi access is also available.

Rooms 7 rms (6 en suite) (1 pri facs) (3 fmly) (2 GF) S £30-£60; D £40-£80 **Facilities** TVB tea/coffee Cen ht Wi-fi available **Parking** 8 **Notes** LB

►►► Powderham Castle Holiday Park

(SX083593)

PL30 5BU

☎ 01208 872277 01208 871236

e-mail: info@powderhamcastletouristpark.co.uk

web: www.powderhamcastletouristpark.co.uk

Dir: *1.5m SW of Lostwithiel on A390 turn right at brown/white sign in 400mtrs*

PETS: Charges £1-£2 per night **Public areas** except children's play area disp bin **Exercise area** on site field set aside **Facilities** walks info vet info **Other** prior notice required **Restrictions** no Dobermans, Rottwielers, German Shepherds or Staffordshire Bull Terriers **Resident Pets:** Pippin (Cairn Terrier)

Open Etr or Apr-Oct Last arrival 22.00hrs Last departure 11.30hrs

A grassy park set in attractive paddocks with mature trees. A gradual upgrading of facilities is well under way, and both buildings and grounds are carefully maintained. This park is ideally located for visiting the Eden Project, the nearby golden beaches and sailing at Fowey. A 12-acre site with 72 touring pitches, 12 hardstandings and 38 statics.

MARAZION MAP 02 SW53

★★ 76% SMALL HOTEL

Godolphin Arms

TR17 0EN

☎ 01736 710202 01736 710171

e-mail: enquiries@godolphinarms.co.uk

web: www.godolphinarms.co.uk

Dir: *from A30 follow Marazion signs for 1m to hotel. At end of causeway to St Michael's Mount*

PETS: Bedrooms (2GF) **Stables** nearby (1m) **Charges** charge for damage **Public areas** except upper deck area (on leads) **Grounds** accessible on leads disp bin **Exercise area** 100yds **Facilities** water bowl dog chews feeding mat walks info vet info **On Request** fridge access torch towels

This 170-year-old waterside hotel is in a prime location where the stunning views of St Michael's Mount provide a backdrop for the restaurant and lounge bar. Bedrooms are colourful, comfortable and spacious. A choice of menu with the emphasis on locally caught seafood is offered in the main restaurant and the Gig Bar.

Rooms 10 en suite (2 fmly) (2 GF) **Facilities** Wi-fi available Direct access to large beach **Parking** 48 **Notes** LB

►►► Wheal Rodney Holiday Park *(SW525315)*

Gwallon Ln TR17 0HL

☎ 01736 710605

e-mail: reception@whealrodney.co.uk

web: www.whealrodney.co.uk

Dir: *Turn off A30 at Crowlas, signed Rospeath. Site 1.5m on right. From Marazion centre turn opposite Fire Engine Inn, site 500mtrs on left.*

PETS: Charges £1.50 per night **Public areas** except buildings disp bin **Exercise area** 200yds **Facilities** on site shop food food bowl water bowl washing facs walks info vet info **Other** prior notice required **Resident Pets:** Citroen, Harry, Badger (Sheep Dogs), Naughty Ralph (cat)

Open Etr-Oct Last arrival 20.00hrs Last departure 11.00hrs

Set in a quiet rural location surrounded by farmland, with level grass pitches and well-kept facilities. Just half a mile away are the beach at Marazion and the causeway or ferry to St Michael's Mount. A cycle route is just 400yds away. A 2.5-acre site with 30 touring pitches.

Notes Quiet after 22.00hrs

MAWNAN SMITH MAP 02 SW72

★★★★ 79% COUNTRY HOUSE HOTEL

Budock Vean - The Hotel on the River

TR11 5LG

☎ 01326 252100 & 0800 833927 01326 250892

e-mail: relax@budockvean.co.uk

web: www.budockvean.co.uk

Dir: *from A39 follow tourist signs to Trebah Gardens. 0.5m to hotel*

PETS: Bedrooms sign **Charges** £7.75 per night £43.75 per week charge for damage **Grounds** accessible on leads disp bin **Exercise area** on site **Facilities** bedding feeding mat dog scoop/disp bags walks info vet info

Set in 65 acres of attractive, well-tended grounds, this peaceful hotel offers an impressive range of facilities. Convenient for visiting the Helford River Estuary and the many local gardens, or simply as a tranquil venue for a leisure break. Bedrooms are spacious and come in a choice of styles; some overlook the grounds and golf course.

Rooms 57 en suite (2 fmly) S £65-£123; D £130-£146 (incl. bkfst & dinner)✳ **Facilities Spa** 9 Fishing Putt green Wi-fi available Outdoor hot tub Private river boat & foreshore Xmas New Year **Services** Lift **Parking** 100 **Notes** Closed 3 wks Jan

★★★ 85% COUNTRY HOUSE HOTEL

Meudon

TR11 5HT

☎ 01326 250541 01326 250543

e-mail: wecare@meudon.co.uk

web: www.meudon.co.uk

Dir: *from Truro A39 towards Falmouth at Hillhead (Anchor & Cannons) rdbt, follow signs to Maenporth Beach. Hotel on left 1m after beach*

PETS: Bedrooms unattended **Charges** £9.50 per night **Grounds** accessible disp bin **Exercise area** on site 8.5 acre gardens & private beach **Facilities** walks info vet info **On Request** fridge access **Resident Pets:** Felix (cat)

This charming late Victorian mansion is a relaxing place to stay, with friendly hospitality and attentive service. It sits in impressive gardens that lead down to a private beach. The spacious and comfortable bedrooms are situated in a more modern building. The cuisine features the best of local Cornish produce and is served in the conservatory restaurant.

Rooms 29 en suite (2 fmly) (15 GF) S £80-£150; D £160-£300 (incl. bkfst & dinner) **Facilities** FTV Fishing Riding Wi-fi available Private beach Hair salon Yacht for skippered charter Sub-tropical gardens Xmas **Services** Lift **Parking** 52 **Notes LB** Closed Jan

See advert on page 39

MEVAGISSEY MAP 02 SX04

►►►►► Seaview International Holiday Park *(SW990412)*

Boswinger PL26 6LL

☎ 01726 843425 🖷 01726 843358

e-mail: holidays@seaviewinternational.com

web: www.seaviewinternational.com

Dir: *From St Austell take B3273 signed Mevagissey. Turn right before entering village. Follow brown tourist signs to site*

PETS: Charges £3 per dog per night **Public areas** except swimming pool area disp bin **Exercise area** on site **Facilities** on site shop food dog chews cat treats dog scoop/disp bags walks info vet info **Restrictions** no dangerous dogs (see page 7)

Open Mar-Oct Last arrival 21.00hrs Last departure 10.00hrs

An attractive holiday park set in a beautiful environment overlooking Veryan Bay, with colourful landscaping including attractive flowers and shrubs. It continues to offer an outstanding holiday experience, with its luxury family pitches, super toilet facilities, takeaway and shop. The beach and sea are just half a mile away. A 28-acre site with 189 touring pitches, 13 hardstandings and 38 statics.

MULLION MAP 02 SW61

★★★ 77% HOTEL

Polurrian

TR12 7EN

☎ 01326 240421 🖷 01326 240083

e-mail: relax@polurrianhotel.com

web: www.polurrianhotel.com

PETS: Bedrooms (8GF) unattended sign **Stables** nearby (2m) **Charges** £8 per night charge for damage **Grounds** accessible on leads disp bin **Exercise area** adjacent **Facilities** dog scoop/disp bags walks info vet info **On Request** fridge access

With spectacular views across St Mount's Bay, this well managed hotel has undergone extensive upgrading. Guests are assured of a warm welcome and a relaxed atmosphere from the friendly team of staff. In addition to the formal eating option, the High Point restaurant offers a more casual approach, open all day and into the evening. The popular leisure club has a good range of equipment. Bedrooms vary in size, and sea view rooms are always in demand.

Rooms 39 en suite (4 fmly) (8 GF) S £56-£175; D £112-£210 (incl. bkfst & dinner)* **Facilities** Gym Wi-fi available Children's games room & outdoor play area ch fac Xmas New Year **Parking** 100

★★★ 75% HOTEL

Mullion Cove Hotel

TR12 7EP

☎ 01326 240328 🖷 01326 240998

e-mail: enquiries@mullion-cove.co.uk

Dir: *A3083 towards The Lizard. Through Mullion towards Mullion Cove. Hotel in approx 1m*

PETS: Bedrooms (3GF) unattended **Stables** nearby (2m) **Charges** £6 per night (free in low season) charge for damage **Public areas** dogs allowed in specific lounge only (on leads) **Grounds** accessible on leads disp bin **Exercise area** **Facilities** dog chews dog scoop/disp bags washing facs dog grooming walks info vet info **On Request** fridge access torch

Built at the turn of the last century and set high above the working harbour of Mullion, this hotel has spectacular views of the rugged coastline; seaward facing rooms are always popular. The stylish restaurant offers some carefully prepared dishes using local produce; an alternative option is to eat less formally in the bar. After dinner guests might like to relax in one of the elegant lounges.

Rooms 30 en suite (7 fmly) (3 GF) S £50-£290; D £100-£290 (incl. bkfst) * **Facilities** Wi-fi available Xmas New Year **Services** Lift **Parking** 60 **Notes** LB

Mullion Holiday Park *(SW699182)*

Ruan Minor TR12 7LJ

☎ 01326 240428 & 0870 444 5344 🖷 01326 241141

e-mail: enquiries@parkdeanholidays.co.uk

web: www.parkdeanholidays.co.uk

Dir: *A30 onto A39 through Truro towards Falmouth. A394 to Helston, A3083 for The Lizard. Site 7m on left*

PETS: Charges £30 up to 4 pets per night **Exercise area**

Open 5 Apr-28 Oct Last arrival 22.00hrs Last departure 10.00hrs

A comprehensively-equipped leisure park geared mainly for self-catering holidays, and set close to the sandy beaches, coves and fishing villages on the Lizard Peninsula. There is plenty of on-site entertainment for all ages, with indoor and outdoor swimming pools. A 49-acre site with 150 touring pitches, 8 hardstandings and 305 statics.

Notes Family site

NEWQUAY MAP 02 SW86

★★★★ 77% HOTEL

Headland

Fistral Beach TR7 1EW
☎ 01637 872211 01637 872212
e-mail: office@headlandhotel.co.uk
web: www.headlandhotel.co.uk

Dir: *off A30 onto A392 at Indian Queens, approaching Newquay follow signs for Fistral Beach, hotel adjacent*

PETS: Bedrooms unattended **Charges** dogs £9-£12 per night **Public areas** except restaurant (on leads) **Grounds** accessible on leads disp bin **Exercise area** beach 50yds **Facilities** food food bowl water bowl bedding dog chews feeding mat dog scoop/disp bags walks info vet info **Resident Pets:** Milly & Twiglet (Airedale Terriers)

This Victorian hotel enjoys a stunning location overlooking the sea on three sides - views can be enjoyed from most of the windows. Bedrooms are comfortable and spacious. Grand public areas, with impressive floral displays, include various lounges and in addition to the formal dining room, Sands Brasserie offers a relaxed alternative. Self-catering cottages are available.

Rooms 104 en suite (40 fmly) S £65-£145; D £79-£360 (incl. bkfst)✻ **Facilities** STV ⓢ ⲧ ⛳9 Wi-fi in bedrooms Harry Potter playroom Surf school ♫ ch fac New Year **Services** Lift **Parking** 400 **Notes LB** Closed 24-27 Dec

★★★ 78% HOTEL

Best Western Hotel Bristol

Best Western

Narrowcliff TR7 2PQ
☎ 01637 875181 01637 879347
e-mail: info@hotelbristol.co.uk
web: www.hotelbristol.co.uk

Dir: *off A30 onto A392, then onto A3058. Hotel 2.5m on left*

PETS: Bedrooms unattended **Public areas** except restaurant & lounge (on leads) **Exercise area** opposite **Facilities** cage storage walks info vet info **On Request** fridge access torch

This hotel is conveniently situated and many of the bedrooms enjoy fine sea views. Staff are friendly and provide a professional and attentive service. There is a range of comfortable lounges, ideal for relaxing prior to eating in the elegant dining room. There are also leisure and conference facilities.

Rooms 74 en suite (23 fmly) S £60-£90; D £107-£137 (incl. bkfst)✻ **Facilities** STV ⓢ Wi fi available Table tennis ch fac New Year **Services** Lift **Parking** 105 **Notes LB** Closed 23-27 Dec & 4-18 Jan

★★★ 68% HOTEL

Hotel California

Pentire Crescent TR7 1PU
☎ 01637 879292 & 872798 01637 875611
e-mail: info@hotel-california.co.uk
web: www.hotel-california.co.uk

Dir: *A392 to Newquay, follow signs for Pentire Hotels & Guest Houses*

PETS: Bedrooms (13GF) unattended **Stables** nearby (1m) **Charges** £8 per night **Grounds** accessible disp bin **Exercise area Facilities** walks info vet info **On Request** fridge access torch

This hotel is tucked away in a delightful location, close to Fistral Beach and adjacent to the River Gannel. Many rooms have views across the river towards the sea, and some have balconies. There is an impressive range of leisure facilities, including indoor and outdoor pools, and ten-pin bowling. Cuisine is enjoyable and menus offer a range of interesting dishes.

Rooms 70 en suite (27 fmly) (13 GF) **Facilities** ⓢ ⲧ Squash 10 pin bowling alley ♫ **Services** Lift **Parking** 66 **Notes LB** Closed 3 wks Jan

NEWQUAY CONTINUED

★★ 78% HOTEL

Whipsiderry

Trevelgue Rd, Porth TR7 3LY

☎ 01637 874777 & 876066 📠 01637 874777

e-mail: info@whipsiderry.co.uk

Dir: *right onto Padstow road (B3276) from Newquay, in 0.5m right at Trevelgue Rd*

PETS: Bedrooms unattended **Stables** nearby (0.5m) **Public areas** except certain areas including restaurant **Grounds** accessible disp bin **Exercise area** 100mtrs **Facilities** dog walking washing facs cage storage walks info vet info **On Request** fridge access torch

Quietly located, overlooking Porth Beach, this friendly hotel offers bedrooms in a variety of sizes and styles, many with superb views. A daily-changing menu offers interesting and well-cooked dishes with the emphasis on fresh, local produce. An outdoor pool is available, and at dusk guests may be lucky enough to watch badgers in the attractive grounds.

Rooms 20 rms (19 en suite) (5 fmly) (3 GF) S £58-£70; D £116-£140 (incl. bkfst & dinner)✳ **Facilities** ⥾ Pool room Xmas **Parking** 30 **Notes LB** Closed Nov-Etr (ex Xmas)

★★★★ GUEST HOUSE

Dewolf Guest House

100 Henver Rd TR7 3BL

☎ 01637 874746

e-mail: holidays@dewolfguesthouse.com

Dir: *A392 onto A3058 at Quintrell Downs Rdbt, guest house on left just past mini-rdbts*

PETS: Bedrooms (3GF) **Charges** charge for damage **Grounds** accessible disp bin **Exercise area** beach, walks less than 5 mins **Facilities** walks info vet info **On Request** towels **Other** one bedroom with private enclosed area

Making you feel welcome and at home is the priority here. The bedrooms in the main house are bright and well equipped, and there are two more in a separate single storey building at the rear. The cosy lounge has pictures and items that reflect the host's interest in wildlife. The guest house is just a short walk from Porth Beach.

Rooms 4 en suite 2 annexe en suite (2 fmly) (3 GF) S £25-£40; D £50-£80 **Facilities** FTV TVB tea/coffee Licensed Cen ht **Parking** 6 **Notes LB** No coaches

★★★ GUEST ACCOMMODATION

The Three Tees

21 Carminow Way TR7 3AY

☎ 01637 872055 📠 01637 872055

e-mail: greg@3tees.co.uk

web: www.3tees.co.uk

Dir: *A30 onto A392 Newquay. Right at Quintrell Downs rdbt signed Porth, over double mini-rdbt & 3rd right*

PETS: Bedrooms (2GF) **Charges** £1 per night **Public areas** except dining room **Grounds** accessible disp bin **Exercise area** 2 mins walk **Facilities** water bowl dog chews cage storage walks info vet info **Restrictions** no very large dogs **Resident Pets:** Poppy (Border Collie), Parker (cat)

Located in a quiet residential area just a short walk from the town and beach, this friendly family-run accommodation is comfortable and well equipped. There is a lounge, bar and a sun lounge for the use of guests. Breakfast is served in the dining room, where snacks are available throughout the day. Light snacks are available in the bar during the evenings.

Rooms 8 rms (7 en suite) (1 pri facs) 1 annexe en suite (4 fmly) (2 GF) D £60-£70✳ **Facilities** TVB tea/coffee Cen ht TVL Wi-fi available **Parking** 11 **Notes LB** Closed Nov-Feb

►►► Trebellan Park *(SW790571)*

Cubert TR8 5PY

☎ 01637 830522 📠 01637 830277 & 830522

e-mail: enquiries@trebellan.co.uk

web: www.trebellan.co.uk

Dir: *4m S of Newquay, turn W off A3075 at Cubert sign. Left in 0.75m onto unclass road*

PETS: Stables nearby (5m) **Charges** £1 per night **Public areas** (on leads) disp bin **Exercise area** adjacent **Facilities** washing facs walks info vet info **Other** prior notice required; max 2 large dogs per pitch **Resident Pets:** Little Ginge, Missus, B.C. & Bob (cats), peacocks, aviary birds

Open May-Oct Last arrival 21.00hrs Last departure 10.00hrs

A terraced grassy rural park within a picturesque valley with views of Cubert Common, and adjacent to the Smuggler's Den, a 16th-century thatched inn. This park has excellent coarse fishing on site. An 8-acre site with 150 touring pitches and 7 statics.

Notes Families and couples only

►►► Treloy Touring Park *(SW858625)*

TR8 4JN

☎ 01637 872063 & 876279 🖷 01637 872063

e-mail: treloy.tp@btconnect.com

web: www.treloy.co.uk

Dir: *Off A3059 (St Columb Major-Newquay road)*

PETS: Stables nearby (0.5m) (loose box) **Charges** £1-£2 per night **Public areas** except bar & pool disp bin **Exercise area** on site dog walking area **Facilities** on site shop food dog chews vet info **Other** prior notice required **Restrictions** Pit Bull Terriers or similar breeds

Open May-15 Sep (rs Apr & Sep pool, takeaway, shop & bar) Last arrival 21.00hrs Last departure 10.00hrs

Attractive site with fine countryside views, within easy reach of resorts and beaches. The pitches are set in four paddocks with mainly level but some slightly sloping grassy areas. Maintenance and cleanliness are very high. An 18-acre site with 223 touring pitches, 24 hardstandings.

►►► Trethiggey Touring Park *(SW846596)*

Quintrell Downs TR8 4QR

☎ 01637 877672 🖷 01637 879706

e-mail: enquiries@trethiggey.co.uk

web: www.trethiggey.co.uk

Dir: *From A30 take A392 signed Newquay at Quintrell Downs rdbt, turn left onto A3058 past pearl centre to site 0.5m on left*

PETS: Charges please phone for details **Public areas** except playground, shop, restaurant disp bin **Exercise area** on site field **Facilities** on site shop food food bowl water bowl dog chews cat treats dog scoop/disp bags vet info **Other** prior notice required **Resident Pets:** Bex (Springer Spaniel), Brook (Border Collie)

Open Mar-Dec Last arrival 22.00hrs Last departure 10.30hrs

A family-owned park in a rural setting that is ideal for touring this part of Cornwall. Pleasantly divided into paddocks with maturing trees and shrubs, and offering coarse fishing and tackle hire. A 15-acre site with 145 touring pitches, 35 hardstandings and 12 statics.

PADSTOW — MAP 02 SW97

★★★★ 70% ® HOTEL

The Metropole

RICHARDSON

Station Rd PL28 8DB

☎ 01841 532486 🖷 01841 532867

e-mail: info@the-metropole.co.uk

web: www.the-metropole.co.uk

Dir: *M5/A30 pass Launceston, follow Wadebridge & N Cornwall signs. Take A39, follow Padstow signs*

PETS: Bedrooms (2GF) unattended sign **Charges** £7 per night **Public areas** except restaurant **Grounds** accessible **Exercise area Facilities** walks info vet info **On Request** torch **Other** contact number must be provided when pets are left unattended in bedrooms

This long-established hotel first opened its doors to guests back in 1904 and there is still an air of the sophistication and elegance of a bygone age. Bedrooms are soundly appointed and well equipped; dining options include the informal Met Café Bar and the main restaurant, with its enjoyable cuisine and wonderful views over the Camel estuary.

Rooms 58 en suite (3 fmly) (2 GF) S £68-£98; D £136-£176 (incl. bkfst) ✻ **Facilities** FTV Wi-fi available Swimming pool open Jul & Aug only Xmas New Year **Services** Lift **Parking** 36 **Notes** LB

★★ 85% ® SMALL HOTEL

St Petroc's Hotel and Bistro

4 New St PL28 8EA

☎ 01841 532700 🖷 01841 532942

e-mail: reservations@rickstein.com

Dir: *A39 onto A389, follow signs to town centre. Follow one-way system, hotel on right on leaving town*

PETS: Bedrooms unattended **Charges** £15 for 1st night, £5 thereafter per night charge for damage **Public areas** except restaurant (on leads) **Exercise area** beach **Facilities** food bowl water bowl bedding pet sitting dog grooming walks info vet info **On Request** fridge access torch towels

One of the oldest buildings in town, this charming establishment is just up the hill from the picturesque harbour. Style, comfort and individuality are all great strengths here, particularly so in the impressively equipped bedrooms. Breakfast, lunch and dinner all

CONTINUED

ENGLAND

PADSTOW CONTINUED

reflect a serious approach to cuisine, and the popular restaurant has a relaxed, bistro style. Comfortable lounges, a reading room and lovely gardens complete the picture.

Rooms 10 en suite 4 annexe en suite (3 fmly) (3 GF) D £135-£265 (incl. bkfst)✳ **Facilities** FTV Wi-fi available Cookery school **Services** Lift **Parking** 12 **Notes** **LB** Closed 1 May & 25-26 Dec

★★ 72% HOTEL

The Old Ship Hotel

Mill Square PL28 8AE

☎ 01841 532357 📠 01841 533211

e-mail: stay@oldshiphotel-padstow.co.uk

web: www.oldshiphotel-padstow.co.uk

Dir: *from M5 take A30 to Bodmin then A389 to Padstow, follow brown tourist signs to car park*

PETS: Bedrooms Charges £5 per night **Public areas** (on leads) **Grounds** accessible on leads disp bin **Exercise area Facilities** water bowl dog chews washing facs walks info vet info **On Request** fridge access torch towels **Resident Pets:** Harley (Boxer), Sox (cat)

This attractive inn is situated in the heart of the old town's quaint and winding streets, just a short walk from the harbour. A warm welcome is assured, accommodation is pleasant and comfortable, and public areas offer plenty of character. Freshly caught fish features on both the bar and restaurant menus. On site parking is a bonus.

Rooms 14 en suite (4 fmly) S £35-£54; D £70-£108 (incl. bkfst)✳ **Facilities** STV Wi-fi in bedrooms ♫ Xmas New Year **Parking** 20

★★★★★ ◎◎◎

RESTAURANT WITH ROOMS

The Seafood Restaurant

Riverside PL28 8BY

☎ 01841 532700 📠 01841 532942

e-mail: reservations@rickstein.com

Dir: *Padstow town centre*

PETS: Bedrooms unattended **Charges** 1st night £15; £5 thereafter per night charge for damage **Public areas** except restaurant (on leads) **Exercise area** beach nearby **Facilities** food bowl water bowl bedding pet sitting dog grooming walks info vet info **On Request** fridge access torch towels

Food lovers continue to beat the well trodden path to this legendary establishment. This famous restaurant-with-rooms is situated on the edge of the harbour and just a stone's throw from the shops. The comfortable bedrooms are stylishly simple, equipped with numerous thoughtful extras, some have views of the estuary, while a couple have use of a stunning balcony. Service is relaxed and friendly, perfect for that break by the sea; booking is essential for both the accommodation and in the restaurant.

Rooms 14 en suite 6 annexe en suite (6 fmly) (3 GF) D £135-£265✳ **Facilities** STV TVB tea/coffee Direct dial from bedrooms Lift Cen ht Dinner Last d 10pm Cookery School **Parking** 12 **Notes** **LB** Closed 24-26 Dec RS 1 May

★★★★ BED & BREAKFAST

Rick Stein's Cafe

10 Middle St PL28 8AP

☎ 01841 532700 📠 01841 532942

e-mail: reservations@rickstein.com

Dir: *A389 into town, one way past church, 3rd right*

PETS: Bedrooms unattended **Charges** 1st night £15, £5 thereafter charge for damage **Public areas** except restaurant (on leads) **Exercise area** on site **Facilities** food bowl water bowl bedding pet sitting dog grooming walks info vet info **On Request** fridge access torch towels

Another Rick Stein success story, this lively café by day, restaurant by night, offers good food, quality accommodation, and is just a short walk from the harbour. Three rooms are available, all quite different but sharing high standards of cosseting comfort. Friendly and personable staff complete the picture.

Rooms 3 en suite (1 fmly) **Facilities** TVB tea/coffee Cen ht Dinner Last d 9.30pm **Notes** Closed 1 May BH RS 24-26 Dec

★★ BED & BREAKFAST

Little Pentyre

6 Moyle Rd PL28 8DG

☎ 01841 532246

e-mail: jujulloyd@aol.com

Dir: *From A389, right onto Dennis Rd, bear right onto Moyle Rd*

PETS: Bedrooms (2GF) unattended **Public areas Grounds** accessible disp bin **Exercise area** 30mtrs **Facilities** food bowl water bowl bedding dog chews leads washing facs cage storage walks info vet info **On Request** fridge access torch towels **Resident Pets:** Smudge (cat), Crosby, Stills & Young (chickens)

Within easy, level walking distance of the town centre, Little Pentyre is situated in a quiet residential area, adjacent to the Camel Estuary and Trail. The comfortable bedrooms are well equipped and guests enjoy a freshly cooked breakfast, featuring eggs from the hens in the rear garden.

Rooms 2 en suite (2 GF) S fr £30; D fr £55✳ **Facilities** FTV TVB tea/coffee Cen ht **Parking** 2 **Notes** ⊗

►►► Dennis Cove Camping *(SW919743)*

Dennis Ln PL28 8DR

☎ 01841 532349

e-mail: denniscove@freeuk.com

web: www.denniscove.co.uk

Dir: *Approach Padstow on A389, turn right at Tesco into Sarah's Lane, 2nd right to Dennis Lane, follow lane to site at end*

PETS: Charges £1.30-£2 per night **Public areas** (on leads) disp bin **Exercise area** adjacent **Facilities** walks info vet info **Other** prior notice required supermarket 0.25m **Restrictions** disciplined dogs only **Resident Pets:** Milly (Border Collie), Fanny (Schnauzer)

Open Apr-end Sep Last arrival 21.00hrs Last departure 11.00hrs

Set in meadowland with mature trees, this site overlooks Padstow Bay, with access to the Camel Estuary and the nearby beach. The centre of town is just a 10 minute walk away, and bike hire is available on site, with the famous Camel Trail beginning right outside. A 3-acre site with 42 touring pitches.

Notes ⊜ Arrivals from 14.00hrs

►►► Padstow Touring Park *(SW913738)*

PL28 8LE

☎ 01841 532061

e-mail: mail@padstowtouringpark.co.uk

web: www.padstowtouringpark.co.uk

Dir: *1m S of Padstow, on E side of A389 (Padstow to Wadebridge road)*

PETS: Charges £1.50 per night £10.50 per week **Public areas** except shop & amenity blocks disp bin **Exercise area** adjacent public footpaths **Facilities** on site shop food food bowl water bowl dog chews cat treats dog scoop/disp bags walks info vet info **Other** prior notice required **Resident Pets:** Lottie (Border Terrier), Tinkie & Poppy (Yorkshire Terriers)

Open all year Last arrival 21.30hrs Last departure 11.00hrs

Set in open countryside above the quaint fishing town of Padstow which can be approached by footpath directly from the park. This level grassy site is divided into paddocks by maturing bushes and hedges to create a peaceful and relaxing holiday atmosphere. A 13.5-acre site with 180 touring pitches, 14 hardstandings.

Notes No groups

PENTEWAN — MAP 02 SX04

►►►►► Sun Valley Holiday Park *(SX005486)*

Pentewan Rd PL26 6DJ

☎ 01726 843266 & 844393 📠 01726 843266

e-mail: reception@sunvalley-holidays.co.uk

web: www.sunvalleyholidays.co.uk

Dir: *From St Austell take B3273 towards Mevagissey. Site 2m on right*

PETS: Charges disp bin **Exercise area** on site separate exercise area **Facilities** on site shop food food bowl water bowl bedding dog chews cat treats dog scoop/disp bags washing facs walks info vet info **Other** prior notice required **Resident Pets:** Jenny & Joe (donkeys), Lilly & Milly (goats), rabbits

Open all year Last arrival 22.00hrs Last departure noon

In a picturesque valley amongst woodland, this neat park is kept to an exceptionally high standard. The extensive amenities include tennis courts, indoor swimming pool, licensed clubhouse and restaurant. The sea is one mile away, and can be accessed via a footpath and cycle path along the river bank. A 20-acre site with 29 touring pitches, 4 hardstandings and 75 statics.

Notes No motorised scooters/skateboards or bikes at night

PENZANCE — MAP 02 SW43

★★★ 83% ®® HOTEL

Hotel Penzance

Britons Hill TR18 3AE

☎ 01736 363117 📠 01736 350970

e-mail: enquiries@hotelpenzance.com

web: www.hotelpenzance.com

Dir: *from A30 pass heliport on right, left at next rdbt for town centre. 3rd right onto Britons Hill and hotel on right*

PETS: Bedrooms Charges £10 per night charge for damage **Public areas** except restaurant **Grounds** accessible **Exercise area** 300mtrs **Facilities** water bowl walks info vet info **Resident Pets:** Thomas & Jerry (Birman cats)

This Edwardian house has been tastefully redesigned, particularly in the contemporary Bay Restaurant. The focus on style is not only limited to the decor, but is also apparent in the award-winning cuisine that is based upon fresh Cornish produce. Bedrooms have been appointed to modern standards and are particularly well equipped; many have views across Mounts Bay.

Rooms 24 en suite (2 GF) S £70-£78; D £110-£160 (incl. bkfst)*
Facilities FTV ⤥ Wi-fi in bedrooms Xmas New Year **Parking** 14
Notes LB

PENZANCE CONTINUED

★★★ 71% HOTEL

Queens

The Promenade TR18 4HG

☎ 01736 362371 01736 350033

e-mail: enquiries@queens-hotel.com

web: www.queens-hotel.com

Dir: *A30 to Penzance, follow signs for seafront pass harbour and into promenade, hotel 0.5m on right*

PETS: Bedrooms Charges £10 per stay per week **Exercise area** beach & walks nearby **Other** please phone for details of pet facilities

With views across Mount's Bay towards Newlyn, this impressive Victorian hotel has a long and distinguished history. Comfortable public areas are filled with interesting pictures and artefacts, and in the dining room guests can choose from the daily-changing menu. Bedrooms, many with sea views, vary in style and size.

Rooms 70 en suite (10 fmly) S £58-£80; D £116-£170 (incl. bkfst)* **Facilities** FTV Wi-fi available Yoga weekends Xmas New Year **Services** Lift **Parking** 50 **Notes** LB

★★★ GUEST ACCOMMODATION

Penmorvah

61 Alexandra Rd TR18 4LZ

☎ 01736 363711

Dir: *A30 to Penzance, at railway station follow along harbour pass Jubilee Pool. At mini-rdbt, right onto Alexandra Rd*

PETS: Bedrooms (3GF) **Charges** charge for damage **Public areas** except dining room (on leads) **Grounds** accessible **Exercise area** 400yds **Facilities** water bowl dog chews feeding mat walks info vet info **On Request** fridge access torch

Resident Pets: Marbles (dog)

A well situated bed and breakfast offering comfortable rooms, all of which are en suite. Penmorvah is just a few minutes walk from the sea front with convenient on-street parking nearby.

Rooms 10 en suite (2 fmly) (3 GF) S £24-£35; D £48-£70 **Facilities** FTV TVB tea/coffee Cen ht TVL **Notes** LB

★★★ INN

Mount View

Longrock TR20 8JJ

☎ 01736 710416 01736 710416

Dir: *Off A30 at Marazion/Penzance rdbt, 3rd exit signed Longrock. On right after pelican crossing*

PETS: Bedrooms unattended **Public areas** bar only **Exercise area** beach & field 50yds **Facilities** walks info vet info

Resident Pets: Muppet (Beagle)

The Victorian inn, just a short walk from the beach and half a mile from the Isles of Scilly heliport, is a good base for exploring West Cornwall. Bedrooms are well equipped, including a hospitality tray, and the bar is popular with locals. Breakfast is served in the dining room and a dinner menu is available.

Rooms 5 rms (3 en suite) (2 fmly) S £20-£27.50; D £40-£55* **Facilities** TVB tea/coffee Dinner Last d 8.30pm Pool Table **Parking** 8 **Notes** RS Sun

★★★ GUEST HOUSE

Southern Comfort

Seafront, 8 Alexandra Ter TR18 4NX

☎ 01736 366333

Dir: *0.5m SW of town centre. Follow seafront road, right after Lidl store, establishment signed*

PETS: Bedrooms Stables nearby (0.5m) **Charges** variable according to size charge for damage **Grounds** accessible on leads disp bin **Exercise area** 20mtrs **Facilities** food (pre-bookable) food bowl water bowl bedding dog chews cat treats feeding mat litter tray etc dog scoop/disp bags leads pet sitting dog walking washing facs dog grooming cage storage walks info vet info **On Request** fridge access torch towels

Resident Pets: Twinkie & Maxwell (dogs)

This grand Victorian house is in a quiet location overlooking the bay and St Michael's Mount. A pleasant welcome awaits all guests, both tourist and business. Breakfast is served in the lower-ground dining room, and guests can enjoy a drink either outside in summer or in the bar or lounge.

Rooms 12 en suite (2 fmly) **Facilities** STV FTV TVB tea/coffee Licensed Cen ht TVL Dinner Last d noon **Parking** 6 **Notes** No coaches

►►►► Higher Chellew Holiday Park

(SW496353)

Higher Trenowin, Nancledra TR20 8BD

☎ 01736 364532

e-mail: higherchellew@btinternet.com

web: www.higherchellewcamping.co.uk

Dir: *From A30 towards St Ives, left at mini-rdbt towards Nancledra. Left at B3311 junct, through Nancledra. Site 0.5m on left*

PETS: Charges £2.50 per night **Exercise area** bridle path, fields **Facilities** vet info **Other** prior notice required

Open Fri before Etr-Oct Last departure 10.30hrs

A small rural park quietly located just four miles from the golden beaches at St Ives, and a similar distance from Penzance. This well sheltered park occupies an elevated location, and all pitches are level. A 1.25-acre site with 30 touring pitches.

Notes

►►► Bone Valley Caravan & Camping Park

(SW472316)

Heamoor TR20 8UJ

☎ 01736 360313 📠 01736 360313

e-mail: enquiries@bonevalleycandcpark.co.uk

Dir: *A30 to Penzance, then towards Land's End, at 2nd rdbt right into Heamoor, 300yds right into Josephs Lane, 1st left, site 500yds on left*

PETS: Exercise area field 100yds **Facilities** on site shop walks info vet info **Other** prior notice required **Resident Pets:** Toby (Lakeland Terrier/Border cross)

Open all year Last arrival 22.00hrs Last departure 11.00hrs

A compact grassy park on the outskirts of Penzance, with well maintained facilities. It is divided into paddocks by mature hedges, and a small stream runs alongside. A 1-acre site with 17 touring pitches, 2 hardstandings and 5 statics.

PERRANPORTH — MAP 02 SW75

►►► Tollgate Farm Caravan & Camping Park *(SW768547)*

Budnick Hill TR6 0AD

☎ 01872 572130 & 0845 1662126

e-mail: enquiries@tollgatefarm.co.uk

web: www.tollgatefarm.co.uk

Dir: *Off A30 onto B3285 to Perranporth. Site on right 1.5m after Goonhavern*

PETS: Stables nearby (loose box) disp bin **Exercise area** on site large heath adjacent **Facilities** on site shop food food bowl water bowl washing facs walks info vet info **Resident Pets:** 4 dogs, 9 goats, 2 pigs, rabbits, guinea pigs, chickens, turkeys

Open Etr-Sep Last arrival 21.00hrs Last departure 11.00hrs

A quiet site in a rural location with spectacular coastal views. Pitches are divided into four paddocks sheltered and screened by mature hedges. Children will enjoy the play equipment and pets' corner. The three miles of sand at Perran Bay are just a walk away through the sand dunes, or a 0.75m drive. A 10-acre site with 102 touring pitches, 10 hardstandings.

Notes No large groups

POLPERRO — MAP 02 SX25

★★★ 83% COUNTRY HOUSE HOTEL

Talland Bay

Porthallow PL13 2JB

☎ 01503 272667

e-mail: reception@tallandbayhotel.co.uk

web: www.tallandbayhotel.co.uk

Dir: *signed from x-rds on A387 (Looe to Polperro road)*

PETS: Bedrooms (6GF) **Charges** £7.50 per night charge for damage **Grounds** accessible on leads disp bin **Exercise area** surrounding countryside **Facilities** bedding feeding mat leads washing facs cage storage walks info vet info **On Request** fridge access torch towels

This hotel has the benefit of a wonderful location, being situated in its own extensive gardens that run down almost to the cliff's edge. The atmosphere is warm and friendly throughout, and some of the bedrooms, available in a number of styles, have sea views and balconies. Accomplished cooking, with an emphasis on carefully prepared local produce, remains a key feature here.

Rooms 20 en suite 3 annexe en suite (6 GF) D £95-£235 (incl. bkfst)* **Facilities** Putt green Xmas New Year **Parking** 23 **Notes** LB

POLPERRO CONTINUED

★★★ GUEST ACCOMMODATION

Penryn House

The Coombes PL13 2RQ

☎ 01503 272157 📠 01503 273055

e-mail: chrispidcock@aol.com

web: www.penrynhouse.co.uk

Dir: *A387 to Polperro, at mini-rdbt left down hill into village (ignore restricted access). 200yds on left*

PETS: Bedrooms unattended **Stables** nearby (5m) **Public areas** except restaurant **Grounds** accessible on leads disp bin **Exercise area** 200yds **Facilities** food bowl water bowl leads pet sitting washing facs cage storage walks info vet info **On Request** fridge access torch towels **Resident Pets:** Ella (Great Dane)

Penryn House has a relaxed atmosphere and offers a warm welcome. Every effort is made to ensure a memorable stay. Bedrooms are neatly presented and reflect the character of the building. After a day exploring, enjoy a drink at the bar and relax in the comfortable lounge.

Rooms 12 rms (11 en suite) (1 pri facs) (3 fmly) S £35-£40; D £70-£90* **Facilities** TVB tea/coffee **Parking** 13 **Notes** LB

POLZEATH — MAP 02 SW97

►►► **Tristram Caravan & Camping Park** *(SW936790)*

PL27 6TP

☎ 01208 862215 📠 01208 862080

e-mail: info@tristramcampsite.co.uk

web: www.polzeathcamping.co.uk

Dir: *From B3314 take unclass road signed Polzeath. Through village, up hill, site 2nd turn on right*

PETS: Charges £2 per night **Exercise area** 100yds **Facilities** vet info **Other** prior notice required

Open Mar-Nov Last arrival 21.00hrs Last departure 10.00hrs

An ideal family site, positioned on a gently sloping cliff with grassy pitches and glorious sea views. There is direct, gated access to the beach, where surfing is very popular. The local amenities of the village are only a few hundred yards away. A 10-acre site with 100 touring pitches.

Notes No ball games, no disposable BBQs, no noise between 23.00hrs-07.00hrs, dogs on leads at all times

PORTHTOWAN — MAP 02 SW64

►►►► **Porthtowan Tourist Park** *(SW693473)*

Mile Hill TR4 8TY

☎ 01209 890256

e-mail: admin@porthtowantouristpark.co.uk

web: www.porthtowantouristpark.co.uk

Dir: *Exit A30 at junct signed Redruth/Porthtowan. Take 3rd exit from rdbt. 2m & right at T-junct. Site on left at top of hill*

PETS: Charges £1 peak season only per night **Public areas** except buildings & children's play area disp bin **Exercise area** on site short walks & fenced area **Facilities** on site shop dog scoop/disp bags walks info vet info **Other** prior notice required

Open Apr-Sep Last arrival 21.30hrs Last departure 11.00hrs

A neat, level grassy site on high ground above Porthtowan, with plenty of shelter from mature trees and shrubs. The superb toilet facilities considerably enhance the appeal of this peaceful rural park, which is almost midway between the small seaside resorts of Portreath and Porthtowan, with their beaches and surfing. A 5-acre site with 80 touring pitches, 4 hardstandings.

Notes ® No bikes/skateboards during Jul-Aug

PORT ISAAC — MAP 02 SW98

★★★★ BED & BREAKFAST

The Corn Mill

Port Isaac Rd, Trelill PL30 3HZ

☎ 01208 851079

Dir: *Off B3314, between Pendoggett & Trelill*

PETS: Bedrooms Grounds accessible on leads **Exercise area Resident Pets:** Digger (Jack Russell), Rosie (Golden Retriever), Millie (cat), geese, ducks

Dating from the 18th century, this mill has been lovingly restored to provide a home packed full of character. The bedrooms are individually styled and personal touches create a wonderfully relaxed and homely atmosphere. The farmhouse kitchen is the venue for a delicious breakfast.

Rooms 2 en suite (1 fmly) D £70-£75* **Facilities** TV1B tea/coffee Cen ht **Parking** 3 **Notes** Closed 24 Dec-5 Jan ®

REDRUTH MAP 02 SW64

★★ 65% HOTEL

Crossroads Lodge

THE INDEPENDENTS HOTEL ASSOCIATION

Scorrier TR16 5BP

☎ 01209 820551 📠 01209 820392

e-mail: crossroads@hotelstruro.com

web: www.hotelstruro.com/crossroads

Dir: *turn off A30 onto A3047 towards Scorrier*

PETS: Bedrooms unattended **Charges** £4.50 per night charge for damage **Public areas** except restaurant (on leads) **Grounds** accessible on leads **Exercise area** adjacent **Facilities** cage storage walks info vet info **On Request** fridge access towels

Situated on an historic stanary site and conveniently located just off the A30, this hotel has a smart appearance. Bedrooms are soundly furnished and include executive and family rooms. Public areas include an attractive dining room, a quiet lounge and a lively bar. Conference, banqueting and business facilities are also available.

Rooms 36 en suite (2 fmly) (8 GF) **Services** Lift **Parking** 140 **Notes** LB

►►► Lanyon Holiday Park *(SW684387)*

Loscombe Ln, Four Lanes TR16 6LP

☎ 01209 313474

e-mail: Info@lanyonholidaypark.co.uk

web: www.lanyonholidaypark.co.uk

Dir: *Signed 0.5m off B2397 on Helston side of Four Lanes village*

PETS: Charges £5 per night **Public areas** disp bin **Exercise area** on site 1 acre area **Facilities** on site shop dog chews cat treats dog scoop/disp bags washing facs walks info vet info **Other** prior notice required **Resident Pets:** Coco, Smudge & Sandy (Cocker Spaniels)

Open Mar-Oct Last arrival 21.00hrs Last departure noon

Small, friendly rural park in an elevated position with fine views to distant St Ives Bay. This family owned and run park is being upgraded in all areas, and is close to a cycling trail. Stithian's Reservoir for fishing, sailing and windsurfing is two miles away. A 14-acre site with 25 touring pitches and 49 statics.

REJERRAH MAP 02 SW75

►►►► Newperran Holiday Park *(SW801555)*

TR8 5QJ

☎ 01872 572407 📠 01872 571254

e-mail: holidays@newperran.co.uk

web: www.newperran.co.uk

Dir: *4m SE of Newquay & 1m S of Rejerrah on A3075. Or A30 Redruth, turn off B3275 Perranporth, at 1st T-junct turn right onto A3075 towards Newquay, site 300mtrs on left*

PETS: Stables nearby (2m) (loose box) **Charges** £2.50 per night **Public areas** except children's play area disp bin **Exercise area** on site dog walks & field **Facilities** on site shop food food bowl water bowl dog chews cat treats litter tray etc dog scoop/disp bags washing facs walks info vet info **Other** prior notice required **Resident Pets:** Hamish (West Highland Terrier)

Open Etr-Oct Last arrival mdnt Last departure 10.00hrs

A family site in a lovely rural position near several beaches and bays. This airy park offers screening to some pitches, which are set in paddocks on level ground. High season entertainment is available in the park's country inn, and the café has an extensive menu. A 25-acre site with 357 touring pitches, 14 hardstandings and 5 statics.

Notes Families & couples only. No skateboards

ROSUDGEON MAP 02 SW52

►►► Kenneggy Cove Holiday Park

(SW562287)

Higher Kenneggy TR20 9AU

☎ 01736 763453

e-mail: enquiries@kenneggycove.co.uk

web: www.kenneggycove.co.uk

Dir: *On A394 between Penzance & Helston, turn S into signed lane to site & Higher Kenneggy*

PETS: Charges dogs £3 per night **Public areas** except children's play area, shop, toilets & laundry disp bin **Exercise area** adjacent **Facilities** on site shop food food bowl water bowl dog scoop/disp bags washing facs walks info vet info **Restrictions** no dangerous breeds (see page 7) **Resident Pets:** Hugo & Tickle (Wire Haired Dachshunds), Ginger & Mollie (cats), Rosie (rabbit)

Open 17 May-4 Oct Last arrival 21.00hrs Last departure 11.00hrs

Set in an Area of Outstanding Natural Beauty with spectacular sea views, this family-owned park is quiet and well kept. A short walk along a country footpath leads to the Cornish Coastal Path, and on to the golden sandy beach at Kenneggy Cove. A 4-acre site with 50 touring pitches and 9 statics.

Notes ⊜ No large groups

ENGLAND

ST AGNES

MAP 02 SW75

★★★ 77% COUNTRY HOUSE HOTEL

Rose-in-Vale Country House

Mithian TR5 0QD

☎ 01872 552202 01872 552700

e-mail: reception@rose-in-vale-hotel.co.uk

web: www.rose-in-vale-hotel.co.uk

Dir: *Take A30 S towards Redruth. At Chiverton Cross at rdbt take B3277 signed St Agnes. In 500mtrs turn at tourist info sign for Rose-in-Vale. Into Mithian, right at Miners Arms, down hill. Hotel on left.*

PETS: Bedrooms (5GF) **Stables** nearby (3m) **Charges** £4.95 per night charge for damage **Public areas** (on leads) **Grounds** accessible on leads disp bin **Exercise area Facilities** walks info vet info **Restrictions** breed accepted only at manager's discretion **Resident Pets:** Hetty (Black Labrador)

Peacefully located in a wooded valley this Georgian manor house has a wonderfully relaxed atmosphere and abundant charm. Guests are assured of a warm welcome. Accommodation varies in size and style; several rooms are situated on the ground floor. An imaginative fixed-price menu featuring local produce is served in the spacious restaurant.

Rooms 17 en suite 2 annexe en suite (2 fmly) (5 GF) S fr £90; D £130-£260 (incl. bkfst)✻ **Facilities** FTV Wi-fi available Xmas New Year **Parking** 52 **Notes LB** No children

★★★★ GUEST ACCOMMODATION

Driftwood Spars

Trevaunance Cove TR5 0RT

☎ 01872 552428 01872 553701

e-mail: driftwoodspars@hotmail.com

Dir: *A30 to Chiverton rdbt, right onto B3277 through village. Establishment 200yds before beach*

PETS: Bedrooms (5GF) **Stables** nearby (3m) **Charges** £3 per night £21 per week charge for damage **Public areas** except restaurant (on leads) **Grounds** accessible **Exercise area** 500yds beach **Facilities** vet info **On Request** fridge access **Resident Pets:** Purdy (cat)

Partly built from ship-wreck timbers, this 18th-century inn attracts locals and visitors alike. The attractive bedrooms, some in an annexe, are decorated in bright, sea-side style and have many interesting features. Local produce served in the informal pub dining room or in the restaurant, ranges from hand-pulled beers to delicious, locally landed seafood.

Rooms 9 en suite 6 annexe en suite (4 fmly) (5 GF) S £45-£66; D £86-£101✻ **Facilities** TVB tea/coffee Direct dial from bedrooms Cen ht TVL Dinner Last d 9.30pm Wi-fi available Pool Table **Parking** 40 **Notes** RS 25 Dec

►►► Beacon Cottage Farm Touring Park

(SW705502)

Beacon Dr TR5 0NU

☎ 01872 552347 & 553381

e-mail: beaconcottagefarm@lineone.net

web: www.beaconcottagefarmholidays.co.uk

Dir: *From A30 at Threeburrows rdbt, take B3277 to St Agnes, left into Goonvrea Road & right into Beacon Drive, follow brown sign to site*

PETS: Charges £2 per night disp bin **Exercise area** on site field available **Facilities** washing facs walks info vet info **Resident Pets:** Rusty (cat), Folly (horse)

Open Apr-Oct (rs Etr-Whit shop closed) Last arrival 20.00hrs Last departure noon

A neat and compact site on a working farm, utilizing a cottage and outhouses, an old orchard and adjoining walled paddock. The unique location on a headland looking NE along the coast comes with stunning views towards St Ives, and the keen friendly family owners keep all areas very well maintained. A 5-acre site with 70 touring pitches.

Notes No large groups

►►► Presingoll Farm Caravan & Camping Park *(SW721494)*

TR5 0PB

☎ 01872 552333 📠 01872 552333

e-mail: pam@presingollfarm.fsbusiness.co.uk

web: www.presingollfarm.fsbusiness.co.uk

Dir: *From A30 Chiverton rdbt take B3277 towards St Agnes. Site 3m on right*

PETS: Stables nearby (1m) disp bin **Exercise area** on site adjacent meadow **Facilities** walks info vet info **Resident Pets:** various farm animals

Open Etr/Apr-Oct Last departure 10.00hrs

An attractive rural park adjoining farmland, with extensive views of the coast beyond. Family owned and run, with level grass pitches, and modernised toilet block in smart converted farm buildings. There is also a campers' room with microwave and free coffee and tea. A 5-acre site with 90 touring pitches.

Notes ⊛ No large groups

ST AUSTELL — MAP 02 SX05

★★★★ BED & BREAKFAST

Cooperage

37 Cooperage Rd, Trewoon PL25 5SJ

☎ 01726 70497 & 07854 960385

e-mail: lcooperage@tiscali.co.uk

web: www.cooperagebb.co.uk

Dir: *1m W of St Austell. On A3058 in Trewoon*

PETS: Bedrooms Public areas except breakfast room **Grounds** accessible disp bin **Exercise area** 500yds **Facilities** dog chews feeding mat leads pet sitting washing facs walks info vet info **On Request** fridge access torch towels **Resident Pets:** Jack (Black Labrador)

Situated on the edge of the town, this late Victorian, semi-detached granite house has been renovated in a contemporary style. The comfortable bedrooms are well equipped and feature beautifully tiled en suites. Guests are assured of a friendly and relaxed welcome here and the property is conveniently positioned for the numerous amenities and attractions locally. Cooperage is suitable for both business and leisure guests. Pets welcome by arrangement.

Rooms 4 rms (3 en suite) (1 pri facs) S £35-£40; D £55-£60 **Facilities** TVB tea/coffee Cen ht Wi-fi available **Parking** 6 **Notes** LB

►►► Court Farm Holidays *(SW953524)*

St Stephen PL26 7LE

☎ 01726 823684 📠 01726 823684

e-mail: truscott@ctfarm.freeserve.co.uk

web: www.courtfarmcornwall.co.uk

Dir: *From St Austell take A3058 towards Newquay. Through St Stephen (pass Peugeot garage). Right at 'St Stephen/Coombe Hay/Langreth/Industrial site' sign. 400yds, site on right*

PETS: disp bin **Exercise area** on site adjacent fields **Facilities** vet info **Other** prior notice required **Resident Pets:** Bess (Sheep dog), Boots (cat)

Open Apr-Sep Last arrival by dark Last departure 11.00hrs

Set in a peaceful rural location, this large camping field offers plenty of space, and is handy for the Eden Project and the Lost Gardens of Heligan. Coarse fishing and use of a large telescope are among the attractions. A 4-acre site with 20 touring pitches, 5 hardstandings.

Notes No noisy behaviour after dark

►►► Old Kerrow Farm Holiday Park *(SX020573)*

Stenalees PL26 8GD

☎ 01726 851651 📠 01726 852826

e-mail: oldkerrowfarmholidaypark@hotmail.com

web: www.oldkerrowfarmholidaypark.co.uk

Dir: *Exit A30 by taking filter lane onto A391 to Bugle. Left at lights onto unclassified road. Site on right approx 1m just after sign for Kerrow Moor*

PETS: Stables nearby (6m) (loose box) **Charges** £1 for 2nd dog per night **Public areas** except pet free area disp bin **Exercise area** on site adjacent walks & woodland **Facilities** on site shop food bowl water bowl dog chews cat treats washing facs walks info vet info **Other** prior notice required

Open all year Last arrival 20.00hrs Last departure 10.30hrs

A rapidly improving park set on a former working farm, with good toilet facilities. The touring area is divided into two paddocks - one especially for dog owners with an extensive dog walk. Cycle hire can be arranged, and there is a cycle track to the Eden Project four miles away. A 20-acre site with 50 touring pitches, 11 hardstandings.

Notes No noise as quiet, peaceful location

ENGLAND

ST BLAZEY GATE MAP 02 SX05

►►► Doubletrees Farm *(SX060540)*

Luxulyan Rd PL24 2EH
☎ 01726 812266
e-mail: doubletrees@eids.co.uk
web: www.eids.co.uk/doubletrees

Dir: *On A390 at Blazey Gate. Turn by Leek Seed Chapel, almost opposite BP filling station. After approx 300yds turn right by public bench into site.*

PETS: disp bin **Exercise area** on site 5 acres **Resident Pets:** Ben (Border Collie), chickens

Open all year Last arrival 22.30hrs Last departure 11.30hrs

A popular park with terraced pitches offering superb sea and coastal views. Close to beaches, and the nearest park to the Eden Project, it is very well maintained by friendly owners. A 1.75-acre site with 32 touring pitches, 6 hardstandings.

Notes

ST COLUMB MAJOR MAP 02 SW96

►►► Southleigh Manor Naturist Park

(SW918623)

TR9 6HY
☎ 01637 880938 📠 01637 881108
e-mail: enquiries@southleigh-manor.com

Dir: *Leave A30 at junct with A39 signed Wadebridge. At Highgate Hill rdbt take A39. At Halloon rdbt take A39. At Trekenning rdbt take 4th exit 500mtrs along on right*

PETS: Charges £1.50 per night **Public areas** dogs only allowed on or adjacent to owners' pitch **Exercise area** dogs must be exercised off site **Facilities** water bowl walks info vet info
Resident Pets: Wenna (Old English Sheep Dog)

Open Etr-Oct shop open peak times only Last arrival 20.00hrs Last departure 10.30hrs

A very well maintained naturist park in the heart of the Cornish countryside, catering for families and couples only. Seclusion and security are very well planned, and the lovely gardens provide a calm setting. A 4-acre site with 50 touring pitches.

Notes Naturist site

ST GENNYS MAP 02 SX19

►►► Bude Camping & Caravanning Club Site *(SX176943)*

Gillards Moor EX23 0BG
☎ 01840 230650
web: www.thefriendlyclub.co.uk

Dir: *From N on A39 site on right in lay-by, 9m from Bude. From S on A39 site on left in lay-by 9m from Camelford. Approx 3m from B3262 junct*

PETS: Public areas except in buildings **Exercise area** 20mtrs **Facilities** walks info vet info **Other** prior notice required

Open 27 Apr-28 Sep Last arrival 21.00hrs Last departure noon

A well-kept, level grass site with good quality facilities. Located midway between Bude and Camelford in an area full of sandy coves and beaches with good surfing. A 6-acre site with 100 touring pitches, 9 hardstandings.

Notes Site gates closed 23.00hrs-07.00hrs

ST IVES MAP 02 SW54

★★★ 77% HOTEL

Garrack Hotel & Restaurant

Burthallan Ln, Higher Ayr TR26 3AA
☎ 01736 796199 📠 01736 798955
e-mail: aa@garrack.com

Dir: *Turn off A30 for St Ives. B3311 follow brown signs for Tate Gallery, then Garrack brown signs*

PETS: Bedrooms unattended **Charges** max £10 per night charge for damage **Grounds** accessible disp bin **Exercise area** country lane & cliffs nearby **Facilities** washing facs cage storage walks info vet info **On Request** fridge access towels **Other** prior notice required; pets allowed in certain bedrooms only

Enjoying a peaceful, elevated position with splendid views across the harbour and Porthmeor Beach, the Garrack sits in its own delightful grounds and gardens. Bedrooms are comfortable and many have sea views. Public areas include a small leisure suite, a choice of lounges and an attractive restaurant, where locally sourced ingredients are used in the enjoyable dishes.

Rooms 16 en suite 2 annexe en suite (2 fmly) S £75-£99; D £124-£198 (incl. bkfst)✻ **Facilities** FTV Gym Wi-fi available New Year **Parking** 30 **Notes** LB

★★★★ GUEST HOUSE

Old Vicarage

Parc-an-Creet TR26 2ES

☎ 01736 796124

e-mail: stay@oldvicarage.com

web: www.oldvicarage.com

Dir: *Off A3074 in town centre onto B3306, 0.5m right into Parc-an-Creet*

PETS: Bedrooms Public areas must be well behaved **Grounds** accessible **Exercise area** on site

This former Victorian rectory stands in secluded gardens in a quiet part of St Ives and is convenient for the seaside, town and the Tate. The bedrooms are enhanced by modern facilities. A good choice of local produce is offered at breakfast, plus home-made yoghurt and preserves.

Rooms 5 en suite (4 fmly) S £60-£65; D £80-£90 **Facilities** TVB tea/coffee Licensed Cen ht TVL ⛳ **Parking** 12 **Notes** No coaches Closed Dec-Jan

►►► Penderleath Caravan & Camping Park *(SW496375)*

Towednack TR26 3AF

☎ 01736 798403

e-mail: holidays@penderleath.co.uk

web: www.penderleath.co.uk

Dir: *From A30 take A3074 towards St Ives. Left at 2nd mini-rdbt, approx 3m to T-junct. Left then immediately right. Left at next fork*

PETS: Charges £1-£2.50 per night **Public areas** except toilets, bar area & shop (on leads) disp bin **Exercise area** on site not available in August **Facilities** on site shop food food bowl water bowl dog scoop/disp bags walks info vet info **Other** prior notice required **Resident Pets:** Buster (Jack Russell)

Open Etr-Oct Last arrival 21.30hrs Last departure 10.30hrs

Set in a rugged rural location, this tranquil park has extensive views towards St Ives Bay and the north coast. Facilities are all housed in modernised granite barns, and include a quiet licensed bar with beer garden, breakfast room and bar meals. The owners are welcoming and helpful. A 10-acre site with 75 touring pitches.

►►► Trevalgan Touring Park *(SW490402)*

Trevalgan TR26 3BJ

☎ 01736 792048 🖹 01736 798797

e-mail: recept@trevalgantouringpark.co.uk

web: www.trevalgantouringpark.co.uk

Dir: *From A30 follow holiday route to St Ives. B3311 through Halsetown to B3306. Left towards Land's End. Site signed 0.5m on right*

PETS: Stables (loose box) **Charges** approx £1.75 per night **Public areas** except children's play area disp bin **Exercise area** 100mtrs **Facilities** on site shop food food bowl water bowl dog scoop/disp bags washing facs walks info vet info

Open Etr-Sep Last arrival 22.00hrs Last departure 10.00hrs

An open park next to a working farm in a rural area on the coastal road from St Ives to Zennor. The park is surrounded by mature hedges, but there are extensive views out over the sea. There are very good toilet facilities including family rooms, and a large TV lounge and recreation room with drinks machine. A 4.75-acre site with 120 touring pitches.

►► Balnoon Camping Site *(SW509382)*

Halsetown TR26 3JA

☎ 01736 795431

e-mail: nat@balnoon.fsnet.co.uk

Dir: *From A30 take A3074, at 2nd mini-rdbt take 1st left signed Tate St Ives. After 3m turn right after Balnoon Inn*

PETS: disp bin **Exercise area Facilities** on site shop walks info vet info **Other** prior notice required **Restrictions** no Staffordshire Bull Terriers or similar breeds

Open Etr-Oct Last arrival 20.00hrs Last departure 11.00hrs

Small, quiet and friendly, this sheltered site offers superb views of the adjacent rolling hills. The two paddocks are surrounded by mature hedges, and the toilet facilities are kept spotlessly clean. The beaches of Carbis Bay and St Ives are about 2 miles away. A 1-acre site with 23 touring pitches.

Notes ⊜

ST JUST (NEAR LAND'S END) — MAP 02 SW33

►►► *Kelynack Caravan & Camping Park*

(SW374301)

Kelynack TR19 7RE

☎ 01736 787633 📠 01736 787633

e-mail: kelynackholidays@tiscali.co.uk

Dir: *1m S of St Just, 5m N of Land's End on B3306*

PETS: Charges £1 per night **Public areas** except children's play area disp bin **Exercise area** adjacent **Facilities** on site shop food food bowl water bowl dog scoop/disp bags washing facs walks info vet info **Other** prior notice required

Resident Pets: Max (King Charles Cavalier Spaniel), Titch (Yorkshire Terrier), Bracken, Carmen, Ned & Scrumpy Jack (donkeys), Pedro (Shetland Pony)

Open Apr-Oct Last arrival 22.00hrs Last departure 10.00hrs

A small secluded park nestling alongside a stream in an unspoilt rural location. The level grass pitches are in two areas, and the park is close to many coves, beaches, and ancient villages. A 3-acre site with 20 touring pitches, 4 hardstandings and 13 statics.

Notes

►►► *Trevaylor Caravan & Camping Park*

(SW368222)

Botallack TR19 7PU

☎ 01736 787016

e-mail: bookings@trevaylor.com

web: www.trevaylor.com

Dir: *On B3306 (St Just-St Ives road), site on right 0.75m from St Just*

PETS: Stables nearby (200mtrs) **Charges** £1 per night in Jul & Aug per night **Public areas** on leads, may not roam free on any part of the site disp bin **Exercise area** 50mtrs **Facilities** on site shop food food bowl water bowl washing facs walks info vet info **Other** prior notice required **Resident Pets:** Border Collie

Open Fri before Etr-Oct Last departure noon

A sheltered grassy site located off the beaten track in a peaceful location at the western tip of Cornwall. The dramatic coastline and the pretty villages nearby are truly unspoilt. Clean, well-maintained facilities and a good shop are offered along with a bar serving bar meals. A 6-acre site with 50 touring pitches.

ST JUST-IN-ROSELAND — MAP 02 SW83

►►► Trethem Mill Touring Park *(SW860365)*

TR2 5JF

☎ 01872 580504 📠 01872 580968

e-mail: reception@trethem.com

web: www.trethem.com

Dir: *From Tregony on A3078 to St Mawes. 2m after Trewithian, follow signs to site*

PETS: Charges £1 per night **Public areas** except in buildings disp bin **Exercise area** on site 5-acre dog walk **Facilities** on site shop food walks info vet info

Open Apr-mid Oct Last arrival 20.00hrs Last departure 11.00hrs

A quality park in all areas, with upgraded amenities including a reception, shop, laundry, and disabled/family room. This carefully-tended and sheltered park is in a lovely rural setting, with spacious pitches separated by young trees and shrubs. The very keen family who own it are continually looking for ways to enhance its facilities. An 11-acre site with 84 touring pitches, 50 hardstandings.

ST KEVERNE — MAP 02 SW72

★★★ GUEST HOUSE

Gallen-Treath Guest House

Porthallow TR12 6PL

☎ 01326 280400 📠 01326 280400

e-mail: gallentreath@btclick.com

Dir: *1.5m S of St Keverne in Porthallow*

PETS: Bedrooms (1GF) unattended **Charges** £2 per night £14 per week charge for damage **Public areas** except restaurant/ dining room **Grounds** accessible disp bin **Exercise area** 2 mins walk to beach, coastal path & fields **Facilities** food (pre-bookable) food bowl water bowl bedding dog chews cat treats dog scoop/ disp bags washing facs walks info vet info **On Request** fridge access torch towels **Other** all pet facilities by prior request only; pets left unattended in bedrooms at breakfast time only

Resident Pets: J.D.(Bearded Collie/Lurcher cross)

Gallen-Treath has super views over the countryside and sea from its elevated position above Porthallow. Bedrooms are individually decorated and feature many personal touches. Guests can relax in the large, comfortable lounge complete with balcony. Hearty breakfasts and dinners (by arrangement) are served in the bright dining room.

Rooms 5 rms (4 en suite) (1 pri facs) (1 fmly) (1 GF) S £25-£30; D £50-£60✻ **Facilities** FTV TVB tea/coffee Licensed Cen ht TVL Dinner Last d at breakfast **Parking** 6

ST MARTIN'S (ISLES OF SCILLY) MAP 02 SV91

★★★HOTEL

St Martin's on the Isle

Lower Town TR25 0QW

☎ 01720 422090 & 422092 📠 01720 422298

e-mail: stay@stmartinshotel.co.uk

web: www.stmartinshotel.co.uk

Dir: *20-minute helicopter flight to St Mary's, then 10-minute launch to St Martin's*

PETS: Bedrooms (14GF) sign **Charges** £15 (including food) per night **Public areas Grounds** accessible disp bin **Exercise area Facilities** food (pre-bookable) food bowl water bowl bedding feeding mat dog scoop/disp bags washing facs walks info vet info **On Request** fridge access torch towels

This attractive hotel, complete with its own sandy beach, enjoys an idyllic position on the waterfront overlooking Tresco and Tean. Bedrooms are brightly appointed, comfortably furnished and overlook the sea or the well-tended gardens. There is an elegant restaurant and a split level lounge bar where guests can relax and enjoy the memorable view. Locally caught fish features significantly on the daily-changing menus. At the time of going to press the rosette award for this hotel was suspended due to a change of chef. Please see the AA website, www.theAA.com, for up-to-date details.

Rooms 30 en suite (10 fmly) (14 GF) S £105-£190; D £210 £420 (incl. bkfst & dinner)✻ **Facilities** Wi-fi available Clay pigeon shooting Boating Bikes Diving Snorkelling ch fac **Notes LB** Closed Nov-Feb

ST MAWES MAP 02 SW83

★★★ 83% ⊛⊛ HOTEL

Idle Rocks

Harbour Side TR2 5AN

☎ 01326 270771 📠 01326 270062

e-mail: reception@idlerocks.co.uk

web: www.idlerocks.co.uk

Dir: *off A390 onto A3078, 14m to St Mawes. Hotel on left*

PETS: Bedrooms (2GF) unattended sign **Charges** £7 per night **Public areas** except dining room & lounge (on leads) **Exercise area Facilities** walks info vet info **On Request** torch **Other** Please telephone for details

This hotel has splendid sea views overlooking the attractive fishing port. The lounge and bar also benefit from the views and in warmer months service is available on the terrace. Bedrooms are individually styled and tastefully furnished to a high standard. The daily-changing menu served in the restaurant features fresh, local produce in imaginative cuisine.

Rooms 23 en suite 4 annexe en suite (6 fmly) (2 GF) **Facilities** Wi-fi available **Parking** 4 (charged)

SALTASH MAP 02 SX45

★★★ GUEST ACCOMMODATION

Crooked Inn

Stoketon Cross, Trematon PL12 4RZ

☎ 01752 848177 📠 01752 843203

e-mail: info@crooked-inn.co.uk

Dir: *1.5m NW of Saltash. A38 W from Saltash, 2nd left to Trematon, sharp right*

PETS: Bedrooms (7GF) unattended **Exercise area** on site 20 acres of dog roaming territory **Other** Please telephone for details **Resident Pets:** Mambo, Mr Wilks & Cassie (dogs) cats, pet pig, pet sheep, ducks

The friendly animals that freely roam the courtyard add to the relaxed country style of this delightful inn. The spacious bedrooms are well equipped, and freshly cooked dinners are available in the bar and conservatory. Breakfast is served in the cottage-style dining room.

Rooms 18 annexe rms (15 en suite) (5 fmly) (7 GF) S fr £52; D fr £80 **Facilities** TVB tea/coffee Cen ht Dinner **Parking** 45 **Notes** Closed 25 Dec

See advert on page 35

SENNEN MAP 02 SW32

►►► Sennen Cove Camping & Caravanning Club Site *(SW378276)*

Higher Tregiffian Farm TR19 6JB

☎ 01736 871588

web: www.thefriendlyclub.co.uk

Dir: *A30 towards Land's End. Right onto A3306 St Just/Pendeen Rd. Site 200yds on left*

PETS: Public areas except in buildings disp bin **Exercise area** on site **Facilities** walks info vet info **Other** prior notice required

Open 27 Apr-28 Sep Last arrival 21.00hrs Last departure noon

Set in a rural area with distant views of Carn Brae and the coast just 2 miles from Land's End, this very good club site is well run with modern, clean facilities. It offers a children's playfield, late arrivals area and a dog-exercising paddock. A 4-acre site with 72 touring pitches, 6 hardstandings.

Notes Site gates closed 23.00hrs-07.00hrs

ENGLAND

SUMMERCOURT MAP 02 SW85

►►►► Carvynick Country Club *(SW878564)*

TR8 5AF

☎ 01872 510716 📠 01872 510172

e-mail: info@carvynick.co.uk

web: www.carvynick.co.uk

Dir: *Off B3058*

PETS: Exercise area adjacent lane **Facilities** walks info vet info

Open all year (rs Jan-early Feb Restricted leisure facilities)

Set within the gardens of an attractive country estate this spacious dedicated American RV Park (also home to the 'Itchy Feet' retail company) provides all full facility pitches on hard standings. The extensive on site amenities, shared by the high quality time share village, include an excellent restaurant with lounge bar, indoor leisure area with swimming pool, fitness suite and badminton court. 32 touring pitches.

Notes Dogs must be exercised off site

TINTAGEL MAP 02 SX08

★★★ INN

Port William Inn

Trebarwith Strand PL34 0HB

☎ 01840 770230 📠 01840 770936

PETS: Bedrooms unattended **Stables** nearby (10 mins) **Charges** £5 per night **Public areas** except conservatory **Exercise area** coastal path **Facilities** cage storage walks info vet info

The Port William has a superb location, perched on the cliff-side just south of Tintagel. The smartly appointed bedrooms all have wonderful sea views with the sound of the waves below ensuring a restful sleep. The spacious bar-restaurant has a conservatory and outside area, where the extensive menu can be enjoyed along with the spectacular scenery.

Rooms 8 en suite (1 fmly) S £69-£85; D £89-£105* **Facilities** TVB tea/coffee Cen ht Dinner Last d 8.45pm Wi-fi available Pool Table **Parking** 45 **Notes** LB

TREGURRIAN MAP 02 SW86

►►► Tregurrian Camping & Caravanning Club Site *(SW847654)*

TR8 4AE

☎ 01637 860448

web: www.thefriendlyclub.co.uk

Dir: *A30 onto A3059, 1.5m turn right signed Newquay Airport. Left at junct after airport, then right at grass triangle, follow signs to Watergate Bay*

PETS: disp bin **Exercise area Facilities** walks info vet info **Other** prior notice required

Open 27 Apr-28 Sep Last arrival 21.00hrs Last departure noon

A level grassy site close to the famous beaches of Watergate Bay, with a modern amenity block. This upgraded club site is an excellent touring centre for the Padstow-Newquay coast. A 4.25-acre site with 90 touring pitches, 8 hardstandings.

Notes Site gates closed 23.00hrs-07.00hrs

TRURO MAP 02 SW84

★★★ 81% @@ HOTEL

Alverton Manor

Tregolls Rd TR1 1ZQ

☎ 01872 276633 📠 01872 222989

e-mail: reception@alvertonmanor.co.uk

web: www.connexions.co.uk/alvertonmanor/index.htm

Dir: *From Carland Cross, take A39 to Truro*

PETS: Bedrooms (3GF) unattended **Charges** £3 per night **Public areas** except restaurant (on leads) **Grounds** accessible on leads **Exercise area** Malpas Park 1m **Facilities** washing facs cage storage walks info vet info **On Request** fridge access torch towels **Resident Pets:** chickens, a beehive

Formerly a convent, this impressive sandstone property stands in six acres of grounds, within walking distance of the city centre. It has a wide range of smart bedrooms, combining comfort with character. Stylish public areas include the library and the former chapel, now a striking function room. An interesting range of dishes, using the very best of local produce (organic whenever possible) is offered in the elegant restaurant.

Rooms 32 en suite (3 GF) **Facilities** ⛳ 18 Wi-fi available **Services** Lift **Parking** 120 **Notes** Closed 28 Dec RS 4 Jan

★★ 72% HOTEL

Carlton

Falmouth Rd TR1 2HL

☎ 01872 272450 🖷 01872 223938

e-mail: reception@carltonhotel.co.uk

Dir: *on A39 straight across 1st & 2nd rdbts onto bypass (Morlaix Ave). At top of sweeping bend/hill turn right at mini rdbt into Falmouth Rd. Hotel 100mtrs on right*

PETS: Bedrooms (4GF) unattended sign **Charges** charge for damage **Exercise area Facilities** food bowl water bowl bedding dog chews feeding mat walks info vet info **On Request** torch towels

This family-run hotel is pleasantly located a short stroll from the city centre. A friendly welcome is assured and both business and leisure guests choose the Carlton on a regular basis. A smart, comfortable lounge is available, along with leisure facilities. A wide selection of home-cooked dishes is offered in the dining room.

Rooms 29 en suite (4 fmly) (4 GF) S £47-£57; D £67-£77 (incl. bkfst)* **Facilities** STV **Parking** 31 **Notes** Closed 20 Dec-5 Jan

★★★ FARM HOUSE

Polsue Manor Farm *(SW858462)*

Tresillian TR2 4BP

☎ 01872 520234 🖷 01872 520616 Mrs G Holliday

e-mail: geraldineholliday@hotmail.com

Dir: *2m NE of Truro. Farm entrance on A390 at S end of Tresillian*

PETS: Bedrooms Grounds accessible **Exercise area** on site **Facilities** walks info vet info **Other** dogs allowed in non en suite bedrooms only **Resident Pets:** Polly & Penny (Yellow Labradors)

The 190-acre sheep farm is in peaceful countryside a short drive from Truro. The farmhouse provides a relaxing break from the city, with hearty breakfasts and warm hospitality. The spacious dining room has pleasant views and three large communal tables. Bedrooms do not offer televisions but there is a homely lounge equipped with a television and video recorder with a selection of videos for viewing.

Rooms 5 rms (2 en suite) (3 fmly) (1 GF) **Facilities** tea/coffee TVL **Parking** 5 **Notes** 190 acres mixed sheep horses working Closed 21 Dec-2 Jan

VERYAN — MAP 02 SW93

►►► **Veryan Camping & Caravanning Club Site** *(SW934414)*

Tretheake Manor TR2 5PP

☎ 01872 501658

web: www.thefriendlyclub.co.uk

Dir: *Left off A3078 at filling station signed Veryan/Portloe on unclass road. Site signed on left*

PETS: Public areas except in buildings disp bin **Exercise area** on site **Facilities** walks info vet info **Other** prior notice required

Open 2 Apr-2 Nov Last arrival 21.00hrs Last departure noon

A quiet park on slightly undulating land with pleasant views of the surrounding countryside. A tranquil fishing lake holds appeal for anglers, and the site is just 2.5 miles from one of Cornwall's finest sandy beaches. A 9-acre site with 150 touring pitches, 24 hardstandings.

Notes Site gates closed 23.00hrs-07.00hrs

WADEBRIDGE — MAP 02 SW97

►►► **The Laurels Holiday Park** *(SW957715)*

Padstow Rd, Whitecross PL27 7JQ

☎ 01209 313474

e-mail: info@thelaurelsholidaypark.co.uk

web: www.thelaurelsholidaypark.co.uk

Dir: *Off A389 (Padstow road) near junct with A39, W of Wadebridge*

PETS: Charges £2 per night **Public areas** except toilets & laundry (on leads) disp bin **Exercise area** on site fenced area **Facilities** walks info vet info **Other** prior notice required

Open Apr/Etr-Oct Last arrival 20.00hrs Last departure 11.00hrs

A very smart and well-equipped park with individual pitches screened by hedges and young shrubs. The dog walk is of great benefit to pet owners, and the Camel cycle trail and Padstow are not far away. A 2.25-acre site with 30 touring pitches, 2 hardstandings.

Notes ⊜ Dogs must be kept on leads

WATERGATE BAY — MAP 02 SW86

►►►► Watergate Bay Tourist Park

(SW850653)

Watergate Bay TR8 4AD

☎ 01637 860387 Fax 0871 661 7549

e-mail: email@watergatebaytouringpark.co.uk

web: www.watergatebaytouringpark.co.uk

Dir: *4m N of Newquay on B3276 (coast road)*

PETS: Charges £2 Jul-Aug only per night **Public areas** except swimming pool area, clubroom, cafeteria, recreational area disp bin **Exercise area** on site 2-acre exercise field **Facilities** on site shop food litter tray etc dog scoop/disp bags walks info vet info **Other** prior notice required

Open Mar-Oct (rs Mar-22 May & 13 Sep-Oct restricted bar, cafe, shop & pool) Last arrival 22.00hrs Last departure noon

A well-established park above Watergate Bay, where acres of golden sand, rock pools and surf are seen as a holidaymaker's paradise. Toilet facilities are to a high standard, and there is a wide range of activities including a regular entertainment programme in the clubhouse. A 30-acre site with 171 touring pitches, 14 hardstandings and 2 statics.

WIDEMOUTH BAY — MAP 02 SS20

Widemouth Bay Caravan Park

(SS199008)

EX23 0DF

☎ 01271 866766 Fax 01271 866791

e-mail: bookings@jfhols.co.uk

web: www.johnfowlerholidays.com

Dir: *Take Widemouth Bay coastal road off A39, turn left. Site on left*

PETS: Charges £20 (short stay) per night £40 per week **Public areas** except in buildings disp bin **Exercise area** on site acres of open grassland **Facilities** on site shop food food bowl water bowl dog chews cat treats walks info vet info **Other** prior notice required

Open Etr-Oct Last arrival dusk Last departure 10.00hrs

A partly sloping rural site set in countryside overlooking the sea and one of Cornwall's finest beaches. Nightly entertainment in high season with emphasis on children's and family club programmes. This park is located less than half a mile from the sandy beaches of Widemouth Bay. A 58-acre site with 220 touring pitches, 90 hardstandings and 200 statics.

ZENNOR — MAP 02 SW43

★★★ @@ INN

The Gurnard's Head

Treen TR26 3DE

☎ 01736 796928

e-mail: enquiries@gurnardshead.co.uk

Dir: *5m from St Ives on B3306, 4.5m from Penzance via New Mill*

PETS: Bedrooms unattended **Public areas** except restaurant **Grounds** accessible **Exercise area** adjacent to fields & footpaths **Facilities** food bowl

Ideally located for enjoying the beautiful coastline, this inn offers atmospheric public areas. The style is relaxed and very popular with walkers, keen to rest their weary legs. A log fire in the bar provides a warm welcome on colder days and on warmer days, outside seating is available. Lunch and dinner, featuring local home cooked food, is available either in the bar or the adjoining restaurant area. The dinner menu is not extensive but there are interesting choices and everything is home made, including the bread. Breakfast is served around a grand farm-house table.

Rooms 7 en suite S £60-£82.50; D £82.50-£140* **Facilities** tea/coffee Dinner Last d 9.30pm Wi-fi available **Parking** 40 **Notes** No coaches Closed 25 Dec

CUMBRIA

ALSTON — MAP 12 NY74

★★★★ GUEST HOUSE

Lowbyer Manor Country House

Hexham Rd CA9 3JX

☎ 01434 381230 Fax 01434 381425

e-mail: stay@lowbyer.com

web: www.lowbyer.com

Dir: *250yds N of village centre on A686. Pass South Tynedale Railway on left, turn right*

PETS: Bedrooms Charges £5 per night **Public areas** except restaurant (on leads) **Grounds** accessible disp bin **Exercise area** 0.5m **Facilities** dog scoop/disp bags washing facs cage storage walks info vet info **On Request** fridge access torch towels

Located on the edge of the village, this Grade II listed Georgian building retains many original features, which are highlighted by the furnishings and decor. Cosy bedrooms are filled with a wealth of thoughtful extras and day rooms include an elegant dining room, a comfortable lounge and bar equipped with lots of historical artefacts.

Rooms 9 en suite (1 fmly) S £33-£45; D £66-£80 **Facilities** TVB tea/coffee Licensed Cen ht **Parking** 9 **Notes LB** No coaches

AMBLESIDE MAP 07 NY30

★★★★TOWN HOUSE HOTEL

Waterhead

Lake Rd LA22 0ER

☎ 015394 32566 015394 31255

e-mail: waterhead@elhmail.co.uk

web: www.elh.co.uk/hotels/waterhead.htm

Dir: *A591 into Ambleside, hotel opposite Waterhead Pier*

PETS: Bedrooms (7GF) **Charges** £15 per night £25 per stay per week **Public areas** bar only (on leads) **Grounds** accessible on leads **Exercise area** 50yds **Facilities** food bowl water bowl walks info vet info **On Request** fridge access torch towels **Restrictions** no dangerous dogs (see page 7) no Rottweilers

With an enviable location opposite the bay, this well-established hotel offers contemporary and comfortable accommodation with CD/DVD players, plasma screens and internet access. There is a bar with a garden terrace overlooking the lake and a stylish restaurant serving classical cuisine with a modern twist. Staff are very attentive and friendly. Guests can enjoy full use of the Low Wood Hotel leisure facilities nearby.

Rooms 41 en suite (3 fmly) (7 GF) **Facilities** FTV Wi-fi available **Parking** 43

★★★ 80% HOTEL

Regent

Waterhead Bay LA22 0ES

☎ 015394 32254 015394 31474

e-mail: info@regentlakes.co.uk

Dir: *1m S on A591*

PETS: Bedrooms unattended **Charges** £6 per night **Public areas** except restaurant, bar & lounges **Exercise area** park by lake

This attractive holiday hotel, situated close to Waterhead Bay, offers a warm welcome. Bedrooms come in a variety of styles, including three suites and five bedrooms in the garden wing. There is a modern swimming pool and the restaurant offers a fine dining experience in a contemporary setting.

Rooms 30 en suite (7 fmly) **Facilities** Wi-fi available **Parking** 39 **Notes** Closed 19-27 Dec

★★★ 75% HOTEL

Skelwith Bridge

Skelwith Bridge LA22 9NJ

☎ 015394 32115 015394 34254

e-mail: info@skelwithbridgehotel.co.uk

web: www.skelwithbridgehotel.co.uk

Dir: *2.5m W on A593 at junct with B5343 to Langdale*

PETS: Bedrooms (1GF) **Charges** £5 per night **Public areas** except restaurant **Grounds** accessible **Exercise area** 100mtrs **Facilities** water bowl pet sitting washing facs cage storage walks info vet info **On Request** torch towels

This 17th-century inn is today a well-appointed tourist hotel located at the heart of the Lake District National Park and renowned for its friendly and attentive service. Bedrooms include two rooms with four-poster beds. Spacious public areas include a choice of lounges and bars and an attractive restaurant overlooking the gardens and bridge from which the hotel takes its name.

Rooms 22 en suite 6 annexe en suite (2 fmly) (1 GF) S £45-£66; D £80-£162 (incl. bkfst)* **Facilities** Xmas New Year **Parking** 60 **Notes** LB

★★★★ GUEST HOUSE

Ambleside Lodge

Rothay Rd LA22 0EJ

☎ 015394 31681 015394 34547

e-mail: enquiries@ambleside-lodge.com

web: www.ambleside-lodge.com

PETS: Bedrooms (8GF) **Charges** charge for damage **Grounds** accessible on leads **Exercise area** 0.5m **Facilities** cage storage walks info vet info

Located close to the centre of this historic market town, this Grade II listed 18th-century residence has a peaceful atmosphere. The stylishly decorated, elegant accommodation includes attractive bedrooms with antique and contemporary pieces, including four-poster beds. Attentive, personal service is provided.

Rooms 18 en suite (8 GF) **Facilities** FTV TVB tea/coffee Cen ht Wi-fi available **Parking** 20

AMBLESIDE CONTINUED

★★★★ GUEST ACCOMMODATION

Brathay Lodge

Rothay Rd LA22 0EE

☎ 015394 32000

e-mail: brathay@globalnet.co.uk

Dir: *One-way system in town centre. Lodge on right opp church*

PETS: Bedrooms (6GF) **Stables** nearby (6m) **Charges** £5 per night £25 per week charge for damage **Exercise area** park 0.5m **Facilities** food bowl water bowl washing facs cage storage vet info **On Request** fridge access torch towels

This traditional property has been refurbished in a bright contemporary style. The pine-furnished bedrooms are mainly very spacious; some share a communal balcony and some of the ground-floor rooms have their own entrance. All rooms have spa baths. Breakfast is continental, self-service in the lounge or can be taken to your bedroom.

Rooms 14 en suite 7 annexe en suite (5 fmly) (6 GF) D £60-£129✳ **Facilities** TVB tea/coffee Cen ht Wi-fi available Use of Langdale Country Club **Parking** 24 **Notes** LB

APPLEBY-IN-WESTMORLAND MAP 12 NY62

★★★★ BED & BREAKFAST

Hall Croft

Dufton CA16 6DB

☎ 017683 52902

e-mail: r.walker@leaseholdpartnerships.co.uk

Dir: *3m N of Appleby. In Dufton by village green*

PETS: Bedrooms Charges charge for damage **Public areas** except dining room at breakfast **Grounds** accessible disp bin **Exercise area** woods nearby **Facilities** food (pre-bookable) food bowl water bowl pet sitting washing facs cage storage walks info vet info **On Request** fridge access torch towels **Other** pet sitting on request **Resident Pets:** Monty (Collie cross), Kester & Shep (Border Collies)

Standing at the end of a lime-tree avenue, Hall Croft, built in 1882, has been restored to its original glory. Bedrooms are comfortably proportioned, traditionally furnished and well equipped. Breakfasts, served in the lounge-dining room, are substantial and include a range of home-made produce. Guests can enjoy the lovely garden, which has views of the Pennines.

Rooms 3 rms (2 en suite) (1 pri facs) **Facilities** TVB tea/coffee Cen ht **Parking** 3 **Notes** Closed 24-26 Dec

►►►►► **Wild Rose Park** *(NY698165)*

Ormside CA16 6EJ

☎ 017683 51077 📠 017683 52551

e-mail: reception@wildrose.co.uk

web: www.wildrose.co.uk

Dir: *Signed on unclass road to Great Ormside, off B6260*

PETS: Charges £1.50 per night disp bin **Exercise area** on site fenced exercise area **Facilities** on site shop food food bowl water bowl bedding dog chews cat treats dog scoop/disp bags leads washing facs walks info vet info **Other** prior notice required **Restrictions** no Rottweilers, Pit Bulls or Dobermans

Open all year (rs Nov-Mar shop & swimming pool closed) Last arrival 22.00hrs Last departure noon

Situated in the Eden Valley, this large family-run park has been carefully landscaped and offers superb facilities maintained to an extremely high standard. There are several individual pitches, and extensive views from most areas of the park. Traditional stone walls and the planting of lots of indigenous trees help it to blend into the environment, and wildlife is actively encouraged. An 85-acre site with 240 touring pitches, 140 hardstandings and 273 statics.

Notes No unaccompanied teenagers, no group bookings

ARMATHWAITE MAP 12 NY54

★★★ INN

The Dukes Head Inn

Front St CA4 9PB

☎ 016974 72226

e-mail: info@dukeshead-hotel.co.uk

web: www.dukeshead-hotel.co.uk

Dir: *In village centre opp post office*

PETS: Bedrooms unattended **Stables** nearby (1m) **Charges** £5 per stay charge for damage **Public areas** except lounge bar & restaurant **Grounds** accessible disp bin **Exercise area** surrounding countryside **Facilities** walks info vet info **Other** day kennels nearby

Located in the peaceful village of Armathwaite close to the River Eden, the Dukes Head offers comfortable accommodation in a warm friendly atmosphere. There is a relaxing lounge bar with open fires and a wide choice of meals are available either here or in the restaurant.

Rooms 5 rms (3 en suite) (2 pri facs) S fr £38.50; D fr £62.50✳ **Facilities** TV4B tea/coffee Cen ht Dinner Last d 9pm **Parking** 20 **Notes** LB Closed 25 Dec

AYSIDE MAP 07 SD38

►►► Oak Head Caravan Park *(SD389839)*

LA11 6JA

☎ 015395 31475

web: www.caravancampingsites.co.uk/cumbria/oakhead.htm

Dir: *M6 junct 36, A590 towards Newby Bridge, 14m. From A590 bypass follow signs for Ayside*

PETS: disp bin **Exercise area Facilities** vet info **Restrictions** no Rottweilers

Open Mar-Oct Last arrival 22.00hrs Last departure noon

A pleasant terraced site with two separate areas - grass for tents and all gravel pitches for caravans and motorhomes. The site is enclosed within mature woodland and surrounded by hills. A 3-acre site with 60 touring pitches, 30 hardstandings and 71 statics.

Notes No open fires

BARROW-IN-FURNESS MAP 07 SD26

★★★ 79% HOTEL

Clarence House Country Hotel & Restaurant

Skelgate LA15 8BQ

☎ 01229 462508 01229 467177

e-mail: clarencehsehotel@aol.com

web: www.clarencehouse-hotel.co.uk

Dir: *A590 through Ulverston & Lindal, 2nd exit at rdbt & 1st exit at next. Follow signs to Dalton, hotel at top of hill on right*

PETS: Bedrooms Charges £10 per night **Exercise area** on site **Other** well behaved dogs, in cottage rooms only

This hotel is peacefully located in ornamental grounds with unrestricted countryside views. Bedrooms are individually themed with those in the main hotel being particularly stylish and comfortable. The public rooms are spacious and also furnished to a high standard. The popular conservatory restaurant offers well-prepared dishes from extensive menus. There is a delightful barn conversion that is ideal for weddings.

Rooms 7 en suite 12 annexe en suite (1 fmly) (5 GF) **Facilities** ♫ **Parking** 40 **Notes LB** Closed 25-26 Dec

BASSENTHWAITE MAP 11 NY23

★★★★ 80% COUNTRY HOUSE HOTEL

Armathwaite Hall

CA12 4RE

☎ 017687 76551 017687 76220

e-mail: reservations@armathwaite-hall.com

web: www.armathwaite-hall.com

Dir: *M6 junct 40/A66 to Keswick rdbt then A591 signed Carlisle. 8m to Castle Inn junct, turn left. Hotel 300yds*

PETS: Bedrooms (8GF) unattended sign **Stables** on site **Charges** £15 per night charge for damage **Grounds** accessible on leads disp bin **Exercise area** 10 min walk **Facilities** food (pre-bookable) bedding dog chews cat treats dog scoop/disp bags pet sitting dog walking washing facs cage storage walks info vet info **On Request** fridge access torch towels

Resident Pets: Ben & Millie (Belgium Shepherd), Chrissy (Labrador)

Enjoying fine views over Bassenthwaite Lake, this impressive mansion, dating from the 17th century, is peacefully situated amid 400 acres of deer park. Comfortably furnished bedrooms are complemented by a choice of public rooms featuring splendid wood panelling and roaring log fires in the cooler months.

Rooms 42 en suite (4 fmly) (8 GF) S £135-£145; D £210-£350 (incl. bkfst) ✻ **Facilities Spa** STV supervised Fishing Gym Putt green Wi-fi available Archery Beauty salon Clayshooting Quad & mountain bikes Falconry Xmas New Year **Services** Lift **Parking** 100 **Notes LB**

ENGLAND

BASSENTHWAITE CONTINUED

★★★ 83% HOTEL

The Pheasant

CA13 9YE

☎ 017687 76234 017687 76002

e-mail: info@the-pheasant.co.uk

web: www.the-pheasant.co.uk

Dir: *Midway between Keswick & Cockermouth, signed from A66*

PETS: Bedrooms (2GF) **Sep Accom** sleeping boxes **Charges** £5 per night **Public areas** except lounge at meal times (on leads) **Grounds** accessible on leads disp bin **Exercise area** on site **Facilities** food (pre-bookable) food bowl water bowl bedding leads cage storage walks info vet info **On Request** fridge access torch towels **Other** please phone for details of pet facilities **Resident Pets:** Scotch & Soda (Golden Retrievers)

Enjoying a rural setting, within well-tended gardens, on the western side of Bassenthwaite Lake, this friendly 500-year-old inn is steeped in tradition. The attractive oak-panelled bar has seen few changes over the years and features log fires and a great selection of malt whiskies. The individually decorated bedrooms are stylish and thoughtfully equipped.

Rooms 13 en suite 2 annexe en suite (2 GF) S £75-£90; D £140-£200 (incl. bkfst)* **Facilities** Wi-fi available New Year **Parking** 40 **Notes** LB No children 12yrs Closed 25 Dec

BOOT MAP 07 NY10

►►► **Eskdale Camping & Caravanning Club Site** *(NY178011)*

Hollins Farm CA19 1TH

☎ 019467 23253

web: www.thefriendlyclub.co.uk

Dir: *Leave A595 at Gosforth or Holmbrook to Eskdale Green and on to Boot. Site on left towards Hardknott Pass after railway*

PETS: Exercise area Facilities washing facs walks info vet info **Other** prior notice required

Open Mar-Oct Last arrival 21.00hrs Last departure noon

A very pleasant site which has been extensively modernised and offers impressive facilities. The re-fitted toilets and showers, laundries and CDP are matched by an extensive reception and well stocked shop. The electric hook-ups are cleverly tucked away. The park is only 0.25m from Boot station on the Ravenglass/Eskdale railway ('Ratty'). An 8-acre site with 80 touring pitches.

Notes Site gates closed 23.00hrs-07.00hrs

BORROWDALE MAP 11 NY21

★★★ 83% HOTEL

Lodore Falls Hotel

CA12 5UX

☎ 017687 77285 017687 77343

e-mail: info@lodorefallshotel.co.uk

web: www.lodorefallshotel.co.uk

Dir: *M6 junct 40 take A66 to Keswick, then B5289 to Borrowdale. Hotel on left*

PETS: Bedrooms unattended **Charges** £10 per night charge for damage **Grounds** accessible on leads disp bin **Exercise area Facilities** food bowl water bowl pet sitting dog walking cage storage walks info vet info **On Request** torch towels

This impressive hotel has an enviable location overlooking Derwentwater. The refurbished bedrooms, many with lake or fell views, are comfortably equipped; family rooms and suites are also available. The dining room, bar and lounge areas were, at the time of inspections, also undergoing refurbishment to a very high standard. One of the treatments in the hotel's Elemis Spa actually makes use of the Lodore Waterfall!

Rooms 69 en suite (11 fmly) S £88-£209; D £149-£365 (incl. bkfst) **Facilities Spa** STV FTV supervised Fishing Squash Gym Wi-fi in bedrooms Xmas New Year **Services** Lift **Parking** 93 **Notes** LB

★★★ 73% HOTEL

Borrowdale

CA12 5UY

☎ 017687 77224 🖷 017687 77338

e-mail: borrowdale@lakedistricthotels.net

Dir: *3m from Keswick, on B5289 at S end of Lake Derwentwater*

PETS: Bedrooms unattended **Sep Accom** kennels **Public areas** except restaurant, and bar at lunch **Grounds** accessible **Exercise area** 50mtrs **Facilities** food (pre-bookable) food bowl water bowl washing facs walks info vet info **On Request** fridge access torch

Situated in the beautiful Borrowdale Valley overlooking Derwentwater, this traditionally styled hotel guarantees a friendly welcome. Extensive public areas include a choice of lounges, traditional dining room, lounge bar and popular conservatory which serves more informal meals. Bedrooms vary in style and size including two that are suitable for less able guests.

Rooms 36 en suite (3 fmly) (3 GF) S £86-£102; D £172-£204 (incl. bkfst & dinner)✳ **Facilities** STV Wi-fi available Leisure facilities available at nearby sister hotel Xmas New Year **Parking** 30 **Notes** LB

BRAITHWAITE — MAP 11 NY22

★★★★ INN

The Royal Oak

CA12 5SY

☎ 017687 78533 🖷 017687 78533

e-mail: theroyaloak@tp-inns.co.uk

web: www.tp-inns.co.uk

Dir: *In village centre*

PETS: Bedrooms unattended **Public areas** except restaurant at food service **Grounds** accessible **Exercise area** **Facilities** water bowl leads washing facs walks info vet info **On Request** fridge access torch towels

The Royal Oak, in the pretty village of Braithwaite, has delightful views of Skiddaw and Barrow, and is a good base for tourists and walkers. Some of the well-equipped bedrooms are furnished with four-poster beds. Hearty meals and traditional Cumbrian breakfasts are served in the restaurant, and there is an atmospheric, well-stocked bar.

Rooms 10 en suite (1 fmly) **Facilities** STV TVB tea/coffee Cen ht Dinner Last d 9pm Wi-fi available **Parking** 20

BRAMPTON — MAP 12 NY56

★★★ ◎◎ HOTEL

Farlam Hall

RELAIS & CHATEAUX.

CA8 2NG

☎ 016977 46234 🖷 016977 46683

e-mail: farlam@relaischateaux.com

web: www.farlamhall.co.uk

Dir: *On A689 (Brampton to Alston). Hotel 2m on left, (not in Farlam village)*

PETS: Bedrooms (2GF) **Sep Accom** field available **Charges** charge for damage **Public areas** except restaurant **Grounds** accessible disp bin **Exercise area** **Facilities** food bowl water bowl leads fresh food by request washing facs cage storage walks info vet info **On Request** torch towels **Resident Pets:** 4 llamas, 4 rare breed sheep

This delightful family-run country house dates back to 1428. Steeped in history, the hotel is set in beautifully landscaped Victorian gardens complete with an ornamental lake and stream. Lovingly restored over many years, it now provides the highest standards of comfort and hospitality. Gracious public rooms invite relaxation, whilst every thought has gone into the beautiful bedrooms, many of which are simply stunning.

Rooms 11 en suite 1 annexe en suite (2 GF) S £155-£180; D £290-£340 (incl. bkfst & dinner)✳ **Facilities** FTV Wi-fi available New Year **Parking** 35 **Notes** LB No children 5yrs Closed 24-30 Dec

ENGLAND

CARLISLE MAP 11 NY45

★★★ 67% HOTEL

The Crown & Mitre

PEEL HOTELS PLC

4 English St CA3 8HZ

☎ 01228 525491 📠 01228 514553

e-mail: info@crownandmitre-hotel-carlisle.com

web: www.peelhotel.com

Dir: *A6 to city centre, pass station & Woolworths on left. Right into Blackfriars St. Rear entrance at end*

PETS: Bedrooms Public areas except restaurant **Exercise area** 5 min walk **Facilities** vet info **On Request** towels

Located in the heart of the city, this Edwardian hotel is close to the cathedral and a few minutes' walk from the castle. Bedrooms vary in size and style, from smart executive rooms to more functional standard rooms. Public rooms include a comfortable lounge area and the lovely bar with its feature stained-glass windows.

Rooms 75 en suite 20 annexe en suite (4 fmly) **Facilities** Wi-fi available **Services** Lift **Parking** 42

★★★ GUEST ACCOMMODATION

Angus House & Almonds Restaurant

14-16 Scotland Rd CA3 9DG

☎ 01228 523546 📠 01228 531895

e-mail: hotel@angus-hotel.co.uk

web: www.angus-hotel.co.uk

Dir: *0.5m N of city centre on A7*

PETS: Bedrooms unattended **Charges** £5 per night **Public areas** except restaurant **Exercise area Facilities** walks info vet info **On Request** fridge access **Restrictions** no Rottweilers or Bull Terriers

Situated just north of the city, this family-run establishment is ideal for business and leisure. A warm welcome is assured and the accommodation is well equipped. Almonds Restaurant provides enjoyable food and home baking, and there is also a lounge and a large meeting room.

Rooms 10 en suite (2 fmly) S £52; D £76 **Facilities** FTV TVB tea/coffee Direct dial from bedrooms Cen ht Dinner Last d 8.45pm Wi-fi available **Notes** LB

►►► **Green Acres Caravan Park** *(NY416614)*

High Knells, Houghton CA6 4JW

☎ 01228 675418

web: www.caravanpark-cumbria.com

Dir: *Leave M6/A74(M) at junct 44, take A689 towards Brampton for 1m. Left at Scaleby sign and site 1m on left*

PETS: disp bin **Exercise area** on site walks & wooded exercise area **Facilities** vet info **Resident Pets:** Kim (mongrel)

Open Etr-Oct Last arrival 21.00hrs Last departure noon

A small family touring park in rural surroundings with distant views of the fells. This pretty park is run by keen, friendly owners who maintain high standards throughout. A 3-acre site with 30 touring pitches, 25 hardstandings.

Notes

CARTMEL MAP 07 SD37

★★ 78% COUNTRY HOUSE HOTEL

Aynsome Manor

LA11 6HH

☎ 015395 36653 📠 015395 36016

e-mail: aynsomemanor@btconnect.com

Dir: *M6 junct 36, A590 signed Barrow-in-Furness towards Cartmel. Left at end of road, hotel before village*

PETS: Bedrooms Charges £2.50 per night **Grounds** accessible on leads disp bin **Exercise area** 0.75m **Facilities** cage storage walks info vet info **On Request** fridge access torch **Resident Pets:** cat

Dating back, in part, to the early 16th century, this manor house overlooks the fells and the nearby priory. Spacious bedrooms, including some courtyard rooms, are comfortably furnished. Dinner in the elegant restaurant features local produce whenever possible, and there is a choice of lounges to relax in afterwards.

Rooms 10 en suite 2 annexe en suite (2 fmly) S £78-£97; D £128-£174 (incl. bkfst & dinner) **Facilities** FTV New Year **Parking** 20 **Notes** LB Closed 2-31 Jan RS Sun

COCKERMOUTH MAP 11 NY13

★★★ 81% HOTEL

The Trout

Crown St CA13 0EJ

01900 823591 01900 827514

e-mail: enquiries@trouthotel.co.uk

web: www.trouthotel.co.uk

Dir: *next to Wordsworth House*

PETS: Bedrooms (15GF) unattended **Charges** £10 per night charge for damage **Grounds** accessible on leads **Exercise area** **Facilities** water bowl walks info vet info

Dating back to 1670, this privately owned hotel has an enviable setting on the banks of the River Derwent. The well-equipped bedrooms, some contained in a wing overlooking the river, are comfortable and mostly spacious. The Terrace Bar and Bistro, serving food all day, has a sheltered patio area. There is also a cosy bar, a choice of lounge areas and an attractive, traditional style dining room that offers a good choice of set-price dishes.

Rooms 47 en suite (4 fmly) (15 GF) S £99-£139; D £115-£155 (incl. bkfst)✳ **Facilities** STV Fishing Wi-fi in bedrooms Xmas New Year **Parking** 40 **Notes** LB

★★★ 70% HOTEL

Shepherds Hotel

Lakeland Sheep & Wool Centre, Egremont Rd CA13 0QX

01900 822673 01900 820129

e-mail: reception@shepherdshotel.co.uk

web: www.shepherdshotel.co.uk

Dir: *at junct of A66 & A5086 S of Cockermouth, entrance off A5086, 200mtrs off rdbt*

PETS: Bedrooms (13GF) unattended **Grounds** accessible disp bin **Exercise area** on site **Facilities** cage storage walks info vet info **Resident Pets:** dogs, sheep, geese, Jersey cow

This hotel is modern in style and offers thoughtfully equipped accommodation. The property also houses the Lakeland Sheep and Wool Centre, with live sheep shows from Easter to mid November. A restaurant serving a wide variety of meals and snacks is open all day.

Rooms 26 en suite (4 fmly) (13 GF) S £50-£80; D £50-£99 (incl. bkfst)✳ **Facilities** FTV Wi-fi in bedrooms Pool table Small childs play area **Services** Lift **Parking** 100 **Notes** LB Closed 25-26 Dec & 5-19 Jan

★★★★ BED & BREAKFAST

Highside Farmhouse

Embleton CA13 9TN

01768 776893

e-mail: enquiries@highsidefarmhouse.co.uk

web: www.highsidefarmhouse.co.uk

Dir: *A66 Keswick to Cockermouth, left at sign Lorton/Buttermere, left at T-junct. 300yds turn right opp church, farm at top of hill*

PETS: Bedrooms **Charges** £2 per night **Public areas** (on leads) **Grounds** accessible on leads disp bin **Exercise area** 20mtrs **Facilities** cage storage walks info vet info **On Request** fridge access torch towels **Resident Pets:** Bess (Border Collie), 2 cats

True to its name, this 17th-century farmhouse stands over 600 feet up Ling Fell with breathtaking views across to the Solway Firth and Scotland. Add warm hospitality, great breakfasts, an inviting lounge-dining room with open fire in winter, and pine-furnished bedrooms, and the trip up the narrow winding road is well worth it.

Rooms 2 en suite S £40-£42; D £60-£64✳ **Facilities** TVB tea/coffee Cen ht **Parking** 2 **Notes** No children 10yrs

★★★★ GUEST HOUSE

Croft Guest House

6-8 Challoner St CA13 9QS

01900 827533

e-mail: info@croft-guesthouse.com

Dir: *In town centre off Main St*

PETS: Bedrooms **Charges** £2.50 per night **Grounds** accessible **Exercise area** 200mtrs to park **Other** dogs allowed in certain bedrooms only

Croft Guest House, one of the town's oldest buildings, lies in the heart of Cockermouth. It has been carefully upgraded to offer generally spacious, stylish accommodation. Bedrooms are comfortable, well equipped and retain some original features. There is a cosy ground-floor lounge next to the spacious dining room, where delicious breakfasts from the extensive blackboard menu are served at individual tables.

Rooms 6 en suite (1 fmly) S fr £38; D fr £60✳ **Facilities** TVB tea/coffee Cen ht **Parking** 5 **Notes** LB No coaches

ENGLAND

COCKERMOUTH CONTINUED

★★★★ GUEST HOUSE

Rose Cottage

Lorton Rd CA13 9DX

☎ 01900 822189 📠 01900 822189

e-mail: bookings@rosecottageguest.co.uk

Dir: *A5292 from Cockermouth to Lorton/Buttermere, Rose Cottage on right*

PETS: Bedrooms (3GF) **Public areas** except dining room (on leads) **Exercise area** 200mtrs **Facilities** food (pre-bookable) food bowl water bowl bedding dog chews cat treats feeding mat dog scoop/disp bags leads washing facs cage storage walks info vet info **On Request** fridge access torch towels

Resident Pets: Fergus (Irish Wolfhound)

This former inn is on the edge of town and has been refurbished to provide attractive, modern accommodation. The smart, well-equipped en suite bedrooms include a self-contained studio room with external access. There is a cosy lounge, and a smart dining room where delicious home-cooked dinners are a highlight.

Rooms 6 en suite 1 annexe en suite (2 fmly) (3 GF) S £42-£60; D £60-£85 **Facilities** TVB tea/coffee Licensed Cen ht Dinner Last d noon Wi-fi available **Parking** 12 **Notes** LB Closed 13-20 Feb RS 24-27 Dec

CROOKLANDS MAP 07 SD58

►►► **Waters Edge Caravan Park** *(SD533838)*

LA7 7NN

☎ 015395 67708

e-mail: dennis@watersedgecaravanpark.co.uk

web: www.watersedgecaravanpark.co.uk

Dir: *From M6 follow signs for Kirkby Lonsdale A65, at 2nd rdbt follow signs for Crooklands/Endmoor. Site 1m on right at Crooklands garage, just beyond 40mph limit*

PETS: Public areas except bar (at manager's discretion) (on leads) **Exercise area** walks and canal banks 300yds **Facilities** on site shop food water bowl dog scoop/disp bags vet info

Open Mar-14 Nov (rs Low season bar not always open on week days) Last arrival 22.00hrs Last departure noon

A peaceful, well-run park close to the M6, pleasantly bordered by streams and woodland. A Lakeland-style building houses a shop and bar, and the attractive toilet block is clean and modern. Ideal either as a stopover or for longer stays. A 3-acre site with 26 touring pitches and 20 statics.

CROSTHWAITE MAP 07 SD49

★★★ 68% HOTEL

Damson Dene

LA8 8JE

☎ 015395 68676 📠 015395 68227

e-mail: info@damsondene.co.uk

web: www.bestlakesbreaks.co.uk

Dir: *M6 junct 36, A590 signed Barrow-in-Furness, 5m right onto A5074. Hotel on right in 5m*

PETS: Bedrooms (9GF) unattended **Public areas** except restaurant & leisure club (on leads) **Grounds** accessible on leads disp bin **Exercise area** **Facilities** walks info vet info **On Request** fridge access torch

A short drive from Lake Windermere, this hotel enjoys a tranquil and scenic setting. Bedrooms include a number with four-poster beds and jacuzzi baths. The spacious restaurant serves a daily-changing menu, with some of the produce coming from the hotel's own kitchen garden. Real fires warm the lounge in the cooler months and leisure facilities are available.

Rooms 37 en suite 3 annexe en suite (7 fmly) (9 GF) S £69-£89; D £108-£148 (incl. bkfst)* **Facilities** **Spa** Ⓢ Gym Beauty salon Xmas New Year **Parking** 45 **Notes** **LB**

★★★★ GUEST HOUSE

Crosthwaite House

LA8 8BP

☎ 015395 68264 015395 68264

e-mail: bookings@crosthwaitehouse.co.uk

web: www.crosthwaitehouse.co.uk

Dir: *A590 onto A5074, 4m right to Crosthwaite, 0.5m turn left*

PETS: Bedrooms unattended **Stables** nearby (4m) **Grounds** accessible disp bin **Exercise area** 100mtrs **Facilities** washing facs cage storage walks info vet info **On Request** fridge access torch towels **Resident Pets:** Pepper (Labrador), Fidge (Labrador/Collie cross), Bertie (cat)

Having stunning views across the Lyth Valley, this friendly Georgian house is a haven of tranquillity. Bedrooms are spacious and offer a host of thoughtful extras. The reception rooms include a comfortable lounge and a pleasant dining room with polished floorboards and individual tables.

Rooms 6 en suite S £26-£30; D £52-£60 **Facilities** FTV TVB tea/coffee Licensed Cen ht TVL **Parking** 10 **Notes** No coaches Closed mid Nov-Dec RS early Nov & Feb-Mar

DALSTON — MAP 11 NY35

►►► **Dalston Hall Holiday Park** *(NY378519)*

Dalston Hall CA5 7JX

☎ 01228 710165

web: www.dalstonholidaypark.com

Dir: *M6 junct 42 signed for Dalston. 2.5m SW of Carlisle, just off B5299*

PETS: Charges £1 per night disp bin **Exercise area** on site fenced area **Facilities** on site shop food food bowl water bowl walks info vet info **Resident Pets:** Billy (German Shepherd)

Open Mar-Jan Last arrival 22.00hrs Last departure noon

A neat, well-maintained site on level grass in the grounds of an estate located between Carlisle and Dalston. All facilities are to a very high standard, and amenities include a 9-hole golf course, a bar and clubhouse serving breakfast and bar meals, and salmon and trout fly fishing. A 5-acre site with 60 touring pitches, 26 hardstandings and 17 statics.

Notes No commercial vans, gates closed 22.00hrs-07.00hrs

ESKDALE GREEN — MAP 06 NY10

►►► **Fisherground Farm Campsite** *(NY152002)*

CA19 1TF

☎ 01946 723349

e-mail: camping@fishergroundcampsite.co.uk

web: www.fishergroundcampsite.co.uk

Dir: *Leave A595 at Gosforth or Holmrook, follow signs on unclass road to Eskdale Green then Boot. Site signed on left*

PETS: Charges £1 per night £7 per week **Public areas** (on leads) disp bin **Exercise area Facilities** walks info vet info

Open Mar-Oct Last arrival 21.00hrs Last departure 11.00hrs

A mainly level grassy site on farmland amidst beautiful scenery, in Eskdale Valley below Hardknott Pass, between Eskdale and Boot. It has its own railway halt on the Eskdale-Ravenglass railway, 'The Ratty'. A large heated boot drying locker offered free in the laundry is an obvious bonus for walkers and climbers. A 9 acre site with 215 touring pitches.

Notes No caravans, no noise after 22.30hrs

GLENRIDDING — MAP 11 NY31

★★★ 81% HOTEL

The Inn on the Lake

Lake Ullswater CA11 0PE

☎ 017684 82444 017684 82303

e-mail: info@innonthelakeullswater.co.uk

web: www.innonthelakeullswater.com

Dir: *M6 junct 40, then A66 to Keswick. At rdbt take A592 to Ullswater Lake. Along lake to Glenridding. Hotel on left on entering village*

PETS: Bedrooms (1GF) unattended **Charges** £10 per night **Public areas** bar/conservatory only (on leads) **Grounds** accessible disp bin **Exercise area** countryside **On Request** fridge access **Other** pets in certain rooms only **Resident Pets:** Chrissy (Black Labrador)

In a picturesque lakeside setting, this restored Victorian hotel is a popular leisure destination as well as catering for weddings and conferences. Superb views may be enjoyed from the bedrooms and from the garden terrace where afternoon teas are served during

CONTINUED

GLENRIDDING CONTINUED

warmer months. There is a popular pub in the grounds, and moorings for yachts are available to guests. Sailing tuition can be arranged.

Rooms 47 en suite (6 fmly) (1 GF) S £81; D £138-£220 (incl. bkfst)✻ **Facilities** 9 Fishing Gym Putt green Wi-fi available Sailing 9-hole pitch & putt Bowls Lake Bathing Xmas New Year **Services** Lift **Parking** 200 **Notes** LB

GRANGE-OVER-SANDS MAP 07 SD47

★★★ 80% HOTEL

Netherwood

Lindale Rd LA11 6ET

☎ 015395 32552 📠 015395 34121

e-mail: enquiries@netherwood-hotel.co.uk

web: www.netherwood-hotel.co.uk

Dir: *on B5277 before station*

PETS: Bedrooms Charges £3.75 per night charge for damage **Public areas** except restaurant **Grounds** accessible **Exercise area** 200mtrs **Facilities** cage storage walks info vet info **On Request** towels

This imposing hotel stands in terraced grounds and enjoys fine views of Morecambe Bay. Though a popular conference and wedding venue, good levels of hospitality and service ensure all guests are well looked after. Bedrooms vary in size but all are well furnished and have smart modern bathrooms. Magnificent woodwork is a feature of the public areas.

Rooms 32 en suite (5 fmly) S £80-£120; D £120-£200 (incl. bkfst)✻ **Facilities Spa** supervised Gym Wi-fi available Beauty salon Steam room Spa bath Sunbed New Year **Services** Lift **Parking** 100 **Notes** LB

★★ 75% HOTEL

Hampsfell House

Hampsfell Rd LA11 6BG

☎ 015395 32567 📠 015395 35995

e-mail: enquiries@hampsfellhouse.co.uk

web: www.hampsfellhouse.co.uk

Dir: *A590 at junct with B5277, signed to Grange-over-Sands. Left at rdbt into Main St, 2nd rdbt right and right at x-rds. Hotel on left*

PETS: Bedrooms Charges £5 per night **Public areas** except restaurant (on leads) **Exercise area** adjacent **Facilities** pet sitting walks info vet info **On Request** fridge access torch towels **Resident Pets:** Maissie & Lucy (small Terriers), Pepsi (Whippet)

Dating back to 1800, this owner managed hotel is peacefully set in two acres of private grounds yet is just a comfortable walk from the town centre. Bedrooms are smartly decorated and well maintained. The two cosy and comfortable lounges, where guests can enjoy pre-dinner drinks, share a central bar. Comprehensive and imaginative dinners are taken in an attractive dining room.

Rooms 8 en suite (1 fmly) S £40-£55; D £55-£85 (incl. bkfst)✻ **Facilities** Wi-fi available Xmas New Year **Parking** 20 **Notes** LB

GRASMERE MAP 11 NY30

★★ 80% HOTEL

Grasmere

Broadgate LA22 9TA

☎ 015394 35277 📠 015394 35277

e-mail: enquiries@grasmerehotel.co.uk

web: www.grasmerehotel.co.uk

Dir: *From Ambleside take A591 N, 2nd left into Grasmere. Over humpback bridge, past playing field. Hotel on left*

PETS: Bedrooms (2GF) unattended **Charges** £5 per stay charge for damage **Grounds** accessible on leads **Exercise area** park 20yds **Facilities** washing facs cage storage walks info vet info **On Request** fridge access torch towels **Other** some bedrooms are not suitable for large dogs **Restrictions** no dangerous dogs - see page 7

Attentive and hospitable service contribute to the atmosphere at this family-run hotel, set in secluded gardens by the River Rothay. There are two inviting lounges (one with residents' bar) and an attractive dining room looking onto the garden. The thoughtfully prepared dinner menu makes good use of fresh ingredients. Pine furniture is featured in most bedrooms, along with welcome personal touches.

Rooms 13 en suite 1 annexe en suite (2 GF) S £60-£75; D £110-£220 (incl. bkfst & dinner)✻ **Facilities** Wi-fi available Full leisure facilities at nearby country club Free fishing permit available Xmas New Year **Parking** 14 **Notes** LB No children 10yrs Closed 3 Jan-early Feb

GRIZEDALE MAP 07 SD39

★★★★ GUEST ACCOMMODATION

Grizedale Lodge

LA22 0QL

☎ 015394 36532 📠 015394 36572

e-mail: enquiries@grizedale-lodge.com

web: www.grizedale-lodge.com

Dir: *From Hawkshead follow signs S to Grizedale. Lodge 2m on right*

PETS: Bedrooms Charges £2.50 (small), £5 (medium), £10 (large) per night **Public areas** except dining room **Grounds** accessible **Exercise area** 250yds **Other** Breakfast doggie bag

Set in the heart of the tranquil Grizedale Forest Park, this charming establishment provides particularly comfortable bedrooms, some with four-poster beds and splendid views. Hearty breakfasts are served in the attractive dining room, which leads to a balcony for relaxing on in summer.

Rooms 8 en suite (1 fmly) (2 GF) **Facilities** TVB tea/coffee Cen ht Dinner Last d 8.30pm **Parking** 20

HAWKSHEAD MAP 07 SD39

★★★ INN

Kings Arms

LA22 0NZ

☎ 015394 36372 🖹 015394 36006

e-mail: info@kingsarmshawkshead.co.uk

web: www.kingsarmshawkshead.co.uk

Dir: *In main square*

PETS: Bedrooms Stables nearby **Public areas** except restaurant (bar only) (on leads) **Exercise area** surrounding area **Facilities** food bowl water bowl washing facs walks info vet info **On Request** fridge access torch towels

A traditional Lakeland inn in the heart of a conservation area. The cosy, thoughtfully equipped bedrooms retain much character and are traditionally furnished. A good choice of freshly prepared food is available in the lounge bar and the neatly presented dining room.

Rooms 9 rms (8 en suite) (3 fmly) **Facilities** TVB tea/coffee Direct dial from bedrooms Cen ht Dinner Last d 9.30pm Fishing **Parking** available **Notes** Closed 25 Dec

HELTON MAP 12 NY52

★★★★ GUEST ACCOMMODATION

Beckfoot Country House

CA10 2QB

☎ 01931 713241 🖹 01931 713391

e-mail: info@beckfoot.co.uk

Dir: *M6 junct 39, A6 through Shap & left to Bampton. Through Bampton Grange and Bampton, house 2m on left*

PETS: Bedrooms (1GF) **Charges** £2.50 per night charge for damage **Grounds** accessible on leads disp bin **Exercise area Facilities** food bowl water bowl bedding dog chews feeding mat dog scoop/disp bags cage storage walks info vet info **On Request** fridge access **Resident Pets:** Turbo & Tweaky (cats), Storm & Fleur (Shetland ponies)

This delightful Victorian country house stands in well-tended gardens surrounded by beautiful open countryside, yet is only a short drive from Penrith. Bedrooms are spacious and particularly well equipped. The four-poster room is particularly impressive. Public areas include an elegant drawing room, where guitar workshops are occasionally held, an oak-panelled dining room and a television lounge.

Rooms 7 en suite 1 annexe en suite (1 fmly) (1 GF) S £35-£39; D £78-£100✻ **Facilities** STV TVB tea/coffee Cen ht TVL Wi-fi available Children's play area **Parking** 12 **Notes LB** Closed Dec-Feb

HOLMROOK MAP 07 SD09

★★★ INN

The Lutwidge Arms

CA19 1UH

☎ 019467 24230 🖹 019467 24100

e-mail: mail@lutwidge.co.uk

Dir: *M6 junct 36 onto A590 towards Barrow. Follow A595 towards Whitehaven/Workington, in centre of Holmrook*

PETS: Bedrooms (5GF) **Charges** charge for damage **Public areas** except at meal times (on leads) **Grounds** accessible on leads **Exercise area** 25mtrs **Facilities** cage storage vet info **On Request** fridge access towels

This Victorian roadside inn is family run and offers a welcoming atmosphere. The name comes from the Lutwidge family of Holmrook Hall, who included Charles Lutwidge Dodgson, better known as Lewis

CONTINUED

ENGLAND

HOLMROOK CONTINUED

Caroll. The bar and restaurant offer a wide range of meals during the evening. Bedrooms are comfortably equipped.

Rooms 11 en suite 5 annexe en suite (5 fmly) (5 GF) S £40-£55; D £65-£75✳ **Facilities** FTV TVB tea/coffee Direct dial from bedrooms Cen ht TVL Dinner Last d 9pm Wi-fi available Pool Table **Parking** 30 **Notes** LB

IREBY MAP 11 NY23

★★★ 80% COUNTRY HOUSE HOTEL

Overwater Hall

CA7 1HH

☎ 017687 76566 017687 76921

e-mail: welcome@overwaterhall.co.uk

Dir: *A591 take turn to Ireby at Castle Inn. Hotel signed after 2m on right.*

PETS: Bedrooms (1GF) unattended **Charges** charge for damage **Public areas** except restaurant & drawing room **Grounds** accessible disp bin **Exercise area** on site 18-acre gardens **Facilities** food bowl water bowl dog scoop/disp bags washing facs cage storage walks info vet info **On Request** fridge access torch towels **Resident Pets:** Oscar & Bafta (Black Labradors)

This privately owed country house dates back to 1811 and is set lovely gardens surrounded by woodlands. The professional owners provide warm hospitality and attentive service in a relaxed manner. The hotel has undergone a refurbishment throughout, and the bedrooms are very tastefully appointed. Creative dishes are served in the traditional-style dining room.

Rooms 11 en suite (2 fmly) (1 GF) S £100-£220; D £150-£270 (incl. bkfst & dinner)✳ **Facilities** FTV Xmas New Year **Parking** 20 **Notes** LB

KENDAL MAP 07 SD59

★★★ 70% HOTEL

Riverside Hotel Kendal

Beezon Rd, Stramongate Bridge LA9 6EL

☎ 01539 734861 01539 734863

e-mail: info@riversidekendal.co.uk

web: www.bestlakesbreaks.co.uk

Dir: *M6 junct 36 Sedburgh, Kendal 7m, left at end of Ann St, 1st right onto Beezon Rd, hotel on left*

PETS: Bedrooms (10GF) unattended **Public areas** except restaurant & leisure areas (on leads) **Exercise area** 100yds **Facilities** walks info vet info **On Request** fridge access torch

Centrally located in this market town, and enjoying a peaceful riverside location, this 17th-century former tannery provides a suitable base for both business travellers and tourists. The comfortable bedrooms are well equipped, and open-plan day rooms include the attractive restaurant and bar. Conference facilities are available, and the state-of-the-art leisure club has a heated pool, sauna, steam room, solarium and gym.

Rooms 47 en suite (18 fmly) (10 GF) S £69-£89; D £108-£148 (incl. bkfst)✳ **Facilities** STV supervised Gym Xmas New Year **Services** Lift **Parking** 60 **Notes** LB

►►► Kendal Camping & Caravanning Club Site *(SD526948)*

Millcrest, Shap Rd LA9 6NY

☎ 01539 741363

web: www.thefriendlyclub.co.uk

Dir: *On A6, 1.5m N of Kendal. Site 100yds N of Skelsmergh sign*

PETS: Public areas except in buildings disp bin **Exercise area** on site **Facilities** walks info vet info **Other** prior notice required

Open 2 Apr-2 Nov Last arrival 21.00hrs Last departure noon

A sloping grass site, set in hilly wood and meadowland, with some level all-weather pitches. Very clean, well kept facilities and attractive flower beds and tubs make a positive impression. The park is handy for nearby Kendal, with its shops and laundry (there is no laundry on site). A 3.5-acre site with 50 touring pitches, 6 hardstandings.

Notes Site gates closed 23.00hrs-07.00hrs

KESWICK MAP 11 NY22

★★★★ GUEST ACCOMMODATION

Hazelmere

Crosthwaite Rd CA12 5PG

☎ 017687 72445 017687 74075

e-mail: info@hazelmerekeswick.co.uk

web: www.hazelmerekeswick.co.uk

Dir: *Off A66 at Crosthwaite rdbt (A591 junct) for Keswick, Hazelmere 400yds on right*

PETS: Bedrooms Charges charge for damage **Exercise area Facilities** cage storage walks info vet info

This large Victorian house is only a short walk from Market Square and within walking distance of Derwentwater and the local fells. The attractive bedrooms are comfortably furnished and well equipped. Hearty Cumbrian breakfasts are served at individual tables in the ground-floor dining room, which has delightful views.

Rooms 6 en suite (1 fmly) S £34-£36; D £68-£72✳ **Facilities** TVB tea/coffee Cen ht Wi-fi available **Parking** 7 **Notes** No children 8yrs

★★★ FARM HOUSE

Low Nest Farm B&B *(NY282224)*

Castlerigg CA12 4TF

☎ 017687 72378 Mrs A True

e-mail: info@lownestfarm.co.uk

Dir: *2m S of Keswick, off A591 Windermere Rd*

PETS: Bedrooms (3GF) unattended sign **Sep Accom** kennel block **Stables** on site **Charges** £5 per stay charge for damage **Public areas Grounds** accessible disp bin **Exercise area** 5-acre adjacent field **Facilities** food food bowl water bowl bedding dog chews dog scoop/disp bags leads pet sitting dog walking washing facs dog grooming cage storage walks info vet info **On Request** fridge access torch towels **Resident Pets:** Sophie, Billie, Erik, Max & Lucy (Weimaraners), Pepsi (Poodle), Jasper (parrot)

Low Nest Farm is a small, family-run farm set in some typically breath taking Cumbrian scenery. Bedrooms are comfortable, en suite and benefit from the lovely views. There are, of course, any number of walks available in the area, and Keswick is just two miles away.

Rooms 3 en suite (3 GF) **Facilities** tea/coffee Cen ht TVL Wi-fi available **Parking** 10 **Notes** No children 16yrs 120 acres Mixed RS Nov-Mar

►►►► Castlerigg Hall Caravan & Camping Park *(NY282227)*

Castlerigg Hall CA12 4TE

☎ 017687 74499 🖹 017687 74499

e-mail: info@castlerigg.co.uk

web: www.castlerigg.co.uk

Dir: *1.5m SE of Keswick on A591, turn right at sign. Site 200mtrs on right past Heights Hotel*

PETS: Public areas except on recreational field **Charges** £1 per night disp bin **Exercise area** on site adjacent to tent field **Facilities** on site shop food food bowl water bowl dog chews cat treats dog scoop/disp bags leads walks info vet info **Restrictions** well behaved dogs only, no dangerous breeds (see page 7); dogs must be on leads at all times and not left unattended **Resident Pets:** Jack, Holly, Bells (dogs), Walter & Toby (cats), Amy (Shetland Pony), goats, pot belly pigs, ducks

Open mid Mar-7 Nov Last arrival 21.00hrs Last departure 11.30hrs

Spectacular views over Derwentwater to the mountains beyond are among the many attractions at this lovely Lakeland park. Old farm buildings have been tastefully converted into excellent toilets with private washing and family bathroom, reception and a well-equipped shop, and there is a kitchen/dining area for campers with a courtyard tearoom which also serves breakfast. An 8-acre site with 48 touring pitches, 48 hardstandings and 30 statics.

►►►► Gill Head Farm Caravan & Camping Park *(NY380269)*

Troutbeck CA11 0ST

☎ 017687 79652 🖹 017687 79130

e-mail: enquiries@gillheadfarm.co.uk

web: www.gillheadfarm.co.uk

Dir: *From M6 junct 40 take A66, then A5091 towards Troutbeck. Turn right after 100yds, then right again*

PETS: Exercise area on site riverside field **Facilities** on site shop washing facs walks info vet info **Resident Pets:** Farm dogs and cats

Open Apr-Oct Last arrival 22.30hrs Last departure noon

A family-run park on a working hill farm with lovely fell views. It has level touring pitches, and a log cabin dining room that is popular with families. Tent pitches are gently sloping in a separate field. A 5.5-acre site with 42 touring pitches, 21 hardstandings and 17 statics.

Notes No fires

►►► Burns Farm Caravan Park *(NY307244)*

St Johns in the Vale CA12 4RR

☎ 017687 79225 & 79112

e-mail: linda@burns-farm.co.uk

web: www.burns-farm.co.uk

Dir: *Exit A66 signed Castlerigg Stone Circle/Youth Centre/Burns Farm. Site on right in 0.5m*

PETS: Exercise area adjacent **Facilities** vet info **Other** prior notice required

Open Mar-4 Nov Last departure noon

Lovely views of Blencathra and Skiddaw can be enjoyed from this secluded park, set on a working farm which extends a warm welcome to families. This is a good choice for exploring the beautiful and interesting countryside. Food can be found in the pub at Threlkeld. A 2.5-acre site with 32 touring pitches.

Notes

KESWICK CONTINUED

►►► Derwentwater Camping & Caravanning Club Site *(NY262232)*

Crow Park Rd CA12 5EN

☎ 01768 772579

web: www.thefriendlyclub.co.uk

Dir: *Signed off B5289 in town centre*

PETS: Public areas except in buildings **Exercise area Facilities** walks info vet info **Other** prior notice required

Open 5 Feb-23 Nov Last arrival 21.00hrs Last departure noon

A peaceful location close to Derwentwater for this well-managed and popular park which is divided into two areas for tourers. Keswick, with its shops and pubs, is just a 5 minute walk away. A 16-acre site with 44 touring pitches, 17 hardstandings and 160 statics.

Notes Site gates closed 23.00hrs-07.00hrs

►►► Keswick Camping & Caravanning Club Site *(NY258234)*

Crow Park Rd CA12 5EP

☎ 01768 772392

web: www.thefriendlyclub.co.uk

Dir: *From Penrith on A66 into Main Street (Keswick), right to pass 'Lakes' bus station, past rugby club, turn right, site on right*

PETS: Exercise area on site dog walks **Facilities** on site shop walks info vet info **Other** prior notice required

Open 5 Feb-23 Nov Last arrival 21.00hrs Last departure noon

A well situated lakeside site within walking distance of the town centre. Boat launching is available from the site onto Derwentwater, and this level grassy park also offers a number of all-weather pitches. A 14-acre site with 250 touring pitches, 95 hardstandings.

Notes Site gates closed 23.00hrs-07.00hrs

KIRKBY LONSDALE MAP 07 SD67

★★★★★ ® INN

The Sun Inn

6 Market St LA6 2AU

☎ 015242 71965 📠 015242 72485

e-mail: email@sun-inn.info

web: www.sun-inn.info

Dir: *From A65, follow signs to Kirkby town centre. Inn on main street.*

PETS: Bedrooms unattended **Charges** £5 per stay **Public areas** except restaurant (on leads) **Exercise area** adjacent

A 17th-century inn situated in a historic market town, overlooking St Mary's Church. The atmospheric bar features stone walls, wooden beams and log fires with real ales available. Delicious meals are served in the bar and more formal, modern restaurant. Traditional and modern styles are blended together in the beautifully appointed rooms with excellent en suites.

Rooms 11 en suite (2 fmly) S £65-£110; D £90-£130* **Facilities** TVB tea/coffee Cen ht Dinner Last d 9-9.30pm Wi-fi available **Notes** No coaches

KIRKBY STEPHEN MAP 12 NY70

★★★★ GUEST HOUSE

Brownber Hall Country House

Newbiggin-on-Lune CA17 4NX

☎ 01539 623208

e-mail: enquiries@brownberhall.co.uk

web: www.brownberhall.co.uk

Dir: *6m SW of Kirkby Stephen. Off A685 signed Great Asby, 60yds right through gatehouse, 0.25m sharp left onto driveway*

PETS: Bedrooms Public areas must be under supervision **Grounds** accessible **Exercise area** on site **Resident Pets:** Sooty & Polar Bear (cats)

Having an elevated position with superb views of the surrounding countryside, Brownber Hall, built in 1860, has been restored to its original glory. The en suite bedrooms are comfortably proportioned, attractively decorated and well equipped. The ground floor has two lovely reception rooms, which retain many original features, and a charming dining room where traditional breakfasts, and by arrangement delicious dinners, are served.

Rooms 6 en suite (1 GF) **Facilities** TVB tea/coffee Lift Cen ht Dinner Last d 24hrs in advance **Parking** 12

★★★ FARM HOUSE

Southview Farm *(NY785105)*

Winton CA17 4HS

☎ 01768 371120 & 07801 432184 Mrs J Marston

e-mail: southviewwinton@hotmail.com

Dir: *1.5m N of Kirkby Stephen. Off A685 signed Winton*

PETS: Bedrooms unattended **Sep Accom** stable **Stables** on site **Public areas** except dining area **Grounds** accessible disp bin **Exercise area** 200yds **Facilities** feeding mat dog scoop/disp bags washing facs cage storage walks info vet info **On Request** fridge access torch towels **Restrictions** no Dobermans

A friendly family home, Southview lies in the centre of Winton village, part of a terrace with the working farm to the rear. Two well-proportioned bedrooms are available, and there is a cosy lounge-dining room where traditional breakfasts are served around one table.

Rooms 2 rms (2 fmly) S £30; D £42* **Facilities** TVB tea/coffee TVL Dinner Last d 8am **Parking** 2 **Notes** 280 acres beef, dairy

LAMPLUGH MAP 11 NY02

►►► Inglenook Caravan Park *(NY084206)*

Fitz Bridge CA14 4SH

☎ 01946 861240 📠 01946 861240

e-mail: enquiry@inglenookcaravanpark.co.uk

web: www.inglenookcaravanpark.co.uk

Dir: *M6 junct 40, A66 signed Keswick/Cockermouth. At large rdbt on outskirts of Cockermouth. Follow A5086 Egremont signs. Approx 7m to Lamplugh Tip public house (on right). Left in 200yds. Site 900yds on right*

PETS: Stables nearby (0.5m) **Public areas** except in shop & shower block (on leads) **Exercise area** fields adjacent **Facilities** on site shop food water bowl vet info

Open all year Last arrival 20.00hrs Last departure noon

An ideal touring site, well-maintained and situated in beautiful surroundings. The picturesque village of Lamplugh is close to the western lakes of Ennerdale, Buttermere and Loweswater, and a short drive from sandy beaches. A 3.5-acre site with 12 touring pitches, 12 hardstandings and 40 statics.

LONGTOWN MAP 11 NY36

►► Camelot Caravan Park *(NY391666)*

CA6 5SZ

☎ 01228 791248 📠 01228 791248

Dir: *Leave M6 junct 44. Site 5m N on A7, 1m S of Longtown*

PETS: Exercise area on site adjacent field **Facilities** washing facs walks info vet info

Open Mar-Oct Last arrival 22.00hrs Last departure noon

Very pleasant level grassy site in a wooded setting near the M6, with direct access from the A7. This park is an ideal stopover site. A 1.5-acre site with 20 touring pitches and 2 statics.

Notes ⊜

LOWESWATER MAP 11 NY12

★★ 69% SMALL HOTEL

Grange Country House

CA13 0SU

☎ 01946 861211 & 861570

e-mail: info@thegrange-loweswater.co.uk

Dir: *left off A5086 for Mockerkin, through village. After 2m left for Loweswater Lake. Hotel at bottom of hill on left*

PETS: Bedrooms (1GF) unattended **Charges** £5-6 per night **Public areas** except dining room **Grounds** accessible disp bin **Exercise area** adjacent **Facilities** food (pre-bookable) food bowl water bowl bedding dog scoop/disp bags leads washing facs cage storage walks info vet info **On Request** fridge access torch towels **Resident Pets:** Toby (Labrador/Collie cross), 3 ducks

This delightful country hotel is set in extensive grounds in a quiet valley at the north-western end of Loweswater, and continues to prove popular with guests seeking peace and quiet. It has a friendly and relaxed atmosphere, and the cosy public areas include a small bar, a residents' lounge and an attractive dining room. The bedrooms are well equipped and comfortable, and include four-poster rooms.

Rooms 8 en suite (2 fmly) (1 GF) S £50-£60; D £80-£100 (incl. bkfst) **Facilities** National Trust boats & fishing Xmas **Parking** 22 **Notes** RS Jan-Feb No credit cards accepted

MEALSGATE MAP 11 NY24

►►►► Larches Caravan Park *(NY205415)*

CA7 1LQ

☎ 016973 71379 & 71803 📠 016973 71782

Dir: *On A595 (Carlisle to Cockermouth road)*

PETS: Stables nearby (6m) (loose box) **Public areas** except in toilet & shops disp bin **Exercise area** on site fenced exercise area **Facilities** on site shop food food bowl water bowl litter tray dog scoop/disp bags washing facs dog grooming walks info vet info **Resident Pets:** Holly (German Shepherd/Labrador cross), Trudy (Belgian Shepherd), Tiger-Lil, Tibby & Blackie (cats)

Open Mar-Oct (rs early & late season) Last arrival 21.30hrs Last departure noon

This over 18s-only park is set in wooded rural surroundings on the fringe of the Lake District National Park. Touring units are spread out over two sections. This friendly family-run park offers well cared for facilities, and a small indoor swimming pool. A 20-acre site with 73 touring pitches, 30 hardstandings.

Notes ⊜

ENGLAND

PATTERDALE MAP 11 NY31

►►► Sykeside Camping Park *(NY403119)*

Brotherswater CA11 0NZ

☎ 017684 82239 🖹 017684 82239

e-mail: info@sykeside.co.uk

web: www.sykeside.co.uk

Dir: *Direct access off A592 (Windermere to Ullswater road) at foot of Kirkstone Pass*

PETS: Stables nearby (loose box) **Charges** £1.50 per night disp bin **Exercise area** on site fenced exercise area **Facilities** on site shop food food bowl water bowl dog chews leads washing facs walks info vet info **Other** prior notice required

Open all year Last arrival 22.30hrs Last departure 14.00hrs

A camper's delight, this family-run park is sited at the foot of Kirkstone Pass, under the 2000ft Hartsop Dodd in a spectacular area with breathtaking views. The park has mainly grass pitches with a few hardstandings, and for those campers without a tent there is bunkhouse accommodation. A small camper's kitchen and bar serves breakfast and bar meals. There is abundant wildlife. A 5-acre site with 86 touring pitches, 5 hardstandings.

RAVENGLASS MAP 06 SD09

►►► Ravenglass Camping & Caravanning Club Site *(SD087964)*

CA18 1SR

☎ 01229 717250

web: www.thefriendlyclub.co.uk

Dir: *From A595 turn W for Ravenglass. Before village turn left into site*

PETS: Public areas except in buildings disp bin **Exercise area** adjacent footpaths **Facilities** on site shop food food bowl water bowl walks info vet info **Other** prior notice required

Open 12 Jan-11 Nov Last arrival 21.00hrs Last departure noon

A pleasant wooded park peacefully located in open countryside, a short stroll from the charming old fishing village of Ravenglass. The Club have improved the park to a high standard with level gravel pitches, upgraded toilet block and smart reception. Muncaster Castle & gardens, the Eskdale/Ravenglass Steam Railway and the coast are all within easy reach. A 5-acre site with 66 touring pitches, 56 hardstandings.

Notes Site gates closed 23.00hrs-07.00hrs, tents must book with site directly

RAVENSTONEDALE MAP 07 NY70

★★ 69% HOTEL

The Fat Lamb

Crossbank CA17 4LL

☎ 015396 23242 🖹 015396 23285

e-mail: fatlamb@cumbria.com

Dir: *on A683, between Kirkby Stephen & Sedbergh*

PETS: Bedrooms (5GF) **Public areas** except restaurant **Grounds** accessible **Exercise area** 100yds **Facilities** leads cage storage vet info **On Request** fridge access torch

Open fires and solid stone walls feature at this 17th-century inn, set on its own nature reserve. There is a choice of dining options with an extensive menu available in the traditional bar and a more formal dining experience in the restaurant. Bedrooms are bright and cheerful, and include family rooms and easily accessible rooms for guests with limited mobility.

Rooms 12 en suite (4 fmly) (5 GF) S £48-£54; D £80-£88 (incl. bkfst)✳ **Facilities** Wi-fi available Private 5-acre nature reserve Xmas **Parking** 60 **Notes** LB

ROSTHWAITE MAP 11 NY21

★ 72% HOTEL

Royal Oak

CA12 5XB

☎ 017687 77214 🖹 017687 77214

e-mail: info@royaloakhotel.co.uk

web: www.royaloakhotel.co.uk

Dir: *6m S of Keswick on B5289 in centre of Rosthwaite*

PETS: Bedrooms (4GF) unattended **Public areas** except dining room **Grounds** accessible **Exercise area** **Facilities** food bowl water bowl leads cage storage walks info vet info **On Request** fridge access torch towels

Set in a village in one of Lakeland's most picturesque valleys, this family-run hotel offers friendly and obliging service. There is a variety of accommodation styles, with particularly impressive rooms being located in a converted barn across the courtyard and backed by a stream. Family rooms are available. The cosy bar is for residents and diners only. A set home-cooked dinner is served at 7pm.

Rooms 8 en suite 4 annexe en suite (5 fmly) (4 GF) S £42-£53; D £82-£116 (incl. bkfst & dinner)✳ **Facilities** no TV in bdrms **Parking** 15 **Notes** LB Closed 6-24 Jan & 7-27 Dec

SILLOTH MAP 11 NY15

★★ 68% HOTEL

Golf Hotel

Criffel St CA7 4AB

☎ 016973 31438 016973 32582

e-mail: golf.hotel@virgin.net

PETS: Bedrooms sign **Stables** nearby **Charges** £2 per night £14 per week charge for damage **Public areas** (on leads) **Exercise area** opposite **Facilities** washing facs cage storage walks info vet info **On Request** fridge access torch

A friendly welcome waits at this hotel which occupies a prime position in the centre of the historic market town; it is a popular meeting place for the local community. Bedrooms are mostly well proportioned and are comfortably equipped. The lounge bar is a popular venue for dining with a wide range of dishes on offer. Refurbishment at the hotel is ongoing.

Rooms 22 en suite (4 fmly) S £49-£67.50; D £82-£105 (incl. bkfst)* **Facilities** Snooker & Games room **Notes LB** Closed 24-26 Dec

►►►► Hylton Caravan Park *(NY113533)*

Eden St CA7 4AY

☎ 016973 31707 & 32666 016973 32555

e-mail: enquiries@stanwix.com

web: www.stanwix.com

Dir: *On entering Silloth on B5302 follow signs Hylton Caravan Park, approx 0.5m on left, (end of Eden St)*

PETS: Public areas except leisure & entertainment complex **Charges** £3 per night £21 per week **Exercise area** 15min walk to beach **Facilities** food food bowl water bowl walks info vet info **Other** prior notice required **Restrictions** well behaved dogs only, max 2 per family

Open Mar-15 Nov Last arrival 21.00hrs Last departure 11.00hrs

A smart, modern touring park with excellent toilet facilities including several bathrooms. This high quality park is a sister site to Stanwix Park, which is just a mile away and offers all the amenities of a holiday centre. An 18-acre site with 90 touring pitches and 213 statics.

Notes Families only

TEBAY MAP 07 NY60

►►► Westmorland Caravan Park *(NY609060)*

Orton CA10 3SB

☎ 01539 711322 015396 24944

e-mail: caravans@westmorland.com

web: www.westmorland.com

Dir: *Exit M6 at Westmorland Services, 1m from junct 38. Site accessed through service area from either N'bound or S'bound carriageways. Follow park signs*

PETS: Stables nearby (3m) disp bin **Exercise area** on site walks around woods & grassland **Facilities** on site shop washing facs walks info vet info

Open Mar-Oct Last arrival anytime Last departure noon

An ideal stopover site adjacent to the Tebay service station on the M6, and handy for touring the Lake District. The park is screened by high grass banks, bushes and trees, and is within walking distance of a shop and restaurant. A 4-acre site with 70 touring pitches, 70 hardstandings and 7 statics.

TROUTBECK (NEAR KESWICK) MAP 11 NY32

►►►► Troutbeck Camping and Caravanning Club Site *(NY364270)*

Hutton Moor End CA11 0SX

☎ 01768 779615

web: www.thefriendlyclub.co.uk

Dir: *On A66 (Penrith to Keswick) turn left at Wallthwaite sign*

PETS: Public areas except in buildings disp bin **Exercise area** on site **Facilities** walks info vet info **Other** prior notice required

Open Mar-15 Nov Last arrival 21.00hrs Last departure noon

Beautifully situated between Penrith and Keswick, this quiet, pleasant Lakeland park offers a sheltered touring field with serviced pitches enjoying extensive views of the surrounding fells. The toilet block has been upgraded to a very high standard including two family cubicles, and the log cabin stocks local and organic produce. A 4.5-acre site with 54 touring pitches, 19 hardstandings and 20 statics.

Notes Site gates closed 23.00hrs-07.00hrs

ENGLAND

ULVERSTON MAP 07 SD27

★★★★ BED & BREAKFAST

Church Walk House

Church Walk LA12 7EW

☎ 01229 582211

e-mail: martinchadd@btinternet.com

Dir: *In town centre opp Stables furniture shop*

PETS: Bedrooms Public areas Grounds accessible disp bin **Exercise area Facilities** dog scoop/disp bags cage storage walks info vet info **On Request** fridge access **Restrictions** no breed larger than St Bernard

This Grade II listed 18th-century residence stands in the heart of the historic market town. Stylishly decorated, the accommodation includes attractive bedrooms with a mix of antiques and contemporary pieces. A peaceful atmosphere prevails with attentive service, and there is a small herbal garden and patio.

Rooms 3 rms (2 en suite) S £25-£40; D £55-£65* **Facilities** tea/coffee Cen ht TVL **Notes LB**

WATERMILLOCK MAP 12 NY42

★★★ HOTEL

Rampsbeck Country House

CA11 0LP

☎ 017684 86442 017684 86688

e-mail: enquiries@rampsbeck.co.uk

web: www.rampsbeck.co.uk

Dir: *M6 junct 40, A592 to Ullswater, at T-junct (with lake in front) turn right, hotel 1.5m*

PETS: Bedrooms (1GF) unattended **Charges** £10 per stay **Public areas** hall & lounge only (on leads) **Grounds** accessible disp bin **Exercise area** meadow adjacent **Facilities** walks info vet info **On Request** fridge access torch towels **Other** dogs allowed in 3 bedrooms only

This fine country house lies in 18 acres of parkland on the shores of Lake Ullswater, and is furnished with many period and antique pieces. There are three delightful lounges, an elegant restaurant and a traditional bar. Bedrooms come in three grades; the most spacious rooms are spectacular and overlook the lake. Service is attentive and the cuisine a real highlight.

Rooms 19 en suite (1 GF) S £85-£150; D £140-£280 (incl. bkfst)* **Facilities** STV FTV Fishing Wi-fi available Xmas New Year **Parking** 30 **Notes LB**

★★★★ INN

Brackenrigg

CA11 0LP

☎ 017684 86206 017684 86945

e-mail: enquiries@brackenrigginn.co.uk

web: www.brackenrigginn.co.uk

Dir: *6m from M6 onto A66 towards Keswick & A592 to Ullswater, right at lake & continue 2m*

PETS: Bedrooms (3 GF) **Charges** £10 per stay charge for damage **Public areas** in bar only (not restaurant) **Grounds** accessible **Exercise area** surrounding area

An 18th-century coaching inn with superb views of Ullswater and the surrounding countryside. Freshly prepared dishes and daily specials are served by friendly staff in the traditional bar and restaurant. The bedrooms include six attractive rooms in the stable cottages.

Rooms 11 en suite 6 annexe en suite (8 fmly) (3 GF) S £53-£63; D £79-£110* **Facilities** TVB tea/coffee Cen ht Dinner Last d 9pm Wi-fi available **Parking** 40 **Notes LB**

►►► Cove Caravan & Camping Park

(NY431236)

Ullswater CA11 0LS

☎ 017684 86549 017684 86549

e-mail: info@cove-park.co.uk

web: www.cove-park.co.uk

Dir: *M6 junct 40 take A592 for Ullswater. Right at lake junct, then right at Brackenrigg Hotel. Site 1.5m on left*

PETS: Charges £1 per dog per night disp bin **Exercise area** on site 2 dog walks **Facilities** washing facs walks info vet info **Restrictions** well behaved dogs only **Resident Pets:** Molly (Springer Spaniel)

Open Mar-Oct Last arrival 21.00hrs Last departure noon

A peaceful family site in an attractive and elevated position with extensive fell views and glimpses of Ullswater Lake. The ground is gently sloping grass, but there are also hardstandings for motorhomes and caravans. A 3-acre site with 50 touring pitches, 17 hardstandings and 39 statics.

Notes No open fires

WINDERMERE MAP 07 SD49

★★★★ COUNTRY HOUSE HOTEL

Holbeck Ghyll Country House

Holbeck Ln LA23 1LU

☎ 015394 32375 015394 34743

e-mail: stay@holbeckghyll.com

Dir: *3m N of Windermere on A591, right into Holbeck Lane (signed Troutbeck), hotel 0.5m on left*

PETS: Bedrooms (6GF) unattended **Stables** nearby (1.5m) **Charges** £8 per night charge for damage **Public areas** front hall only **Grounds** accessible disp bin **Exercise area** adjacent **Facilities** food (pre-bookable) food bowl water bowl bedding dog chews feeding mat dog scoop/disp bags leads pet sitting dog walking washing facs dog grooming cage storage walks info vet info **On Request** fridge access torch towels **Other** dog grooming available nearby **Resident Pets:** Solie & Brook (Black Labradors)

With a peaceful setting in extensive grounds, this beautifully maintained hotel enjoys breathtaking views over Lake Windermere and the Langdale Fells. Public rooms include luxurious, comfortable lounges and two elegant dining rooms, where memorable meals are served. Bedrooms are individually styled, beautifully furnished and many have balconies or patios. Some in an adjacent, more private lodge are less traditional in design and have superb views. The professionalism and attentiveness of the staff is exemplary.

Rooms 14 en suite 14 annexe en suite (4 fmly) (6 GF) S £155-£300; D £250-£550 (incl. bkfst & dinner)* **Facilities Spa** STV Gym Putt green Wi-fi available Steam room Treatment rooms Beauty massage Xmas New Year **Parking** 34 **Notes** LB

★★★★ 76% HOTEL

Storrs Hall

Storrs Park LA23 3LG

☎ 015394 47111 015394 47555

e-mail: storrshall@elhmail.co.uk

web: www.elh.co.uk/hotels/storrshall

Dir: *on A592 2m S of Bowness, on Newby Bridge road*

PETS: Bedrooms Charges dog £15 per night charge for damage **Grounds** accessible on leads disp bin **Exercise area Facilities** water bowl cage storage walks info vet info **On Request** torch

Set in 17 acres of landscaped grounds by the lakeside, this imposing Georgian mansion is delightful. There are numerous lounges to relax in, furnished with fine art and antiques. Individually styled bedrooms are generally spacious and boast impressive bathrooms. Imaginative cuisine is served in the elegant restaurant, which offers fine views across the lawn to the lake and fells beyond.

Rooms 30 en suite S £113-£177; D £176-£304 (incl. bkfst) **Facilities** FTV Fishing Wi-fi in bedrooms Use of nearby sports/beauty facilities Xmas New Year **Parking** 50 **Notes** LB No children 12yrs

★★★ COUNTRY HOUSE HOTEL

Linthwaite House Hotel & Restaurant

Crook Rd LA23 3JA

☎ 015394 88600 015394 88601

e-mail: stay@linthwaite.com

web: www.linthwaite.com

Dir: *A591 towards The Lakes for 8m to large rdbt, take 1st exit (B5284), 6m, hotel on left. 1m past Windermere golf club*

PETS: Sep Accom outdoor kennel & caged run **Grounds** accessible **Exercise area Facilities** water bowl **Other** owners to bring dogs' own bedding; please note dogs are not allowed in the hotel

Linthwaite House is set in 14 acres of hilltop grounds and enjoys stunning views over Lake Windermere. Inviting public rooms include an attractive conservatory and adjoining lounge and an elegant restaurant. Bedrooms, which are individually decorated, combine contemporary furnishings with classical styles; all are thoughtfully equipped and include CD players. Service and hospitality are attentive and friendly.

Rooms 27 en suite (1 fmly) (7 GF) S £120-£165; D £160-£380 (incl. bkfst & dinner)* **Facilities** STV Fishing Putt green Wi-fi in bedrooms Beauty treatments Massage Xmas New Year **Parking** 40 **Notes** LB ®

★★★ COUNTRY HOUSE HOTEL

Miller Howe Hotel

Rayrigg Rd LA23 1EY

☎ 015394 42536 015394 45664

e-mail: lakeview@millerhowe.com

Dir: *M6 junct 36 follow A591 past Windermere village, left at rdbt towards Bowness*

PETS: Bedrooms (1GF) unattended **Charges** £5 per night **Public areas** only at management's discretion (on leads) **Grounds** accessible **Exercise area** 100yds **Facilities** food bowl water bowl cage storage walks info vet info **On Request** fridge access torch towels **Resident Pets:** Betty & Doris (Cocker Spaniels)

This long established hotel of much character enjoys a lakeside setting amidst delightful landscaped gardens. The bright and welcoming day rooms include sumptuous lounges, a conservatory and an opulently decorated restaurant. Imaginative dinners make use of fresh, local produce where possible and there is an extensive, well-balanced wine list. Stylish bedrooms, many with fabulous lake views, include well-equipped cottage rooms and a number with whirlpool baths.

Rooms 12 en suite 3 annexe en suite (1 GF) S £70-£150; D £140-£200 (incl. bkfst)* **Facilities** Xmas New Year **Parking** 35 **Notes** LB No children 8yrs

ENGLAND

WINDERMERE CONTINUED

★★★ 81% HOTEL

Langdale Chase

Langdale Chase LA23 1LW

☎ 015394 32201 015394 32604

e-mail: sales@langdalechase.co.uk

web: www.langdalechase.co.uk

Dir: *2m S of Ambleside and 3m N of Windermere, on A591*

PETS: Bedrooms (9GF) unattended **Charges** £3 per night charge for damage **Public areas** except restaurant/bar (on leads) **Grounds** accessible on leads disp bin **Exercise area** **Facilities** food (pre-bookable) food bowl water bowl pet sitting dog walking washing facs cage storage walks info vet info **On Request** fridge access torch towels **Resident Pets:** Nobby (Boxer)

Enjoying unrivalled views of Lake Windermere, this imposing country manor has been trading as a hotel for over 70 years. Public areas feature beautifully carved fireplaces, oak panelling and an imposing galleried staircase. Bedrooms have stylish, spacious bathrooms and outstanding views.

Rooms 20 en suite 9 annexe en suite (2 fmly) (9 GF) S £80-£140; D £90-£210 (incl. bkfst)✱ **Facilities** Fishing Putt green Mini golf Xmas New Year **Parking** 50 **Notes** LB

★★ 73% HOTEL

Cedar Manor Hotel & Restaurant

Ambleside Rd LA23 1AX

☎ 015394 43192 & 45970 015394 45970

e-mail: info@cedarmanor.co.uk

Dir: *From A591 follow signs to Windermere. Hotel on left just beyond St Mary's Church at bottom of hill*

PETS: Bedrooms (3GF) unattended sign **Stables** nearby (3m) **Charges** £5 per night £30 per week charge for damage **Grounds** accessible disp bin **Exercise area** 0.25m **Facilities** washing facs cage storage walks info vet info **On Request** fridge access torch **Restrictions** no Rottweilers or Pit Bull Terriers

Built in 1854 as a country retreat this lovely old house enjoys a peaceful location that is within easy walking distance of the town centre. Bedrooms, some on the ground floor, are attractive and well equipped, with two bedrooms in the adjacent coach house. There is a comfortable lounge bar where guests can relax before enjoying dinner in the well-appointed dining room.

Rooms 9 en suite 2 annexe en suite (2 fmly) (3 GF) S £63-£80; D £92-£150 (incl. bkfst)✱ **Facilities** FTV Wi-fi in bedrooms New Year **Parking** 11 **Notes** Closed 2-10 Jan

►►►► Windermere Camping & Caravanning Club Site *(SD479964)*

Ashes Ln LA8 9JS

☎ 01539 821119

web: www.thefriendlyclub.co.uk

Dir: *Signed off A591, 0.75m from rdbt with B5284 towards Windermere*

PETS: Public areas except in buildings disp bin **Exercise area** on site **Facilities** walks info vet info **Other** prior notice required

Open 14 Mar-14 Jan Last arrival 21.00hrs Last departure noon

A top Club site in a beautifully landscaped setting bordered by bluebell woods. Many mature trees and shrubs add to the natural beauty, and there are rocky outcrops and lovely views to be enjoyed. First class toilet facilities, good security, a large adventure playground, and a bar (The Whistling Pig) serving breakfasts, snacks and hot meals all add to the popularity of this very well-redeveloped site. A 24-acre site with 250 touring pitches, 88 hardstandings and 75 statics.

Notes Site gates closed 23.00hrs-07.00hrs

DERBYSHIRE

ASHBOURNE — MAP 07 SK14

★★★★ FARM HOUSE

Mercaston Hall *(SK279419)*

Mercaston DE6 3BL

☎ 01335 360263 Mr & Mrs A Haddon

e-mail: mercastonhall@btinternet.com

Dir: *Off A52 in Brailsford onto Luke Ln, 1m turn right at 1st x-rds, house 1m on right*

PETS: Bedrooms Sep Accom barn **Stables** on site **Charges** £2 per night charge for damage **Public areas** except dining room **Grounds** accessible disp bin **Exercise area** adjacent fields **Facilities** food bowl water bowl leads washing facs cage storage walks info vet info **On Request** fridge access torch towels

Located in a pretty hamlet, this medieval building retains many original features. Bedrooms are homely, and additional facilities include an all-weather tennis court and a livery service. This is a good base for visiting local stately homes, the Derwent Valley mills and Dovedale.

Rooms 3 en suite S £40-£45; D £60-£66✱ **Facilities** FTV TVB tea/coffee Cen ht **Parking** 3 **Notes** No children 8yrs 60 acres mixed Closed Xmas

►► Carsington Fields Caravan Park

(SK251493)

Millfields Ln, Nr Carsington Water DE6 3JS

☎ 01335 372872

web: www.carsingtoncaravaning.co.uk

Dir: *From Belper towards Ashbourne on A517 turn right approx 0.25m past Hulland Ward into Dog Lane. 0.75m right at x-roads signed Carsington. Site on right after approx 0.75m*

PETS: Public areas except near toilets disp bin **Exercise area** on site grass dog run **Facilities** vet info **Other** prior notice required

Open end Mar-end Sep Last arrival 21.00hrs Last departure 18.00hrs

A very well presented and spacious park with a good toilet block, open views and a large fenced pond that attracts plenty of wildlife. The popular tourist attraction of Carsington Water is a short stroll away, with its variety of leisure facilities including fishing, sailing, windsurfing and children's play area. The park is also a good base for walkers. A 6 acre site with 10 touring pitches, 10 hardstandings.

Notes No large groups or group bookings

BAKEWELL — MAP 08 SK26

★★★ 70% HOTEL

Rutland Arms

The Square DE45 1BT

☎ 01629 812812 01629 812309

e-mail: rutland@bakewell.demon.co.uk

Dir: *M1 junct 28 to Matlock, A6 to Bakewell. Hotel in town centre*

PETS: Bedrooms unattended **Charges** charge for damage **Public areas** certain times only (on leads) **Exercise area** 100yds **Facilities** vet info **Other** dogs may only be left unattended in bedrooms for short periods **Restrictions** very large dogs not accepted

This 19th-century hotel lies at the very centre of Bakewell and offers a wide range of quality accommodation. The friendly staff are attentive and welcoming, and The Four Seasons candlelit restaurant serves interesting fine dining in elegant surroundings.

Rooms 18 en suite 17 annexe en suite (2 fmly) (7 GF) S £47-£65; D £79-£124 (incl. bkfst)* **Facilities** Wi-fi in bedrooms Xmas New Year **Parking** 25

U

Monsal Head Hotel

Monsal Head DE45 1NL

☎ 01629 640250 01629 640815

e-mail: enquiries@monsalhead.com

web: www.monsalhead.com

Dir: *A6 from Bakewell to Buxton. After 2m turn into Ashford in the Water, take B6465 for 1m*

PETS: Bedrooms Charges £5 per night £35 per week charge for damage **Public areas** except restaurant (on leads) **Grounds** accessible on leads **Exercise area** 50yds **Facilities** walks info vet info **Restrictions** small, well behaved dogs only

At the time of going to press the rating for this establishment was not confirmed. This may be due to a change of ownership or because it has only recently joined the AA rating scheme. For further details please see the AA website: www.theAA.com

Rooms 7 en suite (1 fmly) **Parking** 20 **Notes** RS 25 Dec

★★★★ GUEST HOUSE

Croft Cottages

Coombs Rd DE45 1AQ

☎ 01629 814101

e-mail: croftco@btopenworld.com

Dir: *A619 E from town centre over bridge, right onto Station Rd & Coombs Rd*

PETS: Bedrooms unattended **Grounds** accessible on leads **Exercise area** 100yds **Facilities** walks info vet info **On Request** fridge access towels **Restrictions** no breeds larger than Labrador/Retreiver **Resident Pets:** Steffi (Belgian Shepherd)

A warm welcome is assured at this Grade II listed stone building close to the River Wye and town centre. Thoughtfully equipped bedrooms are available in the main house or in an adjoining converted barn suite. Breakfast is served in a spacious lounge dining room.

Rooms 3 rms (2 en suite) (1 pri facs) 1 annexe en suite (1 fmly) S £35-£45; D £58-£80 **Facilities** TVB tea/coffee Cen ht **Parking** 2 **Notes LB** No coaches

BAKEWELL *CONTINUED*

★★★ INN

Castle Inn

Castle St DE45 1DU

☎ 01629 812103

web: www.oldenglish.co.uk

PETS: Bedrooms Public areas except restaurant **Grounds** accessible disp bin **Exercise area**

A traditional inn built in the 16th century and offering well furnished bedrooms and extensive bars. A wide range of well-prepared dishes is available and real ales are served.

Rooms 4 annexe en suite D £60* (room only) **Facilities** TVB Direct dial from bedrooms Cen ht Dinner Last d 9pm **Parking** 14 **Notes** No coaches

BELPER MAP 08 SK34

★★★★ 70% HOTEL

Makeney Hall Hotel

Makeney, Milford DE56 0RS

☎ 01332 842999 📠 01332 842777

e-mail: makeneyhall@foliohotels.com

web: www.foliohotels.com/makeneyhall

Dir: *off A6 at Milford, signed Makeney. Hotel 0.25m on left*

PETS: Bedrooms Charges £5 per night **Grounds** accessible **Exercise area** fields adjacent **Other** dogs in courtyard rooms only

This restored Victorian mansion stands in six acres of landscaped gardens and grounds above the River Derwent. Bedrooms vary in style and are generally very spacious. They are divided between the main house and the ground floor courtyard. Comfortable public rooms include a lounge, bar and spacious restaurant with views of the gardens.

Rooms 28 en suite 18 annexe en suite (3 fmly) **Facilities** STV Wi-fi available **Services** Lift **Parking** 150

★★★ 78% ® HOTEL

Shottle Hall Country House

White Ln, Shottle DE56 2EB

☎ 01773 550577 📠 01773 551000

e-mail: info@shottlehall.co.uk

Dir: *A517 (Ashbourne to Belper) turn towards Wirksworth on A5097, 1st right, hotel 0.25m on left*

PETS: Bedrooms unattended **Charges** £15 per night charge for damage **Grounds** accessible **Exercise area Facilities** vet info **On Request** torch

This delightfully refurbished hotel stands in extensive and lovely grounds. It offers individually designed bedrooms which have been thoughtfully equipped. The lounge is comfortable and quality cooking is served in the Orangery restaurant. Expect attentive service from dedicated staff.

Rooms 8 en suite (3 fmly) **Facilities** FTV Wi-fi available **Parking** 100

BUXTON MAP 07 SK07

★★★★ 70% HOTEL

Barceló Buxton Palace Hotel

Palace Rd SK17 6AG

☎ 01298 22001 📠 01298 72131

e-mail: palace@barcelo-hotels.co.uk

web: www.barcelo-hotels.co.uk

Dir: *M6 junct 20, follow M56/M60 signs to Stockport then A6 to Buxton, hotel adjacent to railway station*

PETS: Bedrooms unattended sign **Charges** £15 per stay charge for damage **Public areas** except bar & restaurant (on leads) **Grounds** accessible **Exercise area** park 600mtrs **Facilities** cage storage walks info vet info **On Request** fridge access torch towels

This impressive Victorian hotel is located on the hill overlooking the town. Public areas are traditional and elegant in style, and include chandeliers and decorative ceilings. The bedrooms are spacious and equipped with modern facilities, and The Dovedale Restaurant provides modern British cuisine. Good leisure facilities are available.

Rooms 122 en suite (18 fmly) S £65-£130* **Facilities Spa** supervised Gym Wi-fi available Beauty facilities Xmas New Year **Services** Lift **Parking** 180 (charged)

★★★ 79% ® HOTEL

Best Western Lee Wood

The Park SK17 6TQ

☎ 01298 23002 📠 01298 23228

e-mail: leewoodhotel@btconnect.com

web: www.leewoodhotel.co.uk

Dir: *NE on A5004, 300mtrs beyond Devonshire Royal Hospital*

PETS: Bedrooms Charges £8 per night **Exercise area** park opposite **Other** please phone for details of pet facilities

This elegant Georgian hotel offers high standards of comfort and hospitality. Individually furnished bedrooms are generally spacious, with all of the expected modern conveniences. There is a choice of two comfortable lounges and a conservatory restaurant. Quality cooking, good service and fine hospitality are noteworthy.

Rooms 35 en suite 5 annexe en suite (4 fmly) S £69.50-£85; D £110-£145 (incl. bkfst)* **Facilities** Wi-fi in bedrooms New Year **Services** Lift **Parking** 50 **Notes LB**

★★★★★ GUEST HOUSE

Grendon Guest House

Bishops Ln SK17 6UN

☎ 01298 78831

e-mail: grendonguesthouse@hotmail.com

web: www.grendonguesthouse.co.uk

Dir: *0.75m from Buxton centre. Off A53 St Johns Rd, Bishops Ln 1st right after Otter Hole development*

PETS: Bedrooms Public areas Grounds accessible disp bin **Exercise area Facilities** walks info vet info **On Request** torch **Other** only one dog allowed per room

A warm welcome is assured at this non-smoking Edwardian house, set in immaculate grounds just a short walk from the town centre. The spacious, carefully furnished bedrooms are filled with thoughtful extras and lots of local information. Stunning country views can be enjoyed from the elegant lounge-dining room, where imaginative dinners are served. The attractive breakfast room is the setting for comprehensive breakfasts using local produce.

Rooms 5 en suite S £38-£50; D £60-£90✳ **Facilities** TVB tea/coffee Cen ht TVL Dinner Last d 5pm Wi-fi available **Parking** 8 **Notes** LB No children 10yrs No coaches Closed 3 Jan-3 Feb

★★★ BED & BREAKFAST

Wellhead Farm

Wormhill SK17 8SL

☎ 01298 871023 🖷 0871 236 0267

e-mail: wellhead4bunkntrough@cbits.net

Dir: *Between Bakewell and Buxton. Off A6 onto B6049 signed Millers Dale/Tideswell & left to Wormhill*

PETS: Bedrooms Public areas except dining room **Grounds** accessible disp bin **Exercise area** adjacent **Facilities** water bowl feeding mat litter tray leads pet sitting washing facs cage storage walks info vet info **On Request** fridge access torch towels **Resident Pets:** Zack (Retriever), Murphy (Border Terrier), Zoro & Billy (cats)

This 16th-century farmhouse is in a peaceful location, and has low beams and two comfortable lounges. The bedrooms, some with four poster beds, come with radios, beverage trays and many thoughtful extras. The proprietors provide friendly and attentive hospitality in their delightful home.

Rooms 4 en suite (1 fmly) S £40-£48; D £66-£70 **Facilities** tea/coffee Cen ht TVL Dinner Last d 9am **Parking** 4 **Notes** LB ⊜

►►►► Lime Tree Park *(SK070725)*

Dukes Dr SK17 9RP

☎ 01298 22988 🖷 01298 22988

e-mail: info@limetreeparkbuxton.co.uk

web: www.limetreeparkbuxton.co.uk

Dir: *1m S of Buxton, between A515 & A6*

PETS: Charges £2 per night (touring pitches) disp bin **Exercise area** on site field available **Facilities** on site shop food **Other** prior notice required

Open Mar-Oct Last arrival 21.00hrs Last departure noon

A most attractive and well-designed site, set on the side of a narrow valley in an elevated location. Its backdrop of magnificent old railway viaduct and views over Buxton and the surrounding hills make this a sought-after destination. A 10.5-acre site with 99 touring pitches, 8 hardstandings and 43 statics.

►► Cottage Farm Caravan Park *(SK122720)*

Beech Croft, Blackwell in the Peak SK17 9TQ

☎ 01298 85330

e-mail: mail@cottagefarmsite.co.uk

web: www.cottagefarmsite.co.uk

Dir: *Off A6 midway between Buxton and Bakewell. Site signed*

PETS: Public areas except toilets **Exercise area** bridlepath 100yds **Facilities** on site shop food food bowl water bowl walks info vet info

Open mid Mar-Oct (rs Mar hook up & water tap only) Last arrival 21.30hrs

A small terraced site in an attractive farm setting with lovely views. Hardstandings are provided for caravans, and there is a separate field for tents. An ideal site for those touring or walking in the Peak District. A 3-acre site with 30 touring pitches, 25 hardstandings.

Notes ⊜

►► Thornheyes Farm Campsite *(SK084761)*

Thornheyes Farm, Longridge Ln, Peak Dale SK17 8AD

☎ 01298 26421

Dir: *1.5m from Buxton on A6 turn E for Peak Dale. After 0.5m S at x-rds to site on right*

PETS: disp bin **Exercise area** adjacent **Facilities** vet info **Other** prior notice required **Resident Pets:** Bart (Alsation), 4 cats

Open Etr-Oct Last arrival 21.30hrs Last departure noon

A pleasant mainly-sloping farm site run by a friendly family team in the central Peak District. Toilet and other facilities are very simple but extremely clean. A 2-acre site with 10 touring pitches.

Notes ⊜ No ball games

ENGLAND

CALVER MAP 08 SK27

★★★★ GUEST ACCOMMODATION

Valley View

Smithy Knoll Rd S32 3XW

☎ 01433 631407

e-mail: sue@a-place-2-stay.co.uk

web: www.a-place-2-stay.co.uk

Dir: *A623 from Baslow into Calver, 3rd left onto Donkey Ln*

PETS: Bedrooms Exercise area by open fields, dogs can run off lead

This detached stone house is in the heart of the village. It is very well-furnished throughout and delightfully friendly service is provided. A hearty breakfast is served in the cosy dining room, which is well-stocked with local guide books.

Rooms 3 en suite (1 fmly) D £52-£80 **Facilities** TVB tea/coffee Cen ht Wi-fi available **Parking** 6 **Notes LB** No children 5yrs

CASTLETON MAP 07 SK18

★★★★ GUEST ACCOMMODATION

The Rising Sun

Hope Rd S33 0AL

☎ 01433 651323 🖷 01433 651601

e-mail: info@the-rising-sun.org

Dir: *On A625 from Sheffield to Castleton*

PETS: Bedrooms Public areas on lead (on leads) **Grounds** accessible on leads disp bin **Exercise area** surrounding countryside **Facilities** water bowl dog chews cage storage vet info **On Request** fridge access

Located at Thornhill Moor within the Hope Valley, this 18th-century inn has been renovated to provide high standards of comfort and facilities. Spacious luxury bedrooms offer quality furnishings and efficient modern bathrooms, and some have stunning views of the surrounding countryside. The staff are friendly and capable, and imaginative food is offered in the comfortable public areas.

Rooms 12 en suite (2 fmly) S £55.50-£69.50; D £60-£140✻ **Facilities** STV TVB tea/coffee Cen ht Dinner Last d 10pm Wi-fi available **Parking** 120 **Notes LB**

See advert on opposite page

CHESTERFIELD MAP 08 SK37

BUDGET HOTEL

Ibis Chesterfield

Lordsmill St S41 7RW

☎ 01246 221333 🖷 01246 221444

e-mail: h3160@accor.com

web: www.ibishotel.com

Dir: *M1 junct 29/A617 to Chesterfield. 2nd exit at 1st rdbt. Hotel on right at 2nd rdbt*

PETS: Bedrooms Exercise area Facilities vet info

Modern, budget hotel offering comfortable accommodation in bright and practical bedrooms. Breakfast is self-service and dinner is available in the restaurant.

Rooms 86 en suite S £50-£54; D £50-£54✻

CROMFORD MAP 08 SK25

★★★★ GUEST ACCOMMODATION

Alison House

Intake Ln DE4 3RH

☎ 01629 822211 🖷 01629 822316

e-mail: alisonhouse@toch.org.uk

PETS: Bedrooms unattended **Stables** nearby (2m) **Charges** £5 per night £35 per week charge for damage **Public areas** except restaurant (on leads) **Grounds** accessible disp bin **Exercise area** 100yds **Facilities** dog scoop/disp bags washing facs walks info vet info **On Request** fridge access torch towels

This very well furnished and spacious 18th-century house stands in seven acres of grounds just a short walk from the village. Public rooms are comfortable and bedrooms are mostly very spacious.

Rooms 16 en suite (1 fmly) (4 GF) S £49; D £79-£99✻ **Facilities** FTV TVB tea/coffee Direct dial from bedrooms Cen ht Dinner Last d 9pm Wi-fi available **Parking** 30

CROWDEN MAP 07 SK09

►► Crowden Camping & Caravanning Club Site *(SK072992)*

Woodhead Rd SK13 1HZ

☎ 01457 866057

web: www.thefriendlyclub.co.uk

Dir: *A628. At Crowden follow sign for car park/youth hostel & camp site. Site approx 300yds*

PETS: Public areas except in buildings disp bin **Exercise area** adjacent **Facilities** walks info vet info **Other** prior notice required

Open 27 Apr-28 Sep Last arrival 21.00hrs Last departure noon

A beautifully located moorland site, overlooking the reservoirs and surrounded by hills. Tents only, with backpackers' drying room. A 2.5-acre site with 45 touring pitches.

Notes Site gates closed 23.00hrs-07.00hrs

AA ★★★★

The Rising Sun

ETC ◆◆◆◆

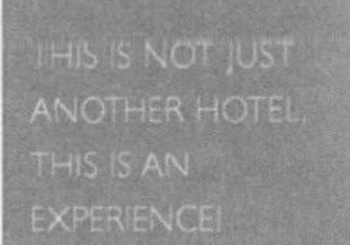

THIS IS NOT JUST ANOTHER HOTEL. THIS IS AN EXPERIENCE!

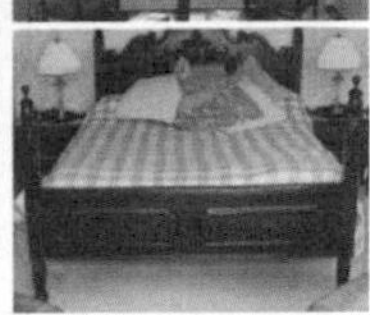

The Rising Sun, an 18th Century Inn situated in the heart of the Peak District National Park, is privately owned and family run. The hotel has been sympathetically restored with 12 individually designed de luxe bedrooms yet maintains its authentic country inn atmosphere. Fresh flowers in abundance and antiques together with friendly and efficient staff make this the place to stay. Quality fresh food, real ales and fine wines served daily in a relaxed and comfortable bar. Civil ceremonies & wedding receptions a speciality.

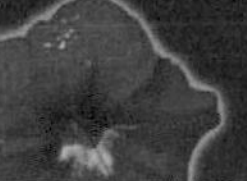

The Rising Sun, Thornhill Moor, Hope Road, Nr. Bamford, Hope Valley, Derbyshire S33 0AL
Telephone: 01433 651323 • Fax: 01433 651601
E-Mail: info@the-rising-sun.org •

"The Inn of the Peaks"

Weddings are our speciality. Hold your Civil Ceremony in our Oak Panelled Chatsworth Suite.

ENGLAND

DERBY SERVICE AREA (A50) MAP 08 SK42

BUDGET HOTEL

Days Inn Donnington

Welcome Break Services, A50 Westbound DE72 2WA

☎ 01332 799666 01332 794166

e-mail: derby.hotel@welcomebreak.co.uk

web: www.welcomebreak.co.uk

Dir: *M1junct 24/24a, onto A50 towards Stoke/Derby. Hotel between juncts 1 & 2*

PETS: Bedrooms (17GF) **Public areas** must be on lead or in carrier **Grounds** accessible on leads **Exercise area**

This modern building offers accommodation in smart, spacious and well-equipped bedrooms, suitable for families and business travellers, and all with en suite bathrooms. Refreshments may be taken at the nearby family restaurant.

Rooms 47 en suite S £39-£59; D £49-£69*

GLOSSOP MAP 07 SK09

★★★ BED & BREAKFAST

The Old House

Woodhead Rd, Torside SK13 1HU

☎ 01457 857527

e-mail: oldhouse@torside.co.uk

Dir: *2m N of Glossop. On B6105 between sailing club & hairpin bend*

PETS: Bedrooms Stables on site **Charges** horse £5; dogs no charge **Public areas Grounds** accessible **Exercise area** 25yds **Facilities** food bowl **Resident Pets:** 12 dogs, horses, chickens

Set on the northwest-facing slopes above a reservoir, this smallholding commands superb views and offers all mod cons, including a drying room for people who are walking the nearby Pennine Way. Oak beams and rough plastered walls date from the 17th century, and hospitality is warm.

Rooms 3 en suite (1 fmly) (1 GF) **Facilities** tea/coffee Cen ht TVL **Parking** 5 **Notes**

GRINDLEFORD MAP 08 SK27

★★★ 78% HOTEL

Maynard

Main Rd S32 2HE

☎ 01433 630321 01433 630445

e-mail: info@themaynard.co.uk

Dir: *from Sheffield take A625 to Castleton. Left into Grindleford on B6521. After Fox House hotel on left*

PETS: Bedrooms sign **Charges** £10 per night **Public areas** except restaurant (on leads) **Grounds** accessible disp bin **Exercise area Facilities** food (pre-bookable) food bowl water bowl bedding dog chews cat treats feeding mat dog scoop/disp bags leads dog walking washing facs cage storage walks info vet info **On Request** fridge access torch towels

This building, dating back over 100 years, is situated in a beautiful and tranquil location yet is within easy reach of Sheffield and the M1. The hotel has undergone a full refurbishment programme, and the bedrooms are contemporary is style and offer a wealth of accessories. The Peak District views from the restaurant and garden are stunning.

Rooms 10 en suite (1 fmly) S £70-£140; D £115-£175 (incl. bkfst)* **Facilities** STV Wi-fi available **Parking** 70 **Notes LB**

HAYFIELD MAP 07 SK08

►► Hayfield Camping & Caravanning Club Site *(SK048868)*

Kinder Rd SK22 2LE

☎ 01663 745394

web: www.thefriendlyclub.co.uk

Dir: *Off A624, Glossop to Chapel-en-le-Frith (Hayfield by-pass). Well signed into village, follow wood-carved signs to site*

PETS: Public areas except in buildings disp bin **Exercise area** adjacent to site **Facilities** walks info vet info **Other** prior notice required **Resident Pets:** Billy (Labrador)

Open 2 Apr-2 Nov Last arrival 21.00hrs Last departure noon

On level ground along the River Sett valley, a peaceful location overlooked on three sides by mature woodland, with the hills of the North Derbyshire moors on the fourth side. The camping area is in two fields with central amenities. A 6-acre site with 90 touring pitches.

Notes Site gates closed 23.00hrs-07.00hrs

HOPE MAP 07 SK18

★★★★ GUEST ACCOMMODATION

Stoney Ridge

Granby Rd, Bradwell S33 9HU

☎ 01433 620538

e-mail: toneyridge@aol.com

web: www.stoneyridge.org.uk

Dir: *From N end of Bradwell, Gore Ln uphill past Bowling Green Inn, turn left onto Granby Rd*

PETS: Bedrooms unattended **Public areas** except dining room (on leads) **Grounds** accessible on leads disp bin **Exercise area** 100mtrs **Facilities** pet sitting walks info vet info **On Request** fridge access torch towels **Resident Pets:** Paddy (cockatiel), chickens (various breeds)

This large, split-level bungalow stands in attractive mature gardens at the highest part of the village and has extensive views. Hens roam freely in the landscaped garden, and their fresh eggs add to the hearty breakfasts. Bedrooms are attractively furnished and thoughtfully equipped, and there is a spacious comfortable lounge and a superb indoor swimming pool.

Rooms 4 rms (3 en suite) (1 pri facs) S £40-£42; D £54-£68* **Facilities** TVB tea/coffee Cen ht TVL Wi-fi available **Parking** 3 **Notes LB** No children 10yrs RS Winter

★★★ BED & BREAKFAST

Round Meadow Barn

Parsons Ln S33 6RB

☎ 01433 621347 & 07836 689422 01433 621347

e-mail: rmbarn@bigfoot.com

Dir: *Off A625 Hope Rd N onto Parsons Ln, over railway bridge, 200yds right into Hay barnyard, through gates, across 3 fields, house on left*

PETS: Bedrooms Stables on site **Charges** dogs £3, horses £10 per night **Public areas** except at breakfast (on leads) **Grounds** accessible disp bin **Exercise area** on site **Facilities** water bowl feeding mat washing facs vet info **On Request** towels **Restrictions** no Staffordshire Bull Terriers **Resident Pets:** Puzzle (Jack Russell), Kayti & Jasmin (Welsh ponies), Floss (horse), Lucy (cat)

This converted barn, with original stone walls and exposed timbers, stands in open fields in the picturesque Hope Valley. The bedrooms are large enough for families and there are two modern bathrooms. Breakfast is served at one large table adjoining the family kitchen.

Rooms 4 rms (1 en suite) (1 fmly) S £30-£35; D £50-£60* **Facilities** TVB tea/coffee Cen ht Golf 18 Riding **Parking** 8 **Notes LB**

MATLOCK MAP 08 SK36

★★★ 79% HOTEL

Riber Hall

DE4 5JU

☎ 01629 582795 01629 580475

e-mail: info@riber-hall.co.uk

web: www.riber-hall.co.uk

Dir: *1m off A615 at Tansley*

PETS: Bedrooms (6GF) **Charges** £5 per night charge for damage **Exercise area** on site **Facilities** water bowl cage storage walks info vet info **On Request** torch towels **Restrictions** small & medium dogs only

This beautiful Elizabethan manor house enjoys an idyllic location in charming grounds overlooking Matlock. Pleasantly furnished, thoughtfully equipped bedrooms, many with oak four-poster beds, are situated in the courtyard. Tastefully appointed public rooms are furnished with period and antique pieces.

Rooms 3 en suite 11 annexe en suite (6 GF) **Facilities** **Parking** 40

★★★ FARM HOUSE

Farley *(SK294622)*

Farley DE4 5LR

☎ 01629 582533 & 07801 756409 01629 584856

Mrs Brailsford

e-mail: eric.brailsford@btconnect.com

Dir: *1m N of Matlock. From A6 rdbt towards Bakewell, 1st right, right at top of hill, left up Farley Hill, 2nd farm on left*

PETS: Bedrooms Sep Accom stables **Stables** on site **Charges** pony £15, horse £20 inc feed/bedding per night **Public areas** except dining room **Grounds** accessible **Exercise area** fields surrounding farm **Facilities** food (pre-bookable) food bowl water bowl bedding leads pet sitting dog walking washing facs dog grooming cage storage vet info **On Request** fridge access torch towels **Resident Pets:** 5 Border Terriers, 1 Labrador, 4 horses, ferrel cats

Guests can expect a warm welcome at this traditional stone farmhouse. In addition to farming, the proprietors also breed dogs and horses. The bedrooms are pleasantly decorated and equipped with many useful extras. Breakfast is served round one large table (dinner is available by arrangement).

Rooms 2 en suite (3 fmly) S £35; D £50-£55 **Facilities** TVB tea/coffee Cen ht TVL Dinner Last d 5pm Riding **Parking** 8 **Notes LB** 165 acres arable beef dairy

ENGLAND

MATLOCK CONTINUED

►►►► Lickpenny Caravan Site *(SK339597)*

Lickpenny Ln, Tansley DE4 5GF

☎ 01629 583040 📠 01629 583040

e-mail: lickpenny@btinternet.com

web: www.lickpennycaravanpark.co.uk

Dir: *From A615 between Alfreton & Matlock, approx 1m N of Tansley. Turn into Lickpenny Lane at x-rds*

PETS: disp bin **Exercise area** on site woodland area **Facilities** on site shop food food bowl water bowl dog scoop/disp bags walks info vet info

Open all year Last arrival 20.00hrs Last departure noon

A picturesque site in the grounds of an old plant nursery with areas broken up and screened by a variety of shrubs, and spectacular views. Pitches, several fully serviced, are spacious and well marked, and facilities are to a very good standard. A bistro/coffee shop is popular with visitors. A 16-acre site with 80 touring pitches, 80 hardstandings.

NEWHAVEN MAP 07 SK16

►►► Newhaven Caravan & Camping Park

(SK167602)

SK17 0DT

☎ 01298 84300 📠 01332 726027

web: www.newhavencaravanpark.co.uk

Dir: *Between Ashbourne & Buxton at A515 & A5012 junct*

PETS: Public areas except in shop disp bin **Exercise area** on site woodland walks **Facilities** on site shop food food bowl water bowl dog chews cat treats dog scoop/disp bags walks info

Resident Pets: Basil (Border Collie), Ned (Golden Retriever)

Open Mar-Oct Last arrival 23.00hrs Last departure anytime

Pleasantly situated within the Peak District National Park, with mature trees screening the three touring areas. Very good toilet facilities cater for touring vans and a large tent field, and there's a restaurant adjacent to the site. A 30-acre site with 125 touring pitches, 18 hardstandings and 73 statics.

REPTON MAP 08 SK32

★★★ INN

The Boot Inn

12 Boot Hill DE65 6FT

☎ 01283 703327

e-mail: susie_goulden@yahoo.co.uk

web: www.thebootinn.co.uk

Dir: *Off A38 or A50, follow signs for Willington and then Repton. Turn left at 'cross' rdbt*

PETS: Bedrooms Charges £10 per night charge for damage **Public areas** (on leads) **Grounds** accessible on leads disp bin **Exercise area** 2m **Facilities** walks info vet info

Resident Pets: Nelson (Labrador)

Situated in the centre of the village, this traditional old inn offers pleasingly furnished bedrooms and busy bars. A wide choice of food is available and the service is friendly and attentive.

Rooms 5 en suite (1 fmly) S £35-£45; D £65-£75* **Facilities** TVB tea/coffee Cen ht Dinner Last d 8.30pm Wi-fi available **Parking** 8

ROSLISTON MAP 08 SK21

►► Beehive Woodland Lakes *(SK249161)*

DE12 8HZ

☎ 01283 763981 📠 01283 763981

e-mail: info@beehivefarm-woodlandlakes.co.uk

web: www.beehivefarm-woodlandlakes.co.uk

Dir: *Turn S off A444 at Castle Gresley onto Mount Pleasant Road, follow Rosliston signs. Site on left at T-junct at end of Linton road*

PETS: Public areas except near lakes **Charges** £1 per night disp bin **Exercise area** 800yds **Facilities** on site shop food bowl water bowl dog chews cat treats litter tray leads washing facs dog grooming walks info vet info **Other** prior notice required

Open Mar-Nov Last arrival 20.00hrs Last departure 10.30hrs

A small, informal caravan area secluded from an extensive woodland park in the heart of The National Forest. Young children will enjoy the on-site animal farm and playground, whilst anglers will appreciate fishing the three lakes within the park. The Honey Pot tearoom provides snacks and is open most days. A 2.5-acre site with 25 touring pitches, 12 hardstandings.

ROWSLEY MAP 08 SK26

★★★ 88% @@ HOTEL

The Peacock at Rowsley

Bakewell Rd DE4 2EB

☎ 01629 733518 📠 01629 732671

e-mail: reception@thepeacockatrowsley.com

web: www.thepeacockatrowsley.com

Dir: *A6, 3m before Bakewell, 6m from Matlock towards Bakewell*

PETS: Bedrooms unattended **Charges** £10 per dog per night charge for damage **Grounds** accessible **Exercise area** 0.25m **Facilities** food (pre-bookable) water bowl walks info vet info **On Request** torch towels

Owned by Haddon Hall this hotel is a smart, contemporary destination although many of the property's original features can still be seen. The menus are well balanced and use local produce. Dry fly fishing is a great attraction here as the hotel owns fishing rights in the area. The staff are delightful and deliver high standards of service.

Rooms 16 en suite (5 fmly) **Facilities** Fishing Wi-fi in bedrooms Free use of Woodlands Fitness Centre Free membership to Bakewell Golf Club **Parking** 25 **Notes** No children 10yrs

SANDIACRE MAP 08 SK43

★★★ 68% HOTEL

Holiday Inn Derby/Nottingham

Bostocks Ln NG10 5NJ

☎ 0870 400 9062 📠 0115 949 0469

e-mail: rachel.shipley@ihg.com

web: www.holidayinn.co.uk

Dir: *M1 junct 25 follow exit to Sandiacre, hotel on right*

PETS: Bedrooms (53GF) unattended **Charges** £10 per night £70 per week charge for damage **Grounds** accessible on leads disp bin **Exercise area Facilities** vet info **On Request** fridge access torch towels

Currently the rating for this establishment is not confirmed. This may be due to a change of ownership or because it has only recently joined the AA rating scheme. For further details please see the AA website: www.theAA.com

Rooms 92 en suite (31 fmly) (53 GF) S £39-£150; D £39-£150 (incl. bkfst) **Facilities** STV Wi-fi available Xmas New Year **Services** air con **Parking** 200

SWADLINCOTE MAP 08 SK21

★★★ BED & BREAKFAST

Overseale House

Acresford Rd, Overseal DE12 6HX

☎ 01283 763741 📠 01283 760015

e-mail: oversealehouse@hotmail.com

web: www.oversealehouse.co.uk

Dir: *On A444 between Burton upon Trent & M42 junct 11*

PETS: Bedrooms (2GF) **Stables** nearby **Grounds** accessible disp bin **Exercise area Facilities** cage storage walks info vet info **On Request** fridge access torch towels **Resident Pets:** Jemini (Old English Bull terrier)

Located in the village, this well-proportioned Georgian mansion, built for a renowned industrialist, retains many original features including a magnificent dining room decorated with ornate mouldings. The period-furnished ground-floor areas include a cosy sitting room, and bedrooms contain many thoughtful extras.

Rooms 4 en suite 1 annexe rms (3 fmly) (2 GF) S £30-£45; D £60-£70* (room only) **Facilities** TVB tea/coffee Cen ht **Parking** 6 **Notes**

THORPE (DOVEDALE) MAP 07 SK15

★★★ 79% @@ HOTEL

Izaak Walton

Dovedale DE6 2AY

☎ 01335 350555 📠 01335 350539

e-mail: reception@izaakwaltonhotel.com

web: www.izaakwaltonhotel.com

Dir: *A515 onto B5054, to Thorpe village, continue straight over cattle grid & 2 small bridges, 1st right & sharp left*

PETS: Bedrooms (8GF) unattended **Charges** £10 per night charge for damage **Public areas** except main restaurant and 1st floor **Grounds** accessible on leads **Exercise area**

This hotel is peacefully situated, with magnificent views over the valley of Dovedale to Thorpe Cloud. Many of the bedrooms have lovely views, and the executive rooms are particularly spacious. Meals are served in the bar area, with more formal dining in the Haddon Restaurant. Staff are friendly and efficient. Fishing on the River Dove can be arranged.

Rooms 35 en suite (6 fmly) (8 GF) S fr £110; D fr £145 (incl. bkfst)* **Facilities** Fishing Wi-fi in bedrooms Xmas New Year **Parking** 80

TIDESWELL MAP 07 SK17

★★★ GUEST ACCOMMODATION

Poppies

Bank Square SK17 8LA

☎ 01298 871083

e-mail: poptidza@dialstart.net

Dir: *On B6049 in village centre opp NatWest bank*

PETS: Bedrooms Charges charge for damage **Public areas** (on leads) **Exercise area** 200yds **Facilities** walks info vet info **On Request** fridge access torch

A friendly welcome is assured at this non-smoking house, located in the heart of a former lead-mining and textile community, a short walk from the 14th-century parish church. Bedrooms are homely and practical.

Rooms 3 rms (1 en suite) (1 fmly) S £22-£25; D £44-£53✻ **Facilities** TVB tea/coffee Cen ht Dinner Last d previous day **Notes** ⊜

YOULGREAVE MAP 08 SK26

► Bakewell Camping & Caravanning Club Site *(SK206632)*

Hopping Farm DE45 1NA

☎ 01629 636555

web: www.thefriendlyclub.co.uk

Dir: *A6/B5056, after 0.5m turn right to Youlgreave. Turn sharp left after church down Bradford Lane, opposite George Hotel. 0.5m to sign turn right*

PETS: Public areas except in buildings disp bin **Exercise area** on site **Facilities** walks info vet info **Other** prior notice required

Open 2 Apr-2 Nov Last arrival 21.00hrs Last departure noon

Ideal for touring and walking in the Peak District National Park, this gently sloping grass site is accessed through narrow streets and along unadopted hardcore. Own sanitary facilities essential. A 14-acre site with 100 touring pitches, 6 hardstandings.

Notes Site gates closed 23.00hrs-07.00hrs

DEVON

ASHBURTON MAP 03 SX77

★★★★ ⊜ INN

The Rising Sun

Woodland TQ13 7JT

☎ 01364 652544

e-mail: admin@therisingsunwoodland.co.uk

Dir: *A38, exit signed Woodland/Denbury, continue straight on for 1.5m Rising Sun on left*

PETS: Bedrooms unattended **Public areas** (on leads) **Grounds** accessible disp bin **Exercise area** 50yds **Facilities** washing facs cage storage walks info vet info

Peacefully situated in scenic south Devon countryside, this inn is just a short drive from the A38. A friendly welcome is extended to all guests, business, leisure and families alike. Bedrooms are comfortable and well equipped. Dinner and breakfast feature much local and organic produce. A good selection of homemade puddings, West Country cheeses, local wines and quality real ales are available.

Rooms 5 en suite (2 fmly) (2 GF) D £75✻ **Facilities** FTV TVB tea/coffee Cen ht Dinner Last d 9.15pm **Parking** 30 **Notes** No coaches

►►►► Parkers Farm Holiday Park *(SX779713)*

Higher Mead Farm TQ13 7LJ

☎ 01364 654869 📠 01364 654004

e-mail: parkersfarm@btconnect.com

web: www.parkersfarm.co.uk

Dir: *From Exeter on A38, take 2nd left after Plymouth 26m sign, at Alston, signed Woodland-Denbury. From Plymouth on A38 take A383 Newton Abbot exit, turn right across bridge and rejoin A38, then as above.*

PETS: Stables nearby (0.5m) **Public areas** except children's play area & main bar **Charges** £1.50 per night (touring pitches) disp bin **Exercise area** on site dog walks, fields **Facilities** on site shop food food bowl water bowl dog chews cat treats dog scoop/disp bags leads washing facs walks info vet info **Other** prior notice required **Resident Pets:** dogs, horses, sheep, goats, pigs, rabbits, chickens, ducks, guinea pigs

Open Etr-end Oct Last arrival 22.00hrs Last departure 10.00hrs

A well-developed site terraced into rising ground. Part of a working farm, this park offers beautifully maintained, quality facilities. Large family rooms with two shower cubicles, a large sink and a toilet are especially appreciated by families with small children. There are regular farm walks when all the family can meet and feed the various animals. A 25-acre site with 100 touring pitches, 5 hardstandings and 18 statics.

►►►► River Dart Country Park *(SX734700)*

Holne Park TQ13 7NP

☎ 01364 652511 📠 01364 652020

e-mail: info@riverdart.co.uk

web: www.riverdart.co.uk

Dir: *From M5 junct 31 take A38 towards Plymouth. At Ashburton at Peartree junction follow brown site signs. Site 1m on left. (NB Peartree junction is 2nd exit at Ashburton - do not exit at Linhay junction as narrow roads are unsuitable for caravans)*

PETS: Public areas except amenity block, shop & café **Charges** £2-£3 per night (seasonal) disp bin **Exercise area** on site marked dog walks **Facilities** on site shop food food bowl water bowl dog scoop/disp bags washing facs walks info vet info **Other** prior notice required **Resident Pets:** Harry (Jack Russell)

Open Apr-Sep (rs low season café bar restricted opening hours) Last arrival 21.00hrs Last departure 11.00hrs

Set in 90 acres of magnificent parkland that was once part of a Victorian estate, with many specimen and exotic trees, and in spring a blaze of colour from the many azaleas and rhododendrons. There are numerous outdoor activities for all ages including abseiling, caving and canoeing, plus high quality, well-maintained facilities. The open moorland of Dartmoor is only a few minutes away. A 90-acre site with 170 touring pitches, 12 hardstandings.

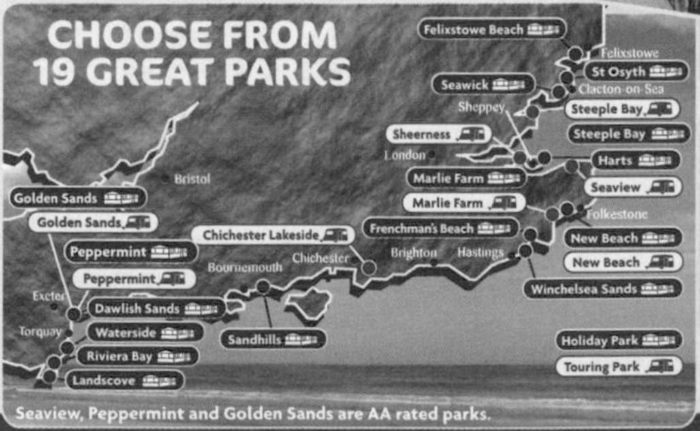

ASHWATER

MAP 02 SX39

★★★ ⊛⊛ HOTEL

Blagdon Manor Hotel & Restaurant

EX21 5DF

☎ 01409 211224 01409 211634

e-mail: stay@blagdon.com

web: www.blagdon.com

Dir: *Take A388 N of Launceston towards Holsworthy. Approx 2m N of Chapman's Well take 2nd right for Ashwater. Next right beside Blagdon Lodge, hotel 0.25m*

PETS: Bedrooms Charges £7.50 per night **Public areas** except restaurant **Grounds** accessible disp bin **Exercise area Facilities** food bowl water bowl bedding dog chews feeding mat dog scoop/disp bags washing facs cage storage walks info vet info **On Request** fridge access torch towels

Resident Pets: Nutmeg & Cassia (Chocolate Labradors)

Located on the borders of Devon and Cornwall within easy reach of the coast, and set in its own beautifully kept yet natural gardens, this small and friendly hotel offers a charming home-from-home atmosphere. The tranquillity of the secluded setting, the character and charm of the house and its unhurried pace ensure calm and relaxation. High levels of service, personal touches and thoughtful extras are all part of a stay here. Steve Morey cooks with passion and his commitment to using only the finest local ingredients speaks volumes.

Rooms 8 en suite S £85; D £135-£180 (incl. bkfst)* **Facilities** FTV Boules Giant chess/draughts **Parking** 13 **Notes** No children 12yrs Closed 2wks Jan/Feb & 2wks Oct/Nov

AXMINSTER

MAP 03 SY29

★★★ 74% ⊛ HOTEL

Fairwater Head Hotel

Hawkchurch EX13 5TX

☎ 01297 678349 01297 678459

e-mail: stay@fairwaterheadhotel.co.uk

web: www.fairwaterheadhotel.co.uk

Dir: *off B3165 (Crewkerne to Lyme Regis road). Hotel signed to Hawkchurch*

PETS: Bedrooms (8GF) unattended **Charges** charge for damage **Public areas** except dining room (on leads) **Grounds** accessible on leads disp bin **Exercise area** surrounding countryside **Facilities** food (pre-bookable) food bowl water bowl dog chews dog scoop/disp bags leads pet sitting cage storage walks info vet info **On Request** fridge access torch towels

Resident Pets: Mocca (Springer/Cocker Spaniel)

This elegant Edwardian country house provides a perfect location for anyone looking for a peaceful break. Surrounded by extensive gardens and rolling countryside, the setting guarantees relaxation. Bedrooms are located both within the main house and the garden wing; all provide good levels of comfort. Public areas have much appeal and include lounge areas, a bar and an elegant restaurant. Food is a highlight with excellent local produce prepared with care and skill.

Rooms 12 en suite 4 annexe en suite (8 GF) S £80-£115; D £140-£210 (incl. bkfst & dinner)* **Facilities** Wi-fi available Xmas New Year **Parking** 30 **Notes** LB Closed 1-30 Jan

See advertisement on page 96

ENGLAND

AXMINSTER CONTINUED

►►►► Andrewshayes Caravan Park

(ST248088)

Dalwood EX13 7DY

☎ 01404 831225 📠 01404 831893

e-mail: info@andrewshayes.co.uk

web: www.andrewshayes.co.uk

Dir: *On A35, 3m from Axminster. Turn N at Taunton Cross signed Stockland/Dalwood. Site 150mtrs on right*

PETS: Charges £1.50-£2 per night (seasonal) **Public areas** except in bar disp bin (on leads) **Exercise area** on site 2 dog walking fields **Facilities** on site shop dog scoop/disp bags walks info vet info **Other** prior notice required

Open Mar-Nov (rs Sep-Nov shop, bar hrs ltd, pool shut Sep-mid May) Last arrival 22.00hrs Last departure 11.00hrs

A friendly family run park set in beautiful East Devon countryside, making an ideal location for touring the west country and within easy reach of Lyme Regis, Charmouth, Branscombe and Sidmouth beach resorts. This popular park has an outdoor heated swimming pool, a bar and takeaway food service, laundry and shop. A 12-acre site with 150 touring pitches, 105 hardstandings and 80 statics.

BAMPTON — MAP 03 SS92

★★★★ GUEST ACCOMMODATION

The Bark House

Oakford Bridge EX16 9HZ

☎ 01398 351236

Dir: *A361 to rdbt at Tiverton onto A396 for Dulverton and onto Oakfordbridge, on right*

PETS: Bedrooms Charges £4 per night charge for damage **Grounds** accessible disp bin **Exercise area** 10mtrs **Facilities** food bowl water bowl feeding mat walks info vet info **On Request** towels **Resident Pets:** Jack & Ellie (dogs)

Located in the stunning Exe Valley, this is a perfect place to relax and unwind, surrounded by wonderful unspoilt countryside. Hospitality is a hallmark here and a cup of tea by the fireside is always on offer. Both breakfast and dinner make use of the excellent local produce, and are served in the attractive dining room, overlooking fields and the river. Bedrooms all have a homely, cottage-style feel with comfy beds to ensure a peaceful night's sleep.

Rooms 6 rms (5 en suite) (1 pri facs) S £48.50-£64; D £77-£128* **Facilities** TVB tea/coffee Cen ht Dinner Last d 7.30pm **Parking** 6 **Notes** LB

BARNSTAPLE — MAP 02 SS53

★★★★★ GUEST ACCOMMODATION

Halmpstone Manor

Bishop's Tawton EX32 0EA

☎ 01271 830321 & 831003 📠 01271 830826

e-mail: jane@halmpstonemanor.co.uk

web: www.halmpstonemanor.co.uk

Dir: *3m SE of Barnstaple. Off A377 E of river & rail bridges*

PETS: Bedrooms Public areas except restaurant **Grounds** accessible disp bin **Exercise area Facilities** washing facs cage storage walks info vet info **On Request** fridge access torch towels **Resident Pets:** Barley (Cocker Spaniel)

The manor was mentioned in the Domesday Book and parts of the later medieval manor house survive. Halmpstone Manor now provides quality accommodation, personal service and fine cuisine. Delightful day rooms include a spacious lounge complete with deep sofas and a roaring fire, and a creative, daily changing menu is offered in the elegant restaurant. Superb hospitality and excellent value make this a great choice for a restful break.

Rooms 4 en suite **Facilities** TVB tea/coffee Dinner Last d 7.30pm **Parking** 12 **Notes** Closed Xmas & New Year

BICKINGTON (NEAR ASHBURTON) — MAP 03 SX87

►►►► Lemonford Caravan Park *(SX793723)*

TQ12 6JR

☎ 01626 821242 & 821263 📠 01626 821263

e-mail: mark@lemonford.co.uk

web: www.lemonford.co.uk

Dir: *From Exeter A38 take A382, then 3rd exit on rdbt , follow Bickington signs*

PETS: Charges £1.20 per dog per night disp bin **Exercise area** 10yds **Facilities** on site shop walks info vet info **Other** prior notice required **Restrictions** breeds only accepted at owner's discretion **Resident Pets:** 3 cats

Open Mar-Oct Last arrival 22.00hrs Last departure 11.00hrs

Small, secluded and well-maintained park with a good mixture of attractively laid out pitches. The friendly owners pay a great deal of attention to detail, and the toilets in particular are kept spotlessly clean. This good touring base is only 1m from Dartmoor and 10m from the seaside at Torbay. A 7-acre site with 82 touring pitches, 55 hardstandings and 44 statics.

BIDEFORD MAP 02 SS42

★★★ 74% HOTEL

Royal

Brend Hotels

Barnstaple St EX39 4AE

☎ 01237 472005 📠 01237 478957

e-mail: reservations@royalbideford.co.uk

web: www.brend-hotels.co.uk

Dir: *at eastern end of Bideford Bridge*

PETS: Bedrooms Stables nearby (3-5m) **Charges** £3 per dog per night **Exercise area Facilities** cage storage vet info

A quiet and relaxing hotel, the Royal is set near the river within five minutes' walk of the busy town centre and quay. The bright, well maintained public areas retain much of the charm and style dating from its 16th-century origins, particularly in the wood-panelled Kingsley Suite. Bedrooms are well equipped and comfortable. Both meals at dinner and lounge snacks are appetising.

Rooms 32 en suite (2 fmly) (2 GF) S £65-£95; D £79-£109* **Facilities** FTV Wi-fi in bedrooms ♫ Xmas New Year **Services** Lift **Parking** 70 **Notes** LB

★★ 81% ❀ HOTEL

Yeoldon Country House

Durrant Ln, Northam EX39 2RL

☎ 01237 474400 📠 01237 476618

e-mail: yeoldonhouse@aol.com

web: www.yeoldonhousehotel.co.uk

Dir: *A39 from Barnstaple over River Torridge Bridge. At rdbt right onto A386 towards Northam, then 3rd right into Durrant Lane*

PETS: Bedrooms Charges £5 per night charge for damage **Public areas** lounge only (under strict control) (on leads) **Grounds** accessible disp bin **Exercise area** N Devon coastal path nearby **Facilities** dog food available (beef & gravy occasionally) washing facs cage storage walks info vet info **On Request** fridge access torch towels **Resident Pets:** Shaz (Collie cross)

In a tranquil location with superb views over the River Torridge and attractive grounds, this is a charming Victorian house. The well-equipped bedrooms are individually decorated and some have balconies with breathtaking views. The public rooms are full of character with many interesting features and artefacts. The daily-changing dinner menu offers imaginative dishes.

Rooms 10 en suite S £75-£80; D £115-£130 (incl. bkfst) **Facilities** FTV Wi-fi available **Parking** 20 **Notes** LB Closed 24-27 Dec

★★★★ GUEST ACCOMMODATION

Pines at Eastleigh

The Pines, Eastleigh EX39 4PA

☎ 01271 860561 📠 01271 861689

e-mail: pirrie@thepinesateastleigh.co.uk

Dir: *A39 onto A386 signed East-The-Water. 1st left signed Eastleigh, 500yds next left, 1.5m to village, house on right*

PETS: Bedrooms (4GF) **Stables** nearby **Charges** charge for damage **Grounds** accessible on leads disp bin **Exercise area** adjacent **Facilities** food bowl water bowl pet sitting dog walking washing facs cage storage walks info vet info **On Request** torch towels **Other** dogs off lead in paddock (if no sheep)

Friendly hospitality is assured at this Georgian farmhouse, set in seven acres of gardens. Two of the comfortable bedrooms are located in the main house, the remainder in converted barns around a charming courtyard, with a pretty pond and well. A delicious breakfast featuring local and home-made produce is served in the dining room and a lounge and honesty bar are also available.

Rooms 6 en suite (1 fmly) (4 GF) S £45; D £75-£100 **Facilities** TVB tea/coffee Direct dial from bedrooms Cen ht Wi-fi available ⛳ Table Tennis, Archery, Table Football **Parking** 20 **Notes** LB No children 9yrs

BISHOPSTEIGNTON MAP 03 SX97

★★ 67% HOTEL

Cockhaven Manor Hotel

THE INDEPENDENTS HOTEL ASSOCIATION

Cockhaven Rd TQ14 9RF

☎ 01626 775252 📠 01626 775572

e-mail: cockhaven@btconnect.com

web: www.cockhavenmanor.com

Dir: *M5/A380 towards Torquay, then A381 towards Teignmouth. Left at Metro Motors. Hotel 500yds on left*

PETS: Bedrooms unattended **Public areas** except restaurant **Grounds** accessible disp bin **Exercise area Facilities** food bowl water bowl dog chews dog scoop/disp bags leads pet sitting dog walking washing facs walks info vet info **On Request** fridge access torch towels **Resident Pets:** Bitsy (dog)

A friendly, family-run inn that dates back to the 16th century. Bedrooms are well equipped and many enjoy views across the beautiful Teign

CONTINUED

BISHOPSTEIGNTON CONTINUED

estuary. A choice of dining options is offered, and traditional and interesting dishes, along with locally caught fish, prove popular.

Rooms 12 en suite (2 fmly) S £46-£55; D £60-£72 (incl. bkfst) **Facilities** Wi-fi available Petanque **Parking** 50 **Notes** LB RS 25-26 Dec

BRANSCOMBE MAP 03 SY18

★★ 79% HOTEL

The Masons Arms

EX12 3DJ

☎ 01297 680300 01297 680500

e-mail: reception@masonsarms.co.uk

Dir: *off A3052 towards Branscombe, hotel at hill bottom*

PETS: Bedrooms Charges £5 per night charge for damage **Public areas** except restaurant (on leads) **Grounds** accessible on leads disp bin **Exercise area** 300yds **Facilities** water bowl washing facs walks info vet info **On Request** fridge access towels **Resident Pets:** Maisy (Parson Russell Terrier)

This delightful 14th-century village inn is just half a mile from the sea. The bedrooms in the thatched annexed cottages tend to be more spacious and have patios with seating; those in the inn reflect much period charm. In the bar, an extensive selection of dishes, which includes many local specialities, is available and the restaurant offers an imaginative range of dishes.

Rooms 7 en suite 14 annexe en suite (1 fmly) S £80-£170; D £80-£170 (incl. bkfst)✻ **Facilities** Wi-fi available Xmas New Year **Parking** 43 **Notes** LB

BRAUNTON MAP 02 SS43

►►►► ***Hidden Valley Park*** *(SS499408)*

EX34 8NU

☎ 01271 813837 01271 814041

e-mail: relax@hiddenvalleypark.com

web: www.hiddenvalleypark.com

Dir: *Direct access off A361, 8m from Barnstaple & 2m from Mullacott Cross*

PETS: Public areas except shop & coffee shop **Charges** max £2 per night disp bin **Exercise area** on site exercise field & woods **Facilities** on site shop food dog scoop/disp bags washing facs walks info vet info

Open all year (rs 15 Nov-15 Mar all weather pitches only) Last arrival 21.30hrs Last departure 10.00hrs

A delightful, well-appointed family site set in a wooded valley, with superb facilities and a cafe. The park is set in a very rural, natural position not far from the beautiful coastline around Ilfracombe. A 25-acre site with 135 touring pitches, 74 hardstandings.

BRIDGERULE MAP 02 SS20

►► Highfield House Camping & Caravanning *(SS279035)*

Holsworthy EX22 7EE

☎ 01288 381480

e-mail: nikki@highfieldholidays.freeserve.co.uk

Dir: *Exit A3072 at Red Post x-rds onto B3254 towards Launceston. Direct access just over Devon border on right*

PETS: disp bin **Exercise area** on site **Facilities** on site shop washing facs walks info vet info **Restrictions** no Staffordshire Bull Terriers, German Shepherds or Rottweilers

Resident Pets: Tilly (West Highland White Terrier), Tara (German Shepherd), Sparky (Cairn Terrier), goats, pigs, chickens, ducks

Open all year

Set in a quiet and peaceful rural location, this park has extensive views over the valley to the sea at Bude, five miles away. The friendly young owners, with small children of their own, offer a relaxing holiday for families, with the simple facilities carefully looked after. A 4-acre site with 20 touring pitches and 4 statics.

Notes

BRIXHAM MAP 03 SX95

★★★ 73% HOTEL

Quayside

41-49 King St TQ5 9TJ

☎ 01803 855751 01803 882733

e-mail: reservations@quaysidehotel.co.uk

web: www.quaysidehotel.co.uk

Dir: *A380, at 2nd rdbt at Kinkerswell towards Brixham on A3022. Hotel overlooks harbour*

PETS: Bedrooms Charges £10 per night charge for damage **Public areas** allowed in bar during the day (on leads) **Exercise area Facilities** food bowl water bowl cage storage walks info vet info **On Request** fridge access torch towels **Restrictions** small dogs only

With views over the harbour and bay, this hotel was formerly six cottages. The owners and their team of local staff provide friendly and attentive service. Public rooms retain a certain cosiness and intimacy, and include the lounge, residents' bar and Ernie Lister's public bar. Freshly landed fish features on menus in the well-appointed restaurant, and snacks are available in the public bar.

Rooms 29 en suite (2 fmly) **Facilities** Wi-fi available **Parking** 30

★★★ 70% HOTEL

Berry Head

THE INDEPENDENTS HOTEL ASSOCIATION

Berry Head Rd TQ5 9AJ

☎ 01803 853225 📠 01803 882084

e-mail: stay@berryheadhotel.com

Dir: *From marina, 1m, hotel on left*

PETS: Bedrooms Charges £10 per night **Public areas** lounge only at certain times **Grounds** accessible **Exercise area** 20yds **Restrictions** small dogs only; by prior arrangement

From its stunning cliff-top location, this imposing property that dates back to 1809, has spectacular views across Torbay. Public areas include two comfortable lounges, an outdoor terrace, a swimming pool, together with a bar serving a range of popular dishes. Many of the bedrooms have the benefit of the splendid sea views.

Rooms 32 en suite (7 fmly) S £50-£74; D £100-£180 (incl. bkfst)✳ **Facilities** STV Wi-fi available Petanque sailing Deep sea fishing Yacht charter ♫ Xmas New Year **Parking** 200 **Notes LB**

BUDLEIGH SALTERTON — MAP 03 SY08

★★★★★ GUEST ACCOMMODATION

Downderry House

10 Exmouth Rd EX9 6AQ

☎ 01395 442663 📠 01395 442663

e-mail: info@downderryhouse.co.uk

web: www.downderryhouse.co.uk

Dir: *From M5 follow Budleigh Salterton signs. From A303 exit at Daisy Mount onto B3180*

PETS: Bedrooms (1GF) **Charges** £5 per night **Grounds** accessible on leads disp bin **Exercise area** adjacent **Facilities** cage storage walks info vet info **On Request** torch towels **Other** dogs in one ground floor bedroom only **Resident Pets:** Bertie (Beagle)

Just a short stroll from the town and seafront, this lovely house stands in an acre of gardens with views across meadows. Quality is the hallmark here with spacious and stylish bedrooms offering impressive levels of comfort. In addition, the luxurious bathrooms come complete with robes and fluffy towels. Breakfast provides a wonderful taste of the local area, served in the attractive dining room overlooking the gardens. An elegant guest lounge is also available, complete with honesty bar.

Rooms 5 en suite (1 GF) S £65-£89; D £79-£99✳ **Facilities** FTV TVB tea/coffee Cen ht Wi-fi available **Parking** 9 **Notes LB** No children 10yrs

★★★★ GUEST ACCOMMODATION

Hansard House

3 Northview Rd EX9 6BY

☎ 01395 442773 📠 01395 442475

e-mail: enquiries@hansardhotel.co.uk

web: www.hansardhousehotel.co.uk

Dir: *500yds W of town centre*

PETS: Bedrooms (3GF) unattended sign **Charges** £7.50 per night £45 per week charge for damage **Grounds** accessible disp bin **Exercise area Facilities** food bowl water bowl bedding feeding mat pet sitting dog walking washing facs cage storage walks info vet info **On Request** fridge access torch towels

Hansard House is quietly situated a short walk from the town centre. Many of the well-presented bedrooms have commanding views across the town to the countryside and estuary beyond. Several are located on the ground floor and have easier access. Guests enjoy a varied selection at breakfast including a range of healthy options. The dining room and lounge are both comfortably furnished and dinners are sometimes available with prior notification.

Rooms 12 en suite (1 fmly) (3 GF) S £39-£47; D £79-£93✳ **Facilities** STV TVB tea/coffee Direct dial from bedrooms Lift Cen ht TVL Dinner Last d noon **Parking** 11 **Notes LB**

CHAGFORD — MAP 03 SX78

★★★★ @@@@ COUNTRY HOUSE HOTEL

Gidleigh Park

RELAIS & CHATEAUX.

TQ13 8HH

☎ 01647 432367 📠 01647 432574

e-mail: gidleighpark@gidleigh.co.uk

web: www.gidleigh.com

Dir: *from Chagford, right at Lloyds Bank into Mill St. After 150yds fork right, follow lane 2m to end*

PETS: Bedrooms (4GF) unattended **Charges** charge for damage **Grounds** accessible disp bin **Exercise area Facilities** food bowl water bowl bedding feeding mat dog scoop/disp bags leads washing facs cage storage walks info vet info **On Request** torch towels **Other** suitable bedrooms 75yds from main house, plus one cottage

Set in 45 acres of lovingly tended grounds this world-renowned hotel retains a timeless charm and a very endearing, homely atmosphere.

CONTINUED

CHAGFORD CONTINUED

Individually styled bedrooms are sumptuously furnished; some with separate seating areas, some with balconies and many enjoying panoramic views. Public areas are spacious featuring antique furniture, beautiful flower arrangements and magnificent artwork. The award-winning cuisine created by Michael Caines, together with the top quality wine list, will make a stay here a truly memorable experience.

Rooms 21 en suite 3 annexe en suite (4 fmly) (4 GF) D £480-£1325 (incl. bkfst & dinner)* **Facilities** Fishing Putt green Wi-fi in bedrooms Bowls Guided walks Xmas New Year **Parking** 25

★★ HOTEL

Mill End

Dartmoor National Park TQ13 8JN

☎ 01647 432282 01647 433106

e-mail: info@millendhotel.com

web: www.millendhotel.com

Dir: *from A30 at Whiddon Down follow A382 to Moretonhampstead. After 3.5m hump back bridge at Sandy Park, hotel on right by river*

PETS: Bedrooms Charges £10 per night charge for damage **Grounds** accessible disp bin **Exercise area** on site **Facilities** food bowl water bowl bedding dog chews leads washing facs cage storage walks info vet info **On Request** fridge access torch towels **Resident Pets:** Harry & Orvis (Labradors), Devon & Poppy (cats)

In an attractive location, Mill End, an 18th-century working water mill sits by the River Teign that offers six miles of angling. The atmosphere is akin to a family home where guests are encouraged to relax and enjoy the peace and informality. Bedrooms are available in a range of sizes and all are stylishly decorated and thoughtfully equipped. Dining is certainly a highlight of a stay here; the menus offer exciting dishes featuring local produce.

Rooms 14 en suite (3 GF) S £90-£160; D £90-£220 (incl. bkfst) **Facilities** FTV Fishing Wi-fi available Xmas New Year **Parking** 25 **Notes** LB

★★ 69% SMALL HOTEL

Three Crowns Hotel

High St TQ13 8AJ

☎ 01647 433444 01647 433117

e-mail: threecrowns@msn.com

web: www.chagford-accom.co.uk

Dir: *exit A30 at Whiddon Down. Hotel in town centre opposite church*

PETS: Bedrooms unattended **Charges** £3 per night **Public areas** except restaurant **Exercise area** 200mtrs to common

This 13th-century inn is located in the heart of the village. Exposed beams, mullioned windows and open fires are all part of the charm which is evident throughout. There is a range of bedrooms; all are comfortable and several have four-poster beds. A choice of bars is available along with a pleasant lounge and separate dining room.

Rooms 17 en suite (1 fmly) **Facilities** Pool table in bar **Parking** 20 **Notes** LB

★★★★ GUEST ACCOMMODATION

Easton Court

Easton Cross TQ13 8JL

☎ 01647 433469

e-mail: stay@easton.co.uk

web: www.easton.co.uk

Dir: *1m NE of Chagford at junct A382 & B3206*

PETS: Bedrooms (2GF) **Charges** £2.50 per night charge for damage **Grounds** accessible disp bin **Exercise area Facilities** feeding mat dog scoop/disp bags washing facs walks info vet info **On Request** fridge access torch towels **Resident Pets:** Cassie (German Shepherd), Libby (Rough Collie)

Set in Dartmoor National Park, the age of this picturesque house is reflected in the oak beams and deep granite walls. Guests can come and go via a separate entrance. Relaxation is obligatory, either in the lovely garden or in the snug surroundings of the lounge. The delightful bedrooms all have country views.

Rooms 5 en suite (2 GF) S £50-£65; D £60-£80* **Facilities** TVB tea/coffee Cen ht Wi-fi available **Parking** 5 **Notes** No children 10yrs

★★★ INN

The Sandy Park Inn

TQ13 8JW

☎ 01647 433267

e-mail: sandyparkinn@aol.com

Dir: *1m NE of Chagford off A382*

PETS: Bedrooms unattended **Grounds** accessible **Exercise area** 20yds **Facilities** food bowl water bowl

This popular, thatched country inn is conveniently located a short drive from the A30. The busy bar is full of character and is well stocked. There is a separate restaurant and smaller cosy rooms. Bedrooms are contemporary in style and well appointed with comfortable furnishings. A good choice of hearty dishes is also available.

Rooms 5 rms (2 en suite) (3 pri facs) S fr £55; D fr £92 **Facilities** TVB tea/coffee Cen ht Dinner Last d 9pm Wi-fi available Fishing Gofl Course nearby **Parking** 4 **Notes** No coaches

CHIVENOR MAP 02 SS53

►►► *Chivenor Caravan Park* *(SS501351)*

EX31 4BN

☎ 01271 812217 🖷 01271 812644

e-mail: chivenorcp@lineone.net

web: www.chivenorcaravanpark.co.uk

Dir: *On rdbt at Chivenor Cross take right exit to park.*

PETS: Charges £1 per night £5 per week **Public areas** except showers & shop **Exercise area** country walks **Facilities** on site shop dog scoop/disp bags walks info vet info **Other** prior notice required dog crèche nearby

Open mid Mar-mid Jan Last arrival 21.00hrs Last departure noon

A nicely maintained grassy park with some hard pitches, set in a good location for touring North Devon, and handy for the bus stop into Barnstaple. The site is about 5 miles from sandy beaches. A 3.5-acre site with 30 touring pitches, 5 hardstandings and 10 statics.

COLYFORD MAP 03 SY29

★★★★ BED & BREAKFAST

Lower Orchard

Swan Hill Rd EX24 6QQ

☎ 01297 553615

e-mail: robin@barnardl.demon.co.uk

Dir: *On A3052 in Colyford, between Lyme Regis & Sidmouth*

PETS: Bedrooms (2GF) unattended **Charges** charge for damage **Public areas** (on leads) **Grounds** accessible on leads disp bin **Exercise area** 200mtrs **Facilities** cage storage walks info vet info **On Request** fridge access **Resident Pets:** Biene & Sasha (Tibetan Terriers)

This modern ranch-style family home looks over the Axe Valley. The spacious ground-floor bedrooms are very well equipped. Breakfast is served in the lounge-dining room with patio doors leading to a private sun terrace, well-tended gardens and splash pool. The owners have also created a motoring memories museum and a classic car showroom nearby.

Rooms 2 rms (1 en suite) (1 pri facs) (2 GF) D £55-£65 **Facilities** TVB tea/coffee Cen ht TVL ⚲ **Parking** 3 **Notes** ⊜

COMBE MARTIN MAP 02 SS54

►►► Newberry Valley Park *(SS576473)*

Woodlands EX34 0AT

☎ 01271 882334

e-mail: relax@newberryvalleypark.co.uk

web: www.newberryvalleypark.co.uk

Dir: *From M5 junct 27, take A361 to North Aller rdbt. Right onto A399, through Combe Martin to sea. Left into site*

PETS: Charges disp bin **Exercise area** on site exercise field **Facilities** on site shop food bowl water bowl dog chews litter tray dog scoop/disp bags walks info vet info **Other** prior notice required **Resident Pets:** Taz (Labrador/Shepherd cross), Amber (German Shepherd), Teyha (Utonagan/wolf dog)

Open Mar-Sep Last arrival 20.45hrs Last departure 10.00hrs

A family owned and run touring park on the edge of Combe Martin, with all its amenities just five minutes walk away. The park is set in a wooded valley with its own coarse fishing lake. The safe beaches of Newberry and Combe Martin are reached by a short footpath opposite the park entrance, where the South West coast path is located. A 20-acre site with 125 touring pitches.

Notes No camp fires

DARTMEET MAP 03 SX67

★★★ GUEST ACCOMMODATION

Brimpts Farm

PL20 6SG

☎ 01364 631450 🖷 01364 631179

e-mail: info@brimptsfarm.co.uk

web: www.brimptsfarm.co.uk

Dir: *Dartmeet at E end of B3357, establishment signed on right at top of hill*

PETS: Bedrooms (7GF) **Stables** on site **Public areas** **Grounds** accessible **Exercise area** adjacent **Facilities** water bowl washing facs walks info vet info **On Request** fridge access torch towels **Resident Pets:** Billy (Border Collie), Kipper (Jack Russell)

A popular venue for walkers and lovers of the great outdoors, Brimpts is peacefully situated in the heart of Dartmoor and has been a Duchy of Cornwall farm since 1307. Bedrooms are simply furnished and many have wonderful views across Dartmoor. Dinner is served by arrangement. Additional facilities include a children's play area and sauna and spa. Brimpts is also home to the Dartmoor Pony Heritage Trust.

Rooms 10 en suite (2 fmly) (7 GF) S fr £30; D £50-£60 **Facilities** TV1B tea/coffee Cen ht TVL Dinner Last d 24hrs notice Wi-fi available Sauna Pool Table Farm walks & trails **Parking** 50 **Notes** LB

DARTMOUTH — MAP 03 SX85

★★★★ 79% @@ HOTEL

The Dart Marina

CLASSIC BRITISH HOTELS

Sandquay Rd TQ6 9PH

☎ 01803 832580 & 837120 🖹 01803 835040

e-mail: reservations@dartmarina.com

web: www.dartmarina.com

Dir: *A3122 from Totnes to Dartmouth. Follow road which becomes College Way, before Higher Ferry. Hotel sharp left in Sandquay Rd*

PETS: Bedrooms (4GF) unattended **Charges** £10 per night charge for damage **Exercise area** 30mtrs **Facilities** walks info vet info

Boasting a stunning riverside location with its own marina, this is a truly special place to stay. Bedrooms vary in style but all have wonderful views, and some have private balconies to sit and soak up the atmosphere. Stylish public areas take full advantage of the waterside setting with opportunities to dine alfresco. In addition to the Wildfire bistro, the River Restaurant is the venue for accomplished cooking.

Rooms 45 en suite 4 annexe en suite (4 fmly) (4 GF) S £95-£155; D £125-£195 (incl. bkfst)✳ **Facilities Spa** Ⓣ Gym Wi-fi available Canoeing Sailing Xmas New Year **Services** Lift **Parking** 50 **Notes LB**

★★★ 75% HOTEL

Royal Castle

11 The Quay TQ6 9PS

☎ 01803 833033 🖹 01803 835445

e-mail: enquiry@royalcastle.co.uk

web: www.royalcastle.co.uk

Dir: *in centre of town, overlooking Inner Harbour*

PETS: Bedrooms unattended **Charges** £10 per stay charge for damage **Public areas** except restaurant **Exercise area** 800mtrs **Facilities** water bowl bedding dog chews dog scoop/disp bags pet sitting walks info vet info **On Request** fridge access torch towels **Resident Pets:** Stella (Springer Spaniel)

At the edge of the harbour, this imposing 17th-century former coaching inn is filled with charm and character. Bedrooms are well equipped and comfortable; many have harbour views. A choice of quiet seating areas is offered in addition to both the traditional and contemporary bars. A variety of eating options is available, including the main restaurant which features accomplished cuisine and lovely views.

Rooms 25 en suite (3 fmly) **Facilities** Wi-fi in bedrooms ♫ **Parking** 17

►►► **Dartmouth Camping & Caravanning Club Site** *(SX864493)*

Dartmouth Rd, Stoke Fleming TQ6 0RF

☎ 01803 770253

web: www.thefriendlyclub.co.uk

Dir: *Direct access from A379 from Dartmouth before Stoke Fleming*

PETS: Exercise area Facilities washing facs walks info vet info **Other** prior notice required

Open Mar-Nov Last arrival 20.00hrs Last departure noon

Set on high ground with extensive sea views over Start Bay, this park is divided into three grassy paddocks. The toilet/shower block has been refurbished with all new fittings, and the parent and child/family room and the unisex disabled suite are also to the same high standard. A new laundry is very well fitted and a very good dishwashing room has been added. A 6-acre site with 83 touring pitches.

Notes Site gate closed between 23.00hrs-07.00hrs

DAWLISH — MAP 03 SX97

★★★ 77% HOTEL

Langstone Cliff

THE INDEPENDENTS HOTEL ASSOCIATION

Dawlish Warren EX7 0NA

☎ 01626 868000 🖹 01626 868006

e-mail: reception@langstone-hotel.co.uk

web: www.langstone-hotel.co.uk

Dir: *1.5m NE off A379 Exeter road to Dawlish Warren*

PETS: Bedrooms (10GF) unattended **Public areas** except restaurant **Exercise area** on site woods **Other** please phone for details of pet facilities

A family owned and run hotel, the Langstone Cliff offers a range of leisure, conference and function facilities. Bedrooms, many with sea views and balconies, are spacious, comfortable and well equipped. There are a number of attractive lounges and a well-stocked bar. Dinner is served, often carvery style, in the restaurant.

Rooms 62 en suite 4 annexe en suite (52 fmly) (10 GF) S £71-£86; D £112-£156 (incl. bkfst)✳ **Facilities** STV FTV Ⓣ ⛳ Gym Wi-fi in bedrooms Table tennis Golf practice area Hair & beauty salon Ballroom ♫ ch fac Xmas New Year **Services** Lift **Parking** 200 **Notes LB**

See advert on page 97

ENGLAND

Golden Sands Holiday Park *(SX968784)*

Week Ln EX7 0LZ

☎ 01626 863099 📠 01626 867149

e-mail: info@goldensands.co.uk

web: www.goldensands.co.uk

Dir: *M5 junct 30 onto A379 signed Dawlish. After 6m pass small harbour at Cockwood, signed on left in 2m*

PETS: Exercise area Other please phone for details

Open 21 Mar-Oct Last arrival noon Last departure 10.00hrs

A holiday centre for all the family, offering a wide range of entertainment. The small touring area is surrounded by mature trees and hedges in a pleasant area, and visitors enjoy free use of the licensed club and heated swimming pools. Organised children's activities are a popular feature, and the facilities of neighbouring Peppermint Park are open to all visitors. A 12-acre site with 23 touring pitches.

Lady's Mile Holiday Park *(SX968784)*

EX7 0LX

☎ 01626 863411 📠 01626 888689

e-mail: info@ladysmile.co.uk

web: www.ladysmile.co.uk

Dir: *1m N of Dawlish on A379*

PETS: Charges £1.50 - £3.50 per night **Public areas** except in shop disp bin **Exercise area** on site fenced area **Facilities** on site shop food walks info vet info

Open 17 Mar-27 Oct Last arrival 20.00hrs Last departure 11.00hrs

A holiday site with all grass touring pitches, and plenty of activities for everyone. Two swimming pools with waterslides, a large adventure playground, 9-hole golf course, and a bar with entertainment in high season all add to the enjoyment of a stay here. Facilities are kept clean, and the surrounding beaches are easily accessed. A 16-acre site with 243 touring pitches and 43 statics.

Peppermint Park *(SX978788)*

Warren Rd EX7 0PQ

☎ 01626 863436 📠 01626 866482

e-mail: info@peppermintpark.co.uk

web: www.peppermintpark.co.uk

Dir: *From A379 at Dawlish follow signs for Dawlish Warren. Site 1m on left at bottom of hill*

PETS: Stables nearby (2m) (loose box) **Public areas** except play area, swimming pool & club house **Charges** disp bin **Exercise area** 750yds **Facilities** on site shop **Other** please phone for further details

Open Etr-end Oct Last arrival 21.00hrs Last departure 10.00hrs

Well managed, attractive park close to the coast, with excellent facilities including club and bar which are well away from pitches. Nestling close to sandy beaches, the park offers individually marked pitches on level terraces in pleasant, sheltered grassland. The many amenities include a heated swimming pool and water chute, coarse fishing and launderette. A 26-acre site with 250 touring pitches, 15 hardstandings and 57 statics.

Notes Families & couples only

See advert on page 97

DREWSTEIGNTON MAP 03 SX79

►►► Woodland Springs Adult Touring Park

(SX695912)

Venton EX6 6PG

☎ 01647 231695

e-mail: enquiries@woodlandsprings.co.uk

web: www.woodlandsprings.co.uk

Dir: *Exit A30 at Whiddon Down Junction, left onto A382 towards Moretonhampstead. Site 1.5m on left*

PETS: Sep Accom day kennels disp bin **Public areas** except toilet block & shop **Exercise area** on site 1-acre open area **Facilities** on site shop walks info vet info **Resident Pets:** Charlie & Suzie (West Highland Whites)

Open all year Last arrival 22.00hrs Last departure 11.00hrs

An attractive park in a rural area within Dartmoor National Park. This site is surrounded by woodland and neighbouring farmland, and is very peaceful. Children are not admitted. A 4-acre site with 85 touring pitches, 39 hardstandings.

Notes No fires, no noise 23.00hrs-08.00hrs

EAST ALLINGTON — MAP 03 SX74

►►► Mounts Farm Touring Park *(SX757488)*

The Mounts TQ9 7QJ

☎ 01548 521591

e-mail: mounts.farm@lineone.net

web: www.mountsfarm.co.uk

Dir: *A381 from Totnes towards Kingsbridge (ignore signs for East Allington). At 'Mounts' site is 0.5m on left*

PETS: disp bin **Exercise area** public footpaths adjacent **Facilities** on site shop food bowl water bowl dog chews cat treats dog scoop/disp bags washing facs walks info vet info **Resident Pets:** 3 cats

Open 15 Mar-Oct Last arrival anytime Last departure anytime

A neat grassy park divided into four paddocks by mature natural hedges. Three of the paddocks house the tourers and campers, and the fourth is the children's play area. The toilet facilities have been refurbished, and the laundry and well-stocked little shop are in converted farm buildings. A 7-acre site with 50 touring pitches.

EAST ANSTEY — MAP 03 SS82

►►►► Zeacombe House Caravan Park

(SS860240)

Blackerton Cross EX16 9JU

☎ 01398 341279

e-mail: enquiries@zeacombeadultretreat.co.uk

web: www.zeacombeadultretreat.co.uk

Dir: *M5 junct 27 onto A361 signed Barnstaple, turn right at next rdbt onto A396 signed Dulverton/Minehead. In 5m at Exeter Inn turn left 1.5m Black Cat junct left onto B3227 towards South Molton, site in 7m on left*

PETS: Public areas except toilet block & shop (on leads) disp bin **Exercise area** on site **Facilities** on site shop dog scoop/disp bags washing facs walks info vet info **Other** prior notice required **Restrictions** no American Pit Bulls

Open 7 Mar-Oct Last arrival 21.00hrs Last departure noon

Set on the southern fringes of Exmoor National Park, this 'garden' park is nicely landscaped in a tranquil location, and enjoys panoramic views towards Exmoor. This adult-only park offers a choice of grass or hardstanding pitches, and a unique restaurant-style delivery service allows you to eat an evening meal in the comfort of your own unit. A 5-acre site with 50 touring pitches, 12 hardstandings.

EXETER — MAP 03 SX99

★★★ 75% HOTEL

Best Western Lord Haldon Country House

Dunchideock EX6 7YF

☎ 01392 832483 🖹 01392 833765

e-mail: enquiries@lordhaldonhotel.co.uk

web: www.lordhaldonhotel.co.uk

Dir: *M5 junct 31, 1st exit off A30, Ide to Dunchideock*

PETS: Bedrooms Stables nearby **Charges** £5 per night charge for damage **Public areas** except restaurant & lounge **Grounds** accessible disp bin **Exercise area Facilities** dog walking cage storage walks info vet info **On Request** fridge access torch towels **Resident Pets:** Jake (cat)

Set amidst rural tranquillity, this attractive country house goes from strength to strength. Guests are assured of a warm welcome from the professional team of staff and the well-equipped bedrooms are comfortable, many with stunning views. The daily-changing menu features skilfully cooked dishes with most of the produce sourced locally.

Rooms 23 en suite (3 fmly) **Facilities** Wi-fi in bedrooms **Parking** 120

★★★ 71% HOTEL

Barton Cross Hotel & Restaurant

Huxham, Stoke Canon EX5 4EJ

☎ 01392 841245 🖹 01392 841942

e-mail: bartonxhuxham@aol.com

Dir: *0.5m off A396 at Stoke Canon, 3m N of Exeter*

PETS: Bedrooms (2GF) unattended sign **Stables** nearby **Grounds** accessible on leads disp bin **Exercise area Facilities** walks info vet info **On Request** fridge access torch towels

17th-century charm combined with 21st-century luxury perfectly sums up the appeal of this lovely country hotel. The bedrooms are spacious, tastefully decorated and well maintained. Public areas include the cosy first-floor lounge and the lounge/bar with its warming log fire. The restaurant offers a seasonally changing menu of consistently enjoyable cuisine.

Rooms 9 en suite (2 fmly) (2 GF) **Parking** 35 **Notes** LB

★★★★ GUEST HOUSE

The Edwardian

30-32 Heavitree Rd EX1 2LQ

☎ 01392 276102

e-mail: michael@edwardianexeter.co.uk

web: www.edwardianexeter.co.uk

Dir: *M5 junct 29, right at lights signed city centre, on left after Exeter University School of Education*

PETS: Bedrooms (4GF) **Charges** £10 per night charge for damage **Public areas** except breakfast room (on leads) **Exercise area** 200yds **Facilities** cage storage walks info vet info **On Request** fridge access torch **Restrictions** small & medium size dogs only **Resident Pets:** Tara (dog)

Friendly proprietors offer a warm welcome at this attractive Edwardian terrace property, which is situated within easy walking distance of the city centre. The bedrooms vary in size, but are well presented and comfortable, and offer a range of extra accessories. Breakfast is served in the spacious dining room, while the separate, inviting lounge offers comfort and relaxation.

Rooms 13 en suite (3 fmly) (4 GF) **Facilities** FTV TVB tea/coffee Direct dial from bedrooms Cen ht Wi-fi available **Parking** 5 **Notes** No coaches

★★★★ FARM HOUSE

Rydon *(SX999871)*

Woodbury EX5 1LB

☎ 01395 232341 📠 01395 232341 Mrs S Glanvill

e-mail: sallyglanvill@aol.com

web: www.rydonfarmwoodbury.co.uk

Dir: *A376 & B3179 from Exeter into Woodbury, right before 30mph sign*

PETS: Bedrooms Grounds accessible disp bin **Exercise area** 20mtrs **Facilities** cage storage walks info vet info **On Request** fridge access torch towels

Dating from the 16th century, this Devon longhouse has been run by the same family for eight generations. A stay here is an opportunity to experience a farming lifestyle complete with patient cows steadfastly waiting to be milked! The spacious bedrooms are equipped with many useful extra facilities and one has a four-poster bed. There is a television lounge and a delightful garden in which to relax. Breakfast is a treat, served in front of an inglenook fireplace.

Rooms 3 rms (2 en suite) (1 pri facs) (1 fmly) S £40-£55; D £62-£74✻ **Facilities** FTV TVB tea/coffee Cen ht TVL **Parking** 3 **Notes** LB 450 acres dairy

EXMOUTH MAP 03 SY08

►► St Johns Caravan & Camping Park

(SY027834)

St Johns Rd EX8 5EG

☎ 01395 263170 📠 01395 273004

e-mail: stjohns.farm@virgin.net

Dir: *M5 junct 30 follow A376/Exmouth signs. Left through Woodbury towards Budleigh Salterton on B3179 & B3180. Turn right 1m after Exmouth exit*

PETS: disp bin **Exercise area** on site bottom of field area **Facilities** on site shop food bowl water bowl dog scoop/disp bags walks info vet info **Other** prior notice required **Resident Pets:** 4 dogs, 2 cats

Open mid Feb-Dec Last arrival 22.00hrs Last departure noon

A quiet rural site with attractive country views, only two miles from Exmouth's sandy beaches, and half a mile from Woodbury Common. The owners offer a warm welcome to visitors. A 6-acre site with 45 touring pitches, 8 hardstandings.

GULWORTHY MAP 02 SX47

★★★ 85% ❀❀❀ HOTEL

Horn of Plenty

PL19 8JD

☎ 01822 832528 📠 01822 834390

e-mail: enquiries@thehornofplenty.co.uk

web: www.thehornofplenty.co.uk

Dir: *from Tavistock take A390 W for 3m. Right at Gulworthy Cross. In 400yds turn left, hotel in 400yds on right*

PETS: Bedrooms unattended **Charges** £10 per night **Exercise area**

With stunning views over the Tamar Valley, The Horn of Plenty maintains its reputation as one of Britain's best country-house hotels. The bedrooms are well equipped and have many thoughtful extras with the garden rooms offering impressive levels of comfort and quality. Cuisine here is also impressive and local produce provides interesting and memorable dining.

Rooms 4 en suite 6 annexe en suite (3 fmly) (4 GF) S £150-£240; D £160-£250 (incl. bkfst)✻ **Facilities** New Year **Parking** 25 **Notes** Closed 24-26 Dec

ENGLAND

HAYTOR VALE MAP 03 SX77

★★ 76% HOTEL

Rock Inn

TQ13 9XP

☎ 01364 661305 & 661465 01364 661242

e-mail: inn@rock-inn.co.uk

web: www.rock-inn.co.uk

Dir: *A38 onto A382 to Bovey Tracey, in 0.5m left onto B3387 to Haytor*

PETS: Bedrooms unattended **Charges** £5.50 per night **Exercise area** woods adjacent **Other** dogs allowed in 3 bedrooms only; not allowed in public rooms

Dating back to the 1750s, this former coaching inn is in a pretty hamlet on the edge of Dartmoor. Each named after a Grand National winner, the individually decorated bedrooms have some nice extra touches. Bars are full of character, with flagstone floors and old beams and offer a wide range of dishes, cooked with imagination and flair.

Rooms 9 en suite (2 fmly) S £66.95-£99; D £76.95-£117 (incl. bkfst) **Facilities** FTV New Year **Parking** 20 **Notes LB** Closed 25-26 Dec

HOLSWORTHY MAP 02 SS30

► Noteworthy Caravan and Campsite

(SS303052)

Noteworthy, Bude Rd EX22 7JB

☎ 01409 253731

e-mail: enquiries@noteworthy-devon.co.uk

web: www.noteworthy-devon.co.uk

Dir: *On A3072 between Holsworthy & Bude. 3m from Holsworthy on right*

PETS: Stables (loose box) **Public areas** except play area **Charges** £2 per week disp bin **Exercise area** on site dog walk **Facilities** washing facs dog grooming walks info vet info **Resident Pets:** 4 British miniature horses, 3 cats, farm animals

Open all year

This campsite is owned by a friendly young couple with their own small children. There are good views from the quiet rural location, and simple toilet facilities. A 5-acre site with 5 touring pitches and 1 static.

Notes No open fires

HONITON MAP 03 ST10

★★★ COUNTRY HOUSE HOTEL

Combe House

Gittisham EX14 3AD

☎ 01404 540400 01404 46004

e-mail: stay@thishotel.com

web: www.thishotel.com

Dir: *off A30 1m S of Honiton, follow Gittisham Heathpark signs*

PETS: Bedrooms unattended sign **Sep Accom** cottage with dog ante room & walled garden **Stables** on site **Charges** £8 per night charge for damage **Public areas** except restaurants **Grounds** accessible on leads disp bin **Exercise area** on site **Facilities** food bowl water bowl bedding dog chews cat treats feeding mat dog scoop/disp bags leads washing facs cage storage walks info vet info **On Request** fridge access torch towels **Resident Pets:** Maverick (cat)

Standing proudly in an elevated position, this Elizabethan mansion enjoys uninterrupted views over acres of its own woodland, meadow and pasture. Bedrooms are a blend of comfort and quality with relaxation being the ultimate objective; the Linen Room suite combines many original features with contemporary style. A range of atmospheric public rooms retain all the charm and history of the old house. Dining is equally impressive - a skilled kitchen brigade maximises the best of local and home-grown produce, augmented by excellent wines.

Rooms 15 en suite 1 annexe en suite S £150-£345; D £170-£375 (incl. bkfst)✻ **Facilities** Wi-fi available Xmas New Year **Parking** 39 **Notes LB** Closed 14-27 Jan

★★★ 72% COUNTRY HOUSE HOTEL

Deer Park Country Hotel

Weston EX14 3PG

☎ 01404 41266 🖹 01404 43958

e-mail: admin@deerparkcountryhotel.co.uk

web: www.deerparkcountryhotel.co.uk

Dir: *M5 junct 28/A373 to Honiton. Right at lights, left to Heathpark Industrial Estate by BP garage, hotel signed*

PETS: Bedrooms (4GF) unattended **Stables** 6-7m **Charges** £3 per night **Public areas** only in grounds - not in main building **Grounds** accessible disp bin **Exercise area** hotel parkland **Facilities** walks info vet info **On Request** fridge access

Peacefully located in 30 acres of wonderful countryside, this Georgian squire's mansion dates back to 1721. There is character here in abundance with elegant public rooms providing ample space for guests to relax and unwind. Bedrooms are split between the main house and The Mews, with a variation in size and style. Additional facilities include outdoor swimming pool, croquet lawn, tennis courts and fishing on the River Otter.

Rooms 16 en suite 6 annexe en suite (4 GF) S £62.50-£115; D £105-£190 (incl. bkfst)✳ **Facilities** Fishing Gym Putt green Archery Games room Shooting Snooker room Xmas New Year **Parking** 50 **Notes** LB

★★★★ GUEST ACCOMMODATION

Ridgeway Farm

Awliscombe EX14 3PY

☎ 01404 841331 🖹 01404 841119

e-mail: jessica@ridgewayfarm.co.uk

Dir: *3m NW of Honiton. A30 onto A373, through Awliscombe to near end of 40mph area, right opp Godford Farm, farm 500mtrs up narrow lane*

PETS: Bedrooms Stables on site **Public areas Grounds** accessible **Exercise area** surrounding farmland **Facilities** cage storage walks info **Other** pets not allowed on beds **Resident Pets:** Lettuce (Border terrier), Chaos (Labrador), 3 horses

This 18th-century farmhouse has a peaceful location on the slopes of Hembury Hill, and is a good base for exploring nearby Honiton and the east Devon coast. Renovations have brought the cosy accommodation to a high standard and the atmosphere is relaxed and homely. The proprietors and their family pets assure a warm welcome.

Rooms 2 en suite S £30-£34; D £52-£58✳ **Facilities** TVB tea/coffee Cen ht TVL Dinner Last d morning **Parking** 4 **Notes** LB

ILFRACOMBE

MAP 02 SS54

★★ 71% HOTEL

Darnley

3 Belmont Rd EX34 8DR

☎ 01271 863955

e-mail: darnleyhotel@yahoo.co.uk

web: www.darnleyhotel.co.uk

Dir: *A361 to Barnstaple & Ilfracombe. Left at Church Hill, 1st left into Belmont Rd. 3rd entrance on left under walled arch*

PETS: Bedrooms (2GF) unattended **Public areas** except restaurant (on leads) **Grounds** accessible on leads disp bin **Exercise area** 400yds **Facilities** water bowl feeding mat cage storage walks info vet info **On Request** fridge access torch towels **Resident Pets:** Pepsi (cat)

Standing within award-winning, mature gardens, with a wooded path to the High Street and the beach (about a five minute stroll away), this former Victorian gentleman's residence offers friendly, informal service. The individually furnished and decorated bedrooms vary in size. Dinners feature honest home-cooking, with 'old fashioned puddings' always proving popular.

Rooms 10 rms (7 en suite) (2 fmly) (2 GF) S £36-£38; D £56-£80 (incl. bkfst)✳ **Facilities** FTV Xmas New Year **Parking** 10 **Notes** LB

★★★★ GUEST ACCOMMODATION

Strathmore

57 St Brannock's Rd EX34 8EQ

☎ 01271 862248 🖹 01271 862248

e-mail: peter@small6374.fsnet.co.uk

web: www.the-strathmore.co.uk

Dir: *A361 from Barnstaple to Ilfracombe, Strathmore 1.5m from Mullacot Cross entering Ilfracombe*

PETS: Bedrooms Charges £5 (breakfast included) per night charge for damage **Public areas** in bar & lounge only (on leads) **Grounds** accessible **Exercise area** 0.25m **Facilities** water bowl dog chews dog scoop/disp bags leads washing facs cage storage walks info vet info **On Request** fridge access torch towels **Resident Pets:** Holly (Sheltie)

Situated within walking distance of the town centre and beach, this charming Victorian property offers a very warm welcome. The attractive bedrooms are comfortably furnished, while public areas include a well-stocked bar, an attractive terraced garden, and an elegant breakfast room.

Rooms 8 en suite (3 fmly) S £32-£35; D £65-£76✳ **Facilities** TVB tea/coffee Cen ht Wi-fi available **Parking** 7 **Notes** LB

ENGLAND

ILFRACOMBE CONTINUED

★★★★ GUEST HOUSE

Marine Court

Hillsborough Rd EX34 9QQ

☎ 01271 862920

e-mail: marinecourthotel@btconnect.com

Dir: *M5 junct 27, A361 to Barnstaple, continue to Ilfracombe*

PETS: Bedrooms Stables nearby **Charges** £5 per stay charge for damage **Exercise area** 25mtrs **Facilities** walks info vet info **Resident Pets:** Poppy (Jack Russell cross), Tilly (cat)

This friendly and welcoming establishment offers comfortable and homely accommodation opposite the Old Thatched Inn. The well-presented bedrooms all provide good levels of comfort with thoughtful extras. Freshly prepared evening meals and breakfast are served in the spacious dining room which is next to the bar. On-site and adjacent parking is a bonus.

Rooms 8 en suite (2 fmly) S £36.50-£42; D £58-£68 **Facilities** TVB tea/coffee Licensed Cen ht Dinner Last d noon **Parking** 3 **Notes** LB No coaches

►►►► **Hele Valley Holiday Park** *(SS533472)*

Hele Bay EX34 9RD

☎ 01271 862460 📠 01271 867926

e-mail: holidays@helevalley.co.uk

web: www.helevalley.co.uk

Dir: *M5 junct 27 onto A361. Through Barnstaple & Braunton to Ilfracombe. Then A399 towards Combe Martin. Follow brown Hele Valley signs. 400mtrs sharp right, then to T-junct. Reception on left.*

PETS: Public areas except children's play area **Charges** £2.85 - £4 per night £20 - £28 per week disp bin **Exercise area** on site dog walking area **Facilities** on site shop food food bowl water bowl dog chews dog scoop/disp bags washing facs walks info vet info **Other** prior notice required **Resident Pets:** Anna (Rottweiler)

Open May-Sep Last arrival 18.00hrs Last departure 11.00hrs

A deceptively spacious park set in a picturesque valley with glorious tree-lined hilly views from most pitches. High quality toilet facilities are provided, and the park is close to a lovely beach, with the harbour and other attractions of Ilfracombe just a mile away. A 17-acre site with 58 touring pitches and 80 statics.

Notes No groups

ILSINGTON — MAP 03 SX77

★★★ 85% ❁❁ COUNTRY HOUSE HOTEL

Ilsington Country House

Ilsington Village TQ13 9RR

☎ 01364 661452 📠 01364 661307

e-mail: hotel@ilsington.co.uk

web: www.ilsington.co.uk

Dir: *M5 onto A38 to Plymouth. Exit at Bovey Tracey. 3rd exit from rdbt to 'Ilsington', then 1st right. Hotel in 5m by Post Office*

PETS: Bedrooms unattended **Stables** on site **Charges** £8 per night **Grounds** accessible on leads **Exercise area** 5 min walk **Restrictions** well behaved dogs only

This friendly, family owned hotel, offers tranquillity and far-reaching views from its elevated position on the southern slopes of Dartmoor. The stylish suites and bedrooms, some on the ground floor, are individually furnished. The restaurant provides a stunning backdrop for the innovative, daily changing menus which feature local fish, meat and game.

Rooms 25 en suite (4 fmly) (8 GF) S £94-£102; D £144-£154 (incl. bkfst) ✳ **Facilities** ⓢ supervised Gym Wi-fi in bedrooms Steam room Xmas New Year **Services** Lift **Parking** 100 **Notes** LB

KENNFORD — MAP 03 SX98

►►►► **Kennford International Caravan Park** *(SX912857)*

EX6 7YN

☎ 01392 833046 📠 01392 833046

e-mail: ian@kennfordint.fsbusiness.co.uk

web: www.kennfordinternational.co.uk

Dir: *At end of M5, take A38, site signed at Kennford slip road*

PETS: Charges £1 per dog per night disp bin **Exercise area** on site small field provided **Facilities** walks info vet info **Resident Pets:** Jade (Rottweiler), Alfie (British bulldog),Tigger (cat), guinea pigs

Open all year Arrival times change during Winter Last arrival 21.00hrs Last departure 11.00hrs

Screened by trees and shrubs from the A38, this park offers many pitches divided by hedging for privacy. A high quality toilet block complements the park's facilities. A good, centrally-located base for touring the coast and countryside of Devon, and Exeter is easily accessible via a nearby bus stop. A 15-acre site with 96 touring pitches and 53 statics.

KENTISBEARE MAP 03 ST00

►►► Forest Glade Holiday Park *(ST100075)*

Cullompton EX15 2DT

☎ 01404 841381 🖷 01404 841593

e-mail: enquiries@forest-glade.co.uk

web: www.forest-glade.co.uk

Dir: *Tent traffic: from A373 signed at Keepers Cottage Inn, (2.5m E of M5 junct 28). Touring caravans: via Honiton/Dunkeswell road: please phone for access details*

PETS: Public areas except swimming pool, shop & toilet **Charges** £1.50 per night disp bin **Exercise area** on site surrounding woodland **Facilities** on site shop food food bowl water bowl dog chews washing facs walks info vet info **Other** prior notice required

Open mid Mar-end Oct (rs low season limited shop hours) Last arrival 21.00hrs

A quiet, attractive park in a forest clearing with well-kept gardens and beech hedge screening. One of the main attractions is the immediate proximity of the forest, which offers magnificent hillside walks with surprising views over the valleys. Please telephone for route details. A 15-acre site with 80 touring pitches, 40 hardstandings and 57 statics.

Notes Families and couples only

LEWDOWN MAP 02 SX48

★★★ ❀❀❀ HOTEL

Lewtrenchard Manor

von Essen hotels
A PRIVATE COLLECTION
www.vonessenhotels.com

EX20 4PN

☎ 01566 783256 & 783222 🖷 01566 783332

e-mail: info@lewtrenchard.co.uk

web: www.vonessenhotels.co.uk

Dir: *A30 from Exeter to Plymouth/Tavistock road. At T-junct turn right, then left onto old A30 (Lewdown road). Left in 6m signed Lewtrenchard*

PETS: Bedrooms Charges £10 per night charge for damage **Public areas** except restaurant **Grounds** accessible on leads disp bin **Exercise area** adjacent **Facilities** water bowl washing facs cage storage vet info **On Request** fridge access torch towels

This Jacobean mansion was built in the 1600s, with many interesting architectural features, and is surrounded by its own idyllic grounds in a quiet valley close to the northern edge of Dartmoor. Public rooms include a fine gallery, as well as magnificent carvings and oak panelling. Meals can be taken in the dining room where imaginative and carefully prepared dishes are served using the best of Devon produce. Bedrooms are comfortably furnished and spacious.

Rooms 14 en suite (2 fmly) (3 GF) S £125-£365; D £155-£395 (incl. bkfst)✳ **Facilities** Fishing Clay pigeon shooting Falconry Beauty therapies Xmas New Year **Parking** 50 **Notes** LB

LIFTON MAP 03 SX38

★★★ 81% ❀❀ HOTEL

Arundell Arms

PL16 0AA

☎ 01566 784666 🖷 01566 784494

e-mail: reservations@arundellarms.com

Dir: *1m off A30, 3m E of Launceston*

PETS: Bedrooms unattended **Stables** nearby (1m) **Charges** £5 per night plus food **Public areas** except restaurant **Grounds** accessible disp bin **Exercise area** 0.5m **Facilities** food water bowl walks info vet info **On Request** fridge access **Other** dogs not allowed on river bank

This former coaching inn, boasting a long history, sits in the heart of a quiet Devon village. It is internationally famous for its country pursuits such as winter shooting and angling. The bedrooms offer individual style and comfort. Public areas are full of character and present a relaxed atmosphere, particularly around the open log fire during colder evenings. Award-winning cuisine is a celebration of local produce.

Rooms 21 en suite (4 GF) S £105-£120, D £170-£200 (incl. bkfst)✳ **Facilities** STV Fishing Wi-fi in bedrooms Skittle alley Game shooting (in winter) Fly fishing school New Year **Parking** 70 **Notes** LB Closed 3 days Xmas

LYDFORD MAP 02 SX58

►►► Lydford Camping & Caravanning Club Site *(SX512853)*

EX20 4BE

☎ 01822 820275

web: www.thefriendlyclub.co.uk

Dir: *A30, A386 (signed Tavistock/Lydford). Past Fox & Hounds on left, right at Lydford sign. Right at war memorial, site in 200yds*

PETS: Public areas except in buildings disp bin **Exercise area** on site marked area, dogs must be on leads **Facilities** walks info vet info **Other** prior notice required

Open 2 Apr-2 Nov Last arrival 21.00hrs Last departure noon

Site on mainly level ground looking towards the western slopes of Dartmoor at the edge of the village, near the spectacular gorge. This popular park is close to the Devon coast to coast cycle route, between Tavistock and Okehampton. A 7.75-acre site with 90 touring pitches, 27 hardstandings.

Notes Site gates closed 23.00hrs-07.00hrs

ENGLAND

LYNMOUTH

MAP 03 SS74

★★★ 73% HOTEL

Tors

EX35 6NA

☎ 01598 753236 01598 752544

e-mail: info@torshotellynmouth.co.uk

web: www.torslynmouth.co.uk

Dir: *adjacent to A39 on Countisbury Hill just before entering Lynmouth from Minehead*

PETS: Bedrooms unattended **Charges** £5 per night **Public areas** except restaurant, luxury suite & pool area **Grounds** accessible disp bin **Exercise area** surrounding woodland **Facilities** food (pre-bookable) food bowl water bowl walks info vet info **On Request** fridge access torch towels

In an elevated position overlooking Lynmouth Bay, this friendly hotel is set in five acres of woodland. The majority of the bedrooms benefit from the superb views, as do the public areas; which are generous and well presented. A fixed-price menu is offered with local, seasonal produce to the fore.

Rooms 31 en suite (6 fmly) S £80-£205; D £118-£264 (incl. bkfst)✻ **Facilities** Table tennis Pool table Xmas New Year **Services** Lift **Parking** 40 **Notes** Closed 4-31 Jan

★★ 68% HOTEL

Bath

Sea Front EX35 6EL

☎ 01598 752238 01598 753894

e-mail: info@bathhotellynmouth.co.uk

Dir: *M5 junct 25, follow A39 to Lynmouth*

PETS: Bedrooms unattended **Charges** charge for damage **Public areas** except restaurant **Exercise area** 200yds **Facilities** food (pre-bookable) food bowl water bowl bedding walks info vet info **On Request** fridge access torch towels

This well-established, friendly hotel is situated near the harbour and offers lovely views from the attractive, sea-facing bedrooms and is an excellent starting point for scenic walks. There are two lounges and a sun lounge. The restaurant menu is extensive and features daily-changing specials that make good use of fresh produce and local fish.

Rooms 22 en suite (9 fmly) S £39-£64; D £78-£140 (incl. bkfst)✻ **Parking** 12 **Notes** Closed Jan & Dec RS Feb-Mar & Nov

★★★ GUEST ACCOMMODATION

Countisbury Lodge

6 Tors Park, Countisbury Hill EX35 6NB

☎ 01598 752388

e-mail: paulpat@countisburylodge.co.uk

Dir: *Off A39 Countisbury Hill just before Lynmouth centre, signed 'Countisbury Lodge'*

PETS: Bedrooms Exercise area on site in grounds **Resident Pets:** Magic & Jessica (Golden Retrievers)

From its peaceful elevated position high above the town, this former Victorian vicarage has spectacular views of the harbour and countryside. The atmosphere is friendly and informal with attentive service. The comfortable bedrooms are attractively decorated, and breakfast is served in the pleasant dining room.

Rooms 4 en suite (1 fmly) **Facilities** FTV TVB tea/coffee Cen ht TVL Dinner Last d breakfast **Parking** 6

LYNTON MAP 03 SS74

★★★ 73% HOTEL

Lynton Cottage

Northwalk EX35 6ED

☎ 01598 752342 📠 01598 754016

e-mail: mail@lyntoncottage.co.uk

Dir: *M5 junct 23 to Bridgewater, then A39 to Minehead & follow signs to Lynton. 1st right after church and right again.*

PETS: Bedrooms (1GF) unattended **Charges** charge for damage **Public areas** except restaurant (on leads) **Grounds** accessible on leads disp bin **Exercise area Facilities** water bowl walks info vet info **Resident Pets:** Mango (Golden Retriever), Chloe & Charlie (cats)

Boasting breathtaking views, this wonderfully relaxing and friendly hotel stands some 500 feet above the sea and makes a peaceful hideaway. Bedrooms are individual in style and size, with the added bonus of the wonderful views; public areas have charm and character in equal measure. Accomplished cuisine is on offer with dishes created with care and considerable skill.

Rooms 16 en suite (1 fmly) (1 GF) **Facilities** FTV **Parking** 20
Notes Closed 2 Dec-12 Jan

★★ 81% SMALL HOTEL

Seawood

North Walk EX35 6HJ

☎ 01598 752272

e-mail: seawoodhotel@aol.com

web: www.seawoodhotel.co.uk

Dir: *turn right at St Mary's Church in Lynton High St for hotel, 2nd on left*

PETS: Bedrooms Stables nearby (1m) **Charges** £3 per night charge for damage **Grounds** accessible on leads disp bin **Exercise area** 20yds National Park **Facilities** dog chews washing facs walks info vet info **On Request** torch towels **Resident Pets:** Libby & Millie (Cocker Spaniels)

Tucked away in a quiet area and spectacularly situated 400 feet above the seashore, the Seawood enjoys magnificent views, and is set in delightful grounds. Bedrooms, many with sea views and some with four-poster beds, are comfortable and well equipped. At dinner, the daily-changing menu provides freshly prepared and appetising dishes.

Rooms 12 en suite **Parking** 12 **Notes** No children 10yrs Closed Dec-Feb

►►►► Channel View Caravan and Camping Park *(SS724482)*

Manor Farm EX35 6LD

☎ 01598 753349 📠 01598 752777

e-mail: relax@channel-view.co.uk

web: www.channel-view.co.uk

Dir: *A39 E for 0.5m on left past Barbrook*

PETS: Exercise area on site exercise field provided **Facilities** on site shop food dog scoop/disp bags washing facs walks info vet info **Other** prior notice required

Open 15 Mar-15 Nov Last arrival 22.00hrs Last departure noon

On the top of the cliffs overlooking the Bristol Channel, a well-maintained park on the edge of Exmoor, and close to both Lynton and Lynmouth. Pitches can be selected from a hidden hedged area, or with panoramic views over the coast. A 6-acre site with 76 touring pitches, 15 hardstandings and 31 statics.

Notes Groups by prior arrangement only

►►► Lynton Camping & Caravanning Club Site *(SS703481)*

Caffyns Cross EX35 6JS

☎ 01598 752379

web: www.thefriendlyclub.co.uk

Dir: *M5 junct 27 onto A361 to Barnstable. Turn right to Blackmoor Gate signed Lynmouth & Lynton. Approx 5m to Caffyns Cross, immediately right to site in 1m*

PETS: Public areas except in buildings disp bin **Exercise area** adjacent walks **Facilities** walks info vet info **Other** prior notice required

Open 2 Apr-28 Sep Last arrival 21.00hrs Last departure noon

Set on high ground with excellent views over the Bristol Channel, and close to the twin resorts of Lynton & Lynmouth. This area is known as Little Switzerland because of its wooded hills, and the park is ideal for walking, and cycling on the nearby National Cycle Network. A 5.5-acre site with 105 touring pitches, 10 hardstandings.

Notes Site gates closed 23.00hrs-07.00hrs

MODBURY — MAP 03 SX65

►►► California Cross Camping & Caravanning Club Site *(SX705530)*

PL21 0SG

☎ 01548 821297

web: www.thefriendlyclub.co.uk

Dir: *Leave A38 at Wrangton Cross onto A3121, continue to x-rds. Cross over onto B3196, left after California Cross sign before petrol station, site on right*

PETS: Public areas except in buildings disp bin **Exercise area Facilities** walks info vet info **Other** prior notice required

Open 2 Apr-2 Nov Last arrival 21.00hrs Last departure noon

A gently sloping site with some terracing, set in a rural location midway between Ivybridge and Kingsbridge. This well ordered site is protected by high hedging, and is an ideal base for exploring the lovely South Devon countryside. A 3.75-acre site with 80 touring pitches, 7 hardstandings.

Notes Site gates closed 23.00hrs-07.00hrs

MORTEHOE — MAP 02 SS44

►►► *Easewell Farm Holiday Parc & Golf Club* *(SS465455)*

EX34 7EH

☎ 01271 871400 🖹 01271 870089

e-mail: goodtimes@woolacombe.com

web: www.woolacombe.com

Dir: *Take B3343 to Mortehoe. Turn right at fork, site 2m on right*

PETS: Stables nearby (1.5m) **Charges** £1.50 per night £10 per week disp bin **Exercise area** on site dog exercise area **Facilities** on site shop food walks info vet info

Open Etr-Oct (rs Etr) Last arrival 22.00hrs Last departure 10.00hrs

A peaceful clifftop park with full facility pitches for caravans and motorhomes, and superb views. The park offers a range of activities including indoor bowling and a golf course, and all the facilities of the three other nearby holiday centres within this group are open to everyone. A 17-acre site with 302 touring pitches, 50 hardstandings and 1 static.

►►► North Morte Farm Caravan & Camping Park *(SS462455)*

North Morte Rd EX34 7EG

☎ 01271 870381 🖹 01271 870115

e-mail: info@northmortefarm.co.uk

web: www.northmortefarm.co.uk

Dir: *From B3343 into Mortehoe, right at post office. Site 500yds on left*

PETS: Charges £1.50-2 per night (seasonal) **Public areas** on leads disp bin **Exercise area** on site dog areas provided **Facilities** on site shop walks info vet info

Open Apr-Oct Last arrival 22.30hrs Last departure noon

Set in spectacular coastal countryside close to National Trust land and 500yds from Rockham Beach. This attractive park is very well run and maintained by friendly family owners, and the quaint village of Mortehoe with its cafés, shops and pubs, is just a 5 minute walk away. A 22-acre site with 180 touring pitches, 18 hardstandings and 73 statics.

Notes No large groups

►►► Warcombe Farm Caravan & Camping Park *(SS478445)*

Station Rd EX34 7EJ

☎ 01271 870690 & 07774 428770 🖹 01271 871070

e-mail: info@warcombefarm.co.uk

web: www.warcombefarm.co.uk

Dir: *N towards Mortehoe from Mullacot Cross rdbt at A361 junct with B3343. Site 2m on right*

PETS: Public areas except play area & toilets **Charges** £1.50 per night disp bin **Exercise area** on site 14-acre field provided **Facilities** on site shop food food bowl water bowl dog chews cat treats dog scoop/disp bags leads walks info vet info **Other** prior notice required

Open 15 Mar-Oct Last arrival 21.00hrs Last departure noon

Extensive views over the Bristol Channel can be enjoyed from the open areas of this attractive park, while other pitches are sheltered in paddocks with maturing trees. The superb sandy beach with Blue Flag award at Woolacombe Bay is only 1.5m away, and there is a fishing lake with direct access from some pitches. A 19-acre site with 250 touring pitches, 10 hardstandings.

Notes No groups unless booked in advance

NEWTON ABBOT MAP 03 SX87

★★★★ FARM HOUSE

Bulleigh Park *(SX860660)*

Ipplepen TQ12 5UA

☎ 01803 872254 01803 872254 Mrs A Dallyn

e-mail: bulleigh@lineone.net

web: www.southdevonaccommodation.co.uk

Dir: *3.5m S of Newton Abbot. Off A381 at Parkhill Cross by Power station for Compton, continue 1m, signed*

PETS: Stables on site **Charges** dog £5, horse £5 per night £30 per week charge for damage **Public areas** except restaurant & lounge **Grounds** accessible disp bin **Exercise area Facilities** food (pre-bookable) food bowl water bowl dog chews dog scoop/disp bags leads washing facs cage storage walks info vet info **On Request** fridge access torch towels **Resident Pets:** Nippy (Jack Russell cross)

Bulleigh Park is a working farm, producing award-winning Aberdeen Angus beef. The owners have also won an award for green tourism by reducing the impact of the business on the environment. Expect a friendly welcome at this family home set in glorious countryside, where breakfasts are notable for the wealth of fresh, local and home-made produce, and the porridge is cooked from a secret recipe.

Rooms 2 en suite 1 annexe en suite S £38-£50; D £70-£76 **Facilities** FTV TVB tea/coffee Cen ht TVL Wi-fi available **Parking** 6 **Notes LB** 60 acres beef, sheep, hens Closed Dec-1 Feb

►►►►► Dornafield *(SX838683)*

Dornafield Farm, Two Mile Oak TQ12 6DD

☎ 01803 812732 01803 812032

e-mail: enquiries@dornafield.com

web: www.dornafield.com

Dir: *Take A381 (Newton Abbot-Totnes) for 2m. At Two Mile Oak Inn turn right, then left at x-roads in 0.5m to site on right*

PETS: Charges £1-£2 per night disp bin **Exercise area** on site 2 exercise areas provided **Facilities** on site shop food food bowl water bowl dog chews cat treats dog scoop/disp bags walks info vet info **Other** prior notice required **Resident Pets:** cat

Open 15 Mar-3 Jan Last arrival 22.00hrs Last departure 11.00hrs

An immaculately kept park in a tranquil wooded valley between Dartmoor and Torbay, offering either de-luxe or fully-serviced pitches. A lovely 15th-century farmhouse sits at the entrance, and the park is divided into three separate areas, served by two superb, ultra-modern toilet blocks. The friendly family owners are always available. A 30-acre site with 135 touring pitches, 97 hardstandings.

►►►►► Ross Park *(SX845671)*

Park Hill Farm, Ipplepen TQ12 5TT

☎ 01803 812983 01803 812983

e-mail: enquiries@rossparkcaravanpark.co.uk

web: www.rossparkcaravanpark.co.uk

Dir: *Off A381, 3m from Newton Abbot towards Totnes, signed opposite Texaco garage towards 'Woodland'*

PETS: Public areas except restaurant disp bin **Exercise area** on site 3 fields & orchard **Facilities** on site shop food washing facs walks info vet info **Other** dog shower room **Restrictions** breeds accepted only at manager's discretion **Resident Pets:** Baloo & Monty (Labradors)

Open Mar-2 Jan (rs Nov-Feb & 1st 3wks of Mar restaurant/bar closed (ex Xmas/New Year)) Last arrival 21.00hrs Last departure 10.00hrs

A top-class park in every way, with large secluded pitches, high quality toilet facilities and lovely floral displays throughout. The beautiful tropical conservatory also offers a breathtaking show of colour. This very rural park enjoys superb views of Dartmoor, and good quality meals to suit all tastes and pockets are served in the restaurant. A 32-acre site with 110 touring pitches, 82 hardstandings.

Notes Bikes, skateboards/scooters only allowed on leisure field

►►► Twelve Oaks Farm Caravan Park *(SX852737)*

Teigngrace TQ12 6QT

☎ 01626 352769 01626 352769

e-mail: info@twelveoaksfarm.co.uk

web: www.twelveoaksfarm.co.uk

Dir: *A38 from Exeter left signed Teigngrace (only), 0.25m before Drumbridges rdbt. 1.5m, through village, site on left. From Plymouth pass Drumbridges rdbt, take slip road for Chudleigh Knighton. Right over bridge, rejoin A38 towards Plymouth. Left for Teigngrace (only), then as above*

PETS: disp bin **Exercise area** on site **Facilities** on site shop walks info vet info **Resident pets** farm animals

Open all year Last arrival 21.00hrs Last departure 11.00hrs

An attractive small park on a working farm close to Dartmoor National Park, and bordered by the River Teign. The tidy pitches are located amongst trees and shrubs, and the modern facilities are very well maintained. Children will enjoy all the farm animals, and nearby is the Templar Way walking route. A 2-acre site with 35 touring pitches, 17 hardstandings.

OTTERY ST MARY — MAP 03 SY19

★★ BED & BREAKFAST

Fluxton Farm

Fluxton EX11 1RJ

☎ 01404 812818 📠 01404 814843

web: www.fluxtonfarm.co.uk

Dir: *2m SW of Ottery St Mary. B3174, W from Ottery over river, left, next left to Fluxton*

PETS: Bedrooms Sep Accom pens for cats only **Public areas** except dining room & lounge **Grounds** accessible on leads **Exercise area** opposite **Facilities** food bowl water bowl washing facs walks info vet info **On Request** fridge access **Other** cat food available on request **Resident Pets:** the farm is a cat rescue sanctuary; ducks, chickens

A haven for cat lovers, Fluxton Farm offers comfortable accommodation with a choice of lounges and a large garden, complete with pond and ducks. Set in peaceful farmland four miles from the coast, this 16th-century longhouse has a wealth of beams and open fireplaces.

Rooms 7 en suite S £27.50; D £55✻ **Facilities** TVB tea/coffee Cen ht TVL **Parking** 15 **Notes LB** No children 8yrs RS Nov-Apr

PAIGNTON — MAP 03 SX86

★★★★ GUEST ACCOMMODATION

The Commodore

14 Esplanade Rd TQ4 6EB

☎ 01803 553107 📠 01803 557040

e-mail: info@commodorepaignton.com

web: www.commodorepaignton.com

Dir: *A379 to Paignton, A3022 to seafront. Pass multiplex cinema, property on right*

PETS: Bedrooms (3GF) **Charges** £5 per night £35 per week charge for damage **Public areas** (on leads) **Exercise area** 20mtrs **Facilities** food (pre-bookable) leads washing facs walks info vet info **On Request** torch towels **Resident Pets:** Robbie (Springer Spaniel)

With an excellent seafront location, all the popular attractions of the town including shopping, the harbour, cinema and restaurants, are all just a short stroll from this family-run accommodation. Bedrooms are generally spacious and well furnished and some enjoy sea views. Guests are welcome to use the lounge and a small downstairs bar is also available.

Rooms 11 en suite (5 fmly) (3 GF) S £36-£70; D £52-£80 **Facilities** FTV TVB tea/coffee Cen ht TVL Dinner Last d 8.45am Wi-fi available **Parking** 10 **Notes LB**

★★★★ GUEST HOUSE

The Wentworth Guest House

18 Youngs Park Rd, Goodrington TQ4 6BU

☎ 01803 557843

e-mail: enquiries@wentworthguesthouse.co.uk

Dir: *Through Paignton on A378, 1m left at rdbt, sharp right onto Roundham Rd, right & right again onto Youngs Park Rd*

PETS: Bedrooms (1GF) unattended **Charges** £4 per night £28 per week charge for damage **Exercise area** park opposite **Facilities** food bowl water bowl bedding feeding mat litter tray etc vet info **On Request** fridge access torch towels

Within 200 yards of the beach, this Victorian house overlooks Goodrington Park and is convenient for many attractions and the town centre. The bedrooms are attractively decorated, well equipped, and feature many thoughtful extras. The traditional English breakfast is a tasty start to the day, and additional facilities include a comfortable bar and a spacious lounge.

Rooms 10 en suite (2 fmly) (1 GF) S £20-£27; D £40-£54✻ **Facilities** TVB tea/coffee Licensed Cen ht TVL **Parking** 4

★★★ GUEST ACCOMMODATION

The Park

Esplanade Rd TQ4 6BQ

☎ 01803 557856 📠 01803 555626

e-mail: stay@parkhotel.me.uk

Dir: *On Paignton seafront, nearly opp pier*

PETS: Bedrooms Charges charge for damage **Public areas** except restaurant (on leads) **Grounds** accessible on leads **Exercise area Facilities** cage storage walks info vet info **On Request** fridge access torch towels

This large establishment has a prominent position on the seafront with excellent views of Torbay. The pleasant bedrooms are all spacious and available in a number of options, and several have sea views. Entertainment is provided on some evenings in the lounge. Dinner and breakfast are served in the spacious dining room, which overlooks the attractive front garden.

Rooms 47 en suite (5 fmly) (3 GF) S £26-£43; D £54-£90✻ **Facilities** TVB tea/coffee Lift Cen ht Dinner Last d 6pm Wi-fi available Pool Table Games room with 3/4 snooker table & table tennis **Parking** 38 **Notes LB**

PLYMOUTH MAP 02 SX45

★★★ 77% ❁ HOTEL

Best Western Duke of Cornwall

Millbay Rd PL1 3LG
☎ 01752 275850 & 275855 🖷 01752 275854
e-mail: dukereservations@hotmail.com
web: www.thedukeofcornwallhotel.com
Dir: *follow city centre, then Plymouth Pavilions Conference & Leisure Centre signs*

PETS: Bedrooms unattended **Charges** charge for damage **Exercise area Facilities** water bowl bedding walks info vet info **On Request** fridge access torch towels

A historic landmark, this city centre hotel is conveniently located. The spacious public areas include a popular bar, comfortable lounge and multi-functional ballroom. Bedrooms, many with far reaching views, are individually styled and comfortably appointed. The range of dining options includes meals in the bar, or guests might choose the elegant dining room for a more formal atmosphere.

Rooms 71 en suite (6 fmly) S £105-£230; D £120-£230 (incl. bkfst) **Facilities** STV Wi-fi available Xmas New Year **Services** Lift **Parking** 50 **Notes** LB

★★★ 71% HOTEL

Novotel Plymouth

Marsh Mills PL6 8NH
☎ 01752 221422 🖷 01752 223922
e-mail: h0508@accor.com
web: www.novotel.com
Dir: *Exit A38 at Marsh Mills, follow Plympton signs, hotel on left*

PETS: Bedrooms (18GF) **Charges** £10 per night charge for damage **Public areas** except restaurant (on leads) **Grounds** accessible on leads disp bin **Exercise area Facilities** water bowl cage storage walks info vet info **On Request** torch towels

Conveniently located on the outskirts of the city, close to Marsh Mills roundabout, this modern hotel offers good value accommodation. All rooms are spacious and designed with flexibility for family use. Public areas are open-plan with meals available throughout the day in either the Garden Brasserie, the bar, or from room service.

Rooms 100 en suite (17 fmly) (18 GF) **Facilities** ⚸ **Services** Lift **Parking** 140 **Notes** LB

★★★ GUEST ACCOMMODATION

The Cranbourne

278-282 Citadel Rd, The Hoe PL1 2PZ
☎ 01752 263858 & 224646 & 661400 🖷 01752 263858
e-mail: cran.hotel@virgin.net
web: www.cranbournehotel.co.uk
Dir: *Behind the Promenade, Plymouth Hoe*

PETS: Bedrooms Public areas except dining room (on leads) **Exercise area** 60yds **Facilities** dog scoop/disp bags leads walks info vet info **On Request** fridge access towels **Resident Pets:** Harry (Golden Retriever), Mickie (Shiba Inu)

This attractive Georgian terrace house has been extensively renovated, and is located just a short walk from The Hoe, The Barbican and the city centre. Bedrooms are practically furnished and well equipped. Hearty breakfasts are served in the elegant dining room and there is also a cosy bar.

Rooms 40 rms (28 en suite) (5 fmly) (1 GF) S £25-£40; D £44-£60* **Facilities** TVB tea/coffee Cen ht TVL **Parking** 14

★★★ GUEST ACCOMMODATION

The Lamplighter

103 Citadel Rd, The Hoe PL1 2RN
☎ 01752 663855 & 07793 360815 🖷 01752 228139
e-mail: stay@lamplighterplymouth.co.uk
web: www.lamplighterplymouth.co.uk
Dir: *Near war memorial*

PETS: Bedrooms Charges £5 minimum per night charge for damage **Public areas** except dining room (on leads) **Exercise area** 50mtrs **Facilities** cage storage walks info vet info

With easy access to The Hoe, The Barbican and the city centre, this comfortable guest house provides a good base for leisure or business. Bedrooms, including family rooms, are light and airy and furnished to a consistent standard. Breakfast is served in the dining room, which has an adjoining lounge area.

Rooms 9 rms (7 en suite) (2 pri facs) (2 fmly) S £30; D £50* **Facilities** TVB tea/coffee Cen ht TVL Wi-fi available **Parking** 4

★★ GUEST ACCOMMODATION

The Firs Guest Accommodation

13 Pier St, West Hoe PL1 3BS
☎ 01752 262870 & 300010
e-mail: thefirsguesthouse@hotmail.co.uk

PETS: Bedrooms Exercise area 100yds **Facilities** walks info vet info **On Request** fridge access torch **Resident Pets:** Rosie, Jessica, Tabitha & Fluffy (cats)

A well-located and-well established house on the West Hoe with convenient on-street parking. Friendly owners and comfortable rooms make it a popular destination.

Rooms 7 rms (2 en suite) (2 fmly) S £20-£30; D £40-£50* **Facilities** FTV TVB tea/coffee Cen ht Dinner Last d Breakfast time **Notes** LB

ENGLAND

PRINCETOWN MAP 02 SX57

►► *The Plume of Feathers Inn* (*SX592734*)

Plymouth PL20 6QQ

☎ 01822 890240

Dir: *Site accessed directly from B3212 rdbt (beside Plume of Feathers Inn) in centre of Princetown*

PETS: Stables on site disp bin **Exercise area** on site paddock & field **Facilities** food food bowl water bowl dog chews washing facs walks info vet info **Other** prior notice required small selection of food available **Resident Pets:** Bonnie (West Highland Terrier), Jeannie (Border Terrier), Dribbles (cat)

Open all year Last arrival 23.30hrs Last departure 11.00hrs

Set amidst the rugged beauty of Dartmoor not far from the notorious prison, this campsite boasts good toilet facilities and all the amenities of the inn. The Plume of Feathers is Princetown's oldest building, and serves all day food in an atmospheric setting. The campsite is mainly for tents. A 3-acre site with 85 touring pitches.

Notes No caravans

SALCOMBE MAP 03 SX73

★★★★ 78% HOTEL

Soar Mill Cove

Soar Mill Cove, Malborough TQ7 3DS

☎ 01548 561566 01548 561223

e-mail: info@soarmillcove.co.uk

web: www.soarmillcove.co.uk

Dir: *3m W of town off A381 at Malborough. Follow Soar signs*

PETS: Bedrooms (21GF) **Grounds** accessible disp bin **Exercise area** on site **Facilities** dog scoop/disp bags cage storage walks info vet info **On Request** fridge access torch towels **Other** 2000 acres NT land & beach without restrictions for walking **Resident Pets:** Rosie (Bichon Frisé), Farley (Golden Labrador)

Situated amid spectacular scenery with dramatic sea views, this hotel is ideal for a relaxing stay. Family-run, with a committed team, keen standards of hospitality and service are upheld. Bedrooms are well equipped and many rooms have private terraces. There are different seating areas where impressive cream teas are served, and for the more active, there's a choice of swimming pools. Local produce and seafood are used to good effect in the restaurant.

Rooms 22 en suite (5 fmly) (21 GF) S £70-£100; D £140-£199 (incl. bkfst) **Facilities** FTV Putt green Wi-fi available Table tennis Games room Xmas New Year **Parking** 30 **Notes LB** Closed 2 Jan-8 Feb

★★★ 81% HOTEL

Tides Reach

South Sands TQ8 8LJ

☎ 01548 843466 01548 843954

e-mail: enquire@tidesreach.com

web: www.tidesreach.com

Dir: *Off A38 at Buckfastleigh to Totnes. Then A381 to Salcombe, follow signs to South Sands*

PETS: Bedrooms unattended **Public areas** except bar, restaurant, 2 lounges **Charges** £8.50 per night **Grounds** accessible (on leads) disp bin **Exercise area Facilities** food (pre-bookable) bedding cage storage walks info vet info **On request** torch towel **Other** dogs accepted by prior arrangement only - please phone for further details

Superbly situated at the water's edge, this personally run, friendly hotel has splendid views of the estuary and beach. Bedrooms, many with balconies, are spacious and comfortable. In the bar and lounge, attentive service can be enjoyed along with the view, and the Garden Room restaurant serves appetising and accomplished cuisine.

Rooms 35 en suite (7 fmly) S £75-£143; D £124-£320 (incl. bkfst & dinner)* **Facilities** FTV supervised Squash Gym Wi-fi available Windsurfing Sailing Kayaking Scuba diving Hair & beauty treatment **Services** Lift **Parking** 100 **Notes LB** No children 8yrs Closed Dec-early Feb

SAMPFORD PEVERELL MAP 03 ST01

►►►► Minnows Touring Park (*SS042148*)

Holbrook Ln EX16 7EN

☎ 01884 821770 01884 829199

web: www.ukparks.co.uk/minnows

Dir: *M5 junct 27 take A361 signed Tiverton & Barnstaple. In 600yds take 1st slip road, then right over bridge, site ahead*

PETS: Public areas except in buildings **Charges** 2 dogs free, £1 per extra dog per night **Exercise area** canal towpath adjacent **Facilities** on site shop walks info vet info **Other** water at reception, dog ties by buildings

Open 9 Mar-9 Nov Last arrival 20.00hrs Last departure 11.30hrs

A small, well-sheltered park, peacefully located amidst fields and mature trees. The toilet facilities are of a high quality in keeping with the rest of the park, and there is a good laundry. The park has direct gated access to the canal towpath. A 5.5-acre site with 45 touring pitches, 45 hardstandings and 1 static.

Notes No cycling, no groundsheets on grass

SIDMOUTH MAP 03 SY18

★★ 79% HOTEL

Kingswood

The Esplanade EX10 8AX

☎ 01395 516367 📠 01395 513185

e-mail: kingswood@hotels-sidmouth.co.uk

web: www.hotels-sidmouth.co.uk

Dir: *take A375 off A3052 towards seafront. Hotel in centre of Esplanade*

PETS: Bedrooms (2GF) unattended **Charges** £6 per night charge for damage **Public areas** except restaurant/lounge (on leads) **Exercise area** 1 min walk

Super standards of hospitality are only surpassed by this hotel's prominent position on the esplanade. All bedrooms have modern facilities and some enjoy the stunning sea views. The two lounges offer comfort and space and the attractive dining room serves good traditional cooking.

Rooms 26 rms (25 en suite) (7 fmly) (2 GF) S £54-£76; D £54-£76 (incl. bkfst & dinner)✻ **Facilities** Guests receive vouchers for local swimming pool Discounts for local golf course Xmas **Services** Lift **Parking** 17 **Notes** Closed 28 Dec-9 Feb

★★ 79% HOTEL

Royal York & Faulkner

The Esplanade EX10 8AZ

☎ 01395 513043 & 0800 220714 📠 01395 577472

e-mail: stay@royalyorkhotel.co.uk

web: www.royalyorkhotel.co.uk

Dir: *M5 junct 30 take A3052, 10m to Sidmouth, hotel in centre of Esplanade*

PETS: Bedrooms (5GF) unattended sign **Charges** £5 per night charge for damage **Exercise area** 250mtrs **Facilities** food (pre-bookable) food bowl water bowl cage storage walks info vet info **On Request** fridge access torch

This seafront hotel, owned and run by the same family for generations, maintains its Regency charm and grandeur. The attractive bedrooms vary in size; many have balconies and sea views. Public rooms are spacious and traditional dining is offered plus Blinis Café-Bar, which is more contemporary in style and offers coffees, lunch and afternoon teas. The spa facilities include a hydrotherapy pool, steam room, sauna and a variety of treatments.

Rooms 68 en suite 2 annexe en suite (8 fmly) (5 GF) S £52-£92; D £104-£184 (incl. bkfst & dinner)✻ **Facilities Spa** Wi-fi available Steam cabin Snooker table Sauna ♫ Xmas New Year **Services** Lift **Parking** 20 **Notes LB** Closed Jan

★★ 72% HOTEL

The Woodlands Hotel

Cotmaton Cross EX10 8HG

☎ 01395 513120 📠 01395 513348

e-mail: info@woodlands-hotel.com

web: www.woodlands-hotel.com

Dir: *follow signs for Sidmouth*

PETS: Bedrooms (8GF) unattended sign **Exercise area** 200yds **Facilities** cage storage walks info vet info **Restrictions** breeds no larger than a Labrador

Located in the heart of the town and ideally situated for exploring Devon and Dorset, this listed property has numerous character features. There is a spacious bar and a lounge where guests may relax. Freshly prepared dinners are enjoyed in the smart dining room. Families with children are made very welcome and may dine early.

Rooms 20 en suite (4 fmly) (8 GF) S £35-£65; D £70-£130 (incl. bkfst)✻ **Facilities** Wi-fi available **Parking** 20 **Notes LB** Closed 20 Dec-15 Jan

★★★★★ ◎◎ RESTAURANT WITH ROOMS

The Salty Monk

Church St, Sidford EX10 9QP

☎ 01395 513174

e-mail: saltymonk@btconnect.com

web: www.saltymonk.biz

Dir: *On A3052 opposite church*

PETS: Bedrooms (3GF) **Charges** £20 per stay charge for damage **Public areas** except restaurant (on leads) **Grounds** accessible on leads disp bin **Exercise area** 50yds **Facilities** food (pre-bookable) food bowl water bowl bedding dog chews dog scoop/disp bags leads washing facs cage storage walks info vet info **On Request** fridge access torch towels **Resident Pets:** Finn & Mardi (Irish Water Spaniels)

Set in the village of Sidford, this attractive property dates from the 16th century. Some of the well-presented bedrooms feature spa baths or special showers, and a ground-floor courtyard room has a king-size water bed. Meals are served in the restaurant, where the two owners both cook. They use fresh local produce to ensure that the food is of a high standard and thoroughly enjoyable.

Rooms 5 en suite (3 GF) S £70-£90; D £110-£180✻ **Facilities** FTV TVB tea/coffee Cen ht Dinner Last d 9pm Wi-fi available **Parking** 20 **Notes LB** Closed 2wks Nov & 3wks Jan

SIDMOUTH CONTINUED

►►►► Oakdown Touring & Holiday Caravan Park *(SY167902)*

Gatedown Ln, Weston EX10 0PT

☎ 01297 680387 📠 01297 680541

e-mail: enquiries@oakdown.co.uk

web: www.oakdown.co.uk

Dir: *Off A3052, 2.5m E of junct with A375*

PETS: Public areas except children's play area **Charges** £2.20 per night (touring pitches) disp bin **Exercise area** on site field trails **Facilities** walks info vet info

Open Apr-Oct Last arrival 22.00hrs Last departure 10.30hrs

Friendly, well-maintained park with good landscaping and plenty of maturing trees. Pitches are grouped in paddocks surrounded by shrubs, and the park is well screened from the A3502. The park's conservation areas with their natural flora and fauna offer attractive walks, and there is a hide by the Victorian reed bed for both casual and dedicated bird watchers. A 13-acre site with 100 touring pitches, 90 hardstandings and 62 statics.

Notes Dogs must be kept on leads, no bikes/skateboards or kite flying

SLAPTON MAP 03 SX84

►►► Slapton Sands Camping & Caravanning Club Site *(SX825450)*

Middle Grounds TQ7 2QW

☎ 01548 580538

web: www.thefriendlyclub.co.uk

Dir: *On A379 from Kingsbridge. Site entrance 0.25m from A379, beyond brow of hill approaching Slapton*

PETS: Public areas except in buildings disp bin **Exercise area** on site **Facilities** walks info vet info **Other** prior notice required

Open 2 Apr-2 Nov Last arrival 21.00hrs Last departure noon

A very attractive location and well-run site overlooking Start Bay, with extensive views from some pitches, and glimpses of the sea from others. The shingle beach of Slapton Sands, and the Blue Flag beach at Blackpool Sands are among attractions, along with a nearby freshwater lake and nature reserve. A 5.5-acre site with 115 touring pitches, 10 hardstandings.

Notes Members' touring caravans only. Site gates closed 23.00hrs-07.00hrs

SOURTON MAP 03 SX59

★★ 78% COUNTRY HOUSE HOTEL

Collaven Manor

EX20 4HH

☎ 01837 861522 📠 01837 861614

e-mail: collavenmanor@supanet.com

Dir: *A30 onto A386 to Tavistock, hotel 2m on right*

PETS: Bedrooms unattended **Stables** nearby (5m) **Charges** £5 per night **Grounds** accessible disp bin **Exercise area** accessed directly from grounds **Facilities** food bowl water bowl cat treats washing facs cage storage walks info vet info **On Request** fridge access torch towels **Other** food by prior arrangement **Restrictions** no Dobermans, Rottweilers or Pit Bulls **Resident Pets:** Willow, Jas & Jack (cats)

This delightful 15th-century manor house is quietly located in five acres of well-tended grounds. The friendly proprietors provide attentive service and ensure a relaxing environment. Charming public rooms have old oak beams and granite fireplaces, and provide a range of comfortable lounges and a well stocked bar. In the restaurant, a daily-changing menu offers interesting dishes.

Rooms 9 en suite (1 fmly) **Facilities** Bowls ch fac **Parking** 50 **Notes** LB

SOURTON CROSS MAP 02 SX59

►►► Bundu Camping & Caravan Park *(SX546916)*

EX20 4HT

☎ 01837 861611 📠 01837 861611

e-mail: frances@bundu.plus.com

web: www.bundu.co.uk

Dir: *W on A30, past Okehampton. Take A386 to Tavistock. Take 1st left & left again*

PETS: disp bin **Exercise area** adjacent **Facilities** on site shop food washing facs walks info vet info **Resident Pets:** Sophie (German Shepherd)

Open all year Last arrival 23.30hrs Last departure 14.00hrs

Welcoming, friendly owners set the tone for this well-maintained site, ideally positioned on the border of the Dartmoor National Park. Along with fine views and level grassy pitches, the Granite Way cycle track from Lydford to Okehampton along the old railway line, part of the

Devon Coast to Coast cycle trail, passes the edge of the park. A 4.5-acre site with 38 touring pitches, 8 hardstandings.

Notes

SOUTH BRENT — MAP 03 SX66

★★ 76% HOTEL

Glazebrook House Hotel

TQ10 9JE

☎ 01364 73322 01364 72350

e-mail: enquiries@glazebrookhouse.com

web: www.glazebrookhouse.com

Dir: *Exit A38 at South Brent, follow brown signs to hotel*

PETS: Bedrooms unattended **Stables** nearby (2m) **Charges** charge for damage **Public areas** except restaurant **Grounds** accessible disp bin **Exercise area** 0.5m **Facilities** leads dog walking washing facs cage storage walks info vet info **On Request** fridge access torch towels **Restrictions** only well behaved dogs accepted **Resident Pets:** Bobby (Pointer/Collie cross), Sly (cat)

Enjoying a tranquil and convenient location next to the Dartmoor National Park and set within four acres of gardens, this 18th-century former gentleman's residence offers a friendly welcome and comfortable accommodation. Elegant public areas offer ample space to relax and enjoy the atmosphere, whilst bedrooms are well appointed and include a number with four-poster beds. Cuisine offers interesting combinations of fresh, locally-sourced produce.

Rooms 10 en suite S £50-£55; D £75-£125 (incl. bkfst)* **Facilities** Wi-fi available Xmas New Year **Parking** 40 **Notes LB** Closed 2-18 Jan RS 1 wk Aug

SOUTH MOLTON — MAP 03 SS72

★★★ RESTAURANT WITH ROOMS

Stumbles

134 East St EX36 3BU

☎ 01769 574145 01769 572558

e-mail: info@stumbles.co.uk

Dir: *M5 junct 27 to South Molton on A361. Establishment in town centre*

PETS: Bedrooms (2GF) sign **Charges** £5 per animal per night £25 per animal per week charge for damage **Public areas** except restaurants (on leads) **Exercise area Facilities** water bowl feeding mat washing facs cage storage walks info vet info **On Request** torch towels

Located in the centre of this bustling town, Stumbles is a charming place with a friendly and welcoming atmosphere. Bedrooms are individual in style and all have lots of character and good levels of comfort. A small conservatory area is also available for guests. The restaurant is a popular venue for locals and visitors alike, with a varied menu on offer both at lunchtime and in the evenings.

Rooms 6 en suite 4 annexe en suite (1 fmly) (2 GF) **Facilities** FTV TVB tea/coffee Direct dial from bedrooms Cen ht Dinner Last d 9pm **Parking** 25

SOUTH ZEAL — MAP 03 SX69

★★ 76% HOTEL

Oxenham Arms

EX20 2JT

☎ 01837 840244 & 840577 01837 840791

e-mail: theoxenhamarms@aol.com

web: www.theoxenhamarms.co.uk

Dir: *off A30, 4m E of Okehampton in centre of village*

PETS: Bedrooms Sep Accom purpose-built kennels **Stables** on site **Charges** £5 per night charge for damage **Public areas** except restaurant **Grounds** accessible disp bin **Exercise area Facilities** food (pre-bookable) food bowl water bowl bedding feeding mat dog scoop/disp bags leads washing facs cage storage walks info vet info **On Request** fridge access torch towels **Resident Pets:** Arti, Desmond, Derek & Gilbert (dogs)

Dating back to the 12th century, this fascinating inn, still very much the village local, was first licensed in 1477. Extensive refurbishment has blended contemporary styling with the historic features. Bedrooms have lots of character and no two are alike. The stylish restaurant offers varied cuisine, often utilising produce from the owner's rare breeds farm. In summer, meals can be taken in the extensive garden with stunning views of Dartmoor.

Rooms 7 en suite S £55-£100; D £85-£165 (incl. bkfst)* **Facilities** Wi-fi in bedrooms Xmas New Year **Parking** 6

STOKE GABRIEL — MAP 03 SX85

►►► **Broadleigh Farm Park** *(SX851587)*

Coombe House Ln, Aish TQ9 6PU

☎ 01803 782309

e-mail: enquiries@broadleighfarm.co.uk

web: www.broadleighfarm.co.uk

Dir: *From Exeter on A38 then A380 towards Tor Bay. Right onto A385 for Totnes. After 0.5m at Parkers Arms left for Stoke Gabriel. Right after Whitehill Country Park to site*

PETS: Exercise area field adjacent **Resident Pets:** 1 dog, 2 cats

Open Mar-Oct Last arrival 21.00hrs Last departure 11.30hrs

Set in a very rural location on a working farm which borders Paignton and Stoke Gabriel. The large sloping field with a timber-clad toilet block in the centre is sheltered and peaceful, surrounded by rolling countryside but handy for the beaches. A 7-acre site with 80 touring pitches.

Notes

ENGLAND

STRETE

MAP 03 SX84

★★★★ GUEST HOUSE

Strete Barton House

Totnes Rd TQ6 0RU

☎ 01803 770364 🖷 01803 771182

e-mail: info@stretebarton.co.uk

web: www.stretebarton.co.uk

Dir: *Off A379 into village centre, just below church*

PETS: Charges £5 per night £35 per week **Grounds** accessible disp bin **Exercise area** on site **Facilities** dog chews cage storage walks info vet info **On Request** fridge access torch towels **Other** pets allowed in cottage suite only

This delightful 16th-century farmhouse has been refurbished to blend stylish accommodation with its original character. Bedrooms are very comfortably furnished and well equipped with useful extras. Breakfast utilises quality local produce and is served in the spacious dining room. Guests are also welcome to use the very comfortable lounge complete with real log burner for the cooler months. The village lies between Dartmouth and Kingsbridge and has easy access to the natural beauty of the South Hams as well as local pubs and restaurants.

Rooms 5 rms (4 en suite) (1 pri facs) 1 annexe en suite (2 fmly) (1 GF) S £65-£90; D £75-£100✳ **Facilities** FTV TVB tea/coffee Cen ht Wi-fi available **Parking** 4 **Notes LB** No children 3yrs No coaches

TAVISTOCK

MAP 02 SX47

★★★ GUEST ACCOMMODATION

The Coach House

PL19 8NS

☎ 01822 617515 🖷 01822 617515

e-mail: estevens255@aol.com

web: www.thecoachousehotel.co.uk

Dir: *2.5m NW of Tavistock. A390 from Tavistock to Gulworthy Cross, at rdbt take 3rd exit towards Chipshop Inn turn right to Ottery, 1st building in village*

PETS: Bedrooms Public areas in bar only (on leads) **Grounds** accessible on leads **Exercise area** 20yds **Facilities** water bowl washing facs walks info vet info

Dating from 1857, this building was constructed for the Duke of Bedford and converted by the current owners. Some bedrooms are on the ground floor and in an adjacent barn conversion. Dinner is available in the cosy dining room or the restaurant, which leads onto the south-facing garden.

Rooms 6 en suite 3 annexe en suite (4 GF) S £47; D £65✳ **Facilities** TVB tea/coffee Direct dial from bedrooms Cen ht Dinner Last d 9pm **Parking** 24 **Notes LB** No children 5yrs

★★★ BED & BREAKFAST

Sampford Manor

Sampford Spiney PL20 6LH

☎ 01822 853442 🖷 01822 855691

e-mail: manor@sampford-spiney.fsnet.co.uk

web: www.sampford-spiney.fsnet.co.uk

Dir: *B3357 towards Princetown, right at 1st x-rds. Next x-rds Warren Cross left for Sampford Spiney. 2nd right, house below church*

PETS: Bedrooms Sep Accom barn **Stables** on site **Charges** £2 per night **Public areas** except dining room (on leads) **Grounds** accessible disp bin **Exercise area** 200yds **Facilities** food bowl water bowl feeding mat leads washing facs cage storage walks info vet info **On Request** fridge access torch towels **Resident Pets:** Spin (Springer/Terrier cross), Cleo (Springer/Collie cross), Woody (Chocolate Labrador), Monty (cat), 31 alpacas, 2 horses

Once owned by Sir Francis Drake, this manor house is tucked away in a tranquil corner of Dartmoor National Park. The family home is full of character, with exposed beams and slate floors, while outside, a herd of award winning alpacas graze in the fields. Genuine hospitality is assured together with scrumptious breakfasts featuring home-produced eggs. Children as well as pets are equally welcome.

Rooms 3 rms (2 pri facs) (1 fmly) S £27-£35; D £50-£70✳ **Facilities** TVB tea/coffee Cen ht Golf 19 **Parking** 3 **Notes** Closed Xmas

►►►► **Woodovis Park** *(SX431745)*

Gulworthy PL19 8NY

☎ 01822 832968 🖷 01822 832948

e-mail: info@woodovis.com

web: www.woodovis.com

Dir: *A390 from Tavistock signed Callington & Gunnislake. At top of hill turn right at rdbt signed Lamerton & 'Chipshop'. Site 1m on left*

PETS: Public areas except buildings & swimming pool (on leads) disp bin **Exercise area** on site dog walks & woods **Facilities** on site shop washing facs walks info vet info **Other** prior notice required ground anchor for lead by tents **Resident Pets:** Border Collie (& at times Springer cross & cat)

Open 28 Mar-Oct Last arrival 22.00hrs Last departure noon

A well-kept park in a remote woodland setting on the edge of the Tamar Valley. This peacefully-located park is set at the end of a half-mile private tree-lined road, and has lots of on-site facilities. The toilets are excellent, and there is an indoor swimming pool, all in a friendly, purposeful atmosphere. A 14.5-acre site with 50 touring pitches, 18 hardstandings and 35 statics.

►►► Langstone Manor Camping & Caravan Park *(SX524738)*

Moortown PL19 9JZ

☎ 01822 613371 ▤ 01822 613371

e-mail: jane@langstone-manor.co.uk

web: www.langstone-manor.co.uk

Dir: *Take B3357 from Tavistock to Princetown. Approx 1.5m turn right at x-rds, follow signs*

PETS: Stables (loose box) disp bin **Exercise area** moor adjacent **Facilities** leads washing facs walks info vet info **Other** prior notice required **Resident Pets:** Cassie (Collie), Mercury (Russian Blue cat)

Open 15 Mar-Oct (rs wkdys in low season restricted hours in bar & restaurant) Last arrival 22.00hrs Last departure 11.00hrs

A secluded site set in the well-maintained grounds of a manor house in Dartmoor National Park. Many attractive mature trees provide a screen within the park, and there is a popular lounge bar with an excellent menu of reasonably priced evening meals. Plenty of activities and places of interest can be found within the surrounding moorland. A 5.5-acre site with 40 touring pitches, 5 hardstandings and 25 statics.

Notes No skateboards, scooters, cycles, ball games

THURLESTONE — MAP 03 SX64

★★★★ 79% HOTEL

Thurlestone

TQ7 3NN

☎ 01548 560382 ▤ 01548 561069

e-mail: enquiries@thurlestone.co.uk

web: www.thurlestone.co.uk

Dir: *A38 take A384 into Totnes, A381 towards Kingsbridge, onto A379 towards Churchstow, onto B3197 turn into lane signed to Thurlestone*

PETS: Bedrooms unattended sign **Stables** nearby **Charges** £6 per night charge for damage **Public areas** front foyer only **Grounds** accessible **Exercise area Facilities** food bowl water bowl pet sitting washing facs cage storage walks info vet info **On Request** fridge access torch towels

This perennially popular hotel has been in the same family-ownership since 1896 and continues to go from strength to strength. A vast range of facilities is available for all the family including indoor and outdoor pools, a golf course and a beauty salon. Bedrooms are equipped to ensure a comfortable stay with many having wonderful views of the South Devon coast. A range of eating options includes the elegant and stylish restaurant with its stunning views.

Rooms 64 en suite (23 fmly) S £61-£135; D £122-£350 (incl. bkfst)✳ **Facilities** STV pool supervised 9 Squash Gym Putt green Wi-fi available Badminton courts Games room Toddler room Snooker room ch fac Xmas New Year **Services** Lift **Parking** 121 **Notes LB** Closed 1-2 wks Jan

TIVERTON — MAP 03 SS91

★★★ 73% HOTEL

Best Western Tiverton

Blundells Rd EX16 4DB

☎ 01884 256120 ▤ 01884 258101

e-mail: sales@tivertonhotel.co.uk

web: www.bw-tivertonhotel.co.uk

Dir: *A396 follow signs for town centre. Right at 2nd rdbt & immediately right into Blundells Rd. Hotel on right.*

PETS: Bedrooms unattended **Stables** nearby (4m) **Charges** £10 per night charge for damage **Grounds** accessible **Exercise area** 200mtrs **Facilities** food bowl water bowl bedding dog chews walks info vet info **On Request** fridge access towels

Conveniently situated on the outskirts of the town, with easy access to the M5, this comfortable hotel has a relaxed atmosphere. The spacious bedrooms are well equipped and decorated in a contemporary style. A formal dining option is offered in the Gallery Restaurant, and lighter snacks are served in the bar area. Room service is extensive, as is the range of conference facilities.

Rooms 69 en suite (4 fmly) (30 GF) S £60-£85; D £80-£120 (incl. bkfst)✳ **Facilities** STV Fishing Wi-fi in bedrooms Xmas New Year **Services** Lift **Parking** 130 **Notes LB**

★★★★ FARM HOUSE

Rhode Farm House *(SS967102)*

Exeter Hill EX16 4PL

☎ 01884 242853 ▤ 01884 242853 Mr & Mrs D Boulton

e-mail: david@rhodefarmhouse.com

web: www.rhodefarmhouse.com

Dir: *Follow signs to Grand Western Canal, right fork signed Exeter Hill, farmhouse 3m on left*

PETS: Stables on site **Charges** stabling £15 per night **Exercise area Resident Pets:** Buster & Kitty (Fox Terriers), Fritz (cat), Miss Mouse & Tess (horses)

Guests receive a very warm welcome at Rhode Farm House. It stands in five acres with stables in the yard, a 30-minute drive from Exeter city centre. Bedrooms are finished with many considerate extras and there is an inviting lounge with a log fire for colder nights. A delicious breakfast, featuring local produce, is served around a communal table in the dining room. Carefully prepared and presented dinners are available by arrangement.

Rooms 2 en suite (2 fmly) S £35-£40; D £65-£70 **Facilities** TVB tea/coffee Cen ht TVL Dinner Last d noon Riding **Parking** 5 **Notes** 4 acres

TORQUAY MAP 03 SX96

★★★★ 79% HOTEL

Barceló Torquay Imperial Hotel

Barceló HOTELS & RESORTS

Park Hill Rd TQ1 2DG

☎ 01803 294301 01803 298293

e-mail: imperialtorquay@barcelo-hotels.co.uk

web: www.barcelo-hotels.co.uk

Dir: *A380 towards the seafront. Turn left. To harbour, at clocktower turn right. Hotel 300yds on right*

PETS: Bedrooms unattended **Charges** £15 per night charge for damage **Grounds** accessible on leads disp bin **Exercise area** 100yds **Facilities** food bowl water bowl dog chews dog scoop/disp bags cage storage walks info vet info **On Request** fridge access torch towels **Restrictions** small to medium dogs only

This hotel has an enviable location with extensive views of the coastline. Traditional in style, the public areas are elegant and offer a choice of dining options, including the informal TQ1 brasserie or the more formal Regatta Restaurant. Bedrooms are spacious, most with private balconies, and the hotel has an extensive range of indoor and outdoor leisure facilities.

Rooms 152 en suite (14 fmly) S £65-£180* **Facilities** supervised Squash Gym Wi-fi available Beauty salon Hairdresser Steam room Xmas New Year **Services** Lift **Parking** 140 (charged)

★★★ 77% HOTEL

Corbyn Head Hotel & Orchid Restaurant

Torbay Rd, Sea Front TQ2 6RH

☎ 01803 213611 01803 296152

e-mail: info@corbynhead.com

web: www.corbynhead.com

Dir: *follow signs to Torquay seafront, turn right on seafront. Hotel on right with green canopies*

PETS: Bedrooms (9GF) unattended **Charges** £7 per night £49 per week charge for damage **Exercise area** 400mtrs **Facilities** vet info **Restrictions** no Pit Bull Terriers, Rottweilers, Dobermans or dangerous breeds (see page 7)

This hotel occupies a prime position overlooking Torbay, and offers well-equipped bedrooms, many with sea views and some with balconies. The staff are friendly and attentive, and a well-stocked bar and comfortable lounge are available. Guests can enjoy fine dining in the award-winning Orchid Restaurant or more traditional dishes in the Harbour View Restaurant.

Rooms 45 en suite (3 fmly) (9 GF) **Facilities** Squash Gym Wi-fi available **Parking** 50 **Notes** LB

★★ 69% HOTEL

Red House Hotel & Maxton Lodge Apartments

Rousdown Rd, Chelston TQ2 6PB

☎ 01803 607811 01803 200592

e-mail: stay@redhouse-hotel.co.uk

web: www.redhouse-hotel.co.uk

Dir: *towards seafront/Chelston, turn into Avenue Rd, 1st lights turn right. Past shops & church, take next left. Hotel on right*

PETS: Bedrooms unattended **Charges** £3 per night charge for damage **Public areas** except restaurant & lounge (on leads) **Exercise area** 100yds **Facilities** vet info **Restrictions** small to medium sized breeds only **Resident Pets:** Jemima (cat)

This friendly hotel enjoys pleasant views over Torbay in a quiet residential area of the town. Bedrooms vary in size but are generally spacious, comfortable and well appointed. Extensive leisure facilities are on offer including an outdoor and indoor pool, a gym and beauty treatment rooms.

Rooms 9 en suite (3 fmly) S £38-£56; D £56-£92 (incl. bkfst & dinner)* **Facilities** Gym Sun shower Beauty room Sauna Xmas New Year **Parking** 9 **Notes** LB

★★ 67% HOTEL

Shelley Court

29 Croft Rd TQ2 5UD

☎ 01803 295642 01803 215793

e-mail: shelleycourthotel@hotmail.com

Dir: *from B3199 up Shedden Hill Rd, 1st left into Croft Rd*

PETS: Bedrooms (6GF) unattended sign **Charges** £10-£15 per week charge for damage **Public areas** except dining room **Grounds** accessible disp bin **Exercise area** adjacent **Facilities** dog scoop/disp bags leads washing facs cage storage walks info vet info **On Request** fridge access torch towels **Resident Pets:** Jack (Parson Jack Russell)

This hotel, popular with groups, is located in a pleasant, quiet area that overlooks the town towards Torbay. With a friendly team of staff, many guests return here time and again. Entertainment is provided most evenings in the season. Bedrooms come in a range of sizes and there is a large and comfortable lounge bar.

Rooms 27 en suite (3 fmly) (6 GF) S £32-£49; D £32-£52.50* **Facilities** Xmas New Year **Parking** 20 **Notes** LB Closed 4 Jan-10 Feb

★★ 65% HOTEL

Bute Court

Belgrave Rd TQ2 5HQ

☎ 01803 213408 01803 213429

e-mail: stay@butecourt.co.uk

Dir: *A3022 into Torquay. Follow signs for seafront*

PETS: Bedrooms (13GF) **Charges** £8 per night charge for damage **Grounds** accessible on leads **Exercise area** park adjacent to garden **Facilities** walks info vet info **Restrictions** no large dogs including Alsatians & Great Danes **Resident Pets:** Sasha (Jack Russell)

This popular hotel is only a short, level walk from the seafront and resort attractions. It still retains many Victorian features, and the comfortable bedrooms offer modern facilities and many have far-reaching views. Public areas include a bar and lounges, while the attractive dining room looks across secluded gardens to the sea. Entertainment is also offered during busier periods.

Rooms 43 en suite (2 fmly) (13 GF) S £32-£49; D £64-£98 (incl. bkfst & dinner)* **Facilities** Xmas New Year **Services** Lift **Parking** 25 **Notes** LB

★★★★ GUEST HOUSE

Kingsholm

539 Babbacombe Rd TQ1 1HQ

☎ 01803 297794

e-mail: enquiries@kingsholmhotel.co.uk

Dir: *A3022 left onto Torquay seafront, left at clock tower rdbt, Kingsholm 400mtrs on left*

PETS: Bedrooms Charges £5 per night **Public areas** except dining room (on leads) **Grounds** accessible on leads **Exercise area** opposite **Facilities** walks info vet info **On Request** fridge access torch

Guests will no doubt enjoy the friendly and welcoming atmosphere created here by the resident proprietors. A range of well furnished and decorated bedrooms and bathrooms provide guests with plenty of comfort and quality. A relaxing guest lounge, small bar area and car park to the rear are all welcome features. Dinner featuring seasonal, home cooking is available by prior arrangement and should not be missed.

Rooms 9 en suite S £27-£35; D £54-£70* **Facilities** FTV TVB tea/coffee Licensed Cen ht Dinner Last d 12 noon **Parking** 4 **Notes** LB No children 10yrs No coaches

★★★ GUEST ACCOMMODATION

Stover Lodge

29 Newton Rd TQ2 5DB

☎ 01803 297287 01803 297287

e-mail: enquiries@stoverlodge.co.uk

web: www.stoverlodge.co.uk

Dir: *Signs to Torquay town centre, at station/Halfords left lane, Lodge on left after lights*

PETS: Bedrooms (2GF) **Grounds** accessible on leads **Exercise area** 100mtrs **Facilities** walks info vet info **On Request** fridge access torch towels **Restrictions** small dogs only

Located close to the town centre, the family-run Stover Lodge is relaxed and friendly. Children and babies are welcome, and a cot and high chair can be provided on request. Hearty breakfasts, with a vegetarian option, are served in the dining room. There is a garden to enjoy in summer

Rooms 9 rms (8 en suite) (1 pri facs) (3 fmly) (2 GF) S £25-£40; D £48-£56* **Facilities** FTV TVB tea/coffee Cen ht Wi-fi available **Parking** 10 **Notes** LB

★★★ GUEST HOUSE

Ashleigh House

61 Meadfoot Ln TQ1 2BP

☎ 01803 294660

e-mail: dawnsmale@btinternet.com

web: www.ashleighhousetorquay.co.uk

PETS: Bedrooms Charges £10 per week charge for damage **Public areas** (on leads) **Exercise area** on site **Facilities** bedding feeding mat dog scoop/disp bags leads pet sitting dog walking washing facs walks info vet info **On Request** fridge access torch towels **Restrictions** very large breeds or untrained puppies not accepted **Resident Pets:** Oscar (Springer Spaniel)

Quietly located in a residential area of Torquay, and only a five minute downhill walk from the town or harbour, this pleasant accommodation includes roadside permit parking. Relaxed and friendly hospitality is provided and guests are welcome to use the large, well furnished lounge. Bedrooms offer a range of shapes and sizes and include some useful extras. A carefully prepared breakfast is served in the bright, comfortable dining room.

Rooms 4 rms (3 en suite) (1 pri facs) (3 fmly) **Facilities** TVB tea/coffee Cen ht TVL Dinner Last d 11am **Notes**

TORQUAY CONTINUED

►►►► Widdicombe Farm Touring Park

(SX880650)

Marldon TQ3 1ST

☎ 01803 558325

e-mail: info@widdicombefarm.co.uk

web: www.widdicombefarm.co.uk

Dir: *On A380, midway between Torquay & Paignton ring road*

PETS: Public areas except in buildings **Charges** £1.50-£2.50 per night £10.50-£16 per week disp bin **Exercise area** on site small field **Facilities** on site shop food food bowl water bowl dog chews dog scoop/disp bags walks info vet info **Other** prior notice required dogs must be on short lead at all times **Restrictions** no Alsatians, Dobermans, Rottweilers, Bull Terriers or Ridgebacks **Resident Pets:** 2 Border Collies, 1 Jack Russell, cat

Open mid Mar-mid Oct Last arrival 20.00hrs Last departure 10.00hrs

A friendly family-run park on a working farm, with good quality facilities and extensive views. The level pitches are terraced to take advantage of the views towards the coast and Dartmoor. This is the only touring park within Torquay, and is also handy for Paignton and Brixham. A large children's play area, a well-stocked shop, a restaurant, and a lounge bar are among the amenities, and there's an adults-only field. An 8-acre site with 180 touring pitches, 180 hardstandings and 3 statics.

Notes Families & couples only, 1 family field, 3 adults only fields

TWO BRIDGES MAP 02 SX67

★★★ 77% ✿ HOTEL

Two Bridges Hotel

PL20 6SW

☎ 01822 890581 🖷 01822 892306

e-mail: enquiries@twobridges.co.uk

web: www.twobridges.co.uk

Dir: *junct of B3212 & B3357*

PETS: Bedrooms (6GF) unattended **Public areas** except restaurant (on leads) **Grounds** accessible on leads disp bin **Exercise area** on dartmoor **Facilities** water bowl dog chews washing facs cage storage walks info vet info **On Request** fridge access torch towels

This wonderfully relaxing hotel is set in the heart of the Dartmoor National Park, in a beautiful riverside location. Three standards of comfortable rooms provide every modern convenience, and include four-poster rooms. There is a choice of lounges and fine dining is available in the restaurant, where menus feature local game and seasonal produce.

Rooms 33 en suite (2 fmly) (6 GF) S fr £70; D fr £140 (incl. bkfst)* **Facilities** STV Fishing Xmas New Year **Parking** 100 **Notes** LB

★★ 85% ✿ COUNTRY HOUSE HOTEL

Prince Hall

PL20 6SA

☎ 01822 890403 🖷 01822 890676

e-mail: info@princehall.co.uk

Dir: *on B3357 1m E of Two Bridges road junct*

PETS: Bedrooms unattended **Stables** nearby (5m) **Public areas** except restaurant **Grounds** accessible disp bin **Exercise area** adjacent **Facilities** food (pre-bookable) water bowl dog chews dog scoop/disp bags leads washing facs walks info vet info **On Request** fridge access torch towels **Resident Pets:** Lily (Retriever Collie cross), Poppy (Retriever)

Charm, peace and relaxed informality pervade at this small hotel, which has a stunning location at the heart of Dartmoor. Bedrooms, each named after a Dartmoor tor, have been equipped with thoughtful extras. The history of this house and its location are reflected throughout the public areas, which are very comfortable. The accomplished cooking is memorable. Dogs are welcomed here as warmly as their owners.

Rooms 9 en suite (1 fmly) D £140-£160 (incl. bkfst)* **Facilities** Fishing Wi-fi available Xmas New Year **Parking** 12 **Notes LB** Closed 3-24 Jan

UMBERLEIGH MAP 03 SS62

►►► Umberleigh Camping & Caravanning Club Site *(SS604241)*

Over Weir EX37 9DU

☎ 01769 560009

web: www.thefriendlyclub.co.uk

Dir: *On A377 from Barnstaple turn right at Umberleigh sign onto B3227. Site on right in 0.25m*

PETS: Public areas except in buildings disp bin **Exercise area** on site **Facilities** walks info vet info **Other** prior notice required

Open 2 Apr-2 Nov Last arrival 21.00hrs Last departure noon

There are fine country views from this compact site set on high ground. The site has the advantage of a games room with table tennis and skittle alley, and two quality tennis courts, with an adjacent wooded area for walks, and a nearby fishing pond. A 3-acre site with 60 touring pitches, 12 hardstandings.

Notes Site gates closed 23.00hrs-07.00hrs

WESTWARD HO! MAP 02 SS42

★★★ GUEST HOUSE

Culloden House

Fosketh Hill EX39 1UL

☎ 01237 479421

e-mail: enquiry@culloden-house.co.uk

web: www.culloden-house.co.uk

Dir: *S of town centre. Off B3236 Stanwell Hill onto Fosketh Hill*

PETS: Bedrooms (1GF) unattended **Public areas** except dining room **Grounds** accessible disp bin **Exercise area** short walk **Facilities** food bowl water bowl pet sitting washing facs cage storage walks info vet info **On Request** fridge access towels **Other** pets allowed unattended in bedrooms by arrrangement only

A warm welcome is assured in this family-friendly Victorian property stands on a wooded hillside with sweeping views over the beach and coast. Guests can relax in the spacious lounge with its log-burning fire and enjoy the wonderful sea views.

Rooms 5 en suite (3 fmly) (1 GF) **Facilities** TVB tea/coffee Cen ht TVL **Parking** available **Notes** No coaches Closed Xmas

WITHERIDGE MAP 03 SS81

►►► West Middlewick Farm Caravan & Camping Site *(SS826136)*

Nomansland EX16 8NP

☎ 01884 861235

e-mail: stay@westmiddlewick.co.uk

web: www.westmiddlewick.co.uk

Dir: *From M5 junct 27, A361 to Tiverton. Then B3137, follow Witheridge signs. Site 1m past Nomansland on right (8m from Tiverton)*

PETS: Stables nearby (loose box) **Charges** 50p per dog per night **Public areas** (on leads) disp bin **Exercise area** on site farm walks **Facilities** washing facs walks info vet info

Resident Pets: 6 cats

Open all year Last arrival 22.00hrs Last departure noon

A working dairy farm on a ridge west of the hamlet of Nomansland, with extensive rural views. This upgraded park offers campers a quiet and relaxing break, and is approximately one mile from the attractive and charming village of Witheridge which has a variety of amenities. A 3.5-acre site with 25 touring pitches, 16 hardstandings.

Notes ⊜ Children must be supervised

YELVERTON MAP 02 SX56

★★★ 74% ⊛ HOTEL

Moorland Links

PL20 6DA

☎ 01822 852245 📠 01822 855004

e-mail: moorland.links@forestdale.com

web: www.forestdale.com

Dir: *A38 from Exeter to Plymouth, then A386 towards Tavistock. 5m onto open moorland, hotel 1m on left*

PETS: Bedrooms unattended sign **Charges** £7.50 per night **Public areas** except restaurant **Grounds** accessible **Exercise area**

Set in nine acres in the Dartmoor National Park, this hotel offers spectacular views from many of the rooms across open moorland and the Tamar Valley. Bedrooms are well equipped and comfortably furnished, and some rooms have open balconies. The stylish restaurant looks out over the oak fringed lawns.

Rooms 44 en suite (4 fmly) (17 GF) S £80-£89; D £109-£125 (incl. bkfst) ✳ **Facilities** ♨ Wi-fi available Xmas New Year **Parking** 120 **Notes LB**

DORSET

ALDERHOLT MAP 04 SU11

►►►► Hill Cottage Farm Camping and Caravan Park *(SU119133)*

Sandleheath Rd SP6 3EG

☎ 01425 650513 📠 01425 652339

e-mail: hillcottagefarmcaravansite@supanet.com

web: hillcottagefarmcampingandcaravanpark.co.uk

Dir: *Take B3078 W of Fordingbridge. Turn off at Alderholt, site 0.25m on left after railway bridge*

PETS: Stables on site (loose box) **Charges** £1 per dog per night disp bin **Exercise area** on site dog walks (except farm fields) **Facilities** on site shop washing facs dog grooming walks info vet info **Other** prior notice required pet shop 0.25m

Open Mar-Oct Last arrival 19.00hrs Last departure 11.00hrs

Set within extensive grounds this rural, beautifully landscaped park offers all fully-serviced pitches set in individual hardstanding bays with mature hedges between giving adequate pitch privacy. A modern toilet block is kept immaculately clean, and there's a good range of leisure facilities. In high season there is an area available for tenting. A 40-acre site with 35 touring pitches, 35 hardstandings.

BEAMINSTER MAP 03 ST40

★★★ 78% HOTEL

BridgeHouse

3 Prout Bridge DT8 3AY

☎ 01308 862200 01308 863700

e-mail: enquiries@bridge-house.co.uk

web: www.bridge-house.co.uk

Dir: *off A3066, 100yds from town square*

PETS: Bedrooms (5GF) **Charges** £15 per stay per week **Grounds** accessible **Exercise area** country walks nearby **Facilities** food

Dating back to the 13th century, this property offers friendly and attentive service. Bedrooms are tastefully furnished and decorated; those in the main house are generally more spacious than those in the adjacent coach house. Smartly presented public areas include the Georgian dining room, cosy bar and adjacent lounge, together with a breakfast room overlooking the attractive garden.

Rooms 9 en suite 5 annexe en suite (1 fmly) (5 GF) S £76-£108; D £116-£200 (incl. bkfst)✳ **Facilities** Wi-fi in bedrooms Xmas New Year **Parking** 20 **Notes LB**

BLANDFORD FORUM MAP 03 ST80

★★★★ INN

The Anvil Inn

Salisbury Rd, Pimperne DT11 8UQ

☎ 01258 453431 01258 480182

e-mail: theanvil.inn@btconnect.com

Dir: *2m NE of Blandford on A354 in Pimperne*

PETS: Bedrooms unattended **Charges** £10 per night **Public areas** only in bar (on leads) **Grounds** accessible on leads **Exercise area Facilities** water bowl dog chews walks info vet info **On Request** fridge access torch towels

Located in a village near Blandford, this 16th-century thatched inn provides a traditional country welcome with plenty of character. Bedrooms have been refurbished to high standards. Dinner is a varied selection of home-made dishes with a tempting variety of hand-pulled ales and wines by the glass.

Rooms 12 en suite S £75-£80; D £100-£130✳ **Facilities** STV TVB tea/coffee Direct dial from bedrooms Cen ht Dinner Last d 9.30pm **Parking** 18 **Notes LB** No coaches

★★★★ BED & BREAKFAST

St Martin's House

Whitecliff Mill St DT11 7BP

☎ 01258 451245 & 07748 887719

e-mail: info@stmartinshouse.co.uk

Dir: *Off Market Pl onto Salisbury St & left onto White Cliff Mill St, on right before traffic island*

PETS: Bedrooms Charges £5 per night charge for damage **Exercise area** 0.25m **Facilities** food bowl water bowl walks info vet info **On Request** torch towels

Dating from 1866, this restored property was once part of the chorister's house for a local church. The bedrooms are comfortable and well equipped. The hosts offer warm hospitality and attentive service. Breakfast, which features local and home-made items, is enjoyed around a communal table. Carefully prepared dinners are available by arrangement.

Rooms 2 rms (2 pri facs) (1 fmly) S £45-£50; D £65-£70✳ **Facilities** TVB tea/coffee Cen ht Dinner Last d 24hrs before Wi-fi available **Parking** 3 **Notes** Closed 22 Dec-6 Jan

►►►► The Inside Park *(ST869046)*

Down House Estate DT11 9AD

☎ 01258 453719 01258 459921

e-mail: inspark@aol.com

web: www.members.aol.com/inspark/inspark

Dir: *From town, over River Stour, follow Winterborne Stickland signs. Site in 1.5m*

PETS: Sep Accom day kennels **Public areas** except dog-free areas **Charges** 60p-£1 per night disp bin **Exercise area** on site private woods & farm walks 6m **Facilities** on site shop food food bowl water bowl walks info vet info **Other** prior notice required

Open Etr-Oct Last arrival 22.00hrs Last departure noon

An attractive, well-sheltered and quiet park, 0.5m off a country lane in a wooded valley. Spacious pitches are divided by mature trees and shrubs, and amenities are housed in an 18th-century coach house and stables. There are some lovely woodland walks within the park.
A 12-acre site with 125 touring pitches.

BOURNEMOUTH MAP 04 SZ09

★★★ 80% HOTEL

Langtry Manor - Lovenest of a King

Derby Rd, East Cliff BH1 3QB

☎ 01202 553887 01202 290115

e-mail: lillie@langtrymanor.com

web: www.langtrymanor.co.uk

Dir: *A31/A338, 1st rdbt by rail station turn left. Over next rdbt, 1st left into Knyveton Rd. Hotel opposite*

PETS: Bedrooms (3GF) **Charges** charge for damage **Grounds** accessible disp bin **Exercise area** beach & gardens 5 mins **Facilities** washing facs dog grooming cage storage walks info vet info **On Request** fridge access torch towels **Resident Pets:** Tyson (Boxer)

Retaining a stately air, this property was originally built in 1877 by Edward VII for his mistress Lillie Langtry. The individually furnished and decorated bedrooms include several with four-poster beds. Enjoyable cuisine is served in the magnificent dining hall, complete with several large Tudor tapestries. There is an Edwardian banquet on Saturday evenings.

Rooms 12 en suite 8 annexe en suite (2 fmly) (3 GF) **Facilities** Free use of local health club ♫ **Parking** 30

★★★ 75% HOTEL

Carrington House

31 Knyveton Rd BH1 3QQ

☎ 01202 369988 01202 292221

e-mail: carrington.house@forestdale.com

web: www.forestdale.com

Dir: *A338 at St Paul's rdbt, 200mtrs & left into Knyveton Rd. Hotel 400mtrs on right*

PETS: Bedrooms unattended **Charges** £7.50 per night **Public areas** except restaurant **Exercise area** **Facilities** food (pre-bookable)

This hotel occupies a prominent position on a tree-lined avenue and a short walk from the seafront. The bedrooms are comfortable, well equipped and include many purpose-built family rooms. There are two dining options, Mortimers restaurant, and the Kings bar which serves light meals and snacks. Guests can relax in the comfortable lounge areas whilst the leisure complex offers a whole host of activities including a heated swimming pool.

Rooms 145 en suite (42 fmly) S £73-£77; D £104-£125 (incl. bkfst)* **Facilities** Wi-fi in bedrooms Children's play area Xmas New Year **Services** Lift **Parking** 85 **Notes** LB

★★★ 75% HOTEL

Wessex

West Cliff Rd BH2 5EU

☎ 01202 551911 01202 297354

e-mail: wessex@forestdale.com

web: www.forestdale.com

Dir: *Follow M27/A35 or A338 from Dorchester & A347 N. Hotel on West Cliff side of town*

PETS: Bedrooms unattended **Charges** £7.50 per night **Public areas** except restaurant **Grounds** accessible **Exercise area** **Facilities** food (pre-bookable) feeding mat

Centrally located and handy for the beach, the Wessex is a popular, relaxing hotel. Bedrooms are well equipped and comfortable with a range of modern amenities. The Lulworth restaurant provides a range of appetizing dishes. The excellent leisure facilities boast both indoor and outdoor pools, sauna, ample function rooms and an open-plan bar and lounge.

Rooms 109 en suite (32 fmly) (17 GF) S £75-£85; D £115-£130 (incl. bkfst)* **Facilities** Gym Wi-fi in bedrooms Table tennis Xmas New Year **Services** Lift **Parking** 160 **Notes** LB

★★★ 74% HOTEL

Suncliff

29 East Overcliff Dr BH1 3AG

☎ 01202 291711 01202 293788

e-mail: info@suncliffbournemouth.co.uk

Dir: *A338/A35 towards East Cliff & beaches, right into Holdenhurst Rd, straight over 2 rdbts, left at junct into East Overcliff Drive*

PETS: Bedrooms (14GF) unattended sign **Charges** £10 per night charge for damage **Exercise area** 0.5m **Facilities** walks info vet info **On Request** torch towels **Restrictions** small and medium dogs only

Enjoying splendid views from the East Cliff and catering mainly for leisure guests, this friendly hotel offers a range of facilities and services. Bedrooms are well equipped and comfortable, and many have sea views. Public areas include a large conservatory, an attractive bar and pleasant lounges.

Rooms 97 en suite (29 fmly) (14 GF) S £59-£99; D £118-£198 (incl. bkfst) * **Facilities** Squash Wi-fi available Use of outdoor pool at sister hotel ♫ Xmas New Year **Services** Lift **Parking** 62 **Notes** LB

ENGLAND

BOURNEMOUTH CONTINUED

★★★ 73% HOTEL

Cliffeside

East Overcliff Dr BH1 3AQ

☎ 01202 555724 01202 314534

e-mail: info@cliffesidebournemouth.co.uk

Dir: *Off A35/A338 to East Cliff & beaches, right into Holdenhurst Rd, over next 2 rdbts, at junct left into East Overcliff Drive, hotel on left*

PETS: Bedrooms unattended **Charges** £10 per night **Grounds** accessible on leads **Exercise area** **On Request** fridge access towels

Benefiting from an elevated position on the seafront and just a short walk to town, it's no wonder that this friendly hotel has many returning guests. Bedrooms and public areas are attractively appointed, many with sea views. The Atlantic Restaurant offers guests a fixed-price menu.

Rooms 62 en suite (5 fmly) (2 GF) S £59-£89; D £118-£178 (incl. bkfst) ✳ **Facilities** Squash Wi-fi in bedrooms Use of pool at sister hotel Xmas New Year **Services** Lift **Parking** 32 **Notes** LB

★★★ 73% HOTEL

The Riviera

Burnaby Rd, Alum Chine BH4 8JF

☎ 01202 763653 01202 768422

e-mail: info@rivierabournemouth.co.uk

web: www.rivierabournemouth.co.uk

Dir: *A338, follow signs to Alum Chine*

PETS: Bedrooms (11GF) **Charges** £7.50 per night £52.50 per week charge for damage **Public areas** except restaurant (on leads) **Exercise area** 5 mins walk **Facilities** vet info

The Riviera offers a range of comfortable, well-furnished bedrooms and bathrooms. Welcoming staff provide efficient service delivered in a friendly manner. In addition to a spacious lounge with regular entertainment, there is an indoor and an outdoor pool, and all just a short walk from the beach.

Rooms 69 en suite 4 annexe en suite (25 fmly) (11 GF) S £35-£75; D £70-£150 (incl. bkfst)✳ **Facilities** Wi-fi available Games room Sauna Xmas New Year **Services** Lift **Parking** 45 **Notes** LB

★★★ 70% HOTEL

Hotel Collingwood

11 Priory Rd, West Cliff BH2 5DF

☎ 01202 557575 01202 293219

e-mail: info@hotel-collingwood.co.uk

web: www.hotel-collingwood.co.uk

Dir: *A338 left at West Cliff sign, over 1st rdbt and left at 2nd rdbt. Hotel 500yds on left*

PETS: Bedrooms (6GF) unattended **Charges** £4 per night £28 per week charge for damage **Exercise area** park & beach 5 mins **Facilities** cage storage walks info vet info **On Request** fridge access towels

This privately owned and managed hotel is situated close to the BIC. Bedrooms are airy, with the emphasis on comfort. An excellent range of leisure facilities is available and the public areas are spacious and welcoming. Pinks Restaurant offers carefully prepared cuisine and a fixed-price, five-course dinner.

Rooms 53 en suite (16 fmly) (6 GF) **Facilities** FTV Gym Steam room Sauna Games room Snooker room **Services** Lift **Parking** 55

★★★ 64% HOTEL

Burley Court

Bath Rd BH1 2NP

☎ 01202 552824 & 556704 01202 298514

e-mail: info@burleycourthotel.co.uk

Dir: *leave A338 at St Paul's rdbt, take 3rd exit at next rdbt into Holdenhurst Rd. 3rd exit at next rdbt into Bath Rd, over crossing, 1st left*

PETS: Bedrooms (4GF) unattended **Charges** £10 per night charge for damage **Exercise area** **Facilities** food (pre-bookable) walks info vet info **On Request** fridge access torch

Located on Bournemouth's West Cliff, this well-established hotel is easily located and convenient for the town and beaches. Bedrooms are pleasantly furnished and decorated in bright colours. A daily-changing menu is served in the spacious dining room.

Rooms 38 en suite (8 fmly) (4 GF) **Facilities** **Services** Lift **Parking** 35 **Notes** Closed 30 Dec-14 Jan RS 15-31 Jan

★★ 78% HOTEL

The Whitehall

Exeter Park Rd BH2 5AX

☎ 01202 554682 📠 01202 292637

e-mail: reservations@thewhitehallhotel.co.uk

web: www.thewhitehallhotel.co.uk

Dir: *follow BIC signs then turn into Exeter Park Rd off Exeter Rd*

PETS: Bedrooms (3GF) unattended **Charges** £2 per night **Grounds** accessible **Exercise area** green 50mtrs

This friendly hotel enjoys an elevated position overlooking the park and is also close to the town centre and seafront. The spacious public areas include a choice of lounges, a cosy bar and a well-presented restaurant. The well-equipped and inviting bedrooms are spread over three floors.

Rooms 46 en suite (5 fmly) (3 GF) **Facilities** ♫ **Services** Lift **Parking** 25 **Notes** LB

★★ 68% HOTEL

Ullswater

West Cliff Gardens BH2 5HW

☎ 01202 555181 📠 01202 317896

e-mail: enquiries@ullswater-hotel.co.uk

web: www.ullswater-hotel.co.uk

Dir: *In Bournemouth follow signs to West Cliff. Hotel just off Westcliff Rd*

PETS: Bedrooms (2GF) unattended **Charges** £4.50 per night charge for damage **Exercise area Facilities** dog walking cage storage walks info vet info **On Request** fridge access

A welcoming family run hotel conveniently located for the city and the seafront. This popular establishment attracts a loyal following. The well-equipped bedrooms vary in size, and the charming lounge bar and dining room are very smart. Cuisine is hearty and homemade, offering a good choice from the daily-changing menu.

Rooms 42 en suite (8 fmly) (2 GF) S £43-£52; D £76-£88 (incl. bkfst) **Facilities** Wi-fi available Snooker room ♫ Xmas New Year **Services** Lift **Parking** 12 **Notes** LB

★★★★ GUEST ACCOMMODATION

Wood Lodge

10 Manor Rd, East Cliff BH1 3EY

☎ 01202 290891 📠 01202 290892

e-mail: enquiries@woodlodgehotel.co.uk

web: www.woodlodgehotel.co.uk

Dir: *A338 to St Pauls rdbt, 1st exit left. Straight over next 2 rdbts, immediate left*

PETS: Bedrooms (4GF) unattended **Charges** £5 per night charge for damage **Public areas** only allowed in halls for access to bedrooms (on leads) **Grounds** accessible on leads **Exercise area** many walks nearby **Facilities** walks info vet info **On Request** fridge access torch towels **Restrictions** small dogs only **Resident Pets:** Lucy (West Highland Terrier)

Expect a warm welcome from this family-run guest house. Set in beautiful gardens minutes from the seafront and a 10 minute walk from the town centre. Bedrooms, which vary in size, are well presented. Home-cooked evening meals and hearty breakfasts are served in the smart dining room.

Rooms 15 rms (14 en suite) (1 pri facs) (1 fmly) (4 GF) S £34-£55; D £68-£110 **Facilities** TVB tea/coffee Cen ht TVL Dinner Last d 1pm Wi-fi available Use of pools, jacuzzi and sauna at nearby hotel **Parking** 12 **Notes** LB

BRIDPORT MAP 03 SY49

★★ 75% HOTEL

Bridge House

THE INDEPENDENTS HOTEL ASSOCIATION

115 East St DT6 3LB

☎ 01308 423371 📠 01308 459573

e-mail: info@bridgehousebridport.co.uk

Dir: *follow signs to town centre from A35 rdbt, hotel 200mtrs on right*

PETS: Bedrooms unattended **Charges** charge for damage **Public areas** except restaurant, must be well behaved (on leads) **Grounds** accessible disp bin **Exercise area** park adjacent **Facilities** walks info vet info **On Request** fridge access

A short stroll from the town centre, this 18th-century Grade II listed property offers well-equipped bedrooms that vary in size. In addition to the main lounge, there is a small bar-lounge and a separate breakfast room. An interesting range of home-cooked meals is provided in the restaurant.

Rooms 10 en suite (3 fmly) S £65-£89; D £89-£134 (incl. bkfst) **Facilities** Wi-fi in bedrooms Complimentary membership to leisure park New Year **Parking** 13 **Notes** LB

ENGLAND

BRIDPORT CONTINUED

★★★★ INN

The Shave Cross Inn

Marshwood Vale DT6 6HW

☎ 01308 868358 📠 01308 867064

e-mail: roy.warburton@virgin.net

web: www.theshavecrossinn.co.uk

Dir: *From B3165 turn at Birdsmoorgate and follow brown signs.*

PETS: Bedrooms (3GF) unattended **Public areas** allowed in bar but not restaurant (on leads) **Grounds** accessible on leads disp bin **Exercise area** walks adjacent **Facilities** washing facs cage storage walks info vet info **On Request** torch towels

A newly-built property in the grounds of an historic inn. Rooms are extremely well appointed and equipped, staff are very friendly, and dinner with a Trinidadian theme is available in the restaurant.

Rooms 7 en suite (1 fmly) (3 GF) **Facilities** STV FTV TVB tea/coffee Direct dial from bedrooms Cen ht Dinner Last d 9pm Wi-fi available Pool Table **Parking** 29 **Notes** No children No coaches RS Mon (ex BH)

★★★★ GUEST ACCOMMODATION

Britmead House

West Bay Rd DT6 4EG

☎ 01308 422941 & 07973 725243

e-mail: britmead@talk21.com

web: www.britmeadhouse.co.uk

Dir: *1m S of town centre, off A35 onto West Bay Rd*

PETS: Bedrooms Public areas except dining room (on leads) **Grounds** accessible on leads **Exercise area** 100mtrs **Facilities** washing facs cage storage walks info vet info **On Request** fridge access towels

Britmead House is located south of Bridport, within easy reach of the town centre and West Bay harbour. Family-run, the atmosphere is friendly and the accommodation well-appointed and comfortable. Suitable for business and leisure, many guests return regularly. A choice of breakfast is served in the light and airy dining room.

Rooms 8 en suite (2 fmly) (2 GF) **Facilities** TVB tea/coffee Cen ht TVL **Parking** 12 **Notes** Closed 24-27 Dec

CERNE ABBAS MAP 03 ST60

►►► ***Lyons Gate Caravan and Camping Park*** *(ST660062)*

Lyons Gate DT2 7AZ

☎ 01300 345260

e-mail: info@lyons-gate.co.uk

web: www.lyons-gate.co.uk

Dir: *Signed with direct access from A352, 3m N of Cerne Abbas*

PETS: Charges 50p per night disp bin **Exercise area** on site bridle path **Facilities** on site shop walks info vet info **Other** prior notice required

Open all year Last arrival 20.00hrs Last departure 11.30hrs

A peaceful park with pitches set out around the four attractive coarse fishing lakes. It is surrounded by mature woodland, with many footpaths and bridleways. Other easily accessible attractions include the Cerne Giant carved into the hills, the old market town of Dorchester, and the superb sandy beach at Weymouth. A 10-acre site with 90 touring pitches, 14 hardstandings.

Notes ⊜

►► **Giant's Head Caravan & Camping Park** *(ST675029)*

Giants Head Farm, Old Sherborne Rd DT2 7TR

☎ 01300 341242

e-mail: holidays@giantshead.co.uk

web: www.giantshead.co.uk

Dir: *From Dorchester into town avoiding by-pass, at Top O'Town rdbt take A352 (Sherborne road), in 500yds right fork at Esso (Loder's) garage, site signed*

PETS: Public areas except dog-free areas **Charges** £1 per night disp bin **Exercise area** on site **Facilities** vet info **Other** prior notice required

Open Etr-Oct (rs Etr shop & bar closed) Last arrival anytime Last departure 13.00hrs

A pleasant though rather basic park set in Dorset downland near the Cerne Giant (the local landmark figure cut into the chalk) with stunning views. A good stopover site, ideal for tenters and backpackers on the Ridgeway route. A 4-acre site with 50 touring pitches.

Notes ⊜

CHARMOUTH MAP 03 SY39

►►►►► Wood Farm Caravan & Camping Park *(SY356940)*

Axminster Rd DT6 6BT

☎ 01297 560697 📄 01297 561243

e-mail: holidays@woodfarm.co.uk

web: www.woodfarm.co.uk

Dir: *Site entered directly off A35 rdbt, on Axminster side of Charmouth*

PETS: Stables nearby (4m) **Charges** £2 per night **Public areas** except buildings & play area (on leads) disp bin **Exercise area** on site 2 acre dog walk **Facilities** on site shop food food bowl water bowl walks info vet info **Resident Pets:** dog, cats, sheep, chickens

Open Etr-Oct Last arrival 19.00hrs Last departure noon

A pleasant, well-established and mature park overlooking Charmouth, the sea and the Dorset hills and valleys. It stands on a high spot, and the four camping fields are terraced, each with its own impressive toilet block. Convenient for Lyme Regis, Axminster, and the famous fossil coastline. A 13-acre site with 216 touring pitches, 175 hardstandings and 81 statics.

Notes No skateboards, scooters or roller skates

►►►► Charmouth Camping & Caravanning Club Site *(SY330965)*

Monkton Wylde Farm DT6 6DB

☎ 01297 32965

web: www.thefriendlyclub.co.uk

Dir: *From Dorchester on A35 turn right onto B3165 signed Hawkchurch, site on left in 0.25m*

PETS: Public areas except in buildings disp bin **Exercise area** on site Charmouth & Lyme Regis beaches **Facilities** walks info vet info **Other** prior notice required

Open 2 Apr-2 Nov Last arrival 21.00hrs Last departure noon

Located in a rural setting almost on the Devon/Dorset border, this attractively terraced park with high quality toilet facilities is ideally placed for visiting the resorts of Charmouth, Lyme Regis and the Jurassic Coast. Friendly managers keep the whole park in tiptop condition. A 12-acre site with 150 touring pitches, 34 hardstandings.

Notes Site gates closed 23.00hrs-07.00hrs

►►►► Monkton Wyld Farm Caravan Park *(SY336964)*

Scotts Ln DT6 6DB

☎ 01297 631131

e-mail: holidays@monktonwyld.co.uk

web: www.monktonwyld.co.uk

Dir: *From Charmouth on A35 towards Axminster, after approx 3m (ignore 1st sign to Monkton Wyld - road very steep) take next right signed Marshwood. Site 500mtrs on left*

PETS: Stables on site (loose box) disp bin **Exercise area** on site dog walk **Facilities** on site shop washing facs walks info vet info **Restrictions** no dangerous dogs (see page 7)

Open Etr-mid Nov Last arrival 22.00hrs Last departure 11.00hrs

An attractive family park in a secluded location yet central for Charmouth, Lyme and the coast. It has been tastefully designed in a maturing landscape, with perimeter trees providing a screen, and every pitch backed by hedges or shrubs. A 20-acre site with 150 touring pitches, 90 hardstandings and 16 statics.

►►► Manor Farm Holiday Centre *(SY368937)*

DT6 6QL

☎ 01297 560226

e-mail: enq@manorfarmholidaycentre.co.uk

web: www.manorfarmholidaycentre.co.uk

Dir: *W on A35 to Charmouth, site 0.75m on right*

PETS: Public areas except swimming pool, shop, bar & restaurant **Charges** £1-£3 per night disp bin **Exercise area** on site Open field available **Facilities** on site shop food vet info **Other** prior notice required

Open all year (rs End Oct-mid Mar statics only) Last arrival 20.00hrs Last departure 10.00hrs

Set just a short walk from the safe sand and shingle beach at Charmouth, this popular family park offers a good range of facilities. Children enjoy the activity area and outdoor swimming pool (so do their parents!), and the park also offers a lively programme in the extensive bar and entertainment complex. A 28-acre site with 400 touring pitches, 80 hardstandings and 29 statics.

Notes No skateboards

CHRISTCHURCH MAP 04 SZ19

★★★★ 80% 🏵🏵 HOTEL

Captain's Club

Wick Ferry, Wick Ln BH23 1HU

☎ 01202 475111 📠 01202 490111

e-mail: enquiries@thecaptainsclub.com

Dir: *B3073 to Christchurch. On Fountain rdbt take 5th exit (Sopers Ln) 2nd left (St Margarets Ave) 1st right onto Wick Ln*

PETS: Bedrooms sign **Charges** £20 per night **Exercise area** 1 min walk **Facilities** food (pre-bookable) food bowl water bowl bedding dog chews dog scoop/disp bags pet sitting dog walking dog grooming walks info vet info **On Request** fridge access torch towels **Restrictions** small-medium dogs only

Situated in the heart of the town on the banks of the River Stour at Christchurch Quay, and only ten minutes from Bournemouth. All bedrooms, including the suites and apartments have views overlooking the river. Guests can relax in the hydrotherapy pool, enjoy a spa treatment or enjoy the cuisine in Tides Restaurant.

Rooms 29 en suite (12 fmly) S £119-£149; D £129-£169* **Facilities** Spa FTV Wi-fi in bedrooms Hydro-therapy pool Sauna ♫ Xmas New Year **Services** Lift air con **Parking** 41 **Notes** LB

CORFE CASTLE MAP 03 SY98

►►► Corfe Castle Camping & Caravanning Club Site *(SY953818)*

Bucknowle BH20 5PQ

☎ 01929 480280

web: www.thefriendlyclub.co.uk

Dir: *From Wareham A351 towards Swanage. In 4m turn right at foot of Corfe Castle signed Church Knowle. 0.75m right to site*

PETS: Exercise area Facilities washing facs walks info vet info **Other** prior notice required

Open Mar-Oct Last arrival 20.00hrs Last departure noon

A quiet family park set in a clearing within a wooded area, with touring pitches spread around the perimeter in secluded areas. The central grass area is kept free as a play space, and there are many walks from the park. A toilet and amenities block provides very good facilities. A 5-acre site with 80 touring pitches.

Notes Site gates closed between 23.00hrs-07.00hrs

DORCHESTER MAP 03 SY69

🏵🏵 U

Yalbury Cottage & Restaurant

Lower Bockhampton DT2 8PZ

☎ 01305 262382

e-mail: yalburyemails@aol.com

Dir: *Off A35 past Thomas Hardys cottage, over x-rds, 400yds on left, past telephone box, opp village pump*

PETS: Bedrooms (6GF) unattended **Stables** nearby **Charges** £6 per night **Public areas** except restaurant (on leads) **Grounds** accessible **Exercise area** open countryside **Facilities** cage storage walks info vet info **On Request** torch towels

At the time of going to press the rating for this establishment was not confirmed. This may be due to a change of ownership or because it has only recently joined the AA rating scheme. For further details please see the AA website: www.theAA.com

Rooms 8 en suite (1 fmly) (6 GF) **Facilities** TVB tea/coffee Direct dial from bedrooms Cen ht Dinner Last d 9pm **Parking** 16

ENGLAND

EVERSHOT MAP 03 ST50

★★★★ ⊛⊛⊛ COUNTRY HOUSE HOTEL

Summer Lodge Country House Hotel, Restaurant & Spa

DT2 0JR

☎ 01935 482000 🖹 01935 482040

e-mail: summer@relaischateaux.com

Dir: *1m W of A37 halfway between Dorchester & Yeovil*

PETS: Bedrooms (2GF) unattended sign **Stables** nearby (5m) **Charges** £20 per night £140 per week charge for damage **Public areas** except restaurant & drawing room **Grounds** accessible disp bin **Exercise area** 20yds **Facilities** food (pre-bookable) food bowl water bowl bedding dog chews feeding mat dog scoop/disp bags leads pet sitting dog walking washing facs dog grooming cage storage walks info vet info **On Request** fridge access torch towels **Resident Pets:** William (cat)

This picturesque hotel is situated in the heart of Dorset and is the ideal retreat for getting away from it all. It's worth arriving in time for afternoon tea. Bedrooms are appointed to a very high standard; they are individually designed with upholstered walls and come with a wealth of luxurious facilities. Delightful public areas include a sumptuous lounge complete with an open fire and the elegant restaurant where the cuisine continues to be the high point of any stay.

Rooms 10 en suite 14 annexe en suite (6 fmly) (2 GF) S £195-£515; D £225-£515 (incl. bkfst)✱ **Facilities Spa** STV FTV Ⓢ Gym Wi-fi in bedrooms Xmas New Year **Services** air con **Parking** 41 **Notes LB**

★★★★ ⊛ INN

The Acorn Inn

DT2 0JW

☎ 01935 83228 🖹 01935 83707

e-mail: stay@acorn-inn.co.uk

web: www.acorn-inn.co.uk

Dir: *0.5m off A37 between Yeovil and Dorchester, signed Evershot, Holywell*

PETS: Bedrooms Charges £10 per night charge for damage **Public areas** except restaurant (on leads) **Grounds** accessible on leads **Exercise area Facilities** water bowl walks info vet info **On Request** torch

This delightful 16th-century coaching inn is located at the heart of the village. Several of the bedrooms feature interesting four-poster beds, and all have been individually decorated and furnished. Public rooms retain many original features including oak panelling, open fires and stone-flagged floors. Fresh local produce is included on the varied menu.

Rooms 10 en suite (2 fmly) **Facilities** STV TVB tea/coffee Direct dial from bedrooms Cen ht TVL Dinner Last d 9pm Pool Table **Parking** 40

HOLTON HEATH MAP 03 SY99

Sandford Holiday Park *(SY939916)*

Organford Rd BH16 6JZ

☎ 01202 622513 🖹 01202 625678

e-mail: bookings@weststarholidays.co.uk

web: www.parkdeantouring.co.uk

Dir: *A35 from Poole towards Dorchester, at lights onto A351 towards Wareham. Right at Holton Heath. Site 100yds on left*

PETS: Public areas except in buildings **Charges** £5 per night £30 per week disp bin **Exercise area** on site large walking area **Facilities** on site shop food walks info vet info **Other** prior notice required **Restrictions** no dangerous dogs (see page 7)

Open Mar-Nov Last arrival 22.00hrs Last departure 10.00hrs

With touring pitches set individually in 20 acres surrounded by woodland, this park offers a full range of leisure activities and entertainment for the whole family. The touring area is neat and well maintained, and there are children's clubs in the daytime and nightly entertainment. A reception area with lounge, bar, café and restaurant creates an excellent and attractive entrance, with a covered area outside with tables and chairs and well landscaped gardens. A 64-acre site with 343 touring pitches and 344 statics.

Notes No unaccompanied minors

HORTON MAP 04 SU00

►►► Meadow View Caravan Park *(SU045070)*

Wigbeth BH21 7JH

☎ 01258 840040 🖹 01258 840040

e-mail: mail@meadowviewcaravanpark.co.uk

web: www.meadowviewcaravanpark.co.uk

Dir: *Follow unclass road from Horton to site, 0.5m from Druscilla pub*

PETS: Charges £1 per night **Exercise area** on site 2-acre paddock **Other** one dog per unit; dogs must be on leads

Open all year Last arrival 20.00hrs Last departure 11.00hrs

A small family-owned park, part of a specialised commercial turf farm, and set in a very rural area with its own lake and nature reserve. This very good park is always neatly trimmed and clean. A 1.5-acre site with 15 touring pitches, 7 hardstandings.

Notes ⊛

LOWER ANSTY MAP 03 ST70

★★★★ INN

The Fox Inn

DT2 7PN

☎ 01258 880328 📠 01258 881440

e-mail: fox@anstyfoxinn.co.uk

web: www.anstyfoxinn.co.uk

Dir: *Off A354 at Millbourne St Andrew, follow brown signs to Ansty*

PETS: Bedrooms unattended **Charges** charge for damage **Public areas** bar only **Grounds** accessible on leads **Exercise area** public footpath 200yds **Facilities** food bowl water bowl cage storage walks info vet info **On Request** fridge access torch towels

This popular inn has a long and interesting history including strong links to the Hall and Woodhouse brewery. Surrounded by beautiful lush Dorset countryside, this is a great base for exploring the area. Bedrooms are smartly appointed and offer generous levels of comfort. The interesting menu focuses upon excellent local produce, with a choice of dining options including the oak-panelled dining room. An extensive garden and patio area is also available.

Rooms 11 en suite (7 fmly) S £40-£70; D £60-£100✻ **Facilities** TVB tea/coffee Cen ht TVL Dinner Last d 9pm **Parking** 30 **Notes** LB

LYME REGIS MAP 03 SY39

★★★★ GUEST HOUSE

The Orchard Country House

Rousdon DT7 3XW

☎ 01297 442972 📠 01297 443670

e-mail: reception@orchardcountryhotel.com

web: www.orchardcountryhotel.com

Dir: *Take B3052 from Lyme Regis towards Sidmouth, on right after garage*

PETS: Bedrooms (1GF) **Charges** charge for damage **Exercise area** walks nearby **Facilities** water bowl walks info vet info **On Request** fridge access torch

Located in the peaceful village of Rousdon and set in attractive orchard gardens, this friendly and comfortable establishment is a good base for exploring the area. The hop-on hop-off bus stop just outside provides relaxed means to visit many of the local attractions. There is a spacious lounge, and breakfast and dinner are served in the pleasant dining room.

Rooms 11 en suite (1 fmly) (1 GF) S £50; D £88-£100✻ **Facilities** FTV TVB tea/coffee Licensed Cen ht Dinner Last d 6pm **Parking** 25

►►► Hook Farm Caravan & Camping Park

(SY323930)

Gore Ln, Uplyme DT7 3UU

☎ 01297 442801 📠 01297 442801

e-mail: information@hookfarm-uplyme.co.uk

web: www.hookfarm-uplyme.co.uk

Dir: *From A35, take B3165 towards Lyme Regis & Uplyme at Hunters Lodge pub. 2m turn right into Gore Lane, site 400yds on right*

PETS: Stables (loose box) **Public areas** except shop, reception & washroom facilities **Charges** £1 per night disp bin **Exercise area** on site apple orchard available **Facilities** on site shop walks info vet info **Restrictions** no Dobermans, Bullmastiffs, Pit Bulls or Rottweilers

Open 15 Mar-Oct shop closed in low season Last arrival 21.30hrs Last departure 11.00hrs

Set in a peaceful and very rural location with views of Lym Valley and just a mile from the seaside at Lyme Regis. The modern toilet facilities are part of an upgrading programme, and there are good on-site amenities. Most pitches are level due to excellent terracing. A 5.5-acre site with 100 touring pitches and 17 statics.

Notes No groups of 6 adults or more

LYTCHETT MINSTER MAP 03 SY99

►►►► South Lytchett Manor *(SY954926)*

Dorchester Rd BH16 6JB

☎ 01202 622577

e-mail: info@southlytchettmanor.co.uk

web: www.southlytchettmanor.co.uk

Dir: *On B3067, off A35, 1m E of Lytchett Minster, 600yds on right after village*

PETS: Charges £1 per night £7 per week disp bin **Exercise area** on site field & wood adjacent **Facilities** on site shop food bowl water bowl dog chews dog scoop/disp bags walks info vet info **Other** prior notice required

Open Etr-11 Oct Last arrival 21.00hrs Last departure noon

A redeveloped park set along the tree-lined driveway of an old manor house with pitches enjoying rural views. All the amenities here are appointed to a very high quality. The park is close to the popular resorts of Poole and Bournemouth. A 20-acre site with 150 touring pitches, 30 hardstandings.

Notes No camp fires

MILTON ABBAS MAP 03 ST80

★★★ FARM HOUSE

Fishmore Hill Farm *(ST799013)*

DT11 0DL

☎ 01258 881122 📠 01258 881122 Mr & Mrs N Clarke

e-mail: neal.clarke@btinternet.com

Dir: *Off A354 signed Milton Abbas, 3m left on sharp bend, up steep hill, 1st left*

PETS: Sep Accom barn **Stables** on site **Grounds** accessible disp bin **Exercise area Facilities** cage storage walks info **On Request** torch **Other** on site veterinary practice, paddock for horses **Resident Pets:** dogs, horses, sheep

This working sheep farm and family home is surrounded by beautiful Dorset countryside and is close to historic Milton Abbey and a short drive from the coast. Bedrooms, which vary in size, are comfortable and finished with considerate extras. The atmosphere is friendly and relaxed. Breakfast is served in the smart dining room around a communal table.

Rooms 3 en suite **Facilities** TVB tea/coffee Cen ht **Parking** 4 **Notes** ⊗ 50 acres Sheep and horses Closed Xmas & New Year

MORETON MAP 03 SY88

►►► Moreton Camping & Caravanning Club Site *(SY782892)*

Station Rd DT2 8BB

☎ 01305 853801

web: www.thefriendlyclub.co.uk

Dir: *From Poole on A35, past Bere Regis, left onto B3390 signed Alfpuddle. Approx 2m, site on left before Moreton Station; next to public house*

PETS: Public areas except in buildings disp bin **Exercise area** on site **Facilities** walks info vet info **Other** prior notice required

Open 2 Apr-16 Nov Last arrival 21.00hrs Last departure noon

Modern purpose-built site on level ground with good amenities. This tidy, well-maintained park offers electric hook-ups to most pitches, and there is a very good play area for children. A 7-acre site with 120 touring pitches, 10 hardstandings.

Notes Site gates closed 23.00hrs-07.00hrs

PIDDLETRENTHIDE MAP 03 SY79

★★★★ INN

The Poachers

DT2 7QX

☎ 01300 348358 📠 01300 348153

e-mail: info@thepoachersinn.co.uk

web: www.thepoachersinn.co.uk

Dir: *N of Dorchester on B3143, inn on left*

PETS: Bedrooms Stables nearby (0.5m) **Charges** £2.50 per night charge for damage **Public areas** except restaurant (on leads) **Grounds** accessible on leads **Exercise area Facilities** cage storage walks info vet info **On Request** fridge access torch towels

This friendly, owner-run inn combines original 16th-century character with contemporary style in the bar and dining areas. Home-cooked meals are a feature, and the smart, en suite bedrooms open onto a courtyard. In fine weather guests can lounge round the swimming pool or relax in the garden.

Rooms 21 en suite (3 fmly) (12 GF) S fr £54; D fr £74* **Facilities** TVB tea/coffee Direct dial from bedrooms Cen ht Dinner Last d 9.30pm Wi-fi available **Parking** 42 **Notes LB**

See advertisement under DORCHESTER

POOLE MAP 04 SZ09

★★★ 68% HOTEL

Salterns Harbourside

38 Salterns Way, Lilliput BH14 8JR

☎ 01202 707321 📠 01202 707488

e-mail: reception@salterns-hotel.co.uk

web: www.salterns-hotel.co.uk

Dir: *in Poole follow B3369 Sandbanks road. 1m at Lilliput shops turn into Salterns Way by Barclays Bank*

PETS: Bedrooms unattended **Charges** £10 per pet per stay **Public areas** except restaurant **Exercise area** 0.5m **Facilities** cage storage vet info

Located next to the marina with superb views across to Brownsea Island, this modernised hotel used to be the headquarters for the flying boats in WWII and was later a yacht club. Bedrooms are spacious and

CONTINUED

POOLE CONTINUED

some have private balconies, whilst the busy bar and restaurant both share harbour views.

Rooms 20 en suite (4 fmly) S £70-£100; D £80-£130 (incl. bkfst) **Facilities** Wi-fi in bedrooms Xmas **Parking** 40 **Notes** LB

★★★ GUEST ACCOMMODATION

The Burleigh

76 Wimborne Rd BH15 2BZ

☎ 01202 673889 01202 685283

Dir: *Off A35 onto A349*

PETS: Bedrooms Charges charge for damage **Exercise area Facilities** walks info vet info **Resident Pets:** Alfie (Tibetan Terrier), Cassie & Jazz (cats)

Suited to business and leisure, this well-kept guest house is close to the town centre and ferry terminal. The individually furnished and decorated bedrooms are of a good standard. Breakfast is served at separate tables and there is a small, attractive lounge.

Rooms 8 rms (4 en suite) (1 fmly) S £27-£35; D £50-£55* **Facilities** TVB tea/coffee Cen ht TVL Wi-fi available **Parking** 5

PUNCKNOWLE MAP 03 SY58

★★★★ GUEST ACCOMMODATION

Offley Bed & Breakfast

Looke Ln DT2 9BD

☎ 01308 897044 & 07792 624977

Dir: *Off B3157 into village centre*

PETS: Bedrooms Grounds accessible disp bin **Exercise area** woods & fields adjacent **Facilities** food bowl water bowl feeding mat leads washing facs cage storage walks info vet info **On Request** fridge access torch towels

With magnificent views over the Bride Valley, this village house provides comfortable, quality accommodation. Guests are assured of a warm, friendly welcome; an ideal venue to enjoy the numerous local attractions. There are several local inns, one in the village, just a gentle stroll away.

Rooms 3 rms (2 en suite) S £40; D £65 **Facilities** TV2B tea/coffee Cen ht TVL **Parking** 3 **Notes** LB

ST LEONARDS MAP 04 SU10

►►►► Back of Beyond Touring Park

(SU103034)

234 Ringwood Rd BH24 2SB

☎ 01202 876968 01202 876968

e-mail: melandsuepike@aol.com

web: www.backofbeyondtouringpark.co.uk

Dir: *From E: on A31 over Little Chef rdbt, pass St Leonard's Hotel, at next rdbt u-turn into lane immediately left to site at end of lane. From W: on A31 pass Texaco garage & Woodsman Inn, immediately left to site*

PETS: Charges £1 per night disp bin **Exercise area** on site 18-acre wood **Facilities** on site shop walks info vet info **Other** prior notice required **Resident Pets:** Holly, Dusty & Gabby (Dalmatians)

Open Mar-Oct Last arrival 19.00hrs Last departure noon

Set well off the beaten track in natural woodland surroundings, with its own river and lake yet close to many attractions. This tranquil park is run by keen, friendly owners, and the quality facilities are for adults only. A 28-acre site with 80 touring pitches.

Notes No commercial vehicles

►►►► Shamba Holidays *(SU105029)*

230 Ringwood Rd BH24 2SB

☎ 01202 873302 01202 873392

e-mail: enquiries@shambaholidays.co.uk

web: www.shambaholidays.co.uk

Dir: *Off A31, from Poole turn left into Eastmoors Lane, 100yds past 2nd rdbt from Texaco garage. Site 0.25m on right (just past Woodman Inn)*

PETS: Public areas except in buildings **Charges** £2.25 per night £15.75 per week disp bin **Exercise area** on site 12-acre field **Facilities** on site shop food walks info vet info

Open Mar-Oct (rs low season some facilities only open at wknds) Last arrival 22.00hrs Last departure 11.00hrs

A relaxed touring park in pleasant countryside between the New Forest and Bournemouth. The park is very well equipped for holidaymakers, with swimming pool, good playground, and bar, shop and takeaway. A 7-acre site with 150 touring pitches.

Notes No large groups, no commercial vehicles

SHAFTESBURY
MAP 03 ST82

★★★ 71% HOTEL

Best Western Royal Chase

Royal Chase Roundabout SP7 8DB

☎ 01747 853355 🖷 01747 851969

e-mail: royalchasehotel@btinternet.com

web: www.theroyalchasehotel.co.uk

Dir: *A303 to A350 signed Blandford Forum. Avoid town centre, follow road to 3rd rdbt*

PETS: Bedrooms (6GF) unattended **Charges** £6.50 per night **Grounds** accessible **Exercise area** many walks nearby

Equally suitable for both leisure and business guests, this well-known local landmark is situated close to the famous Gold Hill. Both Standard and Crown bedrooms offer good levels of comfort and quality. In addition to the fixed-price menu in the Byzant Restaurant, guests have the option of eating more informally in the convivial bar.

Rooms 33 en suite (13 fmly) (6 GF) S £54-£160; D £54-£160* **Facilities** Wi-fi in bedrooms Turkish steam room Xmas New Year **Parking** 100 **Notes** LB

►► Blackmore Vale Caravan & Camping Park *(ST835233)*

Sherborne Causeway SP7 9PX

☎ 01747 851523 & 852573 🖷 01747 851671

e-mail: bmvgroup@ukf.net

web: www.ukcampsite.co.uk

Dir: *From Shaftesbury's Ivy Cross rdbt take A30 signed Sherborne. Site 2m on right*

PETS: Charges £1 per night disp bin **Exercise area** on site large field adjacent **Facilities** vet info **Other** prior notice required **Restrictions** no Rottweilers, Dobermans or Pit Bulls

Open all year Last arrival 21.00hrs

A pleasant touring park with spacious pitches and well-maintained facilities. A fully-equipped gym is the latest addition to this park, and is open to visitors. Blackmore Vale is set behind a caravan sales showground and dealership, and about 2m from Shaftesbury. A 3-acre site with 26 touring pitches, 6 hardstandings.

STURMINSTER NEWTON
MAP 03 ST71

★★★ FARM HOUSE

Honeysuckle House *(ST772102)*

1995 Fifehead St Quintin DT10 2AP

☎ 01258 817896 & 07980 085107 Mrs J Miller

Dir: *Off A357, up Glue Hill signed Hazelbury Bryan. Left after sharp bend, then 2.5m*

PETS: Exercise area Other Please telephone for details

The young proprietors of this 400-acre dairy farm offer a particularly friendly welcome and ensure all guests are very well looked after. The lovely rural setting is a delight, with contented cows grazing in the fields awaiting milking time. Bedrooms are comfortable and include some welcome extras. Breakfasts are enormous, and be sure to book for dinner which is a real highlight.

Rooms 3 en suite (1 fmly) **Facilities** TVB tea/coffee Cen ht TVL Dinner Last d Previous day Fishing Riding Pony rides, farm tours, children's tractor rides **Parking** 6 **Notes** 400 acres Dairy Closed 22 Dec-2 Jan

SWANAGE
MAP 04 SZ07

★★★ 73% HOTEL

The Pines

Burlington Rd BH19 1LT

☎ 01929 425211 🖷 01929 422075

e-mail: reservations@pineshotel.co.uk

web: www.pineshotel.co.uk

Dir: *A351 to seafront, left then 2nd right. Hotel at end of road*

PETS: Bedrooms (6GF) unattended **Stables** nearby (4m) **Grounds** accessible on leads disp bin **Exercise area Facilities** walks info vet info **On Request** fridge access torch towels

Enjoying a peaceful location with spectacular views over the cliffs and sea, The Pines is a pleasant place to stay. Many of the comfortable bedrooms have sea views. Guests can take tea in the lounge, enjoy appetising bar snacks in the attractive bar, and interesting and accomplished cuisine in the restaurant.

Rooms 41 en suite (26 fmly) (6 GF) S £63; D £126-£152 (incl. bkfst)* **Facilities** Xmas New Year **Services** Lift **Parking** 60 **Notes** LB

ENGLAND

SWANAGE CONTINUED

►►► Herston Caravan & Camping Park

(SZ018785)

Washpond Ln BH19 3DJ

☎ 01929 422932 🖹 01929 423888

e-mail: office@herstonleisure.co.uk

web: www.herstonleisure.co.uk

Dir: *From Wareham on A351 towards Swanage. Washpond Lane on left just after 'Welcome to Swanage' sign.*

PETS: Public areas (on leads) disp bin **Exercise area** on site **Facilities** on site shop food food bowl water bowl leads vet info **Other** prior notice required max 2 dogs per family **Restrictions** no Dobermans, Rottweilers, Pit Bull or Staffordshire Terriers

Open all year

Set in a rural area with extensive views of the Purbecks, this tree lined park has many full facility pitches and quality toilet facilities. Herston Halt is within walking distance, a stop for the famous Swanage steam railway between the town centre and Corfe Castle. A 10-acre site with 100 touring pitches, 71 hardstandings and 5 statics.

Notes No noise after 23.00hrs

►►► Ulwell Cottage Caravan Park *(SZ019809)*

Ulwell Cottage, Ulwell BH19 3DG

☎ 01929 422823 🖹 01929 421500

e-mail: enq@ulwellcottagepark.co.uk

web: www.ulwellcottagepark.co.uk

Dir: *From Swanage N for 2m on unclass road towards Studland*

PETS: Public areas except signed areas (on leads) disp bin **Exercise area** 100yds **Facilities** on site shop food food bowl water bowl bedding dog chews cat treats litter tray dog scoop/ disp bags leads walks info vet info

Open Mar-7 Jan (rs Mar-Spring BH & mid Sep-early Jan takeaway closed, shop open variable hrs) Last arrival 22.00hrs Last departure 11.00hrs

Nestling under the Purbeck Hills surrounded by scenic walks and only 2 miles from the beach. This family-run park caters well for families and couples, offering high quality facilities including an indoor heated swimming pool and village inn. A 13-acre site with 77 touring pitches, 19 hardstandings and 140 statics.

TARRANT MONKTON MAP 03 ST90

★★★★ INN

The Langton Arms

DT11 8RX

☎ 01258 830225 🖹 01258 830053

e-mail: info@thelangtonarms.co.uk

Dir: *Off A354 in Tarrant Hinton to Tarrant Monkton, through ford, Langton Arms opp*

PETS: Bedrooms (6GF) **Stables** nearby (1m) **Public areas** except small bar (on leads) **Grounds** accessible **Exercise area** **Facilities** cage storage walks info vet info **On Request** fridge access torch towels

Tucked away in this sleepy Dorset village, the Langton Arms offers light and airy, stylish accommodation and is a good base for touring this attractive area. Bedrooms, all situated at ground level in the modern annexe, are very well equipped and comfortable. There is a choice of dining options, the relaxed bar-restaurant or the more formal Stables restaurant (open Wednesday to Saturday evenings and Sunday lunch time), which offers innovative and appetising dishes. Breakfast is served in the conservatory dining room, just a few steps through the pretty courtyard.

Rooms 6 annexe en suite (6 fmly) (6 GF) S £70; D £90* **Facilities** TVB tea/coffee Direct dial from bedrooms Cen ht Dinner Last d 9.30pm **Parking** 100 **Notes** LB

VERWOOD MAP 04 SU00

►►► Verwood Camping & Caravanning Club Site *(SU069098)*

Sutton Hill, Woodlands BH21 8NQ

☎ 01202 822763

web: www.thefriendlyclub.co.uk

Dir: *Turn left on A354, 13m from Salisbury onto B3081, site is 1.5m W of Verwood*

PETS: Public areas except in buildings disp bin **Exercise area** on site dog walks **Facilities** walks info vet info **Other** prior notice required

Open 2 Apr-2 Nov Last arrival 21.00hrs Last departure noon

Set on rising ground between the woodland of the New Forest and the rolling downs of Cranborne Chase and Salisbury Plains. This comfortable site is well kept by very keen wardens. A 12.75-acre site with 150 touring pitches, 18 hardstandings.

Notes Site gates closed 23.00hrs-07.00hrs

WAREHAM MAP 03 SY98

★★★ 73% HOTEL

Worgret Manor

Worgret Rd BH20 6AB

☎ 01929 552957 01929 554804

e-mail: admin@worgretmanorhotel.co.uk

web: www.worgretmanorhotel.co.uk

Dir: *on A352 (Wareham to Wool), 500mtrs from Wareham rdbt*

PETS: Bedrooms (3GF) **Public areas** bar & lobby only **Grounds** accessible on leads **Exercise area** local walks **Facilities** vet info **Resident Pets:** Tammy (Retriever)

On the edge of Wareham, with easy access to major routes, this privately owned Georgian manor house has a friendly, cheerful atmosphere. The bedrooms come in a variety of sizes. Public rooms are well presented and comprise a popular bar, a quiet lounge and an airy restaurant.

Rooms 12 en suite (1 fmly) (3 GF) S £65-£80; D £110-£120 (incl. bkfst)* **Facilities** Wi-fi available **Parking** 30 **Notes** LB

★★★★★ GUEST ACCOMMODATION

Kemps Country House

East Stoke BH20 6AL

☎ 0845 8620315 0845 8620316

e-mail: info@kempscountryhouse.co.uk

web: www.kempshotel.com

Dir: *Follow A352 W from Wareham, 3m on right in East Stoke*

PETS: Bedrooms (6GF) sign **Charges** £5 per night £35 per week charge for damage **Grounds** accessible on leads disp bin **Exercise area** 1m

Located within easy reach of the Dorset coastline, this former rectory provides a calming, friendly atmosphere and is the perfect base for touring the area. The refurbished bedrooms are spacious and well appointed, and benefit from plenty of modern extras; super king-size beds, flat screen TV and power showers. Breakfast and dinner are served in the elegant dining room and offer an imaginative choice of modern British cuisine.

Rooms 12 annexe en suite (2 fmly) (6 GF) **Facilities** FTV TVB tea/coffee Direct dial from bedrooms Cen ht Dinner Wi-fi available **Parking** 24

★★★ GUEST ACCOMMODATION

Luckford Wood House

East Stoke BH20 6AW

☎ 01929 463098 & 07888 719002

e-mail: johnbarnes@ukipemail.co.uk

web: www.luckfordleisure.co.uk

Dir: *3m W of Wareham. Off A352, take B3070 to Lulworth, turn right onto Holme Ln. 1m right on Church Ln*

PETS: Bedrooms (1GF) **Charges** £5 per night £30 per week **Public areas** except restaurant (on leads) **Exercise area** lane adjacent **Facilities** dog walking cage storage walks info vet info **On Request** fridge access torch **Resident Pets:** Suzie & Sammy (cats)

Rurally situated about three miles west of Wareham, this family home offers comfortable accommodation. Situated on the edge of woodland, wildlife is in abundance. Guests can be assured of a friendly welcome and an extensive choice at breakfast.

Rooms 6 rms (3 en suite) (1 pri facs) (3 fmly) (1 GF) S £25-£55; D £50-£80 **Facilities** TVB tea/coffee Cen ht TVL Wi-fi available **Parking** 6 **Notes** LB

►►►► Wareham Forest Tourist Park

(SY894912)

North Trigon BH20 7NZ

☎ 01929 551393 01929 558321

e-mail: holiday@warehamforest.co.uk

web: www.warehamforest.co.uk

Dir: *Telephone for directions*

PETS: Public areas except in buildings **Charges** £1.50 maximum per night disp bin **Exercise area** on site woodland walks **Facilities** on site shop washing facs walks info vet info **Restrictions** well behaved dogs only

Open all year (rs off-peak season limited services) Last arrival 21.00hrs Last departure 11.00hrs

AA Campsite of the Year for South-west England 2009. A woodland park within the tranquil Wareham Forest, with its many walks and proximity to Poole, Dorchester and the Purbeck coast. Two luxury blocks, with combined washbasin/WCs for total privacy, maintain a high standard of cleanliness. A heated outdoor swimming pool, off licence, shop and games room add to the pleasure of a stay here. A 42-acre site with 200 touring pitches, 70 hardstandings.

Notes Couples & families only, no group bookings

WEST BEXINGTON — MAP 03 SY58

★★ 74% HOTEL

The Manor

Beach Rd DT2 9DF

☎ 01308 897616 📠 01308 897704

e-mail: themanorhotel@btconnect.com

Dir: *B3157 to Burton Bradstock, continue to The Bull public house in Swire. Immediately right to West Bexington.*

PETS: Bedrooms unattended **Charges** £15 per night **Public areas** except restaurant **Grounds** accessible **Exercise area** 5 mins to beach & countryside

Surrounded by scenic splendour and just a short stroll from the magnificent sweep of Chesil Beach, the atmosphere is relaxed and welcoming with snug lounges and crackling wood fires. Bedrooms are individual in style, many with wonderful sea views and the sound of waves in the background. With an abundance of excellent local produce, dining here, in either the convivial Cellar Bar, or the elegant dining room is recommended.

Rooms 13 en suite (2 fmly) **Parking** 80

WEST LULWORTH — MAP 03 SY88

★★ 75% HOTEL

Cromwell House

Lulworth Cove BH20 5RJ

☎ 01929 400253 & 400332 📠 01929 400566

e-mail: catriona@lulworthcove.co.uk

web: www.lulworthcove.co.uk

Dir: *200yds beyond end of West Lulworth, left onto high slip road, hotel 100yds on left opposite beach car park*

PETS: Bedrooms (2GF) unattended sign **Charges** £2 per night **Public areas** except dining room **Grounds** accessible disp bin **Exercise area** adjacent **Facilities** water bowl washing facs cage storage walks info vet info **On Request** fridge access torch towels **Resident Pets:** Jaldi (Springer Spaniel), Douglas (Bearded Collie cross), Lily (cat)

Built in 1881 by the Mayor of Weymouth, specifically as a guest house, this family-run hotel now provides visitors with an ideal base for touring the area and for exploring the beaches and coast. Cromwell House enjoys spectacular views across the sea and countryside.

Bedrooms, many with sea views, are comfortable and some have been specifically designed for family use.

Rooms 17 en suite 1 annexe en suite (3 fmly) (2 GF) S £40-£65; D £80-£105 (incl. bkfst) **Facilities** ⛱ Access to Dorset coastal footpath & Jurassic Coast **Parking** 17 **Notes LB** Closed 22 Dec-3 Jan

WEYMOUTH — MAP 03 SY67

★★ GUEST HOUSE

Charlotte Guest House

5 Commercial Rd DT4 7DW

☎ 01305 772942 & 07719 576744

e-mail: charlottegh1@aol.com

Dir: *On A353 Esplanade, at clock turn right onto Kings St. At rdbt take 1st left, left again onto Commercial Rd*

PETS: Bedrooms Charges £5 per night £25 per week **Exercise area** 150yds

A warm welcome is offered at this small renovated guest house within easy walking distance of the town's amenities. The breakfast room is light and airy and bedrooms vary in size.

Rooms 12 rms (7 en suite) (3 fmly) (1 GF) S £25-£30; D £45-£60* **Facilities** TVB tea/coffee Cen ht **Parking** 3 **Notes LB**

►►►► East Fleet Farm Touring Park

(SY640797)

Chickerell DT3 4DW

☎ 01305 785768

e-mail: enquiries@eastfleet.co.uk

web: www.eastfleet.co.uk

Dir: *On B3157 (Weymouth-Bridport road), 3m from Weymouth*

PETS: Public areas except play area **Charges** 25p-£1 per night disp bin **Exercise area** on site **Facilities** on site shop food food bowl water bowl bedding dog chews cat treats dog scoop/disp bags leads washing facs walks info vet info **Resident Pets:** George & Clem (donkeys)

Open 16 Mar-Oct Last arrival 22.00hrs Last departure 10.30hrs

Set on a working organic farm overlooking Fleet Lagoon and Chesil Beach, with a wide range of amenities and quality toilet facilities in a Scandinavian log cabin. The friendly owners are welcoming and helpful, and their family bar serving meals and take-away food is open from Easter, with glorious views from the patio area. A 21-acre site with 400 touring pitches, 50 hardstandings.

►►► Bagwell Farm Touring Park *(SY627816)*

Knights in the Bottom, Chickerell DT3 4EA
☎ 01305 782575 🖷 01305 780554
e-mail: aa@bagwellfarm.co.uk
web: www.bagwellfarm.co.uk

Dir: *4m W of Weymouth on B3157 (Weymouth-Bridport), past Chickerell, turn left into site 500yds after Victoria Inn*

PETS: Public areas (on leads) **Charges** £1 per night **Exercise area** on site field available (dogs on leads) **Facilities** on site shop food food bowl water bowl dog chews cat treats dog scoop/disp bags leads walks info vet info **Other** prior notice required

Open all year (rs Winter bar closed) Last arrival 21.00hrs Last departure 11.00hrs

An idyllically-placed terraced site on a hillside and a valley overlooking Chesil Beach. The park is well equipped with mini-supermarket, children's play area and pets corner, and a bar and grill serving food in high season. A 14-acre site with 320 touring pitches, 10 hardstandings.

Notes Families only

WIMBORNE MINSTER — MAP 03 SZ09

►►► Charris Camping & Caravan Park *(SY992988)*

Candy's Ln, Corfe Mullen BH21 3EF
☎ 01202 885970 🖷 01202 881281
e-mail: bookings@charris.co.uk
web: www.charris.co.uk

Dir: *From E, exit Wimborne bypass (A31) W end. 300yds after Caravan Sales, follow brown sign. From W on A31, over A350 rdbt, take next turn after B3074, follow brown signs*

PETS: Public areas except toilet & shop disp bin **Exercise area** 0.25m **Facilities** on site shop food bowl water bowl washing facs walks info vet info **Other** prior notice required **Resident Pets:** Spike (cat)

Open Mar-Jan Last arrival 21.00hrs Last departure 11.00hrs

A sheltered park of grassland lined with trees, on the edge of the Stour Valley. The owners are friendly and welcoming, and they maintain the park facilities to a good standard. Barbecues are a popular occasional event. A 3.5-acre site with 45 touring pitches, 12 hardstandings.

Notes ⊜ Earliest arrival time 11.00hrs

CO DURHAM

BARNARD CASTLE — MAP 12 NZ01

►►►► Barnard Castle Camping & Caravanning Club Site *(NZ025168)*

Dockenflatts Ln, Lartington DL12 9DG
☎ 01833 630228
web: www.thefriendlyclub.co.uk

Dir: *From Barnard Castle take B6277 to Middleton-in-Teesdale. 1m left signed Raygill Riding Stables. Site 500mtrs on left*

PETS: disp bin **Exercise area** on site **Facilities** walks info vet info **Other** prior notice required

Open 2 Apr-2 Nov Last arrival 21.00hrs Last departure noon

A peaceful site surrounded by mature woodland and meadowland, with first class facilities. This immaculately maintained park is set in the heart of the countryside. Pitches are well laid out and generous, on mainly level grass with some hardstandings. A 10-acre site with 90 touring pitches, 15 hardstandings.

Notes Site gates closed 23.00hrs-07.00hrs

CONSETT — MAP 12 NZ15

★★★ 73% HOTEL

Best Western Derwent Manor

OXFORD HOTELS & INNS

Allensford DH8 9BB
☎ 01207 592000 🖷 01207 502472
e-mail: gm@derwent-manor-hotel.com
web: www.oxfordhotelsandinns.com

Dir: *on A68*

PETS: Bedrooms Exercise area outside hotel

This hotel, built in the style of a manor house, is set in open grounds overlooking the River Derwent. Spacious bedrooms, including a number of suites, are comfortably equipped. A popular wedding venue, there are also extensive conference facilities and an impressive leisure suite. The Grouse & Claret bar serves a wide range of drinks and light meals, and Guinevere's restaurant offers the fine dining option.

Rooms 48 en suite (3 fmly) (26 GF) S £92; D £122 (incl. bkfst)✳ **Facilities** FTV ⓢ supervised Gym Xmas New Year **Services** Lift **Parking** 100

DARLINGTON MAP 08 NZ21

★★★ 80% HOTEL

Headlam Hall

Headlam, Gainford DL2 3HA

☎ 01325 730238 Fax 01325 730790

e-mail: admin@headlamhall.co.uk

web: www.headlamhall.co.uk

Dir: *2m N of A67 between Piercebridge & Gainford*

PETS: Bedrooms (10GF) unattended **Stables** on site **Charges** charge for damage **Grounds** accessible on leads disp bin **Exercise area** 50yds **Facilities** water bowl washing facs cage storage walks info vet info **On Request** fridge access torch towels **Other** dogs allowed in certain bedrooms only; dogs not to be fed in bedrooms

This impressive Jacobean hall lies in farmland north-east of Piercebridge and has its own 9-hole golf course. The main house retains many historical features, including flagstone floors and a pillared hall. Bedrooms are well proportioned and traditionally styled. A converted coach house contains the more modern rooms, as well as a conference and leisure centre.

Rooms 18 en suite 22 annexe en suite (4 fmly) (10 GF) S £85-£155; D £110-£180 (incl. bkfst)* **Facilities Spa** STV 9 Fishing Gym Putt green Wi-fi in bedrooms New Year **Services** Lift **Parking** 80 **Notes LB** Closed 24-26 Dec

★★★ 78% HOTEL

The Blackwell Grange Hotel

Blackwell Grange DL3 8QH

☎ 0870 609 6121 & 01325 509955 Fax 01325 380899

e-mail: blackwell.grange@forestdale.com

web: www.forestdale.com

Dir: *on A167, 1.5m from central ring road*

PETS: Bedrooms Charges £7.50 per night **Public areas** except restaurant **Exercise area Other** please phone for further details on pet facilities

This beautiful 17th-century mansion is peacefully situated in nine acres of its own grounds yet is convenient for the motorway network. The pick of the bedrooms are in a courtyard building or the impressive feature rooms in the original house. The Havelock restaurant offers a range of traditional and continental menus.

Rooms 99 en suite 11 annexe en suite (3 fmly) (36 GF) D £95-£99 (incl. bkfst)* **Facilities** Gym Beauty room Xmas **Services** Lift **Parking** 250 **Notes LB**

DURHAM MAP 12 NZ24

★★★★ 76% HOTEL

Durham Marriott Hotel, Royal County

Marriott HOTELS & RESORTS

Old Elvet DH1 3JN

☎ 0191 386 6821 Fax 0191 386 0704

e-mail: mhrs.xvudm.frontdesk@marriotthotels.com

web: www.marriott.co.uk

Dir: *from A1(M) junct 62, then A690 to Durham, over 1st rdbt, left at 2nd rdbt left at lights, hotel on left*

PETS: Bedrooms (15GF) **Exercise area Facilities** vet info **Restrictions** small dogs only

In a wonderful position on the banks of the River Wear, the hotel's central location makes it ideal for visiting the attractions of this historic city. The building was developed from a series of Jacobean town houses. The bedrooms are tastefully styled and the County Restaurant and lounge bar have been refurbished.

Rooms 142 en suite 8 annexe en suite (10 fmly) (15 GF) **Facilities** STV supervised Gym Wi-fi available Turkish steam room Plunge pool Sanarium Tropical fun shower **Services** Lift **Parking** 76

★★★ 66% HOTEL

Bowburn Hall

Bowburn DH6 5NH

☎ 0191 377 0311 Fax 0191 377 3459

e-mail: info@bowburnhallhotel.co.uk

Dir: *towards Bowburn. Right at Cooperage Pub, then 0.5m to junct signed Durham. Hotel on left*

PETS: Bedrooms unattended **Grounds** accessible **Exercise area Facilities** vet info

A former country mansion, this hotel lies in five acres of grounds in a residential area, but within easy reach of the A1. The comfortable and spacious lounge bar and conservatory overlook the gardens, and offer both bar and restaurant meals. Bedrooms are not large but are very smartly presented and well equipped.

Rooms 19 en suite (1 fmly) S £75; D £85 (incl. bkfst)* **Facilities** STV Wi-fi available **Parking** 100 **Notes** RS 24-26 Dec & 1 Jan

★★★★ GUEST ACCOMMODATION

Farnley Tower

The Avenue DH1 4DX

☎ 0191 375 0011 & 384 6655 📠 0191 383 9694

e-mail: enquiries@farnley-tower.co.uk

web: www.farnley-tower.co.uk

Dir: *Exit A1(M) junct 62 onto A690, straight over 4 rdbts. After 4th rdbt take 4th right*

PETS: Bedrooms (5GF) sign **Charges** £5 per night £35 per week charge for damage **Public areas** except restaurant, dining room & bar **Grounds** accessible disp bin **Exercise area** 1m **Facilities** walks info vet info **Resident Pets:** Farnley (cat)

Built in 1875, this former manse stands in gardens on the edge of the city, enjoying a quiet location, yet minutes walk away from the City centre. The house is popular with both business and leisure guests. Bedrooms are thoughtfully equipped and vary in size. Food is fast becoming a real feature here with skilfully prepared meals served each evening in the stylish basement Gourmet Spot restaurant.

Rooms 15 rms (13 en suite) (2 fmly) (5 GF) S £60-£65; D £85-£95* **Facilities** STV FTV TVB tea/coffee Direct dial from bedrooms Cen ht Dinner Last d 9.30pm Wi-fi available **Parking** 20 **Notes LB** RS Sun

MIDDLETON-IN-TEESDALE MAP 12 NY92

★★ 65% HOTEL

The Teesdale Hotel

Market Place DL12 0QG

☎ 01833 640264 📠 01833 640651

e-mail: enquiries@teesdalehotel.co.uk

web: www.teesdalehotel.com

Dir: *from Barnard Castle take B6278, follow signs for Middleton-in-Teesdale & Highforce. Hotel in town centre*

PETS: Bedrooms Public areas bar only (on leads) **Exercise area** 50mtrs **Facilities** walks info vet info **Restrictions** small-medium size dogs only

Located in the heart of the popular village, this family-run hotel offers a relaxed and friendly atmosphere. Bedrooms and bathrooms are well equipped and offer a good standard of quality and comfort. Public areas include a residents' lounge on the first floor, a spacious restaurant and a lounge bar which is popular with locals.

Rooms 14 en suite (1 fmly) S £30-£42.50; D £75 (incl. bkfst)* **Facilities** Xmas **Parking** 20 **Notes LB**

REDWORTH MAP 08 NZ22

★★★★ 76% HOTEL

Barceló Redworth Hall Hotel

Barceló HOTELS & RESORTS

DL5 6NL

☎ 01388 770600 📠 01388 770654

e-mail: redworthhall@barcelo-hotels.co.uk

web: www.barcelo-hotels.co.uk

Dir: *from A1(M) junct 58/A68 signed Corbridge. Follow hotel signs*

PETS: Bedrooms Charges £15 per stay per night charge for damage **Public areas** only to gain acess to bedrooms (on leads) **Grounds** accessible disp bin **Exercise area Facilities** food (pre-bookable) food bowl water bowl bedding feeding mat dog grooming walks info vet info **On Request** fridge access **Other** dog pack (inc room service meal & grooming treatment details (charges on request))

This imposing Georgian building includes a health club with state-of-the-art equipment and impressive conference facilities making this a popular destination for business travellers. There are several spacious lounges to relax in along with the Conservatory Restaurant. Bedrooms are very comfortable and well equipped.

Rooms 143 en suite (12 fmly) S £69-£150* **Facilities** Gym Wi-fi available Bodysense Health & Leisure Club Xmas New Year **Services** Lift **Parking** 300

STOCKTON-ON-TEES MAP 08 NZ41

★★★ INN

The Parkwood Inn

64-66 Darlington Rd, Hartburn TS18 5ER

☎ 01642 587933

e-mail: theparkwoodhotel@aol.com

web: www.theparkwoodhotel.com

Dir: *1.5m SW of town centre. A66 onto A137 signed Yarm & Stockton West, left at lights onto A1027, left onto Darlington Rd*

PETS: Bedrooms Public areas except dining areas **Grounds** accessible **Exercise area** park nearby **Facilities** food **Resident Pets:** Charlie (Yorkshire/Terrier cross)

A very friendly welcome awaits at this family-run establishment. The well-equipped en suite bedrooms come with many homely extras and a range of professionally prepared meals are served in the cosy bar lounge, conservatory, or the attractive dining room.

Rooms 6 en suite **Facilities** TVB tea/coffee Cen ht Dinner Last d 9.15pm **Parking** 36 **Notes** No coaches

ENGLAND

ESSEX

BIRCHANGER GREEN MOTORWAY SERVICE AREA (M11) MAP 05 TL52

BUDGET HOTEL

Days Inn London Stansted

DAYS INN

CM23 5QZ

☎ 01279 656477 🖷 01279 656590

e-mail: birchanger.hotel@welcomebreak.co.uk

web: www.welcomebreak.co.uk

Dir: *M11 junct 8*

PETS: Bedrooms Charges £10 per pet deposit **Exercise area** on site grass area

This modern building offers accommodation in smart, spacious and well-equipped bedrooms, suitable for families and business travellers, and all with en suite bathrooms. Refreshments may be taken at the nearby family restaurant.

Rooms 60 en suite S £49-£69; D £69-£89*

CANEWDON MAP 05 TQ99

►►► Riverside Village Holiday Park

(TQ929951)

Creeksea Ferry Rd, Wallasea Island SS4 2EY

☎ 01702 258297 🖷 01702 258555

Dir: *M25 junct 29, A127, towards Southend-on-Sea. Take B1013 towards Rochford. Follow signs for Wallsea Island & Baltic Wharf*

PETS: Charges £1 per night **Public areas** except play area, (on leads) disp bin **Exercise area** on site dog walk area provided **Facilities** on site shop food dog scoop/disp bags walks info vet info **Other** prior notice required **Restrictions** dogs not allowed in tents

Open Mar-Oct

Next to a nature reserve beside the River Crouch, this holiday park is surrounded by wetlands but only eight miles from Southend. A modern toilet block with disabled facilities has been provided for tourers. Several restaurants and pubs are within a short distance. A 25-acre site with 60 touring pitches and 162 statics.

CLACTON-ON-SEA MAP 05 TM11

★★★★ GUEST ACCOMMODATION

The Sandrock

1 Penfold Rd, Marine Pde West CO15 1JN

☎ 01255 428215 🖷 01255 428215

e-mail: thesandrock@btinternet.com

web: www.thesandrock.co.uk

Dir: *A133 to seafront, right, pass lights at pier, then 2nd right*

PETS: Bedrooms (1GF) **Charges** £5 per night £30 per week charge for damage **Exercise area** 50mtrs **Facilities** pet sitting vet info **Restrictions** small & medium dogs only

A warm welcome is offered at this Victorian property, just off the seafront and within easy walking distance of the town centre. The attractive bedrooms vary in size and style, are thoughtfully equipped, and some have sea views. Breakfast is served in the smart bar-restaurant and there is also a cosy lounge.

Rooms 9 en suite (1 fmly) (1 GF) S £40-£42; D £58-£60* **Facilities** TVB tea/coffee Cen ht TVL Wi-fi available **Parking** 5 **Notes** LB

KELVEDON HATCH MAP 05 TQ59

►►► Kelvedon Hatch Camping & Caravanning Club Site *(TQ577976)*

Warren Ln, Doddinghurst CM15 0JG

☎ 01277 372773

web: www.thefriendlyclub.co.uk

Dir: *M25 junct 28. Brentwood 2m left on A128 signed Ongar. After 3m turn right. Site signed*

PETS: Public areas except in buildings disp bin **Exercise area** on site adjacent woodland **Facilities** walks info vet info **Other** prior notice required

Open 2 Apr-2 Nov Last arrival 21.00hrs Last departure noon

A very pretty rural site with many separate areas amongst the trees, and a secluded field for campers. This peaceful site has older-style toilet facilities which are kept very clean, and smart laundry equipment. A 12-acre site with 90 touring pitches, 23 hardstandings.

Notes Site gates closed 23.00hrs-07.00hrs

MERSEA ISLAND — MAP 05 TM01

Waldegraves Holiday Park *(TM033133)*

CO5 8SE

☎ 01206 382898 🖷 01206 385359

e-mail: holidays@waldegraves.co.uk

web: www.waldegraves.co.uk

Dir: *B1025 to Mersea Island across the Strood. Left to East Mersea, 2nd turn on right, follow tourist signs to site*

PETS: Charges £2 per night (touring pitches) disp bin **Exercise area** on site field available **Facilities** on site shop food food bowl water bowl dog chews walks info vet info **Other** prior notice required

Open Mar-Nov Last arrival 22.00hrs Last departure noon

A spacious and pleasant site, located between farmland and its own private beach on the Blackwater Estuary. Facilities include two freshwater fishing lakes, heated swimming pool, club, amusements, café and golf, and there is generally good provision for families. A 25-acre site with 60 touring pitches and 250 statics.

Notes No large groups or under 21's

SOUTHEND-ON-SEA — MAP 05 TQ88

★★★ 78% HOTEL

Balmoral

34 Valkyrie Rd, Westcliff-on-Sea SS0 8BU

☎ 01702 342947 🖷 01702 337828

e-mail: enq@balmoralsouthend.com

web: www.balmoralsouthend.com

Dir: *off A13*

PETS: Bedrooms Charges £10 per night £70 per week charge for damage **Public areas** except outdoor patio (muzzled or on leads) **Grounds** accessible on leads disp bin **Exercise area Restrictions** small breeds only; no dangerous dogs (see page 7)

A delightful property situated just a short walk from the main shopping centre, railway station and the seafront. The attractively decorated bedrooms are tastefully furnished and equipped with many thoughtful touches. Public rooms feature a smart open-plan bar/lounge, a conservatory restaurant and a terrace with a large wooden gazebo.

Rooms 34 rms (14 en suite) (4 fmly) (4 GF) **Facilities** Arrangement with nearby health club **Parking** 32

GLOUCESTERSHIRE

ALDERTON — MAP 03 SP03

★★★★ BED & BREAKFAST

Tally Ho Bed & Breakfast

20 Beckford Rd GL20 8NL

☎ 01242 621482

e-mail: tallyhobb@aol.com

Dir: *3m NW of Winchcombe. Off B4077 into Alderton village*

PETS: Bedrooms (2GF) **Charges** charge for damage **Grounds** accessible **Exercise area** 200yds **Facilities** dog scoop/disp bags leads cage storage walks info vet info

Resident Pets: Springer Spaniels, Fox Terriers

Convenient for the M5, this friendly establishment stands in a delightful quiet village. Bedrooms, including two on the ground floor, offer modern comforts and attractive co-ordinated furnishings. Breakfast is served in the stylish dining room with the village pub just a stroll away for dinner.

Rooms 3 en suite (1 fmly) (2 GF) S £40-£45; D £60-£70 **Facilities** TVB tea/coffee Cen ht **Parking** 3 **Notes** LB ⊜

ALVESTON — MAP 03 ST68

★★★ 80% HOTEL

Alveston House

Davids Ln BS35 2LA

☎ 01454 415050 🖷 01454 415425

e-mail: info@alvestonhousehotel.co.uk

web: www.alvestonhousehotel.co.uk

Dir: *M5 junct 14 from N or junct 16 from S, on A38*

PETS: Bedrooms (6GF) unattended sign **Charges** charge for damage **Grounds** accessible **Exercise area** near bridleway **Facilities** walks info vet info **On Request** fridge access torch towels

In a quiet area with easy access to the city and a short drive from both the M4 and M5, this smartly presented hotel provides an impressive combination of good service, friendly hospitality and a relaxed atmosphere. The comfortable bedrooms are well equipped for both business and leisure guests. The restaurant offers carefully prepared fresh food, and the pleasant bar and conservatory area is perfect for enjoying a pre-dinner drink.

Rooms 30 en suite (1 fmly) (6 GF) S £75-£95; D £99.50-£140 (incl. bkfst)✻ **Facilities** FTV Wi-fi available New Year **Parking** 75 **Notes** LB

ENGLAND

BIBURY MAP 04 SP10

★★★ 82% HOTEL

Swan

GL7 5NW

☎ 01285 740695 01285 740473

e-mail: info@swanhotel.co.uk

web: www.cotswold-inns-hotels.co.uk

Dir: *9m S of Burford A40 onto B4425. 6m N of Cirencester A4179 onto B4425*

PETS: Bedrooms unattended **Charges** £15 per night charge for damage **Public areas** except eating areas **Exercise area Facilities** walks info vet info **On Request** fridge access torch towels

This hotel, built in the 17th century as a coaching inn, is set in peaceful and picturesque surroundings. It provides well-equipped and smartly presented accommodation, including four luxury cottage suites set just outside the main hotel. The elegant public areas are comfortable and have feature fireplaces. There is a choice of dining options to suit all tastes.

Rooms 18 en suite 4 annexe en suite (1 fmly) D £145-£295 (incl. bkfst)* **Facilities** Fishing Wi-fi in bedrooms Xmas New Year **Services** Lift **Parking** 22 **Notes** LB

BOURTON-ON-THE-WATER MAP 04 SP12

★★ 79% HOTEL

Chester House

Victoria St GL54 2BU

☎ 01451 820286 01451 820471

e-mail: info@chesterhousehotel.com

Dir: *A429 between Northleach & Stow-on-Wold.*

PETS: Bedrooms (8GF) unattended **Public areas** except lounge & bar **Grounds** accessible **Exercise area** 300mtrs **Facilities** cage storage walks info vet info **On Request** fridge access torch towels **Resident Pets:** Poppy (Patterdale Terrier)

This hotel occupies a secluded but central location in this delightful Cotswold village. Rooms, some at ground floor level, are situated in the main house and adjoining coach house. The public areas are stylish, light and airy. Breakfast is taken in the main building whereas dinner is served in the attractive restaurant just a few yards away.

Rooms 12 en suite 10 annexe en suite (8 fmly) (8 GF) D £75-£110 (incl. bkfst) **Facilities** Wi-fi available Beauty therapist New Year **Parking** 20 **Notes** Closed 7 Jan-1 Feb

CHELTENHAM MAP 03 SO92

★★★★ 80% HOTEL

Hotel du Vin Cheltenham

Parabola Rd GL50 3AQ

☎ 01242 588450 01242 588455

e-mail: info@cheltenham.hotelduvin.com

web: www.hotelduvin.com

Dir: *M5 junct 11, follow signs for city centre. At rdbt opposite Morgan Estate Agents take 2nd left, 200mtrs to Parabola Rd*

PETS: Bedrooms (5GF) unattended **Charges** £10 per night **Public areas** except bistro **Exercise area** 10 min walk **Facilities** food bowl water bowl bedding walks info

This Hotel du Vin offers spacious public areas that are packed with style and features. The pewter-topped bar has comfortable seating and in the spacious restaurant the characteristic Hotel du Vin style is evident. Service is friendly and attentive, with skilled Sommeliery and bar staff a feature too. Bedrooms are comfortable, many have feature baths and all have comfortable beds. There is some parking and a delightful external smoking area in the well tended grounds.

Rooms 49 en suite (2 fmly) (5 GF) S £145-£360; D £145-£360* **Facilities** Spa STV Wi-fi in bedrooms **Services** Lift air con **Parking** 26 **Notes** LB

★★★ 83% HOTEL

The Greenway

Shurdington GL51 4UG

☎ 01242 862352 01242 862780

e-mail: info@thegreenway.co.uk

web: www.vonessenhotels.co.uk

Dir: *2.5m SW on A46*

PETS: Bedrooms (4GF) unattended **Charges** £5 per night **Grounds** accessible **Exercise area** adjacent countryside **On Request** torch towels

This hotel, with a wealth of history, is peacefully located in a delightful setting close to the A46 and the M5. Within easy reach of the many attractions of the Cotswolds. The Greenway certainly offers something different. The attractive dining room overlooks the sunken garden and is the venue for exciting food, proudly served by dedicated and attentive staff.

Rooms 11 en suite 10 annexe en suite (4 fmly) (4 GF) S £150-£360; D £255-£500 **Facilities** FTV Wi-fi available Clay pigeon shooting Horse riding Mountain biking Beauty treatment Xmas New Year **Parking** 50 **Notes** LB

U

Cotswold Grange

Pittville Circus Rd GL52 2QH

☎ 01242 515119 📠 01242 241537

e-mail: info@cotswoldgrange.co.uk

Dir: *from town centre, follow Prestbury signs. Right at 1st rdbt, next rdbt straight over, hotel 100yds on left*

PETS: Bedrooms Public areas except restaurant **Grounds** accessible **Exercise area** park nearby **Facilities** walks info vet info **On Request** fridge access torch

At the time of going to press the rating for this establishment was not confirmed. This may be due to a change of ownership or because it has only recently joined the AA rating scheme. For further details please see the AA website: www.theAA.com

Rooms 24 en suite (2 fmly) S £55-£65; D £75-£90 (incl. bkfst)✳ **Facilities** Wi-fi in bedrooms **Parking** 20 **Notes LB** Closed 25 Dec-1 Jan

★★★★ GUEST ACCOMMODATION

White Lodge

Hatherley Ln GL51 6SH

☎ 01242 242347 📠 01242 242347

e-mail: pamela@whitelodgebandb.wanadoo.co.uk

Dir: *M5 junct 11, A40 to Cheltenham, 1st rdbt 4th exit Hatherley Ln, White Lodge 1st on right*

PETS: Bedrooms (1GF) unattended **Charges** £5 per night **Public areas** except dining room **Grounds** accessible disp bin **Exercise area**

Built around 1900, this well cared for, smart and friendly establishment is convenient for access to the M5. Bedrooms, of varied size, offer quality and many extra facilities, including fridges and Wi-fi. The very comfortable dining room, where breakfast is served around a grand table, looks out across the pleasant backdrop of White Lodge's extensive gardens.

Rooms 4 en suite (1 GF) S £39-£42; D £55-£60✳ **Facilities** FTV TVB tea/coffee Cen ht Wi-fi available **Parking** 6 **Notes** ⊜

★★★ GUEST ACCOMMODATION

Hope Orchard

Gloucester Rd, Staverton GL51 0TF

☎ 01452 855556 📠 01452 530037

e-mail: info@hopeorchard.com

web: www.hopeorchard.com

Dir: *A40 onto B4063 at Arlecourt rdbt, Hope Orchard 1.25m on right*

PETS: Bedrooms (8GF) unattended **Charges** charge for damage **Grounds** accessible disp bin **Exercise area** on site **Facilities** food bowl water bowl dog scoop/disp bags washing facs cage storage walks info vet info **On Request** fridge access torch towels **Other** local kennel can provide day sitting service

Resident Pets: Bertie (Staffordshire Bull Terrier), Jessie, Jasper & Louis (cats)

Situated midway between Gloucester and Cheltenham, this is a good base for exploring the area. The comfortable bedrooms are next to the main house, and all are on the ground floor and have their own separate entrances. There is a large garden, and ample off-road parking is available.

Rooms 8 en suite (8 GF) **Facilities** FTV TVB tea/coffee Direct dial from bedrooms Cen ht Wi-fi available **Parking** 10

CHIPPING CAMPDEN — MAP 04 SP13

★★★★ ⊛⊛⊛ HOTEL

Cotswold House

The Square GL55 6AN

☎ 01386 840330 📠 01386 840310

e-mail: reception@cotswoldhouse.com

web: www.cotswoldhouse.com

Dir: *A44 take B4081 to Chipping Campden. Right at T-junct into High St. House in The Square*

PETS: Bedrooms unattended **Grounds** accessible on leads **Exercise area** The Common **Facilities** food bowl water bowl bedding cage storage walks info vet info **On Request** fridge access torch towels **Other** dog baskets can be provided

This is at the cutting edge of hotel-keeping, and guests will find it easy to relax at this mellow Cotswold stone, town centre establishment. The individually designed bedrooms, including some spacious suites, are

CONTINUED

ENGLAND

CHIPPING CAMPDEN CONTINUED

impressive and offer a beguiling blend of style, quality and comfort. The restaurant provides a stunning venue to sample accomplished and imaginative cuisine, with local produce at the heart of dishes on offer here. Alternatively, Hicks Brasserie and bar provides a more informal dining experience.

Rooms 21 en suite 8 annexe en suite (1 fmly) (2 GF) S £150-£800; D £150-£800 (incl. bkfst)* **Facilities** STV Wi-fi available Xmas New Year **Parking** 26 **Notes** LB

★★★ 80% HOTEL

Three Ways House

Mickleton GL55 6SB

☎ 01386 438429 01386 438118

e-mail: reception@puddingclub.com

web: www.puddingclub.com

Dir: *in Mickleton centre, on B4632 (Stratford-upon-Avon to Broadway road)*

PETS: Bedrooms unattended **Public areas** except restaurant **Grounds** accessible disp bin **Exercise area** 100mtrs **Facilities** water bowl walks info vet info **On Request** fridge access

Built in 1870, this charming hotel has welcomed guests for over 100 years and is home to the world famous Pudding Club, formed in 1985 to promote traditional English puddings. Individuality is a hallmark here, as reflected in a number of the bedrooms that have been styled around to a pudding theme. Public areas are stylish and include the air-conditioned restaurant, lounges and meeting rooms.

Rooms 48 en suite (7 fmly) (14 GF) S £99-£105; D £140-£220 (incl. bkfst) **Facilities** Wi-fi in bedrooms Xmas New Year **Services** Lift **Parking** 37 **Notes** LB

★★★ 75% HOTEL

Noel Arms

High St GL55 6AT

☎ 01386 840317 01386 841136

e-mail: reception@noelarmshotel.com

web: www.noelarmshotel.com

Dir: *off A44 onto B4081 to Chipping Campden, 1st right down hill into town. Hotel on right opposite Market Hall*

PETS: Bedrooms (6GF) unattended **Charges** £15 per stay **Public areas** bar only **Exercise area** on site car park **Facilities** vet info **Restrictions** Small - medium dogs preferred

This historic 14th-century hotel has a wealth of character and charm, and retains some of its original features. Bedrooms are very individual in style, but all have high levels of comfort and interesting interior design. Such distinctiveness is also evident throughout the public areas, which include the popular bar, conservatory lounge and attractive restaurant.

Rooms 26 en suite (1 fmly) (6 GF) **Facilities** Wi-fi available **Parking** 26

★★★★ BED & BREAKFAST

Staddlestones

7 Aston Rd GL55 6HR

☎ 01386 849288

e-mail: info@staddle-stones.com

web: www.staddle-stones.com

Dir: *B4081 signed to Mickleton, out of Chipping Campden 200mtrs. House on right opp gravel lane*

PETS: Bedrooms Charges charge for damage **Grounds** accessible disp bin **Exercise area** track adjacent **Facilities** walks info vet info **On Request** fridge access torch towels **Other** pets allowed in Garden Room only **Resident Pets:** Casper (Bearded Collie), Phoebe (Border Collie)

A warm welcome can be expected from the host Pauline Kirton at this delightful property, situated just a short walk from the Cotswold village of Chipping Campden and an ideal base for walking, cycling, golf or just relaxing. The accommodation consists of three comfortable bedrooms offering some thoughtful extras for guests use. A hearty breakfast is taken in the dining room around the communal table, and offers a good choice using mostly organic produce from local farms. Dinner can be provided by arrangement.

Rooms 2 en suite 1 annexe en suite (1 fmly) D £65-£85* **Facilities** FTV TVB tea/coffee Cen ht Dinner Last d previous day **Parking** 6 **Notes** No children 12yrs

U

The Kings

The Square GL55 6AW

☎ 01386 840256 & 841056 01386 841598

e-mail: info@kingscampden.co.uk

Dir: *In centre of town square*

PETS: Bedrooms sign **Stables** nearby **Charges** £5 per night **Public areas** except restaurant (on leads) **Grounds** accessible disp bin **Exercise area** 5 mins **Resident Pets:** Ceriad & Spoch (cats)

At the time of going to press the rating for this establishment was not confirmed. This may be due to a change of ownership or because it has only recently joined the AA rating scheme. For further details please see the AA website: www.theAA.com

Rooms 14 en suite (2 fmly) **Facilities** FTV TVB tea/coffee Direct dial from bedrooms Cen ht Dinner Last d 9.30pm Wi-fi available **Parking** 8

CIRENCESTER

MAP 03 SP00

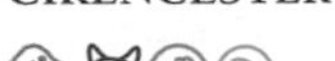

★★★★ 72% HOTEL

The Crown of Crucis

Ampney Crucis GL7 5RS

☎ 01285 851806 🖹 01285 851735

e-mail: reception@thecrownofcrucis.co.uk

web: www.thecrownofcrucis.co.uk

Dir: *A417 to Fairford, hotel 2.5m on left*

PETS: Bedrooms (13GF) unattended **Stables** stable in village, please phone for details **Charges** £6 per night charge for damage **Public areas** in bar only **Grounds** accessible disp bin **Exercise area** over bridge nearby **Facilities** walks info vet info **On Request** fridge access torch

This delightful hotel consists of two buildings; one a 16th-century coaching inn, which now houses the bar and restaurant, and a more modern bedroom block which surrounds a courtyard. Rooms are attractively appointed and offer modern facilities; the restaurant serves a range of imaginative dishes.

Rooms 25 en suite (2 fmly) (13 GF) S £60-£89; D £80-£138 (incl. bkfst)✳ **Facilities** Wi-fi in bedrooms **Parking** 82 **Notes** LB RS 25-26 Dec & 1 Jan

★★★ 79% HOTEL

Best Western Stratton House

Gloucester Rd GL7 2LE

☎ 01285 651761 🖹 01285 640024

e-mail: stratton.house@forestdale.com

web: www.forestdale.com

Dir: *M4 junct 15, A419 to Cirencester. Hotel on left on A417 or M5 junct 11 to Cheltenham onto B4070 to A417. Hotel on right*

PETS: Bedrooms unattended **Charges Public areas** except restaurant **Exercise area**

This attractive 17th-century manor house is quietly situated about half a mile from the town centre. The comfortable bedrooms are well presented and spacious; premier rooms are available. The well appointed drawing rooms and restaurant has beautiful views over walled gardens - the perfect place to enjoy pre-dinner drinks on a summer evening.

Rooms 39 en suite (9 GF) S £94-£105; D £114-£135 (incl. bkfst)✳ **Facilities** Wi-fi available Xmas New Year **Parking** 100 **Notes** LB

★★★ 71% HOTEL

Fleece Hotel

Market Place GL7 2NZ

☎ 01285 658507 🖹 01285 651017

e-mail: relax@fleecehotel.co.uk

web: www.fleecehotel.co.uk

Dir: *A417/A419 Burford road junct, follow signs for town centre. Right at lights into 'The Waterloo', car park 250yds on left*

PETS: Bedrooms (4GF) unattended **Stables** nearby (1m) **Charges** £8 per night charge for damage **Public areas** except restaurant **Exercise area** 200yds **Facilities** walks info vet info **On Request** fridge access

This old, town centre coaching inn, which dates back to the Tudor period, retains many original features such as flagstone-floors and oak beams. Well-equipped bedrooms vary in size and shape, but all offer good levels of comfort and have plenty of character. The bar lounge is a popular venue for morning coffee, and the stylish restaurant offers a range of dishes in an informal and convivial atmosphere.

Rooms 28 en suite (3 fmly) (4 GF) S £59-£119; D £79-£129 (incl. bkfst)✳ **Facilities** Wi-fi available Xmas New Year **Parking** 10

CLEARWELL MAP 03 SO50

★★★ 75% @@ HOTEL

Tudor Farmhouse Hotel & Restaurant

High St GL16 8JS

☎ 01594 833046 📠 01594 837093

e-mail: info@tudorfarmhousehotel.co.uk

web: www.tudorfarmhousehotel.co.uk

Dir: *Off A4136 onto B4228, through Coleford, turn right into Clearwell, hotel on right just before War Memorial Cross*

PETS: Bedrooms (8GF) unattended **Charges** £5 per pet per night charge for damage **Grounds** accessible on leads disp bin **Exercise area Facilities** walks info vet info **On Request** torch towels **Resident Pets:** 2 cats

Dating from the 13th century, this idyllic former farmhouse retains a host of original features including exposed stonework, oak beams, wall panelling and wonderful inglenook fireplaces. Bedrooms have great individuality and style and are located either within the main house or in converted buildings in the grounds. Creative menus offer quality cuisine, served in the intimate, candlelit restaurant.

Rooms 5 en suite 15 annexe en suite (3 fmly) (8 GF) S £60-£65; D £90-£210 (incl. bkfst)* **Facilities** STV FTV Wi-fi in bedrooms New Year **Parking** 30 **Notes** LB Closed 24-27 Dec

★★★ 68% @ HOTEL

Wyndham Arms

GL16 8JT

☎ 01594 833666 📠 01594 836450

e-mail: nigel@thewyndhamhotel.co.uk

Dir: *Off B4228, in centre of village on B4231*

PETS: Bedrooms (6GF) unattended **Stables** on site **Charges** £5 per night charge for damage **Public areas** except at food service (on leads) **Grounds** accessible disp bin **Exercise area** on site fenced gardens **Facilities** washing facs cage storage walks info vet info **On Request** fridge access torch towels **Resident Pets:** Ruby & Poppy (Irish Red Setters)

The history of this charming village inn can be traced back over 600 years. It has exposed stone-walls, original beams and an impressive inglenook fireplace in the friendly bar. Most bedrooms are in a modern extension, whilst rooms in the main house are more traditional in style. A range of dishes is offered in the bar or restaurant.

Rooms 6 en suite 12 annexe en suite (3 fmly) (6 GF) S £50-£65; D £85-£115 (incl. bkfst) **Facilities** Wi-fi available Xmas **Parking** 52 **Notes** LB

COLEFORD MAP 03 SO51

★★★ 66% HOTEL

Speech House

GL16 7EL

☎ 01594 822607 📠 01594 823658

e-mail: relax@thespeechhouse.co.uk

Dir: *M48 junct 2 to Chepstow, A48 to Blakeney, turn left signed Parkend, right, hotel on right*

PETS: Bedrooms (18GF) unattended **Stables** nearby (4m) **Public areas** except dining room (on leads) **Grounds** accessible **Exercise area Facilities** washing facs cage storage walks info vet info

This hotel is located in the heart of the Forest of Dean, and has plenty of history and character. Bedrooms vary considerably in terms of space, from the larger rooms in the main building to a range of smaller rooms in the adjacent courtyard. Popular with walkers, the friendly and relaxed bar offers a range of snacks through the day and evening, while the more formal restaurant provides a good selection of carefully prepared ingredients for an enjoyable dinner.

Rooms 15 en suite 22 annexe rms (11 en suite) (3 fmly) (18 GF) S £55-£75; D £80-£150 (incl. bkfst)* **Facilities** Wi-fi in bedrooms Xmas New Year **Parking** 65

★★★★ FARM HOUSE

Dryslade Farm *(SO581147)*

English Bicknor GL16 7PA

☎ 01594 860259 ▤ 01594 860259 Mrs D Gwilliam

e-mail: daphne@drysladefarm.co.uk

web: www.drysladefarm.co.uk

Dir: *3m N of Coleford. Off A4136 onto B4432, right towards English Bicknor, farm 1m*

PETS: Bedrooms Charges charge for damage **Public areas** except breakfast room **Grounds** accessible disp bin **Exercise area Facilities** dog scoop/disp bags washing facs cage storage walks info vet info **On Request** fridge access torch towels **Resident Pets:** Kay & Milly (Spaniels)

Guests receive a warm welcome at this 184-acre working farm, which dates from 1780 and has been in the same family for almost 100 years. The en suite bedrooms are attractively furnished in natural pine and are well equipped. The lounge leads onto a conservatory where hearty breakfasts are served.

Rooms 3 en suite (1 GF) S £45-£50; D £60-£70 **Facilities** TVB tea/coffee Cen ht TVL **Parking** 6 **Notes LB** 184 acres Beef

★★★ BED & BREAKFAST

Cor Unum

Monmouth Rd, Edge-End GL16 7HB

☎ 01594 837960

e-mail: antony@jones3649.freeserve.co.uk

Dir: *On A4136 in village of Edge End*

PETS: Bedrooms Charges charge for damage **Public areas Grounds** accessible disp bin **Exercise area** 300yds **Facilities** food (pre-bookable) food bowl water bowl bedding dog chews cat treats pet sitting dog walking washing facs cage storage vet info **On Request** fridge access torch towels **Other** pet facilities may be pre-arranged when booking **Restrictions** small-medium dogs only

A genuine welcome is assured at this comfortably appointed bungalow which is located in the heart of the Forest of Dean. Bedrooms are neatly furnished, and the lounge has wonderful views across the garden of the Welsh mountains. Breakfast, served in the cosy dining room, is a tasty and fulfilling start to the day.

Rooms 3 rms (2 en suite) (3 GF) S £25-£35; D £50-£80* **Facilities** TVB tea/coffee Cen ht TVL **Parking** 1 **Notes LB** No children

CORSE LAWN — MAP 03 SO83

★★★ ®® HOTEL

Corse Lawn House

GL19 4LZ

☎ 01452 780771 ▤ 01452 780840

e-mail: enquiries@corselawn.com

web: www.corselawn.com

Dir: *on B4211 5m SW of Tewkesbury*

PETS: Bedrooms (5GF) unattended sign **Public areas** except restaurant (on leads) **Grounds** accessible disp bin **Exercise area** 100yds **Facilities** food (pre-bookable) washing facs walks info vet info **On Request** fridge access torch **Resident Pets:** Sugar & Spice (Black Labradors), Donna & Gigi (horses)

This gracious Grade II listed Queen Anne house has been home to the Hine family since 1978. Aided by an enthusiastic and committed team, the family still presides over all aspects, creating a relaxed and wonderfully comforting environment. Bedrooms offer a reassuring mix of comfort and quality. The restaurant is very much at the heart of this establishment and the impressive cuisine is based upon excellent produce, much of it locally sourced.

Rooms 19 en suite (2 fmly) (5 GF) S £95; D £150 (incl. bkfst)* **Facilities** STV Wi-fi in bedrooms Badminton Table tennis New Year **Parking** 62 **Notes LB** Closed 24-26 Dec

DUMBLETON — MAP 04 SP03

★★★ 75% HOTEL

Dumbleton Hall

WR11 7TS

☎ 01386 881240 ▤ 01386 882142

e-mail: dh@pofr.co.uk

Dir: *M5 junct 9/A46. 2nd exit at rdbt signed Evesham. Through Beckford for 1m, turn right signed Dumbleton. Hotel at S end of village.*

PETS: Bedrooms unattended **Charges** £5 per night **Grounds** accessible **Exercise area** on site grounds

Originally constructed in the 16th century, and re-built in the mid-18th century this mansion is set in 19 acres of landscaped gardens and

CONTINUED

DUMBLETON CONTINUED

parkland. Panoramic views of the Vale of Evesham can be seen from every window. Spacious public rooms make this an ideal venue for weddings, conferences or just as a hideaway retreat - its location makes an ideal touring base. The individually designed bedrooms vary in size and layout; one room is adapted for less able guests.

Rooms 34 en suite (9 fmly) S £125; D £265 (incl. bkfst)* **Facilities** Wi-fi available Xmas New Year **Services** Lift **Parking** 60 **Notes** LB

FAIRFORD MAP 04 SP10

★★ 68% HOTEL

Bull Hotel

The Market Place GL7 4AA

☎ 01285 712535 & 712217 📠 01285 713782

e-mail: info@thebullhotelfairford.co.uk

Dir: *on A417 in market square adjacent to post office*

PETS: Bedrooms (2GF) unattended **Charges** £5 per night £20 per week charge for damage **Public areas** except restaurant (on leads) **Grounds** accessible **Exercise area** 100yds **Facilities** food bowl water bowl dog chews cat treats washing facs cage storage walks info vet info **On Request** fridge access torch towels **Resident Pets:** Foxy '5' (Pomeranian)

Located in a picturesque Cotswold market town, this family-run inn dates back to the 15th century and still retains much period character and charm. A wide range of meals can be enjoyed in the popular bar or alternatively in the bistro restaurant. Bedrooms are individual in style and a number overlook the square.

Rooms 22 rms (20 en suite) 4 annexe en suite (4 fmly) (2 GF) S £59.50-£69.50; D £89.50-£99.50 (incl. bkfst) **Facilities** Fishing Cycle hire New Year **Parking** 10 **Notes** LB

FOSSEBRIDGE MAP 04 SP01

★★★★ INN

The Inn at Fossebridge

GL54 3JS

☎ 01285 720721 📠 01285 720793

e-mail: info@fossebridgeinn.co.uk

Dir: *Situated on A429, 3m S of A40 & 6m N of Cirencester*

PETS: Bedrooms Public areas (on leads) **Grounds** accessible on leads disp bin **Exercise area Facilities** water bowl dog chews feeding mat walks info vet info **On Request** fridge access towels **Resident Pets:** Harry (West Highland Terrier)

The Inn at Fossebridge is around 300 years old, and used to be a coaching inn on the Fosseway. Today, it is a beautiful Cotswold retreat, with wonderful accommodation and grounds, located not too far from Stratford-upon-Avon, Cheltenham and Cirencester. Fine food is served in the character bar and dining areas, and a warm welcome awaits all travellers resting at this delightful inn.

Rooms 8 en suite (1 fmly) S £90-£130; D £100-£140* **Facilities** STV TVB tea/coffee Cen ht TVL Dinner Last d 9.30pm Fishing **Parking** 30 **Notes** LB No coaches

GLOUCESTER MAP 03 SO81

★★★ 80% HOTEL

Hatherley Manor

CLASSIC BRITISH HOTELS

Down Hatherley Ln GL2 9QA

☎ 01452 730217 📠 01452 731032

e-mail: reservations@hatherleymanor.com

web: www.hatherleymanor.com

Dir: *off A38 into Down Hatherley Lane, signed. Hotel 600yds on left*

PETS: Bedrooms unattended **Grounds** accessible **Exercise area**

Within easy striking distance of the M5, Gloucester, Cheltenham and the Cotswolds, this stylish 17th-century manor remains popular with both business and leisure guests. Bedrooms offer contemporary comforts. A range of meeting and function rooms is available.

Rooms 52 en suite S £59-£270; D £59-£270 **Facilities** FTV Wi-fi in bedrooms Xmas New Year **Parking** 250 **Notes** LB

►►► Red Lion Caravan & Camping Park

(SO849258)

Wainlode Hill, Norton GL2 9LW

☎ 01452 730251 📠 01452 730251

web: www.redlioninn-caravancampingpark.co.uk

Dir: *Turn off A38 at Norton and follow road to river*

PETS: Charges 1st dog free, 2nd dog £1.50 per night disp bin **Exercise area** river bank adjacent **Facilities** on site shop food dog chews cat treats walks info vet info **Other** prior notice required; pets must not roam free

Open all year Last arrival 22.00hrs Last departure 11.00hrs

An attractive meadowland park, adjacent to a traditional pub, with the River Severn just across a country lane. This is an ideal touring and fishing base. A 13-acre site with 60 touring pitches, 10 hardstandings and 85 statics.

LAVERTON MAP 04 SP03

★★★★ GUEST ACCOMMODATION

Leasow House

Laverton Meadows WR12 7NA

☎ 01386 584526 📠 01386 584596

e-mail: leasow@hotmail.com

web: www.leasow.co.uk

Dir: *2m SW of Broadway. Off B4632 towards Wormington, 500yds on right*

PETS: Bedrooms (1GF) unattended **Charges** £5 min donation to Guide Dogs or Dogs Trust charge for damage **Grounds** accessible disp bin **Exercise area**

Located in countryside to the south-west of Broadway, this 16th-century former farmhouse has been restored to provide high standards of comfort. Bedrooms have a wealth of extras and the attractive dining room is the setting for comprehensive breakfasts. There is also an elegant library lounge and a warm welcome is assured.

Rooms 5 en suite 2 annexe en suite (2 fmly) (1 GF) **Facilities** TVB tea/coffee Direct dial from bedrooms Cen ht **Parking** 10 **Notes** No children 8yrs Closed Xmas & New Year

LOWER SLAUGHTER MAP 04 SP12

★★★ 79% ❀❀ HOTEL

Washbourne Court

von Essen hotels
A PRIVATE COLLECTION
www.vonessenhotels.com

GL54 2HS

☎ 01451 822143 🖷 01451 821045

e-mail: info@washbournecourt.co.uk

web: www.vonessenhotels.co.uk

Dir: *Exit A429 at 'The Slaughters' sign, between Stow-on-the-Wold & Bourton-on-the-Water. Hotel in village centre*

PETS: Bedrooms (4GF) unattended **Charges** £10 per night £40 per week charge for damage **Public areas** except restaurant (on leads) **Grounds** accessible on leads **Exercise area** 50mtrs **Facilities** food (pre-bookable) food bowl water bowl dog walking dog grooming cage storage walks info vet info **On Request** fridge access torch towels **Other** dog basket available

Beamed ceilings, log fires and flagstone floors are some of the attractive features of this part 17th-century hotel, set in four acres of immaculate grounds beside the River Eye. The smartly decorated bedrooms are situated in the main house and there are also self-contained cottages, many offering lovely views. The riverside terrace is popular during summer months, whilst the elegant dining room serves an interesting menu and a comprehensive wine list.

Rooms 30 en suite (4 GF) **Parking** 40

MICHAEL WOOD MOTORWAY SERVICE AREA (M5) MAP 03 ST79

BUDGET HOTEL

Days Inn Michaelwood

DAYS INN

Michael Wood Service Area, Lower Wick GL11 6DD

☎ 01454 261513 🖷 01454 269150

e-mail: michaelwood.hotel@welcomebreak.co.uk

web: www.welcomebreak.co.uk

Dir: *M5 northbound between junct 13 and 14*

PETS: Bedrooms unattended **Charges** charge for damage **Public areas Grounds** accessible on leads disp bin **Exercise area Facilities** walks info vet info **On Request** fridge access torch towels **Restrictions** no dangerous breeds (see page 7)

This modern building offers accommodation in smart, spacious and well-equipped bedrooms, suitable for families and business travellers, and all with en suite bathrooms. Refreshments may be taken at the nearby family restaurant.

Rooms 38 en suite S £39-£59; D £49-£69*

NEWENT MAP 03 SO72

►►► Pelerine Caravan and Camping

(SO645183)

Ford House Rd GL18 1LQ

☎ 01531 822761

e-mail: pelerine@hotmail.com

web: www.newent.biz

Dir: *1m from Newent*

PETS: Charges £1 per night disp bin **Exercise area** adjacent **Facilities** washing facs vet info **Other** prior notice required **Resident Pets:** Narla & Simba (Spaniels), Buttons (cat)

Open Mar-Nov Last arrival 22.00hrs Last departure 16.00hrs

A pleasant site divided into two areas, one of which is for adults only, with hardstandings and electric hook ups in each area. It is close to several vineyards, and well positioned in the north of the Forest of Dean with Tewkesbury and Cheltenham within easy reach. A 5-acre site with 35 touring pitches.

Notes ®

RANGEWORTHY MAP 03 ST68

★★ 71% HOTEL

Rangeworthy Court

Church Ln, Wotton Rd BS37 7ND

☎ 01454 228347 🖷 01454 228945

e-mail: reception@rangeworthycourt.com

Dir: *Signed from B4058. Hotel at end of Church Lane*

PETS: Bedrooms Charges £3 per night charge for damage **Public areas** except restaurant (on leads) **Grounds** accessible disp bin **Exercise area Facilities** food bowl water bowl walks info vet info **On Request** torch towels **Resident Pets:** Bennie (German Shepherd/Corgi cross)

This welcoming manor house hotel is peacefully located in its own grounds, and is within easy reach of the motorway network. The character bedrooms come in a variety of sizes and there is a choice of comfortable lounges in which to enjoy a drink before dinner. The relaxing restaurant offers a selection of carefully prepared, enjoyable dishes.

Rooms 13 en suite (4 fmly) S fr £82.25; D fr £99.87 (incl. bkfst) **Facilities** FTV Wi-fi available **Parking** 30 **Notes** Closed 24-30 Dec

ENGLAND

SLIMBRIDGE MAP 03 SO70

►►► Tudor Caravan & Camping *(SO728040)*

Shepherds Patch GL2 7BP

☎ 01453 890483

e-mail: aa@tudorcaravanpark.co.uk

web: www.tudorcaravanpark.com

Dir: *From M5 junct 13 follow signs for WWT Wetlands Wildlife Centre-Slimbridge. Site at rear of Tudor Arms pub*

PETS: Stables nearby (2m) **Charges** £1 per night disp bin **Exercise area** on site rally field available when not in use **Facilities** on site shop food bowl water bowl walks info vet info **Other** prior notice required

Open all year Last arrival 20.00hrs Last departure noon

An orchard-style park sheltered by mature trees and shrubs, set in an attractive meadow beside a canal. This tidy site offers both level grass and gravel pitches complete with electric hook-ups, and there is a separate area for adults only. Slimbridge Wetlands Centre is close by, and there is much scope locally for bird-watching. An 8-acre site with 75 touring pitches, 48 hardstandings.

Notes

STOW-ON-THE-WOLD MAP 04 SP12

★★★ 75% SMALL HOTEL

The Unicorn

Sheep St GL54 1HQ

☎ 01451 830257 01451 831090

e-mail: reception@birchhotels.co.uk

Dir: *at junct of A429 & A436*

PETS: Bedrooms unattended **Charges** £10 per night **Public areas** bar only **Grounds** accessible **Exercise area** 1m **Facilities** water bowl cage storage walks info vet info

This attractive limestone hotel dates back to the 17th century. Individually designed bedrooms include some delightful four-poster rooms. Spacious public areas retain much character and include a choice of inviting lounges and a traditional bar offering a good selection of bar meals and ales. The restaurant provides a stylish venue for impressive cuisine.

Rooms 20 en suite S £95-£100; D £125-£190 (incl. bkfst & dinner)* **Facilities** Wi-fi available Xmas New Year **Parking** 40 **Notes** LB

★★★ 74% HOTEL

The Royalist

Digbeth St GL54 1BN

☎ 01451 830670 01451 870048

e-mail: stay@theroyalisthotel.com

web: www.theroyalisthotel.com

Dir: *Off A436*

PETS: Bedrooms (2GF) unattended **Public areas** in Eagle & Child pub only (on leads) **Exercise area** 200mtrs **Facilities** walks info vet info **Resident Pets:** Henry (Black Labrador), Daisy (Flat Coat Retriever)

Verified as the oldest inn in England, this charming hotel has a wealth of history and character. Bedrooms and public areas have been stylishly and sympathetically decorated to ensure high levels of comfort at every turn. Some rooms are in an adjoining annexe. There are two eating options: the restaurant offers high-quality cooking and the Eagle and Child provides a more informal alternative.

Rooms 10 en suite 4 annexe en suite (1 fmly) (2 GF) S £65-£110; D £100-£160 (incl. bkfst)* **Facilities** Wi-fi in bedrooms Xmas New Year **Parking** 8 **Notes** LB

★★ 71% SMALL HOTEL

Old Stocks

The Square GL54 1AF

☎ 01451 830666 01451 870014

e-mail: aa@theoldstockshotel.co.uk

web: www.oldstockshotel.co.uk

Dir: *Exit A429 to town centre. Hotel facing village green*

PETS: Bedrooms (4GF) unattended **Charges** £5 per night **Public areas** except restaurant (on leads) **Grounds** accessible on leads **Exercise area** 500yds **On Request** torch **Other** patio garden bedrooms are most suitable **Restrictions** well behaved dogs only

Overlooking the old market square, this Grade II listed, mellow Cotswold-stone building is a comfortable and friendly base from which to explore this picturesque area. There's lots of character throughout, and the bedrooms offer individuality and charm. Facilities include a guest lounge, restaurant and bar, whilst outside, the patio is a popular summer venue for refreshing drinks and good food.

Rooms 15 en suite 3 annexe en suite (5 fmly) (4 GF) **Parking** 12 **Notes** LB

★★★ GUEST ACCOMMODATION

Limes

Evesham Rd GL54 1EJ

☎ 01451 830034 🖷 01451 830034

e-mail: thelimes@zoom.co.uk

Dir: *500yds from village centre on A424*

PETS: Bedrooms (2GF) **Charges** charge for damage **Public areas** except breakfast room (on leads) **Grounds** accessible on leads disp bin **Exercise area** **Facilities** water bowl dog chews leads walks info vet info **On Request** fridge access torch towels **Resident Pets:** Casey (Doberman)

Just a short walk from the village centre, this Victorian house provides a comfortable base from which to explore this beautiful area. Bedroom styles vary, with four-poster and ground-floor rooms offered. A warm and genuine welcome is extended, and many guests return on a regular basis. A spacious lounge is available and breakfast is served in the light and airy dining room.

Rooms 5 en suite 1 annexe en suite (2 fmly) (2 GF) S £35-£52; D £50-£60* **Facilities** STV TVB tea/coffee Cen ht TVL **Parking** 4 **Notes** Closed Xmas

STROUD MAP 03 SO80

★★★★ BED & BREAKFAST

Hyde Crest

Cirencester Rd GL6 8PE

☎ 01453 731631

e-mail: anthea@hydecrest.demon.co.uk

web: www.hydecrest.co.uk

Dir: *Off A419, 5m E of Stroud, signed Minchinhampton & Aston Down, house 3rd right opp Ragged Cot pub*

PETS: Bedrooms (3GF) unattended **Public areas** **Grounds** accessible disp bin **Exercise area** local walks, 500-acre common within 1m **Facilities** washing facs walks info vet info **On Request** fridge access torch towels **Resident Pets:** Polly (Cocker Spaniel)

Hyde Crest lies on the edge of the picturesque Cotswold village of Minchinhampton. Bedrooms are located at ground floor level, each with a private patio where welcome refreshments are enjoyed upon arrival (weather permitting). Guests are attentively cared for and scrumptious breakfasts are served in the small lounge-dining room around a communal table.

Rooms 3 en suite (3 GF) S fr £40; D fr £65* **Facilities** TVB tea/coffee Cen ht TVL Wi-fi available **Parking** 6 **Notes** No children 10yrs RS Xmas & New Year

TETBURY MAP 03 ST89

★★★ 77% HOTEL

Best Western Hare & Hounds

Best Western

Westonbirt GL8 8QL

☎ 01666 880233 & 881000 🖷 01666 880241

e-mail: enquiries@hareandhoundshotel.com

web: www.hareandhoundshotel.com

Dir: *2.5m SW of Tetbury on A433*

PETS: Bedrooms (13GF) unattended **Charges** £5 per night charge for damage **Public areas** except restaurant (on leads) **Grounds** accessible on leads disp bin **Exercise area** **Facilities** water bowl dog chews cage storage walks info vet info **On Request** fridge access

This popular hotel, set in extensive grounds, is situated close to Westonbirt Arboretum and has remained under the same ownership for over 50 years. Bedrooms are individual in style; those in the main house are more traditional and the stylish cottage rooms are contemporary in design. Public rooms include the informal bar and light, airy lounges - one with a log fire in colder months. Guests can eat either in the bar or the attractive restaurant.

Rooms 24 en suite 21 annexe en suite (8 fmly) (13 GF) S £88-£93; D £110-£125 (incl. bkfst)* **Facilities** FTV Putt green Wi-fi in bedrooms Xmas New Year **Parking** 85 **Notes** LB

ENGLAND

TEWKESBURY MAP 03 SO83

★★★★ 72% HOTEL

Tewkesbury Park Hotel Golf & Country Club

folio Hotels

Lincoln Green Ln GL20 7DN

☎ 0870 609 6101 🖷 01684 292386

e-mail: tewkesburypark@foliohotels.com

web: www.foliohotels.com/tewkesburypark

Dir: *M5 junct 9/A438 through Tewkesbury, A38 (pass Abbey on left), right into Lincoln Green Lane*

PETS: Bedrooms (27GF) sign **Charges** £10 per night charge for damage **Public areas** assist dogs only (on leads) **Exercise area Facilities** vet info **On Request** fridge access

Only two miles from the M5, this extended 18th-century manor house boasts wonderful views across the Malvern Hills from its hilltop position. Bedrooms have contemporary comforts and many enjoy countryside views. In addition to the well-established golf course, an indoor pool, gym, sauna, squash and tennis courts are also available.

Rooms 82 en suite (8 fmly) (27 GF) D £78-£148 (incl. bkfst)✳ **Facilities Spa** STV supervised 18 Squash Gym Putt green Wi-fi available Xmas New Year **Parking** 250 **Notes LB**

THORNBURY MAP 03 ST69

★★★ HOTEL

Thornbury Castle

von Essen hotels A PRIVATE COLLECTION www.vonessenhotels.com

Castle St BS35 1HH

☎ 01454 281182 🖷 01454 416188

e-mail: info@thornburycastle.co.uk

web: www.vonessenhotels.co.uk

Dir: *on A38 N'bound from Bristol take 1st turn to Thornbury. At end of High St left into Castle St, follow brown sign, entrance to Castle on left behind St Mary's Church*

PETS: Bedrooms (4GF) **Charges** £10 per night £70 per week charge for damage **Grounds** accessible on leads **Exercise area** 0.5m **Facilities** washing facs cage storage walks info vet info **On Request** fridge access torch towels

Henry VIII ordered the first owner of this castle to be beheaded! Guests today have the opportunity of sleeping in historical surroundings fitted out with all the modern amenities. Most rooms have four-poster or coronet beds and real fires. Tranquil lounges enjoy views over the gardens, while elegant, wood-panelled dining rooms make memorable settings for a leisurely award-winning meal.

Rooms 27 en suite (3 fmly) (4 GF) S £140-£215; D £155-£435 (incl. bkfst)✳ **Facilities** STV FTV Wi-fi available Archery Helicopter ride Clay pigeon shooting Massage treatment Xmas New Year **Parking** 50 **Notes LB**

TORMARTON MAP 03 ST77

★★ 76% HOTEL

Best Western Compass Inn

Best Western

GL9 1JB

☎ 01454 218242 & 218577 🖷 01454 218741

e-mail: info@compass-inn.co.uk

web: www.compass-inn.co.uk

Dir: *0.5m from M4 junct 18*

PETS: Bedrooms (12GF) unattended **Charges** £3 per night **Public areas** except restaurant **Grounds** accessible **Exercise area** countryside **Resident Pets:** Standard Poodle & cat

Originally a coaching inn dating from the 18th century, this hostelry has grown considerably over the years. Bedrooms are spacious and well equipped, whilst public areas include a choice of bars and varied dining options. A range of conference rooms is also available, providing facilities for varied functions.

Rooms 26 en suite (6 fmly) (12 GF) S £67.50-£98; D £76.50-£130✳ **Facilities** FTV Wi-fi in bedrooms French boules Golf driving nets New Year **Parking** 160 **Notes LB** Closed 24-26 Dec

WINCHCOMBE MAP 04 SP02

►►► Winchcombe Camping & Caravanning Club Site *(SP007324)*

Brooklands Farm, Alderton GL20 8NX

☎ 01242 620259

web: www.thefriendlyclub.co.uk

Dir: *M5 junct 9 onto A46, straight on at rdbt onto B4077 signed Stow-on-the-Wold. Site 3m on right*

PETS: Public areas except in buildings disp bin **Exercise area** on site dog walk **Facilities** walks info vet info **Other** prior notice required

Open 16 Mar-15 Jan Last arrival 21.00hrs Last departure noon

A pleasant rural park with pitches spaced around two attractive lakes offering good fishing, and the benefit of a long season. This flower-filled park is in an area of historic buildings and picturesque villages between Cheltenham and Tewkesbury. A 20-acre site with 80 touring pitches, 63 hardstandings.

Notes Site gates closed 23.00hrs-07.00hrs

GREATER LONDON

HEATHROW AIRPORT (LONDON) MAP 04 TQ07

★★★ 78% HOTEL

Novotel London Heathrow

Cherry Ln UB7 9HB

☎ 01895 431431 🖷 01895 431221

e-mail: H1551-gm@accor.com

web: www.novotel.com

Dir: *M4 junct 4, follow Uxbridge signs on A408. Keep left, take 2nd exit off traffic island into Cherry Ln signed West Drayton. Hotel on left*

PETS: Bedrooms Exercise area Other please contact for further details

Conveniently located for Heathrow Airport and the motorway network, this modern hotel provides comfortable accommodation. The large, airy indoor atrium creates a sense of space to the public areas, which include an all-day restaurant and bar, meeting rooms, fitness centre and swimming pool. Ample secure parking is available.

Rooms 178 en suite (178 fmly) (10 GF) S £65-£180; D £65-£180 **Facilities** STV Gym Wi-fi available **Services** Lift air con **Parking** 100 (charged) **Notes** LB

★★★ GUEST ACCOMMODATION

Harmondsworth Hall

Summerhouse Ln, Harmondsworth Village UB7 0BG

☎ 020 8759 1824 & 07713 104229 🖷 020 8897 6385

e-mail: elaine@harmondsworthhall.com

web: www.harmondsworthhall.com

Dir: *M4 junct 4, A3044 Holloway Ln onto Harmondsworth High St, left after Crown pub*

PETS: Bedrooms Charges £10 per stay charge for damage **Public areas** except breakfast room (on leads) **Grounds** accessible disp bin **Exercise area** Harmondsworth Moor Country Park 2 mins walk **Facilities** cage storage walks info vet info **On Request** fridge access torch towels **Resident Pets:** Connie (Golden Retriever)

Hidden away in the old part of the village, this delightful property has been restored and converted into a spacious guest house. It is well located for the airport and motorways. Breakfast is served in an attractive wood-panelled dining room overlooking the gardens and there is a spacious lounge. The well-equipped bedrooms are all individually furnished.

Rooms 10 en suite (4 fmly) (2 GF) S £65-£70; D £75-£80✻ **Facilities** STV FTV TVB tea/coffee Direct dial from bedrooms Cen ht TVL Dinner Last d by arrangement Wi-fi available **Parking** 10 **Notes** LB

GREATER MANCHESTER

ALTRINCHAM MAP 07 SJ78

★★★ 77% HOTEL

Best Western Cresta Court

Church St WA14 4DP

☎ 0161 927 7272 & 927 2601 🖷 0161 929 6548

e-mail: rooms@cresta-court.co.uk

web: www.cresta-court.co.uk

PETS: Bedrooms unattended sign **Charges** charge for damage **Public areas** except bar & restaurant (on leads) **Grounds** accessible on leads **Exercise area On Request** towels

This modern hotel enjoys a prime location on the A56, close to the station, town centre shops and other amenities. Bedrooms vary in style from spacious four-posters to smaller, traditionally furnished rooms. Public areas include a choice of bars and extensive function and conference facilities.

Rooms 140 en suite (9 fmly) S £49-£89; D £59-£140 **Facilities** FTV Wi-fi in bedrooms **Services** Lift **Parking** 200

BOLTON MAP 07 SD70

★★★ GUEST HOUSE

Broomfield House

33-35 Wigan Rd, Deane BL3 5PX

☎ 01204 61570 🖷 01204 650932

e-mail: chris@broomfield.force9.net

Dir: *M61 junct 5, A58 to 1st lights, straight onto A676, premises on right*

PETS: Bedrooms unattended **Public areas Exercise area** adjacent **Facilities** washing facs cage storage walks info vet info **On Request** fridge access torch towels

A friendly relaxed atmosphere prevails at Broomfield House, close to the motorway and west of the town centre. There is a comfy lounge and separate bar area. Hearty breakfasts are served in the separate dining room.

Rooms 20 en suite (2 fmly) (2 GF) S £40-£44; D fr £54✻ **Facilities** TVB tea/coffee Licensed Cen ht TVL Wi-fi available **Parking** 12

ENGLAND

DELPH MAP 07 SD90

★★★★ GUEST ACCOMMODATION

Wellcroft House

Bleak Hey Nook OL3 5LY

☎ 01457 875017

e-mail: wellcrofthouse@hotmail.co.uk

Dir: *Off A62 on Standedge Foot Rd near A670 junct*

PETS: Bedrooms (1GF) **Charges** £5 per night **Public areas** except kitchen **Grounds** accessible **Exercise area** 100mtrs **Facilities** food (pre-bookable) food bowl water bowl bedding washing facs walks info vet info **On Request** torch towels

Commanding superb views down the valley below this former weaver's cottage offers warm traditional hospitality to walkers on the Pennine Way and those simply touring the Pennine towns and villages. Modern comforts in all bedrooms and transport from local railway or walks is routinely provided by the friendly proprietors.

Rooms 3 rms (2 en suite) (1 GF) S £30-£35; D £50-£60✻ **Facilities** TVB tea/coffee Cen ht TVL Dinner Last d 6pm Pool Table **Parking** 1 **Notes LB**

DIGGLE MAP 07 SE00

★★★★ INN

The Hanging Gate

217 Huddersfield Rd OL3 5PQ

☎ 01457 871164

e-mail: info@thehanginggate.co.uk

Dir: *A627 to Oldham, then A62 to Saddleworth, follow signs for Diggle, in centre of village*

PETS: Bedrooms Charges £5-£10 per night charge for damage **Public areas** except restaurant (on leads) **Grounds** accessible on leads disp bin **Exercise area** 20mtrs **Facilities** cage storage walks info vet info **On Request** fridge access

Resident Pets: Freddie (Miniature Schnauzer), Jaffa (cat)

Located within the village of Diggle in the heart of Saddleworth, this 200-year-old inn, with its award-winning frontage, has been sympathetically renovated to provide high standards of comfort with a warm welcome. Bedrooms combine modern facilities with creature comforts and imaginative food is available in the attractive public areas.

Rooms 4 en suite (1 fmly) **Facilities** TVB tea/coffee Cen ht Dinner Last d 8.30pm Pool Table **Parking** 20

★★ GUEST ACCOMMODATION

Sunfield Accommodation

Diglea OL3 5LA

☎ 01457 874030

e-mail: sunfield.accom@lineone.net

Dir: *Off A670 to Diggle village, off Huddersfield Rd onto Sam Rd to Diggle Hotel & signs for Diggle Ranges*

PETS: Bedrooms (4GF) **Stables** on site **Exercise area Facilities** food bowl water bowl leads cage storage walks info vet info **On Request** fridge access torch

This friendly, family-run operation is located within easy reach of Manchester and the M62, and affords wonderful views over the Pennines; bedrooms are on the ground floor and pets are made welcome. Breakfast is served at one large table and a couple of good pubs serving food are located at the bottom of the lane.

Rooms 4 en suite (1 fmly) (4 GF) S £35-£40; D £50-£60✻ **Facilities** FTV TVB tea/coffee Cen ht TVL **Parking** 11 **Notes**

MANCHESTER MAP 07 SJ89

★★★ 79% HOTEL

Novotel Manchester Centre

21 Dickinson St M1 4LX

☎ 0161 235 2200 Fax 0161 235 2210

e-mail: H3145@accor.com

web: www.novotel.com

Dir: *from Oxford Street, into Portland Street, left into Dickinson Street. Hotel on right*

PETS: Bedrooms unattended **Charges** £10 per night charge for damage **Exercise area Facilities** walks info vet info

This smart, modern property enjoys a central location convenient for theatres, shops, China Town, and Manchester's business district. Spacious bedrooms are thoughtfully equipped and brightly decorated. Open-plan, contemporary public areas include an all-day restaurant and a stylish bar. Extensive conference and meeting facilities are available.

Rooms 164 en suite (15 fmly) S £69-£149; D £69-£149✻ **Facilities** Gym Wi-fi available Steam room Sauna **Services** Lift air con **Notes LB**

BUDGET HOTEL

Ibis Hotel Manchester

Charles St, Princess St M1 7DL

☎ 0161 272 5000 🖹 0161 272 5010

e-mail: H3143@accor-hotels.com

web: www.ibishotel.com

Dir: *M62, M602 towards Manchester Centre, follow signs to UMIST(A34)*

PETS: Bedrooms Charges charge for damage **Public areas** except restaurant (on leads) **Exercise area Facilities** vet info

Modern, budget hotel offering comfortable accommodation in bright and practical bedrooms. Breakfast is self-service and dinner is available in the restaurant.

Rooms 126 en suite D £59-£95✳

BUDGET HOTEL

Ibis Manchester City Centre

96 Portland St M1 4GY

☎ 0161 234 0600 🖹 0161 234 0610

e-mail: H3142@accor.com

Dir: *In city centre, between Princess St & Oxford St. 10min walk from Piccadilly*

PETS: Bedrooms Charges Public areas except restaurant & bars (on leads) **Exercise area**

Modern, budget hotel offering comfortable accommodation in bright and practical bedrooms. Breakfast is self-service and dinner is available in the restaurant.

Rooms 127 en suite S £61-£75; D £61-£75✳

WORSLEY — MAP 07 SD70

★★★ 68% HOTEL

Novotel Manchester West

Worsley Brow M28 2YA

☎ 0161 799 3535 🖹 0161 703 8207

e-mail: H0907@accor.com

web: www.novotel.com

Dir: *adjacent to M60 junct 13*

PETS: Bedrooms (41GF) unattended **Stables** nearby (approx 5m) **Charges** £10 per night charge for damage **Grounds** accessible on leads disp bin **Exercise area** 100yds **Facilities** cage storage walks info vet info **On Request** towels

Well placed for access to the Peak and the Lake District, as well as the City of Manchester, this modern hotel successfully caters for both families and business guests. The spacious bedrooms have sofa beds and a large work area; the hotel boasts an outdoor swimming pool, children's play area, and secure parking.

Rooms 119 en suite (10 fmly) (41 GF) **Facilities** Wi-fi available **Services** Lift **Parking** 95 **Notes LB**

HAMPSHIRE

ALTON — MAP 04 SU73

★★★ 74% HOTEL

Alton Grange

London Rd GU34 4EG

☎ 01420 86565 🖹 01420 541346

e-mail: info@altongrange.co.uk

web: www.altongrange.co.uk

Dir: *from A31 right at rdbt signed Alton/Holybourne/Bordon B3004. Hotel 300yds on left*

PETS: Bedrooms (7GF) unattended **Stables** nearby **Charges** £5 per night charge for damage **Public areas** bar only (on leads) **Grounds** accessible on leads **Exercise area** 100yds **Facilities** walks info vet info **On Request** fridge access torch towels **Resident Pets:** Caramel, Barley, Smartie, Treacle, Honey, Saffron & Cracker (cats)

A friendly family owned hotel, conveniently located on the outskirts of this market town and set in two acres of lovingly tended gardens. The individually styled bedrooms, including three suites, are all thoughtfully equipped. Diners can choose between the more formal Truffles Restaurant or relaxed Muffins Brasserie. The attractive public areas include a function suite.

Rooms 26 en suite 4 annexe en suite (4 fmly) (7 GF) **Facilities** Wi-fi in bedrooms Hot air ballooning **Parking** 48 **Notes LB** No children 3yrs Closed 24 Dec-2 Jan

ANDOVER — MAP 04 SU34

★★★ 78% HOTEL

Esseborne Manor

Hurstbourne Tarrant SP11 0ER

☎ 01264 736444 🖹 01264 736725

e-mail: info@esseborne-manor.co.uk

web: www.esseborne-manor.co.uk

Dir: *halfway between Andover & Newbury on A343, just 1m N of Hurstbourne Tarrant*

PETS: Bedrooms (6GF) unattended sign **Charges** charge for damage **Grounds** accessible disp bin **Exercise area** adjacent **Facilities** food bowl water bowl washing facs cage storage walks info vet info **On Request** fridge access torch towels

Set in two acres of well-tended gardens, this attractive manor house is surrounded by the open countryside of the North Wessex Downs. Bedrooms are delightfully individual and are split between the main house, an adjoining courtyard and separate garden cottage. There's a wonderfully relaxed atmosphere throughout, and public rooms combine elegance with comfort.

Rooms 11 en suite 8 annexe en suite (2 fmly) (6 GF) S £110-£130; D £125-£180 (incl. bkfst)✳ **Facilities** STV Wi-fi in bedrooms **Parking** 50 **Notes LB**

ENGLAND

BASINGSTOKE MAP 04 SU65

★★★★ 74% HOTEL

Barceló Basingstoke Country Hotel

Barceló

Scures Hill, Nately Scures, Hook RG27 9JS

☎ 01256 764161 📠 01256 768341

e-mail: basingstokecountry@barcelo-hotels.co.uk

web: www.barcelo-hotels.co.uk

Dir: *M3 junct 5, A287 towards Newnham. Left at lights. Hotel 200mtrs on right*

PETS: Bedrooms (26GF) sign **Stables** nearby (7m) **Charges** £15 per night charge for damage **Grounds** accessible on leads disp bin **Exercise area** 100mtrs **Facilities** cage storage walks info vet info **On Request** fridge access torch

This popular hotel is close to Basingstoke and its country location ensures a quiet stay. Bedrooms are available in a number of styles, and guests have a choice of dining in the formal restaurant, or for lighter meals and snacks there is a relaxed café and a smart bar. Extensive conference and leisure facilities complete the picture.

Rooms 100 en suite (26 GF) S £65-£160∗ **Facilities** Gym Wi-fi available Sauna Solarium Steam room Dance studio Beauty treatments New Year **Services** Lift air con **Parking** 200 **Notes** RS 24 Dec-2 Jan

BEAULIEU MAP 04 SU30

★★★ 73% ® HOTEL

Beaulieu

Beaulieu Rd SO42 7YQ

☎ 023 8029 3344 📠 023 8029 2729

e-mail: beaulieu@newforesthotels.co.uk

web: www.newforesthotels.co.uk

Dir: *M27 junct 1/A337 towards Lyndhurst. Left at lights, through Lyndhurst, right onto B3056, continue for 3m*

PETS: Bedrooms unattended **Charges** £5 per night **Public areas** except food areas **Grounds** accessible **Exercise area** adjacent

Conveniently located in the heart of the New Forest and close to Beaulieu Road railway station, this popular, small hotel provides an ideal base for exploring this lovely area. Facilities include an indoor swimming pool, an outdoor children's play area and an adjoining pub. A daily changing menu is offered in the restaurant.

Rooms 20 en suite 3 annexe en suite (2 fmly) (3 GF) **Facilities** Steam room **Services** Lift **Parking** 60

BROCKENHURST MAP 04 SU30

★★★ ®®® COUNTRY HOUSE HOTEL

Whitley Ridge Hotel

Beaulieu Rd SO42 7QL

☎ 01590 622354 📠 01590 622856

e-mail: info@whitleyridge.co.uk

web: www.whitleyridge.com

Dir: *At Brockenhurst onto B3055 Beaulieu Road. 1m on left up private road.*

PETS: Stables nearby **Charges** £10 per night charge for damage **Exercise area Facilities** washing facs cage storage walks info vet info **On Request** fridge access torch **Other** small cottage available for guests with dogs **Resident Pets:** sheep, hens

This charming hotel enjoys a secluded picturesque setting in the heart of the New Forest. The newly extended and relaxing public areas, delightful grounds, smart and comfortable bedrooms and a team of helpful and attentive staff all contribute to a memorable stay. The cuisine of the well-established Le Poussin restaurant is a highlight at this venue.

Rooms 18 en suite (2 GF) S £85-£160; D £135-£320 (incl. bkfst & dinner)∗ **Facilities** Wi-fi in bedrooms Xmas New Year **Parking** 40 **Notes** LB

★★★ 85% ® HOTEL

Balmer Lawn

Lyndhurst Rd SO42 7ZB

☎ 01590 623116 📠 01590 623864

e-mail: info@balmerlawnhotel.com

Dir: *just off A337 from Brockenhurst towards Lymington*

PETS: Bedrooms unattended **Stables** nearby (1m) **Charges** £20 (1st night), £10 (subsequent nights) £80 per week charge for damage **Public areas** except restaurant **Grounds** accessible disp bin **Exercise area** direct access to New Forest National Park **Facilities** water bowl dog chews washing facs cage storage walks info vet info **On Request** fridge access torch towels

Situated in the heart of the New Forest, this peacefully located hotel provides comfortable public rooms and a wide range of bedrooms. A selection of carefully prepared and enjoyable dishes is offered in the spacious restaurant. The extensive function and leisure facilities make this popular with both families and conference delegates.

Rooms 55 en suite (10 fmly) S £99-£110; D £150-£180 (incl. bkfst) **Facilities** FTV Squash Gym Wi-fi available Indoor leisure suite Xmas New Year **Services** Lift **Parking** 100 **Notes** LB

★★★ 82% COUNTRY HOUSE HOTEL

New Park Manor

Lyndhurst Rd SO42 7QH

01590 623467 01590 622268

e-mail: info@newparkmanorhotel.co.uk

web: www.vonessenhotels.co.uk

Dir: *M27 junct 1, A337 to Lyndhurst & Brockenhurst. Hotel 1.5m on right*

PETS: Bedrooms unattended **Stables** nearby (2m) **Charges** £10 per night **Grounds** accessible **Exercise area** 100yds **Other** dogs allowed in one bedroom only

Once the favoured hunting lodge of King Charles II, this well presented hotel enjoys a peaceful setting in the New Forest and comes complete with an equestrian centre. The bedrooms are divided between the old house and a purpose-built wing. An impressive spa offers a range of treatments.

Rooms 24 en suite (6 fmly) S £118-£208; D £135-£315 (incl. bkfst)* **Facilities** Spa STV FTV Riding Gym Wi-fi available Mountain biking Xmas New Year **Parking** 70 **Notes** LB

★★★ 73% HOTEL

Forest Park

Rhinefield Rd SO42 7ZG

01590 622844 01590 623948

e-mail: forest.park@forestdale.com

web: www.forestdale.com

Dir: *A337 to Brockenhurst turn into Meerut Rd, follow road through Waters Green. Right at T-junct into Rhinefield Rd*

PETS: Bedrooms unattended **Charges** £7.50 per night **Public areas** except restaurant **Exercise area**

Situated in the heart of the New Forest, this former vicarage and war field hospital is now a hotel which offers a warm and friendly welcome to all its guests. The hotel offers a heated pool, riding, a log cabin sauna and tennis courts. The bedrooms and public areas are comfortable and stylish.

Rooms 38 en suite (2 fmly) (7 GF) S £85-£90; D £123-£129 (incl. bkfst) * **Facilities** Riding Wi-fi available Xmas New Year **Parking** 80 **Notes** LB

★★ 63% HOTEL

Watersplash

The Rise SO42 7ZP

01590 622344

e-mail: bookings@watersplash.co.uk

web: www.watersplash.co.uk

Dir: *M3 junct 13/M27 junct 1/A337 S through Lyndhurst & Brockenhurst. The Rise on left, hotel on left*

PETS: Bedrooms (3GF) unattended **Charges** £4 per night **Grounds** accessible disp bin **Exercise area Facilities** walks info vet info

This popular, welcoming hotel that dates from Victorian times, has been in the same family for over 40 years. Bedrooms have co-ordinated decor and good facilities. The restaurant overlooks the neatly tended garden and there is also a comfortably furnished lounge, separate bar and an outdoor pool.

Rooms 23 en suite (6 fmly) (3 GF) **Facilities** **Parking** 29

BURLEY — MAP 04 SU20

★★★ 75% HOTEL

Burley Manor

Ringwood Rd BH24 4BS

01425 403522 01425 403227

e-mail: burley.manor@forestdale.com

web: www.forestdale.com

Dir: *exit A31at Burley sign, hotel 3m on left*

PETS: Bedrooms unattended **Stables** on site **Charges** £7.50 per night **Public areas** except restaurant **Exercise area**

Set in extensive grounds, this 18th-century mansion house enjoys a relaxed ambience and a peaceful setting. Half of the well-equipped, comfortable bedrooms, including several with four-posters, are located in the main house. The remainder, many with balconies, are in the adjacent converted stable block overlooking the outdoor pool. Cosy public rooms benefit from log fires in winter.

Rooms 21 en suite 17 annexe en suite (2 fmly) (17 GF) D £129-£139 (incl. bkfst)* **Facilities** Riding Wi-fi available Xmas New Year **Parking** 60 **Notes** LB

ENGLAND

BURLEY CONTINUED

★★★ 70% COUNTRY HOUSE HOTEL

Moorhill House

BH24 4AH

☎ 01425 403285 01425 403715

e-mail: moorhill@newforesthotels.co.uk

web: www.newforesthotels.co.uk

Dir: *M27, A31, follow signs to Burley village, through village, up hill, turn right opposite school and cricket grounds*

PETS: Bedrooms (3GF) unattended **Stables** nearby (2m) **Charges** £5 per pet per night £35 per week **Public areas** except restaurant & bar (on leads) **Grounds** accessible **Exercise area** nearby **Facilities** water bowl walks info vet info

Situated deep in the heart of the New Forest and formerly a grand gentleman's residence, this charming hotel offers a relaxed and friendly environment. Bedrooms, of varying sizes, are smartly decorated. A range of facilities is provided and guests can relax by walking around the extensive grounds. Both dinner and breakfast offer a choice of interesting and freshly prepared dishes.

Rooms 31 en suite (13 fmly) (3 GF) S £60-£75; D £120-£156 (incl. bkfst) ✳ **Facilities** Gym Putt green Wi-fi available Badminton (Apr-Sep) Xmas New Year **Parking** 50 **Notes** LB

CADNAM — MAP 04 SU31

★★★ 75% HOTEL

Bartley Lodge

Lyndhurst Rd SO40 2NR

☎ 023 8081 2248 023 8081 2075

e-mail: bartley@newforesthotels.co.uk

web: www.newforesthotels.co.uk

Dir: *M27 junct 1 at 1st rdbt 1st exit, at 2nd rdbt 3rd exit onto A337. Hotel sign on left*

PETS: Bedrooms (2GF) unattended **Stables** nearby **Charges** £5 per night £35 per week **Public areas** except restaurant & lounge (on leads) **Grounds** accessible on leads **Exercise area** **Facilities** water bowl walks info vet info **On Request** fridge access

This 18th-century former hunting lodge is very quietly situated, yet is just minutes from the M27. Bedrooms vary in size but all are well equipped. There is a selection of small lounge areas, a cosy bar and an indoor pool, together with a small fitness suite. The Crystal dining room offers a tempting choice of well prepared dishes.

Rooms 31 en suite (12 fmly) (2 GF) S £60-£78; D £120-£156 (incl. bkfst)✳ **Facilities** Gym Wi-fi in bedrooms Xmas New Year **Parking** 60 **Notes** LB

EAST TYTHERLEY — MAP 04 SU22

★★★★ INN

The Star Inn

SO51 0LW

☎ 01794 340225

e-mail: info@starinn.co.uk

Dir: *1m S of East Tytherley*

PETS: Bedrooms (3GF) unattended **Charges** charge for damage **Public areas** except restaurant (on leads) **Grounds** accessible on leads disp bin **Exercise area** adjacent **Facilities** food (pre-bookable) food bowl water bowl washing facs cage storage walks info vet info **On Request** fridge access torch towels **Resident Pets:** Jake (Jack Russell), 3 cats

This charming coaching inn offers bedrooms in a purpose-built annexe, separate from the main pub. The spacious rooms have high levels of quality and comfort, and an outdoor children's play area is available. The inn has a loyal following of locals and visitors, drawn especially by the excellent food.

Rooms 3 annexe en suite (3 GF) S £50-£75; D £80✳ **Facilities** FTV TVB tea/coffee Cen ht Dinner Last d 9pm Wi-fi available **Parking** 50 **Notes** LB RS Sun eve & Mon

EMSWORTH — MAP 04 SU70

★★★★ BED & BREAKFAST

Hollybank House

Hollybank Ln PO10 7UN

☎ 01243 375502 01243 378118

e-mail: anna@hollybankhouse.com

web: www.hollybankhouse.com

Dir: *1m N of town centre. A259 onto B2148, 1m right onto Southleigh Rd, 3rd left onto Hollybank Ln, house at top*

PETS: Bedrooms Stables 100yds (arrangements can be made) **Charges** charge for damage **Public areas** except dining room **Grounds** accessible disp bin **Exercise area** 100yds **Facilities** cage storage walks info vet info **On Request** fridge access torch towels **Other** pets are accepted by prior arangement only

The Georgian country house stands in a 10-acre woodland garden with a tennis court on the outskirts of Emsworth, and looks out to Chichester Harbour. Emsworth has a variety of restaurants, pubs and harbour walks.

Rooms 4 rms (3 en suite) (1 pri facs) (1 fmly) S £45-£50; D £70-£75✳ **Facilities** TVB tea/coffee Cen ht Wi-fi available **Parking** 85

FAREHAM MAP 04 SU50

★★★ GUEST ACCOMMODATION

Travelrest - Solent Gateway

22 The Avenue PO14 1NS

☎ 01329 232175 🖷 01329 232196

e-mail: solentreservations@travelrest.co.uk

web: www.travelrest.co.uk

Dir: *0.5m from town centre on A27. 500yds from railway station*

PETS: Bedrooms (6GF) unattended **Charges** £5 per night charge for damage **Grounds** accessible on leads disp bin **Exercise area** 1m **Facilities** walks info vet info **Other** pets in 2 bedrooms only

Situated just west of the town centre, this well-presented accommodation is convenient for the ferry terminals and naval heritage sites. The comfortable bedrooms are spacious and well equipped, and one has a four-poster bed. Breakfast is served in the cosy conservatory-dining room and conference rooms are available.

Rooms 19 en suite (3 fmly) (6 GF) S £45-£65; D £49.50-£80* (room only) **Facilities** FTV TVB tea/coffee Direct dial from bedrooms Cen ht Dinner Last d 10pm Wi-fi available **Parking** 27

FLEET MOTORWAY SERVICE AREA (M3) MAP 04 SU75

BUDGET HOTEL

Days Inn Fleet

DAYS INN

Fleet Services GU51 1AA

☎ 01252 815587 🖷 01252 815587

e-mail: fleet.hotel@welcomebreak.co.uk

web: www.welcomebreak.co.uk

Dir: *between junct 4a & 5 southbound on M3*

PETS: Bedrooms Charges charge for damage **Grounds** accessible on leads disp bin **Exercise area Facilities** food bowl water bowl walks info vet info **On Request** fridge access **Other** cats must be caged

This modern building offers accommodation in smart, spacious and well-equipped bedrooms, suitable for families and business travellers, and all with en suite bathrooms. Refreshments may be taken at the nearby family restaurant.

Rooms 58 en suite S £49-£69; D £59-£79*

FORDINGBRIDGE MAP 04 SU11

Sandy Balls Holiday Centre *(SU167148)*

Sandy Balls Estate Ltd, Godshill SP6 2JZ

☎ 0845 270 2248 🖷 01425 653067

e-mail: post@sandy-balls.co.uk

web: www.sandy-balls.co.uk

Dir: *M27 junct 1 onto B3078/B3079, W 8m to Godshill. Site 0.25m after cattle grid*

PETS: Stables nearby (0.5m) **Public areas** except ready tents & Northfield & certain guest facilities **Charges** from £3 (touring & camping pitches) disp bin **Exercise area** on site 120 acres woods & parkland **Facilities** on site shop food food bowl water bowl dog chews litter tray etc dog scoop/disp bags leads washing facs walks info vet info **Other** prior notice required max 2 dogs per booking

Open all year (rs Nov-Feb pitches reduced, no activities) Last arrival 21.00hrs Last departure 11.00hrs

A large, mostly wooded New Forest holiday complex with good provision of touring facilities on terraced, well laid-out fields. Pitches are fully serviced with shingle bases, and groups can be sited beside the river and away from the main site. Excellent sport, leisure and entertainment facilities for the whole family, and now eight ready-erected tents for hire. A 120-acre site with 230 touring pitches, 230 hardstandings and 267 statics.

Notes Groups by arrangement, no gazebos

HAMBLE MAP 04 SU40

►►► Riverside Holidays *(SU481081)*

Satchell Ln SO31 4HR

☎ 023 8045 3220 🖷 023 8045 3611

e-mail: enquiries@riversideholidays.co.uk

web: www.riversideholidays.co.uk

Dir: *M27 junct 8, follow signs to Hamble B3397. Turn left into Satchell Lane, site 1m down lane on left*

PETS: Public areas except in buildings **Charges** £2 per night £14 per week disp bin **Exercise area** 0.5m **Facilities** walks info vet info

Open Mar-Oct Last arrival 22.00hrs Last departure 11.00hrs

A small, peaceful park next to the marina, and close to the pretty village of Hamble. The park is neatly kept, though the toilet facilities are dated. A pub and restaurant are very close by. A 6-acre site with 77 touring pitches and 45 statics.

ENGLAND

HARTLEY WINTNEY MAP 04 SU75

★★★ 79% HOTEL

Elvetham

RG27 8AR

☎ 01252 844871 📠 01252 844161

e-mail: enq@theelvetham.co.uk

web: www.theelvetham.co.uk

Dir: *M3 junct 4A W, junct 5 E (or M4 junct 11, A33, B3011). Hotel signed from A323 between Hartley Wintney & Fleet*

PETS: Bedrooms (7GF) unattended **Charges** £15 per night charge for damage **Grounds** accessible disp bin **Exercise area** on site **Facilities** water bowl feeding mat washing facs cage storage walks info vet info **On Request** fridge access torch towels **Resident Pets:** Harvey (Golden Retriever)

A spectacular 19th-century mansion set in 35 acres of grounds with an arboretum. All bedrooms are individually styled and many have views of the manicured gardens. A popular venue for weddings and conferences, the hotel lends itself to team building events and outdoor pursuits.

Rooms 41 en suite 29 annexe en suite (7 GF) S £110; D £135-£200 (incl. bkfst)* **Facilities** STV Gym Putt green Wi-fi available Badminton Boules Volleyball **Parking** 200 **Notes** Closed 24 Dec-1 Jan

LINWOOD MAP 04 SU10

►►► Red Shoot Camping Park *(SU187094)*

BH24 3QT

☎ 01425 473789 📠 01425 471558

e-mail: enquiries@redshoot-campingpark.com

web: www.redshoot-campingpark.com

Dir: *A31 onto A338 towards Fordingbridge & Salisbury. Right at brown signs for caravan park towards Linwood on unclassified roads, site signed*

PETS: Stables nearby (2m) **Public areas** except shop & toilets (on leads) **Charges** £1 per night £7 per week disp bin **Exercise area** New Forest adjacent **Facilities** on site shop food leads walks info vet info **Other** prior notice required **Restrictions** no Pitt Bull Terriers

Open Mar-Oct Last arrival 20.30hrs Last departure 13.00hrs

Sitting behind the Red Shoot Inn in one of the most attractive parts of the New Forest, this park is in an ideal spot for nature lovers, walkers and tourers. It is personally supervised by friendly owners, and offers many amenities including a children's play area. A 3.5-acre site with 130 touring pitches.

Notes Quiet after 22.30hrs

LYMINGTON MAP 04 SZ39

★★★ 80% HOTEL

Stanwell House

14-15 High St SO41 9AA

☎ 01590 677123 📠 01590 677756

e-mail: enquiries@stanwellhouse.com

Dir: *M27 junct 1, follow signs to Lyndhurst into Lymington centre & High Street*

PETS: Bedrooms (4GF) unattended **Charges** £15 per night **Public areas** except restaurant **Grounds** accessible on leads disp bin **Exercise area** 2 min walk **Facilities** water bowl dog chews dog scoop/disp bags pet sitting dog walking washing facs walks info vet info **On Request** fridge access torch towels **Restrictions** well behaved dogs only **Resident Pets:** Louis (Terrier)

A privately owned Georgian house situated on the wide High Street of Lymington, only a few minutes from the town's marina and a short drive from the stunning New Forest. Accommodation is comfortable and public areas have been redecorated to a high standard. Dining options include the informal Bistro or the intimate atmosphere of the Seafood Restaurant. Service is friendly and attentive. A meeting room is available for hire which benefits from doors leading out onto the attractive garden and patio area.

Rooms 27 en suite (3 fmly) (4 GF) S fr £99; D fr £135 (incl. bkfst)* **Facilities** FTV Wi-fi in bedrooms Xmas New Year **Notes LB**

★★★★ BED & BREAKFAST

1 Honeysuckle Gardens

Everton SO41 0EH

☎ 01590 641282

e-mail: mway286978@aol.com

web: www.newforest-uk.com/honeysucklebandb

Dir: *Off A337 Lymington to Christchurch onto Everton Rd, Honeysuckle Gardens 3rd left*

PETS: Bedrooms Charges £3 per night charge for damage **Exercise area** 100mtrs **Facilities** walks info vet info **On Request** fridge access towels **Restrictions** small dogs preferred

Located in a residential development in the village of Everton, this charming house is a good base for visiting Lymington, New Milton and the New Forest. Bedrooms are well furnished and decorated, and a range of useful extra facilities is provided. Full English breakfasts are served around one large table. The owner has won an award for green tourism by reducing the impact on the environment.

Rooms 3 rms (2 en suite) (1 pri facs) (2 fmly) S £35-£40; D £62 **Facilities** TVB tea/coffee Cen ht Wi-fi available **Parking** 3 **Notes LB** No children 3yrs

★★★★ BED & BREAKFAST

Jevington

47 Waterford Ln SO41 3PT

☎ 01590 672148 📠 01590 672148

e-mail: jevingtonbb@lineone.net

Dir: *From High St at St Thomas's Church onto Church Ln, left fork onto Waterford Ln*

PETS: Bedrooms Exercise area Facilities walks info vet info **Resident Pets:** Lady (Terrier cross)

Situated within walking distance of the town centre and marinas, Jevington offers attractive bedrooms furnished to a high standard with co-ordinated soft furnishings. An appetising breakfast is served at two tables in the dining room, and the friendly proprietors can suggest local places for dinner.

Rooms 3 en suite (1 fmly) S £30-£45; D £58* **Facilities** FTV TVB tea/coffee Cen ht **Parking** 3 **Notes** No children 5yrs

★★★ GUEST HOUSE

Gorse Meadow Country House

Sway Rd SO41 8LR

☎ 01590 673354 📠 01590 673336

e-mail: gorse.meadow.guesthouse@wildmushrooms.co.uk

web: www.gorsemeadowguesthouse.co.uk

Dir: *Off A337 from Brockenhurst, right onto Sway Rd before Toll House pub, Gorse Meadow 1.5m on right*

PETS: Bedrooms Stables on site **Grounds** accessible **Exercise area** on site in garden under supervision **Facilities** food **Resident Pets:** Camilla & Igor (Great Danes), Otto (Black Labrador)

This imposing Edwardian house is situated within 14 acres of grounds and most bedrooms enjoy views across the gardens and paddocks. Situated just one mile from Lymington, this is an excellent base to enjoy the many leisure pursuits that the New Forest has to offer. Meals are also available here, and Mrs Tee often uses the local wild mushrooms in her dishes.

Rooms 5 en suite (2 fmly) (2 GF) **Facilities** TVB tea/coffee Licensed Cen ht Dinner Last d 6pm Wi-fi available **Parking** 20 **Notes** No coaches

LYNDHURST

MAP 04 SU30

★★★ 79% HOTEL

Best Western Forest Lodge

Pikes Hill, Romsey Rd SO43 7AS

☎ 023 8028 3677 📠 023 8028 2940

e-mail: forest@newforesthotels.co.uk

web: www.newforesthotels.co.uk

Dir: *M27 junct 1, A337 towards Lyndhurst. In village, with police station & courts on right, take 1st right into Pikes Hill*

PETS: Bedrooms (6GF) unattended **Charges** £5 per night £35 per week **Public areas** except restaurant & bar (on leads) **Grounds** accessible on leads **Exercise area Facilities** water bowl walks info vet info **On Request** fridge access

Situated on the edge of Lyndhurst, this hotel is set well back from the main road. The smart, contemporary bedrooms include four-poster rooms and family rooms; children are very welcome here and parents will find that the hotel offers many child-friendly facilities. The eating options are the Forest Restaurant and the fine-dining Glasshouse Restaurant. There is an indoor swimming pool and Nordic sauna.

Rooms 28 en suite (7 fmly) (6 GF) **Facilities** Wi-fi in bedrooms **Parking** 50 **Notes** LB

★★★ 75% HOTEL

Best Western Crown

High St SO43 7NF

☎ 023 8028 2922 📠 023 8028 2751

e-mail: reception@crownhotel-lyndhurst.co.uk

web: www.crownhotel-lyndhurst.co.uk

Dir: *in centre of village, opposite church*

PETS: Bedrooms Charges £6 per night **Public areas** lounge only (on leads) **Grounds** accessible on leads disp bin **Exercise area** New Forest 200mtrs **Facilities** water bowl dog chews washing facs cage storage walks info vet info **On Request** fridge access torch towels

The Crown, with its stone mullioned windows, panelled rooms and elegant period decor evokes the style of an Edwardian country house. Bedrooms are generally a good size and offer a useful range of facilities. Public areas have style and comfort and include a choice of function and meeting rooms. The pleasant garden and terrace are havens of peace and tranquillity.

Rooms 39 en suite (8 fmly) S £73-£98; D £95-£185 (incl. bkfst)* **Facilities** FTV Wi-fi in bedrooms Xmas New Year **Services** Lift **Parking** 60 **Notes** LB

LYNDHURST CONTINUED

★★★ 72% HOTEL

Lyndhurst Park

High St SO43 7NL

☎ 023 8028 3923 📠 023 8028 3019

e-mail: lyndhurst.park@forestdale.com

web: www.forestdale.com

Dir: *M27 junct 1-3 to A35 to Lyndhurst. Hotel at bottom of High St*

PETS: Bedrooms unattended **Charges** £7.50 per night **Public areas** except restaurant **Exercise area**

Although it is just by the High Street, this hotel is afforded seclusion and tranquillity from the town due to its five acres of mature grounds. The comfortable bedrooms include home-from-home touches such as ducks in the bath! The bar offers a stylish setting for a snack whilst the oak-panelled Tudor restaurant provides a more formal dining venue.

Rooms 59 en suite (3 fmly) S £90-£95; D £113-£129 (incl. bkfst)* **Facilities** Wi-fi in bedrooms Sauna Xmas New Year **Services** Lift **Parking** 100 **Notes** LB

★★ 68% HOTEL

Knightwood Lodge

THE INDEPENDENTS HOTEL ASSOCIATION

Southampton Rd SO43 7BU

☎ 023 8028 2502 📠 023 8028 3730

e-mail: jackie4r@aol.com

web: www.knightwoodlodge.co.uk

Dir: *M27 junct 1 follow A337 to Lyndhurst. Left at traffic lights in village onto A35 towards Southampton. Hotel 0.25m on left*

PETS: Bedrooms unattended **Exercise area** New Forest over road **Facilities** water bowl bedding washing facs walks info vet info **On Request** fridge access torch towels **Other** pets allowed in annexe bedrooms only

This friendly, family-run hotel is situated on the outskirts of Lyndhurst. Comfortable bedrooms are modern in style and well equipped with many useful extras. The hotel offers an excellent range of facilities including a swimming pool, a jacuzzi and a small gym area. Two separate cottages are available for families or larger groups, and dogs are also welcome to accompany their owners in these units.

Rooms 14 en suite 4 annexe en suite (2 fmly) (3 GF) S £35-£55; D £70-£110 (incl. bkfst)* **Facilities** FTV Gym Steam room Sauna Spa bath **Parking** 15 **Notes** LB

MILFORD ON SEA — MAP 04 SZ29

★★★ ◎◎ COUNTRY HOUSE HOTEL

Westover Hall

Park Ln SO41 0PT

☎ 01590 643044 📠 01590 644490

e-mail: info@westoverhallhotel.com

Dir: *M3 & M27 W onto A337 to Lymington, follow signs to Milford-on-Sea onto B3058, hotel outside village centre towards cliff.*

PETS: Bedrooms unattended **Charges** £12 per night charge for damage **Public areas** except restaurants & bar (on leads) **Grounds** accessible on leads **Exercise area** beach 100mtrs **Facilities** washing facs walks info vet info **On Request** torch towels

Just a few moments' walk from the beach and boasting uninterrupted views across Christchurch Bay to the Isle of Wight in the distance, this late-Victorian mansion offers a relaxed, informal and friendly atmosphere together with efficient standards of hospitality and service. Bedrooms do vary in size and aspect, but all have been decorated with flair and style. Architectural delights include dramatic stained-glass windows, extensive oak panelling and a galleried entrance hall. The cuisine is prepared with much care and attention to detail.

Rooms 12 en suite (2 fmly) S £130-£200; D £190-£340 (incl. bkfst & dinner) **Facilities** Wi-fi available Xmas New Year **Parking** 50 **Notes** LB

►►► Lytton Lawn Touring Park *(SZ293937)*

Lymore Ln SO41 0TX

☎ 01590 648331 📠 01590 645610

e-mail: holidays@shorefield.co.uk

web: www.shorefield.co.uk

Dir: *From Lymington A337 to Christchurch for 2.5m to Everton. Left onto B3058 to Milford on Sea. After 0.25m left onto Lymore Lane*

PETS: Charges £1.50-£3 per night £10.50-£21 per week **Exercise area** on site **Facilities** on site shop food dog scoop/disp bags **Other** prior notice required **Restrictions** no Rottweilers or Staffordshire Bull Terriers

Open 6 Feb-2 Jan (rs Low season Shop/reception ltd hrs. No grass pitches) Last arrival 22.00hrs Last departure 10.00hrs

A pleasant well-run park with good facilities, located near the coast. The park is peaceful and quiet, but the facilities of a sister park 2.5 miles away are available to campers, including swimming pool, tennis courts, bistro and bar/carvery, and large club with family entertainment. Fully-serviced pitches provide good screening, and standard pitches are on gently-sloping grass. An 8-acre site with 136 touring pitches, 53 hardstandings.

Notes Families & couples only. Rallies welcome

OWER MAP 03 SU31

►►► Green Pastures Farm *(SU321158)*

SO51 6AJ

☎ 023 8081 4444

e-mail: enquiries@greenpasturesfarm.com

web: www.greenpasturesfarm.com

Dir: *M27 junct 2. Follow Salisbury signs for 0.5m. Then follow brown tourist signs for Green Pastures. Also signed from A36 & A3090 at Ower*

PETS: Sep Accom day kennels **Stables** (loose box) **Exercise area** on site **Facilities** on site shop food walks info vet info **Other** prior notice required **Resident Pets:** Pudsey (Collie), Molly (cat)

Open 15 Mar-Oct Last departure 11.00hrs

A pleasant site on a working farm, with good screening of trees and shrubs around the perimeter. The touring area is divided by a border of shrubs and, at times, colourful foxgloves. This peaceful location is close to the M27 and New Forest. A 5-acre site with 45 touring pitches, 2 hardstandings.

Notes

PETERSFIELD MAP 04 SU72

★★★ 74% HOTEL

Langrish House

Langrish GU32 1RN

☎ 01730 266941 01730 260543

e-mail: frontdesk@langrishhouse.co.uk

web: www.langrishhouse.co.uk

Dir: *A3 onto A272 towards Winchester. Hotel signed, 2.5m on left*

PETS: Bedrooms (3GF) unattended **Charges** £10 per night **Public areas** except restaurant **Grounds** accessible **Exercise area** surrounding area **Facilities** bedding dog scoop/disp bags **On Request** towels **Other** Pet pack for dogs - welcome letter, blanket, poop scoop, biscuits & towel **Resident Pets:** Tonga (Black Labrador), Constansa & Bunji (cats), chickens, ducks, guineafowl

Located in an idyllic country location just outside Petersfield, this family home dates back to the 17th century. Rooms offer good levels of comfort with beautiful views over the countryside. The public areas consist of a small cosy restaurant, a bar in the vaults, and conference and banqueting rooms that are popular for weddings. Staff throughout are friendly and nothing is too much trouble.

Rooms 13 en suite (1 fmly) (3 GF) S £72-£90; D £104-£155 (incl. bkfst)* **Facilities** Fishing Wi-fi available Xmas New Year **Parking** 80 **Notes LB** Closed 2 weeks in Jan

PORTSMOUTH & SOUTHSEA MAP 04 SU60

★★★ 74% HOTEL

Best Western Royal Beach

Best Western

South Pde, Southsea PO4 0RN

☎ 023 9273 1281 023 9281 7572

e-mail: enquiries@royalbeachhotel.co.uk

web: www.royalbeachhotel.co.uk

Dir: *M27 to M275, follow signs to seafront. Hotel on seafront*

PETS: Bedrooms Public areas except restaurant **Exercise area** nearby park & green **Facilities** vet info

This former Victorian seafront hotel is a smart and comfortable venue suitable for leisure and business guests alike. Bedrooms and public areas are well presented and generally spacious, and the smart Coast Bar is an ideal venue for a relaxing drink.

Rooms 124 en suite (18 fmly) S £60-£95; D £80-£125 (incl. bkfst) **Facilities** Wi-fi in bedrooms Xmas New Year **Services** Lift **Parking** 50 **Notes LB**

RINGWOOD MAP 04 SU10

★★★★ GUEST HOUSE

Little Forest Lodge

Poulner Hill BH24 3HS

☎ 01425 478848 01425 473564

Dir: *1.5m E of Ringwood on A31*

PETS: Bedrooms (1GF) **Charges** £5 per night **Public areas** except dining room **Grounds** accessible disp bin **Exercise area Facilities** dog chews feeding mat washing facs cage storage walks info vet info **On Request** fridge access torch towels **Resident Pets:** Jade (Retriever/Collie cross), Millie (Doberman/Whippet cross), Harry & Spike (cats), ducks, chickens

A warm welcome is given to guests and their pets, at this charming Edwardian house set in two acres of woodland. Bedrooms are

CONTINUED

RINGWOOD CONTINUED

pleasantly decorated and equipped with thoughtful extras. Both the attractive wood-panelled dining room and the delightful lounge, with bar and wood-burning fire, overlook the gardens. Home-cooked evening meals by arrangement.

Rooms 6 en suite (3 fmly) (1 GF) S £45-£50; D £80✳ **Facilities** TVB tea/coffee Licensed Cen ht Dinner Last d 7.30pm badminton **Parking** 10 **Notes** No coaches

ROMSEY MAP 03 SU32

►►►► Hill Farm Caravan Park *(SU287238)*

Branches Ln, Sherfield English SO51 6FH

☎ 01794 340402 🖷 01794 342358

e-mail: gjb@hillfarmpark.com

web: www.hillfarmpark.com

Dir: *Signed from A27 (Salisbury to Romsey road) in Sherfield English, 4m NW of Romsey & M27 junct 2*

PETS: disp bin **Exercise area** on site dog walks **Facilities** on site shop dog scoop/disp bags leads washing facs dog grooming walks info vet info **Other** prior notice required

Open Mar-Oct Last arrival 20.00hrs Last departure noon

A small, well-sheltered park peacefully located amidst mature trees and meadows. The two toilet blocks offer smart unisex showers as well as a fully en suite family/disabled room and plenty of privacy in the wash rooms. The owners are continuing to develop this attractive park, and with its proximity to Salisbury and the New Forest, it makes an appealing holiday location. A 10.5-acre site with 70 touring pitches, 60 hardstandings and 6 statics.

Notes Minimum noise at all times and no noise after 23.00hrs, one unit per pitch

SOUTHAMPTON MAP 04 SU41

★★★ 69% HOTEL

Southampton Park

Cumberland Place SO15 2WY

☎ 023 8034 3343 🖷 023 8033 2538

e-mail: southampton.park@forestdale.com

web: www.forestdale.com

Dir: *at north end of Inner Ring Road, opposite Watts Park & Civic Centre*

PETS: Bedrooms unattended **Charges** £7.50 per night **Public areas** except restaurant **Exercise area**

This modern hotel, in the heart of the city, provides well-equipped, smartly appointed and comfortable bedrooms. It boasts a well equipped spa with all modern facilities and a beauty salon for those who wish to pamper themselves. The public areas are spacious and include the popular MJ's Brassiere. Parking is available in a multi-storey behind the hotel.

Rooms 72 en suite (10 fmly) S £90-£95; D £120-£125 (incl. bkfst)✳ **Facilities Spa** supervised Gym Wi-fi available New Year **Services** Lift **Notes LB** Closed 25 & 26 Dec nights

★★ 76% HOTEL

Elizabeth House

42-44 The Avenue SO17 1XP

☎ 023 8022 4327 🖷 023 8022 4327

e-mail: mail@elizabethhousehotel.com

web: www.elizabethhousehotel.com

Dir: *on A33, hotel on left after Southampton Common, before main lights*

PETS: Bedrooms (8GF) unattended **Grounds** accessible **Exercise area** 200yds **Facilities** walks info **On Request** fridge access torch towels

This hotel is conveniently situated close to the city centre, so provides an ideal base for both business and leisure guests. The bedrooms are well equipped and are attractively furnished with comfort in mind. There is also a cosy and atmospheric bistro in the cellar where evening meals are served.

Rooms 20 en suite 7 annexe en suite (9 fmly) (8 GF) S fr £62; D fr £75 (incl. bkfst)✳ **Facilities** Wi-fi available **Parking** 31

BUDGET HOTEL

Travelodge Southampton

Lodge Rd SO14 6QR

☎ 08719 846 212 🖷 023 8033 4569

web: www.travelodge.co.uk

Dir: *M3 junct 14, A33 to Southampton, on left after 6th lights*

PETS: Bedrooms unattended **Charges** £10 per stay per night charge for damage **Public areas** (on leads) **Grounds** accessible on leads disp bin **Exercise area Facilities** walks info vet info **On Request** fridge access torch towels

Travelodge offers good quality, good value, modern accommodation. Ideal for families, the spacious en suite bedrooms include remote-control TV, tea and coffee-making facilities and comfortable beds. Meals can be taken at the nearby family restaurant.

Rooms 59 en suite S fr £29; D fr £29

ENGLAND

SOUTHSEA

See Portsmouth & Southsea

STOCKBRIDGE MAP 04 SU33

★★★★ BED & BREAKFAST

York Lodge

Five Bells Ln, Nether Wallop SO20 8HE

☎ 01264 781313

e-mail: bradley@york-lodge.co.uk

web: www.york-lodge.co.uk

Dir: *Turn off A30 or A343 onto B3084, turn onto Hosketts Ln, fork left, 1st house on right*

PETS: Bedrooms (2GF) **Charges** £5 per night **Public areas** **Grounds** accessible disp bin **Exercise area** 2 mins walk **Facilities** washing facs cage storage walks info vet info **On Request** fridge access torch towels **Resident Pets:** Polly (Black Labrador)

Located in the picturesque village famous for Agatha Christie's Miss Marple series, this charming house has comfortable accommodation in a self-contained wing. Bedrooms are stylishly presented with many thoughtful extra facilities. The dining room overlooks peaceful gardens, and delicious dinners are available by arrangement.

Rooms 2 en suite (2 GF) S £35-£55; D £70-£75✱ **Facilities** TVB tea/coffee Cen ht Wi-fi available **Parking** 4 **Notes** No children 8yrs

★★★ INN

The Three Cups Inn

High St SO20 6HB

☎ 01264 810527 🖹 08708 913158

e-mail: manager@the3cups.co.uk

PETS: Bedrooms Charges charge for damage **Public areas** bar & lounge only (on leads) **Grounds** accessible **Exercise area** adjacent **Facilities** food bowl water bowl cage storage walks info vet info **On Request** fridge access torch

A former coaching inn on the high street in a popular town, with its own parking. Rooms are comfortable and well equipped, and food is available every evening.

Rooms 8 en suite (3 fmly) S fr £62; D fr £72✱ **Facilities** TVB tea/coffee Cen ht Dinner Last d 9.25pm Wi-fi available **Parking** 15

STRATFIELD TURGIS MAP 04 SU65

★★★ 71% HOTEL

Wellington Arms

RG27 0AS

☎ 01256 882214 🖹 01256 882934

e-mail: wellingtonarmsreception.basingstoke@hall-woodhouse.co.uk

Dir: *A33 between Basingstoke & Reading*

PETS: Bedrooms unattended **Charges** £10 per night **Grounds** accessible **Exercise area** on site in grounds

Situated at an entrance to the ancestral home of the Duke of Wellington. The majority of bedrooms are located in the modern Garden Wing; those in the original building have a period feel and unusual furniture. Public rooms include a brasserie and a comfortable lounge bar with log fire.

Rooms 28 en suite (3 fmly) (11 GF) **Facilities** Wi-fi in bedrooms **Parking** 150

SWAY MAP 04 SZ29

★★★ 75% HOTEL

Sway Manor Restaurant & Hotel

Station Rd SO41 6BA

☎ 01590 682754 🖹 01590 682955

e-mail: info@swaymanor.com

web: www.swaymanor.com

Dir: *exit B3055 (Brockenhurst/New Milton road) into village centre*

PETS: Bedrooms unattended **Charges** £6 per night charge for damage **Public areas** except restaurant (on leads) **Grounds** accessible on leads disp bin **Exercise area** **Facilities** walks info vet info **On Request** fridge access **Resident Pets:** Bobby (Chocolate Labrador), Bernard (Golden Labrador)

Built at the turn of the 20th century, this attractive mansion is set in its own grounds, and conveniently located in the village centre. Bedrooms are well appointed and generously equipped; most have views over the gardens and pool. The bar and conservatory restaurant, both with views over the gardens, are popular with locals.

Rooms 15 en suite (3 fmly) S £63.50-£69.50; D £109-£139 (incl. bkfst)✱ **Facilities** ⛱ ♫ Xmas **Services** Lift **Parking** 40 **Notes** LB

SWAY CONTINUED

★★★★ GUEST ACCOMMODATION

The Nurse's Cottage Restaurant with Rooms

Station Rd SO41 6BA

☎ 01590 683402

e-mail: nurses.cottage@lineone.net

web: www.nursescottage.co.uk

Dir: *Off B3055 in village centre, close to shops*

PETS: Bedrooms (5GF) unattended sign **Stables** nearby (1m) **Charges** charge for damage **Exercise area** 200yds **Facilities** food bowl water bowl vet info **On Request** fridge access **Restrictions** accommodation not suitable for large dogs

Smart and appealing accommodation, excellent hospitality and service, and carefully prepared food contribute to an enjoyable stay at this former district-nurse's cottage. Sight, sound and accessibility facilities further enhance the experience for guests at this delightful establishment. The bedrooms offer comfort with numerous thoughtful extras, and lovely toiletries and fluffy towels are provided in the bathrooms. The conservatory-restaurant is popular with locals and guests.

Rooms 5 en suite (5 GF) S £90; D £170-£190(incl. dinner) **Facilities** FTV TVB tea/coffee Direct dial from bedrooms Cen ht Dinner Last d 8pm Wi-fi available **Parking** 5 **Notes** LB No children 10yrs Closed Feb-Mar & Nov (3 wks)

★★★★ BED & BREAKFAST

Acorn Shetland Pony Stud

Meadows Cottage, Arnewood Bridge Rd SO41 6DA

☎ 01590 682000

e-mail: meadows.cottage@virgin.net

Dir: *M27 junct 1, A337 to Brockenhurst, B3055 to Sway, pass Birchy Hill Nursing Home, over x-rds, 2nd entrance left*

PETS: Bedrooms (3GF) **Stables** on site **Charges** £3 per night charge for damage **Grounds** accessible on leads disp bin **Exercise area** New Forest 1m **Facilities** leads washing facs cage storage walks info vet info **On Request** fridge access torch towels **Resident Pets:** Bill & Sir Bobby (cat), 10 Shetland ponies

Located on the outskirts of Sway, this comfortable establishment is set in over 6 acres of pony paddocks and a water garden. The ground-floor bedrooms are well furnished and have direct access onto patios. The enjoyable, freshly cooked breakfasts use a range of fine produce including delicious home-made bread.

Rooms 3 en suite (1 fmly) (3 GF) S fr £27; D fr £56* **Facilities** TVB tea/coffee Cen ht Carriage driving with Shetland ponies **Parking** 30 **Notes** LB

★★★ INN

The Forest Heath

Station Rd SO41 6BA

☎ 01590 682287 🖹 01590 682626

e-mail: forestheathhotel@hotmail.co.uk

Dir: *M27 junct 1, A337 to Brockenhurst, B3055 to Sway, onto Church Ln & Station Rd*

PETS: Bedrooms unattended **Stables** nearby (5m) **Charges** £5 per night **Public areas** (on leads) **Grounds** accessible on leads disp bin **Exercise area** 1m **Facilities** washing facs cage storage walks info vet info **On Request** fridge access towels **Resident Pets:** Ollie (Patterdale cross), Crystal (Yorkshire Terrier), Bonnie (Black Labrador), Elvis, Tigger & Smudge (cats)

Located in a New Forest village, this late Victorian inn is a popular meeting place for the local community. Bedrooms are well equipped and comfortable, and a range of real ales and imaginative meals is offered in the bars and the conservatory dining room.

Rooms 4 en suite (2 fmly) **Facilities** TVB tea/coffee Cen ht Dinner Last d 8.45pm Wi-fi available Pool Table boules, petanque **Parking** 20

WINCHESTER MAP 04 SU42

★★★★ HOTEL

Lainston House

Sparsholt SO21 2LT

☎ 01962 776088 🖹 01962 776672

e-mail: enquiries@lainstonhouse.com

web: www.exclusivehotels.co.uk

Dir: *2m NW off B3049 towards Stockbridge*

PETS: Bedrooms (18GF) **Charges** £25 per night charge for damage **Public areas** lounge only (on leads) **Grounds** accessible **Exercise area Facilities** food (pre-bookable) food bowl water bowl **Other** dog menu

This graceful example of a William and Mary House enjoys a countryside location amidst mature grounds and gardens. Staff provide good levels of courtesy and care with a polished, professional service. Bedrooms are tastefully appointed and include some spectacular spacious rooms with stylish handmade beds and stunning bathrooms. Public rooms include a cocktail bar built entirely from a single cedar and stocked with an impressive range of rare drinks and cigars.

Rooms 50 en suite (6 fmly) (18 GF) S £75-£125; D £99-£360* **Facilities** Fishing Gym Wi-fi available Archery Clay pigeon shooting Cycling Hot air ballooning Walking Xmas New Year **Parking** 150 **Notes** LB

★★★★ 71% HOTEL

Mercure Wessex

Paternoster Row SO23 9LQ

☎ 01962 861611 📠 01962 841503

web: www.mercure-uk.com

Dir: *M3, follow signs for town centre, at rdbt by King Alfred's statue past Guildhall, next left, hotel on right*

PETS: Bedrooms Charges £10 per night £70 per week charge for damage **Exercise area Facilities** cage storage walks info vet info **On Request** torch

Occupying an enviable location in the centre of this historic city and adjacent to the spectacular cathedral, this hotel is quietly situated on a side street. Inside, the atmosphere is restful and welcoming, with public areas and some bedrooms enjoying unrivalled views of the hotel's centuries-old neighbour.

Rooms 94 en suite (6 fmly) **Facilities** STV Gym Wi-fi in bedrooms **Services** Lift **Parking** 60 (charged)

★★★ 76% HOTEL

The Winchester Royal

Saint Peter St SO23 8BS

☎ 01962 840840 📠 01962 841582

e-mail: winchester.royal@forestdale.com

web: www.forestdale.com

Dir: *M3 junct 9 to Winnall Trading Estate. Follow to city centre, cross river, left, 1st right. Onto one-way system, take 2nd right. Hotel immediately on right*

PETS: Bedrooms Charges £7.50 per night **Public areas** except restaurant **Exercise area Other** please phone for further details on pet facilities

Situated in the heart of the former capital of England, a warm welcome awaits at this friendly hotel, which in parts, dates back to the 16th century. The bedrooms may vary in style but they are all comfortable and well equipped; the modern annexe rooms overlook the attractive well-tended gardens. The conservatory restaurant makes a very pleasant setting for enjoyable meals.

Rooms 19 en suite 56 annexe en suite (1 fmly) (27 GF) D £139-£149 (incl. bkfst)✳ **Facilities** Wi-fi in bedrooms Xmas New Year **Parking** 50 **Notes** LB

HEREFORDSHIRE

HEREFORD — MAP 03 SO54

★★★ 73% HOTEL

Three Counties Hotel

Belmont Rd HR2 7BP

☎ 01432 299955 📠 01432 275114

e-mail: enquiries@threecountieshotel.co.uk

web: www.threecountieshotel.co.uk

Dir: *on A465 Abergavenny Rd*

PETS: Bedrooms (46GF) **Grounds** accessible on leads **Exercise area Facilities** vet info **Other** dogs allowed in certain bedrooms only

A mile west of the city centre, this large, privately owned, modern complex has well-equipped, spacious bedrooms, many of which are located in separate single-storey buildings around the extensive car park. There is a spacious, comfortable lounge, a traditional bar and an attractive restaurant.

Rooms 28 en suite 32 annexe en suite (4 fmly) (46 GF) S £63.50-£80; D £75.50-£103 (incl. bkfst)✳ **Facilities** STV Wi-fi available **Parking** 250 **Notes** LB

★★★★ FARM HOUSE

Holly House Farm *(SO456367)*

Allensmore HR2 9BH

☎ 01432 277294 & 07889 830223 📠 01432 261285

Mrs D Sinclair

e-mail: hollyhousefarm@aol.com

web: www.hollyhousefarm.org.uk

Dir: *A465 S to Allensmore, right signed Cobhall Common, at small x-rds right into lane, house on right*

PETS: Bedrooms Stables on site **Public areas** (on leads) **Grounds** accessible on leads **Exercise area** grounds & bridleway by house **Facilities** water bowl washing facs cage storage walks info vet info **On Request** fridge access torch towels **Other** pet sitting & dog walking occasionally available (ask when booking) **Resident Pets:** Slipper (Labrador), Chappie & Masie (horses), Wilfie & Popsie (cats)

Surrounded by open countryside, this spacious farmhouse is a relaxing base for those visiting this beautiful area. The homely and comfortable bedrooms offer lovely views over the fields. Breakfast makes use of local produce together with home-made jams and marmalade. Pets are very welcome here and the proprietor is happy to look after them during the day if required.

Rooms 2 rms (1 en suite) (1 pri facs) D £56-£76 **Facilities** TVB tea/coffee Cen ht **Parking** 32 **Notes** 11 acres Horses Closed 25-26, 31 Dec & 1 Jan

HEREFORD CONTINUED

★★★★ FARM HOUSE

Sink Green *(SO542377)*

Rotherwas HR2 6LE

☎ 01432 870223 📠 01432 870223 Mr D E Jones

e-mail: enquiries@sinkgreenfarm.co.uk

web: www.sinkgreenfarm.co.uk

Dir: *3m SE of city centre. Off A49 onto B4399 for 2m*

PETS: Bedrooms Public areas Grounds accessible **Exercise area Facilities** cage storage walks info vet info **On Request** fridge access torch towels **Resident Pets:** Bob & Max (dogs)

This charming 16th-century farmhouse stands in attractive countryside and has many original features, including flagstone floors, exposed beams and open fireplaces. Bedrooms are traditionally furnished and one has a four-poster bed. The pleasant garden has a comfortable summer house, hot tub and barbecue.

Rooms 3 en suite S £28-£33; D £54-£67✻ **Facilities** TVB tea/coffee Cen ht TVL Wi-fi available Fishing Hot Tub **Parking** 10 **Notes LB** 180 acres beef

► Ridge Hill Caravan and Campsite *(SO509355)*

HR1 1UN

☎ 01432 351293

e-mail: ridgehill@fsmail.net

web: www.ridgehillcaravanandcampsite.co.uk

Dir: *From Hereford on A49, then B4399 signed Rotherwas. At 1st rdbt follow Dinedor/Little Dewchurch signs, in 1m signed Ridge Hill/Twyford, turn right, then right at phone box, site 200yds on right.*

PETS: Public areas (on leads) disp bin **Exercise area Facilities** walks info vet info

Open Mar-Oct Last departure noon

A simple, basic site set high on Ridge Hill a few miles south of Hereford. This peaceful site offers outstanding views over the surrounding countryside. It does not have toilets or showers, and therefore own facilities are essential. Please do not rely on Sat Nav directions to this site - guide book directions must be used for caravans and motorhomes. A 1.5-acre site with 5 touring pitches.

Notes

LEOMINSTER — MAP 03 SO45

★★★★ FARM HOUSE

Heath House *(SO535552)*

Stoke Prior HR6 0NF

☎ 01568 760385 & 07720 887393 Mr & Mrs Cholerton

e-mail: heathhouse@onetel.com

Dir: *A44 turn right at x-rds, signed Risbury & brown tourist sign for Broadfield vineyard, house located on left after 1m*

PETS: Bedrooms Stables on site **Public areas Grounds** accessible **Exercise area Facilities** leads cage storage walks info vet info **On Request** fridge access torch towels **Other** dogs and horses by prior arrangement only **Resident Pets:** Tommy (Jack Russell), Tallulah (Chocolate Labrador), Jack, Finn, Gizmo, Angel & Seffy (horses), chickens, goldfish

A warm and friendly welcome awaits all guests at this pleasant property, which is situated in a peaceful rural location. This former 17th-century farmhouse has an attractive garden and retains many original features including exposed beams and open fireplace. The bedrooms are spacious and comfortable, and provide some thoughtful guest extras. A carefully prepared breakfast, including eggs from the owners' own hens, can be taken at the communal table in the kitchen. Horses and dogs are welcome by arrangement.

Rooms 1 en suite 1 annexe en suite (1 fmly) S £40; D £65✻ **Facilities** TVB tea/coffee Cen ht **Parking** 3 **Notes LB** No children 5yrs 5 acres Non-Working/Horses Closed Dec-1 Feb

LITTLE TARRINGTON — MAP 03 SO64

►►►► Hereford Camping & Caravanning Club Site *(SO625410)*

The Millpond HR1 4JA

☎ 01432 890243 📠 01432 890243

web: www.thefriendlyclub.co.uk

Dir: *300yds off A438 on Ledbury side of Tarrington, entrance on right, 50yds before railway bridge*

PETS: Exercise area Facilities washing facs walks info vet info

Open Mar-Nov Last arrival 20.00hrs Last departure noon

A spacious grassy park set beside a 3-acre fishing lake in a peaceful location. Well-planted trees and shrubs help to divide and screen the park, and the modern toilet block provides good facilities. A 4.5-acre site with 55 touring pitches.

Notes Site gates closed between 23.00hrs-07.00hrs

ROSS-ON-WYE

MAP 03 SO62

★★★ 80% HOTEL

Wilton Court Hotel

Wilton Ln HR9 6AQ

☎ 01989 562569 ▤ 01989 768460

e-mail: info@wiltoncourthotel.com

web: www.wiltoncourthotel.com

Dir: *M50 junct 4 onto A40 towards Monmouth at 3rd rdbt turn left signed Ross-on-Wye then take 1st right, hotel on right*

PETS: Bedrooms unattended **Charges** £10 per night charge for damage **Public areas** except restaurant **Grounds** accessible disp bin **Exercise area Facilities** washing facs cage storage walks info vet info **On Request** fridge access torch towels **Restrictions** no very large dogs or long haired breeds

Dating back to the 16th century, this hotel has great charm and a wealth of character. Standing on the banks of the River Wye and just a short walk from the town centre, there is a genuinely relaxed, friendly and unhurried atmosphere here. Bedrooms are tastefully furnished and well equipped, while public areas include a comfortable lounge, traditional bar and pleasant restaurant with a conservatory extension overlooking the garden. High standards of food using fresh locally-sourced ingredients is offered.

Rooms 10 en suite (1 fmly) S £80-£125; D £105-£145 (incl. bkfst)✳ **Facilities** FTV Fishing Wi-fi in bedrooms Boule Xmas New Year **Parking** 24 **Notes** LB

★★★ 75% HOTEL

Best Western Pengethley Manor

Best Western

Pengethley Park HR9 6LL

☎ 01989 730211 ▤ 01989 730238

e-mail: reservations@pengethleymanor.co.uk

web: www.pengethleymanor.co.uk

Dir: *4m N on A49 (Hereford road), from Ross-on-Wye*

PETS: Bedrooms unattended **Charges** charge for damage **Public areas** except restaurant & bar (on leads) **Grounds** accessible on leads disp bin **Exercise area Facilities** food bowl water bowl washing facs walks info vet info **On Request** fridge access torch towels

This fine Georgian mansion is set in extensive grounds with glorious views and two successful vineyards that produce over 1,000 bottles a year. The bedrooms are tastefully appointed and come in a wide variety of styles; all are well equipped. The elegant public rooms are furnished in a style that is in keeping with the house's character. Dinner provides a range of enjoyable options and is served in the spacious restaurant.

Rooms 11 en suite 14 annexe en suite (3 fmly) (4 GF) S £79-£115; D £120-£160 (incl. bkfst)✳ **Facilities** 9 Wi-fi available Golf improvement course Xmas New Year **Parking** 70 **Notes** LB

★★★ 73% COUNTRY HOUSE HOTEL

Glewstone Court

Glewstone HR9 6AW

☎ 01989 770367 ▤ 01989 770282

e-mail: glewstone@aol.com

web: www.glewstonecourt.com

Dir: *from Ross-on-Wye Market Place take A40/A49 Monmouth/Hereford, over Wilton Bridge to rdbt, turn left onto A40 to Monmouth, after 1m turn right for Glewstone*

PETS: Bedrooms unattended **Charges** £10 per night £50 per week **Public areas** except dining areas **Grounds** accessible disp bin **Exercise area Facilities** food (pre-bookable) food bowl water bowl bedding feeding mat dog scoop/disp bags cage storage walks info vet info **On Request** fridge access torch towels **Resident Pets:** Buster & Brecon (Golden Retrievers), Barney (Miniature Dachshund), Toots & Tilly (cats)

This charming hotel enjoys an elevated position with views over Ross-on-Wye, and is set in well-tended gardens. Informal service is delivered with great enthusiasm by Bill Reeve-Tucker, whilst the kitchen is the domain of Christine Reeve-Tucker who offers an extensive menu of well executed dishes. Bedrooms come in a variety of sizes and are tastefully furnished and well equipped.

Rooms 8 en suite (2 fmly) S £80-£95; D £118-£135 (incl. bkfst)✳ **Facilities** Wi-fi in bedrooms New Year **Parking** 25 **Notes** LB Closed 25-27 Dec

★★★ 70% COUNTRY HOUSE HOTEL

Pencraig Court Country House Hotel

Pencraig HR9 6HR

☎ 01989 770306 ▤ 01989 770040

e-mail: info@pencraig-court.co.uk

web: www.pencraig-court.co.uk

Dir: *off A40, into Pencraig 4m S of Ross-on-Wye*

PETS: Bedrooms Charges £5 per night £20 per week **Public areas** except dining room (on leads) **Grounds** accessible disp bin **Exercise area** on site **Facilities** food (pre-bookable) walks info vet info **On Request** fridge access torch towels **Resident Pets:** Sam (Sussex Spaniel), Fugley (Tibetan Spaniel), Ross (cat)

This Georgian mansion commands impressive views of the River Wye to Ross-on-Wye beyond. Guests can be assured of a relaxing stay and the proprietors are on hand to ensure personal attention and service. The bedrooms have a traditional feel and include one room with a four-poster bed. The country-house atmosphere is carried through in the lounges and the elegant restaurant.

Rooms 11 en suite (1 fmly) S £49-£65; D £89-£99 (incl. bkfst)✳ **Facilities** Wi-fi available **Parking** 20 **Notes** LB RS 24-27 Dec

ROSS-ON-WYE CONTINUED

★★ 69% SMALL HOTEL

Chasedale

Walford Rd HR9 5PQ

☎ 01989 562423 & 565801 📠 01989 567900

e-mail: chasedale@supanet.com

web: www.chasedale.co.uk

Dir: *from town centre, S on B4234, hotel 0.5m on left*

PETS: Bedrooms (1GF) unattended **Public areas** except restaurant **Grounds** accessible disp bin **Exercise area** 300mtrs **Facilities** food bowl water bowl cage storage walks info vet info **On Request** fridge access towels **Resident Pets:** Marmite (Chocolate Labrador), Cassis (Black Labrador)

This large, mid-Victorian property is situated on the south-west outskirts of the town. Privately owned and personally run, it provides spacious, well-proportioned public areas and extensive grounds. The accommodation is well equipped and includes ground floor and family rooms, whilst the restaurant offers a wide selection of wholesome food.

Rooms 10 en suite (2 fmly) (1 GF) S £41-£42.50; D £82-£85 (incl. bkfst) **Facilities** Wi-fi available Xmas **Parking** 14 **Notes** LB

★★ 68% HOTEL

King's Head

8 High St HR9 5HL

☎ 01989 763174 📠 01989 769578

e-mail: enquiries@kingshead.co.uk

web: www.kingshead.co.uk

Dir: *in town centre, turn right past Royal Hotel*

PETS: Bedrooms unattended **Public areas** bar only (on leads) **Grounds** accessible on leads **Exercise area** 200yds **Facilities** food (pre-bookable) food bowl water bowl cage storage walks info vet info **On Request** torch

This establishment dates back to the 14th century and has a wealth of charm and character. Bedrooms are well equipped and include both four-poster and family rooms. The restaurant doubles as a coffee shop during the day and is a popular venue with locals. There is also a very pleasant bar and comfortable lounge.

Rooms 15 en suite (1 fmly) S £53.50; D £90 (incl. bkfst) **Facilities** Wi-fi available **Parking** 13 **Notes** LB

★★★★ GUEST ACCOMMODATION

Lea House

Lea HR9 7JZ

☎ 01989 750652 📠 01989 750652

e-mail: enquiries@leahouse.co.uk

web: www.leahouse.co.uk

Dir: *4m SE of Ross on A40 towards Gloucester, in Lea village*

PETS: Bedrooms Charges £6 per stay per night **Public areas** except dining room during meals (on leads) **Grounds** accessible on leads disp bin **Exercise area** 30yds **Facilities** washing facs cage storage walks info vet info **On Request** torch towels **Resident Pets:** Cocoa (Terrier)

This former coaching inn near Ross is a good base for exploring the Forest of Dean and the Wye Valley. The individually furnished bedrooms are thoughtfully equipped with many extras and toiletries, and the atmosphere is relaxed and homely. Breakfast in the oak-beamed dining room includes freshly squeezed fruit juices, fish and local sausages.

Rooms 3 rms (2 en suite) (1 pri facs) (1 fmly) S £35-£45; D £60-£70* **Facilities** TVB tea/coffee Cen ht TVL Dinner Last d by prior arrangement Wi-fi available **Parking** 4 **Notes** LB

★★★★ BED & BREAKFAST

Lumleys

Kern Bridge, Bishopswood HR9 5QT

☎ 01600 890040 📠 0870 706 2378

e-mail: helen@lumleys.force9.co.uk

web: www.thelumleys.co.uk

Dir: *Off A40 onto B4229 at Goodrich, over Kern Bridge, right at Inn On The Wye, 400yds opp picnic ground*

PETS: Bedrooms unattended **Public areas** except dining room **Grounds** accessible disp bin **Exercise area** 20yds **Facilities** washing facs cage storage walks info vet info **On Request** fridge access torch towels **Resident Pets:** Megan (Golden Cocker Spaniel)

This pleasant and friendly guest house overlooks the River Wye, and has been a hostelry since Victorian times. It offers the character of a bygone era combined with modern comforts and facilities. Bedrooms are individually and carefully furnished and one has a four-poster bed and its own patio. Comfortable public areas include a choice of sitting rooms.

Rooms 3 en suite D £65-£75 **Facilities** STV FTV TVB tea/coffee Direct dial from bedrooms Cen ht TVL Dinner Last d 7pm Wi-fi available **Parking** 15 **Notes** ⊗

★★★★ GUEST ACCOMMODATION

Sunnymount

Ryefield Rd HR9 5LS

☎ 01989 563880 🖷 01989 566251

e-mail: sunnymount@tinyworld.co.uk

Dir: *M50 junct 4, A449 for Ross, next rdbt onto A40 Gloucester, B4260 for Ross town centre, 2nd right*

PETS: Bedrooms Public areas except restaurant (assist dogs permitted) **Grounds** accessible on leads disp bin **Exercise area Facilities** dog walking washing facs cage storage walks info vet info **On Request** fridge access torch towels **Restrictions** small dogs only

Built in the 1920s, this large house is in a quiet suburb close to the M50 and the A40. Immaculately maintained throughout, the bedrooms are comfortable and well equipped, and the public areas are spacious. A hearty breakfast is provided and served in the pleasant, airy dining room.

Rooms 6 en suite S £35-£40; D £55-£65✻ **Facilities** TVB tea/coffee Cen ht Dinner Last d 4pm **Parking** 7 **Notes LB** RS 21-31 Dec

★★★★ GUEST ACCOMMODATION

Thatch Close

Llangrove HR9 6EL

☎ 01989 770300

e-mail: info@thatchclose.co.uk

web: www.thatchclose.com

Dir: *Off A40 at Symonds Yat West/Whitchurch junct to Llangrove, right at x-rds after Post Office. Thatch Close 0.6m on left*

PETS: Bedrooms Public areas at discretion of other guests **Grounds** accessible disp bin **Exercise area Facilities** food food bowl water bowl dog scoop/disp bags leads washing facs cage storage walks info vet info **On Request** fridge access torch towels **Resident Pets:** Aku & Zippy (African Grey parrots), Oliver & Tilly (Spaniel/Collie cross)

Standing in 13 acres, this sturdy farmhouse dating from 1760 is full of character. There is a wonderfully warm atmosphere here with a genuine welcome from the hosts. The homely bedrooms are equipped for comfort with many thoughtful extras. Breakfast and dinner are served in the elegant dining room, and a lounge is available. The extensive patios and gardens are popular in summer, providing plenty of space to find a quiet corner and relax with a good book.

Rooms 3 en suite **Facilities** TVB tea/coffee Cen ht TVL Dinner Last d 9am **Parking** 8 **Notes** ⊗

SHOBDON — MAP 03 SO46

★★★★ INN

The Bateman Arms

HR6 9LX

☎ 01568 708374 🖷 08701 236418

e-mail: diana@batemanarms.co.uk

web: www.batemanarms.co.uk

Dir: *On B4362 in Shobdon village*

PETS: Bedrooms (3GF) sign **Stables** nearby (0.5m) **Charges** £5 per night £10 per week **Grounds** accessible on leads disp bin **Exercise area** 500yds **Facilities** food (pre-bookable) water bowl washing facs cage storage walks info vet info **On Request** fridge access torch towels **Resident Pets:** Bing & Lui (dogs)

Located in the village, parts of this refurbished inn date back over four hundred years. Now under the new ownership of Bill and Diana Mahood who offer a warm welcome to all their guests as well as accommodation which comprises six modern style bedrooms located in the separate refurbished building and three bedrooms in the main building. All are comfortable and well appointed. Much of the character has been retained with plenty of oak beams and a large log fire adding to the ambience in the public areas. In addition to the friendly welcome, the food here is a key feature with carefully prepared local produce.

Rooms 3 en suite 6 annexe en suite (2 fmly) (3 GF) S £55-£65; D £85-£95✻ **Facilities** FTV TVB tea/coffee Cen ht Dinner Last d 8.45pm Wi-fi available Pool Table Games room **Parking** 40

STANFORD BISHOP — MAP 03 SO65

►►► **Boyce Caravan Park** *(SO692528)*

WR6 5UB

☎ 01886 884248 🖷 01886 884187

e-mail: enquiries@boyceholidaypark.co.uk

web: www.boyceholidaypark.co.uk

Dir: *From B4220 (Malvern road) take sharp turn opposite Herefordshire House pub, then right after 0.25m. Signed Linley Green, then 1st drive on right*

PETS: Public areas except buildings & play areas disp bin **Exercise area** on site dog walking area **Facilities** walks info vet info **Other** prior notice required **Restrictions** no Dobermans, German Shepherds, Bull Terriers, Rottweilers, Japanese Tosa or similar cross breeds

Open Feb-Dec (rs Mar-Oct Tourers) Last arrival 18.00hrs Last departure noon

A friendly and peaceful park with access allowed onto the 100 acres of farmland. Coarse fishing is also available in the grounds, and there are extensive views over the Malvern and Suckley Hills. Many walks available. A 10-acre site with 14 touring pitches, 3 hardstandings and 200 statics.

ENGLAND

SYMONDS YAT (WEST) MAP 03 SO51

★★★★ GUEST ACCOMMODATION

Norton House

Whitchurch HR9 6DJ

☎ 01600 890046 01600 890045

e-mail: su@norton.wyenet.co.uk

web: www.norton-house.com

Dir: *0.5m N of Symonds Yat West. Off A40 into Whitchurch village and left onto Old Monmouth Rd*

PETS: Bedrooms Public areas when no other guests are present (on leads) **Grounds** accessible disp bin **Exercise area** 0.25m **Facilities** food bowl water bowl bedding dog chews feeding mat dog scoop/disp bags leads washing facs cage storage walks info vet info **On Request** fridge access torch towels **Other** welcome pack for dogs; large dog cage for loan **Resident Pets:** Hector & Hamish (Standard Poodles)

Built as a farmhouse, Norton House dates back 300 years and retains a lot of character, with features such as flagstone floors and beamed ceilings. The bedrooms, including a four-poster room, are individually styled and furnished for maximum comfort. Excellent local produce is used to create an imaginative range of breakfast and dinner options. The charming public areas include a snug lounge, with a wood-burning stove. Self-catering cottages are also available.

Rooms 3 en suite S £45-£50; D £60-£90 **Facilities** TVB tea/coffee Cen ht TVL Dinner Last d 9am **Parking** 5 **Notes** No children 12yrs Closed 25-26 Dec

►►► Doward Park Camp Site *(SO539167)*

Great Doward HR9 6BP

☎ 01600 890438

e-mail: enquiries@dowardpark.co.uk

web: www.dowardpark.co.uk

Dir: *2m from A40 between Ross-on-Wye & Monmouth. Take Symonds Yat (West) turn, then Crockers Ash, follow signs to site*

PETS: Public areas except children's play area **Charges** £1 per night **Exercise area** adjacent **Facilities** on site shop food bowl water bowl walks info vet info **Other** prior notice required **Resident Pets:** Woody (dog), Fairy Sprinkle (cat)

Open Mar-Oct Last arrival 20.00hrs Last departure 11.30hrs

This delightful little park is set in peaceful woodlands on the hillside above the Wye Valley. It is ideal for campers and motor homes but not caravans due to the narrow approach roads. A warm welcome awaits and the facilities are kept spotless. A 1.5-acre site with 28 touring pitches.

Notes No caravans or fires, quiet after 22.00hrs, dogs must be on leads

YARKHILL MAP 03 SO64

★★★★ FARM HOUSE

Garford Farm *(SO600435)*

HR1 3ST

☎ 01432 890226 01432 890707 Mrs H Parker

e-mail: garfordfarm@btconnect.com

Dir: *Off A417 at Newtown x-rds onto A4103 for Hereford, farm 1.5m on left*

PETS: Bedrooms Stables on site **Charges** £4 (dogs) per night charge for damage **Grounds** accessible disp bin **Exercise area** on site on farm **Facilities** food bowl water bowl bedding leads washing facs cage storage walks info vet info **On Request** fridge access torch towels **Resident Pets:** Bertie, Millie & Berry (Black Labradors), Cokie & Soda (cats)

This black and white timber-framed farmhouse, set on a large arable holding, dates from the 17th century. Its character is enhanced by period furnishings, and fires burn in the comfortable lounge during colder weather. The traditionally furnished bedrooms, including a family room, have modern facilities.

Rooms 2 en suite (1 fmly) S fr £40; D fr £60* **Facilities** TVB tea/coffee Cen ht Fishing **Parking** 6 **Notes** No children 2yrs 700 acres arable Closed 25-26 Dec

HERTFORDSHIRE

BISHOP'S STORTFORD MAP 05 TL42

★★★★ 76% HOTEL

Down Hall Country House

Hatfield Heath CM22 7AS

☎ 01279 731441 01279 730416

e-mail: reservations@downhall.co.uk

web: www.downhall.co.uk

Dir: *A1060, at Hatfield Heath keep left. Turn right into lane opposite Hunters Meet restaurant & left at end, follow sign*

PETS: Bedrooms (20GF) unattended **Charges** £10 per stay **Grounds** accessible disp bin **Exercise area Facilities** food food bowl water bowl dog chews dog scoop/disp bags cage storage vet info **On Request** fridge access torch **Other** welcome pack on arrival **Resident Pets:** deer & peacocks

Imposing country-house hotel set amidst 100 acres of mature grounds in a peaceful location just a short drive from Stansted Airport. Bedrooms are generally quite spacious; each one is pleasantly decorated, tastefully furnished and equipped with modern facilities. Public rooms include a choice of restaurants, a cocktail bar, two lounges and leisure facilities.

Down Hall Country House

Rooms 99 en suite (20 GF) S £99-£104; D £104-£140 (incl. bkfst)✻ **Facilities** Wi-fi in bedrooms Giant chess Whirlpool Sauna Snooker room Gym equipment Xmas New Year **Services** Lift **Parking** 150 **Notes** LB

See advert on this page

★★★ BED & BREAKFAST

Broadleaf Guest House

38 Broadleaf Av CM23 4JY

☎ 01279 835467

e-mail: b-tcannon@tiscali.co.uk

Dir: *1m SW of town centre. Off B1383 onto Whittinton Way & Friedburge Av, Broadleaf Av 6th left*

PETS: Bedrooms Exercise area surrounding countryside **Facilities** vet info

A delightful detached house situated in a peaceful residential area close to the town centre, and within easy striking distance of the M11 and Stansted Airport. The pleasantly decorated bedrooms are carefully furnished and equipped with many thoughtful touches. Breakfast is served in the smart dining room, which overlooks the pretty garden.

Rooms 2 rms (1 fmly) S £30-£35; D £55-£60✻ **Facilities** TVB tea/coffee Cen ht **Parking** 2 **Notes**

HERTFORD — MAP 04 TL31

►►►► **Hertford Camping & Caravanning Club Site** *(TL334113)*

Mangrove Rd SG13 8QF

☎ 01992 586696

web: www.thefriendlyclub.co.uk

Dir: *From A10 follow A414/Hertford signs to next rdbt (Foxholes), straight over. In 200yds left signed Balls Park & Hertford University. Left at T-junct into Mangrove Road. Site on left*

PETS: Public areas except in buildings disp bin **Exercise area** on site **Facilities** walks info vet info **Other** prior notice required

Open all year Last arrival 21.00hrs Last departure noon

A spacious, well-landscaped club site in a rural setting one mile south of Hertford, with immaculate modern toilet facilities. There are several hedged areas with good provision of hardstandings, and a cosy camping section in an old orchard. All kinds of wildlife flourish around the lake. A 32-acre site with 250 touring pitches, 54 hardstandings.

Notes Site gates closed 23.00hrs-07.00hrs

SOUTH MIMMS SERVICE AREA (M25) — MAP 04 TL20

BUDGET HOTEL

Days Inn South Mimms

Bignells Corner EN6 3QQ

☎ 01707 665440 📠 01707 660189

e-mail: south.mimms@welcomebreak.co.uk

web: www.welcomebreak.co.uk

Dir: *M25 junct 23, at rdbt follow signs*

PETS: Bedrooms unattended **Charges** charge for damage **Public areas** (on leads) **Grounds** accessible on leads **Exercise area**

This modern building offers accommodation in smart, spacious and well-equipped bedrooms, suitable for families and business travellers, and all with en suite bathrooms. Refreshments may be taken at the nearby family restaurant.

Rooms 74 en suite S £49-£69; D £59-£79✻

STEVENAGE MAP 04 TL22

★★★ 77% HOTEL

Novotel Stevenage

Knebworth Park SG1 2AX

☎ 01438 346100 📠 01438 723872

e-mail: H0992@accor.com

web: www.novotel.com

Dir: *A1(M) junct 7, at entrance to Knebworth Park*

PETS: Bedrooms (30GF) **Charges** £6 per night **Public areas** except restaurant (on leads) **Grounds** accessible disp bin **Exercise area**

Ideally situated just off the A1(M) is this purpose built hotel, which is a popular business and conference venue. Bedrooms are pleasantly decorated and equipped with a good range of useful extras. Public rooms include a large open plan lounge bar serving a range of snacks, and a smartly appointed restaurant.

Rooms 101 en suite (20 fmly) (30 GF) **Facilities** ⥼ Wi-fi available Free use of local health club **Services** Lift **Parking** 120

WALTHAM CROSS MAP 05 TL30

►►► Theobalds Park Camping & Caravanning Club Site *(TL344005)*

Theobalds Park, Bulls Cross Ride EN7 5HS

☎ 01992 620604

web: www.thefriendlyclub.co.uk

Dir: *M25 junct 25. A10 towards London, keep in right lane. Right at 1st lights. Right at T-junct, right behind dog kennels. Site towards top of lane on right*

PETS: Public areas except in buildings disp bin **Exercise area** on site **Facilities** walks info vet info **Other** prior notice required

Open 2 Apr-2 Nov Last arrival 21.00hrs Last departure noon

A lovely open site surrounded by mature trees, and set in parkland at Theobalds Hall. The portacabin toilet facilities are freshly painted and extremely clean, and there are two separate glades for tents. A 14-acre site with 90 touring pitches.

Notes Site gates closed 23.00hrs-07.00hrs

WARE MAP 05 TL31

★★★★★ 81% ❀❀

COUNTRY HOUSE HOTEL

Marriott Hanbury Manor Hotel & Country Club

Marriott HOTELS & RESORTS

SG12 0SD

☎ 01920 487722 & 0870 400 7222 📠 01920 487692

e-mail: mhrs.stngs.guestrelations@marriotthotels.com

web: www.marriott.co.uk

Dir: *M25 junct 25, take A10 north for 12m, then A1170 exit, right at rdbt, hotel on left*

PETS: Bedrooms (3GF) **Charges** £40 per stay (cleaning fee) per week charge for damage **Grounds** accessible on leads **Exercise area Facilities** food bowl water bowl walks info vet info **On Request** torch

Set in 200 acres of landscaped grounds, this impressive Jacobean-style mansion boasts an enviable range of leisure facilities, including an excellent health club and championship golf course. Bedrooms are traditionally and comfortably furnished in the country-house style and have lovely marbled bathrooms. There are a number of food and drink options, including the renowned Zodiac and Oakes restaurants.

Rooms 134 en suite 27 annexe en suite (3 GF) **Facilities** supervised 18 Gym Putt green Wi-fi in bedrooms Health & beauty treatments Aerobics Yoga Dance class **Services** Lift **Parking** 200 **Notes LB**

★★★ 74% HOTEL

Roebuck

Baldock St SG12 9DR

☎ 01920 409955 📠 01920 468016

e-mail: roebuck@forestdale.com

web: www.forestdale.com

Dir: *A10 onto B1001, left at rdbt, 1st left behind fire station*

PETS: Bedrooms unattended sign **Charges** £7.50 per night charge for damage **Public areas** except restaurant (on leads) **Exercise area Facilities** food (pre-bookable) food bowl water bowl feeding mat cage storage walks info vet info **On Request** fridge access

The Roebuck is a comfortable and friendly hotel situated close to the old market town of Ware, it is also within easy reach of Stansted Airport, Cambridge and Hertford. The hotel has spacious bedrooms, a comfortable lounge, bar and conservatory restaurant. There is also a range of air-conditioned meeting rooms.

Rooms 50 en suite (1 fmly) (16 GF) S £84-£89; D £114-£125 (incl. bkfst)✳ **Facilities** Wi-fi available **Services** Lift **Parking** 64 **Notes LB**

KENT

ASHFORD MAP 05 TR04

★★★ GUEST ACCOMMODATION

The Croft

Canterbury Rd, Kennington TN25 4DU

☎ 01233 622140 📠 01233 635271

e-mail: info@crofthotel.com

Dir: *M20 junct 10, 2m on A28 signed Canterbury*

PETS: Bedrooms unattended **Charges** £5-£7 per night **Exercise area** heath across road

An attractive red-brick house situated in 2 acres of landscaped grounds just a short drive from Ashford railway station. The generously proportioned bedrooms are in the main house and in pretty cottages; all are pleasantly decorated and thoughtfully equipped. Public rooms include a smart Italian restaurant, a bar, and a cosy lounge.

Rooms 27 en suite (6 fmly) (8 GF) **Facilities** TVB tea/coffee Direct dial from bedrooms Cen ht TVL Dinner Last d 9.30pm **Parking** 30

►►►► **Broad Hembury Caravan & Camping Park** *(TR009387)*

Steeds Ln, Kingsnorth TN26 1NQ

☎ 01233 620859 📠 01233 620918

e-mail: holidaypark@broadhembury.co.uk

web: www.broadhembury.co.uk

Dir: *From M20 junct 10 take A2070. Left at 2nd rdbt signed Kingsnorth, then left at 2nd x-roads in village*

PETS: Public areas except toilets & play area **Exercise area** on site 2 acre meadow **Facilities** on site shop dog scoop/disp bags washing facs walks info vet info **Other** prior notice required **Restrictions** no more 2 per pitch **Resident Pets:** Bruce (German Shepherd), Henry (King Charles Spaniel), Scooby (cross), 4 chickens, Moor Hens

Open all year Last arrival 22.00hrs Last departure noon

AA Campsite of the Year for South-east England 2009. Well-run and maintained small family park surrounded by open pasture and neatly landscaped, with pitches sheltered by mature hedges. Some super pitches have proved a popular addition, and there is a well-equipped campers' kitchen. A 10-acre site with 60 touring pitches, 24 hardstandings and 25 statics.

BRANDS HATCH MAP 05 TQ56

★★★★ 83% ❀❀ HOTEL

Thistle Brands Hatch

thistle

DA3 8PE

☎ 0870 333 9128 📠 0870 333 9228

e-mail: brandshatch@thistle.co.uk

web: www.thistlehotels.com/brandshatch

Dir: *Follow Brands Hatch signs, hotel on left of racing circuit entrance*

PETS: Bedrooms (43GF) unattended **Stables** nearby (2m) **Charges** charge for damage **Public areas** (on leads) **Grounds** accessible **Exercise area Facilities** washing facs cage storage vet info **On Request** torch towels

Ideally situated overlooking Brands Hatch race track and close to the major road networks (M20/M25). The open-plan public areas include a choice of bars, large lounge and an award-winning restaurant. Bedrooms are stylishly appointed and well equipped for both leisure and business guests. Extensive meeting rooms and Otium leisure facilities are also available.

Rooms 121 en suite (4 fmly) (43 GF) **Facilities** Gym Health & beauty treatments Solarium **Parking** 180

CANTERBURY MAP 05 TR15

★★★ 88% HOTEL

Best Western Abbots Barton

Best Western

New Dover Rd CT1 3DU

☎ 01227 760341 📠 01227 785442

e-mail: sales@abbotsbartonhotel.com

Dir: *A2 onto A2050 at bridge, S of Canterbury. Hotel 0.75m past Old Gate Inn on left*

PETS: Bedrooms unattended **Charges** £10 per night **Grounds** accessible on leads **Exercise area** 1m **Facilities** food bowl bedding cage storage walks info vet info **On Request** torch **Restrictions** small dogs only

Delightful property with a country-house hotel feel set amid two acres of pretty landscaped gardens close to the city centre and major road networks. The spacious accommodation includes a range of stylish lounges, a smart bar and the Fountain Restaurant, which serves imaginative food. Conference and banqueting facilities are also available.

Rooms 50 en suite (2 fmly) (6 GF) **Facilities** Wi-fi in bedrooms **Services** Lift air con **Parking** 80 **Notes** LB

ENGLAND

CANTERBURY CONTINUED

★★★★★ GUEST ACCOMMODATION
Yorke Lodge

50 London Rd CT2 8LF

☎ 01227 451243 Fax 01227 462006

e-mail: info@yorkelodge.com

web: www.yorkelodge.com

Dir: *From London M2/A2, 1st exit signed Canterbury. At 1st rdbt left onto London Rd*

PETS: Bedrooms unattended **Exercise area** 100yds **Facilities** walks info vet info **On Request** fridge access torch towels **Resident Pets:** Fleur (Dalmatian/Collie cross)

The charming Victorian property stands in a tree-lined road just ten minutes walk from the town centre and railway station. The spacious bedrooms are thoughtfully equipped and carefully decorated; some rooms have four-poster beds. The stylish dining room leads to a conservatory-lounge, which opens onto a superb terrace.

Rooms 8 en suite (1 fmly) S £52-£58; D £85-£98 **Facilities** FTV TVB tea/coffee Cen ht Wi-fi available **Parking** 5 **Notes** LB

★★★ GUEST ACCOMMODATION
St Stephens Guest House

100 St Stephens Rd CT2 7JL

☎ 01227 767644 Fax 01227 767644

Dir: *A290 from city Westgate & sharp right onto North Ln, 2nd rdbt left onto St Stephens Rd, right onto Market Way, car park on right*

PETS: Bedrooms (3GF) **Charges** £3 per night **Public areas** except dining room **Exercise area Facilities** washing facs walks info vet info **On Request** fridge access torch towels **Resident Pets:** Jack & Molly (Springer Spaniels)

A large, privately-owned guest house situated close to the university and within easy walking distance of the city centre. The pleasant bedrooms are equipped with a good range of useful extras, and there is a cosy lounge. Breakfast is served at individual tables in the smart dining room.

Rooms 12 rms (11 en suite) (2 fmly) (3 GF) S £39-£45; D £59-£68* **Facilities** TVB tea/coffee Cen ht TVL **Parking** 11 **Notes** No children 5yrs Closed 18 Dec-mid Jan

★★★ GUEST ACCOMMODATION
Cathedral Gate

36 Burgate CT1 2HA

☎ 01227 464381 Fax 01227 462800

e-mail: cgate@cgate.demon.co.uk

Dir: *In city centre. Next to main gateway into cathedral precincts*

PETS: Bedrooms unattended **Public areas** except dining room **Exercise area** Westgate Gardens 0.5m, Blean Woods 3m **Facilities** vet info **On Request** fridge access **Other** guests must bring pet's own bedding

Dating from 1438, this house has an enviable central location next to the Cathedral. Old beams and winding corridors are part of the character of the property. Bedrooms are traditionally furnished, equipped to modern standards and many have cathedral views. Luggage can be unloaded at reception before parking in a local car park.

Rooms 13 rms (2 en suite) 12 annexe rms (10 en suite) (5 fmly) S £31.75-£103.50; D £61.50-£103.50 **Facilities** TVB tea/coffee Direct dial from bedrooms Cen ht Dinner Last d 8pm **Notes** LB

►►► **Canterbury Camping & Caravanning Club Site** *(TR172577)*

Bekesbourne Ln CT3 4AB

☎ 01227 463216

web: www.thefriendlyclub.co.uk

Dir: *From Canterbury follow A257 signs (Sandwich), turn right opposite golf course*

PETS: disp bin **Exercise area** on site dog walks **Facilities** walks info vet info **Other** prior notice required

Open all year Last arrival 21.00hrs Last departure noon

An attractive tree-screened site in pleasant rural surroundings yet within walking distance of the city centre. The park is well landscaped, and offers very smart toilet facilities in one block, with another older but well-kept building housing further facilities. A 20-acre site with 200 touring pitches, 21 hardstandings.

►► **Ashfield Farm** *(TR138508)*

Waddenhall, Petham CT4 5PX

☎ 01227 700624

e-mail: mpatterson@ashfieldfarm.freeserve.co.uk

Dir: *7m S of Canterbury on B2068*

PETS: Sep Accom short term dog minding **Exercise area** 100m **Facilities** washing facs walks info vet info

Open Apr-Oct Last arrival anytime Last departure noon

Small rural site with simple facilities and well-drained pitches, set in beautiful countryside and enjoying lovely open views. Located south of Canterbury, and with very security-conscious owners. A 4.5-acre site with 30 touring pitches and 1 static.

Notes

DARTFORD MAP 05 TQ57

BUDGET HOTEL

Campanile Dartford

Campanile HOTEL RESTAURANT

1 Clipper Boulevard West, Crossways Business Park DA2 6QN

☎ 01322 278925 🖹 01322 278948

e-mail: dartford@campanile.com

web: www.envergure.fr

Dir: *follow signs for Ferry Terminal from Dartford Bridge*

PETS: Bedrooms unattended **Exercise area Other** Please telephone for details

This modern building offers accommodation in smart, well-equipped bedrooms, all with en suite bathrooms. Refreshments may be taken at the informal Bistro.

Rooms 125 en suite

DEAL MAP 05 TR35

★★★★★ GUEST ACCOMMODATION

Sutherland House

186 London Rd CT14 9PT

☎ 01304 362853 🖹 01304 381146

e-mail: info@sutherlandhouse.fsnet.co.uk

Dir: *0.5m W of town centre/seafront on A258*

PETS: Bedrooms (1GF) unattended sign **Charges** charge for damage **Public areas** with consideration for other guests' comfort **Grounds** accessible **Exercise area Facilities** water bowl washing facs walks info vet info **On Request** fridge access torch towels **Restrictions** small dogs only

This stylish accommodation demonstrates impeccable taste with its charming, well-equipped bedrooms and a comfortable lounge. Fully stocked bar, books, free Wi-fi, Freeview TV and radio are some of the many amenities offered. The elegant dining room is the venue for a hearty breakfast and dinner is available by prior arrangement.

Rooms 4 en suite (1 GF) S £55-£60; D £65-£70* **Facilities** FTV TVB tea/coffee Direct dial from bedrooms Cen ht Dinner Last d 6.30pm Wi-fi available **Parking** 7 **Notes LB** No children 5yrs

DOVER MAP 05 TR34

★★★★ GUEST ACCOMMODATION

Hubert House

9 Castle Hill Rd CT16 1QW

☎ 01304 202253 🖹 01304 210142

e-mail: huberthouse@btinternet.com

web: www.huberthouse.co.uk

Dir: *On A258 by Dover Castle*

PETS: Bedrooms Charges £7.50 per night charge for damage **Exercise area** 300mtrs **Facilities** food (pre-bookable) food bowl water bowl bedding **Resident Pets:** Lillie (Weimaraner), Tullah (Slovakian Pointer)

This charming Georgian house is within walking distance of the ferry port and the town centre. Bedrooms are sumptuously decorated and furnished with an abundance of practical extras. Breakfast, including full English and healthy options, is served in the smart coffee house, which is open all day. Families are especially welcome.

Rooms 7 en suite (4 fmly) S £40-£50; D £50-£75* (room only) **Facilities** FTV TVB tea/coffee Cen ht Dinner Last d 2pm Wi-fi available **Parking** 6 **Notes LB** Closed Jan-Feb

FOLKESTONE MAP 05 TR23

★★★ 73% HOTEL

The Burlington

Earls Av CT20 2HR

☎ 01303 255301 🖹 01303 251301

e-mail: info@theburlingtonhotel.com

web: www.choicehotelseurope.com

Dir: *M20 junct 13. At rdbt 3rd exit signed A20/Folkstone. At next rdbt 2nd exit into Cherry Garden Lane. To lights, take middle lane into Beachborough Rd, under bridge, left into Shorncliffe Rd. 5th right signed Hythe & Hastings. Hotel at end on right*

PETS: Bedrooms (5GF) **Charges** £10 per night **Public areas** except restaurant (on leads) **Grounds** accessible on leads **Exercise area Facilities** water bowl bedding cage storage walks info vet info **Resident Pets:** Cherit (Golden Retriever), Misty (cat)

Situated close to the beach in a peaceful side road just a short walk from the town centre. The public rooms include a choice of lounges, the Bay Tree restaurant and a large cocktail bar. Bedrooms are pleasantly decorated and equipped with modern facilities; some rooms have superb sea views.

Rooms 50 en suite (6 fmly) (5 GF) S £42-£98; D £54-£123* **Facilities** FTV Putt green Wi-fi available Xmas New Year **Services** Lift **Parking** 20 **Notes LB**

FOLKESTONE CONTINUED

★★★ GUEST ACCOMMODATION

Langhorne Garden

10-12 Langhorne Gardens CT20 2EA

☎ 01303 257233 📠 01303 242760

e-mail: info@langhorne.co.uk

web: www.langhorne.co.uk

Dir: *Exit M20 junct 13 and follow signs for The Leas 2m*

PETS: Bedrooms unattended **Public areas** except restaurant **Exercise area Facilities** cage storage walks info vet info **On Request** fridge access torch towels

Once a Victorian seaside villa, Langhorne Garden is close to the seafront, shops and restaurants. Bright spacious bedrooms are traditionally decorated with plenty of original charm. Public rooms include a choice of comfortable lounges and a bar, a spacious dining room and a popular local bar in the basement with billiards, darts and a fussbol table.

Rooms 29 en suite (8 fmly) S £35-£49; D £59-£65✻ **Facilities** STV FTV TVB tea/coffee Direct dial from bedrooms Lift Cen ht Dinner Last d 7pm Wi-fi available Pool Table **Notes LB** Closed Xmas RS Jan-Etr

►►►► Folkestone Camping & Caravanning Club Site *(TR246376)*

The Warren CT19 6NQ

☎ 01303 255093

web: www.thefriendlyclub.co.uk

Dir: *From A2 or A20 onto A260, left at island into Folkstone. Continue straight over x-rds into Wear Bay Road, 2nd left past Martello Tower, site 0.5m on right*

PETS: Public areas except in buildings disp bin **Exercise area** beach, 60mtrs **Facilities** walks info vet info **Other** prior notice required

Open 2 Apr-2 Nov Last arrival 21.00hrs Last departure noon

This site commands marvellous views across the Strait of Dover, and is well located for the Channel ports. It nestles on the side of the cliff, and is tiered in some areas. The toilet facilities are modern and tasteful, with cubicled wash basins in both blocks. No caravans accepted. A 4-acre site with 80 touring pitches, 9 hardstandings.

Notes Site gates closed 23.00hrs-07.00hrs

►►► Little Satmar Holiday Park *(TR260390)*

Winehouse Ln, Capel Le Ferne CT18 7JF

☎ 01303 251188 📠 01303 251188

e-mail: info@keatfarm.co.uk

web: www.keatfarm.co.uk

Dir: *Signed off B2011*

PETS: Charges £1.50 per night £9.45 per week **Exercise area** 100mtrs **Facilities** on site shop food food bowl water bowl dog chews cat treats dog scoop/disp bags washing facs walks info vet info **Resident Pets:** 2 Rottweilers, 2 West Highland Terriers, Shih tzu

Open Mar-Nov Last arrival 23.00hrs Last departure 14.00hrs

A quiet, well-screened site well away from the road and statics, with clean and tidy facilities. A useful base for visiting Dover and Folkestone, and just a short walk from cliff paths with their views of the Channel, and sandy beaches below. A 5-acre site with 47 touring pitches and 75 statics.

►► Little Switzerland Camping & Caravan Site *(TR248380)*

Wear Bay Rd CT19 6PS

☎ 01303 252168

e-mail: btony328@aol.com

web: www.caravancampingsites.co.uk/kent/littleswitzerland.htm

Dir: *Signed from A20 E of Folkestone. Approaching from A259 or B2011 on E outskirts of Folkestone follow signs for Wear Bay/ Martello Tower, then tourist sign to site, follow signs to country park*

PETS: Stables nearby (1m) disp bin **Exercise area** on site dog walks **Facilities** washing facs walks info vet info **Resident Pets:** Fluffy (cat)

Open Mar-Oct Last arrival mdnt Last departure noon

Set on a narrow plateau below the white cliffs, this unusual site enjoys fine views across Wear Bay and the Strait of Dover. A licensed café with an alfresco area is popular; the basic toilet facilities are unsuitable for the disabled. A 3-acre site with 32 touring pitches and 13 statics.

Notes No open fires

KINGSGATE MAP 05 TR37

★★★ 77% HOTEL

The Fayreness

Marine Dr CT10 3LG
☎ 01843 868641 01843 608750
e-mail: info@fayreness.co.uk
web: www.fayreness.co.uk

Dir: *A28 onto B2051 which becomes B2052. Pass Holy Trinity Church on right and '19th Hole' public house. Next left, down Kingsgate Ave, hotel at end on left*

PETS: Bedrooms (5GF) unattended **Stables** nearby (5m) **Charges** £5 per night £20 per week charge for damage **Public areas** except restaurant & conservatory (on leads) **Grounds** accessible on leads disp bin **Exercise area** clifftop & beach adjacent **Facilities** food bowl water bowl dog chews cage storage walks info vet info **On Request** fridge access torch towels

Situated on the cliff top overlooking the English Channel, just a few steps from a sandy beach and adjacent to the North Foreland Golf Club. The spacious bedrooms are tastefully furnished with many thoughtful touches including free Wi-fi; some rooms have stunning sea views. Public rooms include a large open-plan lounge/bar, a function room, dining room and conservatory restaurant.

Rooms 29 en suite (3 fmly) (5 GF) S £55.50-£143; D £71-£153 (incl. bkfst)✻ **Facilities** STV Wi-fi available New Year **Parking** 70 **Notes** LB

MAIDSTONE MAP 05 TQ75

★★★★ INN

The Black Horse Inn

Pilgrims Way, Thurnham ME14 3LD
☎ 01622 737185 & 630830 01622 739170
e-mail: info@wellieboot.net
web: www.wellieboot.net/home_blackhorse.htm

Dir: *M20 junct 7, N onto A249. Right into Detling, opp pub onto Pilgrims Way for 1m*

PETS: Bedrooms (11GF) unattended **Charges** £6 per night charge for damage **Public areas** except restaurant (on leads) **Grounds** accessible on leads disp bin **Exercise area** Kent Downs adjacent **Facilities** dog scoop/disp bags washing facs cage storage walks info vet info **On Request** fridge access torch **Restrictions** no Pit Bull Terriers **Resident Pets:** Sam (Pointer), Boston (Staffordshire Bull Terrier)

This charming inn dates from the 17th century, and the public areas have a wealth of oak beams, exposed brickwork and open fireplaces. The stylish bedrooms are in a series of cosy cabins behind the premises; each one is attractively furnished and thoughtfully equipped.

Rooms 16 annexe en suite (4 fmly) (11 GF) S £65-£90; D £80-£90✻ **Facilities** FTV TVB tea/coffee Cen ht Dinner Last d 10pm Wi-fi available **Parking** 40 **Notes** LB No coaches

See advert on this page

★★★★ GUEST ACCOMMODATION

Aylesbury House

56-58 London Rd ME16 8QL
☎ 01622 762100 01622 664673
e-mail: mail@aylesburyhouse.co.uk

Dir: *5mins from M20 junct 5 on A20 to Maidstone. Aylesbury House on left before town centre*

PETS: Bedrooms unattended **Charges** charge for damage **Grounds** accessible disp bin **Exercise area** 1m **Facilities** walks info vet info

Located just a short walk from the town centre, this smartly maintained establishment offers a genuine welcome. The carefully decorated bedrooms have co-ordinated soft fabrics and many thoughtful touches. Breakfast is served in the smart dining room overlooking a walled garden.

Rooms 8 en suite S £50-£55; D £60-£75 **Facilities** TVB tea/coffee Cen ht Wi-fi available **Parking** 8

MAIDSTONE CONTINUED

★★★★ GUEST HOUSE

Roslin Villa

11 St Michaels Rd ME16 8BS

☎ 01622 758301 01622 761459

e-mail: info@roslinvillaguesthouse.com

web: www.roslinvillaguesthouse.com

Dir: *0.6m W of town centre. Off A26 Tonbridge Rd, brown tourist signs to Roslin Villa*

PETS: Bedrooms Charges £5 per night charge for damage **Exercise area** 500yds **Facilities** walks info vet info

Expect a warm welcome from the caring hosts at this delightful detached Victorian house, which is within easy walking distance of the town centre and only a short drive from the M20. The smart bedrooms are carefully furnished and equipped with many thoughtful touches. Public rooms include a cosy lounge and an elegant dining room.

Rooms 5 en suite (1 fmly) S £48-£50; D £65-£75* **Facilities** TVB tea/coffee Licensed Cen ht TVL Wi-fi available **Parking** 10 **Notes** No children 12yrs No coaches

NEW ROMNEY — MAP 05 TR02

★★★★ FARM HOUSE

Honeychild Manor Farmhouse *(TR062276)*

St Mary In The Marsh TN29 0DB

☎ 01797 366180 & 07951 237821 01797 366925

Mrs V Furnival

e-mail: honeychild@farming.co.uk

Dir: *2m N of New Romney off A259. S of village centre*

PETS: Bedrooms Stables on site **Charges** £10 (horses) per night **Grounds** accessible on leads disp bin **Exercise area** 100yds **Facilities** cage storage walks info vet info **On Request** fridge access torch towels **Resident Pets:** Georgie (Labrador), Molly (Collie), Charlie (horse)

This imposing Georgian farmhouse is part of a working dairy farm on Romney Marsh. Walkers and dreamers alike will enjoy the stunning views and can relax in the beautifully landscaped gardens or play tennis on the full-sized court. A hearty breakfast is served in the elegant dining room and features quality local produce. Bedrooms are pleasantly decorated, well furnished and thoughtfully equipped.

Rooms 3 rms (1 en suite) (1 fmly) **Facilities** TVB tea/coffee Cen ht Dinner Last d 4pm **Parking** 10 **Notes** 1500 acres Arable & Dairy

SANDWICH — MAP 05 TR35

★★★ INN

The Blue Pigeons Inn

The Street, Worth CT14 0DE

☎ 01304 613245 01304 621177

e-mail: info@bluepigeons.co.uk

web: www.bluepigeons.co.uk

Dir: *From A258 (Deal to Sandwich road), turn right onto The Street, 600mtrs on left*

PETS: Bedrooms (2GF) **Stables** nearby (1.5m) **Charges** charge for damage **Public areas** except restaurant **Grounds** accessible on leads disp bin **Exercise area Facilities** food bowl water bowl cage storage walks info vet info **On Request** torch towels

This popular local inn is close to historic Canterbury and the village of Sandwich. Bedrooms vary in size and all are en suite and comfortably presented. A hearty English breakfast is served in the restaurant and evening dining offers plentiful fresh, local produce. Bar meals are also available. Child-friendly environment.

Rooms 4 en suite 2 annexe en suite (2 fmly) (2 GF) S £39.95-£65; D £49.95-£75 **Facilities** FTV TVB tea/coffee Cen ht TVL Dinner Last d 9.30pm Pool Table **Parking** 10 **Notes** LB

SEVENOAKS — MAP 05 TQ55

►►► Oldbury Hill Camping & Caravanning Club Site *(TQ577564)*

Styants Bottom, Seal TN15 0ET

☎ 01732 762728

web: www.thefriendlyclub.co.uk

Dir: *Take A25 from Sevenoaks towards Borough Green. Left just after Crown Point Inn, on right, down narrow lane to Styants Bottom. Site on left*

PETS: Public areas except in buildings **Exercise area** woods **Facilities** walks info vet info **Other** prior notice required

Open 2 Apr-2 Nov Last arrival 21.00hrs Last departure noon

A remarkably tranquil site in the centre of National Trust woodland, with buildings blending well into the surroundings. Expect the usual high standard of customer care found at all Club sites. A 6-acre site with 60 touring pitches.

Notes Site gates closed 23.00hrs-07.00hrs

SITTINGBOURNE MAP 05 TQ96

★★★ 83% HOTEL

Hempstead House Country Hotel

London Rd, Bapchild ME9 9PP

☎ 01795 428020 📠 01795 436362

e-mail: info@hempsteadhouse.co.uk

web: www.hempsteadhouse.co.uk

Dir: *1.5m from town centre on A2 towards Canterbury*

PETS: Bedrooms (1GF) unattended **Stables** nearby (2m) **Public areas Grounds** accessible disp bin **Exercise area** adjacent **Facilities** food bowl water bowl washing facs cage storage walks info vet info **On Request** fridge access torch towels **Resident Pets:** Jade (Staffordshire Bull Terrier), Megan (Black Labrador), cats

Expect a warm welcome at this charming detached Victorian property, situated amidst four acres of mature landscaped gardens. Bedrooms are attractively decorated with lovely co ordinated fabrics, tastefully furnished and equipped with many thoughtful touches. Public rooms feature a choice of elegant lounges as well as a superb conservatory dining room. In summer guests can eat on the terraces.

Rooms 34 en suite (7 fmly) (1 GF) S £80-£110; D £100-£150 (incl. bkfst) **Facilities Spa** STV FTV Gym Wi-fi in bedrooms Fitness studio Steam room Sauna Hydrotherapy pool Xmas New Year **Services** Lift **Parking** 100 **Notes** LB

TUNBRIDGE WELLS (ROYAL) MAP 05 TQ53

★★★★ TOWN HOUSE HOTEL

Hotel du Vin Tunbridge Wells

Hotel du Vin & Bistro

Crescent Rd TN1 2LY

☎ 01892 526455 📠 01892 512044

e-mail: reception.tunbridgewells@hotelduvin.com

web: www.hotelduvin.com

Dir: *follow town centre to main junct of Mount Pleasant Road & Crescent Road/Church Road. Hotel 150yds on right just past Phillips House*

PETS: Bedrooms unattended **Charges** £10 (only if basket requested) per night **Public areas** except restaurant **Grounds** accessible **Exercise area** park 200yds **Facilities** water bowl cage storage walks info vet info **On Request** fridge access torch towels

This impressive Grade II listed building dates from 1762, and as a princess, Queen Victoria often stayed here. The spacious bedrooms are available in a range of sizes, beautifully and individually appointed, and equipped with a host of thoughtful extras. Public rooms include a bistro-style restaurant, two elegant lounges and a small bar.

Rooms 34 en suite D £115-£325* **Facilities** STV Wi-fi in bedrooms Boules court in garden **Services** Lift **Parking** 30 **Notes** LB

WHITSTABLE MAP 05 TR16

►►► Seaview Holiday Village *(TR145675)*

St John's Rd CT5 2RY

☎ 01227 792246 📠 01227 792247

e-mail: info@parkholidaysuk.com

web: www.parkholidaysuk.com

Dir: *From A299 take A2990 then B2205 to Swalecliffe, site between Herne Bay & Whitstable*

PETS: Public areas except in pet free areas **Stables** nearby (5m) **Charges** £2 per night disp bin **Exercise area** on site **Facilities** on site shop vet info **Other** prior notice required

Open Mar-Oct Last arrival 21.30hrs Last departure noon

A pleasant open site on the edge of Whitstable, set well away from the static area, with a smart, modern toilet block and both super and hardstanding pitches. A 12-acre site with 171 touring pitches, 41 hardstandings and 452 statics.

LANCASHIRE

ACCRINGTON MAP 07 SD72

★★★★ GUEST ACCOMMODATION

The Maple Lodge

70 Blackburn Rd, Clayton-le-Moors BB5 5JH

☎ 01254 301284 📠 0560 112 5380

e-mail: info@stayatmaplelodge.co.uk

Dir: *M65 junct 7, signs for Clayton-le-Moors, right at T-junct onto Blackburn Rd*

PETS: Bedrooms (4GF) **Charges** £5 per stay charge for damage **Exercise area** 100mtrs **Facilities** washing facs cage storage walks info vet info **On Request** fridge access torch towels **Restrictions** small & medium dogs only

This welcoming house is convenient for the M65, and provides comfortable, well-equipped bedrooms. There is an inviting lounge with well-stocked bar, and freshly cooked dinners (by arrangement) and hearty breakfasts are served in the attractive dining room.

Rooms 4 en suite 4 annexe en suite (1 fmly) (4 GF) S £44; D £62* **Facilities** FTV TVB tea/coffee Direct dial from bedrooms Cen ht TVL Dinner Last d 8pm Wi-fi available **Parking** 6 **Notes** LB

ENGLAND

BLACKPOOL MAP 07 SD33

★★★★ 74% HOTEL

Barceló Blackpool Imperial Hotel

North Promenade FY1 2HB

☎ 01253 623971 📠 01253 751784

e-mail: imperialblackpool@barcelo-hotels.co.uk

web: www.barcelo-hotels.co.uk

Dir: *M55 junct 2, take A583 North Shore, follow signs to North Promenade. Hotel on seafront, north of tower.*

PETS: Bedrooms unattended sign **Charges** £15 per stay per night charge for damage **Public areas** only in lobby area (on leads) **Grounds** accessible on leads **Exercise area** beach adjacent **Facilities** vet info **Other** dogs allowed in standard bedrooms only

Enjoying a prime seafront location, this grand Victorian hotel offers smartly appointed, well-equipped bedrooms and spacious, elegant public areas. Facilities include a smart leisure club; a comfortable lounge, the No.10 bar and an attractive split-level restaurant that overlooks the seafront. Conferences and functions are extremely well catered for.

Rooms 180 en suite (16 fmly) S £64-£158* **Facilities Spa** Gym Wi-fi available Xmas New Year **Services** Lift **Parking** 150 (charged)

BURNLEY MAP 07 SD83

★★★ 78% HOTEL

Best Western Higher Trapp Country House

Trapp Ln, Simonstone BB12 7QW

☎ 01282 772781 📠 01282 772782

e-mail: reception@highertrapphotel.co.uk

PETS: Bedrooms unattended **Grounds** accessible on leads **Exercise area** local walks **Facilities** vet info

Set in beautifully maintained gardens with rolling countryside beyond, this hotel offers spacious, comfortable bedrooms, some of which are located in the Lodge, a smart annexe building. Public areas include a pleasant lounge, bar and conservatory restaurant where guests will find service friendly and attentive.

Rooms 19 en suite 10 annexe en suite (3 fmly) (4 GF) S £50-£90; D £58-£98 (incl. bkfst & dinner) **Facilities** Xmas **Parking** 100 **Notes LB**

CHARNOCK RICHARD MOTORWAY SERVICE AREA (M6) MAP 07 SD51

BUDGET HOTEL

Welcome Lodge Charnock Richard

Welcome Break Service Area PR7 5LR

☎ 01257 791746 📠 01257 793596

e-mail: charnockhotel@welcomebreak.co.uk

web: www.welcomebreak.co.uk

Dir: *between junct 27 & 28 of M6 N'bound. 500yds from Camelot Theme Park via Mill Lane*

PETS: Bedrooms (32GF) **Grounds** accessible **Exercise area** on site large field

This modern building offers accommodation in smart, spacious and well-equipped bedrooms, suitable for families and business travellers, and all with en suite bathrooms. Refreshments may be taken at the nearby family restaurant.

Rooms 100 en suite S £39-£59; D £49-£69*

CLITHEROE MAP 07 SD74

►►► Clitheroe Camping & Caravanning Club Site *(SD727413)*

Edisford Rd BB7 3LA

☎ 01200 425294

web: www.thefriendlyclub.co.uk

Dir: *From W follow A671 to Clitheroe. Follow sign for left turn to Longridge/Sports Centre. Into Greenacre Rd approx 25mtrs after pelican crossing. To T-junct. (Sports Centre on right). Site 50mtrs on left*

PETS: Public areas except in buildings **Exercise area Facilities** walks info vet info **Other** prior notice required

Open 2 Apr-2 Nov Last arrival 21.00hrs Last departure noon

Set on the banks of the River Ribble, this park is attractively landscaped with mature trees and shrubs. An ideal spot for walking and fishing, and the site is also adjacent to a park with a café, pitch and putt, leisure centre, swimming pool and miniature steam railway. The Ribble Country Way is nearby. A 6-acre site with 80 touring pitches, 30 hardstandings.

FORTON MOTORWAY SERVICE AREA (M6) — MAP 07 SD55

BUDGET HOTEL

Travelodge Lancaster (M6)

White Carr Ln, Bay Horse LA2 9DU
☎ 08719 846 154 🖷 01524 791703
web: www.travelodge.co.uk

Dir: *between junct 32 & 33 of M6*

PETS: Bedrooms Charges £10 per pet per night charge for damage **Public areas** (on leads) **Grounds** accessible on leads disp bin **Exercise area Facilities** walks info vet info

Travelodge offers good quality, good value, modern accommodation. Ideal for families, the spacious en suite bedrooms include remote-control TV, tea and coffee-making facilities and comfortable beds. Meals can be taken at the nearby family restaurant.

Rooms 53 en suite S fr £29; D fr £29

GARSTANG — MAP 07 SD44

►►►► Claylands Caravan Park *(SD496485)*

Cabus PR3 1AJ
☎ 01524 791242 🖷 01524 792406
e-mail: alan@claylands.com
web: www.claylands.com

Dir: *From M6 junct 33 S to Garstang, approx 6m pass Little Chef, signed off A6 into private road on Lancaster side of Garstang*

PETS: Public areas (on leads) **Charges** £1 per night disp bin **Exercise area Facilities** on site shop dog scoop/disp bags washing facs walks info vet info

Open Mar-4 Jan (rs Jan & Feb holiday park only) Last arrival 23.00hrs Last departure 14.00hrs

A well-maintained site with lovely river and woodland walks and good views over the River Wyre towards the village of Scorton. This friendly park is set in delightful countryside. Guests can enjoy fishing, and the atmosphere is very relaxed. The quality facilities and amenities are of a high standard, and everything is immaculately maintained. A 14-acre site with 30 touring pitches, 30 hardstandings and 68 statics.

Notes No roller blades or skateboards

LANCASTER — MAP 07 SD46

★★★★ 76% ❁ HOTEL

Lancaster House

CLASSIC BRITISH HOTELS

Green Ln, Ellel LA1 4GJ
☎ 01524 844822 🖷 01524 844766
e-mail: lancaster@elhmail.co.uk
web: www.elh.co.uk/hotels/lancaster

Dir: *M6 junct 33 N towards Lancaster. Through Galgate and into Green Ln. Hotel before university on right*

PETS: Bedrooms (44GF) **Charges** £25 per night charge for damage **Grounds** accessible on leads disp bin **Exercise area** 500mtrs **Facilities** walks info vet info **On Request** fridge access towels

This modern hotel enjoys a rural setting south of the city and close to the university. The attractive open-plan reception and lounge boast a roaring log fire in colder months. Bedrooms are spacious, and include 19 rooms that are particularly well equipped for business guests. There are leisure facilities with a hot tub and a function suite.

Rooms 99 en suite (29 fmly) (44 GF) S £74-£120; D £84-£120 (incl. bkfst)✻ **Facilities Spa** STV supervised Gym Wi-fi available Beauty salon Outside hot tub Xmas New Year **Parking** 120 **Notes LB**

★★★ 72% HOTEL

Best Western Royal Kings Arms

OXFORD HOTELS & INNS

Market St LA1 1HP
☎ 01524 32451 🖷 01524 841698
e-mail: reservations.lancaster@ohiml.com
web: www.oxfordhotelsandinns.com

Dir: *M6 junct 33, follow A6 to city centre, turn 1st left, after Market Hotel. Hotel at lights before Lancaster Castle*

PETS: Bedrooms unattended **Charges** charge for damage **Exercise area** 0.5m **Facilities** cage storage walks info vet info **On Request** fridge access torch

A distinctive period building located in the town centre, close to the castle. Bedrooms and bathrooms are comfortable and suitable for both business and leisure guests. Public areas include a small lounge on the ground floor and The Castle Bar and Brasserie Restaurant on the first floor. The hotel also has a private car park.

Rooms 55 en suite (14 fmly) **Services** Lift **Parking** 26

ENGLAND

LEYLAND MAP 07 SD52

★★★★ 77% HOTEL

Best Western Premier Leyland

Leyland Way PR25 4JX

☎ 01772 422922 📠 01772 622282

e-mail: leylandhotel@feathers.uk.com

web: www.feathers.uk.com

Dir: *M6 junct 28 turn left at end of slip road, hotel 100mtrs on left*

PETS: Bedrooms (31GF) unattended **Charges** £10 per night £70 per week charge for damage **Public areas** except restaurant (on leads) **Grounds** accessible on leads disp bin **Exercise area** 20mtrs **Facilities** walks info vet info **On Request** fridge access

This purpose-built hotel enjoys a convenient location, just off the M6, within easy reach of Preston and Blackpool. Spacious public areas include extensive conference and banqueting facilities as well as a smart leisure club.

Rooms 93 en suite (4 fmly) (31 GF) S £94-£104; D £99-£109 (incl. bkfst)✳ **Facilities** STV FTV supervised Gym Wi-fi available Xmas New Year **Parking** 150

MORECAMBE MAP 07 SD46

★★★ 68% HOTEL

Clarendon

76 Marine Rd West, West End Promenade LA4 4EP

☎ 01524 410180 📠 01524 421616

e-mail: clarendon@mitchellshotels.co.uk

Dir: *M6 junct 34 follow Morecambe signs. At rdbt (with 'The Shrimp' on corner) 1st exit to Westgate, follow to seafront. Right at lights, hotel 3rd block*

PETS: Bedrooms Exercise area 30mtrs **Facilities** cage storage walks info vet info **Restrictions** small dogs only

This traditional seafront hotel offers modern facilities, and several long serving key staff ensure guests experience a home-from-home atmosphere. Well maintained throughout, it offers bright, cheerful public areas and ample convenient parking.

Rooms 29 en suite (4 fmly) S fr £60; D fr £90 (incl. bkfst)✳ **Facilities** Wi-fi in bedrooms Xmas New Year **Services** Lift **Parking** 22 **Notes** LB

★ 75% HOTEL

Hotel Prospect

363 Marine Rd East LA4 5AQ

☎ 01524 417819 📠 01524 417819

e-mail: peter@hotel-prospect.fsnet.co.uk

PETS: Bedrooms Charges charge for damage **Public areas Exercise area Facilities** vet info **Other** 1 dog only allowed

Situated on the promenade, this friendly, family-run establishment has panoramic views over the bay to the Lakeland mountains. Bedrooms are comfortably proportioned and thoughtfully furnished, and the bright dining room extends into a small lounge area which has a well-stocked bar and overlooks the sea.

Rooms 13 en suite (4 fmly) (2 GF) S fr £20; D £40 (incl. bkfst)✳ **Facilities** Xmas **Parking** 14

►►► Venture Caravan Park *(SD436633)*

Langridge Way, Westgate LA4 4TQ

☎ 01524 412986 📠 01524 422029

e-mail: mark@venturecaravanpark.co.uk

web: www.venturecaravanpark.co.uk

Dir: *From M6 junct 34 follow Morecambe signs. At rdbt take road towards Westgate & follow site signs. 1st right after fire station*

PETS: disp bin **Exercise area Facilities** on site shop food litter tray etc dog scoop/disp bags vet info **Other** prior notice required

Open all year (rs 6 Jan-22 Feb touring vans only, one toilet block open) Last arrival 22.00hrs Last departure noon

A large park with good modern facilities, including a small indoor heated pool, a licensed clubhouse and a family room with children's entertainment. The site has many statics, and is close to the town centre. A 17.5-acre site with 56 touring pitches, 40 hardstandings and 304 statics.

ORMSKIRK MAP 07 SD40

►►►► Abbey Farm Caravan Park *(SD434098)*

Dark Ln L40 5TX

☎ 01695 572686 📠 01695 572686

e-mail: abbeyfarm@yahoo.com

web: www.abbeyfarmcaravanpark.co.uk

Dir: *M6 junct 27 onto A5209 to Burscough. 4m left onto B5240. Immediate right into Hobcross Ln. Site 1.5m on right*

PETS: Stables nearby (4m) disp bin **Exercise area** on site field available **Facilities** on site shop food walks info vet info

Open all year Last arrival 21.00hrs Last departure noon

Delightful hanging baskets and flower beds brighten this garden-like rural park which is sheltered by hedging and mature trees. Modern, very clean facilities include a family bathroom, and there are special pitches for the disabled near the toilets. A superb recreation field caters for children of all ages, and there is an indoor games room, large library, fishing lake and dog walk. Tents have their own area with BBQ and picnic tables. A 6-acre site with 56 touring pitches and 44 statics.

Notes No camp fires

WHITEWELL MAP 07 SD64

★★★★★ INN

The Inn at Whitewell

Forest of Bowland, Clitheroe BB7 3AT

☎ 01200 448222 01200 448298

e-mail: reception@innatwhitewell.com

Dir: *M6 junct 31a, B6243 to Longridge. Left at mini-rdbt. After 3 rdbts leave Longridge. Approx 3m, sharp left bend (with white railings), then right. Approx 1m left, right at T junct. Next left, 3m to Whitewell*

PETS: Bedrooms (1GF) unattended **Stables** nearby (1m) **Public areas** except restaurant **Grounds** accessible disp bin **Exercise area Facilities** water bowl washing facs walks info vet info **On Request** towels

This long-established culinary destination is hidden away in quintessential Lancashire countryside just 20 minutes from the M6. The fine dining restaurant is complemented by two historic and cosy bars with roaring fires, real ales and polished service. Bedrooms are richly furnished with antiques and eye-catching bijouterie, while many of the bathrooms have Victorian brass showers.

Rooms 19 en suite 4 annexe en suite (1 fmly) (1 GF) S £70-£135; D £96-£172* **Facilities** STV TVB tea/coffee Direct dial from bedrooms Cen ht Dinner Last d 9.30pm Fishing **Parking** 60 **Notes** No coaches

LEICESTERSHIRE

BUCKMINSTER MAP 08 SK82

★★★★ GUEST ACCOMMODATION

The Tollemache Arms

48 Main St NG33 5SA

☎ 01476 860007

e-mail: enquiries@thetollemachearms.com

Dir: *Off A1 Colsterworth rdbt onto B676 to Buckminster*

PETS: Bedrooms Charges charge for damage **Public areas** except restaurant (on leads) **Grounds** accessible on leads **Exercise area Facilities** pet sitting dog walking cage storage vet info **On Request** fridge access torch towels

This revamped village property has a minimalist decor of neutral colours, and strong shades in the pictures, brown leather chairs and crisp white table linen. Its busy restaurant serves high quality food.

Rooms 4 en suite (3 fmly) S £50; D £75* **Facilities** TVB tea/coffee Cen ht Dinner Last d 9.30pm **Parking** 21 **Notes LB** RS Sun-Mon

COALVILLE MAP 08 SK41

★★★★ GUEST HOUSE

Ravenstone Guesthouse

Ravenstone LE67 2AE

☎ 01530 810536

e-mail: annthorne@ravenstone-guesthouse.co.uk

web: www.ravenstone-guesthouse.co.uk

Dir: *1.5m W of Coalville. Off A447 onto Church Ln for Ravenstone, 2nd house on left*

PETS: Bedrooms sign **Stables** on site **Public areas** at proprietor's discretion **Grounds** accessible disp bin **Exercise area** 40yds **Facilities** water bowl feeding mat washing facs cage storage walks info vet info **On Request** fridge access torch towels **Other** no charge but contribution to charity requested **Restrictions** no Pit Bulls or other fighting dogs **Resident Pets:** Faruska (Black Labrador), Saffron (Yellow Labrador)

Situated in the heart of Ravenstone village, this early 18th-century house is full of character. The bedrooms are individually decorated and feature period furniture, and local produce is used for dinner and in the extensive breakfast menu. The beamed dining room has an honesty bar and there is also a cosy lounge.

Rooms 3 en suite **Facilities** TV available tea/coffee Licensed Cen ht TVL Dinner Last d noon Painting tuition **Parking** 6 **Notes** No children 18yrs No coaches Closed 23-30 Dec & 1 Jan

HINCKLEY MAP 04 SP49

★★★★ 79% HOTEL

Sketchley Grange

CLASSIC BRITISH HOTELS

Sketchley Ln, Burbage LE10 3HU

☎ 01455 251133 01455 631384

e-mail: info@sketchleygrange.co.uk

web: www.sketchleygrange.co.uk

Dir: *SE of town, off A5/M69 junct 1, take B4109 to Hinckley. Left at 2nd rdbt. 1st right onto Sketchley Lane*

PETS: Bedrooms (1GF) **Charges** £6 per night charge for damage **Public areas** (on leads) **Grounds** accessible on leads disp bin **Exercise area Facilities** walks info vet info **On Request** torch towels **Restrictions** small dogs only

Close to motorway connections, this hotel is peacefully set in its own grounds, and enjoys open country views. Extensive leisure facilities include a stylish health and leisure spa with a crèche. Modern meeting facilities, a choice of bars, and two dining options, together with comfortable bedrooms furnished with many extras, make this a special hotel.

Rooms 52 en suite (9 fmly) (1 GF) S £65-£130; D £65-£140* **Facilities Spa** supervised Gym Wi-fi in bedrooms Steam room Hairdressing Crèche **Services** Lift **Parking** 200

ENGLAND

KNIPTON MAP 08 SK83

★★★★ ◎ GUEST ACCOMMODATION

The Manners Arms

Croxton Rd NG32 1RH

☎ 01476 879222 🖷 01476 879228

e-mail: info@mannersarms.com

web: www.mannersarms.com

Dir: *Off A607 into Knipton*

PETS: Bedrooms unattended **Stables** nearby (0.25m) **Charges** £7 per night charge for damage **Grounds** accessible **Exercise area Facilities** food (pre-bookable) food bowl water bowl walks info vet info **On Request** torch towels

Part of the Rutland Estate and built as a hunting lodge for the 6th Duke, the Manners Arms has been renovated to provide thoughtfully furnished bedrooms designed by the present Duchess. Public areas include the intimate themed Beater's Bar and attractive Red Coats Restaurant, popular for imaginative dining.

Rooms 10 en suite (1 fmly) S £55-£65; D £80-£120* **Facilities** TVB tea/coffee Direct dial from bedrooms Cen ht TVL Dinner Last d 8.45pm, 7.45pm Sun Wi-fi available **Parking** 60

LEICESTER MAP 04 SK50

BUDGET HOTEL

Campanile Leicester

Campanile HOTEL RESTAURANT

St Matthew's Way, 1 Bedford St North LE1 3JE

☎ 0116 261 6600 🖷 0116 261 6601

e-mail: leicester@campanile.com

web: www.envergure.fr

Dir: *A5460. Right at end of road, left at rdbt on A594. Follow Vaughan Way, Burleys Way then St. Matthews Way. Hotel on left*

PETS: Bedrooms Charges charge for damage **Exercise area**

This modern building offers accommodation in smart, well-equipped bedrooms, all with en suite bathrooms. Refreshments may be taken at the informal Bistro.

Rooms 93 en suite

LEICESTER FOREST MOTORWAY SERVICE AREA (M1) MAP 04 SK50

BUDGET HOTEL

Days Inn Leicester Forest East

DAYS INN

Leicester Forest East, Junction 21 M1 LE3 3GB

☎ 0116 239 0534 🖷 0116 239 0546

e-mail: leicester.hotel@welcomebreak.co.uk

web: www.welcomebreak.co.uk

Dir: *on M1 northbound between junct 21 & 21A*

PETS: Bedrooms unattended **Charges** £5 per night **Public areas** (on leads) **Grounds** accessible on leads **Exercise area**

This modern building offers accommodation in smart, spacious and well-equipped bedrooms, suitable for families and business travellers, and all with en suite bathrooms. Refreshments may be taken at the nearby family restaurant.

Rooms 92 en suite S £39-£59; D £39-£59*

MELTON MOWBRAY MAP 08 SK71

★★★★ ◎◎ COUNTRY HOUSE HOTEL

Stapleford Park

Stapleford LE14 2EF

☎ 01572 787000 🖷 01572 787651

e-mail: reservations@stapleford.co.uk

web: www.staplefordpark.com

Dir: *1m SW of B676, 4m E of Melton Mowbray & 9m W of Colsterworth*

PETS: Bedrooms Stables nearby (10m) **Charges** £15 per night charge for damage **Public areas** except dining areas **Grounds** accessible **Exercise area Facilities** food food bowl water bowl bedding dog chews walks info vet info **On Request** fridge access **Other** treats for cats on request, no dogs on golf course

This stunning mansion, dating back to the 14th century, sits in over 500 acres of beautiful grounds. Spacious, sumptuous public rooms include a choice of lounges and an elegant restaurant; an additional brasserie-style restaurant is located in the golf complex. The hotel also

boasts a spa with health and beauty treatments and gym, plus horse-riding and many other country pursuits. Bedrooms are individually styled and furnished to a high standard. Attentive service is delivered with a relaxed yet professional style. Dinner, in the impressive dining room, is a highlight of any stay.

Rooms 48 en suite 7 annexe en suite (10 fmly) S £225-£275; D £295-£850 (incl. bkfst)✳ **Facilities** **Spa** STV FTV 18 Fishing Riding Gym Putt green Wi-fi available Archery Croquet Falconry Horse riding Petanque Shooting Billiards Xmas New Year **Services** Lift **Parking** 120 **Notes** **LB**

★★★ 75% HOTEL

Sysonby Knoll

Asfordby Rd LE13 0HP

☎ 01664 563563 01664 410364

e-mail: reception@sysonby.com

web: www.sysonby.com

Dir: *0.5m from town centre beside A6006*

PETS: Bedrooms (7GF) **Charges** charge for damage **Public areas** except restaurant (on leads) **Grounds** accessible on leads disp bin **Exercise area** adjacent **Facilities** washing facs cage storage walks info vet info **On Request** fridge access torch towels **Resident Pets:** Stalky & Twiglet (Miniature Dachshunds)

This well-established hotel is on the edge of town and set in attractive gardens. A friendly and relaxed atmosphere prevails and the many returning guests have become friends. Bedrooms, including superior rooms in the annexe, are generally spacious and thoughtfully equipped. There is a choice of lounges, a cosy bar, and a smart a restaurant that offers carefully prepared meals.

Rooms 23 en suite 7 annexe en suite (1 fmly) (7 GF) S £68-£89; D £82-£115 (incl. bkfst)✳ **Facilities** FTV Fishing Wi-fi in bedrooms **Parking** 48 **Notes** **LB** Closed 25 Dec-1 Jan

★★★★ GUEST ACCOMMODATION

Bryn Barn

38 High St, Waltham-on-the-Wolds LE14 4AH

☎ 01664 464783 & 07791 215614

e-mail: glenarowlands@onetel.com

web: www.brynbarn.co.uk

Dir: *4.5m NE of Melton. Off A607 in Waltham village centre*

PETS: Bedrooms (1GF) **Charges** £5 per night charge for damage **Grounds** accessible disp bin **Exercise area** 500mtrs **Facilities** food bowl water bowl feeding mat cage storage vet info **On Request** fridge access torch towels **Other** ground-floor room with garden access available

A warm welcome awaits at this attractive, peacefully located cottage within easy reach of Melton Mowbray, Grantham, Rutland Water and Belvoir Castle. Bedrooms are smartly appointed and comfortably furnished, while public rooms include an inviting lounge overlooking a wonderful courtyard garden. Meals are available at one of the nearby village pubs.

Rooms 4 rms (3 en suite) (1 pri facs) (2 fmly) (1 GF) S £30-£40; D £50-£60 **Facilities** FTV TVB tea/coffee Cen ht TVL Wi-fi available **Parking** 4 **Notes** **LB** Closed 21 Dec-4 Jan RS wknds

★★ INN

Noels Arms

31 Burton St LE13 1AE

☎ 01664 562363

Dir: *On A606 S of town centre at junct Mill St*

PETS: Bedrooms Public areas (on leads) **Exercise area** park 50yds **Facilities** walks info vet info

The traditional inn lies close to the town centre. The bar is the focal point of the inn, where breakfast is served and staff and locals generate a relaxed and friendly atmosphere. Bedrooms come in a variety of co-ordinated styles and sizes, each furnished in pine.

Rooms 6 rms (4 en suite) (2 fmly) S fr £26; D fr £50✳ **Facilities** TVB tea/coffee Cen ht Pool Table **Notes**

LINCOLNSHIRE

ANCASTER MAP 08 SK94

►►► Woodland Waters *(SK979435)*

Willoughby Rd NG32 3RT

☎ 01400 230888 🖹 01400 230888

e-mail: info@woodlandwaters.co.uk

web: www.woodlandwaters.co.uk

Dir: *On A153 W of x-roads with B6403*

PETS: Charges £1 per night £7 per week **Public areas** except bar (on leads) disp bin **Exercise area** on site lake & park walks **Facilities** walks info vet info **Other** dog bowls at outdoor eating areas on request **Resident Pets:** 2 Black Labradors

Open all year Last arrival 21.00hrs Last departure noon

Peacefully set around five impressive fishing lakes, with a few log cabins in a separate area, a pleasant open park. The access road is through mature woodland, and there is a very good heated toilet block, and a pub/club house with restaurant. A 5-acre site with 62 touring pitches.

Notes ⊛

GRANTHAM MAP 08 SK93

★★★ 73% HOTEL

Best Western Kings

North Pde NG31 8AU

☎ 01476 590800 🖹 01476 577072

e-mail: kings@bestwestern.co.uk

web: www.bw-kingshotel.co.uk

Dir: *S on A1, 1st exit to Grantham. Through Great Gonerby, 2m on left*

PETS: Bedrooms (3GF) **Charges** charge for damage **Public areas** except restaurant (on leads) **Exercise area** 200yds **Facilities** cage storage walks info vet info **On Request** fridge access

A friendly atmosphere exists at this extended Georgian house. Modern bedrooms are attractively decorated and furnished, suitably equipped to meet the needs of corporate and leisure guests. Dining options include the formal Victorian restaurant and the popular Orangery, which also operates as an informal coffee shop and breakfast room; a lounge bar and a comfortable open-plan foyer lounge are also available.

Rooms 21 en suite (3 fmly) (3 GF) S £58.50-£84; D £68.50-£94 (incl. bkfst)✳ **Facilities** STV Wi-fi in bedrooms New Year **Parking** 40 **Notes** Closed 25-26 Dec RS 24 Dec

LINCOLN MAP 08 SK97

★★★ 73% HOTEL

Holiday Inn Lincoln

Brayford Wharf North LN1 1YW

☎ 01522 544244 🖹 01522 560805

e-mail: reservations@lincoln.kewgreen.co.uk

web: www.holidayinn.co.uk

Dir: *From A46 onto A57 to Lincoln Central. Left at lights, right, take next right onto Lucy Tower St then right onto Brayford Wharf North for hotel on right*

PETS: Bedrooms (9GF) unattended **Charges** £10 per night **Exercise area** common 1m **Facilities** walks info vet info **On Request** fridge access torch towels **Restrictions** small short-haired dogs only

In a wonderful location of the edge of the Brayford waterside, this hotel is ideally placed for exploring the historic city of Lincoln. All rooms are well equipped with a work desk, data point and many modern extras.

Rooms 97 en suite (32 fmly) (9 GF) S £82-£121; D £82-£121 (incl. bkfst)✳ **Facilities** Gym Wi-fi available **Services** Lift air con **Parking** 100 (charged) **Notes LB**

★★ 79% HOTEL

Castle

Westgate LN1 3AS

☎ 01522 538801 🖹 01522 575457

e-mail: aa@castlehotel.net

web: www.castlehotel.net

Dir: *follow signs for Historic Lincoln. Hotel at NE corner of castle*

PETS: Bedrooms (5GF) **Charges** £5 per night **Exercise area** 10 mins walk **Facilities** food bowl water bowl **Restrictions** small dogs only

Located in the heart of historic Lincoln, this privately owned and run hotel has been carefully restored to offer comfortable, attractive, well-appointed accommodation. Bedrooms are thoughtfully equipped, particularly the deluxe rooms and the spacious Lincoln Suite. Specialising in traditional fayre, Knights Restaurant has an interesting medieval theme.

Rooms 16 en suite 3 annexe en suite (5 GF) S £70-£115; D £89-£150 (incl. bkfst)✳ **Facilities** Wi-fi available **Parking** 20 **Notes LB** No children 8yrs RS 25-26 Dec evening

★★★ GUEST HOUSE

Newport

26-28 Newport Rd LN1 3DF

☎ 01522 528590 📠 01522 542868

e-mail: info@newportguesthouse.co.uk

web: www.newportguesthouse.co.uk

Dir: *On Roman Rd, 600mtrs N of cathedral*

PETS: Bedrooms (2GF) **Charges** charge for damage **Exercise area** 200mtrs **Facilities** walks info vet info **On Request** fridge access

Situated in the quieter upper part of the city and just a few minutes' walk from the cathedral, this double-fronted terrace house offers well-equipped and comfortable bedrooms with broadband access. The pleasing public areas include a very comfortable sitting room and a bright and attractive breakfast room.

Rooms 9 en suite (2 GF) S £37-£60; D £55-£60* **Facilities** FTV TVB tea/coffee Cen ht TVL Wi-fi available **Parking** 4 **Notes** No coaches

LOUTH — MAP 08 TF38

★★★ 79% HOTEL

Best Western Kenwick Park

Kenwick Park Estate LN11 8NR

☎ 01507 608806 📠 01507 608027

e-mail: enquiries@kenwick-park.co.uk

web: www.kenwick-park.co.uk

Dir: *A16 from Grimsby, then A157 Mablethorpe/Manby Rd. Hotel 400mtrs down hill on right*

PETS: Bedrooms Public areas Exercise area on site large grounds **Other** Please telephone for details

This elegant Georgian house is situated on the 320-acre Kenwick Park estate, overlooking its own golf course. Bedrooms are spacious, comfortable and provide modern facilities. Public areas include a restaurant and a conservatory bar that overlook the grounds. There is also an extensive leisure centre and state-of-the-art conference and banqueting facilities.

Rooms 29 en suite 5 annexe en suite (10 fmly) **Facilities** supervised 18 Squash Gym Putt green Wi-fi available Health & beauty centre **Parking** 100 **Notes** LB

★★★ 72% HOTEL

Beaumont

66 Victoria Rd LN11 0BX

☎ 01507 605005 📠 01507 607768

e-mail: beaumonthotel@aol.com

PETS: Bedrooms (6GF) unattended **Charges** £9 per night **Grounds** accessible disp bin **Exercise area** 100yds **Facilities** food bowl water bowl bedding cage storage vet info **On Request** fridge access **Resident Pets:** Dandy (Shih Tzu)

This smart, family-run hotel enjoys a quiet location, within easy reach of the town centre. Bedrooms are spacious and individually designed. Public areas include a smart restaurant serving Mediterranean-influenced cuisine, and an inviting lounge bar with comfortable deep sofas and open fires.

Rooms 16 en suite (2 fmly) (6 GF) S £62-£75; D £88-£98 (incl. bkfst)* **Services** Lift **Parking** 70 **Notes** RS Sun

MABLETHORPE — MAP 09 TF58

►►► Mablethorpe Camping & Caravanning Club Site *(TF499839)*

Highfield, 120 Church Ln LN12 2NU

☎ 01507 472374

web: www.thefriendlyclub.co.uk

Dir: *On outskirts of Mablethorpe, on A1104, just after the 'Welcome to Mablethorpe' sign turn right into Church Lane. 800yds to end of lane. Site on right*

PETS: disp bin **Exercise area Facilities** walks info vet info **Other** prior notice required

Open 2 Apr-2 Nov Last arrival 21.00hrs Last departure noon

Located next to flat agricultural land one mile from the sea, and well away from the road. The camping area is in two hedged fields with rural views, and the modern toilet facilities and laundry are centrally sited. A 6-acre site with 105 touring pitches, 1 hardstanding.

Notes Site gates closed 23.00hrs-07.00hrs

ENGLAND

MARTON (VILLAGE) MAP 08 SK88

★★★★ GUEST ACCOMMODATION

Black Swan Guest House

21 High St DN21 5AH

☎ 01427 718878

e-mail: info@blackswanguesthouse.co.uk

web: www.blackswanguesthouse.co.uk

Dir: *On A156 in village centre at junct A1500*

PETS: Bedrooms (4GF) **Stables** nearby (4m) **Charges** charge for damage **Grounds** accessible disp bin **Exercise area** 300yds **Facilities** cage storage walks info vet info **On Request** fridge access torch **Resident Pets:** TC & Scooby (cats)

Centrally located in the village, this 18th-century former coaching inn retains many original features, and offers good hospitality and homely bedrooms with modern facilities. Tasty breakfasts are served in the cosy dining room and a comfortable lounge with Wi-fi access is available. Transport to nearby pubs and restaurants can be provided.

Rooms 6 en suite 4 annexe en suite (3 fmly) (4 GF) S £45-£55; D £68-£75✻ **Facilities** FTV TVB tea/coffee Cen ht TVL Wi-fi available **Parking** 10 **Notes** LB

OLD LEAKE MAP 09 TF45

►►► *White Cat Caravan & Camping Park*

(TF415498)

Shaw Ln PE22 9LQ

☎ 01205 870121 🖷 01205 870121

e-mail: kevin@klannen.freeserve.co.uk

web: www.whitecatpark.com

Dir: *Just off A52, 7m NE of Boston, opposite B1184*

PETS: Charges 50p per night £3 per week disp bin **Public areas** except toilet, shower & washing facility **Exercise area** on site 1 acre paddock (mown & hedged) **Facilities** on site shop dog chews cat treats dog scoop/disp bags washing facs walks info vet info **Other** prior notice required **Restrictions** no Pit Bulls, Rottweilers or similar breeds **Resident Pets:** Border Collie

Open Apr-Oct Last arrival 20.00hrs Last departure noon

A pleasant, well-maintained small touring park set down a rural lane just off the A52, surrounded by the typical tranquillity of the Fenlands. It makes a peaceful base for exploring Boston and the Lincolnshire coast. A 2.5-acre site with 30 touring pitches, 4 hardstandings and 10 statics.

Notes ⊜

SCUNTHORPE MAP 08 SE81

★★★★ 81% HOTEL

Forest Pines Hotel

QHOTELS

Ermine St, Broughton DN20 0AQ

☎ 01652 650770 🖷 01652 650495

e-mail: forestpines@qhotels.co.uk

web: www.qhotels.co.uk

Dir: *200yds from M180 junct 4, on Brigg-Scunthorpe rdbt*

PETS: Bedrooms (67GF) unattended Exercise area Restrictions small, well behaved dogs only

This smart hotel provides a comprehensive range of leisure facilities. Extensive conference rooms, a modern health and beauty spa, and a championship golf course ensure that it is a popular choice with both corporate and leisure guests. Extensive public areas include a choice of dining options, with fine dining available in The Eighteen 57 fish restaurant, and more informal eating in the Garden Room or Mulligan's Bar. The well-equipped bedrooms are modern, spacious, and refurbished to a good standard.

Rooms 188 en suite (66 fmly) (67 GF) S £89-£149; D £99-£159 (incl. bkfst)✻ **Facilities** Spa STV FTV supervised ⛳ 27 Gym Putt green Wi-fi in bedrooms Mountain bikes Jogging track Xmas New Year **Services** Lift **Parking** 300 **Notes** LB

★★★ 74% HOTEL

Wortley House

Rowland Rd DN16 1SU

☎ 01724 842223 🖷 01724 280646

e-mail: reception@wortleyhousehotel.co.uk

web: www.wortleyhousehotel.co.uk

Dir: *M180 junct 3 take A18. Follow signs for Grimsby/Humberside airport, 2nd left into Brumby Wood Ln, over rdbt into Rowland Rd. Hotel 200yds on right*

PETS: Bedrooms Stables nearby (5m) **Charges** £10 deposit per night charge for damage **Grounds** accessible on leads **Exercise area** 2 mins walk **Facilities** food bowl water bowl cage storage walks info vet info **On Request** torch towels

A friendly hotel with good facilities for conferences, meetings, banquets and other functions. Bedrooms offer modern comfort and facilities. An extensive range of dishes is available in both the formal restaurant and the more relaxed bar.

Rooms 38 en suite 4 annexe en suite (5 fmly) (4 GF) S £55-£75; D £75-£150 (incl. bkfst) **Facilities** FTV Wi-fi in bedrooms Xmas New Year **Parking** 100

SKEGNESS MAP 09 TF56

★★★ 67% HOTEL

Best Western Vine

Vine Rd, Seacroft PE25 3DB

☎ 01754 763018 & 610611 📠 01754 769845

e-mail: info@thevinehotel.com

Dir: *A52 to Skegness, S towards Gibraltar Point, turn right on to Drummond Rd, after 0.5m turn right into Vine Rd*

PETS: Bedrooms unattended **Charges** £5 per night **Grounds** accessible disp bin **Exercise area** surrounding area **Facilities** cage storage walks info vet info **On Request** fridge access torch towels

Reputedly the second oldest building in Skegness, this traditional style hotel offers two character bars that serve excellent local beers. Freshly prepared dishes are served in both the bar and the restaurant; service is both friendly and helpful. The smartly decorated bedrooms are well equipped and comfortably appointed.

Rooms 25 en suite (3 fmly) S £41-£50; D £58-£71* **Facilities** FTV Wi-fi in bedrooms Xmas New Year **Parking** 50 **Notes** LB

STAMFORD MAP 04 TF00

★★★ 86% ® HOTEL

The George of Stamford

71 St Martins PE9 2LB

☎ 01780 750750 & 750700 (res) 📠 01780 750701

e-mail: reservations@georgehotelofstamford.com

web: www.georgehotelofstamford.com

Dir: *A1, 15m N of Peterborough onto B1081, hotel 1m on left*

PETS: Bedrooms Public areas except restaurant (assist dogs only) **Grounds** accessible **Exercise area** meadow 500yds **Facilities** water bowl bedding dog chews feeding mat vet info **On Request** towels **Resident Pets:** Peter & Harry (cats)

Steeped in hundreds of years of history, this delightful coaching inn provides spacious public areas that include a choice of dining options, inviting, lounges, a business centre and a range of quality shops. A highlight is afternoon tea, taken in the colourful courtyard when weather permits. Bedrooms are stylishly appointed and range from traditional to contemporary in design.

Rooms 47 en suite (18 fmly) S £90-£130; D £130-£245 (incl. bkfst)* **Facilities** STV Wi-fi in bedrooms Complimentary membership to local gym Xmas New Year **Parking** 80 **Notes** LB

★★★ 70% HOTEL

Garden House

High St, St Martins PE9 2LP

☎ 01780 763359 📠 01780 763339

e-mail: enquiries@gardenhousehotel.com

web: www.gardenhousehotel.com

Dir: *A1 to South Stamford, B1081, signed Stamford & Burghley House. Hotel on left on entering town*

PETS: Bedrooms (4GF) unattended **Public areas** except restaurant **Grounds** accessible **Exercise area** Burghley Park across road **Facilities** dog walking cage storage walks info vet info **On Request** fridge access torch towels **Resident Pets:** Oliver (Retriever)

Situated within a few minutes' walk of the town centre, this transformed 18th-century town house provides pleasant accommodation. Bedroom styles vary; all are well equipped and comfortably furnished. Public rooms include a charming lounge bar, conservatory restaurant and a smart breakfast room. Service is attentive and friendly throughout.

Rooms 20 en suite (2 fmly) (4 GF) **Parking** 22 **Notes** LB Closed 26-30 Dec RS 1-12 Jan

SUTTON ON SEA MAP 09 TF58

★★★ GUEST ACCOMMODATION

Athelstone Lodge

25 Trusthorpe Rd LN12 2LR

☎ 01507 441521

Dir: *On A52 N of village*

PETS: Bedrooms Exercise area Facilities vet info **Restrictions** small dogs only

Situated between Mablethorpe and Skegness and close to the promenade, Athelstone Lodge has pleasant, soundly maintained bedrooms equipped with many useful extras. Breakfast is served in the dining room and a bar and a lounge are also available. A variety of enjoyable home-cooked dinners is served.

Rooms 6 rms (5 en suite) (1 fmly) S £28-£30; D £56-£60* **Facilities** TVB tea/coffee Cen ht TVL Dinner Last d 4.30pm **Parking** 6 **Notes** LB Closed Nov-Feb

SUTTON ST JAMES MAP 09 TF31

►►► Foremans Bridge Caravan Park

(TF409197)

Sutton Rd PE12 0HU

☎ 01945 440346

e-mail: foremansbridge@btconnect.com

web: www.foremans-bridge.co.uk

Dir: *2m from A17 on B1390*

PETS: Stables nearby (0.5m) **Charges** £1 per night £7 per week disp bin **Public areas** except in buildings (on leads) **Exercise area** on site river bank **Facilities** cat treats walks info vet info **Other** prior notice required **Restrictions** no very large dogs **Resident Pets:** Arfur & Ollie (Shih Tzus), Max (German Shepherd)

Open Mar-Jan Last arrival 21.00hrs Last departure 10.00hrs

A small site set beside the South Holland Main Drain which flows past, and offers good fishing. This quiet park is mainly used by adults. A 2.5-acre site with 40 touring pitches, 22 hardstandings and 22 statics.

Notes No cycling or ball games

WADDINGHAM MAP 08 SK99

►►► *Brandy Wharf Leisure Park* *(TF014968)*

Brandy Wharf DN21 4RT

☎ 01673 818010 🖷 01673 818010

e-mail: brandywharflp@freenetname.co.uk

web: www.brandywharfleisurepark.co.uk

Dir: *From A15 onto B1205 through Waddingham. Site 3m from Waddingham*

PETS: Stables nearby (5m) disp bin **Exercise area** on site river bank **Facilities** washing facs walks info vet info **Other** prior notice required **Resident Pets:** Bess, Fizz & Spike (Border Collies), Jabber (Clumber Spaniel), Ben, Ruby & Junior (Mongrels), 12 cats

Open Etr-Oct Last arrival dusk Last departure 17.00hrs

A delightfully refurbished site in a very rural area on the banks of the River Ancholme, where fishing is available. The unisex facilities offer combined toilet, washbasin and shower, and there is a new laundry. All of the grassy pitches have electricity, and there's a playing/picnic area. The site attracts a lively clientele at weekends, and music is allowed until 1am. Advance booking is necessary for weekend pitches. A 5-acre site with 30 touring pitches.

Notes no disposable BBQs on grass, no music after 01.00hrs

WINTERINGHAM MAP 08 SE92

★★★★★ RESTAURANT WITH ROOMS

Winteringham Fields

DN15 9PF

☎ 01724 733096 🖷 01724 733898

e-mail: wintfields@aol.com

Dir: *In centre of village at x-rds*

PETS: Bedrooms Stables nearby (200mtrs) **Charges** £10 per night charge for damage **Grounds** accessible **Exercise area** 20mtrs **Facilities** food (pre-bookable) food bowl water bowl dog chews dog scoop/disp bags leads walks info vet info **On Request** fridge access torch towels **Other** courtyard bedrooms recommended **Resident Pets:** Juma & Peri (Labradors), Azerah (Great Dane)

This highly regarded restaurant with rooms, located deep in the countryside in Winteringham village, is six miles west of the Humber Bridge. Public rooms and bedrooms, some of which are housed in renovated barns and cottages, are delightfully cosseting. Award-winning food is available in the restaurant.

Rooms 4 en suite 6 annexe en suite (3 GF) S £105-£145; D £145-£215* **Facilities** TVB tea/coffee Direct dial from bedrooms Cen ht Dinner Last d 9pm **Parking** 14 **Notes LB** Closed 25 Dec for 2 wks, last wk Oct, 2 wks Aug

WOODHALL SPA MAP 08 TF16

★★★ 74% HOTEL

Petwood

Stixwould Rd LN10 6QG

☎ 01526 352411 🖷 01526 353473

e-mail: reception@petwood.co.uk

web: www.petwood.co.uk

Dir: *from Sleaford take A153 (signed Skegness). At Tattershall turn left on B1192. Hotel is signed from village*

PETS: Bedrooms (3GF) unattended **Charges** £15 per night charge for damage **Public areas** certain areas only (on leads) **Exercise area Facilities** washing facs walks info vet info **On Request** fridge access torch

This lovely Edwardian house, set in 30 acres of gardens and woodlands, is adjacent to Woodhall Golf Course. Built in 1905, the house was used by 617 Squadron, the famous Dambusters, as an

officers' mess during World War II. Bedrooms and public areas are spacious and comfortable, and retain many original features. Weddings and conferences are well catered for in modern facilities.

Rooms 53 en suite (3 GF) S £99-£124; D £145-£170 (incl. bkfst)* **Facilities** Putt green Complimentary pass to leisure centre Xmas New Year **Services** Lift **Parking** 140 **Notes** LB

►►► Woodhall Spa Camping & Caravanning Club Site *(TF225633)*

Wellsyke Ln, Kirkby-on-Bain LN10 6YU

☎ 01526 352911

web: www.thefriendlyclub.co.uk

Dir: *From Sleaford or Horncastle take A153 to Haltham. At garage turn onto side road. Over bridge, left towards Kirkby-on-Bain. 1st turn right, signed.*

PETS: Public areas except in buildings **Exercise area** on site small area **Facilities** walks info vet info **Other** prior notice required

Open 2 Apr-2 Nov Last arrival 21.00hrs Last departure noon

A pleasant site in silver birch wood and moorland, with pitches laid out around a central lake (no fishing). Facilities include a family room, and a unisex room with en suite facilities. A 6-acre site with 90 touring pitches.

Notes Site gates closed 23.00hrs-07.00hrs

WOOLSTHORPE — MAP 08 SK92

★★★★ INN

The Chequers Inn

Main St NG32 1LU

☎ 01476 870701 📠 01476 870085

e-mail: justinnabar@yahoo.co.uk

Dir: *In village opp Post Office*

PETS: Bedrooms (3GF) unattended **Stables** nearby (next door) **Charges** £5 per stay per night charge for damage **Public areas** except restaurant **Grounds** accessible disp bin **Exercise area** open countryside adjacent **Facilities** washing facs cage storage walks info vet info **On Request** fridge access torch towels **Resident Pets:** Hector & Ruby (English Springer Spaniels)

A 17th-century coaching inn set in the lee of Belvoir Castle next to the village cricket pitch and having its own pétanque pitch. Exposed beams, open fireplaces and original stone and brickwork, with 24 wines by the glass, a gastro menu, and real ales. Comfortable bedrooms are in the former stable block.

Rooms 4 annexe en suite (1 fmly) (3 GF) S £49; D £59 **Facilities** TVB tea/coffee Cen ht TVL Dinner Last d 9.30pm **Parking** 40

LONDON

E16

★★★★ 72% HOTEL

Novotel London ExCel

NOVOTEL HOTELS

7 Western Gateway, Royal Victoria Docks E16 1AA

☎ 020 7540 9700 & 0870 850 4560 📠 020 7540 9710

e-mail: H3656@accor.com

web: www.novotel.com

Dir: *M25 junct 30. A13 towards 'City', exit at Canning Town. Follow signs to 'ExCel West'. Hotel adjacent*

PETS: Bedrooms unattended **Charges** £12 per night charge for damage **Public areas** except restaurant (on leads) **Exercise area** 5mtrs **Facilities** food bowl water bowl cage storage walks info vet info **On Request** fridge access towels

This hotel is situated adjacent to the ExCel exhibition centre and overlooks the Royal Victoria Dock. Design throughout the hotel is contemporary and stylish. Public rooms include a range of meeting rooms, a modern coffee station, indoor leisure facilities and a smart bar and restaurant, both with a terrace overlooking the dock. Bedrooms feature modern décor, a bath and separate shower and an extensive range of extras.

Rooms 257 en suite (211 fmly) **Facilities** Gym Wi-fi available Steam room Relaxation room with massage bed **Services** Lift air con **Parking** 80

EC1

★★★ 86% HOTEL

Malmaison Charterhouse Square

18-21 Charterhouse Square, Clerkenwell EC1M 6AH

☎ 020 7012 3700 📠 020 7012 3702

e-mail: london@malmaison.com

web: www.malmaison.com

Dir: *Exit Barbican Station turn left, take 1st left. Hotel on far left corner of Charterhouse Square*

PETS: Bedrooms (5GF) **Charges** £10 per night charge for damage **Public areas** except restaurant (assist dogs only) (muzzled) (on leads) **Exercise area Facilities** food bowl water bowl bedding cage storage vet info **On Request** fridge access torch towels

Situated in a leafy and peaceful square, Malmaison Charterhouse maintains the same focus on quality service and food as the other hotels in the group. The bedrooms, stylishly decorated in calming tones, have all the expected facilities including power showers, CD players and free internet access. The brasserie and bar at the hotel's centre has a buzzing atmosphere and traditional French cuisine.

Rooms 97 en suite (5 GF) S £125-£250; D £125-£475* **Facilities** STV Gym Wi-fi available **Services** Lift air con **Notes** LB

N9

►►► Lee Valley Camping & Caravan Park

(TQ360945)

Meridian Way N9 0AR

☎ 020 8803 6900 📠 020 8884 4975

e-mail: leisurecomplex@leevalleypark.org.uk

web: www.leevalleypark.org.uk

Dir: *From M25 junct 25, A10 S, 1st left on A1055, approx 5m to Leisure Complex. From A406 (North Circular), N on A1010, left after 0.25m, right (Pickets Lock Lane)*

PETS: Charges £1.70 per night £11.90 per week disp bin **Public areas** except in toilets, showers, laundry & shop **Exercise area** on site **Facilities** on site shop food

Open all year Last arrival 22.00hrs Last departure noon

A pleasant, open site within easy reach of London yet peacefully located close to two large reservoirs. The very good toilet facilities are beautifully kept by dedicated wardens, and the site has the advantage of being adjacent to a restaurant and bar, and a multi-screen cinema. A 4.5-acre site with 160 touring pitches, 41 hardstandings.

Notes No commercial vehicles

NW1

BUDGET HOTEL

Ibis London Euston St Pancras

3 Cardington St NW1 2LW

☎ 020 7388 7777 📠 020 7388 0001

e-mail: H0921@accor-hotels.com

web: www.ibishotel.com

Dir: *From Euston Rd or station, right to Melton St leading to Cardington St*

PETS: Bedrooms unattended **Charges** £5 per night charge for damage **Public areas Exercise area** park nearby **Facilities** water bowl

Modern, budget hotel offering comfortable accommodation in bright and practical bedrooms. Breakfast is self-service and dinner is available in the restaurant.

Rooms 380 en suite S £109-£130; D £109-£130✳

SE1

★★★★ 73% HOTEL

Novotel London City South

Southwark Bridge Rd SE1 9HH

☎ 020 7089 0400 📠 020 7089 0410

e-mail: H3269@accor.com

web: www.novotel.com

Dir: *junct at Thrale St, off Southwark St*

PETS: Bedrooms Charges £8 per night £56 per week charge for damage **Public areas** except restaurant (on leads) **Exercise area Facilities** food bowl water bowl bedding dog chews cat treats feeding mat litter tray etc dog scoop/disp bags leads pet sitting dog walking washing facs dog grooming cage storage walks info vet info **On Request** fridge access towels

Conveniently located for both business and leisure guests, with the City just across the Thames; other major attractions are also easily accessible. The hotel is contemporary in design with smart, modern bedrooms and spacious public rooms. There is a gym, sauna and steam room on the 6th floor, and limited parking is available at the rear of the hotel.

Rooms 182 en suite (139 fmly) S £99-£215; D £109-£235✳ **Facilities** STV FTV Gym Wi-fi available Steam room Sauna **Services** Lift air con **Parking** 80 (charged) **Notes LB**

SW1

★★★★★TOWN HOUSE HOTEL

No 41

41 Buckingham Palace Rd SW1W 0PS

☎ 020 7300 0041 📠 020 7300 0141

e-mail: book41@rchmail.com

web: www.redcarnationhotels.com

Dir: *opp Buckingham Palace Mews entrance*

PETS: Bedrooms sign **Charges** damage deposit required per night **Public areas** assist dogs only **Exercise area** St James's Park & Green Park, 0.5m **Facilities** food (pre-bookable) food bowl water bowl bedding dog chews cat treats feeding mat litter tray etc dog scoop/disp bags leads pet sitting dog walking dog grooming cage storage walks info vet info **On Request** fridge access torch towels **Other** pets are accepted by prior arrangement only; pet menus, dedicated staff member for pets

Small, intimate and very private, this stunning town house is located opposite the Royal Mews. Decorated in stylish black and white, bedrooms successfully combine comfort with state-of-the-art technology. The large lounge is the focal point; food and drinks are available as are magazines and newspapers from around the world plus internet access. Attentive personal service and a host of thoughtful extra touches make No 41 really special.

Rooms 28 en suite (2 fmly) S £345; D £345✳ **Facilities** STV Wi-fi in bedrooms Local health club Beauty treatments Xmas New Year **Services** Lift air con

★★★★★ 88% ❀❀❀ HOTEL

Sheraton Park Tower

101 Knightsbridge SW1X 7RN

☎ 020 7235 8050 🖹 020 7235 8231

e-mail: 00412.central.london.reservations@sheraton.com

web: www.starwood.com

Dir: *Next to Harvey Nichols*

PETS: Bedrooms sign **Charges** charge for damage **Public areas** except food areas & gym (on leads) **Exercise area** 0.5km **Facilities** food bowl water bowl bedding dog chews dog scoop/disp bags walks info vet info **On Request** towels **Restrictions** weight limit 18kg (70lbs)

Superbly located for some of London's most fashionable stores, the Park Tower offers stunning views over the city. Bedrooms combine a high degree of comfort with up-to-date decor and a super range of extras; the suites are particularly impressive. The hotel offers the intimate Knightsbridge lounge, the more formal Piano Bar and extensive conference and banqueting facilities. Restaurant One-O-One is renowned for its seafood.

Rooms 280 en suite (280 fmly) **Facilities** Gym Fitness room ♫ **Services** Lift air con **Parking** 67

★★★★ 85% ❀ HOTEL

The Rubens at the Palace

39 Buckingham Palace Rd SW1W 0PS

☎ 020 7834 6600 🖹 020 7233 6037

e-mail: bookrb@rchmail.com

web: www.redcarnationhotels.com

Dir: *opposite Royal Mews, 100mtrs from Buckingham Palace*

PETS: Bedrooms sign **Charges** damage deposit required per night charge for damage **Exercise area** St James's Park & Green Park 0.5m **Facilities** food (pre-bookable) food bowl water bowl bedding dog chews cat treats feeding mat litter tray etc dog scoop/disp bags leads pet sitting dog walking dog grooming cage storage walks info vet info **On Request** fridge access torch towels **Other** pets are accepted by prior arrangement only; dedicated staff member for pets

This hotel enjoys an enviable location next to Buckingham Palace. Stylish, air-conditioned bedrooms include the pinstripe-walled Savile Row rooms, which follow a tailoring theme, and the opulent Royal rooms, named after different monarchs. Public rooms include the Library fine dining restaurant and a comfortable stylish cocktail bar and lounge. The team here pride themselves on their warmth and friendliness.

Rooms 161 en suite (13 fmly) S £249; D £259✻ **Facilities** STV Wi-fi available ♫ Xmas New Year **Services** Lift air con

SW3

★★★★★ TOWN HOUSE HOTEL

Egerton House

17 Egerton Ter, Knightsbridge SW3 2BX

☎ 020 7589 2412 🖹 020 7584 6540

e-mail: bookeg@rchmail.com

web: www.redcarnationhotels.com

Dir: *Just off Brompton Rd, between Harrods and Victoria & Albert Museum, opposite Brompton Oratory.*

PETS: Bedrooms sign **Charges** charge for damage **Public areas** except dining room (on leads) **Exercise area** 10 mins walk Hyde Park **Facilities** food (pre-bookable) food bowl water bowl bedding dog chews dog scoop/disp bags leads walks info vet info **On Request** fridge access torch towels **Other** all pet facilities are subject to request & availability **Restrictions** small dogs only

This delightful town house enjoys a prestigious Knightsbridge location, a short walk from Harrods and close to the Victoria & Albert museum. Air-conditioned bedrooms and public rooms are appointed to the highest standards, with luxurious furnishings and quality antique pieces; an exceptional range of facilities include iPods, safes, mini bars and flat screen TVs. Staff offer the highest levels of personalised, attentive service.

Rooms 29 en suite (4 fmly) (3 GF) S £255-£495; D £255-£495✻ **Facilities** STV Wi-fi in bedrooms Xmas New Year **Services** Lift air con

SW10

★★★★★ 86% ❀ HOTEL

Wyndham Grand London Chelsea Harbour

Chelsea Harbour SW10 0XG

☎ 020 7823 3000 🖹 020 7351 6525

e-mail: wyndhamlondon@wyndham.com

web: www.wyndham.com

Dir: *A4 to Earls Court Rd S towards river. Right into Kings Rd, left down Lots Rd. Chelsea Harbour in front*

PETS: Bedrooms Stables nearby **Charges** charge for damage **Public areas** except restaurant (on leads) **Grounds** accessible on leads disp bin **Exercise area** 5 min walk **Facilities** food (pre-bookable) food bowl water bowl bedding dog chews cat treats feeding mat pet sitting dog walking dog grooming cage storage walks info vet info **On Request** fridge access towels

Against the picturesque backdrop of Chelsea Harbour's small marina, this modern hotel offers spacious, comfortable accommodation. All rooms are suites, which are superbly equipped; many enjoy splendid views of the marina. In addition, there are also several luxurious penthouse suites. Public areas include a modern bar and restaurant, excellent leisure facilities and extensive meeting and function rooms.

Rooms 160 en suite (39 fmly) **Facilities** STV ⓢ Gym Wi-fi available ♫ ch fac **Services** Lift air con **Parking** 1007 (charged)

ENGLAND

SW19

★★★★ 77% COUNTRY HOUSE HOTEL

Cannizaro House

West Side, Wimbledon Common SW19 4UE

020 8879 1464 020 8879 7338

e-mail: info@cannizarohouse.com

Dir: *from A3 follow A219 signed Wimbledon into Parkside, right onto Cannizaro Rd, sharp right onto Westside Common*

PETS: Bedrooms (5GF) unattended **Stables** nearby (5 min walk) **Charges** charge for damage **Public areas** (on leads) **Grounds** accessible on leads disp bin **Exercise area** 100yds **Facilities** food bowl water bowl bedding pet sitting dog walking cage storage walks info vet info **On Request** fridge access towels **Restrictions** small to medium size dogs only

This unique, elegant 18th-century house has a long tradition of hosting the rich and famous of London society. A few miles from the city centre, the landscaped grounds provide a peaceful escape and a country-house ambience; fine art, murals and stunning fireplaces feature throughout. Spacious bedrooms are individually furnished and equipped to a high standard.

Rooms 46 en suite (10 fmly) (5 GF) D £155-£595 (incl. bkfst)* **Facilities** STV Wi-fi in bedrooms Xmas New Year **Services** Lift **Parking** 95 **Notes** LB

W1

★★★★★ 84% HOTEL

The Metropolitan

Old Park Ln W1K 1LB

020 7447 1000 020 7447 1100

e-mail: res.lon@metropolitan.como.bz

Dir: *on corner of Old Park Ln and Hertford St, within 200mtrs from Hyde Park corner*

PETS: Bedrooms unattended **Public areas** except restaurants **Exercise area** Hyde Park opposite **Facilities** food (pre-bookable) vet info **Restrictions** small - medium dogs only

Overlooking Hyde Park this hotel is located within easy reach of the fashionable stores of Knightsbridge and Mayfair. The hotel's contemporary style allows freedom and space to relax. Understated luxury is the key here with bedrooms enjoying great natural light. There is also a Shambhala Spa, steam room and fully equipped gym. For those seeking a culinary experience, Nobu offers innovative Japanese cuisine with an upbeat atmosphere.

Rooms 150 en suite S £375-£2800; D £375-£2800* **Facilities** Spa STV FTV Gym Wi-fi available Treatments **Services** Lift air con **Parking** 15

★★★★ 84% HOTEL

Chesterfield Mayfair

35 Charles St, Mayfair W1J 5EB

020 7491 2622 020 7491 4793

e-mail: bookch@rchmail.com

web: www.redcarnationhotels.com

Dir: *Hyde Park Corner along Piccadilly, left into Half Moon St. At end left & 1st right into Queens St, then right into Charles St*

PETS: Bedrooms Charges charge for damage **Public areas** (on leads) **Exercise area Facilities** food (pre-bookable) food bowl water bowl bedding dog chews cat treats feeding mat litter tray etc dog scoop/disp bags leads pet sitting dog walking washing facs dog grooming cage storage walks info vet info **On Request** fridge access torch towels **Other** all pet facilities available on request

Quiet elegance and an atmosphere of exclusivity characterise this stylish Mayfair hotel where attentive, friendly service is a highlight. Bedrooms have been decorated in a variety of contemporary styles, some with fabric walls; all are thoughtfully equipped and boast marble-clad bathrooms. Air conditioned throughout.

Rooms 107 en suite (7 fmly) S £135-£346.63; D £170-£381.88 **Facilities** STV Wi-fi in bedrooms Xmas **Services** Lift air con **Notes** LB

W8

★★★★★ HOTEL

Milestone Hotel & Apartments

1 Kensington Court W8 5DL

020 7917 1000 020 7917 1010

e-mail: bookms@rchmail.com

web: www.redcarnationhotels.com

Dir: *From Warwick Rd right into Kensington High St. Hotel 400yds past Kensington underground*

PETS: Bedrooms (2GF) sign **Charges** charge for damage **Public areas** except food service areas **Exercise area** 20yds **Facilities** food (pre-bookable) food bowl water bowl bedding dog chews cat treats feeding mat litter tray etc dog scoop/disp bags leads pet sitting dog walking dog grooming cage storage walks info vet info **On Request** fridge access torch towels **Other** welcome pack; dog sitting & dog walking bookable (24hrs notice required) **Restrictions** no breed larger than Golden Retriever

This delightful town house enjoys a wonderful location opposite Kensington Palace and is near the elegant shops. Individually themed bedrooms include a selection of stunning suites that are equipped with every conceivable extra. Public areas include the luxurious Park Lounge where afternoon tea is served, a delightful panelled bar, a sumptuous restaurant and a small gym and resistance pool.

Rooms 57 en suite (3 fmly) (2 GF) S £275-£311; D £370-£405* **Facilities** STV FTV Gym Wi-fi in bedrooms Health club Xmas New Year **Services** Lift air con **Parking** 1 **Notes** LB

WC1

★★★★ 84% HOTEL

The Montague on the Gardens

Red Carnation HOTELS

15 Montague St, Bloomsbury WC1B 5BJ
☎ 020 7637 1001 020 7637 2516
e-mail: bookmt@rchmail.com
web: www.redcarnationhotels.com

Dir: *just off Russell Square, adjacent to British Museum*

PETS: Bedrooms (19GF) **Charges** charge for damage **Public areas** (on leads) **Exercise area** 100mtrs **Facilities** food bowl water bowl bedding dog chews cat treats pet sitting dog walking cage storage walks info vet info **On Request** fridge access torch towels **Other** please telephone for details

This stylish hotel is situated right next to the British Museum. A special feature is the alfresco terrace overlooking a delightful garden. Other public rooms include the Blue Door Bistro and Chef's Table, a bar, a lounge and a conservatory where traditional afternoon teas are served. The bedrooms are beautifully appointed and range from split-level suites to more compact rooms.

Rooms 100 en suite (19 GF) S £115-£210; D £135-£260* **Facilities** STV Gym Wi-fi available ♫ ch fac Xmas New Year **Services** Lift air con **Notes** LB

LONDON GATEWAY MOTORWAY SERVICE AREA (M1) MAP 04 TQ29

★★★ 67% HOTEL

Days Hotel London North

Welcome Break

Welcome Break Service Area NW7 3HU
☎ 020 8906 7000 020 8906 7011
e-mail: lgw.hotel@welcomebreak.co.uk
web: www.welcomebreak.co.uk

Dir: *on M1 between junct 2/4 northbound & southbound*

PETS: Bedrooms unattended **Charges** charge for damage **Public areas** except restaurant or bar area **Exercise area**

This modern building offers accommodation in smart, spacious and well-equipped bedrooms, suitable for families and business travellers, and all with en suite bathrooms. Continental breakfast is available and other refreshments may be taken at the nearby family restaurant.

Rooms 200 en suite (190 fmly) (80 GF) S £59-£89; D £59-£99* **Facilities** STV Wi-fi available **Services** Lift air con **Parking** 160

MERSEYSIDE

HAYDOCK MAP 07 SJ59

★★★★ 76% HOTEL

Thistle Haydock

thistle

Penny Ln WA11 9SG
☎ 0871 376 9044 & 01942 272000 0871 376 9144
e-mail: haydock@thistle.co.uk
web: www.thistlehotels.com/haydock

Dir: *M6 junct 23, follow Racecourse signs (A49) towards Ashton-in-Makerfield, 1st left, after bridge 1st turn*

PETS: Bedrooms (78GF) **Charges** £20 (dependent on size of pet) per night **Grounds** accessible on leads disp bin **Exercise area**

A smart, purpose-built hotel which offers an excellent standard of thoughtfully equipped accommodation. It is conveniently situated between Liverpool and Manchester, just off the M6. The wide range of leisure and meeting facilities prove popular with guests.

Rooms 137 en suite (13 fmly) (78 GF) S £56-£170; D £66-£170* **Facilities** **Spa** STV supervised Gym Wi-fi in bedrooms Children's play area Xmas New Year **Parking** 200 **Notes** LB

LIVERPOOL MAP 07 SJ39

BUDGET HOTEL

Campanile Liverpool

Campanile HOTEL RESTAURANT

Chaloner St, Queens Dock L3 4AJ
☎ 0151 709 8104 0151 709 8725
e-mail: liverpool@campanile.com
web: www.envergure.fr

Dir: *follow tourist signs marked Albert Dock. Hotel on waterfront*

PETS: Bedrooms (33GF) **Charges** charge for damage **Grounds** accessible on leads disp bin **Exercise area**

This modern building offers accommodation in smart, well-equipped bedrooms, all with en suite bathrooms. Refreshments may be taken at the informal Bistro.

Rooms 100 en suite

ENGLAND

NEWTON-LE-WILLOWS — MAP 07 SJ59

★★ 63% HOTEL

Kirkfield Hotel

2/4 Church St WA12 9SU

☎ 01925 228196 🖹 01925 291540

e-mail: enquiries@kirkfieldhotel.co.uk

Dir: *on A49, opposite St Peter's Church*

PETS: Bedrooms Charges charge for damage **Public areas** except restaurant (on leads) **Grounds** accessible on leads **Exercise area Facilities** food bowl water bowl dog chews cat treats washing facs walks info vet info **On Request** fridge access torch towels **Other** local pet sitting service available **Restrictions** small, quiet dogs only **Resident Pets:** River & Phoenix (cats)

A conveniently located, family-run hotel that offers comfortable accommodation. Guests receive a friendly welcome and there is an informal atmosphere throughout. A set menu is available and there are options for lighter dining in the attractive bar area.

Rooms 15 en suite (3 fmly) (1 GF) **Facilities** Wi-fi available

SOUTHPORT — MAP 07 SD31

★★ 81% HOTEL

Cambridge House

4 Cambridge Rd PR9 9NG

☎ 01704 538372 🖹 01704 547183

e-mail: info@cambridgehouse.co.uk

Dir: *A565 N from town centre, over 2 rdbts*

PETS: Bedrooms unattended **Charges** £5 per night charge for damage **Public areas** except restaurant **Grounds** accessible disp bin **Exercise area** 100yds **Facilities** food water bowl walks info vet info **On Request** fridge access torch towels **Resident Pets:** Samson (Newfoundland cross), Tiger & Thomas (cats)

This delightful house is in a peaceful location close to Hesketh Park, a short drive from Lord Street. The spacious, individually styled bedrooms, including a luxurious honeymoon suite, are furnished to a very high standard. Stylish public areas include a lounge, a cosy bar and a dining room. Attentive service and delicious food complete the picture.

Rooms 16 en suite (2 fmly) S £63-£90; D £78-£118 (incl. bkfst)* **Facilities** Wi-fi available **Parking** 20 **Notes** LB

★★★★ GUEST ACCOMMODATION

Whitworth Falls

16 Lathom Rd PR9 0JH

☎ 01704 530074

e-mail: whitworthfalls@rapid.co.uk

Dir: *A565 N from town centre, over rdbt, 2nd left onto Alexandra Rd, 4th right*

PETS: Bedrooms Public areas Exercise area Resident Pets: Shelby (King Charles Spaniel), Zoe (Labrador), Sherbert (African Grey parrot), Midge (cat)

Located on a mainly residential avenue within easy walking distance of seafront and Lord Street shops, this Victorian house has been renovated to provide a range of practical but homely bedrooms. Breakfasts and pre-theatre dinners are served in the attractive dining room, and a comfortable sitting room and lounge bar are also available.

Rooms 12 en suite (2 fmly) (1 GF) **Facilities** TVB tea/coffee Direct dial from bedrooms Cen ht TVL Dinner Last d noon **Parking** 8

NORFOLK

ATTLEBOROUGH — MAP 05 TM09

★★★★ ◎ RESTAURANT WITH ROOMS

Sherbourne House

8 Norwich Rd NR17 2JX

☎ 01953 454363

e-mail: stay@sherbourne-house.co.uk

web: www.sherbourne-house.co.uk

Dir: *Off B1077*

PETS: Bedrooms (1GF) **Charges** charge for damage **Public areas** except restaurant **Grounds** accessible disp bin **Exercise area** 0.75m **Facilities** food bowl water bowl dog chews dog scoop/disp bags leads cage storage walks info vet info **On Request** fridge access torch towels **Resident Pets:** Chalky (Terrier)

Expect a warm welcome from the caring hosts at this delightful 17th century property situated just a short walk from the centre of this historic market town. Public rooms include a choice of lounges, a sunny conservatory/lounge bar and Taste restaurant. The individually decorated bedrooms are smartly appointed and have many thoughtful touches.

Rooms 8 en suite (1 fmly) (1 GF) S £40-£70; D £70-£80* **Facilities** FTV TVB tea/coffee Cen ht Dinner Last d 8.30pm Wi-fi available **Parking** 30

BELTON MAP 05 TG40

►►►► Rose Farm Touring & Camping Park

(TG488033)

Stepshort NR31 9JS

☎ 01493 780896 🖷 01493 780896

web: www.rosefarmtouringpark.co.uk

Dir: *Follow signs to Belton off A143, right at lane signed Stepshort, site 1st on right*

PETS: disp bin **Exercise area** on site **Facilities** vet info **Other** prior notice required

Open all year

A former railway line is the setting for this very peaceful site which enjoys rural views and is beautifully presented throughout. The ever-improving toilet facilities are spotlessly clean and inviting to use, and the park is brightened with many flower and herb beds. Customer care is truly exceptional. A 10-acre site with 80 touring pitches, 15 hardstandings.

Notes No dog fouling

BLAKENEY MAP 09 TG04

★★★ @@@ HOTEL

Morston Hall

Morston, Holt NR25 7AA

☎ 01263 741041 🖷 01263 740419

e-mail: reception@morstonhall.com

web: www.morstonhall.com

Dir: *1m W of Blakeney on A149 (King's Lynn Cromer road)*

PETS: Bedrooms unattended **Sep Accom** 2 kennels & small run **Charges** £5 per night charge for damage **Grounds** accessible on leads disp bin **Exercise area** 200yds, marshes **Facilities** walks info vet info **On Request** torch towels **Resident Pets:** Phyllis (cat - lives outside)

This delightful 17th-century country-house hotel enjoys a tranquil setting amid well-tended gardens. The comfortable public rooms offer a choice of attractive lounges and a sunny conservatory, while the elegant dining room is the perfect setting to enjoy Galton Blackiston's award-winning cuisine. The spacious bedrooms are individually decorated and stylishly furnished with modern opulence.

Rooms 7 en suite 6 annexe en suite (7 GF) D £260-£300 (incl. bkfst & dinner)✳ **Facilities** STV Wi-fi available New Year **Parking** 40 **Notes LB** Closed 1 Jan-2 Feb & 2 days Xmas

BRANCASTER STAITHE MAP 09 TF74

★★★ 79% @@ HOTEL

White Horse

PE31 8BY

☎ 01485 210262 🖷 01485 210930

e-mail: reception@whitehorsebrancaster.co.uk

web: www.whitehorsebrancaster.co.uk

Dir: *on A149 coast road midway between Hunstanton & Wells-next-the-Sea*

PETS: Bedrooms (8GF) **Charges** £10 per night charge for damage **Public areas** except restaurant **Grounds** accessible disp bin **Exercise area** Norfolk coastal path at end of garden **Facilities** washing facs walks info vet info **On Request** fridge access torch towels **Other** dogs allowed in ground floor bedrooms only

A charming hotel situated on the north Norfolk coast with contemporary bedrooms in two wings, some featuring an interesting cobbled fascia. Each room is attractively decorated and thoughtfully equipped. There is a large bar and a lounge area leading through to the conservatory restaurant, with stunning tidal marshland views across to Scolt Head Island.

Rooms 7 en suite 8 annexe en suite (4 fmly) (8 GF) S £75-£114; D £100-£178 (incl. bkfst)✳ **Facilities** Wi-fi in bedrooms Xmas New Year **Parking** 60 **Notes LB**

BURNHAM MARKET MAP 09 TF84

★★★ 86% @@ HOTEL

Hoste Arms

The Green PE31 8HD

☎ 01328 738777 🖷 01328 730103

e-mail: reception@hostearms.co.uk

web: www.hostearms.co.uk

Dir: *signed on B1155, 5m W of Wells-next-the-Sea*

PETS: Bedrooms (7GF) unattended **Charges** £10 per stay per night **Public areas** bar & lounge only **Grounds** accessible on leads **Exercise area** green opposite **Facilities** food food bowl water bowl bedding walks info vet info **On Request** torch towels

A stylish, privately-owned inn situated in the heart of a bustling village close to the north Norfolk coast. The extensive public rooms feature a

CONTINUED

BURNHAM MARKET *CONTINUED*

range of dining areas that include a conservatory with plush furniture, a sunny patio and a traditional pub. The tastefully furnished and thoughtfully equipped bedrooms are generally very spacious and offer a high degree of comfort.

Rooms 35 en suite (7 GF) S £114-£119; D £145-£160 (incl. bkfst & dinner)✳ **Facilities** STV Wi-fi available Xmas New Year **Services** air con **Parking** 45

See advert on opposite page

CLIPPESBY MAP 09 TG41

►►►►► Clippesby Hall *(TG423147)*

Hall Ln NR29 3BL

☎ 01493 367800 📠 01493 367809

e-mail: holidays@clippesby.com

web: www.clippesby.com

Dir: *From A47 follow tourist signs for The Broads. At Acle rdbt take A1064, after 2m left onto B1152, 0.5m turn left opposite village sign, site 400yds on right*

PETS: Charges £3.50 per night **Public areas** except shop & coffee shop (on leads) disp bin **Exercise area** on site dog walk **Facilities** on site shop food food bowl water bowl dog chews cat treats walks info vet info **Other** prior notice required

Open end Mar-end Oct (rs Etr-23 May no swimming/tennis. Pub/cafe BH wknds) Last arrival 17.30hrs Last departure 11.00hrs

Overall winner of AA Campsite of the Year & AA Campsite of the Year for England 2009. A lovely country house estate with secluded pitches hidden among the trees or in sheltered sunny glades. The toilet facilities have been upgraded to a very good standard, providing a wide choice of cubicle. Amenities include a café, clubhouse and family crazy-golf. A 30-acre site with 120 touring pitches, 9 hardstandings.

CROMER MAP 09 TG24

★★★ 72% HOTEL
The Cliftonville

NR27 9AS

☎ 01263 512543 📠 01263 515700

e-mail: reservations@cliftonvillehotel.co.uk

web: www.cliftonvillehotel.co.uk

Dir: *From A149 (coastal road), 500yds from town centre, northbound on clifftop by sunken gardens*

PETS: Bedrooms unattended **Stables** on site **Charges** £5 per night **Public areas** except restaurants (on leads) **Exercise area Facilities** cage storage walks info vet info

An imposing Edwardian hotel situated on the main coast road with stunning views of the sea. Public rooms feature a magnificent staircase, minstrels' gallery, coffee shop, lounge bar, a further residents' lounge, Boltons Bistro and an additional restaurant. The pleasantly decorated bedrooms are generally quite spacious and have lovely sea views.

Rooms 30 en suite (5 fmly) S £50-£77; D £100-£154 (incl. bkfst)✳ **Facilities** Wi-fi available Xmas New Year **Services** Lift **Parking** 20 **Notes** LB

★★★ GUEST HOUSE
Glendale

33 Macdonald Rd NR27 9AP

☎ 01263 513278

e-mail: glendalecromer@aol.com

Dir: *A149 coast road from Cromer centre, 4th left*

PETS: Bedrooms unattended **Public areas** except breakfast room (on leads) **Grounds** accessible on leads disp bin **Exercise area** 200mtrs **Facilities** walks info vet info **On Request** fridge access torch towels **Resident Pets:** Daisy & Megan (Jack Russells), Jess (Collie/Springer Spaniel)

Victorian property situated in a peaceful side road adjacent to the seafront and just a short walk from the town centre. Bedrooms are pleasantly decorated, well maintained and equipped with a good range of useful extras. Breakfast is served at individual tables in the smart dining room.

Rooms 5 rms (1 en suite) S £23-£32; D £46-£64 **Facilities** TVB tea/coffee **Parking** 2 **Notes** LB No coaches Closed 20 Oct-3 Apr

★★★ GUEST HOUSE
The Sandcliff

Runton Rd NR27 9AS

☎ 01263 512888 📠 01263 512888

e-mail: bookings@sandcliffcromer.co.uk

Dir: *500yds W of town centre on A149*

PETS: Bedrooms Charges £10 per stay per night **Exercise area** 100mtrs

Ideally situated on the seafront overlooking the beach and sea beyond, just a short walk from the town centre. Public rooms include a large lounge bar with comfortable seating and a spacious dining room where breakfast and dinner are served. The bedrooms are pleasantly decorated and thoughtfully equipped, and some have superb sea views.

Rooms 22 rms (16 en suite) (10 fmly) (3 GF) S £47-£55; D £64-£80✳ **Facilities** TVB tea/coffee Licensed TVL Dinner Last d 8pm **Parking** 10 **Notes** LB

►►► *Forest Park* *(TG233405)*

Northrepps Rd NR27 0JR

☎ 01263 513290 📠 01263 511992

e-mail: info@forest-park.co.uk

web: www.forest-park.co.uk

Dir: *A140 from Norwich, left at T-junct signed Cromer, right signed Northrepps, right then immediate left, left at T-junct, site on right*

PETS: Stables nearby (0.75m) (loose box) **Charges** £2.50 per night **Exercise area** on site large woods disp bin **Facilities** on site shop food food bowl water bowl dog chews cat treats dog scoop/disp bags walks info vet info **Other** prior notice required **Resident Pets:** Malacca & Jamila (Black Labradors)

Open 15 Mar-15 Jan Last arrival 21.00hrs Last departure 11.00hrs

Surrounded by forest, this gently sloping park offers a wide choice of pitches. Visitors have the use of a heated indoor swimming pool, and a large clubhouse with entertainment. A 100-acre site with 344 touring pitches and 372 statics.

►►► Manor Farm Caravan & Camping Site

(TG198416)

East Runton NR27 9PR

☎ 01263 512858

e-mail: manor-farm@ukf.net

web: www.manorfarmcaravansite.co.uk

Dir: *1m W of Cromer, turn off A148 or A149 at Manor Farm sign*

PETS: Public areas except dog free areas **Stables** (loose box) **Charges** £1 per night **Exercise area** farmland & public footpaths adjacent **Facilities** walks info vet info **Other** prior notice required **Resident Pets:** Mollie (Border Terrier/Lakeland cross), Titch & Gerbil (ponies)

Open Etr-Sep Last arrival 20.30hrs Last departure noon

A well-established family-run site on a working farm enjoying panoramic sea views. There are good modern facilities across the site, which is elevated above Cromer. A 17-acre site with 250 touring pitches.

Notes ⊜

DOWNHAM MARKET MAP 05 TF60

★★★ BED & BREAKFAST

Crosskeys Riverside House

Bridge St, Hilgay PE38 0LD

☎ 01366 387777 📠 01366 387777

e-mail: crosskeyshouse@aol.com

web: www.crosskeys.info

Dir: *2m S of Downham Market. Off A10 into Hilgay, Crosskeys on bridge*

PETS: Bedrooms (2GF) unattended **Stables** on site **Charges** £3.50 per stay per night **Grounds** accessible disp bin **Exercise area** 500yds **Facilities** leads walks info vet info **On Request** fridge access torch towels **Resident Pets:** 2 Shih Tzus, 3 horses

Situated in the small village of Hilgay on the banks of the River Wissey, this former coaching inn offers comfortable accommodation that includes a number of four-poster bedrooms; many rooms have river views. Public rooms include a dining room with oak beams and inglenook fireplace, plus a small, rustic residents' bar.

Rooms 4 en suite (1 fmly) (2 GF) S £30-£50; D £50-£60*
Facilities TVB tea/coffee Cen ht Fishing Rowing boat for guests use
Parking 10

ENGLAND

FAKENHAM MAP 09 TF92

★★★ FARM HOUSE

Abbott Farm *(TF975390)*

Walsingham Rd, Binham NR21 0AW

☎ 01328 830519 📠 01328 830519 Mrs E Brown

e-mail: abbot.farm@btinternet.com

web: www.abbottfarm.co.uk

Dir: *NE of Fakenham. From Binham SW onto Walsingham Rd, farm 0.6m on left*

PETS: Bedrooms (2GF) sign **Stables** nearby (1m) **Charges** charge for damage **Public areas** **Grounds** accessible disp bin **Exercise area** **Facilities** food bowl water bowl bedding feeding mat litter tray etc dog scoop/disp bags leads washing facs cage storage walks info vet info **On Request** fridge access torch towels **Resident Pets:** Buster (Retriever/Labrador)

A detached red-brick farmhouse set amidst 190 acres of arable farmland and surrounded by open countryside. The spacious bedrooms are pleasantly decorated and thoughtfully equipped; they include a ground-floor room with a large en suite shower. Breakfast is served in the attractive conservatory, which has superb views of the countryside.

Rooms 3 en suite (2 GF) S £26-£30; D £52-£60 **Facilities** TVB tea/coffee Cen ht TVL **Parking** 20 **Notes** 190 acres arable Closed 24-26 Dec

►►► Caravan Club M.V.C. Site *(TF926288)*

Fakenham Racecourse NR21 7NY

☎ 01328 862388 📠 01328 855908

e-mail: caravan@fakenhamracecourse.co.uk

web: www.fakenhamracecourse.co.uk

Dir: *Towards Fakenham follow brown signs for 'racecourse' with tent & caravan symbols, directly to site entrance*

PETS: Stables on site (loose box) disp bin **Exercise area** on site **Facilities** on site shop dog chews walks info

Open all year Last arrival 21.00hrs Last departure noon

A very well laid out site set around the racecourse, with a grandstand offering smart modern toilet facilities. Tourers move to the centre of the course on race days, and enjoy free racing, and there's a wide range of sporting activities in the club house. An 11.5-acre site with 120 touring pitches, 25 hardstandings.

►► Crossways Caravan & Camping Park

(TF961321)

Crossways, Holt Rd, Little Snoring NR21 0AX

☎ 01328 878335

e-mail: joyholland@crosswayscaravanpark.co.uk

web: www.crosswayscaravan.co.uk

Dir: *From Fakenham take A148 towards Cromer. After 3m pass exit for Little Snoring. Site on A148 on left behind Post Office*

PETS: Charges 50p per night **Public areas** (on leads) **Exercise area** 10mtrs disp bin **Facilities** on site shop food food bowl water bowl dog chews cat treats litter tray etc dog scoop/disp bags washing facs walks info vet info **Other** prior notice required

Open all year Last arrival 22.00hrs Last departure noon

Set on the edge of the peaceful hamlet of Little Snoring, this level site enjoys views across the fields towards the North Norfolk coast some seven miles away. Visitors can use the health suite for a small charge, and there is a shop on site, and a good village pub. A 2-acre site with 26 touring pitches, 10 hardstandings and 1 static.

GREAT HOCKHAM MAP 05 TL99

►►► Thetford Forest Camping & Caravanning Club Site *(TL941926)*

Puddledock Farm IP24 1PA

☎ 01953 498455

web: www.thefriendlyclub.co.uk

Dir: *Off A1075 between Norwich & Cambridge*

PETS: Exercise area **Facilities** washing facs walks info vet info **Other** prior notice required

Open all year Last arrival 21.00hrs Last departure noon

This expansive site on the edge of Thetford Forest occupies a central location in East Anglia, providing a multitude of touring options. The 88 pitches are generously proportioned and well sheltered. There is a small fishing lake on site. 80 touring pitches, 80 hardstandings.

Notes Site gates closed 23.00hrs-07.00hrs

GREAT YARMOUTH MAP 05 TG50

★★★★ BED & BREAKFAST

Barnard House

2 Barnard Crescent NR30 4DR

☎ 01493 855139 🖷 01493 843143

e-mail: enquiries@barnardhouse.com

Dir: *0.5m N of town centre. Off A149 onto Barnard Crescent*

PETS: Bedrooms Public areas at other guests' discretion **Exercise area Facilities** walks info vet info **On Request** fridge access torch towels **Resident Pets:** Fergus & Flora (Field Spaniels)

A friendly, family-run guest house, set in mature landscaped gardens in a residential area. The smartly decorated bedrooms have co-ordinated fabrics and many thoughtful touches. Breakfast is served in the stylish dining room and there is an elegant lounge with plush sofas. A warm welcome is assured.

Rooms 3 rms (2 en suite) (1 pri facs) S £40-£42; D £60-£65 **Facilities** FTV TVB tea/coffee Cen ht TVL Wi-fi available **Parking** 3 **Notes LB** Closed Xmas & New Year

★★★ GUEST ACCOMMODATION

Swiss Cottage B&B Just for Non Smokers

31 North Dr NR30 4EW

☎ 01493 855742 & 08450 943949 🖷 0870 2846294

e-mail: info@swiss-cottage.info

web: www.swisscottagebedandbreakfast.co.uk

Dir: *0.5m N of town centre. Off A47 or A12 to to seafront, 750yds N of pier. Turn left at Britannia Pier. Swiss Cottage on left opposite Water Gardens*

PETS: Bedrooms (2GF) **Charges** charge for damage **Public areas** except breakfast room **Exercise area** 30mtrs **On Request** fridge access **Other** dogs must not be left unattended in bedrooms at any time **Restrictions** medium size only no Ridgebacks or Jack Russells

A charming property situated at the quieter end of town overlooking the Venetian waterways and the sea beyond. The comfortable bedrooms are pleasantly decorated with co-ordinated fabrics and have many useful extras. Breakfast is served in the smart dining room and guests have use of an open-plan lounge area.

Rooms 9 en suite (1 fmly) (2 GF) S £27-£38; D £48-£71✻ **Facilities** FTV TVB tea/coffee Cen ht Wi-fi available **Parking** 9 **Notes LB** No children 8yrs Closed Nov-Feb

HUNSTANTON MAP 09 TF64

★★★ 80% HOTEL

Caley Hall

Old Hunstanton Rd PE36 6HH

☎ 01485 533486 🖷 01485 533348

e-mail: mail@caleyhallhotel.co.uk

web: www.caleyhallhotel.co.uk

Dir: *1m from Hunstanton, on A149*

PETS: Bedrooms (30GF) unattended **Charges** £3 per night **Public areas** except bar & restaurant (on leads) **Grounds** accessible on leads disp bin **Exercise area** 50mtrs **Facilities** food bowl water bowl leads washing facs cage storage walks info vet info **On Request** fridge access torch towels **Resident Pets:** Basil (Cocker Spaniel), Sox (cat)

Situated within easy walking distance of the seafront. The tastefully decorated bedrooms are in a series of converted outbuildings; each is smartly furnished and thoughtfully equipped. Public rooms feature a large open-plan lounge/bar with plush leather seating, and a restaurant offering an interesting choice of dishes.

Rooms 40 en suite (20 fmly) (30 GF) S £55-£150; D £78-£199 (incl. bkfst)✻ **Facilities** STV Wi-fi in bedrooms ch fac **Parking** 50 **Notes LB** Closed 18 Dec-20 Jan

Searles Leisure Resort *(TF671400)*

South Beach Rd PE36 5BB

☎ 01485 534211 🖷 01485 533815

e-mail: bookings@searles.co.uk

web: www.searles.co.uk

Dir: *A149 from King's Lynn to Hunstanton. At rdbt follow signs for South Beach. Straight on at 2nd rdbt. Site on left*

PETS: Charges £2.50 per night **Public areas** except buildings **Exercise area** on site Field available for dogs on leads **Facilities** on site shop food food bowl water bowl bedding dog chews cat treats litter tray etc dog scoop/disp bags washing facs walks info vet info **Other** prior notice required **Restrictions** no Rottweilers, Pit Bulls, Staffordshire Bull Terriers, German Shepherds, Dobermans or similar breeds

Open all year (rs 25 Dec & Feb-May Limited entertainment & restaurant) Last arrival 20.45hrs Last departure 11.00hrs

A large seaside holiday complex with well-managed facilities, adjacent to sea and beach. The tourers have their own areas, including two

CONTINUED

HUNSTANTON CONTINUED

excellent toilet blocks, and pitches are individually marked by small maturing shrubs for privacy. The bars and entertainment, restaurant, bistro and takeaway, heated indoor and outdoor pools, golf, fishing and bowling green make this park popular throughout the year. A 50-acre site with 332 touring pitches, 100 hardstandings and 460 statics.

Notes No dangerous breeds

NORTH WALSHAM MAP 09 TG23

★★★ HOTEL

Beechwood

Cromer Rd NR28 0HD

☎ 01692 403231 01692 407284

e-mail: enquiries@beechwood-hotel.co.uk

web: www.beechwood-hotel.co.uk

Dir: *B1150 from Norwich. At North Walsham left at 1st lights, then right at next*

PETS: Bedrooms unattended **Charges** £9 per night **Public areas** except restaurant **Grounds** accessible **Exercise area** park 400yds **Resident Pets:** Emily & Harry (Airedale Terriers)

Expect a warm welcome at this elegant 18th-century house, situated just a short walk from the town centre. The individually styled bedrooms are tastefully furnished with well-chosen antique pieces, attractive co-ordinated soft fabrics and many thoughtful touches. The spacious public areas include a lounge bar with plush furnishings, a further lounge and a smartly appointed restaurant.

Rooms 17 en suite (4 GF) S £72; D £90-£160 (incl. bkfst) **Facilities** Wi-fi available New Year **Parking** 20 **Notes LB** No children 10yrs

►►►► Two Mills Touring Park *(TG291286)*

Yarmouth Rd NR28 9NA

☎ 01692 405829 01692 405829

e-mail: enquiries@twomills.co.uk

web: www.twomills.co.uk

Dir: *1m S of North Walsham on Old Yarmouth road past police station & hospital on left*

PETS: Charges 75p per night **Public areas** except in buildings disp bin **Exercise area** on site dog walks **Facilities** on site shop food food bowl water bowl dog scoop/disp bags vet info

Open Mar-3 Jan Last arrival 20.30hrs Last departure noon

Set in superb countryside in a peaceful spot which is also convenient for touring. Some fully-serviced pitches offer panoramic views over the site, and the layout of pitches and facilities is excellent. The very friendly and helpful owners keep the park in immaculate condition. This park does not accept children. A 5-acre site with 50 touring pitches, 50 hardstandings.

Notes 2 dogs max per pitch

NORWICH MAP 05 TG20

★★ 85% HOTEL

Stower Grange

School Rd, Drayton NR8 6EF

☎ 01603 860210 01603 860464

e-mail: enquiries@stowergrange.co.uk

web: www.stowergrange.co.uk

Dir: *Norwich ring road N to Asda supermarket. Take A1067 (Fakenham road) at Drayton, right at lights into School Rd. Hotel 150yds on right*

PETS: Bedrooms unattended **Public areas** except restaurant **Grounds** accessible disp bin **Exercise area Facilities** food (pre-bookable) pet sitting dog walking washing facs cage storage walks info vet info **On Request** torch towels **Resident Pets:** Saffy (Staffordshire Bull Terrier)

Expect a warm welcome at this 17th-century, ivy-clad property situated in a peaceful residential area close to the city centre and airport. The individually decorated bedrooms are generally quite spacious; each one is tastefully furnished and equipped with many thoughtful touches. Public rooms include a smart open-plan lounge bar and an elegant restaurant.

Rooms 11 en suite (1 fmly) **Facilities** Wi-fi available **Parking** 40 **Notes LB**

★★★★★ GUEST HOUSE

Catton Old Hall

Lodge Ln, Old Catton NR6 7HG

☎ 01603 419379 01603 400339

e-mail: enquiries@catton-hall.co.uk

web: www.catton-hall.co.uk

Dir: *2m N of city centre in Old Catton. A1042 N onto B1150, left onto White Woman Ln, straight over at lights onto Lodge Ln*

PETS: Bedrooms Public areas Grounds accessible disp bin **Exercise area Facilities** food bowl water bowl dog chews pet sitting dog walking cage storage vet info **On Request** fridge access torch towels **Resident Pets:** Fendi (Yorkshire Terrier), chickens

This is a superb Jacobean house which dates back to 1632. The property is situated just a short drive from the city centre and airport. Original features include brick and flint walls, oak timbers and reused

Caen stone. The stylish bedrooms offer a high degree of comfort; each one is individually decorated and tastefully furnished. The elegant public areas include a dining room and a cosy lounge with plush furnishings.

Rooms 7 en suite S fr £75; D £75-£130* **Facilities** TVB tea/coffee Direct dial from bedrooms Licensed Cen ht TVL Dinner Last d 12pm Wi-fi available **Parking** 11 **Notes** LB No children 12yrs No coaches

★★★ GUEST ACCOMMODATION

Edmar Lodge

64 Earlham Rd NR2 3DF

☎ 01603 615599 🖷 01603 495599

e-mail: mail@edmarlodge.co.uk

web: www.edmarlodge.co.uk

Dir: *Off A47 S bypass onto B1108 Earlham Rd, follow university and hospital signs*

PETS: Bedrooms Grounds accessible on leads **Exercise area** approx 200yds **Facilities** walks info vet info **On Request** fridge access towels **Other** Please telephone for details

Located just a ten minute walk from the city centre, this friendly family-run guest house offers a convenient location and ample private parking. Individually decorated bedrooms are smartly appointed and well equipped. Freshly prepared breakfasts are served within the cosy dining room; a microwave and a refrigerator are also available.

Rooms 5 en suite (1 fmly) S £38-£43; D £43-£48* **Facilities** FTV TVB tea/coffee Cen ht Wi-fi available **Parking** 6

★★★ GUEST ACCOMMODATION

The Larches

345 Aylsham Rd NR3 2RU

☎ 01603 415420 🖷 01603 465340

e-mail: lynda@thelarches.com

web: www.thelarches.com

Dir: *On A140 500yds past ring road, on left adjacent to Lloyds Bank*

PETS: Bedrooms (1GF) **Exercise area** 50yds **Facilities** cage storage walks info vet info

A modern, detached property situated only a short drive from the city centre and airport. The spacious, well equipped bedrooms are brightly decorated, pleasantly furnished and have co-ordinated soft fabrics. Breakfast is served at individual tables in the smart lounge-dining room.

Rooms 7 en suite (2 fmly) (1 GF) S fr £30; D fr £50* **Facilities** STV FTV TVB tea/coffee Cen ht TVL Wi-fi available **Parking** 10

►►► Norwich Camping & Caravanning Club Site *(TG237063)*

Martineau Ln NR1 2HX

☎ 01603 620060

web: www.thefriendlyclub.co.uk

Dir: *From A47 onto A146 towards city centre. Left at lights to next lights, under low bridge to Cock pub, turn left. Site 150yds on right*

PETS: Public areas except in buildings disp bin **Exercise area** on site **Facilities** walks info vet info **Other** prior notice required

Open 2 Apr-2 Nov Last arrival 21.00hrs Last departure noon

A very pretty small site on the outskirts of the city, close to the River Yare. The park is built on two levels, with the lower meadow enjoying good rural views, and there is plenty of screening from nearby houses. The older-style toilet block is kept immaculately clean. A 2.5-acre site with 50 touring pitches.

Notes Site gates closed 23.00hrs-07.00hrs

REEPHAM MAP 09 TG12

U

Old Brewery House

OXFORD HOTELS & INNS

Market Place NR10 4JJ

☎ 01603 870881 📠 01603 870969

e-mail: reservations.oldbreweryhouse@ohiml.com

web: www.oxfordhotelsandinns.com

Dir: *A1067, right at Bawdeswell onto B1145 into Reepham, hotel on left in Market Place*

PETS: Bedrooms (7GF) unattended sign **Public areas** except bar & restaurant areas (on leads) **Grounds** accessible on leads **Exercise area** woods 1m **Facilities** water bowl cage storage walks info vet info **On Request** fridge access torch towels

At the time of going to press the rating for this establishment was not confirmed. This may be due to a change of ownership or because it has only recently joined the AA rating scheme. For further details please see the AA website: www.theAA.com

Rooms 23 en suite (2 fmly) (7 GF) S £45-£55; D £65-£85 (incl. bkfst)* **Facilities** Squash Gym Xmas **Parking** 40 **Notes** LB

RINGSTEAD MAP 09 TF74

★★★★ ◎ INN

The Gin Trap Inn

6 High St PE36 5JU

☎ 01485 525264

e-mail: thegintrap@hotmail.co.uk

Dir: *A149 from Kings Lynn towards Hunstanton. In 15m turn right at Heacham for Ringstead into village centre*

PETS: Bedrooms Public areas except conservatory & dining room **Grounds** accessible **Exercise area** 500mtrs **Facilities** dog chews walks info vet info **On Request** fridge access torch

This delightful 17th-century inn is in a quiet village just a short drive from the coast. The public rooms include a large open-plan bar and a cosy restaurant. The accommodation is luxurious. Each individually appointed bedroom has been carefully decorated and thoughtfully equipped.

Rooms 3 en suite S £49-£80; D £78-£140* **Facilities** TVB tea/coffee Cen ht Dinner Last d 9.30pm Fri/Sat Wi-fi available **Parking** 20 **Notes** No children No coaches

ST JOHN'S FEN END MAP 09 TF51

►►►► Virginia Lake Caravan Park *(TF538113)*

Smeeth Rd PE14 8JF

☎ 01945 430332 & 430585

e-mail: louise@virginialake.co.uk

web: www.virginialake.co.uk

Dir: *From A47 E of Wisbech follow tourist signs to Terrington St John. Site on left*

PETS: disp bin **Public areas** except lakeside **Exercise area** on site dog walk **Facilities** on site shop food food bowl water bowl dog chews cat treats feeding mat litter tray etc dog scoop/disp bags leads washing facs walks info vet info **Other** prior notice required **Resident Pets:** 4 Labradors & 2 cats

Open all year Last arrival 23.00hrs Last departure noon

A well-established park beside a 2-acre fishing lake with good facilities for both anglers and tourers. The toilet facilities are very good, and security is carefully observed throughout the park. A clubhouse serves a selection of meals. A 5-acre site with 100 touring pitches, 20 hardstandings.

SANDRINGHAM MAP 09 TF62

►►►► Sandringham Camping & Caravanning Club Site *(TF683274)*

The Sandringham Estate, Double Lodges PE35 6EA

☎ 01485 542555

web: www.thefriendlyclub.co.uk

Dir: *From A148 onto B1440 signed West Newton. Follow signs to site. From A149 turn left & follow site signs*

PETS: disp bin **Public areas** except in buildings **Exercise area** adjacent area **Facilities** on site shop walks info vet info **Other** prior notice required

Open 12 Feb-23 Nov Last arrival 21.00hrs Last departure noon

A prestige park, very well landscaped and laid out in mature woodland, with toilets and other buildings blending in with the scenery. There are plenty of walks from the site, and this is a good touring base for the rest of Norfolk. A 28-acre site with 275 touring pitches, 2 hardstandings.

Notes Site gates closed 23.00hrs-07.00hrs

SWAFFHAM MAP 05 TF80

►►► Breckland Meadows Touring Park

(TF809094)

Lynn Rd PE37 7PT

☎ 01760 721246

e-mail: info@brecklandmeadows.co.uk

web: www.brecklandmeadows.co.uk

Dir: *1m W of Swaffham on old A47*

PETS: Stables (loose box) **Charges** 50p per night disp bin **Exercise area** on site footpath around perimeter **Facilities** washing facs walks info vet info

Open all year Last arrival 21.00hrs Last departure 14.00hrs

An immaculate, well-landscaped little park on the edge of Swaffham. The impressive toilet block is well equipped, and there are hardstandings, full electricity and laundry equipment. Plenty of planting is resulting in attractive screening. A 3-acre site with 45 touring pitches, 29 hardstandings.

Notes ⊜

SYDERSTONE MAP 09 TF83

►►► The Garden Caravan Site *(TF812337)*

Barmer Hall Farm PE31 8SR

☎ 01485 578220 & 578178 📠 01485 578178

e-mail: nigel@gardencaravansite.co.uk

web: www.gardencaravansite.co.uk

Dir: *Signed from B1454 at Barmer between A148 & Docking, 1m W of Syderstone*

PETS: disp bin **Exercise area** 10yds **Facilities** walks info vet info **Other** prior notice required; max 2 dogs per pitch

Open Mar-Nov Last departure noon

In the tranquil setting of a former walled garden beside a large farmhouse, with mature trees and shrubs, a secluded site surrounded by woodland. The site is run mainly on trust, with a daily notice indicating which pitches are available, and an honesty box for basic foods. An ideal site for the discerning camper, and well placed for touring north Norfolk. A 3.5-acre site with 30 touring pitches.

Notes ⊜ Max 2 dogs per pitch

THETFORD MAP 05 TL88

★★ 68% HOTEL

The Thomas Paine Hotel

THE INDEPENDENTS HOTEL ASSOCIATION

White Hart St IP24 1AA

☎ 01842 755631 📠 01842 766505

e-mail: bookings@thomaspainehotel.com

Dir: *N'bound on A11, at rdbt immediately before Thetford take A1075, hotel on right on approach to town*

PETS: Bedrooms unattended **Charges** £2.50 per night charge for damage **Public areas** except bar & restaurant (on leads) **Grounds** accessible on leads disp bin **Exercise area** on site courtyard

This Grade II listed building is situated close to the town centre and Thetford Forest Park is just a short drive away. Public rooms include a large lounge bar, a pleasantly appointed restaurant and a meeting room. Bedrooms vary in size and style; each one is attractively decorated and thoughtfully equipped.

Rooms 13 en suite (2 fmly) S fr £55; D fr £66 (incl. bkfst) **Facilities** Wi-fi available Xmas **Parking** 30 **Notes** LB

THORNHAM MAP 09 TF74

★★ ⊛ HOTEL

Lifeboat Inn

Ship Ln PE36 6LT

☎ 01485 512236 📠 01485 512323

e-mail: reception@lifeboatinn.co.uk

web: www.lifeboatinn.co.uk

Dir: *follow A149 from Hunstanton for approx 6m. 1st left after Thornham sign*

PETS: Bedrooms (1GF) unattended **Exercise area Facilities** dog chews **Other** please telephone for further details

This popular 16th-century smugglers' alehouse enjoys superb views across open meadows to Thornham Harbour. The tastefully decorated bedrooms are furnished with pine pieces and have many thoughtful

CONTINUED

ENGLAND

THORNHAM *CONTINUED*

touches. The public rooms have a wealth of character and feature open fireplaces, exposed brickwork and oak beams.

The Lifeboat Inn

Rooms 13 en suite (3 fmly) (1 GF) S £72-£82; D £104-£124 (incl. bkfst)✳ **Facilities** Wi-fi available Xmas New Year **Parking** 120

THURSFORD — MAP 09 TF93

★★★ RESTAURANT WITH ROOMS

The Old Forge Seafood Restaurant

Seafood Restaurant, Fakenham Rd NR21 0BD

☎ 01328 878345

e-mail: sarah.goldspink@btconnect.com

Dir: *On A148 (Fakenham to Holt road), next to garage at Thursford*

PETS: Bedrooms Stables nearby (2m) **Charges** charge for damage **Public areas** (on leads) **Grounds** accessible on leads **Exercise area** adjacent **Facilities** cage storage walks info vet info **On Request** fridge access torch

Expect a warm welcome at this delightful relaxed restaurant with rooms. The open-plan public areas include a lounge bar area with comfy sofas, and a intimate restaurant with pine tables. Bedrooms are pleasantly decorated and equipped with a good range of useful facilities.

Rooms 2 rms (1 en suite) (1 pri facs) S £25-£35; D £55-£65 **Facilities** FTV TVB tea/coffee Dinner Last d 9pm **Parking** 10 **Notes** No children 6yrs

TITCHWELL — MAP 09 TF74

★★★ 82% HOTEL

Titchwell Manor

PE31 8BB

☎ 01485 210221 📠 01485 210104

e-mail: margaret@titchwellmanor.com

web: www.titchwellmanor.com

Dir: *on A149 coast road between Brancaster and Thornham*

PETS: Bedrooms (16GF) unattended sign **Stables** nearby (2m) **Charges** £8 per night charge for damage **Public areas** except conservatory restaurant (on leads) **Grounds** accessible on leads disp bin **Exercise area** 1m **Facilities** food bowl water bowl bedding dog chews cat treats feeding mat litter tray etc dog scoop/disp bags leads pet sitting dog walking washing facs cage storage walks info vet info **On Request** fridge access torch towels

Friendly family-run hotel ideally placed for touring the north Norfolk coastline. The tastefully appointed bedrooms are very comfortable; some in the adjacent annexe offer ground floor access. Smart public rooms include a lounge area, relaxed informal bar and a delightful conservatory restaurant, overlooking the walled garden. Imaginative menus feature quality local produce and fresh fish.

Rooms 8 en suite 18 annexe en suite (4 fmly) (16 GF) D £100-£200 (incl. bkfst) **Facilities** ch fac Xmas New Year **Parking** 50 **Notes** LB

WEST RUNTON — MAP 09 TG14

►►►► **West Runton Camping & Caravanning Club Site** *(TG189419)*

Holgate Ln NR27 9NW

☎ 01263 837544

web: www.thefriendlyclub.co.uk

Dir: *From King's Lynn on A148 towards West Runton. Left at Roman Camp Inn. Site track on right at crest of hill, 0.5m to site opposite National Trust sign*

PETS: disp bin **Exercise area** on site **Facilities** walks info vet info **Other** prior notice required

Open 2 Apr-2 Nov Last arrival 21.00hrs Last departure noon

A lovely, well-kept site with some gently sloping pitches on pleasantly undulating ground. This peaceful park is surrounded on three sides by woodland, with the fourth side open to fields and the coast beyond. The very well equipped family rooms and toilet blocks are excellent. A 15-acre site with 200 touring pitches, 3 hardstandings.

Notes Site gates closed 23.00hrs-07.00hrs

ENGLAND

WORSTEAD

MAP 09 TG32

★★★★ GUEST HOUSE

The Ollands

Swanns Yard NR28 9RP
☎ 01692 535150 01692 535150
e-mail: theollands@btinternet.com
Dir: *Off A149 to village x-rds, off Back St*

PETS: Bedrooms (1GF) **Charges** £3 per night charge for damage **Public areas** except dining room **Grounds** accessible disp bin **Exercise area Facilities** walks info vet info **On Request** torch **Restrictions** small & medium sized dogs only
Resident Pets: Candy, Dusti, Mouse & Abbs (Burmese cats)

This charming detached property is set in the heart of the picturesque village of Worstead. The well-equipped bedrooms are pleasantly decorated and carefully furnished, and breakfast served in the elegant dining room features local produce.

Rooms 3 en suite (1 GF) S £35.50-£37.50; D £56-£60* **Facilities** TVB tea/coffee Cen ht TVL Dinner Last d 9am **Parking** 8 **Notes** LB No coaches

NORTHAMPTONSHIRE

CRICK

MAP 04 SP57

★★★ 70% HOTEL

Holiday Inn Rugby/Northampton

NN6 7XR
☎ 0870 400 9059 & 0800 405060 01788 823 8955
e-mail: rugbyhi@ihg.com
web: www.holidayinn.co.uk
Dir: *0.5m from M1 junct 18*

PETS: Bedrooms (42GF) sign **Charges** charge for damage **Public areas** except eating areas (on leads) **Grounds** accessible on leads **Exercise area Facilities** walks info vet info

Situated in pleasant surroundings, located just off M1 Junction 18, this modern hotel offers well-equipped and comfortable bedrooms. Public areas include the popular Traders restaurant & a comfortable lounge where a menu is available to guests all day. Spirit Health club provides indoor swimming & a good fitness facility.

Rooms 90 en suite (19 fmly) (42 GF) S £65-£150; D £65-£150* **Facilities** STV Gym Wi-fi available New Year **Services** Lift air con **Parking** 250 **Notes** LB

BUDGET HOTEL

Ibis Rugby East

Parklands NN6 7EX
☎ 01788 824331 01788 824332
e-mail: H3588@accor-hotels.com
web: www.ibishotel.com
Dir: *M1 junct 18, follow Daventry/Rugby A5 signs. At rdbt 3rd exit signed DIRFT East. Hotel on right*

PETS: Bedrooms (12GF) **Charges** £10 per night **Public areas** except restaurant (on leads) **Grounds** accessible on leads **Exercise area Facilities** vet info

Modern, budget hotel offering comfortable accommodation in bright and practical bedrooms. Breakfast is self-service and dinner is available in the restaurant.

Rooms 111 en suite

DAVENTRY

MAP 04 SP56

★★★★ 71% HOTEL

Barceló Daventry Hotel

Barceló

Sedgemoor Way NN11 0SG
☎ 01327 307000 01327 706313
e-mail: daventry@barcelo-hotels.co.uk
web: www.barcelo-hotels.co.uk
Dir: *M1 junct 16/A45 to Daventry, at 1st rdbt turn right to Kilsby/ M1(N). Hotel on right in 1m*

PETS: Bedrooms unattended **Charges** £15 per night charge for damage **Grounds** accessible on leads disp bin **Exercise area** parks **Facilities** washing facs cage storage walks info vet info **On Request** fridge access torch

This modern, striking hotel overlooking Drayton Water boasts spacious public areas that include a good range of banqueting, meeting and leisure facilities. It is a popular venue for conferences. Bedrooms are suitable for both business and leisure guests.

Rooms 155 en suite (14 fmly) S £55-£135* **Facilities** supervised Gym Wi-fi available Steam room Health & beauty salon **Services** Lift **Parking** 350

WELLINGBOROUGH MAP 04 SP86

BUDGET HOTEL

Ibis Wellingborough

Enstone Court NN8 2DR

☎ 01933 228333 📠 01933 228444

e-mail: H3164@accor-hotels.com

web: www.ibishotel.com

Dir: *at junct of A45 & A509 towards Kettering, SW outskirts of Wellingborough*

PETS: Bedrooms (2GF) **Public areas** except lounge & dining room **Grounds** accessible **Exercise area** field nearby **Facilities** vet info

Modern, budget hotel offering comfortable accommodation in bright and practical bedrooms. Breakfast is self-service and dinner is available in the restaurant.

Rooms 78 en suite

NORTHUMBERLAND

ALNWICK MAP 12 NU11

★★★★ GUEST ACCOMMODATION

Rock Farm House B & B

Rock NE66 3SE

☎ 01665 579367

e-mail: stay@rockfarmhouse.co.uk

Dir: *Off A1 into village centre*

PETS: Bedrooms Stables nearby (2m) **Charges** £7.50 per stay per night charge for damage **Grounds** accessible on leads disp bin **Exercise area** on site large grounds **Facilities** water bowl leads pet sitting washing facs cage storage walks info vet info **On Request** fridge access torch towels **Resident Pets:** Wrangler & Milo (Golden Retrievers), Asti & TC (cats)

Do not be misled by the surroundings of this old farmhouse. Inside, a loving restoration has transformed it into a delightful home. The spacious and comfortable bedrooms upstairs look out onto walled gardens, and downstairs there is a cosy lounge with a wood-burning stove and a charming dining room where breakfast (with healthy options) is served at a large pine table.

Rooms 3 en suite (1 fmly) **Facilities** FTV TVB tea/coffee Cen ht **Parking** 10

BAMBURGH MAP 12 NU13

★★★ 78% COUNTRY HOUSE HOTEL

Waren House

Waren Mill NE70 7EE

☎ 01668 214581 📠 01668 214484

e-mail: enquiries@warenhousehotel.co.uk

web: www.warenhousehotel.co.uk

Dir: *2m E of A1 turn onto B1342 to Waren Mill, at T-junct turn right, hotel 100yds on right*

PETS: Bedrooms (1GF) **Charges** charge for damage **Exercise area** 20mtrs **Facilities** vet info **On Request** fridge access torch

This delightful Georgian mansion is set in six acres of woodland and offers a welcoming atmosphere and views of the coast. The individually themed bedrooms and suites include many with large bathrooms. Good, home-cooked food is served in the elegant dining room. A comfortable lounge and library are also available.

Rooms 13 en suite (1 GF) S £85-£143; D £113-£223 (incl. bkfst)✳ **Facilities** FTV Wi-fi available Xmas New Year **Parking** 20 **Notes** No children 14yrs

►►► **Glororum Caravan Park** *(NU166334)*

Glororum Farm NE69 7AW

☎ 01668 214457 📠 01688 214484

web: www.northumbrianleisure.co.uk

Dir: *Exit A1 at junct with B1341 (Purdy's Lodge). In 3.5m left onto unclass road. Site 300yds on left*

PETS: Stables nearby (5m) (loose box) disp bin **Public areas** (on leads) except in children's play area **Exercise area** on site dog walks **Facilities** on site shop food food bowl water bowl dog scoop/disp bags washing facs walks info vet info **Other** prior notice required **Restrictions** friendly dogs only **Resident Pets:** dogs, cats

Open Etr-end Oct Last arrival 18.00hrs Last departure noon

A pleasantly situated site where tourers have their own well-established facilities. The open countryside setting affords good views of Bamburgh Castle and surrounding farmland. A 6-acre site with 100 touring pitches and 150 statics.

Notes No tents

BEADNELL MAP 12 NU22

►► Beadnell Bay Camping & Caravanning Club Site *(NU231297)*

NE67 5BX
☎ 01665 720586
web: www.thefriendlyclub.co.uk

Dir: *A1 onto B1430 signed Seahouses. At Beadnell ignore signs for Beadnell village. Site on left after village, just after left bend*

PETS: Exercise area on site dog walk **Facilities** walks info vet info **Other** prior notice required

Open 27 Apr-28 Sep Last arrival 21.00hrs Last departure noon

A level grassy site in a coastal area just across the road from the sea and sandy beach. Popular with divers, anglers, surfboarders and canoeists, and ideal for visiting many tourist attractions. Motorvans and tents only. A 6-acre site with 150 touring pitches.

Notes Site gates closed 23.00hrs-07.00hrs

BELFORD MAP 12 NU13

★★ 74% HOTEL

Purdy Lodge

Adderstone Services NE70 7JU
☎ 01668 213000 📠 01668 213131
e-mail: stay@purdylodge.co.uk
web: www.purdylodge.co.uk

Dir: *turn off A1 onto B1341 then immediately left*

PETS: Bedrooms (10GF) **Charges** charge for damage **Public areas** except restaurant & bar **Grounds** accessible on leads **Exercise area** adjacent

Situated on the A1, this family-owned lodge provides quiet bedrooms that look out over fields towards Bamburgh Castle. Food is readily available in the attractive restaurant, the smart 24-hour café, and the cosy lounge bar.

Rooms 20 en suite (4 fmly) (10 GF) **Parking** 60

BELLINGHAM MAP 12 NY88

►►►► Bellingham Brown Rigg Camping & Caravanning Club Site *(NY835826)*

Brown Rigg NE48 2JY
☎ 01434 220175
web: www.thefriendlyclub.co.uk

Dir: *From A69 take A68 N. Then B6318 to Chollerford & B6320 to Bellingham. Pass Forestry Commission land, site 0.5m S of Bellingham*

PETS: Exercise area Facilities washing facs walks info vet info **Other** prior notice required

Open Apr-Oct Last arrival 21.00hrs Last departure noon

A beautiful and peaceful site set in the glorious Northumberland National Park. This is a perfect base for exploring this undiscovered part of England, and it is handily placed for visiting the beautiful Northumberland coast. The site has been recently refurbished to a very good standard. A 5-acre site with 64 touring pitches, 64 hardstandings.

Notes Site gates closed 23.00hrs-07.00hrs

BERWICK-UPON-TWEED MAP 12 NT95

★★★ 70% COUNTRY HOUSE HOTEL

Marshall Meadows Country House

TD15 1UT
☎ 01289 331133 📠 01289 331438
e-mail: gm.marshallmeadows@classiclodges.co.uk
web: www.classiclodges.co.uk

Dir: *signed directly off A1, 300yds from Scottish border*

PETS: Bedrooms Charges Grounds accessible **Exercise area Other** dogs accepted by prior arrangement only; certain bedrooms only available

This stylish Georgian mansion is set in wooded grounds flanked by farmland and has convenient access from the A1. A popular venue for weddings and conferences, it offers comfortable and well-equipped bedrooms. Public rooms include a cosy bar, a relaxing lounge and a two-tier restaurant, which serves imaginative dishes.

Rooms 19 en suite (1 fmly) **Facilities** ⚘ **Parking** 87 **Notes** LB

►►►►► Ord House Country Park *(NT982515)*

East Ord TD15 2NS
☎ 01289 305288 📠 01289 330832
e-mail: enquiries@ordhouse.co.uk
web: www.ordhouse.co.uk

Dir: *On A1, Berwick bypass, turn off at 2nd rdbt at East Ord, follow 'Caravan' signs*

PETS: Charges up to £1.50 per night **Public areas** except club house unless assist dog **Exercise area** on site 2km walk **Facilities** walks info vet info **Other** prior notice required **Restrictions** max 1 large & 2 small breed per family no dangerous breeds (see page 7) & no Rottweilers or Dobermans

Open all year Last arrival 23.00hrs Last departure noon

A very well run park set in the pleasant grounds of an 18th-century country house. Touring pitches are marked and well spaced, some of them fully-serviced. The very modern toilet facilities include family bath and shower suites, and first class disabled rooms. There is a six-hole golf course and an outdoor leisure shop with a good range of camping and caravanning spares, as well as clothing and equipment. A 42-acre site with 79 touring pitches, 46 hardstandings and 255 statics.

ENGLAND

CORNHILL-ON-TWEED MAP 12 NT83

★★★ 86% HOTEL

Tillmouth Park Country House

TD12 4UU

☎ 01890 882255 01890 882540

e-mail: reception@tillmouthpark.force9.co.uk

web: www.tillmouthpark.co.uk

Dir: *off A1(M) at East Ord rdbt at Berwick-upon-Tweed. Take A698 to Cornhill and Coldstream. Hotel 9m on left*

PETS: Bedrooms unattended **Public areas** bar only (on leads) **Grounds** accessible on leads disp bin **Exercise area** on site **Facilities** water bowl vet info **Resident Pets:** Carter & Teal (Black Labradors)

An imposing mansion set in landscaped grounds by the River Till. Gracious public rooms include a stunning galleried lounge with a drawing room adjacent. The quiet, elegant dining room overlooks the gardens, whilst lunches and early dinners are available in the bistro. Bedrooms retain much traditional character and include several magnificent master rooms.

Rooms 12 en suite 2 annexe en suite (1 fmly) S £68; D £90-£195 (incl. bkfst)* **Facilities** FTV Wi-fi available Game shooting Fishing New Year **Parking** 50 **Notes** LB Closed 2 Jan-6 Apr 09

CRASTER MAP 12 NU21

►►► Dunstan Hill Camping & Caravanning Club Site *(NU236214)*

Dunstan Hill, Dunstan NE66 3TQ

☎ 01665 576310

web: www.thefriendlyclub.co.uk

Dir: *From A1, just N of Alnwick, take B1340 signed Seahouses. Continue to T-junct at Criston Bank, turn right. 2nd right signed Embleton. Right at x-rds then 1st left signed Craster*

PETS: disp bin **Exercise area** on site dog walk **Facilities** walks info vet info **Other** prior notice required

Open 2 Apr-2 Nov Last arrival 21.00hrs Last departure noon

An immaculately maintained site with pleasant landscaping, close to the beach and Craster harbour. The historic town of Alnwick is nearby, as is the ruined Dunstanburgh Castle. A 14-acre site with 150 touring pitches, 20 hardstandings.

Notes Site gates closed 23.00hrs-07.00hrs

EMBLETON MAP 12 NU22

★★ 76% HOTEL

Dunstanburgh Castle Hotel

NE66 3UN

☎ 01665 576111 01665 576203

e-mail: stay@dunstanburghcastlehotel.co.uk

web: www.dunstanburghcastlehotel.co.uk

Dir: *from A1, take B1340 to Denwick past Rennington & Masons Arms. Take next right signed Embleton, and into village*

PETS: Bedrooms unattended **Grounds** accessible disp bin **Exercise area** 10mtrs **Facilities** dog scoop/disp bags walks info vet info **On Request** fridge access torch towels **Resident Pets:** Uncle Bob (dog)

The focal point of the village, this friendly, family-run hotel has a dining room and grill room that offer different menus, plus a cosy bar and two lounges. In addition to the main bedrooms, a barn conversion houses three stunning suites, each with a lounge and gallery bedroom above.

Rooms 20 en suite (4 fmly) S £37.50-£52.50; D £75-£105 (incl. bkfst)* **Parking** 16 **Notes** LB Closed Dec-Jan

FALSTONE MAP 12 NY78

★★★ INN

The Blackcock Inn

NE48 1AA

☎ 01434 240200 01434 240200

e-mail: thebcinn@yahoo.co.uk

Dir: *In village centre, towards to Kielder Water*

PETS: Bedrooms unattended **Stables** nearby (adjacent) **Charges** charge for damage **Public areas** except restaurant **Grounds** accessible on leads disp bin **Exercise area** adjacent **Facilities** food (pre-bookable) food bowl water bowl bedding dog chews cat treats feeding mat litter tray etc dog scoop/disp bags leads cage storage walks info vet info **On Request** torch **Other** squeaky toys available **Resident Pets:** Pooch (dog), Eyeful, Cello, Banjo & Sno (cats), Rosso (rabbit), Hallo (fish)

This traditional family-run village inn lies close to Kielder Water. A cosy pub, it has a very homely atmosphere, with a welcoming fire in the bar in the colder weather. Evening meals are served here in the cosy restaurant, which is reminiscent of a Victorian parlour. The inn is closed during the day on Tuesdays throughout winter.

Rooms 6 rms (4 en suite) (1 fmly) S fr £40; D fr £70* **Facilities** TVB tea/coffee Cen ht Dinner Last d 8.30pm Fishing Pool Table **Parking** 15 **Notes** LB RS Tue

HALTWHISTLE — MAP 12 NY76

►►► Haltwhistle Camping & Caravanning Club Site *(NY685621)*

Burnfoot Park Village NE49 0JP

☎ 01434 320106

web: www.thefriendlyclub.co.uk

Dir: *From A69 Haltwhistle bypass (NB do not enter town) take Alston Road S signed A689, then right signed Kellan*

PETS: disp bin **Exercise area** on site dog walk **Facilities** walks info vet info **Other** prior notice required

Open 2 Apr-2 Nov Last arrival 21.00hrs Last departure noon

An attractive site on the banks of the River South Tyne amidst mature trees, on the Bellister Castle estate. This peaceful, relaxing site is a good cross country transit stop in excellent walking country. A 3.5-acre site with 50 touring pitches, 15 hardstandings.

Notes Site gates closed 23.00hrs-07.00hrs

MATFEN — MAP 12 NZ07

★★★★ 81% HOTEL

Matfen Hall

CLASSIC BRITISH HOTELS

NE20 0RH

☎ 01661 886500 & 855708 01661 886055

e-mail: info@matfenhall.com

web: www.matfenhall.com

Dir: *off A69 to B6318. Hotel just before village*

PETS: Bedrooms unattended **Charges** £7.50 per night charge for damage **Grounds** accessible on leads disp bin **Exercise area** **Facilities** washing facs cage storage walks info vet info **On Request** fridge access torch towels

This fine mansion lies in landscaped parkland overlooking its own golf course. Bedrooms are a blend of contemporary and traditional, but all are very comfortable and well equipped. Impressive public rooms include a splendid drawing room and the elegant Library and Print Room Restaurant, as well as a conservatory bar and very stylish spa, leisure and conference facilities.

Rooms 53 en suite (11 fmly) S £115-£190; D £175-£270 (incl. bkfst)* **Facilities** Spa STV FTV supervised 27 Gym Putt green Wi-fi available Sauna Steam room Salt grotto Ice fountain Aerobics Driving range Golf academy Xmas **Services** Lift **Parking** 150 **Notes** LB

OTTERBURN — MAP 12 NY89

★★★ 75% HOTEL

The Otterburn Tower Hotel

NE19 1NT

☎ 01830 520620 01830 521504

e-mail: info@otterburntower.com

web: www.otterburntower.com

Dir: *in village, on A696 (Newcastle to Edinburgh road)*

PETS: Bedrooms Stables nearby (at adjacent stud farm) **Charges** £10 per night **Public areas** except restaurant (on leads) **Grounds** accessible on leads disp bin **Exercise area** on site **Facilities** food (pre-bookable) food bowl water bowl dog scoop/ disp bags washing facs cage storage walks info vet info **On Request** fridge access torch towels **Resident Pets:** Pete (Jack Russell)

Built by the cousin of William the Conqueror, this mansion is set in its own wooded grounds. The hotel is steeped in history, and Sir Walter Scott stayed here in 1812. Bedrooms come in a variety of sizes and some have huge ornamental fireplaces; though furnished in period style, they are equipped with all modern amenities. The restaurant features 16th-century oak panelling.

Rooms 18 en suite (2 fmly) (2 GF) S £65; D £130-£190 (incl. bkfst) **Facilities** Fishing Wi-fi in bedrooms Clay target shooting ch fac Xmas New Year **Parking** 70 **Notes** LB

NOTTINGHAMSHIRE

HOLME PIERREPONT — MAP 08 SK63

★★★ GUEST ACCOMMODATION

Holme Grange Cottage

Adbolton Ln NG12 2LU

☎ 0115 981 0413

e-mail: jean.colinwightman@talk21.com

Dir: *Off A52 SE of Nottingham, opp National Water Sports Centre*

PETS: Bedrooms Public areas Grounds accessible disp bin **Exercise area** 100yds **Facilities** cage storage walks info vet info **On Request** fridge access torch **Other** dogs are accepted by arrangement only **Restrictions** only 1 large dog at a time **Resident Pets:** Peggy (Cavalier King Charles Spaniel)

A stone's throw from the National Water Sports Centre, this establishment with its own all-weather tennis court is ideal for the active guest. Indeed, when not providing warm hospitality and freshly cooked breakfasts, the proprietor is usually on the golf course.

Rooms 3 rms (1 en suite) (1 fmly) S £28-£34; D £48-£54* **Facilities** TVB tea/coffee Cen ht TVL **Parking** 6 **Notes** LB Closed Xmas

ENGLAND

NOTTINGHAM MAP 08 SK54

★★★★ 82% HOTEL

Hart's

Standard Hill, Park Row NG1 6FN
☎ 0115 988 1900 0115 947 7600
e-mail: ask@hartshotel.co.uk
web: www.hartsnottingham.co.uk

Dir: *at junct of Park Row & Rope Walk, close to city centre*

PETS: Bedrooms (7GF) **Charges** £5 per night charge for damage **Exercise area** local walks **Facilities** food (pre-bookable) walks info vet info **On Request** fridge access torch towels **Restrictions** some breeds may not be accepted, please telephone for details

This outstanding modern building stands on the site of the ramparts of the medieval castle, overlooking the city. Many of the bedrooms enjoy splendid views. Rooms are well appointed and stylish, while the Park Bar is the focal point of the public areas; service is professional and caring. Fine dining is offered at nearby Hart's Restaurant. Secure parking and private gardens are an added bonus.

Rooms 32 en suite (1 fmly) (7 GF) S £120; D £120-£170* **Facilities** STV FTV Gym Wi-fi in bedrooms Small unsupervised exercise room Xmas New Year **Services** Lift **Parking** 19 (charged)

★★★★ TOWN HOUSE HOTEL

Lace Market

29-31 High Pavement NG1 1HE
☎ 0115 852 3232 0115 852 3223
e-mail: stay@lacemarkethotel.co.uk
web: www.lacemarkethotel.co.uk

Dir: *follow tourist signs for Galleries of Justice. Hotel opposite*

PETS: Bedrooms Charges £15 per night charge for damage **Public areas** in gastro-pub only (on leads) **Exercise area** 100mtrs **Facilities** water bowl cage storage walks info vet info **On Request** fridge access torch towels **Restrictions** small dogs only

This smart town house, a conversion of two Georgian houses, is located in the trendy Lace Market area of the city. Smart public areas, including the stylish and very popular Merchants Restaurant and Saints Bar, are complemented by the 'Cock and Hoop', a traditional pub offering real ales and fine wines. Accommodation is stylish and contemporary and includes spacious superior rooms and split-level suites; are all thoughtfully equipped with a host of extras including CD players and mini bars.

Rooms 42 en suite **Facilities** Wi-fi in bedrooms Complimentary use of nearby health club, including indoor pool. ♫ **Services** Lift **Notes** LB

ENGLAND

★★★ 71% HOTEL

Best Western Bestwood Lodge

Bestwood Country Park, Arnold NG5 8NE

☎ 0115 920 3011 ▤ 0115 964 9678

e-mail: bestwoodlodge@btconnect.com

web: www.bw-bestwoodlodge.co.uk

Dir: *3m N off A60. Left at lights into Oxclose Ln, right at next lights into Queens Bower Rd. 1st right. Keep right at fork in road*

PETS: Bedrooms unattended **Charges** £10 per night **Grounds** accessible **Exercise area** nearby country park **Other** Please telephone for details

Set in 700 acres of parkland this Victorian building, once a hunting lodge, has stunning architecture that includes Gothic features and high vaulted ceilings. Bedrooms include all modern comforts, suitable for both business and leisure guests, and the popular restaurant serves an extensive menu.

Rooms 39 en suite (5 fmly) **Facilities** Riding Wi-fi in bedrooms Guided walks **Parking** 120 **Notes** RS 25 Dec & 1 Jan

★★★ 70% HOTEL

Rutland Square Hotel

St James St NG1 6FJ

☎ 0115 941 1114 ▤ 0115 941 0014

e-mail: rutland.square@forestdale.com

web: www.forestdale.com

Dir: *follow signs to castle. Hotel on right 50yds beyond castle*

PETS: Bedrooms sign **Charges** £7.50 per night **Public areas** except bar & restaurant (muzzled) (on leads) **Exercise area Facilities** food (pre-bookable) food bowl water bowl vet info **On Request** fridge access towels

The enviable location in the heart of the city adjacent to the castle makes this hotel a popular choice with both leisure and business travellers. The hotel is modern and comfortable with excellent business facilities. Bedrooms offer a host of thoughtful extras to guests and the penthouse has its own jacuzzi. The contemporary Woods Restaurant offers a full range of dining options.

Rooms 87 en suite (3 fmly) S £79-£85; D £105-£109 (incl. bkfst)✳ **Facilities** Wi-fi in bedrooms Discounted day passes to nearby gym Xmas **Services** Lift **Parking** 30 (charged) **Notes** LB

★★★ 67% HOTEL

Nottingham Gateway

Nuthall Rd, Cinderhill NG8 6AZ

☎ 0115 979 4949 ▤ 0115 979 4744

e-mail: sales@nottinghamgatewayhotel.co.uk

web: www.nottinghamgatewayhotel.co.uk

Dir: *M1 junct 26, A610, hotel on 3rd rdbt on left*

PETS: Bedrooms unattended **Charges** charge for damage **Exercise area Facilities** cage storage walks info vet info **On Request** fridge access torch towels

Located approximately three miles from the city centre, and with easy access to the M1. This modern hotel provides spacious public areas, with a popular restaurant and lounge bar, and the contemporary accommodation is suitably well equipped. Ample parking is a bonus.

Rooms 108 en suite (18 fmly) S £50-£85; D £55-£100 (incl. bkfst) **Facilities** STV FTV Wi-fi available Xmas New Year **Services** Lift **Parking** 250 **Notes** LB

RADCLIFFE ON TRENT — MAP 08 SK63

►►► Thornton's Holt Camping Park

(SK638377)

Stragglethorpe Rd, Stragglethorpe NG12 2JZ

☎ 0115 933 2125 & 933 4204 ▤ 0115 933 3318

e-mail: camping@thorntons-holt.co.uk

web: www.thorntons-holt.co.uk

Dir: *Take A52, 3m E of Nottingham. Turn S at lights towards Cropwell Bishop. Site 0.5m on left. Or A46 SE of Nottingham. N at lights. Site 2.5m on right*

PETS: Public areas except swimming pool & central toilet block **Exercise area** on site public footpaths **Facilities** on site shop washing facs walks info vet info **Resident Pets:** Pickle (Border Terrier), Sprocket, Perkins & Scrabble (cats), Eric (horse)

Open all year (rs 2 Nov-24 Mar no pool, shop or games room) Last arrival 21.00hrs Last departure 13.00hrs

A well-run family site in former meadowland, with pitches located among young trees and bushes for a rural atmosphere and outlook. The toilets are housed in converted farm buildings, and an indoor swimming pool is a popular attraction. A 13-acre site with 155 touring pitches, 35 hardstandings.

Notes Noise curfew at 22.00hrs

RETFORD (EAST) MAP 08 SK78

★★★ 74% HOTEL

Best Western West Retford

24 North Rd DN22 7XG

☎ 01777 706333 & 0870 609 6162

📠 01777 709951

e-mail: reservations@westretfordhotel.co.uk

web: www.westfordhotel.co.uk

Dir: *From A1 take A620 to Ranby/Retford. Left at rdbt into North Rd (A638). Hotel on right*

PETS: Bedrooms (32GF) unattended **Stables** nearby (3m) **Charges** £10 per night charge for damage **Grounds** accessible on leads disp bin **Exercise area** adjacent **Facilities** walks info vet info **Restrictions** dogs accepted only at manager's discretion

Stylishly appointed throughout, and set in very attractive gardens close to the town centre, this 18th-century manor house offers a good range of well-equipped meeting facilities. The spacious, well-laid out bedrooms and suites are located in separate buildings and all offer modern facilities and comforts.

Rooms 63 en suite (32 GF) S £75-£97; D £85-£104 (incl. bkfst)✻ **Facilities** FTV Wi-fi available Xmas New Year **Parking** 150

SOUTHWELL MAP 08 SK65

★★★ GUEST HOUSE

The Old Forge

Burgage Ln NG25 0ER

☎ 01636 812809 📠 01636 816302

e-mail: theoldforgesouthwell@yahoo.co.uk

Dir: *Off A612 past Minster, Church St, left onto Newark Rd, 2nd left onto Burgage Ln*

PETS: Bedrooms (1GF) **Charges** £2 per night **Public areas** except dining room **Exercise area** 0.5m **Facilities** walks info vet info **Restrictions** no large dogs **Resident Pets:** 2 dogs

An interesting house packed with pictures and antique furniture, the Old Forge is central and handy for the Minster, while its own parking also makes this a good touring base. Bedrooms are comfortable and a secluded conservatory-lounge and spacious breakfast room are available.

Rooms 3 en suite 1 annexe en suite (1 GF) S £48-£60; D £78✻ **Facilities** TVB tea/coffee Direct dial from bedrooms Cen ht **Parking** 4 **Notes** No coaches

TEVERSAL MAP 08 SK46

►►►► **Teversal Camping & Caravanning Club Site** *(SK472615)*

Silverhill Ln NG17 3JJ

☎ 01623 551838

web: www.thefriendlyclub.co.uk

Dir: *M1 junct 28 onto A38 towards Mansfield. Left at lights onto B6027. At top of hill straight over at lights & left at Peacock Hotel. Right onto B6014, left at Craven Arms, site on left*

PETS: disp bin **Exercise area Facilities** on site shop walks info vet info **Other** prior notice required

Open all year Last arrival 21.00hrs Last departure noon

A top notch park with excellent purpose-built facilities, set in a rural former mining area. Each pitch is spacious, and there are views of and access to the surrounding countryside and nearby Silverhill Community Woods. The attention to detail and all-round quality are truly exceptional. A 6-acre site with 126 touring pitches, 58 hardstandings and 1 static.

Notes Site gates closed 23.00hrs-07.00hrs

WORKSOP MAP 08 SK57

★★★ 78% HOTEL

Best Western Lion

112 Bridge St S80 1HT

☎ 01909 477925 📠 01909 479038

e-mail: reception@thelionworksop.co.uk

web: www.thelionworksop.co.uk

Dir: *A57 to town centre, turn at Walkers Garage on right, follow to Norfolk Arms, turn left*

PETS: Bedrooms (7GF) unattended sign **Charges** £8 per night charge for damage **Grounds** accessible on leads disp bin **Exercise area** 2 mins **Facilities** walks info vet info **On Request** torch towels

This former coaching inn lies on the edge of the main shopping precinct, with a car park to the rear. It has been extended to offer modern accommodation that includes excellent executive rooms. A wide range of interesting dishes is offered in both the restaurant and bar.

Rooms 46 en suite (3 fmly) (7 GF) S £65-£75; D £75-£105 (incl. bkfst)✻ **Facilities** STV FTV Wi-fi in bedrooms Xmas New Year **Services** Lift **Parking** 50 **Notes** LB

►►► **Riverside Caravan Park** *(SK582790)*

Central Av S80 1ER

☎ 01909 474118

web: www.riversideworksop.co.uk

Dir: *From A57 E of town follow international camping sign to site.*

PETS: Public areas (on leads) disp bin **Exercise area** 0.25m

Open all year Last arrival 20.00hrs Last departure 14.00hrs

A very well maintained park within the attractive market town of Worksop and next door to the cricket/bowls club where Riverside customers are made welcome. This is an ideal park for those wishing to be within walking distance of all amenities yet within a 10 minute car journey of the extensive Clumber Park and numerous good garden centres. The towpath of the adjacent Chesterfield Canal provides excellent walking opportunities. A 4-acre site with 60 touring pitches, 59 hardstandings.

Notes

OXFORDSHIRE

BANBURY MAP 04 SP44

★★★ 73% HOTEL

Best Western Wroxton House

Wroxton St Mary OX15 6QB
01295 730777 01295 730800
e-mail: reservations@wroxtonhousehotel.com
web: www.maypolehotels.com
Dir: *A422 signed Banbury & Wroxton. Approx 3m, hotel on right on entering village.*

PETS: Bedrooms (7GF) unattended **Charges** £5 per night **Public areas** except restaurant (on leads) **Grounds** accessible on leads **Exercise area** 100yds **Facilities** walks info vet info **On Request** fridge access torch towels **Resident Pets:** Cocoa (Chocolate Labrador)

Dating in parts from 1647, this partially thatched hotel is set just off the main road. Bedrooms, which have either been created out of converted cottages or are situated in a more modern wing, are comfortable and well equipped. The public areas are open plan and consist of a reception lounge and a bar, and the low-beamed Inglenook Restaurant has a peaceful atmosphere for dining.

Rooms 32 en suite (1 fmly) (7 GF) S £60-£110, D £90-£134 (incl. bkfst)* **Facilities** FTV Wi-fi available Xmas New Year **Parking** 50 **Notes** LB

★★★ GUEST ACCOMMODATION

Fairlawns

60 Oxford Rd OX16 9AN
01295 262461 & 07831 330220 01295 261296
e-mail: fairlawnsgh@aol.com
Dir: *0.5m S of town centre on A4260 near hospital*

PETS: Bedrooms (9GF) **Grounds** accessible **Exercise area** park nearby **Facilities** vet info **On Request** fridge access torch towels **Resident Pets:** Rosie (Boxer), Harley (cat)

This extended Edwardian house retains many original features and has a convenient location. Bedrooms are mixed in size, and all are neatly furnished, some with direct access to the car park. A comprehensive breakfast is served in the traditional dining room and a selection of soft drinks and snacks is also available.

Rooms 12 rms (11 en suite) 6 annexe en suite (5 fmly) (9 GF) S £48; D £58* **Facilities** TVB tea/coffee Direct dial from bedrooms Cen ht Wi-fi available **Parking** 18

►►►► **Bo Peep Farm Caravan Park**

(SP481348)

Bo Peep Farm, Aynho Rd, Adderbury OX17 3NP
01295 810605 01295 810605
e-mail: warden@bo-peep.co.uk
web: www.bo-peep.co.uk
Dir: *1m E of Adderbury & A4260, on B4100 (Aynho road)*

PETS: Stables (loose box) **Charges** £1 per dog per stay per week **Exercise area** on site extensive walks disp bin **Facilities** on site shop food food bowl water bowl dog chews cat treats dog scoop/disp bags leads washing facs walks info vet info **Resident Pets:** 3 cats

Open Mar-Oct Last arrival 20.00hrs Last departure noon

A delightful park with good views and a spacious feel. Four well laid out camping areas including two with hardstandings and a separate tent field are all planted with maturing shrubs and trees. The two facility blocks are in attractive Cotswold stone. Unusually there is a bay in which you can clean your caravan or motorhome. A 13-acre site with 98 touring pitches.

Notes

BLETCHINGDON MAP 04 SP51

U

The Oxfordshire Inn

Heathfield Village OX5 3DX
01869 351444 01869 351555
e-mail: staff@oxfordshireinn.co.uk
web: www.oxfordshireinn.co.uk
Dir: *From M40 junct 9 take A34 towards Oxford, and A4027 towards Bletchingdon. Hotel signed 0.7m on right*

PETS: Bedrooms (15GF) unattended **Stables** nearby (adjacent) **Charges** £10 per night £30 per week charge for damage **Grounds** accessible disp bin **Exercise area** on site 255 acre-grounds **Facilities** walks info vet info **Other** horses can be accommodated on adjacent premises

At the time of going to press the rating for this establishment was not confirmed. This may be due to a change of ownership or because it has only recently joined the AA rating scheme. For further details please see the AA website: www.theAA.com

Rooms 28 en suite (4 fmly) (15 GF) S £65-£99; D £79-£160 (incl. bkfst)* **Facilities** Putt green Wi-fi available Golf driving range Xmas New Year **Parking** 50 **Notes** LB

ENGLAND

BURFORD MAP 04 SP21

★★★ 81% SMALL HOTEL

The Lamb Inn

CLASSIC BRITISH HOTELS

Sheep St OX18 4LR

☎ 01993 823155 01993 822228

e-mail: info@lambinn-burford.co.uk

web: www.cotswold-inns-hotels.co.uk

Dir: *Exit A40 into Burford, downhill, take 1st left into Sheep St, hotel last on right*

PETS: Bedrooms (4GF) **Charges** charge for damage **Public areas** except eating areas **Grounds** accessible on leads **Exercise area Facilities** cage storage walks info vet info **On Request** fridge access torch towels

This enchanting old inn is just a short walk from the centre of a delightful Cotswold village. An abundance of character and charm is found inside with a cosy lounge and log fire, and in intimate bar with flagged floors. An elegant restaurant offers locally sourced produce in carefully prepared dishes. Bedrooms, some with original features, are comfortable and well appointed.

Rooms 17 en suite (1 fmly) (4 GF) S £145; D £145-£255 (incl. bkfst)* **Facilities** Wi-fi in bedrooms Xmas New Year

★★★ 79% HOTEL

The Bay Tree Hotel

CLASSIC BRITISH HOTELS

Sheep St OX18 4LW

☎ 01993 822791 01993 823008

e-mail: info@baytreehotel.info

web: www.cotswold-inns-hotels.co.uk/bay-tree

Dir: *A40 or A361 to Burford. From High St turn into Sheep St, next to old market square. Hotel on right.*

PETS: Bedrooms Charges charge for damage **Public areas** except eating areas **Grounds** accessible **Exercise area Facilities** cage storage walks info vet info **On Request** fridge access torch towels

The modern decorative style combines seamlessly with features from this delightful inn's long history. Bedrooms are tastefully furnished and some have four-poster and half-tester beds. Public areas consist of a character bar, a sophisticated airy restaurant, a selection of meeting rooms and an attractive walled garden.

Rooms 8 en suite 13 annexe en suite (2 fmly) S £129; D £165-£250 (incl. bkfst)* **Facilities** Wi-fi available Xmas New Year **Parking** 50 **Notes** LB

★★ 75% HOTEL

The Inn For All Seasons

THE INDEPENDENTS HOTEL ASSOCIATION

The Barringtons OX18 4TN

☎ 01451 844324 01451 844375

e-mail: sharp@innforallseasons.com

web: www.innforallseasons.com

Dir: *3m W of Burford on A40 towards Cheltenham*

PETS: Charges £5 per night **Grounds** accessible **Exercise area** woods nearby **Other** prior notice required Please telephone for details **Resident Pets:** Bob (Black Labrador)

This 16th-century coaching inn is conveniently located near Burford. Bedrooms are comfortable, and public areas retain much period charm with original fireplaces and oak beams still remaining. A good selection of bar meals is available at lunchtime, while the evening menu includes an appetising selection of fresh fish.

Rooms 9 en suite 1 annexe en suite (2 fmly) (1 GF) S £68-£90; D £90-£115 (incl. bkfst)* **Facilities** Wi-fi available Xmas New Year **Parking** 62 **Notes** LB

BUDGET HOTEL

Travelodge Burford Cotswolds

Bury Barn OX18 4JF

☎ 08719 846 018 🖹 01993 822699

web: www.travelodge.co.uk

Dir: *A40/A361*

PETS: Bedrooms Charges £10 per stay per night **Public areas** (on leads) **Grounds** accessible on leads **Exercise area** 10 min walk **On Request** fridge access towels

Travelodge offers good quality, good value, modern accommodation. Ideal for families, the spacious en suite bedrooms include remote-control TV, tea and coffee-making facilities and comfortable beds. Meals can be taken at the nearby family restaurant.

Rooms 40 en suite S fr £29; D fr £29

★★★★ RESTAURANT WITH ROOMS

The Angel at Burford

14 Witney St OX18 4SN

☎ 01993 822714 🖹 01993 822069

e-mail: paul@theangelatburford.co.uk

web: www.theangelatburford.co.uk

Dir: *Off A40 at Burford rdbt, down hill, 1st right onto Swan Ln, 1st left to Pytts Ln, left at end onto Witney St*

PETS: Bedrooms Charges £5 per night **Public areas** except restaurant (on leads) **Grounds** accessible on leads disp bin **Exercise area** 500yds **Facilities** food bowl water bowl dog chews feeding mat dog scoop/disp bags washing facs walks info vet info **On Request** fridge access torch towels **Restrictions** no Pit Bull Terriers

Once a coaching inn in the 16th century, this establishment is situated in the centre of Burford, the Gateway to The Cotswolds. Three attractively decorated en suite bedrooms offer plentiful accessories and share a cosy resident's lounge. The award-winning restaurant is open for lunch and dinner. The peaceful courtyard and walled garden are perfect for relaxing in the summer.

Rooms 3 en suite S £70-£85; D £93-£110* **Facilities** TVB tea/coffee Direct dial from bedrooms Cen ht Dinner Last d 9pm Wi-fi available **Notes** No children 9yrs RS Mon & Sun eve

CHARLBURY — MAP 04 SP31

★★ 68% HOTEL

The Bell at Charlbury

Church St OX7 3PP

☎ 01608 810278 🖹 01608 811447

e-mail: info@bellhotel-charlbury.com

web: www.bellhotel-charlbury.com

Dir: *turn off A44 onto B4437. Once in Charlbury, 2nd left (signed Centre). Past church, hotel top of hill on right*

PETS: Bedrooms unattended **Charges** £10 per night charge for damage **Public areas** except restaurant **Grounds** accessible on leads **Exercise area** 2 mins walk **Facilities** food bowl water bowl pet sitting dog walking cage storage walks info vet info **On Request** fridge access torch towels

This mellow Cotswold-stone inn dates back to the 16th century, when it was home to Customs & Excise, and sits close to the town centre. Popular with locals, the bar has an enjoyable and relaxed atmosphere and comes complete with flagstone floors and log fires. The well-equipped bedrooms are situated in the main building and the adjacent converted barn.

Rooms 8 en suite 4 annexe en suite (6 fmly) **Facilities** Wi-fi in bedrooms **Parking** 25 **Notes** RS 25 Dec

CHIPPING NORTON — MAP 04 SP32

►►► Chipping Norton Camping & Caravanning Club Site *(SP315244)*

Chipping Norton Rd, Chadlington OX7 3PE

☎ 01608 641993

web: www.thefriendlyclub.co.uk

Dir: *Take A44 to Chipping Norton onto A361 Burford road. After 1.5m bear left at fork signed Chadlington*

PETS: disp bin **Exercise area Facilities** walks info vet info **Other** prior notice required

Open 2 Apr-2 Nov Last arrival 21.00hrs Last departure noon

A hilltop site surrounded by trees but close to a busy main road. The toilets are very clean and visitors are given the usual warm Club welcome. A 4-acre site with 105 touring pitches.

Notes Site gates closed 23.00hrs-07.00hrs

FARINGDON MAP 04 SU29

★★★ 75% HOTEL

Best Western Sudbury House Hotel & Conference Centre

London St SN7 8AA

01367 241272 01367 242346

e-mail: stay@sudburyhouse.co.uk

web: www.sudburyhouse.co.uk

Dir: *off A420, signed Folly Hill*

PETS: Bedrooms (10GF) unattended **Charges** £10 per night charge for damage **Grounds** accessible disp bin **Exercise area Facilities** food bowl water bowl washing facs cage storage walks info vet info **On Request** fridge access torch towels

Situated on the edge of the Cotswolds and set in nine acres of pleasant grounds, this hotel offers spacious and well-equipped bedrooms that are attractively decorated in warm colours. Dining options include the comfortable restaurant for a good selection of carefully presented dishes, and the bar for lighter options. A comprehensive room service menu is also available.

Rooms 49 en suite (2 fmly) (10 GF) S £50-£90; D £60-£100 (incl. bkfst)✳ **Facilities** STV Gym Wi-fi available Badminton Boules New Year **Services** Lift **Parking** 100 **Notes LB**

★★★★ FARM HOUSE

Chowle Farmhouse Bed & Breakfast

(SU272925)

Great Coxwell SN7 7SR

01367 241688 07775 669102 Mr & Mrs Muir

e-mail: info@chowlefarmhouse.co.uk

web: www.chowlefarmhouse.co.uk

Dir: *From Faringdon rdbt on A420, 2m W on right. From Watchfield rdbt 1.5m E on left*

PETS: Bedrooms (1GF) **Stables** on site **Charges** £5 per night on application per week **Grounds** accessible on leads disp bin **Exercise area** fields adjacent **Facilities** leads washing facs cage storage walks info vet info **On Request** fridge access torch towels **Other** pets allowed in one bedroom only

Resident Pets: Winston (Black Labrador), Angus, Moozer, Marvin, Denzel, Lola & Timmy (cats), guinea pig, rabbits, ferrets, tropical fish, chickens, guinea fowl

Chowle is a delightful, friendly and quiet modern farmhouse just off the A420. Bedrooms are very well equipped with a charming and airy downstairs breakfast room. There is ample parking, and the location is ideal for visiting Oxford and Swindon. Great breakfasts, and dinner is available; pre-booking preferred.

Rooms 4 en suite (1 GF) S fr £55; D fr £75✳ **Facilities** FTV TVB tea/coffee Cen ht Dinner Last d 4pm Wi-fi available Fishing Clay pigeon shooting **Parking** 10 **Notes LB** 10 acres Pedigree Beef Cattle

HENLEY-ON-THAMES MAP 04 SU78

★★★★ TOWN HOUSE HOTEL

Hotel du Vin Henley-on-Thames

Hotel du Vin & Bistro

New St RG9 2BP

01491 848400 01491 848401

e-mail: info@henley.hotelduvin.com

web: www.hotelduvin.com

Dir: *M4 junct 8/9 signed High Wycombe, take 2nd exit and onto A404 in 2m. A4130 into Henley, over bridge, through lights, up Hart St, right onto Bell St, right onto New St, hotel on right*

PETS: Bedrooms (4GF) **Charges** £10 per night £70 per week **Public areas** except restaurant (on leads) **Grounds** accessible on leads **Exercise area Facilities** food bowl water bowl bedding vet info **On Request** torch

Situated just 50 yards from the water's edge, this hotel retains the character and much of the architecture of the former Brakspears brewery. Food, and naturally wine, take on a strong focus here and guests will find an interesting mix of dishes to choose from; there are three private dining rooms where the fermentation room and old malt house used to be; alfresco dining is popular when the weather permits. Bedrooms provide comfort, style and a good range of facilities including power showers. Parking is available and there is a drop-off point in the courtyard.

Rooms 43 en suite (4 fmly) (4 GF) D £145-£160✳ **Facilities** STV Wi-fi available Use of local spa & gym Xmas New Year **Services** air con **Parking** 36 **Notes LB**

HOOK NORTON MAP 04 SP33

★★★★ INN

The Gate Hangs High

OX15 5DF

01608 737387 01608 737870

e-mail: gatehangshigh@aol.com

Dir: *0.6m N of village on x-rds*

PETS: Bedrooms (4GF) unattended **Stables** nearby **Charges** charge for damage **Public areas** except restaurant **Grounds** accessible on leads disp bin **Exercise area Facilities** food bowl water bowl walks info vet info **On Request** fridge access towels

This delightful inn located between Banbury and Chipping Norton is convenient for Oxford and the Cotswolds. Stylish spacious bedrooms are situated around a courtyard in a carefully converted barn. They are comfortably furnished and extremely well-equipped. Carefully prepared food is served in the bar or the attractive restaurant.

Rooms 4 en suite (1 fmly) (4 GF) **Facilities** FTV TVB tea/coffee Direct dial from bedrooms Cen ht Dinner Last d 10pm Golf Riding **Parking** 40

KINGHAM MAP 04 SP22

★★★ 81% ⊛⊛ HOTEL

Mill House Hotel & Restaurant

OX7 6UH

☎ 01608 658188 🖹 01608 658492

e-mail: stay@millhousehotel.co.uk

web: www.millhousehotel.co.uk

Dir: *off A44 onto B4450. Hotel indicated by tourist sign*

PETS: Bedrooms (7GF) unattended **Stables** nearby (4m) **Charges** charge for damage **Grounds** accessible disp bin **Exercise area** on site 7-acre grounds **Facilities** food (pre-bookable) food bowl water bowl dog chews dog scoop/disp bags cage storage walks info vet info **On Request** fridge access torch towels **Resident Pets:** Ben (Labrador)

This Cotswold-stone, former mill house has been carefully converted into a comfortable and attractive hotel. It is set in well-kept grounds bordered by its own trout stream. Bedrooms are comfortable and provide thoughtfully equipped accommodation. There is a peaceful lounge and bar, plus an atmospheric restaurant where the imaginative, skilfully cooked dishes are a highlight of any stay.

Rooms 21 en suite 2 annexe en suite (1 fmly) (7 GF) S £85-£95; D £120-£140 (incl. bkfst) **Facilities** STV FTV Fishing Wi-fi available Xmas New Year **Parking** 62

★★★★ ⊛ INN

The Kingham Plough

The Green OX7 6YD

☎ 01608 658327 🖹 01608 658327

e-mail: book@thekinghamplough.co.uk

Dir: *On village green*

PETS: Bedrooms unattended **Stables** nearby (opposite & 0.5m) **Charges** £10 per night charge for damage **Public areas** bar only **Grounds** accessible disp bin **Exercise area** adjacent **Facilities** food bowl water bowl bedding dog chews feeding mat dog scoop/disp bags cage storage walks info vet info **On Request** fridge access torch towels **Resident Pets:** Monkey & Ooti (Terriers)

Situated on the village green, in 'Englands favourite village', Kingham, this quintessential Cotswold inn has seven boutique en suite bedrooms that have been beautifully created for maximum comfort. The restaurant is housed in the historic tithe barn leading on from the bar area. A great countryside retreat for good food in a welcoming, relaxed environment

Rooms 4 en suite 3 annexe en suite S £70-£80; D £85-£110 **Facilities** TVB tea/coffee Cen ht Dinner Last d 8.45pm **Parking** 25 **Notes** No coaches Closed 25 Dec RS Mon & Sun eve

★★★★ INN

The Tollgate Inn & Restaurant

Church St OX7 6YA

☎ 01608 658389

e-mail: info@thetollgate.com

PETS: Bedrooms unattended **Charges** £10 per stay per night **Public areas** except restaurant & lounge **Grounds** accessible disp bin **Exercise area** on site **Facilities** washing facs walks info vet info **On Request** fridge access torch towels **Other** other facilities - please phone for details **Resident Pets:** Guinness (Black Labrador)

Situated in the idyllic Cotswold village of Kingham, this Grade II-listed Georgian building has been lovingly restored to provide a complete home-from-home among some of the most beautiful and historic countryside in Britain. The Tollgate provides comfortable, well-equipped accommodation in pleasant surroundings. A good choice of menu for lunch and dinner is available with fine use made of

CONTINUED

KINGHAM CONTINUED

fresh and local produce. You can also be sure of a hearty breakfast provided in the modern, well-equipped dining room.

Rooms 5 en suite 4 annexe en suite (1 fmly) (4 GF) **Facilities** TVB tea/ coffee Cen ht Dinner Last d 9/9.30pm Fri/Sat **Parking** 12

OXFORD MAP 04 SP50

★★★★ 76% HOTEL

Barceló Oxford Hotel

Godstow Rd, Wolvercote Roundabout OX2 8AL

☎ 01865 489988 🖷 01865 489952

e-mail: oxford@barcelo-hotels.co.uk

web: www.barcelo-hotels.co.uk

Dir: *adjacent to A34/A40, 2m from city centre*

PETS: Bedrooms (89GF) unattended sign **Charges** £15 per night charge for damage **Grounds** accessible on leads **Exercise area** at rear of hotel **Facilities** walks info vet info

Conveniently located on the northern edge of the city centre, this purpose-built hotel offers bedrooms that are bright, modern and well equipped. Guests can eat in the 'Medio' restaurant or try the Cappuccino bar menu. The hotel offers impressive conference, business and leisure facilities.

Rooms 168 en suite (11 fmly) (89 GF) S £69-£145✻ **Facilities** supervised Squash Gym Wi-fi available Steam room New Year **Parking** 250 (charged)

★★★★ ❁ TOWN HOUSE HOTEL

Old Parsonage

1 Banbury Rd OX2 6NN

☎ 01865 310210 🖷 01865 311262

e-mail: info@oldparsonage-hotel.co.uk

web: www.oldparsonage-hotel.co.uk

Dir: *from Oxford ring road to city centre via Summertown. Hotel last building on right next to St Giles Church before city centre*

PETS: Bedrooms (10GF) unattended **Charges** charge for damage **Public areas** except restaurant (on leads) **Grounds** accessible **Exercise area** 2 mins walk **Facilities** food (pre-bookable) food bowl water bowl bedding leads pet sitting dog walking cage storage walks info vet info **On Request** torch towels **Other** dog baskets available

Dating back in parts to the 16th century, this stylish hotel offers great character and charm and is conveniently located at the northern edge of the city centre. Bedrooms are attractively styled and particularly well appointed. The focal point of the operation is the busy all-day bar and restaurant; the small garden areas and terraces prove popular in summer months.

Rooms 30 en suite (4 fmly) (10 GF) S £150-£185; D £170-£185✻ **Facilities** FTV Wi-fi in bedrooms Beauty treatments Free use of nearby leisure facilities, punt & house bikes ♫ Xmas **Services** air con **Parking** 14

★★ 57% METRO HOTEL

Bath Place

4-5 Bath Place, Holywell St OX1 3SU

☎ 01865 791812 🖷 01865 791834

e-mail: info@bathplace.co.uk

Dir: *on S side of Holywell St running parallel to High St*

PETS: Bedrooms (3GF) **Charges** charge for damage **Exercise area** park 500mtrs **Facilities** walks info vet info **On Request** fridge access **Resident Pets:** Hamish (Border Terrier)

The hotel has been created from a group of 17th-century cottages originally built by Flemish weavers who were permitted to settle outside the city walls. This lovely hotel is very much at the heart of the city today and offers individually designed bedrooms, including some with four-posters.

Rooms 14 en suite (2 fmly) (3 GF) S £75-£125; D £105-£150 (incl. bkfst)✻ **Facilities** FTV Wi-fi in bedrooms **Parking** 14 (charged) **Notes** LB

BUDGET HOTEL

Travelodge Oxford Wheatley

London Rd, Wheatley OX33 1JH

☎ 0871 984 6207 🖷 01865 875905

web: www.travelodge.co.uk

Dir: *off A40 next to The Harvester on outskirts of Wheatley*

PETS: Bedrooms unattended **Charges** £10 per pet per stay per night **Public areas** (on leads) **Grounds** accessible **Exercise area Facilities** walks info vet info **On Request** fridge access torch towels

Travelodge offers good quality, good value, modern accommodation. Ideal for families, the spacious en suite bedrooms include remote-control TV, tea and coffee-making facilities and comfortable beds. Meals can be taken at the nearby family restaurant.

Rooms 36 en suite S fr £29; D fr £29

►►► Oxford Camping & Caravanning Club Site *(SP519039)*

426 Abingdon Rd OX1 4XG

☎ 01865 244088

web: www.thefriendlyclub.co.uk

Dir: *From M40 onto A34, exit at A423 for Oxford. Turn left immediately after junct into Abingdon Road, site on left behind Touchwood Sports*

PETS: Public areas disp bin **Exercise area Facilities** walks info vet info **Other** prior notice required

Open all year Last arrival 21.00hrs Last departure noon

A very busy town site with handy park-and-ride into Oxford. All pitches are on grass, and most offer electric hook-ups. A 5-acre site with 85 touring pitches.

Notes Site gates closed 23.00hrs-07.00hrs

OXFORD MOTORWAY SERVICE AREA (M40) — MAP 04 SP60

BUDGET HOTEL

Days Inn Oxford

M40 junction 8A, Waterstock OX33 1LJ

☎ 01865 877000 🖹 01865 877016

e-mail: oxford.hotel@welcomebreak.co.uk

web: www.welcomebreak.co.uk

Dir: *M40 junct 8a, at Welcome Break service area*

PETS: Bedrooms unattended **Public areas** must be kept on lead **Grounds** accessible **Exercise area**

This modern building offers accommodation in smart, spacious and well-equipped bedrooms, suitable for families and business travellers, and all with en suite bathrooms. Refreshments may be taken at the nearby family restaurant.

Rooms 59 en suite S £39-£59; D £49-£69✱

STANDLAKE — MAP 04 SP30

►►►►► Lincoln Farm Park Oxfordshire

(SP395028)

High St OX29 7RH

☎ 01865 300239 🖹 01865 300127

e-mail: lincolnfarmpark@btconnect.com

web: www.lincolnfarmpark.co.uk

Dir: *In village off A415 between Abingdon & Witney, 5m SE of Witney*

PETS: Charges £1.25 per night **Public areas** except children's play area (on leads) **Exercise area** on site 2 small dog runs disp bin **Facilities** on site shop food food bowl water bowl bedding dog chews cat treats litter tray etc dog scoop/disp bags leads walks info vet info **Other** prior notice required **Resident Pets:** Chance (Border Collie), 2 giant continental rabbits, free range chickens

Open Feb-Nov Last arrival 20.00hrs Last departure noon

An attractively landscaped park in a quiet village setting, with superb facilities and a high standard of maintenance. Family rooms, fully-serviced pitches, two indoor swimming pools and a fully-equipped gym are part of the comprehensive amenities. A 9-acre site with 90 touring pitches, 75 hardstandings and 19 statics.

Notes No gazebos, no noise after 23.00hrs

WALLINGFORD — MAP 04 SU68

★★★ 80% HOTEL

The Springs Hotel & Golf Club

Wallingford Rd, North Stoke OX10 6BE

☎ 01491 836687 🖹 01491 836877

e-mail: info@thespringshotel.com

web: www.thespringshotel.com

Dir: *off A4074 (Oxford-Reading road) onto B4009 (Goring). Hotel approx 1m on right*

PETS: Bedrooms (8GF) **Charges** £10 per night charge for damage **Grounds** accessible on leads **Exercise area** **Other** dogs allowed in certain bedrooms only

Set on its own golf course, this Victorian mansion has a timeless and peaceful atmosphere. The generously equipped bedrooms vary in size but many are spacious. The elegant restaurant enjoys splendid views over the spring-fed lake where a variety of wildfowl enjoy the natural surroundings. There is also a comfortable lounge with original features, and a cosy bar to relax in.

Rooms 32 en suite (4 fmly) (8 GF) S £95-£120; D £115-£135 (incl. bkfst)✱ **Facilities** STV FTV 18 Fishing Putt green Wi-fi in bedrooms Clay pigeon shooting nearby Horse riding Xmas New Year **Parking** 150 **Notes** LB

★★★ 74% HOTEL

Shillingford Bridge

Shillingford OX10 8LZ

☎ 01865 858567 🖹 01865 858636

e-mail: shillingford.bridge@forestdale.com

web: www.forestdale.com

Dir: *M4 junct 10, A329 through Wallingford towards Thame, then B4009 through Watlington. Right on A4074 at Benson, then left at Shillingford rdbt (unclass road) Wallingford Road*

PETS: Bedrooms (9GF) unattended sign **Charges** £7.50 per night charge for damage **Public areas** except restaurant (on leads) **Grounds** accessible on leads disp bin **Exercise area** **Facilities** food (pre-bookable) food bowl water bowl washing facs cage storage walks info vet info **On Request** fridge access torch towels

This hotel enjoys a superb position right on the banks of the River Thames, and benefits from private moorings and has a waterside open-air swimming pool. Public areas are stylish with a contemporary feel and have large picture windows making the best use of the view. Bedrooms are well equipped and furnished with guest comfort in mind.

Rooms 32 en suite 8 annexe en suite (6 fmly) (9 GF) S £89-£95; D £119-£130 (incl. bkfst)✱ **Facilities** pool supervised Fishing Wi-fi available Table tennis Xmas New Year **Parking** 100 **Notes** LB

WOODSTOCK MAP 04 SP41

★★★ 83% HOTEL

Feathers

Market St OX20 1SX

☎ 01993 812291 01993 813158

e-mail: enquiries@feathers.co.uk

Dir: *from A44 (Oxford to Woodstock), 1st left after lights. Hotel on left*

PETS: Bedrooms (2GF) unattended **Stables** nearby (1m) **Charges** £10 per night **Public areas** except restaurant & bar (on leads) **Grounds** accessible on leads disp bin **Exercise area** 0.5m **Facilities** food (pre-bookable) food bowl water bowl bedding dog chews washing facs cage storage walks info vet info **On Request** fridge access torch towels
Resident Pets: Johann (African Grey parrot)

This intimate and unique hotel enjoys a town centre location with easy access to nearby Blenheim Palace. Public areas are elegant and full of traditional character from the cosy drawing room to the atmospheric restaurant. Individually styled bedrooms are appointed to a high standard and are furnished with attractive period and reproduction furniture.

Rooms 15 en suite 5 annexe en suite (4 fmly) (2 GF) S £99-£169; D £169-£279 (incl. bkfst) **Facilities** FTV Wi-fi in bedrooms 1 suite has steam room Xmas New Year **Notes LB**

RUTLAND

CLIPSHAM MAP 08 SK91

★★★★ INN

Beech House

Main St LE15 7SH

☎ 01780 410355 01780 410000

e-mail: rooms@theolivebranchpub.com

Dir: *From A1 take B668 junct signed to Stretton and Clipsham*

PETS: Bedrooms (3GF) **Charges** £10 per night charge for damage **Public areas** bar only (on leads) **Grounds** accessible on leads **Exercise area** field 200mtrs **Facilities** water bowl washing facs walks info vet info **On Request** fridge access towels **Other** dogs allowed in ground-floor bedrooms only

This well furnished house stands over the road from the Olive Branch restaurant. It offers very well furnished bedrooms which include DVD players. Breakfasts are served in the Olive Branch. Excellent lunches and dinners are also available.

Rooms 5 en suite 1 annexe en suite (2 fmly) (3 GF) S £85-£150; D £100-£170* **Facilities** TVB tea/coffee Direct dial from bedrooms Cen ht Dinner Last d 9.30pm **Parking** 10 **Notes** No coaches Closed 24-26 Dec & 1 Jan

EMPINGHAM MAP 04 SK90

★★★ INN

The White Horse Inn

Main St LE15 8PS

☎ 01780 460221 01780 460521

e-mail: info@whitehorserutland.co.uk

web: www.whitehorserutland.co.uk

Dir: *On A606 (Oakham to Stamford road)*

PETS: Bedrooms (5GF) unattended **Charges** £5 per night **Grounds** accessible **Exercise area** 10 min walk **Facilities** cage storage walks info vet info **On Request** fridge access
Resident Pets: Tia (Chocolate Labrador)

This attractive stone-built inn, offering bright, comfortable accommodation, is conveniently located just minutes from the A1. Bedrooms in the main building are spacious and include a number of family rooms. Public areas include a well-stocked bar, a bistro and restaurant where a wide range of meals is served.

Rooms 4 en suite 9 annexe en suite (3 fmly) (5 GF) **Facilities** TVB tea/coffee Direct dial from bedrooms **Parking** 60 **Notes** Closed 25 Dec

MORCOTT — MAP 04 SK90

BUDGET HOTEL

Travelodge Uppingham Morcott

Uppingham LE15 8SA

☎ 0871 984 6113 🖹 01572 747719

web: www.travelodge.co.uk

Dir: *on A47, eastbound*

PETS: Bedrooms Charges £10 per stay charge for damage **Public areas** (on leads) **Grounds** accessible disp bin **Exercise area** Rutland Water 3m **Facilities** vet info

Travelodge offers good quality, good value, modern accommodation. Ideal for families, the spacious en suite bedrooms include remote-control TV, tea and coffee-making facilities and comfortable beds. Meals can be taken at the nearby family restaurant.

Rooms 40 en suite S fr £29; D fr £29

NORMANTON — MAP 04 SK90

★★★ 73% HOTEL

Best Western Normanton Park

Oakham LE15 8RP

☎ 01780 720315 🖹 01780 721086

e-mail: info@normantonpark.co.uk

web: www.normantonpark.com

Dir: *From A1 follow A606 towards Oakham, 1m. Turn left, 1.5m. Hotel on right*

PETS: Bedrooms (11GF) sign **Charges** £10 per night £50 per week charge for damage **Public areas** except restaurant (on leads) **Grounds** accessible on leads disp bin **Exercise area Facilities** food bowl water bowl bedding dog chews cat treats feeding mat litter tray etc dog scoop/disp bags leads walks info vet info **On Request** fridge access torch towels

This delightful hotel, on Rutland Water's south shore, is appointed to a high standard and there are two dining styles available including an extensive Chinese menu. Bedrooms are well furnished and there are ample public rooms for guest to relax in.

Rooms 23 en suite 7 annexe en suite (6 fmly) (11 GF) S £80-£90; D £80-£140 (incl. bkfst)* **Facilities** FTV Wi-fi in bedrooms Xmas New Year **Parking** 100 **Notes** LB

OAKHAM — MAP 04 SK80

★★★★ @@@@ COUNTRY HOUSE HOTEL

Hambleton Hall

Hambleton LE15 8TH

RELAIS & CHATEAUX.

☎ 01572 756991 🖹 01572 724721

e-mail: hotel@hambletonhall.com

web: www.hambletonhall.com

Dir: *3m E off A606*

PETS: Bedrooms Stables nearby (15 mins) **Charges** £10 per night £70 per week charge for damage **Grounds** accessible on leads **Exercise area Facilities** vet info

Established over 25 years ago by Tim and Stefa Hart this delightful country house enjoys tranquil and spectacular views over Rutland Water. The beautifully manicured grounds are a delight to walk in. The bedrooms in the main house are stylish, individually decorated and equipped with a range of thoughtful extras. A two-bedroom folly, with its own sitting and breakfast room, is only a short walk away. Day rooms include a cosy bar and a sumptuous drawing room, both featuring open fires. The elegant restaurant serves skilfully prepared, award-winning cuisine with menus highlighting locally sourced, seasonal produce - some grown in the hotel's own grounds.

Rooms 15 en suite 2 annexe en suite S £170-£200; D £200-£600 (incl. bkfst)* **Facilities** STV Wi-fi available Private access to lake Xmas New Year **Services** Lift **Parking** 40 **Notes** LB

ENGLAND

OAKHAM CONTINUED

★★★ 78% HOTEL

Barnsdale Lodge

The Avenue, Rutland Water, North Shore LE15 8AH

☎ 01572 724678 01572 724961

e-mail: enquiries@barnsdalelodge.co.uk

web: www.barnsdalelodge.co.uk

Dir: *off A1 onto A606. Hotel 5m on right, 2m E of Oakham*

PETS: Bedrooms (15GF) unattended **Charges** £10 per night **Public areas** in bar area only **Grounds** accessible disp bin **Exercise area Facilities** food bowl water bowl walks info vet info **On Request** fridge access torch towels **Resident Pets:** Coco & Maisie (Norfolk Terriers)

A popular and interesting hotel converted from a farmstead overlooking Rutland Water. The public areas are dominated by a very successful food operation with a good range of appealing meals on offer for either formal or informal dining. Bedrooms are comfortably appointed with excellent beds enhanced by contemporary soft furnishings and thoughtful extras.

Rooms 44 en suite (2 fmly) (15 GF) S £68.25-£89.25; D £84-£120.75 (incl. bkfst) **Facilities** STV Fishing Archery Beauty treatments Golf Shooting Xmas New Year **Parking** 200 **Notes** LB

SHROPSHIRE

CHURCH STRETTON MAP 07 SO49

★★ 75% HOTEL

Longmynd Hotel

Cunnery Rd SY6 6AG

☎ 01694 722244 01694 722718

e-mail: info@longmynd.co.uk

web: www.longmynd.co.uk

Dir: *A49 into town centre on Sandford Ave, left at Lloyds TSB, over mini-rdbt, 1st right into Cunnery Rd, hotel at top of hill on left*

PETS: Bedrooms unattended **Charges** £4 per night charge for damage **Grounds** accessible disp bin **Exercise area** on site **Facilities** food (pre-bookable) dog scoop/disp bags washing facs cage storage walks info vet info **On Request** fridge access torch towels

This family-run hotel overlooks this country town and the views from many of the rooms are breathtaking. Bedrooms are generally spacious, comfortable and well equipped. Facilities include a range of comfortable lounges and the hotel is set in attractive grounds and gardens.

Rooms 50 en suite (6 fmly) S £50-£65; D £100-£130 (incl. bkfst) **Facilities** Putt green Wi-fi available Pitch and putt Sauna Xmas New Year **Services** Lift **Parking** 100 **Notes** LB

★★★★ GUEST HOUSE

Belvedere

Burway Rd SY6 6DP

☎ 01694 722232 01694 722232

e-mail: info@belvedereguesthouse.co.uk

Dir: *Off A49 into town centre, over x-rds onto Burway Rd*

PETS: Bedrooms Grounds accessible on leads disp bin **Exercise area** 100mtrs **Facilities** food bowl water bowl washing facs cage storage walks info vet info **On Request** fridge access torch towels

Located on the lower slopes of the Long Mynd, this impressive, well-proportioned Edwardian house has a range of homely bedrooms, equipped with practical extras and complemented by modern bathrooms. Ground-floor areas include a cottage-style dining room overlooking the pretty garden and a choice of lounges.

Rooms 7 rms (6 en suite) (2 fmly) **Facilities** tea/coffee Cen ht TVL Wi-fi available **Parking** 9 **Notes** No coaches

★★★★ BED & BREAKFAST

North Hill Farm

Cardington SY6 7LL

☎ 01694 771532

e-mail: cbrandon@btinternet.com

Dir: *From Cardington village S onto Church Stretton road, right signed Cardington Moor, farm at top of hill on left*

PETS: Bedrooms (1GF) **Sep Accom** unheated, outdoor kennel with inner bench & run barn, stables **Stables** on site **Charges** £2 per night charge for damage **Public areas** except dining room **Grounds** accessible disp bin **Exercise area** on site fields adjacent **Facilities** food bowl water bowl dog scoop/disp bags leads washing facs cage storage walks info vet info **On Request** fridge access torch towels **Other** large breeds must stay in kennels **Restrictions** no Rottweilers or American Pit Bull Terriers **Resident Pets:** Saffron, Connie & Bryony (Gordon Setters), Bonnie & Millie (English Springer Spaniels), Sam (cat), Sonny & Opal (horses)

This delightful house has been modernised to provide comfortable accommodation. It is located on a fairly remote 20-acre sheep-rearing holding amid the scenery of the Shropshire hills. The lounge, with exposed beams, has log fires in cold weather. Guests share one large table in the breakfast room.

Rooms 2 rms (2 pri facs) 1 annexe en suite (1 GF) S £30; D £50-£60* **Facilities** TVB tea/coffee Cen ht **Parking** 6 **Notes LB** No children 10yrs Closed Xmas

CRAVEN ARMS — MAP 07 SO48

★★★★ BED & BREAKFAST

Castle View

Stokesay SY7 9AL

☎ 01588 673712

e-mail: castleviewb_b@btinternet.com

Dir: *On A49 S of Craven Arms opp turning to Stokesay Castle*

PETS: Bedrooms unattended **Public areas** assist dogs in dining room only **Grounds** accessible disp bin **Exercise area** **Facilities** food bowl water bowl feeding mat walks info vet info **On Request** fridge access torch towels **Resident Pets:** Cindy (Bearded Collie)

The Victorian cottage, extended about 20 years ago, stands in delightful gardens on the southern outskirts of Craven Arms, close to Stokesay Castle. Bedrooms are thoughtfully furnished, and breakfasts, featuring local produce, are served in the cosy, traditionally-furnished dining room.

Rooms 3 rms (1 en suite) (2 pri facs) S £35-£40; D £55-£60* **Facilities** TVB tea/coffee Cen ht **Parking** 4 **Notes LB** No children 3yrs

HAUGHTON — MAP 07 SJ51

► Ebury Hill Camping & Caravanning Club Site *(SJ546164)*

Ebury Hill, Ring Bank SY4 4GB

☎ 01743 709334

web: www.thefriendlyclub.co.uk

Dir: *2.5m through Shrewsbury on A53. Turn right signed Haughton & Upton Magna. Continue 1.5m site on right*

PETS: disp bin **Exercise area** on site dog walk **Facilities** walks info vet info **Other** prior notice required

Open 2 Apr-2 Nov Last arrival 21.00hrs Last departure noon

A wooded hill fort with a central lake overlooking the countryside. The site is well screened by mature trees, and there is good fishing in a disused quarry. Though there are no toilet or shower facilities, this lovely park is very popular with discerning visitors. An 18-acre site with 100 touring pitches, 21 hardstandings.

Notes Site gates closed 23.00hrs-07.00hrs

IRONBRIDGE — MAP 07 SJ60

★★★★ BED & BREAKFAST

Woodlands Farm Guest House

Beech Rd TF8 7PA

☎ 01952 432741 📠 01952 432741

e-mail: woodlandsfarm@ironbridge68.fsnet.co.uk

web: www.woodlandsfarmguesthouse.co.uk

Dir: *Off B4373 rdbt in Ironbridge onto Church Hill & Beech Rd, house on private lane 0.5m on right*

PETS: Bedrooms (3GF) sign **Charges** £5 per night charge for damage **Public areas** except dining room (on leads) **Grounds** accessible disp bin **Exercise area** 10yds **Facilities** cage storage walks info vet info **On Request** fridge access torch **Resident Pets:** Bobby & Billy (Rabbits)

Originally a brick works and then a working farm before conversion to spacious comfortable en suite bedrooms. Stylish furnishing and comfortable beds feature alongside warm hospitality. Wholesome breakfast is taken overlooking the pretty garden.

Rooms 5 en suite (1 fmly) (3 GF) S £35-£70; D £60-£80 **Facilities** STV FTV TVB tea/coffee Cen ht **Parking** 8 **Notes LB** No children 5yrs Closed 24 Dec-1 Jan

ENGLAND

KINNERLEY MAP 07 SJ32

►►► Oswestry Camping & Caravanning Club Site *(SJ366211)*

Cranberry Moss SY10 8DY

☎ 01743 741118 📠 01743 741118

web: www.thefriendlyclub.co.uk

Dir: *Turn off A5 at Wolfshead rdbt signed B4396 Knockin.*

PETS: Exercise area Facilities washing facs walks info vet info **Other** prior notice required

Open all year Last arrival 21.00hrs Last departure noon

This developing park is well positioned for visiting nearby Oswestry or Shrewsbury, and is very much the gateway to Wales. The park has excellent access from the A5. It provides excellent, well cared for facilities. A 4-acre site with 65 touring pitches, 39 hardstandings.

Notes Site gates closed 23.00hrs-07.00hrs

KNOCKIN MAP 07 SJ32

★★★★ GUEST HOUSE

Top Farm House

SY10 8HN

☎ 01691 682582 📠 01691 682070

e-mail: p.a.m@knockin.freeserve.co.uk

web: www.topfarmknockin.co.uk

Dir: *Off B4396 in village centre*

PETS: Bedrooms unattended **Charges** charge for damage **Public areas** except dining room **Grounds** accessible disp bin **Exercise area** 200mtrs **Facilities** pet sitting washing facs cage storage walks info vet info **On Request** fridge access torch **Restrictions** Telephone for details

This impressive half-timbered Tudor house, set amid pretty gardens, retains many original features including a wealth of exposed beams and open fires. Bedrooms are equipped with many thoughtful extras, and the open-plan ground-floor area includes a comfortable sitting room and elegant dining section, where imaginative comprehensive breakfasts are served.

Rooms 3 en suite (1 fmly) S £35-£45; D £65-£75* **Facilities** TVB tea/coffee Cen ht TVL **Parking** 6 **Notes LB** No coaches

LUDLOW MAP 07 SO57

★★★ 80% SMALL HOTEL

Fishmore Hall

Fishmore Rd SY8 3DP

☎ 01584 875148 & 07919 174595 📠 01584 877907

e-mail: laura@fishmorehall.co.uk

web: www.fishmorehall.co.uk

Dir: *A49 onto Henley Rd. Follow until mini rdbt, right onto Fishmore Rd, hotel on right.*

PETS: Bedrooms (1GF) unattended **Charges** charge for damage **Public areas** except restaurant **Grounds** accessible **Exercise area** adjacent **Facilities** water bowl washing facs cage storage walks info vet info **On Request** fridge access torch towels **Resident Pets:** Derek (cat)

Located in a rural area within easy reach of town centre, this Palladian styled Georgian house has been sympathetically renovated and extended to provide high standards of comfort and facilities. A contemporary styled interior highlights the many retained period features and public areas include a comfortable lounge and restaurant, the setting for imaginative cooking.

Rooms 15 en suite (1 GF) S £70-£210; D £100-£250 (incl. bkfst) **Facilities** FTV Wi-fi available Xmas New Year **Services** Lift **Parking** 48 **Notes LB**

★★ 75% SMALL HOTEL

Cliffe

Dinham SY8 2JE

☎ 01584 872063 📠 01584 873991

e-mail: thecliffehotel@hotmail.com

web: www.thecliffehotel.co.uk

Dir: *in town centre turn left at castle gates to Dinham, follow over bridge. Take right fork, hotel 200yds on left*

PETS: Bedrooms Charges £5 per night **Exercise area Resident Pets:** Megan (Black Labrador), Sally (Yellow Labrador)

Built in the 19th century and standing in extensive grounds and gardens, this privately owned and personally run hotel is quietly located close to the castle and the river. It provides well-equipped accommodation, and facilities include a lounge bar, a pleasant restaurant and a patio overlooking the garden.

Rooms 9 en suite (2 fmly) S £50-£60; D £80-£100 (incl. bkfst) **Parking** 22 **Notes LB**

★★★★ BED & BREAKFAST

Angel House

Bitterley SY8 3HT

☎ 01584 891377

e-mail: lockett1956@yahoo.co.uk

Dir: *On A4117 towards Kidderminster*

PETS: Bedrooms Charges £5 per stay **Public areas Grounds** accessible disp bin **Exercise area** local walks **Facilities** food bowl water bowl washing facs cage storage vet info **On Request** fridge access torch towels

Formally "The Angel Inn", this sympathetically renovated 17th-century establishment, located four miles east of town centre, provides comfortable bedrooms, with stunning views of the surrounding countryside. Breakfast is taken in an attractive dining room and a comfortable lounge and valley facing conservatory sitting area is also available.

Rooms 2 en suite (1 fmly) **Facilities** TVB tea/coffee Cen ht Dinner **Parking** 30 **Notes** No children 5yrs

★★★★ BED & BREAKFAST

Bromley Court B & B

58 Bridgewood Rise SY8 2ND

☎ 01584 876996

e-mail: phil@ludlowhotels.com

Dir: *Off B4361 at bridge into town centre*

PETS: Bedrooms Grounds accessible disp bin **Exercise area** 300mtrs **Facilities** washing facs walks info vet info **On Request** fridge access torch towels **Other** please phone for further details; pets allowed in certain suites only

Located close to the river and attractions of this historic town, this award-winning renovation of Georgian cottages provides split-level suites. All have comfortable sitting areas and kitchenettes; the carefully furnished bedrooms are filled with thoughtful extras and a peaceful patio garden is also available. Comprehensive continental breakfasts are available in each suite and cooked English breakfasts are available at the town centre Bull Hotel, (which is under the same ownership).

Rooms 3 en suite S £75-£115; D £75-£115 **Facilities** TVB tea/coffee Cen ht TVL **Notes LB**

★★★★ INN

Church Inn

The Buttercross SY8 1AW

☎ 01584 872174 🖷 01584 877146

web: www.thechurchinn.com

Dir: *In town centre at top of Broad St*

PETS: Bedrooms unattended **Public areas Exercise area Facilities** water bowl dog chews **Other** owners must bring dog's own bedding if required

Set right in the heart of the historic town, this Grade II listed inn has been renovated to provide quality accommodation with smart modern bathrooms, some with spa baths. Other areas include a small lounge, a well-equipped meeting room, and cosy bar areas where imaginative food and real ales are served.

Rooms 8 en suite (3 fmly) S £40-£90; D £70-£90* **Facilities** TVB tea/coffee Direct dial from bedrooms Cen ht TVL Dinner Last d 9pm **Notes** No coaches

★★★★ GUEST HOUSE

Moor Hall

Cleedownton SY8 3EG

☎ 01584 823209 🖷 08715 041324

e-mail: enquiries@moorhall.co.uk

Dir: *A4117 Ludlow to Kidderminster, left to Brignorth. B4364, follow for 3.5m, Moor Hall on right*

PETS: Bedrooms Public areas except dining room **Grounds** accessible disp bin **Exercise area** fields **Facilities** food bowl water bowl washing facs cage storage walks info vet info **Resident Pets:** 1 dog & 5 cats

This impressive Georgian house, once the home of Lord Boyne, is surrounded by extensive gardens and farmland. Bedrooms are richly decorated, well equipped, and one room has a sitting area. Public areas are spacious and comfortably furnished. There is a choice of sitting rooms and a library bar. Guests dine family-style in an elegant dining room.

Rooms 3 en suite (1 fmly) S £40-£45; D £60-£70* **Facilities** TVB tea/coffee Licensed Cen ht Dinner Last d day before Fishing **Parking** 7 **Notes LB** No coaches Closed 25-26 Dec

LUDLOW CONTINUED

★★★ FARM HOUSE

Haynall Villa *(SO543674)*

Little Hereford SY8 4BG

☎ 01584 711589 📠 01584 711589 Mrs R Edwards

e-mail: rachelmedwards@hotmail.com

web: www.haynallvilla.co.uk

Dir: *A49 onto A456, at Little Hereford turn right signed Leysters and Middleton on the Hill, 1m on right*

PETS: Bedrooms Stables nearby (300yds) **Charges** £5 per night **Public areas** except dining room & lounge **Grounds** accessible **Exercise area** adjacent **Facilities** leads washing facs cage storage walks info vet info **On Request** torch **Resident Pets:** Jerry (Springer Spaniel)

Located in immaculate gardens in the pretty hamlet of Little Hereford, this Victorian house retains many original features, which are enhanced by the furnishings and décor. Bedrooms are filled with lots of homely extras and the lounge has an open fire.

Rooms 3 rms (2 en suite) (1 fmly) S fr £30; D fr £56✱ **Facilities** TVB tea/coffee Cen ht TVL Dinner Last d 3pm Fishing **Parking** 3 **Notes** No children 6yrs 72 acres arable Closed mid Dec-mid Jan

LYNEAL (NEAR ELLESMERE) MAP 07 SJ43

►►►► Fernwood Caravan Park *(SJ445346)*

SY12 0QF

☎ 01948 710221 📠 01948 710324

e-mail: enquiries@fernwoodpark.co.uk

web: www.fernwoodpark.co.uk

Dir: *From A495 in Welshampton take B5063, over canal bridge, turn right as signed*

PETS: disp bin **Exercise area** on site adjacent woods **Facilities** on site shop food dog scoop/disp bags walks info vet info **Other** prior notice required **Resident Pets:** Poppy (Border Collie)

Open Mar-Nov Last arrival 21.00hrs Last departure 17.00hrs

A peaceful park set in wooded countryside, with a screened, tree-lined touring area and coarse fishing lake. The approach is past flower beds, and the static area which is tastefully arranged around an attractive children's playing area. There is a small child-free touring area for those wanting complete relaxation, and the park has 20 acres of woodland walks. A 26-acre site with 60 touring pitches, 8 hardstandings and 165 statics.

MUCH WENLOCK MAP 07 SO69

★★★★ FARM HOUSE

Yew Tree *(SO543958)*

Longville In The Dale TF13 6EB

☎ 01694 771866 Mr & Mrs A Hilbery

e-mail: hilbery@tiscali.co.uk

Dir: *5m SW of Much Wenlock. N off B4371 at Longville, left at pub, right at x-rds, farm 1.2m on right*

PETS: Bedrooms Sep Accom Stables nearby (6m) **Charges** charge for damage **Public areas** except dining room **Grounds** accessible disp bin **Exercise area** adjacent **Facilities** food bowl water bowl feeding mat dog scoop/disp bags leads pet sitting washing facs cage storage walks info vet info **On Request** fridge access torch towels **Restrictions** no giant breeds **Resident Pets:** Saffy & Tuli (Norfolk Terriers/Jack Russell cross), sheep, chickens

Peacefully located between Much Wenlock and Church Stretton in ten acres of unspoiled countryside, where pigs, sheep and chickens are reared, and own produce is a feature on the comprehensive breakfast menu. Bedrooms are equipped with thoughtful extras and a warm welcome is assured.

Rooms 2 rms (1 en suite) (1 pri facs) S £30-£35; D £50-£60✱ **Facilities** TVB tea/coffee Cen ht TVL **Parking** 4 **Notes LB** 10 acres small holding, sheep, pigs

OSWESTRY MAP 07 SJ22

★★★ 82% ❀❀ HOTEL

Pen-y-Dyffryn Country Hotel

WELSH RAREBITS

Rhydycroesau SY10 7JD

☎ 01691 653700 📠 01978 211004

e-mail: stay@peny.co.uk

web: www.peny.co.uk

Dir: *from A5 into Oswestry town centre. Follow signs to Llansilin on B4580, hotel 3m W of Oswestry before Rhydycroesau village*

PETS: Bedrooms (1GF) unattended **Stables** on site **Public areas** not after 6pm **Grounds** accessible disp bin **Exercise area Facilities** food bowl water bowl dog scoop/disp bags leads washing facs cage storage walks info vet info **On Request** fridge access torch towels

Peacefully situated in five acres of grounds, this charming old house dates back to around 1840, when it was built as a rectory. The tastefully appointed public rooms have real fires during cold weather, and the accommodation includes several mini-cottages, each with its own patio. This hotel attracts many guests for its food and attentive, friendly service.

Rooms 8 en suite 4 annexe en suite (1 fmly) (1 GF) S £86; D £114-£186 (incl. bkfst)✱ **Facilities** STV Riding Wi-fi in bedrooms Guided walks Xmas New Year **Parking** 18 **Notes LB** No children 3yrs Closed 18 Dec-19 Jan

★★★★ INN

The Bradford Arms

Llanymynech SY22 6EJ

☎ 01691 830582 01691 839009

e-mail: cateloo@tesco.net

Dir: *5.5m S of Oswestry on A483 in Llanymynech*

PETS: Bedrooms (2GF) **Stables** nearby (2m) **Charges** charge for damage **Public areas** except restaurant & conservatory (on leads) **Grounds** accessible on leads disp bin **Exercise area** 200yds **Facilities** water bowl washing facs cage storage walks info vet info **On Request** fridge access torch towels **Resident Pets:** Charlie (cat)

Once a coaching inn on the Earl of Bradford's estate, the Bradford Arms provides a range of carefully furnished bedrooms with a wealth of thoughtful extras. The elegant ground-floor areas include lounges, bars, and a choice of formal or conservatory restaurants, the settings for imaginative food and fine wines.

Rooms 5 en suite (2 fmly) (2 GF) S £35-£40; D £60-£70* **Facilities** TVB tea/coffee Direct dial from bedrooms Cen ht Dinner Last d 9pm Golf 18 Fishing Riding Pool Table **Parking** 20 **Notes** RS Mon

SHIFNAL — MAP 07 SJ70

★★★★ 75% HOTEL

Park House

Park St TF11 9BA

☎ 01952 460128 01952 461658

e-mail: reception@parkhousehotel.net

Dir: *M54 junct 4 follow A464 (Wolverhampton road) for approx 2m, under railway bridge, hotel 100yds on left*

PETS: Bedrooms (8GF) unattended **Charges** £20 per night **Grounds** accessible **Exercise area** 500yds **Facilities** walks info vet info **On Request** fridge access

This hotel was created from what were originally two country houses of very different architectural styles. Located on the edge of the historic market town, it offers guests easy access to motorway networks, a choice of banqueting and meeting rooms, and leisure facilities.

Rooms 38 en suite 16 annexe en suite (4 fmly) (8 GF) S £75-£90; D £90-£200 (incl. bkfst)* **Facilities** STV FTV Gym Wi-fi available Steam room Sauna Beauty room Xmas New Year **Services** Lift **Parking** 90 **Notes** LB

SHREWSBURY — MAP 07 SJ41

★★★★ 73% HOTEL

Albright Hussey Manor Hotel & Restaurant

Ellesmere Rd SY4 3AF

☎ 01939 290571 & 290523 01939 291143

e-mail: info@albrighthussey.co.uk

web: www.albrighthussey.co.uk

Dir: *2.5m N of Shrewsbury on A528, follow signs for Ellesmere*

PETS: Bedrooms unattended **Charges** £10 per night **Exercise area**

First mentioned in the Domesday Book, this enchanting medieval manor house is complete with a moat. Bedrooms are situated in either the sumptuously appointed main house or in the more modern wing. The intimate restaurant displays an abundance of original features and there is also a comfortable cocktail bar and lounge.

Rooms 26 en suite (4 fmly) (8 GF) **Facilities** Wi-fi in bedrooms **Parking** 100

★★★ 77% HOTEL

Mytton & Mermaid

Atcham SY5 6QG

☎ 01743 761220 01743 761292

e-mail: admin@myttonandmermaid.co.uk

web: www.myttonandmermaid.co.uk

Dir: *from Shrewsbury over old bridge in Atcham. Hotel opposite main entrance to Attingham Park*

PETS: Bedrooms unattended **Charges** £10 per night **Grounds** accessible disp bin **Exercise area** **Facilities** food bowl water bowl cage storage walks info vet info **On Request** fridge access **Resident Pets:** dogs

Convenient for Shrewsbury, this ivy-clad former coaching inn enjoys a pleasant location beside the River Severn. Some bedrooms, including family suites, are in a converted stable block adjacent to the hotel. There is a large lounge bar, a comfortable lounge, and a brasserie that has gained a well-deserved local reputation for the quality of its food.

Rooms 11 en suite 7 annexe en suite (1 fmly) S £80-£85; D £105-£165 (incl. bkfst)* **Facilities** Fishing Wi-fi in bedrooms New Year **Parking** 50 **Notes** Closed 25 Dec

SHREWSBURY CONTINUED

★★ 65% HOTEL

Lion & Pheasant

49-50 Wyle Cop SY1 1XJ

☎ 01743 236288 🖹 01743 244475

e-mail: lionandpheasant@aol.com

Dir: *In town centre*

PETS: Bedrooms unattended **Charges** £5 per night **Public areas** except restaurant & breakfast room (on leads) **Exercise area** 8 mins

Located close to The English Bridge and within easy walking distance of the historic centre, this traditional coaching hotel provides a range of bedrooms, some of which are situated in an extension. Public areas include a cottage style restaurant, a café bar and a cosy foyer lounge.

Rooms 27 rms (25 en suite) (2 fmly) **Parking** 22 **Notes** Closed Xmas

★★★ GUEST HOUSE

Shenandoah Guest House

Sparrow Ln, Off Abbey Ln SY2 5EP

☎ 01743 363015 🖹 01743 244918

web: www.shenandoah.org.uk

Dir: *A5 onto A5064, turn onto Abbey Foregate after 100yds right onto Sparrow Ln*

PETS: Bedrooms Charges £1 per night £5 per week charge for damage **Exercise area** 100yds **Facilities** bedding feeding mat washing facs cage storage walks info vet info **On Request** fridge access torch towels **Other** food & water bowl on request **Restrictions** small breeds only

Located between The Lord Hill Monument and Abbey, and within easy walking distance of town centre, this peacefully located modern house provides a range of thoughtfully furnished bedrooms with en suite shower rooms. Hearty breakfasts are taken in an attractive dining room and a warm welcome is assured.

Rooms 4 en suite (3 fmly) S £35; D £50-£55 **Facilities** TVB tea/coffee Cen ht **Parking** 6 **Notes LB** No coaches

►►►► Oxon Hall Touring Park *(SJ455138)*

Welshpool Rd SY3 5FB

☎ 01743 340868 🖹 01743 340869

e-mail: oxon@morris-leisure.co.uk

web: www.morris-leisure.co.uk

Dir: *Leave A5 ring road at junct with A458. Site shares entrance with 'Oxon Park & Ride'*

PETS: Charges £1 per night **Exercise area** on site 2 dog walks disp bin **Facilities** on site shop food food bowl water bowl dog chews cat treats dog scoop/disp bags leads washing facs walks info vet info **Other** prior notice required max 2 dogs per pitch

Open all year Last arrival 21.00hrs

A delightful park with quality facilities, and a choice of grass and fully-serviced pitches. An adults-only section is very popular with those wanting a peaceful holiday, and there is an inviting patio area next to reception and the shop, overlooking a small lake. This site is ideally located for visiting Shrewsbury and the surrounding countryside, and there is always a warm welcome here. A 15-acre site with 124 touring pitches, 72 hardstandings and 42 statics.

TELFORD — MAP 07 SJ60

★★★★ BED & BREAKFAST

Avenue Farm

Uppington TF6 5HW

☎ 01952 740253 & 07711 219453 🖹 01952 740401

e-mail: jones@avenuefarm.fsnet.co.uk

web: www.virtual-shropshire.co.uk/avenuefarm

Dir: *M54 junct 7, B5061 for Atcham, 2nd left signed Uppington. Right after sawmill, farm 400yds on right*

PETS: Bedrooms Sep Accom large pen **Stables** on site **Charges** £5 per night **Grounds** accessible on leads **Exercise area** 200yds **Facilities** washing facs vet info **On Request** fridge access torch **Resident Pets:** Spike (Lucas Terrier), Rosie (cat)

This impressive, well-proportioned house stands within immaculate mature gardens in the hamlet of Uppington. Quality furnishings and décor highlight the many original features, and the bedrooms are homely. A comfortable sitting room is also available.

Rooms 3 en suite (1 fmly) S £35-£40; D £55-£60* **Facilities** TV2B tea/coffee TVL Riding **Parking** 4 **Notes** Closed Xmas

TELFORD SERVICE AREA (M54) — MAP 07 SJ70

BUDGET HOTEL

Days Inn Telford

Telford Services, Priorslee Rd TF11 8TG

☎ 01952 238400 🖹 01952 238410

e-mail: telford.hotel@welcomebreak.co.uk

web: www.welcomebreak.co.uk

Dir: *M54 junct 4*

PETS: Bedrooms Public areas must be kept on lead **Grounds** accessible **Exercise area**

This modern building offers accommodation in smart, spacious and well-equipped bedrooms, suitable for families and business travellers, and all with en suite bathrooms. Refreshments may be taken at the nearby family restaurant.

Rooms 48 en suite S £39-£59; D £49-£69*

WEM MAP 07 SJ52

★★★★ GUEST ACCOMMODATION

Soulton Hall

Soulton SY4 5RS

☎ 01939 232786 🖷 01939 234097

e-mail: enquiries@soultonhall.co.uk

web: www.soultonhall.co.uk

Dir: *A49 between Shrewsbury & Whitchurch turn onto B5065 towards Wem. Soulton Hall 2m NE of Wem on B5065*

PETS: Bedrooms (3GF) **Sep Accom** dogs accepted in Coach House rooms only **Charges** £10 per night £70 per week **Grounds** accessible on leads disp bin **Exercise area** 500 acres of open land adjacent **Facilities** washing facs walks info vet info **On Request** torch towels **Resident Pets:** dog

Located two miles from historic Wem, this late 17th-century former manor house incorporates part of an even older building. The house stands in 560 acres and provides high levels of comfort. Bedrooms are equipped with homely extras and the ground-floor areas include a spacious hall sitting room, lounge-bar and an attractive dining room, the setting for imaginative dinners.

Rooms 4 en suite 3 annexe en suite (2 fmly) (3 GF) S £56.50-£74.75; D £83-£119.50* **Facilities** FTV TVB tea/coffee Direct dial from bedrooms Cen ht Dinner Last d 8.30pm Wi-fi available Fishing Birdwatching in 50 acre private woodland **Parking** 52 **Notes** LB

WENTNOR MAP 07 SO39

►►► The Green Caravan Park *(SO380932)*

SY9 5EF

☎ 01588 650605

e-mail: karen@greencaravanpark.co.uk

web: www.greencaravanpark.co.uk

Dir: *1m NE of Bishop's Castle on A489. Turn right at brown tourist sign*

PETS: Stables nearby (1.5m) (loose box) **Charges** £1 per dog per night £6.30 per week **Public areas** on leads **Exercise area** on site disp bin **Facilities** on site shop food dog scoop/disp bags walks info vet info **Resident Pets:** Englebert, Ronnie, Reggie (Pygmy goats), Sophie, Lily, Tommy & Molly (cats)

Open Etr-Oct Last arrival 21.00hrs Last departure 13.00hrs

A pleasant site in a peaceful setting convenient for visiting Ludlow or Shrewsbury. The grassy pitches are mainly level. A 15-acre site with 140 touring pitches, 4 hardstandings and 20 statics.

SOMERSET

BATH MAP 03 ST76

★★★★★ 82% HOTEL

The Royal Crescent

von Essen hotels A PRIVATE COLLECTION www.vonessenhotels.com

16 Royal Crescent BA1 2LS

☎ 01225 823333 🖷 01225 339401

e-mail: info@royalcrescent.co.uk

web: www.vonessenhotels.co.uk

Dir: *from A4, right at lights. 2nd left onto Bennett St. Continue into The Circus, 2nd exit onto Brock St*

PETS: Bedrooms (7GF) unattended **Charges** charge for damage **Public areas** except restaurant **Grounds** accessible **Exercise area** park adjacent **Facilities** food (pre-bookable) food bowl water bowl bedding pet sitting dog walking cage storage walks info vet info **Resident Pets:** Charlie (cat)

John Wood's masterpiece of fine Georgian architecture provides the setting for this elegant hotel in the centre of the world famous Royal Crescent. Spacious, air-conditioned bedrooms are individually designed and furnished with antiques. Delightful central grounds lead to a second house, which is home to further rooms, the award-winning Dower House restaurant and the Bath House which offers therapies and treatments.

Rooms 45 en suite (8 fmly) (7 GF) D £225-£320 (incl. bkfst)* **Facilities Spa** STV FTV Gym Wi-fi available 1920s river launch Xmas New Year **Services** Lift air con **Parking** 27 **Notes** LB

★★★ 84% HOTEL

Best Western Cliffe

Best Western

Cliffe Dr, Crowe Hill, Limpley Stoke BA2 7FY

☎ 01225 723226 🖷 01225 723871

e-mail: cliffe@bestwestern.co.uk

Dir: *A36 S from Bath onto B3108 at lights left towards Bradford-on-Avon, 0.5m. Right before bridge through village, hotel on right*

PETS: Bedrooms (4GF) **Charges** £8 per night charge for damage **Public areas** except food areas (on leads) **Grounds** accessible on leads **Exercise area Facilities** water bowl washing facs walks info vet info **On Request** fridge access torch towels

With stunning countryside views, this attractive country house is just a short drive from the City of Bath. Bedrooms vary in size and style but

CONTINUED

BATH CONTINUED

are well equipped; several are particularly spacious and a number of rooms are on the ground floor. The restaurant overlooks the well-tended garden and offers a tempting selection of carefully prepared dishes. Wi-fi is available throughout.

Rooms 8 en suite 3 annexe en suite (2 fmly) (4 GF) S £102-£130; D £124-£160 (incl. bkfst)* **Facilities** Wi-fi in bedrooms Xmas New Year **Parking** 20 **Notes** LB

★★★ 72% HOTEL

Pratt's

South Pde BA2 4AB

☎ 01225 460441 01225 448807

e-mail: pratts@forestdale.com

web: www.forestdale.com

Dir: *A46 into city centre. Left at 1st lights (Curfew Pub), right at next lights. 2nd exit at next rdbt, right at lights, left at next lights, 1st left into South Pde*

PETS: Bedrooms Charges £7.50 per night **Exercise area**

Built in 1743 this popular Georgian hotel still has many original features and is centrally placed to explore Bath. The hotel's bedrooms each with their own individual character and style offer great comfort. The lounge has original open fire places and offers a relaxing venue for afternoon tea.

Rooms 46 en suite (2 fmly) S £90-£95; D £129-£139 (incl. bkfst)* **Facilities** Wi-fi available Xmas New Year **Services** Lift **Notes** LB

★★★★ GUEST ACCOMMODATION

Eagle House

Church St, Bathford BA1 7RS

☎ 01225 859946 01225 859430

e-mail: jonap@eagleho.demon.co.uk

web: www.eaglehouse.co.uk

Dir: *Off A363 onto Church St*

PETS: Bedrooms (2GF) **Stables** nearby (2m) **Charges** £4 per night **Public areas** with consent of other guests **Grounds** accessible disp bin **Exercise area** 300yds **Facilities** food bowl water bowl cage storage walks info vet info **On Request** fridge access torch towels **Resident Pets:** Aquilla (Labrador), Inka (cat), Twitch (rabbit)

Set in attractive gardens, this delightful Georgian house is pleasantly located on the outskirts of the city. Bedrooms are individually styled, and each has a thoughtful range of extra facilities. The impressive lounge is adorned with attractive pictures, and the dining room has views of the grounds and tennis court.

Rooms 6 en suite 2 annexe en suite (2 fmly) (2 GF) S £48-£88.50; D £56-£112* **Facilities** TVB tea/coffee Direct dial from bedrooms Cen ht **Parking** 10 **Notes** LB Closed 12 Dec-8 Jan

★★★★ GUEST ACCOMMODATION

Marlborough House

1 Marlborough Ln BA1 2NQ

☎ 01225 318175 01225 466127

e-mail: mars@manque.dircon.co.uk

web: www.marlborough-house.net

Dir: *450yds W of city centre, at A4 junct*

PETS: Bedrooms Charges £5 per night **Public areas** must be under control **Exercise area** 2 mins walk **Facilities** water bowl walks info vet info **Restrictions** no Alsatians, Dobermans, Pit Bull Terriers or Rottweilers

Marlborough House is situated opposite Royal Victoria Park and close to the Royal Crescent. Some original features remain and the rooms are decorated with period furniture and pictures. The atmosphere is relaxed, and service is attentive and friendly. The breakfast, served from an open-plan kitchen, is vegetarian and organic.

Rooms 6 en suite (2 fmly) (1 GF) S £75-£95; D £85-£135* **Facilities** TVB tea/coffee Direct dial from bedrooms Cen ht Wi-fi available **Parking** 3 **Notes** LB Closed 24-25 Dec

►►►► Newton Mill Caravan and Camping Park *(ST715649)*

Newton Rd BA2 9JF

☎ 01225 333909

e-mail: newtonmill@hotmail.com

web: www.campinginbath.co.uk

Dir: *From Bath W on A4 to rdbt by Globe Inn, immediate left, site 1m on left*

PETS: Charges 75p per night **Public areas** except restaurant, bar & food shop **Exercise area** on site disp bin **Facilities** on site shop food walks info vet info

Open all year Last arrival 21.00hrs Last departure noon

An attractive, high quality park set in a sheltered valley and surrounded by woodland, with a stream running through. It offers excellent toilet facilities with private cubicles and rooms, and there is an appealing restaurant and bar offering a wide choice of menus throughout the year. The city is easily accessible by bus or via the Bristol to Bath cycle path. A 42-acre site with 195 touring pitches, 85 hardstandings.

BAWDRIP MAP 03 ST33

►►► The Fairways International Touring C & C Park *(ST349402)*

Bath Rd TA7 8PP

☎ 01278 685569 & 685433 🖷 01278 685569

e-mail: holiday@fairwaysinternational.co.uk

web: www.fairwaysinternational.co.uk

Dir: *A39 onto B3141, site 100yds on right*

PETS: Charges £2 per night £12 per week **Exercise area** on site disp bin **Facilities** on site shop dog scoop/disp bags leads washing facs walks info vet info

Open all year Last arrival 22.00hrs Last departure 22.00hrs

This family orientated site is well positioned for visiting the many attractions in the area including Burnham-on-Sea, Weston-Super-Mare and Glastonbury. The park also makes a convenient overnight stop off the M5. A 5.75-acre site with 200 touring pitches, 90 hardstandings and 1 static.

BREAN MAP 03 ST25

Warren Farm Holiday Centre *(ST297564)*

Brean Sands TA8 2RP

☎ 01278 751227

e-mail: enquiries@warren-farm.co.uk

web: www.warren-farm.co.uk

Dir: *M5 junct 22 onto B3140 through Burnham-on-Sea to Berrow and Brean. Centre 1.5m past Brean Leisure Park*

PETS: Public areas except buildings, Sunnyside area & field 6 **Exercise area** on site farm walk disp bin **Facilities** on site shop food food bowl water bowl dog chews litter tray etc dog scoop/disp bags walks info vet info **Other** prior notice required

Open Apr-Oct Last arrival 20.00hrs Last departure noon

A large family-run holiday park close to the beach, divided into several fields each with its own designated facilities. Pitches are spacious and level, and enjoy panoramic views of the Mendip Hills and Brean Down. A bar and restaurant are part of the complex, which provide entertainment for all the family, and there is also separate entertainment for children. A 100-acre site with 575 touring pitches and 800 statics.

Notes No commerical vehicles

►►►► Northam Farm Caravan & Touring Park *(ST299556)*

TA8 2SE

☎ 01278 751244 🖷 01278 751150

e-mail: enquiries@northamfarm.co.uk

web: www.northamfarm.co.uk

Dir: *From M5 junct 22 to Burnham-on-Sea. In Brean, Northam Farm on right 0.5m past Brean leisure park*

PETS: Public areas on leads no dogs in fields **Exercise area** on site dog walks & exercise field disp bin **Facilities** on site shop food food bowl water bowl dog chews cat treats dog scoop/disp bags leads washing facs walks info vet info **Other** prior notice required

Open Mar-Oct (rs Mar & Oct shop/cafe/takeaway open limited hours) Last arrival 21.00hrs Last departure 10.30hrs

An attractive site a short walk from the sea with game, coarse fishing and sea fishing close by. The quality park also has lots of children's play areas, and is near a long sandy beach. It also runs the Seagull Inn about 600yds away, which includes a restaurant and entertainment. A 30-acre site with 350 touring pitches, 156 hardstandings and 112 statics.

Notes Families & couples only, no motorcycles or commercial vans

BRIDGETOWN MAP 03 SS93

►►► Exe Valley Caravan Site *(SS923333)*

Mill House TA22 9JR

☎ 01643 851432

e-mail: paul@paulmatt.fsnet.co.uk

web: www.exevalleycamping.co.uk

Dir: *Take A396 (Tiverton to Minehead road). Turn W in centre of Bridgetown, site 40yds on right*

PETS: Stables nearby (3m) **Charges** £1 per night £6 per week **Public areas** except buildings **Exercise area** on site riverside walks disp bin **Facilities** on site shop food food bowl water bowl dog chews dog scoop/disp bags leads walks info vet info

Open 13 Mar-12 Oct Last arrival 22.00hrs

Set in the Exmoor National Park, this 'adults only' park occupies an enchanting, peaceful spot in a wooded valley alongside the River Exe. There is free fly fishing, and an abundance of wildlife, with excellent walks directly from the park. The inn opposite serves lunchtime and evening meals. A 4-acre site with 50 touring pitches, 10 hardstandings.

Notes ⊜

BRIDGWATER — MAP 03 ST23

★★★★ GUEST ACCOMMODATION

Model Farm

Perry Green, Wembdon TA5 2BA

☎ 01278 433999

e-mail: info@modelfarm.com

web: www.modelfarm.com

Dir: *2.5m NW of Bridgwater. Off junct A39 & B3339 to Perry Green, at T-junct follow sign No Through Road, farm 2nd drive on left*

PETS: Bedrooms Charges charge for damage **Grounds** accessible **Exercise area** surrounding countryside **Facilities** cage storage walks info vet info **On Request** torch

This extensive Victorian house enjoys a peaceful rural setting and has glorious country views. Guests are assured of a warm welcome and friendly hospitality throughout their stay. Bedrooms are very spacious and include thoughtful touches with a good selection of extras. By arrangement, the proprietors join their guests around the large dining room table for a carefully prepared three-course dinner using fresh local ingredients. A suite of conference is located in the original cider press barn.

Rooms 3 en suite (1 fmly) S fr £42.50; D £75✱ **Facilities** tea/coffee Cen ht TVL Dinner Last d noon **Parking** 6 **Notes** No children 3yrs

BURTLE — MAP 03 ST34

► Orchard Camping *(ST397434)*

Ye Olde Burtle Inn, Catcott Rd TA7 8NG

☎ 01278 722269 & 722123 🖹 01278 722269

e-mail: food@theinn.eu

web: www.theinn.eu

Dir: *From M5 junct 23 onto A39, approx 4m turn left onto unclass road to Burtle, site by pub in village centre*

PETS: Public areas except restaurant **Stables** nearby (adjacent) (loose box) **Exercise area** surrounding open countryside **Facilities** food bowl water bowl washing facs walks info vet info **Other** prior notice required

Open all year Last arrival anytime

A simple campsite set in an orchard at the rear of a lovely 17th-century family inn in the heart of the Somerset Levels. The restaurant offers a wide range of meals, and breakfast can be pre-ordered by campers. A shower and disabled toilet have been added and these facilities are available to campers outside pub opening hours. A 0.75-acre site with 30 touring pitches.

Notes no cars by tents

CHARD — MAP 03 ST30

★★★ GUEST HOUSE

Watermead

83 High St TA20 1QT

☎ 01460 62834 🖹 01460 67448

e-mail: trudy@watermeadguesthouse.co.uk

web: www.watermeadguesthouse.co.uk

Dir: *On A30 in town centre*

PETS: Bedrooms Charges £5 per night charge for damage **Public areas** except dining room (on leads) **Grounds** accessible disp bin **Exercise area** 100mtrs **Facilities** water bowl dog scoop/disp bags leads washing facs cage storage walks info vet info **On Request** torch towels **Resident Pets:** Jasper (Black Labrador), Charlie (cat)

Guests will feel at home at this family-run house, a smart establishment in a convenient location. Hearty breakfasts are served in the dining room overlooking the garden. Bedrooms are neat, and the spacious, self-contained suite is popular with families. Free Wi-fi access is available.

Rooms 9 rms (6 en suite) 1 annexe en suite (1 fmly) S £29-£50; D £59-£62✱ **Facilities** TVB tea/coffee Cen ht TVL Wi-fi available **Parking** 10 **Notes LB** No coaches

►►► Alpine Grove Touring Park *(ST342071)*

Forton TA20 4HD

☎ 01460 63479 🖹 01460 63479

e-mail: stay@alpinegrovetouringpark.com

web: www.alpinegrovetouringpark.com

Dir: *Turn off A30 between Chard & Crewkerne towards Cricket St Thomas, follow signs. Site 2m on right*

PETS: Sep Accom single kennel for dog sitting **Stables** nearby (adjacent) (loose box) **Charges** £1.50 per night £10.50 per week **Public areas** except play area on leads **Exercise area** on site woodland trail disp bin **Facilities** (on leads) on site shop dog scoop/disp bags pet sitting washing facs walks info vet info **Other** prior notice required **Resident Pets:** Freddie (American Cocker Spaniel), Murphy (Springer/Collie cross)

Open 1 wk before Etr-Sep Last arrival 21.00hrs Last departure 10.30hrs

A warm welcome awaits at this attractive, quiet wooded park with both hardstandings and grass pitches, close to Cricket St Thomas Wildlife

Park. The refurbished facilities are kept spotlessly clean. Families particularly enjoy the small swimming pool and terrace in summer. Log cabins are also available for hire on this park. An 8.5-acre site with 40 touring pitches, 15 hardstandings.

Notes No open fires

CLEVEDON MAP 03 ST47

★★★ 73% HOTEL

Best Western Walton Park

Best Western

Wellington Ter BS21 7BL

☎ 01275 874253 📠 01275 343577

e-mail: info@waltonparkhotel.eclipse.co.uk

web: www.latonahotels.com

Dir: *M5 junct 20, follow signs for seafront. Stay on coast road, past pier into Wellington Terrace, hotel on left*

PETS: Bedrooms Charges £7 per night **Grounds** accessible on leads **Exercise area Facilities** pet sitting dog walking walks info vet info **On Request** torch towels **Resident Pets:** Charlie (cat)

Quietly located with spectacular views across the Bristol Channel to Wales, this popular Victorian hotel offers a relaxed atmosphere. Bedrooms are well decorated and equipped to meet the demands of both business and leisure guests. A high standard of home-cooked food is served in the comfortable restaurant, and lighter meals are available in the convivial bar at lunchtime.

Rooms 40 en suite (4 fmly) S £75-£95; D £95-£135 (incl. bkfst)* **Facilities** STV Wi-fi in bedrooms **Services** Lift **Parking** 50 **Notes LB**

CLUTTON MAP 03 ST65

★★★★ INN

The Hunters Rest

King Ln, Clutton Hill BS39 5QL

☎ 01761 452303 📠 01761 453308

e-mail: paul@huntersrest.co.uk

web: www.huntersrest.co.uk

Dir: *Off A37 onto A368 towards Bath, 100yds right onto lane, left at T-junct, inn 0.25m on left*

PETS: Bedrooms unattended **Stables** nearby (100yds) **Charges** £10 per stay per night charge for damage **Public areas** (on leads) **Grounds** accessible disp bin **Exercise area** adjacent **Facilities** food (pre-bookable) food bowl water bowl dog chews feeding mat dog scoop/disp bags leads washing facs cage storage walks info vet info **On Request** fridge access torch **Other** dogs allowed in certain bedrooms only **Resident Pets:** Reg (Black Labrador), Blacks (Greyhound)

The Hunters Rest was originally built around 1750 as a hunting lodge for the Earl of Warwick. Set in delightful countryside, it is ideally located for Bath, Bristol and Wells. Bedrooms and bathrooms are furnished and equipped to excellent standards, and the ground floor combines the character of a real country inn with an excellent range of home-cooked meals.

Rooms 5 en suite (1 fmly) S £62.50-£79.50; D £87.50-£125* **Facilities** TVB tea/coffee Direct dial from bedrooms Cen ht Dinner Last d 9.45pm Wi-fi available **Parking** 90 **Notes LB**

CREWKERNE MAP 03 ST40

★★★ GUEST ACCOMMODATION

Manor Farm

Wayford TA18 8QL

☎ 01460 78865 & 0776 7620031 📠 01460 78865

web: www.manorfarm.biz

Dir: *B3165 from Crewkerne to Lyme Regis, 3m in Clapton right onto Dunsham Ln, Manor Farm 0.5m up hill on right*

PETS: Sep Accomm kennels **Stables** on site **Public areas Grounds** accessible disp bin **Exercise area Facilities** food bowl water bowl bedding leads washing facs cage storage walks info vet info **On Request** fridge access torch **Other** pet food on request **Resident Pets:** Charlie & Ginger (cats)

Located off the beaten track, this fine Victorian country house has extensive views over Clapton towards the Axe Valley. The comfortably furnished bedrooms are well equipped, and front-facing rooms enjoy splendid views. Breakfast is served at separate tables in the dining room, and a spacious lounge is also provided.

Rooms 4 en suite 1 annexe en suite S £35-£40; D £65-£70* **Facilities** STV TV4B tea/coffee Cen ht TVL Fishing Riding **Parking** 14 **Notes**

DULVERTON MAP 03 SS92

★★★★★ INN

Tarr Farm Inn

Tarr Steps, Exmoor National Park TA22 9PY

☎ 01643 851507 📠 01643 851111

e-mail: enquiries@tarrfarm.co.uk

web: www.tarrfarm.co.uk

Dir: *4m NW of Dulverton. Off B3223 signed Tarr Steps, signs to Tarr Farm Inn*

PETS: Bedrooms (4GF) **Stables** nearby (0.5m) **Charges** £8 per night £56 per week **Public areas** except restaurant & lounge (on leads) **Grounds** accessible on leads disp bin **Exercise area** 100mtrs **Facilities** food bowl water bowl bedding dog chews leads cage storage walks info vet info **On Request** fridge access torch towels

Tarr Farm, dating from the 16th century, nestles on the lower slopes of Exmoor overlooking the famous old clapper bridge, Tarr Steps. The majority of rooms are in the bedroom block that provides very stylish and comfortable accommodation with an impressive selection of thoughtful touches. Tarr Farm Inn, with much character and traditional charm, draws the crowds for cream teas and delicious dinners which are prepared from good local produce.

Rooms 9 en suite (4 GF) D fr £150* **Facilities** STV TVB tea/coffee Direct dial from bedrooms Cen ht Dinner Last d 9.30pm Wi-fi available Fishing Riding **Parking** 10 **Notes LB** No children 14yrs No coaches

ENGLAND

DULVERTON *CONTINUED*

★★★★ GUEST ACCOMMODATION

Threadneedle

EX16 9JH

☎ 01398 341598

e-mail: stay@threadneedlecottage.co.uk

web: www.threadneedlecottage.co.uk

Dir: *On Devon/Somerset border just off B3227 between Oldways End & East Anstey*

PETS: Bedrooms Sep Accom stable **Stables** on site **Charges** £8 horse per night charge for damage **Public areas** by arrangement; must be on lead **Grounds** accessible disp bin **Exercise area** 40yds **Facilities** food (pre-bookable) food bowl water bowl bedding dog chews dog scoop/disp bags leads washing facs cage storage walks info vet info **On Request** fridge access torch towels **Resident Pets:** Scamp & Charlie (Shetland Sheepdogs), Sparkie (horse)

Situated on the edge of Exmoor near Dulverton, Threadneedle is built in the style of a Devon longhouse. The spacious, well-appointed family home offers comfortable, en suite accommodation. Traditional West Country dishes are served, by arrangement, in the light airy dining room, which overlooks the garden and surrounding countryside.

Rooms 2 en suite (1 fmly) D £70-£80* **Facilities** FTV TVB tea/coffee Cen ht Dinner Last d 9am **Parking** 12 **Notes LB**

DUNSTER MAP 03 SS94

★★★ 73% HOTEL

The Luttrell Arms Hotel

High St TA24 6SG

☎ 01643 821555 📠 01643 821567

e-mail: info@luttrellarms.fsnet.co.uk

web: www.luttrellarms.co.uk/main.htm

Dir: *A39/A396 S toward Tiverton. Hotel on left opposite Yarn Market*

PETS: Bedrooms unattended **Charges** £5 for dogs per night **Public areas** except restaurant **Grounds** accessible on leads **Exercise area** adjacent **Facilities** walks info vet info **On Request** fridge access torch

Occupying an enviable position on the high street, this 15th-century hotel looks up towards the town's famous castle. Beautifully renovated and decorated, high levels of comfort can be found throughout. Some of the spacious bedrooms have four-poster beds. The warm and friendly staff provide attentive service in a relaxed atmosphere.

Rooms 28 en suite (3 fmly) S £70-£102; D £104-£140 (incl. bkfst)* **Facilities** Exmoor safaris Historic tours Walking tours New Year **Notes LB**

EXFORD MAP 03 SS83

★★★ 75% HOTEL

Crown

TA24 7PP

☎ 01643 831554 📠 01643 831665

e-mail: info@crownhotelexmoor.co.uk

web: www.crownhotelexmoor.co.uk

Dir: *M5 junct 25, follow Taunton signs. Take A358 from Taunton, then B3224 via Wheddon Cross to Exford*

PETS: Bedrooms unattended **Sep Accom** stables **Stables** on site **Charges** £8 up to 5 days per night £16 5 days per week charge for damage **Public areas** except restaurant **Grounds** accessible **Exercise area** 25mtrs **Facilities** water bowl dog chews washing facs walks info vet info **On Request** fridge access torch towels **Resident Pets:** Oscar (Patterdale Terrier)

Guest comfort is certainly the hallmark here. Afternoon tea is served in the lounge beside a roaring fire and tempting menus in the bar and restaurant are all part of the charm of this delightful old coaching inn that specialises in breaks for shooting and other country sports. Bedrooms retain a traditional style yet offer a range of modern comforts and facilities, many with views of this pretty moorland village.

Rooms 17 en suite (3 fmly) S £70; D £110-£140 (incl. bkfst)* **Facilities** Riding Wi-fi available Xmas New Year **Parking** 30 **Notes LB**

ENGLAND

GORDANO SERVICE AREA (M5) MAP 03 ST57

BUDGET HOTEL

Days Inn Bristol West

BS20 7XJ

☎ 01275 373709 & 373624 📠 01275 374104

e-mail: gordano.hotel@welcomebreak.co.uk

web: www.welcomebreak.co.uk

Dir: *M5 junct 19, follow signs for Gordano Services*

PETS: Bedrooms Grounds accessible on leads disp bin **Exercise area Facilities** vet info **On Request** torch towels **Other** please contact for details of pet facilities

This modern building offers accommodation in smart, spacious and well-equipped bedrooms, suitable for families and business travellers, and all with en suite bathrooms. Refreshments may be taken at the nearby family restaurant.

Rooms 60 en suite S £39-£59; D £49-£69*

HIGHBRIDGE MAP 03 ST34

★★ 68% SMALL HOTEL

Sundowner

74 Main Rd, West Huntspill TA9 3QU

☎ 01278 784766 📠 01278 794133

e-mail: runnalls@msn.com

Dir: *from M5 junct 23, 3m N on A38*

PETS: Bedrooms Public areas except restaurant (on leads) **Grounds** accessible on leads **Exercise area** adjacent bridle path **Restrictions** small dogs only

Friendly service and an informal atmosphere are just two of the highlights of this small hotel. The open-plan lounge/bar is a comfortable, homely area in which to relax after a busy day exploring the area or working in the locality. An extensive menu, featuring freshly cooked, imaginative dishes, is offered in the popular restaurant.

Rooms 8 en suite (1 fmly) S £50-£55; D £65-£70 (incl. bkfst)* **Facilities** Wi-fi available **Parking** 18 **Notes** Closed 26-31 Dec & 1 Jan RS 25 Dec

HINTON CHARTERHOUSE MAP 03 ST75

★★★ 86% HOTEL

Homewood Park

BA2 7TB

☎ 01225 723731 📠 01225 723820

e-mail: info@homewoodpark.co.uk

web: www.vonessenhotels.co.uk

Dir: *6m SE of Bath on A36, turn left at 2nd sign for Freshford*

PETS: Bedrooms (2GF) **Charges** £15 for 1st 3 nights charge for damage **Public areas** except restaurant (on leads) **Grounds** accessible disp bin **Exercise area Facilities** food (pre-bookable) food bowl water bowl bedding dog chews feeding mat dog scoop/disp bags leads pet sitting washing facs cage storage walks info vet info **On Request** fridge access torch towels **Resident Pets:** Chi Chi (cat)

Homewood Park, an unassuming yet stylish Georgian house set in delightful grounds, offers relaxed surroundings and maintains high standards of quality and comfort throughout. Bedrooms, all individually decorated, include thoughtful extras to ensure a comfortable stay. The hotel has a reputation for excellent cuisine - offering an imaginative interpretation of classical dishes.

Rooms 19 en suite (3 fmly) (2 GF) S fr £105, D £155-£315 (incl. bkfst)* **Facilities** FTV Wi-fi available Xmas New Year **Parking** 30 **Notes** LB

ENGLAND

HOLFORD MAP 03 ST14

★★ 82% HOTEL

Combe House

TA5 1RZ

☎ 01278 741382 & 741213 01278 741322

e-mail: enquiries@combehouse.co.uk

web: www.combehouse.co.uk

Dir: *from A39 W left in Holford then left at T-junct. Left at fork, 0.25m to Holford Combe*

PETS: Bedrooms (1GF) unattended **Charges** £3 per night charge for damage **Public areas** in bar & grounds only **Grounds** accessible disp bin **Exercise area Facilities** food (pre-bookable) food bowl water bowl leads washing facs cage storage walks info vet info **On Request** fridge access torch towels **Resident Pets:** Roger & Flo (Springer Spaniel/Collie cross)

Located in a peaceful wooded valley with four acres of tranquil gardens to explore, the atmosphere here is relaxed and welcoming. The individually styled bedrooms have lots of comfort - all are designed for a cosseted and pampered stay! Public areas have equal charm with traditional features interwoven with contemporary style. Food comes highly recommended with a dedicated kitchen team producing accomplished, seasonal dishes.

Rooms 17 en suite 2 annexe en suite (1 fmly) (1 GF) S £55-£80; D £80-£160 (incl. bkfst)* **Facilities** Wi-fi available Xmas New Year **Parking** 36 **Notes** LB

HUNSTRETE MAP 03 ST66

★★★ 82% COUNTRY HOUSE HOTEL

Hunstrete House

von Essen hotels
A PRIVATE COLLECTION
www.vonessenhotels.com

BS39 4NS

☎ 01761 490490 01761 490732

e-mail: info@hunstretehouse.co.uk

web: www.vonessenhotels.co.uk

Dir: *from Bath take A4 to Bristol. At Globe Inn rdbt 2nd left onto A368 to Wells. 1m after Marksbury turn right for Hunstrete. Hotel next left*

PETS: Bedrooms (8GF) **Charges** charge for damage **Grounds** accessible **Exercise area** adjacent **Facilities** walks info vet info **Other** please contact for further details

This delightful Georgian house enjoys a stunning setting in 92 acres of deer park and woodland on the edge of the Mendip Hills. Elegant bedrooms in the main building and coach house are both spacious and comfortable. Public areas feature antiques, paintings and fine china. The restaurant enjoys a well-deserved reputation for its fine cuisine that utilises much home-grown produce.

Rooms 25 en suite (2 fmly) (8 GF) S £140-£265; D £190-£315 (incl. bkfst)* **Facilities** Wi-fi available Xmas New Year **Parking** 50

ILMINSTER MAP 03 ST31

★★★ 78% HOTEL

Best Western Shrubbery

Best Western

TA19 9AR

☎ 01460 52108 01460 53660

e-mail: stuart@shrubberyhotel.com

web: www.shrubberyhotel.com

Dir: *0.5m from A303 towards Ilminster town centre*

PETS: Bedrooms unattended **Charges** charge for damage **Public areas** except restaurant (on leads) **Grounds** accessible on leads **Exercise area** nature reserve 0.25m **Facilities** food bowl water bowl walks info vet info **On Request** fridge access **Resident Pets:** Oscar (Collie)

Set in attractive terraced gardens, the Shrubbery is a well established hotel in this small town. Bedrooms are well equipped and bright, they include three ground-floor rooms and impressive executive rooms. Bar meals or full meals are available in the bar, lounges and restaurant. Additional facilities include a range of function rooms.

Rooms 21 en suite (3 fmly) S £80-£120; D £105-£140 (incl. bkfst)* **Facilities** STV Wi-fi in bedrooms New Year **Parking** 80 **Notes** LB Closed 24-26 Dec

BUDGET HOTEL

Travelodge Ilminster

Southfields Roundabout, Horton Cross TA19 9PT

☎ 08719 846 229 🖹 01460 53748

web: www.travelodge.co.uk

Dir: *on A303/A358 at junct with Ilminster bypass*

PETS: Bedrooms Charges £10 per night charge for damage **Public areas** (on leads) **Exercise area Facilities** vet info

Travelodge offers good quality, good value, modern accommodation. Ideal for families, the spacious en suite bedrooms include remote-control TV, tea and coffee-making facilities and comfortable beds. Meals can be taken at the nearby family restaurant.

Rooms 32 en suite S fr £29; D fr £29

LANGPORT MAP 03 ST42

►►► Thorney Lakes Caravan Park *(ST430237)*

Thorney Lakes, Muchelney TA10 0DW

☎ 01458 250811

e-mail: enquiries@thorneylakes.co.uk

web: www.thorneylakes.co.uk

Dir: *From A303 at Podimore rdbt take A372 to Langport. At Huish Episcopi Church turn left for Muchelney. In 100yds left (signed Muchelney & Crewkerne). Site 300yds after John Leach Pottery*

PETS: Stables on site (loose box) **Exercise area** on site 2m around farm & site **Facilities** vet info

Open Etr-Oct

A small, basic but very attractive park set in a cider apple orchard, with coarse fishing in the three well-stocked on-site lakes. The famous John Leach pottery shop is nearby. A 6-acre site with 36 touring pitches.

Notes

MINEHEAD MAP 03 SS94

★★★ 74% HOTEL

Best Western Northfield

Northfield Rd TA24 5PU

☎ 01643 705155 0845 1302678 🖹 01643 707715

e-mail: reservations@northfield-hotel.co.uk

web: www.northfield-hotel.co.uk

Dir: *M5 junct 23, follow A38 to Bridgwater then A39 to Minehead*

PETS: Bedrooms sign **Stables** nearby **Charges** £8 per night **Grounds** accessible on leads disp bin **Exercise area** 200mtrs **Facilities** walks info vet info **On Request** fridge access torch

Located conveniently close to the town centre and the seafront, this hotel is set in delightfully maintained gardens and has a loyal following. A range of comfortable sitting rooms and leisure facilities, including an indoor, heated pool is provided. A fixed-price menu is served every evening in the oak-panelled dining room. The attractively co-ordinated bedrooms vary in size and are equipped to a good standard.

Rooms 30 en suite (7 fmly) (4 GF) S £59-£68; D £118-£136 (incl. bkfst & dinner)* **Facilities** STV FTV Gym Putt green Wi-fi in bedrooms Steam room Xmas New Year **Services** Lift **Parking** 44 **Notes** LB

★★ 85% HOTEL

Alcombe House

Bircham Rd, Alcombe TA24 6BG

☎ 01643 705130 🖹 01643 705130

e-mail: alcombe.house@virgin.net

web: www.alcombehouse.co.uk

Dir: *On A39 on outskirts of Minehead opposite West Somerset Community College.*

PETS: Bedrooms unattended **Stables** nearby (2m) **Grounds** accessible on leads disp bin **Exercise area** 0.25m **Facilities** water bowl cage storage walks info vet info **On Request** fridge access torch towels

Located midway between Minehead and Dunster on the coastal fringe of Exmoor National Park, this Grade II listed, Georgian hotel offers a delightful combination of efficient service and genuine hospitality delivered by the very welcoming resident proprietors. Public areas include a comfortable lounge and a candlelit dining room where a range of carefully prepared dishes is offered from a daily changing menu.

Rooms 7 en suite S £42; D £64 (incl. bkfst)* **Facilities** Xmas **Parking** 9 **Notes** No children 15yrs Closed 8 Nov-18 Mar

►►► Minehead Camping & Caravanning Club Site *(SS958471)*

Hill Rd, North Hill TA24 5LB

☎ 01643 704138

web: www.thefriendlyclub.co.uk

Dir: *From A39 towards town centre. In main street turn opposite W H Smith to Blenheim Rd. Left in 50yds (by pub) into Martlet Rd. Up hill, site on right*

PETS: Public areas except in buildings **Exercise area** disp bin **Facilities** walks info vet info **Other** prior notice required

Open 27 Apr-28 Sep Last arrival 21.00hrs Last departure noon

A secluded site on a hilltop with glorious views of the Bristol Channel and the Quantocks. Good clean facilities plus a laundry and information room make this a popular choice for those seeking an isolated holiday. A 3.75-acre site with 60 touring pitches, 10 hardstandings.

Notes Site gates closed 23.00hrs-07.00hrs

ENGLAND

ENGLAND

MINEHEAD CONTINUED

►►► Minehead & Exmoor Caravan & Camping Site *(SS950457)*

Porlock Rd TA24 8SW

☎ 01643 703074

web: www.mineheadandexmoorcamping.co.uk

Dir: *1m W of Minehead centre, take A39 towards Porlock. Site on right.*

PETS: Public areas except children's play area & toilet block **Exercise area** disp bin **Facilities** walks info vet info **Other** vet available on-site on certain days

Open all year (rs Nov-Feb reduced no. of pitches) Last arrival 22.00hrs Last departure noon

A small terraced park on the edge of Exmoor, spread over five paddocks and screened by the mature trees that surround it. The level pitches provide a comfortable space for each unit on this family-run park. There is a laundrette in nearby Minehead. A 3-acre site with 50 touring pitches, 10 hardstandings.

Notes ⊜

MUCHELNEY MAP 03 ST42

►►► Muchelney Caravan & Camping Site

(ST429249)

Abbey Farm TA10 0DQ

☎ 01458 250112 🖷 01458 250112

Dir: *From A303 at Podimore rdbt take A372 towards Langport. At church in Huish Episcopi follow Muchelney Abbey sign. In Muchelney left at village cross. Site in 50mtrs*

PETS: Stables (loose box) **Charges** £1.50 for dogs per night **Public areas** except dog-free area of site; dogs and cats on leads **Exercise area** on site dog walk disp bin **Facilities** washing facs vet info **Other** prior notice required

Open all year

This small developing site is situated opposite Muchelney Abbey, an English Heritage property. This quiet and peaceful site will appeal to all lovers of the countryside, and is well positioned for visiting the Somerset Levels. A 3-acre site with 40 touring pitches, 5 hardstandings.

Notes ⊜

NETHER STOWEY MAP 03 ST13

★★★★★ GUEST ACCOMMODATION

Castle of Comfort Country House

TA5 1LE

☎ 01278 741264 🖷 01278 741144

e-mail: reception@castle-of-comfort.co.uk

web: www.castle-of-comfort.co.uk

Dir: *On A39 1.3m W of Nether Stowey on left*

PETS: Bedrooms unattended **Sep Accom** stables **Stables** on site **Charges** charge for damage **Public areas** except lounge & restaurant (on leads) **Grounds** accessible on leads disp bin **Exercise area** on site **Facilities** food bowl water bowl washing facs cage storage walks info vet info **On Request** fridge access torch towels **Resident Pets:** Humbug & Treacle (cats)

Dating in part from the 16th century, this former inn is situated beside the A39 on the northern slopes of the Quantock Hills in an Area of Outstanding Natural Beauty. Bedrooms and bathrooms are well equipped, and the public rooms are smart and comfortable. The delightful gardens and a heated swimming pool are available to guests in the summer. An imaginative choice of dishes, using good local produce, is offered at dinner.

Rooms 5 en suite 1 annexe en suite (2 fmly) (1 GF) S £42-£92; D £104-£142* **Facilities** TVB tea/coffee Direct dial from bedrooms Cen ht Dinner Last d 8pm Stabling with access to bridle paths **Parking** 10 **Notes LB** Closed 24 Dec-2 Jan

PORLOCK MAP 03 SS84

►►►► Porlock Caravan Park *(SS882469)*

TA24 8ND

☎ 01643 862269 🖷 01643 862269

e-mail: info@porlockcaravanpark.co.uk

web: www.porlockcaravanpark.co.uk

Dir: *Through village fork right signed Porlock Weir, site on right*

PETS: Charges £1 per night £7 per week **Public areas** except toilets, shower, dishwasher, laundry & nature garden **Exercise area** on site enclosed dog walk disp bin **Facilities** walks info vet info **Other** prior notice required organised walks with dogs **Resident Pets:** Sid & Alfie (cats)

Open 15 Mar-Oct Last arrival 22.00hrs Last departure noon

A sheltered touring park in the centre of lovely countryside on the edge of the village, with Exmoor right on the doorstep. The toilet facilities are superb, and there's a popular kitchen area with microwave and freezer. A 3-acre site with 40 touring pitches, 14 hardstandings and 55 statics.

Notes No fires

►►► Burrowhayes Farm Caravan & Camping Site *(SS897460)*

West Luccombe TA24 8HT

☎ 01643 862463

e-mail: info@burrowhayes.co.uk

web: www.burrowhayes.co.uk

Dir: *A39 from Minehead towards Porlock for 5m. Left at Red Post to Horner & West Lucombe, site 0.25m on right, immediately before humpback bridge*

PETS: Stables nearby (2m) disp bin **Exercise area** adjacent woods **Facilities** on site shop food dog scoop/disp bags leads walks info vet info **Other** prior notice required

Open 15 Mar-Oct (rs Sat before Etr shop closed) Last arrival 22.00hrs Last departure noon

A delightful site on the edge of Exmoor, sloping gently down to Horner Water. The farm buildings have been converted into riding stables which offers escorted rides on the moors, and the excellent toilet facilities are housed in timber-clad buildings. There are many walks directly into the countryside. An 8-acre site with 120 touring pitches, 3 hardstandings and 20 statics.

PRIDDY — MAP 03 ST55

►►►► Cheddar, Mendip Heights Camping & Caravanning Club Site *(ST522519)*

Townsend BA5 3BP

☎ 01749 870241

web: www.thefriendlyclub.co.uk

Dir: *From A39 take B3135 to Cheddar. After 4.5m turn left. Site 200yds on right*

PETS: disp bin **Exercise area** on site dog walk **Facilities** on site shop walks info vet info **Other** prior notice required

Open Mar-15 Nov Last arrival 21.00hrs Last departure noon

A gently sloping site set high on the Mendip Hills and surrounded by trees. This excellent site offers good self-catered facilities especially for families, and fresh bread is baked daily. The site is well positioned for visiting local attractions like Cheddar, Wookey Hole, Wells and Glastonbury, and is popular with walkers. A 3.5-acre site with 90 touring pitches, 30 hardstandings and 2 statics.

Notes Site gates closed 23.00hrs-07.00hrs

RUDGE — MAP 03 ST85

★★★ INN

The Full Moon Inn

BA11 2QF

☎ 01373 830936

e-mail: info@thefullmoon.co.uk

Dir: *From A36 S from Bath, 10m, left at Standerwick by The Bell pub. 1m from Warminster*

PETS: Bedrooms (2GF) unattended **Charges** £5 per night **Public areas** except restaurant (on leads) **Grounds** accessible on leads **Exercise area** local walks **Facilities** vet info

Peacefully located in the quiet village of Rudge, this traditional inn offers a warm welcome and a proper country pub atmosphere. In the bar area, guests mix well with the locals to enjoy a selection of real ales and a log fire in the colder months. In addition to bar meals, a comfortable restaurant serving excellent home cooked dishes is also available. Bedrooms include some at the main inn and more in an adjacent annexe - all are comfortable and well equipped.

Rooms 5 en suite 11 annexe en suite (1 fmly) (2 GF) **Facilities** TVB tea/coffee Cen ht Dinner Last d 9pm ⊗ **Parking** 25

SEDGEMOOR MOTORWAY SERVICE AREA (M5) — MAP 03 ST35

BUDGET HOTEL

Days Inn Sedgemoor

DAYS INN

Sedgemoor BS24 0JL

☎ 01934 750831 📠 01934 750808

e-mail: sedgemoor.hotel@welcomebreak.co.uk

web: www.welcomebreak.co.uk

Dir: *M5 northbound junct 21/22*

PETS: Bedrooms Public areas Grounds accessible **Exercise area**

This modern building offers accommodation in smart, spacious and well-equipped bedrooms, suitable for families and business travellers, and all with en suite bathrooms. Refreshments may be taken at the nearby family restaurant.

Rooms 40 en suite S £39-£59; D £49-£69*

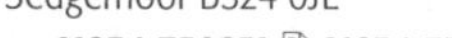

STANTON DREW MAP 03 ST56

★★★★ FARM HOUSE

Greenlands *(ST597636)*

BS39 4ES

☎ 01275 333487 📠 01275 331211 Mrs J Cleverley

Dir: *A37 onto B3130, on right before Stanton Drew Garage*

PETS: Bedrooms unattended **Public areas** except dining room (on leads) **Grounds** accessible disp bin **Exercise area** adjacent **Facilities** washing facs cage storage walks info vet info **On Request** fridge access torch **Resident Pets:** Spoof & Magic (Labradors)

Situated near the ancient village of Stanton Drew in the heart of the Chew Valley, Greenlands is convenient for Bristol Airport and Bath, Bristol and Wells. There are comfortable, well-equipped bedrooms and a downstairs lounge, and breakfast is the highlight of any stay here.

Rooms 4 en suite S £25-£30; D £50✳ **Facilities** STV FTV TVB tea/coffee Cen ht TVL **Parking** 8 **Notes** No children 12yrs 3 acres Hobby Farming - Poultry

STON EASTON MAP 03 ST65

★★★★ 89% COUNTRY HOUSE HOTEL

Ston Easton Park

von Essen hotels
A PRIVATE COLLECTION
www.vonessenhotels.com

BA3 4DF

☎ 01761 241631 📠 01761 241377

e-mail: info@stoneaston.co.uk

web: www.vonessenhotels.co.uk

Dir: *on A37*

PETS: Bedrooms Stables nearby (0.5m) **Charges** £10 per night charge for damage **Public areas** except restaurant; at manager's discretion **Grounds** accessible disp bin **Exercise area** on site **Facilities** food (pre-bookable) food bowl water bowl bedding dog chews feeding mat dog scoop/disp bags leads washing facs dog grooming cage storage walks info vet info **On Request** fridge access torch towels **Resident Pets:** Sweep (Cocker Spaniel)

This outstanding Palladian mansion lies in extensive parklands that were landscaped by Humphrey Repton. The architecture and decorative features are stunning and the Saloon is considered to be one of Somerset's finest rooms. The helpful and attentive team provide a very efficient service, and good, award-winning cuisine is on offer. Refurbished public areas, bedrooms and bathrooms are all appointed to a very high standard.

Rooms 19 en suite 3 annexe en suite (2 fmly) (2 GF) S £170-£255; D £195-£480 (incl. bkfst)✳ **Facilities** STV Fishing Wi-fi available Archery Clay pigeon shooting Quad bikes Hot air balloon Xmas New Year **Parking** 120 **Notes** LB

TAUNTON MAP 03 ST22

★★★ 73% SMALL HOTEL

Farthings Country House Hotel and Restaurant

Village Rd, Hatch Beauchamp TA3 6SG

☎ 01823 480664 & 0785 668 8128 📠 01823 481118

e-mail: info@farthingshotel.co.uk

web: www.farthingshotel.co.uk

Dir: *from A358, between Taunton and Ilminster turn into Hatch Beauchamp for hotel in village centre*

PETS: Bedrooms (2GF) **Public areas** (on leads) **Grounds** accessible on leads **Exercise area** adjacent **Facilities** leads **Other** please contact for further details

This delightful hotel, set in its own extensive gardens in a peaceful village location, offers comfortable accommodation, combined with all the character and charm of a building dating back over 200 years. The calm atmosphere makes this a great place to relax and unwind. Dinner service is attentive, and menus feature best quality local ingredients prepared and presented with care.

Rooms 11 en suite (1 fmly) (2 GF) S £110-£155; D £130-£175 (incl. bkfst)✳ **Facilities** FTV Wi-fi available Xmas New Year **Parking** 20 **Notes** LB

BUDGET HOTEL

Express by Holiday Inn Taunton, M5 Jct 25

Blackbrook Business Park, Blackbrook Park Av TA1 2PX

☎ 01823 624000 📠 01823 624024

e-mail: managertaunton@expressholidayinn.co.uk

web: www.hiexpress.com/taunton

Dir: *M5 junct 25. Follow signs for Blackbrook Business Park. 100yds on right*

PETS: Bedrooms Charges charge for damage **Grounds** accessible on leads disp bin **Exercise area** **On Request** torch

A modern hotel ideal for families and business travellers. Fresh and uncomplicated, the spacious bedrooms include Sky TV, power shower and tea and coffee-making facilities. Continental buffet breakfast is included in the room rate; other meals may be taken at the nearby family pub or restaurant. See also the Hotel Groups pages.

Rooms 92 en suite

★★★ INN

The Hatch Inn

Village Rd, Hatch Beauchamp TA3 6SG

☎ 01823 480245

e-mail: gemma@thehatchinn.co.uk

web: www.thehatchinn.co.uk

Dir: *M5 junct 25, 3m S off A358*

PETS: Bedrooms unattended **Charges** charge for damage **Public areas** except lounge bar (on leads) **Exercise area** country walks **Facilities** food bowl water bowl washing facs cage storage walks info vet info **On Request** fridge access torch towels

With easy access to both the A303 and M5, this 18th-century, family-run coaching inn is very much the village local, complete with crackling logs fires and a convivial atmosphere. Bedrooms offer good levels of comfort with well appointed bathrooms. Public areas include a choice of bars serving local ales, and the menu features honest, home-cooked cuisine with a focus upon local produce.

Rooms 5 en suite (1 fmly) S £35; D £70-£80* **Facilities** TVB tea/coffee Cen ht Dinner Last d 9pm Wi-fi available Pool Table skittle alley **Notes** No coaches

►►►► **Cornish Farm Touring Park** *(ST235217)*

Shoreditch TA3 7BS

☎ 01823 327746 📠 01823 354946

e-mail: info@cornishfarm.com

web: www.cornishfarm.com

Dir: *M5 junct 25 towards Taunton. Left at lights. 3rd left into Ilminster Road (follow Corfe signs). Right at rdbt, left at next. Right at T-junct, left into Killams Drive, 2nd left into Killams Ave. Follow road over motorway bridge. Site on left, take 2nd entrance*

PETS: Charges 50p per night £3.50 per week **Exercise area** public footpath adjacent **Facilities** walks info vet info **Resident Pets:** German Shepherd & cats

Open all year Last arrival anytime Last departure 11.30hrs

This smart park provides really top quality facilities throughout. Although only two miles from Taunton, the park is set in open countryside and is a very convenient base for visiting the many attractions of the area such as Clarks Village, Glastonbury and Cheddar Gorge. A 3.5-acre site with 50 touring pitches, 25 hardstandings.

WELLINGTON

MAP 03 ST12

★★★ 67% HOTEL

The Cleve Hotel & Country Club

Mantle St TA21 8SN

☎ 01823 662033 📠 01823 660874

e-mail: reception@clevehotel.com

web: www.clevehotel.com

Dir: *M5 junct 26 follow signs to Wellington. Left before Total petrol station*

PETS: Bedrooms Charges £15 per night charge for damage **Public areas** except restaurant or bar (during service) (on leads) **Grounds** accessible on leads **Exercise area Facilities** food bowl water bowl vet info

Offering comfortable bedrooms and public areas, this hotel is quietly located in an elevated position above the town. The atmosphere is relaxed and guests can enjoy Mediterranean influenced cuisine in the stylish restaurant. Extensive leisure facilities are available, including a heated indoor pool, a well-equipped gym, sauna and snooker table.

Rooms 20 en suite (5 fmly) (3 GF) S £65-£79.50; D £80-£110 (incl. bkfst) **Facilities** FTV ⓢ Gym Wi-fi available Steam room Sauna Fitness studio Xmas **Parking** 100

►►► **Gamlins Farm Caravan Park** *(ST083195)*

Gamlins Farm House, Greenham TA21 0LZ

☎ 01823 672859 & 07986 832516 📠 01823 673391

Dir: *M5 junct 26, A38 towards Tiverton & Exeter. 4m turn right for Greenham, site 1m on right*

PETS: Stables on site (loose box) **Charges** cats & dogs 50p, horses £6-£10 per night **Public areas** except laundry & wash rooms (on leads) **Exercise area** on site field available **Facilities** washing facs walks info vet info **Other** prior notice required sand school (80x20mtrs) available

Open Etr-Oct Last arrival 20.00hrs

A well-planned site in a secluded position with panoramic views. The friendly owners keep the toilet facilities to a good standard of cleanliness. A 3-acre site with 25 touring pitches, 6 hardstandings and 3 statics.

Notes ⊜ No loud noise after 22.00hrs

ENGLAND

WELLS

MAP 03 ST54

★★ 78% HOTEL

Crown at Wells

Market Place BA5 2RP

☎ 01749 673457 📠 01749 679792

e-mail: stay@crownatwells.co.uk

web: www.crownatwells.co.uk

Dir: *on entering Wells follow signs for Hotels & Deliveries. Hotel in Market Place*

PETS: Bedrooms Charges £5 per night **Exercise area** 50yds **Facilities** cage storage walks info vet info **On Request** fridge access torch **Other** Please telephone for details **Restrictions** Telephone for details

Retaining its original features and period charm, this historic inn is situated in the heart of the city, just a short stroll from the cathedral. The building's frontage has been used for film sets. Bedrooms, all with modern facilities, vary in size and style. Public areas focus around Anton's, the popular bistro, which offers a light and airy environment and relaxed atmosphere. The Penn Bar offers an alternative eating option and real ales.

Rooms 15 en suite (2 fmly) S £60-£90; D £90-£110 (incl. bkfst) **Facilities** Beauty treatments **Parking** 15 **Notes LB** RS 25 Dec

★★ 72% HOTEL

Coxley Vineyard

Coxley BA5 1RQ

☎ 01749 670285 📠 01749 679708

e-mail: max@orofino.freeserve.co.uk

Dir: *A39 from Wells signed Coxley. Village halfway between Wells & Glastonbury. Hotel off main road at end of village*

PETS: Bedrooms (8GF) unattended **Stables** nearby (3m) **Public areas** except restaurant & lounge bar **Grounds** accessible disp bin **Exercise area** surrounding area **Facilities** water bowl washing facs cage storage walks info vet info **On Request** fridge access towels

This privately owned and personally run hotel was built on the site of an old cider farm. It was later part of a commercial vineyard and some of the vines are still in evidence. It provides well equipped, modern bedrooms; most are situated on the ground floor. There is a comfortable bar and a spacious restaurant with an impressive lantern ceiling. The hotel is a popular venue for conferences and other functions.

Rooms 9 en suite (5 fmly) (8 GF) **Facilities** ⫯ **Parking** 50

★★★★ BED & BREAKFAST

Infield House

36 Portway BA5 2BN

☎ 01749 670989 📠 01749 679093

e-mail: infield@talk21.com

web: www.infieldhouse.co.uk

Dir: *500yds W of city centre on A371 Portway*

PETS: Bedrooms Grounds accessible on leads disp bin **Exercise area** 0.5m **Facilities** leads washing facs walks info vet info **On Request** fridge access torch towels **Restrictions** no dogs under 1year **Resident Pets:** Pepper (Pembroke Corgi)

This charming Victorian house offers comfortable, spacious rooms of elegance and style. The friendly hosts are very welcoming and provide a relaxing home from home. Guests may bring their pets, by arrangement. Dinners, also by arrangement, are served in the pleasant dining room where good home cooking ensures an enjoyable and varied range of options.

Rooms 3 en suite D £58-£60* **Facilities** TVB tea/coffee Cen ht Dinner Last d 10.30am Wi-fi available **Parking** 3 **Notes** No children 12yrs

★★★ GUEST ACCOMMODATION

Birdwood House

Birdwood, Bath Rd BA5 3EW

☎ 01749 679250

e-mail: info@birdwood-bandb.co.uk

web: www.birdwood-bandb.co.uk

Dir: *1.5m NE of city centre. On B3139 between South & West Horrington*

PETS: Bedrooms Sep Accom large kennel with run **Stables** nearby (4m) **Public areas** except dining room (on leads) **Grounds** accessible on leads disp bin **Exercise area** 100mtrs **Facilities** food (pre-bookable) food bowl water bowl bedding dog chews feeding mat dog scoop/disp bags leads dog walking washing facs cage storage walks info vet info **On Request** fridge access towels **Restrictions** no Pit Bull Terriers **Resident Pets:** Florrie (Springer Spaniel), Daisy (cat), cows, peahen

Set in extensive grounds and gardens just a short drive from the town centre, this imposing detached house dates from the 1850s. The bedrooms are comfortable and equipped with a number of extra facilities. Breakfast is served around a communal table in the pleasant dining room or conservatory, which is also available for guest use and enjoyment throughout the day.

Rooms 3 rms (2 en suite) (1 pri facs) (1 fmly) **Facilities** TVB tea/coffee Cen ht TVL **Parking** 12 **Notes**

►► Homestead Park *(ST532474)*

Wookey Hole BA5 1BW

☎ 01749 673022 01749 673022

e-mail: homesteadpark@onetel.com

web: www.homesteadpark.co.uk

Dir: *0.5m NW off A371 (Wells to Cheddar road) (weight limit on bridge into touring area now 1 tonne)*

PETS: Charges 50p per night **Exercise area** disp bin **Facilities** on site shop food vet info **Resident Pets:** Jasper (Golden Retriever)

Open Etr-Sep Last arrival 20.00hrs Last departure noon

This attractive, small site for tents only is by a stream and has mature trees. Set in hilly woods and meadowland with access to the river and Wookey Hole. This park is for adults only. A 2-acre site with 30 touring pitches and 28 statics.

Notes Tents only

WESTON-SUPER-MARE MAP 03 ST36

★★★★ BED & BREAKFAST

Camellia Lodge

76 Walliscote Rd BS23 1ED

☎ 01934 613534 01934 613534

e-mail: dachefscamellia@aol.com

Dir: *200yds from seafront*

PETS: Bedrooms unattended **Charges** charge for damage **Public areas** except food areas (on leads) **Exercise area** 200mtrs **Facilities** walks info vet info **On Request** torch **Resident Pets:** Jack (dog), Rosie & Riley (cats)

Guests return regularly for the warm welcome they receive at this immaculate Victorian family home, which is just off the seafront and within walking distance of the town centre. Bedrooms have a range of thoughtful touches, and carefully prepared breakfasts are served in the relaxing dining room. Home-cooked dinners are also available by prior arrangement.

Rooms 5 rms (4 en suite) (1 pri facs) (2 fmly) S £27.50-£35; D £55-£65* **Facilities** TVB tea/coffee Cen ht Dinner Last d 10.30am **Notes**

★★★ BED & BREAKFAST

Ynishir B&B

74 Uphill Way BS23 4TN

☎ 01934 412703 & 0771 495 0023

e-mail: simon.bilkus@homecall.co.uk

Dir: *A370 follow signs to hospital (Grange Rd), right at mini-rdbt, left onto Uphill Way*

PETS: Bedrooms (1GF) unattended **Exercise area** opposite **Facilities** feeding mat washing facs walks info vet info **On Request** fridge access torch towels **Other** pets allowed in one bedroom only **Resident Pets:** 2 Labradors, 2 Jack Russells, 1 cat, 2 goats, 1 horse

Set in pleasant countryside in the quiet village of Uphill, just a short distance from the Channel, Ynishir has one bedroom with private facilities, and would be ideal for anyone who wants to walk the Mendip Way.

Rooms 1 en suite (1 fmly) (1 GF) S £30; D £50-£60* **Facilities** FTV TVB tea/coffee Cen ht TVL **Parking** 1 **Notes**

►►► Country View Holiday Park *(ST335647)*

Sand Rd, Sand Bay BS22 9UJ

☎ 01934 627595

e-mail: giles@cvhp.co.uk

web: www.cvhp.co.uk

Dir: *M5 junct 21, A370 towards Weston-Super-Mare. Immediately into left lane, follow Kewstoke/Sand Bay signs. Straight over 3 rdbts onto Lower Norton Ln. At Sand Bay right into Sand Rd, site on right*

PETS: Stables nearby (1m) **Charges** £1 per night £7 per week **Public areas** except in shop & bar **Exercise area** 200yds disp bin **Facilities** on site shop walks info vet info **Other** prior notice required

Open Mar-Jan Last arrival 20.00hrs Last departure noon

A pleasant open site in a rural area a few hundred yards from Sandy Bay and beach. The park is also well placed for energetic walks along the coast at either end of the beach. The refurbished toilet facilities are excellent and well maintained. An 8-acre site with 120 touring pitches, 90 hardstandings and 65 statics.

Notes

WHEDDON CROSS MAP 03 SS94

★★★★ FARM HOUSE

North Wheddon Farm *(SS923385)*

TA24 7EX

☎ 01643 841791 Mrs R Abraham

e-mail: rachael@go-exmoor.co.uk

web: www.go-exmoor.co.uk

Dir: *500yds S of village x-rds on A396. Pass Moorland Hall on left, driveway next right*

PETS: Bedrooms Stables on site **Charges** dogs £5 per night charge for damage **Public areas** except dining areas at meal times (on leads) **Grounds** accessible disp bin **Exercise area** 0.25m **Facilities** washing facs cage storage walks info vet info **On Request** torch **Resident Pets:** Poppy & Mingming (Border/ Lakeland Terrier cross), sheep, pigs, chickens, ducks

North Wheddon Farm is a delightfully friendly and comfortable environment with great views. The tranquil grounds include a pleasant garden, and the memorable dinners and breakfasts feature local and the farm's own fresh produce. The bedrooms are thoughtfully equipped, and beds are most comfortable.

Rooms 3 rms (2 en suite) (1 pri facs) S £35-£37.50; D £70-£75 **Facilities** TVB tea/coffee Licensed Cen ht Dinner Last d 10am Wi-fi available Riding **Parking** 5 **Notes LB** 17 acres Mixed

WILLITON MAP 04 ST04

★★★★ GUEST HOUSE

The White House

11 Long St TA4 4QW

☎ 01984 632306

e-mail: thewhitehouse@stefanroberts.orangehome.co.uk

Dir: *A39 Bridgwater to Minehead, In Williton on right prior to Watchet turning*

PETS: Bedrooms (4GF) unattended **Charges** £5 surcharge per night charge for damage **Exercise area** 2min **Facilities** washing facs cage storage walks info vet info **On Request** fridge access torch towels

A relaxed and easy-going atmosphere is the hallmark of this charming Georgian property. Bedrooms in the main building are more spacious than those in the courtyard, but all are well equipped with extra touches that make the White House a home-from-home.

Rooms 6 rms (5 en suite) (1 pri facs) 4 annexe en suite (3 fmly) (4 GF) S £37.50-£42.50; D £65-£75* **Facilities** TVB tea/coffee Licensed Cen ht Dinner Last d 2pm **Parking** 12 **Notes LB** No coaches

WINCANTON MAP 03 ST72

★★★ 79% COUNTRY HOUSE HOTEL

Holbrook House

Holbrook BA9 8BS

☎ 01963 824466 & 828844 01963 32681

e-mail: enquiries@holbrookhouse.co.uk

web: www.holbrookhouse.co.uk

Dir: *from A303 at Wincanton, turn left on A371 towards Castle Cary & Shepton Mallet*

PETS: Charges £10 per night charge for damage **Public areas** except restaurant areas (on leads) **Grounds** accessible on leads **Exercise area** 50mtrs **Facilities** food bowl water bowl leads cage storage walks info vet info **On Request** fridge access torch towels **Resident Pets:** Pepsi (cat)

This handsome country house offers a unique blend of quality and comfort combined with a friendly atmosphere. Set in 17 acres of peaceful gardens and wooded grounds, Holbrook House makes a perfect retreat. The restaurant provides a selection of innovative dishes prepared with enthusiasm and served by a team of caring staff.

Rooms 16 en suite 5 annexe en suite (2 fmly) (5 GF) S £100-£190; D £140-£320 (incl. bkfst & dinner)* **Facilities Spa** FTV Gym Wi-fi available Beauty treatment Exercise classes Sauna Steam room Xmas New Year **Parking** 100

WINSFORD MAP 03 SS93

★★★★ GUEST HOUSE

Karslake House

Halse Ln TA24 7JE

☎ 01643 851242 01643 851242

e-mail: enquiries@karslakehouse.co.uk

web: www.karslakehouse.co.uk

Dir: *In village centre, past the pub and up the hill*

PETS: Bedrooms (1GF) unattended **Stables** nearby (0.25m) **Charges** £10 per night charge for damage **Public areas** **Exercise area** 50yds **Facilities** washing facs cage storage vet info **On Request** fridge access torch towels **Resident Pets:** Sally (Staffordshire cross), Molly (cats)

The 15th-century Karslake House stands in a peaceful Exmoor village. Its public rooms feature original beams and fireplaces, and an interesting menu of delicious meals is available in the dining room. Bedrooms are thoughtfully furnished and have a number of extra touches.

Rooms 6 rms (5 en suite) (1 pri facs) (1 GF) S £60-£80; D £85-£120✳ **Facilities** TVB tea/coffee Licensed Cen ht Dinner Last d 8.15pm Aromatherapist & Masseuse **Parking** 15 **Notes** No children 12yrs No coaches Closed Feb & Mar RS Nov-Jan

►►► Halse Farm Caravan & Camping Park

(SS894344)

TA24 7JL

☎ 01643 851259 01643 851592

e-mail: enquiries@halsefarm.co.uk

web: www.halsefarm.co.uk

Dir: *Signed from A396 at Bridgetown. In Winsford turn left and bear left past pub. 1m up hill, entrance on left immediately after cattle grid*

PETS: Stables nearby (2m) (loose box) **Charges** charge for horses by arrangement per night **Exercise area** extensive walks **Facilities** vet info

Open 22 Mar-Oct Last arrival 22.00hrs Last departure noon

A peaceful little site on Exmoor overlooking a wooded valley with glorious views. This moorland site is quite remote, but it provides good modern toilet facilities which are kept immaculately clean. A 3-acre site with 44 touring pitches, 11 hardstandings.

WITHYPOOL MAP 03 SS83

★★★★★ BED & BREAKFAST

Kings Farm

TA24 7RE

☎ 01643 831381 01643 831381

e-mail: info@kingsfarmexmoor.co.uk

Dir: *Off B3223 to Withypool, over bridge & sharp left to farm*

PETS: Stables on site **Charges** from £10 per night **Grounds** accessible on leads **Exercise area** **Facilities** food food bowl water bowl cage storage walks info vet info **On Request** torch **Resident Pets:** 4 dogs & 6 horses

Over two acres of landscaped gardens beside the river form the backdrop of this delightful farmhouse, set in an idyllic valley beside the Barle. It combines all the character and charm of its 19th-century origins with every modern comfort. From the carefully planned bedrooms to the sumptuously furnished sitting room, delicious home-cooked breakfasts and the warmest of welcomes, top quality is most definitely the hallmark of Kings Farm. Stabling and fishing available.

Rooms 2 rms (1 en suite) (1 pri facs) S £55; D £79-£89✳ **Facilities** STV TVB tea/coffee Cen ht Wi-fi available Fishing **Parking** 3 **Notes** No children 14yrs

WITHYPOOL CONTINUED

★★★★ INN

The Royal Oak Inn

TA24 7QP

☎ 01643 831506 01643 831659

e-mail: enquiries@royaloakwithypool.co.uk

Dir: *7m N of Dulverton, off B3223*

PETS: Bedrooms Sep Accom 1 outdoor kennel **Stables** nearby (1m) **Charges** £8 per night £56 per week **Public areas** except restaurant (on leads) **Exercise area** 500mtrs **Facilities** food bowl water bowl bedding dog chews leads walks info vet info **On Request** torch towels

Set in the heart of the beautiful Exmoor landscape, this long established and popular inn has been providing rest and sustenance for weary travellers for many years. The atmosphere is warm and engaging with the bar always frequented by cheery locals with a story to tell! Bedrooms and bathrooms are stylish and very well appointed with added touches of luxury such as Egyptian cotton linen, bath robes and cosseting towels. Menus feature local produce and can be enjoyed either in the bars or in the elegant restaurant.

Rooms 8 rms (7 en suite) (1 pri facs) S £75; D £120✻ **Facilities** TVB tea/coffee Direct dial from bedrooms Cen ht Dinner Last d 9.30pm **Parking** 10 **Notes LB** No children 10yrs No coaches

WIVELISCOMBE MAP 03 ST02

►►►► **Waterrow Touring Park** *(ST053251)*

TA4 2AZ

☎ 01984 623464 01984 624280

web: www.waterrowpark.co.uk

Dir: *From M5 junct 25 take A358 (signed Minehead) around Taunton, then B3227 through Wiveliscombe. Site after 3m at Waterrow, 0.25m past Rock Inn*

PETS: Charges £1.20 per night £8.40 per week **Public areas** except amenity block disp bin **Exercise area** on site dog exercise field & river walks **Facilities** walks info vet info **Other** prior notice required max 2 dogs per unit **Resident Pets:** Sophie (Labrador), Basil & Smokey (cats), Muscovy ducks

Open all year Last arrival 19.00hrs Last departure 11.30hrs

A pretty park for adults only with individual pitches and plenty of hardstandings. The River Tone runs along a valley beneath the park, accessed by steps to a nature area created by the owners, where fly fishing is permitted. Painting workshops and other activities are available, and the local pub is a short walk away. A 6-acre site with 45 touring pitches, 38 hardstandings and 1 static.

Notes No children

YEOVIL MAP 03 ST51

★★★★ INN

The Masons Arms

41 Lower Odcombe BA22 8TX

☎ 01935 862591 01935 862591

e-mail: paula@masonsarmsodcombe.co.uk

web: www.masonsarmsodcombe.co.uk

Dir: *From A303 take A3088 to Yeovil, follow signs to Montacute after village, 3rd turning on right*

PETS: Bedrooms (5GF) **Stables** nearby (0.5m) **Charges** charge for damage **Public areas** (on leads) **Grounds** accessible disp bin **Exercise area** on site **Facilities** food (pre-bookable) food bowl water bowl bedding dog chews litter tray etc dog scoop/disp bags leads washing facs cage storage walks info vet info **On Request** fridge access torch towels **Resident Pets:** Royce (Springer Spaniel), Ruff (Border Collie), Blake (Jack Russell / Chihuahua cross), Rolo (Jack Russell/Poodle cross), Harley, Dut & Morgan (cats), PJ, Moppet & Fiver (rabbits), chickens

Dating back to the 16th century, this charming inn claims to be the oldest building in this small country village on the outskirts of Yeovil. The spacious bedrooms are contemporary in style, with clean lines, high level of comfort and a wide range of considerate extras. The friendly hosts run their own micro-brewery, and their ales are available at the bar along with others. Public areas include the bar/restaurant, which offers a full menu of freshly prepared dishes, along with a choice of lighter snacks. There is a small caravan/touring park at the rear of the inn.

Rooms 5 en suite (5 GF) S £70; D £85✻ **Facilities** FTV TVB tea/coffee Direct dial from bedrooms Cen ht Dinner Last d 9.30pm Wi-fi available **Parking** 35 **Notes** No coaches

★★★★ ◎ INN

The Helyar Arms

Moor Ln, East Coker BA22 9JR

☎ 01935 862332 01935 864129

e-mail: info@helyar-arms.co.uk

Dir: *3m S of Yeovil. Off A30 or A37 into East Coker*

PETS: Bedrooms unattended **Stables** nearby (1m) **Charges** charge for damage **Public areas** (on leads) **Grounds** accessible disp bin **Exercise area** 1m **Facilities** food bowl water bowl cage storage walks info vet info **On Request** torch towels

A charming 15th-century inn, serving real food in the heart of a pretty Somerset village. The traditional friendly bar with hand-drawn ales retains many original features while the bedrooms offer well equipped, attractive accommodation and modern facilities.

Rooms 6 en suite (3 fmly) **Facilities** TVB tea/coffee Direct dial from bedrooms Cen ht Dinner Last d 9.30pm Wi-fi available Skittle alley **Parking** 40 **Notes** RS 25 Dec

★★★ INN

The Halfway House Inn Country Lodge

Ilchester Rd BA22 8RE

☎ 01935 840350 🖷 01935 849006

e-mail: paul@halfwayhouseinn.com

web: www.halfwayhouseinn.com

Dir: *A303 onto A37 Yeovil road at Ilchester, inn 2m on left*

PETS: Bedrooms (10GF) sign **Charges** £5 per night charge for damage **Public areas** except restaurant (assist dogs only) (on leads) **Grounds** accessible on leads disp bin **Exercise area** 2m **Facilities** walks info vet info **On Request** fridge access **Resident Pets:** Paddy (German Shepherd)

This roadside inn offers comfortable accommodation, which consists of bedrooms in the main house and other contemporary style rooms, each having its own front door, in the annexe. All rooms are bright and well equipped. Meals of generous portion are available in the cosy restaurant and bar, where friendly staff ensure a warm welcome.

Rooms 11 en suite 10 annexe en suite (6 fmly) (10 GF) **Facilities** STV TVB tea/coffee Cen ht TVL Dinner Last d 9pm Wi-fi available Fishing Pool Table **Parking** 49

STAFFORDSHIRE

AUDLEY — MAP 07 SJ75

★★★★ FARM HOUSE

Domvilles Farm *(SJ776516)*

Barthomley Rd ST7 8HT

☎ 01782 720378 🖷 01782 720883 Mrs E E Oulton

e-mail: eileen.oulton@virgin.net

Dir: *M6 junct 16, B5078 towards Alsager, 0.5m left to Barthomley, left at White Lion, Domvilles 0.5m on left*

PETS: Bedrooms (3GF) **Stables** on site **Charges** dog £10; horse £20 per night charge for damage **Grounds** accessible on leads disp bin **Exercise area** on site fields **Facilities** walks info vet info **On Request** fridge access torch **Other** dogs can be fed in yard, or downstairs halls (tiled floor)

This 260-acre dairy farm is a short drive from major roads, and is delightfully presented throughout. Quality décor, antiques and memorabilia highlight the original features of the elegant Georgian property, and bedrooms feature fine Victorian four-poster, half-tester and brass beds. Imaginative food is served and a warm welcome is assured.

Rooms 5 en suite (1 fmly) (3 GF) S £35; D £60✻ **Facilities** TVB tea/coffee Cen ht TVL Dinner Last d 7pm Fishing **Parking** 10 **Notes** LB 260 acres Dairy/sheep

BURTON UPON TRENT — MAP 08 SK22

★★★ 78% COUNTRY HOUSE HOTEL

Newton Park RAMADA

Newton Solney DE15 0SS

☎ 01283 703568 🖷 01283 709235

e-mail: sales.newtonpark@ramadajarvis.co.uk

web: www.ramadajarvis.co.uk

Dir: *B5008 follow road past Repton to Newton Solney. Hotel on left.*

PETS: Bedrooms (7GF) **Charges** £10 per night charge for damage **Grounds** accessible on leads **Exercise area Facilities** vet info **On Request** torch

Set in well tended gardens, this country-house hotel is a popular venue for conferences and meetings. Bedrooms are comfortably appointed for both business and leisure guests.

Rooms 50 en suite (5 fmly) (7 GF) S £79-£186; D £79-£202 (incl. bkfst) **Facilities** FTV Wi-fi available Xmas New Year **Services** Lift **Parking** 120 **Notes** LB

BUDGET HOTEL

Express by Holiday Inn Burton upon Trent

2nd Av, Centrum 100 DE14 2WF

☎ 01283 504300 🖷 01283 504301

e-mail: info@exhiburton.co.uk

web: www.hiexpress.com/burton-n-trent

Dir: *From A38 Branston exit take A5121 signed Town Centre. At McDonalds rdbt, turn left into 2nd Avenue. Hotel on left*

PETS: Bedrooms Stables nearby (0.5m) **Charges** charge for damage **Grounds** accessible on leads disp bin **Exercise area** on site **Facilities** walks info vet info **On Request** torch towels

A modern hotel ideal for families and business travellers. Fresh and uncomplicated, the spacious bedrooms include Sky TV, power shower and tea and coffee-making facilities. Continental buffet breakfast is included in the room rate; other meals may be taken at the nearby family pub or restaurant.

Rooms 82 en suite

CANNOCK MAP 07 SJ91

U

Roman Way

folio Hotels

Watling St WS11 1SH

☎ 01543 572121 📠 01543 502749

e-mail: reservations.romanway@foliohotels.com

web: www.foliohotels.com

Dir: *M6 junct 11, A460 to Cannock, at 1st island turn left, hotel 200yds on left*

PETS: Bedrooms (23GF) sign **Charges** £10 per night charge for damage **Exercise area** adjacent **Facilities** walks info vet info

At the time of going to press the rating for this establishment was not confirmed. This may be due to a change of ownership or because it has only recently joined the AA rating scheme. For further details please see the AA website: www.theAA.com

Rooms 56 en suite (17 fmly) (23 GF) S £49-£95; D £49-£95✳ **Facilities** Wi-fi available Xmas New Year **Parking** 125 **Notes** LB

►►► Cannock Chase Camping & Caravanning Club Site *(SK039145)*

Old Youth Hostel, Wandon WS15 1QW

☎ 01889 582166

web: www.thefriendlyclub.co.uk

Dir: *on A460 to Hednesford, right at Rawnsley/Hazelslade sign, then 1st left. Site 0.5m past golf club*

PETS: Public areas except in buildings **Exercise area** on site disp bin **Facilities** walks info vet info **Other** prior notice required

Open 2 Apr-2 Nov Last arrival 21.00hrs Last departure noon

Very popular and attractive site in an excellent location in the heart of the Chase, with gently sloping ground and timber-built facilities. Walks from the site into this Area of Outstanding Natural Beauty are a pleasant feature of this park, just 2.5 miles from Rugeley. A 5-acre site with 60 touring pitches, 6 hardstandings.

Notes Site gates closed 23.00hrs-07.00hrs

LEEK MAP 07 SJ95

►►► Leek Camping & Caravanning Club Site *(SK004591)*

Blackshaw Grange, Blackshaw Moor ST13 8TL

☎ 01538 300285

web: www.thefriendlyclub.co.uk

Dir: *2m from Leek on A53 Leek to Buxton road. Site 200yds past sign for 'Blackshaw Moor' on left*

PETS: Public areas except in buildings **Exercise area** on site dog walks disp bin **Facilities** walks info vet info **Other** prior notice required

Open all year Last arrival 21.00hrs Last departure noon

A beautifully located club site with well-screened pitches. The very good facilities are kept in pristine condition, and children will enjoy the enclosed play area. A 6-acre site with 70 touring pitches, 39 hardstandings.

Notes Site gates closed 23.00hrs-07.00hrs

LONGNOR MAP 07 SK06

►►►► Longnor Wood Caravan & Camping Park *(SK072640)*

SK17 0NG

☎ 01298 83648 📠 01298 83648

e-mail: info@longnorwood.co.uk

web: www.longnorwood.co.uk

Dir: *1.25m from Longnor (off Longnor to Leek road), signed from village*

PETS: Public areas except toilets & shop/reception **Exercise area** on site 4-acre field **Facilities** on site shop food bowl water bowl dog scoop/disp bags leads washing facs walks info vet info

Open Mar-10 Jan Last arrival 21.00hrs Last departure noon

This spacious adult only park enjoys a secluded setting in the Peak National Park, an Area of Outstanding Natural Beauty. It is surrounded by beautiful rolling countryside and sheltered by woodland, with wildlife encouraged. The nearby village of Longnor offers pub food, restaurants and shops. A 10.5-acre site with 47 touring pitches, 26 hardstandings and 14 statics.

STOKE-ON-TRENT MAP 07 SJ84

★★★ 67% ❁ HOTEL

Haydon House

Haydon St, Basford ST4 6JD

☎ 01782 711311 & 753690 📠 01782 717470

e-mail: enquiries@haydon-house-hotel.co.uk

Dir: *A500/A53 (Hanley/Newcastle), turn left at rdbt, 2nd left at brow of hill, into Haydon St. Hotel on left*

PETS: Bedrooms Charges charge for damage **Public areas** assist dogs only (on leads) **Exercise area Facilities** water bowl

A Victorian property, within easy reach of Newcastle-under-Lyme. The public rooms are furnished in a style befitting the age and character of the house; several rooms are located in a separate house across the road. The hotel has a good reputation for its food and is popular with locals.

Rooms 17 en suite (1 fmly) S £47.50-£75; D £57.50-£85 (incl. bkfst)✳ **Parking** 52

SUFFOLK

ALDEBURGH MAP 05 TM45

★★★ 88% ❀❀ HOTEL

Wentworth

Wentworth Rd IP15 5BD

☎ 01728 452312 📠 01728 454343

e-mail: stay@wentworth-aldeburgh.co.uk

web: www.wentworth-aldeburgh.com

Dir: *off A12 onto A1094, 6m to Aldeburgh, with church on left, left at bottom of hill*

PETS: Bedrooms (5GF) unattended **Charges** £2 per night charge for damage **Public areas** except restaurant **Grounds** accessible **Exercise area** 300mtrs **Facilities** food bowl water bowl walks info vet info **On Request** fridge access torch **Restrictions** no breeds larger than Labrador

A delightful privately owned hotel overlooking the beach. The attractive, well-maintained public rooms include three stylish lounges as well as a cocktail bar and elegant restaurant. Bedrooms are smartly decorated with co-ordinated fabrics and have many thoughtful touches; some rooms have superb sea views. Several very spacious Mediterranean-style rooms are located across the road.

Rooms 28 en suite 7 annexe en suite (5 GF) S £56-£100; D £96-£224 (incl. bkfst)✳ **Facilities** FTV Wi-fi available Xmas New Year **Parking** 30 **Notes** LB

★★★ 86% ❀❀ HOTEL

The Brudenell

The Parade IP15 5BU

☎ 01728 452071 📠 01728 454082

e-mail: info@brudenellhotel.co.uk

web: www.brudenellhotel.co.uk

Dir: *A12/A1094, on reaching town, turn right at junct into High St. Hotel on seafront adjoining Fort Green car park*

PETS: Bedrooms unattended **Charges** £7.50 per night charge for damage **Public areas** except bar or restaurant (assist dogs only) (on leads) **Exercise area Facilities** food (pre-bookable) food bowl water bowl dog chews vet info **On Request** fridge access torch **Restrictions** well behaved dogs only

Situated at the far end of the town centre just a step away from the beach, this hotel has a contemporary appearance, enhanced by subtle lighting and quality soft furnishings. Many of the bedrooms have superb sea views; they include deluxe rooms with king-sized beds and superior rooms suitable for families.

Rooms 42 en suite (15 fmly) S £64-£117; D £104-£232 (incl. bkfst)✳ **Facilities** Wi-fi in bedrooms Xmas New Year **Services** Lift **Parking** 16 **Notes** LB

★★★ 82% ❀ HOTEL

Best Western White Lion

Best Western

Market Cross Place IP15 5BJ

☎ 01728 452720 📠 01728 452986

e-mail: info@whitelion.co.uk

web: www.whitelion.co.uk

Dir: *A12 onto A1094, follow signs to Aldeburgh at junct on left. Hotel on right*

PETS: Bedrooms unattended **Stables** nearby (2m) **Charges** £7.50 per night **Public areas** except restaurant (on leads) **Exercise area** beach adjacent (Oct-Apr only) **Facilities** food bowl water bowl washing facs walks info vet info **On Request** fridge access torch

A popular 15th-century hotel situated at the quiet end of town overlooking the sea. Bedrooms are pleasantly decorated and thoughtfully equipped, many rooms have lovely sea views. Public areas include two lounges and an elegant restaurant, where locally-caught fish and seafood are served. There is also a modern brasserie.

Rooms 38 en suite (1 fmly) S £61.50-£88.50; D £98-£148 (incl. bkfst)✳ **Facilities** STV Wi-fi available Xmas New Year **Parking** 15

BECCLES MAP 05 TM48

►► **Beulah Hall Caravan Park** *(TM478892)*

Dairy Ln, Mutford NR34 7QJ

☎ 01502 476609

e-mail: beulah.hall@btinternet.com

Dir: *0.5m from A146, midway between Beccles & Lowestoft. At Barnby exit A146 into New Road, right at T-junct, site 2nd on right (300yds)*

PETS: disp bin **Exercise area** on site **Facilities** walks info vet info **Other** prior notice required **Resident Pets:** Newfoundland dogs

Open Apr-Oct Last arrival 22.00hrs Last departure noon

Small secluded site in well kept grounds with mature trees and hedging. The neat pitches and pleasant tent area are beneath large trees opposite the swimming pool, and there are clean and well maintained portaloo toilets. This park is now for adults only. A 2.5-acre site with 30 touring pitches.

Notes 

BILDESTON MAP 05 TL94

★★★ 88% ❀❀❀ HOTEL

Bildeston Crown

104 High St IP7 7EB

☎ 01449 740510 🖷 01449 741843

e-mail: hayley@thebildestoncrown.co.uk

web: www.thebildestoncrown.co.uk

Dir: *A12 junct 31, turn right onto B1070 & follow signs to Hadleigh. At T-junct turn left onto A1141, then immediately right onto B1115. Hotel 0.5m*

PETS: Bedrooms unattended **Charges** £10 per stay per night **Public areas** except restaurant **Exercise area** on site courtyard & side terrace

Charming inn situated in a peaceful village close to the historic town of Lavenham. Public areas feature beams, exposed brickwork and oak floors, with contemporary style decor; they include a choice of bars, a lounge and a restaurant. The tastefully decorated bedrooms have lovely co-ordinated fabrics and modern facilities that include a Yamaha music system and LCD TVs. Food here is the real focus and draw; guests can expect fresh, high-quality local produce and accomplished technical skills in both modern and classic dishes.

Rooms 10 en suite **Facilities** Riding Wi-fi in bedrooms **Services** Lift **Parking** 30

BUNGAY MAP 05 TM38

★★★★ FARM HOUSE

Earsham Park Farm *(TM304883)*

Old Railway Rd, Earsham NR35 2AQ

☎ 01986 892180 🖷 01986 894796 Mrs B Watchorn

e-mail: aa@earsham-parkfarm.co.uk

web: www.earsham-parkfarm.co.uk

Dir: *3m SW of Bungay on A143*

PETS: Bedrooms Sep Accom horse stables with straw **Stables** on site **Charges** £5, £10 horses per night charge for damage **Public areas** except dining room (on leads) **Grounds** accessible on leads disp bin **Exercise area** 100mtrs **Facilities** food bowl water bowl feeding mat dog scoop/disp bags leads washing facs cage storage walks info vet info **On Request** fridge access torch towels **Resident Pets:** Widget (Jack Russell), Woggle (Weimeraner), George (horse)

A superb detached Victorian property overlooking open countryside and forming part of a working farm. The property has been restored by the enthusiastic owners and retains many original features. Bedrooms and public areas are attractively furnished, and the excellent breakfasts feature home-made produce including sausages and bacon from the organically reared pigs.

Rooms 3 en suite S £46-£68; D £70-£92 **Facilities** FTV TVB tea/coffee Cen ht Wi-fi available **Parking** 11 **Notes** 589 acres arable, pigs (outdoor)

►►► ***Outney Meadow Caravan Park***

(TM333905)

Outney Meadow NR35 1HG

☎ 01986 892338 🖷 01986 896627

e-mail: c.r.hancy@ukgateway.net

web: www.outneymeadow.co.uk

Dir: *At Bungay site signed from rdbt junction of A143 & A144*

PETS: Public areas except pet free area (on leads) **Exercise area** on site dog walks disp bin **Facilities** walks info vet info **Other** prior notice required

Open Mar-Oct Last arrival 21.00hrs Last departure 16.00hrs

Three pleasant grassy areas beside the River Waveney, with screened pitches. The central toilet block offers good modern facilities, especially in the ladies, and is open at all times. The views from the site across the wide flood plain could be straight out of a Constable painting. Canoeing and boating, coarse fishing and cycling are all available here. A 6-acre site with 45 touring pitches, 5 hardstandings and 30 statics.

Notes ⊜ Dogs must be kept on leads

BURY ST EDMUNDS MAP 05 TL86

★★★★ ◎◎ TOWN HOUSE HOTEL

Angel

Angel Hill IP33 1LT

☎ 01284 714000 🖹 01284 714001

e-mail: staying@theangel.co.uk

web: www.theangel.co.uk

Dir: *from A134, left at rdbt into Northgate St. Continue to lights, right into Mustow St, left into Angel Hill. Hotel on right*

PETS: Bedrooms (15GF) unattended **Charges** charge for damage **Public areas** lounge only (on leads) **Exercise area** Abbey Gardens, 1 min walk **Facilities** walks info vet info

An impressive building situated just a short walk from the town centre. One of the Angel's more notable guests over the last 400 years was Charles Dickens who is reputed to have written part of the Pickwick Papers whilst in residence. The hotel offers a range of individually designed bedrooms that includes a selection of four-poster rooms and a suite.

Rooms 75 en suite (7 fmly) (15 GF) S £110-£150; D £119-£159 (incl. bkfst)✳ **Facilities** Wi-fi available Xmas New Year **Services** Lift **Parking** 20 **Notes** LB

★★★ 87% ◎◎ COUNTRY HOUSE HOTEL

Ravenwood Hall

Rougham IP30 9JA

☎ 01359 270345 🖹 01359 270788

e-mail: enquiries@ravenwoodhall.co.uk

web: www.ravenwoodhall.co.uk

Dir: *3m E off A14, junct 45. Hotel on left*

PETS: Exercise area Facilities water bowl **Other** please telephone for details of pet facilities

Delightful 15th-century property set in seven acres of woodland and landscaped gardens. The building has many original features including carved timbers and inglenook fireplaces. The spacious bedrooms are attractively decorated, tastefully furnished with well-chosen pieces and equipped with many thoughtful touches. Public rooms include an elegant restaurant and a smart lounge bar with an open fire.

Rooms 7 en suite 7 annexe en suite (5 GF) D £120-£195 (incl. bkfst)✳ **Facilities** Wi-fi available Shooting & fishing Hunting can be arranged h fac Xmas New Year **Parking** 150 **Notes** LB

★★★★ INN

The Fox & Hounds

Felsham Rd, Bradfield St George IP30 0AB

☎ 01284 386379

e-mail: bradfieldfox@aol.com

Dir: *Off A134 Bury onto Sudbury Rd, at Sicklesmere turning to Little Welnetham & Bradfield St George*

PETS: Bedrooms (2GF) **Sep Accom** large lockable cage **Stables** nearby (300mtrs) **Charges** charge for damage **Public areas** except eating areas (on leads) **Grounds** accessible on leads disp bin **Exercise area** on site **Facilities** water bowl cage storage walks info vet info **On Request** towels **Resident Pets:** Sacha & Izzy (Labradors), Dennis (Persian cat)

Delightful inn set in a peaceful rural location surrounded by open countryside. The spacious bedrooms are in a converted barn to the rear of the inn; each one has pine furniture and a good range of useful extras. Public areas include a smart restaurant, a cosy bar and a small conservatory.

Rooms 2 annexe en suite (2 GF) **Facilities** TVB tea/coffee Cen ht Dinner Last d 9pm Petanque pitch **Parking** 30 **Notes** Closed 2-9 Jan

DUNWICH MAP 05 TM47

►► Haw Wood Farm Caravan Park

(TM421717)

Hinton IP17 3QT

☎ 01986 784248

Dir: *Turn right off A12, 1.5m N of Darsham level crossing at Little Chef. Site 0.5m on right*

PETS: disp bin **Exercise area** on site large field **Facilities** on site shop food food bowl water bowl dog chews dog scoop/disp bags leads washing facs walks info vet info **Resident Pets:** Benjy (Black Labrador), Tigger (cat)

Open Mar-14 Jan Last arrival 21.00hrs Last departure noon

An unpretentious family-orientated park set in two large fields surrounded by low hedges. The toilets are clean and functional, and there is plenty of space for children to play. An 8-acre site with 65 touring pitches and 25 statics.

Notes ⊜

ENGLAND

ELMSWELL MAP 05 TL96

★★★★ GUEST HOUSE

Kiln Farm

Kiln Ln IP30 9QR

☎ 01359 240442

e-mail: davejankilnfarm@btinternet.com

Dir: *Exit A14 junct 47 for A1088. Entrance to Kiln Ln off east bound slip road.*

PETS: Bedrooms (6GF) **Charges** charge for damage **Public areas Grounds** accessible **Exercise area** 10mtrs **Facilities** feeding mat cage storage vet info **On Request** fridge access torch towels **Resident Pets:** Barney & MummaPuss (cats)

A delightful Victorian farmhouse situated in a peaceful rural location amid three acres of landscaped grounds. The bedrooms are housed in converted farm buildings; each one is smartly decorated and furnished in country style. Breakfast is served in the smart conservatory and there is also a cosy lounge and bar area.

Rooms 2 en suite 6 annexe en suite (2 fmly) (6 GF) S £40-£50; D £80-£100✻ **Facilities** TVB tea/coffee Licensed Cen ht TVL Dinner Last d 6pm Wi-fi available **Parking** 20 **Notes** No coaches

FELIXSTOWE MAP 05 TM33

►►► ***Peewit Caravan Park*** *(TM290338)*

Walton Av IP11 2HB

☎ 01394 284511

web: www.peewitcaravanpark.co.uk

Dir: *Signed from A14 in Felixstowe, 100mtrs past dock gate 1, 1st on left*

PETS: Public areas except in shower/toilet block **Exercise area** on site grass walkway disp bin **Facilities** walks info vet info **Restrictions** well behaved breeds only

Open Apr or Etr-Oct Last arrival 21.00hrs Last departure 11.00hrs

A grass touring area fringed by trees, with well-maintained grounds and a colourful floral display. This handy urban site is not overlooked by houses, and the toilet facilities are clean and well cared for. A function room contains a TV and library. The beach is a few minutes away by car. A 13-acre site with 45 touring pitches, 4 hardstandings and 200 statics.

Notes ⊜ Only foam footballs

FRAMLINGHAM MAP 05 TM26

★★★ GUEST ACCOMMODATION

Church Farm

Church Rd, Kettleburgh IP13 7LF

☎ 01728 723532

e-mail: jbater@suffolkonline.net

Dir: *Off A12 to Wickham Market, signs to Easton Farm Park & Kettleburgh 1.25m, house behind church*

PETS: Bedrooms (1GF) **Charges** £1 per night **Public areas** if other guests approve (on leads) **Grounds** accessible on leads **Exercise area Facilities** feeding mat leads cage storage walks info vet info **On Request** fridge access torch towels **Resident Pets:** Minnie (Jack Russell), Jessie (Labrador), Boots (Border/Jack Russell)

A charming 300-year-old farmhouse situated close to the village church amid superb grounds with a duck pond, mature shrubs and sweeping lawns. The converted property retains exposed beams and open fireplaces. Bedrooms are pleasantly decorated and equipped with useful extras, and a ground-floor bedroom is available.

Rooms 3 rms (1 en suite) (1 GF) S £32-£34; D £64-£68 **Facilities** tea/coffee Cen ht TVL Dinner Last d 7.30pm Fishing **Parking** 10 **Notes** ⊜

HINTLESHAM MAP 05 TM04

★★★★ ⊛⊛ HOTEL

Hintlesham Hall

George St IP8 3NS

☎ 01473 652334 📠 01473 652463

e-mail: reservations@hintleshamhall.com

web: www.hintleshamhall.com

Dir: *4m W of Ipswich on A1071 to Hadleigh & Sudbury*

PETS: Bedrooms (10GF) **Grounds** accessible on leads disp bin **Exercise area Facilities** water bowl feeding mat dog scoop/disp bags pet sitting dog walking cage storage walks info vet info **On Request** torch towels **Other** dogs to be muzzled at owner's discretion

Hospitality and service are key features at this imposing Grade I listed country-house hotel, situated in 175 acres of grounds and landscaped gardens. Individually decorated bedrooms offer a high degree of comfort; each one is tastefully furnished and equipped with many thoughtful touches. The spacious public rooms include a series of comfortable lounges and an elegant restaurant, which serves fine classical cuisine.

Rooms 33 en suite (10 GF) **Facilities** 18 Gym Putt green Health & Beauty services Clay pigeon shooting **Parking** 60 **Notes** LB RS Sat

HORRINGER MAP 05 TL86

★★★★ 75% HOTEL

The Ickworth Hotel & Apartments

von Essen hotels
A PRIVATE COLLECTION
www.vonessenhotels.com

IP29 5QE

☎ 01284 735350 01284 736300

e-mail: info@ickworthhotel.com

web: www.vonessenhotels.co.uk

Dir: *A14 exit for Bury St Edmunds, follow brown signs for Ickworth House, 4th exit at rdbt, to staggered x-rds. Then onto T-junct, left into village, almost immediately right into Ickworth Estate*

PETS: Bedrooms Stables on site **Charges Public areas** except restaurant & food areas **Grounds** accessible **Exercise area Other** please contact for further details

Gifted to the National Trust in 1956 this stunning property is in part a luxurious hotel that combines the glorious design and atmosphere of the past with a reputation for making children very welcome. The staff are friendly and easy going, there is a children's play area, crèche, horses and bikes to ride, and wonderful 'Capability' Brown gardens to roam in. Plus tennis, swimming, beauty treatments and two dining rooms.

Rooms 27 en suite 11 annexe en suite (35 fmly) (4 GF) D £200-£320 (incl. bkfst & dinner)* **Facilities** Spa FTV Riding Wi-fi available Children's crèche Massage Manicures Adventure playground Vineyard Xmas New Year **Services** Lift **Parking** 40

IPSWICH MAP 05 TM14

★★★ 73% HOTEL

Novotel Ipswich Centre

NOVOTEL HOTELS

Greyfriars Rd IP1 1UP

☎ 01473 232400 01473 232414

e-mail: h0995@accor.com

web: www.novotel.com

Dir: *from A14 towards Felixstowe. Left onto A137, follow for 2m into town centre. Hotel on double rdbt by Stoke Bridge*

PETS: Bedrooms unattended sign **Charges** £7.50 per night charge for damage **Public areas** except restaurant (on leads) **Grounds** accessible on leads **Exercise area** Marina & parks nearby **Facilities** cage storage walks info vet info

A modern, red brick hotel perfectly placed in the centre of town close to shops, bars and restaurants. The open-plan public areas include a Mediterranean-style restaurant and a bar with a small games area. The bedrooms are smartly appointed and have many thoughtful touches; three rooms are suitable for less mobile guests.

Rooms 101 en suite (8 fmly) S £59-£119; D £59-£119* **Facilities** Gym Wi-fi in bedrooms Pool table Sauna Xmas New Year **Services** Lift air con **Parking** 53 (charged) **Notes** LB

KESSINGLAND MAP 05 TM58

►►►► Kessingland Camping & Caravanning Club Site *(TM520860)*

Suffolk Wildlife Park, Whites Ln NR33 7TF

☎ 01502 742040

web: www.thefriendlyclub.co.uk

Dir: *On A12 from Lowestoft at Kessingland rdbt, follow Wildlife Park signs, turn right through park entrance*

PETS: Public areas except in buildings disp bin **Exercise area** on site **Facilities** walks info vet info **Other** prior notice required

Open 2 Apr-2 Nov Last arrival 21.00hrs Last departure noon

A well screened open site next to Suffolk Wildlife Park, where concessions are available for visitors. An extensive renovation has created superb facilities, including three family rooms, a disabled unit, and smart reception. A well-equipped laundry and covered dishwashing sinks add to the quality amenities. A 5-acre site with 90 touring pitches.

Notes Site gates closed 23.00hrs-7.00hrs

LAVENHAM MAP 05 TL94

★★★★ 81% HOTEL

The Swan

"bespoke" HOTELS

High St CO10 9QA

☎ 01787 247477 01787 248286

e-mail: info@theswanatlavenham.co.uk

web: www.bespokehotels.com

Dir: *from A12 or A14 onto A134, then B1071 to Lavenham*

PETS: Bedrooms unattended **Charges** £10 per night charge for damage **Public areas** except food service areas (on leads) **Grounds** accessible **Exercise area** 400yds **Facilities** water bowl walks info vet info **On Request** fridge access torch towels

A delightful collection of listed buildings dating back to the 14th century, lovingly restored to retain their original charm. Public rooms include comfortable lounge areas, a charming rustic bar, an informal brasserie and a fine-dining restaurant. Bedrooms are tastefully furnished and equipped with many thoughtful touches. The friendly staff are helpful, attentive and offer professional service.

Rooms 46 en suite (4 fmly) (11 GF) S £85-£105; D £95-£115 (incl. bkfst & dinner)* **Facilities** STV FTV Wi-fi available Xmas **Parking** 62

ENGLAND

LEISTON MAP 05 TM46

►►► Cakes & Ale *(TM432637)*

Abbey Ln, Theberton IP16 4TE

☎ 01728 831655 🖷 01728 831998

e-mail: cakesandalepark@gmail.com

web: www.cakesandale.net

Dir: *From Saxmundham E on B1119. 3m follow minor road over level crossing, turn right, in 0.5m straight on at x-rds, entrance 0.5m on left*

PETS: Charges £2 per night £14 per week disp bin **Exercise area** on site small wooded area **Facilities** on site shop washing facs walks info vet info **Other** prior notice required **Resident Pets:** Jasper (Blue Merle Border Collie)

Open Apr-Oct (rs low season club, shop & reception limited hours) Last arrival 20.00hrs Last departure 13.00hrs

A large, well spread out site with many trees and bushes on a former Second World War airfield. The spacious touring area includes plenty of hardstandings and super pitches, and there is a good bar and a well-maintained toilet block. Wireless internet access is available on site. A 45-acre site with 50 touring pitches, 50 hardstandings and 200 statics.

Notes No group bookings, no noise between 21.00hrs-08.00hrs

LONG MELFORD MAP 05 TL84

★★★ 81% ⊛ HOTEL

The Black Lion

Church Walk, The Green CO10 9DN

☎ 01787 312356 🖷 01787 374557

e-mail: enquiries@blacklionhotel.net

web: www.blacklionhotel.net

Dir: *at junct of A134 & A1092*

PETS: Bedrooms Charges charge for damage **Public areas** except restaurant (on leads) **Grounds** accessible on leads **Exercise area** opposite **Facilities** water bowl walks info vet info **On Request** fridge access torch **Other** food by prior arrangement

This charming 15th-century hotel is situated on the edge of this bustling town overlooking the green. Bedrooms are generally spacious and each is attractively decorated, tastefully furnished and equipped with useful extras. An interesting range of dishes is served in the lounge bar or guests may choose to dine from the same innovative menu in the more formal restaurant.

Rooms 10 en suite (1 fmly) D £120-£195 (incl. bkfst)* **Facilities** Wi-fi available ch fac Xmas New Year **Parking** 10 **Notes LB**

LOWESTOFT MAP 05 TM59

★★★ 82% ⊛⊛ HOTEL

Ivy House Country Hotel

Ivy Ln, Beccles Rd, Oulton Broad NR33 8HY

☎ 01502 501353 & 588144 🖷 01502 501539

e-mail: aa@ivyhousecountryhotel.co.uk

web: www.ivyhousecountryhotel.co.uk

Dir: *on A146 SW of Oulton Broad turn into Ivy Ln beside Esso petrol station. Over railway bridge, follow private drive*

PETS: Bedrooms (17GF) sign **Charges** £17.50 per stay per week **Public areas** except restaurant (on leads) **Grounds** accessible on leads disp bin **Exercise area** on site **Facilities** water bowl bedding dog chews feeding mat dog scoop/disp bags leads washing facs walks info vet info **On Request** fridge access torch towels **Resident Pets:** Tammie (Jack Russell), Patch (Labrador)

Peacefully located, family-run hotel set in three acres of mature landscaped grounds just a short walk from Oulton Broad. Public rooms include an 18th-century thatched barn restaurant where an interesting choice of dishes is served. The attractively decorated bedrooms are housed in garden wings, and many have lovely views of the grounds to the countryside beyond.

Rooms 20 annexe en suite (1 fmly) (17 GF) S £99-£115; D £135-£170 (incl. bkfst)* **Facilities** FTV Wi-fi available Reduced rates at nearby leisure club **Parking** 50 **Notes LB** Closed 23 Dec-6 Jan

★★★★ GUEST ACCOMMODATION

Somerton House

7 Kirkley Cliff NR33 0BY

☎ 01502 565665 🖹 01502 501176

e-mail: pippin.somerton@btinternet.com

Dir: *On the old A12, 100yds from Claremont Pier*

PETS: Bedrooms (1GF) **Charges** £5 per visit charge for damage **Public areas** except dining room **Exercise area** beach opposite **Facilities** walks info vet info

Somerton House is a Grade II Victorian terrace situated in a peaceful area of town overlooking the sea. Bedrooms are smartly furnished in a period style and have many thoughtful touches; some rooms have four poster or half-tester beds. Breakfast is served in the smart dining room and guests have the use of a cosy lounge.

Rooms 7 rms (5 en suite) (2 pri facs) (1 fmly) (1 GF) S £35-£36; D £40-£41✻ **Facilities** STV FTV TVB tea/coffee Cen ht TVL Dinner Last d noon Wi-fi available **Notes LB** Closed 25-26 Dec

★★★ GUEST ACCOMMODATION

Katherine

49 Kirkley Cliff Rd NR33 0DF

☎ 01502 567858 🖹 01502 581341

e-mail: beauthaicuisine@aol.com

web: www.beauthaikatherine.co.uk

Dir: *On A12 seafront road next to Kensington Garden*

PETS: Bedrooms Stables nearby (1m) **Charges** by arrangement per night charge for damage **Exercise area** adjacent **Restrictions** small dogs only (max 10kg)

This large Victorian property lies opposite the beach in the quiet part of town. The spacious public rooms include a smart lounge bar with plush leather sofas and an intimate restaurant serving authentic Thai cuisine. The pleasant bedrooms have coordinated fabrics and many thoughtful touches.

Rooms 10 en suite (5 fmly) S £35-£50; D £55-£65✻ **Facilities** TVB tea/coffee Direct dial from bedrooms Cen ht Dinner Last d 10.30pm **Parking** 4 **Notes LB**

★★★ GUEST HOUSE

Coventry House

8 Kirkley Cliff NR33 0BY

☎ 01502 573865 🖹 01502 573865

Dir: *On A12 opp Claremont Pier, 0.25m S from Harbour Bridge*

PETS: Bedrooms (1GF) **Charges** charge for damage **Public areas** except dining room **Exercise area** 100yds

An impressive Victorian terrace house, situated on the seafront opposite the pier. The pleasant bedrooms are thoughtfully equipped and many rooms have lovely sea views. Breakfast is served in the carefully appointed dining room and there is a comfortable lounge.

Rooms 7 rms (5 en suite) (2 pri facs) (3 fmly) (1 GF) S £25-£35; D £55-£60✻ **Facilities** TVB tea/coffee Cen ht TVL **Parking** 4 **Notes LB** No coaches Closed 24-27 Dec

★★★ GUEST HOUSE

Fairways

398 London Rd South NR33 0BQ

☎ 01502 572659

e-mail: amontali@netmatters.co.uk

Dir: *S of town centre on A12, 1m from railway and bus station*

PETS: Bedrooms Stables nearby (1m) **Charges** charge for damage **Exercise area Facilities** vet info

A friendly, family-run guest house located at the southern end of the town. Bedrooms come in a variety of sizes and styles; each room is pleasantly decorated and thoughtfully equipped. Breakfast is served in the smart dining room and there is also a cosy lounge.

Rooms 7 rms (4 en suite) (2 fmly) S fr £20✻ **Facilities** TVB tea/coffee Licensed Cen ht TVL

NEWMARKET — MAP 05 TL66

★★★ 78% HOTEL

Best Western Heath Court

Moulton Rd CB8 8DY

☎ 01638 667171 🖹 01638 666533

e-mail: quality@heathcourthotel.com

Dir: *leave A14 at Newmarket & Ely exit onto A142. Follow town centre signs over mini rdbt. At clocktower left into Moulton Rd*

PETS: Bedrooms unattended sign **Stables** nearby (3m) **Charges** charge for damage **Grounds** accessible on leads disp bin **Exercise area** 100yds **Facilities** food (pre-bookable) food bowl water bowl pet sitting dog walking washing facs cage storage walks info vet info **On Request** fridge access torch towels

Modern red-brick hotel situated close to Newmarket Heath and perfectly placed for the town centre. Public rooms include a choice of dining options - informal meals can be taken in the lounge bar or a modern carte menu is offered in the restaurant. The smartly presented bedrooms are mostly spacious and some have air conditioning.

Rooms 41 en suite (2 fmly) S £55-£105; D £60-£120✻ **Facilities** STV Wi-fi in bedrooms Health & beauty salon New Year **Services** Lift **Parking** 60 **Notes LB**

ENGLAND

NEWMARKET CONTINUED

★★★★ BED & BREAKFAST

The Garden Lodge

11 Vicarage Ln, Woodditton CB8 9SG

☎ 01638 731116

e-mail: swedishgardenlodge@hotmail.com

web: www.gardenlodge.net

Dir: *3m S of Newmarket in Woodditton village*

PETS: Bedrooms (3GF) unattended **Grounds** accessible **Exercise area Facilities** food bowl water bowl **Restrictions** no Bull Terriers

A warm welcome is assured in this home-from-home, not far from the famous racecourse. The accommodation, within quality chalets, is very well equipped and features a wealth of thoughtful extras. Freshly prepared home-cooked breakfasts are served in an elegant dining room in the main house.

Rooms 3 en suite (3 GF) S £30-£35; D £50-£60✻ **Facilities** TVB tea/coffee Cen ht Dinner Last d noon **Parking** 6 **Notes**

ORFORD — MAP 05 TM45

★★ 85% HOTEL

The Crown & Castle

IP12 2LJ

☎ 01394 450205

e-mail: info@crownandcastle.co.uk

web: www.crownandcastle.co.uk

Dir: *turn right from B1084 on entering village, towards castle*

PETS: Bedrooms (11GF) unattended **Charges** £10 per dog, per stay charge for damage **Public areas** allowed in bar & at table 30 only (on leads) **Grounds** accessible on leads disp bin **Exercise area** 100yds **Facilities** food (pre-bookable) dog chews dog scoop/disp bags washing facs walks info vet info **On Request** fridge access torch towels **Restrictions** no very large dogs; no more than 2 dogs per room **Resident Pets:** Jack & Annie (Wire-Haired Fox Terriers), Holly (cat)

Delightful inn situated adjacent to the Norman castle keep. Contemporary style bedrooms are spilt between the main house and the garden wing; the latter are more spacious and have patios with access to the garden. The restaurant has an informal atmosphere with polished tables and local artwork; the menu features quality, locally sourced produce.

Rooms 7 en suite 12 annexe en suite (1 fmly) (11 GF) S £92-£124; D £115-£155 (incl. bkfst)✻ **Facilities** Wi-fi available Xmas New Year **Parking** 20 **Notes LB** No children 9yrs Closed 5-8 Jan

SAXMUNDHAM — MAP 05 TM36

★★★★ BED & BREAKFAST

Sandpit Farm

Bruisyard IP17 2EB

☎ 01728 663445

e-mail: smarshall@aldevalleybreaks.co.uk

web: www.aldevalleybreaks.co.uk

Dir: *4m W of Saxmundham. A1120 onto B1120, 1st left for Bruisyard, house 1.5m on left*

PETS: Bedrooms sign **Sep Accom** outbuildings by barn **Stables** on site **Charges** £5 per night £35 per week charge for damage **Grounds** accessible on leads disp bin **Exercise area Facilities** cage storage walks info vet info **On Request** fridge access **Other** pets allowed in one bedroom only **Resident Pets:** Twiggy & Inca (Black Labradors), chickens, guinea fowl

Sandpit Farm is a delightful Grade II listed farmhouse set in 20 acres of grounds. Bedrooms have many thoughtful touches and lovely country views, and there are two cosy lounges to enjoy. Breakfast features quality local produce and freshly laid free-range eggs.

Rooms 2 en suite S £40-£60; D £65-£80✻ **Facilities** tea/coffee Cen ht TVL Riding **Parking** 4 **Notes LB** Closed 24-26 Dec

SOUTHWOLD — MAP 05 TM57

★★★ 81% HOTEL

Swan

Market Place IP18 6EG

☎ 01502 722186 01502 724800

e-mail: swan.hotel@adnams.co.uk

Dir: *A1095 to Southwold. Hotel in town centre. Parking via archway to left of building*

PETS: Bedrooms (17GF) **Charges** £5 per night charge for damage **Grounds** accessible disp bin **Exercise area Facilities** food bowl water bowl bedding dog chews feeding mat dog scoop/disp bags washing facs cage storage vet info **On Request** fridge access

A charming 17th-century coaching inn situated in the heart of this bustling town centre overlooking the market place. Public rooms feature an elegant restaurant, a comfortable drawing room, a cosy bar and a lounge where guests can enjoy afternoon tea. The spacious bedrooms are attractively decorated, tastefully furnished and thoughtfully equipped.

Rooms 25 en suite 17 annexe en suite (17 GF) S £50-£98; D £80-£220 (incl. bkfst) **Facilities** Xmas New Year **Services** Lift **Parking** 35 **Notes LB**

★★ 85% SMALL HOTEL

Blyth

Station Rd IP18 6AY

☎ 01502 722632 & 0845 348 6867 📠 01502 724123

e-mail: reception@blythhotel.com

PETS: Bedrooms unattended **Charges** £5 per night charge for damage **Public areas** except restaurant & lounge (on leads) **Grounds** accessible on leads disp bin **Exercise area** 5 mins

Expect a warm welcome at this delightful family run hotel which is situated just a short walk from the town centre. The spacious public rooms include a smart residents' lounge, an open-plan bar and a large restaurant. Bedrooms are tastefully appointed with co-ordinated fabrics and have many thoughtful touches.

Rooms 13 en suite S £65-£75; D £100-£140 (incl. bkfst)✳ **Facilities** FTV Wi-fi available Xmas New Year **Parking** 8 **Notes** LB

WESTLETON MAP 05 TM46

★★★ 77% 🏵🏵 HOTEL

Westleton Crown

The Street IP17 3AD

☎ 01728 648777 📠 01728 648239

e-mail: reception@westletoncrown.co.uk

web: www.westletoncrown.co.uk

Dir: *A12 N, turn right for Westleton just after Yoxford. Hotel opposite on entering Westleton*

PETS: Bedrooms Charges £5 per night **Public areas** except main dining room **Grounds** accessible disp bin **Exercise area** outside hotel **Facilities** food bowl water bowl dog chews walks info vet info **On Request** fridge access torch **Resident Pets:** Stopit (Lurcher)

Charming coaching inn situated in a peaceful village location just a few minutes from the A12. Public rooms include a smart, award-winning restaurant, comfortable lounge, and busy bar with exposed beams and open fireplaces. The stylish bedrooms are tastefully decorated and equipped with many thoughtful little extras.

Rooms 22 en suite 3 annexe en suite (3 fmly) (8 GF) S £85-£95; D £95-£160 (incl. bkfst) **Facilities** Wi-fi available Xmas New Year **Parking** 26 **Notes** Closed 25 Dec

YOXFORD MAP 05 TM36

★★★ 86% 🏵🏵 COUNTRY HOUSE HOTEL

Satis House

IP17 3EX

☎ 01728 668418 📠 01728 668640

e-mail: enquiries@satishouse.co.uk

web: www.satishouse.co.uk

Dir: *off A12 between Ipswich & Lowestoft. 9m E Aldeburgh & Snape*

PETS: Bedrooms (1GF) **Charges** £5 per night £20 per week charge for damage **Public areas** except restaurant & lounge (on leads) **Grounds** accessible on leads **Exercise area** walled garden adjacent **Facilities** food (pre-bookable) food bowl water bowl cage storage walks info vet info **On Request** fridge access torch towels **Restrictions** small & medium sized dogs only

Expect a warm welcome from the caring hosts at this delightful 18th-century, Grade II listed property set in three acres of parkland. The stylish public areas have a really relaxed atmosphere; they include a choice of dining rooms, a smart bar and a cosy lounge. The individually decorated bedrooms are tastefully appointed and thoughtfully equipped.

Rooms 7 en suite 1 annexe en suite (1 fmly) (1 GF) S £60-£125; D £90-£155 (incl. bkfst)✳ **Facilities** STV FTV Xmas New Year **Parking** 30 **Notes** LB

SURREY

BAGSHOT MAP 04 SU96

★★★★★ 🏵🏵🏵 COUNTRY HOUSE HOTEL

Pennyhill Park Hotel & The Spa

EXCLUSIVE HOTELS

London Rd GU19 5EU

☎ 01276 471774 📠 01276 473217

e-mail: enquiries@pennyhillpark.co.uk

web: www.exclusivehotels.co.uk

Dir: *on A30 between Bagshot & Camberley*

PETS: Bedrooms (26GF) unattended **Stables** nearby (5m) **Charges** £50 per stay charge for damage **Public areas** except restaurant, bar & spa **Grounds** accessible **Exercise area** 2m **Facilities** food (pre-bookable) food bowl water bowl bedding dog chews cat treats feeding mat leads pet sitting dog walking washing facs cage storage walks info vet info **On Request** fridge access torch towels

This delightful country-house hotel set in 120-acre grounds provides every modern comfort. The stylish bedrooms are individually designed and have impressive bathrooms. The award-winning Latymer Restaurant is among the range of dining options and there is a choice of lounges and bars. Leisure facilities include a jogging trail, a golf course and a state-of-the-art spa with a thermal sequencing experience, ozone treated swimming and hydrotherapy pools along with a comprehensive range of therapies and treatments.

Rooms 26 en suite 97 annexe en suite (6 fmly) (26 GF) D £250-£925✳ **Facilities Spa** STV 9 Fishing Gym Wi-fi in bedrooms Archery Clay shooting Plunge pool Turkish steam room Rugby/football pitch Xmas New Year **Services** Lift **Parking** 500 **Notes** LB

ENGLAND

CHERTSEY MAP 04 TQ06

►►►► Chertsey Camping & Caravanning Club Site *(TQ052667)*

Bridge Rd KT16 8JX

☎ 01932 562405

web: www.thefriendlyclub.co.uk

Dir: *M25 junct 11, follow A317 to Chertsey. At rdbt take 1st exit to lights. Straight over at next lights. Turn right 400yds, turn left into site*

PETS: Public areas disp bin **Exercise area** on site dog walk **Facilities** walks info vet info **Other** prior notice required

Open all year Last arrival 21.00hrs Last departure noon

A pretty Thames-side site set amongst trees and shrubs in well-tended grounds, ideally placed for the M3/M25 and for visiting London. Some attractive riverside pitches are very popular, and fishing and boating is allowed from the site on the river. The toilet facilities are very good. A 12-acre site with 200 touring pitches, 50 hardstandings.

Notes Site gates closed 23.00hrs-07.00hrs

CHOBHAM MAP 04 SU96

★★★★ GUEST ACCOMMODATION

Pembroke House

Valley End Rd GU24 8TB

☎ 01276 857654 📠 01276 858445

e-mail: pembroke_house@btinternet.com

Dir: *A30 onto B383 signed Chobham, 3m right onto Valley End Rd, 1m on left*

PETS: Bedrooms Public areas except dining room & kitchen **Grounds** accessible disp bin **Exercise area** adjacent **Facilities** food bowl water bowl bedding leads pet sitting washing facs cage storage walks info vet info **On Request** fridge access torch towels **Resident Pets:** Puzzle, Carrie, Pandora (Jack Russells)

Proprietor Julia Holland takes obvious pleasure in treating you as a friend at her beautifully appointed and spacious home. The elegantly proportioned public areas include an imposing entrance hall and dining room with views over the surrounding countryside. Bedrooms are restful and filled with thoughtful extras.

Rooms 4 rms (2 en suite) (2 pri facs) S £40-£70; D £100-£140✻ **Facilities** STV TVB tea/coffee Cen ht Wi-fi available **Parking** 10 **Notes** No children 6yrs

EAST HORSLEY MAP 04 TQ05

►►► Horsley Camping & Caravanning Club Site *(TQ083552)*

Ockham Rd North KT24 6PE

☎ 01483 283273

web: www.thefriendlyclub.co.uk

Dir: *M25 junct 10. S & take 1st major turn signed Ockham/Southend/Ripley. Left & site 2.5m on right. From S take A3 past Guildford & take B2215 towards Ripley*

PETS: Public areas except in buildings disp bin **Exercise area** on site **Facilities** walks info vet info **Other** prior notice required

Open 2 Apr-2 Nov Last arrival 21.00hrs Last departure noon

A beautiful lakeside site with plenty of trees and shrubs and separate camping fields, providing a tranquil base within easy reach of London. Toilet facilities are well maintained and clean. A 9.5-acre site with 130 touring pitches, 41 hardstandings.

Notes Site gates closed 23.00hrs-07.00hrs

HASLEMERE MAP 04 SU93

★★★★ 77% HOTEL

Lythe Hill Hotel and Spa

Petworth Rd GU27 3BQ

☎ 01428 651251 📠 01428 644131

e-mail: lythe@lythehill.co.uk

web: www.lythehill.co.uk

Dir: *left from High St onto B2131. Hotel 1.25m on right*

PETS: Bedrooms (18GF) unattended **Stables** nearby (10 mins) **Charges** charge for damage **Grounds** accessible **Exercise area** 5 mins **Facilities** dog grooming vet info **On Request** torch towels

This privately owned hotel sits in 30 acres of attractive parkland with lakes, complete with roaming geese. The hotel has been described as a hamlet of character buildings, each furnished in a style that complements the age of the property; the oldest one dating back to 1475. Cuisine in the adjacent 'Auberge de France' offers interesting, quality dishes, whilst breakfast is served in the hotel dining room. The bedrooms are split between a number of 15th-century buildings and vary in size. The stylish spa includes a 16-metre swimming pool.

Rooms 41 en suite (8 fmly) (18 GF) S £165-£300; D £165-£300 (incl. bkfst)✻ **Facilities Spa** FTV Fishing Gym Wi-fi in bedrooms Boules Xmas New Year **Parking** 200 **Notes LB**

SUSSEX, EAST

ALFRISTON MAP 05 TQ50

★★★ 82% HOTEL

Deans Place

Seaford Rd BN26 5TW

☎ 01323 870248 01323 870918

e-mail: mail@deansplacehotel.co.uk

web: www.deansplacehotel.co.uk

Dir: *off A27, signed Alfriston & Drusillas Zoo Park. Continue south through village*

PETS: Bedrooms (8GF) unattended **Charges** £5 per night **Public areas** except restaurant & function rooms (on leads) **Grounds** accessible **Exercise area Facilities** water bowl washing facs cage storage walks info vet info **On Request** fridge access torch towels

Situated on the southern fringe of the village, this friendly hotel is set in attractive gardens. Bedrooms vary in size and are well appointed with good facilities. A wide range of food is offered including an extensive bar menu and a fine dining option in Harcourt's Restaurant.

Rooms 36 en suite (4 fmly) (8 GF) S £78-£120; D £100-£210 (incl. bkfst) **Facilities** STV FTV Putt green Wi-fi in bedrooms Boules Xmas New Year **Parking** 100 **Notes** LB

★★★ 77% HOTEL

Star Inn

BN26 5TA

☎ 01323 870495 01323 870922

e-mail: bookings@star-inn-alfriston.com

Dir: *2m off A27, at Drusillas rdbt follow Alfriston signs. Hotel on right in centre of High Street*

PETS: Bedrooms (11GF) unattended sign **Charges** £25 per stay charge for damage **Public areas** except restaurant (on leads) **Exercise area** 0.2m **Facilities** cage storage vet info **On Request** fridge access torch towels

Built in the 13th century and reputedly one of the country's oldest inns, this charming establishment is ideally situated for walking the South Down or exploring the East Sussex coast. Bedrooms are traditionally decorated but with comfortable, modern facilities. Public areas include cosy lounges with open log fires, a bar and a popular restaurant serving a wide choice of dishes using mainly local produce. Guests can also enjoy luxury spa treatments by appointment.

Rooms 37 en suite (1 fmly) (11 GF) S £69-£99; D £98-£140 (incl. bkfst)* **Facilities** Xmas New Year **Parking** 35

BATTLE MAP 05 TQ71

★★★ 79% HOTEL

Powder Mills

Powdermill Ln TN33 0SP

☎ 01424 775511 01424 774540

e-mail: powdc@aol.com

web: www.powdermillshotel.com

Dir: *pass Abbey on A2100. 1st right, hotel 1m on right*

PETS: Bedrooms (3GF) unattended sign **Stables** on site **Charges** £10 per stay per night charge for damage **Public areas** except restaurant **Grounds** accessible disp bin **Exercise area Facilities** leads washing facs cage storage walks info vet info **On Request** fridge access torch towels **Resident Pets:** Jessica, Holly & Jenny (Springer Spaniels)

A delightful 18th-century country-house hotel set amidst 150 acres of landscaped grounds with lakes and woodland. The individually decorated bedrooms are tastefully furnished and thoughtfully equipped; some rooms have sun terraces with lovely views over the lake. Public rooms include a cosy lounge bar, music room, drawing room, library, restaurant and conservatory.

Rooms 30 en suite 10 annexe en suite (3 GF) S £105; D £130-£160 (incl. bkfst)* **Facilities** Fishing Wi-fi in bedrooms Jogging trails Woodland walks Clay pigeon shooting Xmas New Year **Parking** 101 **Notes** LB

BEXHILL MAP 05 TQ70

★★★ 78% HOTEL

Cooden Beach Hotel

TN39 4TT

☎ 01424 842281 01424 846142

e-mail: jk@thecoodenbeachhotel.co.uk

web: www.thecoodenbeachhotel.co.uk

Dir: *A259 towards Cooden. Signed at rdbt in Little Common Village. Hotel at end of road*

PETS: Bedrooms (4GF) unattended **Public areas** tavern/bar only **Grounds** accessible disp bin **Exercise area** adjacent **Facilities** water bowl walks info vet info **On Request** fridge access

This privately owned hotel is situated within two acres of private gardens directly accessing the beach. With a train station within walking distance the location is perfectly suited for both business and leisure guests. Bedrooms are comfortably appointed, and public areas include a spacious restaurant, lounge, bar and leisure centre with swimming pool.

Rooms 33 en suite 8 annexe en suite (10 fmly) (4 GF) **Facilities** FTV Gym Wi-fi in bedrooms Sauna Steam room **Parking** 60

ENGLAND

BRIGHTON & HOVE

MAP 04 TQ30

★★★★ 73% HOTEL

Barceló Brighton Old Ship Hotel

King's Rd BN1 1NR

☎ 01273 329001 01273 820718

e-mail: oldship@barcelo-hotels.co.uk

web: www.barcelo-hotels.co.uk

Dir: *A23 to seafront, right at rdbt along Kings Rd. Hotel 200yds on right*

PETS: Bedrooms unattended sign **Charges** £15 per night charge for damage **Public areas** except food & beverage areas (on leads) **Exercise area** seafront adjacent **Facilities** cage storage vet info **On Request** torch towels

This historic hotel enjoys a stunning seafront location and offers guests elegant surroundings to relax in. Bedrooms are well designed, with modern facilities ensuring comfort. Many original features have been retained, including the newly renovated Paganini Ballroom. Facilities include a sleek bar, alfresco dining and a variety of conference rooms.

Rooms 152 en suite S £65-£200✱ **Facilities** Wi-fi available Xmas New Year **Services** Lift **Parking** 40

★★★ 75% HOTEL

Best Western Princes Marine

153 Kingsway BN3 4GR

☎ 01273 207660 01273 325913

e-mail: princesmarine@bestwestern.co.uk

Dir: *right at Brighton Pier, follow seafront for 2m. Hotel 200yds from King Alfred leisure centre*

PETS: Bedrooms Stables nearby (4m) **Public areas** except restaurant (on leads) **Grounds** accessible on leads disp bin **Exercise area Facilities** food (pre-bookable) water bowl feeding mat washing facs walks info vet info **On Request** fridge access torch towels

This friendly hotel enjoys a seafront location and offers spacious, comfortable bedrooms equipped with a good range of facilities including free Wi-fi. There is a stylish restaurant, modern bar and selection of roof-top meeting rooms with sea views. Limited parking is available at the rear.

Rooms 48 en suite (4 fmly) **Services** Lift **Parking** 30 **Notes** LB

★★★ 68% HOTEL

The Granville

124 King's Rd BN1 2FA

☎ 01273 326302 01273 728294

e-mail: granville@brighton.co.uk

web: www.granvillehotel.co.uk

Dir: *opposite West Pier next to Hilton Metropole*

PETS: Bedrooms (2GF) unattended **Charges** charge for damage **Public areas** (on leads) **Exercise area** park **Facilities** bedding **On Request** towels

This stylish hotel is located on Brighton's busy seafront. Bedrooms are carefully furnished and decorated with great style. Contemporary bathrooms, some with spa baths are a focal point of many rooms. A trendy cocktail bar that also serves food is located in the cellar which has street access and a terrace for outdoor dining.

Rooms 24 en suite (2 fmly) (2 GF) **Facilities** Wi-fi in bedrooms **Services** Lift **Parking Notes** LB

★★★ 64% HOTEL

Preston Park Hotel

216 Preston Rd BN1 6UU

☎ 01273 507853 01273 540039

e-mail: manager@prestonparkhotel.co.uk

Dir: *on A23 towards Brighton town centre*

PETS: Bedrooms Charges £5 per night £30 per week charge for damage **Public areas** except food & beverage areas **Grounds** accessible on leads **Exercise area** park 2min **Facilities** walks info vet info **On Request** fridge access torch towels

This hotel enjoys a convenient roadside location on the outskirts of Brighton. Bedrooms are modern in style and well provisioned for both the leisure and business guest. Freshly prepared meals are offered in the spacious Sussex Bar (open 24 hours to residents) and in the more intimate and relaxing restaurant. Guests can enjoy a drink on the patio in summer.

Rooms 33 en suite (4 fmly) **Facilities** supervised Gym **Parking** 60

★★★★ GUEST ACCOMMODATION

Brighton Pavilions

7 Charlotte St BN2 1AG

☎ 01273 621750 📠 01273 622477

e-mail: sanchez-crespo@lineone.net

web: www.brightonpavilions.com

Dir: *A23 to Brighton Pier, left onto A259 Marine Parade, Charlotte St 15th left*

PETS: Bedrooms (1GF) unattended **Charges** £10 per night charge for damage **Public areas** except dining room (on leads) **Exercise area** 5 mins walk **Facilities** walks info vet info **On Request** fridge access **Restrictions** very large breeds not accepted **Resident Pets:** Fluffy (budgie)

This well-run operation is in one of Brighton's Regency streets, a short walk from the seafront and town centre. Bedrooms have themes such as Mikado or Pompeii, and are very smartly presented with many thoughtful extras including room service breakfast in superior rooms and free WiFi. The bright breakfast room is styled after a Titanic garden restaurant.

Rooms 10 rms (7 en suite) (1 fmly) (1 GF) S £46-£65; D £92-£152*
Facilities TVB tea/coffee Direct dial from bedrooms Cen ht **Notes** LB

★★★★ GUEST ACCOMMODATION

Ambassador Brighton

22-23 New Steine, Marine Pde BN2 1PD

☎ 01273 676869 📠 01273 689988

e-mail: info@ambassadorbrighton.co.uk

web: www.ambassadorbrighton.co.uk

Dir: *A23 to Brighton Pier, left onto A259, 9th left, onto Garden Sq, 1st left*

PETS: Bedrooms Charges charge for damage **Public areas** allowed in bar only **Exercise area** adjacent **Facilities** feeding mat dog walking walks info **On Request** fridge access torch

At the heart of bustling Kemp Town, overlooking the attractive garden square next to the seaside, this well-established property has a friendly and relaxing atmosphere. Bedrooms are well equipped and vary in size, with the largest having the best views. A small lounge with a separate bar is available.

Rooms 24 en suite (9 fmly) (3 GF) S £40-£75; D £65-£115*
Facilities TVB tea/coffee Direct dial from bedrooms Cen ht **Notes** LB

★★★ GUEST ACCOMMODATION

Avalon

7 Upper Rock Gardens BN2 1QE

☎ 01273 692344 📠 01273 692344

e-mail: info@avalonbrighton.co.uk

Dir: *A23 to Brighton Pier, left onto Marine Parade, 300yds at lights left onto Lower Rock Gdns, over lights Avalon on left*

PETS: Bedrooms (1GF) unattended **Charges** charge for damage **Public areas** (on leads) **Exercise area** 25mtrs **Facilities** food bowl water bowl dog chews feeding mat dog scoop/disp bags leads walks info vet info **On Request** fridge access torch towels

A warm welcome is assured at this guest house just a short walk from the seafront and The Lanes. Ensuite bedrooms vary in size and style but all are attractively presented with plenty of useful accessories including free WiFi. Parking vouchers are available for purchase from the proprietor.

Rooms 7 en suite (1 fmly) (1 GF) S £35-£39; D £65-£115*
Facilities FTV TVB tea/coffee Cen ht

CROWBOROUGH — MAP 05 TQ53

►►► **Crowborough Camping & Caravanning Club Site** *(TQ520315)*

Goldsmith Recreation Ground TN6 2TN

☎ 01892 664827

web: www.thefriendlyclub.co.uk

Dir: *Turn off A26 into entrance to 'Goldsmiths Ground', signed Leisure Centre. At top of road right onto site lane*

PETS: disp bin **Exercise area** on site **Facilities** walks info vet info **Other** prior notice required

Open 2 Apr-2 Nov Last arrival 21.00hrs Last departure noon

A spacious terraced site with stunning views across the Weald to the North Downs in Kent. This good quality site has clean, modern toilets, a kitchen and eating area for campers, a recreation room, and good provision of hardstandings. An excellent leisure centre is adjacent to the park. A 13-acre site with 90 touring pitches, 26 hardstandings.

Notes Site gates closed 23.00hrs-07.00hrs

EASTBOURNE MAP 05 TV69

★★★★★ 81% HOTEL

The Grand Hotel

King Edward's Pde BN21 4EQ

☎ 01323 412345 01323 412233

e-mail: reservations@grandeastbourne.com

web: www.grandeastbourne.com

Dir: *on seafront W of Eastbourne, 1m from railway station*

PETS: Bedrooms Charges £7 per night **Exercise area** park adjacent

This famous Victorian hotel offers high standards of service and hospitality. The extensive public rooms feature a magnificent Great Hall, with marble columns and high ceilings, where guests can relax and enjoy afternoon tea. The spacious bedrooms provide high levels of comfort and some rooms have balconies with stunning sea views. There is a choice of restaurants and bars as well as superb leisure facilities.

Rooms 152 en suite (20 fmly) (4 GF) S £160-£505; D £190-£535 (incl. bkfst)* **Facilities Spa** STV pool supervised Gym Putt green Hairdressing Beauty therapy ch fac Xmas New Year **Services** Lift **Parking** 80 **Notes LB**

★★★ 70% HOTEL

Courtlands

3-5 Wilmington Gardens BN21 4JN

☎ 01323 723737 01323 732902

e-mail: bookings@courtlandseastbourne.com

Dir: *Exit Grand Parade at Carlisle Rd*

PETS: Bedrooms Charges £5.99 per night **Grounds** accessible on leads **Exercise area** nearby park

Situated opposite the Congress Theatre, this hotel is just a short walk from both the seafront and Devonshire Park. Bedrooms are comfortably furnished and pleasantly decorated. Public areas are smartly appointed and include a cosy bar, a separate lounge and an attractive dining room.

Rooms 46 en suite (4 fmly) (3 GF) **Facilities** **Services** Lift **Parking** 36

★★ 68% HOTEL

Congress

31-41 Carlisle Rd BN21 4JS

☎ 01323 732118 01323 720016

e-mail: reservations@congresshotel.co.uk

web: www.congresshotel.co.uk

Dir: *From Eastbourne seafront W towards Beachy Head. Right at Wishtower into Wilmington Sq, cross Compton St, hotel on left*

PETS: Bedrooms (8GF) unattended sign **Grounds** accessible **Exercise area** 200yds **Facilities** walks info vet info **On Request** fridge access

Attractive Victorian property ideally located close to seafront, Wish Tower and Congress Theatre. The bedrooms are bright and spacious. Family rooms are available plus facilities for less able guests. Entertainment is provided in a large dining room that has a dance floor and bar.

Rooms 61 en suite (6 fmly) (8 GF) S £33-£47; D £66-£94 (incl. bkfst) **Facilities** Wi-fi available Games room Xmas New Year **Services** Lift **Parking** 12 **Notes** RS Jan-Feb

★★★★ GUEST ACCOMMODATION

Arden House

17 Burlington Place BN21 4AR

☎ 01323 639639 01323 417840

e-mail: info@theardenhotel.co.uk

web: www.theardenhotel.co.uk

Dir: *Eastbourne seafront, head W, 5th turning after the pier*

PETS: Bedrooms Charges charge for damage **Exercise area** 100mtrs **Facilities** food bowl water bowl dog scoop/disp bags leads walks info vet info **On Request** torch towels

This attractive Regency property sits just minutes away from the seafront and town centre. Bedrooms are comfortable and bright, many with new en suite bathrooms. Guests can enjoy a hearty breakfast at the beginning of the day then relax in the cosy lounge in the evening.

Rooms 11 rms (10 en suite) (1 pri facs) (1 fmly) S £30-£37; D £50-£60* **Facilities** TVB tea/coffee Cen ht TVL Wi-fi available **Parking** 5 **Notes LB**

★★★★ GUEST ACCOMMODATION

The Gladwyn

16 Blackwater Rd BN21 4JD

☎ 01323 733142

e-mail: contact@thegladwyn.com

web: www.thegladwyn.com

Dir: *250yds S of town centre. Off A259 South St onto Hardwick Rd & 1st right*

PETS: Bedrooms (2GF) unattended sign **Charges** charge for damage **Public areas** except breakfast room (on leads) **Grounds** accessible disp bin **Exercise area** 500yds **Facilities** food food bowl water bowl dog chews cat treats walks info vet info **On Request** fridge access torch towels

A warm welcome is guaranteed at this delightful guest house located opposite the famous tennis courts. Art work and interesting collectables feature throughout the property, including public areas and bedrooms. Freshly prepared breakfasts are served in the cosy dining room overlooking the attractive garden, which is available during the summer.

Rooms 10 en suite (1 fmly) (2 GF) S £40-£45; D £70-£80 **Facilities** TVB tea/coffee TVL Wi-fi available **Notes** LB

FURNER'S GREEN — MAP 05 TQ42

►► **Heaven Farm** *(TQ403264)*

TN22 3RG

☎ 01825 790226 🖷 01825 790881

e-mail: heavenfarmleisure@btinternet.com

web: www.heavenfarm.co.uk

Dir: *On A275 between Lewes & East Grinstead, 1m N of Sheffield Park Gardens*

PETS: Public areas except near toilet block **Exercise area** adjacent meadows **Facilities** on site shop vet info **Other** prior notice required; dogs must not worry resident poultry & ducks **Resident Pets:** 3 cats

Open Apr-Oct Last arrival 21.00hrs Last departure noon

Delightful small rural site on a popular farm complex incorporating a farm museum, craft shop, tea room and nature trail. Good clean facilities in well-converted outbuildings. A 1.5-acre site with 25 touring pitches, 2 hardstandings.

Notes Prefer no children between 6-18yrs

HAILSHAM — MAP 05 TQ50

★★ 75% HOTEL

The Olde Forge Hotel & Restaurant

Magham Down BN27 1PN

☎ 01323 842893 🖷 01323 842893

e-mail: theoldeforgehotel@tesco.net

web: www.theoldeforgehotel.co.uk

Dir: *off Boship rdbt on A271 to Bexhill & Herstmonceux. Hotel 3m on left*

PETS: Bedrooms Charges £5 per night charge for damage **Grounds** accessible on leads disp bin **Exercise area** outside hotel **Facilities** washing facs cage storage walks info vet info **On Request** fridge access torch towels **Other** Please phone for information **Resident Pets:** Diesel (Boxer)

In the heart of the countryside, this family-run hotel offers a friendly welcome and an informal atmosphere. The bedrooms are attractively decorated with thoughtful extras. The restaurant, with its timbered beams and log fires, was a forge in the 16th century; today it has a good local reputation for both its cuisine and service.

Rooms 7 en suite S £48; D £80 (incl. bkfst)✳ **Facilities** Wi-fi available **Parking** 11 **Notes** LB

HASTINGS & ST LEONARDS MAP 05 TQ80

★★★ 72% HOTEL

Best Western Royal Victoria

Marina, St Leonards-on-Sea TN38 0BD

☎ 01424 445544 📠 01424 721995

e-mail: reception@royalvichotel.co.uk

web: www.royalvichotel.co.uk

Dir: *on A259 (seafront road) 1m W of Hastings pier*

PETS: Bedrooms unattended **Stables** nearby **Charges** £10 per night charge for damage **Exercise area** 100mtrs **Facilities** food bowl **On Request** fridge access torch towels

This imposing 18th-century property is situated in a prominent position overlooking the sea. A superb marble staircase leads up from the lobby to the main public areas on the first floor which has panoramic views of the sea. The spacious bedrooms are pleasantly decorated and well equipped, and include duplex and family suites.

Rooms 50 en suite (15 fmly) **Services** Lift **Parking** 6 **Notes** LB

HOVE

See Brighton & Hove

NEWICK MAP 05 TQ42

★★★ ®®® HOTEL

Newick Park Hotel & Country Estate

BN8 4SB

☎ 01825 723633 📠 01825 723969

e-mail: bookings@newickpark.co.uk

web: www.newickpark.co.uk

Dir: *Exit A272 at Newick Green, 1m, pass church & pub. Turn left, hotel 0.25m on right*

PETS: Bedrooms (1GF) unattended sign **Charges** £5 per night **Grounds** accessible **Exercise area Facilities** food (pre-bookable) food bowl water bowl washing facs cage storage walks info vet info **On Request** fridge access torch towels **Other** ground floor bedrooms only; pet food available by prior arrangement

Resident Pets: Ellie & Maddy (Black Labradors)

Delightful Grade II listed Georgian country house set amid 250 acres of Sussex parkland and landscaped gardens. The spacious, individually decorated bedrooms are tastefully furnished, thoughtfully equipped and have superb views of the grounds; many rooms have huge American king-size beds. The comfortable public rooms include a study, a sitting room, lounge bar and an elegant restaurant.

Rooms 13 en suite 3 annexe en suite (5 fmly) (1 GF) S £125-£245; D £165-£285 (incl. bkfst) **Facilities** FTV Fishing Wi-fi available Badminton Clay pigeon shooting Helicopter rides Quad biking Tank driving Xmas **Parking** 52

NORMAN'S BAY MAP 05 TQ60

►►► Norman's Bay Camping & Caravanning Club Site *(TQ682055)*

BN24 6PR

☎ 01323 761190

web: www.thefriendlyclub.co.uk

Dir: *From rdbt junct of A27/A259 follow A259 signed Eastbourne. In Pevensey Bay village take 1st left signed Beachlands only. 1.25m site on left*

PETS: Public areas except in buildings disp bin **Exercise area** on site **Facilities** on site shop walks info vet info **Other** prior notice required

Open 2 Apr-2 Nov Last arrival 20.00hrs Last departure noon

A well kept site with immaculate toilet block, right beside the sea. This popular family park enjoys good rural views towards Rye and Pevensey. A 13-acre site with 200 touring pitches, 5 hardstandings.

Notes Site gates closed 23.00hrs-07.00hrs

PEASMARSH MAP 05 TQ82

★★★ 79% HOTEL

Best Western Flackley Ash

TN31 6YH

☎ 01797 230651 📠 01797 230510

e-mail: enquiries@flackleyashhotel.co.uk

web: www.flackleyashhotel.co.uk

Dir: *exit A21 onto A268 to Newenden, next left A268 to Rye. Hotel on left on entering Peasmarsh*

PETS: Bedrooms (19GF) unattended **Charges** £8.50 per night **Public areas** except restaurant, leisure centre & bar (on leads) **Grounds** accessible disp bin **Exercise area** 10mtrs **Facilities** walks info vet info **On Request** torch

Five acres of beautifully kept grounds make a lovely backdrop to this elegant Georgian country house. The hotel is superbly situated for exploring the many local attractions, including the ancient Cinque Port of Rye. Stylishly decorated bedrooms are comfortable and boast many thoughtful touches. A sunny conservatory dining room, luxurious beauty spa and a swimming pool are available.

Rooms 45 en suite (5 fmly) (19 GF) D £144-£190 (incl. bkfst & dinner)* **Facilities Spa** STV supervised Gym Putt green Wi-fi in bedrooms Beauty salon Steam room Saunas ch fac Xmas New Year **Parking** 80 **Notes** LB

RYE **MAP 05 TQ92**

★★★ 75% HOTEL

Rye Lodge

Hilders Cliff TN31 7LD

☎ 01797 223838 01797 223585

e-mail: info@ryelodge.co.uk

web: www.ryelodge.co.uk

Dir: *one-way system in Rye, follow signs for town centre, through Landgate arch, hotel 100yds on right*

PETS: Bedrooms Charges £8 per night charge for damage **Public areas** except restaurant **Exercise area** 150yds **Facilities** food (pre-bookable)

Standing in an elevated position, Rye Lodge has panoramic views across Romney Marshes and the Rother Estuary. Traditionally styled bedrooms come in a variety of sizes; they are attractively decorated and thoughtfully equipped. Public rooms feature indoor leisure facilities and the Terrace Room Restaurant where home-made dishes are offered. Lunch and afternoon tea are served on the flower-filled outdoor terrace in warmer months.

Rooms 18 en suite (5 GF) S £70-£160; D £120-£220 (incl. bkfst)* **Facilities** STV Aromatherapy Steam cabinet Sauna Exercise machines Xmas **Parking** 20 **Notes** LB

★★★★★ GUEST ACCOMMODATION

Jeake's House

Mermaid St TN31 7ET

☎ 01797 222828 01797 222623

e-mail: stay@jeakeshouse.com

web: www.jeakeshouse.com

Dir: *Approach from High St or The Strand*

PETS: Bedrooms Charges £5 per night **Public areas** except dining room (welcome in bar) **Exercise area** 5-10 mins walk **Facilities** walks info vet info **On Request** fridge access torch towels **Resident Pets:** Princess Yum Yum & Monte (Tonkinese cats)

Previously a 17th-century wool store and then a 19th-century Baptist school, this delightful house stands on a cobbled street in one of the most beautiful parts of this small, bustling town. The individually decorated bedrooms combine elegance and comfort with modern facilities. Breakfast is served at separate tables in the galleried dining room, and there is an oak-beamed lounge as well as a stylish book-lined bar with old pews.

Rooms 11 rms (10 en suite) (1 pri facs) (2 fmly) S £70-£79; D £90-£126 **Facilities** TVB tea/coffee Direct dial from bedrooms Cen ht **Parking** 21 **Notes** No children 8yrs

ENGLAND

RYE continued

★★★★ GUEST ACCOMMODATION

Little Saltcote

22 Military Rd TN31 7NY

☎ 01797 223210 📠 01797 224474

e-mail: info@littlesaltcote.co.uk

web: www.littlesaltcote.co.uk

Dir: *0.5m N of town centre. Off A268 onto Military Rd signed Appledore, house 300yds on left*

PETS: Bedrooms (1GF) **Charges** £5 per night charge for damage **Exercise area** 0.5m **Facilities** food bowl water bowl cage storage walks info vet info **On Request** fridge access torch towels **Restrictions** the largest breeds are not accepted

This delightful family-run guest house stands in quiet surroundings within walking distance of Rye town centre. The bright and airy en suite bedrooms are equipped with modern facilities including Wi-fi, and you can enjoy afternoon tea in the garden conservatory. A hearty breakfast is served at individual tables in the dining room.

Rooms 4 en suite (2 fmly) (1 GF) S £40-£65; D £63-£80 **Facilities** TVB tea/coffee Cen ht Wi-fi available **Parking** 5 **Notes** LB

ST LEONARDS

See Hastings & St Leonards

WADHURST — MAP 05 TQ63

★★★★ FARM HOUSE

Little Tidebrook Farm *(TQ621304)*

Riseden TN5 6NY

☎ 01892 782688 Mrs Sally Marley-Ward

e-mail: info@littletidebrook.co.uk

web: www.littletidebrook.co.uk

Dir: *A267 from Tunbridge Wells to Mark Cross, left onto B2100, 2m turn right at Best Beech Inn, left after 1m, farm on left*

PETS: Bedrooms Stables on site **Charges** £5 per night charge for damage **Public areas** except breakfast times (on leads) **Grounds** accessible on leads disp bin **Exercise area** on site farm **Facilities** washing facs cage storage walks info vet info **On Request** fridge access torch towels **Resident Pets:** 2 Labradors, 1 Jack Russell, 2 cats, 17 horses

This traditional farmhouse has cosy log fires in winter and wonderful garden dining in warm months. The imaginative décor combines with modern amenities such as Wi-fi to provide leisure and business travellers with the ideal setting. Close to Bewl Water and Royal Tunbridge Wells.

Rooms 4 rms (2 en suite) (1 pri facs) D £50-£80* **Facilities** TVB tea/coffee Cen ht TVL Wi-fi available **Parking** 8 **Notes** No children 12yrs 40 acres Horses

SUSSEX, WEST

ARUNDEL — MAP 04 TQ00

★★★ 75% HOTEL

Norfolk Arms

High St BN18 9AB

☎ 01903 882101 📠 01903 884275

e-mail: norfolk.arms@forestdale.com

web: www.forestdale.com

Dir: *On High St in city centre*

PETS: Bedrooms unattended **Charges** £7.50 per night **Public areas** except restaurant **Exercise area**

Built by the 10th Duke of Norfolk, this Georgian coaching inn enjoys a superb setting beneath the battlements of Arundel Castle. Bedrooms vary in sizes and character - all are comfortable and well equipped. Public areas include two bars serving 'real ale', comfortable lounges with roaring log fires, a traditional English restaurant and a range of meeting and function rooms.

Rooms 21 en suite 13 annexe en suite (4 fmly) (8 GF) S £72-£79; D £117-£129 (incl. bkfst)* **Facilities** Wi-fi available Xmas New Year **Parking** 34 **Notes** LB

★★ 67% HOTEL

Comfort Inn

Crossbush BN17 7QQ

☎ 01903 840840 📠 01903 849849

e-mail: reservations@comfortinnarundel.co.uk

Dir: *A27/A284, 1st right into services*

PETS: Bedrooms (25GF) **Charges** £5 per night **Public areas** except restaurant & bar **Grounds** accessible disp bin **Exercise area Facilities** dog scoop/disp bags vet info **On Request** fridge access

This modern, purpose-built hotel provides a good base for exploring the nearby historic town. Good access to local road networks and a range of meeting rooms, all air-conditioned, also make this an ideal venue for business guests. Bedrooms are spacious, smartly decorated and well equipped.

Rooms 53 en suite (4 fmly) (25 GF) S £50-£120; D £55-£120 (incl. bkfst) **Facilities** STV FTV Wi fi in bedrooms Xmas New Year **Parking** 53 **Notes** LB

►► Ship & Anchor Marina *(TQ002040)*

Station Rd, Ford BN18 0BJ

☎ 01243 551262 📠 01243 555256

e-mail: enquiries@shipandanchormarina.co.uk

Dir: *From A27 at Arundel take road S signed Ford. Site 2m from Arundel on left after level crossing*

PETS: Stables (loose box) disp bin **Exercise area** on site riverside walks **Facilities** on site shop food dog chews cat treats walks info vet info **Other** please phone for information on accommodating horses **Resident Pets:** 2 dogs & 5 cats

Open Mar-Oct Last arrival 21.00hrs Last departure noon

A neat and tidy site in a pleasant position beside the Ship & Anchor pub and the tidal River Arun. There are good walks from the site both to Arundel and to the coast. A 12-acre site with 120 touring pitches, 11 hardstandings and 40 statics.

Notes ⊜

BARNS GREEN — MAP 04 TQ12

►►► *Sumners Ponds Fishery & Campsite*

(TQ125268)

Chapel Rd RH13 0PR

☎ 01403 732539

e-mail: sumnersponds@dsl.co.uk

web: www.sumnersponds.co.uk

Dir: *From A272 at Coolham x-rds, N towards Barns Green. In 1.5m take 1st left at small x-rds. 1m, over level crossing. Site on left just after right bend*

PETS: Stables nearby (2m) disp bin **Exercise area** on site **Facilities** on site shop food food bowl water bowl walks info vet info **Resident Pets:** Basil (Shih Tzu), Pickles & Chutney (Jack Russells)

Open all year Last arrival 20.00hrs Last departure 17.00hrs

A touring area on a working farm on the edge of the quiet village of Barnes Green, with purpose built facilities of a high standard. There are three well-stocked fishing lakes set in attractive surroundings, and a woodland walk with direct access to miles of footpaths. Horsham and Brighton are within easy reach. A 40-acre site with 61 touring pitches, 31 hardstandings.

Notes Only one car per pitch

BILLINGSHURST — MAP 04 TQ02

►► Limeburners Arms Camp Site *(TQ072255)*

Lordings Rd, Newbridge RH14 9JA

☎ 01403 782311

e-mail: chippy.sawyer@virgin.net

Dir: *From A29 turn W onto A272 for 1m, then left onto B2133. Site 300yds on left*

PETS: Exercise area adjacent walks **Facilities** vet info

Open Apr-Oct Last arrival 22.00hrs Last departure 14.00hrs

A secluded site in rural West Sussex, at the rear of the Limeburners Arms public house, and surrounded by fields. It makes a pleasant base for touring the South Downs and the Arun Valley. The toilets are basic but very clean. A 2.75-acre site with 40 touring pitches.

BOGNOR REGIS MAP 04 SZ99

★★★ 72% HOTEL

Royal Norfolk

The Esplanade PO21 2LH

☎ 01243 826222 🖹 01243 826325

e-mail: accommodation@royalnorfolkhotel.com

web: www.royalnorfolkhotel.com

Dir: *from A259 follow Longford Rd through lights to Canada Grove to T-junct. Right, take 2nd exit at rdbt. Hotel on right*

PETS: Bedrooms sign **Charges** £20 per stay **Public areas** except restaurant **Grounds** accessible **Exercise area** local fields & beach **Facilities** walks info

On the Esplanade, but set back behind lawns and gardens, this fine-looking hotel has been welcoming guests since Regency times. Today the traditionally furnished bedrooms, four with four-poster beds, are well provided with all the modern comforts. Public areas offer sea views from the elegant restaurant and comfortable lobby lounge.

Rooms 43 en suite (4 fmly) S £55-£70; D £100-£130 (incl. bkfst)✳ **Facilities** Wi-fi available ♫ Xmas New Year **Services** Lift **Parking** 60 **Notes** LB

CHICHESTER MAP 04 SU80

★★★ 79% ❁ HOTEL

Crouchers Country Hotel & Restaurant

Birdham Rd PO20 7EH

☎ 01243 784995 🖹 01243 539797

e-mail: crouchers@btconnect.com

Dir: *off A27 to A286, 1.5m from Chichester centre opposite Black Horse pub*

PETS: Bedrooms (12GF) **Charges** £10 per night £70 per week charge for damage **Grounds** accessible **Exercise area** **Facilities** walks info vet info **On Request** fridge access torch towels

This friendly, family-run hotel, situated in open countryside, is just a short drive from the harbour. The comfortable and well-equipped bedrooms include some in a separate barn and coach house, and the open-plan public areas have pleasant views.

Rooms 3 en suite 17 annexe en suite (2 fmly) (12 GF) S £75-£110; D £110-£140 (incl. bkfst) **Facilities** FTV Wi-fi available Xmas New Year **Parking** 80 **Notes** LB

★★★★ INN

Horse and Groom

East Ashling PO18 9AX

☎ 01243 575339 🖹 01243 575560

e-mail: info@thehorseandgroomchichester.co.uk

web: www.thehorseandgroomchichester.co.uk

Dir: *On B2178 3m N of Chichester on road to Rowlands Castle*

PETS: Bedrooms (11GF) unattended **Public areas** except restaurant **Grounds** accessible **Exercise area** adjacent **Facilities** water bowl leads walks info vet info **On Request** torch towels

The Horse and Groom is a unique 17th-century country pub and restaurant offering spacious and comfortable accommodation, and warm, friendly hospitality. Substantial freshly prepared breakfasts, lunches and dinners are available making good use of freshly caught fish and locally sourced ingredients.

Rooms 11 en suite (11 GF) S £45-£55; D £70-£80 **Facilities** TVB tea/coffee Cen ht Dinner Last d 9.15pm **Parking** 40 **Notes** RS Sun eve

★★★★ BED & BREAKFAST

Old Chapel Forge

Lower Bognor Rd, Lagness PO20 1LR

☎ 01243 264380

e-mail: info@oldchapelforge.co.uk

Dir: *4m SE of Chichester. Off A27 Chichester bypass at Bognor rdbt signed Pagham/Runcton, onto B2166 Pagham Rd & Lower Bognor Rd, Old Chapel Forge on right*

PETS: Bedrooms (4GF) **Stables** nearby (0.25m) **Charges** donation to nature reserve (min £10 per stay) charge for damage **Public areas** except breakfast area (on leads) **Grounds** accessible on leads disp bin **Exercise area** 80 acres adjacent **Facilities** walks info vet info **On Request** fridge access torch towels **Other** all pets accepted by prior arrangement only **Restrictions** no dogs under 1 year; dogs must be house-trained **Resident Pets:** Jade (Labrador), Alphie (Bengal cat), Eddie & Ellie (geese), 4 donkeys

Great local produce features in the hearty breakfasts at this comfortable, eco-friendly property, an idyllic 17th-century house and chapel set in mature gardens with panoramic views of the South Downs. Old Chapel Forge is a short drive from Chichester, Goodwood, Pagham Harbour Nature Reserve and the beach. Bedrooms, including suites in the chapel, are luxurious, and all have internet access.

Rooms 4 annexe en suite (2 fmly) (4 GF) S £35-£55; D £50-£110 **Facilities** TVB tea/coffee Cen ht Dinner Last d Breakfast Wi-fi available **Parking** 6 **Notes** LB

►►► ***Ellscott Park*** *(SU829995)*

Sidlesham Ln, Birdham PO20 7QL

☎ 01243 512003 🖷 01243 512003

e-mail: camping@ellscottpark.co.uk

web: www.ellscottpark.co.uk

Dir: *Take A286 (Chichester/Wittering road) for approx 4m, left at Butterfly Farm sign, site 500yds right*

PETS: Stables nearby (1m) (loose box) disp bin **Exercise area** on site 3-acre field **Facilities** washing facs walks info vet info **Other** prior notice required **Resident Pets:** Lockie (Springer Spaniel)

Open Mar-Oct

A well kept park set in meadowland behind the owners' nursery and van storage area. The park attracts a peace-loving clientele, and is handy for the beach and other local attractions. Home-grown produce and eggs are for sale. A 2.5-acre site with 50 touring pitches.

Notes

CHILGROVE — MAP 04 SU81

U

The Fish House (formerly White Horse)

PO18 9HX

☎ 01243 535219 & 519444 🖷 01243 519499

e-mail: info@fishhouse.co.uk

Dir: *From Chichester take A286 N, turn left onto B2141 to village*

PETS: Bedrooms (11GF) **Charges** charge for damage **Public areas** except restaurant (on leads) **Grounds** accessible on leads **Exercise area** 30yds **Facilities** washing facs cage storage vet info **On Request** fridge access torch towels **Resident Pets:** Barney (Bulldog)

At the time of going to press the rating for this establishment was not confirmed. This may be due to a change of ownership or because it has only recently joined the AA rating scheme. For further details please see the AA website: www.theAA.com

Rooms 17 en suite (11 GF) S £90-£150; D £120-£220* **Facilities** STV FTV TVB tea/coffee Direct dial from bedrooms Cen ht Dinner Last d 9.45pm Wi-fi available Sauna **Parking** 50 **Notes LB**

CLIMPING — MAP 04 SU90

★★★ 83% HOTEL

Bailiffscourt Hotel & Spa

Climping St BN17 5RW

☎ 01903 723511 🖷 01903 718987

e-mail: bailiffscourt@hshotels.co.uk

web: www.hshotels.co.uk

Dir: *A259, follow Climping Beach signs. Hotel 0.5m on right*

PETS: Bedrooms (16GF) unattended **Charges** £12 per night **Public areas Grounds** accessible disp bin **Exercise area** 200mtrs **Facilities** food (pre-bookable) food bowl water bowl dog chews feeding mat dog scoop/disp bags washing facs cage storage walks info vet info **On Request** fridge access torch towels **Other** room service menu

This delightful 'medieval manor' dating back only to the 1920s has the appearance of having been in existence for centuries. Bedrooms vary from atmospheric feature rooms with log fires, oak beams and four-poster beds to spacious, stylish and contemporary rooms located in the grounds. Classic European cooking is a highlight, and a stylish spa plus a choice of cosy lounges complete the package.

Rooms 9 en suite 30 annexe en suite (25 fmly) (16 GF) S £190-£465; D £210-£525 (incl. bkfst) **Facilities Spa** STV pool supervised Gym Wi-fi available Xmas New Year **Parking** 100 **Notes LB**

CUCKFIELD — MAP 04 TQ32

★★★ HOTEL

Ockenden Manor

Ockenden Ln RH17 5LD

☎ 01444 416111 🖷 01444 415549

e-mail: reservations@ockenden-manor.com

web: www.hshotels.co.uk

Dir: *A23 towards Brighton. 4.5m left onto B2115 towards Haywards Heath. Cuckfield 3m. Ockendon Lane off High St. Hotel at end*

PETS: Bedrooms (4GF) unattended **Charges** £10 per night charge for damage **Grounds** accessible **Exercise area** countryside walks **Facilities** cage storage walks info vet info

This charming 16th-century hotel enjoys fine views of the South Downs. Bedrooms offer high standards of accommodation, some with historic features. Public rooms, retaining much original character, include an elegant sitting room with all the elements for a relaxing afternoon in front of the fire. Imaginative, noteworthy cuisine is a highlight to any stay.

Rooms 22 en suite (4 fmly) (4 GF) S £105-£195; D £170-£360 (incl. bkfst)* **Facilities** STV FTV Wi-fi available Xmas New Year **Parking** 43 **Notes LB**

ENGLAND

GRAFFHAM MAP 04 SU91

►►► Graffham Camping & Caravanning Club Site *(SU941187)*

Great Bury GU28 0QJ

☎ 01798 867476

web: www.thefriendlyclub.co.uk

Dir: *From Petworth on A285 pass Badgers pub on left & BP garage on right. Next right signed Selham Graffham. Follow sign to site*

PETS: Public areas except in buildings disp bin **Exercise area** on site dog walks **Facilities** walks info vet info **Other** prior notice required

Open 2 Apr-2 Nov Last arrival 21.00hrs Last departure noon

A superb woodland site with some pitches occupying their own private, naturally-screened areas. A peaceful retreat, or base for touring the South Downs, Chichester and the south coast. A 20-acre site with 90 touring pitches.

Notes Site gates closed 23.00hrs-07.00hrs

MIDHURST MAP 04 SU82

★★★ 79% ®® HOTEL

Spread Eagle Hotel and Spa

South St GU29 9NH

☎ 01730 816911 🖷 01730 815668

e-mail: spreadeagle@hshotels.co.uk

web: www.hshotels.co.uk/spread/spreadeagle-main.htm

Dir: *M25 junct 10, A3 to Milford, take A286 to Midhurst. Hotel adjacent to market square*

PETS: Bedrooms unattended **Stables** nearby (3m) **Charges** £15 per night charge for damage **Public areas** except restaurant **Grounds** accessible **Exercise area Facilities** food (pre-bookable) food bowl water bowl bedding walks info vet info **On Request** fridge access torch **Other** dogs must not be allowed on beds **Restrictions** very large breeds not accepted

Offering accommodation since 1430, this historic property is full of character, evident in its sloping floors and inglenook fireplaces. Individually styled bedrooms provide modern comforts; those in the main house have oak panelling and include some spacious feature rooms. The hotel also boasts a well-equipped spa and offers noteworthy food in the oak beamed restaurant.

Rooms 35 en suite 4 annexe en suite (8 GF) S £80-£385; D £99-£385 (incl. bkfst)✻ **Facilities Spa** STV FTV ⓣ Gym Wi-fi available Health & beauty treatment rooms Steam room Sauna Fitness trainer Xmas New Year **Parking** 75 **Notes LB**

SELSEY MAP 04 SZ89

★★★★ GUEST ACCOMMODATION

St Andrews Lodge

Chichester Rd PO20 0LX

☎ 01243 606899 🖷 01243 607826

e-mail: info@standrewslodge.co.uk

web: www.standrewslodge.co.uk

Dir: *B2145 into Selsey, on right just before the church*

PETS: Bedrooms (5GF) unattended **Charges** £3 per stay **Public areas** except restaurant/lounge **Grounds** accessible disp bin **Exercise area** 200yds **Facilities** food bowl water bowl cage storage walks info vet info **On Request** fridge access torch towels **Resident Pets:** Pepper (cat)

This friendly lodge is just half a mile from the seafront. The refurbished bedrooms are bright and spacious, and have a range of useful extras. Five ground-floor rooms, one with easier access, overlook the large south-facing garden, which is perfect for a drink on a summer evening.

Rooms 5 en suite 5 annexe en suite (3 fmly) (5 GF) S £36-£50; D £62.50-£85 **Facilities** TVB tea/coffee Direct dial from bedrooms Cen ht TVL **Parking** 14 **Notes LB** Closed 21 Dec-11 Jan

SLINDON MAP 04 SU90

► Slindon Camping & Caravanning Club Site *(SU958084)*

Slindon Park BN18 0RG

☎ 01243 814387

web: www.thefriendlyclub.co.uk

Dir: *From A27 Fontwell to Chichester turn right at sign for Brittons Lane & 2nd right to Slindon. Site on this road*

PETS: Public areas except in buildings disp bin **Exercise area** on site interesting walks around site **Facilities** walks info vet info **Other** prior notice required

Open 2 Apr-28 Nov Last arrival 21.00hrs Last departure noon

A beautiful former orchard, completely screened by National Trust trees, and very quiet. It is ideal for the self-contained camper, and own sanitary facilities are essential. The entrance gate is narrow and on a bend, and touring units are advised to take a wide sweep on approach from private gravel roadway. A 2-acre site with 40 touring pitches.

Notes Site gates closed 23.00hrs-07.00hrs

SOUTHBOURNE MAP 04 SU70

►►► Chichester Camping & Caravanning Club Site *(SU774056)*

Main Rd PO10 8JH
☎ 01243 373202
web: www.thefriendlyclub.co.uk
Dir: *From Chichester take A259 to Southampton, site on right past Inlands Road*
PETS: Public areas disp bin **Exercise area Facilities** walks info vet info **Other** prior notice required
Open 5 Feb-16 Nov Last arrival 21.00hrs Last departure noon

Situated in open meadow and orchard, a very pleasant, popular site with well looked after, clean facilities. Well placed for Chichester, South Downs and the ferry ports. A 3-acre site with 58 touring pitches, 42 hardstandings.

Notes Site gates closed 23.00hrs-07.00hrs

WORTHING MAP 04 TQ10

★★ 64% HOTEL

Cavendish

THE INDEPENDENTS HOTEL ASSOCIATION

115 Marine Pde BN11 3QG
☎ 01903 236767 🖷 01903 823840
e-mail: reservations@cavendishworthing.co.uk
web: www.cavendishworthing.co.uk
Dir: *On seafront, 600yds W of pier*
PETS: Bedrooms (1GF) unattended **Public areas** except restaurant (on leads) **Exercise area** countryside walks & beach opposite **Facilities** walks info vet info

This popular, family-run hotel enjoys a prominent seafront location. Bedrooms are well equipped and soundly decorated. Guests have an extensive choice of meal options, with a varied bar menu, and carte and daily menus offered in the restaurant. Limited parking is available at the rear of the hotel.

Rooms 17 en suite (4 fmly) (1 GF) S £45-£49; D £69.50-£85 (incl. bkfst)✳ **Facilities** STV Wi-fi available **Services** air con **Parking** 5

TYNE & WEAR

NEWCASTLE UPON TYNE MAP 12 NZ26

★★★★ 76% HOTEL

Newcastle Marriott Hotel Gosforth Park

Marriott HOTELS & RESORTS

High Gosforth Park, Gosforth NE3 5HN
☎ 0191 236 4111 🖷 0191 236 8192
web: www.marriott.co.uk
Dir: *onto A1056 to Killingworth & Wideopen. 3rd exit to Gosforth Park, hotel ahead*
PETS: Bedrooms Exercise area on site 12.5 acres of woodland **Facilities** vet info

Set within its own grounds, this modern hotel offers extensive conference and banqueting facilities, along with indoor and outdoor leisure and a choice of formal and informal dining. Many of the air-conditioned bedrooms have views over the park; executive rooms feature extras such as CD players. The hotel is conveniently located for the by-pass, airport and racecourse.

Rooms 178 en suite S £99-£129; D £99-£156✳ **Facilities Spa** STV supervised Squash Gym Wi-fi available Jogging trail New Year **Services** Lift air con **Parking** 340 **Notes LB** RS Xmas & New Year

WHICKHAM MAP 12 NZ26

★★★ 70% HOTEL

Gibside

Front St NE16 4JG
☎ 0191 488 9292 🖷 0191 488 8000
e-mail: reception@gibside-hotel.co.uk
web: www.gibside-hotel.co.uk
Dir: *off A1(M) towards Whickham on B6317, onto Front St, 2m on right*
PETS: Bedrooms (13GF) unattended **Exercise area** on site paved area

Conveniently located in the village centre, this hotel is close to the Newcastle by-pass and its elevated position affords views over the Tyne Valley. Bedrooms come in two styles, classical and contemporary. Public rooms include the Egyptian-themed Sphinx bar and a more formal restaurant. Secure garage parking is available.

Rooms 45 en suite (2 fmly) (13 GF) S £62.50-£75; D £72.50-£85✳ **Facilities** FTV Wi-fi in bedrooms Golf Academy at The Beamish Park New Year **Services** Lift **Parking** 28

ENGLAND

WARWICKSHIRE

BAGINTON MAP 04 SP37

★★★ INN

The Oak

Coventry Rd CV8 3AU

☎ 024 7651 8855 📠 024 7651 8866

e-mail: thebagintonoak@aol.com

web: http://theoak.greatpubs.net

PETS: Bedrooms (6GF) unattended **Stables** nearby (0.5m) **Charges** £5 per night £30 per week charge for damage **Public areas** (on leads) **Grounds** accessible disp bin **Exercise area** adjacent **Facilities** water bowl dog chews washing facs walks info vet info **On Request** fridge access torch towels **Other** pet washing facilities on request **Resident Pets:** Beau & Jasper (Border Collies)

Located close to major road links and Coventry Airport, this popular inn provides a wide range of food throughout the themed open plan public areas. Families are especially welcome. Modern well equipped bedrooms are situated within a separate accommodation building.

Rooms 13 annexe en suite (1 fmly) (6 GF) S £40-£60; D £40-£60 **Facilities** FTV TVB tea/coffee Cen ht Dinner Last d 9pm Wi-fi available Free use of local gym **Parking** 110

COLESHILL MAP 04 SP28

★★★ 70% COUNTRY HOUSE HOTEL

Grimstock Country House

Gilson Rd, Gilson B46 1LJ

☎ 01675 462121 & 462161 📠 01675 467646

e-mail: enquiries@grimstockhotel.co.uk

web: www.grimstockhotel.co.uk

Dir: *off A446 at rdbt onto B4117 to Gilson, hotel 100yds on right*

PETS: Bedrooms (13GF) unattended sign **Charges** charge for damage **Grounds** accessible on leads **Exercise area** **Facilities** dog walking walks info vet info

This privately owned hotel is convenient for Birmingham International Airport and the NEC, and benefits from a peaceful rural setting. Bedrooms are spacious and comfortable. Public rooms include two restaurants, a wood-panelled bar, good conference facilities and a gym featuring the latest cardiovascular equipment.

Rooms 44 en suite (1 fmly) (13 GF) **Facilities** Gym Wi-fi available **Parking** 100

CORLEY MOTORWAY SERVICE AREA (M6) MAP 04 SP38

BUDGET HOTEL

Days Inn Corley - NEC (M6)

Junction 3-4, M6 North, Corley CV7 8NR

☎ 01676 543800 & 540111 📠 01676 540128

e-mail: corley.hotel@welcomebreak.co.uk

web: www.welcomebreak.co.uk

PETS: Bedrooms Exercise area Other please contact for further details

This modern building offers accommodation in smart, spacious and well-equipped bedrooms, suitable for families and business travellers, and all with en suite bathrooms. Refreshments may be taken at the nearby family restaurant.

Rooms 50 en suite

GREAT WOLFORD MAP 04 SP23

★★★★ INN

The Fox & Hounds Inn

CV36 5NQ

☎ 01608 674220

e-mail: enquiries@thefoxandhoundsinn.com

Dir: *Off A3400, 1.5m to Great Wolford*

PETS: Bedrooms unattended **Public areas** if well behaved **Grounds** accessible **Exercise area** 50yds

Very much a focal point of the local community, this 16th-century inn retains many original features, which are enhanced by rustic furniture and memorabilia. The thoughtfully furnished bedrooms are in converted outbuildings, and a warm welcome is assured.

Rooms 3 annexe en suite S £50; D £80 **Facilities** TVB tea/coffee Cen ht Dinner Last d 9pm Wi-fi available **Parking** 12 **Notes** RS Sun & Mon

KENILWORTH MAP 04 SP27

★★★★ 80% HOTEL

Chesford Grange

QHOTELS

Chesford Bridge CV8 2LD

☎ 01926 859331 🖹 01926 859272

e-mail: chesfordgrangereservations@qhotels.co.uk

web: www.qhotels.co.uk

Dir: *0.5m SE of junct A46/A452. At rdbt turn right signed Leamington Spa, then follow signs to hotel*

PETS: Bedrooms (43GF) unattended **Charges** £10 per night **Grounds** accessible **Exercise area** on site acres of grounds **Other** well behaved dogs only

This much-extended hotel set in 17 acres of private grounds is well situated for Birmingham International Airport, the NEC and major routes. Bedrooms range from traditional style to contemporary rooms featuring state-of-the-art technology. Public areas include a leisure club and extensive conference and banqueting facilities.

Rooms 209 en suite (20 fmly) (43 GF) S £90-£150; D £100-£160 (incl. bkfst) **Facilities** **Spa** STV supervised Gym Wi-fi in bedrooms Steam room Xmas New Year **Services** Lift **Parking** 650 **Notes** **LB**

KINGSBURY MAP 04 SP29

►►►► Kingsbury Water Park Camping & Caravanning Club Site *(SP202968)*

Kingsbury Water Park, Bodymoor, Heath Ln B76 0DY

☎ 01827 874101

web: www.thefriendlyclub.co.uk

Dir: *From M42 junct 9 take B4097 Kingsbury road. Left at rdbt, past main entrance to water park, over motorway, take next right. Follow lane for 0.5m to site*

PETS: Public areas except in buildings disp bin **Exercise area** **Facilities** walks info vet info **Other** prior notice required

Open all year Last arrival 21.00hrs Last departure noon

A very upmarket site providing high standards in every area. Along with private washing facilities in the quality toilets, there is good security on this attractive former gravel pit, with its complex of lakes, canals, woods and marshland, with good access roads. An 18-acre site with 150 touring pitches, 75 hardstandings.

Notes Site gates closed 23.00hrs-07.00hrs

LEAMINGTON SPA (ROYAL) MAP 04 SP36

★★★ 72% HOTEL

Best Western Falstaff

Best Western

16-20 Warwick New Rd CV32 5JQ

☎ 01926 312044 🖹 01926 450574

e-mail: sales@falstaffhotel.com

web: www.falstaffhotel.com

Dir: *M40 junct 13 or 14, follow Leamington Spa signs. Over 4 rdbts, under bridge. Left into Princes Dr, right at mini-rdbt*

PETS: Bedrooms (16GF) unattended **Charges** £10 per night **Grounds** accessible on leads **Exercise area** parks nearby **Facilities** vet info **On Request** fridge access towels

Bedrooms at this hotel come in a variety of sizes and styles and are well equipped, with many thoughtful extras. Snacks can be taken in the relaxing lounge bar, and an interesting selection of English and continental dishes is offered in the restaurant; 24-hour room service is also available. Conference and banqueting facilities are extensive.

Rooms 63 en suite (2 fmly) (16 GF) S £65-£115; D £75-£125 (incl. bkfst) **Facilities** FTV Wi-fi in bedrooms Arrangement with local health club Xmas New Year **Parking** 50 **Notes** **LB**

★★★★ GUEST ACCOMMODATION

Bubbenhall House

Paget's Ln CV8 3BJ

☎ 024 7630 2409 & 07746 282541 🖹 024 7630 2409

e-mail: wharrison@bubbenhallhouse.freeserve.co.uk

Dir: *5m NE of Leamington. Off A445 at Bubbenhall S onto Paget's Ln, 1m on single-track lane (over 4 speed humps*

PETS: Bedrooms Public areas except dining room (on leads) **Grounds** accessible disp bin **Exercise area** **Facilities** food (pre-bookable) food bowl water bowl dog chews pet sitting washing facs cage storage walks info vet info **On Request** fridge access torch towels **Resident Pets:** Zippy (Black Labrador), Budweiser (Jack Russell), Kitty (cat)

Located between Leamington Spa and Coventry in extensive mature grounds with an abundance of wildlife, this impressive late Edwardian house was once the home of Alexander Issigonis, designer of the Mini. It contains many interesting features including a Jacobean-style staircase. Thoughtful extras are provided in the bedrooms, and public

CONTINUED

LEAMINGTON SPA (ROYAL) CONTINUED

areas include an elegant dining room and choice of sumptuous lounges.

Rooms 5 en suite (1 GF) S £50; D £70-£75* **Facilities** FTV TVB tea/coffee Cen ht TVL Wi-fi available **Parking** 12 **Notes** LB

NUNEATON — MAP 04 SP39

★★★ 72% HOTEL

Best Western Weston Hall

Weston Ln, Bulkington CV12 9RU

☎ 024 7631 2989 024 7664 0846

e-mail: info@westonhallhotel.co.uk

Dir: *M6 junct 2, B4065 through Ansty. Left in Shilton, follow Nuneaton signs from Bulkington, turn into Weston Ln at 30mph sign*

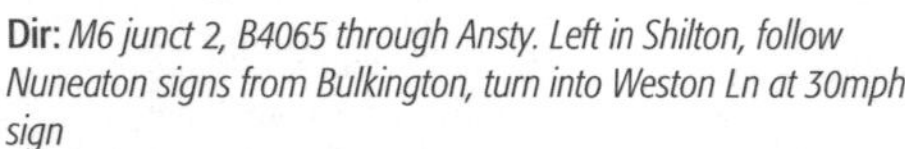

PETS: Bedrooms (14GF) **Charges** £10 per night charge for damage **Public areas** only front bar (on leads) **Grounds** accessible **Exercise area Facilities** food bowl water bowl bedding washing facs cage storage walks info vet info **On Request** fridge access torch towels **Other** food by prior arrangement

This Grade II listed hotel, whose origins date back to the reign of Elizabeth I, sits within seven acres of peaceful grounds. The original three-gabled building retains many original features, such as the carved wooden fireplace in the library. Friendly service is provided; and the bedrooms, that vary in size, are thoughtfully equipped.

Rooms 40 en suite (1 fmly) (14 GF) S £60-£74; D £70-£100 (incl. bkfst) **Facilities** FTV Wi-fi available New Year **Parking** 300 **Notes** LB

RUGBY — MAP 04 SP57

►► Lodge Farm Campsite *(SP476748)*

Bilton Ln, Long Lawford CV23 9DU

☎ 01788 560193

e-mail: alec@lodgefarm.com

web: www.lodgefarm.com

Dir: *From Rugby take A428 (Lawford Road) 1.5m towards Coventry. At Sheaf & Sickle pub left into Bilton Lane, site 500yds*

PETS: Stables nearby (3m) (loose box) disp bin **Exercise area** 200yds **Facilities** washing facs walks info vet info **Other** dogs must be exercised off site **Resident Pets:** 1 Collie, 2 cats

Open Etr-Nov Last arrival 22.00hrs

A small, simple farm site set behind the friendly owner's home and self-catering cottages, with converted stables housing the toilet facilities. Rugby is only a short drive away, and the site is tucked well away from the main road. A 2.5-acre site with 35 touring pitches, 3 hardstandings and 10 statics.

STRATFORD-UPON-AVON — MAP 04 SP25

★★★★ 77% HOTEL

Barceló Billesley Manor Hotel

Billesley, Alcester B49 6NF

☎ 01789 279955 01789 764145

e-mail: billesleymanor@barcelo-hotels.co.uk

web: www.barcelo-hotels.co.uk

Dir: *A46 towards Evesham. Over 3 rdbts, right for Billesley after 2m*

PETS: Bedrooms (5GF) unattended **Charges** £15 per night charge for damage **Grounds** accessible disp bin **Exercise area Facilities** cage storage vet info **On Request** fridge access torch towels

This 16th-century manor is set in peaceful grounds and parkland with a delightful yew topiary garden and fountain. The spacious bedrooms and suites, most in traditional country-house style, are thoughtfully designed and well equipped. Conference facilities and some of the bedrooms are found in the cedar barns. Public areas retain many original features, such as oak panelling, fireplaces and exposed stone.

Rooms 43 en suite 29 annexe en suite (5 GF) S £75-£159* **Facilities** Gym Steam room Beauty treatments Yoga studio Xmas New Year **Parking** 100

★★★★ 71% HOTEL

Mercure Shakespeare

Chapel St CV37 6ER

☎ 01789 294997 📠 01789 415411

e-mail: h6630@accor.com

web: www.mercure-uk.com

Dir: *M40 junct 15. Follow signs for Stratford town centre on A439. Follow one-way system onto Bridge St. Left at rdbt, hotel 200yds on left opp HSBC bank*

PETS: Bedrooms Charges £10 per night charge for damage **Exercise area** parks 300yds

Dating back to the early 17th century, The Shakespeare is one of the oldest hotels in this historic town. The hotel name represents one of the earliest exploitations of Stratford as the birthplace of one of the world's leading poets and playwrights. With exposed beams and open fires, the public rooms retain an ambience reminiscent of this era. Bedrooms are appointed to a good standard and remain in keeping with the style of the property.

Rooms 63 en suite 11 annexe en suite (3 GF) **Facilities** Wi-fi available **Services** Lift **Parking** 34 (charged)

★★★ 81% HOTEL

Thistle Stratford-upon-Avon

Waterside CV37 6BA

☎ 0871 376 9035 📠 0871 376 9135

e-mail: stratforduponavon@thistle.co.uk

web: www.thistlehotels.com/stratforduponavon

Dir: *M40 junct 15, A46 to Stratford-upon-Avon, take 1st exit at rdbt towards town centre, A439.*

PETS: Bedrooms unattended **Charges** £10 per night charge for damage **Public areas** except restaurant (on leads) **Grounds** accessible disp bin **Exercise area** gardens adjacent **Facilities** walks info vet info **On Request** torch towels

The hotel is located just a very short walk from the town centre, sitting directly opposite the world famous Shakespeare and Swan theatres and is fronted by award-winning gardens. Service throughout the day rooms is both friendly and professional, offering separate bar and lounge areas, with the dining room providing interesting menu selections. Bedrooms are well equipped and comfortably appointed.

Rooms 63 en suite (4 fmly) S £70-£175; D £90-£205 (incl. bkfst)✳ **Facilities** STV Wi-fi in bedrooms Xmas New Year **Parking** 55 (charged) **Notes** LB

★★★ 75% HOTEL

Charlecote Pheasant Hotel

Charlecote CV35 9EW

☎ 0870 609 6159 📠 01789 470222

e-mail: charlecote@foliohotels.com

web: www.foliohotels.com/charlcotepheasant

Dir: *M40 junct 15, A429 towards Cirencester through Barford. In 2m right into Charlecote, hotel opposite Charlecote Park*

PETS: Bedrooms unattended **Charges** £10 per night **Grounds** accessible on leads **Exercise area** on site **Facilities** vet info

Located just outside Stratford, this hotel is set in extensive grounds and is a popular conference venue. Various bedroom styles are available within the annexe wings, ranging from standard rooms to executive suites. The main building houses the restaurant and a lounge bar area.

Rooms 70 en suite (39 fmly) S £70-£120; D £90-£140✳ **Facilities** FTV Wi fi available Children's play area Xmas New Year **Parking** 100 **Notes** LB

WARWICK — MAP 04 SP26

★★★★ GUEST HOUSE

Croft

Haseley Knob CV35 7NL

☎ 01926 484447 📠 01926 484447

e-mail: david@croftguesthouse.co.uk

web: www.croftguesthouse.co.uk

Dir: *4.5m NW of Warwick. Off A4177 into Haseley Knob, follow B&B signs*

PETS: Bedrooms (4GF) **Charges** £3 per night **Public areas** only sitting area **Grounds** accessible **Exercise area Facilities** food bowl water bowl feeding mat cage storage walks info vet info **On Request** fridge access torch

Friendly proprietors provide homely accommodation at this modern detached house, set in peaceful countryside and convenient for Warwick and the NEC, Birmingham. The conservatory dining room overlooks large well-kept gardens. Fresh eggs from home-reared chickens are used for memorable English breakfasts.

Rooms 7 rms (5 en suite) (2 pri facs) 2 annexe rms (1 en suite) (1 annexe pri facs) (2 fmly) (4 GF) S £40-£45; D £60-£65✳ **Facilities** TVB tea/coffee Cen ht TVL Wi-fi available **Parking** 9 **Notes** No coaches Closed Xmas wk

WARWICK MOTORWAY SERVICE AREA (M40) MAP 04 SP35

BUDGET HOTEL

Days Inn Warwick North

Warwick Services, M40 Northbound Junction 12-13, Banbury Rd CV35 0AA

☎ 01926 651681 📠 01926 651634

e-mail: warwick.north.hotel@welcomebreak.co.uk

web: www.welcomebreak.co.uk

Dir: *M40 northbound between junct 12 & 13*

PETS: Bedrooms Public areas (on leads) **Grounds** accessible on leads disp bin **Exercise area** on site large grassed area **Other** prior notice required **Restrictions** small to medium dogs only

This modern building offers accommodation in smart, spacious and well-equipped bedrooms, suitable for families and business travellers, and all with en suite bathrooms. Refreshments may be taken at the nearby family restaurant.

Rooms 54 en suite S £39-£59; D £49-£69✳

BUDGET HOTEL

Days Inn Warwick South

Warwick Services, M40 Southbound, Banbury Rd CV35 0AA

☎ 01926 650168 📠 01926 651601

e-mail: warwick.south.hotel@welcomebreak.co.uk

Dir: *M40 southbound between junct 14 & 12*

PETS: Bedrooms sign **Charges** charge for damage **Public areas** (on leads) **Grounds** accessible on leads disp bin **Exercise area** 5m

This modern building offers accommodation in smart, spacious and well-equipped bedrooms, suitable for families and business travellers, and all with en suite bathrooms. Refreshments may be taken at the nearby family restaurant.

Rooms 40 en suite S £39-£59; D £49-£69✳

WOLVEY MAP 04 SP48

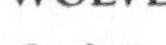

►►► Wolvey Villa Farm Caravan & Camping Site *(SP428869)*

LE10 3HF

☎ 01455 220493 & 220630

web: www.wolveycaravanpark.itgo.com

Dir: *From M6 junct 2 take B4065 follow Wolvey signs. Or M69 junct 1 & follow Wolvey signs*

PETS: Charges 50p per dog per night **Exercise area** on site field **Facilities** on site shop food vet info

Open all year Last arrival 22.00hrs Last departure noon

A level grass site surrounded by trees and shrubs, on the borders of Warwickshire and Leicestershire. This quiet country site has its own popular fishing lake, and is convenient for visiting the major cities of Coventry and Leicester. A 7-acre site with 110 touring pitches, 24 hardstandings.

Notes No twin axles

WEST MIDLANDS

BIRMINGHAM MAP 07 SP08

★★★★ TOWN HOUSE HOTEL

Hotel du Vin Birmingham

25 Church St B3 2NR

☎ 0121 200 0600 📠 0121 236 0889

e-mail: info@birmingham.hotelduvin.com

web: www.hotelduvin.com

Dir: *M6 junct 6/A38(M) to city centre, over flyover. Keep left & exit at St Chads Circus signed Jewellery Quarter. At lights & rdbt take 1st exit, follow signs for Colmore Row, opposite cathedral. Right into Church St, across Barwick St. Hotel on right*

PETS: Bedrooms unattended **Charges** £10 per night charge for damage **Public areas** except bar & bistro (on leads) **Exercise area Facilities** food bowl water bowl bedding cage storage walks info vet info **Other** dog bed, blanket & bowls available

The former Birmingham Eye Hospital has become a chic and sophisticated hotel. The stylish, high-ceilinged rooms, all with a wine theme, are luxuriously appointed and feature stunning bathrooms, sumptuous duvets and Egyptian cotton sheets. The Bistro offers relaxed dining and a top-notch wine list, while other attractions include a champagne bar, a wine boutique and a health club.

Rooms 66 en suite D £150-£425✳ **Facilities** **Spa** STV Gym Wi-fi in bedrooms Treatment rooms Steam room Sauna Xmas New Year **Services** Lift air con **Notes** LB

★★★★ 70% HOTEL

Novotel Birmingham Centre

70 Broad St B1 2HT

☎ 0121 643 2000 0121 643 9796

e-mail: h1077@accor.com

web: www.novotel.com

Dir: *A38/A456, hotel on right beyond International Convention Centre*

PETS: Bedrooms Charges £5 per night **Exercise area** canal walks **Other** Please telephone for further details

This large, modern, purpose-built hotel benefits from an excellent city centre location, with the bonus of secure parking. Bedrooms are spacious, modern and well equipped especially for business users; four rooms have facilities for less able guests. Public areas include the Garden Brasserie, function rooms and a fitness room.

Rooms 148 en suite (148 fmly) S £155-£175; D £155-£185✻ **Facilities** Gym Wi-fi in bedrooms Fitness room Cardio-vascular equipment Spa bath **Services** Lift air con **Parking** 53 **Notes** LB

★★ 75% HOTEL

Copperfield House

60 Upland Rd, Selly Park B29 7JS

☎ 0121 472 8344 0121 415 5655

e-mail: info@copperfieldhousehotel.fsnet.co.uk

Dir: *M6 junct 6/A38 through city centre. After tunnels, right at lights into Belgrave Middleway. Right at rdbt onto A441. At Selly Park Tavern, right into Upland Rd*

PETS: Bedrooms (2GF) **Charges** £5 per night charge for damage **Grounds** accessible disp bin **Exercise area** 0.25km **Facilities** walks info vet info **On Request** torch towels

A delightful Victorian hotel, situated in a leafy suburb, close to the BBC's Pebble Mill Studios and within easy reach of the centre. Accommodation is smartly presented and well equipped, and the executive rooms are particularly spacious. There is a lounge with an honesty bar and the restaurant offers carefully prepared, seasonally-inspired food accompanied by a well-chosen wine list.

Rooms 17 en suite (1 fmly) (2 GF) S £50-£82.50; D £70-£100 (incl. bkfst)✻ **Facilities** FTV Wi-fi available **Parking** 11 **Notes** LB Closed 24 Dec - 2 Jan

BUDGET HOTEL

Campanile Birmingham

Chester St, Aston B6 4BE

☎ 0121 359 3330 0121 359 1223

e-mail: birmingham@campanile.com

web: www.envergure.fr

Dir: *next to rdbt at junct of A4540/A38*

PETS: Bedrooms unattended **Stables** on site **Charges** charge for damage **Public areas Grounds** accessible disp bin **Exercise area** 5 min walk **Facilities** food (pre-bookable) food bowl water bowl bedding dog chews cat treats feeding mat litter tray dog scoop/disp bags leads pet sitting dog walking washing facs dog grooming cage storage walks info vet info **On Request** fridge access torch towels

This modern building offers accommodation in smart, well-equipped bedrooms, all with en suite bathrooms. Refreshments may be taken at the informal Bistro.

Rooms 109 en suite

BUDGET HOTEL

Express by Holiday Inn Birmingham

1200 Chester Rd, Castle Bromwich B35 7AF

☎ 0121 747 6633 0121 747 6644

e-mail: castlebromwich@holidayinnexpress.co.uk

web: www.hiexpress.com/birminghamex

Dir: *M6 junct 5/6/A38 for Tyburn, right into Chester Rd, follow Park signs*

PETS: Bedrooms (12GF) **Charges** £10 per night charge for damage **Public areas** except bar & restaurant (on leads) **Grounds** accessible on leads **Exercise area Facilities** walks info vet info **On Request** fridge access towels

A modern hotel ideal for families and business travellers. Fresh and uncomplicated, the spacious bedrooms include Sky TV, power shower and tea and coffee-making facilities. Continental buffet breakfast is included in the room rate; other meals may be taken at the nearby family pub or restaurant.

Rooms 110 en suite

BIRMINGHAM CONTINUED

BUDGET HOTEL

Ibis Birmingham Bordesley Circus

1 Bordesley Park Rd, Bordesley B10 0PD

☎ 0121 506 2600 🖷 0121 506 2610

e-mail: H2178@accor-hotels.com

web: www.ibishotel.com

PETS: Bedrooms unattended sign **Grounds** accessible on leads **Exercise area Facilities** food bowl water bowl **On Request** torch

Modern, budget hotel offering comfortable accommodation in bright and practical bedrooms. Breakfast is self-service and dinner is available in the restaurant.

Rooms 87 en suite

BUDGET HOTEL

Ibis Birmingham City Centre

Arcadian Centre, Ladywell Walk B5 4ST

☎ 0121 622 6010 🖷 0121 622 6020

e-mail: h1459@accor-hotels.com

Dir: *From motorways follow city centre signs. Then follow Bullring or Indoor Market signs. Hotel next to market*

PETS: Bedrooms unattended **Charges** no charge except during Crufts Week (March) charge for damage **Public areas** (on leads) **Exercise area** canals 7 min walk **Facilities** cage storage walks info vet info **On Request** towels **Other** dogs to be muzzled at owner's discretion

Modern, budget hotel offering comfortable accommodation in bright and practical bedrooms. Breakfast is self-service and dinner is available in the restaurant.

Rooms 159 en suite

★★ GUEST ACCOMMODATION

Rollason Wood

130 Wood End Rd, Erdington B24 8BJ

☎ 0121 373 1230 🖷 0121 382 2578

e-mail: rollwood@globalnet.co.uk

Dir: *M6 junct 6, A5127 to Erdington, right onto A4040, 0.25m on left*

PETS: Bedrooms sign **Exercise area** 200yds **Facilities** cage storage walks info vet info

Well situated for routes and the city centre, this owner-managed establishment is popular with contractors. The choice of three different bedroom styles suits most budgets, and rates include full English breakfasts. Ground-floor areas include a popular bar, cosy television lounge and a dining room.

Rooms 35 rms (11 en suite) (5 fmly) **Facilities** TVB tea/coffee Cen ht TVL Dinner Last d 8.30pm Pool Table **Parking** 35

BIRMINGHAM AIRPORT — MAP 07 SP18

★★★ 74% HOTEL

Novotel Birmingham Airport

B26 3QL

☎ 0121 782 7000 & 782 4111 🖷 0121 782 0445

e-mail: H1158@accor.com

web: www.novotel.com

Dir: *M42 junct 6/A45 to Birmingham, signed to airport. Hotel opposite main terminal.*

PETS: Bedrooms Charges £15 per night charge for damage **Exercise area Other** Please telephone for details

This large, purpose-built hotel is located opposite the main passenger terminal. Bedrooms are spacious, modern in style and well equipped, including Playstations to keep the children busy. Several rooms have facilities for less able guests. The Garden Brasserie is open from noon until midnight, the bar is open 24 hours and a full room service is available.

Rooms 195 en suite (36 fmly) S £75-£159; D £75-£159* **Facilities** STV Wi-fi in bedrooms **Services** Lift **Notes LB**

BIRMINGHAM (NATIONAL EXHIBITION CENTRE) — MAP 07 SP18

★★★ 71% HOTEL

Arden Hotel & Leisure Club

Coventry Rd, Bickenhill B92 0EH

☎ 01675 443221 🖷 01675 445604

e-mail: enquiries@ardenhotel.co.uk

Dir: *M42 junct 6/A45 towards Birmingham. Hotel 0.25m on right, just off Birmingham International railway island*

PETS: Bedrooms Charges £10 per night charge for damage **Grounds** accessible on leads disp bin **Exercise area Facilities** vet info **On Request** fridge access

This smart hotel neighbouring the NEC offers modern rooms and well-equipped leisure facilities. After dinner in the formal restaurant, the place to relax is the spacious lounge area. A buffet breakfast is served in the bright and airy Meeting Place.

Rooms 216 en suite (6 fmly) (6 GF) **Facilities** supervised Gym Wi-fi in bedrooms Sports therapy Beautician **Services** Lift **Parking** 300 **Notes LB** RS 25-28 Dec

COVENTRY — MAP 04 SP37

★★★ 72% HOTEL

Novotel Coventry

Wilsons Ln CV6 6HL

☎ 024 7636 5000 📠 024 7636 2422

e-mail: h0506@accor-hotels.com

web: www.novotel.com

Dir: *M6 junct 3. Follow signs for B4113 towards Longford and Bedworth. 3rd exit on large rdbt*

PETS: Bedrooms (25GF) **Stables** nearby (3m) **Charges** £12 per night £84 per week charge for damage **Public areas** foyer only (on leads) **Grounds** accessible on leads disp bin **Exercise area Facilities** walks info vet info **On Request** fridge access torch towels **Other** disposal bags available

A modern hotel convenient for Birmingham, Coventry and the motorway network, offering spacious, well-equipped accommodation. The bright brasserie has extended dining hours, and alternatively there is an extensive room-service menu. Family rooms and a play area make this a child-friendly hotel, and there is also a selection of meeting rooms.

Rooms 98 en suite (33 fmly) (25 GF) S £55-£150; D £55-£150✻ **Facilities** STV Wi-fi available **Services** Lift **Parking** 120 **Notes** LB

HAMPTON-IN-ARDEN — MAP 04 SP28

★★★★ GUEST HOUSE

The Cottage Guest House

Kenilworth Rd B92 0LW

☎ 01675 442323 📠 01675 443323

e-mail: cottage.roger88@virgin.net

web: www.cottageguesthouse.net

Dir: *2m SE of Hampton on A452*

PETS: Bedrooms Charges £1 per night charge for damage **Exercise area** 100yds **Facilities** water bowl walks info vet info **Resident Pets:** North & South (Longhaired German Shepherds), Lovebirds & Peacocks

A fine collection of antique memorabilia adorns the public areas of this delightful cottage, which is convenient for visiting the NEC, Birmingham, or exploring the area. Many guests return for the friendly and relaxing atmosphere and the attentive service. Freshly cooked traditional breakfasts, served in the cottage dining room, provide a good start to the day.

Rooms 9 en suite (2 GF) S £35-£50; D £50-£70✻ **Facilities** TVB tea/coffee Cen ht TVL **Parking** 14 **Notes** Closed Xmas

MERIDEN — MAP 04 SP28

★★★ 82% HOTEL

Manor

Main Rd CV7 7NH

☎ 01676 522735 📠 01676 522186

e-mail: reservations@manorhotelmeriden.co.uk

web: www.manorhotelmeriden.co.uk

Dir: *M42 junct 6, A45 towards Coventry then A452 signed Leamington. At rdbt take B4102 signed Meriden, hotel on left*

PETS: Bedrooms unattended **Public areas** assist dogs only (on leads) **Grounds** accessible on leads disp bin **Exercise area Facilities** vet info **On Request** fridge access

A sympathetically extended Georgian manor in the heart of a sleepy village is just a few minutes away from the M6, M42 and National Exhibition Centre. The Regency Restaurant offers modern dishes, while the Triumph Buttery serves lighter meals and snacks. The bedrooms are smart and well equipped.

Rooms 110 en suite (20 GF) S £70-£140; D £90-£180 (incl. bkfst)✻ **Facilities** Wi-fi in bedrooms **Services** Lift **Parking** 200 **Notes** LB RS 24 Dec-2 Jan

►►►► Somers Wood Caravan Park

(SP225824)

Somers Rd CV7 7PL

☎ 01676 522978 📠 01676 522978

e-mail: enquiries@somerswood.co.uk

web: www.somerswood.co.uk

Dir: *M42 junct 6, A45 signed Coventry. Keep left (do not take flyover). Then right onto A452 signed Meriden/Leamington. At next rdbt left onto B4102, Hampton Lane. Site in 0.5m on left*

PETS: Exercise area adjacent **Facilities** walks info vet info **Other** prior notice required **Resident Pets:** Jodie (dog), Tiddles (cat)

Open Feb-2 Jan

A peaceful adults-only park set in the heart of England with spotless facilities. The park is well positioned for visiting the National Exhibition Centre (NEC) or the NEC Arena and National Indoor Arena (NIA), and Birminghan is only 12 miles away. The park also makes and ideal touring base for Warwick, Coventry and Stratford-on-Avon just 22 miles away. A 4-acre site with 48 touring pitches, 48 hardstandings.

Notes No tents

ENGLAND

SOLIHULL MAP 07 SP17

★★★ 77% HOTEL

Ramada Solihull/Birmingham

RAMADA

The Square B91 3RF

☎ 0121 711 2121 🖷 0121 711 3374

e-mail: sales.solihull@ramadajarvis.co.uk

web: www.ramadajarvis.co.uk/solihull

Dir: *M42 junct 5, A41 towards Solihull. 1st left on slip road. Right at island, left at 2 sets of lights. Hotel 600yds on right*

PETS: Bedrooms (36GF) unattended **Stables** nearby **Charges** £5 per night **Public areas** except bar & restaurant (on leads) **Grounds** accessible on leads **Exercise area** park 200mtrs **Facilities** food bowl water bowl walks info vet info **On Request** fridge access torch towels

Within a few minutes walk of the central attractions, this modern hotel provides a range of well-equipped bedrooms, with studio rooms being particularly attractive. Extensive conference facilities are available and public areas include Arts Restaurant, overlooking one of the world's oldest bowling greens, and cosy bars dating from the 16th century, which retain many original features.

Rooms 145 en suite (14 fmly) (36 GF) S £67-£187; D £67-£199 (incl. bkfst)✻ **Facilities** FTV Wi-fi available Crown Green bowling Xmas New Year **Services** Lift **Parking** 180 (charged) **Notes** LB

★★★ 70% HOTEL

Corus hotel Solihull

Stratford Rd, Shirley B90 4EB

☎ 0844 736 8605 & 0121 745 0400 🖷 0121 733 3801

e-mail: solihull@corushotels.com

web: www.corushotels.com

Dir: *M42 junct 4 onto A34 for Shirley, cross 1st 3 rdbts, then double back along dual carriageway, hotel on left*

PETS: Bedrooms (13GF) **Charges** £5 per night charge for damage **Public areas** reception only (on leads) **Grounds** accessible on leads **Exercise area Facilities** walks info vet info

A large, friendly hotel attracting both corporate and leisure guests. It is ideally located within a few minutes of the major transportation links and benefits from its own extensive leisure centre that includes a lagoon pool, sauna and gym.

Rooms 111 en suite (11 fmly) (13 GF) S £120-£135; D £120-£135✻ **Facilities** Gym Wi-fi available Steam room Plunge pool Sauna New Year **Services** Lift **Parking** 275 **Notes** LB RS Xmas

SUTTON COLDFIELD MAP 07 SP19

★★★ 72% HOTEL

Ramada Hotel & Resort Birmingham

RAMADA HOTEL & RESORT

Penns Ln, Walmley B76 1LH

☎ 0121 351 3111 🖷 0844 815 9022

e-mail: sales.birmingham@ramadajarvis.co.uk

web: www.ramadajarvis.co.uk

Dir: *A5127 towards Sutton Coldfield for 2m, through lights, 4th right into Penns Lane. Hotel 1m on right follow brown tourist signs*

PETS: Bedrooms (20GF) **Grounds** accessible on leads **Exercise area Facilities** vet info

Conveniently located for both M42 and M6 this large hotel is set in private grounds overlooking a lake. Bedrooms are comfortably appointed for both business and leisure guests. Public areas include the Club Restaurant and bar, a leisure club and extensive conference facilities.

Rooms 157 en suite 13 annexe en suite (20 fmly) (20 GF) S £67-£181; D £67-£193 (incl. bkfst)✻ **Facilities Spa** supervised Fishing Squash Gym Wi-fi in bedrooms Hairdressing salon Xmas New Year **Services** Lift **Parking** 500 **Notes** LB

WOLVERHAMPTON MAP 07 SO99

★★★ 75% HOTEL

Novotel Wolverhampton

NOVOTEL

Union St WV1 3JN

☎ 01902 871100 🖷 01902 870054

e-mail: H1188@accor.com

web: www.novotel.com

Dir: *6m from M6 junct 10. A454 to Wolverhampton. Hotel on main ring road*

PETS: Bedrooms unattended **Charges** £5 per night charge for damage **Public areas** bar/lounge only (on leads) **Exercise area** 5 mins walk **Facilities** walks info vet info **On Request** towels

This large, modern, purpose-built hotel stands close to the town centre. It provides spacious, smartly presented and well-equipped bedrooms, all of which contain convertible bed settees for family occupancy. In addition to the open-plan lounge and bar area, there is an attractive brasserie-style restaurant, which overlooks the small outdoor swimming pool.

Rooms 132 en suite (9 fmly) S £55-£125; D £55-£125✻ **Facilities** Wi-fi available **Services** Lift **Parking** 120 **Notes** LB RS 23 Dec-4 Jan

WIGHT, ISLE OF

ARRETON

MAP 04 SZ58

★★★★ BED & BREAKFAST

Blandings

Horringford PO30 3AP

☎ 01983 865720 & 865331 📠 01983 862099

e-mail: robin.oulton@horringford.com

web: www.horringford.com/bedandbreakfast.htm

Dir: *S through Arreton (B3056), pass Stickworth Hall on right, 300yds on left farm entrance signed Horringford Gdns. Take U-turn to left, drive to end of poplar trees, turn right. Blandings on left*

PETS: Bedrooms (1GF) **Stables** nearby **Charges** charge for damage **Public areas Grounds** accessible on leads disp bin **Exercise area Facilities** washing facs cage storage walks info vet info

This newly-built detached home stands in the grounds of Horringford Gardens. The bedroom has private access and a decking area for warm summer evenings. Breakfast is a highlight with local island produce gracing the table.

Rooms 1 en suite (1 GF) D £60* **Facilities** FTV TVB tea/coffee Cen ht **Parking** 3 **Notes** LB

BONCHURCH

MAP 04 SZ57

★★★★★ GUEST HOUSE

Winterbourne Country House

Bonchurch Village Rd PO38 1RQ

☎ 01983 852535 📠 01983 857529

e-mail: info@winterbournehouse.co.uk

Dir: *1m E of Ventnor. Off A3055 into Bonchurch village*

PETS: Bedrooms Charges £9 per night charge for damage **Public areas** except breakfast room (on leads) **Grounds** accessible on leads disp bin **Exercise area Facilities** food bowl water bowl feeding mat cage storage walks info vet info **On Request** fridge access torch towels

During his stay in 1849, Charles Dickens described Winterbourne as 'the prettiest place I ever saw in my life, at home or abroad'. Today, the comfortable bedrooms are well equipped and differ in size, and include luxurious rooms with sea views. There are two lounges and a secluded terrace.

Rooms 7 rms (6 en suite) (1 pri facs) S £65-£150; D £110-£190* **Facilities** TVB tea/coffee Direct dial from bedrooms Licensed Cen ht TVL **Parking** 8 **Notes** No children 10yrs No coaches Closed Xmas

COWES

MAP 04 SZ49

★★★ 70% HOTEL

Best Western New Holmwood

Queens Rd, Egypt Point PO31 8BW

☎ 01983 292508 📠 01983 295020

e-mail: reception@newholmwoodhotel.co.uk

Dir: *from A3020 at Northwood Garage lights, left & follow road to rdbt. 1st left then sharp right into Baring Rd, 4th left into Egypt Hill. At bottom turn right, hotel on right*

PETS: Bedrooms unattended **Charges** charge for damage **Public areas** except restaurant **Exercise area** 2 mins walk to beach **Facilities** water bowl **Resident Pets:** Mya (German Shepherd)

Just by the Esplanade, this hotel has an enviable outlook. Bedrooms are comfortable and very well equipped, and the light and airy, glass-fronted restaurant looks out to sea and serves a range of interesting meals. The sun terrace is delightful in the summer and there is a small pool area.

Rooms 26 en suite (1 fmly) (9 GF) **Facilities** STV Wi-fi in bedrooms **Parking** 20

★★★ BED & BREAKFAST

Medina Post Office

5-7 York St PO31 7BS

☎ 01983 292665 📠 01983 292665

e-mail: info@medinapost.co.uk

web: www.medinapost.co.uk

Dir: *Off A3020 Mill Hill Rd in West Cowes, 200yds from floating bridge*

PETS: Bedrooms Charges charge for damage **Public areas** (on leads) **Exercise area Facilities** food bowl water bowl dog chews feeding mat dog scoop/disp bags cage storage walks info vet info **On Request** fridge access torch towels

A warm welcome is to be expected at this charming terrace property, which is situated close to the town centre and ferry terminal. Bedrooms are pleasantly decorated with co-ordinated fabrics and have a good range of facilities. Breakfast is served at separate tables in the sunny conservatory.

Rooms 2 rms (1 en suite) (1 pri facs) D £50-£75* **Facilities** TVB tea/coffee Cen ht TVL Wi-fi available **Notes** Closed Nov-Feb

ENGLAND

COWES CONTINUED

★★★ GUEST ACCOMMODATION

Windward House

69 Mill Hill Rd PO31 7EQ

☎ 01983 280940 & 07771 573580 📠 01983 280940

e-mail: sueogston1@tiscali.co.uk

Dir: *A320 Cowes-Newport, halfway up Mill Hill Rd on right from floating bridge from E Cowes (Red Funnel Ferries)*

PETS: Bedrooms sign **Stables** nearby (1.5m) **Public areas** except dining room **Grounds** accessible disp bin **Exercise area** on site garden **Facilities** food bowl water bowl bedding dog chews feeding mat dog scoop/disp bags leads dog walking washing facs cage storage walks info vet info **On Request** fridge access torch towels **Other** Pet food by request

Resident Pets: Gem (German Shepherd)

A friendly atmosphere prevails at this comfortable Victorian house, located close to the centre of Cowes. Bedrooms are bright and neat, and downstairs there is a spacious lounge equipped with satellite television, video and music systems. Breakfast is served in a separate dining room around a shared table.

Rooms 6 rms (3 en suite) (2 fmly) (1 GF) S £25-£40; D £50-£70✻ **Facilities** TVB tea/coffee Cen ht TVL **Parking** 4 **Notes**

FRESHWATER — MAP 04 SZ38

★★★ 76% HOTEL

Farringford

Bedbury Ln PO40 9PE

☎ 01983 752500 📠 01983 756515

e-mail: enquiries@farringford.co.uk

web: www.farringford.co.uk

Dir: *A3054, left to Norton Green down Pixlie Hill. Left to Freshwater Bay. At bay turn right into Bedbury Lane, hotel on left*

PETS: Bedrooms (4GF) **Stables** nearby **Charges** £7 per night charge for damage **Grounds** accessible on leads disp bin **Exercise area Facilities** water bowl dog scoop/disp bags walks info vet info

Upon seeing Farringford, Alfred Lord Tennyson is said to have remarked "we will go no further, this must be our home" and so it was for some forty years. Some 150 years later, the hotel provides bedrooms ranging in style and size, from large rooms in the main house to adjoining chalet-style rooms. The atmosphere is relaxed, and dinner features fresh local produce.

Rooms 14 en suite 4 annexe en suite (5 fmly) (4 GF) **Facilities** 9 Putt green Beauty treatment room Bowling Green **Parking** 55 **Notes LB**

►►►► **Heathfield Farm Camping** *(SZ335879)*

Heathfield Rd PO40 9SH

☎ 01983 756756

e-mail: web@heathfieldcamping.co.uk

web: www.heathfieldcamping.co.uk

Dir: *2m W from Yarmouth ferry port on A3054, left to Heathfield Rd, entrance 200yds on right*

PETS: Stables nearby (600mtrs) (loose box) **Charges** £1.50 per night **Public areas** except playing field & dog-free pitches disp bin **Exercise area** on site adjacent meadow **Facilities** vet info

Open May-Sep Last arrival 20.00hrs Last departure 22.00hrs

A good quality park with friendly owners and lovely views across the Solent to Hurst Castle. The toilet facilities, amenities and grounds are very well maintained, and this park is constantly improving to meet the needs of campers and caravanners. A 10-acre site .

Notes Family camping only

NEWBRIDGE — MAP 04 SZ48

►►►►► **Orchards Holiday Caravan Park**

(SZ411881)

PO41 0TS

☎ 01983 531331 & 531350 📠 01983 531666

e-mail: info@orchards-holiday-park.co.uk

web: www.orchards-holiday-park.co.uk

Dir: *4m E of Yarmouth; 6m W of Newport on B3401*

PETS: Charges £1.50-£2.50 per night disp bin **Exercise area** on site fenced field **Facilities** on site shop food food bowl water bowl dog chews cat treats leads washing facs walks info vet info **Other** prior notice required

Open 11 Feb-2 Jan (rs Nov-Jan & Feb-mid Mar) Last arrival 23.00hrs Last departure 11.00hrs

A really excellent, well-managed park set in a peaceful village location amid downs and meadowland, with glorious downland views. Pitches are terraced, and offer a good provision of hardstandings, including super pitches. A new high quality toilet block is planned to be opened by Easter 2009 offering excellent private facilities. The park has indoor and outdoor swimming pools, a shop, takeaway and licensed coffee shop. There is disabled access to all facilities on site, plus disabled toilets. A 15-acre site with 171 touring pitches, 74 hardstandings and 65 statics.

NEWCHURCH MAP 04 SZ58

►►►►► Southland Camping Park *(SZ557847)*

PO36 0LZ

☎ 01983 865385 📠 01983 867663

e-mail: info@southland.co.uk

web: www.southland.co.uk

Dir: *A3056 towards Sandown. 2nd left after Fighting Cocks pub towards Newchurch. Site 1m on left*

PETS: Charges £1.20 per night (dogs) **Public areas** except shop, toilet, laundrette (on leads) disp bin **Exercise area** on site small enclosed areas **Facilities** on site shop dog scoop/disp bags walks info vet info **Other** dog tethers **Restrictions** no dangerous dog breeds (see page 7)

Open 5 Apr-Sep Last arrival 21.30hrs Last departure 11.00hrs

Beautifully maintained site, peacefully located and impressively laid out on the outskirts of the village in the Arreton Valley. Good quality sanitary facilities including spacious family rooms enhance the park. Pitches are well screened by lovely trees and shrubs. A 9-acre site with 120 touring pitches.

RYDE MAP 04 SZ59

►►►► Whitefield Forest Touring Park

(SZ604893)

Brading Rd PO33 1QL

☎ 01983 617069

e-mail: pat&louise@whitefieldforest.co.uk

web: www.whitefieldforest.co.uk

Dir: *From Ryde follow A3055 towards Brading, after Tesco rdbt site 0.5m on left.*

PETS: Public areas except toilets **Charges** £1-£1.50 per night disp bin **Exercise area Facilities** walks info vet info **Other** prior notice required **Resident Pets:** Izzy (West Highland White Terrier), Scooby (Black Labrador)

Open Etr-Oct Last arrival 21.00hrs Last departure 11.00hrs

This park is beautifully laid out in Whitefield Forest, and offers a wide variety of pitches, all of which have electricity. It offers excellent modern facilities which are spotlessly clean. The park takes great care in retaining the natural beauty of the forest, and is a haven for wildlife, including the red squirrel. A 23-acre site with 80 touring pitches, 20 hardstandings.

SANDOWN MAP 04 SZ58

★★ 74% HOTEL

The Wight Montrene

11 Avenue Rd PO36 8BN

☎ 01983 403722 📠 01983 405553

e-mail: enquiries@wighthotel.co.uk

web: www.wighthotel.co.uk

Dir: *100yds after mini-rdbt between High St and Avenue Rd*

PETS: Bedrooms (21GF) unattended sign **Stables** nearby (8m) **Charges** charge for damage **Grounds** accessible on leads **Exercise area** 300yds **Facilities** cage storage walks info vet info **Other** dogs must be taken off site to exercise

Resident Pets: Magnum (Great Pyrenian Mountain Dog), Oyette (cat)

A family hotel set in secluded grounds that is only a short walk from Sandown's beach and high street shops. Bedrooms provide comfort and are either on the ground or first floor. Guests can relax in the heated swimming pool or enjoy evening entertainment in the bar. The dinner menu changes nightly, and a plentiful breakfast is served in the colourful dining room.

Rooms 41 en suite (18 fmly) (21 GF) **Facilities** ⓢ Gym Wi-fi in bedrooms Pool table Steam room Table tennis ♫ ch fac **Parking** 40 **Notes** LB

See advert on page 297

SANDOWN CONTINUED

★★★★ GUEST HOUSE

Carisbrooke House

11 Beachfield Rd PO36 8NA

☎ 01983 402257 🖷 01983 402257

e-mail: wmch583@aol.com

Dir: *2 minutes from Sandown town, beach and leisure centre, opposite Ferncliff Gardens*

PETS: Bedrooms Charges £5 per stay charge for damage **Public areas** except dining areas **Grounds** accessible **Exercise area** adjacent

Expect a friendly welcome at this family run guest-house situated opposite Ferncliff Gardens and within walking distance of the town centre and seafront. A full English breakfast is served in the dining room overlooking the sun terrace. Enjoy a drink in the bar/lounge. Dinner by arrangement

Rooms 11 rms (9 en suite) (2 pri facs) (3 fmly) (3 GF) S £27-£30; D £54-£70✳ **Facilities** TVB tea/coffee Licensed Cen ht TVL Dinner Last d breakfast same day Wi-fi available **Parking** 3 **Notes LB**

►►►► **Adgestone Camping & Caravanning Club Site** *(SZ590855)*

Lower Adgestone Rd PO36 0HL

☎ 01983 403432

web: www.thefriendlyclub.co.uk

Dir: *Turn off A3055 (Sandown/Shanklin road) at Manor House pub, in Lake. Past school & golf course on left, turn right at T-junct, site 200yds on right*

PETS: disp bin **Exercise area** on site dog walk **Facilities** on site shop walks info vet info **Other** prior notice required

Open 2 Apr-2 Nov Last arrival 21.00hrs Last departure noon

A popular, well-managed park in a quiet, rural location not far from Sandown. The level pitches are imaginatively laid out, and surrounded by beautiful flower beds and trees set close to a small river. This planting offers good screening as well as enhancing the appearance of the park. There is excellent provision for families in general. A 22-acre site with 270 touring pitches.

Notes Site gates closed 23.00hrs-07.00hrs

SHANKLIN MAP 04 SZ58

★★ 76% HOTEL

Melbourne Ardenlea

4-6 Queens Rd PO37 6AP

☎ 01983 862283 🖷 01983 862865

e-mail: reservations@melbourneardenlea.co.uk

Dir: *A3055 to Shanklin. Then follow signs to Ventnor via B3328 (Queens Rd). Hotel just before end of road on right*

PETS: Bedrooms (6GF) unattended sign **Charges** £4 per night **Public areas** except dining room (on leads) **Grounds** accessible disp bin **Exercise area** 500mtrs **Facilities** food (pre-bookable) food bowl water bowl feeding mat dog scoop/disp bags leads washing facs cage storage walks info vet info **On Request** fridge access torch towels

This quietly located hotel is within easy walking distance of the town centre and the lift down to the promenade. Bedrooms are traditionally furnished and guests can enjoy the various spacious public areas including a welcoming bar and a large heated indoor swimming pool.

Rooms 54 en suite (5 fmly) (6 GF) S £39-£79; D £70-£120 (incl. bkfst)✳ **Facilities** Wi-fi available Sauna ♫ New Year **Services** Lift **Parking** 26 **Notes LB** Closed 21-28 Dec

★★★★ GUEST ACCOMMODATION

Hayes Barton

7 Highfield Rd PO37 6PP

☎ 01983 867747 🖷 01983 862104

e-mail: williams.2000@virgin.net

web: www.hayesbarton.co.uk

Dir: *A3055 onto A3020 Victoria Av, 3rd left*

PETS: Bedrooms (2GF) unattended **Charges** £3.50 per night £22 per week charge for damage **Public areas** except dining room **Grounds** accessible disp bin **Exercise area** 200yds **Facilities** feeding mat dog scoop/disp bags pet sitting washing facs cage storage walks info vet info **On Request** fridge access torch towels **Resident Pets:** Katy (Labrador cross)

Hayes Barton has the relaxed atmosphere of a family home and provides well-equipped bedrooms and a range of comfortable public areas. Dinner is available from a short selection of home-cooked dishes and there is a cosy bar lounge. The old village, beach and promenade are all within walking distance.

Rooms 9 en suite (4 fmly) (2 GF) D £52-£68✳ **Facilities** TVB tea/coffee Cen ht TVL Dinner Last d noon **Parking** 8 **Notes LB** Closed Nov-Mar

★★★★ GUEST ACCOMMODATION

Rowborough

32 Arthurs Hill PO37 6EX

☎ 01983 866072 & 863070 📠 01983 867703

e-mail: mister.paulwood@virgin.net

web: www.rowborough-hotel.com

Dir: *Between Sandown and Shanklin*

PETS: Bedrooms (1GF) **Charges** £10 per stay charge for damage **Public areas** except restaurant at meal times (on leads) **Grounds** accessible disp bin **Exercise area** 300yds **Facilities** walks info vet info **On Request** fridge access torch towels **Resident Pets:** Penny (Lhasa Apso)

Located on the main road into town, this charming, family-run establishment provides comfortable bedrooms with many extra facilities. The conservatory overlooks the garden, along with a lounge and a bar. Dinner is available by arrangement.

Rooms 9 en suite (5 fmly) (1 GF) S £28-£32; D £56-£64* **Facilities** TVB tea/coffee Cen ht TVL Dinner Last d 4pm Wi-fi available DVD players in all rooms **Parking** 5 **Notes** LB

TOTLAND BAY — MAP 04 SZ38

★★★ 74% HOTEL

Sentry Mead

Madeira Rd PO39 0BJ

☎ 01983 753212 📠 01983 754710

e-mail: info@sentrymead.co.uk

web: www.sentrymead.co.uk

Dir: *off A3054 onto B3322. At 1st rdbt right into Madeira Rd. Hotel 250mtrs on right*

PETS: Bedrooms unattended sign **Charges** £3 per night £15 per week charge for damage **Public areas** except dining room (on leads) **Grounds** accessible disp bin **Exercise area** 50yds **Facilities** food bowl water bowl bedding dog chews dog scoop/disp bags washing facs cage storage walks info vet info **On Request** fridge access torch towels

Just two minutes' walk from the sea at Totland Bay, this well-kept Victorian villa has a comfortable lounge and separate bar, as well as a conservatory that looks out over the delightful garden. Bedrooms feature co-ordinated soft furnishings and welcome extras such as mineral water and biscuits.

Rooms 13 en suite (1 fmly) S £45-£60; D £90-£120 (incl. bkfst)* **Facilities** Wi-fi in bedrooms **Parking** 9 **Notes** LB

TOTLAND BAY CONTINUED

★★★ GUEST ACCOMMODATION

The Hermitage

Cliff Rd PO39 0EW

☎ 01983 752518

e-mail: blake_david@btconnect.com

web: www.thehermitagebnb.co.uk

Dir: *Church Hill B3322, right onto Eden Rd, left onto Cliff Rd, 0.5m on right*

PETS: Bedrooms unattended **Charges** charge for damage **Public areas** except dining area **Grounds** accessible **Exercise area Facilities** water bowl washing facs cage storage walks info vet info **On Request** fridge access torch towels **Resident Pets:** 3 cats, 2 lovebirds

The Hermitage is an extremely pet and people friendly establishment which occupies a stunning and unspoilt location near to the cliff top in Totland Bay. Extensive gardens are well maintained and off road parking is a bonus. Accommodation is comfortable and guests are assured of a genuinely warm welcome and friendly service at this traditionally styled establishment. A range of delicious items at breakfast provide a substantial start to the day.

Rooms 4 rms (3 en suite) (1 pri facs) (1 fmly) S £30-£40; D £50-£70* **Facilities** TVB tea/coffee TVL Dinner Last d at breakfast **Parking** 6 **Notes** LB

VENTNOR MAP 04 SZ57

★★★ 68% HOTEL

Eversley

Park Av PO38 1LB

☎ 01983 852244 & 852462 📠 01983 856534

e-mail: eversleyhotel@yahoo.co.uk

web: www.eversleyhotel.com

Dir: *on A3055 W of Ventnor, next to Ventnor Park*

PETS: Bedrooms (2GF) **Charges Public areas** except restaurant (on leads) **Grounds** accessible **Exercise area** private access to Ventor Park & coastal walks

Located west of Ventnor, this hotel enjoys a quiet location and has some rooms with garden and pool views. The spacious restaurant is sometimes used for functions, and there is a bar, television room, lounge area, a card room as well as a jacuzzi and gym. Bedrooms are generally a good size.

Rooms 30 en suite (8 fmly) (2 GF) **Facilities** ⛳ Gym Pool table **Parking** 23 **Notes** Closed 30 Nov-22 Dec & 2 Jan-8 Feb

See advert on page 297

★★★★ GUEST ACCOMMODATION

The Lake

Shore Rd, Bonchurch PO38 1RF

☎ 01983 852613

e-mail: enquiries@lakehotel.co.uk

Dir: *0.5m E of Ventnor. Off A3055 to Bonchurch, opp village pond*

PETS: Bedrooms Charges £5 per night **Grounds** accessible on leads disp bin **Exercise area** 400yds **Facilities** vet info **On Request** fridge access torch towels **Other** Pet food on request

A warm welcome is assured at this friendly, family-run property set in two acres of well-tended gardens close to the sea. Bedrooms are equipped with modern facilities and the elegant public rooms offer a high standard of comfort. A choice of menus is offered at dinner and breakfast.

Rooms 11 en suite 9 annexe en suite (7 fmly) (4 GF) S £44; D £72-£88* **Facilities** TVB tea/coffee Cen ht TVL Dinner Last d 6.30pm **Parking** 20 **Notes** LB No children 3yrs RS Nov-Feb

★★★★ GUEST ACCOMMODATION

The Hillside

Mitchell Av PO38 1DR

☎ 01983 852271 📠 01983 852271

e-mail: aa@hillside-hotel.co.uk

web: www.hillsideventnor.co.uk

Dir: *Exit A3055 onto B3327, premises 600yds on right behind tennis courts*

PETS: Bedrooms (1GF) **Charges** charge for damage **Public areas** except dining room (on leads) **Grounds** accessible **Exercise area Facilities** food (pre-bookable) food bowl water bowl bedding feeding mat dog scoop/disp bags washing facs cage storage walks info vet info **On Request** fridge access torch towels **Other** pets can only be left unattended in bedrooms by arrangement **Resident Pets:** Hamish (cat)

Hospitality is an important factor at this friendly establishment. Built as an inn during the 18th century, it enjoys some beautiful views of the sea and back onto St Boniface Downs. Bedrooms are individually furnished and are all en suite. Guests can relax in the cosy bar, elegant lounge and plant-filled conservatory. Breakfast is served at an unhurried pace in the bright dining room.

Rooms 12 en suite (1 fmly) (1 GF) S £40-£43; D £80-£86 **Facilities** TVB tea/coffee Cen ht Green Island Award Gold Standard **Parking** 12 **Notes LB** No children 5yrs Closed Xmas

WILTSHIRE

BRADFORD-ON-AVON MAP 03 ST86

★★★ 82% HOTEL

Woolley Grange

von Essen hotels
A PRIVATE COLLECTION
www.vonessenhotels.com

Woolley Green BA15 1TX

☎ 01225 864705 01225 864059

e-mail: info@woolleygrangehotel.co.uk

web: www.vonessenhotels.co.uk

Dir: *A4 onto B3109. Bradford Leigh, left at x-roads, hotel 0.5m on right at Woolley Green*

PETS: Bedrooms unattended **Charges Public areas** except dining areas **Grounds** accessible disp bin **Exercise area** on site 14-acre grounds **Facilities** food bowl water bowl bedding dog chews dog scoop/disp bags leads walks info vet info **On Request** fridge access torch towels **Other** dog owners are advised to keep dogs on leads due to children staying at hotel

This splendid Cotswold manor house is set in beautiful countryside. Children are made especially welcome; there is a trained nanny on duty in the nursery. Bedrooms and public areas are charmingly furnished and decorated in true country-house style, with many thoughtful touches and luxurious extras. The hotel offers a varied and well-balanced menu selection, including ingredients from the hotel's own garden.

Rooms 12 en suite 14 annexe en suite (8 fmly) **Facilities** Putt green Wi-fi available Badminton Beauty treatments Football games room Table tennis ch fac **Parking** 40

CALNE MAP 03 ST97

►►► Blackland Lakes Holiday & Leisure Centre *(ST973687)*

Stockley Ln SN11 0NQ

☎ 01249 810943 01249 811346

e-mail: blacklandlakes.bookings@btconnect.com

web: www.blacklandlakes.co.uk

Dir: *From Calne take A4 E for 1.5m, right at camp sign. Site 1m on left*

PETS: Stables nearby **Charges** £1.50 per night £10.50 per week disp bin **Exercise area** on site dog walks **Facilities** on site shop food dog scoop/disp bags washing facs vet info **Other** prior notice required

Open all year (rs Nov-mid Mar pre paid bookings only) Last arrival 22.00hrs Last departure noon

A rural site surrounded by the North and West Downs. The park is divided into several paddocks separated by hedges, trees and fences, and there are two well-stocked carp fisheries for the angling enthusiast. Some excellent walks close by, and the interesting market town of Devizes is a few miles away. A 15-acre site with 180 touring pitches, 25 hardstandings.

CASTLE COMBE MAP 03 ST87

★★★★ COUNTRY HOUSE HOTEL

Manor House Hotel and Golf Club

EXCLUSIVE HOTELS

SN14 7HR

☎ 01249 782206 01249 782159

e-mail: enquiries@manor-housecc.co.uk

web: www.exclusivehotels.co.uk

Dir: *M4 junct 17 follow Chippenham signs onto A420 Bristol, then right onto B4039. Through village, right after bridge*

PETS: Bedrooms (12GF) unattended **Charges** £50 per stay **Public areas** except food service areas **Grounds** accessible on leads **Exercise area** on site **Facilities** cage storage walks info vet info **On Request** fridge access **Resident Pets:** 1 cat, 6 pigs, 6 chickens

This delightful hotel is situated in a secluded valley adjacent to a picturesque village, where there have been no new buildings for 300 years. There are 365 acres of grounds to enjoy, complete with an Italian garden and an 18-hole golf course. Bedrooms, some in the main house and some in a row of stone cottages, have been superbly furnished, and public rooms include a number of cosy lounges with roaring fires. Service is a pleasing blend of professionalism and friendliness. The food offered utilises top quality local produce.

Rooms 22 en suite 26 annexe en suite (8 fmly) (12 GF) S £150-£800; D £180-£800* **Facilities** STV 18 Fishing Putt green Wi-fi available Jogging track Hot air ballooning Xmas New Year **Parking** 100 **Notes LB**

DEVIZES MAP 04 SU06

►►►► Devizes Camping & Caravanning Club Site *(ST951619)*

Spout Ln, Nr Seend, Melksham SN12 6RN

☎ 01380 828839

web: www.thefriendlyclub.co.uk

Dir: *From Devizes on A361 turn right onto A365, over canal, next left down lane beside 3 Magpies pub. Site on right*

PETS: Public areas except in buildings disp bin **Exercise area** on site **Facilities** walks info vet info **Other** prior notice required

Open all year Last arrival 21.00hrs Last departure noon

An excellent club site with well designed, quality facilities and a high level of staff commitment. This popular park is set beside the Kennet and Avon Canal, with a gate to the towpath for walking and cycling, and with fishing available in the canal. Well situated for exploring Salisbury Plain and the Marlborough Downs. A 13.5-acre site with 90 touring pitches, 70 hardstandings.

Notes Site gates closed 23.00hrs-07.00hrs

ENGLAND

HINDON — MAP 03 ST93

★★★★ INN

The Lamb Inn

SP3 6DP

☎ 01747 820573 📠 01747 820605

e-mail: manager@lambathindon.co.uk

Dir: *Off B3089 in village centre*

PETS: Bedrooms unattended sign **Charges** charge for damage **Public areas** bar area only **Grounds** accessible on leads disp bin **Exercise area** 100mtrs **Facilities** food bowl water bowl cage storage walks info vet info **On Request** fridge access torch

The 17th-century coaching inn is in a pretty village within easy reach of Salisbury and Bath. It has been refurbished in an eclectic style, and some of the well-equipped bedrooms have four-poster beds. Enjoyable, freshly prepared dishes are available at lunch and dinner in the restaurant or bar, where log fires provide a welcoming atmosphere on colder days.

Rooms 14 en suite (1 fmly) S £70; D £99-£135* **Facilities** STV TVB tea/coffee Direct dial from bedrooms Cen ht Dinner Last d 9.30pm **Parking** 16 **Notes** **LB**

LACOCK — MAP 03 ST96

★★★★ GUEST ACCOMMODATION

At the Sign of the Angel

6 Church St SN15 2LB

☎ 01249 730230 📠 01249 730527

e-mail: angel@lacock.co.uk

web: www.lacock.co.uk

Dir: *Off A350 into Lacock, follow Local Traffic sign*

PETS: Bedrooms (4GF) unattended sign **Charges** charge for damage **Public areas** except restaurant **Grounds** accessible on leads **Exercise area** walks in surrounding area **Facilities** water bowl walks info vet info **On Request** fridge access torch towels **Resident Pets:** Felix (cat)

Visitors will be impressed by the character of this 15th-century former wool merchant's house, set in the National Trust village of Lacock. Bedrooms come in a range of sizes and styles including the atmospheric rooms in the main house and others in an adjacent new building. Excellent dinners and breakfasts are served in the beamed dining rooms, and there is also a first-floor lounge and a pleasant rear garden.

Rooms 6 en suite 5 annexe en suite (1 fmly) (4 GF) S £72-£85; D £132-£155* **Facilities** FTV TVB tea/coffee Direct dial from bedrooms Cen ht Dinner Last d 9pm **Parking** 7 **Notes** Closed 23-30 Dec RS Mon (ex BHs)

LANDFORD — MAP 04 SU21

►►► Greenhill Farm Camping & Caravan Park *(SU266183)*

Greenhill Farm, New Rd SP5 2AZ

☎ 01794 324117 & 023 8081 1506 📠 023 8081 3209

e-mail: greenhillcamping@btconnect.com

web: www.newforest-uk.com/greenhill.htm

Dir: *M27 junct 2, A36 towards Salisbury, approx 3m after Hants/Wilts border, (Shoe Inn pub on right, BP garage on left) take next left into New Rd, signed Nomansland, 2nd site on left*

PETS: Stables (loose box) **Public areas** except fish-breeding lake area (on leads) **Charges** 1st dog free, £1 per additional pet per night disp bin **Exercise area** on site footpath to Common & New Forest **Facilities** vet info **Other** grazing for horses only (no stables) **Resident Pets:** 2 Golden Retrievers, horses

Open 16 Jan-21 Dec Last arrival 21.30hrs Last departure 10.30hrs

A tranquil, well-landscaped park hidden away in unspoilt countryside on the edge of the New Forest. Pitches overlooking the fishing lake include hardstandings. Facilities are housed in portable type buildings. This park is for adults only. A 13-acre site with 80 touring pitches, 30 hardstandings.

Notes No kites/flags

LOWER CHICKSGROVE — MAP 03 ST92

★★★★ INN

Compasses Inn

SP3 6NB

☎ 01722 714318 📠 01722 714318

e-mail: thecompasses@aol.com

web: www.thecompassesinn.com

Dir: *Off A30 signed Lower Chicksgrove, 1st left onto Lagpond Ln, single-track lane to village*

PETS: Bedrooms unattended **Public areas** **Grounds** accessible disp bin **Exercise area** adjacent **Facilities** food bowl water bowl cage storage walks info vet info **On Request** fridge access torch towels

This charming 17th-century inn, within easy reach of Bath, Salisbury, Glastonbury and the Dorset coast, offers comfortable accommodation in a peaceful setting. Carefully prepared dinners are enjoyed in the warm atmosphere of the bar-restaurant, while breakfast is served in a separate dining room.

Rooms 5 en suite (1 fmly) S £65-£90; D £85-£90 **Facilities** FTV TVB tea/coffee Cen ht Dinner Last d 9.30pm **Parking** 40 **Notes** **LB** Closed 25-26 Dec

MALMESBURY MAP 03 ST98

★★★★★ @@@@ HOTEL

Whatley Manor

Easton Grey SN16 0RB

☎ 01666 822888 🖹 01666 826120

e-mail: reservations@whatleymanor.com

web: www.whatleymanor.com

Dir: *M4 junct 17, follow signs to Malmesbury, over 2 rdbts. Follow B4040 & signs for Sherston, hotel 2m on left*

PETS: Bedrooms unattended **Charges** £25 per night **Grounds** accessible on leads disp bin **Exercise area** **Facilities** food (pre-bookable) food bowl water bowl bedding dog chews dog scoop/disp bags **On Request** towels **Other** welcome letter, guidelines, luxury dog basket, treats, walk routes & maps

Sitting in 12 acres of beautiful countryside, this impressive country house provides the most luxurious surroundings. Spacious bedrooms, most with views over the attractive gardens, are individually decorated with splendid features. Several eating options are available: Le Mazot, a Swiss-style brasserie, The Dining Room that serves classical French cuisine with a contemporary twist, plus the Kitchen Garden Terrace for alfresco breakfasts, lunches and dinners. The old Loggia Barn is ideal for wedding ceremonies, and the Aquarius Spa is magnificent.

Rooms 23 en suite (4 GF) D £290-£850 (incl. bkfst) **Facilities Spa** STV Fishing Gym Wi-fi available Cinema Hydro pool Xmas New Year **Services** Lift **Parking** 100 **Notes LB** No children 12yrs

★★★ 80% @@ HOTEL

Old Bell

Abbey Row SN16 0BW

☎ 01666 822344 🖹 01666 825145

e-mail: info@oldbellhotel.com

web: www.oldbellhotel.com

Dir: *M4 junct 17, follow A429 north. Left at first rdbt. Left at T-junct. Hotel next to Abbey*

PETS: Bedrooms (7GF) unattended sign **Charges** £10 per night charge for damage **Public areas** except restaurants (on leads) **Grounds** accessible **Exercise area** 250mtrs **Facilities** water bowl bedding pet sitting cage storage walks info vet info **Restrictions** no large dogs (eg Newfoundland, Great Dane, Irish Wolfhound)

Dating back to 1220, the Old Bell is reputed to be the oldest purpose-built hotel in England. Bedrooms vary in size and style; those in the main house are traditionally furnished with antiques, while the newer bedrooms have a contemporary feel. Guests have a choice of comfortable sitting areas and dining options.

Rooms 16 en suite 16 annexe en suite (7 GF) S fr £87.50; D £125-£235 (incl. bkfst) **Facilities** FTV Wi-fi available Aromatherapy massages Xmas New Year **Parking** 32 **Notes LB**

★★★ 72% @ HOTEL

Best Western Mayfield House

Crudwell SN16 9EW

☎ 01666 577409 🖹 01666 577977

e-mail: reception@mayfieldhousehotel.co.uk

web: www.mayfieldhousehotel.co.uk

Dir: *M4 junct 17. Follow A429 to Cirencester. 3m N of Malmesbury on right in Crudwell.*

PETS: Bedrooms (6GF) unattended **Stables** nearby (0.25m) **Charges** £15 per stay charge for damage **Exercise area** paddock opposite & bridleway **Facilities** washing facs cage storage walks info vet info **On Request** torch towels

This popular hotel is in an ideal location for exploring many of the nearby attractions of Wiltshire and The Cotswolds. Bedrooms come in a range of shapes and sizes, and include some on the ground-floor level in a cottage adjacent to the main hotel. In addition to outdoor seating, guests can relax with a drink in the comfortable lounge area where orders are taken for the carefully prepared dinner to follow.

Rooms 21 en suite 3 annexe en suite (3 fmly) (6 GF) S £70-£90; D £80-£133 (incl. bkfst) **Facilities** Wi-fi in bedrooms Xmas New Year **Parking** 50 **Notes LB**

MELKSHAM MAP 03 ST96

★★ 76% SMALL HOTEL

Shaw Country

Bath Rd, Shaw SN12 8EF

☎ 01225 702836 & 790321 🖹 01225 790275

e-mail: info@shawcountryhotel.com

web: www.shawcountryhotel.com

Dir: *1m from Melksham, 9m from Bath on A365*

PETS: Bedrooms Exercise area

Located within easy reach of both Bath and the M4, this relaxed and friendly hotel sits in its own gardens and includes a patio area ideal for enjoying a drink during the summer months. The house boasts some very well-appointed bedrooms, a comfortable lounge and bar and the Mulberry Restaurant, where a wide selection of innovative dishes make up both carte and set menus. A spacious function room is a useful addition.

Rooms 13 en suite (2 fmly) S £58-£80; D £80-£99 (incl. bkfst)* **Facilities** FTV Wi-fi in bedrooms **Parking** 30 **Notes LB** RS 26-27 Dec & 1 Jan

MELKSHAM *CONTINUED*

U

Beechfield House

Beanacre SN12 7PU

☎ 01225 703700 📠 01225 790118

e-mail: reception@beachfieldhouse.co.uk

web: www.beechfieldhouse.co.uk

Dir: *1m N via A350*

PETS: Bedrooms (2GF) unattended **Charges** £10 per night charge for damage **Grounds** accessible **Exercise area** **Facilities** cage storage walks info vet info **Restrictions** no large dogs **Resident Pets:** Misty (Black Labrador), Lola & Daisy (cats)

At the time of going to press the rating for this establishment was not confirmed. This may be due to a change of ownership or because it has only recently joined the AA rating scheme. For further details please see the AA website: www.theAA.com

Rooms 18 en suite (5 fmly) (2 GF) S £90-£95; D £125-£150 (incl. bkfst)✻ **Facilities** FTV Wi-fi available Table tennis ch fac Xmas **Parking** 50 **Notes** LB

ORCHESTON MAP 04 SU04

►►► Stonehenge Touring Park *(SU061456)*

SP3 4SH

☎ 01980 620304

e-mail: stay@stonehengetouringpark.com

web: www.stonehengetouringpark.com

Dir: *From A360 turn right, follow lane, site at bottom of village on right*

PETS: Public areas except facility block & shop **Exercise area** 50mtrs **Facilities** on site shop food dog scoop/disp bags walks info vet info **Other** prior notice required

Open all year Last arrival 21.00hrs Last departure 11.00hrs

A quiet site adjacent to the small village of Orcheston near the centre of Salisbury Plain and 4m from Stonehenge. A 2-acre site with 30 touring pitches, 12 hardstandings.

PURTON MAP 04 SU08

★★★ 80% HOTEL

The Pear Tree at Purton

PRIDE OF BRITAIN HOTELS

Church End SN5 4ED

☎ 01793 772100 📠 01793 772369

e-mail: stay@peartreepurton.co.uk

Dir: *M4 junct 16 follow signs to Purton, at Spar shop turn right. Hotel 0.25m on left*

PETS: Bedrooms Public areas except restaurant **Grounds** accessible disp bin **Exercise area** adjacent **Facilities** food bowl water bowl dog chews cat treats dog scoop/disp bags leads washing facs walks info vet info **On Request** fridge access torch towels **Resident Pets:** Smudge (dog), Poppy & Buzz (cats)

A charming 15th-century, former vicarage set amidst extensive landscaped gardens in a peaceful location in the Vale of the White Horse and near the Saxon village of Purton. The resident proprietors and staff provide efficient, dedicated service and friendly hospitality. The spacious bedrooms are individually decorated and have a good range of thoughtful extras such as fresh fruit, sherry and shortbread. Fresh ingredients feature on the award-winning menus.

Rooms 17 en suite (2 fmly) (6 GF) S £115-£150; D £115-£150 (incl. bkfst) **Facilities** STV Wi-fi in bedrooms Outdoor giant chess Vineyard **Parking** 60 **Notes** LB Closed 26-30 Dec

SALISBURY MAP 04 SU12

★★★ 68% HOTEL

Grasmere House Hotel

Harnham Rd SP2 8JN

☎ 01722 338388 📠 01722 333710

e-mail: info@grasmerehotel.com

web: www.grasmerehotel.com

Dir: *on A3094 on S side of Salisbury next to All Saints Church in Harnham*

PETS: Bedrooms (9GF) **Charges** £10 per night **Grounds** accessible **Exercise area** adjacent to park **Other** Please telephone for further details

This popular hotel, dating from 1896, has gardens that overlook the water meadows and the cathedral. The attractive bedrooms vary in size, some offer excellent quality and comfort, and some rooms are specially equipped for less mobile guests. In summer there is the option of dining on the pleasant outdoor terrace.

Rooms 7 en suite 31 annexe en suite (16 fmly) (9 GF) S £79.50 £105.50; D £95.50-£165.50 (incl. bkfst)✻ **Facilities** Fishing Wi-fi in bedrooms Xmas New Year **Parking** 64 **Notes** LB

★★★ GUEST ACCOMMODATION

Byways Guest House

31 Fowlers Rd SP1 2QP

☎ 01722 328364 📠 01722 322146

e-mail: info@bywayshouse.co.uk

web: www.bywayshouse.co.uk

Dir: *500yds E of city centre. A30 onto A36 signed Southampton, follow Youth Hostel signs to hostel, Fowlers Rd opp*

PETS: Bedrooms (13GF) unattended **Exercise area Facilities** food bowl water bowl vet info **On Request** fridge access torch towels **Resident Pets:** cat

Located in a quiet street with off-road parking, Byways is within walking distance of the town centre. Several bedrooms have been decorated in a Victorian style and another two have four-poster beds. All rooms offer good levels of comfort, with one adapted for easier access.

Rooms 23 rms (19 en suite) (6 fmly) (13 GF) S £39-£60; D £55-£80✻ **Facilities** TVB tea/coffee Cen ht Wi-fi available **Parking** 15 **Notes** Closed Xmas & New Year

►►►► Coombe Touring Park *(SU099282)*

Race Plain, Netherhampton SP2 8PN

☎ 01722 328451 📠 01722 328451

Dir: *A36 onto A3094, then 2m SW, adjacent to Salisbury racecourse*

PETS: Public areas except toilet block, shower block & laundry block **Charges** 20p per night disp bin **Exercise area Facilities** on site shop washing facs walks info vet info **Resident Pets:** Alfie (Labrador/Collie cross), Tigger & Blackie (cats)

Open 3 Jan-20 Dec (rs Oct-May shop closed) Last arrival 21.00hrs Last departure noon

A very neat and attractive site adjacent to the racecourse with views over the downs. The park is well landscaped with shrubs and maturing trees, and the very colourful beds are stocked from the owner's greenhouse. A comfortable park with a superb luxury toilet block. A 3-acre site with 50 touring pitches and 2 statics.

Notes no disposable BBQs or fires, no mini motorbikes

►►►► Salisbury Camping & Caravanning Club Site *(SU140320)*

Hudsons Field, Castle Rd SP1 3RR

☎ 01722 320713

web: www.thefriendlyclub.co.uk

Dir: *1.5m from Salisbury on A345. (Large open field next to Old Sarum)*

PETS: Public areas except in buildings disp bin **Exercise area** adjacent to site **Facilities** walks info vet info **Other** prior notice required

Open 2 Apr-2 Nov Last arrival 21.00hrs Last departure noon

Well placed within walking distance of Salisbury, this tidy site has friendly and helpful wardens, and immaculate toilet facilities with cubicled wash basins. A 4.5-acre site with 150 touring pitches, 16 hardstandings.

Notes Site gates closed 23.00hrs-07.00hrs

ENGLAND

SWINDON MAP 04 SU18

Campanile Swindon

Campanile HOTEL RESTAURANT

Delta Business Park, Great Western Way SN5 7XG

☎ 01793 514777 ▤ 01793 514570

e-mail: swindon@campanile.com

web: www.envergure.fr

Dir: *M4 junct 16 onto A3102 towards Swindon. After 2nd rdbt, 2nd exit onto Welton Road (Delta Business Park) and 1st left*

PETS: Bedrooms (20GF) **Charges** charge for damage **Public areas** except restaurant & bar (on leads) **Grounds** accessible on leads disp bin **Exercise area Facilities** cage storage walks info vet info

At the time of going to press the rating for this establishment was not confirmed. This may be due to a change of ownership or because it has only recently joined the AA rating scheme. For further details please see the AA website: www.theAA.com

Rooms 120 en suite (6 fmly) (20 GF) D £54.95-£85* **Facilities** STV Wi-fi available **Services** Lift **Parking** 95 **Notes** LB

★★★★ GUEST ACCOMMODATION

Portquin

Broadbush, Broad Blunsdon SN26 7DH

☎ 01793 721261

e-mail: portquin@msn.com

Dir: *A419 onto B4019 at Blunsdon signed Highworth, continue 0.5m*

PETS: Bedrooms (4GF) **Charges** charge for damage **Public areas** except dining room **Grounds** accessible disp bin **Exercise area Facilities** walks info vet info **On Request** fridge access torch **Restrictions** no dogs of similar size to Great Danes **Resident Pets:** Basil & Diva (horses)

This friendly guest house near Swindon provides a warm welcome and views of the Lambourn Downs. The rooms vary in shape and size, with six in the main house and three in an adjacent annexe. Full English breakfasts are served at two large tables in the kitchen-dining area.

Rooms 6 en suite 3 annexe en suite (2 fmly) (4 GF) S £40-£45; D £50-£70 **Facilities** TVB tea/coffee Cen ht Wi-fi available **Parking** 12

★★★ GUEST ACCOMMODATION

Fir Tree Lodge

17 Highworth Rd, Stratton St Margaret SN3 4QL

☎ 01793 822372 ▤ 01793 822372

e-mail: info@firtreelodge.com

Dir: *1.5m NE of town centre. A419 onto B4006 signed Stratton/ Town Centre, premises 200yds opp Rat Trap pub*

PETS: Bedrooms (5GF) **Charges** £3 per night £21 per week charge for damage **Grounds** accessible on leads **Exercise area Resident Pets:** Bratch (Golden Retriever)

Fir Tree Lodge is a modern guest house offering a range of comfortable bedrooms including rooms on the ground floor. The resident proprietors provide a relaxed and friendly welcome. The guest house benefits from a large secure car park.

Rooms 12 en suite 2 annexe rms (2 annexe pri facs) (1 fmly) (5 GF) S £35-£40; D £55-£60* **Facilities** FTV TVB tea/coffee Cen ht **Parking** 13

WARMINSTER MAP 03 ST84

★★★★ 77% HOTEL

Bishopstrow House

von Essen hotels A PRIVATE COLLECTION www.vonessenhotels.com

BA12 9HH

☎ 01985 212312 ▤ 01985 216769

e-mail: info@bishopstrow.co.uk

web: www.vonessenhotels.co.uk

Dir: *A303, A36, B3414, hotel 2m on right*

PETS: Bedrooms unattended **Charges Public areas** except restaurant, conservatory, pool area **Exercise area Other** please contact for further details

This is a fine example of a Georgian country home, situated in 27 acres of grounds. Public areas are traditional in style and feature antiques and open fires. Most bedrooms offer DVD players. A spa, a tennis court and several country walks ensure there is something for all guests. The restaurant serves quality, contemporary cuisine.

Rooms 30 en suite 2 annexe en suite (2 fmly) (7 GF) S £120-£375; D £149-£395 (incl. bkfst)* **Facilities Spa** Fishing Gym Wi-fi available Clay pigeon shooting Archery Cycling Xmas New Year **Parking** 100 **Notes** LB

WESTBURY MAP 03 ST85

★★★ 70% HOTEL

The Cedar

Warminster Rd BA13 3PR

☎ 01373 822753 📠 01373 858423

e-mail: info@cedarhotel-wiltshire.co.uk

Dir: *on A350, 0.5m S of town towards Warminster*

PETS: Bedrooms (10GF) **Stables** nearby (2m) **Charges** £10 per night £70 per week charge for damage **Exercise area** 500yds **Facilities** water bowl cage storage walks info vet info **On Request** torch towels

This 18th-century hotel is an ideal base for exploring Bath and the surrounding area and is popular with both leisure and corporate guests. The bedrooms are attractive and well equipped; some are located at ground-floor level in an annexe. An interesting selection of meals is available in both the lounge bar and conservatory, and the Regency Restaurant is the venue for more formal dining.

Rooms 8 en suite 12 annexe en suite (5 fmly) (10 GF) S £65; D £78-£88 (incl. bkfst)✱ **Facilities** FTV **Parking** 30 **Notes** LB

►►►► Brokerswood Country Park *(ST836523)*

Brokerswood BA13 4EH

☎ 01373 822238 📠 01373 858474

e-mail: info@brokerswood.co.uk

web: www.brokerswood.co.uk

Dir: *From M4 junct 17 south on A350. Right at Yarnbrook to Rising Sun pub at North Bradley, then left at rdbt. Left on bend approaching Southwick, follow lane for 2.5m, site on right*

PETS: Public areas except toilet/shower facility, shop & café **Charges** £1 per dog per night disp bin **Exercise area** on site 80-acre country park **Facilities** on site shop food bowl water bowl dog scoop/disp bags leads walks info vet info **Other** prior notice required

Open all year Last arrival 21.30hrs Last departure 11.00hrs

A popular park on the edge of an 80-acre woodland park with nature trails and fishing lakes. An adventure playground offers plenty of fun for all ages, and there is a miniature railway, an indoor play centre, and a café. The toilet block offers high quality facilities. A 5-acre site with 69 touring pitches, 21 hardstandings.

Notes Families only, no cycling

WORCESTERSHIRE

ABBERLEY MAP 07 SO76

★★★ INN

The Manor Arms at Abberley

Netherton Ln WR6 6BN

☎ 01299 896507 📠 01299 896723

e-mail: info@themanorarms.co.uk

web: www.themanorarms.co.uk

Dir: *From A443 at Abberley follow brown signs to Manor Arms*

PETS: Bedrooms (3GF) **Stables** nearby (100yds) **Charges** charge for damage **Public areas** bar only (on leads) **Grounds** accessible disp bin **Exercise area** village green 100yds **Facilities** water bowl walks info vet info **On Request** fridge access torch **Restrictions** no dangerous breeds (see page 7)

Resident Pets: Belle (Labrador), Bramble (cat)

The Manor Arms has been part of the village for over 300 years, and was originally owned by the Lord of the Manor. While a number of changes have been made to the interior of the inn over a period of years, it still retains much of its original status and interest. Bedrooms are individually furnished, and all offer en suite facility. The traditional lounge bar offers cask marque ales and a good choice of meals from bar snacks to a carte menu.

Rooms 10 en suite (1 fmly) (3 GF) S £45-£55; D £60-£70✱ **Facilities** TVB tea/coffee Direct dial from bedrooms Cen ht Dinner Last d 9pm **Parking** 20 **Notes** LB

BEWDLEY MAP 07 SO77

★★★★ 🍽 INN

Royal Forester Country Inn

Callow Hill DY14 9XW

☎ 01299 266286

e-mail: contact@royalforesterinn.co.uk

PETS: Bedrooms sign **Stables** on site **Charges** £10 (dog), £30 (horse) per night charge for damage **Grounds** accessible on leads disp bin **Exercise area Facilities** food (pre-bookable) food bowl water bowl bedding dog chews cat treats feeding mat litter tray etc dog scoop/disp bags dog walking washing facs dog grooming cage storage walks info vet info **On Request** fridge access torch towels

Located opposite The Wyre Forest on the town's outskirts, this inn dates back to 1411 and has been sympathetically restored to provide high standards of comfort. Stylish modern bedrooms are complemented by smart bathrooms and equipped with many thoughtful extras. Décor styles throughout the public areas highlight the many retained period features and the restaurant serves imaginative food featuring locally sourced produce.

Rooms 7 en suite (2 fmly) S £55-£75; D £79-£99✱ **Facilities** STV FTV TVB tea/coffee Cen ht Dinner Last d 9.30pm Wi-fi available **Parking** 40 **Notes** LB No coaches

ENGLAND

BEWDLEY CONTINUED

★★★ BED & BREAKFAST

Pewterers' House

Pewterers' Alley DY12 1AE

☎ 01299 401956

e-mail: pewterershouse@tiscali.co.uk

web: www.pewterershouse.co.uk

Dir: *250yds NE of town centre. On B4190 E of bridge, opp Black Boy Hotel*

PETS: Bedrooms Charges charge for damage **Public areas** except dining room **Exercise area Facilities** water bowl bedding feeding mat cage storage walks info vet info **On Request** fridge access torch towels

A short walk from the River Severn and historic centre, this deceptively spacious period cottage has been sympathetically renovated to provide high standards of comfort and facilities. Bedrooms are equipped with a wealth of thoughtful extras and efficient modern shower rooms. Comprehensive breakfasts feature local produce and a warm welcome is assured.

Rooms 3 rms (2 en suite) **Facilities** TVB tea/coffee Cen ht **Parking** 2 **Notes**

BROADWAY MAP 04 SP03

★★★★ 78% HOTEL

Barceló The Lygon Arms

High St WR12 7DU

☎ 01386 852255 01386 854470

e-mail: thelygonarms@barcelo-hotels.co.uk

web: www.barcelo-hotels.co.uk

Dir: *From Evesham take A44 signed Oxford, 5m. Follow Broadway signs. Hotel on left*

PETS: Bedrooms (9GF) unattended **Stables** nearby (3m) **Charges** £15 per night £105 per week charge for damage **Public areas** except dining room (on leads) **Grounds** accessible on leads disp bin **Exercise area Facilities** food bowl water bowl bedding walks info vet info **On Request** fridge access towels

A hotel with a wealth of historic charm and character, the Lygon Arms dates back to the 16th century. There is a choice of restaurants, a stylish cosy bar, an array of lounges and a smart spa and leisure club. Bedrooms vary in size and style, but all are thoughtfully equipped and include a number of stylish contemporary rooms as well as a cottage in the grounds.

Rooms 77 en suite (9 GF) S £109-£229* **Facilities Spa** Gym Xmas New Year **Parking** 200

★★★ 77% HOTEL

Broadway

CLASSIC BRITISH HOTELS

The Green, High St WR12 7AA

☎ 01386 852401 01386 853879

e-mail: info@broadwayhotel.info

web: www.cotswold-inns-hotels.co.uk

Dir: *Follow signs to Evesham, then Broadway*

PETS: Bedrooms (3GF) unattended **Charges** charge for damage **Public areas** except eating areas **Grounds** accessible **Exercise area Facilities** food bowl water bowl cage storage walks info vet info **On Request** fridge access torch towels

A half-timbered Cotswold stone property, built in the 15th century as a retreat for the Abbots of Pershore. The hotel combines modern, attractive decor with original charm and character. Bedrooms are tastefully furnished and well equipped while public rooms include a relaxing lounge, cosy bar and charming restaurant; alfresco all-day dining in summer months proves popular.

Rooms 19 en suite (1 fmly) (3 GF) S £95-£140; D £140-£200 (incl. bkfst)* **Facilities** Wi-fi available Xmas New Year **Parking** 20 **Notes** LB

★★★★ GUEST ACCOMMODATION

Cowley House

Church St WR12 7AE

☎ 01386 858148

e-mail: cowleyhouse.broadway@tiscali.co.uk

Dir: *Follow signs for Broadway village, Church St adjacent to village green, 3rd on left*

PETS: Bedrooms (2GF) **Charges** £5 per night charge for damage **Grounds** accessible disp bin **Exercise area** approx 100yds **Facilities** dog chews feeding mat dog scoop/disp bags leads washing facs walks info vet info **On Request** fridge access torch towels **Restrictions** small, well behaved dogs only

Resident Pets: Holly & Tuppence (West Highland Terriers)

A warm welcome is assured at this 18th-century Cotswold-stone house, just a stroll from the village green. Fine period furniture enhances the interiors, and the elegant hall has a polished flagstone floor. Tastefully equipped bedrooms include thoughtful extras, smart modern shower rooms and the comprehensive breakfasts feature local produce.

Rooms 6 rms (5 en suite) (1 pri facs) (1 fmly) (2 GF) S £45-£50; D £58-£85* **Facilities** TVB tea/coffee Cen ht Wi-fi available **Parking** 6 **Notes** LB

★★★★ INN

Horse & Hound

54 High St WR12 7DT

☎ 01386 852287 🖷 01386 853784

e-mail: k2mtk@aol.com

Dir: *Off A46 to Evesham*

PETS: Bedrooms unattended **Charges** £10 per night **Public areas** except restaurant **Exercise area** **Resident Pets:** Talisker (Springer Spaniel)

The Horse & Hound is at the heart of this beautiful Cotswold village. A warm welcome is guaranteed whether dining in the inviting pub or staying overnight in the attractive and well-appointed bedrooms. Breakfast and dinner should not to be missed - both use carefully prepared local produce.

Rooms 5 en suite (1 fmly) D £80✳ **Facilities** TVB tea/coffee Cen ht Dinner Last d 9pm **Parking** 15 **Notes** RS Winter

EVESHAM MAP 04 SP04

★★★ 79% ❀ HOTEL

The Evesham

Coopers Ln, Off Waterside WR11 1DA

☎ 01386 765566 & 0800 716969 (Res) 🖷 01386 765443

e-mail: reception@eveshamhotel.com

web: www.eveshamhotel.com

Dir: *Coopers Lane is off road by River Avon*

PETS: Bedrooms (11GF) unattended sign **Grounds** accessible **Exercise area** **Facilities** vet info

Dating from 1540 and set in extensive grounds, this delightful hotel has well-equipped accommodation that includes a selection of quirkily themed rooms - Alice in Wonderland, Egyptian, and Aquarium (which has a tropical fish tank in the bathroom). A reputation for food is well deserved, with a particularly strong choice for vegetarians. Children are welcome and toys are always available.

Rooms 39 en suite 1 annexe en suite (3 fmly) (11 GF) S £73-£83; D £117 (incl. bkfst)✳ **Facilities** Putt green New Year **Parking** 50 **Notes LB** Closed 25-26 Dec

HANLEY SWAN MAP 03 SO84

►►►► Blackmore Camping & Caravanning Club Site *(SO812440)*

Blackmore Camp Site No 2 WR8 0EE

☎ 01684 310280

web: www.thefriendlyclub.co.uk

Dir: *A38 to Upton on Severn. Turn north over river bridge. 2nd left, then 1st left signed Hanley Swan. Site 1m on right*

PETS: Public areas except in buildings disp bin **Exercise area** on site **Facilities** walks info vet info **Other** prior notice required

Open all year Last arrival 21.00hrs Last departure noon

Blackmore is a well-established, level wooded park, ideally located for exploring the Malvern Hills and Worcester. The excellent toilet facilities are spotlessly maintained. A 17-acre site with 200 touring pitches, 66 hardstandings.

Notes Site gates closed 23.00hrs-07.00hrs

KEMPSEY MAP 03 SO84

★★★ INN

Walter de Cantelupe Inn

Main Rd (A38) WR5 3NA

☎ 01905 820572

e-mail: walter.depub@fsbdial.co.uk

web: www.walterdecantelupeinn.com

Dir: *On A38 in village centre*

PETS: Bedrooms sign **Stables** nearby (2m) **Charges** charge for damage **Public areas** except restaurant area (on leads) **Grounds** accessible on leads **Exercise area** 0.5m **Facilities** water bowl dog chews feeding mat washing facs cage storage walks info vet info **On Request** fridge access torch towels **Other** dog grooming available nearby

This inn provides cosy bedrooms with smart bathrooms, and is convenient for the M5 and Worcester. The intimate, open-plan public areas are the setting for a range of real ales, and imaginative food featuring local produce and a fine selection of British cheeses.

Rooms 3 rms (2 en suite) (1 pri facs) **Facilities** TVB tea/coffee Cen ht Dinner Last d 9pm (Fri/Sat 10pm) Wi-fi available **Parking** 24 **Notes** No coaches

ENGLAND

MALVERN MAP 03 SO74

★★★ 85% HOTEL

The Cottage in the Wood Hotel

Holywell Rd, Malvern Wells WR14 4LG

01684 588860 01684 560662

e-mail: reception@cottageinthewood.co.uk

web: www.cottageinthewood.co.uk

Dir: *3m S of Great Malvern off A449, 500yds N of B4209, on opposite side of road*

PETS: Bedrooms (9GF) unattended **Charges** £7.50 per night charge for damage **Grounds** accessible disp bin **Exercise area** adjacent **Facilities** food bowl water bowl bedding dog chews cage storage walks info vet info **On Request** fridge access torch

Sitting high up on a wooded hillside, this delightful, family-run hotel boasts lovely views over the Severn Valley. The bedrooms are divided between the main house, Beech Cottage and the Pinnacles. The public areas are very stylishly decorated, and imaginative food is served in an elegant dining room, overlooking the immaculate grounds.

Rooms 7 en suite 23 annexe en suite (9 GF) S £79-£112; D £99-£185 (incl. bkfst) **Facilities** Wi-fi available Direct access to Malvern Hills Xmas New Year **Parking** 40 **Notes** LB

See advert on opposite page

★★ 82% HOTEL

Holdfast Cottage

Marlbank Rd, Welland WR13 6NA

01684 310288 01684 311117

e-mail: enquiries@holdfast-cottage.co.uk

web: www.holdfast-cottage.co.uk

Dir: *A438 to Tewkesbury, at War Memorial rdbt turn right signed A438, at mini rdbt left for Ledbury*

PETS: Bedrooms Stables nearby **Charges** £5 per night **Public areas** except lounge & restaurant (on leads) **Grounds** accessible on leads disp bin **Exercise area** 200yds **Facilities** vet info **On Request** torch

At the base of the Malvern Hills this delightful wisteria-covered hotel sits in attractive manicured grounds. Charming public areas include an intimate bar, a log fire enhanced lounge and an elegant dining room. Bedrooms vary in size but all are comfortable and well appointed. Fresh local and seasonal produce are the basis for award-winning cuisine.

Rooms 8 en suite (3 fmly) **Facilities** **Parking** 15 **Notes** LB

★★★ GUEST ACCOMMODATION

Sidney House

40 Worcester Rd WR14 4AA

01684 574994 01684 574994

e-mail: info@sidneyhouse.co.uk

web: www.sidneyhouse.co.uk

Dir: *On A449, 200yds N from town centre*

PETS: Bedrooms Charges £5 per stay **Public areas** (on leads) **Grounds** accessible **Exercise area** 100yds **Facilities** walks info vet info **On Request** fridge access torch towels **Restrictions** bedroom sizes vary so please ask if suitable when booking **Resident Pets:** 2 dogs (Kelpies)

This impressive Grade II Georgian house is close to the central attractions and has stunning views. Bedrooms are filled with thoughtful extras, and some have small shower rooms en suite. The spacious dining room overlooks the Cotswold escarpment and a comfortable lounge is also available.

Rooms 8 rms (6 en suite) (1 fmly) S £25-£55; D £59-£75* **Facilities** TVB tea/coffee Cen ht TVL **Parking** 9 **Notes** Closed 24 Dec-3 Jan

★★ GUEST ACCOMMODATION

Four Hedges

The Rhydd, Hanley Castle WR8 0AD

01684 310405

e-mail: fredgies@aol.com

Dir: *4m E of Malvern at junct of B4211 & B4424*

PETS: Bedrooms unattended **Public areas Grounds** accessible disp bin **Exercise area** adjoining **Facilities** food bowl water bowl leads pet sitting washing facs cage storage walks info vet info **On Request** fridge access torch towels **Resident Pets:** Machu & Pichu (cats)

Situated in a rural location, this detached house stands in mature grounds with wild birds in abundance. The bedrooms are equipped with thoughtful extras. Tasty English breakfasts, using free-range eggs, are served in a cosy dining room at a table made from a 300-year-old elm tree.

Rooms 4 rms (2 en suite) S fr £20; D fr £40 **Facilities** TV1B tea/coffee Cen ht TVL Fishing **Parking** 5 **Notes** Closed Xmas

REDDITCH MAP 07 SP06

BUDGET HOTEL

Campanile Redditch

Far Moor Ln, Winyates Green B98 0SD

☎ 01527 510710 📠 01527 517269

e-mail: redditch@campanile.com

web: www.envergure.fr

Dir: *A435 towards Redditch, then A4023 to Redditch & Bromsgrove*

PETS: Bedrooms unattended **Charges** charge for damage **Grounds** accessible on leads disp bin **Exercise area** 15 min walk **Facilities** walks info vet info **On Request** torch

This modern building offers accommodation in smart, well-equipped bedrooms, all with en suite bathrooms. Refreshments may be taken at the informal Bistro.

Rooms 46 annexe

ROMSLEY MAP 07 SO98

►►►► Clent Hills Camping & Caravanning Club Site (SO955795)

Fieldhouse Ln B62 0NH

☎ 01562 710015

web: www.thefriendlyclub.co.uk

Dir: *M5 junct 3, A456. Left on B4551 to Romsley. Turn right past Sun Hotel, take 5th left, then next left. Site 330yds on left*

PETS: Public areas except in buildings disp bin **Exercise area** on site **Facilities** walks info vet info **Other** prior notice required

Open 2 Apr-2 Nov Last arrival 21.00hrs Last departure noon

A very pretty, well tended park surrounded by wooded hills. The site offers excellent facilities, including hardstandings to provide flat pitches for motorhomes. Lovely views of the Clent Hills can be enjoyed from this park, and there are plenty of local scenic walks. A 7.5-acre site with 95 touring pitches, 27 hardstandings.

Notes Site gates closed 23.00hrs-07.00hrs

UPTON UPON SEVERN MAP 03 SO84

★★★ 71% ❁ HOTEL

White Lion

21 High St WR8 0HJ

☎ 01684 592551 📠 01684 593333

e-mail: reservations@whitelionhotel.biz

Dir: *A422, A38 towards Tewkesbury. In 8m take B4104, after 1m cross bridge, turn left to hotel, past bend on left*

PETS: Bedrooms (2GF) unattended **Charges** £5 per night **Exercise area** on site car park **Other** Please telephone for details of pet facilities **Resident Pets:** Oscar (Giant Schnauzer), 2 cats

Famed for being the inn depicted in Henry Fielding's novel *Tom Jones*, this 16th-century hotel is a reminder of 'Old England' with features such exposed beams and wall timbers still remaining. The quality furnishing and the decor throughout all enhance its character; the bedrooms are smart and include one four-poster room.

Rooms 11 en suite 2 annexe en suite (2 fmly) (2 GF) S £65-£70; D £99-£125 (incl. bkfst)* **Facilities** FTV Wi-fi available **Parking** 14 **Notes LB** Closed 1 Jan RS 25 Dec

ENGLAND

WOLVERLEY MAP 07 SO87

►►► **Wolverley Camping & Caravanning Club Site** *(SO833792)*

Brown Westhead Park DY10 3PX

☎ 01562 850909

web: www.thefriendlyclub.co.uk

Dir: *From Kidderminster A449 to Wolverhampton, turn left at lights onto B4189 signed Wolverley. Follow brown camping signs, turn right. Site on left*

PETS: Public areas except in buildings disp bin **Exercise area** on site **Facilities** walks info vet info **Other** prior notice required

Open 2 Apr-2 Nov Last arrival 21.00hrs Last departure noon

A very pleasant grassy site on the edge of the village, with the canal lock and towpath close to the entrance, and a pub overlooking the water. The site has good access to and from nearby motorways. A 12-acre site with 120 touring pitches.

Notes Site gates closed 23.00hrs-07.00hrs

YORKSHIRE, EAST RIDING OF

BRIDLINGTON MAP 08 TA16

★★★★★ GUEST ACCOMMODATION

Marton Grange

Flamborough Rd, Marton cum Sewerby YO15 1DU

☎ 01262 602034 01262 602034

e-mail: martongrange@talk21.com

web: www.marton-grange.co.uk

Dir: *2m NE of Bridlington. On B1255, 600yds W of Links golf club*

PETS: Bedrooms (3GF) **Charges** £5 per night charge for damage **Public areas** conservatory only (on leads) **Grounds** accessible on leads disp bin **Exercise area Facilities** cage storage walks info vet info **On Request** fridge access torch **Other** no more than 2 small dogs or 1 medium sized dog **Restrictions** no large dogs **Resident Pets:** chickens

There is a welcoming atmosphere at this country guest house and the bedrooms are all of high quality, with a range of extra facilities; ground-floor rooms are available. There are attractive lounges with views over the immaculate gardens while substantial breakfasts are served in the delightful dining room.

Rooms 11 en suite (3 GF) S £45-£52; D £70-£84* **Facilities** TVB tea/coffee Lift Cen ht **Parking** 11 **Notes** No children 12yrs Closed Dec-Feb

★★★ GUEST HOUSE

Shearwater

22 Vernon Rd YO15 2HE

☎ 01262 679883

e-mail: shearwaterhotel@amserve.com

Dir: *In town centre. Off B1254 Promenade onto Trinity Rd & Vernon Rd*

PETS: Bedrooms Charges £5 per stay **Public areas** except dining room, lounge **Exercise area** 5 mins to sea, 20 mins to park **Facilities** food bedding

A friendly welcome awaits at this well-furnished house in a residential area near the seafront. Bedrooms are very comfortably furnished and equipped. There is a cosy lounge, and quality home-cooked meals are provided in the modern dining room.

Rooms 7 en suite (3 fmly) (1 GF) S £30; D £50* **Facilities** TVB tea/coffee Cen ht Dinner Last d 4.30pm **Notes LB**

★★★ GUEST ACCOMMODATION

The Tennyson

19 Tennyson Av YO15 2EU

☎ 01262 604382 & 07729 149729

e-mail: dianew2@live.co.uk

web: www.thetennysonhotel.co.uk

Dir: *500yds NE of town centre. B1254 Promenade from town centre towards Flamborough, Tennyson Av on left*

PETS: Bedrooms Charges £2.50 per stay **Public areas** except dining room (on leads) **Exercise area** 300yds **Facilities** food bowl water bowl bedding feeding mat dog scoop/disp bags leads walks info vet info **On Request** fridge access towels **Resident Pets:** Shandy & Jerry (dogs)

Situated in a quiet side road close to the town centre and attractions, this friendly guest house offers attentive service, comfortable bedrooms and a cosy bar.

Rooms 7 rms (6 en suite) (1 pri facs) (1 fmly) S £26-£35; D £52-£60* **Facilities** TVB tea/coffee Cen ht TVL Dinner Last d 10am **Notes LB**

★★ GUEST HOUSE

The Chimes Guest House

9 Wellington Rd YO15 2BA

☎ 01262 401659

e-mail: sandsbb@aol.com

Dir: *A165 into town centre, Quay Rd, 3rd left after level crossing at Christchurch*

PETS: Bedrooms Charges charge for damage **Exercise area** approx 3 mins walk **Facilities** food bowl water bowl bedding feeding mat dog scoop/disp bags washing facs cage storage walks info vet info **On Request** fridge access torch towels **Other** certain breeds must be muzzled

Resident Pets: G.S. (dog)

With a town centre location close to beach and shops, yet in a quiet side road, this family home provides family accommodation and well-equipped cosy bedrooms. A fresh breakfast is carefully prepared to order, and friendliness is both sincere and helpful.

Rooms 8 rms (1 en suite) (2 fmly) **Facilities** FTV TVB tea/coffee Cen ht TVL Dinner Last d Lunchtime **Parking** 3

►► The Poplars Touring Park *(TA194701)*

45 Jewison Ln, Sewerby YO15 1DX

☎ 01262 677251

web: www.the-poplars.co.uk

Dir: *B1255 towards Flamborough, at 2nd bend off Z-bend, 1st left after Marton Hall, site 0.33m on left*

PETS: Charges dogs 50p per night **Exercise area** 1m **Facilities** walks info vet info

Open Mar-Oct Last arrival 21.00hrs Last departure noon

A small, peaceful and mainly adult park with immaculate facilities including a well-appointed toilet block. The friendly owners also run a B & B next door, and there is a good pub close by. A 1.25-acre site with 30 touring pitches, 10 hardstandings.

Notes ® No large groups

KINGSTON UPON HULL — MAP 08 TA02

★★★★ 71% HOTEL

Portland

Paragon St HU1 3JP

☎ 01482 326462 🖷 01482 213460

e-mail: info@portland-hotel.co.uk

web: www.portland-hull.com

Dir: *M62 onto A63, to 1st main rdbt. Left at 2nd lights and over x-rds. Right at next junct onto Carr Ln, follow one-way system*

PETS: Bedrooms Exercise area Facilities vet info **On Request** fridge access torch

A modern hotel situated next to the City Hall providing a good range of accommodation. Most of the public rooms are on the first floor and Wi-fi is available. In addition, the Bay Tree Café, at street level, is open during the day and evening. Staff are friendly and helpful and take care of car parking for hotel guests.

Rooms 126 en suite (4 fmly) S £58-£160; D £58-£160* **Facilities** STV FTV Wi-fi available Complimentary use of nearby health & fitness centre Xmas New Year **Services** Lift

MARKET WEIGHTON — MAP 08 SE84

★★★ GUEST ACCOMMODATION

Robeanne House

Driffield Ln, Shiptonthorpe YO43 3PW

☎ 01430 873312 🖷 01430 879142

e-mail: enquiries@robeannehouse.co.uk

web: www.robeannehouse.co.uk

Dir: *1.5m NW on A614*

PETS: Bedrooms (2GF) **Sep Accom** stables **Stables** on site **Charges** £5 (dogs) £15 (horses) per night charge for damage **Public areas** except dining room (on leads) **Grounds** accessible on leads disp bin **Exercise area** on site **Facilities** food (pre-bookable) food bowl water bowl bedding dog chews cat treats feeding mat litter tray etc dog scoop/disp bags leads pet sitting dog walking washing facs cage storage walks info vet info **On Request** fridge access torch towels **Resident Pets:** Beatty & Josie, Nina (horses), Megan & Dylan (ponies), Moulder (cat), (Jack, Guinness & Poppy - visiting dogs)

Set back off the A614 in a quiet location, this delightful modern family home was built as a farmhouse. York, the coast, and the Yorkshire Moors and Dales are within easy driving distance. All bedrooms have country views and include a large family room. A charming wooden chalet is available in the garden.

Rooms 2 en suite 5 annexe en suite (2 fmly) (2 GF) S £30-£45; D fr £60* **Facilities** TVB tea/coffee Cen ht TVL Dinner Last d 24hrs prior **Parking** 10 **Notes** LB

YORKSHIRE, NORTH

ALDBROUGH ST JOHN — MAP 08 NZ21

★★★ GUEST ACCOMMODATION

Lucy Cross Farm

DL11 7AD

☎ 01325 374319 & 07931 545985

e-mail: sally@lucycross.co.uk

web: www.lucycross.co.uk

Dir: *A1 junct 56 onto B6275 at Barton, white house 3m from Barton rdbt on left towards Piercebridge*

PETS: Bedrooms (1GF) **Sep Accom** outside kennel & stable available **Stables** on site **Charges** £6 (dog & cat), £25 (horse) per night £30 per week charge for damage **Grounds** accessible on leads disp bin **Exercise area Facilities** food (pre-bookable) food bowl water bowl bedding dog chews cat treats feeding mat litter tray etc dog scoop/disp bags leads pet sitting dog walking washing facs dog grooming cage storage walks info vet info **On Request** fridge access torch towels **Other** dogs must sleep in own basket; pets allowed in ground-floor bedroom only **Resident Pets:** Spud (Jack Russell)

Located close to major road links, a relaxed atmosphere and friendly welcome is assured. Traditionally furnished bedrooms are very comfortably equipped; one is on the ground floor. A lounge is available and hearty breakfasts are served in the pleasant dining room.

Rooms 5 rms (3 en suite) (2 pri facs) (1 fmly) (1 GF) S £30-£40; D £56-£65 **Facilities** FTV TVB tea/coffee Cen ht TVL Dinner Last d 8pm Wi-fi available Fishing Riding **Parking** 10 **Notes** LB

ALLERSTON — MAP 08 SE88

►►►► Vale of Pickering Caravan Park

(SE879808)

Carr House Farm YO18 7PQ

☎ 01723 859280 🖷 01723 850060

e-mail: tony@valeofpickering.co.uk

web: www.valeofpickering.co.uk

Dir: *On B1415, 1.75m off A170 (Pickering-Scarborough road)*

PETS: Charges 50p per dog per night disp bin **Exercise area** on site large dog walk **Facilities** on site shop food dog scoop/disp bags leads walks info vet info **Other** prior notice required

Open Mar-4 Jan (rs Mar) Last arrival 21.00hrs Last departure noon

A well-maintained, spacious family park with excellent facilities including a well-stocked shop. Younger children will enjoy the attractive play area, while the large ball sports area will attract older ones. The park is set in open countryside bounded by hedges, and is handy for the North Yorkshire Moors and the attractions of Scarborough. A 13-acre site with 120 touring pitches, 80 hardstandings.

ASKRIGG — MAP 07 SD99

★★ 72% SMALL HOTEL

White Rose

Main St DL8 3HG

☎ 01969 650515 🖷 01969 650176

e-mail: stay@thewhiterosehotelaskrigg.co.uk

Dir: *M6 or A1onto A684. Follow signs to Askrigg, hotel in centre of village*

PETS: Bedrooms Charges £5 per night charge for damage **Public areas** except restaurant, & bar at food service (on leads) **Grounds** accessible on leads **Exercise area** field 100yds **Facilities** vet info **Restrictions** no dog larger than Labrador

Dating from the 19th century this former private house has been carefully and sympathetically refurbished to create a family-run hotel. It is situated in the heart of Askrigg which was the fictional town of Darrowby in the BBC's *All Creatures Great and Small* series. The friendliness of the staff is noteworthy. The accommodation is tastefully decorated and comfortably furnished, and home cooked food is served in the conservatory overlooking the beer garden.

Rooms 11 en suite S £45; D £70-£80 (incl. bkfst)* **Facilities** New Year **Parking** 20 **Notes** Closed 24-25 Dec

★★★★ BED & BREAKFAST

Whitfield

Helm DL8 3JF

☎ 01969 650565 🖷 01969 650565

e-mail: bookings@askrigg-cottages.co.uk

web: www.askrigg-cottages.co.uk

Dir: *Off A684 at Bainbridge signed Askrigg, right at T-junct, 150yds to No Through Rd sign, left up hill 0.5m*

PETS: Bedrooms Charges £10 per stay **Public areas Grounds** accessible **Exercise area** adjacent **Facilities** leads washing facs cage storage walks info vet info **On Request** fridge access torch towels **Resident Pets:** Molly & Sally (Border Collies)

Set high in the fells, this smart accommodation is in a carefully converted barn, built of Yorkshire limestone. Both bedrooms are homely, and have stunning views of the Wensleydale countryside. Hearty breakfasts are served around a communal table in the inviting lounge-dining room.

Rooms 2 en suite S £45; D fr £58 **Facilities** TVB tea/coffee Cen ht TVL **Parking** 1 **Notes** LB Closed 23 Dec-2 Jan

AUSTWICK MAP 07 SD76

★★ 84% SMALL HOTEL

The Austwick Traddock

LA2 8BY

☎ 015242 51224 015242 51796

e-mail: info@austwicktraddock.co.uk

Dir: *Off A65 into village centre, 3m NW of Settle*

PETS: Bedrooms unattended **Grounds** accessible disp bin **Exercise area Facilities** water bowl dog scoop/disp bags washing facs walks info vet info **On Request** fridge access torch towels

Situated within the Yorkshire Dales National Park and in a peaceful village environment, this Georgian country house with well-tended gardens offers a haven of calm. There are two comfortable lounges, with real fires and fine furnishings, as well as a cosy bar and an elegant dining room serving good food. Bedrooms are all individually styled with many homely touches.

Rooms 10 en suite (1 fmly) S £85-£100; D £140-£190 (incl. bkfst)* **Facilities** Wi-fi available Xmas New Year **Parking** 20 **Notes** LB

AYSGARTH MAP 07 SE08

★★ 79% HOTEL

The George & Dragon Inn

DL8 3AD

☎ 01969 663358 01969 663773

e-mail: info@georgeanddragonaysgarth.co.uk

Dir: *A684 on main road in village*

PETS: Bedrooms Stables nearby (0.5m) **Charges** £10 per night charge for damage **Public areas** except restaurant (on leads) **Exercise area** 0.5m **Facilities** food (pre-bookable) food bowl water bowl leads washing facs cage storage walks info vet info **On Request** fridge access torch **Other** other pets by arrangement only **Resident Pets:** Duke (dog), Charlie Boy (horse), Buster (pigeon)

This 17th-century coaching inn offers spacious, comfortably appointed rooms. Popular with walkers, the cosy bar has a real fire and a good selection of local beers. The beamed restaurant serves hearty breakfasts and interesting meals using fresh local produce. Service is very friendly and attentive.

Rooms 7 en suite (2 fmly) S £40-£60; D £72-£120 (incl. bkfst)* **Facilities** FTV Xmas New Year **Parking** 35 **Notes** LB

BEDALE MAP 08 SE28

★★★★ INN

Castle Arms

Snape DL8 2TB

☎ 01677 470270 01677 470837

e-mail: castlearms@aol.com

Dir: *2m S of Bedale. Off B6268 into Snape*

PETS: Bedrooms (8GF) **Charges** £5 per night charge for damage **Public areas** except restaurant (on leads) **Grounds** accessible on leads disp bin **Exercise area** 100mtrs **Facilities** walks info vet info

Nestled in the quiet village of Snape, this former coaching inn is full of character. Bedrooms are in a converted barn, and each room is very comfortable and carefully furnished. The restaurant and public bar offer a good selection of fine ales, along with an interesting selection of freshly-prepared dishes.

Rooms 9 annexe en suite (8 GF) S £55-£58; D £75-£85* **Facilities** TVB tea/coffee Cen ht Dinner Last d 8.30pm **Parking** 15 **Notes** LB No coaches

BISHOP MONKTON MAP 08 SE36

►►► Church Farm Caravan Park *(SE328660)*

Knaresborough Rd HG3 3QQ

☎ 01765 677668 & 07932 158924 📠 01765 677668

e-mail: churchfarmcaravans@uwclub.net

Dir: *Left at Boroughbridge off A1, or right off A61. Site opposite church.*

PETS: Stables nearby (1m) (loose box) **Public areas** (on leads) **Exercise area** adjacent **Facilities** washing facs walks info vet info **Other** prior notice required **Resident Pets:** Cocker Spaniel, cat, 3 horses

Open Mar-Oct Last arrival 22.30hrs Last departure 15.30hrs

A very pleasant rural site on a working farm, on the edge of the attractive village of Bishop Monkton with its well-stocked shop and pubs. Whilst very much a place to relax, there are many attractions close by including Fountains Abbey, Newby Hall, Ripon and Harrogate. A 4-acre site with 45 touring pitches, 3 hardstandings and 3 statics.

Notes ⊜ No ball games

BOLTON ABBEY MAP 07 SE05

★★★★ HOTEL

Devonshire Arms Country House Hotel & Spa

BD23 6AJ

☎ 01756 710441 & 718111 📠 01756 710564

e-mail: res@thedevonshirehotels.co.uk

web: www.devonshirehotels.co.uk

Dir: *on B6160, 250yds N of junct with A59*

PETS: Bedrooms (17GF) unattended sign **Stables** nearby (1m) **Public areas** except restaurants & health spa **Grounds** accessible disp bin **Exercise area** adjacent **Facilities** food bowl water bowl bedding dog chews cat treats feeding mat dog scoop/disp bags leads dog walking washing facs cage storage walks info vet info **On Request** fridge access torch towels **Other** dog goodie bag inc feeding bowls, treat & bio-degradable scoop; food on request; dogs greeted by name! **Resident Pets:** Pip (Lurcher), Poppy (Black Labrador), Cindy (Yorkshire Terrier)

With stunning views of the Wharfedale countryside, this beautiful hotel, owned by the Duke and Duchess of Devonshire, dates back to the 17th century. Bedrooms are elegantly furnished; those in the old part of the house are particularly spacious, complete with four-posters and fine antiques. The sitting rooms are delightfully cosy with log fires, and the dedicated staff deliver service with a blend of friendliness and professionalism. The Burlington Restaurant offers highly accomplished cuisine, while the brasserie provides a lighter alternative. At the time of going to press the AA Rosette award had been suspended due to a change of head chef. Please see the AA website (www.theAA.com) for up-to-date information.

Devonshire Arms Country House Hotel & Spa

Rooms 40 en suite (1 fmly) (17 GF) S fr £180; D fr £250 (incl. bkfst)✳ **Facilities Spa** STV supervised Fishing Gym Wi-fi in bedrooms Classic cars Falconry Laser pigeon shooting Fly fishing Cricket Xmas New Year **Parking** 150 **Notes LB**

BOROUGHBRIDGE MAP 08 SE36

►►►► Boroughbridge Camping & Caravanning Club Site *(SE384662)*

Bar Ln, Roecliffe YO51 9LS

☎ 01423 322683

web: www.thefriendlyclub.co.uk

Dir: *From A1(M) junct 48 follow signs for Bar Lane Ind Est & Roecliffe. Site 0.25m from rdbt*

PETS: Public areas except in buildings disp bin **Exercise area** on site **Facilities** walks info vet info **Other** prior notice required

Open all year Last arrival 21.00hrs Last departure noon

A quiet riverside site with direct access onto the River Ure, with fishing and boating available. Close enough to the A1(M) but far enough away to hear little traffic noise, this site is a perfect stopover for longer journeys. Ripon, Knaresborough, Harrogate and York are within easy reach, and Boroughbridge offers plenty of facilities just a short walk away. A 5-acre site with 85 touring pitches, 13 hardstandings.

Notes Site gates closed 23.00hrs-07.00hrs

BURNSALL MAP 07 SE06

★★★★ RESTAURANT WITH ROOMS

Devonshire Fell

BD23 6BT

☎ 01756 729000 📠 01756 729009

e-mail: manager@devonshirefell.co.uk

web: www.devonshirefell.co.uk

Dir: *On B6160, 6m from Bolton Abbey rdbt A59 junct*

PETS: Bedrooms Charges charge for damage **Grounds** accessible on leads **Exercise area Other** dogs allowed in certain bedrooms only; goody bag available

Located on the edge of the attractive village of Burnsall, Devonshire Fell offers comfortable, well equipped accommodation in a relaxing atmosphere. There is an extensive menu featuring local produce, and meals can be taken either in the bar area or the more formal restaurant. A function room with views over the valley is also available.

Rooms 12 en suite D £130-£265* **Facilities** STV FTV TVB tea/coffee Direct dial from bedrooms Cen ht Dinner Last d 7.30pm Wi-fi available Fishing **Parking** 30 **Notes** LB

CATTERICK MAP 08 SE29

★★★ GUEST ACCOMMODATION

Rose Cottage

26 High St DL10 7LJ

☎ 01748 811164

Dir: *Off A1 in village centre, opp newsagents*

PETS: Bedrooms unattended **Exercise area** 5 min walk to river, 10 mins to racecourse **Facilities** walks info vet info **On Request** torch

Convenient for exploring the Dales and Moors, this well-maintained guest house lies in the middle of Catterick. Bedrooms are nicely presented and comfortable. The cosy public rooms include a cottage-style dining room adorned with Mrs Archer's paintings, and a lounge. Dinner is available by arrangement during the summer.

Rooms 4 rms (2 en suite) (1 fmly) S £29-£35; D £46-£52 **Facilities** TVB tea/coffee Cen ht Dinner Last d 9.30am **Parking** 4 **Notes** Closed 24-26 Dec

FILEY MAP 08 TA18

★★★★ GUEST HOUSE

Gables

2A Rutland St YO14 9JB

☎ 01723 514750

e-mail: thegablesfiley@aol.com

Dir: *Off A165 signs for town centre, right onto West Av, 2nd left onto Rutland St, the Gables opp church on corner*

PETS: Bedrooms Charges £2.50 per night charge for damage **Public areas** except dining room (on leads) **Grounds** accessible on leads disp bin **Exercise area** on site opposite **Facilities** food bowl water bowl cage storage vet info **On Request** fridge access torch towels **Resident Pets:** Boots (Old English Sheepdog), Topsy (Yorkshire Terrier), Psycho & Smokey (cats)

Located in a quiet residential area, just a stroll from the centre and promenade, this smart Edwardian house extends a warm welcome. Bedrooms are brightly decorated and well equipped and some are suitable for families. Breakfasts are substantial and a varied evening menu is available.

Rooms 5 en suite (2 fmly) D £60-£76* **Facilities** TVB tea/coffee Cen ht Dinner Last d noon Wi-fi available Golf 18 **Parking** 2 **Notes** LB No coaches

GREAT AYTON MAP 08 NZ51

★★★ INN

Royal Oak

123 High St TS9 6BW

☎ 01642 722361 & 723270 📠 01642 724047

e-mail: info@royaloak-hotel.co.uk

Dir: *Off A173, on High Street*

PETS: Bedrooms unattended **Public areas** assist dogs only (on leads) **Grounds** accessible on leads **Exercise area** local walks **Facilities** water bowl washing facs cage storage walks info vet info **On Request** fridge access torch towels **Other** pet food on request

This 18th-century former coaching inn is very popular with locals and visitors to the village. Bedrooms are all comfortably equipped. The restaurant and public bar retain many original features and offer a good selection of fine ales; an extensive range of food is available all day and is served in the bar or the dining room.

Rooms 5 en suite S £35-£45; D £70* **Facilities** TVB tea/coffee Direct dial from bedrooms Cen ht Dinner Last d 9.30pm **Notes** No coaches

HARROGATE

MAP 08 SE35

★★★★ HOTEL

Rudding Park Hotel & Golf

Rudding Park, Follifoot HG3 1JH

01423 871350 01423 872286

e-mail: reservations@ruddingpark.com

web: www.ruddingpark.com

Dir: *from A61 at rdbt with A658 take York exit and follow signs to Rudding Park*

PETS: Bedrooms (19GF) **Charges** £20 per night £140 per week **Public areas** except restaurant (on leads) **Grounds** accessible **Exercise area** on site **Facilities** food bowl water bowl bedding dog chews vet info **On Request** fridge access torch towels

In the heart of 200-year-old landscaped parkland, this modern hotel is elegant and stylish. Bedrooms, including two luxurious suites, are very smartly presented and thoughtfully equipped. Carefully prepared meals and Yorkshire tapas are served in the Clocktower, with its striking, contemporary decor. The stylish bar leads to the conservatory with a generous terrace for alfresco dining. The grandeur of the mansion house and the grounds make this a very popular venue for weddings. There is an adjoining 18-hole, par 72 golf course and an 18-bay floodlit, covered driving range; this hotel also provides extensive facilities for corporate activities.

Rooms 49 en suite (19 GF) S £155-£385; D £185-£385 (incl. bkfst)* **Facilities** STV 18 Putt green Wi-fi in bedrooms Driving range Jogging trail Membership of local gym Xmas New Year **Services** Lift **Parking** 150 **Notes** LB

★★★★ 75% HOTEL

Barceló Harrogate Majestic Hotel

Ripon Rd HG1 2HU

01423 700300 01423 502283

e-mail: majestic@barcelo-hotels.co.uk

web: www.barcelo-hotels.co.uk

Dir: *from M1 onto A1(M) at Wetherby. Take A661 to Harrogate. Hotel in town centre adjacent to Royal Hall*

PETS: Bedrooms Charges £15 per night £105 per week charge for damage **Grounds** accessible on leads **Exercise area Facilities** vet info **Restrictions** some bedrooms may not be suitable for larger breeds (please check when booking); no Rottweilers, Dobermans or Pitt Bull Terriers

Popular for conferences and functions, this grand Victorian hotel is set in 12 acres of landscaped grounds that is within walking distance of the town centre. It benefits from spacious public areas, and the comfortable bedrooms, including some spacious suites, come in a variety of sizes.

Rooms 174 en suite (8 fmly) S £69-£140* **Facilities Spa** supervised Gym Wi-fi available Golf practice net Xmas New Year **Services** Lift **Parking** 250 (charged)

★★★ 75% HOTEL

Ascot House

53 Kings Rd HG1 5HJ

01423 531005 01423 503523

e-mail: admin@ascothouse.com

web: www.ascothouse.com

Dir: *follow Town Centre/Conference/Exhibition Centre signs into Kings Rd, hotel on left after park*

PETS: Bedrooms (4GF) **Charges** £10 per week **Grounds** accessible on leads disp bin **Exercise area** 20yds **Facilities** washing facs cage storage walks info vet info **On Request** fridge access torch towels

This late-Victorian house is situated a short distance from the International Conference Centre and provides comfortable, well-equipped bedrooms with smartly presented bathrooms. The attractive public areas include an inviting lounge, bar, elegant dining room and a beautiful stained-glass window on the main staircase.

Rooms 18 en suite (2 fmly) (4 GF) S £67-£78; D £98-£128 (incl. bkfst) **Facilities** Wi-fi in bedrooms Xmas **Parking** 14 **Notes** LB Closed New Year, 25 Jan-8 Feb

★★★★ GUEST HOUSE

Alexa House & Stable Cottages

26 Ripon Rd HG1 2JJ

01423 501988 01423 504086

e-mail: enquires@alexa-house.co.uk

web: www.alexa-house.co.uk

Dir: *On A61, 0.25m from junct A59*

PETS: Bedrooms (4GF) **Charges** charge for damage **Grounds** accessible on leads disp bin **Exercise area** 200yds **Facilities** walks info vet info **On Request** fridge access torch

This popular establishment has stylish, well-equipped bedrooms split between the main house and cottage rooms. All rooms come with homely extras. The opulent day rooms include an elegant lounge with honesty bar, and a bright dining room. The hands-on proprietors ensure high levels of customer care.

Rooms 9 en suite 4 annexe en suite (2 fmly) (4 GF) S £55-£65; D £85-£95* **Facilities** TVB tea/coffee Licensed Cen ht Wi-fi available **Parking** 10 **Notes** No coaches Closed 23-26 Dec

►► *Bilton Park* *(SE317577)*

Village Farm, Bilton Ln HG1 4DH

☎ 01423 863121

Dir: *Turn E off A59 at Skipton Inn into Bilton Lane. Site approx 1m*

PETS: Exercise area on site 8 acres of fields & walks **Facilities** on site shop food bowl water bowl vet info **Other** kennels within 100yds

Open Apr-Oct

An established family-owned park in open countryside yet only two miles from the shops and tearooms of Harrogate. The spacious grass pitches are complemented by a well appointed toilet block with private facilities. The Nidd Gorge is right on the doorstep. A 4-acre site with 50 touring pitches.

Notes

HAWNBY — MAP 08 SE58

★★★★ GUEST ACCOMMODATION

Laskill Grange

YO62 5NB

☎ 01439 798268

e-mail: laskillgrange@tiscali.co.uk

web: www.laskillgrange.co.uk

Dir: *6m N of Helmsley on B1257*

PETS: Bedrooms (3GF) **Public areas** except dining room & lounge **Grounds** accessible disp bin **Exercise area** adjacent **Facilities** food bowl water bowl feeding mat washing facs cage storage walks info vet info **On Request** fridge access torch towels **Resident Pets:** ducks, peacocks & chickens

Country lovers will enjoy this charming 19th-century farmhouse. Guests can take a walk in the surrounding countryside, fish the River Seph which runs through the grounds, or visit nearby Rievaulx Abbey. Comfortable bedrooms are in the main house and are well furnished and supplied with many thoughtful extras.

Rooms 3 annexe rms (2 en suite) (1 annexe pri facs) (3 GF) S £35-£40; D £70-£80* **Facilities** FTV TVB tea/coffee Cen ht TVL Fishing Riding **Parking** 20 **Notes** LB Closed 25 Dec

HELMSLEY — MAP 08 SE68

★★★★ 78% HOTEL

Black Swan Hotel

Market Place YO62 5BJ

☎ 01439 770466 📠 01439 770174

e-mail: enquiries @blackswan-helmsley.co.uk

web: www.blackswan-helmsley.co.uk

Dir: *A1 junct 49, A168, A170 east, hotel 14m from Thirsk*

PETS: Bedrooms unattended sign **Charges** £10 per night **Grounds** accessible on leads **Exercise area** 200mtrs **Facilities** food bowl water bowl bedding dog chews dog walking dog grooming cage storage walks info vet info **On Request** fridge access torch towels

People have been visiting this establishment for over 200 years and it has become a landmark that dominates the market square. The hotel is renowned for its hospitality and friendliness; many of the staff are long-serving and dedicated. The bedrooms are stylish and include a junior suite and feature rooms. The award-winning cuisine uses the freshest local produce. The hotel also has a Tearoom & Patisserie that is open daily. At the time of our inspection there was a planned refurbishment.

Rooms 45 en suite (4 fmly) D £170-£240 (incl. bkfst)* **Facilities** STV Wi-fi available Use of leisure facilities at nearby sister hotel Xmas New Year **Parking** 50 **Notes** LB

★★★ 83% HOTEL

Feversham Arms Hotel & Verbena Spa

PRIDE OF BRITAIN HOTELS

1 High St YO62 5AG

☎ 01439 770766 📠 01439 770346

e-mail: info@fevershamarmshotel.com

web: www.fevershamarmshotel.com

Dir: *A168 (signed Thirsk) from A1 then A170 or A64 (signed York) from A1 to York North, then B1363 to Helmsley. Hotel 125mtrs from Market Place*

PETS: Bedrooms (8GF) unattended sign **Stables** nearby **Charges** charge for damage **Grounds** accessible on leads **Exercise area** 100yds **Facilities** food bowl water bowl washing facs walks info vet info **On Request** fridge access torch towels

This long established hotel lies just round the corner from the main square, and under its caring ownership proves to be a refined operation, yet without airs and graces. There are several lounge areas and a conservatory restaurant where good local ingredients are prepared with skill and minimal fuss. The bedrooms, including four poolside suites, have their own individual character and decor.

Rooms 23 en suite (9 fmly) (8 GF) S £125-£285; D £135-£295 (incl. bkfst)* **Facilities** Spa STV FTV Wi-fi available Sauna Saunarium Spa Xmas New Year **Services** Lift **Parking** 50 **Notes** LB

HELMSLEY CONTINUED

★★★ 79% HOTEL

Pheasant

Harome YO62 5JG

☎ 01439 771241 📠 01439 771744

e-mail: reservations@thepheasanthotel.com

web: www.thepheasanthotel.com

Dir: *From Helmsley take A170 towards Kirkbymoorside for 0.25m. Follow sign on right for Harome. 2m, hotel opposite church*

PETS: Bedrooms (1GF) **Exercise area** 200yds **Facilities** water bowl washing facs cage storage walks info vet info **On Request** fridge access torch towels

Guests can expect a family welcome at this popular hotel which has spacious, comfortable bedrooms and enjoys a delightful setting next to the village pond. The beamed, flagstone bar leads into the charming lounge and conservatory dining room, where very enjoyable English food is served. A separate building contains the swimming pool. Dinner-inclusive tariffs are available.

Rooms 12 en suite 2 annexe en suite (1 GF) S £85-£95; D £170-£190 (incl. bkfst & dinner) **Facilities** FTV ⓢ **Parking** 20 **Notes** No children 12yrs Closed Xmas & Jan-Feb

►►► Foxholme Caravan Park *(SE658828)*

Harome YO62 5JG

☎ 01439 771241 📠 01439 771744

Dir: *A170 from Helmsley towards Scarborough, right signed Harome, left at church, through village, follow signs*

PETS: disp bin **Exercise area** on site dog walking area **Facilities** on site shop washing facs vet info

Open Etr-Oct Last arrival 23.00hrs Last departure noon

A quiet park set in secluded wooded countryside, with well-shaded pitches in individual clearings divided by mature trees. The facilities are well maintained, and the site is ideal as a touring base or a place to relax. Please note caravans are prohibited on the A170 at Sutton Bank between Thirsk and Helmsley. A 6-acre site with 60 touring pitches.

Notes ⊜

HIGH BENTHAM — MAP 07 SD66

► Lowther Hill Caravan Park *(SD696695)*

LA2 7AN

☎ 015242 61657

web: www.caravancampingsites.co.uk/northyorkshire/lowtherhill.htm

Dir: *From A65 at Clapham onto B6480 signed Bentham. 3m to site on right*

PETS: disp bin **Exercise area** **Facilities** vet info
Resident Pets: Lady Di (Maine Coon cat)

Open Mar-Nov Last arrival 21.00hrs Last departure 14.00hrs

A simple site with stunning panoramic views from every pitch. Peace reigns on this little park, though the tourist villages of Ingleton, Clapham and Settle are not far away. All pitches have electricity, and there is a heated toilet/washroom. A 1-acre site with 9 touring pitches, 4 hardstandings.

Notes ⊜

HINDERWELL — MAP 08 NZ71

►►► Serenity Touring and Camping Park *(NZ792167)*

26A High St TS13 5JH

☎ 01947 841122

e-mail: patandni@aol.com

web: www.serenitycaravanpark.co.uk

Dir: *Off A174 in village of Hinderwell*

PETS: Public areas except laundry, washroom & toilet area **Charges** 50p per night disp bin **Exercise area** cliff walks 0.5m **Facilities** walks info vet info **Other** prior notice required
Resident Pets: D.J. (Black Labrador)

Open Mar-Oct Last arrival 21.00hrs Last departure noon

A charming park mainly for adults, being developed by enthusiastic owners. It lies behind the village of Hinderwell with its two pubs and store, and is handy for backpackers on the Cleveland Way. The sandy Runswick Bay and old fishing port of Staithes are close by, whilst Whitby is a short drive away. A 5.5-acre site with 20 touring pitches, 3 hardstandings.

Notes ⊜ Mainly adult site, no ball games, kites or frisbees

HOVINGHAM MAP 08 SE67

★★★ 71% HOTEL

Worsley Arms

High St YO62 4LA

☎ 01653 628234 🖷 01653 628130

e-mail: worsleyarms@aol.com

Dir: *A64, signed York, towards Malton. At dual carriageway left to Hovingham. At Slingsby left, then 2m*

PETS: Bedrooms (4GF) unattended **Stables** nearby **Charges** £5 per night **Public areas** lounge only **Grounds** accessible disp bin **Exercise area Facilities** food bowl water bowl dog chews feeding mat leads pet sitting walks info vet info **On Request** fridge access torch towels **Other** welcome dog biscuit on arrival! **Resident Pets:** Badger (Black Labrador)

Overlooking the village green, this hotel has relaxing and attractive lounges with welcoming open fires. Bedrooms are also comfortable and several are contained in cottages across the green. The restaurant provides interesting quality cooking, with less formal dining in the Cricketers' Bar and Bistro to the rear.

Rooms 12 en suite 8 annexe en suite (2 fmly) (4 GF) **Facilities** Shooting **Parking** 25

HUBY MAP 08 SE56

★★★ GUEST ACCOMMODATION

The New Inn Motel

Main St YO61 1HQ

☎ 01347 810219 🖷 01347 810219

e-mail: enquiries@newinnmotel.freeserve.co.uk

web: www.newinnmotel.co.uk

Dir: *Off A19 E into village centre, motel on left*

PETS: Bedrooms (8GF) sign **Charges** £5 per night (reduced rate for multipal nights stay) charge for damage **Public areas** except dining room (on leads) **Grounds** accessible on leads **Exercise area** 150mtrs **Facilities** leads washing facs cage storage walks info vet info **On Request** fridge access torch towels **Other** pets accepted by prior arrangement only **Restrictions** well behaved dogs only

Located behind the New Inn, this modern motel-style accommodation has a quiet location in the village of Huby, nine miles north of York. Comfortable bedrooms are spacious and neatly furnished, and breakfast is served in the cosy dining room. The reception area hosts an array of tourist information and the resident owners provide a friendly and helpful service.

Rooms 8 en suite (3 fmly) (8 GF) S £35-£50; D £60-£70✳ **Facilities** TVB tea/coffee Cen ht **Parking** 8 **Notes LB** Closed mid Nov-mid Dec & part Feb

INGLETON MAP 07 SD67

★★★★ BED & BREAKFAST

Gale Green Cottage

Westhouse LA6 3NJ

☎ 015242 41245 & 077867 82088

e-mail: jill@galegreen.com

Dir: *2m NW of Ingleton. S of A65 at Masongill x-rds*

PETS: Bedrooms Public areas except dining room (on leads) **Grounds** accessible disp bin **Exercise area** adjacent **Facilities** food bowl water bowl bedding feeding mat dog scoop/disp bags leads washing facs cage storage walks info vet info **On Request** fridge access torch towels **Resident Pets:** Jaffa (Red Border Collie), Beau (Golden Retriever), Lottie (cat), ducks, hens

Peacefully located in a rural hamlet, this 300-year-old house has been lovingly renovated to provide modern facilities without compromising original charm and character. Thoughtfully furnished bedrooms feature smart modern en suite shower rooms and a guest lounge is also available.

Rooms 3 en suite (1 fmly) S £29; D £58 **Facilities** FTV TVB tea/coffee Cen ht TVL **Parking** 6 **Notes**

KNARESBOROUGH MAP 08 SE35

★★★ 77% HOTEL

Best Western Dower House

Best Western

Bond End HG5 9AL

☎ 01423 863302 🖷 01423 867665

e-mail: enquiries@dowerhouse-hotel.co.uk

Dir: *A1(M) onto A59 Harrogate Rd. Through Knaresborough, hotel on right after lights at end of high street*

PETS: Bedrooms (3GF) unattended **Stables** nearby (2m) **Charges** £7.50 per stay charge for damage **Public areas** except restaurant (on leads) **Grounds** accessible disp bin **Exercise area** 0.5m **Facilities** food (pre-bookable) food bowl water bowl bedding cat treats walks info vet info **On Request** fridge access torch towels **Other** pets allowed in certain bedrooms only **Resident Pets:** 2 cats

This attractive 15th-century house stands in pleasant gardens on the edge of the town. Welcoming real fires enhance its charm and character. Restaurant 48 has a relaxed and comfortable atmosphere and overlooks the garden, plus there is a cosy bar and comfortable lounge. Other facilities include two function rooms and a popular health and leisure club.

Rooms 28 en suite 3 annexe en suite (2 fmly) (3 GF) S £65-£85; D £80-£130 (incl. bkfst)✳ **Facilities** FTV supervised Gym Wi-fi in bedrooms Sauna Steam room Spa pool Aerobics studio Xmas New Year **Parking** 100 **Notes LB**

ENGLAND

KNARESBOROUGH CONTINUED

★★★★★ GUEST HOUSE

Gallon House

47 Kirkgate HG5 8BZ

☎ 01423 862102

e-mail: gallon-house@ntlworld.com

web: www.gallon-house.co.uk

Dir: *Adjacent to railway station*

PETS: Bedrooms Public areas Grounds accessible disp bin **Exercise area** 100mtrs **Facilities** food (pre-bookable) food bowl water bowl bedding dog chews feeding mat cage storage walks info vet info **On Request** fridge access torch towels

Resident Pets: Lucy (Springer Spaniel)

This delightful building has spectacular views over the River Nidd, and offers very stylish accommodation and a homely atmosphere. The bedrooms are all individual with many homely extras. Rick's culinary delights are not to be missed. Dinner (by arrangement) and breakfast, feature quality local and home-made produce. Sue and Rick Hodgson were finalists for the AA Friendliest Landlady of the Year 2008 Award.

Rooms 3 en suite S £60-£85; D £90-£120✱ **Facilities** FTV TVB tea/coffee Licensed Cen ht Dinner Last d 24hrs notice Wi-fi available **Notes LB** No coaches

★★★★ GUEST ACCOMMODATION

Newton House

5-7 York Place HG5 0AD

☎ 01423 863539 🖷 01423 869748

e-mail: newtonhouse@btinternet.com

web: www.newtonhouseyorkshire.com

Dir: *On A59 in Knaresborough, 500yds from town centre*

PETS: Bedrooms (3GF) **Public areas** except breakfast room **Exercise area** 150mtrs **Facilities** food bowl water bowl bedding dog chews feeding mat washing facs cage storage walks info vet info **On Request** fridge access torch towels

Resident Pets: Keema (dog)

The delightful 18th-century former coaching inn is only a short walk from the river, castle and market square. The property is entered by an archway into a courtyard. The attractive, very well-equipped bedrooms include some four-posters and also king-size doubles. There is a charming lounge, and memorable breakfasts feature local and homemade produce.

Rooms 9 rms (8 en suite) (1 pri facs) 2 annexe en suite (3 fmly) (3 GF) S £50-£85; D £75-£100✱ **Facilities** FTV TVB tea/coffee Direct dial from bedrooms Cen ht TVL Wi-fi available **Parking** 10 **Notes LB** Closed 1wk Xmas

See advertisement on page 313

LEYBURN — MAP 07 SE19

★ 72% HOTEL

Golden Lion Hotel & Restaurant

Market Place DL8 5AS

☎ 01969 622161 🖷 01969 623836

e-mail: info@goldenlionleyburn.co.uk

web: www.thegoldenlion.co.uk

Dir: *on A684 in market square*

PETS: Bedrooms sign **Stables** nearby (3m) **Charges** charge for damage **Public areas** except restaurant **Exercise area** 100yds **Facilities** washing facs cage storage walks info vet info **On Request** fridge access torch towels

Dating back to 1765, this traditional inn overlooks the cobbled market square where weekly markets still take place. Bedrooms, including some family rooms, offer appropriate levels of comfort. A wide choice of delicious homemade meals are served in the restaurant or bar.

Rooms 14 rms (13 en suite) (5 fmly) (5 GF) **Facilities** FTV Wi-fi available **Services** Lift **Notes** Closed 25-26 Dec

MALHAM — MAP 07 SD96

★★★★ GUEST HOUSE

River House

BD23 4DA

☎ 01729 830315

e-mail: info@riverhousehotel.co.uk

web: www.riverhousehotel.co.uk

Dir: *Off A65, N to Malham*

PETS: Bedrooms (1GF) **Charges** £5 per stay charge for damage **Public areas** except lounge bar & restaurant **Grounds** accessible on leads disp bin **Exercise area** 50yds **Facilities** leads washing facs cage storage walks info vet info **On Request** fridge access torch towels **Other** dogs accepted by arrangement only

Resident Pets: Poppy (Weimaraner), Heidi (English Shorthair cat)

A warm welcome awaits at this attractive house, which dates from 1664. The bedrooms are bright and comfortable, with one on the ground floor. Public areas include a cosy lounge and a large, well-appointed dining room. Breakfasts and evening meals offer choice and quality above expectation and are well worthy of the Breakfast and Dinner Awards held.

Rooms 8 en suite (1 GF) S £45-£60; D £60-£100 **Facilities** TVB tea/coffee Licensed Cen ht Dinner Last d 8pm Wi-fi available **Parking** 5 **Notes LB** No children 9yrs No coaches

★★★ GUEST HOUSE

Beck Hall

Cove Rd BD23 4DJ

☎ 01729 830332

e-mail: alice@beckhallmalham.com

web: www.beckhallmalham.com

Dir: *A65 to Gargrave, turn right to Malham. Beck Hall 100yds on right after mini rdbt*

PETS: Bedrooms (4GF) unattended sign **Stables** nearby (100yds) **Public areas** with other guests' permission **Grounds** accessible disp bin **Exercise area** 10yds **Facilities** food bowl water bowl pet sitting dog walking washing facs cage storage walks info vet info **On Request** fridge access torch towels **Resident Pets:** Harvey (cat)

A small stone bridge over Malham Beck leads to this delightful property. Dating from 1710, the house has true character, with bedrooms carefully furnished with four-poster beds. Delicious afternoon teas are available in the colourful garden in warmer months, while roaring log fires welcome guests in the winter.

Rooms 10 rms (9 en suite) (1 pri facs) 7 annexe en suite (4 fmly) (4 GF) S £25-£60; D £54-£80* **Facilities** STV TV15B tea/coffee Licensed Cen ht Dinner Last d 6pm Wi-fi available Fishing Riding **Parking** 40 **Notes** LB

MARKINGTON MAP 08 SE26

★★★ 82% COUNTRY HOUSE HOTEL

Hob Green

HG3 3PJ

☎ 01423 770031 🖷 01423 771589

e-mail: info@hobgreen.com

web: www.hobgreen.com

Dir: *from A61, 4m N of Harrogate, left at Wormald Green, follow hotel signs*

PETS: Bedrooms Exercise area on site 800 acres of woodland **Facilities** food bowl water bowl **Other** please telephone for details of pet facilities **Resident Pets:** Dieffer (Labrador/Spaniel cross)

This hospitable country house is set in delightful gardens amidst rolling countryside midway between Harrogate and Ripon. The inviting lounges boast open fires in season and there is an elegant restaurant with a small private dining room. The individual bedrooms are very comfortable and come with a host of thoughtful extras.

Rooms 12 en suite (1 fmly) S £100-£115; D £120-£135 (incl. bkfst) **Facilities** Xmas New Year **Parking** 40 **Notes** LB

MASHAM MAP 08 SE28

★★★★ ®®® HOTEL

Swinton Park

HG4 4JH

☎ 01765 680900 🖷 01765 680901

e-mail: enquiries@swintonpark.com

web: www.swintonpark.com

Dir: *A1 onto B6267/8 to Masham. Follow signs through town centre & turn right into Swinton Terrace. 1m past golf course, over bridge, up hill. Hotel on right*

PETS: Bedrooms Stables on site **Charges** £25 per night **Grounds** accessible **Exercise area Facilities** bedding **Other** please telephone for further details

Although extended during the Victorian and Edwardian eras, the original part of this welcoming castle dates from the 17th century. Bedrooms are luxuriously furnished and come with a host of thoughtful extras. Samuel's restaurant (built by the current owner's

CONTINUED

MASHAM CONTINUED

great-great-great grandfather) is very elegant and serves imaginative dishes using local produce, much being sourced from the Swinton estate itself.

Rooms 30 en suite (4 fmly) S £160-£350; D £160-£350 (incl. bkfst)* **Facilities Spa** FTV 9 Fishing Riding Gym Putt green Wi-fi in bedrooms Shooting Falconry Pony trekking Cookery school Off-road driving Xmas New Year **Services** Lift **Parking** 50 **Notes LB**

►►► *Old Station Caravan Park* *(SE232812)*

Old Station Yard, Low Burton HG4 4DF

☎ 01765 689569 📠 01765 689569

e-mail: oldstation@tiscali.co.uk

web: www.oldstation-masham.co.uk

Dir: *Exit A1 onto B6267 signed Masham & Thirsk. In 8m left onto A6108. In 100yds left into site*

PETS: Stables (loose box) disp bin **Exercise area** on site **Facilities** on site shop walks info vet info

Open Mar-Nov Last arrival 20.00hrs Last departure noon

An interesting site on a former station. The enthusiastic and caring family owners have maintained the railway theme in creating a park with high quality facilities. The small town of Masham with its Theakston and Black Sheep breweries are within easy walking distance of the park. The reception/café in a carefully restored wagon shed is the latest feature of this park. A 3.75-acre site with 50 touring pitches and 12 statics.

Notes No fast cycling around site, no campfires

MIDDLESBROUGH — MAP 08 NZ41

★★★★ GUEST ACCOMMODATION

The Grey House

79 Cambridge Rd, Linthorpe TS5 5NL

☎ 01642 817485 📠 01642 817485

e-mail: denistaylor-100@btinternet.com

web: www.greyhousehotel.co.uk

Dir: *A19 N onto A1130 & A1032 Acklam Rd, right at lights*

PETS: Bedrooms Charges £5 per night £35 per week charge for damage **Public areas** (muzzled or on leads) **Grounds** accessible on leads **Exercise area Facilities** cage storage vet info **On Request** fridge access towels

This Edwardian mansion stands in mature gardens in a quiet residential area, and is lovingly maintained to provide a relaxing retreat. The master bedrooms are well sized, and the upper rooms, though smaller, also offer good comfort. Downstairs there is an attractive lounge and the breakfast room.

Rooms 9 en suite (1 fmly) S £48; D £65* **Facilities** FTV TVB tea/coffee Direct dial from bedrooms Cen ht TVL Wi-fi available **Parking** 10 **Notes LB**

MONK FRYSTON — MAP 08 SE52

★★★ 81% COUNTRY HOUSE HOTEL

Monk Fryston Hall

LS25 5DU

☎ 01977 682369 📠 01977 683544

e-mail: reception@monkfrystonhallhotel.co.uk

web: www.monkfrystonhallhotel.co.uk

Dir: *A1(M) junct 42/A63 towards Selby. Monk Fryston village in 2m, hotel on left*

PETS: Bedrooms unattended **Charges** £5 per night **Public areas** except restaurant **Grounds** accessible **Exercise area** on site **Facilities** cage storage vet info **On Request** fridge access torch towels

This delightful 16th-century mansion house enjoys a peaceful location in 30 acres of grounds, yet is only minutes' drive from the A1. Many original features have been retained and the public rooms are furnished with antique and period pieces. Bedrooms are individually styled and thoughtfully equipped for both business and leisure guests.

Rooms 29 en suite (2 fmly) (5 GF) S £75-£105; D £110-£175 (incl. bkfst)* **Facilities** STV Wi-fi available Xmas New Year **Parking** 80 **Notes LB**

NORTHALLERTON — MAP 08 SE39

★★★ 71% HOTEL

Solberge Hall

Newby Wiske DL7 9ER

☎ 01609 779191 📠 01609 780472

e-mail: reservations@solbergehall.co.uk

web: www.solbergehall.co.uk

Dir: *Exit A1 at Leeming Bar, follow A684, turn right at x-rds, hotel in 2m on right*

PETS: Bedrooms (5GF) **Charges** £10 per stay charge for damage **Grounds** accessible on leads disp bin **Exercise area Facilities** food bowl water bowl washing facs cage storage walks info vet info **On Request** fridge access torch towels

This Grade II listed Georgian country house is set in 16 acres of parkland and commands panoramic views over open countryside. Spacious bedrooms, some with four-poster beds, vary in style. Public areas include a comfortable lounge bar and an elegant drawing room. The restaurant offers an interesting range of carefully prepared dishes.

Rooms 24 en suite (7 fmly) (5 GF) S £50-£80; D £95-£130 (incl. bkfst)* **Facilities** STV FTV Wi-fi in bedrooms Clay Pigeon Shooting (charges apply), Walks Xmas **Parking** 100 **Notes LB**

NORTH STAINLEY MAP 08 SE27

►►► Sleningford Water Mill Caravan Camping Park *(SE280783)*

HG4 3HQ

☎ 01765 635201

e-mail: sleningford@hotmail.co.uk

web: www.sleningfordwatermill.co.uk

Dir: *Adjacent to A6108. 5m N of Ripon & 1m N of North Stainley*

PETS: Public areas except in buildings **Charges** £1 per night disp bin **Exercise area** adjacent **Facilities** food food bowl water bowl dog scoop/disp bags walks info vet info **Other** prior notice required **Resident Pets:** Poppy (Springer Spaniel/Border Collie cross), Boots, Murphy & Rosie (cats)

Open Etr & Apr-Oct Last arrival 21.00hrs Last departure 12.30hrs

The old watermill and the River Ure make an attractive setting for this touring park which is laid out in two areas. Pitches are placed in meadowland and close to mature woodland, and the park has two enthusiastic managers. Popular place with canoeists. A 14-acre site with 40 touring pitches, 9 hardstandings.

Notes Youth groups by prior arrangement only

OSMOTHERLEY MAP 08 SE49

►►►► Cote Ghyll Caravan & Camping Park

(SE459979)

DL6 3AH

☎ 01609 883425

e-mail: hills@coteghyll.com

web: www.coteghyll.com

Dir: *Exit A19 dual carriageway at A684 (Northallerton junct). Follow signs to Osmotherley. Left in village centre. Site entrance 0.5m on right*

PETS: Public areas on leads at all times disp bin **Exercise area** on site dog walk **Facilities** on site shop food food bowl water bowl washing facs walks info vet info

Open Mar-Oct Last arrival 22.00hrs Last departure noon

A quiet, peaceful site in a pleasant valley on the edge of moors, close to the village. The park is divided into terraces bordered by woodland, and the well-appointed amenity block is a welcome addition to this attractive park. There are pubs and shops nearby. A 7-acre site with 77 touring pitches, 12 hardstandings and 18 statics.

Notes Family park

PICKERING MAP 08 SE78

★★★ 80% ❀ HOTEL

The White Swan Inn

Market Place YO18 7AA

☎ 01751 472288 📠 01751 475554

e-mail: welcome@white-swan.co.uk

web: www.white-swan.co.uk

Dir: *in town, between church & steam railway station*

PETS: Bedrooms (8GF) unattended **Stables** nearby **Charges** £12.50 per stay per night **Public areas** except restaurant **Grounds** accessible disp bin **Exercise area** 200mtrs **Facilities** food bowl water bowl dog scoop/disp bags washing facs cage storage walks info vet info **On Request** fridge access torch

This 16th-century coaching inn offers well-equipped, comfortable bedrooms, including suites, either of a more traditional style in the main building or modern rooms in the annexe. Service is friendly and attentive. Good food is served in the attractive restaurant, in the cosy bar and the lounge, where a log fire burns in cooler months. A comprehensive wine list focuses on many fine vintages. A private dining room is also available.

Rooms 12 en suite 9 annexe en suite (3 fmly) (8 GF) D £145-£250 (incl. bkfst)✳ **Facilities** FTV Wi-fi available Xmas New Year **Parking** 45 **Notes** LB

★★ 78% ❀ HOTEL

Fox & Hounds Country Inn

Main St, Sinnington YO62 6SQ

☎ 01751 431577 📠 01751 432791

e-mail: foxhoundsinn@easynet.co.uk

web: www.thefoxandhoundsinn.co.uk

Dir: *3m W of Pickering, off A170*

PETS: Bedrooms (4GF) **Stables** nearby **Charges** £5 per night **Public areas** except restaurant & lounge bar **Grounds** accessible disp bin **Exercise area Facilities** washing facs walks info vet info **On Request** fridge access torch towels **Resident Pets:** Bracken (Hungarian Vizsla), Flax (Labrador)

This attractive inn lies in the quiet village of Sinnington just off the main road. The smartly maintained, yet traditional public areas are cosy and inviting. The menu offers a good selection of freshly cooked, modern British dishes and is available in the restaurant or informally in the bar. Bedrooms and bathrooms are well equipped and offer a good standard of quality and comfort. Service throughout is friendly and attentive.

Rooms 10 en suite (4 GF) S £49-£69; D £70-£130 (incl. bkfst)✳ **Facilities** New Year **Parking** 40 **Notes** LB Closed 25-26 Dec

PICKERING *CONTINUED*

★★ 72% HOTEL

Old Manse

19 Middleton Rd YO18 8AL

☎ 01751 476484 📠 01751 477124

e-mail: info@oldmansepickering.com

web: www.oldmansepickering.co.uk

Dir: *A169, left at rdbt, through lights, 1st right into Potter Hill. Follow road to left. From A170 left at 'local traffic only' sign*

PETS: Bedrooms (2GF) sign **Grounds** accessible on leads disp bin **Exercise area** 200mtrs **Facilities** washing facs cage storage walks info vet info **On Request** towels **Resident Pets:** Benji (Dachshund), Millie (Doberman/Setter cross)

A peacefully located house standing in mature grounds close to the town centre. It offers a combined dining room and lounge area and comfortable bedrooms that are also well equipped. Expect good hospitality from the resident owners.

Rooms 10 en suite (2 fmly) (2 GF) S £47.50-£69; D £82-£110 (incl. bkfst) **Facilities** Wi-fi available New Year **Parking** 12 **Notes** LB

RAVENSCAR — MAP 08 NZ90

★★★ 73% HOTEL

Raven Hall Country House

YO13 0ET

☎ 01723 870353 📠 01723 870072

e-mail: enquiries@ravenhall.co.uk

web: www.ravenhall.co.uk

Dir: *A171 towards Whitby. At Cloughton turn right onto unclassified road to Ravenscar*

PETS: Bedrooms (5GF) **Stables** nearby **Charges** £5 per night £30 per week charge for damage **Public areas** except lounge, bar & restaurant (on leads) **Grounds** accessible on leads disp bin **Exercise area** 50yds **Facilities** food (pre-bookable) food bowl water bowl bedding feeding mat dog scoop/disp bags leads washing facs cage storage walks info vet info **On Request** fridge access torch towels

This impressive cliff top mansion enjoys breathtaking views over Robin Hood's Bay. Extensive well-kept grounds include tennis courts, putting green, swimming pools and historic battlements. The bedrooms vary in size but all are comfortably equipped, many offer panoramic views. Public rooms are extensive while the restaurant enjoys fine views over the bay.

Rooms 52 en suite (20 fmly) (5 GF) S £49-£95; D £98-£193 (incl. bkfst & dinner)✻ **Facilities** 🎾 ⛳9 🏊 Riding Gym 🏌 Putt green Archery Bowls Table tennis Xmas New Year **Services** Lift **Parking** 200 **Notes** LB

RICCALL — MAP 08 SE63

★★★★ GUEST ACCOMMODATION

The Park View

20 Main St YO19 6PX

☎ 01757 248458 📠 01757 249211

e-mail: mail@parkviewriccall.co.uk

web: www.parkviewriccall.co.uk

Dir: *A19 from Selby, left for Riccall by water tower, 100yds on right*

PETS: Bedrooms Charges £5 per night **Grounds** accessible disp bin **Exercise area** 100mtrs **Facilities** vet info **On Request** torch towels **Resident Pets:** Merti & Elki (Mini Schnauzer), Dougie (Lhasa Apso)

The well-furnished and comfortable Park View stands in grounds and offers well-equipped bedrooms. There is a cosy lounge plus a small bar, while breakfasts are served in the dining room. Dinner is available midweek.

Rooms 7 en suite (1 fmly) S £49-£51; D £71-£74✻ **Facilities** TVB tea/coffee Cen ht TVL Dinner Last d at booking Mon-Thu Wi-fi available **Parking** 10

RICHMOND — MAP 07 NZ10

►►►► **Brompton Caravan Park** *(NZ199002)*

Brompton-on-Swale DL10 7EZ

☎ 01748 824629 📠 01748 826383

e-mail: brompton.caravanpark@btinternet.com

web: www.bromptoncaravanpark.co.uk

Dir: *Exit A1 signed Catterick, continue on B6271 to Brompton-on-Swale, site 1m on left*

PETS: Charges £1 per night disp bin **Exercise area** on site field **Facilities** on site shop food dog chews dog scoop/disp bags walks info vet info **Other** prior notice required pet shop adjacent **Restrictions** 2 dogs per pitch **Resident Pets:** Marmie(cat), Deefur (Bassett Hound), Mickey (Barber Terrier), Mr Tortoise (Tortoise), Petal (Hamster)

Open mid Mar-Oct Last arrival 21.00hrs Last departure noon

An attractive and well-managed family park where pitches have an open outlook across the River Swale. There is a good children's playground and fishing is available on the river. A 14-acre site with 177 touring pitches, 2 hardstandings and 22 statics.

Notes No gazebos, no motor or electric cars/scooters, quiet at midnight

RIPON MAP 08 SE37

★★★ 79% HOTEL

Best Western Ripon Spa

Park St HG4 2BU

☎ 01765 602172 🖷 01765 690770

e-mail: spahotel@bronco.co.uk

web: www.bw-riponspa.com

Dir: *From A61 to Ripon, follow Fountains Abbey signs. Hotel on left after hospital. Or from A1(M) junct 48, B6265 to Ripon, straight on at 2 rdbts. Right at lights towards city centre. Left at hill top. Left at Give Way sign. Hotel on left*

PETS: Bedrooms (4GF) unattended **Public areas** except food areas (on leads) **Grounds** accessible on leads disp bin **Exercise area** 25yds **Facilities** cage storage walks info vet info **On Request** torch towels

This privately owned hotel is set in extensive and attractive gardens just a short walk from the city centre. The bedrooms are well equipped to meet the needs of leisure and business travellers alike, while the comfortable lounges are complemented by the convivial atmosphere of the Turf Bar.

Rooms 40 en suite (5 fmly) (4 GF) S fr £80; D £97-£135 (incl. bkfst)* **Facilities** STV Wi-fi in bedrooms Free use of nearby gym Xmas New Year **Services** Lift **Parking** 60 **Notes LB**

ROSEDALE ABBEY MAP 08 SE79

★★★ 70% HOTEL

Blacksmith's Country Inn

Hartoft End YO18 8EN

☎ 01751 417331 🖷 01751 417167

e-mail: info@hartoft-bci.co.uk

Dir: *off A170 in village of Wrelton, N to Hartoft*

PETS: Bedrooms (4GF) unattended **Stables** nearby (5m) **Charges** £5 per night charge for damage **Public areas** bar only **Grounds** accessible on leads disp bin **Exercise area Facilities** dog chews cat treats walks info vet info **On Request** fridge access torch **Other** food by prior arrangement

Set amongst the wooded valleys and hillsides of the Yorkshire Moors, this charming hotel offers a choice of popular bars and intimate, cosy lounges, and retains the friendly atmosphere of a country inn. Food is available either in the bars or the spacious restaurant, while bedrooms vary in size all equipped to comfortable modern standards.

Rooms 19 en suite (2 fmly) (4 GF) **Facilities** Fishing **Parking** 100 **Notes LB** RS Oct-Mar

SALTBURN-BY-THE-SEA MAP 08 NZ62

★★★ 73% HOTEL

Rushpool Hall Hotel

Saltburn Ln TS12 1HD

☎ 01287 624111 🖷 01287 625255

e-mail: enquiries@rushpoolhallhotel.co.uk

web: www.rushpoolhallhotel.co.uk

Dir: *A174 Redcar & Whitby, straight over 5 rdbts, at 6th rdbt take 3rd exit for Skelton, left at next 2 rdbts, hotel 0.5m on left*

PETS: Bedrooms unattended **Stables** nearby (2m) **Public areas** except restaurants (on leads) **Grounds** accessible on leads disp bin **Exercise area** on site 90-acre estate **Facilities** washing facs walks info vet info **On Request** fridge access torch towels **Other** pets allowed in chalets only **Resident Pets:** Shalca (Rhodesian Ridgeback), Humphrey (Miniature Shetland Pony), peacocks

A grand Victorian mansion located in its own grounds and woodlands. Stylish, elegant bedrooms are well equipped and spacious; many enjoy excellent sea views. The interesting public rooms are full of charm and character, and roaring fires welcome guests in cooler months. The hotel boasts an excellent reputation as a wedding venue thanks to its superb location and experienced event management.

Rooms 21 en suite S £65-£90; D £135-£165 (incl. bkfst)* **Facilities** STV FTV Fishing Bird watching Walking Jogging track ch fac Xmas New Year **Parking** 120

ENGLAND

SCARBOROUGH

MAP 08 TA08

★★★ 80% HOTEL

Best Western Ox Pasture Hall Country Hotel

Lady Edith's Dr, Raincliffe Woods YO12 5TD

☎ 01723 365295 📠 01723 355156

e-mail: oxpasturehall@btconnect.com

web: www.oxpasturehall.com

Dir: *A171, left onto Lady Ediths Drive, 1.5m, hotel on right*

PETS: Bedrooms (14GF) **Stables** nearby **Charges** £10 per night charge for damage **Public areas** except restaurant **Grounds** accessible disp bin **Exercise area Facilities** vet info **Resident Pets:** Homee (Border Collie cross), Buster & Boxer (Welsh Cobb horses)

This charming country hotel is set in the North Riding Forest Park and has a very friendly atmosphere. Bedrooms (split between the main house, townhouse and the delightful courtyard) are stylish, comfortable and well equipped. Public areas include a split-level bar, quiet lounge and an attractive restaurant. There is also an extensive banqueting area licensed for civil weddings.

Rooms 22 en suite (1 fmly) (14 GF) **Facilities** Wi-fi in bedrooms **Parking** 100 **Notes** LB

★★ 63% HOTEL

Delmont

18/19 Blenheim Ter YO12 7HE

☎ 01723 364500 📠 01723 363554

e-mail: enquiries@delmonthotel.co.uk

Dir: *Follow signs to North Bay. At seafront to top of cliff. Hotel near castle*

PETS: Bedrooms (5GF) unattended **Charges** charge for damage **Public areas** except restaurant (on leads) **Exercise area** adjacent **Facilities** walks info vet info **On Request** fridge access torch

Popular with groups, a friendly welcome is found at this hotel on the North Bay. Bedrooms are comfortable, and many have sea views. There are two lounges, a bar and a spacious dining room in which good-value, traditional food is served along with entertainment on most evenings.

Rooms 51 en suite (18 fmly) (5 GF) S £25-£27; D £50-£70 (incl. bkfst & dinner) **Facilities** Games Room with table tennis etc ♫ Xmas New Year **Services** Lift **Parking** 2

★★★ GUEST ACCOMMODATION

Scarborough Fayre

143-147 Queens Pde YO12 7HU

☎ 01723 361677

e-mail: info@scarboroughfayrehotel.com

Dir: *Off N Marine Road, near cricket ground*

PETS: Bedrooms (1GF) **Charges** £5 per night charge for damage **Public areas** except restaurant & bar (on leads) **Exercise area** opposite **Facilities** vet info **Restrictions** small dogs only

Overlooking the North Bay, a warm welcome is assured at Scarborough Fayre, and guests have use of a comfortable lounge, fully licensed bar and spacious restaurant. Bedrooms are well equipped, most benefiting from compact en suites and some with stunning sea views.

Rooms 24 rms (23 en suite) (1 pri facs) (4 fmly) (1 GF) S £30-£45; D £60-£90 **Facilities** TVB tea/coffee Cen ht TVL Dinner Last d noon Wi-fi available **Parking** 23 **Notes** LB

►►►►► *Jacobs Mount Caravan Park*

(TA021868)

Jacobs Mount, Stepney Rd YO12 5NL

☎ 01723 361178 📠 01723 361178

e-mail: jacobsmount@yahoo.co.uk

web: www.jacobsmount.co.uk

Dir: *Direct access from A170*

PETS: Public areas except toilet block & public house (on leads) **Stables** nearby (1.5m) **Charges** £2.50 per night £17.50 per week disp bin **Exercise area** on site woods & field walks **Facilities** on site shop food food bowl water bowl dog chews cat treats dog scoop/disp bags washing facs walks info vet info **Resident Pets:** 2 Dobermans (working dogs)

Open Mar-Nov (rs Mar-May & Oct limited hours at shop/bar) Last arrival 22.00hrs Last departure noon

An elevated family-run park surrounded by woodland and open countryside, yet only two miles from the beach. Touring pitches are terraced gravel stands with individual services. A licensed bar and family room provide meals and snacks, and there is a separate well-equipped games room for teenagers. An 18-acre site with 156 touring pitches, 131 hardstandings and 60 statics.

►►►► Scarborough Camping & Caravanning Club Site *(TA025911)*

Field Ln, Burniston Rd YO13 0DA

☎ 01723 366212

web: www.thefriendlyclub.co.uk

Dir: *On W side of A165, 1m N of Scarborough*

PETS: Exercise area on site dog walk **Facilities** walks info vet info **Other** prior notice required

Open Apr-2 Nov Last arrival 21.00hrs Last departure noon

This spacious site is appointed to a high standard. The majority of pitches are hardstandings of plastic webbing which allow the grass to grow through naturally. This is an excellent family-orientated park with its own shop and takeaway, within easy reach of the resort of Scarborough. A 20-acre site with 300 touring pitches, 100 hardstandings.

►►► Killerby Old Hall *(TA063829)*

Killerby YO11 3TW

☎ 01723 583799 📠 01723 581608

e-mail: killerbyhall@btconnect.com

web: www.killerbyoldhall.com

Dir: *Direct access via B1261 at Killerby, near Cayton*

PETS: Charges £1 per night disp bin **Exercise area** on site adjacent field **Facilities** vet info

Open Mar-Oct Last departure noon

A small secluded park, well sheltered by mature trees and shrubs, located at the rear of the old hall. Use of the small indoor swimming pool is shared by visitors to the hall's holiday accommodation. A children's play area has been added. A 2-acre site with 20 touring pitches, 20 hardstandings.

Notes no cars by tents

SCOTCH CORNER — MAP 08 NZ20

►►► Scotch Corner Caravan Park *(NZ210054)*

DL10 6NS

☎ 01748 822530 📠 01748 822530

e-mail: marshallleisure@aol.com

web: www.scotchcornercaravanpark.co.uk

Dir: *From Scotch Corner junct of A1 & A66 take A6108 towards Richmond. 250mtrs then cross central reservation, return 200mtrs to site entrance*

PETS: Charges disp bin **Exercise area** on site 3-acre dog walk **Facilities** on site shop dog scoop/disp bags vet info **Other** prior notice required **Resident Pets:** Labrador

Open Etr-Oct Last arrival 22.30hrs Last departure noon

A well-maintained site with good facilities, ideally situated as a stopover, and an equally good location for touring. The Vintage Hotel which serves food can be accessed from the rear of the site. A 7-acre site with 96 touring pitches, 4 hardstandings.

Notes

SHERIFF HUTTON — MAP 08 SE66

►►► Sheriff Hutton Camping & Caravanning Club Site *(SE638652)*

Bracken Hill YO60 6QG

☎ 01347 878660

web: www.thefriendlyclub.co.uk

Dir: *From York follow 'Earswick Strensall' signs. Keep left at filling station & Ship Inn. Follow signs for Sheriff Hutton. Turn left in village of Strensall, site 2nd on right*

PETS: disp bin **Exercise area** on site dog walk **Facilities** walks info vet info **Other** prior notice required

Open 2 Apr-2 Nov Last arrival 21.00hrs Last departure noon

A quiet rural site in open meadowland within easy reach of York. This well-established park is friendly and welcoming, and the landscaping is attractive and mature. A 10-acre site with 90 touring pitches, 16 hardstandings.

SKIPTON — MAP 07 SD95

★★★ 79% HOTEL

The Coniston

Coniston Cold BD23 4EB

☎ 01756 748080 📠 01756 749487

e-mail: info@theconistonhotel.com

Dir: *on A65, 6m NW of Skipton*

PETS: Bedrooms (25GF) unattended **Charges** £10 per stay **Public areas** except restaurant areas **Grounds** accessible **Exercise area Facilities** food bowl water bowl cage storage walks info vet info **On Request** fridge access towels **Resident Pets:** Cloud (Lurcher)

Privately owned and situated on a 1,400 acre estate centred around a beautiful 24-acre lake, this hotel offers guests many exciting outdoor activities. The modern bedrooms are comfortable and most have king-size beds. Macleod's Bar and the main restaurant serve all-day meals, and fine dining is available in the evening from both carte and fixed-price menus. Staff are very friendly and nothing is too much trouble.

Rooms 50 en suite (13 fmly) (25 GF) **Facilities** Fishing Wi-fi available Clay pigeon shooting Falconry Off-road Land Rover driving **Parking** 120

SLINGSBY MAP 08 SE67

►►► Slingsby Camping & Caravanning Club Site *(SE699755)*

Railway St YO62 4AA

☎ 01653 628335

web: www.thefriendlyclub.co.uk

Dir: *0.25m N of Slingsby. Also signed from Helmsley/Malton on B1257*

PETS: disp bin **Exercise area** **Facilities** walks info vet info **Other** prior notice required

Open 2 Apr-2 Nov Last arrival 21.00hrs Last departure noon

A well cared for park in a traditional North Yorkshire village. Pitches are a mixture of grass and hardstanding, and there is a well-appointed toilet block with cubicled facilities. The village pub serving food is a few minutes walk away. Please note caravans are prohibited on the A170 at Sutton Bank between Thirsk and Helmsley. A 3-acre site with 60 touring pitches, 16 hardstandings.

Notes Site gates closed 23.00hrs-07.00hrs

STILLINGFLEET MAP 08 SE54

►►► Home Farm Caravan & Camping

(SE595427)

Moreby YO19 6HN

☎ 01904 728263 🖷 01904 720059

e-mail: home_farm@hotmail.co.uk

Dir: *6m from York on B1222, 1.5m N of Stillingfleet*

PETS: Public areas (on leads) disp bin **Exercise area** on site fields & woodland **Facilities** washing facs walks info vet info **Other** prior notice required **Resident Pets:** cats

Open Feb-Dec Last arrival 22.00hrs

A traditional meadowland site on a working farm bordered by parkland on one side and the River Ouse on another. Facilities are in converted farm buildings, and the family owners extend a friendly welcome to tourers. An excellent site for relaxing and unwinding, yet only a short distance from the attractions of York. A 5-acre site with 25 touring pitches and 2 statics.

Notes ⊜

THIRSK MAP 08 SE48

►►► Sowerby Caravan Park *(SE437801)*

Sowerby YO7 3AG

☎ 01845 522753 🖷 01845 574520

e-mail: sowervanpark@tiscali.co.uk

web: www.ukparks.co.uk/sowerby

Dir: *From A19 approx 3m S of Thirsk, turn W for Sowerby. Turn right at junct. Site 1m on left*

PETS: Public areas except children's play area **Exercise area** adjacent **Facilities** on site shop food vet info

Open Mar-Oct Last arrival 22.00hrs

A grassy site beside a tree-lined river bank, with basic but functional toilet facilities. Tourers enjoy a separate grassed area with an open outlook, away from the statics. A 1-acre site with 25 touring pitches, 5 hardstandings and 85 statics.

Notes ⊜

►► *Thirkleby Hall Caravan Park* *(SE472794)*

Thirkleby YO7 3AR

☎ 01845 501360 & 07799 641815

e-mail: greenwood.parks@virgin.net

web: www.greenwoodparks.com

Dir: *3m S of Thirsk on A19. Turn E through arched gatehouse into site*

PETS: Stables (loose box) **Public areas** (on leads) **Exercise area** on site adjacent wood and field **Facilities** water bowl washing facs walks info vet info **Resident Pets:** Dogs, cats

Open Mar-Oct Last arrival 20.00hrs Last departure 16.30hrs

A long-established site in the grounds of the old hall, with statics in wooded areas around a fishing lake and tourers based on slightly sloping grassy pitches. Toilet facilities are basic but clean and functional, and this well-screened park has superb views of the Hambledon Hills. A 53-acre site with 50 touring pitches and 185 statics.

Notes ⊜

THORNTON WATLASS MAP 08 SE28

★★★ INN

Buck Inn

HG4 4AH

☎ 01677 422461 📠 01677 422447

e-mail: innwatlass1@btconnect.com

Dir: *From A1 at Leeming Bar take A684 towards Bedale, B6268 towards Masham 2m, turn right at x-rds to Thornton Watlass*

PETS: Bedrooms unattended **Charges** £5 per night **Public areas** in residents' lounge only **Grounds** accessible disp bin **Exercise area** 300yds **Facilities** water bowl cage storage walks info vet info **On Request** fridge access torch towels **Resident Pets:** Tess (Border Collie)

This traditional country inn is situated on the edge of the village green overlooking the cricket pitch. Cricket prints and old photographs are found throughout and an open fire in the bar adds to the warm and intimate atmosphere. Wholesome lunches and dinners, from an extensive menu, are served in the bar or dining room. Bedrooms are brightly decorated and well equipped.

Rooms 7 rms (5 en suite) (1 fmly) (1 GF) S £55-£60; D £75-£85* **Facilities** TVB tea/coffee Cen ht TVL Dinner Last d 9.15pm Wi-fi available Fishing Pool Table Quoits **Parking** 10 **Notes** LB RS 24-25 Dec

WEST WITTON MAP 07 SE08

★★ 82% ® HOTEL

Wensleydale Heifer

Main St DL8 4LS

☎ 01969 622322 & 622725 📠 01969 624183

e-mail: info@wensleydaleheifer.co.uk

web: www.wensleydaleheifer.co.uk

Dir: *A1 to Leeming Bar junct, A684 towards Bedale for approx 10m to Leyburn, then towards Hawes 3.5m to West Witton*

PETS: Bedrooms unattended **Charges** £10 per night charge for damage **Public areas Grounds** accessible **Exercise area Facilities** food food bowl water bowl bedding dog chews walks info **On Request** torch

Describing itself as a boutique hotel, this 17th-century coaching inn has been transformed in recent years. The bedrooms (a four-poster room and junior suite included) are each designed with a unique and interesting theme - for example, Chocolate, Malt Whisky, James Herriott and Shooter. Food is very much the focus here - the informal fish bar and the contemporary style restaurant. The kitchen prides itself on sourcing the freshest fish and locally reared meats.

Rooms 9 en suite (3 fmly) S £90; D £110-£140 (incl. bkfst)* **Facilities** Xmas New Year **Parking** 40 **Notes** LB

WHITBY MAP 08 NZ81

★★ 80% HOTEL

Cliffemount

Bank Top Ln, Runswick Bay TS13 5HU

☎ 01947 840103 📠 01947 841025

e-mail: info@cliffemounthotel.co.uk

Dir: *exit A174, 8m N of Whitby, 1m to end*

PETS: Bedrooms (5GF) **Charges** £7.50 per night charge for damage **Public areas** bar only & not during food service (on leads) **Grounds** accessible on leads disp bin **Exercise area** adjacent **Facilities** walks info vet info **On Request** towels **Restrictions** no large breeds

Enjoying an elevated position above the cliff-side village and with splendid views across the bay, this hotel offers a warm welcome. The cosy bar leads to the restaurant where locally caught fish features on the extensive menus. The bedrooms, many with sea-view balconies, are well equipped with both practical and homely extras.

Rooms 20 en suite (4 fmly) (5 GF) S £50-£65; D £90-£135 (incl. bkfst)* **Facilities** Wi-fi available Xmas New Year **Parking** 25 **Notes** LB

►►►► Ladycross Plantation Caravan Park

(NZ821080) Egton YO21 1UA

☎ 01947 895502

e-mail: enquiries@ladycrossplantation.co.uk

web: www.ladycrossplantation.co.uk

Dir: *On unclassified road (signed) off A171 (Whitby-Teesside road)*

PETS: Public areas except reception, toilets & showers disp bin **Exercise area** on site **Facilities** on site shop food bowl water bowl walks info vet info **Other** prior notice required

Open end Mar-Oct Last arrival 20.30hrs Last departure noon

A delightful woodland setting with pitches sited in small groups in clearings around an amenities block. An additional amenity block has been completed. The site is well placed for Whitby and the Moors. Children will enjoy exploring the woodland around the site. A 12-acre site with 130 touring pitches, 18 hardstandings.

►►► *Rigg Farm Caravan Park* *(NZ915061)*

Stainsacre YO22 4LP

☎ 01947 880430

Dir: *From A171 onto B1416 signed Ruswarp. Right in 3.25m onto unclass road signed Hawsker. Left in 1.25m. Site in 0.5m*

PETS: disp bin **Exercise area Facilities** washing facs walks info vet info **Other** prior notice required

Open Mar-Oct Last arrival 22.00hrs Last departure noon

A neat rural site with distant views of the coast and Whitby Abbey, set in peaceful surroundings. The former farm buildings are used to house reception and a small games room. A 3-acre site with 14 touring pitches, 14 hardstandings and 15 statics.

Notes No ball games, cycling, skateboards, roller skating or kite flying

ENGLAND

YORK

MAP 08 SE65

★★★★ 77% HOTEL

The Grange

1 Clifton YO30 6AA

01904 644744 01904 612453

e-mail: info@grangehotel.co.uk

web: www.grangehotel.co.uk

Dir: *on A19 York/Thirsk road, approx 500yds from city centre*

PETS: Bedrooms (6GF) unattended **Charges** charge for damage **Exercise area** 5 mins walk **Facilities** cage storage walks info vet info **On Request** fridge access torch towels

This bustling Regency town house is just a few minutes' walk from the centre of York. A professional service is efficiently delivered by caring staff in a very friendly and helpful manner. Public rooms are comfortable and have been stylishly furnished; these include two dining options, the popular and informal Cellar Bar, and main hotel restaurant The Ivy Brasserie, which offers fine dining in a lavishly decorated environment. The individually designed bedrooms are comfortably appointed and have been thoughtfully equipped.

Rooms 36 en suite (6 GF) S £117-£188; D £130-£225 (incl. bkfst)✳ **Facilities** Wi-fi in bedrooms Use of nearby health club Xmas New Year **Parking** 26 **Notes** LB

★★★ 79% HOTEL

Best Western Monkbar

Monkbar YO31 7JA

01904 638086 01904 629195

e-mail: june@monkbarhotel.co.uk

Dir: *A64 onto A1079 to city, turn right at city walls, take middle lane at lights. Hotel on right*

PETS: Bedrooms (2GF) unattended sign **Charges** £7.50 per night charge for damage **Public areas** except bar/restaurant (on leads) **Grounds** accessible on leads disp bin **Exercise area** 100yds **Facilities** food (pre-bookable) food bowl water bowl bedding dog chews cat treats dog scoop/disp bags leads pet sitting dog walking cage storage walks info vet info **On Request** fridge access torch towels **Resident Pets:** Bonnie (Black Labrador)

This smart hotel enjoys a prominent position adjacent to the city walls, and just a few minutes' walk from the cathedral. Individually styled bedrooms are well equipped for both business and leisure guests. Spacious public areas include comfortable lounges, an American-style bar, an airy restaurant and impressive meeting and training facilities.

Rooms 99 en suite (8 fmly) (2 GF) S £110-£125; D £145-£175 (incl. bkfst)✳ **Facilities** FTV Wi-fi in bedrooms Xmas New Year **Services** Lift **Parking** 70 **Notes** LB

★★★ 75% HOTEL

Novotel York Centre

Fishergate YO10 4FD

01904 611660 01904 610925

e-mail: H0949@accor.com

web: www.novotel.com

Dir: *A19 north to city centre, hotel set back on left*

PETS: Bedrooms Charges £10 per night **Exercise area** riverside walks **Facilities** food bowl water bowl **Other** Please telephone for further details

Set just outside the ancient city walls, this modern, family-friendly hotel is conveniently located for visitors to the city. Bedrooms feature bathrooms with separate toilet room, plus excellent desk space and sofa beds. Four rooms are equipped for less able guests. The hotel's facilities include indoor and outdoor children's play areas and an indoor pool.

Rooms 124 en suite (124 fmly) **Facilities** STV Wi-fi available **Services** Lift **Parking** 150 (charged)

BUDGET HOTEL

Travelodge York Central

90 Piccadilly YO1 9NX

0871 984 6187 01904 652171

web: www.travelodge.co.uk

Dir: *A1(M) follow A64, 3rd turn for A19 & York*

PETS: Bedrooms unattended **Charges** £10 per night charge for damage **Public areas** (on leads) **Exercise area** 500mtrs **Facilities** walks info vet info

Travelodge offers good quality, good value, modern accommodation. Ideal for families, the spacious en suite bedrooms include remote-control TV, tea and coffee-making facilities and comfortable beds. Meals can be taken at the nearby family restaurant.

Rooms 90 en suite S fr £29; D fr £29

★★★★ GUEST ACCOMMODATION

Ascot House

80 East Pde YO31 7YH

☎ 01904 426826 📠 01904 431077

e-mail: admin@ascothouseyork.com

web: www.ascothouseyork.com

Dir: *0.5m NE of city centre. Off A1036 Heworth Green onto Mill Ln, 2nd left*

PETS: Bedrooms (2GF) unattended **Public areas** except dining room **Grounds** accessible disp bin **Exercise area** 300yds **Facilities** dog chews feeding mat leads pet sitting washing facs cage storage walks info vet info **On Request** fridge access torch towels **Resident Pets:** Gemma & Millie (Black Labradors)

June and Keith Wood provide friendly service at the 1869 Ascot House, a 15-minute walk from the town centre. Bedrooms are thoughtfully equipped, many with four-poster or canopy beds and other period furniture. Reception rooms include a cosy lounge that also retains its original features.

Rooms 13 rms (12 en suite) (1 pri facs) (3 fmly) (2 GF) S £55-£70; D £70-£80 **Facilities** TVB tea/coffee Cen ht TVL Wi-fi available Sauna **Parking** 14 **Notes** LB Closed 21-28 Dec

★★★ GUEST HOUSE

Greenside

124 Clifton YO30 6BQ

☎ 01904 623631 📠 01904 623631

e-mail: greenside@surfree.co.uk

web: www.greensideguesthouse.co.uk

Dir: *A19 N towards city centre, over lights for Greenside, on left opp Clifton Green*

PETS: Bedrooms (3GF) unattended **Exercise area** **Facilities** food bowl water bowl

Overlooking Clifton Green, this detached house is just within walking distance of the city centre. Accommodation consists of simply furnished bedrooms and there is a cosy lounge and a dining room, where dinners by arrangement and traditional breakfasts are served. It is a family home, and other families are welcome.

Rooms 6 rms (3 en suite) (2 fmly) (3 GF) S fr £28; D fr £48* **Facilities** TVB tea/coffee Cen ht TVL Wi-fi available **Parking** 6 **Notes** LB No coaches Closed Xmas & New Year

★★★ GUEST ACCOMMODATION

St Georges

6 St Georges Place, Tadcaster Rd YO24 1DR

☎ 01904 625056 📠 01904 625009

e-mail: sixstgeorg@aol.com

web: www.stgeorgesyork.com

Dir: *A64 onto A1036 N to city centre, as racecourse ends, St Georges Place on left*

PETS: Bedrooms **Public areas** except dining areas **Grounds** accessible **Exercise area** 50yds **Resident Pets:** George, Ebony, Bob, Coral & Leo (dogs), Kitson (cat)

Located near the racecourse, this family-run establishment is within walking distance of the city. The attractive bedrooms are equipped with modern facilities, and some rooms have four-poster beds and others can accommodate families. A cosy lounge is available and hearty breakfasts are served in the delightful dining room.

Rooms 10 en suite (5 fmly) (1 GF) S £30-£50; D £58-£65* **Facilities** TVB tea/coffee Cen ht Wi-fi available **Parking** 7 **Notes** LB Closed 20 Dec-2 Jan

ENGLAND

YORKSHIRE, SOUTH

BARNSLEY MAP 08 SE30

★★★ 78% HOTEL

Best Western Ardsley House Hotel

Doncaster Rd, Ardsley S71 5EH

☎ 01226 309955 📠 01226 205374

e-mail: ardsley.house@forestdale.com

web: www.forestdale.com

Dir: *on A635, 0.75m from Stairfoot rdbt*

PETS: Bedrooms unattended **Charges** **Public areas** except restaurant **Exercise area**

This late 18th-century building has retained many of its original Georgian features. Bedrooms are both comfortable and well equipped. The excellent leisure facilities including a gym, pool and beauty salon. The Allendale restaurant with views of the nearby woodlands offers an extensive menu.

Rooms 75 en suite (12 fmly) (14 GF) S £99-£110; D £119-£140 (incl. bkfst)* **Facilities** **Spa** supervised Gym Wi-fi in bedrooms Beauty spa 3 treatment rooms ♫ Xmas New Year **Parking** 200 **Notes** **LB**

DONCASTER MAP 08 SE50

★★★ 74% HOTEL

Regent

Regent Square DN1 2DS

☎ 01302 364180 & 381960 📠 01302 322331

e-mail: reservations@theregenthotel.co.uk

web: www.theregenthotel.co.uk

Dir: *on corner of A630 & A638, 1m from racecourse*

PETS: Bedrooms unattended **Charges** charge for damage **Exercise area** opposite **Facilities** water bowl vet info **On Request** fridge access torch towels **Restrictions** small dogs only

This town centre hotel overlooks a delightful small square. Public rooms include the modern bar and delightful restaurant, where an interesting range of dishes is offered. Service is friendly and attentive. Modern bedrooms have been furnished in a contemporary style and offer high levels of comfort.

Rooms 53 en suite (6 fmly) (8 GF) S £65-£95; D £80-£105 (incl. bkfst)* **Facilities** FTV Wi-fi available ♫ **Services** Lift **Parking** 20 **Notes** Closed 25 Dec & 1 Jan RS BH

BUDGET HOTEL

Campanile Doncaster

Doncaster Leisure Park, Bawtry Rd DN4 7PD

☎ 01302 370770 📠 01302 370813

e-mail: doncaster@campanile.com

web: www.envergure.fr

Dir: *follow signs to Doncaster Leisure Centre, left at rdbt before Dome complex*

PETS: Bedrooms unattended sign **Stables** nearby (1m) **Charges** charge for damage **Public areas** except restaurant (assist dogs only) (on leads) **Grounds** accessible disp bin **Exercise area** surrounding area **Facilities** walks info vet info **On Request** fridge access

This modern building offers accommodation in smart, well-equipped bedrooms, all with en suite bathrooms. Refreshments may be taken at the informal Bistro.

Rooms 50 en suite

ROTHERHAM MAP 08 SK49

★★★ 77% HOTEL

Best Western Elton

Main St, Bramley S66 2SF

☎ 01709 545681 📠 01709 549100

e-mail: bestwestern.eltonhotel@btinternet.com

web: www.bw-eltonhotel.co.uk

Dir: *M18 junct 1 follow A631 Rotherham, turn right to Ravenfield, hotel at end of Bramley village, follow brown signs*

PETS: Bedrooms (11GF) unattended **Grounds** accessible on leads **Exercise area** **Facilities** food (pre-bookable) cage storage walks info vet info **On Request** fridge access

Within easy reach of the M18, this welcoming, stone-built hotel is set in well-tended gardens. The Elton offers good modern accommodation, with larger rooms in the extension that are particularly comfortable and well equipped. A civil licence is held for wedding ceremonies and conference rooms are available.

Rooms 13 en suite 16 annexe en suite (4 fmly) (11 GF) S £55-£82; D £73-£96 (incl. bkfst) **Facilities** FTV Wi-fi in bedrooms **Parking** 48 **Notes** **LB**

SHEFFIELD MAP 08 SK38

★★★★ 71% HOTEL

Novotel Sheffield

50 Arundel Gate S1 2PR

☎ 0114 278 1781 🖹 0114 278 7744

e-mail: h1348-re@accor.com

web: www.novotel.com

Dir: *between Registry Office and Crucible/Lyceum Theatres, follow signs to Town Hall/Theatres & Hallam University*

PETS: Bedrooms unattended **Charges** charge for damage **Public areas** (on leads) **Exercise area**

In the heart of the city centre, this new generation Novotel has stylish public areas including a very modern restaurant, indoor swimming pool and a range of meeting rooms. Spacious bedrooms are suitable for family occupation, and the Novation rooms are ideal for business users.

Rooms 144 en suite (40 fmly) **Facilities** Local gym facilities free for residents **Services** Lift air con **Parking** 60 **Notes** LB

BUDGET HOTEL

Ibis Sheffield

Shude Hill S1 2AR

☎ 0114 241 9600 🖹 0114 241 9610

e-mail: H2891@accor.com

web: www.ibishotel.com

Dir: *M1 junct 33, follow signs to Sheffield City Centre(A630/A57), at rdbt take 5th exit, signed Ponds Forge, for hotel*

PETS: Bedrooms (3GF) **Charges** charge for damage **Public areas** certain areas restricted (on leads) **Exercise area On Request** towels

Modern, budget hotel offering comfortable accommodation in bright and practical bedrooms. Breakfast is self-service and dinner is available in the restaurant.

Rooms 95 en suite S £54-£64; D £54-£64*

WOODALL MOTORWAY SERVICE AREA (M1) MAP 08 SK48

BUDGET HOTEL

Days Inn Sheffield

Woodall Service Area S26 7XR

☎ 0114 248 7992 🖹 0114 248 5634

e-mail: woodall.hotel@welcomebreak.co.uk

web: www.welcomebreak.co.uk

Dir: *M1 southbound, at Woodall Services, between juncts 30/31*

PETS: Bedrooms unattended **Charges** charge for damage **Public areas** (on leads) **Grounds** accessible **Exercise area Facilities** food bowl water bowl walks info vet info

This modern building offers accommodation in smart, spacious and well-equipped bedrooms, suitable for families and business travellers, and all with en suite bathrooms. Refreshments may be taken at the nearby family restaurant.

Rooms 38 en suite S £39-£59; D £49-£69*

WORSBROUGH MAP 08 SE30

►► Greensprings Touring Park *(SE330020)*

Rockley Abbey Farm, Rockley Ln S75 3DS

☎ 01226 288298 🖹 01226 288298

Dir: *M1 junct 36, A61 to Barnsley. Turn left after 0.25m signed Pilley. Site 1m at bottom of hill*

PETS: Stables nearby (0.25m) (loose box) disp bin **Exercise area** on site dog walking area **Facilities** walks info vet info **Other** prior notice required **Restrictions** no more that 2 dogs per caravan

Open Apr-Oct Last arrival 21.00hrs Last departure noon

A secluded and attractive farm site set amidst woods and farmland, with access to the river and several good local walks. There are two touring areas, one gently sloping. Although not far from the M1, there is almost no traffic noise, and this site is convenient for exploring the area's industrial heritage, as well as the Peak District. A 4-acre site with 65 touring pitches, 13 hardstandings.

Notes

ENGLAND

YORKSHIRE, WEST

BARDSEY MAP 08 SE34

►►► Glenfield Caravan Park *(SE351421)*

120 Blackmoor Ln LS17 9DZ

☎ 01937 574657 🖹 01937 579529

e-mail: glenfieldcp@aol.com

web: www.ukparks.co.uk/glenfield/

Dir: *From A58 at Bardsey turn into Church Lane, past church, up hill. Continue 0.5m, site on right*

PETS: Charges £1 per night **Exercise area** 2m **Facilities** vet info

Open all year Last arrival 23.00hrs Last departure noon

A quiet family-owned rural site in a well-screened, tree-lined meadow. The site has an excellent toilet block complete with family room. A convenient touring base for Leeds and the surrounding area. Discounted golf, and food are both available at the local golf club. A 4-acre site with 30 touring pitches, 30 hardstandings and 1 static.

Notes ⊜

BINGLEY MAP 07 SE13

★★★ 77% HOTEL

Ramada Bradford/Leeds

RAMADA

Bradford Rd BD16 1TU

☎ 01274 567123 & 0844 815 9004 🖹 01274 551331

e-mail: sales.bradford@ramadajarvis.co.uk

web: www.ramadajarvis.co.uk

Dir: *From M62 junct 26 onto M606, at rdbt follow signs for A650 Skipton/Keighley, hotel 2m from Shipley.*

PETS: Bedrooms unattended sign **Charges** charge for damage **Grounds** accessible on leads **Exercise area** 1m **Facilities** cage storage **On Request** fridge access towels **Restrictions** small to medium sized dogs only

This large hotel is set in private landscaped grounds with views over the Aire Valley. Bedrooms, split between various wings, are neatly appointed for both business and leisure guests. Public areas include the Arts Restaurant, the Club Bar and a substantial conference centre. Extensive parking is available.

Rooms 103 en suite (14 fmly) (2 GF) S £67-£152; D £67-£164 (incl. bkfst)* **Facilities** STV FTV Fishing Xmas New Year **Services** Lift **Parking** 300 **Notes** LB

★★ 72% HOTEL

Five Rise Locks Hotel & Restaurant

Beck Ln BD16 4DD

☎ 01274 565296 🖹 01274 568828

e-mail: info@five-rise-locks.co.uk

Dir: *Off Main St onto Park Rd, 0.5m left onto Beck Ln*

PETS: Bedrooms unattended **Charges** £5 per night **Grounds** accessible disp bin **Exercise area** 300yds **Facilities** dog scoop/disp bags washing facs cage storage walks info vet info **On Request** fridge access torch towels **Resident Pets:** Charlie (Border Collie), Ruby & Tilly (Bassett Hounds)

A warm welcome and comfortable accommodation await at this impressive Victorian building. Bedrooms are of a good size and feature homely extras. The restaurant offers imaginative dishes and the bright breakfast room overlooks open countryside.

Rooms 9 en suite (2 GF) S £50-£59.95; D £75 (incl. bkfst)* **Facilities** Wi-fi available Xmas **Parking** 20

BRADFORD MAP 07 SE13

★★★ 79% HOTEL

Midland Hotel

Forster Square BD1 4HU

☎ 01274 735735 🖹 01274 720003

e-mail: info@midland-hotel-bradford.com

web: www.peelhotel.com

Dir: *M62 junct 26/M606, left opp Asda, left at rdbt onto A650. Through 2 rdbts & 2 lights. Follow A6181/Haworth signs. Up hill, next left into Manor Row. Hotel 400mtrs.*

PETS: Bedrooms Charges charge for damage **Exercise area** 20 mins walk **Restrictions** small dogs only

Ideally situated in the heart of the city, this grand Victorian hotel provides modern, very well equipped accommodation and comfortable, spacious day rooms. Ample parking is available in what used to be the city's railway station, and a preserved walkway dating from Victorian times linking the hotel to the old platform can still be used today.

Rooms 90 en suite (4 fmly) **Facilities** Wi-fi in bedrooms ♫ **Services** Lift **Parking** 50

★★★ 74% HOTEL

Best Western Guide Post Hotel

Common Rd, Low Moor BD12 0ST

☎ 0845 409 1362 🖹 01274 671085

e-mail: sales@guideposthotel.net

web: www.guideposthotel.net

Dir: *from M606 rdbt take 2nd exit (Little Chef on right). At next rdbt take 1st exit (Cleckheaton Rd). 0.5m, turn right at bollard into Common Rd*

PETS: Bedrooms (13GF) unattended **Public areas Exercise area Facilities** walks info vet info **On Request** towels **Resident Pets:** William (Springer Spaniel)

Situated south of the city, this hotel offers attractively styled, modern, comfortable bedrooms. The restaurant offers an extensive range of food using fresh, local produce; lighter snack meals are served in the bar. There is also a choice of well-equipped meeting and function rooms.

Rooms 42 en suite (6 fmly) (13 GF) S £61-£81; D £67-£87 (incl. bkfst)✳ **Facilities** STV FTV Wi-fi in bedrooms Complimentary use of nearby gym facilities **Parking** 100

★★★ 70% HOTEL

Campanile Bradford

6 Roydsdale Way, Euroway Estate BD4 6SA

☎ 01274 683683 🖹 01274 651342

e-mail: bradford@campanile.com

web: www.envergure.fr

Dir: *M62 junct 26 onto M606. Exit Euroway Estate onto Merrydale Road and right onto Roydsdale Way.*

PETS: Bedrooms (9GF) **Charges** £5 per night charge for damage **Grounds** accessible on leads disp bin **Exercise area On Request** fridge access torch towels **Other** Please telephone for further details

This modern building offers accommodation in smart, well-equipped bedrooms, all with en suite bathrooms. Refreshments may be taken at the informal bistro.

Rooms 119 en suite (37 fmly) (9 GF) **Facilities** Wi-fi available **Services** Lift **Parking** 200 **Notes** LB

GOMERSAL — MAP 08 SE22

★★★ 78% HOTEL

Gomersal Park

Moor Ln BD19 4LJ

☎ 01274 869386 🖹 01274 861042

e-mail: enquiries@gomersalparkhotel.com

web: www.gomersalparkhotel.com

Dir: *A62 to Huddersfield. At junct with A65, by Greyhound Pub right, after 1m take 1st right after Oakwell Hall*

PETS: Bedrooms (32GF) unattended **Charges** charge for damage **Grounds** accessible disp bin **Exercise area** 100yds **Facilities** food bowl water bowl washing facs cage storage walks info vet info **On Request** fridge access torch towels **Resident Pets:** Teal (English Pointer)

Constructed around a 19th-century house, this stylish, modern hotel enjoys a peaceful location and pleasant grounds. Deep sofas ensure comfort in the open-plan lounge and imaginative meals are served in the popular Brasserie 101. The well-equipped bedrooms provide high quality and comfort. Extensive public areas include a well-equipped leisure complex and pool, and a wide variety of air-conditioned conference rooms.

Rooms 100 en suite (3 fmly) (32 GF) **Facilities** supervised Gym Wi-fi available **Services** Lift **Parking** 150

HALIFAX — MAP 07 SE02

★★★ 83% ⚘⚘ HOTEL

Holdsworth House

Holdsworth HX2 9TG

☎ 01422 240024 🖹 01422 245174

e-mail: info@holdsworthhouse.co.uk

web: www.holdsworthhouse.co.uk

Dir: *from town centre take A629 (Keighley road). Right at garage up Shay Ln after 1.5m. Hotel on right after 1m*

PETS: Bedrooms (15GF) **Charges** £10 per night charge for damage **Public areas** except restaurant area (on leads) **Grounds** accessible on leads **Exercise area** 500yds **Facilities** walks info vet info **On Request** fridge access **Restrictions** small/medium sized dogs only

This delightful 17th-century Jacobean manor house, set in well tended gardens, offers individually decorated, thoughtfully equipped bedrooms. Public rooms, adorned with beautiful paintings and antique pieces, include a choice of inviting lounges and superb conference and function facilities. Dinner provides the highlight of any stay and is served in the elegant restaurant by friendly, attentive staff.

Rooms 40 en suite (2 fmly) (15 GF) S £95; D £140 (incl. bkfst)✳ **Facilities** STV Wi-fi in bedrooms New Year **Parking** 60 **Notes** LB

ENGLAND

HARTSHEAD MOOR MOTORWAY SERVICE AREA (M62) MAP 08 SE12

BUDGET HOTEL

Days Inn Bradford

Hartshead Moor Service Area, Clifton HD6 4JX

☎ 01274 851706 📠 01274 855169

e-mail: hartshead.hotel@welcomebreak.co.uk

web: www.welcomebreak.co.uk

Dir: *M62 between junct 25 and 26*

PETS: Bedrooms unattended **Charges** charge for damage **Public areas Exercise area** surrounding fields **Facilities** vet info **On Request** fridge access

This modern building offers accommodation in smart, spacious and well-equipped bedrooms, suitable for families and business travellers, and all with en suite bathrooms. Refreshments may be taken at the nearby family restaurant.

Rooms 38 en suite S £39-£59; D £49-£69✻

HUDDERSFIELD MAP 07 SE11

★★★ 68% HOTEL

The Old Golf House Hotel

New Hey Rd, Outlane HD3 3YP

☎ 0844 736 8609 & 01422 379311

📠 01422 372694

e-mail: oldgolfhouse@corushotels.com

web: www.corushotels.com

Dir: *M62 junct 23 (eastbound only), or junct 24. Follow A640 to Rochdale. Hotel on A640*

PETS: Bedrooms (19GF) unattended sign **Charges** charge for damage **Grounds** accessible on leads disp bin **Exercise area Facilities** water bowl bedding washing facs cage storage walks info vet info **On Request** fridge access torch towels

Situated close to the M62, this traditionally styled hotel offers well-equipped bedrooms. A wide choice of dishes is offered in the restaurant, and lighter meals are available in the lounge bar. The hotel, with lovely grounds, is a popular venue for weddings.

Rooms 52 en suite (4 fmly) (19 GF) S £69-£89; D £69-£89✻ **Facilities** STV Putt green Wi-fi available Mini golf Xmas New Year **Parking** 100 **Notes LB** RS Xmas

U

Cedar Court

Ainley Top HD3 3RH

☎ 01422 375431 📠 01422 314050

e-mail: huddersfield@cedarcourthotels.co.uk

web: www.cedarcourthotels.co.uk

Dir: *500yds from M62 junct 24*

PETS: Bedrooms Charges charge for damage **Public areas** (on leads) **Grounds** accessible on leads disp bin **Exercise area Facilities** cage storage vet info **On Request** fridge access towels

At the time of going to press the rating for this establishment was not confirmed. This may be due to a change of ownership or because it has only recently joined the AA rating scheme. For further details please see the AA website: www.theAA.com

Rooms 114 en suite (6 fmly) (10 GF) **Facilities** supervised Gym Steam room **Services** Lift **Parking** 250 **Notes LB**

★★★ GUEST HOUSE

Griffin Lodge Guest House

273 Manchester Rd HD4 5AG

☎ 01484 431042 📠 01484 431043

e-mail: info@griffinlodge.co.uk

web: www.griffinlodge.co.uk

PETS: Bedrooms (6GF) **Grounds** accessible on leads disp bin **Exercise area** 200yds **Facilities** feeding mat litter tray dog scoop/disp bags leads pet sitting dog walking washing facs cage storage walks info vet info **On Request** fridge access torch towels

Located on the outskirts of Huddersfield and close to the villages of Holmfirth and Marsden, Griffin Lodge is family run and offers comfortable well appointed accommodation. Hearty breakfasts are served in the small dining room and there is secure parking to the rear.

Rooms 6 en suite (4 fmly) (6 GF) S fr £35; D fr £45✻ (room only) **Facilities** FTV TVB tea/coffee Cen ht Wi-fi available **Parking** 10

ILKLEY MAP 07 SE14

★★★ 83% HOTEL

Best Western Rombalds Hotel & Restaurant

11 West View, Wells Rd LS29 9JG

☎ 01943 603201 🖹 01943 816586

e-mail: reception@rombalds.demon.co.uk

web: www.rombalds.co.uk

Dir: *A65 from Leeds. Left at 3rd main lights, follow Ilkley Moor signs. Right at HSBC Bank onto Wells Rd. Hotel 600yds on left*

PETS: Bedrooms Stables nearby (6m) **Charges** £10 per night £50 per week **Grounds** accessible **Exercise area** adjacent **Facilities** water bowl walks info vet info **On Request** fridge access torch

This elegantly furnished Georgian townhouse is located in a peaceful terrace between the town and the moors. Delightful day rooms include a choice of comfortable lounges and an attractive restaurant that provides a relaxed venue in which to sample the skilfully prepared, imaginative meals. The bedrooms are tastefully furnished, well equipped and include several spacious suites.

Rooms 15 en suite (4 fmly) S £75-£100; D £95-£120 (incl. bkfst)* **Facilities** STV Wi-fi in bedrooms Xmas **Parking** 28 **Notes LB** Closed 28 Dec-2 Jan

KEIGHLEY MAP 07 SE04

★★ 70% HOTEL

Dalesgate

406 Skipton Rd, Utley BD20 6HP

☎ 01535 664930 🖹 01535 611253

e-mail: stephen.e.atha@btinternet.com

Dir: *In town centre follow A629 over rdbt onto B6265. Right after 0.75m into St. John's Rd. 1st right into hotel car park*

PETS: Bedrooms (3GF) unattended **Charges** charge for damage **Public areas** except bar & restaurant **Exercise area** 300yds **Facilities** leads washing facs cage storage **On Request** fridge access torch towels **Other** pet food on request

Resident Pets: Max (German Shepherd cross)

Originally the residence of a local chapel minister, this modern, well-established hotel provides well-equipped, comfortable bedrooms. It also boasts a cosy bar and pleasant restaurant, serving an imaginative range of dishes. A large car park is provided to the rear.

Rooms 20 en suite (2 fmly) (3 GF) S £40-£45; D £60-£65 (incl. bkfst) **Parking** 25 **Notes** RS 22 Dec-4 Jan

LEEDS MAP 08 SE33

★★★★ 80% HOTEL

Queens

City Square LS1 1PL

☎ 0113 243 1323 🖹 0113 242 5154

e-mail: queensreservations@qhotels.co.uk

web: www.qhotels.co.uk

Dir: *M621 junct 3. Follow signs for city centre, under railway bridge. Left at 2nd lights, hotel on left.*

PETS: Bedrooms Charges charge for damage **Public areas** at General Manager's discretion (on leads) **Exercise area Facilities** walks info vet info

A legacy from the golden age of railways and located in the heart of the city, overlooking City Square. This grand Victorian hotel retains much of its original splendour. Public rooms include the spacious lounge bar, a range of conference and function rooms along with the grand ballroom. Bedrooms vary in size but all are very well equipped, and there is a choice of suites available.

Rooms 217 en suite (25 fmly) **Facilities** Wi-fi in bedrooms Free access to local gym **Services** Lift **Parking** 80 **Notes LB**

★★★ 80% HOTEL

Novotel Leeds Centre

4 Whitehall, Whitehall Quay LS1 4HR

☎ 0113 242 6446 🖹 0113 242 6445

e-mail: H3270@accor.com

web: www.novotel.com

Dir: *M621 junct 3, follow signs to train station. Turn into Aire Street & left at lights*

PETS: Bedrooms Charges £10 per night charge for damage **Exercise area Restrictions** very large dogs not accepted

With a minimalist style, this contemporary hotel provides a quality, value-for-money experience close to the city centre. Spacious, climate-controlled bedrooms are provided, whilst public areas offer deep leather sofas and an eye-catching water feature in reception. Light snacks are provided in the airy bar, and the restaurant doubles as a bistro. Staff are committed to guest care and nothing is too much trouble.

Rooms 195 en suite (50 fmly) **Facilities** Gym Playstation in rooms Play area Steam room **Services** Lift air con **Parking** 90 (charged)

LEEDS CONTINUED

★★★ 72% HOTEL

Golden Lion

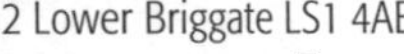

PEEL HOTELS PLC

2 Lower Briggate LS1 4AE

☎ 0113 243 6454 📠 0113 243 4241

e-mail: info@goldenlion-hotel-leeds.com

web: www.peelhotel.com

Dir: *M621 junct 3. Keep in right lane. Follow until road splits into 4 lanes. Keep right & right at lights. (Asda House on left). Left at lights. Over bridge, turn left, hotel opposite. Parking 150mtrs further on*

PETS: Bedrooms unattended **Charges** charge for damage **Exercise area Facilities** vet info **On Request** fridge access torch towels **Restrictions** no large dogs

This smartly presented, Victorian building is located on the south side of the city. The well-equipped bedrooms offer a choice of standard or executive grades. Staff are friendly and helpful ensuring a warm and welcoming atmosphere. Free overnight parking is provided in the adjacent 24-hour car park.

Rooms 89 en suite (5 fmly) **Facilities** Wi-fi in bedrooms **Services** Lift

★★★ 66% HOTEL

Ramada Leeds North

RAMADA

Mill Green View, Ring Rd, Seacroft LS14 5QF

☎ 0113 273 2323 & 0844 815 9095 📠 0113 232 3222

e-mail: sales.leedsnorth@ramadajarvis.co.uk

web: www.ramadajarvis.co.uk

Dir: *M1 junct 46 towards Leeds/Airport. Follow A6120 over several rdbts to Crossgates. Hotel 1m on right - double back at next rdbt*

PETS: Bedrooms (21GF) **Public areas** (on leads) **Grounds** accessible on leads **Exercise area On Request** torch

Located on the outskirts of the city, this modern hotel is within easy reach of the city centre, A1/M1 and M62. Bedrooms vary in size and style but are all comfortably appointed for both business and leisure guests. Events and meeting facilities are available with ample parking proving a bonus.

Rooms 102 en suite (22 fmly) (21 GF) S £55-£137; D £55-£149 (incl. bkfst)✳ **Facilities** Wi-fi available New Year **Services** Lift **Parking** 150 **Notes** LB

OTLEY — MAP 07 SE24

★★★ 74% ® HOTEL

Chevin Country Park Hotel

CRERAR HOTELS

Yorkgate LS21 3NU

☎ 01943 467818 📠 01943 850335

e-mail: chevin@crerarhotels.com

web: www.crerarhotels.com

Dir: *From Leeds/Bradford Airport rdbt take A658 N, towards Harrogate, for 0.75m to 1st lights. Turn left, then 2nd left onto 'Yorkgate'. Hotel 0.5m on left*

PETS: Bedrooms (45GF) unattended **Charges** £10 per night **Grounds** accessible on leads **Exercise area Facilities** walks info vet info **On Request** torch towels **Other** pet allowed in lodge rooms only; 44 acres of woodland available

This hotel, peacefully situated in its own woodland yet conveniently located for major road links and the airport, offers comfortable accommodation. Rooms are split between the original main log building and chalet-style accommodation, situated in the extensive grounds. Public areas are spacious and well equipped. The Lakeside restaurant provides views over the small lake and good leisure facilities are also available.

Rooms 19 en suite 30 annexe en suite (7 fmly) (45 GF) **Facilities** Fishing Gym Wi-fi in bedrooms Mountain bikes **Parking** 100

PUDSEY — MAP 07 SE23

BUDGET HOTEL

Travelodge Bradford

Travelodge

1 Mid Point, Dick Ln BD3 8QD

☎ 08719 846 124 📠 01274 665436

web: www.travelodge.co.uk

Dir: *M62 junct 26 (M606), take A6177 towards Leeds, A647. Lodge 2m on left*

PETS: Bedrooms Charges £10 per night **Public areas Grounds** accessible on leads **Exercise area Facilities** bedding **On Request** towels

Travelodge offers good quality, good value, modern accommodation. Ideal for families, the spacious en suite bedrooms include remote-control TV, tea and coffee-making facilities and comfortable beds. Meals can be taken at the nearby family restaurant.

Rooms 48 en suite S fr £29; D fr £29

ENGLAND

WAKEFIELD MAP 08 SE32

★★★ 71% HOTEL

Holiday Inn Leeds - Wakefield

Queen's Dr, Ossett WF5 9BE

☎ 0870 400 9082 📠 01924 230684

e-mail: wakefield@ichotelsgroup.com

web: www.holidayinn.co.uk

Dir: *M1 junct 40 following signs for Wakefield. Hotel is on right after 200yds*

PETS: Bedrooms (35GF) sign **Charges** charge for damage **Grounds** accessible on leads **Exercise area** field adjacent

Situated close to major motorway networks, this modern hotel offers well-equipped and comfortable bedrooms. Public areas include the popular Traders restaurant and a comfortable lounge where a menu is available throughout the day. Conference facilities are also available.

Rooms 104 en suite (32 fmly) (35 GF) S £49-£109; D £49-£109 (incl. bkfst)✻ **Facilities** STV Wi-fi available Xmas New Year **Services** Lift air con **Parking** 105 **Notes** LB

BUDGET HOTEL

Campanile Wakefield

Campanile HOTEL RESTAURANT

Monckton Rd WF2 7AL

☎ 01924 201054 📠 01924 290976

e-mail: wakefield@campanile.com

web: www.envergure.fr

Dir: *M1 junct 39, A636, 1m towards Wakefield, left into Monckton Rd, hotel on left*

PETS: Bedrooms unattended sign **Charges** charge for damage **Public areas** except buffet section of restaurant (on leads) **Grounds** accessible on leads disp bin **Exercise area** canalside nearby **Facilities** food bowl water bowl bedding feeding mat cage storage walks info vet info **On Request** torch towels

This modern building offers accommodation in smart, well-equipped bedrooms, all with en suite bathrooms. Refreshments may be taken at the informal Bistro.

Rooms 76 annexe en suite

★★★ GUEST HOUSE

Stanley View

226-230 Stanley Rd WF1 4AE

☎ 01924 376803 📠 01924 369123

e-mail: enquiries@stanleyviewguesthouse.co.uk

Dir: *M62 junct 30, follow Aberford Rd 3m. Signed on left*

PETS: Bedrooms (7GF) **Public areas** except dining area **Exercise area** **Other** dogs in ground floor bedrooms only

Part of an attractive terrace, this well established guest house is just half a mile from the city centre and has private parking at the rear. The well equipped bedrooms are brightly decorated, and there is a licensed bar and comfortable lounge. Hearty home cooked meals are served in the attractive dining room.

Rooms 17 rms (13 en suite) (6 fmly) (7 GF) S £25-£34; D £40-£45✻ **Facilities** STV TVB tea/coffee Direct dial from bedrooms Licensed Cen ht TVL Dinner Last d 8.30pm **Parking** 10 **Notes** No coaches

CHANNEL ISLANDS

Guernsey

CASTEL MAP 16

►►► **Fauxquets Valley Campsite**

GY5 7QA

☎ 01481 236951 & 07781 413333

e-mail: info@fauxquets.co.uk

web: www.fauxquets.co.uk

Dir: *Off pier. 2nd exit off rdbt. Top of hill left onto Queens Rd. Continue for 2m. Turn right onto Candie Rd. Opposite sign for German Occupation Museum*

PETS: Stables (loose box) **Public areas** (on leads) disp bin **Exercise area** fields adjacent **Facilities** on site shop washing facs walks info vet info **Other** prior notice required

Resident Pets: Bracken (Jack Russell), Morley (Chocolate Labrador), Blackie (Black Labrador)

Open mid Jun-Aug (rs Etr-mid Jun Haybarn restaurant & bar closed)

A beautiful, quiet farm site in a hidden valley close to the sea. Friendly helpful owners, who understand campers' needs, offer good quality facilities and amenities, including an outdoor swimming pool, bar/restaurant, nature trail and sports areas. A 3-acre site with 100 touring pitches.

ENGLAND

Jersey

GROUVILLE MAP 16

★★★ 71% HOTEL

Beausite

Les Rue des Pres, Grouville Bay JE3 9DJ

☎ 01534 857577 📠 01534 857211

e-mail: beausite@jerseymail.co.uk

web: www.southernhotels.com

Dir: *Opposite Royal Jersey Golf Course*

PETS: Bedrooms unattended **Charges** charge for damage **Public areas** except restaurant (on leads) **Exercise area** 200mtrs **Facilities** water bowl **Resident Pets:** Benjy (Terrier)

Close to the Royal Jersey Golf Club, this hotel is situated on the south-east side of the island; a short distance from the picturesque harbour at Gorey. With parts dating back to 1636, the public rooms retain original character and charm; bedrooms are generally spacious and modern in design. The indoor swimming pool, fitness room, saunas and spa bath are an added bonus.

Rooms 75 en suite (5 fmly) (18 GF) **Facilities** Gym **Parking** 60 **Notes** Closed Nov-Mar

ST BRELADE MAP 16

★★★★ 73% HOTEL

Hotel La Place

Route du Coin, La Haule JE3 8BT

☎ 01534 744261 📠 01534 745164

e-mail: reservations@hotellaplacejersey.com

Dir: *Off main St Helier/St Aubin coast road at La Haule Manor (B25). Up hill, 2nd left (to Red Houses), 1st right. Hotel 100mtrs on right*

PETS: Bedrooms (10GF) **Stables** nearby (5kms) **Charges** £10 per night charge for damage **Grounds** accessible on leads disp bin **Exercise area Facilities** food bowl water bowl bedding feeding mat pet sitting dog walking washing facs cage storage walks info vet info **On Request** fridge access torch towels

Developed around a 17th-century farmhouse and well placed for exploration of the island. Attentive, friendly service is the ethos here. A range of bedroom types is provided, some having private patios and direct access to the pool area. The cocktail bar is popular for pre-dinner drinks and a traditional lounge has a log fire in colder months. An interesting menu is offered.

Rooms 42 en suite (1 fmly) (10 GF) **Facilities** Wi-fi available Discount at Les Ormes Country Club, including golf, gym & indoor tennis **Parking** 100

★★ 72% HOTEL

Hotel Miramar

Mont Gras D'Eau JE3 8ED

☎ 01534 743831 📠 01534 745009

e-mail: miramarjsy@localdial.com

Dir: *From airport take B36 at lights, turn left onto A13, 1st right into Mont Gras D'Eau*

PETS: Bedrooms (14GF) unattended **Exercise area** 100yds **Facilities** cage storage walks info vet info

A friendly welcome awaits at this family-run hotel set in delightful sheltered gardens, overlooking the beautiful bay. Accommodation is comfortable with well appointed bedrooms; some are on the ground floor, and there are two on the lower ground with their own terrace overlooking the outdoor heated pool. The restaurant offers a varied set menu.

Rooms 38 en suite (2 fmly) (14 GF) S £30-£46.75; D £60-£93.50 (incl. bkfst)✳ **Facilities** **Parking** 30 **Notes** Closed Oct-mid Apr

ST MARTIN MAP 16

►►►►► **Beuvelande Camp**

SiteBeuvelande JE3 6EZ

☎ 01534 853575 📠 01534 857788

e-mail: info@campingjersey.com

web: www.campingjersey.com

Dir: *Take A6 from St Helier to St Martin & follow signs to site before St Martins Church*

PETS: Charges £2 per dog per night disp bin **Exercise area** on site **Facilities** on site shop food food bowl water bowl dog scoop/disp bags vet info **Other** prior notice required **Restrictions** no Staffordshire Bull Terriers or Rottweilers

Open Apr-Sep (rs Apr-May & Sep pool & restaurant closed, shop hours limited)

A well-established site with excellent toilet facilities, accessed via narrow lanes in peaceful countryside close to St Martin. An attractive bar/restaurant is the focal point of the park, especially in the evenings, and there is a small swimming pool and playground. Motorhomes and towed caravans will be met at the ferry and escorted to the site if requested when booking. A 6-acre site with 150 touring pitches and 75 statics.

ST OUEN MAP 16

►►► Bleu Soleil Campsite

La Route de Vinchelez, Leoville JE3 2DB

☎ 01534 481007 01534 481525

e-mail: info@bleusoleilcamping.com

web: www.bleusoleilcamping.com

Dir: *From St Helier ferry port take A2 towards St Aubin then turn right onto A12 passing airport to Leoville. Site on right of La Route de Vinchelez*

PETS: Public areas except café, shop & TV lounge **Exercise area** beach nearby **Facilities** on site shop food bowl water bowl vet info **Other** prior notice required; owners must clean up after dogs **Resident Pets:** 1 dog, cats

Open all year Last arrival 23.00hrs Last departure 10.00hrs

A compact tent park set in the NW corner of the island and surrounded by beautiful countryside. Greve-de-Lacq beach is close by, and the golden beaches at St Ouen's Bay and St Brelade's Bay are only a short drive away. There are 45 ready-erected tents for hire. A 1.5-acre site with 55 touring pitches, 8 hardstandings and 45 statics.

Notes No noise after 22.00hrs

ST SAVIOUR MAP 16

★★★★★ ®®® HOTEL

Longueville Manor

JE2 7WF

☎ 01534 725501 01534 731613

e-mail: info@longuevillemanor.com

web: www.longuevillemanor.com

Dir: *A3 E from St Helier towards Gorey. Hotel 1m on left*

PETS: Bedrooms (7GF) unattended **Grounds** accessible disp bin **Exercise area** beach 0.5m **Facilities** feeding mat cage storage walks info vet info **On Request** fridge access torch towels

Dating back to the 13th century, there is something very special about Longueville Manor, which is why so many guests return. It is set in 17 acres of grounds including woodland walks, a spectacular rose garden and a lake. Bedrooms have great style and individuality boasting fresh flowers, fine embroidered bed linen and a host of extras. The committed team of staff create a welcoming atmosphere and every effort is made to ensure a memorable stay. The accomplished cuisine is also a highlight.

Rooms 29 en suite 1 annexe en suite (7 GF) S £175-£360; D £200-£570 (incl. bkfst)✱ **Facilities** STV Wi-fi in bedrooms Xmas New Year **Services** Lift **Parking** 40 **Notes** LB

ISLE OF MAN

PORT ERIN MAP 06 SC16

★★ 69% HOTEL

Falcon's Nest

The Promenade IM9 6AF

☎ 01624 834077 01624 835370

e-mail: falconsnest@enterprise.net

web: www.falconsnesthotel.co.uk

Dir: *follow coastal road, S from airport or ferry. Hotel on seafront, immediately after steam railway station*

PETS: Bedrooms unattended **Exercise area** 50mtrs to beach/park **Facilities** walks info vet info **On Request** fridge access towels

Situated overlooking the bay and harbour, this Victorian hotel offers generally spacious bedrooms. There is a choice of bars, one of which attracts many locals. Meals can be taken in the lounge bar, the conservatory or in the attractively decorated main restaurant.

Rooms 35 en suite (9 fmly) S £35-£42.50; D £70-£85 (incl. bkfst)✱ **Facilities** Wi-fi available Xmas New Year **Parking** 40

Scotland

CITY OF ABERDEEN

ABERDEEN MAP 15 NJ90

★★★★ 77% HOTEL

Aberdeen Patio

Beach Boulevard AB24 5EF

☎ 01224 633339 & 380000 01224 638833

e-mail: info@patiohotels.com

web: www.patiohotels.com

Dir: *from A90 follow signs for city centre, then for beach. On Beach Blvd, turn left at lights, hotel on right*

PETS: Bedrooms unattended **Grounds** accessible on leads disp bin **Exercise area** 100yds **Facilities** food bowl water bowl vet info **On Request** towels

This modern, purpose-built hotel lies close to the seafront. Bedrooms come in two different styles - the retro-style Classics and spacious Premiers. In addition the Platinum Club offers a unique experience of 44 superb high-spec bedrooms that have their own reception bar, lounge and dinner and breakfast room. The restaurant and striking Atrium bar are housed in the main building.

Rooms 124 en suite 44 annexe en suite (8 fmly) (22 GF) S £160-£165; D £170-£175* **Facilities Spa** STV Gym Wi-fi available Steam room Treatment room Sauna Solarium Fitness Studio New Year **Services** Lift **Parking** 172

ABERDEENSHIRE

ABOYNE MAP 15 NO59

►►► Aboyne Loch Caravan Park *(NO538998)*

AB34 5BR

☎ 013398 86244 & 01330 811351 013398 86244

Dir: *On A93, 1m E of Aboyne*

PETS: disp bin **Exercise area** on site dog walks **Facilities** walks info vet info

Open 31 Mar-Oct Last arrival 20.00hrs Last departure 11.00hrs

Attractively sited caravan park set amidst woodland on the shores of the lovely Aboyne Loch in scenic Deeside. The facilities are modern and immaculately maintained, and amenities include boat-launching, boating and fishing. An ideally situated park for touring Royal Deeside and the Aberdeenshire uplands. A 6-acre site with 25 touring pitches, 25 hardstandings and 100 statics.

Notes

BALLATER MAP 15 NO39

★★★ SMALL HOTEL

Darroch Learg

Braemar Rd AB35 5UX

☎ 013397 55443 013397 55252

e-mail: enquiries@darrochlearg.co.uk

web: www.darrochlearg.co.uk

Dir: *on A93, at western side of Ballater*

PETS: Bedrooms (1GF) **Grounds** accessible disp bin **Exercise area Facilities** food bowl water bowl litter tray etc dog scoop/disp bags walks info vet info **On Request** fridge access torch **Resident Pets:** Holly (Golden Labrador), Isla (Black Labrador)

Set high above the road in extensive wooded grounds, this long-established hotel offers superb views over the hills and countryside of Royal Deeside. Nigel and Fiona Franks are caring and attentive hosts who improve their hotel every year. Bedrooms, some with four-poster beds, are individually styled, bright and spacious. Food is a highlight of any visit, whether it is a freshly prepared breakfast or the fine cuisine served in the delightful conservatory restaurant.

Rooms 12 en suite 5 annexe en suite (1 GF) S £120-£165; D £190-£280 (incl. bkfst & dinner)* **Facilities** New Year **Parking** 25 **Notes** Closed Xmas & Jan (ex New Year)

FORDOUN MAP 15 NO77

►►► Brownmuir Caravan Park *(NO740772)*

AB30 1SJ

☎ 01561 320786 01561 320786

e-mail: brownmuircaravanpark@talk21.com

web: www.brownmuircaravanpark.co.uk

Dir: *From N on A90 take B966 signed Fettercairn & site 1.5m on left. From S take A90, turn off 4m N of Laurencekirk signed Fordoun, site 1m on right*

PETS: Public areas except children's play area disp bin **Exercise area** on site **Facilities** walks info vet info

Open Apr-Oct Last arrival 23.00hrs Last departure noon

A mainly static site set in a rural location with level pitches and good touring facilities. The area is ideal for cyclists, walkers and golfers, as well as those wanting to visit Aberdeen, Banchory, Ballater, Balmoral, Glamis and Dundee. A 7-acre site with 11 touring pitches, 4 hardstandings and 49 statics.

Notes

HUNTLY MAP 15 NJ53

★★ 64% HOTEL

Gordon Arms Hotel

The Square AB54 8AF

☎ 01466 792288 📠 01466 794556

e-mail: reception@gordonarms.demon.co.uk

Dir: *off A96 (Aberdeen to Inverness road) at Huntly. Hotel immediately on left after entering town square*

PETS: Bedrooms Stables nearby (2m) **Charges** £5 per night charge for damage **Exercise area Facilities** cage storage walks info vet info **On Request** fridge access torch towels

This friendly, family-run hotel is located in the town square and offers a good selection of tasty, well-portioned dishes served in the bar, and also in the restaurant at weekends or midweek by appointment. Bedrooms come in a variety of sizes, but all have a good range of accessories.

Rooms 13 en suite (3 fmly) S £40-£50; D £50-£60 (incl. bkfst)* **Facilities** FTV ♫ **Notes** LB

NORTH WATER BRIDGE MAP 15 NO66

►►► Dovecot Caravan Park *(NO648663)*

AB30 1QL

☎ 01674 840630 📠 01674 840630

e-mail: adele@dovecotcaravanpark.co.uk

web: www.dovecotcaravanpark.co.uk

Dir: *Take A90, 5m S of Laurencekirk. At Edzell Woods sign turn left. Site 500yds on left*

PETS: disp bin **Exercise area** on site riverside dog walk **Facilities** walks info vet info

Open Apr-Oct Last arrival 20.00hrs Last departure noon

A level grassy site in a country area close to the A90, with mature trees screening one side and the River North Esk on the other. The immaculate toilet facilities make this a handy overnight stop in a good touring area. A 6-acre site with 25 touring pitches, 8 hardstandings and 44 statics.

Notes ⊜

TARLAND MAP 15 NJ40

►►► Tarland Camping & Caravanning Club Site *(NJ477044)*

AB34 4UP

☎ 01339 881388

web: www.thefriendlyclub.co.uk

Dir: *A93 from Aberdeen right in Aboyne onto B9094. 6m next right, then left before bridge, site 600yds on left*

PETS: Public areas except in buildings **Exercise area** on site **Facilities** walks info vet info **Other** prior notice required

Open 2 Apr-2 Nov Last arrival 21.00hrs Last departure noon

A pretty park on the edge of the village, laid out on two levels. The upper area has hardstandings and electric hook-ups, and views over hills and moorland, while the lower level is well screened with mature trees and is grassy. An 8-acre site with 58 touring pitches, 32 hardstandings and 40 statics.

ARGYLL & BUTE

ARDUAINE MAP 10 NM71

★★★ 82% ®® HOTEL

Loch Melfort

PA34 4XG

☎ 01852 200233 📠 01852 200214

e-mail: reception@lochmelfort.co.uk

web: www.lochmelfort.co.uk

Dir: *on A816, midway between Oban & Lochgilphead*

PETS: Bedrooms (10GF) unattended **Charges** £5 per night charge for damage **Grounds** accessible **Exercise area Facilities** washing facs cage storage walks info vet info **On Request** fridge access torch towels **Resident Pets:** Rosie (Beagle), Evie & Bethan (horses)

Enjoying one of the finest locations on the West Coast, this popular, family-run hotel has outstanding views across Asknish Bay towards the Islands of Jura, Scarba and Shuna. Accommodation is provided in either the balconied rooms in the Cedar wing or the more traditional rooms in the main hotel. Skilfully cooked dinners are the highlight of any visit.

Rooms 5 en suite 20 annexe en suite (2 fmly) (10 GF) **Parking** 65 **Notes** LB Closed 3 Jan-15 Feb

SCOTLAND

BARCALDINE — MAP 10 NM94

►►► Oban Camping & Caravanning Club Site *(NM966420)*

PA37 1SG

☎ 01631 720348

web: www.thefriendlyclub.co.uk

Dir: *N on A828, 7m from Connel Bridge, turn into site at Club sign on right (opposite Marine Resource Centre)*

PETS: Public areas except in buildings disp bin **Exercise area** on site adjacent woodland **Facilities** walks info vet info **Other** prior notice required

Open 2 Apr-2 Nov Last arrival 21.00hrs Last departure noon

A sheltered site within a walled garden, bordered by Barcaldine Forest, close to Loch Creran. Tourers are arranged against the old garden walls. There are pleasant woodland walks from the park, including the Sutherland memorial woods close by. A 4.5-acre site with 75 touring pitches, 24 hardstandings and 18 statics.

Notes Site gates closed 23.00hrs-07.00hrs

CARRADALE — MAP 10 NR83

►►► *Carradale Bay Caravan Park*

(NR815385)

PA28 6QG

☎ 01583 431665

e-mail: info@carradalebay.com

web: www.carradalebay.com

Dir: *A83 from Tarbert towards Campbeltown, left onto B842 (Carradale road), right onto B879. Site 0.5m*

PETS: Charges 1st pet free, 2nd pet £1 per night disp bin **Exercise area** on site walks & beach **Facilities** washing facs walks info vet info

Open Apr-Sep Last arrival 22.00hrs Last departure noon

A beautiful, natural site on the sea's edge with superb views over Kilbrannan Sound to the Isle of Arran. Pitches are landscaped into small bays broken up by shrubs and bushes, and backed by dunes close to the long sandy beach. An 8-acre site with 75 touring pitches and 12 statics.

CLACHAN — MAP 10 NR75

★★★ 72% ❁ COUNTRY HOUSE HOTEL

Balinakill Country House

PA29 6XL

☎ 01880 740206 🖷 01880 740298

e-mail: info@balinakill.com

Dir: *access from A83, 50mtrs beyond Thames Garage*

PETS: Bedrooms (1GF) **Stables** nearby (approx 10m) **Charges** charge for damage **Public areas** except restaurant **Exercise area Facilities** washing facs cage storage walks info vet info **On Request** fridge access torch **Resident Pets:** Sprocket & Shadow (Black Labradors)

This imposing listed country mansion is set in grounds on the Kintyre peninsula. Graced with antiques and period pieces it boasts beautiful wood panelling and plasterwork. Many bedrooms reflect the Victorian era, with the larger ones featuring real fires. Service by the hands-on owners is friendly and attentive. Meals focus on interesting menus and well-sourced produce.

Rooms 10 en suite (1 GF) S £50; D £90-£100 (incl. bkfst)✳
Facilities Fishing Aromatherapy Reflexology Stalking Xmas New Year
Parking 20 **Notes** LB

CLACHAN-SEIL — MAP 10 NM71

★★ 85% ❁❁ SMALL HOTEL

Willowburn

PA34 4TJ

☎ 01852 300276

e-mail: willowburn.hotel@virgin.net

web: www.willowburn.co.uk

Dir: *0.5m from Atlantic Bridge, on left*

PETS: Bedrooms (1GF) unattended **Sep Accom** crate available **Charges** charge for damage **Public areas** bar only **Grounds** accessible disp bin **Exercise area** 0.5m **Facilities** food bowl water bowl bedding dog scoop/disp bags leads washing facs walks info vet info **On Request** fridge access torch towels **Resident Pets:** Sisko (Black Labrador), Odo (cat), Tussock (Hovawart), Mooi (Appaloosa horse), Danny (horse)

This welcoming small hotel enjoys a peaceful setting, with grounds stretching down to the shores of Clachan Sound. Friendly unassuming service, a relaxed atmosphere and fine food are key to its success.

Bedrooms are bright, cheerful and thoughtfully equipped. Guests can watch the wildlife from the dining room, lounge or cosy bar.

Rooms 7 en suite (1 GF) S £85; D £170 (incl. bkfst & dinner)✳ **Facilities** Wi-fi in bedrooms **Parking** 20 **Notes LB** No children 8yrs Closed Nov-Mar

CONNEL — MAP 10 NM93

★★★ 77% HOTEL

Falls of Lora

PA37 1PB

☎ 01631 710483 📠 01631 710694

e-mail: enquiries@fallsoflora.com

web: www.fallsoflora.com

Dir: *set back from A85 from Glasgow, 0.5m past Connel sign*

PETS: Bedrooms (4GF) **Charges** charge for damage **Public areas** except dining areas or lounge (on leads) **Grounds** accessible disp bin **Exercise area** 100mtrs **Facilities** washing facs cage storage vet info **On Request** fridge access torch towels

Personally run and welcoming, this long-established and thriving holiday hotel enjoys inspiring views over Loch Etive. The spacious ground floor takes in a comfortable, traditional lounge and a cocktail bar with over a hundred whiskies and an open log fire. Guests can eat in the popular, informal bistro, which is open all day. Bedrooms come in a variety of styles, ranging from the cosy standard rooms to high quality luxury rooms.

Rooms 30 en suite (4 fmly) (4 GF) S £47.50-£59.50; D £55-£139 (incl. bkfst)✳ **Facilities** Wi-fi available ch fac **Parking** 40 **Notes LB** Closed mid Dec & Jan

ERISKA — MAP 10 NM94

★★★★★ ❀❀❀ COUNTRY HOUSE HOTEL

Isle of Eriska

PRIDE OF BRITAIN HOTELS

Eriska, Ledaig PA37 1SD

☎ 01631 720371 📠 01631 720531

e-mail: office@eriska-hotel.co.uk

Dir: *Exit A85 at Connel, onto A828, follow for 4m, then follow hotel signs from N of Benderloch*

PETS: Bedrooms (2GF) **Charges** charge for damage **Grounds** accessible disp bin **Exercise area Facilities** food (pre-bookable) food bowl water bowl dog chews cage storage walks info vet info **On Request** fridge access torch towels **Resident Pets:** Torsten, Marti, Dibley & Glen (Labradors)

Situated on its own private island with delightful beaches and walking trails, this hotel offers a tranquil, personal setting for total relaxation. Spacious bedrooms are comfortable and boast some fine antique pieces. Local seafood, meats and game feature on the award-winning menu, as do vegetables and herbs grown in the hotel's kitchen garden. Leisure facilities include an indoor swimming pool, gym, spa treatment rooms and a small golf course.

Rooms 23 en suite (2 GF) S £155-£230; D £310-£420 (incl. bkfst)✳ **Facilities Spa** FTV supervised 6 Fishing Gym Putt green Wi-fi available Steam room Skeet shooting Nature trails Xmas **Parking** 40 **Notes LB** Closed Jan

GLENDARUEL — MAP 10 NR98

►►► **Glendaruel Caravan Park** *(NR005865)*

PA22 3AB

☎ 01369 820267 📠 01369 820367

e-mail: mail@glendaruelcaravanpark.com

web: www.glendaruelcaravanpark.com

Dir: *From A83 take A815 to Strachur, then 13m to site on A886. By ferry from Gourock to Dunoon then B836, then A886 for approx 4m N. (NB this route not recommended for towing vehicles - 1:5 uphill gradient on B836)*

PETS: Public areas except games room, shop, toilets & children's play area (on leads) disp bin **Exercise area** on site woodland walk **Facilities** on site shop food food bowl water bowl dog chews dog scoop/disp bags washing facs walks info vet info **Other** prior notice required **Resident Pets:** Black Labrador

Open Apr-Oct Last arrival 22.00hrs Last departure noon

A very pleasant, well-established site in the beautiful Victorian gardens of Glendaruel House. The level grass and hardstanding pitches are set in 23 acres of wooded parkland in a valley surrounded by mountains, with many rare specimen trees. The owners are hospitable and friendly. A 3-acre site with 25 touring pitches, 15 hardstandings and 33 statics.

KILCHRENAN — MAP 10 NN02

★★★ 86% ❀❀ COUNTRY HOUSE HOTEL

The Ardanaiseig

by Loch Awe PA35 1HE

☎ 01866 833333 📠 01866 833222

e-mail: ardanaiseig@clara.net

Dir: *turn S off A85 at Taynuilt onto B845 to Kilchrenan. Left in front of pub (road very narrow) signed 'Ardanaiseig Hotel' & 'No Through Road'. Continue for 3m.*

PETS: Bedrooms (5GF) unattended **Charges** £10 per stay **Grounds** accessible disp bin **Exercise area Facilities** pet sitting washing facs walks info vet info **On Request** fridge access torch towels **Resident Pets:** Patch (Jack Russell)

Set amid lovely gardens and breathtaking scenery beside the shore of Loch Awe, this peaceful country-house hotel was built in a Scottish baronial style in 1834. Many fine pieces of furniture are evident in the bedrooms and charming day rooms, which include a drawing room, a library bar, and an elegant dining room. Dinner provides the highlight of any visit with skilfully cooked dishes making excellent use of local, seasonal produce.

Rooms 18 en suite (4 fmly) (5 GF) S £61-£202; D £122-£404 (incl. bkfst) **Facilities** FTV Fishing Wi-fi available Boating Clay pigeon shooting Bikes for hire Xmas New Year **Parking** 20 **Notes** Closed 2 Jan-1 Feb

KILCHRENAN CONTINUED

★★★ 82% COUNTRY HOUSE HOTEL

Taychreggan

PA35 1HQ

☎ 01866 833211 & 833366 01866 833244

e-mail: info@taychregganhotel.co.uk

Dir: *W from Crianlarich on A85 to Taynuilt, S for 7m on B845 to Kilchrenan & Taychreggan*

PETS: Bedrooms Charges £10 per night charge for damage **Grounds** accessible disp bin **Exercise area Facilities** walks info vet info **On Request** torch towels

Surrounded by stunning Highland scenery this stylish and superbly presented hotel enjoys an idyllic setting, in 40 acres of grounds, on the shores of Loch Awe. Ground floor areas include a smart bar with adjacent Orangery and a choice of quiet lounges with deep, luxurious sofas. A well earned reputation has been achieved by the kitchen for the skilfully prepared dinners that showcase the local and seasonal Scottish larder.

Rooms 18 en suite **Facilities** FTV Fishing Wi-fi available **Parking** 40

LUSS — MAP 10 NS39

►►► Luss Camping & Caravanning Club Site *(NS360936)*

G83 8NT

☎ 01436 860658

web: www.thefriendlyclub.co.uk

Dir: *From Erskine bridge take A82 N towards Tarbet. (NB ignore 1st sign for Luss). After workshops take next right at Lodge of Loch Lomond & International Camping sign. Site 200yds*

PETS: Public areas except in buildings disp bin **Exercise area** on site **Facilities** walks info vet info **Other** prior notice required

Open 2 Apr-2 Nov Last arrival 21.00hrs Last departure noon

A lovely tenting site on the grassy western shore of Loch Lomond. The site has two well equipped toilet blocks, including a parent and child facility, and a good laundry. Club members' caravans and motorvans only permitted. A 12-acre site with 90 touring pitches, 30 hardstandings.

Notes Caravan pitches for members only, site gates closed 23.00hrs-07.00hrs

OBAN — MAP 10 NM83

★★★ 75% HOTEL

Oban Bay Hotel and Spa

CRERAR HOTELS

The Esplanade PA34 5AG

☎ 0870 950 6273 01631 564006

e-mail: obanbay@crerarhotels.com

web: www.crerarhotels.com

Dir: *Follow A85 into Oban. Straight at 1st rdbt & right at 2nd, hotel 200yds on right.*

PETS: Bedrooms (3GF) **Charges** £10 per stay charge for damage **Public areas** except meal times (on leads) **Exercise area Facilities** walks info vet info **On Request** fridge access torch

Situated on the esplanade, this hotel enjoys splendid views across the bay to nearby islands. Smart and comfortable lounges set the scene, along with the stylish bedrooms. There are also two very impressive suites.

Rooms 80 en suite (3 GF) **Facilities** Wi-fi in bedrooms Steam room Sauna **Services** Lift **Parking** 16 (charged)

★★ GUEST ACCOMMODATION

Lancaster

Corran Esplanade PA34 5AD

☎ 01631 562587 01631 562587

e-mail: john@lancasteroban.com

Dir: *On seafront next to Columba's Cathedral*

PETS: Bedrooms unattended **Public areas** except dining room **Exercise area** beach & woods adjacent **Facilities** cage storage walks info vet info **On Request** fridge access torch towels **Resident Pets:** Tara (Springer Spaniel), Yoshi (Shih Tzu), Salem (cat), ferrets, goldfish

There are lovely views over the bay towards the Isle of Mull from this welcoming, family-run establishment on the Esplanade. Public areas include a choice of lounges and bars.

Rooms 27 rms (24 en suite) (3 fmly) S £35-£40; D £74-£82* **Facilities** TVB tea/coffee Cen ht TVL Sauna Pool Table Jacuzzi, steam room **Parking** 20 **Notes** LB

PORT APPIN — MAP 14 NM94

★★★★ ◎◎◎ SMALL HOTEL

Airds

PA38 4DF

☎ 01631 730236 📠 01631 730535

e-mail: airds@airds-hotel.com

web: www.airds-hotel.com

Dir: *from A828 (Oban to Fort William road), turn at Appin signed Port Appin. Hotel 2.5m on left*

PETS: Bedrooms (2GF) unattended **Charges** £10 per night charge for damage **Grounds** accessible **Exercise area** surrounding area **Facilities** bedding walks info vet info **On Request** torch towels

The views are stunning from this small, luxury hotel on the shores of Loch Linnhe and where the staff are delightful and nothing is too much trouble. The well-equipped bedrooms provide style and luxury whilst many bathrooms are furnished in marble and have power showers. Expertly prepared dishes, utilising the finest of ingredients, are served in the elegant dining room. Comfortable lounges with deep sofas and roaring fires provide the ideal retreat for relaxation. A real get-away-from-it-all experience.

Rooms 11 en suite (3 fmly) (2 GF) S £181-£351; D £245-£415 (incl. bkfst & dinner)✱ **Facilities** FTV Putt green Wi-fi in bedrooms Xmas New Year **Parking** 20 **Notes** LB RS Nov-Jan

TIGHNABRUAICH — MAP 10 NR97

★★★ 88% ◎◎ SMALL HOTEL

An Lochan

Shore Rd PA21 2BE

☎ 01700 811239 📠 01700 811300

e-mail: info@anlochan.co.uk

web: www.anlochan.co.uk

Dir: *from Strachur on A886 right onto A8003 to Tighnabruaich. Hotel on right at bottom of hill*

PETS: Bedrooms Public areas except restaurant areas (on leads) **Grounds** accessible **Exercise area** 100yds **Facilities** pet sitting dog walking washing facs cage storage walks info vet info **On Request** fridge access torch towels

This outstanding family-run hotel provides high levels of personal care from the proprietors and their locally recruited staff. Set just yards from the loch shore, stunning views are guaranteed from many rooms, including the elegant Crustacean Restaurant, and the more informal Deck Restaurant. Seafood and game, sourced on the doorstep, feature strongly on the menus. Guest can expect to find Egyptian cotton sheets, fluffy towels and locally produced toiletries in the individually-styled, luxuriously appointed bedrooms.

Rooms 11 en suite S £125-£190; D £125-£190 (incl. bkfst)✱ **Facilities** Wi-fi available Sailing Fishing Windsurfing Riding New Year **Parking** 20 **Notes** LB Closed 4 days Xmas

CLACKMANNANSHIRE

DOLLAR — MAP 11 NS99

★★★ 73% SMALL HOTEL

Castle Campbell Hotel

11 Bridge St FK14 7DE

☎ 01259 742519 📠 01259 743742

e-mail: bookings@castle-campbell.co.uk

web: www.castle-campbell.co.uk

Dir: *on A91 (Stirling to St Andrews road), in centre of Dollar, by bridge overlooking Dollar Burn & Clock Tower*

PETS: Bedrooms Charges £5 per night charge for damage **Public areas** except restaurant **Exercise area Facilities** walks info vet info **Resident Pets:** Jasper & Prudence (Cocker Spaniels)

Set in the centre of a delightful country town, this hotel is popular with both local people and tourists. Accommodation ranges in size, though all rooms are thoughtfully equipped. Inviting public rooms feature a delightful lounge with real fire, a well-stocked whisky bar and a stylish restaurant.

Rooms 9 en suite (2 fmly) S £67.50; D £105 (incl. bkfst)✱ **Facilities** Wi-fi available Xmas New Year **Parking** 8 **Notes** LB

SCOTLAND

SCOTLAND

DUMFRIES & GALLOWAY

AUCHENCAIRN MAP 11 NX75

★★★ 85% HOTEL

Balcary Bay

DG7 1QZ

☎ 01556 640217 & 640311 📠 01556 640272

e-mail: reservations@balcary-bay-hotel.co.uk

web: www.balcary-bay-hotel.co.uk

Dir: *on A711 between Dalbeattie & Kirkcudbright, hotel 2m from village*

PETS: Bedrooms (3GF) unattended **Grounds** accessible disp bin **Exercise area** beach adjacent **Facilities** food bowl water bowl dog scoop/disp bags leads washing facs cage storage walks info vet info **On Request** fridge access torch towels

Resident Pets: Rusty (Irish Red Setter)

Taking its name from the bay on which it lies, this hotel has lawns running down to the shore. The larger bedrooms enjoy stunning views over the bay, whilst others overlook the gardens. Comfortable public areas invite relaxation. Imaginative dishes feature at dinner, accompanied by a good wine list.

Rooms 20 en suite (1 fmly) (3 GF) S £69; D £124-£154 (incl. bkfst) **Facilities** FTV **Parking** 50 **Notes LB** Closed 1st Sun Dec-1st Fri Feb

CASTLE DOUGLAS MAP 11 NX76

★★ 68% HOTEL

Imperial

35 King St DG7 1AA

☎ 01556 502086 📠 01556 503009

e-mail: david@thegolfhotel.co.uk

web: www.thegolfhotel.co.uk

Dir: *exit A75 at sign for Castle Douglas, hotel opposite library*

PETS: Bedrooms unattended **Public areas** except eating areas **Grounds** accessible disp bin **Exercise area Facilities** food bowl water bowl washing facs cage storage walks info vet info **On Request** fridge access torch towels

Situated in the main street, this former coaching inn, popular with golfers, offers guests well-equipped and cheerfully decorated bedrooms. There is a choice of bars and good-value meals are served either in the foyer bar or the upstairs dining room.

Rooms 12 en suite (1 fmly) S £47-£49; D £75-£78 (incl. bkfst)* **Facilities** STV **Parking** 29 **Notes LB** Closed 23-26 Dec & 1-3 Jan

CROCKETFORD MAP 11 NX87

►►►► **Park of Brandedleys** *(NX830725)*

DG2 8RG

☎ 01387 266700 📠 01556 690681

e-mail: brandedleys@holgates.com

web: www.holgates.com

Dir: *In village on A75, from Dumfries towards Stranraer site on left up minor road, entrance 200yds on right*

PETS: Public areas except in buildings (except assist dogs) **Stables** nearby (2km) (loose box) **Charges** £2 per night £14 per week disp bin **Exercise area** on site dog trail around park **Facilities** walks info vet info **Restrictions** no dangerous breeds (see page 7)

Open all year (rs Nov-Mar bar/restaurant open Fri-Sun afternoon) Last arrival 22.00hrs Last departure noon

A well-maintained site in an elevated position off the A75, with fine views of Auchenreoch Loch and beyond. This comfortable park offers a wide range of amenities, including a fine games room and a tastefully-designed bar with adjoining bistro. Well placed for enjoying walking, fishing, sailing and golf. A 24-acre site with 80 touring pitches, 40 hardstandings and 63 statics.

Notes Guidelines issued on arrival

ECCLEFECHAN MAP 11 NY17

►►►►► **Hoddom Castle Caravan Park**

(NY154729)

Hoddom DG11 1AS

☎ 01576 300251 📠 01576 300757

e-mail: hoddomcastle@aol.com

web: www.hoddomcastle.co.uk

Dir: *M74 junct 19, follow signs to site. From A75 W of Annan take B723 for 5m, follow signs to site*

PETS: Charges £1.50 per night disp bin **Exercise area** on site woodland walk **Facilities** on site shop food food bowl water bowl walks info vet info **Other** prior notice required

Open Etr or Apr-Oct (rs early season cafeteria closed) Last arrival 21.00hrs Last departure 14.00hrs

The peaceful, well-equipped park can be found on the banks of the River Annan, and offers a good mix of grassy and hard pitches, beautifully landscaped and blending into the surroundings. There are signed nature trails, maintained by the park's countryside ranger, a 9-hole golf course, trout and salmon fishing, and plenty of activity ideas for children. A 28-acre site with 200 touring pitches, 150 hardstandings and 54 statics.

GATEHOUSE OF FLEET MAP 11 NX55

►►► Mossyard Caravan & Camping Park

(NX546518)

Mossyard DG7 2ET

☎ 01557 840226 🖷 01557 840226

e-mail: enquiry@mossyard.co.uk

web: www.mossyard.co.uk

Dir: *0.75m off A75 on private tarmaced farm road, 4.5m W of Gatehouse of Fleet*

PETS: Stables nearby (1.5m) (loose box) disp bin **Exercise area** on site beach walks **Facilities** washing facs walks info vet info **Resident Pets:** Sophie (Black Labrador), Jay & Pip (working Collies), Archie & Alice (cats), sheep & cows

Open Etr/Apr-Oct Last departure noon

A grassy park with its own beach, located on a working farm, and offering an air of peace and tranquillity. Stunning sea and coastal views from touring pitches, and the tenting field is almost on the beach. A 6.5-acre site with 37 touring pitches and 32 statics.

GRETNA MAP 11 NY36

►►► Bruce's Cave Caravan & Camping Park *(NY266705)*

Cove Estate, Kirkpatrick Fleming DG11 3AT

☎ 01461 800285 & 07779 138694 🖷 01461 800269

e-mail: enquiries@brucescave.co.uk

web: www.brucescave.co.uk

Dir: *Exit A74(M) junct 21 for Kirkpatrick Fleming follow N through village, pass Station Inn, at Bruce's Court turn left. Over rail crossing to site entrance.*

PETS: Stables (loose box) disp bin **Public areas** except toilet block, shop & children's play area (on leads) **Exercise area** on site river walk **Facilities** on site shop food dog scoop/disp bags washing facs walks info vet info **Resident Pets:** Scamp, Cally, Bruce & Bruno (dogs), Silver & Buttercup (cats), Daisy (Shetland pony), Silver & Prince (horses), ducks

Open all year (rs Nov-Mar Shop closed, water restriction) Last arrival 23.00hrs Last departure 19.00hrs

The lovely wooded grounds of an old castle and mansion are the setting for this pleasant park. The mature woodland is a haven for wildlife, and there is a riverside walk to Robert the Bruce's Cave. A toilet block with en suite facilities is of special appeal to families. An 80-acre site with 75 touring pitches, 60 hardstandings and 35 statics.

GRETNA SERVICE AREA (A74(M)) MAP 11 NY36

BUDGET HOTEL

Days Inn Gretna Green

DAYS INN

Welcome Break Service Area DG16 5HQ

☎ 01461 337566 🖷 01461 337823

e-mail: gretna.hotel@welcomebreak.co.uk

web: www.welcomebreak.co.uk

Dir: *between junct 21/22 on M74 - accessible from both N'bound & S'bound carriageway*

PETS: Bedrooms (64GF) **Grounds** accessible on leads disp bin **Exercise area** 20yds **Facilities** walks info vet info **On Request** torch

This modern building offers accommodation in smart, spacious and well-equipped bedrooms, suitable for families and business travellers, and all with en suite bathrooms. Refreshments may be taken at the nearby family restaurant.

Rooms 64 en suite S £39-£59; D £45-£55✳

KIRKBEAN MAP 11 NX95

★★ ❀ COUNTRY HOUSE HOTEL

Cavens

DG2 8AA

☎ 01387 880234 🖷 01387 880467

e-mail: enquiries@cavens.com

web: www.cavens.com

Dir: *on entering Kirkbean on A710, hotel signed*

PETS: Bedrooms Charges £10 per stay **Grounds** accessible on leads **Exercise area Facilities** walks info vet info **Resident Pets:** Rosco (Border Terrier), Hamish (Labrador)

Set in parkland gardens, Cavens encapsulates all the virtues of an intimate country-house hotel. Quality is the keynote, and the proprietors spared no effort in completing a fine renovation of the house. Bedrooms are delightfully individual and very comfortably equipped, and a choice of lounges invites peaceful relaxation. A set dinner offers the best of local and home-made produce.

Rooms 6 en suite (1 GF) **Facilities** Shooting Fishing Horse riding **Parking** 12 **Notes** No children 12yrs

SCOTLAND

KIRKCUDBRIGHT MAP 11 NX65

★★★ 75% HOTEL

Best Western Selkirk Arms

Old High St DG6 4JG

☎ 01557 330402 📠 01557 331639

e-mail: reception@selkirkarmshotel.co.uk

web: www.selkirkarmshotel.co.uk

Dir: *On A71, 5m S of A75.*

PETS: Bedrooms (1GF) **Charges** £5 per night charge for damage **Public areas** except restaurant & bars (on leads) **Grounds** accessible on leads disp bin **Exercise area** 2 min walk **Facilities** water bowl dog chews leads dog grooming cage storage walks info vet info **On Request** fridge access torch

The Selkirk Arms is aptly named, as it was originally the hostelry where Robert Burns wrote the Selkirk Grace. It is now a smart and stylish hotel set in secluded gardens just off the town centre. Inviting public areas include the attractive Artistas restaurant, bistro, air conditioned lounge bar and the Burns lounge.

Rooms 14 en suite 3 annexe en suite (2 fmly) (1 GF) S £69-£75; D £70-£104 (incl. bkfst)✳ **Facilities** STV FTV Wi-fi in bedrooms New Year **Parking** 10 **Notes** LB Closed 24-26 Dec

★★ 67% HOTEL

Arden House Hotel

Tongland Rd DG6 4UU

☎ 01557 330544 📠 01557 330742

Dir: *off A57, 4m W of Castle Douglas onto A711. Follow Kirkcudbright, over Telford Bridge. Hotel 400mtrs on left*

PETS: Bedrooms unattended sign **Grounds** accessible disp bin **Exercise area** **Facilities** vet info

Set well back from the main road in extensive grounds on the northeast side of town, this spotlessly maintained hotel offers attractive bedrooms, a lounge bar and adjoining conservatory serving a range of popular dishes, which are also available in the dining room. It boasts an impressive function suite in its grounds.

Rooms 9 en suite (7 fmly) S £50; D £70 (incl. bkfst)✳ **Parking** 70 **Notes** No credit cards accepted

►►► Silvercraigs Caravan & Camping Site

(NX686508)

Silvercraigs Rd DG6 4BT

☎ 01557 330123 & 01556 503806 📠 01557 330123

e-mail: scottg2@dumgal.gov.uk

web: www.dumgal.gov.uk/caravanandcamping

Dir: *In Kirkcudbright off Silvercraigs Rd. Access via A711, follow signs to site*

PETS: Public areas (on leads) disp bin **Exercise area** woods adjacent **Facilities** vet info

Open Etr-Oct Last arrival 19.30hrs Last departure noon

A well-maintained municipal park in an elevated position with extensive views overlooking the picturesque, unspoilt town and harbour to the countryside beyond. Toilet facilities are of a very good standard, and the town centre is just a short stroll away. A 6-acre site with 50 touring pitches.

Notes 🚭

LOCHMABEN MAP 11 NY08

►► Kirk Loch Caravan & Camping Site

(NY082825)

DG11 1PZ

☎ 01556 503806 & 07746 123783 📠 01556 503806

e-mail: scottg2@dumgal.gov.uk

web: www.dumgal.gov.uk/caravanandcamping

Dir: *In Lochmaben enter via Kirkloch Brae*

PETS: Public areas (on leads) disp bin **Exercise area** footpath adjacent **Facilities** dog walking vet info **Other** pet supplies available within walking distance

Open Etr-Oct Last arrival 22.00hrs Last departure noon

A grassy lochside site with superb views and well-maintained facilities. Some hard pitches are available at this municipal park, which is adjacent to a golf club, and close to three lochs. A 1.5-acre site with 30 touring pitches, 14 hardstandings.

Notes 🚭

SCOTLAND

LOCKERBIE MAP 11 NY18

★★★★ 75% HOTEL

Dryfesdale Country House

Dryfebridge DG11 2SF

☎ 01576 202427 01576 204187

e-mail: reception@dryfesdalehotel.co.uk

web: www.dryfesdalehotel.co.uk

Dir: *from M74 junct 17 take 'Lockerbie North', 3rd left at 1st rdbt, 1st exit left at 2nd rdbt, hotel 200yds on left*

PETS: Bedrooms (19GF) unattended **Charges** £5 per night **Grounds** accessible disp bin **Exercise area Facilities** food (pre-bookable) food bowl bedding dog chews feeding mat dog scoop/disp bags cage storage walks info vet info **On Request** fridge access torch towels **Other** pets are welcome with prior notice only; doggy welcome pack

Conveniently situated for the M74, yet discreetly screened from it, this friendly hotel provides attentive service. Bedrooms, some with access to patio areas, vary in size and style; all offer good levels of comfort and are well equipped. Creative, good value dinners make use of local produce and are served in the airy restaurant that overlooks the manicured gardens and rolling countryside.

Rooms 28 en suite (5 fmly) (10 GF) S £75-£95; D £89-£140 (incl. bkfst)✳ **Facilities** STV FTV Putt green Wi-fi available Clay pigeon shooting Fishing Xmas New Year **Parking** 60 **Notes** LB

★★ 76% HOTEL

Kings Arms Hotel

High St DG11 2JL

☎ 01576 202410 01576 202410

e-mail: reception@kingsarmshotel.co.uk

web: www.kingsarmshotel.co.uk

Dir: *A74(M), 0.5m into town centre, hotel opposite town hall*

PETS: Bedrooms unattended **Public areas** except restaurant & 1 bar (on leads) **Exercise area** 1 min walk **Facilities** food bowl water bowl washing facs cage storage walks info vet info **On Request** fridge access torch towels **Resident Pets:** Bailey (Yellow Labrador)

Dating from the 17th century this former inn lies in the town centre. Now a family-run hotel, it provides attractive well-equipped bedrooms now with Wi-fi access. At lunch a menu ranging from snacks to full meals is served in both the two cosy bars and the restaurant at dinner.

Rooms 13 en suite (2 fmly) S £47.50; D £80 (incl. bkfst) **Facilities** FTV Wi-fi available Xmas New Year **Parking** 8

★★ 68% HOTEL

Ravenshill House

12 Dumfries Rd DG11 2EF

☎ 01576 202882 01576 202882

e-mail: aaenquiries@ravenshillhotellockerbie.co.uk

web: www.ravenshillhotellockerbie.co.uk

Dir: *from A74(M) Lockerbie junct onto A709. Hotel 0.5m on right*

PETS: Bedrooms Grounds accessible on leads disp bin **Exercise area** 100yds **Facilities** water bowl walks info vet info **On Request** fridge access

Set in spacious gardens on the fringe of the town, this friendly, family-run hotel offers cheerful service and good value, home-cooked meals. Bedrooms are generally spacious and comfortably equipped, including an ideal two-room family unit.

Rooms 8 en suite (2 fmly) S £50-£65; D £70-£80 (incl. bkfst)✳ **Parking** 35 **Notes** LB Closed 1-3 Jan

MOFFAT MAP 11 NT00

U

Best Western Moffat House

High St DG10 9HL

☎ 01683 220039 01683 221288

e-mail: reception@moffathouse.co.uk

Dir: *M74 junct 15 into town centre.*

PETS: Bedrooms (4GF) unattended **Stables** nearby **Charges** £5 per night charge for damage **Grounds** accessible disp bin **Exercise area Facilities** food bowl water bowl cage storage walks info vet info **On Request** fridge access torch towels

At the time of going to press the rating for this establishment was not confirmed. This may be due to a change of ownership or because it has only recently joined the AA rating scheme. For further details please see the AA website: www.theAA.com

Rooms 21 en suite (4 fmly) (4 GF) S £59-£79; D £79-£99 (incl. bkfst)✳ **Facilities** Wi-fi in bedrooms Xmas New Year **Parking** 30 **Notes** LB

MOFFAT CONTINUED

★★ GUEST ACCOMMODATION

Barnhill Springs Country

DG10 9QS

☎ 01683 220580

Dir: *A74(M) junct 15, A701 towards Moffat, Barnhill Rd 50yds on right*

PETS: Bedrooms unattended **Public areas** except dining room **Grounds** accessible disp bin **Exercise area** on site 1.5 acre grounds **Facilities** food bowl water bowl dog chews dog scoop/disp bags leads washing facs cage storage walks info vet info **On Request** fridge access torch towels **Resident Pets:** Kim (Collie cross)

This former farmhouse has a quiet rural location south of the town and within easy reach of the M74. Bedrooms are well proportioned; one having a bathroom en suite. There is a comfortable lounge and separate dining room.

Rooms 5 rms (1 en suite) (2 pri facs) (1 fmly) (1 GF) S £30; D £60 **Facilities** tea/coffee Cen ht TVL Dinner Last d 9am **Parking** 10 **Notes** ⊜

►►► Moffat Camping & Caravanning Club Site *(NT085050)*

Hammerlands Farm DG10 9QL

☎ 01683 220436

web: www.thefriendlyclub.co.uk

Dir: *From A74 follow Moffat sign. After 1m turn right by Bank of Scotland, right again in 200yds. Sign for site on right*

PETS: Public areas except in buildings disp bin **Exercise area** on site dog walk **Facilities** vet info

Open 2 Apr-2 Nov Last arrival 21.00hrs Last departure noon

Well-maintained level grass touring site, with extensive views of the surrounding hilly countryside from many parts of the park. This busy stopover site is always well maintained, and looks bright and cheerful thanks to meticulous wardens. A 10-acre site with 180 touring pitches, 42 hardstandings.

Notes Site gates closed 23.00hrs-07.00hrs

PARTON MAP 11 NX67

►►► Loch Ken Holiday Park *(NX687702)*

DG7 3NE

☎ 01644 470282

e-mail: penny@lochkenholidaypark.co.uk

web: www.lochkenholidaypark.co.uk

Dir: *On A713, N of Parton*

PETS: Public areas except shop **Charges** £2 per night disp bin **Exercise area** on site field provided **Facilities** on site shop food food bowl water bowl dog scoop/disp bags leads walks info vet info **Other** prior notice required **Resident Pets:** 12 ducks

Open Mar-mid Nov (rs Mar/Apr (ex Etr) & late Sep-Nov restricted shop hours) Last departure noon

A busy and popular park with a natural emphasis on water activities, set on the eastern shores of Loch Ken, with superb views. Family owned and run, it is in a peaceful and beautiful spot opposite the RSPB reserve, with direct access to the loch for boat launching. The park offers a variety of water sports, as well as farm visits and nature trails. A 7-acre site with 52 touring pitches, 4 hardstandings and 35 statics.

PORTPATRICK — MAP 10 NW95

★★★ HOTEL

Knockinaam Lodge

DG9 9AD

☎ 01776 810471 01776 810435

e-mail: reservations@knockinaamlodge.com

web: www.knockinaamlodge.com

Dir: *from A77 or A75 follow signs to Portpatrick. Through Lochans. After 2m left at signs for hotel*

PETS: Bedrooms Charges Public areas assist dogs only **Exercise area Other** dogs allowed in certain bedrooms only; owners to bring dog bedding

Any tour of Dumfries & Galloway would not be complete without a night or two at this haven of tranquillity and relaxation. Knockinaam Lodge is an extended Victorian house, set in an idyllic cove with its own pebble beach and sheltered by majestic cliffs and woodlands. A warm welcome is assured from the proprietors and their committed team, and much emphasis is placed on providing a sophisticated but intimate home-from-home experience. The cooking is a real treat and showcases superb local produce. Dinner is a set meal, but choices can be discussed in advance.

Rooms 10 en suite (1 fmly) S £165-£300; D £270-£400 (incl. bkfst & dinner)✳ **Facilities** FTV Fishing Wi-fi in bedrooms Shooting Walking Sea fishing Clay pigeon shooting ch fac Xmas New Year **Parking** 20 **Notes** LB

★★★ 80% HOTEL

Fernhill

Heugh Rd DG9 8TD

☎ 01776 810220 01776 810596

e-mail: info@fernhillhotel.co.uk

web: www.fernhillhotel.co.uk

Dir: *from Stranraer A77 to Portpatrick, 100yds past Portpatrick village sign, turn right before war memorial. Hotel 1st on left*

PETS: Bedrooms Exercise area wooded area **Facilities** cage storage walks info vet info **On Request** towels

Set high above the village, this hotel looks out over the harbour and Irish Sea; many of the bedrooms take advantage of the views. A modern wing offers particularly spacious and well-appointed rooms; some have balconies. The smart conservatory restaurant offers interesting, freshly prepared dishes.

Rooms 27 en suite 9 annexe en suite (3 fmly) (8 GF) S £58-£83; D £110-£114 (incl. bkfst & dinner)✳ **Facilities** FTV Wi-fi available Leisure facilities available at sister hotel in Stranraer Xmas New Year **Parking** 45 **Notes** LB Closed mid Jan-mid Feb

PORT WILLIAM — MAP 10 NX34

►►► **Kings Green Caravan Site** *(NX340430)*

South St DG8 9SG

☎ 01988 700489

web: www.portwilliam.com

Dir: *Direct access from A747 at junct with B7085, towards Whithorn*

PETS: Public areas except toilet & shower block **Exercise area** beach **Facilities** walks info vet info **Other** pet supplies available at shop, 500yds

Open Etr-Oct Last arrival 20.00hrs Last departure noon

Set beside the unspoilt village with all its amenities and the attractive harbour, this level grassy park is community owned and run. Approached via the coast road, the park has views reaching as far as the Isle of Man. A 3-acre site with 30 touring pitches.

Notes No golf or fireworks on site

STRANRAER — MAP 10 NX06

★★★ 77% HOTEL

Corsewall Lighthouse Hotel

Corsewall Point, Kirkcolm DG9 0QG

☎ 01776 853220 01776 854231

e-mail: lighthousehotel@btinternet.com

web: www.lighthousehotel.co.uk

Dir: *A718 from Stranraer to Kirkcolm (approx 8m). Follow hotel signs for 4m*

PETS: Charges dog £10 per night **Public areas** except restaurant **Grounds** accessible disp bin **Exercise area** adjacent **Facilities** food walks info vet info **On Request** torch towels **Other** dogs allowed in 2 annexe suites only

Looking for something completely different? A unique hotel converted from buildings that adjoin a listed 19th-century lighthouse set on a rocky coastline. Bedrooms come in a variety of sizes, some reached by a spiral staircase, and like the public areas, are cosy and atmospheric. Cottage suites in the grounds offer greater space.

Rooms 6 en suite 4 annexe en suite (4 fmly) (2 GF) S £130-£230; D £150-£250 (incl. bkfst & dinner)✳ **Facilities** FTV Xmas New Year **Parking** 20 **Notes** LB

SCOTLAND

STRANRAER CONTINUED

►►►► Aird Donald Caravan Park *(NX075605)*

London Rd DG9 8RN

☎ 01776 702025

e-mail: enquiries@aird-donald.co.uk

web: www.aird-donald.co.uk

Dir: *Turn left off A75 on entering Stranraer, (signed). Opposite school, site 300yds*

PETS: disp bin **Exercise area** on site wooded area **Facilities** vet info

Open all year Last departure 16.00hrs

A spacious touring site, mainly grass but with tarmac hardstanding area, with pitches large enough to accommodate a car and caravan overnight without unhitching. On the fringe of town screened by mature shrubs and trees. Ideal stopover en route to Northern Irish ferry ports. A 12-acre site with 100 touring pitches, 30 hardstandings.

Notes Tents Apr-Sep

WIGTOWN MAP 10 NX45

►►► Drumroamin Farm Camping & Touring Site *(NX445507)*

1 South Balfern DG8 9DB

☎ 01988 840613 & 07752 471456

e-mail: enquiry@drumroamin.co.uk

web: www.drumroamin.co.uk

Dir: *A75 towards Newton Stewart, turn onto A714 for Wigtown. Left on B7005 through Bladnock, A746 through Kirkinner. Take B7004 Garlieston, 2nd left opposite Kilsture Forest, site 0.75m at end of lane*

PETS: Public areas except toilet block & play room disp bin **Exercise area** on site field perimiter walk **Facilities** washing facs walks info vet info **Resident Pets:** Maggie (Chocolate Labrador)

Open all year Last arrival 21.00hrs Last departure noon

An open, spacious park in a quiet spot a mile from the main road, and close to Wigtown Bay. A superb toilet block offers spacious showers, and there's a lounge/games room and plenty of room for children to play. A 5-acre site with 48 touring pitches and 3 statics.

Notes No fires

EAST LOTHIAN

DUNBAR MAP 12 NT67

►►►►► Thurston Manor Holiday Home Park *(NT712745)*

Innerwick EH42 1SA

☎ 01368 840643 📠 01368 840261

e-mail: mail@thurstonmanor.co.uk

web: www.thurstonmanor.co.uk

Dir: *4m S of Dunbar, signed off A1*

PETS: Public areas except buildings & children's play area disp bin **Exercise area Facilities** on site shop food food bowl water bowl dog chews cat treats litter tray dog scoop/disp bags leads vet info **Other** prior notice required; max 2 dogs per unit

Open Mar-8 Jan Last arrival 23.00hrs Last departure noon

A pleasant park set in 250 acres of unspoilt countryside. The touring and static areas of this large park are in separate areas. The main touring area occupies an open, level position, and the toilet facilities are modern and exceptionally well maintained. The park boasts a well-stocked fishing loch, a heated indoor swimming pool, steam room, sauna, jacuzzi, mini-gym and fitness room and seasonal entertainment. A 250-acre site with 100 touring pitches, 45 hardstandings and 420 statics.

►►►► Dunbar Camping & Caravanning Club Site *(NT700780)*

Oxwellmains EH42 1WG

web: www.thefriendlyclub.co.uk

PETS: Public areas except in buildings **Exercise area Facilities** washing facs walks info vet info

Open Mar-Nov Last arrival 20.00hrs Last departure noon

A brand new clifftop site with fine views over Dunbar towards Bass Rock, on a coastline noted for its natural and geological history. The site is well placed for visits to Edinburgh and the beautiful Borders, as well as the north Northumberland countryside. 90 touring pitches.

Notes Site gates closed between 23.00hrs-07.00hrs

►►► Belhaven Bay Caravan & Camping Park *(NT661781)*

Belhaven Bay EH42 1TS

☎ 01368 865956 📠 01368 865022

e-mail: belhaven@meadowhead.co.uk

web: www.meadowhead.co.uk

Dir: *A1087 towards Dunbar. Site (1m) in John Muir Park*

PETS: Stables (loose box) **Public areas** except play area (on leads) **Charges** £1.50 per night disp bin **Exercise area** on site lakeside grass area **Facilities** food bowl water bowl washing facs walks info vet info **Other** prior notice required **Restrictions** no dangerous breeds (see page 7)

Open Mar-30 Oct Last arrival 20.00hrs Last departure noon

Small, well-maintained park in a sheltered location and within walking distance of the beach. This is an excellent spot for seabird watching, and there is a good rail connection with Edinburgh from Dunbar. A 40-acre site with 52 touring pitches, 11 hardstandings and 64 statics.

MUSSELBURGH MAP 11 NT37

►►►► Drum Mohr Caravan Park *(NT373734)*

Levenhall EH21 8JS

☎ 0131 665 6867 📠 0131 653 6859

e-mail: bookings@drummohr.org

web: www.drummohr.org

Dir: *Leave A1 at junct with A199 towards Musselburgh, at rdbt turn right onto B1361 signed Prestonpans, take 1st left & site 400yds*

PETS: Stables nearby (1km) **Public areas** except children's play area **Charges** £1 per night disp bin **Exercise area** on site perimeter walk **Facilities** on site shop food vet info **Other** max 2 dogs per pitch

Open Mar-Oct Last arrival 20.00hrs Last departure noon

This attractive park is sheltered by mature trees on all sides, and carefully landscaped within. The park is divided into separate areas by mature hedging and planting of trees and ornamental shrubs. Pitches are generous in size, and there are a number of fully serviced pitches plus first-class amenities. A 9-acre site with 120 touring pitches, 50 hardstandings and 12 statics.

CITY OF EDINBURGH

EDINBURGH MAP 11 NT27

★★★★ 75% HOTEL
Novotel Edinburgh Centre

Lauriston Place, Lady Lawson St EH3 9DE

☎ 0131 656 3500 📠 0131 656 3510

e-mail: H3271@accor.com

web: www.novotel.com

Dir: *from Edinburgh Castle right onto George IV Bridge from Royal Mile. Follow to junct, then right onto Lauriston Place. Hotel 700mtrs on right*

PETS: Bedrooms unattended **Charges** £10 per night charge for damage **Public areas** in lobby area only **Exercise area Facilities** walks info vet info

One of the new generations of Novotels, this modern hotel is located in the centre of the city, close to Edinburgh Castle. Smart and stylish public areas include a cosmopolitan bar, brasserie-style restaurant and indoor leisure facilities. The air-conditioned bedrooms feature a comprehensive range of extras and bathrooms with baths and separate shower cabinets.

Rooms 180 en suite (146 fmly) **Facilities** STV Gym Wi-fi available **Services** Lift air con **Parking** 15

★★★ 81% HOTEL
Dalhousie Castle and Aqueous Spa

Bonnyrigg EH19 3JB

☎ 01875 820153 📠 01875 821936

e-mail: info@dalhousiecastle.co.uk

web: www.vonessenhotels.co.uk

Dir: *A7 S from Edinburgh through Lasswade/Newtongrange, right at Shell Garage (B704), hotel 0.5m from junct*

PETS: Bedrooms Stables nearby (2m) **Charges** charge for damage **Grounds** accessible on leads disp bin **Exercise area Facilities** cage storage walks info vet info **On Request** fridge access torch

A popular wedding venue, this imposing medieval castle sits amid lawns and parkland and even has a falconry. Bedrooms offer a mix of styles and sizes, including richly decorated themed rooms named after various historical figures. The Dungeon restaurant provides an atmospheric setting for dinner, and the less formal Orangery serves food all day. The spa offers many relaxing and therapeutic treatments and hydro facilities.

Rooms 29 en suite 7 annexe en suite (3 fmly) S £110-£230; D £135-£365 (incl. bkfst)✳ **Facilities Spa** Fishing Wi-fi in bedrooms Falconry Clay pigeon shooting Archery Laserday Xmas New Year **Parking** 110 **Notes LB**

★★★ 79% HOTEL
Best Western Kings Manor

100 Milton Rd East EH15 2NP

☎ 0131 669 0444 & 468 8003 📠 0131 669 6650

e-mail: reservations@kingsmanor.com

web: www.kingsmanor.com

Dir: *A720 E to Old Craighall junct, left into city, right att A1/A199 junct, hotel 400mtrs on right*

PETS: Bedrooms (13GF) **Public areas** except dining areas (on leads) **Grounds** accessible on leads **Exercise area** on site **Facilities** cage storage walks info vet info **On Request** fridge access torch **Other** Guide Dogs for the Blind Association use this hotel as a residential training centre

Lying on the eastern side of the city and convenient for the by-pass, this hotel is popular with business guests, tour groups and for conferences. It boasts a fine leisure complex and a bright modern bistro, which complements the quality, creative cooking in the main restaurant.

Rooms 95 en suite (8 fmly) (13 GF) S £55-£109; D £65-£165✳ **Facilities** STV FTV Gym Wi-fi in bedrooms Health & beauty salon Steam room Xmas New Year **Services** Lift **Parking** 120 **Notes LB**

EDINBURGH CONTINUED

★★★ 75% HOTEL

Quality Hotel Edinburgh Airport

Ingliston EH28 8AU

☎ 0131 333 4331 🖹 0131 333 4124

e-mail: info@qualityhoteledinburgh.com

Dir: *from M8, M9 & Forth Road Bridge follow signs for airport*

PETS: Bedrooms (35GF) unattended **Charges** £20 per night charge for damage **Exercise area**

Just 20 minutes from the city centre, this modern hotel is convenient for Edinburgh International Airport, which is only two minutes away by courtesy minibus. The spacious executive bedrooms are the pick of the accommodation, and there is a bright restaurant offering a range of contemporary dishes.

Rooms 95 en suite (15 fmly) (35 GF) S £75-£225; D £75-£225 **Facilities** FTV Wi-fi in bedrooms **Services** Lift **Parking** 100 **Notes** LB

★★★ GUEST HOUSE

Arden Guest House

126 Old Dalkeith Rd EH16 4SD

☎ 0131 664 3985 🖹 0131 621 0866

e-mail: ardenedinburgh@aol.com

Dir: *2m SE of city centre nr Craigmillar Castle. On A7 200yds W of hospital*

PETS: Bedrooms (6GF) unattended **Public areas Grounds** accessible disp bin **Exercise area** 0.25m **Facilities** food (pre-bookable) food bowl water bowl bedding dog chews dog scoop/disp bags leads pet sitting dog walking washing facs cage storage walks info vet info **On Request** fridge access torch towels

Colourful flowering baskets adorn the front of this welcoming, personally-run guest house situated on the south side of the city, convenient for leisure and business travellers. The modern bedrooms offer good overall freedom of space. Traditional Scottish breakfasts are served at individual tables in the conservatory dining room. Off-road parking is a bonus.

Rooms 11 en suite (3 fmly) (6 GF) S £35-£90; D £50-£110* **Facilities** STV TVB tea/coffee Cen ht Wi-fi available Golf **Parking** 12 **Notes** LB

★★★ GUEST HOUSE

Garfield Guest House

264 Ferry Rd EH5 3AN

☎ 0131 552 2369

e-mail: enquiries@garfieldguesthouse.co.uk

PETS: Bedrooms Exercise area 50mtrs

Friendly hospitality and good value, no-frills accommodation offering modern comfortable bedrooms. Well situated within easy striking distance of the centre of Edinburgh and well serviced by a regular bus service.

Rooms 7 rms (6 en suite) (1 pri facs) (1 GF) **Facilities** TVB tea/coffee Cen ht

FIFE

ANSTRUTHER MAP 12 NO50

★★★★ GUEST HOUSE

The Spindrift

Pittenweem Rd KY10 3DT

☎ 01333 310573 🖹 01333 310573

e-mail: info@thespindrift.co.uk

web: www.thespindrift.co.uk

Dir: *Enter town from W on A917, 1st building on left*

PETS: Bedrooms Exercise area 2 mins **Facilities** water bowl bedding vet info **On Request** towels

This immaculate Victorian villa stands on the western edge of the village. The attractive bedrooms offer a wide range of extra touches; the Captain's Room, a replica of a wood-panelled cabin, is a particular feature. The inviting lounge has an honesty bar, while imaginative breakfasts, and enjoyable home-cooked meals by arrangement, are served in the cheerful dining room.

Rooms 8 rms (7 en suite) (1 pri facs) (2 fmly) S £40-£48; D £60-£76 **Facilities** FTV TVB tea/coffee Direct dial from bedrooms Licensed Cen ht TVL Dinner Last d noon Wi-fi available **Parking** 12 **Notes** LB No children 10yrs No coaches Closed Xmas-late Jan

DUNFERMLINE MAP 11 NT08

★★★ 75% HOTEL

Pitbauchlie House

Aberdour Rd KY11 4PB

☎ 01383 722282 📠 01383 620738

e-mail: info@pitbauchlie.com

web: www.pitbauchlie.com

Dir: *M90 junct 2, onto A823, then B916. Hotel 0.5m on right*

PETS: Bedrooms (19GF) unattended **Grounds** accessible **Exercise area** on site 3-acre wooded grounds **Facilities** walks info vet info **On Request** fridge access torch towels

Situated in three acres of wooded grounds this hotel is just a mile south of the town and has a striking modern interior. The bedrooms are well equipped, and the deluxe rooms now have 32-inch LDC satellite TVs and CD micro systems; there is one bedroom designed for less able guests. The eating options include Harvey's Conservatory bistro and Restaurant 47 with Scottish and French influenced cuisine.

Rooms 50 en suite (3 fmly) (19 GF) S £62-£102; D £110-£120 (incl. bkfst)✳ **Facilities** STV Gym Wi-fi in bedrooms **Parking** 80 **Notes** LB

LADYBANK MAP 11 NO30

★★★ 74% HOTEL

Fernie Castle

Letham KY15 7RU

☎ 01337 810381 📠 01337 810422

e-mail: mail@ferniecastle.demon.co.uk

Dir: *M90 junct 8 take A91 E (Tay Bridge/St Andrews) to Melville Lodges rdbt. Left onto A92 signed Tay Bridge. Hotel 1.2m on right*

PETS: Bedrooms unattended sign **Stables** nearby (3m) **Charges** charge for damage **Public areas** (on leads) **Grounds** accessible on leads disp bin **Exercise area** 50yds **Facilities** food bowl water bowl dog chews cat treats leads washing facs cage storage walks info vet info **On Request** fridge access torch towels **Other** food by prior arrangement **Resident Pets:** Cinderella (Great Dane), Buttons & Minnie (Chihuahuas), Apollo (Dalmatian), Paco (Chinchilla), Heather (Highland cow) & Hamish (Highland bull)

A historic, turreted castle set in 17 acres of wooded grounds in the heart of Fife, that is an extremely popular venue for weddings.

Bedrooms range from King and Queen rooms, to the more standard-sized Squire and Lady rooms. The elegant Auld Alliance Restaurant presents a formal setting for dining, but guests can also eat in the bar which has impressive vaulted stone walls and ceiling.

Rooms 20 en suite (2 fmly) **Facilities**  Wi-fi available **Parking** 80

LUNDIN LINKS MAP 12 NO40

►►► Woodland Gardens Caravan & Camping Site *(NO418031)*

Blindwell Rd KY8 5QG

☎ 01333 360319

e-mail: enquiries@woodland-gardens.co.uk

web: www.woodland-gardens.co.uk

Dir: *Off A915 (coast road) at Largo. At E end of Lundin Links, turn N off A915, 0.5m signed*

PETS: Charges £5 per week **Public areas** (on leads) disp bin **Exercise area** 100yds **Facilities** dog scoop/disp bags walks info vet info **Other** prior notice required; 1 dog per unit **Restrictions** no dangerous breeds (see page 7) **Resident Pets:** Bramble (Golden Retriever)

Open Apr-Oct Last arrival 21.00hrs Last departure noon

A secluded and sheltered 'little jewel' of a site in a small orchard under the hill called Largo Law. This very attractive site is family owned and run to an immaculate standard, and pitches are grouped in twos and threes by low hedging and gorse. A 1-acre site with 20 touring pitches, 3 hardstandings and 5 statics.

Notes 

ST ANDREWS MAP 12 NO51

U

St Andrews Golf

40 The Scores KY16 9AS

☎ 01334 472611 📠 01334 472188

e-mail: reception@standrews-golf.co.uk

web: www.standrews-golf.co.uk

Dir: *follow 'Golf Course' signs into Golf Place, 200yds turn right into The Scores*

PETS: Bedrooms Charges £5 per night charge for damage **Public areas** assist dogs only (on leads) **Exercise area**

At the time of going to press the rating for this establishment was not confirmed. This may be due to a change of ownership or because it has only recently joined the AA rating scheme. For further details please see the AA website: www.theAA.com

Rooms 22 en suite **Facilities** Wi-fi in bedrooms **Services** Lift **Parking** 6 **Notes** Closed 26-28 Dec

SCOTLAND

ST ANDREWS CONTINUED

★★★★ INN

The Inn at Lathones

Largoward KY9 1JE

☎ 01334 840494 01334 840694

e-mail: lathones@theinn.co.uk

web: www.theinn.co.uk

Dir: *5m S of St Andrews on A915, 0.5m before village of Largoward on left just after hidden dip*

PETS: Bedrooms (11GF) unattended **Charges** £10 per stay charge for damage **Grounds** accessible on leads **Exercise area Facilities** walks info vet info **On Request** fridge access torch

This lovely country inn, parts of which are 400 years old, is full of character and individuality. The friendly staff help to create a relaxed atmosphere. Smart contemporary bedrooms are in two separate wings. The colourful, cosy restaurant is the main focus, the menu offering modern interpretations of Scottish and European dishes.

Rooms 13 annexe en suite (1 fmly) (11 GF) **Facilities** STV TVB tea/coffee Direct dial from bedrooms Cen ht TVL Dinner Last d 9.30pm Wi-fi available **Parking** 35 **Notes** Closed 26 Dec & 3-16 Jan RS 24 Dec

CITY OF GLASGOW

GLASGOW — MAP 11 NS56

★★★ 83% HOTEL

Malmaison Glasgow

278 West George St G2 4LL

☎ 0141 572 1000 0141 572 1002

e-mail: glasgow@malmaison.com

web: www.malmaison.com

Dir: *from S & E - M8 junct 18 (Charing Cross), from W & N - M8 city centre*

PETS: Bedrooms (19GF) unattended **Charges** £10 per night charge for damage **Public areas** except food service areas (on leads) **Exercise area** 50yds **Facilities** food (pre-bookable) food bowl water bowl bedding **On Request** fridge access torch towels **Other** dog walking available if sufficient notice given

Built around a former church in the historic Charing Cross area, this hotel is a smart, contemporary establishment offering impressive levels of service and hospitality. Bedrooms are spacious and feature a host of modern facilities, such as CD players and mini bars. Dining is a treat here, with French brasserie-style cuisine, backed up by an excellent wine list, served in the original crypt.

Rooms 72 en suite (4 fmly) (19 GF) **Facilities** STV Gym Wi-fi available Cardiovascular equipment **Services** Lift

★★★ GUEST HOUSE

Botanic Guest House

1 Alfred Ter, Great Western Rd G12 8RF

☎ 0141 337 7007 0141 337 7070

e-mail: info@botanichotel.co.uk

Dir: *15 mins by car from Glasgow airport and 10 mins from city centre train station.*

PETS: Bedrooms Charges £15 per night **Public areas Exercise area Facilities** walks info

The Botanic is located just off the Great Western Road alongside other guest accommodation and residential properties only two miles from the heart of the city centre. Comfortable bedrooms and well-presented bathrooms provide good value for money. A generous breakfast makes a good start to the day.

Rooms 16 rms (13 en suite) (5 fmly) (3 GF) S £20-£50; D £40-£70* **Facilities** TVB tea/coffee Direct dial from bedrooms **Notes** LB No coaches

★★★ GUEST HOUSE

Kelvin

15 Buckingham Ter, Great Western Rd, Hillhead G12 8EB

☎ 0141 339 7143 📠 0141 339 5215

e-mail: enquiries@kelvinhotel.com

web: www.kelvinhotel.com

Dir: *M8 junct 17, A82 Kelvinside/Dumbarton, 1m on right before Botanic Gardens*

PETS: Bedrooms (2GF) **Charges** charge for damage **Grounds** accessible disp bin **Exercise area Facilities** food bowl water bowl walks info vet info **On Request** fridge access torch

Two substantial Victorian terrace houses on the west side of the city have been combined to create this friendly establishment close to the Botanical Gardens. The attractive bedrooms are comfortably proportioned and well equipped. The dining room on the first floor is the setting for hearty traditional breakfasts served at individual tables.

Rooms 21 rms (9 en suite) (4 fmly) (2 GF) S £28-£45; D £48-£62✳ **Facilities** FTV TVB tea/coffee Cen ht **Parking** 5

HIGHLAND

BOAT OF GARTEN — MAP 14 NH91

★★★ 81% HOTEL

Boat

PH24 3BH

☎ 01479 831258 & 831696 📠 01479 831414

e-mail: info@boathotel.co.uk

Dir: *off A9 N of Aviemore onto A95, follow signs to Boat of Garten*

PETS: Bedrooms unattended **Charges** £5 per night **Public areas** except restaurant (on leads) **Grounds** accessible on leads **Exercise area Facilities** walks info vet info **Other** dogs accommodated in certain rooms only

This well established, refurbished hotel is situated in the heart of the pretty village of Boat of Garten. The public areas include a choice of comfortable lounges and a small public bar, and the restaurant has a well deserved reputation for fine dining; in addition the bistro serves meals until late. Individually styled bedrooms are well equipped and have a host of thoughtful extras.

Rooms 30 en suite (2 fmly) S £50-£110; D £60-£160 (incl. bkfst)✳ **Facilities** Wi-fi available Xmas New Year **Parking** 36 **Notes** LB

CARRBRIDGE — MAP 14 NH92

★★★ 74% SMALL HOTEL

Dalrachney Lodge

PH23 3AT

☎ 01479 841252 📠 01479 841383

e-mail: dalrachney@aol.com

web: www.dalrachney.co.uk

Dir: *follow Carrbridge signs off A9. In village on A938*

PETS: Bedrooms Charges £5 per night £10 per week charge for damage **Grounds** accessible disp bin **Exercise area** on site **Facilities** food bowl water bowl washing facs cage storage walks info vet info **On Request** fridge access torch towels

A traditional Highland lodge, Dalrachney lies in grounds by the River Dulnain on the edge of the village. Spotlessly maintained public areas include a comfortable and relaxing sitting room and a cosy well-stocked bar, which has a popular menu providing an alternative to the dining room. Bedrooms are generally spacious and furnished in period style.

Rooms 11 en suite (3 fmly) S £80-£120; D £80-£160 (incl. bkfst) **Facilities** Fishing Wi-fi in bedrooms Xmas New Year **Parking** 40 **Notes** LB

★★★ BED & BREAKFAST

Pines Country House

Duthil PH23 3ND

☎ 01479 841220 📠 01479 841220

e-mail: lynn@thepines-duthil.co.uk

Dir: *2m E of Carrbridge in Duthil on A938*

PETS: Bedrooms (1GF) unattended sign **Charges** charge for damage **Grounds** accessible on leads disp bin **Exercise area Facilities** food bowl water bowl dog chews dog scoop/disp bags leads pet sitting dog walking washing facs cage storage walks info vet info **On Request** fridge access torch towels **Resident Pets:** Corrie (English Springer Spaniel), Rhea (Golden Labrador)

A warm welcome is assured at this comfortable home in the Cairngorms National Park. The bright bedrooms are traditionally furnished and offer good amenities. Enjoyable home-cooked fare is served around a communal table. Relax in the conservatory-lounge and watch squirrels feed in the nearby wood.

Rooms 4 en suite (1 fmly) (1 GF) S £35-£40; D £50-£55 **Facilities** STV TVB tea/coffee Cen ht Dinner Last d 4pm **Parking** 5 **Notes** LB

SCOTLAND

CONTIN — MAP 14 NH45

★★★ 76% COUNTRY HOUSE HOTEL

Coul House

IV14 9ES

☎ 01997 421487 01997 421945

e-mail: stay@coulhousehotel.com

Dir: *Exit A9 north onto A835. Hotel on right*

PETS: Bedrooms (4GF) unattended **Charges** £5 per night **Public areas** except dining areas **Grounds** accessible disp bin **Exercise area** adjacent **Facilities** cage storage walks info vet info **On Request** fridge access torch

This imposing mansion house is set back from the road in extensive grounds. A number of the generally spacious bedrooms have superb views of the distant mountains and all are thoughtfully equipped. The Octagonal Restaurant offers guests the chance to enjoy contemporary Scottish cuisine.

Rooms 20 en suite (3 fmly) (4 GF) S £65-£85; D £110-£150 (incl. bkfst)✻ **Facilities** Wi-fi in bedrooms 9 hole pitch & putt ch fac New Year **Parking** 60 **Notes LB** Closed 24-26 Dec

CORPACH — MAP 14 NN07

►►►►► **Linnhe Lochside Holidays**

(NN074771)

PH33 7NL

☎ 01397 772376 01397 772007

e-mail: relax@linnhe-lochside-holidays.co.uk

web: www.linnhe-lochside-holidays.co.uk

Dir: *On A830, 1m W of Corpach, 5m from Fort William*

PETS: Charges £5 per night £25 per week **Public areas** except pet-free areas disp bin **Exercise area** on site dog walk area & long beach **Facilities** on site shop food food bowl water bowl dog chews cat treats dog scoop/disp bags washing facs walks info vet info **Other** prior notice required **Resident Pets:** dogs, cats, ferrets, ducks & chickens

Open Etr-Oct Last arrival 21.00hrs Last departure 11.00hrs

An excellently maintained site in a beautiful setting on the shores of Loch Eil, with Ben Nevis to the east and the mountains and Sunart to the west. The owners have worked in harmony with nature to produce an idyllic environment, where they offer the highest standards of design and maintenance. A 5.5-acre site with 85 touring pitches, 63 hardstandings and 20 statics.

Notes no cars by tents

DINGWALL — MAP 14 NH55

►►► **Dingwall Camping & Caravanning Club Site** *(NH555588)*

Jubilee Park Rd IV15 9QZ

☎ 01349 862236

web: www.thefriendlyclub.co.uk

Dir: *A862 to Dingwall, right onto Hill Street, past filling station. Right onto High Street, 1st left after railway bridge. Site ahead*

PETS: disp bin **Exercise area Facilities** walks info vet info **Other** prior notice required

Open 2 Apr-2 Nov Last arrival 21.00hrs Last departure noon

A quiet park with attractive landscaping and very good facilities maintained to a high standard. A convenient touring centre, close to the historic market town of Dingwall. A 6.5-acre site with 83 touring pitches.

Notes Site gates closed 23.00hrs-07.00hrs

FORT AUGUSTUS — MAP 14 NH30

★★★ 86% HOTEL

Lovat Arms

Loch Ness Side PH32 4DU

☎ 0845 450 1100 & 01456 459250 01320 366677

e-mail: info@lovatarms-hotel.com

web: www.lovatarms-hotel.com

Dir: *in town centre on A82*

PETS: Bedrooms (7GF) **Charges** £5 per night charge for damage **Public areas** only in bar area (on leads) **Grounds** accessible on leads disp bin **Exercise area Facilities** food (pre-bookable) food bowl water bowl bedding dog chews cat treats feeding mat dog scoop/disp bags leads cage storage walks info vet info **On Request** fridge access torch towels **Other** 1 bedroom available only

This charming country-house hotel enjoys an elevated position in the pretty town of Fort Augustus. It has impressively styled bedrooms with a host of thoughtful extras. Inviting public areas include a comfortable lounge with a log fire, a stylish bar, and contemporary restaurant were food is cooked with skill and care. The hospitality and commitment to guest care will leave a lasting impression.

Rooms 23 en suite 6 annexe en suite (4 fmly) (7 GF) S £65-£150; D £80-£270 (incl. bkfst)✻ **Facilities** FTV Wi-fi in bedrooms Xmas New Year **Services** Lift **Parking** 30

FORT WILLIAM MAP 14 NN17

★★★ 79% HOTEL

Moorings

Banavie PH33 7LY

☎ 01397 772797 01397 772441

e-mail: reservations@moorings-fortwilliam.co.uk

web: www.moorings-fortwilliam.co.uk

Dir: *take A380 (N from Fort William), cross Caledonian Canal, 1st right*

PETS: Bedrooms (1GF) unattended **Charges** £5 per stay **Public areas** except during food service (on leads) **Grounds** accessible disp bin **Exercise area** 100yds **Facilities** bedding washing facs cage storage walks info vet info **On Request** torch towels **Other** pet blanket provided

Located on the Caledonian Canal next to a series of locks known as Neptune's Staircase and close to Thomas Telford's house, this hotel with its dedicated, young team offers friendly service. Accommodation comes in two distinct styles and the newer rooms are particularly appealing. Meals can be taken in the bars or the spacious dining room.

Rooms 27 en suite (1 fmly) (1 GF) S £84-£106; D £98-£142 (incl. bkfst) * **Facilities** STV Wi-fi available New Year **Parking** 60 **Notes** LB

★★★ 78% SMALL HOTEL

Lime Tree Hotel & Restaurant

Lime Tree Studio, Achintore Rd PH33 6RQ

☎ 01397 701806 01397 701806

e-mail: info@limetreefortwilliam.co.uk

Dir: *On A82 at entrance to Fort William*

PETS: Bedrooms Charges £7.50 per night charge for damage **Public areas** except restaurant (on leads) **Grounds** accessible disp bin **Exercise area** 100mtrs

The Lime Tree is a charming small hotel with a super art gallery on the ground floor, with lots of original artwork displayed throughout. Evening meals can be enjoyed in the restaurant which has a loyal following. The hotel's comfortable lounges with their real fires are ideal for pre or post dinner drinks or maybe just to relax in. Individually designed bedrooms are spacious with some nice little personal touches courtesy of the artist owner.

Rooms 9 en suite (4 fmly) (4 GF) S £60-£75; D £80-£100 (incl. bkfst)* **Facilities** Wi-fi in bedrooms New Year **Parking** 9 **Notes LB** Closed Nov

►►►► *Glen Nevis Caravan & Camping Park* *(NN124722)*

Glen Nevis PH33 6SX

☎ 01397 702191 01397 703904

e-mail: holidays@glen-nevis.co.uk

web: www.glen-nevis.co.uk

Dir: *In northern outskirts of Fort William follow A82 to mini-rdbt. Exit for Glen Nevis. Site 2.5m on right*

PETS: disp bin **Exercise area** on site area available **Facilities** on site shop food dog chews cat treats dog scoop/disp bags walks info vet info

Open 15 Mar-Oct (rs Mar & mid-end Oct limited shop & restaurant facilities) Last arrival 22.00hrs Last departure noon

A tasteful site with well-screened enclosures, at the foot of Ben Nevis in the midst of some of the Highlands' most spectacular scenery; an ideal area for walking and touring. The park boasts a restaurant which offers a high standard of cooking and provides good value for money. A 30-acre site with 380 touring pitches, 150 hardstandings and 30 statics.

Notes Closed to vehicle entry 23.00hrs, quiet 23.00hrs-08.00hrs

FOYERS MAP 14 NH42

★★★★ RESTAURANT WITH ROOMS

Craigdarroch House

IV2 6XU

☎ 01456 486400 01456 486444

e-mail: info@hotel-loch-ness.co.uk

Dir: *Take B862 from either end of loch, then B852 signed Foyers*

PETS: Bedrooms Charges £10 per week charge for damage **Grounds** accessible on leads disp bin **Exercise area** 20mtrs **Facilities** walks info vet info **On Request** towels

Resident Pets: dogs

Opened in 1994 Craigdarroch commands an elevated position high above Loch Ness on the south side of the Loch. Bedrooms vary in style and size but all are comfortable and well equipped with front facing having wonderful Loch views. Dinner and breakfasts should not to be missed.

Rooms 10 en suite S £70-£120; D £100-£180* (room only) **Facilities** FTV TVB tea/coffee Direct dial from bedrooms Cen ht Dinner Last d 8pm Wi-fi available **Parking** 24 **Notes** No children 12yrs

GAIRLOCH MAP 14 NG87

★★★ INN

The Old Inn

Flowerdale Glen IV21 2BD

☎ 01445 712006 01445 712445

e-mail: info@theoldinn.net

web: www.theoldinn.co.uk

Dir: *A832 into Gairloch, establishment on right opp harbour*

PETS: Bedrooms Charges £5 per night **Public areas** except dining areas **Grounds** accessible **Exercise area Facilities** food bowl water bowl bedding cage storage walks info vet info **On Request** fridge access torch **Resident Pets:** Muscovy ducks

Situated close to the harbour, this well-established and lively inn has an idyllic location overlooking the burn and the old bridge. A good range of meals, many featuring seafood, are served in the bars and dining areas, and outside at picnic tables on finer days. Live music is a feature several evenings a week. Bedrooms are well equipped and attractively decorated.

Rooms 14 en suite (3 fmly) (2 GF) **Facilities** STV TVB tea/coffee Direct dial from bedrooms Cen ht Dinner Last d 9.30pm Wi-fi available Pool Table **Parking** 40 **Notes** No coaches

GLENCOE MAP 14 NN15

►►► Glencoe Camping & Caravanning Club Site *(NN111578)*

PH49 4LA

☎ 01855 811397

web: www.thefriendlyclub.co.uk

Dir: *1m SE from Glencoe village on A82, follow Glencoe visitors' centre sign*

PETS: disp bin **Exercise area** on site **Facilities** on site shop walks info vet info **Other** prior notice required

Open 2 Apr-2 Nov Last arrival 21.00hrs Last departure noon

A partly sloping site with separate areas of grass and gravel hardstands. Set in mountainous woodland one mile from the village, and adjacent to the visitors' centre. A 40-acre site with 120 touring pitches, 55 hardstandings.

Notes Site gates closed 23.00hrs-07.00hrs

GLENFINNAN MAP 14 NM98

★★ 78% SMALL HOTEL

The Prince's House

PH37 4LT

☎ 01397 722246 01397 722323

e-mail: princeshouse@glenfinnan.co.uk

web: www.glenfinnan.co.uk

Dir: *on A830, 0.5m on right past Glenfinnan Monument. 200mtrs from railway station*

PETS: Bedrooms Charges £5 per stay charge for damage **Public areas** except restaurant **Grounds** accessible disp bin **Exercise area Facilities** food bowl walks info vet info **On Request** torch **Resident Pets:** Floren (cat)

This delightful hotel enjoys a well deserved reputation for fine food and excellent hospitality. The hotel has inspiring views and sits close to where 'Bonnie' Prince Charlie raised the Jacobite standard. Comfortably appointed bedrooms offer pleasing decor. Excellent local game and seafood can be enjoyed in the restaurant and the bar.

Rooms 9 en suite (1 fmly) S £55-£70; D £90-£130 (incl. bkfst)* **Facilities** Fishing New Year **Parking** 18 **Notes** Closed Xmas & Jan-Feb (ex New Year) RS Nov-Dec & Mar

INVERGORDON MAP 14 NH76

★★★★ 77% COUNTRY HOUSE HOTEL

Kincraig House

IV18 0LF

☎ 01349 852587 01349 852193

e-mail: info@kincraig-house-hotel.co.uk

web: www.kincraig-house-hotel.co.uk

Dir: *off A9 past Alness towards Tain. Hotel on left 0.25m past Rosskeen Church*

PETS: Bedrooms (1GF) **Charges** £5 per night charge for damage **Grounds** accessible on leads disp bin **Exercise area Facilities** washing facs cage storage walks info vet info **On Request** fridge access torch towels **Restrictions** Please phone for details

This mansion house is set in well-tended grounds in an elevated position with views over the Cromarty Firth. It offers smart well-equipped bedrooms and inviting public areas that retain the original features of the house. However it is the friendly service and commitment to guest care that will leave lasting impression.

Rooms 15 en suite (1 fmly) (1 GF) S £65-£150; D £80-£300 (incl. bkfst)* **Facilities** STV Wi-fi in bedrooms Xmas **Parking** 30 **Notes** LB

INVERNESS MAP 14 NH64

★★★ 74% HOTEL

Royal Highland

Station Square, Academy St IV1 1LG

☎ 01463 231926 & 251451 📠 01463 710705

e-mail: info@royalhighlandhotel.co.uk

web: www.royalhighlandhotel.co.uk

Dir: *from A9 into town centre. Hotel next to rail station & Eastgate Retail Centre*

PETS: Bedrooms (2GF) **Charges** charge for damage **Exercise area Facilities** vet info **Other** cats in carriers only **Restrictions** small & medium dogs only; only accept well behaved, non-threatening dogs

Built in 1858 adjacent to the railway station, this hotel has the typically grand foyer of the Victorian era with comfortable seating. The contemporary ASH Brasserie and bar offers a refreshing style for both eating and drinking throughout the day. The generally spacious bedrooms are comfortably equipped for the business traveller.

Rooms 85 en suite (12 fmly) (2 GF) S £80-£130; D £99-£180 (incl. bkfst) **Facilities** FTV Gym Wi-fi in bedrooms Xmas New Year **Services** Lift **Parking** 8 **Notes** LB

BUDGET HOTEL

Express by Holiday Inn Inverness

Express by Holiday Inn

Stoneyfield IV2 7PA

☎ 01463 732700 📠 01463 732732

e-mail: inverness@expressholidayinn.co.uk

web: www.hiexpress.com/inverness

Dir: *from A9 follow A96 & Inverness Airport signs, hotel on right*

PETS: Bedrooms Charges charge for damage **Grounds** accessible on leads disp bin **Exercise area Facilities** walks info vet info **Other** selected rooms available for pets **Restrictions** small & medium-sized dogs only

A modern hotel ideal for families and business travellers. Fresh and uncomplicated, the spacious bedrooms include Sky TV, power shower and tea and coffee-making facilities. Continental buffet breakfast is included in the room rate; other meals may be taken at the nearby family pub or restaurant.

Rooms 94 en suite

JOHN O'GROATS MAP 15 ND37

►►► John O'Groats Caravan Site *(ND382733)*

KW1 4YR

☎ 01955 611329 & 07762 336359

e-mail: info@johnogroatscampsite.co.uk

web: www.johnogroatscampsite.co.uk

Dir: *At end of A99*

PETS: Exercise area 50mtrs **Facilities** washing facs walks info vet info

Open Apr-Sep Last arrival 22.00hrs Last departure 11.00hrs

An attractive site in an open position above the seashore and looking out towards the Orkney Islands. The passenger ferry which makes day trips to the Orkneys is nearby, and there are grey seals to watch; sea angling can be organised by the site owners. A 4-acre site with 90 touring pitches, 20 hardstandings.

Notes

LOCHINVER MAP 14 NC02

★★★★ HOTEL

Inver Lodge

CLASSIC BRITISH HOTELS

IV27 4LU

☎ 01571 844496 📠 01571 844395

e-mail: stay@inverlodge.com

web: www.inverlodgehotel.com

Dir: *A835 to Lochinver, through village, left after village hall, follow private road for 0.5m*

PETS: Bedrooms (11GF) unattended **Charges** charge for damage **Public areas** front foyer lounge only **Grounds** accessible **Exercise area Facilities** washing facs cage storage walks info vet info **On Request** fridge access torch towels **Resident Pets:** Sam (Cairn Terrier)

Genuine hospitality is a real feature at this delightful, purpose-built hotel. Set high on the hillside above the village all bedrooms and public rooms enjoy stunning views. There is a choice of lounges and a restaurant where chefs make use of the abundant local produce. Bedrooms are spacious, stylish and come with an impressive range of accessories. There is no night service between 11pm and 7am.

Rooms 20 en suite (11 GF) S £130; D £200 (incl. bkfst)* **Facilities** Fishing Wi-fi in bedrooms **Parking** 30 **Notes** LB Closed Nov-Apr

SCOTLAND

MALLAIG MAP 13 NM69

★★ 70% HOTEL

West Highland

PH41 4QZ

☎ 01687 462210 📠 01687 462130

e-mail: westhighland.hotel@virgin.net

Dir: *from Fort William turn right at rdbt then 1st right up hill, from ferry left at rdbt then 1st right uphill*

PETS: Bedrooms Grounds accessible on leads disp bin **Exercise area Facilities** food bowl water bowl washing facs cage storage walks info vet info **On Request** torch

Originally the town's station hotel the original building was destroyed by fire and the current hotel built on the same site in the early 20th century. Fine views over to Skye are a real feature of the public rooms which include a bright airy conservatory, whilst the attractive bedrooms are thoughtfully equipped and generally spacious.

Rooms 34 en suite (6 fmly) S £40-£46; D £72-£85 (incl. bkfst)* **Facilities** FTV Wi-fi available ♫ **Parking** 40 **Notes LB** Closed 16 Oct-15 Mar RS 16 Mar-1 Apr

MUIR OF ORD MAP 14 NH55

★★ 72% ❀ SMALL HOTEL

Ord House

IV6 7UH

☎ 01463 870492 📠 01463 870297

e-mail: admin@ord-house.co.uk

Dir: *off A9 at Tore rdbt onto A832. 5m, through Muir of Ord. Left towards Ullapool (still A832). Hotel 0.5m on left*

PETS: Bedrooms (3GF) unattended **Charges** charge for damage **Public areas** except restaurant **Grounds** accessible disp bin **Exercise area Facilities** food (pre-bookable) food bowl water bowl dog scoop/disp bags leads washing facs walks info vet info **On Request** fridge access torch towels **Resident Pets:** Tatty (Black Labrador)

Dating back to 1637, this country-house hotel is situated peacefully in wooded grounds and offers brightly furnished and well-proportioned accommodation. Comfortable day rooms reflect the character and charm of the house, with inviting lounges, a cosy snug bar and an elegant dining room where wide-ranging, creative menus are offered.

Rooms 12 en suite (3 GF) S £40-£60; D £100-£120 (incl. bkfst)* **Facilities** no TV in bdrms Putt green Wi-fi in bedrooms Clay pigeon shooting **Parking** 30 **Notes LB** Closed Nov-Apr

NAIRN MAP 14 NH85

★★★ ❀❀❀❀ HOTEL

Boath House

Auldearn IV12 5TE

☎ 01667 454896 📠 01667 455469

e-mail: wendy@boath-house.com

web: www.boath-house.com

Dir: *2m past Nairn on A96, E towards Forres, signed on main road*

PETS: Bedrooms Stables nearby (1m) **Charges** charge for damage **Grounds** accessible disp bin **Exercise area** 1m **Facilities** water bowl washing facs cage storage walks info vet info **On Request** fridge access torch **Other** pet policy which owners are required to sign **Restrictions** very large dogs are not accepted **Resident Pets:** Pippin (Jack Russell)

Standing in its own grounds, this splendid Georgian mansion has been lovingly restored. Hospitality is first class. The owners are passionate about what they do, and have an ability to establish a special relationship with their guests that will be particularly remembered. The food is also memorable here - the five-course dinners are a culinary adventure, matched only by the excellence of breakfasts. The house itself is delightful, with inviting lounges and a dining room overlooking a trout loch. Bedrooms are striking, comfortable, and include many fine antique pieces.

Rooms 8 en suite (1 fmly) (1 GF) S £180; D £190-£300 (incl. bkfst)* **Facilities** Spa FTV Fishing Gym Beauty salon New Year **Parking** 20 **Notes** Closed Xmas

►►► Nairn Camping & Caravanning Club Site *(NH847551)*

Delnies Wood IV12 5NX

☎ 01667 455281

web: www.thefriendlyclub.co.uk

Dir: *Off A96 (Inverness to Aberdeen road). 2m W of Nairn*

PETS: Public areas except in buildings disp bin **Exercise area** on site dog walks **Facilities** vet info

Open 2 Apr-2 Nov Last arrival 21.00hrs Last departure noon

An attractive site set amongst pine trees, with facilities maintained to a good standard. The park is close to Nairn with its beaches, shopping, golf and leisure activities. A 14-acre site with 75 touring pitches.

Notes Site gates closed 23.00hrs-07.00hrs

NEWTONMORE MAP 14 NN79

★★ 69% HOTEL

Highlander

PH20 1AY

☎ 01540 673341 📠 01540 673708

e-mail: generalmanager.highlander@ohiml.com

web: www.oxfordhotelsandinns.com

Dir: *3m from A9 at N end of village on main street*

PETS: Bedrooms (43GF) unattended **Grounds** accessible on leads disp bin **Exercise area Facilities** pet sitting dog walking washing facs cage storage walks info vet info **On Request** torch towels **Resident Pets:** Shelley & Tinkerbell (cats)

A modern, purpose built hotel that enjoys a prominent position in the quaint town of Newtonmore. Bedrooms are comfortable, bright and spacious. Public areas include a cosy bar and a spacious residents' lounge. Guests are assured of a warm welcome at this friendly hotel. Ample secure parking is an added benefit.

Rooms 85 annexe en suite (9 fmly) (43 GF) **Facilities** Wi-fi available ♫ **Parking** 60

★★★★ GUEST HOUSE

Crubenbeg House

Falls of Truim PH20 1BE

☎ 01540 673300

e-mail: enquiries@crubenbeghouse.com

web: www.crubenbeghouse.com

Dir: *4m S of Newtonmore. Off A9 for Crubenmore, over railway bridge & right, signed*

PETS: Bedrooms (1GF) **Public areas Grounds** accessible disp bin **Exercise area** adjacent **Facilities** food (pre-bookable) food bowl water bowl dog chews feeding mat dog scoop/disp bags leads pet sitting dog walking washing facs cage storage walks info vet info **On Request** fridge access torch towels **Resident Pets:** Rajah (Saluki-Alsatian)

Set in peaceful rural location, Crubenbeg House has stunning country views and is well located for touring the Highlands. The attractive bedrooms are individually styled and well equipped, while the ground-floor bedroom provides easier access. Guests can enjoy a dram in front of the fire in the inviting lounge, while breakfast features the best of local produce in the adjacent dining room.

Rooms 4 rms (3 en suite) (1 pri facs) (1 GF) S £30-£36; D £50-£80 **Facilities** STV TVB tea/coffee Licensed Cen ht Dinner Last d 4pm Wi-fi available **Parking** 10 **Notes LB** No children No coaches

ONICH MAP 14 NN06

★★★ 81% ❁ HOTEL

Onich

PH33 6RY

☎ 01855 821214 📠 01855 821484

e-mail: enquiries@onich-fortwilliam.co.uk

web: www.onich-fortwilliam.co.uk

Dir: *beside A82, 2m N of Ballachulish Bridge*

PETS: Bedrooms unattended **Charges** £5 per night £25 per week charge for damage **Public areas** except food service areas (on leads) **Grounds** accessible disp bin **Exercise area Facilities** washing facs cage storage walks info vet info **On Request** fridge access torch towels **Resident Pets:** Denzel (Black Labrador)

Genuine hospitality is part of the appeal of this hotel, which lies right beside Loch Linnhe with gardens extending to its shores. Nicely presented public areas include a choice of inviting lounges and contrasting bars, and views of the loch can be enjoyed from the attractive restaurant. Bedrooms, with pleasing colour schemes, are comfortably modern.

Rooms 26 en suite (6 fmly) S £49-£63; D £98-£142 (incl. bkfst)* **Facilities** Wi-fi available Games room Xmas **Parking** 50 **Notes** Closed 22-27 Dec

POOLEWE MAP 14 NG88

►►► Inverewe Camping & Caravanning Club Site *(NG862812)*

Inverewe Gardens IV22 2LF

☎ 01445 781249

web: www.thefriendlyclub.co.uk

Dir: *On A832, N of Poolewe village*

PETS: Public areas except in buildings disp bin **Exercise area Facilities** walks info vet info **Other** prior notice required

Open 2 Apr-2 Nov Last arrival 21.00hrs Last departure noon

A well-run site located in Loch Ewe Bay, not far from Inverewe Gardens. The Club has improved this site in the past few years, and continues to upgrade the facilities. The warm waters of the Gulf Stream attract otters and seals. A 3-acre site with 55 touring pitches, 8 hardstandings.

Notes Site gates closed 23.00hrs-07.00hrs

SCOTLAND

SCOTLAND

RESIPOLE (LOCH SUNART) MAP 13 NM76

►►►► Resipole Farm *(NM725639)*

PH36 4HX

☎ 01967 431235 🖹 01967 431777

e-mail: info@resipole.co.uk

web: www.resipole.co.uk

Dir: *From Corran Ferry take A861. Site 8m W of Strontian*

PETS: Public areas (on leads) **Exercise area** on site walks through woods **Facilities** on site shop food dog chews cat treats dog scoop/disp bags walks info vet info

Open Apr-Oct Last arrival 22.00hrs Last departure 11.00hrs

A quiet, relaxing park in beautiful surroundings, with deer frequently sighted, and of great interest to naturalists. Situated on the saltwater Loch Sunart in the Ardnamurchan Peninsula, and offering a great deal of space and privacy. An 8-acre site with 85 touring pitches, 30 hardstandings and 9 statics.

ROSEMARKIE MAP 14 NH75

►►► Rosemarkie Camping & Caravanning Club Site *(NH739569)*

Ness Rd East IV10 8SE

☎ 01381 621117

web: www.thefriendlyclub.co.uk

Dir: *Take A832. A9 at Tore rdbt. Through Avoch, Fortrose then right at police house. Down Ness Rd. 1st left, small turn signed Golf & Caravan site*

PETS: Public areas except in buildings disp bin **Exercise area** on site **Facilities** walks info vet info **Other** prior notice required

Open 2 Apr-2 Nov Last arrival 21.00hrs Last departure noon

A superb club site set along the water's edge, with beautiful views over the bay where resident dolphins swim. Two excellent toilet blocks, including a disabled room, and a family room with combined facilities, have greatly enhanced the facilities here. A smart reception area sets the standard for this very clean and well-maintained site. A 4-acre site with 60 touring pitches.

Notes Site gates closed 23.00hrs-07.00hrs

ROY BRIDGE MAP 14 NN28

★★★ 78% HOTEL

Best Western Glenspean Lodge Hotel

PH31 4AW

☎ 01397 712223 🖹 01397 712660

e-mail: reservations@glenspeanlodge.co.uk

web: www.glenspeanlodge.com

Dir: *2m E of Roy Bridge, right off A82 at Spean Bridge onto A86*

PETS: Bedrooms Stables nearby (3m) **Charges** £15 per night charge for damage **Public areas** bar area only (on leads) **Grounds** accessible on leads disp bin **Exercise area** adjacent **Facilities** water bowl washing facs walks info vet info **On Request** fridge access torch **Resident Pets:** Zac (German Shepherd) & Oscar (Macaw)

With origins as a hunting lodge dating back to the Victorian era, this hotel sits in gardens in an elevated position in the Spean Valley. Accommodation is provided in well laid out bedrooms, some suitable for families. Inviting public areas include a comfortable lounge bar and a restaurant that enjoys stunning views of the valley.

Rooms 17 en suite (4 fmly) **Facilities** Gym Wi-fi available Sauna **Parking** 60

SCOURIE MAP 14 NC14

★★★ 73% SMALL HOTEL

Scourie

IV27 4SX

☎ 01971 502396 🖹 01971 502423

e-mail: patrick@scourie-hotel.co.uk

Dir: *N'bound on A894. Hotel in village on left*

PETS: Bedrooms (5GF) unattended **Charges** charge for damage **Public areas** except dining areas **Grounds** accessible disp bin **Exercise area** 200yds **Facilities** cage storage walks info vet info **On Request** fridge access **Resident Pets:** Molly (Springer Spaniel), Jessie & Clemmie (cats), Minstrel & Angus (horses)

This well-established hotel is an angler's paradise with extensive fishing rights available on a 25,000-acre estate. Public areas include a choice of comfortable lounges, a cosy bar and a smart dining room offering wholesome fare. The bedrooms are comfortable and generally spacious. The resident proprietors and their staff create a relaxed and friendly atmosphere.

Rooms 18 rms (17 en suite) 2 annexe en suite (2 fmly) (5 GF) S £60-£71; D £110-£130 (incl. bkfst & dinner)✻ **Facilities** no TV in bdrms Fishing Wi-fi available **Parking** 30 **Notes LB** Closed mid Oct-end Mar RS winter evenings

SHIELDAIG MAP 14 NG85

★ 75% SMALL HOTEL

Tigh an Eilean

IV54 8XN

☎ 01520 755251 01520 755321

e-mail: tighaneilean@keme.co.uk

Dir: *off A896 onto village road signed Shieldaig, hotel in centre*

PETS: Bedrooms unattended sign **Stables** nearby (400yds) **Grounds** accessible disp bin **Exercise area** 50yds **Facilities** food (pre-bookable) food bowl water bowl bedding dog chews dog scoop/disp bags leads washing facs cage storage walks info vet info **On Request** fridge access torch towels **Resident Pets:** Ella & Katy (Black Labradors), Woody (cat)

A splendid location by the sea, with views over the bay, is the icing on the cake for this delightful small hotel. It can be a long drive to reach Sheildaig but guests remark that the journey is more than worth the effort. The brightly decorated bedrooms are comfortable though don't expect television, except in one of the lounges. For many, it's the food that attracts, with fish and seafood featuring strongly.

Rooms 11 en suite (1 fmly) S £75; D £160 (incl. bkfst)✻ **Facilities** no TV in bdrms Wi-fi in bedrooms Birdwatching Kayaks **Parking** 15 **Notes** LB Closed late Oct-mid Mar

SOUTH BALLACHULISH MAP 14 NN05

★★★★ GUEST HOUSE

Lyn-Leven

West Laroch PH49 4JP

☎ 01855 811392 01855 811600

e-mail: macleodcilla@aol.com

web: www.lynleven.co.uk

Dir: *Off A82 signed on left West Laroch*

PETS: Bedrooms Charges Exercise area

Genuine Highland hospitality and high standards are part of the appeal of this comfortable guest house. The attractive bedrooms vary in size, are well equipped, and offer many thoughtful extra touches. There is a spacious lounge and a smart dining room where delicious home-cooked evening meals and breakfasts are served at individual tables.

Rooms 8 en suite 4 annexe en suite (3 fmly) (12 GF) **Facilities** TVB tea/coffee Licensed Cen ht TVL Dinner Last d 7pm **Parking** 12 **Notes** Closed Xmas

SPEAN BRIDGE MAP 14 NN28

★★★★ RESTAURANT WITH ROOMS

The Smiddy House

Roy Bridge Rd PH34 4EU

☎ 01397 712335 01397 712043

e-mail: enquiry@smiddyhouse.co.uk

web: www.smiddyhouse.co.uk

Dir: *In village centre, A82 onto A86*

PETS: Bedrooms Charges £5 per night charge for damage **Exercise area** 200yds **Facilities** walks info vet info **Other** pet food & water/food bowls on request **Restrictions** small dogs only **Resident Pets:** Cara (King Charles Cavalier)

Set within the 'Great Glen', which stretches from Fort William to Inverness, this was once the village smithy, and is now a friendly establishment. The attractive bedrooms, which are named after Scottish places, are comfortably furnished and well equipped. A relaxing garden room is available for guest use. Delicious evening meals are served in Russell's restaurant.

Rooms 4 en suite (1 fmly) S £60-£75; D £60-£80✻ **Facilities** TVB tea/coffee Dinner Last d 9.30pm **Parking** 15

★★★ FARM HOUSE

Achnabobane *(NN195811)*

PH34 4EX

☎ 01397 712919 Mr and Mrs N Ockenden

e-mail: enquiries@achnabobane.co.uk

web: www.achnabobane.co.uk

Dir: *2m S of Spean Bridge on A82*

PETS: Bedrooms Charges charge for damage **Public areas** except lounge & restaurant (on leads) **Grounds** accessible on leads disp bin **Exercise area Facilities** dog scoop/disp bags cage storage walks info vet info **On Request** fridge access torch towels **Resident Pets:** Morse (Cavalier King Charles Spaniel), Bea, Korky & Dyllon (cats), chickens, 1 cockerel

With breathtaking views of Ben Nevis, Aonach Mhor and the Grey Corries, the farmhouse offers comfortable, good-value accommodation in a friendly family environment. Bedrooms are traditional in style and well equipped. Breakfast and evening meals are served in the conservatory-dining room.

Rooms 4 rms (1 en suite) (1 fmly) (1 GF) S £28; D £56✻ **Facilities** TVB tea/coffee Cen ht TVL Dinner Last d 1pm Wi-fi available **Parking** 5 **Notes** Closed Xmas

SCOTLAND

STRATHPEFFER MAP 14 NH45

★★★ 77% HOTEL

Ben Wyvis Hotel

CRERAR HOTELS

IV14 9DN

☎ 0870 950 6264 📠 01997 421228

e-mail: benwyvis@crerarhotels.com

web: www.crerarhotels.com

Dir: *From S A862 to Dingwall, then A834 to Strathpeffer. Hotel 3rd exit on left*

PETS: Bedrooms (8GF) unattended **Charges** £10 per stay charge for damage **Grounds** accessible on leads disp bin **Exercise area** **Facilities** walks info vet info **On Request** torch towels

This imposing hotel built in 1877 lies in its own extensive landscaped grounds in the centre of the Victorian spa village of Strathpeffer. It offers spacious lounges with open log fires, sparkling chandeliers and even has its own 32-seat cinema. The hotel is popular for meetings and conferences.

Rooms 92 en suite (5 fmly) (8 GF) **Facilities** Putt green Wi-fi available Cinema ♫ **Services** Lift **Parking** 40

STRONTIAN MAP 14 NM86

★★★ ◎◎ COUNTRY HOUSE HOTEL

Kilcamb Lodge

PH36 4HY

☎ 01967 402257 📠 01967 402041

e-mail: enquiries@kilcamblodge.co.uk

web: www.kilcamblodge.co.uk

Dir: *off A861, via Corran Ferry*

PETS: Bedrooms sign **Charges** £5 per night (dogs) £30 per week charge for damage **Grounds** accessible disp bin **Exercise area** on site 22 acres of grounds & lochside **Facilities** food (pre-bookable) dog chews feeding mat dog scoop/disp bags washing facs cage storage walks info vet info **On Request** fridge access torch towels

This historic house on the shores of Loch Sunart was one of the first stone buildings in the area and was used as military barracks around the time of the Jacobite uprising. Accommodation is provided in tastefully decorated rooms with high quality fabrics. Accomplished cooking, utilising much local produce, can be enjoyed in the stylish dining room. Warm hospitality is assured.

Rooms 10 en suite (2 fmly) S £95-£140; D £130-£320 (incl. bkfst)* **Facilities** FTV Fishing Wi-fi available Boating Hiking Bird, Whale & Otter watching Island hopping Stalking Xmas New Year **Parking** 18 **Notes LB** No children 12yrs Closed 2 Jan-1 Feb RS Nov & Feb

TONGUE MAP 14 NC55

★★★ 70% ◎ SMALL HOTEL

Ben Loyal

Main St IV27 4XE

☎ 01847 611216 📠 01847 611212

e-mail: benloyalhotel@btinternet.com

web: www.benloyal.co.uk

Dir: *at junct of A838/A836. Hotel by Royal Bank of Scotland*

PETS: Bedrooms unattended **Stables** nearby (10m) **Charges** charge for damage **Public areas** bar only, not at meal times **Grounds** accessible disp bin **Exercise area** **Facilities** walks info vet info **Resident Pets:** Jasper (Cocker Spaniel), Beanie (cat)

Enjoying a super location close to Ben Loyal and with views of the Kyle of Tongue, this hotel more often that not marks the welcome completion of a stunning highland and coastal drive. Bedrooms are thoughtfully equipped and brightly decorated whilst day rooms extend to a traditionally styled dining room and a cosy bar. Extensive menus ensure there's something for everyone. Staff are especially friendly and provide useful local information.

Rooms 11 en suite S £40; D £70-£80 (incl. bkfst)* **Facilities** FTV Fishing Fly fishing tuition and equipment **Parking** 20 **Notes** Closed 30 Nov-1 Mar

★★ 76% ◎ HOTEL

Borgie Lodge Hotel

Skerray KW14 7TH

☎ 01641 521332 📠 01641 521889

e-mail: info@borgielodgehotel.co.uk

Dir: *A836 between Tongue & Bettyhill. 0.5m from Skerray junct*

PETS: Bedrooms (1GF) **Stables** nearby **Charges** charge for damage **Grounds** accessible on leads disp bin **Exercise area** **Facilities** walks info vet info **On Request** fridge access torch

This small outdoor-sport orientated hotel lies in a glen close to the river of the same name. Whilst fishing parties predominate, those who are not anglers are made equally welcome, and indeed the friendliness and commitment to guest care is paramount. Cosy public rooms offer a choice of lounges and an anglers' bar - they all boast welcoming log fires. The dinner menu is short but well chosen.

Rooms 8 rms (7 en suite) (1 GF) **Facilities** Fishing Shooting Stalking Boating **Parking** 20 **Notes LB** No children 12yrs RS 25 Dec

ULLAPOOL MAP 14 NH19

►►► Broomfield Holiday Park *(NH123939)*

West Shore St IV26 2UT

☎ 01854 612020 & 612664 📠 01854 613151

e-mail: sross@broomfieldhp.com

web: www.broomfieldhp.com

Dir: *Take 2nd right past harbour*

PETS: Public areas except toilets & children's play area (on leads) disp bin **Exercise area** on site beach **Facilities** washing facs walks info vet info

Open Etr/Apr-Sep Last departure noon

Set right on the water's edge of Loch Broom and the open sea, with lovely views of the Summer Isles. The park is close to the harbour and town centre with their restaurants, bars and shops. A 12-acre site with 140 touring pitches.

Notes No noise at night

WHITEBRIDGE MAP 14 NH41

★★ 68% HOTEL

Whitebridge

IV2 6UN

☎ 01456 486226 📠 01456 486413

e-mail: info@whitebridgehotel.co.uk

Dir: *off A9 onto B851, follow signs to Fort Augustus. Off A82 onto B862 at Fort Augustus*

PETS: Bedrooms Public areas except restaurant (on leads) **Grounds** accessible **Exercise area Facilities** water bowl walks info vet info

Close to Loch Ness and set amid rugged mountain and moorland scenery this hotel is popular with tourists, fishermen and deerstalkers. Guests have a choice of more formal dining in the restaurant or lighter meals in the popular cosy bar. Bedrooms are thoughtfully equipped and brightly furnished.

Rooms 12 en suite (3 fmly) S £40-£44; D £60-£66 (incl. bkfst) **Facilities** Fishing Wi-fi in bedrooms **Parking** 32 **Notes** Closed 11 Dec-9 Jan

MIDLOTHIAN

ROSLIN MAP 11 NT26

★★★★ INN

The Original Roslin Inn

4 Main St EH25 9LE

☎ 0131 440 2384 📠 0131 440 2514

e-mail: enquiries@theoriginalhotel.co.uk

Dir: *Off city bypass at Straiton for A703, inn is close to Roslin Chapel*

PETS: Bedrooms Charges charge for damage **Grounds** accessible on leads **Exercise area** on site 10yds **Facilities** food bowl water bowl cage storage walks info vet info **On Request** torch towels

This property is within easy distance of the famous Roslin Chapel which is well worth a visit. This delightful village inn offers well-equipped bedrooms with upgraded en suites. Four of the rooms have four-poster beds. The Grail Restaurant, the lounge and conservatory offer a comprehensive selection of dining options.

Rooms 6 en suite (2 fmly) S £65-£75; D £85-£100* **Facilities** STV TVB tea/coffee Cen ht Dinner Last d 9.30pm **Parking** 8 **Notes** LB

SCOTLAND

MORAY

ARCHIESTOWN — MAP 15 NJ24

★★★ 77% ❁ SMALL HOTEL

Archiestown

AB38 7QL

☎ 01340 810218 📠 01340 810239

e-mail: jah@archiestownhotel.co.uk

web: www.archiestownhotel.co.uk

Dir: *A95 Craigellachie, follow B9102 to Archiestown, 4m*

PETS: Bedrooms Charges £5 per night charge for damage **Grounds** accessible on leads disp bin **Exercise area** adjacent **Facilities** food bowl water bowl washing facs cage storage walks info vet info **On Request** fridge access torch towels **Other** guests are required to bring own bedding for pets **Resident Pets:** Dax (cat)

Set in the heart of this Speyside village this small hotel is popular with anglers and locals alike. It is rightly noted for its great hospitality, attentive service and good food. Cosy and comfortable public rooms include a choice of lounges (there is no bar as such) and a bistro offering an inviting choice of dishes at both lunch and dinner.

Rooms 11 en suite (1 fmly) S £35-£65; D £70-£130 (incl. bkfst)✻ **Facilities** Wi-fi in bedrooms New Year **Parking** 20 **Notes LB** Closed 24-27 Dec & 3 Jan-9 Feb

CRAIGELLACHIE — MAP 15 NJ24

★★★ 80% ❁ HOTEL

Craigellachie

OXFORD HOTELS & INNS

AB38 9SR

☎ 01340 881204 📠 01340 881253

e-mail: info@craigellachie.com

web: www.oxfordhotelsandinns.com

Dir: *On A95 between Aberdeen & Inverness*

PETS: Bedrooms (6GF) unattended **Public areas** except restaurant & bar **Grounds** accessible on leads **Exercise area** 20yds **Facilities** cage storage walks info vet info **On Request** fridge access torch

This impressive and popular hotel is located in the heart of Speyside, so it is no surprise that malt whisky takes centre stage in the Quaich bar with over 600 featured. Bedrooms come in various sizes, all are tastefully decorated and bathrooms are of a high specification. Creative dinners showcase local ingredients in the traditionally styled dining room.

Rooms 26 en suite (1 fmly) (6 GF) **Facilities** Gym Wi-fi available **Parking** 30

►►► Speyside Camping & Caravanning Club Site *(NJ257449)*

AB38 9SL

☎ 01340 810414

web: www.thefriendlyclub.co.uk

Dir: *From S exit A9 at Carrbridge, A95 to Grantown-on-Spey, leave Aberlour on A941. Take next left onto B9102 signed Archiestown. Site 3m on left*

PETS: Public areas except in buildings disp bin **Exercise area** on site **Facilities** walks info vet info **Other** prior notice required

Open 2 Apr-2 Nov Last arrival 21.00hrs Last departure noon

A very nice rural site with views across meadowland towards Speyside, and the usual high Club standards. Hardstandings are well screened on an upper level, and grass pitches with more open views are sited lower down. A 7-acre site with 75 touring pitches, 13 hardstandings.

Notes Site gates closed 23.00hrs-07.00hrs

CULLEN — MAP 15 NJ56

★★★ 68% HOTEL

The Seafield Arms Hotel

Seafield St AB56 4SG

☎ 01542 840791 📠 01542 840736

e-mail: info@theseafieldarms.co.uk

Dir: *in centre of Cullen on A98*

PETS: Bedrooms Charges £5 per night **Public areas** except food areas **Grounds** accessible **Exercise area** beach 0.75m **Facilities** walks info vet info

Centrally located and benefiting from off-road car parking, this is a small but friendly hotel. Bedrooms differ in size and style but all are comfortable. The popular restaurant serves well cooked meals using the very best of Scottish produce including the famous Cullen Skink.

Rooms 23 en suite (1 fmly) S £50-£55; D £75-£130 (incl. bkfst)✻ **Facilities** FTV Wi-fi available Xmas New Year **Parking** 17 **Notes LB**

FORRES MAP 14 NJ05

★★★ 74% HOTEL

Ramnee

Victoria Rd IV36 3BN

☎ 01309 672410 🖹 01309 673392

e-mail: info@ramneehotel.com

Dir: *off A96 at rdbt on E side of Forres, hotel 200yds on right*

PETS: Bedrooms unattended **Grounds** accessible on leads disp bin **Exercise area** 200mtrs **Facilities** cage storage walks info vet info **On Request** towels

Genuinely friendly staff ensure this well-established hotel remains popular with business travellers. Bedrooms, including a family suite, vary in size, although all are well presented. Hearty bar food provides a less formal dining option to the imaginative restaurant menu.

Rooms 19 en suite (4 fmly) S £80-£120; D £90-£160 (incl. bkfst)* **Facilities** STV Wi-fi in bedrooms **Parking** 50 **Notes LB** Closed 25 Dec & 1-3 Jan

NORTH LANARKSHIRE

CUMBERNAULD MAP 11 NS77

★★★★ 76% HOTEL

The Westerwood

QHOTELS

1 St Andrews Dr, Westerwood G68 0EW

☎ 01236 457171 🖹 01236 738478

e-mail: westerwood@qhotels.co.uk

web: www.qhotels.co.uk

PETS: Bedrooms unattended **Charges** **Grounds** accessible **Exercise area** on site **Other** pet food on request **Restrictions** small breeds only

This stylish, contemporary hotel enjoys an elevated position within 400 acres at the foot of the Camspie Hills. Accommodation is provided in spacious, bright bedrooms, many with super bathrooms, and day rooms include sumptuous lounges and an airy restaurant; extensive golf, fitness and conference facilities are available.

Rooms 148 en suite (14 fmly) (49 GF) **Facilities** 18 Gym Putt green Wi-fi in bedrooms Beauty salon Hairdresser Relaxation room Sauna Steam room **Services** Lift air con **Parking** 200 **Notes LB**

★★★ 73% HOTEL

Castlecary House

Castlecary Rd, Castlecary G68 0HD

☎ 01324 840233 🖹 01324 841608

e-mail: enquiries@castlecaryhotel.com

web: www.castlecaryhotel.com

Dir: *off A80 onto B816 between Glasgow & Stirling. Hotel by Castlecary Arches*

PETS: Bedrooms unattended **Charges** charge for damage **Grounds** accessible on leads **Exercise area** 100yds **Facilities** dog walking walks info **Resident Pets:** 3 dogs (Boxer, Labrador, West Highland Terrier)

Close to the Forth Clyde Canal and convenient for the M80, this popular hotel provides a versatile range of accommodation, within purpose-built units in the grounds and also in an extension to the original house. The attractive and spacious restaurant offers a short fixed-price menu, and enjoyable meals are also served in the busy bars.

Rooms 60 rms (55 en suite) (3 fmly) (20 GF) S £70-£90; D £70-£100 (incl. bkfst)* **Facilities** FTV Wi-fi available **Services** Lift **Parking** 100 **Notes** RS 1 Jan

PERTH & KINROSS

ALYTH MAP 15 NO24

★★★★★ GUEST ACCOMMODATION

Tigh Na Leigh Guesthouse

22-24 Airlie St PH11 8AJ

☎ 01828 632372 🖹 01828 632279

e-mail: bandcblack@yahoo.co.uk

web: www.tighnaleigh.co.uk

Dir: *In town centre on B952*

PETS: Bedrooms (1GF) **Charges** £7.50 per night **Public areas** except dining room **Grounds** accessible on leads **Exercise area** 200yds **Facilities** food bowl water bowl dog chews dog scoop/disp bags washing facs cage storage walks info vet info **On Request** fridge access torch towels **Resident Pets:** Tom & Eddie (cats)

Situated in the heart of this country town, Tigh Na Leigh is Gaelic for "The house of the Doctor or Physician". Its location and somewhat sombre façade are in stunning contrast to what lies inside. The house has been completely restored to blend its Victorian architecture with contemporary interior design. Bedrooms include a superb suite and state-of-the-art bathrooms. Public rooms offer three entirely different lounges, while delicious meals are served in the conservatory/dining room overlooking a spectacular landscaped garden.

Rooms 5 en suite (1 GF) S £40; D £80-£110* **Facilities** FTV TVB tea/coffee Cen ht TVL Dinner Last d 8pm Wi-fi available **Parking** 5 **Notes** No children 12yrs Closed Dec-Feb

SCOTLAND

BLAIR ATHOLL MAP 14 NN86

★★★ 74% HOTEL

Atholl Arms

Old North Rd PH18 5SG

☎ 01796 481205 📠 01796 481550

e-mail: hotel@athollarms.co.uk

web: www.athollarmshotel.co.uk

Dir: *off A9 to B8079, 1m into Blair Atholl, hotel near entrance to Blair Castle*

PETS: Bedrooms Stables nearby (1m) **Charges** £5 per night £35 per week charge for damage **Public areas** except restaurant (on leads) **Grounds** accessible on leads disp bin **Exercise area** village green adjacent **Facilities** cage storage walks info vet info

Situated close to Blair Castle and conveniently adjacent to the railway station, this stylish hotel has historically styled public rooms that include a choice of bars, and a splendid baronial-style dining room. Bedrooms vary in size and style. Staff throughout are friendly and very caring.

Rooms 30 en suite (3 fmly) S £45-£75; D £60-£90 (incl. bkfst)✳ **Facilities** Fishing Rough shooting ♫ New Year **Parking** 103 **Notes LB**

►►►►► Blair Castle Caravan Park

(NN874656)

PH18 5SR

☎ 01796 481263 📠 01796 481587

e-mail: mail@blaircastlecaravanpark.co.uk

web: www.blaircastlecaravanpark.co.uk

Dir: *From A9 junct with B8079 at Aldclune, then NE to Blair Atholl. Site on right after crossing bridge in village*

PETS: Charges £1 per night **Public areas** except reception, toilet blocks & children's play areas disp bin **Exercise area** on site dog walk adjacent **Facilities** on site shop food food bowl water bowl dog chews dog scoop/disp bags walks info vet info **Other** prior notice required **Restrictions** no dangerous breeds (see page 7)

Open Mar-Nov Last arrival 21.30hrs Last departure noon

Attractive site set in impressive seclusion within the Atholl estate, surrounded by mature woodland and the River Tilt. Although a large park, the various groups of pitches are located throughout the extensive parkland, and each has its own sanitary block with all-cubicled facilities of a very high standard. There is a choice of grass pitches, hardstandings, or fully-serviced pitches. This park is particularly suitable for the larger type of motorhome. A 32-acre site with 280 touring pitches and 101 statics.

COMRIE MAP 11 NN72

★★★ 83% ❁ HOTEL

Royal

Melville Square PH6 2DN

☎ 01764 679200 📠 01764 679219

e-mail: reception@royalhotel.co.uk

web: www.royalhotel.co.uk

Dir: *off A9 on A822 to Crieff, then B827 to Comrie. Hotel in main square on A85*

PETS: Bedrooms unattended **Stables** nearby (3m) **Charges** charge for damage **Public areas Grounds** accessible disp bin **Exercise area** 500yds **Facilities** food bowl water bowl dog scoop/disp bags leads washing facs walks info vet info **On Request** fridge access torch towels **Resident Pets:** Abby & Ella (Labradors)

A traditional façade gives little indication of the style and elegance inside this long-established hotel located in the village centre. Public areas include a bar and library, a bright modern restaurant and a conservatory-style brasserie. Bedrooms are tastefully appointed and furnished with smart reproduction antiques.

Rooms 11 en suite 2 annexe en suite S £85-£105; D £140-£180 (incl. bkfst) **Facilities** STV Fishing Wi-fi in bedrooms Shooting arranged New Year **Parking** 22 **Notes LB** Closed 25-26 Dec

GLENDEVON MAP 11 NN90

★★★★ ❁ INN

An Lochan Tormaukin

FK14 7JY

☎ 0845 371 1414

e-mail: info@anlochan.co.uk

PETS: Bedrooms Stables nearby (6m) **Charges** charge for damage **Public areas** except restaurant (on leads) **Grounds** accessible on leads disp bin **Exercise area** 100yds **Facilities** pet sitting dog walking washing facs cage storage walks info vet info **On Request** fridge access torch towels

A delightful country inn dating back to the 17th century, located in a secluded idyllic setting not far from the famous Gleneagles Championship golf courses. This well-presented property is currently enjoying a rolling programme of refurbishment. Open log fires and bare stone walls add to the character of this property where the small team are friendly and welcoming. Food is a strong aspect of this inn with the best made of locally sourced foods.

Rooms 13 en suite **Facilities** TV available Direct dial from bedrooms Cen ht Dinner Last d 9pm Wi-fi available **Parking** 50

KENMORE MAP 14 NN74

★★★ 74% HOTEL

Kenmore Hotel

The Square PH15 2NU

01887 830205 01887 830262

e-mail: reception@kenmorehotel.co.uk

web: www.kenmorehotel.com

Dir: *off A9 at Ballinluig onto A827, through Aberfeldy to Kenmore for hotel in village centre*

PETS: Bedrooms (7GF) **Stables** nearby (1m) **Charges** charge for damage **Public areas** except restaurant (on leads) **Grounds** accessible on leads disp bin **Exercise area** 0.5m **Facilities** food (pre-bookable) food bowl water bowl dog chews cat treats dog scoop/disp bags washing facs cage storage walks info vet info **On Request** fridge access torch towels **Restrictions** no dangerous dogs (see page 7)

Dating back to 1572, this riverside hotel is Scotland's oldest inn and has a rich and interesting history. Bedrooms have tasteful decor, and meals can be enjoyed in the restaurant which has panoramic views of the River Tay. The choice of bars includes one with real fires.

Rooms 27 en suite 13 annexe en suite (4 fmly) (7 GF) D £50-£119 (incl. bkfst)* **Facilities** STV Fishing Wi-fi available Salmon fishing on River Tay Xmas New Year **Services** Lift **Parking** 30 **Notes** LB

KINCLAVEN MAP 11 NO13

★★★★ COUNTRY HOUSE HOTEL

Ballathie House

PH1 4QN

01250 883268 01250 883396

e-mail: email@ballathiehousehotel.com

web: www.ballathiehousehotel.com

Dir: *from A9 2m N of Perth, B9099 through Stanley & signed, or from A93 at Beech Hedge follow signs for Ballathie, 2.5m*

PETS: Bedrooms (10GF) **Charges** £10 per pet per stay charge for damage **Grounds** accessible disp bin **Exercise area** **Facilities** food bowl water bowl dog chews vet info **On Request** fridge access towels

Set in delightful grounds, this splendid Scottish mansion house combines classical grandeur with modern comfort. Bedrooms range from well-proportioned master rooms to modern standard rooms, and many boast antique furniture and art deco bathrooms. For the ultimate, request one of the Riverside Rooms, a purpose-built development right on the banks of the river, complete with balconies and terraces. The elegant restaurant has views over the River Tay.

Rooms 25 en suite 16 annexe en suite (2 fmly) (10 GF) S £120-£130; D £240-£260 (incl. bkfst & dinner)* **Facilities** FTV Fishing Putt green Wi-fi available Xmas New Year **Services** Lift **Parking** 50 **Notes** LB

KINLOCH RANNOCH MAP 14 NN65

★★★ 77% HOTEL

Dunalastair

PH16 5PW

01882 632323 & 632218 01882 632371

e-mail: robert@dunalastair.co.uk

web: www.dunalastair.co.uk

Dir: *A9 to Pitlochry, at northern end take B8019 to Tummel Bridge then A846 to Kinloch Rannoch*

PETS: Bedrooms (9GF) unattended sign **Charges** £5 per night charge for damage **Public areas** except restaurant **Grounds** accessible disp bin **Exercise area** on site **Facilities** food (pre-bookable) food bowl water bowl dog chews feeding mat dog scoop/disp bags walks info vet info

A traditional Highland hotel with inviting public rooms that are full of character - log fires, stags heads, wood panelling and an extensive selection of malt whiskies. Standard and superior bedrooms are on offer. However, it is the friendly attentive service by delightful staff, as well as first-class dinners that will leave lasting impressions.

Rooms 28 en suite (4 fmly) (9 GF) S £50-£75; D £110-£170 (incl. bkfst) **Facilities** Fishing Riding 4x4 safaris Rafting Clay pigeon shooting Bike hire Archery ch fac Xmas New Year **Parking** 33 **Notes** LB

KINROSS MAP 11 NO10

★★★★ 75% HOTEL

The Green Hotel

2 The Muirs KY13 8AS

01577 863467 01577 863180

e-mail: reservations@green-hotel.com

web: www.green-hotel.com

Dir: *M90 junct 6 follow Kinross signs, onto A922 for hotel*

PETS: Bedrooms (14GF) **Stables** nearby (4m) **Public areas** except restaurant, lounge & bar **Grounds** accessible on leads **Exercise area** opposite **Facilities** cage storage walks info vet info **On Request** fridge access towels

Resident Pets: Samantha & Shuna (Cocker Spaniels)

A long-established hotel offering a wide range of indoor and outdoor activities. Public areas include a classical restaurant, a choice of bars and a well-stocked gift shop. The comfortable, well-equipped bedrooms, most of which are generously proportioned, boast attractive colour schemes and smart modern furnishings.

Rooms 46 en suite (3 fmly) (14 GF) S £65-£105; D £90-£170 (incl. bkfst) * **Facilities** STV supervised 36 Fishing Squash Gym Putt green Wi-fi in bedrooms Petanque Curling (Sep-Apr) New Year **Parking** 60 **Notes** LB Closed 23-24 & 26-28 Dec RS 25 Dec

SCOTLAND

SCOTLAND

PERTH

MAP 11 NO12

★★★★ BED & BREAKFAST

Westview

49 Dunkeld Rd PH1 5RP

☎ 01738 627787 📠 01738 447790

e-mail: angiewestview@aol.com

Dir: *On A912, 0.5m NW from town centre opp Royal Bank of Scotland*

PETS: Bedrooms Public areas except lounge & dining room (on leads) **Exercise area** 5 min walk **Other** many guests bring tropical fish for showing in local competition
Resident Pets: William Wallace & Flora McDonald (Yorkshire Terriers)

Expect a warm welcome from enthusiastic owner Angie Livingstone. She is a fan of Victoriana, and her house captures that period, one feature being the teddies on the stairs. Best use is made of available space in the bedrooms, which are full of character. Public areas include an inviting lounge and a dining room.

Rooms 5 rms (3 en suite) (1 fmly) (1 GF) **Facilities** STV TVB tea/coffee Cen ht TVL Dinner Last d 12.30pm **Parking** 4 **Notes**

PITLOCHRY

MAP 14 NN95

★★★★ 73% COUNTRY HOUSE HOTEL

Pine Trees

Strathview Ter PH16 5QR

☎ 01796 472121 📠 01796 472460

e-mail: info@pinetreeshotel.co.uk

web: www.pinetreeshotel.co.uk

Dir: *from main street (Atholl Rd), into Larchwood Rd, follow hotel signs*

PETS: Bedrooms unattended **Charges** £5 per night charge for damage **Public areas** lounge only (on leads) **Grounds** accessible on leads disp bin **Exercise area** 0.75m **Facilities** water bowl bedding dog chews cage storage walks info vet info
On Request fridge access torch towels

Set in ten acres of tree-studded grounds high above the town, this fine Victorian mansion retains many fine features including wood panelling, ornate ceilings and a wonderful marble staircase. The atmosphere is refined and relaxing, with public rooms looking onto the lawns. Bedrooms come in a variety of sizes and many are well proportioned. Staff are friendly and keen to please.

Rooms 20 en suite (3 fmly) S £40-£62; D £80-£134 (incl. bkfst)✻ **Facilities** STV Wi-fi available Xmas New Year **Parking** 40 **Notes LB** No children 12yrs

★★★ 85% COUNTRY HOUSE HOTEL

Green Park

Clunie Bridge Rd PH16 5JY

☎ 01796 473248 📠 01796 473520

e-mail: bookings@thegreenpark.co.uk

web: www.thegreenpark.co.uk

Dir: *turn off A9 at Pitlochry, follow signs 0.25m through town*

PETS: Bedrooms (16GF) unattended **Grounds** accessible disp bin **Exercise area** adjacent **Facilities** dog scoop/disp bags washing facs cage storage walks info vet info **On Request** fridge access torch towels

Guests return year after year to this lovely hotel that is situated in a stunning setting on the shores of Loch Faskally. Most of the thoughtfully designed bedrooms, including a splendid wing, the restaurant and the comfortable lounges enjoy these views. Dinner utilises fresh produce, much of it grown in the kitchen garden.

Rooms 51 en suite (16 GF) S £69-£92; D £138-£184 (incl. bkfst & dinner) **Facilities** Putt green Wi-fi available New Year **Parking** 51

★★★ 77% HOTEL

Scotland's Hotel & Leisure Club

CRERAR HOTELS

40 Bonnethill Rd PH16 5BT

☎ 0870 950 6276 📠 01796 473284

e-mail: scotlands@crerarhotels.com

web: www.crerarhotels.com

Dir: *follow A924 (Perth road) into town until War Memorial then take next right for hotel 200mtrs on right*

PETS: Bedrooms unattended **Charges** £10 per stay **Exercise area Facilities** walks info vet info

Enjoying a convenient town centre location, this long-established hotel is a popular base for tourists. Bedrooms, including family rooms and some with four-poster beds, come in a variety of styles with several situated in three period properties close by.

Rooms 57 en suite 15 annexe en suite (21 fmly) (8 GF) S £65-£105; D £95-£160 (incl. bkfst) **Facilities** Gym Wi-fi available Beauty & Therapy treatments Aromatherapy Reflexology Sports massage Xmas New Year **Services** Lift **Parking** 100 **Notes** LB

►►►► Milton of Fonab Caravan Site

(NN945573)

Bridge Rd PH16 5NA

☎ 01796 472882 01796 474363

e-mail: info@fonab.co.uk

web: www.fonab.co.uk

Dir: *0.5m S of town off A924*

PETS: disp bin **Exercise area** on site area provided **Facilities** on site shop food dog chews cat treats dog scoop/disp bags walks info vet info

Open Apr-Oct Last arrival 21.00hrs Last departure 13.00hrs

Set on the banks of the River Tummel, with extensive views down the river valley to the mountains, this park is close to the centre of Pitlochry, adjacent to the Pitlochry Festival Theatre. The sanitary facilities are exceptionally good, with most contained in combined shower/wash basin and toilet cubicles. A 15 acre site with 154 touring pitches and 36 statics.

Notes Couples & families only, no motor cycles

ST FILLANS **MAP 11 NN62**

★★★ 83% HOTEL

The Four Seasons Hotel

Loch Earn PH6 2NF

☎ 01764 685333 01764 685444

e-mail: info@thefourseasonshotel.co.uk

web: www.thefourseasonshotel.co.uk

Dir: *on A85, towards W of village*

PETS: Bedrooms unattended **Charges** charge for damage **Public areas** except restaurants **Grounds** accessible on leads disp bin **Exercise area** behind hotel **Facilities** food (pre-bookable) food bowl water bowl dog chews leads cage storage walks info vet info **On Request** fridge access torch towels **Resident Pets:** Sham & Pagne (Münsterlanders)

Set on the edge of Loch Earn, this welcoming hotel and many of its bedrooms benefit from fine views. There is a choice of lounges, including a library, warmed by log fires during winter. Local produce is used to good effect in both the Meall Reamhar restaurant and the more informal Tarken Room.

The Four Seasons Hotel

Rooms 12 en suite 6 annexe en suite (7 fmly) S £55-£100; D £110-£150 (incl. bkfst)* **Facilities** Wi-fi available Xmas New Year **Parking** 40 **Notes** LB Closed 2 Jan-Feb RS Nov, Dec, Mar

★★★ 74% SMALL HOTEL

Achray House

PH6 2NF

☎ 01764 685231 01764 685320

e-mail: info@achray-house.co.uk

web: www.achray-house.co.uk

Dir: *follow A85 towards Crainlarich, from Stirling follow A9 then B822 at Braco, B827 to Comrie. Turn left onto A85 to St Fillans*

PETS: Bedrooms (3GF) unattended **Charges** £5 per night charge for damage **Public areas** except eating areas **Grounds** accessible disp bin **Exercise area** opposite **Facilities** food (pre-bookable) food bowl water bowl leads pet sitting dog walking cage storage walks info vet info **On Request** fridge access torch towels **Resident Pets:** Corrie & Millie (Retrievers)

A friendly holiday hotel set in gardens overlooking picturesque Loch Earn, Achray House offers smart, attractive and well-equipped bedrooms. An interesting range of freshly prepared dishes is served both in the conservatory and in the adjoining dining rooms.

Rooms 8 en suite 2 annexe en suite (2 fmly) (3 GF) S £40-£60; D £70-£90 (incl. bkfst)* **Facilities** Wi-fi available Xmas New Year **Parking** 30 **Notes** Closed 3-24 Jan

SCONE MAP 11 NO12

►►► Scone Camping & Caravanning Club Site *(NO108274)*

Scone Palace PH2 6BB

☎ 01738 552323

web: www.thefriendlyclub.co.uk

Dir: *Follow signs for Scone Palace, through Perth continue for 2m. Turn left, follow site signs. 1m left onto Racecourse Road. Site entrance from car park*

PETS: Exercise area Facilities walks info vet info **Other** prior notice required

Open 2 Apr-2 Nov Last arrival 21.00hrs Last departure noon

A delightful woodland site, sheltered and well screened from the adjacent Scone racecourse. The two amenity blocks are built of timber and blend in well with the surroundings of mature trees. Super pitches add to the park's appeal. A 16-acre site with 150 touring pitches, 40 hardstandings.

Notes Site gates closed 23.00hrs-07.00hrs

SCOTTISH BORDERS

BROUGHTON MAP 11 NT13

★★★ GUEST ACCOMMODATION

The Glenholm Centre

ML12 6JF

☎ 01899 830408

e-mail: info@glenholm.co.uk

Dir: *1m S of Broughton. Off A701 to Glenholm*

PETS: Bedrooms (2GF) unattended **Grounds** accessible **Exercise area** adjacent **Facilities** water bowl leads cage storage walks info vet info **On Request** torch towels **Resident Pets:** Tarry & Minty (Bearded Collies)

Surrounded by peaceful farmland, this former schoolhouse has a distinct African theme. The home-cooked meals and baking have received much praise and are served in the spacious lounge-dining room. The bright airy bedrooms are thoughtfully equipped, and the service is friendly and attentive. Computer courses are available.

Rooms 3 en suite 1 annexe en suite (1 fmly) (2 GF) S £33-£43; D £54-£66* **Facilities** TVB tea/coffee Cen ht TVL Dinner Last d 10am Wi-fi available **Parking** 14 **Notes LB** Closed 20 Dec-1 Feb

CRAILING MAP 12 NT62

★★★★ GUEST HOUSE

Crailing Old School Guest House

TD8 6TL

☎ 01835 850382

e-mail: jean.player@virgin.net

web: www.crailingoldschool.co.uk

Dir: *A698 onto B6400 signed Nisbet, Crailing Old School also signed*

PETS: Sep Accom large kennel with run **Stables** nearby (0.5m) **Charges** £2 per night charge for damage **Grounds** accessible disp bin **Exercise area** 0.2m **Facilities** food (pre-bookable) food bowl water bowl bedding dog chews dog scoop/disp bags leads dog walking washing facs cage storage walks info vet info **On Request** fridge access torch towels **Other** pets not allowed in main house bedrooms **Resident Pets:** Lurcher (Scottish Deer Hound cross)

This delightful rural retreat, built in 1887 as the village school, has been imaginatively renovated to combine Victorian features with modern comforts. The spacious bedrooms are beautifully maintained and decorated, and filled with homely extras. The lodge annexe suite located 10 yards from the house offers easier ground-floor access. The best of local produce produces tasty breakfasts, served in the stylish lounge-dining room (evening meals by arrangement).

Rooms 3 rms (1 en suite) 1 annexe en suite (1 GF) S £37.50-£45; D £60-£70 **Facilities** TVB tea/coffee Cen ht TVL Dinner Last d 7.30pm Wi-fi available **Parking** 7 **Notes** ⊗ No children 9yrs No coaches Closed 24 Dec-2 Jan, 1 wk Feb & 2wks Autumn

GALASHIELS MAP 12 NT43

★★★ 75% SMALL HOTEL

Kingsknowes

Selkirk Rd TD1 3HY

☎ 01896 758375 📠 01896 750377

e-mail: enq@kingsknowes.co.uk

web: www.kingsknowes.co.uk

Dir: *off A7 at Galashiels/Selkirk rdbt*

PETS: Bedrooms Public areas except meal times **Grounds** accessible **Exercise area Resident Pets:** Isla & Hector (Labradors)

An imposing turreted mansion, this hotel lies in attractive gardens on the outskirts of town close to the River Tweed. It boasts elegant public areas and many spacious bedrooms, some with excellent views. There is a choice of bars, one with a popular menu to supplement the restaurant.

Rooms 12 en suite (2 fmly) **Facilities** Wi-fi available **Parking** 65 **Notes** LB

JEDBURGH MAP 12 NT62

★★ GUEST HOUSE

Ferniehirst Mill Lodge

TD8 6PQ

☎ 01835 863279

e-mail: ferniehirstmill@aol.com

web: www.ferniehirstmill.co.uk

Dir: *2.5m S on A68, onto private track to end*

PETS: Bedrooms (1GF) unattended **Stables** on site **Charges** £6-£12 per night for horses **Grounds** accessible disp bin **Exercise area Facilities** washing facs cage storage walks info vet info **On Request** fridge access torch towels **Resident Pets:** Arctic-maremma (Sheepdog), Flight (Whippet), 11 horses

Reached by a narrow farm track and a rustic wooden bridge, this chalet-style house has a secluded setting by the River Jed. Bedrooms are small and functional but there is a comfortable lounge in which to relax. Home-cooked dinners are available by arrangement, and hearty breakfasts are served in the cosy dining room.

Rooms 7 en suite (1 GF) S £22-£27; D £44-£54 **Facilities** tea/coffee Direct dial from bedrooms Licensed Cen ht TVL Dinner Last d 5pm Fishing Riding **Parking** 10 **Notes** No coaches

►►► Jedburgh Camping & Caravanning Club Site *(NT658219)*

Elliot Park, Edinburgh Rd TD8 6EF

☎ 01835 863393

web: www.thefriendlyclub.co.uk

Dir: *Site opposite Edinburgh & Jedburgh Woollen Mills. N of Jedburgh on A68 (Newcastle-Edinburgh road)*

PETS: disp bin **Exercise area Facilities** walks info vet info **Other** prior notice required

Open 2 Apr-2 Nov Last arrival 21.00hrs Last departure noon

A touring site on the northern edge of town, nestling at the foot of cliffs close to Jed Water. Hardstandings are a welcome feature for caravans. A 3-acre site with 60 touring pitches, 13 hardstandings.

Notes Site gates closed 23.00hrs-07.00hrs

KELSO MAP 12 NT73

★★★ 85% ® COUNTRY HOUSE HOTEL

The Roxburghe Hotel & Golf Course

Heiton TD5 8JZ

☎ 01573 450331 📠 01573 450611

e-mail: hotel@roxburghe.net

web: www.roxburghe.net

Dir: *from A68 Jedburgh take A698 to Heiton, 3m SW of Kelso*

PETS: Bedrooms Sep Accom 2 outdoor kennels **Public areas** courtyard annexe only **Grounds** accessible **Exercise area Facilities** food bowl water bowl **Other** Courtyard rooms only

Outdoor sporting pursuits are popular at this impressive Jacobean mansion owned by the Duke of Roxburghe, and set in 500 acres of woods and parkland bordering the River Teviot. Gracious public areas are the perfect settings for afternoon teas and carefully prepared meals. The elegant bedrooms are individually designed, some by the Duchess herself, and include superior rooms, some with four posters and log fires.

Rooms 16 en suite 6 annexe en suite (3 fmly) (3 GF) S £147-£170; D £185-£390 (incl. bkfst)✳ **Facilities Spa** STV ⛳ 18 Fishing Putt green Clay shooting Health & beauty salon Mountain bike hire Falconry Archery Xmas New Year **Parking** 150 **Notes** LB

LAUDER

MAP 12 NT54

★★★★ INN

The Black Bull

Market Place TD2 6SR

☎ 01578 722208 📠 01578 722419

e-mail: enquiries@blackbull-lauder.com

web: www.blackbull-lauder.com

Dir: *On A68 in village centre*

PETS: Bedrooms Charges £5 per stay charge for damage **Public areas** bar & reception only (on leads) **Grounds** accessible on leads **Exercise area Facilities** food bowl water bowl cage storage walks info vet info **On Request** fridge access torch towels **Restrictions** no Rottweilers

This 18th-century coaching inn has been completely transformed. The lovely bedrooms are furnished in the period character and thoughtfully equipped with modern amenities. All with wooden floors, the cosy bar and four dining areas are charming, the main dining room being a former chapel. The tremendous range of food makes this a destination gastro-pub.

Rooms 8 en suite (2 fmly) **Facilities** TVB tea/coffee Direct dial from bedrooms Cen ht Dinner Last d 9pm **Parking** 8 **Notes** Closed 1st 3 wks of Feb

►►► Lauder Camping & Caravanning Club Site *(NT509535)*

Carfraemill, Oxton TD2 6RA

☎ 01578 750697

web: www.thefriendlyclub.co.uk

Dir: *From Lauder, right at rdbt onto A697, then left at Lodge Hotel (signed). Site on right behind Carfraemill Hotel*

PETS: Public areas except in buildings disp bin **Exercise area** on site by river **Facilities** walks info vet info **Other** prior notice required

Open 2 Apr-2 Nov Last arrival 21.00hrs Last departure noon

A meadowland site with good facilities housed in pine lodge buildings, and pleasant surroundings. Ideal either as a touring base or transit site, it is extremely well maintained. There are four wooden chalets for hire. A 5-acre site with 60 touring pitches, 9 hardstandings.

Notes Site gates closed 23.00hrs-07.00hrs

►►► Thirlestane Castle Caravan & Camping Site *(NT536473)*

Thirlestane Castle TD2 6RU

☎ 01578 718884 & 07976 231032

e-mail: thirlestanepark@btconnect.com

web: www.thirlestanecastlepark.co.uk

Dir: *Signed off A68 & A697, just S of Lauder*

PETS: disp bin **Exercise area Facilities** walks info vet info **Restrictions** no Pit Bull Terriers

Open Apr-1 Oct Last arrival 21.00hrs Last departure noon

Set in the grounds of the impressive Thirlestane Castle, with mainly level grassy pitches. The park and facilities are kept in sparkling condition. A 5-acre site with 60 touring pitches and 21 statics.

Notes

PEEBLES

MAP 11 NT24

★★★★ COUNTRY HOUSE HOTEL

Cringletie House

PRIDE OF BRITAIN HOTELS

Edinburgh Rd EH45 8PL

☎ 01721 725750 📠 01721 725751

e-mail: enquiries@cringletie.com

web: www.cringletie.com

Dir: *2m N on A703*

PETS: Bedrooms unattended **Charges** £10 per night **Grounds** accessible **Exercise area** on site **Other** all dogs welcomed with a dog biscuit **Resident Pets:** Daisy (cat)

This long-established hotel is a romantic baronial mansion set in 28 acres of gardens and woodland with stunning views from all rooms. Delightful public rooms include a cocktail lounge with adjoining conservatory, whilst the first-floor restaurant is graced by a magnificent hand-painted ceiling. Bedrooms, many of them particularly spacious, are attractively furnished.

Rooms 13 en suite (2 GF) S £165-£325; D £220-£375 (incl. bkfst)* **Facilities** STV Putt green Wi-fi in bedrooms Petanque Giant chess & draughts Xmas New Year **Services** Lift **Parking** 30 **Notes** LB

★★★★ 77% ❁ HOTEL

Macdonald Cardrona Hotel Golf & Country Club

Cardrona Mains EH45 6LZ

☎ 01896 833600 01896 831166

e-mail: general.cardrona@macdonald-hotels.co.uk

web: www.macdonald-hotels.co.uk

Dir: *On A72 between Peebles & Innerleithen, 3m S of Peebles.*

PETS: Bedrooms (17GF) unattended **Stables** nearby (2m) **Charges** charge for damage **Public areas** lounge only (on leads) **Grounds** accessible on leads disp bin **Exercise area** on site **Facilities** washing facs cage storage walks info vet info **On Request** fridge access torch towels

The rolling hills of the Scottish Borders are a stunning backdrop for this modern, purpose-built hotel. Spacious bedrooms are traditional in style, equipped with a range of extras, and most enjoy fantastic countryside. The hotel features some impressive leisure facilities, including an 18-hole golf course, 18-metre indoor pool and state-of-the-art gym.

Rooms 99 en suite (24 fmly) (17 GF) S £25-£30; D £75-£159 (incl. bkfst) ✳ **Facilities Spa** STV 18 Gym Putt green Wi-fi in bedrooms Sauna Steam room Xmas New Year **Services** Lift **Parking** 200

★★★ 82% ❁ COUNTRY HOUSE HOTEL

Castle Venlaw

Edinburgh Rd EH45 8QG

☎ 01721 720384 01721 724066

e-mail: stay@venlaw.co.uk

web: www.venlaw.co.uk

Dir: *off A703 Peebles/Edinburgh road, 0.75m N of Peebles*

PETS: Bedrooms unattended **Stables** nearby (3m) **Charges** £10 per night charge for damage **Grounds** accessible disp bin **Exercise area** 20mtrs **Facilities** washing facs cage storage walks info vet info **On Request** fridge access torch

This 18th-century castle is set in four acres of landscaped gardens, set high above the town. Most bedrooms are spacious and all have smart modern bathrooms. Those in the Romantic and four-poster rooms are stunning and worth asking for. There is a cosy library bar and classically elegant restaurant. Service is friendly and obliging.

Rooms 12 en suite (3 fmly) S £103.50-£178.50; D £178.50 (incl. bkfst & dinner)✳ **Facilities** FTV Wi-fi available Xmas New Year **Parking** 17

★★★ 77% HOTEL

Tontine

High St EH45 8AJ

☎ 01721 720892 01721 729732

e-mail: info@tontinehotel.com

web: www.tontinehotel.com

Dir: *in town centre*

PETS: Bedrooms Charges charge for damage **Public areas** assist dogs only **Exercise area** Tweed Green behind hotel **Other** certain bedrooms only **Restrictions** small, well behaved dogs only

Conveniently situated in the main street, this long-established hotel offers comfortable public rooms including an elegant Adam restaurant, inviting lounge and 'clubby' bar. Bedrooms, contained in the original house and the river-facing wing, offer a smart, classical style of accommodation. The lasting impression is of the excellent level of hospitality and guest care.

Rooms 36 en suite (3 fmly) S £45-£75; D £80-£130 (incl. bkfst)✳ **Facilities** Wi-fi in bedrooms Xmas New Year **Parking** 24 **Notes LB**

★★★ 74% HOTEL

Park

Innerleithen Rd EH45 8BA

☎ 01721 720451 01721 723510

e-mail: reserve@parkpeebles.co.uk

Dir: *in town centre opposite filling station*

PETS: Bedrooms unattended sign **Stables** nearby (2m) **Public areas** except when food is served **Grounds** accessible disp bin **Exercise area** 30yds **Facilities** dog scoop/disp bags walks info vet info **On Request** fridge access torch

This hotel offers pleasant, well-equipped bedrooms of various sizes - those in the original house are particularly spacious. Public areas enjoy views of the gardens and include a tartan-clad bar, a relaxing lounge and a spacious wood-panelled restaurant. Guests can use the extensive leisure facilities on offer at the sister hotel, The Hydro.

Rooms 24 en suite **Facilities** STV Putt green Wi-fi available Use of facilities at Peebles Hotel Hydro **Services** Lift **Parking** 50

SCOTLAND

SCOTLAND

PEEBLES CONTINUED

►►►► Crossburn Caravan Park *(NT248417)*

Edinburgh Rd EH45 8ED

☎ 01721 720501 🖷 01721 720501

e-mail: enquiries@crossburncaravans.co.uk

web: www.crossburncaravans.co.uk

Dir: *0.5m N of Peebles on A703*

PETS: Public areas except shop (on leads) disp bin **Exercise area** on site dog walk **Facilities** on site shop walks info vet info **Other** max 2 dogs per pitch **Resident Pets:** Zara (Rhodesian Ridgeback), Ginty (Jack Russell)

Open Apr-Oct Last arrival 21.00hrs Last departure 14.00hrs

A peaceful site in a relatively quiet location, despite the proximity of the main road which partly borders the site, as does the Eddleston Water. There are lovely views, and the park is well stocked with trees, flowers and shrubs. Facilities are maintained to a high standard, and fully-serviced pitches are available. A large caravan dealership is on the same site. A 6-acre site with 45 touring pitches, 15 hardstandings and 85 statics.

ST BOSWELLS — MAP 12 NT53

★★★ 72% SMALL HOTEL

Buccleuch Arms

The Green TD6 0EW

☎ 01835 822243 🖷 01835 823965

e-mail: info@buccleucharms.com

web: www.buccleucharms.com

Dir: *on A68, 8m N of Jedburgh*

PETS: Bedrooms Sep Accom kennel suitable for 2 dogs **Stables** nearby (2m) **Charges** £5 per night **Public areas** except restaurant **Grounds** accessible **Exercise area** on site **Facilities** washing facs cage storage walks info vet info **On Request** fridge access towels **Resident Pets:** Jasper & Monty (Black Labradors), Kelly (Springer Spaniel), Becca & Jasper (Golden Labradors)

Formerly a coaching inn, this long-established hotel stands is the ideal spot for relaxation. Each bedroom is individually designed with striking fabrics and colour combinations. The lounge bar is a popular eating venue and complements the attractive restaurant. Morning coffees and afternoon teas are served in the comfortable lounge with its open fire.

Rooms 19 en suite (1 fmly) S £76-£85; D £95-£105 (incl. bkfst) **Facilities** New Year **Parking** 50 **Notes LB** Closed 25 Dec

SOUTH AYRSHIRE

BALLANTRAE — MAP 10 NX08

★★★★★ ®®® HOTEL

Glenapp Castle

RELAIS & CHATEAUX.

KA26 0NZ

☎ 01465 831212 🖷 01465 831000

e-mail: enquiries@glenappcastle.com

web: www.glenappcastle.com

Dir: *1m from A77 near Ballantrae*

PETS: Bedrooms Grounds accessible disp bin **Exercise area** on site **Facilities** food bowl water bowl feeding mat dog scoop/disp bags leads pet sitting washing facs cage storage walks info vet info **On Request** fridge access torch towels **Resident Pets:** Midge (Springer Spaniel)

Friendly hospitality and attentive service prevail at this stunning Victorian castle, set in extensive private grounds to the south of the village. Impeccably furnished bedrooms are graced with antiques and period pieces. Breathtaking views of Arran and Ailsa Craig can be enjoyed from the delightful, sumptuous day rooms and from many of the bedrooms. Accomplished cooking, using quality local ingredients, is a feature of all meals; dinner is offered on a well crafted and imaginative, no-choice, five course menu. Make a point of walking round the wonderful grounds, to include the azalea lake and walled vegetable gardens with their fine restored greenhouses.

Rooms 17 en suite (2 fmly) (7 GF) S £255-£455; D £375-£575 (incl. bkfst & dinner)* **Facilities** STV FTV Wi-fi available New Year **Services** Lift **Parking** 20 **Notes LB** Closed Jan & Feb

BARRHILL — MAP 10 NX28

►►►► *Barrhill Holiday Park* *(NX216835)*

KA26 0PZ

☎ 01465 821355 🖷 01465 821355

e-mail: barrhill@surfree.co.uk

web: www.barrhillholidaypark.com

Dir: *On A714 (Newton Stewart to Girvan road). 1m N of Barrhill*

PETS: Public areas (on leads) **Exercise area** on site end of park **Facilities** on site shop food bowl water bowl dog scoop/disp bags washing facs walks info vet info **Resident Pets:** Sophie & Sparkie (cats)

Open Mar-Jan

A small, friendly park in a tranquil rural location, screened from the A714 by trees. The park is terraced and well landscaped, and a high quality amenity block includes disabled facilities. A 6-acre site with 30 touring pitches, 9 hardstandings and 29 statics.

Notes ⊜

MAYBOLE — MAP 10 NS20

►►► Culzean Castle Camping & Caravanning Club Site *(NS247103)*

Culzean Castle KA19 8JX

☎ 01655 760627

web: www.thefriendlyclub.co.uk

Dir: *From N on A77 in Maybole turn right onto B7023 (signed Culzean & Maidens), left in 100yds. Site 4m on right*

PETS: disp bin **Exercise area** on site dog walks **Facilities** walks info vet info **Other** prior notice required

Open 2 Apr-2 Nov Last arrival 21.00hrs Last departure noon

A mainly level grass park with some gently sloping pitches and hard stands along the bed of an old railway, situated at the entrance to the castle and country park. The park is surrounded by trees on three sides and has lovely views over Culzean Bay. A 10-acre site with 90 touring pitches, 27 hardstandings.

Notes Site gates closed 23.00hrs-07.00hrs

TROON — MAP 10 NS33

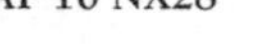

★★★★ 73% HOTEL

Barceló Troon Marine Hotel

Barceló

Crosbie Rd KA10 6HE

☎ 01292 314444 🖷 01292 316922

e-mail: marine@barcelo-hotels.co.uk

web: www.barcelo-hotels.co.uk

Dir: *A77, A78, A79 onto B749. Hotel on left after golf course*

PETS: Bedrooms unattended sign **Stables** nearby (5m) **Charges** £15 per week charge for damage **Grounds** accessible on leads disp bin **Exercise area** 100yds **Facilities** food (pre-bookable) food bowl water bowl bedding pet sitting dog walking cage storage walks info vet info **On Request** fridge access torch towels

A favourite with conference and leisure guests, this hotel overlooks Royal Troon's 18th fairway. The cocktail lounge and split-level restaurant enjoy panoramic views of the Firth of Clyde across to the Isle of Arran. Bedrooms and public areas are attractively appointed.

Rooms 89 en suite S £60-£170✻ **Facilities Spa** ⓢ supervised Squash Gym Wi-fi available Steam room Beauty room Xmas New Year **Services** Lift **Parking** 200

TURNBERRY — MAP 10 NS20

★★★★★ ◎◎ HOTEL

Westin Turnberry Resort

KA26 9LT

☎ 01655 331000 🖷 01655 331706

e-mail: turnberry@westin.com

web: www.westin.com/turnberry

Dir: *from Glasgow take A77/M77 S towards Stranraer, 2m past Kirkoswald, follow signs for A719/Turnberry. Hotel 500mtrs on right*

PETS: Bedrooms sign **Public areas** foyer only **Grounds** accessible **Exercise area** on site **Facilities** food bowl water bowl bedding feeding mat **Other** welcome kit

This famous hotel enjoys magnificent views over to Arran, Ailsa Craig and the Mull of Kintyre. Facilities include a world-renowned golf course, the excellent Colin Montgomerie Golf Academy, a luxurious spa and a host of outdoor and country pursuits. Elegant bedrooms and suites are located in the main hotel, while adjacent lodges provide spacious, well-equipped accommodation. The Ailsa lounge is very welcoming, and in addition to the elegant main restaurant for dining, there is a Mediterranean Terrace Brasserie and the relaxed Clubhouse.

Rooms 130 en suite 89 annexe en suite (9 fmly) (16 GF) S £230-£375; D £250-£395 (incl. bkfst)✻ **Facilities Spa** STV ⓢ supervised ⛳ 36 ♨ Fishing Riding Gym Putt green Wi-fi available Leisure club Outdoor activity centre Colin Montgomerie Golf Academy New Year **Services** Lift **Parking** 200 **Notes LB** Closed 25 Dec

SCOTLAND

SOUTH LANARKSHIRE

ABINGTON MAP 11 NS92

►►► Mount View Caravan Park *(NS935235)*

ML12 6RW

☎ 01864 502808 🖹 01864 502808

e-mail: info@mountviewcaravanpark.co.uk

web: www.mountviewcaravanpark.co.uk

Dir: *M74 junct 13 onto A702 S into Abington. Left into Station Road, over river & railway. Site on right*

PETS: Public areas except static pitches (on leads) **Exercise area** public walks adjacent **Facilities** vet info **Other** prior notice required **Resident Pets:** Hollie (Retriever)

Open Mar-Oct

A developing park, surrounded by the Southern Uplands and handily located between Carlisle and Glasgow. It is an excellent stopover site for those travelling between Scotland and the South. The West Coast railway passes beside the park. A 5.5-acre site with 51 touring pitches, 51 hardstandings and 20 statics.

Notes No cars by tents. Dogs must be walked off the park. 5mph speed limit

ABINGTON MOTORWAY SERVICE AREA (M74) MAP 11 NS92

BUDGET HOTEL

Days Inn Abington

ML12 6RG

☎ 01864 502782 🖹 01864 502759

e-mail: abington.hotel@welcomebreak.co.uk

web: www.welcomebreak.co.uk

Dir: *M74 junct 13, accessible from N'bound and S'bound carriageways*

PETS: Bedrooms unattended **Public areas** (on leads) **Grounds** accessible **Exercise area**

This modern building offers accommodation in smart, spacious and well-equipped bedrooms, suitable for families and business travellers, and all with en suite bathrooms. Refreshments may be taken at the nearby family restaurant.

Rooms 52 en suite S £39-£59; D £49-£69*

BIGGAR MAP 11 NT03

★★★★ 71% ◎◎ COUNTRY HOUSE HOTEL

Shieldhill Castle

Quothquan ML12 6NA

☎ 01899 220035 🖹 01899 221092

e-mail: enquiries@shieldhill.co.uk

web: www.shieldhill.co.uk

Dir: *A702 onto B7016 (Biggar to Carnwath road), after 2m left into Shieldhill Road. Hotel 1.5m on right*

PETS: Bedrooms unattended **Stables** nearby (5m) **Charges** charge for damage **Grounds** accessible on leads disp bin **Exercise area Facilities** washing facs cage storage walks info vet info **On Request** fridge access torch towels **Resident Pets:** Mutley (Springer/Cocker Spaniel)

The focus on food and wine are important at this imposing fortified country mansion that dates back almost 800 years. Public room are atmospheric and include the classical Chancellors' Restaurant, oak-panelled lounge and the Gun Room bar that offers its own menu. Bedrooms, many with feature baths, are spacious and comfortable. A friendly welcome is assured, even from the estate's own dog!

Rooms 16 en suite 10 annexe en suite (10 GF) S £85-£248; D £100-£248 (incl. bkfst) **Facilities** FTV Wi-fi available Cycling Clay shoot Hot air ballooning Falconry Laser & game bird shooting Xmas New Year **Parking** 50

NEW LANARK MAP 11 NS84

★★★ 82% HOTEL

New Lanark Mill Hotel

Mill One, New Lanark Mills ML11 9DB

☎ 01555 667200 🖹 01555 667222

e-mail: hotel@newlanark.org

web: www.newlanark.org

Dir: *signed from all major roads, M74 junct 7 & M8*

PETS: Bedrooms unattended **Charges** £5 per night charge for damage **Grounds** accessible **Exercise area Facilities** cage storage vet info

Originally built as a cotton mill in the 18th-century, this hotel forms part of a fully restored village, now a UNESCO World Heritage Site. There's a bright modern style throughout which contrasts nicely with features from the original mill. There is a comfortable foyer-lounge with a galleried restaurant above. The hotel enjoys stunning views over the River Clyde.

Rooms 38 en suite (5 fmly) S £79.50; D £119-£144 (incl. bkfst)* **Facilities** STV Gym Wi-fi available Beauty room Steam room Sauna Aerobics studios Xmas New Year **Services** Lift **Parking** 75 **Notes** LB

STIRLING

BALMAHA MAP 10 NS49

►►►► Milarrochy Bay Camping & Caravanning Club Site *(NN407927)*

Milarrochy Bay G63 0AL

☎ 01360 870236

web: www.thefriendlyclub.co.uk

Dir: *A811 (Balloch to Stirling road) take Drymen turn. In Drymen take B837 for Balmaha. In 5m road turns sharp right up steep hill. Site in 1.5m*

PETS: Public areas except in buildings disp bin **Exercise area** on site **Facilities** walks info vet info **Other** prior notice required

Open 2 Apr-2 Nov Last arrival 21.00hrs Last departure noon

On the quieter side of Loch Lomond next to the 75,000-acre Queen Elizabeth Forest, this attractive site offers very good facilities. Disabled toilets and family rooms are appointed to a high standard. Towing vehicles should engage low gear immediately at steep hill warning sign in Balmaha. A 12-acre site with 150 touring pitches, 23 hardstandings.

Notes Site gates closed 23.00hrs-07.00hrs

BLAIRLOGIE MAP 11 NS89

►►►► Witches Craig Caravan & Camping Park *(NS821968)*

FK9 5PX

☎ 01786 474947 01786 447286

e-mail: info@witchescraig.co.uk

web: www.witchescraig.co.uk

Dir: *3m NE of Stirling on A91 (Hillfoots-St Andrews road)*

PETS: Public areas except amenity block & children's play area disp bin **Exercise area** on site woods **Facilities** vet info

Open Apr-Oct Last arrival 21.00hrs Last departure 13.00hrs

In an attractive setting with direct access to the lower slopes of the dramatic Ochil Hills, this is a well-maintained family-run park. It is in the centre of 'Braveheart' country, with easy access to historical sites and many popular attractions. A 5-acre site with 60 touring pitches, 26 hardstandings.

LOCHEARNHEAD MAP 11 NN52

★★★★ GUEST HOUSE

Mansewood Country House

FK19 8NS

☎ 01567 830213

e-mail: stay@mansewoodcountryhouse.co.uk

Dir: *A84 N to Lochearnhead, 1st building on left*

PETS: Bedrooms Grounds accessible on leads disp bin **Exercise area Facilities** food bowl water bowl walks info vet info **On Request** fridge access **Other** dogs accepted in log cabin only

This house is a spacious former manse that dates back to the 18th century and lies in a well-tended garden to the south of the village. Bedrooms are well appointed and equipped and offer high standards of comfort. Refreshments can be enjoyed in the cosy bar or the elegant lounge, and meals prepared with flair are served in the attractive restaurant.

Rooms 6 en suite (1 GF) S £40; D £60* **Facilities** TVB tea/coffee Licensed Cen ht TVL Dinner Last d 7.15pm Wi-fi available **Parking** 6 **Notes** LB No coaches RS Nov-Mar

STIRLING MAP 11 NS79

★★★★ 76% HOTEL

Barceló Stirling Highland Hotel

Spittal St FK8 1DU

☎ 01786 272727 01786 272829

e-mail: stirling@barcelo-hotels.co.uk

web: www.barcelo-hotels.co.uk

Dir: *A84 into Stirling. Follow Stirling Castle signs as far as Albert Hall. Left, left again, follow Castle signs*

PETS: Bedrooms unattended **Charges** £15 per week **Public areas** except restaurant (on leads) **Exercise area** 5 min walk **Facilities** food bowl water bowl bedding walks info vet info

Enjoying a location close to the castle and historic old town, this atmospheric hotel was previously the High School. Public rooms have been converted from the original classrooms and retain many interesting features. Bedrooms are more modern in style and comfortably equipped. Scholars Restaurant serves traditional and international dishes, and the Headmaster's Study is the ideal venue for enjoying a drink.

Rooms 96 en suite (4 fmly) S £60-£140* **Facilities** Spa Squash Gym Wi-fi available Steam room Dance studio Beauty therapist Xmas New Year **Services** Lift **Parking** 96

STIRLING CONTINUED

BUDGET HOTEL

Travelodge Stirling (M80)

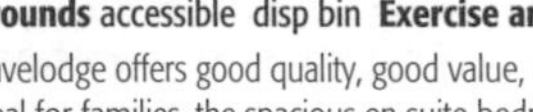

Pirnhall Roundabout, Snabhead FK7 8EU

☎ 0871 9846178 🖷 01786 817646

web: www.travelodge.co.uk

Dir: *M9/M80 junct 9*

PETS: Bedrooms unattended **Charges** £10 per stay **Public areas Grounds** accessible disp bin **Exercise area** 20mtrs

Travelodge offers good quality, good value, modern accommodation. Ideal for families, the spacious en suite bedrooms include remote-control TV, tea and coffee-making facilities and comfortable beds. Meals can be taken at the nearby family restaurant.

Rooms 37 en suite S fr £29; D fr £29

★★★★ GUEST HOUSE

Linden Guest House

22 Linden Av FK7 7PQ

☎ 01786 448850 & 07974 116573 🖷 01786 448850

e-mail: fay@lindenguesthouse.co.uk

web: www.lindenguesthouse.co.uk

Dir: *0.5m SE of city centre off A9*

PETS: Bedrooms (1GF) **Charges** charge for damage **Grounds** accessible on leads disp bin **Exercise area** 50mtrs **Facilities** dog scoop/disp bags leads cage storage walks info vet info **On Request** fridge access torch towels

Situated within walking distance of the town centre, this friendly guest house offers attractive and very well-equipped bedrooms, including a large family room that sleeps five comfortably. There is a bright dining room where delicious breakfasts are served at individual tables.

Rooms 4 en suite (2 fmly) (1 GF) S £50-£60; D £60-£70✻
Facilities STV TVB tea/coffee Cen ht Wi-fi available **Parking** 2
Notes LB No coaches

STRATHYRE — MAP 11 NN51

★★★★★ ❀❀ RESTAURANT WITH ROOMS

Creagan House

FK18 8ND

☎ 01877 384638 🖷 01877 384319

e-mail: eatandstay@creaganhouse.co.uk

web: www.creaganhouse.co.uk

Dir: *0.25m N of Strathyre on A84*

PETS: Bedrooms (1GF) unattended **Grounds** accessible disp bin **Exercise area** part of National Park accessible from car park **Facilities** food bowl water bowl leads washing facs cage storage walks info vet info **On Request** fridge access torch towels **Resident Pets:** Budd (Gordon Setter), Raffles (visiting African Grey Parrot)

Originally a farmhouse dating from the 17th century, Creagan House has operated as a restaurant with rooms for many years. The baronial-style dining room provides a wonderful setting for sympathetic cooking. Warm hospitality and attentive service are the highlights of any stay.

Rooms 5 en suite (1 fmly) (1 GF) S £70-£85; D £120-£130
Facilities FTV TVB tea/coffee Cen ht Dinner Last d 8.30pm **Parking** 26
Notes LB Closed 21 Jan-5 Mar & 1-19 Nov RS Wed & Thu

WEST DUNBARTONSHIRE

BALLOCH MAP 10 NS38

★★★ BED & BREAKFAST

Sunnyside

35 Main St G83 9JX

☎ 01389 750282 & 07717 397548

e-mail: enquiries@sunnysidebb.co.uk

Dir: *From A82 take A811 then A813 for 1m, over mini-rdbt 150mtrs on left*

PETS: Bedrooms (1GF) unattended **Charges** £5 per stay £10 per week charge for damage **Grounds** accessible disp bin **Exercise area** 350yds **Facilities** food (pre-bookable) food bowl water bowl bedding dog chews dog scoop/disp bags leads washing facs cage storage walks info vet info **On Request** fridge access torch towels

Set in its own grounds well back from the road by Loch Lomond, Sunnyside is an attractive, traditional detached house, parts of which date back to the 1830s. Bedrooms are attractively decorated and provide comfortable modern accommodation. The dining room is located on the ground floor, and is an appropriate setting for hearty Scottish breakfasts.

Rooms 6 en suite (2 fmly) (1 GF) S £25-£40; D £40-£60* **Facilities** TVB tea/coffee Cen ht **Parking** 8

►►►► Lomond Woods Holiday Park

(NS383816)

Old Luss Rd G83 8QP

☎ 01389 755000 📠 01389 755563

e-mail: lomondwoods@holiday-parks.co.uk

web: www.holiday-parks.co.uk

Dir: *From A82, 17m N of Glasgow, take A811(Stirling to Balloch road). Left at 1st rdbt, follow holiday park signs, 150yds on left*

PETS: Charges 50p per night disp bin **Public areas** except children's play area **Exercise area** on site perimeter walk **Facilities** walks info vet info **Other** prior notice required **Restrictions** no dangerous breeds (see page 7) **Resident Pets:** Jack & Cody (Labradors)

Open all year Last arrival 21.00hrs Last departure noon

A mature park with well-laid out pitches screened by trees and shrubs, surrounded by woodland and hills. The park is within walking distance of 'Loch Lomond Shores', a leisure and retail complex which is the main gateway to Scotland's first national park. Amenities include the Loch Lomond Aquarium, an Interactive Exhibition and loch cruises. A 13-acre site with 110 touring pitches, 110 hardstandings and 35 statics.

Notes No tents, no jet skis

WEST LOTHIAN

EAST CALDER MAP 11 NT06

►►► Linwater Caravan Park *(NT104696)*

West Clifton EH53 0HT

☎ 0131 333 3326 📠 0131 333 1952

e-mail: linwater@supanet.com

web: www.linwater.co.uk

Dir: *M9 junct 1, signed from B7030 or from Wilkieston on A71*

PETS: Public areas except toilet block disp bin **Exercise area** on site walks to parks & canal **Facilities** walks info vet info **Other** prior notice required **Resident Pets:** Mimi (Black Labrador), Minnow (Cocker Spaniel), Treagh (Deerhound), Beth (Golden Retriever), Cobbles (cat), sheep, pigs, ducks, hens

Open late Mar-late Oct Last arrival 21.00hrs Last departure noon

A farmland park in a peaceful rural area within easy reach of Edinburgh. The very good facilities are housed in a Scandinavian-style building, and are well maintained by resident owners. Nearby are plenty of pleasant woodland walks. A 5-acre site with 60 touring pitches, 14 hardstandings.

LINLITHGOW MAP 11 NS97

★★★★ GUEST HOUSE

Bomains Farm

Bo'Ness EH49 7RQ

☎ 01506 822188 & 822861 📠 01506 824433

e-mail: bunty.kirk@onetel.net

web: www.bomains.co.uk

Dir: *A706 1.5m N towards Bo Ness, left at golf course x-rds, 1st farm on right*

PETS: Bedrooms unattended **Stables** on site **Charges** £5 per night **Grounds** accessible **Exercise area** adjacent **Other** pets may be left unattended by arrangement only **Resident Pets:** Minnie (Bichon Frise), Penny (Mini Schnauzer)

From its elevated location this friendly farmhouse has stunning views of the Firth of Forth. The bedrooms which vary in size are beautifully decorated, well equipped and enhanced by quality fabrics, with many thoughtful extra touches. Delicious home-cooked fare featuring the best of local produce is served a stylish lounge-dining room.

Rooms 5 rms (4 en suite) (1 pri facs) S £35-£40; D £50-£70 **Facilities** STV TVB tea/coffee Cen ht TVL Dinner Last d 5.30pm Golf 18 **Parking** 12 **Notes** No coaches

LIVINGSTON **MAP 11 NT06**

BUDGET HOTEL

Travelodge Livingston

Almondvale Cresent EH54 6QX

☎ 08719 846 288 🖷 0121 521 6026

web: www.travelodge.co.uk

Dir: *M8 junct 3 onto A899 towards Livingston. At 2nd rdbt right onto A779. At 2nd rdbt left. Lodge on left*

PETS: Bedrooms unattended **Charges** £10 per stay charge for damage **Public areas Grounds** accessible disp bin **Exercise area** 200yds **Facilities** walks info vet info **On Request** fridge access torch towels

Travelodge offers good quality, good value, modern accommodation. Ideal for families, the spacious en suite bedrooms include remote-control TV, tea and coffee-making facilities and comfortable beds. Meals can be taken at the nearby family restaurant.

Rooms 60 en suite S fr £29; D fr £29

SCOTTISH ISLANDS

Isle of Arran

LOCHRANZA **MAP 10 NR95**

►►► Lochranza Caravan & Camping Site

(NR942500)

KA27 8HL

☎ 01770 830273

e-mail: office@lochgolf.demon.co.uk

web: www.lochranzagolf.com

Dir: *On A841 at N of island, beside Kintyre ferry & 14m N of Brodick for ferry to Ardrossan*

PETS: Exercise area on site **Facilities** on site shop food vet info

Open Mar-30 Oct Last arrival 22.00hrs Last departure 13.00hrs

Attractive park in a beautiful location, run by friendly family owners. The park is adjacent to an 18-hole golf course, opposite the famous Arran Distillery, between tree-lined hills on the edge of the village. Golf and ferry packages can be arranged. A 2.5-acre site with 60 touring pitches, 10 hardstandings.

Notes No fires

Isle of Harris

SCARISTA **MAP 13 NG09**

★★★★ ◎◎ RESTAURANT WITH ROOMS

Scarista House

HS3 3HX

☎ 01859 550238 🖷 01859 550277

e-mail: timandpatricia@scaristahouse.com

Dir: *On A859, 15m S of Tarbert*

PETS: Bedrooms (2GF) unattended **Public areas** Library only **Grounds** accessible on leads disp bin **Exercise area** 200yds **Facilities** food bowl water bowl pet sitting washing facs cage storage walks info vet info **On Request** fridge access torch towels **Resident Pets:** Molly (Cavalier King Charles Spaniel), Misty & Pip (cats)

A former manse, Scarista House is now a haven for food lovers who seek to explore this magnificent island. The house enjoys breathtaking views of the Atlantic and is just a short stroll from miles of golden sandy beaches. It is run in a relaxed country-house manner by the friendly hosts. Expect wellies in the hall and masses of books and CDs in one of two lounges. Bedrooms are cosy, and delicious set dinners and memorable breakfasts are provided.

Rooms 3 en suite 2 annexe en suite (2 GF) S £125-£150; D £175-£199 **Facilities** tea/coffee Direct dial from bedrooms Cen ht Dinner Last d 8pm **Parking** 12 **Notes LB** Closed Xmas, Jan & Feb

Isle of Mull

TOBERMORY **MAP 13 NM55**

★★★ ◎◎ SMALL HOTEL

Highland Cottage

Breadalbane St PA75 6PD

☎ 01688 302030

e-mail: davidandjo@highlandcottage.co.uk

web: www.highlandcottage.co.uk

Dir: *A848 Craignure/Fishnish ferry terminal, pass Tobermory signs, straight on at mini rdbt across narrow bridge, turn right. Hotel on right opposite fire station*

PETS: Bedrooms Charges charge for damage **Exercise area** 3 mins walk **Facilities** washing facs cage storage walks info vet info **On Request** fridge access torch towels **Restrictions** no large hairy dogs (German Shepherd, St.Bernard etc)

Providing the highest level of natural and unassuming hospitality, this delightful little gem lies high above the island's capital. Don't be fooled by its side street location, a stunning view over the bay is just a few metres away. 'A country house hotel in town' it is an Aladdin's Cave of collectables and treasures, as well as masses of books and magazines. There are two inviting lounges, one with an honesty bar. The cosy dining room offers memorable dinners and splendid breakfasts.

Bedrooms are individual; some have four-posters and all are comprehensively equipped to include TVs and music centres.

Rooms 6 en suite (1 GF) S £120-£165; D £140-£185 (incl. bkfst)* **Facilities** Wi-fi available **Parking** 6 **Notes** LB No children 10yrs Closed Nov-Feb

★★ 76% HOTEL

Tobermory

53 Main St PA75 6NT

☎ 01688 302091 📠 01688 302254

e-mail: tobhotel@tinyworld.co.uk

web: www.thetobermoryhotel.com

Dir: *on waterfront, overlooking Tobermory Bay*

PETS: Bedrooms (2GF) **Charges** charge for damage **Exercise area** 200yds **Facilities** cage storage walks info vet info **On Request** fridge access

This friendly hotel, with its pretty pink frontage, sits on the seafront amid other brightly coloured, picture-postcard buildings. There is a comfortable and relaxing lounge where drinks are served (there is no bar) prior to dining in the stylish restaurant. Bedrooms come in a variety of sizes; all are bright and vibrant.

Rooms 16 rms (15 en suite) (3 fmly) (2 GF) **Notes** LB Closed Xmas

Isle of Skye

PORTREE MAP 13 NG44

★★★ 80% HOTEL

Bosville

Bosville Ter IV51 9DG

☎ 01478 612846 📠 01478 613434

e-mail: bosville@macleodhotels.co.uk

web: www.macleodhotels.com

Dir: *A87 signed Portree, then A855 into town. Cross over zebra crossing, follow road to left.*

PETS: Bedrooms Grounds accessible **Exercise area** 200yds **Facilities** water bowl

This stylish, popular hotel enjoys fine views over the harbour. Bedrooms are furnished to a high specification and have a fresh, contemporary feel. Public areas include a smart bar, bistro and the Chandlery restaurant where fantastic local produce is treated with respect and refreshing restraint.

Rooms 19 en suite (2 fmly) S £59-£120; D £79-£250 (incl. bkfst)* **Facilities** STV Wi-fi in bedrooms Use of nearby leisure club payable Xmas New Year **Parking** 10

★★★ 73% HOTEL

Rosedale

Beaumont Crescent IV51 9DB

☎ 01478 613131 📠 01478 612531

e-mail: rosedalehotelsky@aol.com

web: www.rosedalehotelskye.co.uk

Dir: *follow directions to village centre & harbour*

PETS: Bedrooms (3GF) **Exercise area Facilities** cage storage walks info vet info **On Request** fridge access torch

The atmosphere is wonderfully warm at this delightful family-run waterfront hotel. A labyrinth of stairs and corridors connects the comfortable lounges, bar and charming restaurant, which are set on different levels. The restaurant offers fine views of the bay. Modern bedrooms offer a good range of amenities.

Rooms 18 en suite (1 fmly) (3 GF) S £30-£60; D £60-£130 (incl. bkfst)* **Parking** 2 **Notes** LB Closed Nov-mid Mar

STAFFIN MAP 13 NG46

►► **Staffin Camping & Caravanning**

(NG492670)

IV51 9JX

☎ 01470 562213 📠 01470 562213

e-mail: staffincampsite@btinternet.com

web: www.staffincampsite.co.uk

Dir: *On A855, 16m N of Portree. Turn right before 40mph signs*

PETS: disp bin Exercise area adjacent **Facilities** walks info vet info **Resident Pets:** Henry (Briard), Peasan (cat)

Open Apr-Oct Last arrival 22.00hrs Last departure 11.00hrs

A large sloping grassy site with level hardstandings for motor homes and caravans, close to the village of Staffin. The toilet block is appointed to a very good standard. A 2.5-acre site with 50 touring pitches, 18 hardstandings.

Notes No music after 22.00hrs

Wales

ANGLESEY, ISLE OF

AMLWCH MAP 06 SH49

★★ 76% SMALL HOTEL

Lastra Farm

Penrhyd LL68 9TF

☎ 01407 830906 01407 832522

e-mail: booking@lastra-hotel.com

web: www.lastra-hotel.com

Dir: *after 'Welcome to Amlwch' sign turn left. Straight across main road, left at T-junct on to Rhosgoch Rd*

PETS: Bedrooms (3GF) unattended **Charges** £2.50 per night charge for damage **Grounds** accessible disp bin **Exercise area Facilities** food bowl water bowl dog chews cage storage walks info vet info **On Request** fridge access torch towels

This 17th-century farmhouse offers pine-furnished, colourfully decorated bedrooms. There is also a comfortable lounge and a cosy bar. A wide range of good-value food is available either in the restaurant or Granary's Bistro. The hotel can cater for functions in a separate purpose-built suite.

Rooms 5 en suite 3 annexe en suite (1 fmly) (3 GF) **Facilities** Wi-fi available **Parking** 40

BEAUMARIS MAP 06 SH67

★★★ 77% HOTEL

Best Western Bulkeley Hotel

Best Western

Castle St LL58 8AW

☎ 01248 810415 01248 810146

e-mail: reception@bulkeleyhotel.co.uk

web: www.bulkeleyhotel.co.uk

Dir: *From A55 junct 8a to Beaumaris. Hotel in town centre*

PETS: Bedrooms unattended **Charges** £10 per night charge for damage **Public areas** lounge & bar only (on leads) **Grounds** accessible on leads disp bin **Exercise area** 2 mins walk **Facilities** water bowl walks info vet info **On Request** torch towels **Other** please telephone for details of pet facilities

A Grade I listed hotel built in 1832, the Bulkeley is just 100 yards from the 13th-century Beaumaris Castle in the centre of the town. The hotel commands fine views from many rooms, and the friendly staff create a relaxed atmosphere. Well-equipped bedrooms are generally spacious, with pretty fabrics and wallpapers. There is a choice of bars and an all-day coffee lounge.

Rooms 43 en suite (5 fmly) S £50-£90; D £90-£140 (incl. bkfst) **Facilities** Wi-fi in bedrooms New Year **Services** Lift **Parking** 25 **Notes** LB

WALES

★★ 84% SMALL HOTEL

Bishopsgate House

54 Castle St LL58 8BB

☎ 01248 810302 01248 810166

e-mail: hazel@bishopsgatehotel.co.uk

Dir: *from Menai Bridge onto A545 to Beaumaris. Hotel on left in main street*

PETS: Bedrooms Charges £5 per night £35 per week charge for damage **Exercise area** 200yds **Facilities** dog scoop/disp bags leads pet sitting dog walking washing facs cage storage walks info vet info **On Request** fridge access torch towels **Resident Pets:** Pollyann Jane (cat)

This immaculately maintained, privately owned and personally run small hotel dates back to 1760. It features fine examples of wood panelling and a Chinese Chippendale staircase. Thoughtfully furnished bedrooms are attractively decorated and two have four-poster beds. Quality cooking is served in the elegant restaurant and guests have a comfortable lounge and cosy bar to relax in.

Rooms 9 en suite S £55; D £88-£100 (incl. bkfst)* **Parking** 8 **Notes** LB

DULAS MAP 06 SH48

►►►► **Tyddyn Isaf Caravan Park** *(SH486873)*

Lligwy Bay LL70 9PQ

☎ 01248 410203 01248 410667

e-mail: enquiries@tyddynisaf.demon.co.uk

web: www.tyddynisaf.co.uk

Dir: *Take A5025 through Benllech to Moelfre rdbt, left towards Amlwch to Brynrefail village. Turn right opposite craft shop. Site 0.5m down lane on right*

PETS: Stables (loose box) **Public areas** except shop, bar & children's play area (on leads) disp bin **Exercise area** on site surrounding walks **Facilities** on site shop food bowl water bowl dog scoop/disp bags walks info vet info **Other** prior notice required **Resident Pets:** Labrador, cat, sheep & cattle

Open Mar-Oct (rs Mar-Jul & Sep-Oct bar & shop opening limited) Last arrival 21.30hrs Last departure 11.00hrs

A beautifully situated, very spacious family park on rising ground adjacent to a sandy beach, with magnificent views overlooking Lligwy Bay. Access to the beach is by private footpath (lengthy from some pitches), or by car for the less energetic. The park has very good toilet facilities, a well-stocked shop, and a clubhouse serving meals and takeaway food. A 16-acre site with 30 touring pitches, 4 hardstandings and 106 statics.

Notes No groups - maximum 3 units together

HOLYHEAD MAP 06 SH28

★★ GUEST HOUSE

Wavecrest

93 Newry St LL65 1HU

☎ 01407 763637 01407 764862

e-mail: cwavecrest@aol.com

web: www.holyheadhotels.com

Dir: *Left at end A55, 600yds turn by railings, premises 100yds up hill on right*

PETS: Bedrooms Charges charge for damage **Exercise area** 50yds **Facilities** food (pre-bookable) walks info vet info **On Request** torch towels **Resident Pets:** Purdi (Staffordshire Bull Terrier)

Well located for the Irish ferry terminals and within easy walking distance of the town centre, the Wavecrest is proving to be a popular overnight stop-off. Pretty bedrooms are equipped with satellite television and other modern facilities. There is a comfortable lounge and evening meals may be booked in advance.

Rooms 4 rms (2 en suite) (3 fmly) **Facilities** STV TVB tea/coffee Cen ht TVL Dinner Last d 3pm **Parking** 1 **Notes** No coaches Closed 24-31 Dec

LLANBEDRGOCH MAP 06 SH58

►►► **Ty Newydd Leisure Park** *(SH508813)*

LL76 8TZ

☎ 01248 450677 01248 450711

e-mail: mike@tynewydd.com

web: www.tynewydd.com

Dir: *A5025 from Brittania Bridge. Through Pentraeth, bear left at layby. Site 0.75m on right*

PETS: Public areas except swimming pool, bar & restaurant disp bin **Exercise area** on site **Facilities** on site shop food dog scoop/disp bags washing facs dog grooming walks info vet info

Open Mar-Oct (rs Mar-Whit & mid Sep-Oct club/shop wknds only,outdoor pool closed) Last arrival 23.30hrs Last departure 10.00hrs

A low-density park with many facilities including a club with restaurant, and a good playground for children. The park is close to Benllech Bay, and is set in four acres of lovely countryside. A 4-acre site with 48 touring pitches, 15 hardstandings and 62 statics.

WALES

PENTRAETH — MAP 06 SH57

►►► Rhos Caravan Park *(SH517794)*

Rhos Farm LL75 8DZ

☎ 01248 450214 🖹 01248 450214

e-mail: rhosfarm@googlemail.com

web: www.rhoscaravanpark.co.uk

Dir: *Site on A5025, 1m N of Pentraeth*

PETS: Charges 50p per night **Public areas** except toilets & children's play area **Exercise area** on site 4-acre field **Facilities** walks info vet info **Other** prior notice required **Resident Pets:** Tess (Springer Spaniel), Jack (Chocolate Labrador)

Open Etr-Oct Last arrival 22.00hrs Last departure 16.00hrs

A warm welcome awaits families at this spacious park on level, grassy ground with easy access to the main road to Amlwch. This 200-acre working farm has a games room, two play areas and farm animals to keep children amused, with good beaches, pubs, restaurants and shops nearby. The two toilet blocks are kept to a good standard by enthusiastic owners, who are constantly improving the facilities. A 15-acre site with 98 touring pitches and 66 statics.

RHOSNEIGR — MAP 06 SH37

►►► Ty Hen *(SH323737)*

Station Rd LL64 5QZ

☎ 01407 810331 🖹 01407 810331

e-mail: bernardtyhen@hotmail.com

web: www.tyhen.com

Dir: *A55 exit 5 follow signs to Rhosneigr, at clock turn right. Entrance 50mtrs before Rhosneigr railway station*

PETS: Public areas except toilet block, swimming pool & children's play area disp bin **Exercise area** on site **Facilities** washing facs walks info vet info **Resident Pets:** Twix, Thomas & Suzie (cats), Phebe & Maisey (Shetland ponies), Percy & Petal (donkeys)

Open mid Mar-Oct Last arrival 21.00hrs Last departure noon

Attractive seaside position near a large fishing lake and riding stables, in lovely countryside. A smart toilet block offers a welcome amenity at this popular family park, where friendly owners are always on hand. A 7.5-acre site with 38 touring pitches, 5 hardstandings and 42 statics.

Notes 1 motor vehicle per pitch, dogs on leads, children in tents/tourers/statics by 22.00hrs

BRIDGEND

BRIDGEND — MAP 03 SS97

★★★ 73% HOTEL

Best Western Heronston

Ewenny Rd CF35 5AW

☎ 01656 668811 & 666085 🖹 01656 767391

e-mail: reservations@bestwesternheronstonhotel.co.uk

web: www.bw-heronstonhotel.co.uk

Dir: *M4 junct 35, follow signs for Porthcawl, at 5th rdbt turn left towards Ogmore-by-Sea (B4265), hotel 200yds on left*

PETS: Bedrooms Charges £10 per night charge for damage **Public areas** except bar/restaurant (on leads) **Grounds** accessible on leads **Exercise area Facilities** walks info vet info

Situated within easy reach of the town centre and the M4, this large modern hotel offers spacious well-equipped accommodation, including ground floor rooms. Public areas include an open-plan lounge/bar, attractive restaurant and a smart leisure and fitness club. The hotel also has a choice of function/conference rooms and ample parking is available.

Rooms 75 en suite (4 fmly) (37 GF) **Facilities** STV Gym Wi-fi in bedrooms Steam room Sauna Solarium **Services** Lift **Parking** 160

SARN PARK MOTORWAY SERVICE AREA (M4) — MAP 03 SS98

BUDGET HOTEL

Days Inn Cardiff West

Sarn Park Services CF32 9RW

☎ 01656 659218 🖹 01656 768665

e-mail: sarn.hotel@welcomebreak.co.uk

web: www.welcomebreak.co.uk

Dir: *M4 junct 36*

PETS: Bedrooms (20GF) **Grounds** accessible disp bin **Exercise area** country walks nearby **Facilities** vet info

This modern building offers accommodation in smart, spacious and well-equipped bedrooms, suitable for families and business travellers, and all with en suite bathrooms. Refreshments may be taken at the nearby family restaurant.

Rooms 40 en suite S £39-£59; D £49-£69*

CARDIFF

CARDIFF **MAP 03 ST17**

★★★★ 72% HOTEL

Copthorne Hotel Cardiff-Caerdydd

Copthorne Way, Culverhouse Cross CF5 6DA
☎ 029 2059 9100 📠 029 2059 9080
e-mail: reservations.cardiff@millenniumhotels.co.uk
web: www.millenniumhotels.co.uk
Dir: *M4 junct 33, A4232 for 2.5m towards Cardiff West. Then A48 W to Cowbridge*

PETS: Bedrooms (27GF) **Public areas** except restaurant (on leads) **Grounds** accessible on leads **Exercise area** lakeside walk nearby **Facilities** cage storage walks info vet info **On Request** fridge access torch towels

A comfortable, popular and modern hotel, conveniently located for the airport and city. Bedrooms are a good size and some have a private lounge. Public areas are smartly presented and include a gym, pool, meeting rooms and a comfortable restaurant with views of the adjacent lake.

Rooms 135 en suite (7 fmly) (27 GF) S £59-£250; D £59-£250 **Facilities** STV Gym Wi-fi available Sauna Steam room New Year **Services** Lift **Parking** 225 **Notes** LB

★★★★ 70% HOTEL

Barceló Cardiff Angel Hotel

Castle St CF10 1SZ
☎ 029 2064 9200 📠 029 2039 6212
e-mail: angel@barcelo-hotels-co.uk
web: www.barcelo-hotels.co.uk/hotels/wales/barcelo-cardiff-angel-hotel
Dir: *opposite Cardiff Castle*

PETS: Bedrooms unattended sign **Charges** £15 per stay **Exercise area** **Facilities** vet info **On Request** fridge access torch

This well-established hotel is in the heart of the city overlooking the famous castle and almost opposite the Millennium Stadium. All bedrooms offer air conditioning and are appointed to a good standard. Public areas include an impressive lobby, a modern restaurant and a selection of conference rooms. There is limited parking at the rear of the hotel.

Rooms 102 en suite (3 fmly) S £65-£145* **Facilities** Wi-fi available Xmas New Year **Services** Lift air con **Parking** 60 (charged)

★★★ 72% HOTEL

Best Western St Mellons Hotel & Country Club

Castleton CF3 2XR
☎ 01633 680355 📠 01633 680399
e-mail: reservations.stmellons@ohiml.com
web: www.oxfordhotelsandinns.com
Dir: *M4 junct 28 follow A48 Castleton/St Mellons. Hotel on left past garage*

PETS: Bedrooms (5GF) **Charges** charge for damage **Grounds** accessible on leads disp bin **Exercise area** **Facilities** cage storage walks info vet info **On Request** fridge access torch towels **Restrictions** no large dogs; no Great Danes, Rottweilers or Bull Terriers

This former Regency mansion has been tastefully converted into an elegant hotel with an adjoining leisure complex that attracts a strong local following. Bedrooms, some in purpose-built wings, are spacious and smart. The public areas retain their pleasing architectural proportions and include relaxing lounges and a restaurant serving a varied choice of carefully prepared and enjoyable dishes.

Rooms 21 en suite 20 annexe en suite (9 fmly) (5 GF) **Facilities** **Spa** Squash Gym Beauty salon **Parking** 100

BUDGET HOTEL

Campanile Cardiff

Caxton Place, Pentwyn CF23 8HA
☎ 029 2054 9044 📠 029 2054 9900
e-mail: cardiff@campanile.com
web: www.envergure.fr
Dir: *take Pentwyn exit from A489(M), follow signs for hotel*

PETS: Bedrooms **Charges** charge for damage **Grounds** accessible on leads disp bin **Exercise area** **Facilities** water bowl walks info vet info **On Request** fridge access towels

This modern building offers accommodation in smart, well-equipped bedrooms, all with en suite bathrooms. Refreshments may be taken at the informal Bistro.

Rooms 47 annexe en suite

WALES

CARDIFF CONTINUED

★★★★ GUEST ACCOMMODATION

The Big Sleep Cardiff

Bute Ter CF10 2FE

☎ 029 2063 6363 📠 029 2063 6364

e-mail: bookings.cardiff@thebigsleephotel.com

Dir: *Opp Cardiff International Arena*

PETS: Bedrooms Exercise area

Part of the Cardiff skyline, this city-centre establishment offers well-equipped bedrooms ranging from standard to penthouse, with spectacular views over the city towards the bay. There is a bar on the ground floor and secure parking. Choose between a continental breakfast or Breakfast to Go, an alternative for travellers making an early start.

Rooms 81 en suite (8 fmly) D £45-£120 **Facilities** FTV TVB tea/coffee Direct dial from bedrooms Lift Cen ht Wi-fi available **Parking** 20 **Notes LB** Closed 24 & 25 Dec

WALES

CARMARTHENSHIRE

CWMDUAD MAP 02 SN33

★★★ GUEST HOUSE

Neuadd-Wen

SA33 6XJ

☎ 01267 281438 📠 01267 281438

e-mail: goodbourn@neuaddwen.plus.com

Dir: *On A484, 9m N of Carmarthen, towards Cardigan*

PETS: Bedrooms (2GF) **Charges** charge for damage **Public areas** except dining room **Grounds** accessible disp bin **Exercise area** field adjacent **Facilities** water bowl bedding feeding mat washing facs walks info vet info **On Request** fridge access torch towels

Excellent customer care is assured at this combined Post Office and house situated in pretty gardens in an unspoiled village. Bedrooms are filled with thoughtful extras and there is a choice of lounges. One bedroom is in a carefully renovated Victorian toll cottage across the road. There is an attractive dining room that serves imaginative dinners using fresh local produce.

Rooms 9 rms (6 en suite) 1 annexe en suite (2 fmly) (2 GF) S £22-£26; D £44-£52 **Facilities** TV9B tea/coffee Direct dial from bedrooms Licensed Cen ht TVL Dinner Last d 5pm **Parking** 12 **Notes LB** No coaches

HARFORD MAP 03 SN64

►►► Springwater Lakes *(SN637430)*

SA19 8DT

☎ 01558 650788 📠 01558 650788

web: www.springwaterlakes.com

Dir: *4m E of Lampeter on A482, entrance well signed on right*

PETS: Charges 1st dog free, £1.50 per extra dog per night **Public areas** (on leads) disp bin **Exercise area** on site 2 dog walks & exercise areas **Facilities** walks info vet info **Other** prior notice required

Open Mar-Oct Last arrival 20.00hrs Last departure 11.00hrs

In a rural setting overlooked by the Cambrian Mountains, this park is adjoined on each side by four spring-fed and well-stocked fishing lakes. All pitches have hardstandings, electricity and TV hook-ups, and there is a small and very clean toilet block and a shop. A 20-acre site with 20 touring pitches, 12 hardstandings.

Notes ⊛ Children must be supervised around lakes

LLANDOVERY MAP 03 SN73

►►► Erwlon Caravan & Camping Park

(SN776343)

Brecon Rd SA20 0RD

☎ 01550 721021 & 720332

e-mail: peter@erwlon.co.uk

web: www.erwlon.co.uk

Dir: *0.5m E of Llandovery on A40*

PETS: Stables nearby (1m) (loose box) **Charges** max £1 per night disp bin **Exercise area** on site fenced area provided **Facilities** washing facs walks info vet info

Open all year Last arrival anytime Last departure noon

Long-established family-run site set beside a brook in the Brecon Beacons foothills. The town of Llandovery and the hills overlooking the Towy Valley are a short walk away. A superb facilities block with cubicled washrooms, family and disabled rooms is part of ongoing improvements. An 8-acre site with 75 touring pitches, 15 hardstandings.

Notes ⊛ Quiet after 22.30hrs

LLANELLI MAP 02 SN50

★★★ 77% HOTEL

Best Western Diplomat Hotel

Felinfoel SA15 3PJ

☎ 01554 756156 📠 01554 751649

e-mail: reservations@diplomat-hotel-wales.com

web: www.diplomat-hotel-wales.com

Dir: *M4 junct 48 onto A4138 then B4303, hotel 0.75m on right*

PETS: Bedrooms unattended **Charges** £5 per night charge for damage **Grounds** accessible on leads disp bin **Exercise area** **Facilities** cage storage walks info vet info **On Request** fridge access torch towels **Resident Pets:** Heidi & Duke (Alsatian/Collie cross)

This Victorian mansion, set in mature grounds, has been extended over the years to provide a comfortable and relaxing hotel. The well-appointed bedrooms are located in the main house and there is also a wing of comfortable modern bedrooms. Public areas include Trubshaw's Restaurant, a large function suite and a modern leisure centre.

Rooms 42 en suite 8 annexe en suite (2 fmly) (4 GF) S £70-£80; D £95-£100 (incl. bkfst)✳ **Facilities** supervised Gym Wi-fi available Sauna Steam room Sun beds Xmas New Year **Services** Lift **Parking** 250 **Notes** LB

See advert on this page

NEWCASTLE EMLYN MAP 02 SN34

►►► Argoed Meadow Caravan and Camping Site *(SN268415)*

Argoed Farm SA38 9JL

☎ 01239 710690

web: www.cenarthcamping.co.uk

Dir: *From Newcastle Emlyn on A484 towards Cenarth, take B4332. Site 300yds on right.*

PETS: Stables nearby (3m) (loose box) **Public areas** (on leads) disp bin **Exercise area** on site 7-acre field **Facilities** washing facs walks info vet info **Other** prior notice required

Open all year Last arrival anytime Last departure noon

Pleasant open meadowland on the banks of the River Teifi, very close to Cenarth Falls gorge. A modern toilet block adds to the general appeal. A 3-acre site with 30 touring pitches, 5 hardstandings.

Notes No bikes/skateboards

►►► *Dolbryn Camping & Caravanning*

(SN296386)

Capel Iwan Rd SA38 9LP

☎ 01239 710683

e-mail: dolbryn@btinternet.com

web: www.dolbryn.co.uk

Dir: *A484 (Carmarthen to Cardigan road). At Newcastle Emlyn (signed) turn to Capel Iwan. Follow signs. For larger vehicles go via Newcastle Emlyn.*

PETS: Stables nearby (3m) **Public areas** (on leads) disp bin **Exercise area** on site large field **Facilities** walks info vet info **Other** prior notice required **Restrictions** well behaved dogs only

Open Mar-Nov Last arrival 22.30hrs Last departure 13.00hrs

A secluded park set in a peaceful valley with a stream, ponds, mature trees and an abundance of wildlife in 13 acres, that include a vineyard and plenty of nature walks. The enthusiastic owners have tastefully refurbished the toilets and showers which are located in rustic farm outbuildings. The cosy bar offers a chance to get together with fellow campers, or take part in family activities. A 13.5-acre site with 60 touring pitches, 2 hardstandings.

Notes Dogs must be kept on leads, quiet after 23.30hrs

WALES

NEWCASTLE EMLYN CONTINUED

►►► Moelfryn Caravan & Camping Site

(SN321370)

Ty-Cefn, Pant-y-Bwlch SA38 9JE

☎ 01559 371231

e-mail: moelfryn@moelfryncaravanpark.co.uk

web: www.moelfryncaravanpark.co.uk

Dir: *A484 from Carmarthen towards Cynwyl Elfed. Pass Blue Bell Inn on right, 200yds take left fork onto B4333 towards Hermon. In 7m brown sign on left. Turn left, site on right*

PETS: Public areas except shower block & play area disp bin **Exercise area Facilities** on site shop food bowl water bowl vet info **Resident Pets:** Kai (German Shepherd), Ginger & Patch (cats), Tara & Sultan (horses)

Open Mar-10 Jan Last arrival 22.00hrs Last departure noon

A small family-run park in an elevated location overlooking the valley of the River Teifi. Pitches are level and spacious, and well screened by hedging and mature trees. Facilities are well maintained, clean and tidy, and the playing field is well away from the touring area. A 3-acre site with 25 touring pitches, 13 hardstandings.

WALES

RHANDIRMWYN MAP 03 SN74

►►► Rhandirmwyn Camping & Caravanning Club Site *(SN779435)*

SA20 0NT

☎ 01550 760257

web: www.thefriendlyclub.co.uk

Dir: *From Llandovery take A483, turn left signed Rhandirmwyn for 7m, left at post office, site on left before river*

PETS: disp bin **Exercise area** on site dog walks **Facilities** walks info vet info **Other** prior notice required

Open 2 Apr-2 Nov Last arrival 21.00hrs Last departure noon

On the banks of the Afon Tywi near Towy Forest and the Llyn Brianne reservoir, this secluded park has superb views from all pitches. The park is divided into paddocks by mature hedging, and facilities and grounds are very well tended. An 11-acre site with 90 touring pitches, 17 hardstandings.

Notes Site gates closed 23.00hrs-07.00hrs

CEREDIGION

ABERYSTWYTH MAP 06 SN58

★★★ 73% HOTEL

Marine Hotel & Leisure Suite

The Promenade SY23 2BX

☎ 01970 612444 🖷 01970 617435

e-mail: marinehotel1@btconnect.com

web: www.marinehotelaberystwyth.co.uk

Dir: *from W on A44. From N or S Wales on A487. On seafront, west of pier*

PETS: Bedrooms Charges £5 per night **Public areas** in lounge only (on leads) **Exercise area** park **Facilities** cage storage walks info vet info

Located on the central promenade overlooking Cardigan Bay, this long established privately owed hotel has been sympathetically renovated to provide a range of well equipped bedrooms with modern bathrooms. Spacious public areas include a choice of lounges and an elegant dining room. A fitness suite is also available.

Rooms 48 rms (47 en suite) (9 fmly) S £35-£75; D £65-£110 (incl. bkfst) **Facilities** FTV Gym Wi-fi in bedrooms Steam room Xmas New Year **Services** Lift **Parking** 27 (charged) **Notes** LB

★★★★ GUEST HOUSE

Llety Ceiro Country House

Peggy Ln, Bow St, Llandre SY24 5AB

☎ 01970 821900 🖷 01970 820966

e-mail: marinehotel1@btconnect.com

Dir: *4m NE of Aberystwyth. Off A487 onto B4353 for 300yds*

PETS: Bedrooms unattended **Stables** nearby **Charges** £5 per night £35 per week charge for damage **Public areas** except restaurant (on leads) **Grounds** accessible disp bin **Exercise area** 100yds **Facilities** food bowl water bowl cage storage walks info vet info **On Request** fridge access

Located north of Aberystwyth, this house is immaculately maintained throughout. Bedrooms are equipped with a range of thoughtful extras in addition to smart modern bathrooms. A spacious conservatory lounge is available in addition to an attractive dining room; bicycle hire is also available.

Rooms 11 en suite (2 fmly) (3 GF) S £35-£75; D £50-£95 **Facilities** TVB tea/coffee Direct dial from bedrooms Licensed Cen ht TVL Dinner Last d 8pm Free use of facilities at sister hotel **Parking** 21 **Notes** LB

CROSS INN — MAP 02 SN35

►►► Cardigan Bay Camping & Caravanning Club Site *(SN383566)*

Llwynhelyg SA44 6LW

☎ 01545 560029

web: www.thefriendlyclub.co.uk

Dir: *Left from A487 (Cardigan-Aberystwyth) at Synod Inn.Take A486 signed New Quay. In village of Cross Inn, left after Penrhiwgaled Arms Pub. Site 0.75m on right*

PETS: Public areas except in buildings disp bin **Exercise area** on site dog walk **Facilities** walks info vet info **Other** prior notice required

Open 27 Apr-28 Sep Last arrival 21.00hrs Last departure noon

An excellent, attractive touring site in an elevated rural position with extensive country views. A footpath from the site joins the coastal walk, and the pretty village of New Quay is only a short drive away. A 14-acre site with 90 touring pitches, 6 hardstandings.

Notes Site gates closed 23.00hrs-07.00hrs

DEVIL'S BRIDGE — MAP 06 SN77

★★★ 72% ❀ HOTEL

The Hafod Hotel

SY23 3JL

☎ 01970 890232 🖹 01970 890394

e-mail: hafodhotel@btconnect.com

Dir: *Exit A44 in Ponterwyd signed Devil's Bridge/Pontarfynach onto A4120 for 3m, over bridge. Hotel facing.*

PETS: Bedrooms Charges charge for damage **Public areas** bar only with consent of other customers **Grounds** accessible **Exercise area** 20yds **Facilities** washing facs cage storage walks info vet info **On Request** torch towels

This former hunting lodge dates back to the 17th century and is situated in six acres of grounds. Now a family-owned and run hotel, it provides accommodation suitable for both business people and tourists. Family rooms and a four-poster room are available. In addition to the dining area and lounge, there are tea rooms.

Rooms 17 rms (16 en suite) (2 fmly) S £47.50-£55; D £72-£83 (incl. bkfst)✻ **Facilities** Wi-fi available Xmas New Year **Parking** 200

EGLWYSFACH — MAP 06 SN69

★★★ ❀❀❀ COUNTRY HOUSE HOTEL

Ynyshir Hall

von Essen hotels
A PRIVATE COLLECTION
www.vonessenhotels.com

SY20 8TA

☎ 01654 781209 & 781268 🖹 01654 781366

e-mail: ynyshir@relaischateaux.com

web: www.vonessenhotels.co.uk

Dir: *off A487, 5.5m S of Machynlleth, signed from main road*

PETS: Bedrooms unattended sign **Sep Accom** outside kennel **Charges** £3 per night £21 per week charge for damage **Grounds** accessible disp bin **Exercise area Facilities** food (pre-bookable) food bowl water bowl walks info vet info **On Request** torch towels **Other** dogs allowed in ground-floor rooms only **Resident Pets:** Oscar (Burmese Mountain Dog)

Set in beautifully landscaped grounds and surrounded by a RSBP reserve, Ynyshir Hall is a haven of calm. Lavishly styled bedrooms, each individually themed around a great painter, provide high standards of luxury and comfort. The lounge and bar have different moods, and both feature abundant fresh flowers. The dining room offers outstanding cooking using best ingredients with modern flair.

Rooms 7 en suite 2 annexe en suite S £110-£310; D £275-£375 (incl. bkfst)✻ **Facilities** ⛳ Xmas New Year **Parking** 20 **Notes** LB No children 9yrs

GWBERT-ON-SEA — MAP 02 SN15

★★★ 77% HOTEL

The Cliff Hotel

SA43 1PP

☎ 01239 613241 01239 615391

e-mail: reservations@cliffhotel.com

Dir: *off A487 into Cardigan, follow signs to Gwbert, 3m to hotel*

PETS: Bedrooms (5GF) **Charges** £5 per night charge for damage **Grounds** accessible on leads **Exercise area** 20yds **Facilities** washing facs cage storage walks info vet info **On Request** fridge access towels

Set in 30 acres of grounds with a 9-hole golf course, and enjoying a cliff-top location overlooking Cardigan Bay, this hotel commands superb sea views. Bedrooms in the main building offer excellent views and there is also a wing of 22 modern rooms. Public areas are spacious and comprise a choice of bars, lounges and the fine dining restaurant. The spa offers a wide range of up-to-the-minute leisure facilities.

Rooms 70 en suite (6 fmly) (5 GF) S £59-£85; D £75-£130 (incl. bkfst) **Facilities Spa** FTV 9 Fishing Gym Xmas New Year **Services** Lift **Parking** 150 **Notes LB**

WALES

LAMPETER — MAP 02 SN54

★★★ 86% COUNTRY HOUSE HOTEL

Best Western Falcondale Mansion

SA48 7RX

☎ 01570 422910 01570 423559

e-mail: info@falcondalehotel.com

web: www.falcondalehotel.com

Dir: *800yds W of High St A475 or 1.5m NW of Lampeter A482*

PETS: Bedrooms unattended sign **Charges** £10 per night charge for damage **Public areas** except restaurants/other guests' comfort **Grounds** accessible disp bin **Exercise area** on site hotel grounds **Facilities** food (pre-bookable) food bowl water bowl bedding dog scoop/disp bags leads dog walking washing facs cage storage walks info vet info **On Request** fridge access torch towels **Resident Pets:** Pudgeley & Major (Cocker Spaniels), Chloe & Truffles (cats)

Built in the Italianate style, this charming Victorian property is set in extensive grounds and beautiful parkland. The individually-styled bedrooms are generally spacious, well equipped and tastefully decorated. Bars and lounges are similarly well appointed with additional facilities including a conservatory and function room. Guests have a choice of either the Valley Restaurant for fine dining or the less formal Peterwells Brasserie.

Rooms 19 en suite (2 fmly) S £99-£178; D £139-£200 (incl. bkfst)* **Facilities** FTV Wi-fi in bedrooms Xmas New Year **Services** Lift **Parking** 60 **Notes LB**

CONWY

BETWS-Y-COED — MAP 06 SH75

★★★ 78% COUNTRY HOUSE HOTEL

Craig-y-Dderwen Riverside Hotel

LL24 0AS

☎ 01690 710293 01690 710362

e-mail: info@snowdoniahotel.com

web: www.snowdoniahotel.com

Dir: *A5 to town, cross Waterloo Bridge, take 1st left*

PETS: Bedrooms (1GF) unattended **Stables** nearby (3m) **Charges** £7.50 per night charge for damage **Public areas** except restaurant (on leads) **Grounds** accessible disp bin **Exercise area** on site 16 acres of fields **Facilities** food (pre-bookable) food bowl water bowl cat treats feeding mat litter tray etc dog scoop/disp bags washing facs cage storage walks info vet info **On Request** fridge access torch towels

This Victorian country-house hotel is set in well-maintained grounds alongside the River Conwy, at the end of a tree-lined drive. Very pleasant views can be enjoyed from many rooms, and two of the bedrooms have four-poster beds. There are comfortable lounges and the atmosphere throughout is tranquil and relaxing.

Rooms 16 en suite (2 fmly) (1 GF) S £70-£150; D £80-£160 (incl. bkfst)* **Facilities** STV FTV Wi-fi in bedrooms Badminton Volleyball New Year **Parking** 50 **Notes LB** Closed 23-26 Dec, 2 Jan-1 Feb

COLWYN BAY — MAP 06 SH87

★★ 72% HOTEL

Lyndale

410 Abergele Rd, Old Colwyn LL29 9AB

☎ 01492 515429 01492 518805

e-mail: lyndale@tinyworld.co.uk

Dir: *A55 junct 22 Old Colwyn, turn left. At rdbt through village, then 1m on A547*

PETS: Bedrooms Charges charge for damage **Exercise area Facilities** washing facs walks info vet info **On Request** fridge access torch towels **Restrictions** no dangerous breeds (see page 7)

A range of accommodation is available at this friendly, family-run hotel, including suites that are suitable for family use and a four-poster bedroom. There is a cosy bar and a comfortable foyer lounge, and weddings and other functions can be catered for.

Rooms 14 en suite (1 fmly) S £39-£49; D £59-£69 (incl. bkfst) **Facilities** STV **Parking** 20

★★★ GUEST HOUSE

The Northwood

47 Rhos Rd, Rhos-on-Sea LL28 4RS

☎ 01492 549931

e-mail: welcome@thenorthwood.co.uk

web: www.thenorthwood.co.uk

Dir: *A55 onto B5115 Brompton Av, over rdbt, 2nd right*

PETS: Bedrooms (2GF) unattended sign **Charges** £2.50-£5.50 per night charge for damage **Public areas** except dining room or lounge (on leads) **Grounds** accessible disp bin **Exercise area** 10mtrs **Facilities** food (pre-bookable) food bowl water bowl dog chews cat treats feeding mat litter tray dog scoop/disp bags leads pet sitting dog walking washing facs cage storage walks info vet info **On Request** fridge access torch towels **Resident Pets:** Sticky and Fluffy (lovebirds), Sam (cat)

A short walk from the seafront and shops, the Northwood has a warm and friendly atmosphere and welcomes back many regular guests. Bedrooms are furnished in modern style and freshly prepared meals can be enjoyed in the spacious dining room/bar while light refreshments are offered in the lounge.

Rooms 11 rms (10 en suite) (1 pri facs) (3 fmly) (2 GF) S £25-£35; D £50-£70 **Facilities** TVB tea/coffee Licensed Cen ht TVL Dinner Last d 7pm Wi-fi available **Parking** 12 **Notes** LB No coaches

CONWY — MAP 06 SH77

★★★ 80% ❀❀ HOTEL

Castle Hotel Conwy

WELSH RAREBITS

High St LL32 8DB

☎ 01492 582800 📠 01492 582300

e-mail: mail@castlewales.co.uk

web: www.castlewales.co.uk

Dir: *A55 junct 18, follow town centre signs, cross estuary (castle on left). Right then left at mini-rdbts onto one-way system. Right at Town Wall Gate, right onto Berry St then High St*

PETS: Bedrooms Charges £5 per night **Exercise area** 50mtrs **Facilities** food (pre-bookable) pet sitting dog walking dog grooming cage storage walks info vet info **On Request** fridge access torch towels **Restrictions** no breeds larger than Labrador **Resident Pets:** Tizzy (Cocker Spaniel)

This family-run, 16th-century hotel is one of Conwy's most distinguished buildings and offers a relaxed and friendly atmosphere. Bedrooms are appointed to an impressive standard and include a stunning suite. Public areas include a popular modern bar and the award-winning Shakespeare's restaurant.

Rooms 28 en suite (2 fmly) S £77-£105; D £110-£250 (incl. bkfst) **Facilities** Wi-fi in bedrooms New Year **Parking** 34 **Notes** LB

★★★ 78% ❀ HOTEL

Groes Inn

WELSH RAREBITS

Tyn-y-Groes LL32 8TN

☎ 01492 650545 📠 01492 650855

e-mail: enquiries@thegroes.com

web: www.groesinn.com

Dir: *A55, over Old Conwy Bridge, 1st left through Castle Walls on B5106 (Trefriw road), hotel 2m on right.*

PETS: Bedrooms unattended **Stables** nearby (stabling can be arranged) **Charges** £10 per night **Exercise area** adjacent **Other** pets allowed in two bedrooms only

This inn dates back in part to the 16th century and has charming features. It offers a choice of bars and has a beautifully appointed restaurant, with a conservatory extension opening on to the lovely rear garden. The comfortable, well-equipped bedrooms are contained in a separate building; some have balconies or private terraces. The inn has a deservedly good reputation for its food.

Rooms 14 en suite (1 fmly) (6 GF) S £85-£157; D £103-£189 (incl. bkfst)* **Facilities** Wi-fi in bedrooms New Year **Parking** 100 **Notes** LB Closed Xmas

★★★★★ ❀ GUEST ACCOMMODATION

Sychnant Pass Country House

Sychnant Pass Rd LL32 8BJ

☎ 01492 585486 📠 01492 585486

e-mail: info@sychnantpasscountryhouse.co.uk

web: www.sychnantpasscountryhouse.co.uk

Dir: *1.75m W of Conwy. Off A547 Bangor Rd in town onto Mount Pleasant & Sychnant Pass Rd, 1.75m on right near top of hill*

PETS: Bedrooms (2GF) unattended **Charges** charge for damage **Public areas** except restaurant & leisure area **Grounds** accessible disp bin **Exercise area Facilities** food (pre-bookable) water bowl bedding dog chews dog scoop/disp bags washing facs walks info vet info **On Request** fridge access torch towels **Resident Pets:** Maisie & Millie (dogs), Peter (cat)

Fine views are to be had from this Edwardian house set in landscaped grounds. Bedrooms, including suites and four poster rooms, are individually furnished and equipped with a range of thoughtful extras. Lounges, warmed by open fires in the chillier months, are comfortable and inviting, and imaginative dinners and suppers are served in the attractive dining room.

Rooms 12 en suite (3 fmly) (2 GF) S £75-£160; D £95-£180* **Facilities** TVB tea/coffee Cen ht Dinner Last d 8.30pm Wi-fi available Sauna Solarium Gymnasium **Parking** 30 **Notes** LB Closed 24-26 Dec & Jan

WALES

CONWY CONTINUED

★★★★★ GUEST ACCOMMODATION

The Old Rectory Country House

Llanrwst Rd, Llansanffraid Glan Conwy LL28 5LF

☎ 01492 580611

e-mail: info@oldrectorycountryhouse.co.uk

web: www.oldrectorycountryhouse.co.uk

Dir: *0.5m S from A470/A55 junct on left, by 30mph sign*

PETS: Bedrooms unattended **Grounds** accessible on leads disp bin **Exercise area** adjacent **Facilities** washing facs cage storage walks info vet info **On Request** fridge access torch towels **Other** pets allowed in Coach House only **Restrictions** no breeds larger than Labrador

This very welcoming accommodation has fine views over the Conwy estuary and towards Snowdonia. The elegant day rooms are luxurious and afternoon tea is available in the lounge. Bedrooms share the delightful views and are thoughtfully furnished, while the genuine hospitality creates a real home from home.

Rooms 4 en suite 2 annexe en suite **Facilities** TVB tea/coffee Direct dial from bedrooms Cen ht **Parking** 10 **Notes** No children 5yrs Closed 14 Dec-15 Jan

LLANDDULAS — MAP 06 SH97

►►►► **Bron-Y-Wendon Caravan Park**

(SH903785)

Wern Rd LL22 8HG

☎ 01492 512903 🖷 01492 512903

e-mail: stay@northwales-holidays.co.uk

web: www.northwales-holidays.co.uk

Dir: *Take A55 W. Turn right at sign for Llanddulas A547 junct 23, then sharp right. 200yds, under A55 bridge. Park on left*

PETS: Charges £1 per night disp bin **Exercise area** on site at rear of site **Facilities** walks info vet info

Open all year Last arrival anytime Last departure 11.00hrs

A good quality site with sea views from every pitch, and excellent purpose-built toilet facilities. Staff are helpful and friendly, and everything from landscaping to maintenance has a stamp of excellence. An ideal seaside base for touring Snowdonia, with lots of activities available nearby. An 8-acre site with 130 touring pitches, 85 hardstandings.

LLANDUDNO — MAP 06 SH78

★★★ 80% HOTEL

Dunoon

Gloddaeth St LL30 2DW

☎ 01492 860787 🖷 01492 860031

e-mail: reservations@dunoonhotel.co.uk

web: www.dunoonhotel.co.uk

Dir: *exit Promenade at war memorial by pier onto wide avenue. 200yds on right*

PETS: Bedrooms unattended sign **Charges** £9 per night £63 per week charge for damage **Grounds** accessible on leads **Exercise area Facilities** washing facs cage storage walks info vet info **On Request** fridge access torch towels **Restrictions** small dogs only

This smart, privately owned hotel is centrally located and offers a variety of styles and sizes of attractive, well-equipped bedrooms. The elegant public areas include a tastefully appointed restaurant, where competently prepared dishes are served along with a good choice of carefully selected, good-value wines. The caring, attentive service is noteworthy.

Rooms 49 en suite (7 fmly) S £60-£126; D £90-£126 (incl. bkfst)✳ **Facilities** Pool table ♫ **Services** Lift **Parking** 24 **Notes** LB Closed 22 Dec-early Mar

★★★★ GUEST ACCOMMODATION

Can-Y-Bae

10 Mostyn Crescent, Central Promenade LL30 1AR

☎ 01492 874188 🖷 01492 868376

e-mail: canybae@btconnect.com

Dir: *A55 junct 10 onto A470, signed Llandudno/promenade. Can-Y-Bae on seafront promenade between Venue Cymru Theatre & Band Stand*

PETS: Bedrooms (2GF) sign **Charges** £5 (1st night), £3 (extra nights) £23 per week charge for damage **Public areas** except restaurant (assist dogs only) (on leads) **Exercise area** 10mtrs (beach-restrictions apply) **Facilities** food bowl water bowl feeding mat dog grooming walks info vet info **Other** dog grooming by appointment (charged) **Resident Pets:** Rolo (Airedale Terrier)

A warm welcome is assured at this tastefully renovated house, centrally located on the Promenade. Bedrooms are equipped with both practical and homely extras and upper floors are serviced by a modern lift. Day rooms include a panoramic lounge, cosy bar and attractive basement dining room.

Rooms 16 en suite (1 fmly) (2 GF) S £35-£45; D £70-£80 **Facilities** TVB tea/coffee Direct dial from bedrooms Lift Cen ht Dinner Last d 6pm Wi-fi available **Notes** LB

LLANRWST MAP 06 SH86

★★★ 77% HOTEL

Maenan Abbey

Maenan LL26 0UL

☎ 01492 660247 📠 01492 660734

e-mail: reservations@manab.co.uk

Dir: *3m N on A470*

PETS: Bedrooms unattended **Charges** £5 per night **Public areas** except dining area **Grounds** accessible **Exercise area** surrounding area **Facilities** food **Resident Pets:** Poppy (Staffordshire cross)

Set in its own spacious grounds, this privately owned hotel was built as an abbey in 1850 on the site of a 13th-century monastery. It is now a popular venue for weddings as the grounds and magnificent galleried staircase make an ideal backdrop for photographs. Bedrooms include a large suite and are equipped with modern facilities. Meals are served in the bar and restaurant.

Rooms 14 en suite (3 fmly) S £60; D £95 (incl. bkfst)✱ **Facilities** Fishing Wi-fi available Guided mountain walks Xmas New Year **Parking** 60 **Notes** LB

►►► Bodnant Caravan Park *(SH805609)*

Nebo Rd LL26 0SD

☎ 01492 640248

e-mail: ermin@bodnant-caravan-park.co.uk

web: www.bodnant-caravan-park.co.uk

Dir: *S in Llanrwst, turn off A470 opposite Birmingham garage onto B5427 signed Nebo. Site 300yds on right*

PETS: Charges 50p per dog per night disp bin **Public areas** except children's play area **Exercise area** on site fenced area, short illuminated dog walk **Facilities** walks info vet info **Other** prior notice required pet store 0.25m, kennels nearby (day boarding) **Resident Pets:** Besi, Bobi & Loli (working dogs), cats, sheep, geese, ducks, guinea fowl

Open Mar-end Oct (rs Mar only 1 toilet block open if weather bad) Last arrival 21.00hrs Last departure 11.00hrs

This stunningly attractive park is filled with flower beds, and the landscape includes shrubberies and trees. The statics are unobtrusively sited, and the toilet blocks are very well kept. There is a separate playing field and rally field. A 5-acre site with 54 touring pitches, 10 hardstandings and 2 statics.

Notes Main gates locked 23.00hrs-08.00hrs, no noise after 23.00hrs

TAL-Y-BONT (NEAR CONWY) MAP 06 SH76

► Tynterfyn Touring Caravan Park *(SH768692)*

LL32 8YX

☎ 01492 660525

Dir: *5m S of Conwy on B5106, road sign Tal-y-Bont, 1st on left*

PETS: Public areas except children's play area **Charges** 70p per night disp bin **Exercise area** on site large field **Facilities** food bowl water bowl walks info vet info **Other** prior notice required **Resident Pets:** Nel & Suzie (Border Collies)

Open Mar-Oct tent pitches only for 28 days in year Last arrival 22.00hrs Last departure noon

A quiet, secluded little park set in the beautiful Conwy Valley, and run by family owners. The grounds are tended with care, and the older-style toilet facilities sparkle. There is lots of room for children and dogs to run around. A 2-acre site with 15 touring pitches, 4 hardstandings.

Notes ⊜

TREFRIW

MAP 06 SH76

★★★★ GUEST ACCOMMODATION

Hafod Country House

LL27 0RQ

☎ 01492 640029 📠 01492 641351

e-mail: stay@hafod-house.co.uk

Dir: *On B5106 entering Trefriw from S, house on right*

PETS: Bedrooms unattended **Charges** £6 per night £37.50 per week **Public areas** bar only **Grounds** accessible disp bin **Exercise area** 100yds **Facilities** food (pre-bookable) food bowl water bowl dog chews dog scoop/disp bags leads washing facs cage storage walks info vet info **On Request** fridge access torch towels **Resident Pets:** Isla (Deerhound), Ricky (Greyhound)

This former farmhouse is personally run and friendly with a wealth of charm and character. The tasteful bedrooms feature period furnishings and thoughtful extras such as fresh fruit. There is a comfortable sitting room and a cosy bar. The fixed-price menu is imaginative and makes good use of fresh, local produce while the breakfast menu offers a wide choice.

Rooms 6 en suite **Facilities** TVB tea/coffee Direct dial from bedrooms Cen ht Dinner Last d 9pm **Parking** 14 **Notes** No children 11yrs Closed Jan RS Feb-Mar

DENBIGHSHIRE

CORWEN

MAP 06 SJ04

►► Llawr-Betws Farm Caravan Park

(SJ016424)

LL21 0HD

☎ 01490 460224 & 460296

web: www.ukparks.co.uk/llawrbetws

Dir: *3m W of Corwen off A494 (Bala road)*

PETS: Exercise area Facilities walks info vet info

Open Mar-Oct Last arrival 23.00hrs Last departure noon

A quiet grassy park with mature trees and gently sloping pitches. The friendly owners keep the facilities in good condition. A 12.5-acre site with 35 touring pitches and 68 statics.

Notes

LLANDRILLO

MAP 06 SJ03

★★★★★ RESTAURANT WITH ROOMS

Tyddyn Llan

LL21 0ST

☎ 01490 440264 📠 01490 440414

e-mail: tyddynllan@compuserve.com

web: www.tyddynllan.co.uk

Dir: *Take B4401 from Corwen to Llandrillo. Tyddyn Llan on right leaving village*

PETS: Bedrooms (1GF) unattended **Charges** £5 per night charge for damage **Grounds** accessible disp bin **Exercise area** walks nearby **Facilities** pet sitting cage storage walks info vet info **On Request** fridge access torch towels **Resident Pets:** Sheba, Tiger & Bruno (cats)

An elegant Georgian house set in its own grounds in a peaceful and relaxing location. Bedrooms vary in size but all are comfortably furnished and include some welcome extras. The restaurant and lounges are quite delightful and offer pleasant views over the surrounding gardens. Emphasis is on local produce, carefully prepared by the chef/proprietor and his team.

Rooms 13 en suite (1 GF) S £100-£130; D £200-£340* (incl. dinner) **Facilities** FTV TVB tea/coffee Direct dial from bedrooms Cen ht Dinner Last d 9.30pm **Parking** 20 **Notes LB** Closed 2 wks Jan RS Nov-Mar

WALES

LLANDYRNOG MAP 06 SJ16

★★★★★ GUEST ACCOMMODATION

Pentre Mawr Country House

LL16 4LA

☎ 01824 790732 📠 01492 585486

e-mail: info@pentremawrcountryhouse.co.uk

Dir: *From Denbigh follow signs to Bodfari/Llandyrnog. Left at rdbt to Bodfari, after 50yds turn left onto country lane, follow road and Pentre Mawr on left*

PETS: Bedrooms unattended **Charges** charge for damage **Public areas** except restaurant & pool areas **Grounds** accessible on leads disp bin **Exercise area Facilities** food (pre-bookable) water bowl bedding dog chews dog scoop/disp bags leads washing facs walks info vet info **On Request** fridge access torch towels **Resident Pets:** Molly (Collie), Morris & Oscar (cats), 4 ponies

Expect a warm welcome from Graham and Bre at this superb family country house set in nearly 200 acres of meadows, park and woodland. The property has been in Graham's family for over 400 years. Bedrooms are individually decorated, very spacious and each is thoughtfully equipped. Breakfast is served in either the morning room or, on warmer mornings, on the Georgian terrace. Dinner is served in the formal dining room. There is a salt water swimming pool in the walled garden.

Rooms 5 en suite S £75-£100; D £90-£120* **Facilities** TVB tea/coffee Cen ht Dinner Last d 7pm Wi-fi available Fishing **Parking** 8 **Notes LB** No children 13yrs Closed Nov-Feb

LLANGOLLEN MAP 07 SJ24

►► *Penddol Caravan Park* *(SJ209427)*

Abbey Rd LL20 8SS

☎ 01978 861851

Dir: *From Llangollen on A542, Abbey Rd, turn into Eisteddfodd Pavilion, then over humpback bridge. Site on left*

PETS: disp bin **Exercise area** adjacent field **Facilities** vet info

Open Mar-Oct Last arrival 22.00hrs Last departure 16.00hrs

An elevated adults-only park enjoying panoramic views across the beautiful Vale of Llangollen. The Llangollen Canal runs alongside this tidy park, offering scenic walks and horse drawn barge trips. Nearby is the Eisteddfod Pavilion, and the Llangollen steam railway. A 2.25-acre site with 30 touring pitches.

Notes

RHUALLT MAP 06 SJ07

►►► Penisar Mynydd Caravan Park

(SJ093770)

Caerwys Rd LL17 0TY

☎ 01745 582227 📠 01745 582227

e-mail: penisarmynydd@yahoo.co.uk

web: www.penisarmynydd.co.uk

Dir: *From Llandudno take 1st left at top of Rhuallt Hill (junct 29). From Chester take junct 29, follow signs for Dyserth, site 500yds on right*

PETS: Charges £1 per night disp bin **Public areas** dogs must be on leads except in dog walk area **Exercise area** on site rally field available when not in use **Facilities** food bowl water bowl dog chews washing facs walks info vet info **Resident Pets:** Meg (Parsons Jack Russell), George (Border Terrier)

Open Mar-15 Jan Last arrival 21.00hrs Last departure 21.00hrs

A very tranquil, attractively laid-out park set in three grassy paddocks with superb facilities block including a disabled room and dishwashing area. The majority of pitches are super pitches. Everything is immaculately maintained, and the amenities of the seaside resort of Rhyll are close by. A 6.75-acre site with 75 touring pitches, 75 hardstandings.

Notes No cycling

RUABON MAP 07 SJ34

►►► James' Caravan Park *(SJ300434)*

LL14 6DW

☎ 01978 820148 01978 820148

e-mail: ray@carastay.demon.co.uk

Dir: *0.5m W of the A483/A539 junct to Llangollen*

PETS: Charges £2 per night disp bin **Exercise area** on site **Facilities** walks info vet info

Open all year Last arrival 21.00hrs Last departure 11.00hrs

A well-landscaped park on a former farm, with modern heated toilet facilities. Old farm buildings house a collection of restored original farm machinery, and the village shop, four pubs, take away and launderette are a ten-minute walk away. A 6-acre site with 40 touring pitches, 4 hardstandings.

Notes

RUTHIN MAP 06 SJ15

★★★★ GUEST ACCOMMODATION

Eyarth Station

Llanfair Dyffryn Clwyd LL15 2EE

☎ 01824 703643 01824 707464

e-mail: stay@eyarthstation.com

Dir: *1m S of Ruthin. Off A525 onto lane, 600yds to Eyarth Station*

PETS: Bedrooms (4GF) **Charges** £8 per night charge for damage **Public areas** except dining room & lounge (on leads) **Grounds** accessible on leads disp bin **Exercise area** 20yds **Facilities** food bowl water bowl feeding mat dog scoop/disp bags leads washing facs cage storage walks info vet info **On Request** fridge access torch towels **Restrictions** no Rottweilers or Pit Bull Terriers **Resident Pets:** cat

Until 1964 and the Beeching cuts, this was a sleepy country station. A comfortable lounge and outdoor swimming pool occupy the space once taken up by the railway and platforms. Bedrooms are carefully decorated and full of thoughtful extras. Family rooms are available, and two rooms are in the former stationmaster's house adjoining the main building.

Rooms 4 en suite 2 annexe en suite (2 fmly) (4 GF) S £50; D £72* **Facilities** TV1B tea/coffee Cen ht TVL Dinner Last d 7pm **Parking** 6 **Notes LB** Closed 2 wks Jan

★★★★ RESTAURANT WITH ROOMS

The Wynnstay Arms

Well St LL15 1AN

☎ 01824 703147

e-mail: resevations@wynnstayarms.com

web: www.wynnstayarms.com

Dir: *In town centre*

PETS: Bedrooms Charges £5 per night charge for damage **Exercise area** park nearby **Facilities** washing facs cage storage walks info vet info **On Request** fridge access torch **Restrictions** small dogs only

This former town centre period inn has been sympathetically renovated to provide good quality accommodation and a smart café-bar. Imaginative food is served in Fusions Brasserie, where a contemporary decor style highlights the many retained period features.

Rooms 7 en suite (1 fmly) S £45-£65; D £70-£110* **Facilities** FTV TVB tea/coffee Cen ht Dinner Last d 9.30pm Wi-fi available **Parking** 14 **Notes LB**

FLINTSHIRE

MOLD MAP 07 SJ26

★★★ 74% HOTEL

Beaufort Park Hotel

Alltami Rd, New Brighton CH7 6RQ

☎ 01352 758646 01352 757132

e-mail: info@beaufortparkhotel.co.uk

web: www.beaufortparkhotel.co.uk

Dir: *A55/A494. Through Alltami lights, over mini rdbt by petrol station towards Mold, A5119. Hotel 100yds on right*

PETS: Bedrooms Charges £15 per night charge for damage **Exercise area Facilities** walks info vet info **On Request** towels **Restrictions** small, well behaved dogs only

This large, modern hotel is conveniently located a short drive from the North Wales Expressway and offers various styles of spacious accommodation. There are extensive public areas, and several meeting and function rooms are available. There is a wide choice of meals in the formal restaurant and in the popular Arches bar.

Rooms 105 en suite (8 fmly) (32 GF) **Facilities** FTV Squash Wi-fi available **Parking** 200

NORTHOP HALL — MAP 07 SJ26

★★★ 77% HOTEL

Northop Hall Country House

THE INDEPENDENTS HOTEL ASSOCIATION

Chester Rd CH7 6HJ

☎ 01244 816181 🖷 01244 814661

e-mail: northop@hotel-chester.com

web: www.hotel-chester.com

Dir: *From Buckley/St David's Park 3rd exit at rdbt, 1st right to Northop Hall 2m. Left at mini-rdbt, 200yds on left*

PETS: Bedrooms sign **Charges** charge for damage **Public areas** except restaurant (on leads) **Grounds** accessible **Exercise area** 1m **Facilities** cage storage walks info vet info **On Request** fridge access torch towels

Located within large grounds and woodland, this sympathetically renovated and extended period house retains many original features within public areas and is a popular conference and wedding venue. Bedrooms provide both practical and thoughtful extras and a warm welcome is assured.

Rooms 39 en suite (15 fmly) S £55-£65; D £85-£125 (incl. bkfst)* **Facilities** FTV Wi-fi available ch fac New Year **Parking** 70 **Notes** LB

GWYNEDD

ABERSOCH — MAP 06 SH32

★★★ 80% ❀❀ COUNTRY HOUSE HOTEL

Porth Tocyn

Bwlch Tocyn LL53 7BU

☎ 01758 713303 🖷 01758 713538

e-mail: bookings@porthtocyn.fsnet.co.uk

web: www.porth-tocyn-hotel.co.uk

Dir: *2.5m S follow Porth Tocyn signs after Sarnbach*

PETS: Bedrooms (3GF) unattended **Charges** charge for damage **Grounds** accessible **Exercise area** adjacent **Resident Pets:** 1 dog, 2 cats

Located above Cardigan Bay with fine views over the area, Porth Tocyn is set in attractive gardens. Several elegantly furnished sitting rooms are provided and bedrooms are comfortably furnished. Children are especially welcome and have a playroom. Award-winning food is served in the restaurant.

Rooms 17 en suite (1 fmly) (3 GF) S £65-£90; D £90-£170 (incl. bkfst)* **Facilities** ⛱ ♨ Wi-fi available Table tennis **Parking** 50 **Notes** LB Closed mid Nov-wk before Etr RS some off season nights

►►► Deucoch Touring & Camping Park

(SH301269)

Sarn Bach LL53 7LD

☎ 01758 713293

e-mail: info@deucoch.com

web: www.deucoch.com

Dir: *From Abersoch take Sarn Bach road, at x-rds turn right, site on right in 800yds*

PETS: Public areas except shower block **Stables** nearby disp bin **Exercise area** 1m **Facilities** walks info vet info **Other** prior notice required **Resident Pets:** Chara (Samoyed)

Open Mar-Oct Last arrival 22.00hrs Last departure 11.00hrs

A sheltered site with sweeping views of Cardigan Bay and the mountains, just a mile from Abersoch and a long sandy beach. The facilities block is well maintained, and this site is of special interest to watersports enthusiasts and those touring the Llyn Peninsula. A 5-acre site with 70 touring pitches, 10 hardstandings.

Notes ⊛ Families only

►►► *Rhydolion* *(SH284275)*

Rhydolion, LLangian LL53 7LR

☎ 01758 712342

e-mail: enquiries@rhydolion.co.uk

web: www.rhydolion.co.uk/caravan_camping.htm

Dir: *From A499 take unclassified road to Llangian for 1m, turn left into & through Llangian. Site 1.5m after road fork towards Hell's Mouth/Porth Neigwl*

PETS: Stables (loose box) **Charges** £20 (per horse) per week disp bin **Exercise area** lane adjacent **Facilities** vet info **Other** prior notice required, field available for horses

Open Mar-Oct Last arrival 22.00hrs Last departure noon

A peaceful park with good views, on a working farm close to the long sandy surfers beach at Hell's Mouth. The toilet block is kept to a high standard by the friendly owners, and nearby Abersoch is a mecca for boat owners and water sports enthusiasts. A 1.5-acre site with 28 touring pitches.

Notes ⊛ Families and couples only

BALA MAP 06 SH93

►►►► Pen-y-Bont *(SH932350)*

Llangynog Rd LL23 7PH

☎ 01678 520549 🖷 01678 520006

e-mail: penybont-bala@btconnect.com

web: www.penybont-bala.co.uk

Dir: *From A494 take B4391. Site 0.75m on right*

PETS: Charges £1 per night disp bin **Exercise area Facilities** on site shop food food bowl water bowl dog chews cat treats dog scoop/disp bags leads washing facs walks info vet info

Open Mar-Oct Last arrival 21.00hrs Last departure noon

A family run attractively landscaped park in a woodland country setting. Set close to Bala Lake and the River Dee, with plenty of opportunities for water sports including kayaking and white water rafting. The park offers good facilities including Wi-fi, and many pitches have water and electricity. A 7-acre site with 95 touring pitches, 59 hardstandings.

Notes No camp fires, quiet after 22.30hrs

►►► Bala Camping & Caravanning Club Site *(SH962391)*

Crynierth Caravan Park, Cefn-Ddwysarn LL23 7LN

☎ 01678 530324

web: www.thefriendlyclub.co.uk

Dir: *A5 onto A494 to Bala. Through Bethal & Sarnau. Right at sign onto unclassified road, site 400yds on left*

PETS: Public areas except in buildings disp bin **Exercise area** on site **Facilities** walks info vet info **Other** prior notice required

Open 2 Apr-2 Nov Last arrival 21.00hrs Last departure noon

A quiet pleasant park with interesting views and high class facilities, set back from the main road in a very secluded position. Lake Bala offers great appeal for the water sports enthusiast, as does the nearby River Tryweryn, a leading slalom course in white-water rafting. A 4-acre site with 50 touring pitches, 8 hardstandings.

Notes Site gates closed 23.00hrs-07.00hrs

►►► Tyn Cornel Camping & Caravan Park

(SH895400)

Frongoch LL23 7NU

☎ 01678 520759 🖷 01678 520759

e-mail: peter.tooth@talk21.com

web: www.tyncornel.co.uk

Dir: *From Bala take A4212 (Porthmadog road) for 4m. Site on left before National Whitewater Centre*

PETS: Stables nearby (4m) (loose box) **Public areas** except shop & near toilet block **Charges** £2 per night disp bin **Exercise area** on site 4-acre field **Facilities** on site shop walks info vet info **Other** prior notice required **Resident Pets:** China (Labrador), Mrs Cat (cat)

Open Mar-Oct Last arrival 21.00hrs Last departure noon

A delightful riverside park with mountain views, popular with those seeking a base for river kayaks and canoes, with access to the nearby White Water Centre and riverside walk with tearoom. The helpful, resident owners keep the modern facilities, including a laundry and dishwashing room, very clean. A 10-acre site with 37 touring pitches.

Notes Quiet after 23.00hrs, silence after mdnt, no cycling & no fires

BARMOUTH MAP 06 SH61

★★★★ GUEST ACCOMMODATION Llwyndu Farmhouse

Llanaber LL42 1RR

☎ 01341 280144

e-mail: Intouch@llwyndu-farmhouse.co.uk

web: www.llwyndu-farmhouse.co.uk

Dir: *A496 towards Harlech where street lights end, on outskirts of Barmouth, take next right*

PETS: Bedrooms Grounds accessible on leads disp bin **Exercise area** 0.25m **Facilities** washing facs cage storage walks info vet info **On Request** fridge access torch towels **Resident Pets:** Juke (Jack Russell), Holly, Melody & Khalilah (horses)

This converted 16th-century farmhouse retains many original features including inglenook fireplaces, exposed beams and timbers. There is a cosy lounge and meals are enjoyed at individual tables in the character dining room. Bedrooms are modern and well equipped, and some have four-poster beds. Four rooms are in nearby buildings.

Rooms 3 en suite 4 annexe en suite (2 fmly) D £80-£94* **Facilities** TVB tea/coffee Cen ht TVL Dinner Last d 6pm **Parking** 10 **Notes** LB Closed 25-26 Dec RS Sun

►►►► Trawsdir Touring Caravans & Camping Park *(SH596198)*

Llanaber LL42 1RR

☎ 01341 280999 & 280611 📠 01341 280740

e-mail: enquiries@barmouthholidays.co.uk

web: www.barmouthholidays.co.uk

Dir: *3m N of Barmouth on A496, just past Wayside pub on right*

PETS: Stables (loose box) **Exercise area** on site dog field provided **Facilities** on site shop food food bowl water bowl dog chews cat treats litter tray etc dog scoop/disp bags washing facs vet info

Open Mar-Jan Last arrival 20.00hrs Last departure noon

AA Campsite of the Year for Wales 2009. A quality park with spectacular views to the sea and hills, and very accessible to motor traffic. The facilities have been completely redeveloped to a very high standard, and now include spacious cubicles containing showers and washbasins, individual showers, smart toilets with sensor operated flush, and underfloor heating. Tents and caravans have their own designated areas divided by dry-stone walls, and the site is very convenient for large recreational vehicles. A 15-acre site with 170 touring pitches, 40 hardstandings.

Notes Families & couples only

BEDDGELERT — MAP 06 SH54

★★★ 75% HOTEL

The Royal Goat

THE CIRCLE
Selected Individual Hotels
GREAT BRITAIN

LL55 4YE

☎ 01766 890224 📠 01766 890422

e-mail: info@royalgoathotel.co.uk

web: www.royalgoathotel.co.uk

Dir: *On A498 at Beddgelert*

PETS: Bedrooms Charges £10 per night charge for damage **Grounds** accessible on leads **Exercise area** 100yds **Facilities** walks info vet info **Restrictions** small dogs only

An impressive building steeped in history, the Royal Goat provides well-equipped accommodation. Attractively appointed, comfortable public areas include a choice of bars and restaurants, a residents' lounge and function rooms.

Rooms 32 en suite (4 fmly) **Facilities** Fishing **Services** Lift **Parking** 100 **Notes LB** Closed Jan-1 Mar RS Nov-1 Jan

CAERNARFON — MAP 06 SH46

►►► Plas Gwyn Caravan Park *(SH520633)*

Llanrug LL55 2AQ

☎ 01286 672619

e-mail: info@plasgwyn.co.uk

web: www.plasgwyn.co.uk

Dir: *A4086, 3m E of Caernarfon*

PETS: Charges 50p per night disp bin **Exercise area** on site field available **Facilities** on site shop walks info vet info **Other** prior notice required **Resident Pets:** Megan (Labrador), Kiri (Bichon Frise), Millie (Springer Spaniel), Beth (Cocker Spaniel)

Open Mar-Oct Last arrival 22.00hrs Last departure 11.30hrs

A secluded park handy for the beaches, historic Caernarfon, and for walking. The site is set within the grounds of Plas Gwyn House, a Georgian property with colonial additions, and the friendly owners are constantly improving the facilities. A 1.5-acre site with 27 touring pitches, 4 hardstandings and 18 statics.

►►► Riverside Camping *(SH505630)*

Seiont Nurseries, Pont Rug LL55 2BB

☎ 01286 678781 📠 01286 677223

e-mail: brenda@riversidecamping.co.uk

web: www.riversidecamping.co.uk

Dir: *2m from Caernarfon on right of A4086 towards Llanberis, also signed Seiont Nurseries*

PETS: Charges £2 per night £14 per week **Public areas** except restaurant & garden centre (on leads) disp bin **Exercise area** on site walk along disused railway **Facilities** vet info **Other** prior notice required

Open Etr-end Oct Last arrival anytime Last departure noon

Set in the grounds of a large garden centre beside the small River Seiont, this park is approached by an impressive tree-lined drive. Facilities are very good, and include a café/restaurant and laundry. A 4.5-acre site with 60 touring pitches, 8 hardstandings.

Notes No fires, no loud music

CRICCIETH MAP 06 SH43

★★★★ GUEST HOUSE

Min y Gaer

Porthmadog Rd LL52 0HP

☎ 01766 522151 01766 523540

e-mail: info@minygaer.co.uk

Dir: *On A497 200yds E of junct with B4411*

PETS: Bedrooms Charges £2.50 per night **Public areas** except dining room **Grounds** accessible on leads disp bin **Exercise area** 200mtrs **Facilities** feeding mat dog scoop/disp bags leads cage storage vet info **On Request** fridge access torch towels **Restrictions** no breeds larger than a labrador **Resident Pets:** Daisy (Cocker Spaniel)

The friendly, family-run Min y Gaer has superb views from many of the rooms. The smart, modern bedrooms are furnished in pine, and the welcoming proprietors also provide a bar and a traditionally furnished lounge.

Rooms 10 en suite (2 fmly) S £30-£33; D £60-£70 **Facilities** TVB tea/coffee Licensed Cen ht TVL Wi-fi available **Parking** 12 **Notes** No coaches Closed 17 Dec-14 Mar

►►►► **Eisteddfa** *(SH518394)*

Eisteddfa Lodge, Pentrefelin LL52 0PT

☎ 01766 522696

e-mail: eisteddfa@criccieth.co.uk

web: www.eisteddfapark.co.uk

Dir: *From Porthmadog take A497 towards Criccieth. Approx 3.5m, through Pentrefelin, site signed 1st right after Plas Gwyn Nursing Home*

PETS: Charges 50p per night disp bin **Exercise area** on site **Facilities** walks info vet info **Other** prior notice required

Open Mar-Oct Last arrival 22.30hrs Last departure 11.00hrs

A quiet, secluded park on elevated ground, sheltered by the Snowdonia Mountains and with lovely views of Cardigan Bay. The owners are carefully improving the park whilst preserving its unspoilt beauty, and are keen to welcome families, who will appreciate the cubicled facilities. There's a field and play area, and woodland walks, with Criccieth nearby. An 11-acre site with 100 touring pitches, 17 hardstandings.

DOLGELLAU MAP 06 SH71

★★★ COUNTRY HOUSE HOTEL

Penmaenuchaf Hall

WELSH RAREBITS

Penmaenpool LL40 1YB

☎ 01341 422129 01341 422787

e-mail: relax@penhall.co.uk

web: www.penhall.co.uk

Dir: *off A470 onto A493 to Tywyn. Hotel approx 1m on left*

PETS: Bedrooms Charges £10 per night **Public areas** in hall lounge only **Grounds** accessible on leads disp bin **Exercise area** 50yds **Facilities** food (pre-bookable) food bowl water bowl dog chews cat treats washing facs cage storage walks info vet info **On Request** fridge access torch towels

Built in 1860, this impressive hall stands in 20 acres of formal gardens, grounds and woodland, and enjoys magnificent views across the River Mawddach. Sympathetic restoration has created a comfortable and welcoming hotel with spacious day rooms and thoughtfully furnished bedrooms, some with private balconies. Fresh produce cooked in modern British style is served in an elegant conservatory restaurant, overlooking the countryside.

Rooms 14 en suite (2 fmly) S £95-£145; D £150-£240 (incl. bkfst) **Facilities** STV FTV Fishing Complimentary salmon & trout fishing Xmas New Year **Parking** 30 **Notes LB** No children 6yrs

★★★ 81% HOTEL

Dolserau Hall

LL40 2AG

☎ 01341 422522 01341 422400

e-mail: welcome@dolserau.co.uk

web: www.dolserau.co.uk

Dir: *1.5m outside Dolgellau between A494 to Bala & A470 to Dinas Mawddy*

PETS: Bedrooms (3GF) unattended **Grounds** accessible disp bin **Exercise area** adjacent **Facilities** walks info vet info **On Request** fridge access torch **Resident Pets:** Charlie (Golden Retriever)

This privately owned, friendly hotel lies in attractive grounds that extend to the river and are surrounded by green fields. Several comfortable lounges are provided and welcoming log fires are lit during cold weather. The smart bedrooms are spacious, well equipped and comfortable. A varied menu offers very competently prepared dishes.

Rooms 15 en suite 5 annexe en suite (1 fmly) (3 GF) S £73-£82; D £136-£198 (incl. bkfst & dinner) **Facilities** Fishing Xmas New Year **Services** Lift **Parking** 40 **Notes** No children 10yrs Closed Dec-Jan (ex Xmas & New Year)

FFESTINIOG MAP 06 SH74

★★★★ BED & BREAKFAST

Ty Clwb

The Square LL41 4LS

☎ 01766 762658 📠 01766 762658

e-mail: tyclwb@talk21.com

web: www.tyclwb.co.uk

Dir: *On B4391 in of Ffestiniog, opp church*

PETS: Bedrooms unattended **Public areas** except dining room **Grounds** accessible disp bin **Exercise area** 100yds **Facilities** water bowl dog chews dog scoop/disp bags washing facs cage storage walks info vet info **On Request** fridge access torch towels **Resident Pets:** Ben (Lurcher/Old English Sheepdog cross), Caspar (Border Collie)

Located opposite the historic church, this elegant house has been carefully modernised and is immaculately maintained throughout. Bedrooms are thoughtfully furnished and in addition to an attractive dining room, a spacious lounge with sun patio provides stunning views of the surrounding mountain range.

Rooms 3 en suite D £50-£60 **Facilities** tea/coffee Cen ht TVL

★★★ GUEST ACCOMMODATION

Morannedd

Blaenau Rd LL41 4LG

☎ 01766 762734

e-mail: morannedd@talk21.com

Dir: *At edge of village on A470 towards Blaenau Ffestiniog*

PETS: Bedrooms Public areas except dining room **Grounds** accessible **Exercise area** surrounding countryside **Resident Pets:** Tessa (cat)

This guest house is set in the Snowdonia National Park and is well located for touring north Wales. A friendly welcome is offered and the atmosphere is relaxed and informal. Bedrooms are smart and modern and a cosy lounge is available. Hearty home cooking is a definite draw.

Rooms 4 en suite **Facilities** TVB tea/coffee Cen ht
Notes Closed Xmas

HARLECH MAP 06 SH53

★★★ 80% ®® COUNTRY HOUSE HOTEL

Maes y Neuadd Country House

WELSH RAREBITS

LL47 6YA

☎ 01766 780200 📠 01766 780211

e-mail: maes@neuadd.com

web: www.neuadd.com

Dir: *3m NE of Harlech, signed on unclassified road, off B4573*

PETS: Bedrooms (3GF) **Charges** £7.50 per night charge for damage **Grounds** accessible on leads disp bin **Exercise area** **Facilities** bedding dog scoop/disp bags pet sitting washing facs walks info vet info **On Request** fridge access torch towels **Resident Pets:** Lili (Cocker Spaniel), Felix & Arthur (cats)

This 14th-century hotel enjoys fine views over the mountains and across the bay to the Lleyn Peninsula. The team here is committed to restoring some of the hidden features of the house. Bedrooms, some in an adjacent coach house, are individually furnished and many boast fine antique pieces. Public areas display a similar welcoming charm, including the restaurant, which serves many locally-sourced and home-grown ingredients.

Rooms 15 en suite (5 fmly) (3 GF) S fr £58; D £119-£200 (incl. bkfst)* **Facilities** Wi-fi available Clay pigeon Cooking tuition Garden breaks Xmas New Year **Parking** 50 **Notes** LB

WALES

LLANBEDR MAP 06 SH52

★★ 69% SMALL HOTEL

Ty Mawr

LL45 2NH

☎ 01341 241440 01341 241440

e-mail: tymawrhotel@onetel.com

web: www.tymawrhotel.org.uk

Dir: *from Barmouth A496 (Harlech road). In Llanbedr turn right after bridge, hotel 50yds on left, brown tourist signs on junct*

PETS: Bedrooms unattended **Public areas** except dining room **Grounds** accessible disp bin **Exercise area** 200yds **Facilities** water bowl cage storage walks info vet info **On Request** fridge access towels **Resident Pets:** Carlo (Welsh Sheepdog), Chelly (Border Collie), Tara (Sheepdog), Lola & Boyzie (rabbits), Prada (budgie)

Located in a picturesque village, this family-run hotel has a relaxed, friendly atmosphere. The pleasant grounds opposite the River Artro makes a popular beer garden during fine weather. The attractive, cane-furnished bar offers a blackboard selection of food and a good choice of real ales. A more formal menu is available in the restaurant. Bedrooms are smart and brightly decorated.

Rooms 10 en suite (2 fmly) S £40-£45; D £70-£80 (incl. bkfst)✳ **Facilities** STV **Parking** 30 **Notes** LB Closed 24-26 Dec

LLANDWROG MAP 06 SH45

►►►► White Tower Caravan Park *(SH453582)*

LL54 5UH

☎ 01286 830649 & 07802 562785 01286 830649

e-mail: whitetower@supanet.com

web: www.whitetower.supanet.com

Dir: *1.5m from village on Tai'r Eglwys road. From Caernarfon take A487 (Porthmadog road). Cross rdbt, 1st right. Site 3m on right*

PETS: disp bin **Exercise area** 100mtrs **Facilities** walks info vet info

Open Mar-10 Jan (rs Mar-mid May & Sep-Oct bar open wknds only) Last arrival 23.00hrs Last departure noon

There are lovely views of Snowdonia from this park located just two miles from the nearest beach at Dinas Dinlle. A well-maintained toilet block has key access, and the hard pitches have water and electricity. Popular amenities include an outdoor heated swimming pool, a lounge bar with family room, and a games and TV room. A 6-acre site with 104 touring pitches, 80 hardstandings and 54 statics.

LLANRUG MAP 06 SH56

►►► Llys Derwen Caravan & Camping Site

(SH539629)

Ffordd Bryngwyn LL55 4RD

☎ 01286 673322

e-mail: llysderwen@aol.com

web: www.llysderwen.co.uk

Dir: *From A55 junct 13 (Caernarfon) take A4086 to Llanberis, through Llanrug, turn right at pub, site 60yds on right*

PETS: Public areas only in caravan fields disp bin **Exercise area Facilities** walks info vet info **Resident Pets:** Else, Rosy, Lacey, Buffy, Brenna, Ria, Odin (Bernese Mountain Dogs), Sian (Jack Russell)

Open Mar-Oct Last departure noon

A pleasant site set in woodland within easy reach of Caernarfon, Snowdon, Anglesey and the Lleyn Peninsula. The keen owners continue to plan improvements to the site. A 5-acre site with 30 touring pitches and 2 statics.

Notes No open fires

LLANYSTUMDWY MAP 06 SH43

►►► Llanystumdwy Camping & Caravanning Club Site *(SH469384)*

Tyddyn Sianel LL52 0LS

☎ 01766 522855

web: www.thefriendlyclub.co.uk

Dir: *From Criccieth take A497 W, 2nd right to Llanystumdwy, site on right*

PETS: Exercise area Facilities walks info vet info **Other** prior notice required

Open 2 Apr-2 Nov Last arrival 21.00hrs Last departure noon

An attractive site close to one of many beaches in the area, and with lovely mountain and sea views. There is a good range of well-maintained facilities, and the mainly sloping site is handy for walking in the Snowdonia National Park or on the local network of quiet country lanes. A 4-acre site with 70 touring pitches, 4 hardstandings.

Notes Site gates closed 23.00hrs-07.00hrs

PORTHMADOG MAP 06 SH53

★★★ 75% HOTEL

Royal Sportsman

131 High St LL49 9HB

☎ 01766 512015 01766 512490

e-mail: enquiries@royalsportsman.co.uk

Dir: *by rdbt, at A497 & A487 junct*

PETS: Bedrooms (9GF) unattended **Stables** nearby **Charges** £3.50 per night charge for damage **Public areas** except dining room **Grounds** accessible disp bin **Exercise area** countryside **Facilities** food (pre-bookable) food bowl water bowl pet sitting dog walking dog grooming walks info vet info **On Request** fridge access torch towels **Resident Pets:** Gelert (Sheepdog)

Ideally located in the centre of Porthmadog, this former coaching inn dates from the Victorian era and has been restored into a friendly, privately owned and personally run hotel. Rooms are tastefully decorated and well equipped, and some are in an annexe close to the hotel. There is a large comfortable lounge and a wide range of meals is served in the bar or restaurant.

Rooms 19 en suite 9 annexe en suite (7 fmly) (9 GF) S £52-£77; D £81-£92 (incl. bkfst)✳ **Facilities** STV FTV Wi-fi in bedrooms Xmas New Year **Parking** 18 **Notes** LB

TYWYN MAP 06 SH50

★★★★ FARM HOUSE

Eisteddfa *(SH651055)*

Eisteddfa, Abergynolwyn LL36 9UP

☎ 01654 782385 01654 782228 Mrs G Pugh

Dir: *5m NE of Tywyn on B4405 nr Dolgoch Falls*

PETS: Bedrooms (3GF) **Charges** £10 per stay **Public areas** **Grounds** accessible disp bin **Exercise area** on site **Facilities** cage storage walks info **On Request** torch

Eisteddfa is a modern stone bungalow situated less than a mile from Abergynolwyn, in a spot ideal for walking or for visiting the local historic railway. Rooms are well equipped and stunning views are a feature from the attractive dining room.

Rooms 3 rms (2 en suite) (3 GF) **Facilities** STV TVB tea/coffee Cen ht TVL **Notes** 1200 acres mixed Closed Dec-Feb

MONMOUTHSHIRE

ABERGAVENNY MAP 03 SO21

★★★ 79% COUNTRY HOUSE HOTEL

Llansantffraed Court

WELSH RAREBITS

Llanvihangel Gobion, Clytha NP7 9BA

☎ 01873 840678 01873 840674

e-mail: reception@llch.co.uk

web: www.llch.co.uk

Dir: *at A465/A40 Abergavenny junct take B4598 signed Usk (NB do not join A40). Continue towards Raglan, hotel on left in 4.5m*

PETS: Bedrooms unattended **Stables** (loose box) **Charges** £20 per night **Public areas** except dining area **Exercise area** on site 20 acres of grounds **Facilities** food food bowl water bowl bedding dog walking walks info vet info **Other** turnout paddock available for horses

In a commanding position and in its own extensive grounds, this very impressive property, now a privately owned country-house hotel, has enviable views of the Brecon Beacons. Extensive public areas include a relaxing lounge and a spacious restaurant offering imaginative and enjoyable dishes. Bedrooms are comfortably furnished and have modern facilities.

Rooms 21 en suite (1 fmly) S £86-£130; D £115-£170 (incl. bkfst) **Facilities** STV FTV Fishing Putt green Wi-fi in bedrooms Clay pigeon shooting school **Services** Lift **Parking** 250 **Notes** LB

★★★ 75% HOTEL

Angel

15 Cross St NP7 5EN

☎ 01873 857121 01873 858059

e-mail: mail@angelhotelabergavenny.com

web: www.angelhotelabergavenny.com

Dir: *follow town centre signs from rdbt S of Abergavenny, past rail and bus stations. Turn left by hotel*

PETS: Bedrooms unattended **Charges** £10 per night **Public areas** except restaurant (on leads) **Grounds** accessible on leads **Exercise area** 50mtrs **Facilities** water bowl bedding pet sitting dog walking cage storage walks info vet info **On Request** towels

Once a coaching inn this has long been a popular venue for both local people and visitors; the two traditional function rooms and a ballroom are in regular use. In addition there is a comfortable lounge, a relaxed bar and a smart, award-winning restaurant. In warmer weather there is a central courtyard that is ideal for alfresco eating. The bedrooms include a four-poster room and some that are suitable for families.

Rooms 29 en suite (2 fmly) S £65-£90; D £85-£130 (incl. bkfst)✳ **Facilities** Wi-fi in bedrooms Xmas New Year **Parking** 30 **Notes** LB Closed 25 Dec RS 24, 26 & 27 Dec

WALES

ABERGAVENNY CONTINUED

►►► Pyscodlyn Farm Caravan & Camping Site *(SO266155)*

Llanwenarth Citra NP7 7ER

☎ 01873 853271 01873 853271

e-mail: pyscodlyn.farm@virgin.net

web: www.pyscodlyncaravanpark.com

Dir: *From Abergavenny take A40 (Brecon road), site 1.5m from entrance of Nevill Hall Hospital, on left 50yds past phone box*

PETS: Stables on site (loose box) **Exercise area** on site adjacent field **Facilities** washing facs walks info vet info **Other** prior notice required

Open Apr-Oct

With its outstanding views of the mountains, this quiet park in the Brecon Beacons National Park makes a pleasant venue for country lovers. The Sugarloaf Mountain and the River Usk are within easy walking distance, and despite being a working farm, dogs are welcome. A 4.5-acre site with 60 touring pitches and 6 statics.

Notes

MONMOUTH — MAP 03 SO51

★★★ GUEST HOUSE

Church Farm

Mitchel Troy NP25 4HZ

☎ 01600 712176

e-mail: info@churchfarmguesthouse.eclipse.co.uk

Dir: *From A40 S, left onto B4293 for Trelleck before tunnel, 150yds turn left and follow signs to Mitchel Troy. Guest House on main road, on left 200yds beyond campsite*

PETS: Bedrooms Public areas except dining room **Grounds** accessible disp bin **Exercise area Facilities** cage storage walks info vet info **On Request** fridge access

Resident Pets: Ollie (Labrador)

Located in the village of Mitchel Troy, this 16th-century former farmhouse retains many original features including exposed beams and open fireplaces. There is a range of bedrooms and a spacious lounge, and breakfast is served in the traditionally furnished dining room. Dinner is available by prior arrangement.

Rooms 9 rms (7 en suite) (2 pri facs) (3 fmly) S £29-£31; D £58-£62 **Facilities** TV2B tea/coffee Cen ht TVL Dinner Last d noon **Parking** 12 **Notes LB** No coaches Closed Xmas

SKENFRITH — MAP 03 SO42

★★★★★ RESTAURANT WITH ROOMS

The Bell at Skenfrith

NP7 8UH

☎ 01600 750235 01600 750525

e-mail: enquiries@skenfrith.co.uk

web: www.skenfrith.co.uk

Dir: *On B4521 in Skenfrith, opposite castle*

PETS: Bedrooms Charges £5 per dog per night **Public areas** except restaurant **Grounds** accessible **Exercise area** surrounding countryside **Facilities** water bowl walks info vet info **On Request** torch

The Bell is a beautifully restored, 17th-century former coaching inn which still retains much of its original charm and character. It is peacefully situated on the banks of the Monnow, a tributary of the River Wye, and is ideally placed for exploring the numerous delights of the area. Natural materials have been used to create a relaxing atmosphere, while the bedrooms, which include full suites and rooms with four-poster beds, are stylish, luxurious and equipped with DVD players.

Rooms 11 en suite S £75-£120; D £110-£220* **Facilities** TVB tea/coffee Direct dial from bedrooms Cen ht Dinner Last d 9.30pm Wi-fi available **Parking** 36 **Notes** No children 8yrs Closed last wk Jan-1st wk Feb RS Oct-Mar

TINTERN PARVA — MAP 03 SO50

★★★ 73% HOTEL

Best Western Royal George

Best Western

Wye Valley Rd NP16 6SF

☎ 01291 689205 01291 689448

e-mail: royalgeorgetintern@hotmail.com

web: www.royalgeorgetintern.com

Dir: *off M48/A466, 4m to Tintern, 2nd on left*

PETS: Bedrooms (10GF) **Charges** £12.50 per night charge for damage **Grounds** accessible on leads disp bin **Exercise area** 50yds **Facilities** water bowl cage storage walks info vet info **On Request** fridge access torch

This privately owned and personally run hotel provides comfortable, spacious accommodation, including bedrooms with balconies overlooking the well-tended garden and there are a number of ground-floor bedrooms. The public areas include a lounge bar and a large function room. A varied and popular menu choice is available in either the bar or restaurant. An ideal place to stay for exploring the counties of Monmouthshire and Herefordshire.

Rooms 2 en suite 14 annexe en suite (6 fmly) (10 GF) S £75-£95; D £90-£120 (incl. bkfst)* **Facilities** STV Wi-fi available Xmas New Year **Parking** 50 **Notes LB**

★★★★ GUEST HOUSE

Parva Farmhouse Riverside Guest House

Monmouth Rd NP16 6SQ

☎ 01291 689411 01291 689941

e-mail: parvahoteltintern@fsmail.net

Dir: *On A466 at N edge of Tintern. Next to St Michael's Church on the riverside*

PETS: Bedrooms Charges £3 per night **Public areas** except restaurant **Grounds** accessible disp bin **Exercise area** on site **Facilities** water bowl washing facs vet info **On Request** fridge access torch **Restrictions** small dogs only **Resident Pets:** Frodo (Border Terrier cross)

This relaxed and friendly family-run guest house is situated on a sweep of the River Wye with far reaching views of the valley. Originally a farmhouse dating from the 17th century, many features have been retained, providing character and comfort in an informal atmosphere. The Inglenook Restaurant has a cosy atmosphere where quality ingredients are prepared for dinner and breakfast. The individually designed bedrooms are tastefully decorated and enjoy pleasant views; one has a four-poster.

Rooms 8 en suite S £45-£60; D £65-£80* **Facilities** TVB tea/coffee Cen ht Dinner Last d Same day **Parking** 8 **Notes** No children 12yrs No coaches

---

USK — MAP 03 SO30

★★★ 78% HOTEL

Glen-yr-Afon House

Pontypool Rd NP15 1SY

☎ 01291 672302 & 673202 01291 672597

e-mail: enquiries@glen-yr-afon.co.uk

web: www.glen-yr-afon.co.uk

Dir: *A472 through High Street, over river bridge, follow to right. Hotel 200yds on left*

PETS: Bedrooms Charges £10 per night charge for damage **Grounds** accessible on leads **Exercise area Facilities** walks info vet info

On the edge of this delightful old market town, Glen-yr-Afon, a unique Victorian villa, offers all the facilities expected of a modern hotel combined with the warm atmosphere of a family home. Bedrooms are furnished to a high standard and several overlook the well-tended gardens. There is a choice of comfortable sitting areas and a stylish and spacious banqueting suite.

Rooms 27 en suite (2 fmly) S £94-£118; D £136-£159 (incl. bkfst)* **Facilities** STV FTV Wi-fi in bedrooms Complimentary access to Usk Tennis Club New Year **Services** Lift **Parking** 101 **Notes** LB

NEATH PORT TALBOT

PORT TALBOT — MAP 03 SS79

★★★ 74% HOTEL

Best Western Aberavon Beach

Best Western

SA12 6QP

☎ 01639 884949 01639 897885

e-mail: sales@aberavonbeach.com

web: www.bespokehotels.com

Dir: *M4 junct 41/A48 & follow signs for Aberavon Beach & Hollywood Park*

PETS: Bedrooms unattended **Charges** charge for damage **Public areas** except restaurant (on leads) **Grounds** accessible on leads **Exercise area** Aberavon Beach 100yds **Facilities** water bowl walks info vet info **On Request** fridge access **Restrictions** no dangerous dogs (see page 7)

This friendly, purpose-built hotel enjoys a prominent position on the seafront overlooking Swansea Bay. Bedrooms, many with sea views, are comfortably appointed and thoughtfully equipped. Public areas include a leisure suite with swimming pool, open plan bar and restaurant plus a choice of function rooms.

Rooms 52 en suite (6 fmly) S £69-£120; D £79-£130 (incl. bkfst) **Facilities** FTV Wi-fi in bedrooms All weather leisure centre Sauna Xmas New Year **Services** Lift **Parking** 150 **Notes** LB

NEWPORT

NEWPORT — MAP 03 ST38

★★★ 68% HOTEL

Newport Lodge

THE INDEPENDENTS HOTEL ASSOCIATION

Bryn Bevan, Brynglas Rd NP20 5QN

☎ 01633 821818 01633 856360

e-mail: info@newportlodgehotel.co.uk

web: www.newportlodgehotel.co.uk

Dir: *M4 junct 26 follow signs Newport. Left after 0.5m onto Malpas Rd, up hill, 0.5m to hotel*

PETS: Bedrooms (11GF) **Grounds** accessible on leads disp bin **Exercise area Facilities** walks info vet info **On Request** fridge access torch towels **Resident Pets:** Ralphy (Yorkshire Terrier)

On the edge of the town centre and convenient for the M4, this purpose-built, friendly hotel provides comfortable and well-maintained bedrooms, with modern facilities. A room with a four-poster bed is available, as are ground floor bedrooms. The bistro-style restaurant offers a wide range of freshly prepared dishes, often using local ingredients.

Rooms 27 en suite (11 GF) S £76-£90; D £96-£135 (incl. bkfst) **Facilities** FTV Wi-fi available **Parking** 63 **Notes** LB

WALES

PEMBROKESHIRE

BROAD HAVEN MAP 02 SM81

►►► Creampots Touring Caravan & Camping Park *(SM882131)*

Broadway SA62 3TU

☎ 01437 781776

web: www.creampots.co.uk

Dir: *From Haverfordwest take B4341 to Broadway. Turn left, follow brown tourist signs for Creampots*

PETS: Public areas except children's play area disp bin **Exercise area** beach 1.5m **Facilities** walks info vet info **Other** prior notice required **Restrictions** no Bull Terriers

Open Mar-Jan Last arrival 21.00hrs Last departure noon

Set just outside the Pembrokeshire National Park, this quiet site is just 1.5 miles from a safe sandy beach at Broad Haven, and the coastal footpath. The park is well laid out and carefully maintained, and the toilet block offers a good standard of facilities. The owners welcome families. An 8-acre site with 71 touring pitches, 9 hardstandings and 1 static.

FISHGUARD MAP 02 SM93

★★ 63% HOTEL

Cartref

15-19 High St SA65 9AW

☎ 01348 872430 & 0781 330 5235 🖹 01348 873664

e-mail: cartrefhotel@btconnect.com

web: www.cartrefhotel.co.uk

Dir: *on A40 in town centre*

PETS: Bedrooms unattended **Charges** £5 per night **Public areas** (on leads) **Exercise area** 100mtrs **Facilities** cage storage walks info vet info **On Request** fridge access torch towels **Resident Pets:** Tofie (Terrier)

Personally run by the proprietor, this friendly hotel offers convenient access to the town centre and ferry terminal. Bedrooms are well maintained and include some family bedded rooms. There is also a cosy lounge bar and a welcoming restaurant that looks out onto the high street.

Rooms 10 en suite (2 fmly) S £35-£41; D £60-£65 (incl. bkfst)✳ **Parking** 4 **Notes** LB

►►► Gwaun Vale Touring Park *(SM977356)*

Llanychaer SA65 9TA

☎ 01348 874698

e-mail: margaret.harries@talk21.com

web: www.gwaunvale.co.uk

Dir: *From Fishguard take B4313. Site 1.5m on right*

PETS: Public areas except toilet block, laundry area, children's play area & other pitches (on leads) disp bin **Exercise area** on site fenced area provided **Facilities** on site shop walks info vet info

Open Apr-Oct Last arrival anytime Last departure 11.00hrs

Located at the opening of the beautiful Gwaun Valley, this well-kept park is set on the hillside with pitches tiered on two levels. There are lovely views of the surrounding countryside, and good facilities. A 1.75-acre site with 29 touring pitches, 5 hardstandings and 1 static.

Notes ⊜ No skateboards

HASGUARD CROSS MAP 02 SM80

►►► Redlands Touring Caravan & Camping Park *(SM853109)*

SA62 3SJ

☎ 01437 781300

e-mail: info@redlandscamping.co.uk

web: www.redlandstouring.co.uk

Dir: *From Haverfordwest take B4327 towards Dale. Site 7m on right*

PETS: Charges 1st dog free, 2nd dog 80p per night **Public areas** on leads (not to roam free) disp bin **Exercise area** on site dog walk area small fenced area **Facilities** on site shop walks info vet info **Other** dog tethers **Restrictions** no dangerous dogs (see page 7); no more than 2 pets per pitch

Open Mar-Dec Last arrival 21.00hrs Last departure 11.30hrs

A family owned and run park set in five acres of level grassland with tree-lined borders, close to many sandy beaches and the famous coastal footpath. Ideal for exploring the Pembrokeshire National Park. A 6-acre site with 60 touring pitches, 20 hardstandings.

Notes ⊜ No commercial vans

HAVERFORDWEST MAP 02 SM91

★★ 69% HOTEL

Hotel Mariners

THE INDEPENDENTS HOTEL ASSOCIATION

Mariners Square SA61 2DU

☎ 01437 763353 🖹 01437 764258

e-mail: hotelmariners@aol.com

Dir: *follow town centre signs, over bridge, up High St, 1st right, hotel at end*

PETS: Bedrooms Grounds accessible on leads **Exercise area** 1m

Located a few minutes walk from the town centre, this privately owned and friendly hotel is said to date back to 1625. The bedrooms are equipped with modern facilities and are soundly maintained. A good range of food is offered in the popular bar, which is a focus for the local community. Facilities include a choice of meeting rooms.

Rooms 28 en suite (5 fmly) S £61-£71; D £82-£90 (incl. bkfst)✳ **Facilities** STV Wi-fi available **Parking** 50 **Notes** Closed 25-Dec-2 Jan

WALES

★★★★ GUEST HOUSE

College Guest House

93 Hill St, St Thomas Green SA61 1QL

☎ 01437 763710 🖹 01437 763710

e-mail: colinlarby@aol.com

Dir: *In town centre, along High St, pass church, keep in left lane. Take 1st exit by Stonemason Arms pub, follow signs for St Thomas Green. 300mtrs on left by No Entry sign*

PETS: Bedrooms Charges charge for damage **Public areas** except restaurant **Grounds** accessible disp bin **Exercise area** 90mtrs **Facilities** food bowl water bowl feeding mat dog scoop/disp bags leads pet sitting washing facs cage storage walks info vet info **On Request** fridge access torch towels **Resident Pets:** Bartie (Jack Russell/Collie cross), Zag (cat)

Located in a mainly residential area within easy walking distance of the attractions, this impressive Georgian house has been upgraded to offer good levels of comfort and facilities. There is range of practically equipped bedrooms, along with public areas that include a spacious lounge (with internet access) and an attractive pine-furnished dining room, the setting for comprehensive breakfasts.

Rooms 8 en suite (4 fmly) S £45-£50; D £65-£70* **Facilities** TVB tea/coffee Cen ht TVL Wi-fi available **Parking** 2

MANORBIER MAP 02 SS09

★★ 71% HOTEL

Castle Mead

SA70 7TA

☎ 01834 871358 🖹 01834 871358

e-mail: castlemeadhotel@aol.com

web: www.castlemeadhotel.com

THE CIRCLE Selected Individual Hotels GREAT BRITAIN

Dir: *A4139 towards Pembroke, onto B4585 into village & follow signs to beach & castle. Hotel on left above beach*

PETS: Bedrooms (3GF) **Grounds** accessible disp bin **Exercise area** 500yds beach **Facilities** washing facs cage storage walks info vet info **On Request** fridge access torch towels **Resident Pets:** Rosie (Border Collie), Max & Polly (cats)

Benefiting from a superb location with spectacular views of the bay, the Norman church and Manorbier Castle, this family-run hotel is friendly and welcoming. Bedrooms which include some in a converted former coach house, are generally quite spacious and have modern facilities. Public areas include a sea-view restaurant, bar and residents' lounge, as well as an extensive garden.

Rooms 5 en suite 3 annexe en suite (2 fmly) (3 GF) **Parking** 20 **Notes LB** Closed Dec-Feb RS Nov

See advert on this page

ROSEBUSH MAP 02 SN02

►► **Rosebush Caravan Park** *(SN073293)*

Rhoslwyn SA66 7QT

☎ 01437 532206 & 07831 223166 🖹 01437 532206

Dir: *From A40 near Narbeth take B4313, between Haverfordwest and Cardigan B4329, site 1m*

PETS: disp bin **Exercise area** on site **Facilities** on site shop food walks info vet info **Other** prior notice required

Open 14 Mar-Oct Last arrival 23.00hrs Last departure noon

A most attractive park with a large ornamental lake at its centre and good landscaping. Set off the main tourist track, it offers lovely views of the Presely Hills which can be reached by a scenic walk. Rosebush is a quiet village with a handy pub, and the park owner also runs the village shop. Due to the deep lake on site, children are not accepted. A 12-acre site with 65 touring pitches and 15 statics.

Notes ⊜

WALES

ST DAVID'S MAP 02 SM72

★★★ 80% ❀❀ COUNTRY HOUSE HOTEL

Warpool Court

WELSH RAREBITS

SA62 6BN

☎ 01437 720300 📠 01437 720676

e-mail: info@warpoolcourthotel.com

web: www.warpoolcourthotel.com

Dir: *At Cross Square left by Cartref Restaurant (Goat St). Pass Farmers Arms pub, after 400mtrs left, follow hotel signs, entrance on right*

PETS: Bedrooms unattended **Charges** £10 per night **Grounds** accessible disp bin **Exercise area** on site **Facilities** water bowl washing facs cage storage walks info vet info **On Request** fridge access torch towels

Originally the cathedral choir school, this hotel is set in landscaped gardens looking out to sea and is within easy walking distance of the Pembrokeshire Coastal Path. The lounges are spacious and comfortable, and the bedrooms are well furnished and equipped with modern facilities. The restaurant offers delightful cuisine.

Rooms 25 en suite (3 fmly) S £105-£120; D £180-£290 (incl. bkfst)* **Facilities** Wi-fi available Table tennis Xmas New Year **Parking** 100 **Notes LB** Closed Jan

►► St David's Camping & Caravanning Club Site *(SM805310)*

Dwr Cwmdig, Berea SA62 6DW

☎ 01348 831376

web: www.thefriendlyclub.co.uk

Dir: *S on A487, right at Glyncheryn Farmers Stores in Croesgoch. After 1m turn right follow signs to Abereiddy. At x-roads left. Site 75yds on left*

PETS: Public areas except in buildings disp bin **Exercise area Facilities** walks info vet info **Other** prior notice required

Open 27 Apr-28 Sep Last arrival 21.00hrs Last departure noon

An immaculately kept small site in open country near the Pembrokeshire Coastal Path. The slightly sloping grass has a few hardstandings for motor homes, and plenty of electric hook-ups. A 4-acre site with 40 touring pitches, 4 hardstandings.

Notes Site gates closed 23.00hrs-07.00hrs

SAUNDERSFOOT MAP 02 SN10

★★★★ GUEST HOUSE

Vine Cottage

The Ridgeway SA69 9LA

☎ 01834 814422

e-mail: enquiries@vinecottageguesthouse.co.uk

web: www.vinecottageguesthouse.co.uk

Dir: *A477 S onto A478, left onto B4316, after railway bridge right signed Saundersfoot, cottage 100yds beyond 30mph sign*

PETS: Bedrooms (1GF) **Charges** £5 per stay charge for damage **Public areas** except dining room **Grounds** accessible disp bin **Exercise area Facilities** dog chews feeding mat dog scoop/disp bags leads washing facs cage storage walks info vet info **On Request** fridge access torch towels **Restrictions** no Pit Bull Terriers or Bullmastiffs **Resident Pets:** Ruby & Megan (English Springer Spaniels)

A warm welcome awaits guests at this pleasant, former farmhouse, conveniently located on the outskirts of Saundersfoot, yet within easy walking distance of this delightful village. There are extensive mature gardens which display some rare and exotic plants, also a summer house at the rear of the garden where guests can sit and relax in the warmer evenings. Bedrooms, which include a ground-floor room, are modern and well equipped, and some are suitable for families. There is a comfortable, airy lounge. Dinner (available on request) and breakfast are served in the cosy dining room.

Rooms 5 en suite (2 fmly) (1 GF) S £35-£70; D £56-£70* **Facilities** TVB tea/coffee Cen ht Dinner Last d 10am **Parking** 10 **Notes LB** No children 6yrs No coaches

SOLVA MAP 02 SM82

★★★★★ FARM HOUSE

Lochmeyler Farm Guest House *(SM855275)*

Llandeloy SA62 6LL

☎ 01348 837724 01348 837622 Mrs M Jones

e-mail: stay@lochmeyler.co.uk

web: www.lochmeyler.co.uk

Dir: *From Haverfordwest A487 to Penycwm, right to Llandeloy*

PETS: Bedrooms Grounds accessible disp bin **Exercise area Resident Pets:** George (Labrador), Patch (Collie), Sooty (Cocker Spaniel)

Located on a 220-acre dairy farm in an Area of Outstanding Natural Beauty, Lochmeyler provides high levels of comfort and excellent facilities. The spacious bedrooms, some in converted outbuildings, are equipped with a wealth of thoughtful extras and four have private sitting rooms. Comprehensive breakfasts are served in the dining room as well as dinner on request, and a sumptuous lounge is also available.

Rooms 12 en suite (6 GF) S £30-£50; D £60-£70 **Facilities** TVB tea/coffee Direct dial from bedrooms Licensed Cen ht Dinner Last d 2pm **Parking** 12 **Notes LB** No children 14yrs 220 acres dairy

TAVERNSPITE MAP 02 SN11

►►► Pantglas Farm Caravan Park *(SN175122)*

SA34 0NS

☎ 01834 831618 01834 831193

e-mail: pantglasfarm@btinternet.com

web: www.pantglasfarm.co.uk

Dir: *Leave A477 to Tenby at Red Roses x-roads onto B4314 to Tavernspite. Take middle road at village pumps. Site 0.5m on left*

PETS: Stables nearby (4m) (loose box) **Charges** £1.50 per night £10.50 per week **Public areas** except shower blocks & children's play area disp bin **Exercise area** on site large, mowed grass field available **Facilities** dog scoop/disp bags washing facs walks info vet info **Other** prior notice required **Restrictions** certain breeds may not be allowed if children are on adjacent pitches, please check when booking **Resident Pets:** aviary on site

Open Mar-end Oct Last arrival 19.00hrs Last departure 10.30hrs

A quiet site in a rural location with pitches located in three enclosures, and views across the rolling countryside towards Carmarthen Bay. There is a large activity play area for children, an indoor games room, and a licensed bar, and the toilet facilities are well maintained. The park is well situated for exploring the beautiful surrounding area and the coastline. A 14-acre site with 86 touring pitches, 70 hardstandings and 49 statics.

Notes No kites, halogen heaters, skateboards. Families and couples only.

TENBY MAP 02 SN10

★★ 62% HOTEL

Clarence House

Esplanade SA70 7DU

☎ 01834 844371 01834 844372

e-mail: clarencehotel@freeuk.com

Dir: *Off South Parade by town walls onto St Florance Parade & Esplanade*

PETS: Bedrooms unattended **Charges** £3 per pet per night **Public areas** except restaurant (on leads) **Grounds** accessible disp bin **Exercise area** beach 5 min walk **Facilities** walks info vet info **On Request** fridge access torch towels

Owned by the same family for over 50 years, this hotel has superb views from its elevated position. Many of the bedrooms have sea views and all are comfortably furnished. The bar leads to a sheltered rose garden or a number of lounges. Entertainment is provided in high season, and this establishment is particularly popular with coach tour parties.

Rooms 68 rms (6 fmly) **Notes** Closed 18-28 Dec

★★★★ GUEST HOUSE

Rosendale

Lydstep SA70 7SQ

☎ 01834 870040

e-mail: rosendalewales@yahoo.com

web: www.rosendalepembrokeshire.co.uk

Dir: *3m SW of Tenby. A4139 W towards Pembroke, Rosendale on the right after Lydstep village*

PETS: Bedrooms (3GF) **Charges** £2 per night charge for damage **Grounds** accessible on leads disp bin **Exercise area** Lydstep Headland 0.5m **Facilities** food bowl water bowl feeding mat washing facs cage storage walks info vet info **On Request** fridge access torch **Restrictions** no large dogs accepted (eg Great Danes, St Bernards)

A warm welcome awaits all guests at this family-run guest accommodation, ideally located on the outskirts of the pretty village of Lydstep, not far from the seaside town of Tenby. Rosendale provides modern, well-equipped bedrooms, some with coast or country views. Three rooms are on the ground floor of a separate building to the rear of the main house. The attractive dining room is the setting for breakfast, and there is also a large, comfortable lounge.

Rooms 6 en suite (3 GF) **Facilities** TVB tea/coffee Cen ht **Parking** 6 **Notes** No children 16yrs No coaches Closed Dec-Jan

TENBY CONTINUED

★★★★ GUEST ACCOMMODATION

Esplanade

The Esplanade SA70 7DU

☎ 01834 842760 & 843333 📠 01834 845633

e-mail: esplanade.tenby@virgin.net

web: www.esplanadetenby.co.uk

Dir: *Signs to South Beach, premises on seafront next to town walls*

PETS: Bedrooms (1GF) **Public areas** except restaurant at meal times (on leads) **Exercise area** 20mtrs **Facilities** washing facs cage storage walks info vet info **On Request** fridge access torch towels

Located beside the historic town walls of Tenby and with stunning views over the sea to Caldey Island, the Esplanade provides a range of standard and luxury bedrooms, some ideal for families. Breakfast is offered in the elegant front-facing dining room, which contains a comfortable lounge-bar area.

Rooms 14 en suite (3 fmly) (1 GF) S £50-£85; D £70-£130 **Facilities** TVB tea/coffee Direct dial from bedrooms Cen ht Wi-fi available **Notes LB** Closed 23-27 Dec

►►►► **Trefalun** *(SN093027)*

Devonshire Dr, St Florence SA70 8RD

☎ 01646 651514 & 0500 655314 📠 01646 651746

e-mail: trefalun@aol.com

web: www.trefalunpark.co.uk

Dir: *1.5m NW of St Florence & 0.5m N of B4318*

PETS: Charges £1 per night touring & camping pitches disp bin **Exercise area** on site field available **Facilities** walks info vet info **Other** prior notice required **Resident Pets:** Hobie (Great Dane), Buzz (Miniature Schnauzer), Amber (German Shepherd), Lizzie (donkey)

Open Etr-Oct Last arrival 19.00hrs Last departure noon

Set within 12 acres of sheltered, well-kept grounds, this quiet country park offers well-maintained level grass pitches separated by bushes and trees, with plenty of space to relax in. Children can feed the park's friendly pets. Plenty of activities are available at the nearby Heatherton Country Sports Park, including go-karting, indoor bowls, golf and bumper boating. A 12-acre site with 90 touring pitches, 29 hardstandings and 10 statics.

Notes No motorised scooters

WOLF'S CASTLE MAP 02 SM92

★★★ 78% ❁ COUNTRY HOUSE HOTEL

Wolfscastle Country Hotel

WELSH RAREBITS

SA62 5LZ

☎ 01437 741688 & 741225 📠 01437 741383

e-mail: enquiries@wolfscastle.com

web: www.wolfscastle.com

Dir: *on A40 in village at top of hill. 6m N of Haverfordwest*

PETS: Bedrooms unattended **Grounds** accessible on leads disp bin **Exercise area** 200mtrs **Facilities** washing facs cage storage walks info vet info **On Request** fridge access towels **Other** dogs not allowed in executive bedrooms

This large stone house, a former vicarage, dates back to the mid-19th century and is now a friendly, privately owned and personally run hotel. It provides stylish, modern, well-maintained and well-equipped bedrooms. There is a pleasant bar and an attractive restaurant, which has a well-deserved reputation for its food.

Rooms 20 en suite 2 annexe en suite (2 fmly) S £70-£90; D £100-£135 (incl. bkfst)✳ **Facilities** FTV Wi-fi in bedrooms New Year **Parking** 60 **Notes LB** Closed 24-26 Dec

POWYS

BRECON MAP 03 SO02

★★ 65% SMALL HOTEL

Lansdowne Hotel & Restaurant

The Watton LD3 7EG

☎ 01874 623321 📠 01874 610438

e-mail: reception@lansdownehotel.co.uk

Dir: *A40/A470 onto B4601*

PETS: Bedrooms Charges £2.50 per night **Public areas** except restaurant **Exercise area** 2 min walk **Facilities** washing facs walks info vet info **On Request** torch towels

Now a privately owned and personally run hotel, this Georgian house is conveniently located close to the town centre. The accommodation is well equipped and includes family rooms and a bedroom on ground floor level. There is a comfortable lounge and an attractive split-level dining room containing a bar.

Rooms 9 en suite (2 fmly) (1 GF) S £40-£50; D £60-£70 (incl. bkfst)✳ **Notes LB** No children 5yrs

★★★★ ®® INN

The Felin Fach Griffin

Felin Fach LD3 0UB

☎ 01874 620111 📠 01874 620120

e-mail: enquiries@eatdrinksleep.ltd.uk

web: www.eatdrinksleep.ltd.uk

Dir: *4m NE of Brecon on A470*

PETS: Bedrooms unattended **Public areas** except dining room **Grounds** accessible **Exercise area** on site **Facilities** food bowl water bowl bedding dog chews walks info vet info **On Request** towels **Resident Pets:** Max (Kelpie Collie)

This delightful inn stands in an extensive garden at the northern end of Felin Fach village. The public areas have a wealth of rustic charm and provide the setting for the excellent food. Service and hospitality are commendable. The bedrooms are carefully appointed and have modern equipment and facilities.

Rooms 7 en suite (1 fmly) **Facilities** tea/coffee Direct dial from bedrooms Cen ht Dinner Last d 9.30pm **Parking** 61 **Notes** No coaches Closed 25-26 Dec RS Mon (ex BH's)

★★★ GUEST ACCOMMODATION

Borderers

47 The Watton LD3 7EG

☎ 01874 623559

e-mail: info@borderers.com

web: www.borderers.com

Dir: *200yds SE of town centre on B4601, opp church*

PETS: Bedrooms unattended **Exercise area Facilities** food bowl water bowl pet sitting washing facs walks info vet info **On Request** fridge access torch towels **Resident Pets:** Ella (Black Labrador), Breagh (Chocolate Labrador)

This house was originally a 17th-century drovers' inn. The courtyard, now a car park, is surrounded by many of the bedrooms, and pretty hanging baskets are seen everywhere. The non-smoking bedrooms are attractively decorated with rich floral fabrics. A room suitable for easier access is available.

Rooms 4 rms (3 en suite) (1 pri facs) 5 annexe en suite (2 fmly) (4 GF) S £40-£60; D £60-£70 **Facilities** TVB tea/coffee Cen ht **Parking** 6

BUILTH WELLS

MAP 03 SO05

★★★ 75% COUNTRY HOUSE HOTEL

Caer Beris Manor

THE INDEPENDENTS HOTEL ASSOCIATION

LD2 3NP

☎ 01982 552601 📠 01982 552586

e-mail: caerberis@btconnect.com

web: www.caerberis.com

Dir: *from town centre follow A483/Llandovery signs. Hotel on left*

PETS: Bedrooms unattended **Sep Accom** paddock for horses **Charges** £5 per night charge for damage **Public areas** except main restaurant **Grounds** accessible **Exercise area** on site

Guests can expect a relaxing stay at this friendly and privately owned hotel that has extensive landscaped grounds. Bedrooms are individually decorated and furnished to retain an atmosphere of a bygone era. The spacious and comfortable lounge and a lounge bar continue this theme, and there's an elegant restaurant, complete with 16th-century panelling.

Rooms 23 en suite (1 fmly) (3 GF) S fr £67.95; D fr £115 (incl. bkfst) **Facilities** FTV Fishing Riding Gym Wi-fi available Clay pigeon shooting Xmas New Year **Parking** 100 **Notes LB**

►►► Fforest Fields Caravan & Camping Park *(SO100535)*

Hundred House LD1 5RT

☎ 01982 570406

e-mail: office@fforestfields.co.uk

web: www.fforestfields.co.uk

Dir: *From town follow New Radnor signs on A481. 4m to signed entrance on right, 0.5m before Hundred House village*

PETS: Public areas except toilets disp bin **Exercise area** on site **Facilities** washing facs walks info vet info **Other** prior notice required **Restrictions** no noisy or badly behaved dogs

Open Etr & Apr-Oct Last arrival 21.00hrs Last departure 18.00hrs

A sheltered park in a hidden valley with wonderful views and plenty of wildlife. Set in unspoilt countryside, this is a peaceful park with delightful hill walks beginning on site. The historic town of Builth Wells and the Royal Welsh Showground are only four miles away, and there are plenty of outdoor activities in the vicinity. A 12-acre site with 60 touring pitches, 17 hardstandings.

Notes No loud music or revelry

CRICKHOWELL MAP 03 SO21

★★★ 77% HOTEL

Bear

WELSH RAREBITS

NP8 1BW

☎ 01873 810408 01873 811696

e-mail: bearhotel@aol.com

Dir: *on A40 between Abergavenny & Brecon*

PETS: Bedrooms (6GF) unattended **Public areas** except restaurant (on leads) **Grounds** accessible on leads **Exercise area** **Facilities** food bowl water bowl dog chews washing facs walks info vet info **On Request** fridge access towels **Other** freshly cooked chicked offered to all visiting dogs **Resident Pets:** Magic (cat)

A favourite with locals as well as visitors, the character and friendliness of this 15th-century coaching inn are renowned. The bedrooms come in a variety of sizes and standards including some with four-posters. The bar and restaurant are furnished in keeping with the style of the building and provide comfortable areas in which to enjoy some of the very popular dishes that use the finest locally-sourced ingredients.

Rooms 21 en suite 13 annexe en suite (6 fmly) (6 GF) S £70-£117; D £86-£153 (incl. bkfst) **Facilities** STV FTV Wi-fi in bedrooms Xmas New Year **Parking** 45 **Notes** RS 25 Dec

★★★ 74% HOTEL

Manor

Brecon Rd NP8 1SE

☎ 01873 810212 01873 811938

e-mail: info@manorhotel.co.uk

web: www.manorhotel.co.uk

Dir: *on A40, Crickhowell/Brecon, 0.5m from Crickhowell*

PETS: Bedrooms unattended **Stables** nearby (7m to establishment's own farm) **Charges** £10 per night charge for damage **Public areas** except restaurant **Grounds** accessible disp bin **Exercise area** adjoining footpaths **Facilities** food bowl water bowl bedding dog chews feeding mat dog scoop/disp bags leads pet sitting washing facs cage storage walks info vet info **On Request** fridge access torch towels **Other** pets allowed in certain bedrooms only **Resident Pets:** Honey & Henry (Golden Retrievers), Cerys (Welsh Cob)

This impressive manor house, set in a stunning location, was the birthplace of Sir George Everest. The bedrooms and public areas are elegant, and there are extensive leisure facilities. The restaurant, with panoramic views, is the setting for exciting modern cooking. Guests can also dine informally at the nearby Nantyffin Cider Mill, a sister operation of the hotel.

Rooms 22 en suite (1 fmly) S £65-£90; D £75-£120 (incl. bkfst)* **Facilities** Gym Wi-fi available Fitness assessment Sunbed Xmas New Year **Parking** 200

CRIGGION MAP 07 SJ21

★★★★ FARM HOUSE

Brimford House *(SJ310150)*

SY5 9AU

☎ 01938 570235 Mrs Dawson

e-mail: info@brimford.co.uk

Dir: *Off B4393 after Crew Green turn left for Criggion Brimford 1st on left after pub*

PETS: Bedrooms **Public areas** **Grounds** accessible **Exercise area** **Facilities** cage storage vet info **On Request** fridge access torch towels **Resident Pets:** Emma (Black Labrador)

This elegant Georgian house stands in lovely open countryside and is a good base for touring central Wales and the Marches. Bedrooms are spacious, and thoughtful extras enhance guest comfort. A cheery log fire burns in the lounge during colder weather and the hospitality is equally warm, providing a relaxing atmosphere throughout.

Rooms 3 en suite S £45-£60; D £55-£70* **Facilities** TVB tea/coffee Cen ht TVL Fishing **Parking** 4 **Notes** LB 250 acres Arable, beef, sheep

WALES

ERWOOD MAP 03 SO04

★★★★ BED & BREAKFAST

Hafod-Y-Garreg

LD2 3TQ

☎ 01982 560400

e-mail: john-annie@hafod-y.wanadoo.co.uk

web: www.hafodygarreg.co.uk

Dir: *1m S of Erwood. Off A470 at Trericket Mill, sharp right, up track past cream farmhouse towards pine forest, through gate*

PETS: Bedrooms Public areas Grounds accessible on leads **Exercise area Facilities** walks info vet info **On Request** torch **Restrictions** no puppies **Resident Pets:** Ginger (cat), Rosie (goat), chickens

This remote Grade II listed farmhouse dates in part from 1401 and is the oldest surviving traditional house in Wales. It has tremendous character and has been furnished and decorated to befit its age, while the bedrooms have modern facilities. There is an impressive dining room and a lounge with an open fireplace. Warm hospitality from John and Annie McKay is a major strength here.

Rooms 2 en suite (1 fmly) D £65 **Facilities** STV TVB tea/coffee Cen ht Dinner Last d Day before Wi-fi available **Parking** 6 **Notes LB** Closed Xmas

HAY-ON-WYE MAP 03 SO24

★★★ 72% HOTEL

The Swan-at-Hay

WELSH RAREBITS

Church St HR3 5DQ

☎ 01497 821188 01497 821424

e-mail: info@theswanathay.co.uk

Dir: *on B4350 in town centre*

PETS: Bedrooms Charges £6 per night **Public areas** public bar only (on leads) **Grounds** accessible on leads **Exercise area** 20yds **Facilities** food food bowl water bowl walks info vet info

This former coaching inn dates back to the 1800s and is only a short walk from the town centre. Bedrooms are well equipped and some are located in either the main hotel or in converted cottages across the courtyard. Spacious, relaxing public areas include a comfortable lounge, a choice of bars and a more formal restaurant. There is also a large function room and a smaller meeting room.

Rooms 14 en suite 4 annexe en suite (1 fmly) (2 GF) S £75; D £99-£125 (incl. bkfst)* **Facilities** Fishing Wi-fi available New Year **Parking** 18 **Notes LB**

★★★ INN

Baskerville Arms

Clyro HR3 5RZ

☎ 01497 820670 0870 705 8427

e-mail: info@baskervillearms.co.uk

Dir: *From Hereford follow A438 into Clyro, signed*

PETS: Bedrooms Charges £4 per night **Public areas** except restaurant **Exercise area** on site

Situated near Hay-on-Wye in the peaceful village of Clyro, this former Georgian coaching inn is personally run by its friendly and enthusiastic owners. Bedrooms offer a range of styles while public areas include a bar with a village inn atmosphere, a separate restaurant and a comfortable residents' lounge. There is also a large function room, plus a meeting room.

Rooms 13 en suite (1 fmly) S £45-£55; D £65-£85 **Facilities** TVB tea/coffee Cen ht TVL Dinner Last d 8.30pm Wi-fi available Pool Table **Parking** 12 **Notes LB**

LLANDRINDOD WELLS MAP 03 SO06

►►► **Disserth Caravan & Camping Park**

(SO035583)

Disserth, Howey LD1 6NL

☎ 01597 860277

e-mail: disserthcaravan@btconnect.com

web: www.disserth.com

Dir: *1m off A483, between Howey & Newbridge-on-Wye, by church. Brown signs from A483 or A470*

PETS: Public areas except reception & bar disp bin **Exercise area** adjacent fields with footpaths **Facilities** food food bowl water bowl vet info **Other** prior notice required; horses accepted by arrangement **Resident Pets:** Jake (Lakeland/Terrier cross), Jack & Oscar (cats), Mildred (Berkshire sow)

Open Mar-Oct Last arrival 22.00hrs Last departure noon

A delightfully secluded and predominantly adult park nestling in a beautiful valley on the banks of the River Ithon, a tributary of the River Wye. This little park is next to a 13th-century church, and has a small bar open at weekends and busy periods. The chalet toilet block offers spacious combined cubicles. A 4-acre site with 30 touring pitches and 23 statics.

Notes

WALES

LLANFYLLIN MAP 06 SJ11

★★ 78% HOTEL

Cain Valley

High St SY22 5AQ

☎ 01691 648366 📠 01691 648307

e-mail: info@cainvalleyhotel.co.uk

Dir: *at end of A490. Hotel in town centre, car park at rear*

PETS: Bedrooms unattended **Charges** £5 per night **Exercise area Facilities** vet info **On Request** fridge access torch towels

This Grade II listed coaching inn has a lot of charm and character including features such as exposed beams and a Jacobean staircase. The comfortable accommodation includes family rooms and a wide range of food is available in a choice of bars, or in the restaurant, which has a well-deserved reputation for its locally sourced steaks.

Rooms 13 en suite (2 fmly) S £42-£50; D £67-£80 (incl. bkfst)✳ **Parking** 10 **Notes LB**

LLANGAMMARCH WELLS MAP 03 SN94

★★★ ◎◎ COUNTRY HOUSE HOTEL

The Lake Country House & Spa

LD4 4BS

☎ 01591 620202 & 620474 📠 01591 620457

e-mail: info@lakecountryhouse.co.uk

web: www.lakecountryhouse.co.uk

Dir: *W from Builth Wells on A483 to Garth (approx 6m). Left for Llangammarch Wells, follow hotel signs*

PETS: Bedrooms Charges £6 per night **Grounds** accessible **Exercise area** on site **Resident Pets:** Belle (Labrador), Cassie (Collie/Labrador)

Expect good old-fashioned values and hospitality at this Victorian country house hotel. In fact, the service is so traditionally English, guests may believe they have a butler! The establishment offers a 9-hole, par 3 golf course, 50 acres of wooded grounds and a spa where the hot tub overlooks the lake. Bedrooms, some located in an annexe, and some at ground-floor level, are individually styled and have many extra comforts. Traditional afternoon teas are served in the lounge and award-winning cuisine is provided in the spacious and elegant restaurant.

Rooms 30 en suite (7 GF) S £115-£180; D £170-£250 (incl. bkfst)✳ **Facilities Spa** FTV ⛳9 Fishing Gym Putt green Wi-fi available Archery Horse riding Mountain biking Quad biking Xmas **Parking** 72 **Notes LB**

LLANGURIG MAP 06 SN97

★★★★ GUEST HOUSE

The Old Vicarage

SY18 6RN

☎ 01686 440280 📠 01686 440280

e-mail: info@theoldvicaragellangurig.co.uk

Dir: *A470 onto A44, signed*

PETS: Bedrooms Charges £1 per night **Public areas** except dining areas (on leads) **Grounds** accessible on leads disp bin **Exercise area** 100yds **Facilities** water bowl feeding mat washing facs cage storage walks info vet info **On Request** torch towels **Resident Pets:** Polly (Red Chow)

Located on pretty mature grounds, which feature a magnificent holly tree, this elegant Victorian house provides a range of thoughtfully furnished bedrooms, some with fine period items. Breakfast is served in a spacious dining room and a comfortable guest lounge is also available. Afternoon teas are served in the garden during the warmer months.

Rooms 4 en suite (1 fmly) S £30-£40; D £48-£54✳ **Facilities** TVB tea/coffee Licensed Cen ht TVL Dinner Last d 5pm Wi-fi available **Parking** 6 **Notes LB** No coaches

LLANWDDYN MAP 06 SJ01

★★★ 79% ❀ COUNTRY HOUSE HOTEL

Lake Vyrnwy

CLASSIC BRITISH HOTELS

Lake Vyrnwy SY10 0LY

☎ 01691 870692 🖹 01691 870259

e-mail: info@lakevyrnwyhotel.co.uk

web: www.lakevyrnwyhotel.co.uk

Dir: *on A4393, 200yds past dam turn sharp right into drive*

PETS: Bedrooms Sep Accom heated kennels **Charges** £10 per night charge for damage **Grounds** accessible on leads **Exercise area** countryside walks **Facilities** cage storage walks info vet info **On Request** fridge access torch towels **Other** designated bedrooms only **Resident Pets:** 3 Black Labradors

This fine country-house hotel lies in 26,000 acres of woodland above Lake Vyrnwy. It provides a wide range of bedrooms, most with superb views and many with four-poster beds and balconies. The extensive public rooms are elegantly furnished and include a terrace, a choice of bars serving meals and the more formal dining in the restaurant.

Rooms 52 en suite (4 fmly) S £95-£185; D £120-£210 (incl. bkfst)* **Facilities Spa** STV FTV Fishing Gym Wi-fi available Archery Birdwatching Canoeing Kayaking Clay shooting Sailing Fly fishing Cycling Xmas New Year **Services** Lift **Parking** 70 **Notes LB**

LLANWRTYD WELLS MAP 03 SN84

★★★★ ❀❀❀ RESTAURANT WITH ROOMS

Carlton Riverside

Irfon Crescent LD5 4SP

☎ 01591 610248

e-mail: info@carltonrestaurant.co.uk

Dir: *In town centre next to bridge*

PETS: Bedrooms unattended **Charges** charge for damage **Exercise area** 500mtrs **Facilities** walks info vet info **On Request** towels

Guests become part of the family at this character property, set beside the river in Wales's smallest town. Carlton Riverside offers award-winning cuisine for which Mary Ann Gilchrist relies on the very best of local ingredients. The set menu is complemented by a well-chosen wine list, and dinner is served in the delightfully stylish restaurant which offers a memorable blend of traditional comfort, modern design and river views. Four comfortable bedrooms have tasteful combinations of antique and contemporary furniture, along with welcome personal touches.

Rooms 4 en suite S £40-£50; D £65-£100* **Facilities** TVB tea/coffee Cen ht Dinner Last d 8.30pm **Notes LB** Closed Dec

★★★★ ❀❀ RESTAURANT WITH ROOMS

Lasswade Country House

Station Rd LD5 4RW

☎ 01591 610515 🖹 01591 610611

e-mail: info@lasswadehotel.co.uk

Dir: *Off A483 into Irfon Terrace, right into Station Rd, 350yds on right*

PETS: Sep Accom indoor kennels (no charge) **Stables** nearby (0.25m) **Exercise area** walks & forest nearby **Facilities** walks info vet info **On Request** torch **Other** grazing for horses available only by prior arrangement

This friendly establishment on the edge of the town has impressive views over the countryside. Bedrooms are comfortably furnished and well equipped, while the public areas consist of a tastefully decorated lounge, an elegant restaurant with a bar, and an airy conservatory which looks out on to the neighbouring hills. The kitchen utilises fresh, local produce to provide an enjoyable dining experience.

Rooms 8 en suite **Facilities** TVB

LLYSWEN MAP 03 SO13

★★★★ 85% ❀❀ COUNTRY HOUSE HOTEL

Llangoed Hall

WELSH RAREBITS

LD3 0YP

☎ 01874 754525 🖹 01874 754545

e-mail: enquiries@llangoedhall.com

web: www.llangoedhall.com

Dir: *On A470, 2m from Llyswen towards Builth Wells*

PETS: Sep Accom heated kennels; paddock for horses **Charges** £10 kennels per night charge for damage **Grounds** accessible on leads disp bin **Exercise area** 17-acres of parkland **Facilities** food (pre-bookable) food bowl water bowl bedding dog scoop/disp bags cage storage walks info vet info **On Request** fridge access torch towels **Other** please note pets are not allowed inside hotel; dog/horse/cat walkers available **Resident Pets:** Mr Spotty & Mr Blackie (cats)

Set against the stunning backdrop of the Black Mountains and the Wye Valley, this imposing country house is a haven of peace and quiet. The interior is no less impressive, with a noteworthy art collection complementing the many antiques featured in day rooms and bedrooms. Comfortable, spacious bedrooms and suites are matched by equally inviting lounges.

Rooms 23 en suite S £175-£350; D £210-£400 (incl. bkfst)* **Facilities** Fishing Wi-fi available Maze Clay pigeon shooting Xmas New Year **Parking** 80 **Notes LB** No children 8yrs

WALES

MONTGOMERY MAP 07 SO29

★★ 79% HOTEL

Dragon

SY15 6PA

☎ 01686 668359 0870 011 8227

e-mail: reception@dragonhotel.com

web: www.dragonhotel.com

Dir: *behind town hall*

PETS: Bedrooms unattended **Stables** nearby (0.5m) **Charges** charge for damage **Public areas** except dining areas (on leads) **Grounds** accessible on leads **Exercise area** countryside nearby **Facilities** pet sitting dog walking vet info **On Request** torch towels

This fine 17th-century coaching inn stands in the centre of Montgomery. Beams and timbers from the nearby castle, which was destroyed by Cromwell, are visible in the lounge and bar. A wide choice of soundly prepared, wholesome food is available in both the restaurant and bar. Bedrooms are well equipped and family rooms are available.

Rooms 20 en suite (6 fmly) S £51-£61; D £87.50-£97.50 (incl. bkfst)* **Facilities** Wi-fi available Xmas New Year **Parking** 21 **Notes** LB

WALES

RHONDDA CYNON TAFF

MISKIN MAP 03 ST08

★★★★ 74% COUNTRY HOUSE HOTEL

Miskin Manor Country Hotel

Pendoylan Rd CF72 8ND

☎ 01443 224204 01443 237606

e-mail: ben.rosenberg@miskin-manor.co.uk

web: www.miskin-manor.co.uk

Dir: *M4 junct 34, exit onto A4119, signed Llantrisant, hotel 300yds on left*

PETS: Bedrooms (7GF) unattended **Charges** £20 per pet per night charge for damage **Public areas** except restaurant & dining areas (on leads) **Grounds** accessible on leads disp bin **Exercise area** 20yds **Facilities** water bowl walks info vet info **Other** pets allowed in certain bedrooms only **Resident Pets:** Rosie Lee (Boxer)

This historic manor house is peacefully located in 20-acre grounds yet only minutes away from the M4. Bedrooms are furnished to a high standard and include some located in converted stables and cottages. Public areas are spacious and comfortable and include a variety of function rooms. The relaxed atmosphere and the surroundings ensure this hotel remains popular for wedding functions as well as with business guests.

Rooms 34 en suite 9 annexe en suite (2 fmly) (7 GF) **Facilities** supervised Squash Gym Wi-fi available **Parking** 200

PONTYPRIDD MAP 03 ST08

★★★ 74% COUNTRY HOUSE HOTEL

Llechwen Hall

Llanfabon CF37 4HP

☎ 01443 742050 & 743020 01443 742189

e-mail: steph@llechwen.co.uk

Dir: *A470 N towards Merthyr Tydfil. At large rdbt take 3rd exit. At mini rdbt take 3rd exit, hotel signed 0.5m on left*

PETS: Bedrooms (4GF) unattended **Stables** nearby (2m) **Grounds** accessible on leads disp bin **Exercise area** **Facilities** cage storage walks info vet info **On Request** fridge access torch towels

Set on top of a hill with a stunning approach, this country house hotel has served many purposes in its 200-year-old history including being a private school and a magistrates' court. Bedrooms are spacious, individually decorated and well equipped, and some are situated in the separate comfortable coach house nearby. There are bedrooms ground-floor, twin, double and family rooms on offer. The Victorian-style public areas are attractively appointed and the hotel is a popular venue for weddings.

Rooms 12 en suite 8 annexe en suite (6 fmly) (4 GF) **Facilities** FTV Wi-fi available **Parking** 150 **Notes** Closed 24-30 Dec

SWANSEA

LLANGENNITH MAP 02 SS49

★★★★ INN

Kings Head

Town House SA3 1HX

☎ 01792 386212 📠 01792 386477

e-mail: info@kingsheadgower.co.uk

PETS: Bedrooms (4GF) sign **Stables** nearby (150yds) **Charges** £5 per dog, £15 per horse per night charge for damage **Public areas** (on leads) **Grounds** accessible on leads disp bin **Exercise area** beach 1m (access all year) **Facilities** water bowl walks info vet info **Resident Pets:** Skinny (Greyhound) & Oscar (German Shepherd)

The Kings Head is made up from three 17th-century buildings set behind a splendid rough stone wall, and stands opposite Llangennith Church in this coastal village on the Gower peninsula. In a separate building are the seven well equipped and comfortable bedrooms. This is an ideal base for exploring the Gower peninsula, whether for walking, cycling or surfing. Evening meals and breakfasts can be taken in the pub.

Rooms 7 en suite (3 fmly) (4 GF) D £70-£90✳ **Facilities** FTV TVB tea/coffee Cen ht Dinner Last d 9pm Pool Table **Parking** 10 **Notes** LB

PORT EINON MAP 02 SS48

►►► Carreglwyd Camping & Caravan Park

(SS465863)

SA3 1NL

☎ 01792 390795 📠 01792 390796

Dir: *A4118 to Port Einon, site adjacent to beach*

PETS: Exercise area on site **Facilities** on site shop food food bowl water bowl dog chews cat treats dog scoop/disp bags vet info **Resident Pets:** Brono (Black Labrador), Dave (German Shepherd), Emma-Jane (cat)

Open Mar-Dec Last arrival 18.00hrs Last departure 16.00hrs

Set in an unrivalled location alongside the safe sandy beach of Port Einon on the Gower Peninsula, this popular park is an ideal family holiday spot. Close to an attractive village with pubs and shops, most pitches offer sea views. The sloping ground has been partly terraced, and facilities are excellent. A 12-acre site with 150 touring pitches.

Notes Dogs must be kept on leads at all times

RHOSSILI MAP 02 SS48

►►► Pitton Cross Caravan & Camping Park

(SS434877)

SA3 1PH

☎ 01792 390593 📠 01792 391010

e-mail: admin@pittoncross.co.uk

web: www.pittoncross.co.uk

Dir: *2m W of Scurlage on B4247*

PETS: Stables nearby (3m) (loose box) **Charges** £1 per night £7 per week **Public areas** except dog-free area (on leads) disp bin **Exercise area** on site connecting field **Facilities** on site shop food food bowl water bowl dog scoop/disp bags leads washing facs walks info vet info **Other** prior notice required **Resident Pets:** Buster (dog), Tipsy & Minnie (cats)

Open all year Last arrival 20.00hrs Last departure 11.00hrs

Surrounded by farmland close to sandy Menslade Bay, which is within walking distance across the fields. This grassy park is divided by hedging into paddocks. Nearby Rhossili Beach is popular with surfers. Performance kites are sold, and instruction in flying is given. A 6-acre site with 100 touring pitches, 21 hardstandings.

Notes Quiet at all times

SWANSEA

MAP 03 SS69

★★★ 77% HOTEL

Ramada Swansea

RAMADA

Phoenix Way, Swansea Enterprise Park SA7 9EG

☎ 01792 310330 📠 01792 797535

e-mail: sales.swansea@ramadajarvis.co.uk

web: www.ramadajarvis.co.uk

Dir: *M4 junct 44, A48 (Llansamlet), left at 3rd lights, right at 1st mini rdbt, left into Phoenix Way at 2nd mini rdbt. Hotel 800mtrs on right*

PETS: Bedrooms (50GF) unattended sign **Charges** charge for damage **Grounds** accessible disp bin **Exercise area** **Facilities** dog walking cage storage walks info vet info **On Request** fridge access torch towels

This large, modern hotel is conveniently situated on the outskirts of the city with easy access to the M4. Bedrooms are comfortably appointed for both business and leisure guests. Public areas include the Arts Restaurant, Arts Bar and elegant lounges. 24-hour room service is also available.

Rooms 119 en suite (12 fmly) (50 GF) S £63-£162; D £63-£174 (incl. bkfst)✻ **Facilities** STV FTV supervised Gym Wi-fi available Sauna New Year **Parking** 180 **Notes** LB

WALES

VALE OF GLAMORGAN

BARRY

MAP 03 ST16

★★★ 80% COUNTRY HOUSE HOTEL

Egerton Grey Country House

WELSH RAREBITS

Porthkerry CF62 3BZ

☎ 01446 711666 📠 01446 711690

e-mail: info@egertongrey.co.uk

web: www.egertongrey.co.uk

Dir: *M4 junct 33 follow signs for airport, left at rdbt for Porthkerry, after 500yds turn left down lane between thatched cottages*

PETS: Bedrooms unattended **Charges** charge for damage **Public areas** conservatory only **Grounds** accessible **Exercise area** country park & seaside nearby **Facilities** food bowl water bowl walks info vet info **Resident Pets:** Louis (Cavalier King Charles Spaniel), Puss (cat)

This former rectory enjoys a peaceful setting and views over delightful countryside with distant glimpses of the sea. The bedrooms are spacious and individually furnished. Public areas offer charm and elegance, and include an airy lounge and restaurant, which has been sympathetically converted from the billiards room.

Rooms 10 en suite (4 fmly) S £100-£120; D £140-£170 (incl. bkfst)✻ **Facilities** FTV Putt green Wi-fi in bedrooms Xmas New Year **Parking** 40 **Notes** LB

WREXHAM

EYTON

MAP 07 SJ34

►►►►► **The Plassey Leisure Park** *(SJ353452)*

The Plassey LL13 0SP

☎ 01978 780277 📠 01978 780019

e-mail: enquiries@theplassey.co.uk

web: www.theplassey.co.uk

Dir: *From A483 at Bangor-on-Dee exit onto B5426 for 2.5m. Site entrance signed on left*

PETS: Charges £2 per dog per night £14 per dog per week **Public areas** except bars, restaurants & shops (on leads) disp bin **Exercise area** on site 1-acre grounds, 2m of walks **Facilities** on site shop food dog chews cat treats dog scoop/disp bags vet info **Other** prior notice required **Restrictions** no dangerous breeds (see page 7)

Open Jan-Nov Last arrival 20.30hrs Last departure 18.00hrs

A lovely park set in several hundred acres of quiet farm and meadowland in the Dee Valley. The superb toilet facilities include individual cubicles for total privacy and security, while the Edwardian farm buildings have been converted into a restaurant, coffee shop, beauty studio, and various craft outlets. There is plenty here to entertain the whole family, from scenic walks and swimming pool to free fishing, and use of the 9-hole golf course. A 10-acre site with 110 touring pitches, 45 hardstandings.

Notes No footballs, bikes or skateboards

HANMER

MAP 07 SJ43

★★★★ INN

The Hanmer Arms

SY13 3DE

☎ 01948 830532 📠 0148 830740

e-mail: info@hanmerarms.co.uk

web: www.hanmerarms.co.uk

Dir: *On A539, just off A525 Whitchurch/Wrexham road*

PETS: Bedrooms (5GF) **Charges** £5 per night charge for damage **Public areas** bar only (on leads) **Grounds** accessible on leads **Exercise area** 5 min walk **Facilities** walks info vet info **On Request** fridge access **Resident Pets:** Sidney (Labrador)

Located in the centre of the village and also home to the local crown green bowling club, this former farm has been sympathetically renovated to provide a good range of facilities. Well equipped bedrooms are situated in the former stables or barns, and rustic furniture styles highlight the many period features within public areas, which also feature an attractive first floor function room.

Rooms 12 annexe en suite (2 fmly) (5 GF) S £49.50-£59.50; D £79.50-£89.50✻ **Facilities** FTV TVB tea/coffee Cen ht Dinner Last d 9pm **Parking** 50 **Notes** LB

LLANARMON DYFFRYN CEIRIOG — MAP 07 SJ13

★★★ 87% HOTEL

West Arms

WELSH RAREBITS

LL20 7LD

☎ 01691 600665 & 600612 01691 600622

e-mail: gowestarms@aol.com

Dir: *Off A483/A5 at Chirk, take B4500 to Ceiriog Valley. Llanarmon 11m at end of B4500*

PETS: Bedrooms (3GF) unattended **Sep Accom** kennels with hay **Stables** nearby (4m) **Charges** £6 per night charge for damage **Public areas** except restaurant (on leads) **Grounds** accessible disp bin **Exercise area** 300yds **Facilities** water bowl bedding litter tray etc dog scoop/disp bags leads washing facs cage storage walks info vet info **On Request** fridge access torch towels **Resident Pets:** Marmite (Black Labrador)

Set in the beautiful Ceiriog Valley, this delightful hotel has a wealth of charm and character. There is a comfortable lounge, a room for private dining and two bars, as well as a pleasant, award-winning restaurant offering a set-price menu of freshly cooked dishes. The attractive bedrooms have a mixture of modern and period furnishings.

Rooms 15 en suite (2 fmly) (3 GF) S £53.50-£118; D £87-£225 (incl. bkfst)✻ **Facilities** Fishing Wi-fi available ch fac Xmas New Year **Parking** 22 **Notes** LB

★★★★ INN

The Hand at Llanarmon

LL20 7LD

☎ 01691 600666 01691 600262

e-mail: reception@thehandhotel.co.uk

Dir: *Exit A5 at Chirk onto B4500 signed Ceiriog Valley, continue for 11m*

PETS: Bedrooms unattended **Stables** on site **Public areas** except restaurant **Exercise area** adjacent, country lane **Other** prior notice required; dogs allowed in certain bedrooms only

This small, pleasant, privately owned and run accommodation is located in the village centre and has a wealth of charm and character. Apart from warm and friendly hospitality, it provides a variety of bedroom styles, including rooms on ground floor level and two in a separate building. A large wood-carved hand extends a welcome at front entrance and a good choice of competently prepared food is provided.

Rooms 13 en suite (4 GF) S £40-£70; D £80-£110✻ **Facilities** TVB tea/coffee Direct dial from bedrooms Cen ht Dinner Last d 8.45pm Wi-fi available **Parking** 19 **Notes** LB RS 24-26 Dec

WALES

Ireland

NORTHERN IRELAND

CO ANTRIM

BALLYMONEY MAP 01 C6

►►►► Drumaheglis Marina & Caravan Park *(C 901254)*

36 Glenstall Rd BT53 7QN

☎ 028 2766 0280 & 2766 0227 📠 028 2766 0222

e-mail: helen.neill@ballymoney.gov.uk

web: www.ballymoney.gov.uk

Dir: *Signed off A26, approx 1.5m outside Ballymoney towards Coleraine, & also off B66 S of Ballymoney*

PETS: Public areas (on leads) disp bin **Exercise area** on site **Facilities** vet info

Open 17 Mar-Oct Last arrival 20.00hrs Last departure 13.00hrs

Exceptionally well-designed and laid out park beside the Lower Bann River, with very spacious pitches and two quality toilet blocks. Ideal base for touring Antrim or for watersports enthusiasts. A 16-acre site with 55 touring pitches, 55 hardstandings.

CARRICKFERGUS MAP 01 D5

★★ 65% HOTEL

Dobbins Inn

6-8 High St BT38 7AP

☎ 028 9335 1905 📠 028 9335 1905

e-mail: bookingdobbins@btconnect.com

Dir: *M2 from Belfast, right at rdbt onto A2 to Carrickfergus. Left opposite castle*

PETS: Bedrooms Charges £5 per night charge for damage **Exercise area Facilities** walks info vet info **On Request** fridge access

Colourful window boxes adorn the front of this popular inn near the ancient castle and seafront. Public areas are furnished to a modern standard without compromising the inn's interesting, historical character. Bedrooms vary in size and style, all provide modern comforts. Staff throughout are very friendly and attentive to guests needs.

Rooms 15 en suite (2 fmly) S £50-£52; D £72-£76 (incl. bkfst)✻ **Facilities** STV ♫ New Year **Notes** Closed 25-26 Dec & 1 Jan RS Good Fri

LARNE MAP 01 D5

★★★★ GUEST ACCOMMODATION

Derrin House

2 Princes Gardens BT40 1RQ

☎ 028 2827 3269 📠 028 2827 3269

e-mail: info@derrinhouse.co.uk

Dir: *Off A8 Harbour Highway onto A2 coast route, 1st left after lights at Main St*

PETS: Bedrooms (2GF) **Exercise area** 5 min walk **Facilities** cage storage walks info

Just a short walk from the town centre, and a short drive from the harbour, this comfortable Victorian house offers a very friendly welcome. The bedrooms are gradually being refurbished to offer smartly presented modern facilities. Public areas are light and inviting, hearty breakfasts are offered in the stylish dining room.

Rooms 7 rms (6 en suite) (1 pri facs) (2 fmly) (2 GF) S £35-£38; D £55-£60 **Facilities** TVB tea/coffee Cen ht TVL Wi-fi available **Parking** 6 **Notes** LB

CO DOWN

BANGOR MAP 01 D5

★★★ GUEST ACCOMMODATION

Tara Guest House

49/51 Princetown Rd BT20 3TA

☎ 028 9145 8820 📠 028 9146 8924

e-mail: taraguesthouse@lineone.net

Dir: *A2 to Bangor, down Main St, left onto Queens Parade to mini-rdbt (Gray Hill) right onto Princetown Rd*

PETS: Bedrooms unattended **Grounds** accessible on leads **Exercise area**

Located just a short walk from the town centre this traditionally styled house provides spacious, well-equipped bedrooms, many for which are suitable for families. Some bedrooms also boast sea views while spa baths are provided in others. There is a comfortable lounge and bright dining room.

Rooms 13 en suite (4 fmly) S fr £35; D fr £60 **Facilities** TVB tea/coffee Direct dial from bedrooms Cen ht TVL Wi-fi available **Parking** 8 **Notes** Closed 25-30 Dec

IRELAND

KILLYLEAGH MAP 01 D5

►►►► Delamont Country Park Camping & Caravanning Club Site *(J 511512)*

Delamont Country Park, Downpatrick Rd BT30 9TZ

☎ 028 4482 1833

web: www.thefriendlyclub.co.uk

Dir: *From Belfast take A22. Site 1m S of Killyleagh & 4m N of Downpatrick*

PETS: disp bin **Exercise area** **Facilities** walks info vet info **Other** prior notice required

Open 12 Mar-9 Nov Last arrival 21.00hrs Last departure noon

A spacious park enjoying superb views and walks, in a lovely and interesting part of the province. The facilities are of a very high order, and include fully-serviced pitches and excellent toilets. The site is close to Strangford Loch Marine Water reserve, a medieval fairy fort, and a blue flag beach. A 4.5-acre site with 63 touring pitches, 63 hardstandings.

Notes Site gates closed 23.00hrs-07.00hrs

CO LONDONDERRY

AGHADOWEY MAP 01 C6

★★ 76% HOTEL

Brown Trout Golf & Country Inn

IRISH COUNTRY HOTELS

209 Agivey Rd BT51 4AD

☎ 028 7086 8209 🖹 028 7086 8878

e-mail: jane@browntroutinn.com

Dir: *at junct of A54 & B66 junct on road to Coleraine*

PETS: Bedrooms unattended sign **Charges** charge for damage **Public areas** except restaurant (on leads) **Grounds** accessible disp bin **Exercise area** **Facilities** dog scoop/disp bags leads washing facs dog grooming cage storage walks info vet info **On Request** fridge access torch towels **Resident Pets:** Muffin & Lucy (Chocolate Labrador)

Set alongside the Agivey River and featuring its own 9-hole golf course, this welcoming inn offers a choice of spacious accommodation. Comfortably furnished bedrooms are situated around a courtyard area whilst the cottage suites also have lounge areas. Home-cooked meals are served in the restaurant and lighter fare is available in the charming lounge bar which has entertainment at weekends.

Rooms 15 en suite (11 fmly) S £60-£70; D £80-£110 (incl. bkfst)✳ **Facilities** ⛳ 9 Fishing Gym Putt green Wi-fi available Game fishing ♫ Xmas New Year **Parking** 80 **Notes** LB

LONDONDERRY MAP 01 C5

★★★ 79% ֍ HOTEL

Beech Hill Country House Hotel

MANOR HOUSE HOTELS

32 Ardmore Rd BT47 3QP

☎ 028 7134 9279 🖹 028 7134 5366

e-mail: info@beech-hill.com

web: www.beech-hill.com

Dir: *from A6 take Faughan Bridge turn, 1m to hotel opposite Ardmore Chapel*

PETS: Bedrooms unattended **Stables** nearby (1m) **Public areas** except restaurant (on leads) **Grounds** accessible on leads disp bin **Exercise area** **Facilities** cage storage walks info vet info **On Request** fridge access torch towels **Other** dogs allowed in certain bedrooms only; other pets may be accepted by prior arrangement

Dating back to 1729, Beech Hill is an impressive mansion, standing in 32 acres of glorious woodlands and gardens. Traditionally styled day rooms provide deep comfort, and meals are served in the attractively extended dining room. The splendid bedroom wing provides spacious, well equipped rooms in addition to the more classically designed bedrooms in the main house.

Rooms 17 en suite 10 annexe en suite (4 fmly) S £90-£100; D £110-£200 (incl. bkfst)✳ **Facilities** ♨ Gym Wi-fi available New Year **Services** Lift **Parking** 75 **Notes** LB Closed 24-25 Dec

IRELAND

REPUBLIC OF IRELAND

CO CORK

BANDON — MAP 01 B2

★★★★ BED & BREAKFAST

Glebe Country House

Ballinadee

☎ 021 4778294 📠 021 4778456

e-mail: glebehse@indigo.ie

Dir: *Off N71 at Innishannon Bridge signed Ballinadee, 8km along river bank, left after village sign*

PETS: Bedrooms Grounds accessible disp bin **Exercise area Facilities** food (pre-bookable) food bowl water bowl bedding dog chews cat treats feeding mat dog scoop/disp bags leads washing facs cage storage vet info **On Request** fridge access torch towels **Other** Please telephone for further details **Resident Pets:** Tarka (Dalmatian), Ginder (cat), Harry (wild hedgehog)

This lovely guest house stands in well-kept gardens, and is run with great attention to detail. Antique furnishings predominate throughout this comfortable house, which has a lounge and an elegant dining room. An interesting breakfast menu offers unusual options, and a country-house style dinner is available by arrangement.

Rooms 4 en suite (2 fmly) S €60-€70; D €90-€110✱ **Facilities** tea/coffee Direct dial from bedrooms Cen ht TVL Dinner Last d noon Wi-fi available **Parking** 10 **Notes** LB Closed 21 Dec-3 Jan

BLARNEY — MAP 01 B2

★★★★★ GUEST HOUSE

Ashlee Lodge

Tower

☎ 021 4385346 📠 021 4385726

e-mail: info@ashleelodge.com

Dir: *4km from Blarney on R617*

PETS: Bedrooms (6GF) sign **Grounds** accessible on leads disp bin **Exercise area** on site **Facilities** washing facs walks info vet info **On Request** fridge access towels

Ashley Lodge is a purpose-built guest house, situated in the village of Tower, close to Blarney and local pubs and restaurants. Bedrooms are decorated with comfort and elegance in mind, some with whirlpool baths, and one room has easier access. The extensive breakfast menu is memorable for Ann's home baking. Guests can unwind in the sauna or the outdoor hot tub. Transfers to the nearest airport and railway station can be arranged, and tee times can be booked at many of the nearby golf courses.

Rooms 10 en suite (2 fmly) (6 GF) S €75-€200; D €100-€250✱ **Facilities** STV FTV TVB tea/coffee Direct dial from bedrooms Licensed Cen ht TVL Dinner Last d 8.30pm Wi-fi available Sauna Hot tub **Parking** 12 **Notes** LB

CASTLEMARTYR — MAP 01 C2

U

Capella Hotel at Castlemartyr Resort

☎ 021 4644050 📠 021 4219002

e-mail: reservations.castlemartyr@capellahotels.com

Dir: *N25, 3rd exit signed Rosslare. Continue past Carrigtwohill & Midleton exits. At rdbt take 2nd exit into Castlemartyr*

PETS: Bedrooms (30GF) unattended **Stables** on site **Exercise area Facilities** food (pre-bookable) food bowl water bowl bedding washing facs **Restrictions** only dogs less than 50lb accepted

At the time of going to press the rating for this establishment was not confirmed. This may be due to a change of ownership or because it has only recently joined the AA rating scheme. For further details please see the AA website: www.theAA.com

Rooms 103 en suite (6 fmly) (30 GF) S €225-€2750; D €225-€2750 (incl. bkfst)✱ **Facilities** Spa STV ⓢ ⛳18 Gym Wi-fi available Fitness studio Steam room Sauna Xmas New Year **Services** Lift air con **Parking** 200 **Notes** LB

CLONAKILTY — MAP 01 B2

★★ FARM HOUSE

Desert House *(W 390411)*

Coast Rd

☎ 023 33331 📠 023 33048 Mrs D Jennings

e-mail: deserthouse@eircom.net

Dir: *1km E of Clonakilty. Signed on N71 at 1st rdbt, house 500 mtrs on left*

PETS: Bedrooms Grounds accessible on leads disp bin **Exercise area** adjacent **Facilities** cage storage walks info vet info **On Request** fridge access **Resident Pets:** Holly & Sophie (Golden Cockers), Tess (Sheepdog), Gwen (Springer Spaniel)

This comfortable Georgian farmhouse overlooks Clonakilty Bay and is within walking distance of the town. The estuary is of great interest to bird watching enthusiasts. It is a good base for touring west Cork and Kerry.

Rooms 5 rms (4 en suite) **Facilities** TVB tea/coffee Cen ht **Parking** 10 **Notes** 100 acres dairy mixed

IRELAND

KINSALE MAP 01 B2

★★★★★ GUEST HOUSE

Friar's Lodge

5 Friars St

☎ 086 289 5075 & 021 4777384 📠 021 4774363

e-mail: mtierney@indigo.ie

Dir: *In town centre next to parish church*

PETS: Bedrooms (4GF) unattended **Charges Exercise area Facilities** walks info vet info **On Request** fridge access towels

This purpose built property near the Friary, has been developed with every comfort in mind. Bedrooms are particularly spacious. Located on a quiet street within minutes walk of the town centre, with secure parking to the rear. A very good choice is offered from the breakfast menu.

Rooms 18 en suite (2 fmly) (4 GF) S €60-€80; D €90-€150* **Facilities** STV TVB tea/coffee Direct dial from bedrooms Licensed Lift Cen ht Wi-fi available **Parking** 20 **Notes** Closed Xmas

MACROOM MAP 01 B2

★★★ 78% HOTEL

Castle

IRISH COUNTRY HOTELS

Main St

☎ 026 41074 📠 026 41505

e-mail: castlehotel@eircom.net

Dir: *on N22 midway between Cork & Killarney*

PETS: Bedrooms unattended **Charges** £35 per night charge for damage **Exercise area Facilities** food bowl water bowl dog chews dog scoop/disp bags cage storage walks info vet info **On Request** fridge access towels

This town centre property offers excellent service provided by the Buckley Family and their team. Bedrooms are very comfortable, as are the extensive public areas. Secure parking is available to the rear.

Rooms 58 en suite (6 fmly) S €75-€125; D €150-€199 (incl. bkfst) **Facilities** STV supervised Gym Wi-fi available Steam room New Year **Services** Lift air con **Parking** 30 **Notes** LB Closed 24-28 Dec

CO DONEGAL

DONEGAL MAP 01 B5

★★★★ 86% HOTEL

Harvey's Point Country Hotel

Lough Eske

☎ 074 9722208 📠 074 9722352

e-mail: sales@harveyspoint.com

web: www.harveyspoint.com

Dir: *N56 from Donegal, then 1st right (Loch Eske/Harvey's Point)*

PETS: Bedrooms (16GF) unattended sign **Sep Accom** on request **Stables** on site **Grounds** accessible **Exercise area Facilities** food bowl water bowl cage storage walks info vet info **On Request** fridge access torch towels **Resident Pets:** Paddy (Labrador) & geese

Situated by the lakeshore, this hotel is an oasis of relaxation. Comfort and attentive guest care are the norm here. A range of particularly spacious suites are available; they all make the best use of the views. The kitchen brigade maintains consistently high standards in the dining room, with a very popular Sunday buffet lunch served each week.

Rooms 64 en suite (16 GF) S €129-€420; D €198-€640 (incl. bkfst) **Facilities** Wi-fi available Treatment rooms Pitch 'n' putt Bicycle hire Xmas New Year **Services** Lift **Parking** 300 **Notes** LB Closed Mon & Tue Nov-Mar

RATHMULLAN MAP 01 C6

★★★★ 79% COUNTRY HOUSE HOTEL

Rathmullan House

☎ 074 9158188 📠 074 9158200

e-mail: info@rathmullanhouse.com

Dir: *From Letterkenny, then Ramelton then Rathmullan R243. Left at Mace shop, through village, hotel gates on right*

PETS: Bedrooms (9GF) unattended sign **Stables** nearby (500yds) **Charges** £10 per night **Grounds** accessible on leads disp bin **Exercise area** 500yds **Facilities** food (pre-bookable) food bowl water bowl bedding dog chews dog scoop/disp bags cage storage walks info vet info **On Request** fridge access torch towels **Restrictions** breeds max 80cm in height; no Pit Bull Terriers **Resident Pets:** Suzy (Labrador) & Odie (Jack Russell)

Dating from the 18th-century, this fine property has been operating as a country-house hotel for the last 40 years under the stewardship of the Wheeler family. Guests are welcome to wander around the well-planted grounds and the walled garden, from where much of the ingredients for the Weeping Elm Restaurant are grown. The many lounges are relaxing and comfortable, while many of the bedrooms benefit from balconies and patio areas.

Rooms 34 en suite (4 fmly) (9 GF) S €110-€210; D €220-€330 (incl. bkfst)* **Facilities** Spa Wi-fi available ch fac New Year **Parking** 80 **Notes** LB Closed 11 Jan-5 Feb RS 15 Nov-12 Mar

IRELAND

DUBLIN

DUBLIN — MAP 01 D4

★★★★ GUEST ACCOMMODATION

Glenshandan Lodge

Dublin Rd, Swords

☎ 01 8408838 🖷 01 8408838

e-mail: glenshandan@eircom.net

Dir: *Beside Statoil on airport side of Swords Main St*

PETS: Bedrooms (5GF) unattended **Stables** nearby (1m) **Charges** charge for damage **Public areas** except restaurant & lounge **Grounds** accessible disp bin **Exercise area** 20mtrs **Facilities** washing facs cage storage walks info vet info **On Request** fridge access torch towels **Resident Pets:** 2 Boxers

Family and dog-friendly house with hospitable owners and good facilities including e-mail access. Bedrooms are comfortable and one room has easier access. Secure parking available. Close to pubs, restaurants, golf, airport and the Kennel Club.

Rooms 9 en suite (5 fmly) (5 GF) S €35-€65; D €80-€90 **Facilities** TVB tea/coffee Cen ht TVL Wi-fi available **Parking** 10 **Notes LB** Closed Xmas/New Year

CO GALWAY

CASHEL — MAP 01 A4

★★★ 86% ❁❁ COUNTRY HOUSE HOTEL

Cashel House

☎ 095 31001 🖷 095 31077

e-mail: info@cashel-house-hotel.com

web: www.cashel-house-hotel.com

Dir: *S off N59, 1.5km W of Recess, well signed*

PETS: Bedrooms unattended **Stables** on site **Charges** €20 per horse per night charge for damage **Grounds** accessible on leads disp bin **Exercise area Facilities** washing facs cage storage walks info vet info **On Request** fridge access torch towels

Cashel House is a mid-19th century property, standing at the head of Cashel Bay, in the heart of Connemara. Quietly secluded in award-winning gardens with woodland walks. Attentive service comes with the perfect balance of friendliness and professionalism from McEvilly family and their staff. The comfortable lounges have turf fires and antique furnishings. The restaurant offers local produce such as the famous Connemara lamb, and fish from the nearby coast.

Rooms 32 en suite (4 fmly) (6 GF) S €107-€270; D €214-€304 (incl. bkfst)✳ **Facilities** ⛹ Xmas New Year **Parking** 40 **Notes LB** Closed 4 Jan-4 Feb

CLIFDEN — MAP 01 A4

★★★ 77% ❁❁ HOTEL

Ardagh

IRISH COUNTRY HOTELS

Ballyconneely Rd

☎ 095 21384 🖷 095 21314

e-mail: ardaghhotel@eircom.net

Dir: *N59 (Galway to Clifden), signed to Ballyconneely*

PETS: Bedrooms Public areas except restaurant **Grounds** accessible **Exercise area** 5 mins from beach **Resident Pets:** Rocky (Staffordshire), cat

Situated at the head of Ardbear Bay, this family-run hotel takes full advantage of the spectacular scenery. The restaurant is renowned for its cuisine, which is complemented by friendly and knowledgeable service. Many of the spacious and well-appointed bedrooms have large picture windows and plenty of comfort.

Rooms 19 en suite (2 fmly) S €120-€140; D €180-€210 (incl. bkfst) **Facilities** Wi-fi available Pool room ♫ **Parking** 35 **Notes LB** Closed Nov-Mar

GALWAY — MAP 01 B3

★★★★ 79% ❁ HOTEL

Ardilaun Hotel & Leisure Club

Taylor's Hill

☎ 091 521433 🖷 091 521546

e-mail: info@theardilaunhotel.ie

web: www.theardilaunhotel.ie

Dir: *N6 to Galway City West, then follow signs for N59 Clifden, then N6 towards Salthill*

PETS: Bedrooms (8GF) **Charges** £10 per night **Grounds** accessible on leads disp bin **Exercise area Facilities** walks info vet info **On Request** fridge access towels

The Ardilaun is located on five acres of landscaped gardens and has undergone a major refurbishment. Bedrooms have been thoughtfully equipped and furnished and the new wing of executive rooms and suites are particularly spacious. Public areas include Camilaun Restaurant overlooking the garden, comfortable lounges and Blazers bar, and there extensive banqueting and leisure facilities.

Rooms 125 en suite (17 fmly) (8 GF) S €95-€165; D €110-€350 (incl. bkfst)✳ **Facilities Spa** STV 🏊 supervised Gym Wi-fi available Treatment & analysis rooms Beauty salon Spinning room ♫ New Year **Services** Lift **Parking** 380 **Notes LB** Closed 24-26 Dec RS Closed pm 23 Dec

RECESS MAP 01 A4

★★★ 83% COUNTRY HOUSE HOTEL

Lough Inagh Lodge

Inagh Valley

☎ 095 34706 & 34694 095 34708

e-mail: inagh@iol.ie

Dir: *from Recess take R344 towards Kylemore*

PETS: Bedrooms (4GF) unattended **Public areas** except when food is being served **Grounds** accessible **Exercise area** countryside walks nearby **Other** Please telephone for further details **Resident Pets:** Rex (Cocker Spaniel) Sasha (cat)

This 19th-century, former fishing lodge is akin to a family home where guests are encouraged to relax and enjoy the peace. It is situated between the Connemara Mountains and fronted by a good fishing lake. Bedrooms are smartly decorated and comfortable, there is a choice of lounges with turf fires and a cosy traditional bar. The delightful restaurant specialises in dishes of the local lamb and lake caught fish.

Rooms 13 en suite (1 fmly) (4 GF) **Facilities** Fishing Hill walking Fly fishing Cycling **Services** air con **Parking** 16 **Notes LB** Closed mid Dec-mid Mar

CO KERRY

CASTLEGREGORY MAP 01 A2

★★★ BED & BREAKFAST

Griffin's Palm Beach Country House

Goulane, Conor Pass Rd

☎ 066 7139147 066 7139073

e-mail: griffinspalmbeach@eircom.net

Dir: *1.5km from Stradbally village*

PETS: Bedrooms (1GF) **Charges** €5 per night **Grounds** accessible on leads disp bin **Exercise area** beach 0.5m **Facilities** water bowl washing facs cage storage walks info vet info **On Request** fridge access torch **Resident Pets:** Rose (Sheepdog), Cocoa (Fox Terrier)

This farmhouse is a good base for exploring the Dingle Peninsula and unspoiled beaches. The comfortable bedrooms have fine views over Brandon Bay, and the delightful garden can be enjoyed from the dining room and sitting room. Mrs Griffin offers a warm welcome and her home baking is a feature on the breakfast menu.

Rooms 8 rms (6 en suite) (2 pri facs) (3 fmly) (1 GF) S €48-€51; D €90-€100* **Facilities** tea/coffee Cen ht TVL **Parking** 10 **Notes LB** Closed Nov-Feb

IRELAND

KILLARNEY MAP 01 B2

★★★★ 81% HOTEL

Randles Court

Muckross Rd

☎ 064 6635333 📠 064 6635206

e-mail: info@randlescourt.com

Dir: *N22 towards Muckross, turn tight at T-junct on right. From N72 take 3rd exit on 1st rdbt into town & follow signs for Muckross, hotel on left*

PETS: Bedrooms unattended **Stables** nearby **Charges** charge for damage **Public areas** except restaurants & bars (on leads) **Grounds** accessible on leads disp bin **Exercise area Facilities** cage storage walks info vet info **On Request** towels

Close to all the town's attractions, this is a friendly family-run hotel with an emphasis on customer care. Bedrooms are particularly comfortable. Guests can enjoy a relaxing drink in the cosy bar then dine in the chic Checkers bistro restaurant where good food is served in the evenings. A swimming pool and other leisure facilities are available.

Rooms 52 en suite **Facilities** Gym Putt green **Services** Lift **Parking** 39 **Notes** Closed 23-27 Dec

★★★★★ GUEST HOUSE

Earls Court House

Woodlawn Junction, Muckross Rd

☎ 064 6634009 📠 064 6634366

e-mail: info@killarney-earlscourt.ie

Dir: *Left at lights on Muckross Rd, house 100mtrs on left*

PETS: Bedrooms (8GF) **Stables** nearby **Charges** charge for damage **Grounds** accessible disp bin **Exercise area Facilities** food (pre-bookable) food bowl water bowl cage storage walks info vet info **Resident Pets:** Cuddles (Shetland Sheepdog)

This is a charming guest house situated within walking distance of the town centre and National Park. Bedrooms are spacious and individually furnished with luxury and guest comfort in mind, some with four poster beds, jacuzzi baths and balconies. The relaxing lounges have open fires and guests can enjoy the sun patio and garden. There is ample off-street parking.

Rooms 30 en suite (3 fmly) (8 GF) **Facilities** STV TVB tea/coffee Direct dial from bedrooms Licensed Lift Cen ht TVL Wi-fi available **Parking** 30 **Notes** Closed 13 Nov-11 Feb RS 6 Nov-Feb (group bookings 8+)

CO KILDARE

ATHY MAP 01 C3

★★★★★ BED & BREAKFAST

Coursetown Country House

Stradbally Rd

☎ 059 8631101 📠 059 8632740

e-mail: coursetown@hotmail.com

Dir: *3km from Athy. N78 at Athy onto R428*

PETS: Sep Accom Sep accom **Stables** nearby (6m) **Charges** charge for damage **Grounds** accessible on leads disp bin **Exercise area Facilities** washing facs cage storage vet info **On Request** fridge access towels **Resident Pets:** Casper & Leopold (cats)

This charming Victorian country house stands on a 100-hectare tillage farm and bird sanctuary. It has been extensively refurbished, and all bedrooms are furnished to the highest standards. Convalescent or disabled guests are especially welcome, and Iris and Jim Fox are happy to share their knowledge of the Irish countryside and its wildlife.

Rooms 5 en suite (1 GF) **Facilities** TVB tea/coffee Direct dial from bedrooms Cen ht TVL **Parking** 22 **Notes** No children 12yrs Closed 15 Nov-15 Mar

CO MAYO

ACHILL ISLAND MAP 01 A4

★★★★ GUEST HOUSE

Gray's

Dugort

☎ 098 43244 & 43315

Dir: *11km NW of Achill Sound. Off R319 to Doogort*

PETS: Bedrooms (2GF) **Grounds** accessible disp bin **Exercise area Facilities** vet info **Resident Pets:** Cuddles (Corgi), Huggy Bear & Phoebe (cats)

This welcoming guest house is in Doogort, on the northern shore of Achill Island, at the foot of the Slievemore Mountains. There is a smart conservatory and various lounges, the cosy bedrooms are well appointed, and dinner is served nightly by arrangement in the cheerful dining room. A self-contained villa, ideal for families, is also available.

Rooms 5 en suite 10 annexe en suite (4 fmly) (2 GF) S €55-€61; D €110 **Facilities** TVB tea/coffee Licensed Cen ht TVL Dinner Last d 6pm Pool Table **Parking** 30 **Notes** Closed Oct-Feb

CO ROSCOMMON

ROSCOMMON MAP 01 B4

★★★ RESTAURANT WITH ROOMS

Gleesons Townhouse & Restaurant

Market Square

☎ 090 6626954 🖷 090 6627425

e-mail: info@gleesonstownhouse.com

Dir: *in town centre next to tourist office*

PETS: Bedrooms unattended **Sep Accom** 1 outdoor kennel **Exercise area Resident Pets:** Millie (Cavalier King Charles Spaniel)

This 19th-century cut-limestone town house has been very tastefully restored. The bedrooms and suites are decorated and furnished to a high standard. Dinner is served nightly in the Manse Restaurant and there is an extensive lunch and afternoon tea menu in the café or in the beautifully landscaped front courtyard. Conference facilities and secure parking are available.

Rooms 19 rms (17 en suite) (2 pri facs) (1 fmly) **Facilities** STV FTV TVB tea/coffee Direct dial from bedrooms Lift Cen ht TVL Dinner Last d 8.45pm Wi-fi available **Parking** 25 **Notes** Closed 25-26 Dec

CO SLIGO

ACLARE MAP 01 B4

★★★ BED & BREAKFAST

Haggart Lodge

Lislea

☎ 071 9181954 & 00 353 8797 1339

e-mail: mleheny@eircom.net

PETS: Sep Accom outdoor kennels & run, high fencing & security lighting; barns available by arrangement **Stables** nearby (3km) **Charges** €10 per night (dogs) charge for damage **Public areas** (on leads) **Grounds** accessible disp bin **Exercise area** 6-acre field adjacent **Facilities** food (pre-bookable) food bowl water bowl dog chews cat treats dog scoop/disp bags leads pet sitting dog walking washing facs cage storage walks info vet info **On Request** fridge access torch towels **Other** dog grooming available in Ballina (30-minute drive) **Restrictions** no dangerous breeds (see page 7) **Resident Pets:** Tyra & Tyke (small dogs), Levity & Lakeland (Old English Foxhounds)

Maeve Leheny welcomes guests to her comfortable home overlooking the Ox Mountains in west Sligo, near the Mayo border. Traditional country-cooked dinners are available if booked before midday, and home baking is a feature of breakfast. The resident dogs Tyke and Tyra will vacate their kennels for visiting dogs if required!

Rooms 4 rms (3 en suite) S €45-€51 **Facilities** TVB Cen ht TVL Dinner Last d 1pm Wi-fi available **Parking** 12 **Notes** LB ⊗

BALLYMOTE MAP 01 B4

★★★★ BED & BREAKFAST

Church View

Main St, Gurteen

☎ 071 9182935

e-mail: info@thechurchview.com

Dir: *From Ballymote at x-rds head towards Gurteen, on left beside church*

PETS: Sep Accom outdoor kennel with flap door **Grounds** accessible disp bin **Exercise area** park nearby **Facilities** food food bowl water bowl bedding leads pet sitting washing facs cage storage walks info vet info **On Request** torch towels **Other** only small caged pets are allowed in bedrooms **Resident Pets:** Cotton (dog)

Located in the centre of Gurteen village, a half hour's drive from Knock Airport, this architect designed townhouse is home to Jacci Conlon and her family. Bedrooms are spacious and individually decorated. A wide selection of breakfast options is available, served in the smart dining room.

Rooms 5 en suite (2 fmly) (1 GF) S €40-€46; D €70-€72* **Facilities** STV TVB tea/coffee Cen ht TVL Wi-fi available **Parking** 5

COLLOONEY MAP 01 B5

★★★ 75% HOTEL

Markree Castle

MANOR HOUSE

☎ 071 9167800 🖷 071 9167840

e-mail: markree@iol.ie

Dir: *off N4 at Collooney rdbt, take R290 towards Dromahaire. Just N of junct with N17, 11km S of Sligo, hotel gates on right after 1km*

PETS: Bedrooms unattended **Grounds** accessible **Exercise area Facilities** walks info vet info **On Request** fridge access towels

The castle, which has been in the Cooper family for over 370 years, is a gem of Irish Victorian architecture. The bedrooms vary in size and style, and all in keeping with the character of the building. Dinner is served in the spectacular Louis XIV-styled dining room. Horse riding, archery and clay-pigeon shooting can be arranged on the estate.

Rooms 30 en suite (1 fmly) (3 GF) S €100-€165; D €150-€260 (incl. bkfst)* **Facilities** STV FTV Fishing Riding Wi-fi available Hiking Archery Clay pigeon shooting **Services** Lift **Parking** 120 **Notes** LB

IRELAND

CO TIPPERARY

NENAGH MAP 01 B3

★★★★ BED & BREAKFAST

Ashley Park House

☎ 067 38223 & 38013 📠 067 38013

e-mail: margaret@ashleypark.com

web: www.ashleypark.com

Dir: *6.5km N of Nenagh. Off N52 across lake, signed on left & left under arch*

PETS: Bedrooms Sep Accom stables **Stables** on site **Charges** horses €20 per night horses €120 per week **Public areas** except restaurant **Grounds** accessible disp bin **Exercise area** 20yds **Facilities** food bowl water bowl bedding cage storage walks info vet info **On Request** fridge access torch **Resident Pets:** horses, ducks, peacocks, hens, lambs in spring

The attractive, colonial style farmhouse was built in 1770. Set in gardens that run down to Lake Ourna, it has spacious bedrooms with quality antique furnishings. Breakfast is served in the dining room overlooking the lake, and dinner is available by arrangement. There is a delightful walled garden, and a boat for the fishing on the lake is available.

Rooms 5 en suite (3 fmly) **Facilities** TVB tea/coffee Cen ht TVL Dinner Last d 9pm Wi-fi available Golf 18 Fishing Rowing boat on lake **Parking** 30 **Notes**

IRELAND

CO WATERFORD

ARDMORE MAP 01 C2

U

Cliff House

☎ 024 87800 📠 024 87820

e-mail: info@thecliffhousehotel.com

Dir: *N25 to Ardmore. Hotel at end of village via The Middle Road*

PETS: Sep Accom kennel & dog run **Stables** nearby (5km) **Public areas** only on outdoor terrace (on leads) **Grounds** accessible on leads disp bin **Exercise area** 500mtrs **Facilities** cage storage walks info vet info **On Request** fridge access torch towels

At the time of going to press the rating for this establishment was not confirmed. This may be due to a change of ownership or because it has only recently joined the AA rating scheme. For further details please see the AA website: www.theAA.com

Rooms 39 en suite (8 fmly) (7 GF) S €180-€450; D €180-€450 (incl. bkfst) **Facilities Spa** STV FTV supervised Fishing Gym Wi-fi available Sauna Steam room Relaxation room ch fac **Services** Lift air con **Parking** 52 **Notes LB** Closed Jan-14 Feb

DUNGARVAN MAP 01 C2

★★★★★ FARM HOUSE

Castle Country House *(S 192016)*

Millstreet, Cappagh

☎ 058 68049 Mrs J Nugent

e-mail: castlefm@iol.ie

Dir: *15km off N25 between Dungarvan & Cappoquin. House signed on N72 & R671. From N72, take R671 for 3.5m; turn right at Millstreet.*

PETS: Sep Accom Sep accom **Stables** nearby (1m) **Grounds** accessible **Exercise area Facilities** water bowl bedding washing facs cage storage walks info vet info **On Request** fridge access torch towels **Resident Pets:** Kerry (Collie)

This delightful house is in the west wing of a 15th-century castle. Guests are spoiled by host Joan Nugent who loves to cook and hunt out antiques for her visitors to enjoy. She is helped by her husband Emmett who takes pride in his high-tech dairy farm and is a fount of local knowledge. Bedrooms are spacious and have lovely views. There is a river walk and a beautiful garden to relax in.

Rooms 5 en suite (1 fmly) S €65; D €105* **Facilities** FTV TVB tea/coffee Licensed Cen ht Dinner Last d 5pm Fishing Farm tour **Parking** 11 **Notes LB** 170 acres dairy & beef Closed Dec-Feb

CO WICKLOW

DUNLAVIN MAP 01 C3

★★★★★ GUEST HOUSE

Rathsallagh House

☎ 045 403112 📠 045 403343

e-mail: info@rathsallagh.com

Dir: *10.5km after end of M9 left signed Dunlavin, house signed 5km*

PETS: Sep Accom various sizes; with heat lamps; 2 heated indoor pens **Stables** nearby (6km) **Charges** charge for damage **Public areas** except restaurant & drawing rooms **Grounds** accessible disp bin **Exercise area Facilities** food (pre-bookable) food bowl water bowl bedding dog chews dog scoop/disp bags leads washing facs cage storage walks info vet info **On Request** fridge access torch towels **Other** over 500 acres of grounds available to walk in **Restrictions** no Rottweilers or Bull Terriers **Resident Pets:** Becket & Tilly (Labradors), Tiki, Todi, Truffel, Tigger & Treacle (Terriers)

Surrounded by its own 18-hole championship golf course this delightful house was converted from Queen Ann stables in 1798 and now has the addition of spacious and luxurious bedrooms with conference and leisure facilities. Food is country-house cooking at its best, and there is a cosy bar and comfortable drawing room to relax in. Close to Curragh and Punchestown racecourses.

Rooms 29 en suite (11 GF) S €195, D €270-€320* **Facilities** FTV TVB tea/coffee Direct dial from bedrooms Licensed Cen ht TVL Dinner Last d 9pm Wi-fi available Golf 18 Snooker Sauna Golf academy with driving range **Parking** 150 **Notes LB** No children 12yrs Closed 3 Jan-13 Feb

★★★★ FARM HOUSE

Tynte House *(N 870015)*

☎ 045 401561 📠 045 401586 Mr & Mrs J Lawler

e-mail: info@tyntehouse.com

web: www.tyntehouse.com

Dir: *N81 at Hollywood Cross, right at Dunlavin, follow finger signs for Tynte House, past market house in town centre*

PETS: Bedrooms Grounds accessible on leads disp bin **Exercise area Facilities** cage storage walks info vet info **On Request** fridge access torch towels **Resident Pets:** Suki (Maltese), Sasha (West Yorkshire Terrier)

The 19th-century farmhouse stands in the square of this quiet country village. The friendly hosts have carried out a lot of restoration resulting in comfortable bedrooms and a relaxing guest sitting room. Breakfast is a highlight of a visit to this house, which features Caroline's home baking.

Rooms 7 en suite (2 fmly) S €44-€54; D €70-€90 **Facilities** TVB tea/coffee Direct dial from bedrooms Cen ht TVL Wi-fi available Golf 18 Pool Table Playground Games room **Parking** 16 **Notes LB** 200 acres Beef & Tillage Closed 16 Dec-9 Jan

MACREDDIN MAP 01 D3

★★★★ 86% HOTEL

The Brooklodge Hotel & Wells Spa

MANOR HOUSE

☎ 0402 36444 📠 0402 36580

e-mail: brooklodge@macreddin.ie

web: www.brooklodge.com

Dir: *N11 to Rathnew, R752 to Rathdrum, R753 to Aughrim follow signs to Macreddin Village*

PETS: Bedrooms (4GF) unattended **Sep Accom** stables & barn **Stables** on site **Public areas** small dogs only (on leads) **Grounds** accessible on leads **Exercise area Facilities** vet info **On Request** towels **Resident Pets:** Rudi, Lilly & Sam (Golden Retrievers)

A luxury country-house hotel complex, in a village setting, which includes Acton's pub, Orchard Café and retail outlets. Bedrooms in the original house are very comfortable, and mezzanine suites are situated in the landscaped grounds. Newly added is Brook Hall with ground-floor and first floor bedrooms overlooking the 18th green of the golf course. The award-winning Strawberry Tree Restaurant is a truly romantic setting, specialising in organic and wild foods. The Wells Spa Centre offers extensive treatments and leisure facilities.

Rooms 58 en suite 32 annexe en suite (27 fmly) (4 GF) **Facilities** Spa STV FTV 18 Riding Gym Putt green Wi-fi available Archery Clay pigeon shooting Falconry Shiatsu Massage Off road driving **Services** Lift **Parking** 200

WICKLOW MAP 01 D3

★★★★ FARM HOUSE

Kilpatrick House *(T2257808)*

Redcross

☎ 0404 47137 & 087 6358325 📠 0404 47866

Mr Howard Kingston

e-mail: info@kilpatrickhouse.com

Dir: *13km S, 3.2km off N11, signed from Jack Whites pub*

PETS: Sep Accom farm buildings **Grounds** accessible on leads disp bin **Exercise area Facilities** dog walking cage storage walks info vet info **On Request** torch **Restrictions** no dangerous breeds (see page 7) **Resident Pets:** Betsey (Jack Russell), Megan (Sheep dog), Judy (Labrador)

This elegant 18th-century Georgian residence is set on a beef and tillage farm just north of Arklow. Bedrooms are carefully furnished and thoughtfully equipped. Dinner is available on request and the extensive breakfast menu includes Shirley's home baking and country produce. Nearby at Brittas Bay, there is a choice of golf courses and also horse riding.

Rooms 4 rms (3 en suite) (1 pri facs) (2 fmly) S €55-€65; D €80-€96* **Facilities** TVB tea/coffee Cen ht TVL Fishing **Parking** 20 **Notes** 150 acres Beef Closed Oct-Apr

IRELAND

DOG-FRIENDLY PUBS

Below is a list of pubs that have told us that they allow dogs on the premises

ENGLAND

BEDFORDSHIRE
Knife & Cleaver Inn, BEDFORD
The Three Tuns, BEDFORD
The Plough at Bolnhurst, BOLNHURST
The Cock, BROOM
The Globe Inn, LINSLADE
The Crown, NORTHILL
The Five Bells, STANBRIDGE
John O'Gaunt Inn, SUTTON

BERKSHIRE
The Bell Inn, ALDWORTH
The Bell at Boxford, BOXFORD
The Ibex, CHADDLEWORTH
The Crab at Chieveley, CHIEVELEY
The Horns, CRAZIES HILL
The Bunk Inn, CURRIDGE
The Queen's Arms Country Inn, EAST GARSTON
The White Horse of Hermitage, HERMITAGE
Bird In Hand Country Inn, KNOWL HILL
The Stag, LECKHAMPSTEAD
The Belgian Arms, MAIDENHEAD
The White Hart, MAIDENHEAD
The Yew Tree Inn, NEWBURY
The Flowing Spring, READING
The Bull Country Inn, STANFORD DINGLEY
The Old Boot Inn, STANFORD DINGLEY
The George & Dragon, SWALLOWFIELD
The Bladebone Inn, THATCHAM
Thatchers Arms, THEALE
The Bell, WALTHAM ST LAWRENCE
Carnarvon Arms, WHITWAY
The Winterbourne Arms, WINTERBOURNE
The Langley Hall Inn, WORLD'S END

BRISTOL
Cornubia, BRISTOL

BUCKINGHAMSHIRE
Hit or Miss Inn, AMERSHAM
The Royal Standard of England, BEACONSFIELD
The Lions of Bledlow, BLEDLOW
The Peacock, BOLTER END
The Royal Oak, BOVINGDON GREEN
The Red Lion, BRILL
The Wheatsheaf, BUCKINGHAM
The Old Thatched Inn, BUCKINGHAM
The Ivy House, CHALFONT ST GILES
The Greyhound Inn, CHALFONT ST PETER
The Old Swan, CHEDDINGTON
The Red Lion, CHENIES
The Black Horse Inn, CHESHAM
The Full Moon, CHOLESBURY
The Swan Inn, DENHAM
The Foresters, FARNHAM COMMON
The Yew Tree, FRIETH
The Prince Albert, FRIETH
The Hampden Arms, GREAT HAMPDEN
The Rising Sun, GREAT MISSENDEN
The Nags Head, GREAT MISSENDEN
The White Horse, HEDGERLEY
Il Maschio @ The Stag, MENTMORE
The Black Boy, OVING
The Three Horseshoes Inn, RADNAGE
The Frog, SKIRMETT
The Bull & Butcher, TURVILLE
The Old Queens Head, TYLERS GREEN
The George and Dragon Hotel, WEST WYCOMBE
The Chequers, WHEELEREND COMMON
Red Lion, WHITELEAF

CAMBRIDGESHIRE
The Crown, BROUGHTON
The White Hart, BYTHORN
Cambridge Blue, CAMBRIDGE
The Anchor, CAMBRIDGE
The Leeds Arms, ELTISLEY
The Black Horse, ELTON
The Crown Inn, ELTON
Ancient Shepherds, FEN DITTON
King William IV, FENSTANTON
Woodmans Cottage, GOREFIELD
The Pheasant, GREAT CHISHILL
The Cock Pub and Restaurant, HEMINGFORD GREY
The Pear Tree, HILDERSHAM
The Red Lion, HINXTON
The New Sun Inn, KIMBOLTON
Hole in the Wall, LITTLE WILBRAHAM
Waggon & Horses, MILTON
The Queen's Head, NEWTON
Charters Bar & East Restaurant, PETERBOROUGH
The Brewery Tap, PETERBOROUGH
Dyke's End, REACH

CHESHIRE
The Grosvenor Arms, ALDFORD
The Bhurtpore Inn, ASTON
The White Lion Inn, BARTHOMLEY
The Dysart Arms, BUNBURY
The Combermere Arms, BURLEYDAM
The Pheasant Inn, BURWARDSLEY
Albion Inn, CHESTER
Old Harkers Arms, CHESTER
The Cholmondeley Arms, CHOLMONDELEY
The Calveley Arms, HANDLEY
The Nags Head, HAUGHTON MOSS
Stuart's Table at the Farmer's Arms, HUXLEY
The Dog Inn, KNUTSFORD
The Old Harp, LITTLE NESTON
Chetwode Arms, LOWER WHITLEY
The Windmill Inn, MACCLESFIELD
The Ferry Tavern, PENKETH
The Golden Pheasant Hotel, PLUMLEY
The Boot Inn, TARPORLEY
Blue Bell Inn, TUSHINGHAM CUM GRINDLEY
The Dusty Miller, WRENBURY
The Swan Inn, WYBUNBURY

CORNWALL
The Blisland Inn, BLISLAND
Old Ferry Inn, BODINNICK
The Wellington Hotel, BOSCASTLE
Cadgwith Cove Inn, CADGWITH
The Coachmakers Arms, CALLINGTON
Trengilly Wartha Inn, CONSTANTINE
Coombe Barton Inn, CRACKINGTON HAVEN
The Smugglers' Den Inn, CUBERT
Ye Olde Plough House Inn, DULOE
The Borough Arms, DUNMERE
The Punch Bowl & Ladle, FEOCK
The Ship Inn, FOWEY
The Trevelyan Arms, GOLDSITHNEY
The Rising Sun Inn, GUNNISLAKE
The Gweek Inn, GWEEK
The Halfway House Inn, KINGSAND
Lamorna Wink, LAMORNA
The Crown Inn, LANLIVERY
The Royal Oak, LOSTWITHIEL
White Hart, LUDGVAN
The Heron Inn, MALPAS
The New Inn, MANACCAN
Godolphin Arms, MARAZION
The Rising Sun Inn, MEVAGISSEY
The Ship Inn, MEVAGISSEY
The Bush Inn, MORWENSTOW
The Pandora Inn, MYLOR BRIDGE
The Turks Head Inn, PENZANCE
Dolphin Tavern, PENZANCE
The Victoria Inn, PERRANUTHNOE
Old Mill House Inn, POLPERRO
Port Gaverne Hotel, PORT GAVERNE
The Ship Inn, PORTHLEVEN
Basset Arms, PORTREATH
The Kings Head, RUAN LANIHORNE
The Crooked Inn, SALTASH
The Old Success Inn, SENNEN
Driftwood Spars, ST AGNES
Turks Head, ST AGNES
The Old Inn & Restaurant, ST BREWARD
The Crown Inn, ST EWE
Star Inn, ST JUST [NEAR LAND'S END]
The Rising Sun, ST MAWES

The Victory Inn, ST MAWES
The Falcon Inn, ST MAWGAN
The London Inn, ST NEOT
The Port William, TINTAGEL
Edgcumbe Arms, TORPOINT
The Mill House Inn, TREBARWITH
The Springer Spaniel, TREBURLEY
Eliot Arms (Square & Compass), TREGADILLETT
The Wig & Pen Inn, TRURO
The Royal Inn, TYWARDREATH
Swan, WADEBRIDGE
The Quarryman Inn, WADEBRIDGE
Bay View Inn, WIDEMOUTH BAY
The Gurnards Head, ZENNOR
The Tinners Arms, ZENNOR

CUMBRIA

Wateredge Inn, AMBLESIDE
The Royal Oak, APPLEBY-IN-WESTMORLAND
Tufton Arms Hotel, APPLEBY-IN-WESTMORLAND
The Dukes Head Inn, ARMATHWAITE
Mardale Inn, BAMPTON
The Barbon Inn, BARBON
The Pheasant, BASSENTHWAITE LAKE
The Boot Inn, BOOT
The White Hart Inn, BOUTH
Coledale Inn, BRAITHWAITE
The Royal Oak, BRAITHWAITE
Blacksmiths Arms, BROUGHTON-IN-FURNESS
Oddfellows Arms, CALDBECK
The Cavendish Arms, CARTMEL
The Black Bull Inn & Hotel, CONISTON
Sun Hotel & 16th Century Inn, CONISTON
The Sun Inn, CROOK
The Punch Bowl Inn, CROSTHWAITE
The Britannia Inn, ELTERWATER
The Shepherd's Arms Hotel, ENNERDALE BRIDGE
King George IV Inn, ESKDALE
Bower House Inn, ESKDALE GREEN
The George & Dragon Inn, GARRIGILL
The Globe Hotel, GOSFORTH
The Travellers Rest Inn, GRASMERE
The New Dungeon Ghyll Hotel, GREAT LANGDALE
The Highland Drove Inn and Kyloes Restaurant, GREAT SALKELD
Kings Arms, HAWKSHEAD
The Old Crown, HESKET NEWMARKET
Blue Bell Hotel, HEVERSHAM
Gateway Inn, KENDAL
The Kings Head, KESWICK
The Horse & Farrier Inn, KESWICK
The Swinside Inn, KESWICK
The Whoop Hall, KIRKBY LONSDALE
The Sun Inn, KIRKBY LONSDALE
The Bay Horse, KIRKBY STEPHEN
Kirkstile Inn, LOWESWATER
The Shepherds Inn, MELMERBY
The Mill Inn, MUNGRISDALE
Tower Bank Arms, NEAR SAWREY
The Screes Inn, NETHER WASDALE
Outgate Inn, OUTGATE
The Fat Lamb Country Inn, RAVENSTONEDALE
The Black Swan, RAVENSTONEDALE
King's Head, RAVENSTONEDALE
Queen's Head Inn, TIRRIL
Wasdale Head Inn, WASDALE HEAD
Brackenrigg Inn, WATERMILLOCK
Eagle & Child Inn, WINDERMERE
The Yanwath Gate Inn, YANWATH

DERBYSHIRE

Dog & Partridge Country Inn, ASHBOURNE
Barley Mow Inn, ASHBOURNE
The Monsal Head Hotel, BAKEWELL
Yorkshire Bridge Inn, BAMFORD
The Tickled Trout, BARLOW
The Red Lion, BIRCHOVER
Ye Olde Gate Inne, BRASSINGTON
Ye Olde Nag's Head, CASTLETON
The Peaks Inn, CASTLETON
The Alexandra Hotel, DERBY
Miners Arms, EYAM
Bentley Brook Inn, FENNY BENTLEY
The Maynard, GRINDLEFORD
Millstone Inn, HATHERSAGE
The Red Lion Inn, HOLLINGTON
Cheshire Cheese Inn, HOPE
Red Lion Inn, LITTON
The Nettle Inn, MILLTOWN
The Old Crown, SHARDLOW
The George Hotel, TIDESWELL
Three Stags' Heads, TIDESWELL
The Three Horseshoes, WESSINGTON

DEVON

The Rising Sun, ASHBURTON
The Turtley Corn Mill, AVONWICK
The Ship Inn, AXMOUTH
The Harbour Inn, AXMOUTH
The Beggars Roost, BARBROOK
Olde Plough Inn, BERE FERRERS
Pilchard Inn, BIGBURY-ON-SEA
The Masons Arms, BRANSCOMBE
Rockford Inn, BRENDON
The Monks Retreat Inn, BROADHEMPSTON
Drake Manor Inn, BUCKLAND MONACHORUM
The Butterleigh Inn, BUTTERLEIGH
Ring o'Bells, CHAGFORD
The Sandy Park Inn, CHAGFORD
Three Crowns Hotel, CHAGFORD
The George Inn, CHARDSTOCK
The Old Thatch Inn, CHERITON BISHOP
The Merry Harriers, CLAYHIDON
The Skylark Inn, CLEARBROOK
The Anchor Inn, COCKWOOD
Hunters Lodge Inn, CORNWORTHY
Culm Valley Inn, CULMSTOCK
Royal Castle Hotel, DARTMOUTH
The Union Inn, DENBURY
The Ferry Boat, DITTISHAM
The Nobody Inn, DODDISCOMBSLEIGH
The Union Inn, DOLTON
Rams Head Inn, DOLTON
The Drewe Arms, DREWSTEIGNTON
Fortescue Arms, EAST ALLINGTON
The Church House Inn, HARBERTON
The Mildmay Colours Inn, HOLBETON
The Otter Inn, HONITON
The Elephant's Nest Inn, HORNDON
The Hoops Inn & Country Hotel, HORNS CROSS
The Royal Inn, HORSEBRIDGE
The George & Dragon, ILFRACOMBE
The Anchor Inn, IVYBRIDGE
The Grove Inn, KING'S NYMPTON
The Crabshell Inn, KINGSBRIDGE
Bickley Mill Inn, KINGSKERSWELL
The Ship, KINGSWEAR
The Harris Arms, LEWDOWN
The Arundell Arms, LIFTON
Tally Ho Inn, LITTLEHEMPSTON
The Elizabethan Inn, LUTON (NEAR CHUDLEIGH)
Dartmoor Inn, LYDFORD
The Globe Inn, LYMPSTONE
The Bridge Inn, LYNTON
The Church House Inn, MARLDON
The Royal Oak Inn, MEAVY
California Country Inn, MODBURY
The London Inn, MOLLAND
The White Hart Hotel, MORETONHAMPSTEAD
The Beer Engine, NEWTON ST CYRES
The Ring of Bells Inn, NORTH BOVEY
The Ship Inn, NOSS MAYO
The Talaton Inn, OTTERY ST MARY
The Fox & Goose, PARRACOMBE
Church House Inn, RATTERY
The Victoria Inn, SALCOMBE
Dukes, SIDMOUTH
The Tower Inn, SLAPTON
The Highwayman Inn, SOURTON
The Millbrook Inn, SOUTH POOL
Oxenham Arms, SOUTH ZEAL
The Kings Arms Inn, STOCKLAND
The Green Dragon Inn, STOKE FLEMING
The Tradesman's Arms, STOKENHAM
Kings Arms, STRETE
The Village Inn, THURLESTONE
Bridge Inn, TOPSHAM
Royal Seven Stars Hotel, TOTNES
The Maltsters Arms, TUCKENHAY
The Rising Sun Inn, UMBERLEIGH
The Old Inn, WIDECOMBE IN THE MOOR
The Duke of York, WINKLEIGH
The Kings Arms, WINKLEIGH
Rose & Crown, YEALMPTON

DORSET

Ilchester Arms, ABBOTSBURY
Best Western Crown Hotel, BLANDFORD FORUM
The Anvil Inn, BLANDFORD FORUM
The White Lion Inn, BOURTON
The George Hotel, BRIDPORT
The Shave Cross Inn, BRIDPORT
Stapleton Arms, BUCKHORN WESTON
Fox & Hounds Inn, CATTISTOCK
The Royal Oak, CERNE ABBAS
The Anchor Inn, CHIDEOCK
Fishermans Haunt, CHRISTCHURCH
The Ship In Distress, CHRISTCHURCH
The Greyhound Inn, CORFE CASTLE
The Coventry Arms, CORFE MULLEN
The Cock & Bottle, EAST MORDEN
The Acorn Inn, EVERSHOT
The Museum Inn, FARNHAM
The Kings Arms Inn, GILLINGHAM
The Drovers Inn, GUSSAGE ALL SAINTS
The Greenman, KING'S STAG
Loders Arms, LODERS
Pilot Boat Inn, LYME REGIS
The Coppleridge Inn, MOTCOMBE
Marquis of Lorne, NETTLECOMBE
The Three Elms, NORTH WOOTTON
The Smugglers Inn, OSMINGTON MILLS
The Thimble Inn, PIDDLEHINTON
The Piddle Inn, PIDDLETRENTHIDE
The Poachers Inn, PIDDLETRENTHIDE
The Brace of Pheasants, PLUSH
Three Horseshoes Inn, POWERSTOCK
The Crown Inn, PUNCKNOWLE
White Hart, SHERBORNE
The Digby Tap, SHERBORNE
Queen's Head, SHERBORNE
The New Inn, STOKE ABBOTT
The White Horse Inn, STOURPAINE
Saxon Arms, STRATTON
The Bankes Arms Hotel, STUDLAND
Rose & Crown Inn, TRENT
The Manor Hotel, WEST BEXINGTON
The Castle Inn, WEST LULWORTH
The Old Ship Inn, WEYMOUTH
Botany Bay Inne, WINTERBORNE ZELSTON

COUNTY DURHAM

Victoria Inn, DURHAM
The Oak Tree Inn, HUTTON MAGNA
Ship Inn, MIDDLESTONE
The Teesdale Hotel, MIDDLETON-IN-TEESDALE
Rose & Crown, ROMALDKIRK
The Bird in Hand, TRIMDON

ESSEX

Ye Olde White Harte Hotel, BURNHAM-ON-CROUCH
The Bell Inn, CASTLE HEDINGHAM
The Swan Inn, CHAPPEL
The Sun Inn, DEDHAM
The Crown, ELSENHAM
The Sun Inn, FEERING
The Swan at Felsted, FELSTED
The Whalebone, FINGRINGHOE
The Green Man, GOSFIELD
Bell Inn & Hill House, HORNDON ON THE HILL
The Shepherd and Dog, LANGHAM
The Green Man, LITTLE BRAXTED
Flitch of Bacon, LITTLE DUNMOW
The Mistley Thorn, MANNINGTREE
The Ferry Boat Inn, NORTH FAMBRIDGE
The Compasses at Pattiswick, PATTISWICK
The Plough Inn, RADWINTER
The Hoop, STOCK
The Mitre, WICKHAM BISHOPS
Hurdle Makers Arms, WOODHAM MORTIMER

GLOUCESTERSHIRE

The Royal Oak Inn, ANDOVERSFORD
The Old Passage Inn, ARLINGHAM
The Red Hart Inn at Awre, AWRE
The Village Pub, BARNSLEY
Catherine Wheel, BIBURY
The Golden Heart, BIRDLIP
The Bear Inn, BISLEY
Seven Tuns, CHEDWORTH
Hare & Hounds, CHEDWORTH
Eight Bells Inn, CHIPPING CAMPDEN
Noel Arms Hotel, CHIPPING CAMPDEN
The Bakers Arms, CHIPPING CAMPDEN
The Volunteer Inn, CHIPPING CAMPDEN
The Kings, CHIPPING CAMPDEN
The New Inn, CINDERFORD
The Crown of Crucis, CIRENCESTER
The Yew Tree, CLIFFORD'S MESNE
The Tunnel House Inn, COATES
The Colesbourne Inn, COLESBOURNE
The Green Dragon Inn, COWLEY
The Kings Arms, DIDMARTON
The Inn at Fossebridge, FOSSEBRIDGE
The White Horse, FRAMPTON MANSELL
The Fox, GREAT BARRINGTON
The Lamb Inn, GREAT RISSINGTON
The Harvest Home, GREET
The Hollow Bottom, GUITING POWER
The Bull Inn, HINTON
The Trout Inn, LECHLADE ON THAMES
The Hobnails Inn, LITTLE WASHBOURNE
White Hart, LITTLETON-ON-SEVERN
The Catherine Wheel, MARSHFIELD
The Lord Nelson Inn, MARSHFIELD
The Masons Arms, MEYSEY HAMPTON
The Old Lodge, MINCHINHAMPTON
The Weighbridge Inn, MINCHINHAMPTON
The Britannia, NAILSWORTH
Tipputs Inn, NAILSWORTH
The Black Horse, NAUNTON
The Westcote Inn, NETHER WESTCOTE
The Ostrich Inn, NEWLAND
Bathurst Arms, NORTH CERNEY
The Puesdown Inn, NORTHLEACH
The Butcher's Arms, OAKRIDGE LYNCH
The Falcon Inn, PAINSWICK
The Falcon Inn, POULTON
The Bell at Sapperton, SAPPERTON
The Butchers Arms, SHEEPSCOMBE
The Bakers Arms, SOMERFORD KEYNES
The Swan at Southrop, SOUTHROP
The Eagle and Child, STOW-ON-THE-WOLD
The Unicorn, STOW-ON-THE-WOLD
The Ram Inn, STROUD
Rose & Crown Inn, STROUD
Bear of Rodborough Hotel, STROUD
The Woolpack Inn, STROUD
The Trouble House, TETBURY
The Farriers Arms, TODENHAM
Best Western Compass Inn, TORMARTON
The White Hart Inn and Restaurant, WINCHCOMBE
The Mill Inn, WITHINGTON
The Old Fleece, WOODCHESTER

GREATER MANCHESTER

The Queen's Arms, MANCHESTER
The Oddfellows Arms, MELLOR
The Roebuck Inn, OLDHAM,
Stalybridge Station Buffet Bar, STALYBRIDGE
The Royal Oak, STALYBRIDGE,
The Nursery Inn, STOCKPORT
The Arden Arms, STOCKPORT
Bird I'th Hand, WIGAN

HAMPSHIRE

The Crown at Axford, AXFORD
Hoddington Arms, BASINGSTOKE
The Milburys, BEAUWORTH
The Bull Inn, BENTLEY
The Sun Inn, BENTWORTH
The Red Lion, BOLDRE
The Burley Inn, BURLEY
The Red Lion, CHALTON
The White Hart Inn, CHARTER ALLEY
The Greyfriar, CHAWTON
The Flower Pots Inn, CHERITON
The Compasses Inn, DAMERHAM
The East End Arms, EAST END
Ye Olde George Inn, EAST MEON
The Star Inn Tytherley, EAST TYTHERLEY
Cricketers Inn, EASTON
The Chestnut Horse, EASTON
The Sussex Brewery, EMSWORTH
The Golden Pot, EVERSLEY
The Augustus John, FORDINGBRIDGE
The Royal Oak, FRITHAM
The Vine at Hambledon, HAMBLEDON
The Vine at Hannington, HANNINGTON
The Phoenix Inn, HARTLEY WINTNEY
The Royal Oak, HAVANT
Crooked Billet, HOOK
John O'Gaunt Inn, HORSEBRIDGE
The Trout, ITCHEN ABBAS
The High Corner Inn, LINWOOD

The Running Horse, LITTLETON
The Plough Inn, LONGPARISH
The Yew Tree, LOWER WIELD
Mayflower Inn, LYMINGTON
The Trusty Servant, LYNDHURST
New Forest Inn, LYNDHURST
The Oak Inn, LYNDHURST
The Gamekeepers, MAPLEDURWELL
Half Moon & Spread Eagle, MICHELDEVER
The Black Swan, MONXTON
The Red Lion, MORTIMER WEST END
The Fox, NORTH WALTHAM
The Millstone, OLD BASING
The Bush, OVINGTON
The Ship Inn, OWSLEBURY
The White Horse Inn, PETERSFIELD
The Good Intent, PETERSFIELD
The Fleur de Lys, PILLEY
The Wine Vaults, PORTSMOUTH
The Alice Lisle, ROCKFORD
The Dukes Head, ROMSEY
The Three Tuns, ROMSEY
The Castle Inn, ROWLAND'S CASTLE
The Fountain Inn, ROWLAND'S CASTLE
The Selborne Arms, SELBORNE
Calleva Arms, SILCHESTER
The Plough Inn, SPARSHOLT
The Bourne Valley Inn, ST MARY BOURNE
Harrow Inn, STEEP
Mayfly, STOCKBRIDGE
The Peat Spade, STOCKBRIDGE
The Wellington Arms, STRATFIELD TURGIS
The Fox Inn, TANGLEY
The Tichborne Arms, TICHBORNE
The Hen & Chicken Inn, UPPER FROYLE
The Jolly Farmer Country Inn, WARSASH
The Chequers Inn, WELL
The White Lion, WHERWELL
The Cartwheel Inn, WHITSBURY
The Wykeham Arms, WINCHESTER
The Westgate Inn, WINCHESTER

HEREFORDSHIRE

The Penny Farthing Inn, ASTON CREWS
The Riverside Inn, AYMESTREY
England's Gate Inn, BODENHAM
The Bulls Head, CRASWALL
The Pandy Inn, DORSTONE
The Bunch of Carrots, HAMPTON BISHOP
The Crown & Anchor, HEREFORD
Stockton Cross Inn, KIMBOLTON
The Stagg Inn and Restaurant, KINGTON
The Farmers Arms, LEDBURY
The Trumpet Inn, LEDBURY
The Royal Oak Hotel, LEOMINSTER
The Comet Inn, MADLEY
The Bridge Inn, MICHAELCHURCH ESCLEY
The Boot Inn, ORLETON
The Moody Cow, ROSS-ON-WYE
The Lough Pool Inn at Sellack, SELLACK
The Bell, TILLINGTON
The Wellington, WELLINGTON

HERTFORDSHIRE

The Greyhound Inn, ALDBURY
The Valiant Trooper, ALDBURY
The Three Tuns, ASHWELL
The Fox & Hounds, BARLEY
The Sword Inn Hand, BUNTINGFORD
The Bricklayers Arms, FLAUNDEN
Alford Arms, HEMEL HEMPSTEAD
The Fox and Hounds, HUNSDON
The Lytton Arms, OLD KNEBWORTH
The Rose and Crown, RICKMANSWORTH
The Cabinet Free House and Restaurant, ROYSTON
Rose & Crown, ST ALBANS
Papillon Woodhall Arms, STAPLEFORD
The Plume of Feathers, TEWIN
The White Lion, WALKERN
The Rising Sun, WESTON
The Fox, WILLIAN

KENT

The Three Chimneys, BIDDENDEN
Froggies At The Timber Batts, BODSHAM GREEN
The Hop Pocket, BOSSINGHAM
The Five Bells, BRABOURNE
Woolpack Inn, BROOKLAND
The Royal Oak, BROOKLAND
The Dove Inn, CANTERBURY
The Chapter Arms, CANTERBURY
The Red Lion, CANTERBURY
The Granville, CANTERBURY
The Bowl Inn, CHARING
Castle Inn, CHIDDINGSTONE
The King's Head, DEAL
The Clyffe Hotel, DOVER
Shipwrights Arms, FAVERSHAM
Chafford Arms, FORDCOMBE
The Cock Inn, GRAVESEND
The Pepper Box Inn, HARRIETSHAM
The Wheatsheaf, HEVER
The Green Man, HODSOLL STREET
The Peacock, IDEN GREEN
The Swan at the Vineyard, LAMBERHURST
The Greyhound Charcott, LEIGH
The Bull Inn, LINTON
The Black Horse Inn, MAIDSTONE
The Kentish Horse, MARKBEECH
The Bottle House Inn, PENSHURST
The Spotted Dog, PENSHURST
The Leicester Arms, PENSHURST
The Dering Arms, PLUCKLEY
The Mundy Bois, PLUCKLEY
The Hare on Langton Green, ROYAL TUNBRIDGE WELLS
The Crown Inn, ROYAL TUNBRIDGE WELLS
George & Dragon Inn, SANDWICH
The Rose and Crown, SELLING
The Chequers Inn, SMARDEN
The Bell, SMARDEN
George & Dragon, SPELDHURST
The Coastguard, ST MARGARET'S AT CLIFFE
White Lion Inn, TENTERDEN
The Fox & Hounds, WESTERHAM
The Sportsman, WHITSTABLE
The New Flying Horse, WYE

LANCASHIRE

Owd Nell's Tavern, BILSBORROW
Clog and Billycock, BLACKBURN
The Highwayman, BURROW
Old Station Inn, CARNFORTH
The Assheton Arms, CLITHEROE
The Shireburn Arms, CLITHEROE
Ye Old Sparrow Hawk Inn, FENCE
Farmers Arms, HESKIN GREEN
The Stork Inn, LANCASTER
Ye Olde John O'Gaunt, LANCASTER
Eureka, ORMSKIRK
The Eagle & Child, PARBOLD
Hark to Bounty Inn, SLAIDBURN
The Lunesdale Arms, TUNSTALL
The Three Fishes, WHALLEY
The Inn At Whitewell, WHITEWELL
The New Inn, YEALAND CONYERS

LEICESTERSHIRE

The Queen's Head, BELTON
The Old Crown, FLECKNEY
The Black Horse, GRIMSTON
The Fox & Hounds, KNOSSINGTON
The Swan in the Rushes, LOUGHBOROUGH
The Swan Inn, MOUNTSORREL
Cow and Plough, OADBY
The Crown Inn, OLD DALBY
Peacock Inn, REDMILE
Red Lion Inn, STATHERN
The Wheatsheaf Inn, WOODHOUSE EAVES

LINCOLNSHIRE

The Tally Ho Inn, ASWARBY
The Bell Inn, COLEBY
The Black Horse Inn, DONINGTON ON BAIN
Wig & Mitre, LINCOLN
Pyewipe Inn, LINCOLN
The Red Lion, NEWTON
Red Lion Inn, RAITHBY
Best Western Vine Hotel, SKEGNESS
Blue Cow Inn & Brewery, SOUTH WITHAM
The George of Stamford, STAMFORD
The Bull & Swan Inn, STAMFORD
The Chequers Inn, WOOLSTHORPE

LONDON

Town of Ramsgate, E1
The Grapes, E14
The Peasant, EC1
The Eagle, EC1
The Duke of Cambridge, N1
The Crown, N1
The Compton Arms, N1
The Northgate, N1
The Drapers Arms, N1
The House, N1
The Flask, N6
The Landseer, N19
The Lansdowne, NW1
The Queens, NW1
The Chapel, NW1
The Engineer, NW1
Spaniards Inn, NW3
The Holly Bush, NW3
Dartmouth Arms, NW5
The Junction Tavern, NW5
The Lord Palmerston, NW5
The Salusbury Pub and Dining Room, NW6
The Salt House, NW8
The Greyhound, NW10
The Anchor & Hope, SE1
The Sun and Doves, SE5
Greenwich Union Pub, SE10
The Mayflower, SE16
The Crown & Greyhound, SE21
Franklins, SE22
The Orange Brewery, SW1
The Buckingham Arms, SW1
The Grenadier, SW1
The Coopers of Flood Street, SW3
The Phene Arms, SW3
The Builders Arms, SW3
The Royal Oak, SW4
The Coach & Horses, SW4
The White Horse, SW6
The Salisbury Tavern, SW6
Swag and Tails, SW7
The Anglesea Arms, SW7
The Masons Arms, SW8
The Chelsea Ram, SW10
The Sporting Page, SW10
Lots Road Pub and Dining Room, SW10
The Hollywood Arms, SW10
The Castle, SW11
The Fox & Hounds, SW11
The Bull's Head, SW13
The Spencer Arms, SW15
The Alma Tavern, SW18
The Ship Inn, SW18
The Old Sergeant, SW18
The Freemasons, SW18
The Cat's Back, SW18
The Brewery Tap, SW19
The Prince Bonaparte, W2
The Westbourne, W2
The Devonshire House, W4
The Swan, W4
The Wheatsheaf, W5
The Red Lion, W5
The Dartmouth Castle, W6
The Churchill Arms, W8
The Windsor Castle, W8
The Scarsdale, W8
Mall Tavern, W8
The Waterway, W9
The North Pole, W10
Golborne Grove, W10
The Fat Badger, W10
Portobello Gold, W11

GREATER LONDON

The White Swan, TWICKENHAM

MERSEYSIDE

Fox and Hounds, BARNSTON
The Berkeley Arms, SOUTHPORT

NORFOLK

The Kings Arms, BLAKENEY
The White Horse, BRANCASTER STAITHE
The Hoste Arms, BURNHAM MARKET
The Lord Nelson, BURNHAM THORPE
The George Hotel, CLEY NEXT THE SEA
The Butchers Arms, EAST RUSTON
The Hill House, HAPPISBURGH
Victoria at Holkham, HOLKHAM
Nelson Head, HORSEY
Recruiting Sergeant, HORSTEAD
The King William IV, HUNSTANTON
Walpole Arms, ITTERINGHAM
The Canary and Linnet, LITTLE FRANSHAM
The Black Lion Hotel, LITTLE WALSINGHAM
Crown Hotel, MUNDFORD
The Old Brewery House Hotel, REEPHAM
The Gin Trap Inn, RINGSTEAD
The Dun Cow, SALTHOUSE
The Rose & Crown, SNETTISHAM
Darbys Freehouse, SWANTON MORLEY
Chequers Inn, THOMPSON
Lifeboat Inn, THORNHAM
The Orange Tree, THORNHAM
Green Farm Restaurant & Hotel, THORPE MARKET
Titchwell Manor Hotel, TITCHWELL
Three Horseshoes, WARHAM ALL SAINTS
The Crown, WELLS-NEXT-THE-SEA
Carpenter's Arms, WELLS-NEXT-THE-SEA
The Wheatsheaf, WEST BECKHAM
Fishermans Return, WINTERTON-ON-SEA
Wiveton Bell, WIVETON

NORTHAMPTONSHIRE

The Windmill Inn, BADBY
The Queen's Head, BULWICK
George and Dragon, CHACOMBE
The Bulls Head, CLIPSTON
The Red Lion Inn, CRICK
The Kings Arms, FARTHINGSTONE
The Fox & Hounds, NORTHAMPTON
The Boat Inn, STOKE BRUERNE
The King's Head, WADENHOE
The Crown, WESTON

NORTHUMBERLAND

The Allenheads Inn, ALLENHEADS
Masons Arms, ALNWICK
The Lord Crewe Arms, BLANCHLAND
The Manor House Inn, CARTERWAY HEADS
Jolly Fisherman Inn, CRASTER
Tankerville Arms, EGLINGHAM
The Pheasant Inn, FALSTONE
The Blackcock Inn, FALSTONE
The General Havelock Inn, HAYDON BRIDGE
Miners Arms Inn, HEXHAM
Battlesteads Hotel & Restaurant, HEXHAM
The Anglers Arms, LONGFRAMLINGTON
The Ship Inn, LOW NEWTON BY THE SEA
The Boatside Inn, WARDEN

NOTTINGHAMSHIRE

Victoria Hotel, BEESTON
Fox & Hounds, BLIDWORTH
Caunton Beck, CAUNTON
Black Horse Inn, CAYTHORPE
The Martins Arms Inn, COLSTON BASSETT
Bottle & Glass, HARBY
The Nelson & Railway Inn, KIMBERLEY
The Dovecote Inn, LAXTON
The Full Moon Inn, MORTON
Cock & Hoop, NOTTINGHAM
Three Crowns, RUDDINGTON
The Mussel & Crab, TUXFORD

OXFORDSHIRE

The Merry Miller, ABINGDON
The Romany, BAMPTON
The George Inn, BANBURY
The Wykham Arms, BANBURY
Chilli Pepper, BROADWELL
Saye and Sele Arms, BROUGHTON
The Inn for All Seasons, BURFORD
The Lamb Inn, BURFORD
The Tite Inn, CHADLINGTON
The Red Lion Inn, CHALGROVE
The Highwayman, CHECKENDON
The Fox and Hounds, CHRISTMAS COMMON
The Crown Inn, CHURCH ENSTONE
Duke of Cumberland's Head, CLIFTON
The White Lion, CRAYS POND
Bat & Ball Inn, CUDDESDON
The Vine Inn, CUMNOR
The Half Moon, CUXHAM
Fleur De Lys, DORCHESTER
The Wheatsheaf, EAST HENDRED

The Trout at Tadpole Bridge, FARINGDON
Merrymouth Inn, FIFIELD
The Five Alls, FILKINS
The Butchers Arms, FRINGFORD
Miller of Mansfield, GORING
The Falkland Arms, GREAT TEW
The Five Horseshoes, HENLEY-ON-THAMES
Three Tuns Foodhouse, HENLEY-ON-THAMES
The Gate Hangs High, HOOK NORTON
The Plough Inn, KELMSCOTT
The Leathern Bottel, LEWKNOR
The Baskerville Arms, LOWER SHIPLAKE
Victoria Arms, MARSTON
The Black Boy Inn, MILTON
The Nut Tree Inn, MURCOTT
Turf Tavern, OXFORD
The Royal Oak, RAMSDEN
Home Sweet Home, ROKE
The Bell, SHENINGTON
The Shaven Crown Hotel, SHIPTON-UNDER-WYCHWOOD
The Crown Inn, SOUTH MORETON
The Perch and Pike, SOUTH STOKE
The Talkhouse, STANTON ST JOHN
Star Inn, STANTON ST JOHN
Stag's Head, SWALCLIFFE
The Lampet Arms, TADMARTON
The Old Red Lion, TETSWORTH
The Swan Hotel, THAME
The Hare, WANTAGE
The White Horse, WOOLSTONE

RUTLAND
Exeter Arms, BARROWDEN
The Olive Branch, CLIPSHAM
The Sun Inn, COTTESMORE
The White Horse Inn, EMPINGHAM
Fox & Hounds, EXTON
The Blue Ball, OAKHAM
Barnsdale Lodge Hotel, OAKHAM
The Old Plough, OAKHAM
The Grainstore Brewery, OAKHAM
The Coach House Inn, SOUTH LUFFENHAM
The Jackson Stops Inn, STRETTON

SHROPSHIRE
The Three Tuns Inn, BISHOP'S CASTLE
The Sun Inn, CLUN
The Sun Inn, CRAVEN ARMS
The Riverside Inn, CRESSAGE
The Church Inn, LUDLOW
Unicorn Inn, LUDLOW
The Roebuck Inn, LUDLOW
All Nations Inn, MADELEY
The George & Dragon, MUCH WENLOCK
Longville Arms, MUCH WENLOCK
Wenlock Edge Inn, MUCH WENLOCK
Bottle & Glass Inn, PICKLESCOTT
Fighting Cocks, STOTTESDON
The Travellers Rest Inn, UPPER AFFCOT
Swan at Woore, WOORE

SOMERSET
The Ashcott Inn, ASHCOTT
Square & Compass, ASHILL
Lamb Inn, AXBRIDGE
Red Lion, BABCARY
Pack Horse Inn, BATH
The Star Inn, BATH
King William, BATH
Woolpack Inn, BECKINGTON
The Bicknoller Inn, BICKNOLLER
The New Inn, BLAGDON
The Smugglers, BLUE ANCHOR
White Horse Inn, BRADFORD-ON-TONE
The Rose & Portcullis, BUTLEIGH
The Bear and Swan, CHEW MAGNA
The Cat Head Inn, CHISELBOROUGH
The Crown Inn, CHURCHILL
The Black Horse, CLAPTON-IN-GORDANO
The Hunters Rest, CLUTTON
The Wheatsheaf, COMBE HAY
The Queens Arms, CORTON DENHAM
Strode Arms, CRANMORE
The Bull Terrier, CROSCOMBE
Dinnington Docks, DINNINGTON
The Manor House Inn, DITCHEAT
The Luttrell Arms, DUNSTER
The Helyar Arms, EAST COKER
The Crown Hotel, EXFORD
Tuckers Grave, FAULKLAND
The Inn at Freshford, FRESHFORD
The Horse & Groom, FROME
Ring O'Bells, HINTON BLEWETT
The Lord Poulett Arms, HINTON ST GEORGE
The Holcombe Inn, HOLCOMBE
New Inn, ILMINSTER
The Hood Arms, KILVE
Kingsdon Inn, KINGSDON
Rose & Crown, LANGPORT
The Old Pound Inn, LANGPORT
The Bell Inn, LEIGH UPON MENDIP
The Pilgrims, LOVINGTON
The Royal Oak Inn, LUXBOROUGH
The Nag's Head Inn, MARTOCK
The Notley Arms, MONKSILVER
The Phelips Arms, MONTACUTE
The Kings Arms Inn, MONTACUTE
The Bird in Hand, NORTH CURRY
George Inn, NORTON ST PHILIP
The Royal Oak, OVER STRATTON
The Halfway House, PITNEY
The Ship Inn, PORLOCK
The Anchor Hotel & Ship Inn, PORLOCK
New Inn, PRIDDY
The Full Moon at Rudge, RUDGE
Duke of York, SHEPTON BEAUCHAMP
The Three Horseshoes Inn, SHEPTON MALLET
The Waggon and Horses, SHEPTON MALLET
The Montague Inn, SHEPTON MONTAGUE
The Sparkford Inn, SPARKFORD
The Greyhound Inn, STAPLE FITZPAINE
The White Horse, STOGUMBER
Queens Arms, TAUNTON
The Hatch Inn, TAUNTON
The Blue Ball Inn, TRISCOMBE
The Washford Inn, WASHFORD
The Rock Inn, WATERROW
The Pheasant Inn, WELLS
The City Arms, WELLS
The Rising Sun Inn, WEST BAGBOROUGH
Crossways Inn, WEST HUNTSPILL
The Stags Head Inn, YARLINGTON

STAFFORDSHIRE
The Gresley Arms, ALSAGERS BANK
The George, ALSTONEFIELD
Burton Bridge Inn, BURTON UPON TRENT
Yew Tree Inn, CAULDON
The George, ECCLESHALL
Royal Oak, KING'S BROMLEY
The Junction Inn, NORBURY JUNCTION
Horseshoe Inn, TATENHILL
Ye Olde Royal Oak, WETTON
The Hand & Trumpet, WRINEHILL

SUFFOLK
The Mill Inn, ALDEBURGH
The Bildeston Crown, BILDESTON
The Queens Head, BRANDESTON
The Nutshell, BURY ST EDMUNDS
The Linden Tree, BURY ST EDMUNDS
Bull Inn, CAVENDISH
The Ship Inn, DUNWICH
Victoria, EARL SOHAM
The Station Hotel, FRAMLINGHAM
Red Lion, GREAT BRICETT
The Crown Inn, GREAT GLEMHAM
The Queen's Head, HALESWORTH
The White Horse Inn, HITCHAM
The Swan, HOXNE
Pykkerell Inn, IXWORTH
The Chequers Inn, KETTLEBURGH
The Kings Head, LAXFIELD
Jolly Sailor Inn, ORFORD
King's Head, ORFORD
The Cock Inn, POLSTEAD
The Crown Inn, SNAPE
The Golden Key, SNAPE
Plough & Sail, SNAPE
The Crown, STOKE-BY-NAYLAND
The Buxhall Crown, STOWMARKET
The Ivy House, STRADBROKE
Moon & Mushroom Inn, SWILLAND
The Dolphin Inn, THORPENESS
Bell Inn, WALBERSWICK
The Westleton Crown, WESTLETON

SURREY
William IV, ALBURY
The Plough at Blackbrook, BLACKBROOK
The Villagers Inn, BLACKHEATH
Jolly Farmer Inn, BRAMLEY
The Crown Inn, CHIDDINGFOLD
Pride of the Valley, CHURT
Swan Inn & Lodge, CLAYGATE
The Cricketers, COBHAM
The Plough Inn, COLDHARBOUR
The Withies Inn, COMPTON
The Stephan Langton, DORKING
The Sun Inn, DUNSFOLD
The Fox and Hounds, EGHAM
The Woolpack, ELSTEAD
White Horse, EPSOM
The Bat & Ball Freehouse, FARNHAM
The Parrot Inn, FOREST GREEN
The White Horse, HASCOMBE
The Plough, LEIGH
Hare and Hounds, LINGFIELD
The Running Horses, MICKLEHAM
The Surrey Oaks, NEWDIGATE
Bryce's at The Old School House, OCKLEY
The Royal Oak, PIRBRIGHT
Fox & Hounds, SOUTH GODSTONE
The Swan Hotel, STAINES
Onslow Arms, WEST CLANDON
The Inn @ West End, WEST END
The King William IV, WEST HORSLEY
The White Hart, WITLEY

EAST SUSSEX
Rose Cottage Inn, ALCISTON
George Inn, ALFRISTON
Ash Tree Inn, ASHBURNHAM PLACE
The Cricketers Arms, BERWICK
The Blackboys Inn, BLACKBOYS
The Greys, BRIGHTON
The Market Inn, BRIGHTON
The Basketmakers Arms, BRIGHTON
The Chimney House, BRIGHTON
The Five Bells Restaurant and Bar, CHAILEY
The Six Bells, CHIDDINGLY
The Merrie Harriers, COWBEECH
The Coach and Horses, DANEHILL
The Bull, DITCHLING
The Jolly Sportsman, EAST CHILTINGTON
The Golden Galleon, EXCEAT
Anchor Inn, HARTFIELD
The Hatch Inn, HARTFIELD
The Juggs, KINGSTON NEAR LEWES
The Snowdrop, LEWES
The Cock, RINGMER
Horse & Groom, RUSHLAKE GREEN
The Globe Inn, RYE
The Peacock Inn, SHORTBRIDGE
The Bull, THREE LEG CROSS
The Plough, UPPER DICKER
The Best Beech Inn, WADHURST
The War-Bill-in-Tun Inn, WARBLETON
The Giants Rest, WILMINGTON
The New Inn, WINCHELSEA
The Dorset Arms, WITHYHAM

WEST SUSSEX
The Bridge Inn, AMBERLEY
Black Horse, AMBERLEY
The Fountain Inn, ASHURST
The Murrell Arms, BARNHAM
George & Dragon, BURPHAM
The Fox Goes Free, CHARLTON
Horse and Groom, CHICHESTER
Crown and Anchor, CHICHESTER
The Fish House, CHILGROVE
Coach & Horses, COMPTON
The Cricketers, DUNCTON
The Three Horseshoes, ELSTED
The Red Lion, FERNHURST
The King's Arms, FERNHURST
The Foresters Arms, GRAFFHAM
The Anglesey Arms at Halnaker, HALNAKER
Unicorn Inn, HEYSHOTT
The Black Jug, HORSHAM
The Dog and Duck, KINGSFOLD
The Lamb Inn, LAMBS GREEN
The Lickfold Inn, LICKFOLD
The Hollist Arms, LODSWORTH
The Noah's Ark, LURGASHALL
The White Horse, MAPLEHURST
The Angel Hotel, MIDHURST
Black Horse Inn, NUTHURST
The Gribble Inn, OVING
The Green Man Inn and Restaurant, PARTRIDGE GREEN
The Halfway Bridge Inn, PETWORTH
The Black Horse, PETWORTH
Royal Oak Inn, POYNINGS
Neals Restaurant at The Chequers Inn, ROWHOOK
The Fox Inn, RUDGWICK
George & Dragon, SHIPLEY
The Partridge Inn, SINGLETON
The Spur, SLINDON
The Ship Inn, SOUTH HARTING
Hamilton Arms/Nava Thai Restaurant, STEDHAM
The Keepers Arms, TROTTON
The Barley Mow, WALDERTON
The Greets Inn, WARNHAM
The Half Moon, WARNINGLID
The Royal Oak, WINEHAM
Cricketers Arms, WISBOROUGH GREEN

WARWICKSHIRE
The Bell, ALDERMINSTER
The Baraset Barn, ALVESTON
King's Head, ASTON CANTLOW
Broom Tavern, BROOM
The Houndshill, ETTINGTON
The Inn at Farnborough, FARNBOROUGH
The Fox & Hounds Inn, GREAT WOLFORD
The Boot Inn, LAPWORTH
The Bridge at Napton, NAPTON-ON-THE-HILL
The Crabmill, PRESTON BAGOT
The Hollybush Inn, PRIORS MARSTON
The Rose and Crown, RATLEY
The Red Lion, SHIPSTON ON STOUR
The Cherington Arms, SHIPSTON ON STOUR
The Dirty Duck, STRATFORD-UPON-AVON
The One Elm, STRATFORD-UPON-AVON
The Rose & Crown, WARWICK
The Pheasant Eating House, WITHYBROOK

WEST MIDLANDS
The Orange Tree, CHADWICK END
Beacon Hotel & Sarah Hughes Brewery, SEDGLEY

ISLE OF WIGHT
The White Lion, ARRETON
The Crab & Lobster Inn, BEMBRIDGE
The Pilot Boat Inn, BEMBRIDGE
The Bonchurch Inn, BONCHURCH
The Folly, COWES
The Red Lion, FRESHWATER
Buddle Inn, NITON
Travellers Joy, NORTHWOOD
The Chequers, ROOKLEY
The New Inn, SHALFLEET
Fisherman's Cottage, SHANKLIN
The Crown Inn, SHORWELL
The Spyglass Inn, VENTNOR
Bugle Coaching Inn, YARMOUTH

WILTSHIRE
The Green Dragon, ALDERBURY
The Crown, ALVEDISTON
The Quarrymans Arms, BOX
The Northey, BOX
The Kings Arms, BRADFORD-ON-AVON
The Tollgate Inn, BRADFORD-ON-AVON
The Three Crowns, BRINKWORTH
The Ship Inn, BURCOMBE
The Old House at Home, BURTON
The Rising Sun, CHRISTIAN MALFORD
The Shears Inn & Country Hotel, COLLINGBOURNE DUCIS
The Flemish Weaver, CORSHAM
The Dove Inn, CORTON
The Bear Hotel, DEVIZES
The Forester Inn, DONHEAD ST ANDREW
The Fox and Hounds, EAST KNOYLE
The Beckford Arms, FONTHILL GIFFORD
The Bell Inn, GREAT CHEVERELL
The Neeld Arms, GRITTLETON
The Jolly Tar, HANNINGTON
The Angel Coaching Inn, HEYTESBURY
The Lamb at Hindon, HINDON
Angel Inn, HINDON
The Bridge Inn, HORTON

The Red Lion Inn, KILMINGTON
The George Inn, LACOCK
Red Lion Inn, LACOCK
The Rising Sun, LACOCK
The Hop Pole Inn, LIMPLEY STOKE
The Owl, LITTLE CHEVERELL
Compasses Inn, LOWER CHICKSGROVE
The Grove Arms, LUDWELL
The Smoking Dog, MALMESBURY
Horse & Groom, MALMESBURY
The Vine Tree, MALMESBURY
The Millstream, MARDEN
The Malet Arms, NEWTON TONEY
The Radnor Arms, NUNTON
The Wheatsheaf Inn, OAKSEY
The Seven Stars, PEWSEY
The Silver Plough, PITTON
The Bell, RAMSBURY
The George & Dragon, ROWDE
Bell Inn, SEEND
The Lamb on the Strand, SEMINGTON
Carpenters Arms, SHERSTON
The Sun Inn, SWINDON
King John Inn, TOLLARD ROYAL
The Bath Arms, WARMINSTER
The Three Crowns, WHADDON
The Pear Tree Inn, WHITLEY
The Woodfalls Inn, WOODFALLS
Royal Oak, WOOTTON RIVERS
The Bell Inn, WYLYE

WORCESTERSHIRE
The Manor Arms at Abberley, ABBERLEY
The Beckford, BECKFORD
Little Pack Horse, BEWDLEY
The Mug House Inn & Angry Chef Restaurant, BEWDLEY
The Bell & Cross, CLENT
The Colliers Arms, CLOWS TOP
The Chequers, DROITWICH
The Old Cock Inn, DROITWICH
The Boot Inn, FLYFORD FLAVELL
Walter de Cantelupe Inn, KEMPSEY
The Red Hart, KINGTON
The Talbot, KNIGHTWICK
The Anchor Inn, MALVERN
Admiral Rodney Inn, MARTLEY
The Crown Inn, MARTLEY
The Peacock Inn, TENBURY WELLS

EAST RIDING OF YORKSHIRE
The Seabirds Inn, FLAMBOROUGH
The Old Star Inn, KILHAM
The Gold Cup Inn, LOW CATTON

ORTH YORKSHIRE
The Moors Inn, APPLETON-LE-MOORS
The Craven Arms, APPLETREEWICK
Crab & Lobster, ASENBY
Kings Arms, ASKRIGG
The George & Dragon Inn, AYSGARTH
The Black Bull Inn, BOROUGHBRIDGE
The Bull, BROUGHTON
The Red Lion, BURNSALL
New Inn, CLAPHAM
The White Lion Inn, CRAY
The Durham Ox, CRAYKE
The New Inn, CROPTON
The Blue Lion, EAST WITTON
The Wheatsheaf Inn, EGTON
Horseshoe Hotel, EGTON BRIDGE
Birch Hall Inn, GOATHLAND
The Bay Horse Inn, GREEN HAMMERTON
The Bridge Inn, GRINTON
The Moorcock Inn, HAWES
The Worsley Arms Hotel, HOVINGHAM
The Forresters Arms, KILBURN
The Bay Horse Inn, KIRK DEIGHTON
George & Dragon Hotel, KIRKBYMOORSIDE
Sandpiper Inn, LEYBURN
The Old Horn Inn, LEYBURN
Queens Arms, LITTON
Maypole Inn, LONG PRESTON
Black Swan Hotel, MIDDLEHAM
Crown Hotel, MIDDLESMOOR
The Farmers Arms, MUKER
Queen Catherine, OSMOTHERLEY
The Golden Lion, OSMOTHERLEY
The Stone House Inn, PADSIDE
The White Swan Inn, PICKERING
Fox & Hounds Country Inn, PICKERING
Horseshoe Inn, PICKERING
Nags Head Country Inn, PICKHILL
Laurel Inn, ROBIN HOOD'S BAY
The Milburn Arms Hotel, ROSEDALE ABBEY
The Anvil Inn, SAWDON
The New Inn, THORNTON LE DALE
The Buck Inn, THORNTON WATLASS
The Angel Inn, TOPCLIFFE
Fox & Hounds, WEST BURTON
The Bruce Arms, WEST TANFIELD
Lysander Arms, YORK
Blue Bell, YORK

SOUTH YORKSHIRE
The Strines Inn, BRADFIELD
Cadeby Inn, CADEBY
Waterfront Inn, DONCASTER
The Fat Cat, SHEFFIELD
The Cricket Inn, TOTLEY

WEST YORKSHIRE
The Fleece, ADDINGHAM
The Black Horse Inn, CLIFTON
The Rock Inn Hotel, HALIFAX
Shibden Mill Inn, HALIFAX
The Chequers Inn, LEDSHAM
Whitelocks, LEEDS
The Sair Inn, LINTHWAITE
The Windmill Inn, LINTON
Shoulder of Mutton, MYTHOLMROYD
The Spite Inn, NEWALL
The Travellers Rest, SOWERBY
Pack Horse Inn, WIDDOP

ISLE OF MAN
Falcon's Nest Hotel, PORT ERIN

CHANNEL ISLANDS
GUERNSEY
Hotel Hougue du Pommier, CASTEL
Fleur du Jardin, CASTEL

SCOTLAND
ABERDEENSHIRE
The Lairhillock Inn, NETHERLEY

ARGYLL & BUTE
Loch Melfort Hotel, ARDUAINE
Tigh an Truish Inn, CLACHAN-SEIL
Crinan Hotel, CRINAN
The Pierhouse Hotel & Seafood Restaurant, PORT APPIN
Creggans Inn, STRACHUR
Tayvallich Inn, TAYVALLICH

CITY OF DUNDEE
The Royal Arch Bar, BROUGHTY FERRY
Speedwell Bar, DUNDEE

CITY OF EDINBURGH
The Bow Bar, EDINBURGH
The Shore Bar & Restaurant, EDINBURGH

CITY OF GLASGOW
Rab Ha's, GLASGOW,

CLACKMANNANSHIRE
Castle Campbell Hotel, DOLLAR

DUMFRIES & GALLOWAY
The Steam Packet Inn, ISLE OF WHITHORN
Selkirk Arms Hotel, KIRKCUDBRIGHT
Criffel Inn, NEW ABBEY
Cross Keys Hotel, NEW GALLOWAY
Creebridge House Hotel, NEWTON STEWART

EAST AYRSHIRE
The Kirkton Inn, DALRYMPLE

EAST LOTHIAN
The Drovers Inn, EAST LINTON

FIFE
The Dreel Tavern, ANSTRUTHER
The Golf Hotel, CRAIL
The Ship Inn, ELIE
The Crusoe Hotel, LOWER LARGO
The Inn at Lathones, ST ANDREWS

HIGHLAND
Summer Isles Hotel & Bar, ACHILTIBUIE
Altnaharra Hotel, ALTNAHARRA
Ardvasar Hotel, ARDVASAR

The Badachro Inn, BADACHRO
The Old Inn, CARBOST
Cawdor Tavern, CAWDOR
Moorings Hotel, FORT WILLIAM
The Old Inn, GAIRLOCH
Glenelg Inn, GLENELG
The Old Forge, INVERIE
Hotel Eilean Iarmain, ISLE ORNSAY
Portland Arms, LYBSTER
Loch Leven Hotel, NORTH BALLACHULISH
Plockton Inn & Seafood Restaurant, PLOCKTON
Shieldaig Bar & Coastal Kitchen, SHIELDAIG
Stein Inn, STEIN
The Torridon Inn, TORRIDON
The Ceilidh Place, ULLAPOOL

MORAY
Gordon Arms Hotel, FOCHABERS

NORTH LANARKSHIRE
Castlecary House Hotel, CUMBERNAULD

PERTH & KINROSS
The Tormaukin Country Inn and Restaurant, GLENDEVON
The Famous Bein Inn, GLENFARG
Anglers Inn, GUILDTOWN
Killiecrankie House Hotel, KILLIECRANKIE
Lomond Country Inn, KINNESSWOOD

RENFREWSHIRE
Fox & Hounds, HOUSTON

SCOTTISH BORDERS
Allanton Inn, ALLANTON
Tushielaw Inn, ETTRICK
Kingsknowes Hotel, GALASHIELS
Corner House, INNERLEITHEN
The Black Bull, LAUDER
Burts Hotel, MELROSE
Buccleuch Arms Hotel, ST BOSWELLS
The Gordon Arms, WEST LINTON

STIRLING
The Ardeonaig Hotel, ARDEONAIG
The Lade Inn, CALLANDER
The Clachan Inn, DRYMEN
Cross Keys Hotel, KIPPEN
The Inn at Kippen, KIPPEN

WALES

BRIDGEND
Prince of Wales Inn, KENFIG

CARDIFF
Caesars Arms, CREIGIAU
Gwaelod-y-Garth Inn, CREIGIAU

CARMARTHENSHIRE
The Black Lion, ABERGORLECH

CEREDIGION
The Crown Inn & Restaurant, LLWYNDAFYDD

CONWY
White Horse Inn, BETWS-Y-COED
Cobdens Hotel, CAPEL CURIG

DENBIGHSHIRE
Ye Olde Anchor Inn, RUTHIN
White Horse Inn, RUTHIN

FLINTSHIRE
White Horse Inn, CILCAIN
Glasfryn, MOLD

GWYNEDD
Penhelig Arms Hotel & Restaurant, ABERDYFI
The Miners Arms, BLAENAU FFESTINIOG
Victoria Inn, LLANBEDR
Brigands Inn, MALLWYD
Pen-Y-Gwryd Hotel, NANTGWYNANT
Snowdonia Parc Brewpub & Campsite, WAUNFAWR

MONMOUTHSHIRE
Clytha Arms, ABERGAVENNY
Castle View Hotel, CHEPSTOW
The Woodland Restaurant & Bar, LLANVAIR DISCOED
Horseshoe Inn, MAMHILAD
The Boat Inn, PENALLT
The Carpenters Arms, SHIRENEWTON
The Bell at Skenfrith, SKENFRITH
Fountain Inn, TINTERN PARVA
The Lion Inn, TRELLECH
The Nags Head Inn, USK

PEMBROKESHIRE
Nags Head Inn, ABERCYCH
The New Inn, AMROTH
Carew Inn, CAREW
Salutation Inn, NEWPORT
Tafarn Sinc, ROSEBUSH
Webley Waterfront Inn & Hotel, ST DOGMAELS
The Stackpole Inn, STACKPOLE

POWYS
The Felin Fach Griffin, BRECON
The Old Hand and Diamond Inn, COEDWAY
Nantyffin Cider Mill, CRICKHOWELL
The Bear Hotel, CRICKHOWELL
Star Inn, DYLIFE
The Royal Oak Inn, GLADESTRY
Kilverts Hotel, HAY-ON-WYE
Cain Valley Hotel, LLANFYLLIN
The Radnor Arms, LLOWES
Wynnstay Hotel, MACHYNLLETH
Red Lion Inn, NEW RADNOR
Star Inn, TALYBONT-ON-USK

VALE OF GLAMORGAN
The Bush Inn, ST HILARY

WREXHAM
The Boat Inn, ERBISTOCK
The West Arms Hotel, LLANARMON DYFFRYN CEIRIOG
The Hand at Llanarmon, LLANARMON DYFFRYN CEIRIOG

County Maps

The county map shown here will help you identify the counties within each country. You can look up each county in the guide using the county names at the top of each page. To find towns featured in the guide use the atlas and the index.

England

1 Bedfordshire
2 Berkshire
3 Bristol
4 Buckinghamshire
5 Cambridgeshire
6 Greater Manchester
7 Herefordshire
8 Hertfordshire
9 Leicestershire
10 Northamptonshire
11 Nottinghamshire
12 Rutland
13 Staffordshire
14 Warwickshire
15 West Midlands
16 Worcestershire

Scotland

17 City of Glasgow
18 Clackmannanshire
19 East Ayrshire
20 East Dunbartonshire
21 East Renfrewshire
22 Perth & Kinross
23 Renfrewshire
24 South Lanarkshire
25 West Dunbartonshire

Wales

26 Blaenau Gwent
27 Bridgend
28 Caerphilly
29 Denbighshire
30 Flintshire
31 Merthyr Tydfil
32 Monmouthshire
33 Neath Port Talbot
34 Newport
35 Rhondda Cynon Taff
36 Torfaen
37 Vale of Glamorgan
38 Wrexham

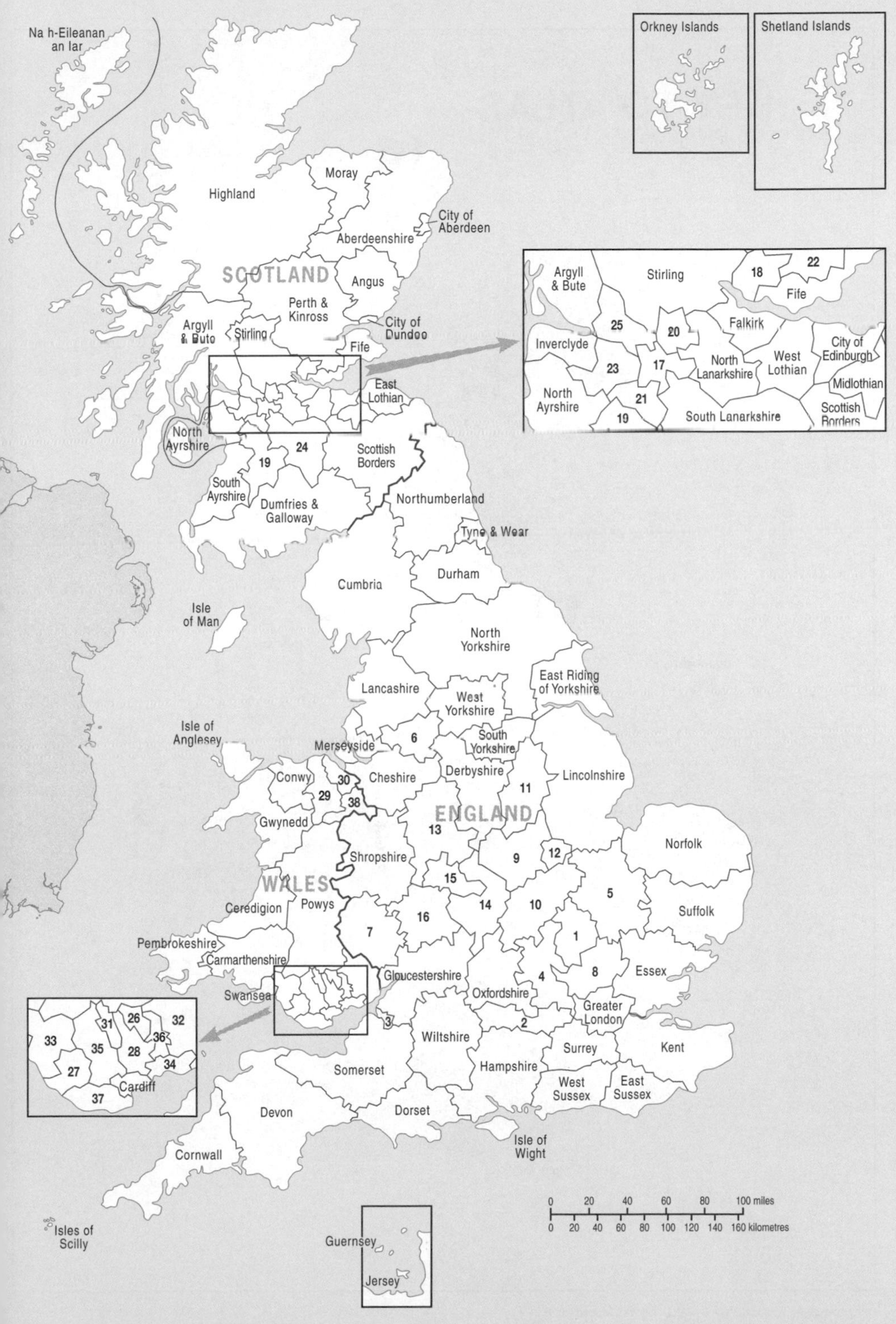
Na h-Eileanan an Iar
Orkney Islands
Shetland Islands
Highland
Moray
City of Aberdeen
Aberdeenshire
SCOTLAND
Angus
Perth & Kinross
City of Dundee
Argyll & Bute
Stirling
Fife
East Lothian
North Ayrshire
24
19
Scottish Borders
South Ayrshire
Dumfries & Galloway
Northumberland
Tyne & Wear
Cumbria
Durham
Isle of Man
North Yorkshire
East Riding of Yorkshire
Lancashire
West Yorkshire
Isle of Anglesey
Merseyside
6
South Yorkshire
Conwy
30
29
38
Cheshire
Derbyshire
11
Lincolnshire
Gwynedd
ENGLAND
13
Shropshire
9
12
Norfolk
WALES
15
Ceredigion
Powys
14
10
5
16
Suffolk
7
1
Pembrokeshire
Carmarthenshire
4
8
Essex
Gloucestershire
Swansea
Oxfordshire
Greater London
3
2
Wiltshire
Surrey
Kent
Somerset
Hampshire
West Sussex
East Sussex
Devon
Dorset
Isle of Wight
Cornwall
Isles of Scilly
Guernsey
Jersey
0 20 40 60 80 100 miles
0 20 40 60 80 100 120 140 160 kilometres
Argyll & Bute
Stirling
18
22
Fife
25
20
Falkirk
Inverclyde
City of Edinburgh
23
17
North Lanarkshire
West Lothian
Midlothian
North Ayrshire
21
19
South Lanarkshire
Scottish Borders
33
31
26
32
35
28
36
34
27
Cardiff
37

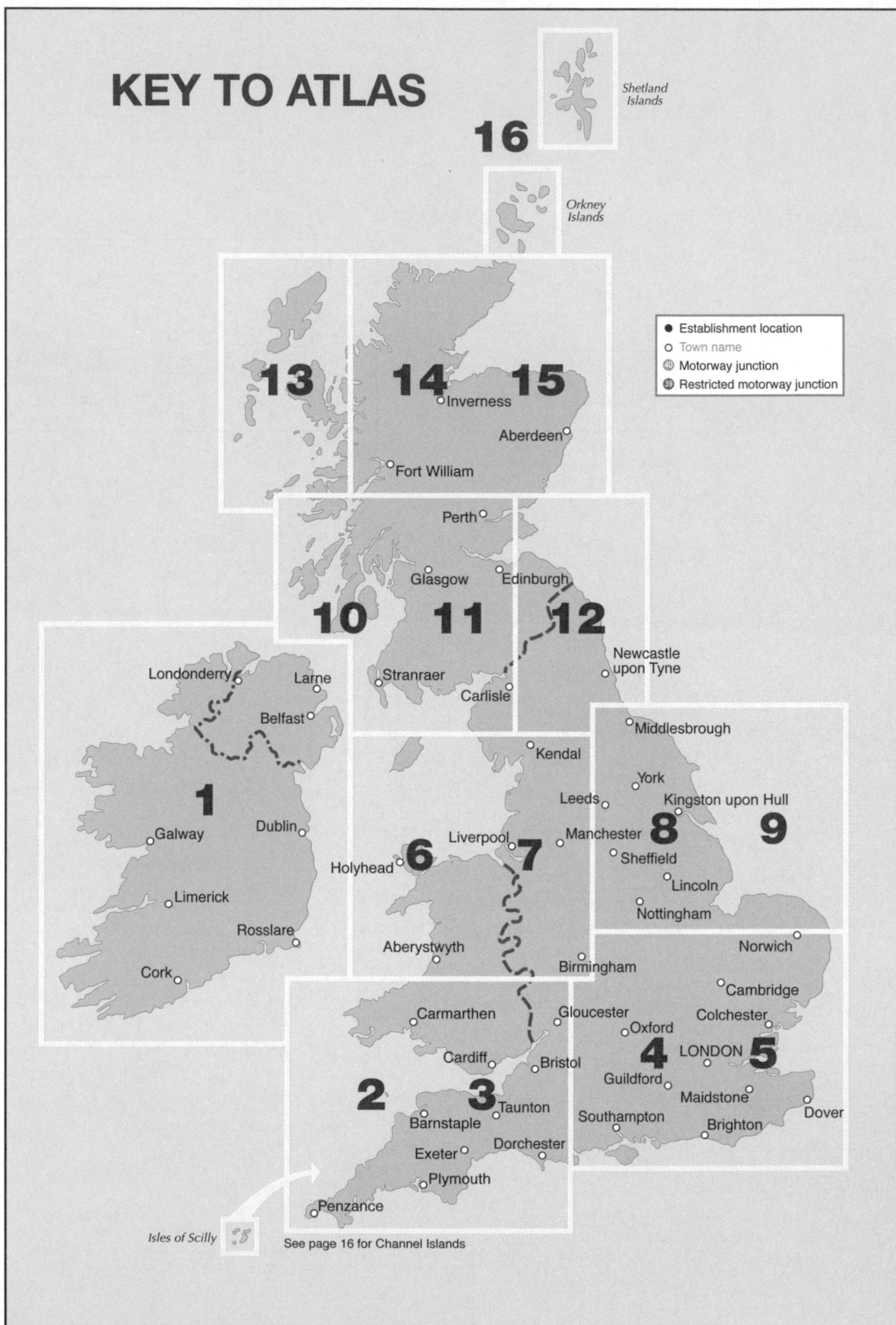
KEY TO ATLAS
16
Shetland Islands
Orkney Islands
Establishment location
Town name
Motorway junction
Restricted motorway junction
13
14
15
Inverness
Aberdeen
Fort William
Perth
Glasgow
Edinburgh
10
11
12
Newcastle upon Tyne
Londonderry
Larne
Belfast
Stranraer
Carlisle
Middlesbrough
Kendal
York
1
Leeds
Kingston upon Hull
Galway
Dublin
Liverpool
Manchester
8
9
6
7
Holyhead
Sheffield
Lincoln
Limerick
Nottingham
Rosslare
Aberystwyth
Norwich
Cork
Birmingham
Cambridge
Carmarthen
Gloucester
Colchester
Oxford
Cardiff
Bristol
LONDON
4
5
Guildford
2
3
Maidstone
Taunton
Dover
Barnstaple
Southampton
Brighton
Dorchester
Exeter
Plymouth
Penzance
Isles of Scilly
See page 16 for Channel Islands

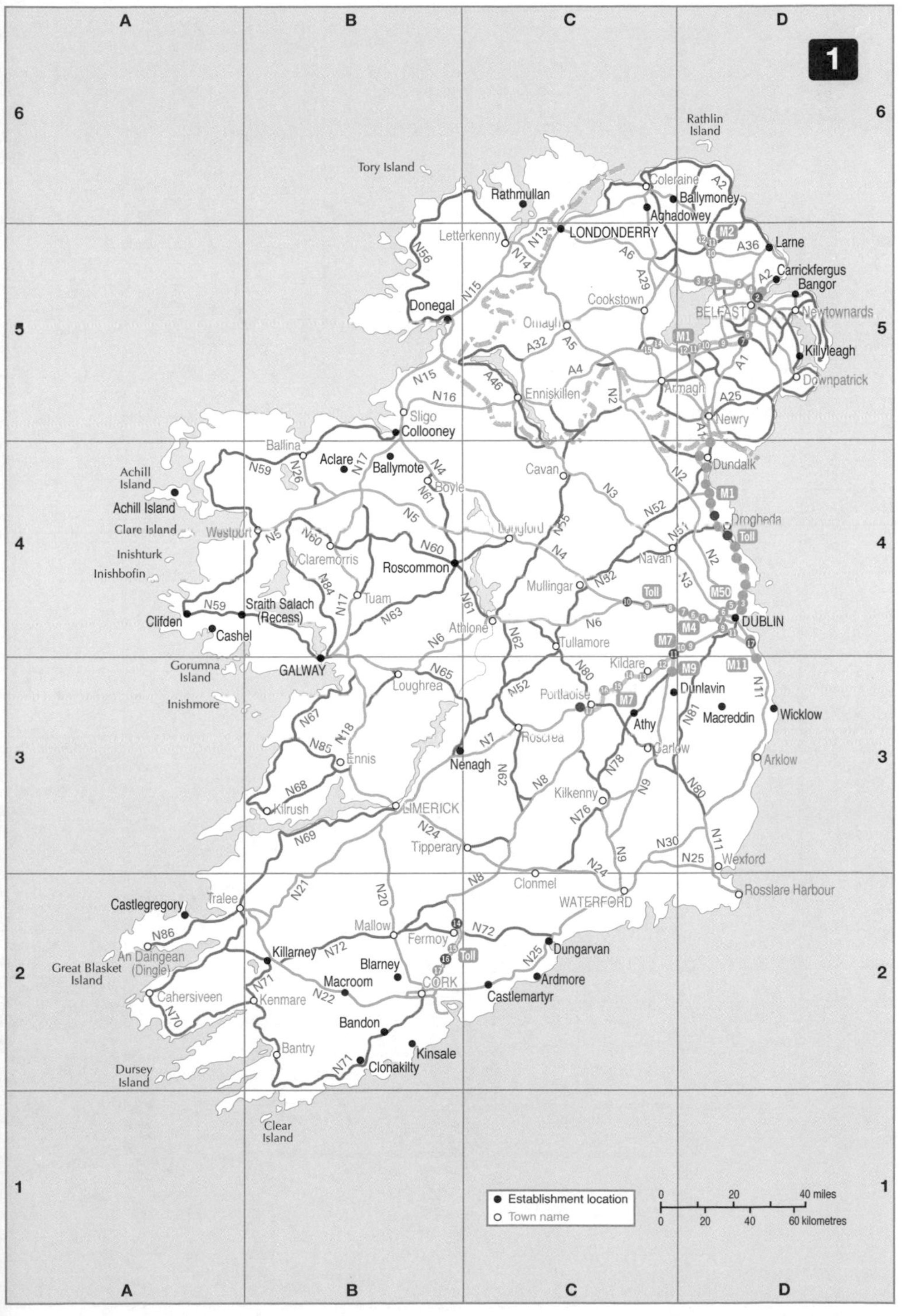

1
A
B
C
D
6
5
4
3
2
1
Rathlin Island
Tory Island
Rathmullan
Coleraine
Ballymoney
Aghadowey
LONDONDERRY
Letterkenny
Larne
Carrickfergus
Bangor
Donegal
Cookstown
Omagh
BELFAST
Newtownards
Killyleagh
Downpatrick
Enniskillen
Armagh
Newry
Sligo
Collooney
Ballina
Aclare
Ballymote
Boyle
Cavan
Dundalk
Achill Island
Achill Island
Clare Island
Westport
Inishturk
Inishbofin
Claremorris
Longford
Drogheda
Roscommon
Navan
Mullingar
Tuam
Clifden
Sraith Salach (Recess)
Cashel
Athlone
DUBLIN
Tullamore
Gorumna Island
GALWAY
Inishmore
Loughrea
Kildare
Dunlavin
Portlaoise
Macreddin
Wicklow
Athy
Roscrea
Carlow
Ennis
Nenagh
Arklow
Kilkenny
Kilrush
LIMERICK
Tipperary
Wexford
Clonmel
Tralee
WATERFORD
Rosslare Harbour
Castlegregory
Mallow
Fermoy
Dungarvan
An Daingean (Dingle)
Great Blasket Island
Killarney
Blarney
Macroom
CORK
Ardmore
Castlemartyr
Cahersiveen
Kenmare
Bandon
Kinsale
Bantry
Clonakilty
Dursey Island
Clear Island
Establishment location
Town name
0 20 40 miles
0 20 40 60 kilometres

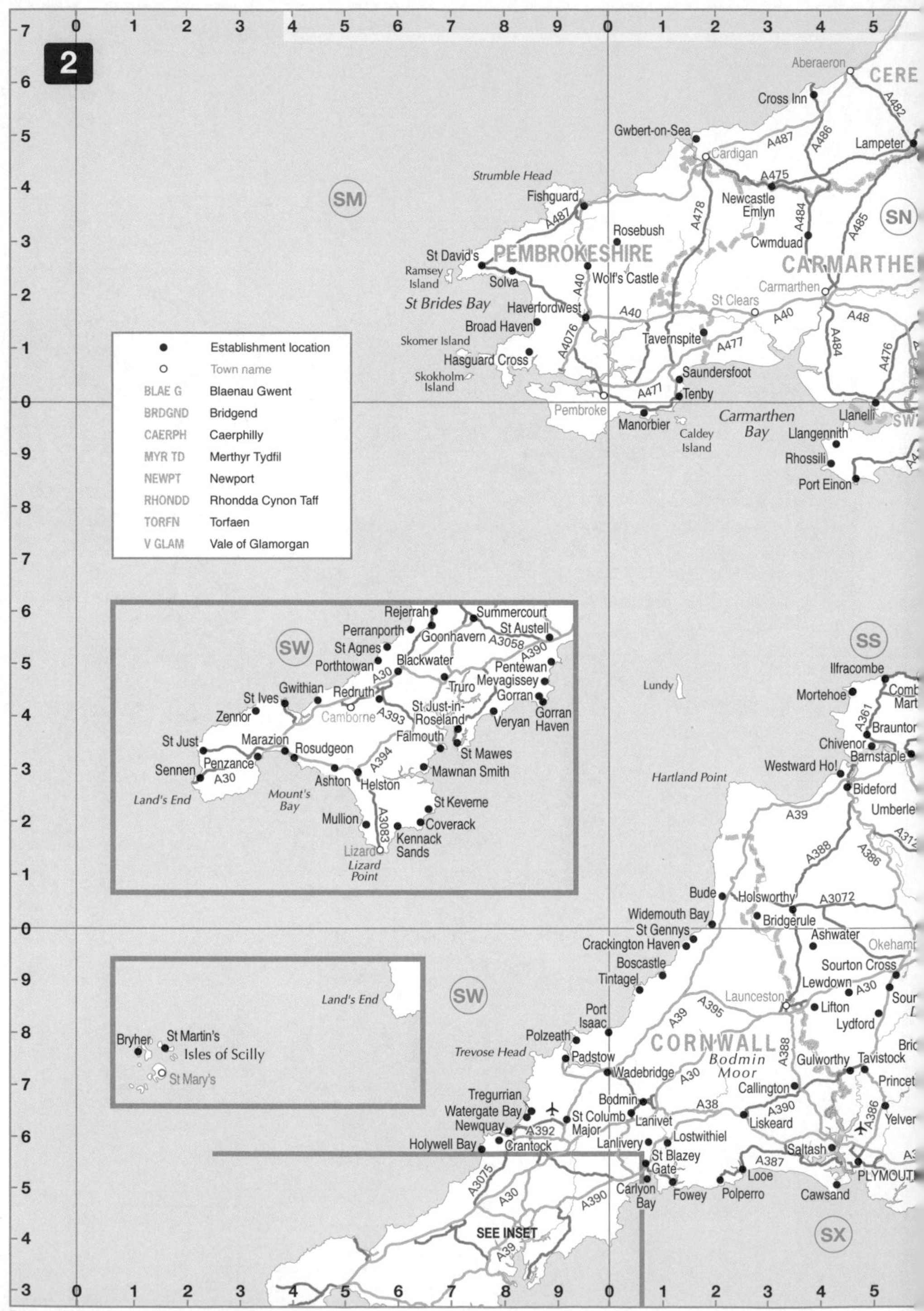

For continuation pages refer to numbered arrows

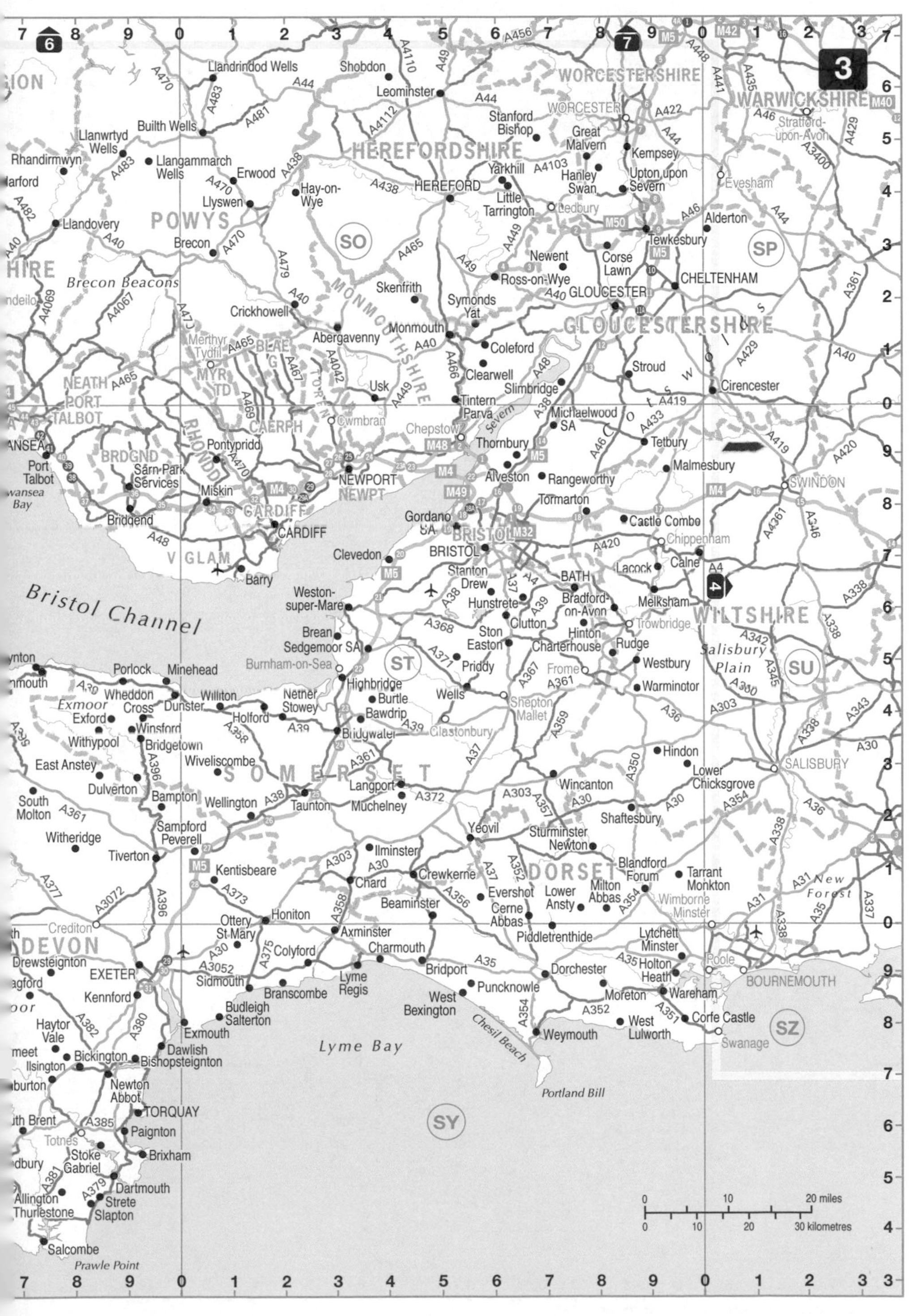
3
WORCESTERSHIRE
WARWICKSHIRE
HEREFORDSHIRE
POWYS
MONMOUTHSHIRE
GLOUCESTERSHIRE
WILTSHIRE
SOMERSET
DORSET
DEVON
Brecon Beacons
Bristol Channel
Exmoor
Salisbury Plain
New Forest
Lyme Bay
Chesil Beach
Portland Bill
Prawle Point
Swansea Bay
Severn
Llandrindod Wells
Shobdon
Leominster
Builth Wells
Stanford Bishop
Great Malvern
WORCESTER
Stratford-upon-Avon
Llanwrtyd Wells
Llangammarch Wells
Rhandirmwyn
Erwood
Hay-on-Wye
HEREFORD
Yarkhill
Little Tarrington
Hanley Swan
Kempsey
Upton upon Severn
Evesham
Llyswen
Llandovery
Ledbury
Alderton
Brecon
Newent
Corse Lawn
Tewkesbury
Ross-on-Wye
CHELTENHAM
Skenfrith
Symonds Yat
GLOUCESTER
Crickhowell
Abergavenny
Monmouth
Coleford
Merthyr Tydfil
Clearwell
Stroud
Slimbridge
Usk
Tintern Parva
Cirencester
NEATH PORT TALBOT
Cwmbran
Michaelwood SA
Chepstow
Thornbury
Tetbury
Pontypridd
CAERPH
SWANSEA
Port Talbot
BRDGND
Sarn Park Services
RHONDD
NEWPORT
NEWPT
Alveston
Malmesbury
Rangeworthy
SWINDON
Miskin
Bridgend
CARDIFF
Tormarton
Gordano SA
Castle Combe
Chippenham
BRISTOL
Clevedon
V GLAM
Barry
Lacock
Calne
Stanton Drew
BATH
Weston-super-Mare
Hunstrete
Bradford-on-Avon
Melksham
Clutton
Trowbridge
Brean
Ston Easton
Hinton Charterhouse
Rudge
Sedgemoor SA
Burnham-on-Sea
Priddy
Frome
Westbury
Porlock
Minehead
Highbridge
Wells
Warminster
Wheddon Cross
Dunster
Williton
Nether Stowey
Burtle
Shepton Mallet
Exford
Winsford
Holford
Bawdrip
Glastonbury
Withypool
Bridgetown
Bridgwater
Hindon
Wiveliscombe
East Anstey
Dulverton
Langport
Wincanton
Lower Chicksgrove
SALISBURY
South Molton
Bampton
Wellington
Taunton
Muchelney
Shaftesbury
Witheridge
Sampford Peverell
Yeovil
Sturminster Newton
Tiverton
Ilminster
Blandford Forum
Tarrant Monkton
Kentisbeare
Chard
Crewkerne
Evershot
Lower Ansty
Milton Abbas
Beaminster
Cerne Abbas
Wimborne Minster
Crediton
Honiton
Ottery St Mary
Axminster
Piddletrenthide
Lytchett Minster
Drewsteignton
Colyford
Charmouth
EXETER
Bridport
Dorchester
Holton Heath
Poole
BOURNEMOUTH
Kennford
Sidmouth
Branscombe
Lyme Regis
West Bexington
Puncknowle
Moreton
Wareham
Haytor Vale
Budleigh Salterton
Corfe Castle
Exmouth
Weymouth
West Lulworth
Swanage
Dawlish
Bickington
Bishopsteignton
Ilsington
Newton Abbot
TORQUAY
Paignton
Totnes
Stoke Gabriel
Brixham
Dartmouth
Allington
Strete
Thurlestone
Slapton
Salcombe
SO
SP
ST
SU
SY
SZ
0 10 20 miles
0 10 20 30 kilometres

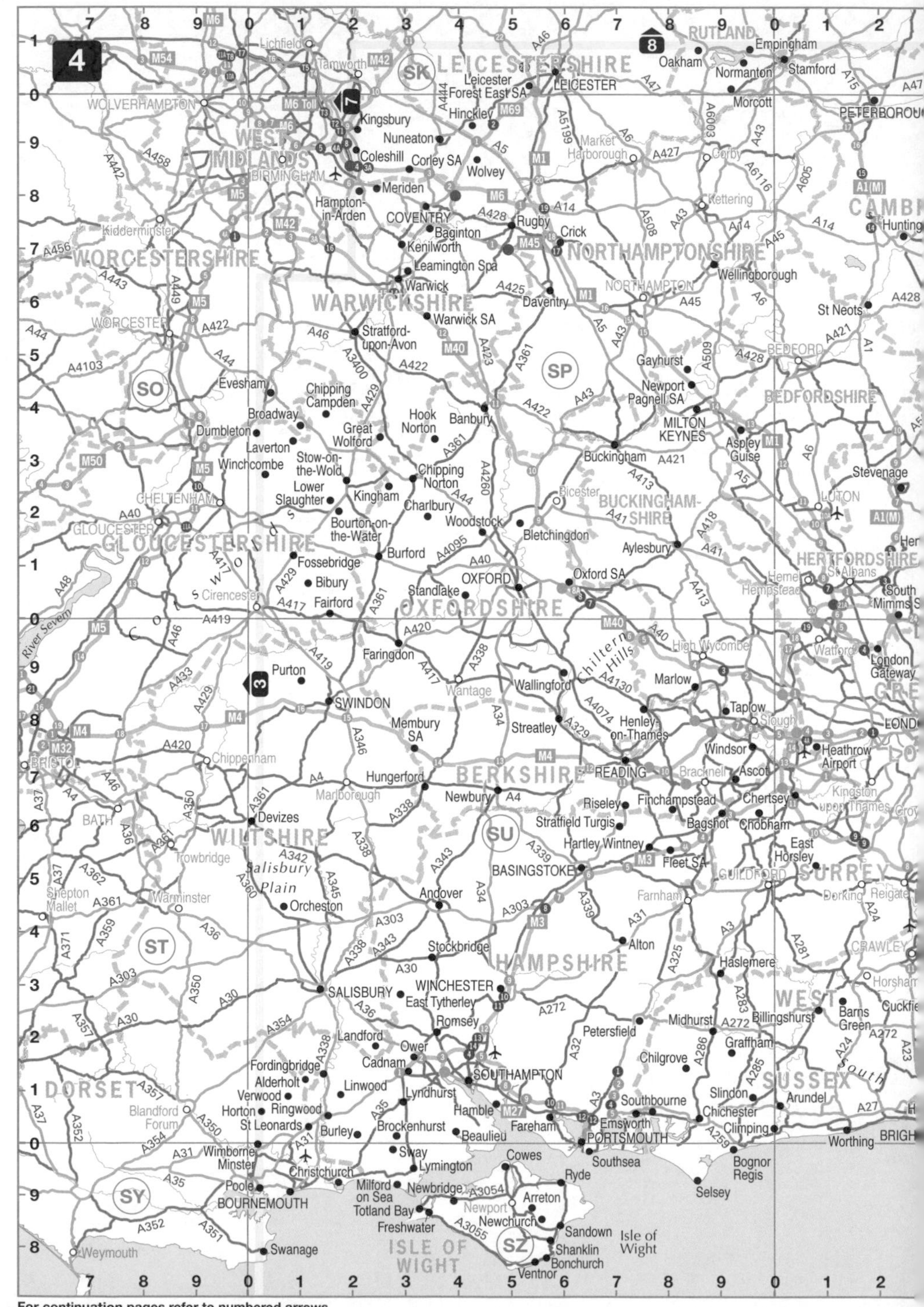

For continuation pages refer to numbered arrows

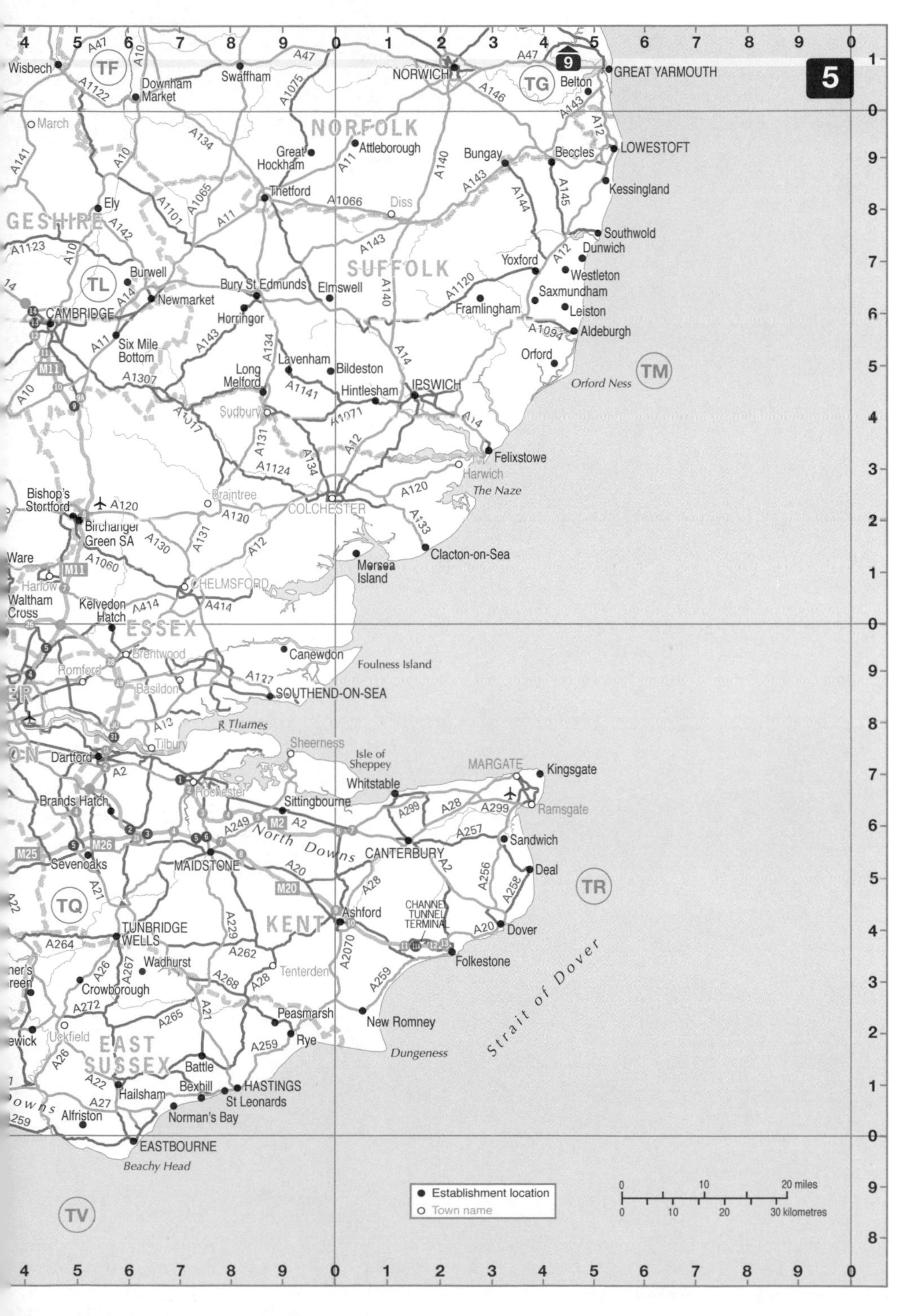

5
NORFOLK
SUFFOLK
ESSEX
KENT
EAST SUSSEX
Wisbech
Downham Market
Swaffham
NORWICH
GREAT YARMOUTH
Belton
March
Great Hockham
Attleborough
Bungay
Beccles
LOWESTOFT
Kessingland
Thetford
Diss
Ely
Southwold
Dunwich
Yoxford
Westleton
Burwell
Bury St Edmunds
Elmswell
Saxmundham
Newmarket
CAMBRIDGE
Horringer
Framlingham
Leiston
Aldeburgh
Six Mile Bottom
Lavenham
Bildeston
Orford
Long Melford
Hintlesham
IPSWICH
Orford Ness
Sudbury
Felixstowe
Harwich
The Naze
Bishop's Stortford
Braintree
COLCHESTER
Birchanger Green SA
Clacton-on-Sea
Mersea Island
Ware
Harlow
CHELMSFORD
Waltham Cross
Kelvedon Hatch
Brentwood
Canewdon
Foulness Island
Romford
Basildon
SOUTHEND-ON-SEA
R Thames
Tilbury
Sheerness
Isle of Sheppey
Dartford
MARGATE
Kingsgate
Whitstable
Rochester
Ramsgate
Brands Hatch
Sittingbourne
North Downs
Sandwich
CANTERBURY
Sevenoaks
MAIDSTONE
Deal
Ashford
CHANNEL TUNNEL TERMINAL
Dover
TUNBRIDGE WELLS
Folkestone
Wadhurst
Tenterden
Crowborough
Strait of Dover
Peasmarsh
Uckfield
Rye
New Romney
Dungeness
Battle
Hailsham
Bexhill
HASTINGS
St Leonards
Alfriston
Norman's Bay
EASTBOURNE
Beachy Head
TF
TG
TL
TM
TQ
TR
TV
Establishment location
Town name
20 miles
30 kilometres

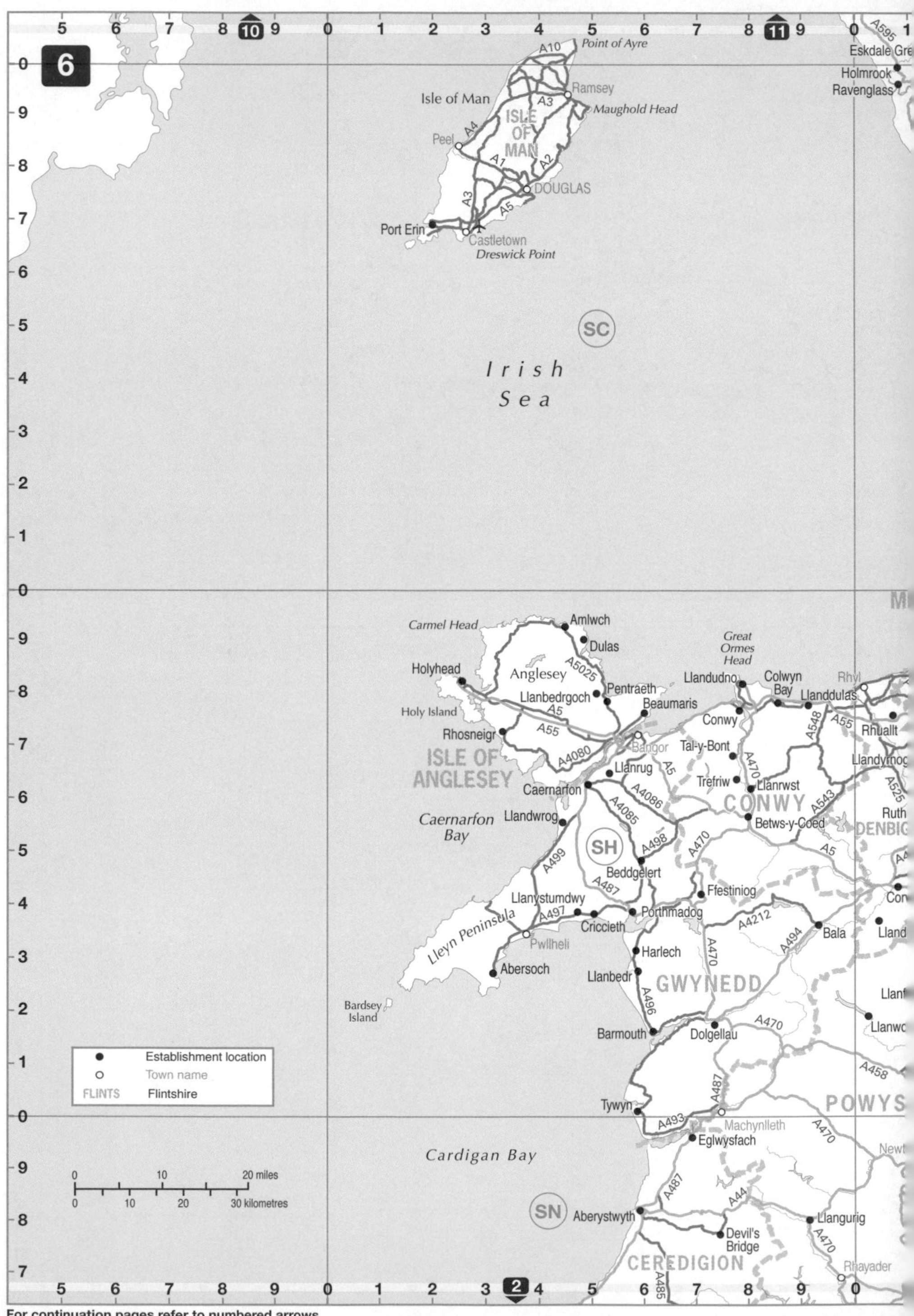

For continuation pages refer to numbered arrows

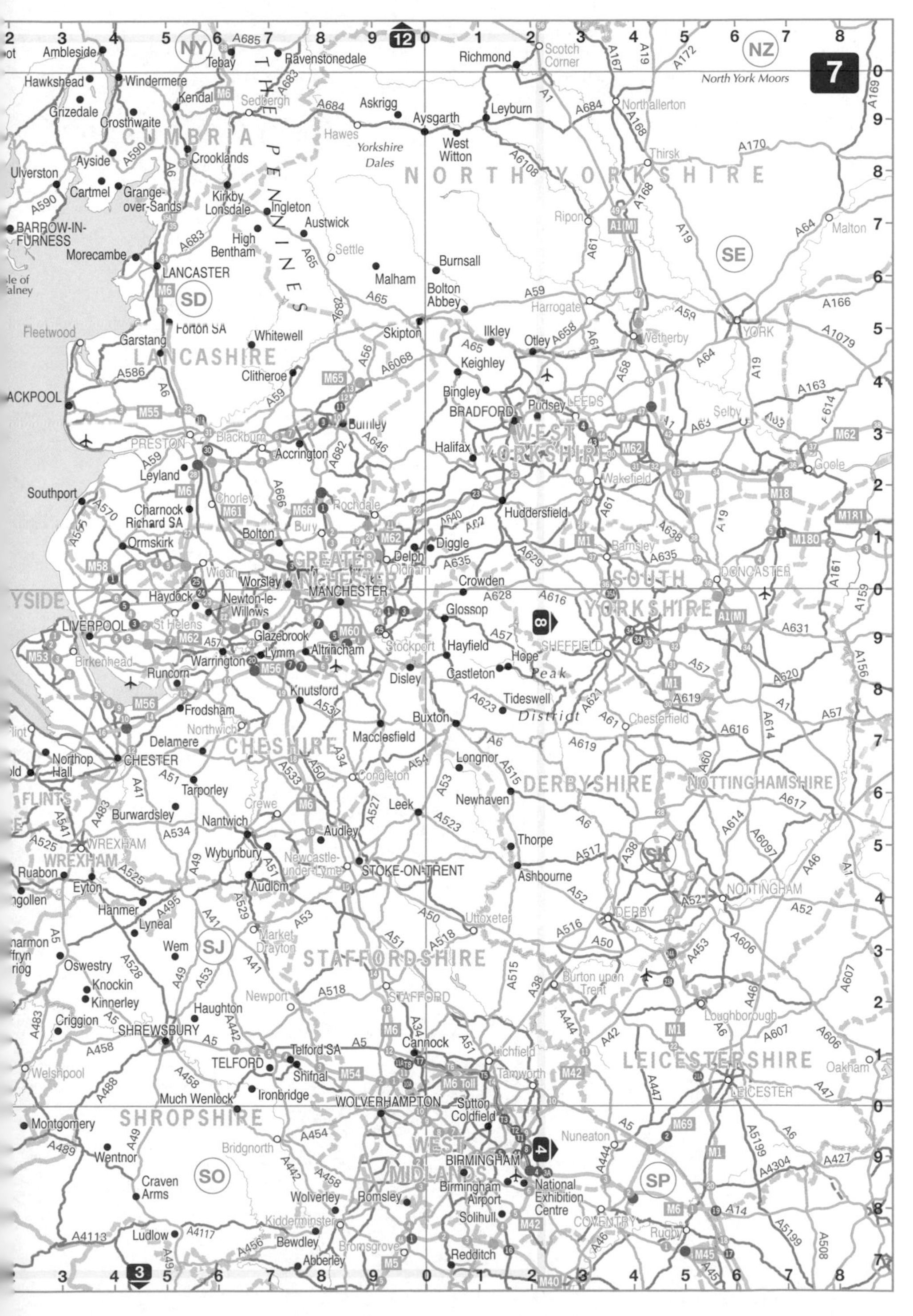
7
CUMBRIA
LANCASHIRE
NORTH YORKSHIRE
WEST YORKSHIRE
SOUTH YORKSHIRE
GREATER MANCHESTER
CHESHIRE
DERBYSHIRE
NOTTINGHAMSHIRE
STAFFORDSHIRE
SHROPSHIRE
WEST MIDLANDS
LEICESTERSHIRE
THE PENNINES
Yorkshire Dales
North York Moors
Peak District
Ambleside
Windermere
Kendal
Tebay
Ravenstonedale
Richmond
Scotch Corner
Northallerton
Leyburn
Askrigg
Aysgarth
West Witton
Hawes
Sedbergh
Thirsk
Ripon
Malton
York
Harrogate
Wetherby
Skipton
Ilkley
Otley
Keighley
Bingley
Bradford
Leeds
Pudsey
Halifax
Huddersfield
Wakefield
Selby
Goole
Barnsley
Doncaster
Sheffield
Chesterfield
Lancaster
Morecambe
Fleetwood
Blackpool
Preston
Blackburn
Burnley
Accrington
Clitheroe
Garstang
Southport
Wigan
Bolton
Bury
Rochdale
Oldham
Manchester
Liverpool
Birkenhead
St Helens
Warrington
Runcorn
Chester
Stockport
Macclesfield
Buxton
Glossop
Crewe
Nantwich
Congleton
Leek
Stoke-on-Trent
Newcastle-under-Lyme
Wrexham
Shrewsbury
Telford
Stafford
Uttoxeter
Derby
Nottingham
Loughborough
Leicester
Burton upon Trent
Lichfield
Tamworth
Cannock
Wolverhampton
Birmingham
Sutton Coldfield
Solihull
Coventry
Nuneaton
Rugby
Redditch
Bromsgrove
Kidderminster
Bridgnorth
Ludlow
Welshpool
Montgomery
Oakham

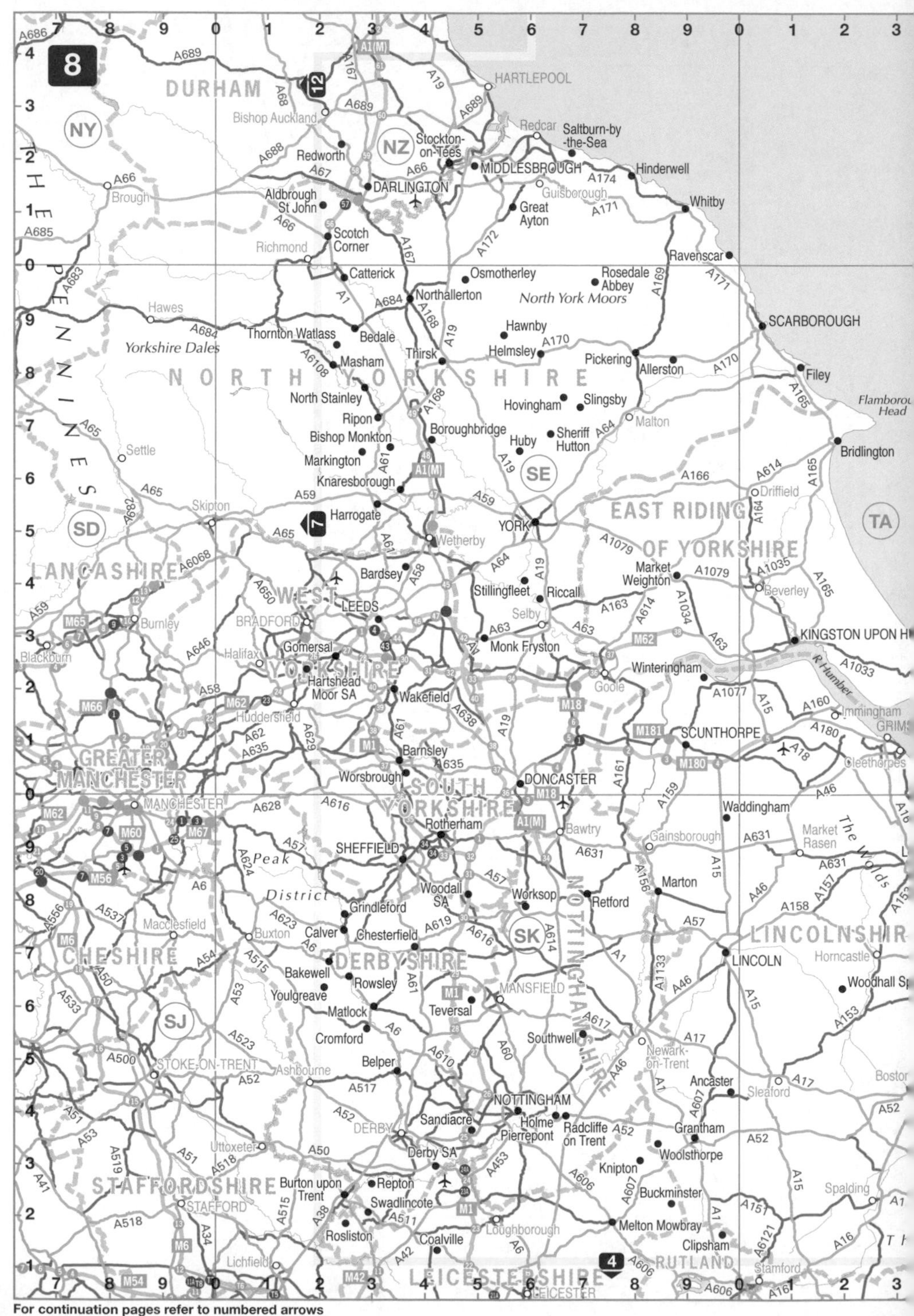

For continuation pages refer to numbered arrows

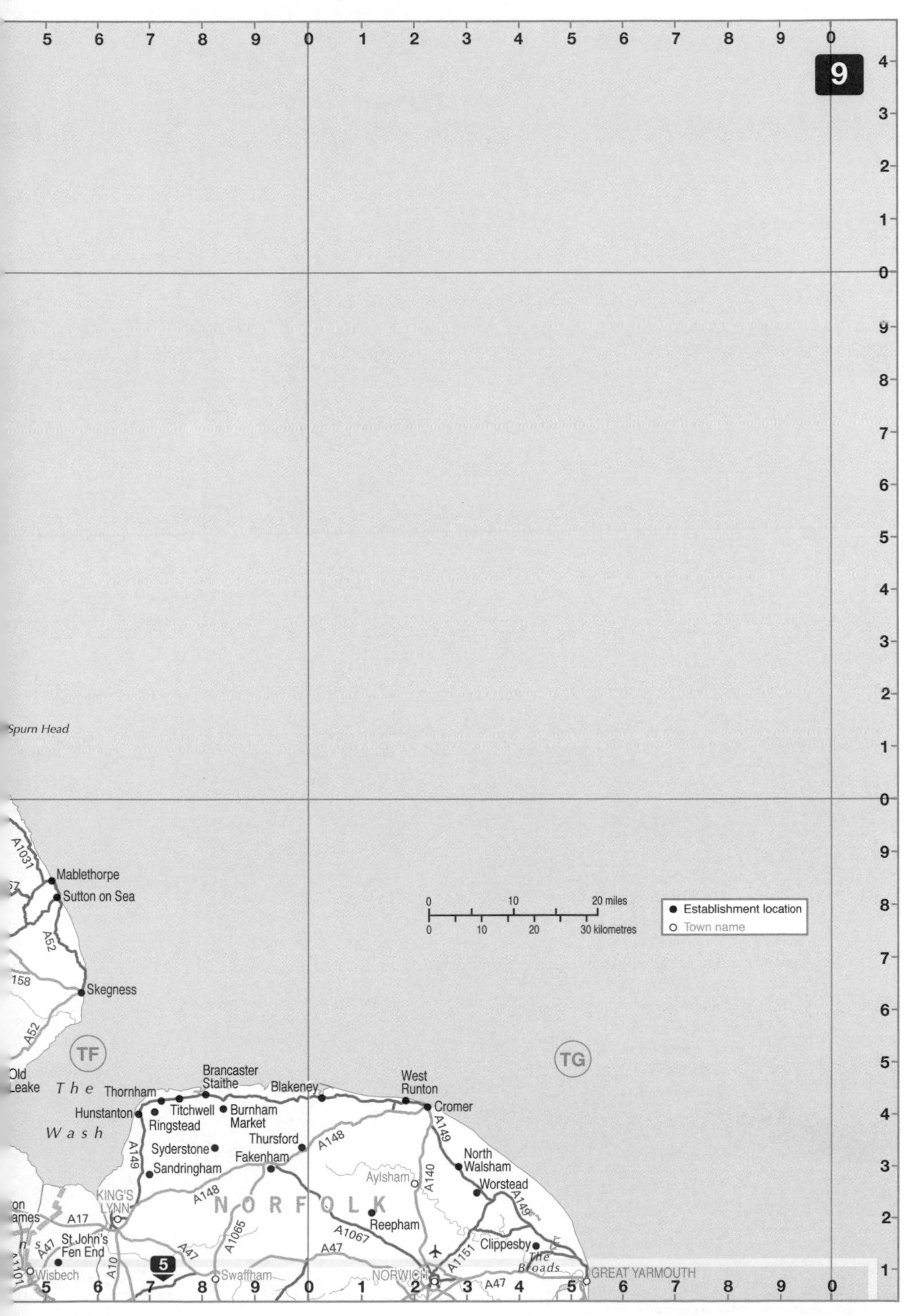
9
Spurn Head
Mablethorpe
Sutton on Sea
Skegness
TF
TG
Old Leake
The Wash
Thornham
Brancaster Staithe
Blakeney
West Runton
Cromer
Hunstanton
Titchwell
Burnham Market
Ringstead
Thursford
Syderstone
Fakenham
Sandringham
North Walsham
Aylsham
Worstead
KING'S LYNN
NORFOLK
Reepham
St John's Fen End
Wisbech
Swaffham
NORWICH
Clippesby
The Broads
GREAT YARMOUTH
A1031
A52
A158
A149
A148
A17
A47
A10
A1065
A1067
A140
A1151
A1101
0
10
20 miles
0
10
20
30 kilometres
Establishment location
Town name

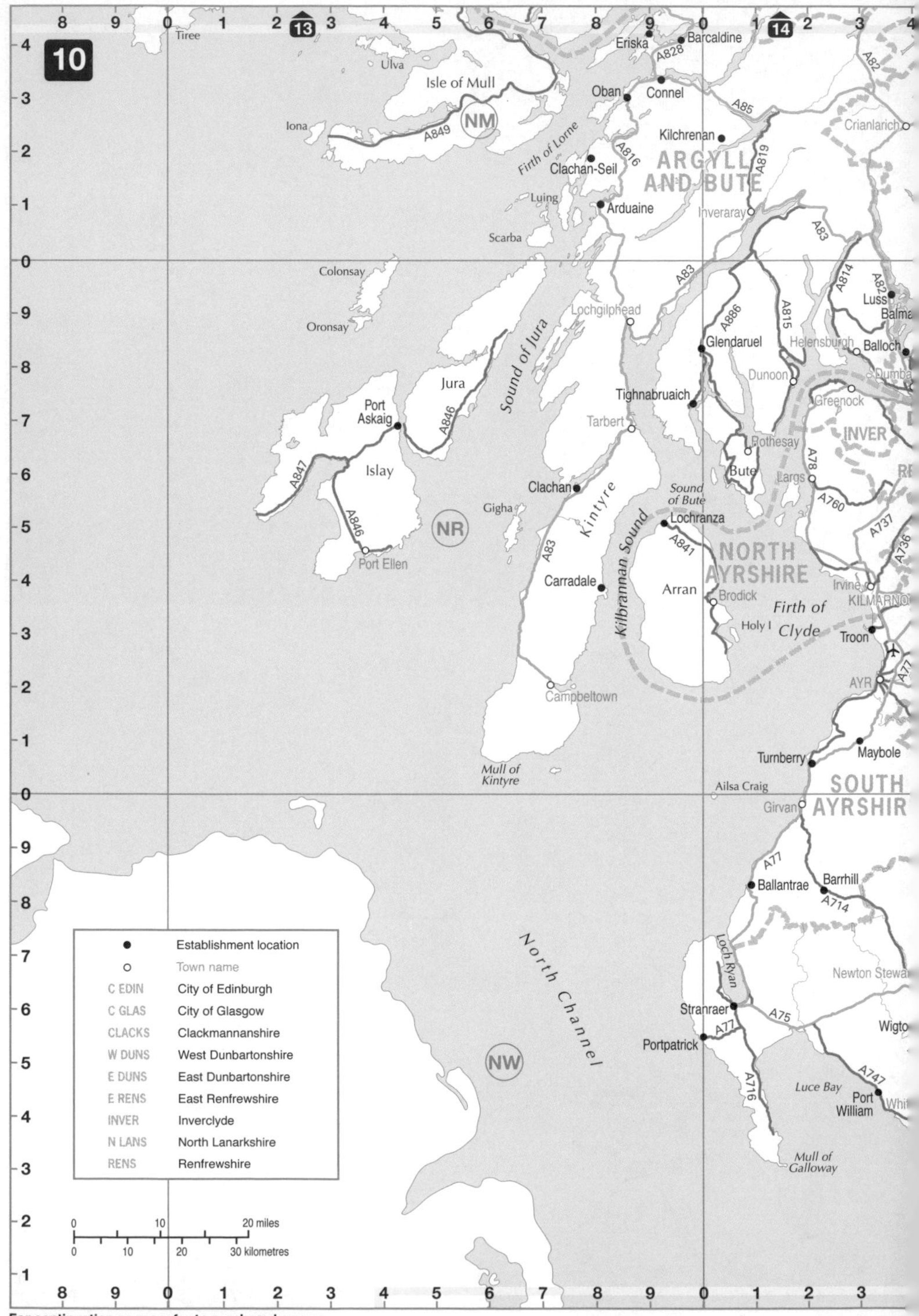

For continuation pages refer to numbered arrows

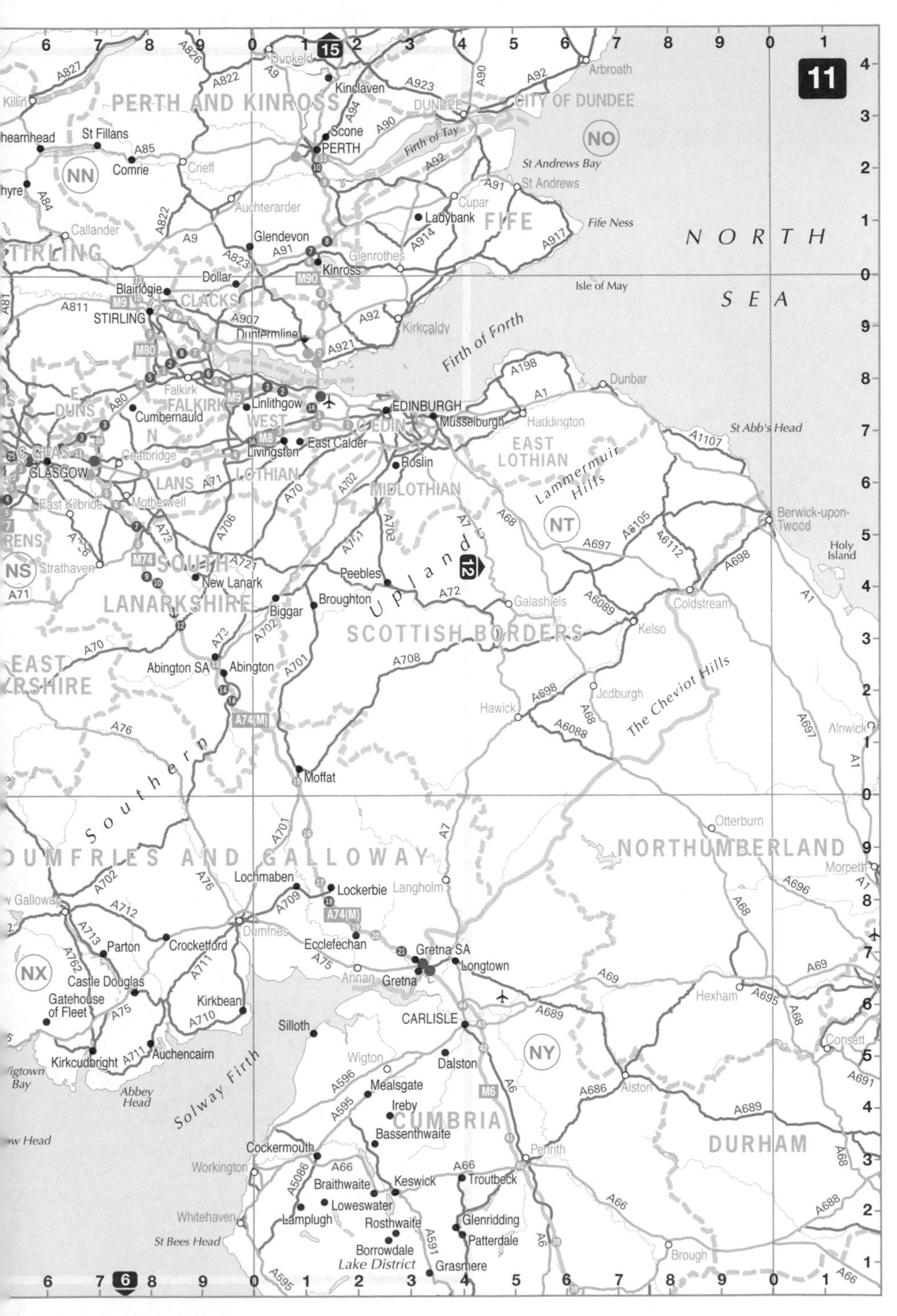

11
15
12
6
PERTH AND KINROSS
CITY OF DUNDEE
Dunkeld
Kinclaven
Killin
St Fillans
Comrie
Crieff
Scone
PERTH
DUNDEE
Arbroath
Firth of Tay
St Andrews Bay
St Andrews
Cupar
Auchterarder
Ladybank
FIFE
Fife Ness
Callander
Glendevon
Glenrothes
Kinross
NORTH
SEA
Isle of May
Dollar
Blairlogie
CLACKS
STIRLING
Dunfermline
Kirkcaldy
Firth of Forth
Falkirk
FALKIRK
Linlithgow
Cumbernauld
WEST
LOTHIAN
EDINBURGH
Musselburgh
Haddington
Dunbar
St Abb's Head
Livingston
East Calder
Coatbridge
GLASGOW
Roslin
EAST
LOTHIAN
MIDLOTHIAN
Lammermuir
Hills
Motherwell
East Kilbride
LANS
Berwick-upon-Tweed
Holy
Island
Strathaven
SOUTH
LANARKSHIRE
New Lanark
Peebles
Uplands
Galashiels
Coldstream
Kelso
Broughton
Biggar
SCOTTISH BORDERS
Abington SA
Abington
EAST
AYRSHIRE
Jedburgh
The Cheviot Hills
Hawick
Alnwick
Moffat
Southern
Otterburn
NORTHUMBERLAND
DUMFRIES AND GALLOWAY
Lochmaben
Lockerbie
Langholm
Morpeth
Dumfries
Ecclefechan
Gretna SA
Longtown
Parton
Crocketford
Castle Douglas
Annan
Gretna
Gatehouse
of Fleet
Kirkbean
Silloth
CARLISLE
Hexham
Kirkcudbright
Auchencairn
Wigton
Dalston
Consett
Abbey
Head
Solway Firth
Mealsgate
Ireby
Alston
CUMBRIA
Bassenthwaite
Cockermouth
DURHAM
Penrith
Workington
Braithwaite
Keswick
Troutbeck
Loweswater
Lamplugh
Whitehaven
Rosthwaite
Glenridding
Patterdale
St Bees Head
Borrowdale
Lake District
Grasmere
Brough
NN
NO
NS
NT
NX
NY

For continuation pages refer to numbered arrows

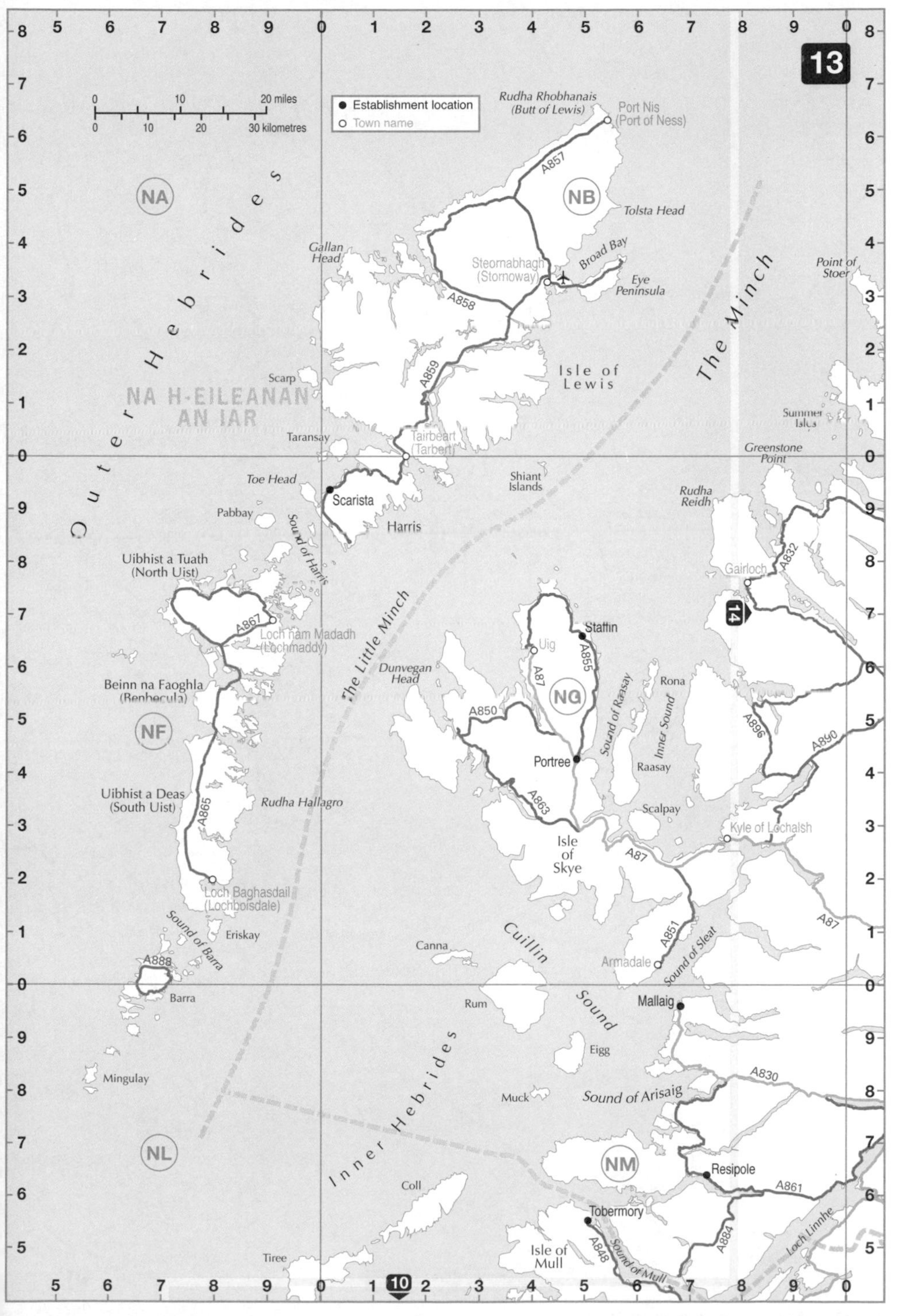

13
Establishment location
Town name
0 10 20 miles
0 10 20 30 kilometres
Rudha Rhobhanais (Butt of Lewis)
Port Nis (Port of Ness)
NA
NB
NF
NG
NL
NM
Outer Hebrides
NA H-EILEANAN AN IAR
Tolsta Head
Gallan Head
Steornabhagh (Stornoway)
Broad Bay
Eye Peninsula
Point of Stoer
The Minch
Isle of Lewis
Scarp
Taransay
Tairbeart (Tarbert)
Summer Isles
Greenstone Point
Toe Head
Scarista
Shiant Islands
Rudha Reidh
Pabbay
Sound of Harris
Harris
Uibhist a Tuath (North Uist)
Gairloch
14
Loch nam Madadh (Lochmaddy)
The Little Minch
Staffin
Uig
Dunvegan Head
Beinn na Faoghla (Benbecula)
Sound of Raasay
Rona
Inner Sound
Portree
Raasay
Uibhist a Deas (South Uist)
Rudha Hallagro
Scalpay
Kyle of Lochalsh
Isle of Skye
Loch Baghasdail (Lochboisdale)
Sound of Barra
Eriskay
Cuillin Sound
Canna
Armadale
Sound of Sleat
Barra
Rum
Mallaig
Eigg
Mingulay
Inner Hebrides
Muck
Sound of Arisaig
Resipole
Coll
Tobermory
Isle of Mull
Sound of Mull
Loch Linnhe
Tiree
10
A857
A858
A859
A867
A865
A888
A855
A87
A850
A863
A851
A832
A896
A890
A830
A861
A884
A848

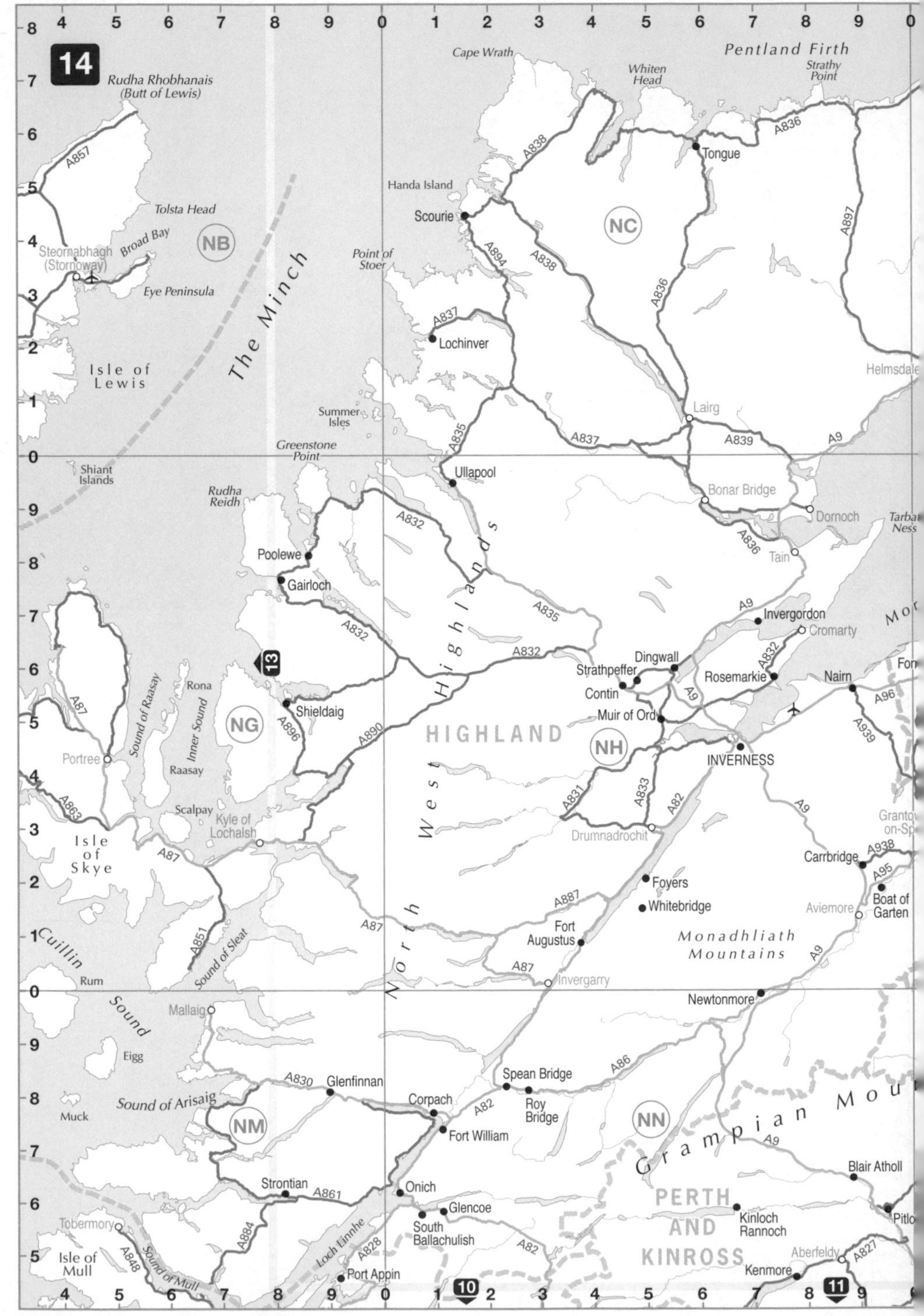

For continuation pages refer to numbered arrows

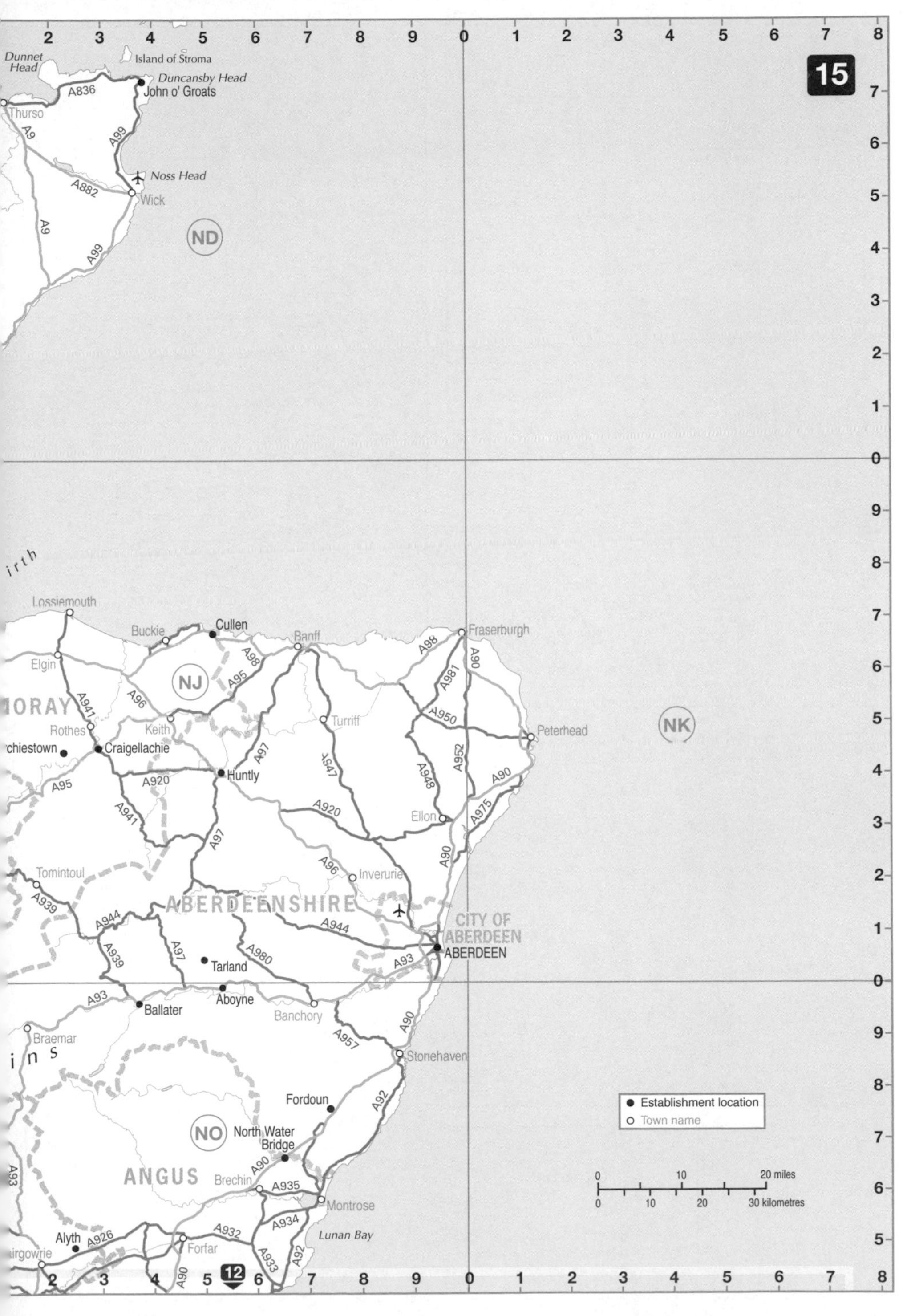

15
Dunnet Head
Island of Stroma
Duncansby Head
John o' Groats
Thurso
A836
A9
A99
Noss Head
A882
Wick
ND
NJ
NK
NO
Lossiemouth
Buckie
Cullen
Banff
Fraserburgh
Elgin
MORAY
Rothes
Keith
Turriff
Craigellachie
Huntly
Peterhead
Ellon
Tomintoul
Inverurie
ABERDEENSHIRE
CITY OF ABERDEEN
ABERDEEN
Tarland
Ballater
Aboyne
Banchory
Braemar
Stonehaven
Fordoun
North Water Bridge
ANGUS
Brechin
Montrose
Lunan Bay
Alyth
Forfar
Establishment location
Town name
0 10 20 miles
0 10 20 30 kilometres
12

16
0 10 20 miles
0 10 20 30 kilometres
Establishment location
Town name
HY
ND
Westray
Sanday
Rousay
Eday
Stronsay
Mainland
Shapinsay
Kirkwall
Stromness
Hoy
South Ronaldsay
Orkney Islands
2 3 4 5 6 7 8
9 8 7 6 5 4 3 2 1 0 9 8

0 10 20 miles
0 10 20 30 kilometres
HP
Unst
Yell
Fetlar
Whalsay
Mainland
Lerwick
Bressay
HU
Shetland Islands
2 3 4 5 6 7
2 1 0 9 8 7 6 5 4 3 2 1

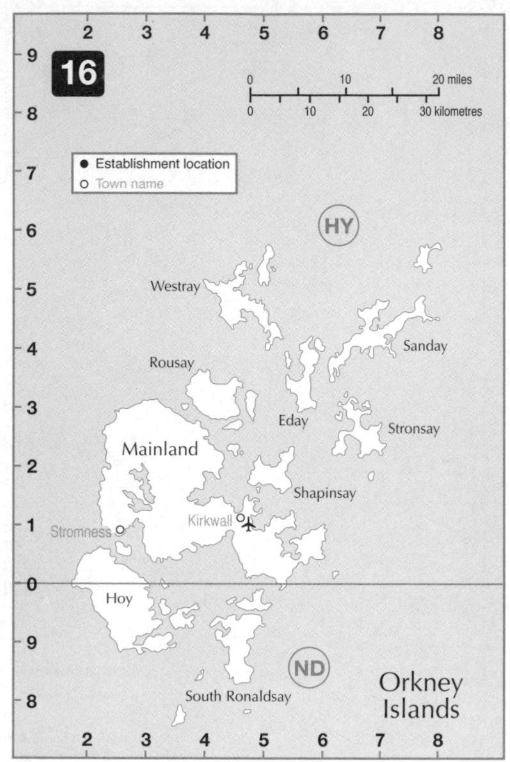

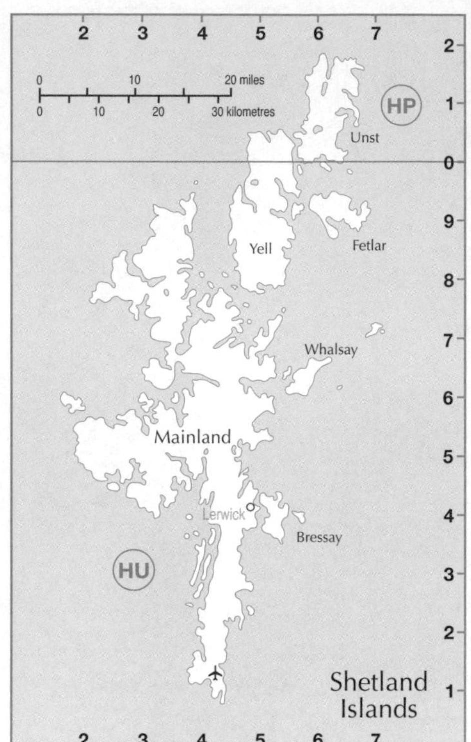

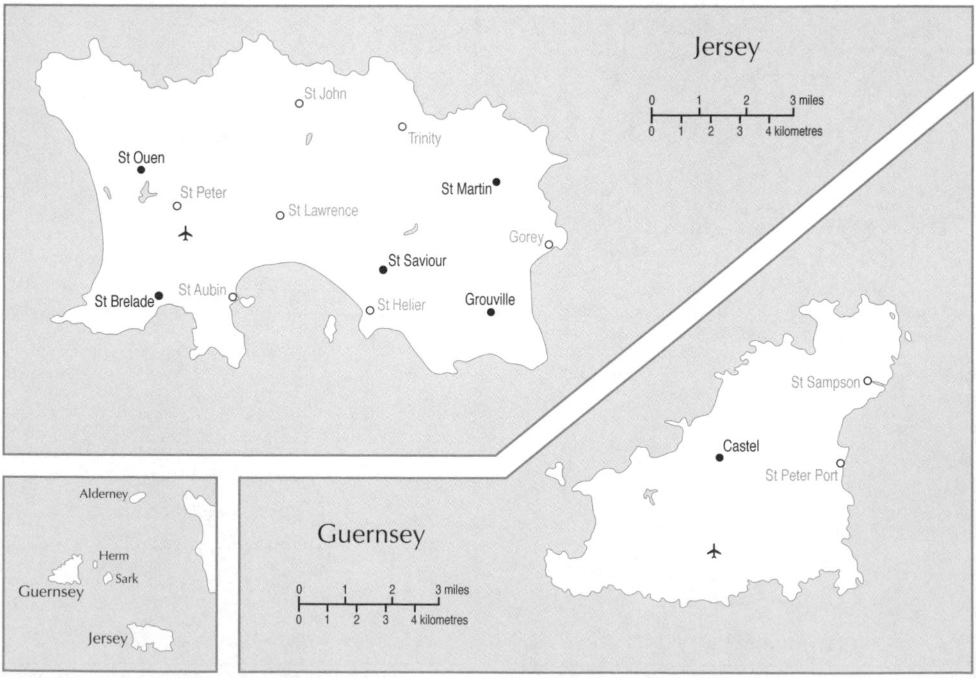

Jersey
0 1 2 3 miles
0 1 2 3 4 kilometres
St John
Trinity
St Ouen
St Peter
St Lawrence
St Martin
Gorey
St Saviour
St Brelade
St Aubin
St Helier
Grouville
St Sampson
Castel
St Peter Port
Guernsey
0 1 2 3 miles
0 1 2 3 4 kilometres
Alderney
Herm
Sark
Guernsey
Jersey

Index

B

I

J

K

M

N

R

S